8/25 - 1-41

8/27 - 1-41

9/1 - 151-69

9/3 - 169-202

9/8 - 202-27

9/10 - 45-89

9/15 - 45-89

9/22 - 89-147

9/24 - 235-74 - more on ACA

9/29 - 281-317 - corporate formation (235-74)

10/6 - TBD 281-317

10/7 - 319-54

10/8 - 375-407

10/14 - 354-74

10/16 - 341-54; IIRT ex rel USA v. Sign Line; 3:16-cv-06205 (USDC, N.D. Texas)

10/21 - TBD

10/23 - TBD

10/28 - 235-52

10/30 - 409-64

11/4 - TBD

11/6 - TBD

11/11 - 467-529

11/13 - 611-59

11/19 - 659-734

2/15 355-374

ASPEN CASEBOOK SERIES

The Law of AMERICAN HEALTH CARE

Second Edition

Nicole Huberfeld

Professor of Health Law, Ethics & Human Rights
Boston University School of Public Health
Professor of Law
Boston University School of Law

Elizabeth Weeks

J. Alton Hosch Professor of Law
Associate Dean for Faculty Development
University of Georgia School of Law

Kevin Outterson

N. Neil Pike Professor of Health Law & Disability Law
Boston University School of Law

Published by Wolters Kluwer in New York.

Wolters Kluwer Legal & Regulatory U.S. serves customers worldwide with CCH, Aspen Publishers, and Kluwer Law International products. (www.WKLegaledu.com)

To contact Customer Service, e-mail customer.service@wolterskluwer.com, call 1-800-234-1660, fax 1-800-901-9075, or mail correspondence to:

    Wolters Kluwer
    Attn: Order Department
    PO Box 990
    Frederick, MD 21705

Printed in the United States of America.

1 2 3 4 5 6 7 8 9 0

ISBN 978-1-4548-9279-3

Library of Congress Cataloging-in-Publication Data

Names: Huberfeld, Nicole, author. | Leonard, Elizabeth Weeks, author. |
    Outterson, Kevin, author.
Title: The law of American health care / Nicole Huberfeld, Professor of
    Health Law, Ethics & Human Rights, BU School of Public Health, Professor
    of Law, BU School of Law ; Elizabeth Weeks, J. Alton Hosch Professor of
    Law, University of Georgia School of Law; Kevin Outterson, N. Neil Pike
    Professor of Health Law & Disability Law, Boston University School of Law.
Description: Second edition. | New York : Wolters Kluwer, [2018] | Series:
    Aspen casebook series | Includes index.
Identifiers: LCCN 2018027406 | ISBN 9781454892793
Subjects: LCSH: Medical care—Law and legislation—United States. | LCGFT:
    Casebooks (Law)
Classification: LCC KF3821 .H83 2018 | DDC 344.7304/1—dc23
LC record available at https://lccn.loc.gov/2018027406

For our students, who inspired us;
our families, who supported us;
and our colleagues, who taught us.

SUMMARY OF CONTENTS

CONTENTS

PREFACE

At its inception, health care law was primarily state-based common law, rooted in 'Law and Medicine,' the original term for the field. Over time, private health insurance became the dominant payment mechanism, and its close cousin, managed care, became the leading cost control tool, but regulatory developments still continued to be largely state-based. Meanwhile, the role of the federal government in health care has grown slowly but consistently, both in public programs like Medicare and Medicaid, and through major federal laws that preempted some state-based rules. Traditionally, health care law has been taught as state-based case law with a significant federal overlay, and administrative law was merely a relevant detail.

The time had come to shift the emphasis and fully recognize that health care is a highly regulated industry with a substantial federal administrative law superstructure, just like railroad and airline transportation, financial services, oil and gas, and telecommunications, to name a few examples. After the passage of the Patient Protection and Affordable Care Act of 2010 (ACA), federal statutory and administrative law dominate the field of health care law. You will learn in the following pages about the ACA's rather complicated history, yet for all the challenges and objections, the law remains largely in place and represents the most sweeping transformation of U.S health care in a generation. The ACA was the farthest reaching in a long line of federal laws that enshrines choices about America's long-debated approaches to health insurance — private versus public provision of care, medical assistance eligibility, and the state-federal relationship in health care, among other themes. Likewise, most of the challenges to the law have operated in federal courts, Congress, and federal agency rule and policymaking, reflecting the increasingly dominant role of federal health care law. This book is the first health care law casebook to reflect that gravitational shift to the federal domain.

This second edition reflects important changes and key updates that have occurred since the 2016 election, including an adjusted framework for Chapter 1's introductory material; adding federal endorsement of work requirements in the Medicaid program in Chapter 2 (public insurance); and addressing repeal of the tax penalty associated with the individual health insurance mandate in Chapter 3 (private insurance). The individual mandate and Medicaid work requirements are significant, because they have spillover effects on other parts of the ACA, and they represent a philosophical shift regarding the role of government and individual responsibility for health. In addition to the reframing and updating of Chapters 1, 2, and 3, other updates include Chapter 5 (tax-exempt organizations) to reflect recent IRS enforcement activity around 501(r) Community Health Needs Assessment compliance; Chapter 6 (fraud and abuse) to include the U.S. Supreme Court's *Universal Health Services v. United States ex rel. Escobar* opinion, issued just after our first edition went to press; Chapter 9 (regulating the beginning and end of life), to incorporate the U.S. Supreme Court opinion in *Whole Woman's Health v. Hellerstedt* and related developments.

The book retains its distinctive features, including its emphasis on primary source materials beyond appellate cases, which are the bread and butter of most first-year law school courses. Health care law abounds with other forms of legal authority, including statutory, regulatory, and sub-regulatory guidance. We use secondary sources sparingly, including only canonical commentary on the field and data-driven empirical research, which are uniquely important for the practicing health care lawyer. The primary source materials are the focal point, with longer excerpts and light editing, providing an experience that foreshadows the work that our students must do when they become practicing lawyers.

We do not attempt to cover all topics comprehensively. Instead, we chose our key topics carefully, making use of guidelines suggested by practicing attorneys and health law professors in the American Health Lawyers Association, the preeminent professional organization for health law practitioners. While surveying fewer topics than some other health law casebooks, we engage the selected topics in more depth, so students emerge with an understanding of the most important features for the practice of health care law. The result is a three- or four-credit-hour book that is shorter but leaves room for professors to supplement with additional topics they are keen to teach.

Finally, we have listened carefully to students' comments about classroom materials over the years and have used that feedback in structuring the book. First, we avoided extensive notes, moving most references to scholarly articles and other secondary sources to the teachers' manual. Second, we use three different kinds of problems throughout the book: 'Questions,' which engage an excerpt directly; 'Problems,' which offer a practice-like scenario, hypothetical, or policy question to consider; and 'Capstone Problems,' which are designed to facilitate integrative and summative mastery of the chapter. While we firmly believe that the sometimes tedious, technical reading of statutes, regulations, cases, and other sources is the real work of health care lawyers, for pedagogical purposes, we highlight key issues, background, and other points of interest through boxed side notes, which enrich understanding in the moment of digesting a key source.

Health care law is complex, but teaching it needn't be. We hope you enjoy our labor of love.

ACKNOWLEDGMENTS

The authors gratefully acknowledge permission from the following sources to use excerpts from their works:

Books & Articles
Arrow, Kenneth J. Uncertainty and the Welfare Economics of Medical Care, 53 *American Economic Review* 941. Copyright © 1963 American Economic Association. Reprinted by permission.
Daniels, Norman. *Health-Care Needs and Distributive Justice*, 166-167. Copyright © 1981 Springer. Reprinted by permission.
Lagnado, Lucette. Jeanette White Is Long Dead But Her Hospital Bill Lives On. *The Wall Street Journal*, March 13, 2003. Copyright © 2003 Dow Jones and Company, Inc. Reprinted by permission.
de Brantes, Francois, Guy D'Andrea, and Meredith B. Rosenthal. Should Health Care Come with a Warranty?, 28 *Health Affairs* 4. Copyright © 2009 Project Hope. Reprinted by permission.

Photographs & Illustrations
Jack Kevorkian and his "suicide machine." Copyright © 1991 Richard Sheinwald/AP Photo. Reprinted by permission.
Paul Gelsinger before the Senate Public Health subcommittee. Copyright © 2000 Douglas Graham/Congressional Quarterly/Getty Images. Reprinted by permission.

The Law of
AMERICAN HEALTH CARE

CHAPTER 1

Introduction to American Health Care Law

A. INTRODUCTION

Health care is a vast, complex industry that will soon approach one-fifth of the U.S. economy, with more than $4 trillion in total spending expected in 2020. The United States is projected to spend on average more than $12,000 per capita on total health care expenses in 2020. Of course, this does not mean that each person in the United States will actually receive $12,000 in health care during the course of the year. Actual health care expenditures vary dramatically by age, sex, and other factors such as health status.

Health care is a growth industry, with costs steadily rising over time and accounting for an ever-increasing share of our nation's gross domestic product (GDP). In 2020, health care spending is projected to reach 18.4 percent of GDP, compared to just 5.5 percent of GDP in 1965 when Medicare and Medicaid began. Government spending on health care is projected to be 45 percent of total national health expenditures by 2020, though that does not account for federal tax benefits to private entities that provide health insurance as an employment benefit. The following chart shows U.S. health care spending, compared to certain other wealthy countries.

Total health expenditures per capita, U.S. dollars, PPP adjusted, 2016

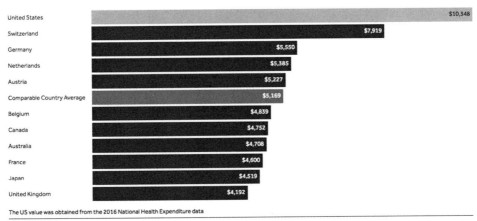

United States	$10,348
Switzerland	$7,919
Germany	$5,550
Netherlands	$5,385
Austria	$5,227
Comparable Country Average	$5,169
Belgium	$4,839
Canada	$4,752
Australia	$4,708
France	$4,600
Japan	$4,519
United Kingdom	$4,192

The US value was obtained from the 2016 National Health Expenditure data

Source: Kaiser Family Foundation analysis of data from OECD (2017), "OECD Health Data: Health expenditure and financing: Health expenditure indicators", OECD Health Statistics (database) (Accessed on March 19, 2017). • Get the data • PNG

Peterson Kaiser
Health System Tracker

Those data might lead to the conclusion that the United States has an especially robust health care sector. Perhaps we value health care more highly than other comparable countries and spend accordingly. But what are we getting for our money? Health care law often operates within the larger sphere of health policy, which means that statistical methods are increasingly prominent in discussions on health care law. Two common ways to measure the relative health of a population are infant mortality and life expectancy. On both those measures, the United States performs poorly compared to other wealthy countries.

First, on infant mortality:

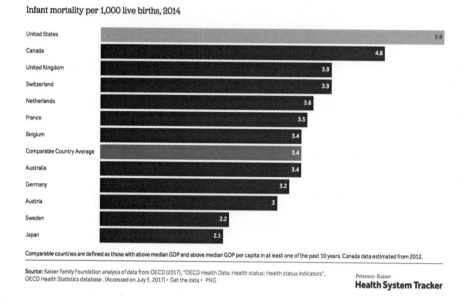

Infant mortality per 1,000 live births, 2014

United States	5.8
Canada	4.8
United Kingdom	3.9
Switzerland	3.9
Netherlands	3.6
France	3.5
Belgium	3.4
Comparable Country Average	3.4
Australia	3.4
Germany	3.2
Austria	3
Sweden	2.2
Japan	2.1

Comparable countries are defined as those with above median GDP and above median GDP per capita in at least one of the past 10 years. Canada data estimated from 2012.

Source: Kaiser Family Foundation analysis of data from OECD (2017), "OECD Health Data: Health status: Health status indicators". OECD Health Statistics database . (Accessed on July 5, 2017) • Get the data • PNG

Peterson-Kaiser
Health System Tracker

U.S. life expectancy at birth also lags by several years:

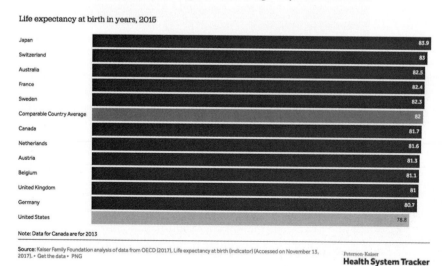

The U.S. has the lowest life expectancy at birth among comparable countries

Life expectancy at birth in years, 2015

Japan	83.9
Switzerland	83
Australia	82.5
France	82.4
Sweden	82.3
Comparable Country Average	82
Canada	81.7
Netherlands	81.6
Austria	81.3
Belgium	81.1
United Kingdom	81
Germany	80.7
United States	78.8

Note: Data for Canada are for 2013

Source: Kaiser Family Foundation analysis of data from OECD (2017), Life expectancy at birth (indicator) (Accessed on November 13, 2017). • Get the data • PNG

Peterson-Kaiser
Health System Tracker

In addition, for all of that spending, the United States also has the highest rate of deaths that could be prevented by basic health care and preventive services, a measure called "mortality amenable to health care." The rate of mortality amenable to health care is even higher than the graphic below depicts, when measured based on demographic factors such as race and poverty. The United States has been ranked last among high-income nations on this measure since 2003.

Amenable mortality per 100,000 population, 2002 - 2003 and 2006 - 2007

■ 2002-2003   ■ 2006-2007

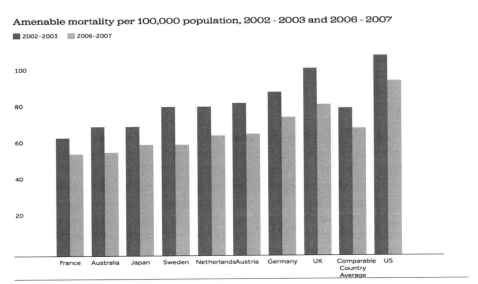

Source: Nolte E and McKee CM. "Measuring the Health of Nations: Updating an Earlier Analysis." Health Affairs, Jan 2008, 27(1):58-71. • Get the data • PNG

Peterson-Kaiser
Health System Tracker

The Affordable Care Act (ACA) succeeded in its central objective of greatly reducing the percentage of uninsured Americans, but even near-universal insurance coverage does not ensure better health. Rates of insurance coverage in the United States reached their highest levels so far in 2016 at 91.1 percent and are projected to fall somewhat (to 89.3 percent) by 2026 under the Trump Administration's reduced enrollment efforts. But the direct health impact of insurance coverage should not be overstated. Insurance facilitates access to health care; but, it guarantees neither access nor affordability. Studies show that even those who have health insurance coverage are likely to struggle with the cost of medical care and to make sacrifices to pay for medical care.

Even more fundamentally, access to health care does not automatically lead to improved health. Many other socioeconomic factors such as wealth, employment, and housing may have greater direct effect on health, as do relatively inexpensive public health programs.

As you consider the snapshot of America's health care landscape on the next page and learn more details of its operation in the following chapters, it is important to recognize that America does not really have a health care "system," although that terminology is often used. In reality, the United States is better described as having a health care "non-system," or health care business "sector" or "space," which is complex, multifaceted, fragmented, and often poorly coordinated.

This fragmentation exists in part because the U.S. Constitution does not contain a right to health care or anything that looks like it, which can be contextualized by

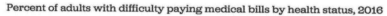

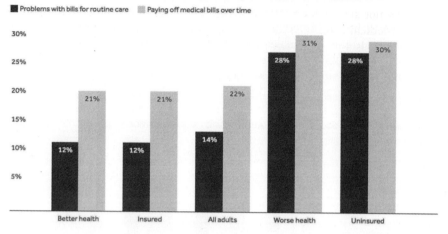

Percent of adults with difficulty paying medical bills by health status, 2016

Problems with bills for routine care ■   Paying off medical bills over time ▫

Source: Kaiser Family Foundation analysis of National Health Interview Survey • Get the data • PNG

Peterson-Kaiser
Health System Tracker

history — such a right would have meant a "right" to bloodletting, fatal surgeries, and other remedies that today are considered barbaric. Medicine looked very different in 1787. This helps to explain why the Constitution does not squarely address the question of an affirmative right to health care, except in the prison context, where the Supreme Court of the United States held that total deprivation of medical care may violate the Eighth Amendment's prohibition on cruel and unusual treatment.

Estelle v. Gamble

429 U.S. 97 (1976)

Mr. Justice MARSHALL delivered the opinion of the Court.

. . . We therefore conclude that deliberate indifference to serious medical needs of prisoners constitutes the "unnecessary and wanton infliction of pain," Gregg v. Georgia, proscribed by the Eighth Amendment. This is true whether the indifference is manifested by prison doctors in their response to the prisoner's needs or by prison guards in intentionally denying or delaying access to medical care or intentionally interfering with the treatment once prescribed. Regardless of how evidenced, deliberate indifference to a prisoner's serious illness or injury states a cause of action under §1983.

> For prisoners, the Constitution guarantees only a minimal right to health care, with quality decisions left to state law.

This conclusion does not mean, however, that every claim by a prisoner that he has not received adequate medical treatment states a violation of the Eighth Amendment. An accident, although it may produce added anguish, is not on that basis alone to be characterized as wanton infliction of unnecessary pain. . . . [I]n the medical context, an inadvertent failure to provide adequate medical care cannot be said to constitute "an unnecessary and wanton infliction of pain" or to be "repugnant to the conscience of mankind." Thus, a complaint that a physician has been negligent in diagnosing or treating a medical condition does not state a valid claim of medical mistreatment under the Eighth Amendment. Medical malpractice does not become a constitutional violation merely because the victim is a prisoner. In order to state a cognizable claim, a prisoner must allege acts or omissions sufficiently harmful to evidence deliberate indifference to serious medical needs. It is only such indifference that can offend "evolving standards of decency" in violation of the Eighth Amendment.

Gamble's claims against Dr. Gray, both in his capacity as treating physician and as medical director of the Corrections Department, are not cognizable. . . . Gamble was seen by medical personnel on 17 occasions spanning a 3-month period: by Dr. Astone five times; by Dr. Gray twice; by Dr. Heaton three times; by an unidentified doctor and inmate nurse on the day of the injury; and by medical assistant Blunt six times. They treated his back injury, high blood pressure, and heart problems. Gamble has disclaimed any objection to the treatment provided for his high blood pressure and his heart problem; his complaint is "based solely on the lack of diagnosis and inadequate treatment of his back injury." The doctors diagnosed his injury as a lower back strain and treated it with bed rest, muscle relaxants and pain relievers. Respondent contends that more should have been done by way of diagnosis and treatment, and suggests a number of options that were not pursued. The Court of Appeals agreed, stating: "Certainly an x-ray of (Gamble's) lower back might have been in order and other tests conducted that would have led to appropriate diagnosis and treatment for the daily pain and suffering he was experiencing." But the question whether an X-ray or additional diagnostic techniques or forms of treatment is [sic] indicated is a classic example of a matter for medical judgment. A medical decision not to order an X-ray, or like measures, does not represent cruel and unusual punishment. At most it is medical malpractice, and as such the proper forum is the state court under the Texas Tort Claims Act.

QUESTION

Should everyone have the same constitutional right of access to health care enjoyed by prisoners?

The lack of a unifying right to health care facilitates complexity and fragmentation, both of which invite legal regulation. Thus, we will see that the health care sector is heavily regulated through statutes, regulations, common law, and other authority, leading to the set of legal doctrines commonly called health care law.

B. COMMON THEMES IN HEALTH CARE LAW

Health care law is one of the more complex subjects taught in law school, given that it contains a high degree of interaction with nonlegal actors and institutions, including doctors, patients, health insurers, hospitals, drug and device companies, and federal and state governments. Each of these groups has interests to defend, and many have highly specialized knowledge that uses special language, which a health care lawyer must be able to understand. As you approach this course and the materials included in this casebook, appreciate that they may be unfamiliar and challenging at times. The objective, however, is to give you ample opportunity to practice reading and digesting the wide range of sources that you might encounter practicing this area of law.

One way to facilitate an ongoing understanding of the disparate field of health care law, despite its often rapidly changing landscape, is to introduce its consistent themes. These themes include:

- **Federalism** (the relationship between the federal government and states);
- **Individual rights** (protected by the U.S. Constitution, state constitutions, and common law, but limited by certain governmental powers and societal needs);
- **Fiduciary relationships** (between patients and providers, insurers and insureds, corporate officers and directors and the public, to name a few);
- **The modern administrative state** (including inherent tensions between coordinate legislative, executive, and judicial branches of government); and
- **Markets and regulation** (operating from the premise that health care markets are marred by various "imperfections" that invite legal interventions).

We offer the following three examples to elucidate these themes and introduce some substantive topics that we will consider more systematically throughout the course. Our purpose here is not to cover these topics exhaustively but rather to offer a brief introduction to laws and concepts that animate the field of health care law. We close the chapter with two theoretical approaches to health care, rooted first in economics and then in distributive justice. These insights and vocabulary will reappear in your studies as well.

1. INDIVIDUAL RIGHTS AND GOVERNMENTAL POWERS

The following case illustrates two inherent tensions in health law: the interests of individuals versus society at large, and the overlapping spheres of state and federal law that regulate health care. The U.S. Constitution recognizes certain individual rights, including liberty, property, free speech, freedom of religion, and privacy. But these rights are not absolute; the government may intrude upon them for justifiable reasons. Throughout the course, you will see numerous examples testing the scope of government power vis-à-vis individual rights. The federal government's powers are enumerated in the Constitution, while all other powers are reserved to the states. The states' reserved powers have long been called the "police powers," which includes authority to protect public health and safety. In the field of health care, it can have a great impact on individual autonomy. For example, in 2014, governors from New Jersey and Maine limited the freedom of a Doctors Without Borders nurse, Kaci Hickox, who returned from treating Ebola patients in West Africa. Global outbreaks of Ebola spurred fears and provoked the states' governors to exert their police powers to quarantine Hickox, despite lack of a clear medical or epidemiological basis for believing that she was infected. Quarantines are just one example of direct state control over a person, ostensibly to protect the public's health.

This early U.S. Supreme Court decision in the realm of medicine is still good law, frequently cited for the propositions it contains.

Jacobson v. Commonwealth of Massachusetts

197 U.S. 11 (1905)

Mr. Justice HARLAN delivered the opinion of the court:

This case involves the validity, under the Constitution of the United States, of certain provisions in the statutes of Massachusetts relating to vaccination.

The Revised Laws of that commonwealth provide that "the board of health of a city or town, if, in its opinion, it is necessary for the public health or safety, shall require and enforce the vaccination and revaccination of all the inhabitants thereof, and shall provide them with the means of free vaccination. Whoever, being over twenty-one years of age and not under guardianship, refuses or neglects to comply with such requirement shall forfeit $5."

An exception is made in favor of "children who present a certificate, signed by a registered physician, that they are unfit subjects for vaccination."

. . . Jacobson[ ] was proceeded against by a criminal complaint in one of the inferior courts of Massachusetts. The complaint charged that on the 17th day of July, 1902, the board of health of Cambridge, being of the opinion that it was necessary for the public health and safety, required the vaccination and revaccination of all the inhabitants thereof who had not been successfully vaccinated since the 1st day of March, 1897, and provided them with the means of free vaccination; and that the defendant, being over twenty-one years of age and not under guardianship, refused and neglected to comply with such requirement.

The defendant, having been arraigned, pleaded not guilty. The government put in evidence the above regulations adopted by the board of health, and made proof tending to show that its chairman informed the defendant that, by refusing to be vaccinated, he would incur the penalty provided by the statute, and would be prosecuted therefor; that he offered to vaccinate the defendant without expense to him; and that the offer was declined, and defendant refused to be vaccinated. . . .

A verdict of guilty was thereupon returned . . . and thereafter, pursuant to the verdict of the jury, he was sentenced by the court to pay a fine of $5. And the court ordered that he stand committed until the fine was paid. . . .

> There is some evidence that Reverend Jacobson refused to be vaccinated because he had already suffered a bad reaction to a vaccine.

Is the statute . . . inconsistent with the liberty which the Constitution of the United States secures to every person against deprivation by the state?

The authority of the state to enact this statute is to be referred to what is commonly called the police power, a power which the state did not surrender when becoming a member of the Union under the Constitution. Although this court has refrained from any attempt to define the limits of that power, yet it has distinctly recognized the authority of a state to enact quarantine laws and "health laws of every description"; indeed, all laws that relate to matters completely within its territory and which do not by their necessary operation affect the people of other states. According to settled principles, the police power of a state must be held to embrace, at least, such reasonable regulations established directly by legislative enactment as will protect the public health and the public safety. . . .

We come, then, to inquire whether any right given or secured by the Constitution is invaded by the statute as interpreted by the state court. The defendant insists that his liberty is invaded when the state subjects him to fine or imprisonment for neglecting or refusing to submit to vaccination; that a compulsory vaccination law is unreasonable, arbitrary, and oppressive, and, therefore, hostile to the inherent right of every freeman to care for his own body and health in such way as to him seems best; and that the execution of such a law against one who objects to vaccination, no matter for what reason, is nothing short of an assault upon his person. But the liberty secured by the Constitution of the United States to every person within its jurisdiction does not import an absolute right in each person to be, at all times and in all circumstances, wholly freed from restraint. There are manifold restraints to which every person is necessarily subject for the common good. On any other basis organized society could not exist with safety to its members. Society based on the rule that each one is a law unto himself would soon be confronted with disorder and anarchy. Real liberty for all could not exist under the operation of a principle which recognizes the right of each individual person to use his own, whether in respect of his person or his property, regardless of the injury that may be done to others. This court has more than once recognized it as a fundamental principle that "persons and property are subjected to all kinds of restraints and burdens in order to secure the general comfort, health, and prosperity of the state; of the perfect right of the legislature to do which no question ever was, or upon acknowledged general principles ever can be, made, so far as natural persons are concerned." In Crowley v. Christensen, 137 U.S. 86, 89, we said:

> The possession and enjoyment of all rights are subject to such reasonable conditions as may be deemed by the governing authority of the country essential to the safety, health, peace, good order, and morals of the community. Even liberty itself, the greatest of all rights, is not unrestricted license to act according to one's own will. It is only freedom from restraint under conditions essential to the equal enjoyment of the same right by others. It is, then, liberty regulated by law.

In the Constitution of Massachusetts adopted in 1780 it was laid down as a fundamental principle of the social compact that the whole people covenants with each citizen, and each citizen with the whole people, that all shall be governed by certain laws for "the common good," and that government is instituted "for the common good, for the protection, safety, prosperity, and happiness of the people, and not for the profit, honor, or private interests of any one man, family, or class of men." The good and welfare of the commonwealth, of which the legislature is primarily the judge, is the basis on which the police power rests in Massachusetts.

Applying these principles to the present case, it is to be observed that the legislature of Massachusetts required the inhabitants of a city or town to be vaccinated only when, in the opinion of the board of health, that was necessary for the public health or the public safety. . . . To invest such a body with authority over such matters was not an unusual, nor an unreasonable or arbitrary, requirement. Upon the principle of self-defense, of paramount necessity, a community has the right to protect itself against an epidemic of disease which threatens the safety of its members. . . .

> There is, of course, a sphere within which the individual may assert the supremacy of his own will, and rightfully dispute the authority of any human government, especially of any free government existing under a written constitution, to interfere with the exercise of that will. But it is equally true that in every well-ordered society charged with the duty of conserving the safety of its members the rights of the individual in

respect of his liberty may at times, under the pressure of great dangers, be subjected to such restraint, to be enforced by reasonable regulations, as the safety of the general public may demand. An American citizen arriving at an American port on a vessel in which, during the voyage, there had been cases of yellow fever or Asiatic cholera, he, although apparently free from disease himself, may yet, in some circumstances, be held in quarantine against his will on board of such vessel or in a quarantine station, until it be ascertained by inspection, conducted with due diligence, that the danger of the spread of the disease among the community at large has disappeared. The liberty secured by the 14th Amendment, this court has said, consists, in part, in the right of a person "to live and work where he will"; and yet he may be compelled, by force if need be, against his will and without regard to his personal wishes or his pecuniary interests, or even his religious or political convictions, to take his place in the ranks of the army of his country, and risk the chance of being shot down in its defense. It is not, therefore, true that the power of the public to guard itself against imminent danger depends in every case involving the control of one's body upon his willingness to submit to reasonable regulations established by the constituted authorities, under the sanction of the state, for the purpose of protecting the public collectively against such danger. . . .

Looking at the propositions embodied in the defendant's rejected offers of proof, it is clear that they are more formidable by their number than by their inherent value. Those offers in the main seem to have had no purpose except to state the general theory of those of the medical profession who attach little or no value to vaccination as a means of preventing the spread of smallpox, or who think that vaccination causes other diseases of the body. What everybody knows the court must know, and therefore the state court judicially knew, as this court knows, that an opposite theory accords with the common belief, and is maintained by high medical authority. We must assume that, when the statute in question was passed, the legislature of Massachusetts was not unaware of these opposing theories, and was compelled, of necessity, to choose between them. It was not compelled to commit a matter involving the public health and safety to the final decision of a court or jury. It is no part of the function of a court or a jury to determine which one of two modes was likely to be the most effective for the protection of the public against disease. That was for the legislative department to determine in the light of all the information it had or could obtain. It could not properly abdicate its function to guard the public health and safety. The state legislature proceeded upon the theory which recognized vaccination as at least an effective, if not the best-known, way in which to meet and suppress the evils of a smallpox epidemic that imperiled an entire population. Upon what sound principles as to the relations existing between the different departments of government can the court review this action of the legislature? If there is any such power in the judiciary to review legislative action in respect of a matter affecting the general welfare, it can only be when that which the legislature has done comes within the rule that, if a statute purporting to have been enacted to protect the public health, the public morals, or the public safety, has no real or substantial relation to those objects, or is, beyond all question, a plain, palpable invasion of rights secured by the fundamental law, it is the duty of the courts to so adjudge, and thereby give effect to the Constitution.

Whatever may be thought of the expediency of this statute, it cannot be affirmed to be, beyond question, in palpable conflict with the Constitution. Nor, in view of the methods employed to stamp out the disease of smallpox, can anyone confidently

> The Court sidestepped the factual issue of whether these vaccinations are safe and effective.

assert that the means prescribed by the state to that end has no real or substantial relation to the protection of the public health and the public safety. Such an assertion would not be consistent with the experience of this and other countries whose authorities have dealt with the disease of smallpox.[1] And the principle of vaccination as a means to prevent the spread of smallpox has been enforced in many states by statutes making the vaccination of children a condition of their right to enter or remain in public schools.

The latest case upon the subject of which we are aware is *Viemester v. White*, decided very recently by the court of appeals of New York. That case involved the validity of a statute excluding from the public schools all children who had not been vaccinated. One contention was that the statute and the regulation adopted in exercise of its provisions was [*sic*] inconsistent with the rights, privileges, and liberties of the citizen. The contention was overruled, the court saying, among other things:

> Smallpox is known of all to be a dangerous and contagious disease. If vaccination strongly tends to prevent the transmission or spread of this disease, it logically follows that children may be refused admission to the public schools until they have been vaccinated. The appellant claims that vaccination does not tend to prevent smallpox, but tends to bring about other diseases, and that it does much harm, with no good. It must be conceded that some laymen, both learned and unlearned, and some physicians of great skill and repute, do not believe that vaccination is a preventive of smallpox. The common belief, however, is that it has a decided tendency to prevent the spread of this fearful disease, and to render it less dangerous to those who contract it. While not accepted by all, it is accepted by the mass of the people, as well as by most members of the medical profession. It has been general in our state, and in most civilized nations for generations. It is generally accepted in theory, and generally applied in practice, both by the voluntary action of the people, and in obedience to the command of law. Nearly every state in the Union has statutes to encourage, or

---

1. "State-supported facilities for vaccination began in England in 1808 with the National Vaccine Establishment. In 1840 vaccination fees were made payable out of the rates. The first compulsory act was passed in 1853, the guardians of the poor being intrusted with the carrying out of the law; in 1854 the public vaccinations under one year of age were 408,824 as against an average of 180,960 for several years before. In 1867 a new act was passed, rather to remove some technical difficulties than to enlarge the scope of the former act; and in 1871 the act was passed which compelled the boards of guardians to appoint vaccination officers. The guardians also appoint a public vaccinator, who must be duly qualified to practise medicine, and whose duty it is to vaccinate (for a fee of one shilling and sixpence) any child resident within his district brought to him for that purpose, to examine the same a week after, to give a certificate, and to certify to the vaccination officer the fact of vaccination or of insusceptibility. . . . Vaccination was made compulsory in Bavarla in 1807, and subsequently in the following countries: Denmark (1810), Sweden (1814), Wu«rttemberg, Hesse, and other German states (1818), Prussia (1835), Roumania (1874), Hungary (1876), and Servia (1881). It is compulsory by cantonal law in 10 out of the 22 Swiss cantons; an attempt to pass a Federal compulsory law was defeated by a plebiscite in 1881. In the following countries there is no compulsory law, but governmental facilities and compulsion on various classes more or less directly under governmental control, such as soldiers, state employees, apprentices, school pupils, etc.: France, Italy, Spain, Portugal, Belgium, Norway, Austria, Turkey. . . . Vaccination has been compulsory in South Australia since 1872, in Victoria since 1874, and in Western Australia since 1878. In Tasmania a compulsory act was passed in 1882. In New South Wales there is no compulsion, but free facilities for vaccination. Compulsion was adopted at Calcutta in 1880, and since then at 80 other towns of Bengal, at Madras in 1884, and at Bombay and elsewhere in the presidency a few years earlier. Revaccination was made compulsory in Denmark in 1871, and in Roumania in 1874; in Holland it was enacted for all school pupils in 1872. The various laws and administrative orders which had been for many years in force as to vaccination and revaccination in the several German states were consolidated in an imperial statute of 1874." 24 Encyclopaedia Britannica (1894), *Vaccination*.

directly or indirectly to require, vaccination; and this is true of most nations of Europe. . . . A common belief, like common knowledge, does not require evidence to establish its existence, but may be acted upon without proof by the legislature and the courts. . . . The fact that the belief is not universal is not controlling, for there is scarcely any belief that is accepted by everyone. The possibility that the belief may be wrong, and that science may yet show it to be wrong, is not conclusive; for the legislature has the right to pass laws which, according to the common belief of the people, are adapted to prevent the spread of contagious diseases. In a free country, where the government is by the people, through their chosen representatives, practical legislation admits of no other standard of action, for what the people believe is for the common welfare must be accepted as tending to promote the common welfare, whether it does in fact or not. Any other basis would conflict with the spirit of the Constitution, and would sanction measures opposed to a Republican form of government. While we do not decide, and cannot decide, that vaccination is a preventive of smallpox, we take judicial notice of the fact that this is the common belief of the people of the state, and, with this fact as a foundation, we hold that the statute in question is a health law, enacted in a reasonable and proper exercise of the police power.

Since, then, vaccination, as a means of protecting a community against smallpox, finds strong support in the experience of this and other countries, no court, much less a jury, is justified in disregarding the action of the legislature simply because in its or their opinion that particular method was — perhaps, or possibly — not the best either for children or adults. . . .

It seems to the court that [Jacobson's arguments] would practically strip the legislative department of its function to care for the public health and the public safety when endangered by epidemics of disease. Such an answer would mean that compulsory vaccination could not, in any conceivable case, be legally enforced in a community, even at the command of the legislature, however widespread the epidemic of smallpox, and however deep and universal was the belief of the community and of its medical advisers that a system of general vaccination was vital to the safety of all.

We are not prepared to hold that a minority, residing or remaining in any city or town where smallpox is prevalent, and enjoying the general protection afforded by an organized local government, may thus defy the will of its constituted authorities, acting in good faith for all, under the legislative sanction of the state. If such be the privilege of a minority, then a like privilege would belong to each individual of the community, and the spectacle would be presented of the welfare and safety of an entire population being subordinated to the notions of a single individual who chooses to remain a part of that population. We are unwilling to hold it to be an element in the liberty secured by the Constitution of the United States that one person, or a minority of persons, residing in any community and enjoying the benefits of its local government, should have the power thus to dominate the majority when supported in their action by the authority of the state. While this court should guard with firmness every right appertaining to life, liberty, or property as secured to the individual by the supreme law of the land, it is of the last importance that it should not invade the domain of local authority except when it is plainly necessary to do so in order to enforce that law. The safety and the health of the people of Massachusetts are, in the first instance, for that commonwealth to guard and protect. They are matters that do not ordinarily concern the national government. So far as they can be reached by any government, they depend, primarily, upon such action as the state, in its wisdom, may take; and we do not perceive that this legislation has invaded any right secured by the Federal Constitution.

Before closing this opinion we deem it appropriate, in order to prevent misapprehension as to our views, to observe—perhaps to repeat a thought already sufficiently expressed, namely—that the police power of a state, whether exercised directly by the legislature, or by a local body acting under its authority, may be exerted in such circumstances, or by regulations so arbitrary and oppressive in particular cases, as to justify the interference of the courts to prevent wrong and oppression. Extreme cases can be readily suggested. Ordinarily such cases are not safe guides in the administration of the law. It is easy, for instance, to suppose the case of an adult who is embraced by the mere words of the act, but yet to subject whom to vaccination in a particular condition of his health or body would be cruel and inhuman in the last degree. We are not to be understood as holding that the statute was intended to be applied to such a case, or, if it was so intended, that the judiciary would not be competent to interfere and protect the health and life of the individual concerned. "All laws," this court has said, "should receive a sensible construction. General terms should be so limited in their application as not to lead to injustice, oppression, or an absurd consequence. It will always, therefore, be presumed that the legislature intended exceptions to its language which would avoid results of this character. The reason of the law in such cases should prevail over its letter." Until otherwise informed by the highest court of Massachusetts, we are not inclined to hold that the statute establishes the absolute rule that an adult must be vaccinated if it be apparent or can be shown with reasonable certainty that he is not at the time a fit subject of vaccination, or that vaccination, by reason of his then condition, would seriously impair his health, or probably cause his death. No such case is here presented. It is the cause of an adult who, for aught that appears, was himself in perfect health and a fit subject of vaccination, and yet, while remaining in the community, refused to obey the statute and the regulation adopted in execution

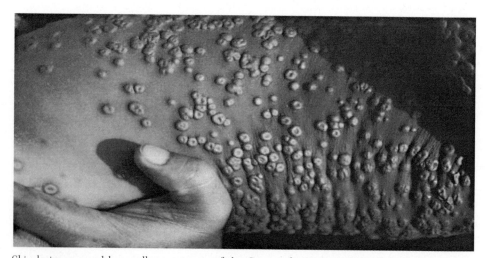

Skin lesions caused by smallpox, courtesy of the Centers for Disease Control and Prevention.

of its provisions for the protection of the public health and the public safety, confessedly endangered by the presence of a dangerous disease.

We now decide only that the statute covers the present case, and that nothing clearly appears that would justify this court in holding it to be unconstitutional and inoperative in its application to the plaintiff in error.

The judgment of the court below must be affirmed.

It is so ordered.

QUESTIONS

1. Did Massachusetts force Jacobson to be vaccinated?
2. Justice Harlan deferred to state legislative judgments about the efficacy of smallpox vaccination as an appropriate exercise of state police power. Why then did the Court review the dominant views in the United States and Europe?
3. Would the Court have decided the case differently if Jacobson had convinced the justices he had a well-founded fear of harm from vaccination?

One justification for the result in *Jacobson* is that the police power can intrude on cognizable individual liberty when the benefit to the public outweighs the risk of harm to the individual. Vaccination hinders the spread of infectious disease. Each vaccination carries a small risk of side effects for the individual, but society is better off with mass vaccination that reaches a high enough level to protect the population (sometimes called "herd immunity"). An unvaccinated individual exposes the entire community to a risk, a negative externality in the language of economics. Even though epidemiologists find that vaccinating 100 percent of the population is rarely necessary, it is also difficult to know when enough of the population has been vaccinated to ensure protection from further disease. The safest path from a population perspective is to attempt to achieve very high levels of vaccination compliance lest a dread disease like smallpox, measles, or polio be permitted to flower into an epidemic.

PROBLEM

You represent a client in Boston, Massachusetts, who believes that the measles vaccine causes autism and, therefore, has not vaccinated his school-aged child. Relying on the guidance below, the Massachusetts Department of Public Health has blocked the child from attending school until he has received all scheduled vaccinations, including measles. What advice do you have for your client about whether he will succeed in challenging the constitutionality of the state's regulations?

MASSACHUSETTS DEPARTMENT OF PUBLIC HEALTH

Immunization Exemptions and
Vaccine Preventable Disease Exclusion Guidelines in School Settings

Definition of Allowable Exemptions

There are two situations in which children who are not appropriately immunized may be admitted to school:

1) a **medical exemption** is allowed if a physician submits documentation attesting that an immunization is medically contraindicated; and
2) a **religious exemption** is allowed if a parent or guardian submits a written statement that immunizations conflict with their sincere religious beliefs.

The law states that medical exemptions must be presented at the beginning of each school year. MDPH recommends also requesting religious exemptions on an annual basis, in writing, at the beginning of each school year.

> **Philosophical exemptions are not allowed by law in Massachusetts, even if signed by a physician. Only medical and religious exemptions are acceptable. These exemptions must be kept in the students' files at school (105 CMR 220.000 and M.G.L. c.76, ss. 15, 15C and 15D).**

Policies for Exclusion at School Entry

While the laws and regulations state that **unimmunized** children who do not meet criteria for medical or religious exemption "shall **not** be admitted to school," policies around enforcement of exclusion for unimmunized or partially immunized children are developed by individual schools/school districts.

The only exception for exclusion of unimmunized or partially immunized children who do not have documentation of a medical or religious exemption is in the case of homeless children, whereby they cannot be denied entry to school if they do not have their immunization records. The federal McKinney-Vento Homeless Assistance Act states that if a homeless student does not have proper documentation of immunizations or any medical records, the Homeless Education Liaison at your school must immediately assist in obtaining them, and the student must be enrolled and permitted to attend school in the interim (as cited in the McKinney-Vento Homeless Assistance Act of 2001).

Exclusion During Disease Outbreaks

In situations when one or more cases of a vaccine-preventable or any other communicable disease are present in a school, all susceptibles, **including those with medical or religious exemptions**, are subject to exclusion as described in the Reportable Diseases and Isolation and Quarantine Requirements (105 CMR 300.000).

The reporting and control of diseases identified as posing a risk to the public health is prescribed by state regulation and law. The Isolation and Quarantine Requirements establish isolation and quarantine requirements for cases of certain diseases and their contacts in certain high-risk situations, including the school setting. The following table outlines several of the more common childhood vaccine-preventable diseases identified in the requirements that may occur in schools and the corresponding exclusion requirements.

2. HEALTH CARE RELATIONSHIPS AND FIDUCIARY DUTIES

Patients visit doctors for expert advice and treatment. But because the doctor is an expert who almost certainly knows much more about available treatments for the patient's medical condition, the patient is vulnerable and must trust the advice that a physician offers. While trust is a core element of the doctor-patient relationship, it is also a major topic in health care law. Under common law, an agent cannot have an undisclosed conflict of interest against his or her principal. But health care is big business, and therefore a wide range of considerations influences health care providers, including insurance company administrators, government regulators, health care corporate officers and directors, and even shareholders, in some cases. Many health care laws attempt to police the actions of providers when they face potential or actual financial conflicts of interest. Some of the most important health care practice areas, including fraud and abuse, regulate financial self-interest by providers, prohibiting financial and other arrangements that are perfectly acceptable in other industries. When a physician recommends surgery, patients understandably want that advice to be based on best medical advice, not the surgeon's desire to make money. By contrast, most consumers recognize that a salesperson's recommendation regarding which car to purchase includes a host of considerations irrelevant to the customer's driving pleasure.

The following example of fiduciary duties and market regulation in health law is illustrated with a collection of materials, including a media report, a court opinion, and an empirical research study. Together, these documents introduce the dynamic interplay of fiduciary rules and their various legal vehicles in the context of questionably necessary heart surgery.

Tenet Physicians Settle Case over Unnecessary Heart Procedures at Redding Medical Center, USA

Med. News Today, Nov. 17, 2005

Federal prosecutors on Tuesday said they have settled civil claims against physicians at Redding Medical Center—formerly owned by Dallas-based Tenet Healthcare—accused of performing unnecessary heart surgeries, the Los Angeles Times reports. In October 2002, federal officials launched an investigation into Drs. Chae Hyun Moon and Fidel Realyvasquez, two physicians at Redding Medical Center who allegedly performed unnecessary surgeries and defrauded Medicare. Federal officials alleged that the physicians participated in a "scheme to cause patients to undergo unnecessary invasive coronary procedures," such as artery bypass and heart valve replacement surgeries. In August 2003, Tenet agreed to pay $54 million to settle the federal case. In addition, the company in December 2004 announced plans to establish a $395 million fund for more than 769 cardiac patients and their families to settle a civil lawsuit filed over the allegations. The latest settlement pertains to Realyvasquez, Moon and two other doctors accused of performing the unnecessary heart procedures. According to the Sacramento Bee, FBI officials had sought to bring criminal charges against the doctors, but federal prosecutors "conceded [on Tuesday] they could not prove a criminal case and settled the matter with a series of civil fines."

Settlement Terms

Under the terms of the settlement, Moon and Realyvasquez each agreed to pay $1.4 million in fines. Kent Brusett, another surgeon in Realyvasquez's group, agreed to pay $250,000 over 10 years. Moon and Realyvasquez also agreed not to perform any procedures or surgeries on patients covered by Medicare, TRICARE or Medi-Cal, California's Medicaid program. In addition, Realyvasquez, Brusett and Ricardo Javier Moreno-Cabral agreed to ask their insurer to pay out $24 million to victims in the case, who have brought a civil lawsuit against the doctors in Shasta County Superior Court. The insurer will decide whether to pay the $24 million or contest the litigation, the San Francisco Chronicle reports. Tenet also agreed to pay an additional $5.5 million to settle claims against the company, U.S. Attorney McGregor Scott said. Tenet also will pay $1 million to California to settle a related state case filed by two of the whistleblowers in the federal investigation. Scott valued the overall settlement at $32.5 million. Tenet has admitted no wrongdoing in the case. The settlement does not resolve a civil lawsuit brought by 647 plaintiffs saying they underwent unnecessary heart surgeries. The first trial in the lawsuit is scheduled to begin on Tuesday.

Reaction

Assistant U.S. Attorney Michael Hirst said, "The evidence shows these doctors ran a high turnover, high volume surgery mill. While the evidence did not establish beyond a reasonable doubt that the doctors intended to perform unnecessary heart surgeries, the evidence was convincing that the doctors showed a reckless disregard for whether those surgeries were necessary or in their patients' best interests." Scott said, "The question at the end of the day becomes, 'Can you convict?' We came to the conclusion that we could not in good conscience go forward." Tenet said in a statement, "Tenet and its subsidiaries have expressly denied that Redding Medical Center submitted false claims to government health care programs for cardiac procedures at Redding." "This settles all significant litigation and investigations having to do with Redding," Tenet spokesperson Harry Anderson, said. Malcolm Segal, Realyvasquez's lawyer, said, "Today's outcome reflects what we have said all along and what renowned heart specialists across the country have testified to under oath — Dr. Realyvasquez provided only necessary surgical care to save and prolong the lives of his patients." Moon's attorneys issued a statement saying, "[W]e appreciate the objectivity of the U.S. attorney for coming to the conclusion that Dr. Moon has no criminal liability."

QUESTIONS

1. Did the government prove that Dr. Moon performed unnecessary surgeries?
2. Did Dr. Moon physically or financially harm patients?
3. Although Dr. Moon avoided criminal prosecution, should he be allowed to continue to practice medicine in California?

The Redding-related litigation proceeded under several statutes, including the False Claims Act, which forbids anyone from submitting a false bill (or claim) to the federal government (discussed in greater detail in Chapter 6). The law applies to any government contractor and has become a key component of the government's oversight of federal health care programs such as Medicare and Medicaid. Private health care providers, including hospitals, physicians, clinical laboratories, pharmacies, and nursing homes, contract with the government to provide care and treatment to individual citizens enrolled in those programs. Each time that a provider submits a bill to the government for services rendered to those patients, significant penalties may be imposed due to violation of the Act.

The False Claims Act also offers substantial rewards to successful whistleblowers, known as *qui tam* relators. *Qui tam* relators receive a share of any money the government recovers as a "bounty" for bringing the matter forward. Accordingly, strong incentives exist for these individuals, and their attorneys, to identify wrongdoers, but the whistleblowers may be wrongdoers as well. The following opinion did not address the merits of the allegations regarding Dr. Moon. Rather, the court was sorting out which whistleblowers qualified for rewards.

Campbell v. Redding Medical Center

421 F.3d 817 (9th Cir. 2005)

I. Factual and Procedural Background

This lawsuit arises out of a scheme involving the performance of thousands of unnecessary invasive cardiac procedures at the Redding Medical Center ("RMC") for the purposes of fraudulently billing Medicare. On October 30, 2002, Magistrate Judge Peter Nowinski issued a medical records search warrant authorizing the FBI to investigate RMC and the medical offices of the defendant doctors. The FBI executed the search warrant at RMC that same day. The U.S. Attorney's Office also released the Search Warrant Affidavit to the public and the press on October 30.

On November 5, 2002, John Corapi, a former RMC patient, and Joseph Zerga, his friend, filed a sealed qui tam complaint pursuant to the False Claims Act, 31 U.

S.C. §3729-3733 ("FCA"), and the California False Claims Act in the United States District Court for the Eastern District of California against RMC; Tenet Healthcare Corporation; Chae Moon, RMC's director of Cardiology; and Fidel Realyvasquez, the Chairman of RMC's Cardiac Surgery Program. The Corapi/Zerga complaint alleged that the defendants had submitted false claims to federal and state medical insurance programs and stated that they had direct and independent knowledge of the facts underlying the complaint and had brought that information to the attention of the United States government. The Corapi/Zerga suit was assigned to Judge William Shubb.

Three days later, on November 8, 2002, Patrick Campbell, a local physician, filed his own complaint under the FCA and the California statute in the same court against the same defendants. Campbell later amended his complaint to accuse the defendants of engaging in a scheme to defraud state- and federally-funded health care insurance programs, including Medicare, Medicaid, and MediCal, by submitting claims for cardiac care that the defendants knew to be medically unnecessary or inappropriate. The complaint alleged that the defendants had performed medically unjustified invasive diagnostic coronary artery imaging tests and then misrepresented the results of these tests to patients so that they would undergo invasive cardiac procedures. . . .

> Both cases were filed after the Oct. 30, 2002 press release.

The United States subsequently announced that it had settled its civil claims against RMC and Tenet Healthcare Corporation for payment of $54 million. . . .

III. Discussion

A. The False Claims Act

The False Claims Act imposes liability on those who submit a false or fraudulent claim for payment to the United States Government. The qui tam provisions of the False Claims Act encourage private parties who are aware of fraud against the government to sue for a civil penalty on behalf of the government. If the government intervenes and the action is successful, such parties will share in up to 25% of the government's recovery.

A private party, referred to as the "relator," may bring a civil action in the name of the government to recover damages against a person who has defrauded the government. . . .

Section 3730(e)(4)(A) states that "[n]o court shall have jurisdiction over an action under this section based upon the public disclosure of allegations or transactions . . . unless . . . the person bringing the action is an original source of the information." This subsection prevents opportunistic individuals from bringing qui tam actions — and sharing in the government's recovery — when they have done nothing to expose the allegations of fraud. For a court to have jurisdiction over a FCA case brought by a private party after the allegations have been made public, the relator must have been "an original source" of the allegations. An "original source" is someone who has "direct and independent knowledge of the information on which the allegations are based" and has voluntarily provided it to the government before filing suit.

. . . This is the first-to-file bar, which encourages prompt disclosure of fraud by creating a race to the courthouse among those with knowledge of fraud. We previously have held that §3730(b)(5) bars without exception a subsequent related action, even if the first action had been dismissed on the merits. The question before us is whether the first-to-file bar also precludes the filing of a subsequent related action when the first complaint is subject to dismissal solely on jurisdictional grounds — i.e., because the relator is not an original source of allegations that already have been publicly disclosed.

B. The First-to-File Bar

. . . .

2. Legislative History and Underlying Purpose of the False Claims Act

. . . The legislative history also does not resolve the dispute before us, although the congressional intent to encourage whistleblowers to come forward is clear. Because that example is not instructive with respect to the case before us, we consider the history of the FCA.

The FCA was originally enacted in 1863 to address fraud by defense contractors during the civil war. . . . Congress . . . amended the statute again in 1986. "[T]he purpose of the 1986 amendments was to repeal overly-restrictive court interpretations of the qui tam statute, which had prohibited not only suits by private citizens based on information obtained by the government, but also suits brought by those who had information independently of the government." The 1986 Amendments also sought to "encourage more private enforcement suits."

3. Section 3730(b)(5) Does Not Create an Absolute First-to-File Bar When the First Complaint Is Jurisdictionally Defective

Both the history of the FCA and the legislative history of the 1986 Amendments demonstrate the effort to achieve "the golden mean between adequate incentives for whistle-blowing insiders with genuinely valuable information and discouragement of opportunistic plaintiffs who have no significant information to contribute of their own."

Even where allegations have already been publicly disclosed, the original source requirement seeks to reward those who came to the government with information about fraud before the public disclosure.

The FCA reflects the strong congressional policy of encouraging whistleblowers to come forward by rewarding the first to do so. In amending the FCA, Congress sought to create incentives for insiders with information that would be particularly valuable to the government.

> The 1986 amendments succeeded in encouraging more private enforcement suits.

Construing §3730(b)(5) to create an absolute bar would permit opportunistic plaintiffs with no inside information to displace actual insiders with knowledge of the fraud. The government conceded at oral argument that under its interpretation of §3730(b)(5), a purely frivolous sham complaint filed in an instance where the allegations had been publicly disclosed would bar a subsequently filed action by an original source. This cannot be what Congress intended. We have previously noted that, "[i]n earlier versions of the FCA, the statute was abused by qui tam suits brought by private plaintiffs who had no independent knowledge of fraud." Although the addition of §3730(e)(4) would now prevent these plaintiffs from recovering in a public disclosure case, the simple fact that the sham complaint was filed before a meritorious complaint brought by a real original source would effectively prevent anyone from bringing a qui tam suit related to those claims. Such an interpretation would have the effect of reducing the number of qui tam suits in public disclosure cases, directly contravening the express intent of Congress. . . .

To summarize: . . . we hold that in a public disclosure case, the first-to-file rule of §3730(b)(5) bars only subsequent complaints filed after a complaint that fulfills the jurisdictional prerequisites of §3730(e)(4).

As noted previously, the district court assumed for purposes of the motion to dismiss that Corapi and Zerga were not original sources, ruling that all that matters was whether Corapi and Zerga were the first to file. As we have shown, that is not all that matters. Accordingly, we remand so that the district court can determine if Corapi and Zerga were, indeed, original sources. . . .

REVERSED AND REMANDED.

QUESTIONS

1. How large is the potential reward for the *qui tam* relators in this case?
2. Should a doctor who participates in unnecessary heart surgeries be permitted to act as a whistleblower under the False Claims Act? Do you think physicians would be motivated to be more or less attentive to their fiduciary responsibilities in light of your answer?

Many surgeries in the United States occur in ambulatory surgery centers (ASCs), which is an outpatient care setting. Surgeons who practice in ASCs frequently own part of the company, which enables the surgeon to make money from both their professional fees (the surgery itself) and also from the facility fee (the separate charge for the ASC's operating room, equipment, and the like). Researchers have found empirical evidence that physician ownership changes referral patterns and that physicians refer differently when the facility fee is at stake. Federal and state lawmakers have enacted many laws, including fraud and abuse laws, in response to such empirical data. As you read an example of the research supporting limitations on physician referral behavior, pay close attention to the numbers in the chart demonstrating changes in referral patterns depending on ownership, which includes bias (intentional or implicit) against certain types of patients.

Jon R. Gabel et al., Where Do I Send Thee? Does Physician-Ownership Affect Referral Patterns to Ambulatory Surgery Centers?

27 Health Aff. w165 (2008)

Background. Recent congressional unease about physician financial conflict of interest has focused on specialty hospitals, but historically, Congress has also turned its attention to physicians' ownership of laboratories, imaging centers, pharmacies, and other facilities. One concern is whether physician-ownership leads to unfair competitive advantages relative to nonphysician-owned facilities. At issue is whether physician-owners refer more-lucrative patients to their own facilities and less-lucrative patients to their competitors. A second issue is that when physicians receive payment for nonprofessional services, they have added incentives to induce demand for these services, without the constraint of their own time as they would when they provide services in their own offices. Proponents of physician ownership see direct ownership of facilities leading to more-efficient management and scheduling.

This paper examines the first of these concerns: physicians' referral patterns when physicians own health care facilities. Current law prohibits physicians from referring their patients to facilities that they own in ten different categories. One ... exception is ambulatory surgery centers (ASCs), where the rationale for the exemption is that ASCs deliver services at a lower cost than hospitals.

ASCs play an important and growing role in the U.S. health care delivery system. An estimated 3,800 ASCs were operational in 2003, with more than 40 percent of them owned by physicians and another 40 percent owned in joint physician-hospital or physician-corporate ventures. These ASCs competed with 3,998 hospital outpatient departments. From 2000 to 2006, the number of ASCs grew 55 percent, and total Medicare payments to ASCs rose 13.3 percent per year.

This paper explores how physician-ownership of ASCs affects referral patterns to ASCs. For a set of Pennsylvania physicians and ASCs, we analyzed whether physicians who are leading referrers to ASCs are more likely to send Medicaid and uninsured patients to hospital outpatient departments and refer privately insured patients to physician-owned facilities. We compared the referral patterns of "high referrers" to physician-owned ASCs, a proxy for physician-ownership, with patterns for physicians who are "high referrers" to non-physician-owned ASCs. . . .

Other patient characteristics. African Americans constituted 16 percent of the population in the study regions in 2003. Nearly 4 percent of patients cared for in

EXHIBIT 3
Distribution Among Payers, For Physicians Who Accounted For The Top 50 Percent Of Physician Referrals To Hospital Outpatient Departments, Not-For-Profit Ambulatory Surgery Centers (ASCs), For-Profit ASCs, And Physician-Owned ASCs In Pennsylvania, 2003

Category	Hospital outpatient department (%)	Not-for-profit ASC (%)	For-profit ASC (%)[a]	Physician-owned ASC (%)
Top 50% of referrals to physician-owned ASCs				
Total (n = 26,249)	8.7	0.0	0.2	91.3
Medicaid (n = 368)	44.6	0.0	0.0	55.4
Uninsured/self-pay (n = 447)	1.6	0.0	0.0	98.2
Commercial/Blue Cross (n = 17,321)	7.9	0.0	0.0	92.1
Medicare (n = 7,969)	9.1	0.0	0.0	90.8
Top 50% of referrals to hospital outpatient departments				
Total (n = 336,527)	95.5	1.7	0.5	2.0
Medicaid (n = 26,526)	97.6	1.0	0.3	0.2
Uninsured/self-pay (n = 12,026)	98.0	0.1	0.1	1.8
Commercial/Blue Cross (n = 191,789)	95.5	1.5	0.3	2.3
Medicare (n = 103,103)	94.5	2.6	0.9	1.9
Top 50% of physician referrals to not-for-profit ASCs				
Total (n = 17,712)	27.8	54.7	4.4	1.2
Medicaid (n = 1,578)	41.5	26.4	0.4	0.1
Uninsured/self-pay (n = 110)	44.6	23.6	5.5	10.0
Commercial/Blue Cross (n = 9,601)	23.8	56.9	1.3	1.6
Medicare (n = 6,293)	30.3	59.2	9.9	0.6
Top 50% of physician referrals to for-profit ASCs				
Total (n = 10,148)	20.0	5.7	73.9	0.3
Medicaid (n = 154)	38.3	0.0	61.0	0.7
Uninsured/self-pay (n = 19)	31.6	0.0	63.2	0.0
Commercial/Blue Cross (n = 6,151)	20.4	1.5	77.7	0.3
Medicare (n = 3,710)	18.8	13.1	67.7	0.3

Source: Pennsylvania Health Cost Containment Commission, Outpatient File, 2003.
[a] ASCs owned by for-profit corporations with no identified physician ownership.

physician-owned ASCs were African Americans, compared to 13 percent in hospital outpatient departments. . . .

. . . .

Discussion

Role of patients' payer status. This study analyzed more than one million discharge abstracts from hospital outpatient departments and ASCs located in the Pittsburgh and Philadelphia metropolitan areas. Our most important findings pertain to physicians who referred many patients to physician-owned ASCs. These physicians referred very few Medicaid patients at all — about 1.2 percent of their total referrals. However, when these physicians referred a Medicaid patient, that patient was referred to the physician-owned ASC about 55 percent of the time and to the outpatient department about 45 percent of the time. In contrast, this same set of physicians referred other patients — commercial/Blue Cross, Medicare, and self-pay/indigent — 90-98 percent of the time to the physician-owned facility. . . .

QUESTIONS

1. Why are the racial characteristics of the physician-owned ASC patients different?
2. Does the study suggest that Congress should prohibit physician ownership of ASCs?
3. Are patients in danger if they are referred to physician-owned facilities? If not, what is the concern?
4. Would a requirement that physicians disclose to their patients their ownership interests in the facilities to which they refer address these concerns?

3. THE MODERN ADMINISTRATIVE HEALTH CARE STATE

As this chapter has already demonstrated, health care law does not evolve solely through judge-made common law, the approach to legal study which traditionally dominates the first-year curriculum. Rather, much of the law exists in a complex and iterative process including legislative debate and enactment, administrative rulemaking and guidance, and sometimes but not always judicial or administrative adjudication.

In the following pages, you will follow the saga of the so-called "contraceptive coverage mandate" regulations. Administrative law develops over time and, as here, may involve complex interplay of the executive, legislative, and judicial branches. We will return to employer-sponsored health insurance and coverage mandates in more detail in Chapter 3. For now, the example is here to expose you to the complexity of the modern health care administrative state. While the particular legal principles discussed below are important, it is also vital to see how the larger machine operates.

The ACA was the most comprehensive reform of U.S. health insurance in a generation. Passage of the ACA triggered many regulatory processes but also political reactions. One example is the federal law that, effective 2014, required most health insurance plans to cover certain preventive health care services without any cost (no copayments or deductibles) to the insured, other than their monthly premiums. Congress did not specify which preventive services must be covered but rather delegated to executive branch agencies the task of fleshing out the details of the new statutory requirement. One of these delegated questions involved whether to require coverage for contraception. After an expert-driven administrative rulemaking process, all forms of contraception approved by the federal Food and Drug Administration (FDA) for women were included, including birth control pills, tubal ligation (which involves a medical device), and emergency contraception.

Some churches and other religious organizations objected to the executive branch's inclusion of contraceptive coverage within the ACA's preventive care coverage requirements. The ACA expressly exempted churches and houses of worship from the requirement to cover contraceptive methods and counseling for their employees. But the rules were not as clear for religiously affiliated employers such as hospitals and universities with religious missions, including Catholic hospitals and universities. In response, federal agencies promulgated rules allowing an expanded group of "religious organizations" to refuse to cover contraceptives by submitting a form to the Department of Health and Human Services (HHS). The Preamble to that February 15, 2012, rule explains the multistep regulatory process.

Group Health Plans and Health Insurance Issuers Relating to Coverage of Preventive Services Under the Patient Protection and Affordable Care Act

T.D. 9578, 77 Fed. Reg. 8725-01 (Feb. 15, 2012)

RULES and REGULATIONS
DEPARTMENT OF THE TREASURY
DEPARTMENT OF LABOR
DEPARTMENT OF HEALTH AND HUMAN SERVICES

I. Background

. . . Section 2713 of the PHS Act, as added by the Affordable Care Act and incorporated into ERISA and the Code, requires that non-grandfathered group health plans and health insurance issuers offering group or individual health insurance coverage provide benefits for certain preventive health services without the imposition of cost sharing. These preventive health services include, with respect to women, preventive care and screening provided for in the comprehensive guidelines supported by the Health Resources and Services Administration (HRSA) that were issued on August 1, 2011 (HRSA Guidelines). As relevant here, the HRSA Guidelines require coverage, without cost sharing, for "[a]ll Food and Drug Administration [(FDA)] approved contraceptive methods, sterilization procedures, and patient education and counseling for all women with reproductive capacity," as prescribed by a provider. Except as discussed below, non-grandfathered group health plans and health insurance issuers are required to provide coverage consistent with the HRSA Guidelines, without cost sharing, in plan years (or, in the individual market, policy years) beginning on or after August 1, 2012. These guidelines were based on recommendations of the independent Institute of Medicine, which undertook a review of the evidence on women's preventive services.

The Departments of Health and Human Services, Labor, and the Treasury (the Departments) published interim final regulations implementing PHS Act section

2713 on July 19, 2010 (75 FR 41726). In the preamble to the interim final regulations, the Departments explained that HRSA was developing guidelines related to preventive care and screening for women that would be covered without cost sharing pursuant to PHS Act section 2713(a)(4), and that these guidelines were expected to be issued no later than August 1, 2011. Although comments on the anticipated guidelines were not requested in the interim final regulations, the Departments received considerable feedback regarding which preventive services for women should be covered without cost sharing. Some commenters, including some religiously-affiliated employers, recommended that these guidelines include contraceptive services among the recommended women's preventive services and that the attendant coverage requirement apply to all group health plans and health insurance issuers. Other commenters, however, recommended that group health plans sponsored by religiously-affiliated employers be allowed to exclude contraceptive services from coverage under their plans if the employers deem such services contrary to their religious tenets, noting that some group health plans sponsored by organizations with a religious objection to contraceptives currently contain such exclusions for that reason.

In response to these comments, the Departments amended the interim final regulations to provide HRSA with discretion to establish an exemption for group health plans established or maintained by certain religious employers (and any group health insurance coverage provided in connection with such plans) with respect to any requirement to cover contraceptive services that they would otherwise be required to cover without cost sharing consistent with the HRSA Guidelines. The amended interim final regulations were issued and effective on August 1, 2011. The amended interim final regulations specified that, for purposes of this exemption, a religious employer is one that: (1) Has the inculcation of religious values as its purpose; (2) primarily employs persons who share its religious tenets; (3) primarily serves persons who share its religious tenets; and (4) is a non-profit organization described in section 6033(a)(1) and section 6033 (a)(3)(A)(i) or (iii) of the Code. Section 6033(a)(3)(A)(i) and (iii) of the Code refers to churches, their integrated auxiliaries, and conventions or associations of churches, as well as to the exclusively religious activities of any religious order. In the HRSA Guidelines, HRSA exercised its discretion under the amended interim final regulations such that group health plans established and maintained by these religious employers (and any group health insurance coverage provided in connection with such plans) are not required to cover contraceptive services.

> To assist in the regulatory process, the agencies commissioned a report from the Institute of Medicine (now the National Academy of Medicine), an independent, nonprofit, private association with significant influence on health care policy.

In the preamble to the amended interim final regulations, the Departments explained that it was appropriate that HRSA take into account the religious beliefs of certain religious employers where coverage of contraceptive services is concerned. The Departments noted that a religious exemption is consistent with the policies in some States that currently both require contraceptive services coverage under State law and provide for some type of religious exemption from their contraceptive services coverage requirement. Comments were requested on the amended interim final regulations, specifically with respect to the definition of religious employer, as well as alternative definitions.

II. Overview of the Public Comments on the Amended Interim Final Regulations

The Departments received over 200,000 responses to the request for comments on the amended interim final regulations. . . .

Some commenters recommended that the exemption for the group health plans of a limited group of religious organizations as formulated in the amended interim final regulations be maintained. Other commenters urged that the definition of religious employer be broadened so that more sponsors of group health plans would qualify for the exemption. Others urged that the exemption be rescinded in its entirety. The Departments summarize below the major issues raised in the comments that were received.

> Public comments are an important aspect of rulemaking under the Administrative Procedure Act. The entire process is made transparent by being posted at http://www.regulations.gov. Anyone can comment on proposed regulations.

Some commenters supported the inclusion of contraceptive services in the HRSA Guidelines and urged that the religious employer exemption be rescinded in its entirety due to the importance of extending these benefits to as many women as possible. For example, one provider association commented that all group health plans and group health insurance issuers should offer the same benefits to plan participants, without a religious exemption for some plans, and that religious beliefs are more appropriately taken into account by individuals when making personal health care decisions. Others urged that the exemption be eliminated because making contraceptive services available to all women would satisfy a basic health care need and would significantly reduce long-term health care costs associated with unplanned pregnancies. . . .

Commenters opposing any exemption stated that, if the exemption were to be retained, clear notice should be provided to the affected plan participants that their group health plans do not include benefits for contraceptive services. In addition, they urged the Departments to monitor plans to ensure that the exemption is not claimed more broadly than permitted.

On the other hand, a number of comments asserted that the religious employer exemption is too narrow. These commenters included some religiously-affiliated educational institutions, health care organizations, and charities. Some of these commenters expressed concern that the exemption for religious employers will not allow them to continue their current exclusion of contraceptive services from coverage under their group health plans. Others expressed concerns about paying for such services and stated that doing so would be contrary to their religious beliefs.

Commenters also claimed that Federal laws, including the Affordable Care Act, have provided for conscience clauses and religious exemptions broader than that provided for in the amended interim final regulations. Some commenters asserted that the narrower scope of the exemption raises concerns under the First Amendment and the Religious Freedom Restoration Act.

Other commenters, however, disputed claims that the contraceptive coverage requirement infringes on rights protected by the First Amendment or the Religious Freedom Restoration Act. These commenters noted that the requirement is neutral and generally applicable. They also explained that the requirement does not substantially burden religious exercise and, in any event, serves compelling governmental interests and is the least restrictive means to achieve those interests.

Some religiously-affiliated employers warned that, if the definition of religious employer is not broadened, they could cease to offer health coverage to their employees in order to avoid having to offer coverage to which they object on religious grounds.

Commenters supporting a broadening of the definition of religious employer proposed a number of options, generally intended to expand the scope of the exemption to include religiously-affiliated educational institutions, health care organizations, and charities. In some instances, in place of the definition that was adopted in the amended interim final regulations, commenters suggested other State insurance law definitions of religious employer. In other instances, commenters referenced alternative standards, such as tying the exemption to the definition of "church plan" under section 414(e) of the Code or to status as a nonprofit organization under section 501(c)(3) of the Code.

III. Overview of the Final Regulations

In response to these comments, the Departments carefully considered whether to eliminate the religious employer exemption or to adopt an alternative definition of religious employer, including whether the exemption should be extended to a broader set of religiously-affiliated sponsors of group health plans and group health insurance coverage. For the reasons discussed below, the Departments are adopting the definition in the amended interim final regulations for purposes of these final regulations while also creating a temporary enforcement safe harbor, discussed below. During the temporary enforcement safe harbor, the Departments plan to develop and propose changes to these final regulations that would meet two goals — providing contraceptive coverage without cost-sharing to individuals who want it and accommodating non-exempted, non-profit organizations' religious objections to covering contraceptive services as also discussed below.

PHS Act section 2713 reflects a determination by Congress that coverage of recommended preventive services by non-grandfathered group health plans and health insurance issuers without cost sharing is necessary to achieve basic health care coverage for more Americans. Individuals are more likely to use preventive services if they do not have to satisfy cost sharing requirements (such as a copayment, coinsurance, or a deductible). Use of preventive services results in a healthier population and reduces health care costs by helping individuals avoid preventable conditions and receive treatment earlier. Further, Congress, by amending the Affordable Care Act during the Senate debate to ensure that recommended preventive services for women are covered adequately by non-grandfathered group health plans and group health insurance coverage, recognized that women have unique health care needs and burdens. Such needs include contraceptive services.

> Because nearly *half* of all pregnancies in the United States are unintended, the findings about the need for contraception and planning for prenatal care were especially important.

As documented in a report of the Institute of Medicine, "Clinical Preventive Services for Women, Closing the Gaps," women experiencing an unintended pregnancy may not immediately be aware that they are pregnant, and thus delay prenatal care. They also may not be as motivated to discontinue behaviors that pose pregnancy-related risks (e.g., smoking, consumption of alcohol). Studies show a greater risk of preterm birth and low birth weight among unintended pregnancies compared with pregnancies that were planned. Contraceptives also have medical benefits for women who are contraindicated for pregnancy, and there are demonstrated preventive health benefits from contraceptives relating to conditions other than pregnancy (e.g., treatment of menstrual disorders, acne, and pelvic pain).

In addition, there are significant cost savings to employers from the coverage of contraceptives. A 2000 study estimated that it would cost employers 15 to 17 percent more not to provide contraceptive coverage in employee health plans than to provide such coverage, after accounting for both the direct medical costs of pregnancy and the indirect costs such as employee absence and reduced productivity. In fact, when contraceptive coverage was added to the Federal Employees Health Benefits Program, premiums did not increase because there was no resulting health care cost increase. Further, the cost savings of covering contraceptive services have already been recognized by States and also within the health insurance industry. Twenty-eight States now have laws requiring health insurance issuers to cover contraceptives. A 2002 study found that more than 89 percent of insured plans cover contraceptives. A 2010 survey of employers revealed that 85 percent of large employers and 62 percent of small employers offered coverage of FDA-approved contraceptives. . . .

Nothing in these final regulations precludes employers or others from expressing their opposition, if any, to the use of contraceptives, requires anyone to use contraceptives, or requires health care providers to prescribe contraceptives if doing so is against their religious beliefs. These final regulations do not undermine the important protections that exist under conscience clauses and other religious exemptions in other areas of Federal law. Conscience protections will continue to be respected and strongly enforced.

This approach is consistent with the First Amendment and Religious Freedom Restoration Act. The Supreme Court has held that the First Amendment right to free exercise of religion is not violated by a law that is not specifically targeted at religiously motivated conduct and that applies equally to conduct without regard to whether it is religiously motivated — a so-called neutral law of general applicability. The contraceptive coverage requirement is generally applicable and designed to serve the compelling public health and gender equity goals described above, and is in no way specially targeted at religion or religious practices. Likewise, this approach complies with the Religious Freedom Restoration Act, which generally requires a federal law to not substantially burden religious exercise, or, if it does substantially burden religious exercise, to be the least restrictive means to further a compelling government interest. . . .

QUESTIONS

1. Why did the regulations narrowly define the scope of religious employers entitled to the exemption?
2. Does the information regarding cost savings appear to fit within the charge given to the administrative agencies?
3. How does the rule support the government's interest in requiring coverage of contraception as preventive care?

Despite federal agencies' conclusion that the final regulations balanced religious freedom and congressional intent to maximize access to core preventive health services, a group of small for-profit businesses owned by religious families challenged the rule, which culminated in the following Supreme Court case.

Burwell v. Hobby Lobby Stores, Inc.

134 S. Ct. 2751 (2014)

Justice ALITO delivered the opinion of the Court.

We must decide in these cases whether the Religious Freedom Restoration Act of 1993 (RFRA), 42 U.S.C. §2000bb et seq., permits the United States Department of Health and Human Services (HHS) to demand that three closely held corporations provide health-insurance coverage for methods of contraception that violate the sincerely held religious beliefs of the companies' owners. We hold that the regulations that impose this obligation violate RFRA, which prohibits the Federal Government from taking any action that substantially burdens the exercise of religion unless that action constitutes the least restrictive means of serving a compelling government interest.

In holding that the HHS mandate is unlawful, we reject HHS's argument that the owners of the companies forfeited all RFRA protection when they decided to organize their businesses as corporations rather than sole proprietorships or general partnerships. The plain terms of RFRA make it perfectly clear that Congress did not discriminate in this way against men and women who wish to run their businesses as for-profit corporations in the manner required by their religious beliefs.

Since RFRA applies in these cases, we must decide whether the challenged HHS regulations substantially burden the exercise of religion, and we hold that they do. The owners of the businesses have religious objections to abortion, and according to their religious beliefs the four contraceptive methods at issue are abortifacients. If the owners comply with the HHS mandate, they believe they will be facilitating abortions, and if they do not comply, they will pay a very heavy price—as much as $1.3 million per day, or about $475 million per year, in the case of one of the companies. If these consequences do not amount to a substantial burden, it is hard to see what would.

Under RFRA, a Government action that imposes a substantial burden on religious exercise must serve a compelling government interest, and we assume that the HHS regulations satisfy this requirement. But in order for the HHS mandate to be sustained, it must also constitute the least restrictive means of serving that interest, and the mandate plainly fails that test. There are other ways in which Congress or HHS could equally ensure that every woman has cost-free access to the particular contraceptives at issue here and, indeed, to all FDA-approved contraceptives.

In fact, HHS has already devised and implemented a system that seeks to respect the religious liberty of religious nonprofit corporations while ensuring that the employees of these entities have precisely the same access to all FDA-approved contraceptives as employees of companies whose owners have no religious objections to providing such coverage. The employees of these religious nonprofit corporations still have access to insurance coverage without cost sharing for all FDA-approved contraceptives; and according to HHS, this system imposes no net economic burden on the insurance companies that are required to provide or secure the coverage.

Although HHS has made this system available to religious nonprofits that have religious objections to the contraceptive mandate, HHS has provided no reason why the same system cannot be made available when the owners of for-profit corporations have similar religious objections. We therefore conclude that this system constitutes an alternative that achieves all of the Government's aims while providing greater respect for religious liberty. And under RFRA, that conclusion means that enforcement of the HHS contraceptive mandate against the objecting parties in these cases is unlawful.

As this description of our reasoning shows, our holding is very specific. We do not hold, as the principal dissent alleges, that for-profit corporations and other commercial enterprises can "opt out of any law (saving only tax laws) they judge incompatible with their sincerely held religious beliefs." Nor do we hold, as the dissent implies, that such corporations have free rein to take steps that impose "disadvantages . . . on others" or that require "the general public [to] pick up the tab." And we certainly do not hold or suggest that "RFRA demands accommodation of a for-profit corporation's religious beliefs no matter the impact that accommodation may have on . . . thousands of women employed by Hobby Lobby." The effect of the HHS-created accommodation on the women employed by Hobby Lobby and the other companies involved in these cases would be precisely zero. Under that accommodation, these women would still be entitled to all FDA-approved contraceptives without cost sharing. . . .

B

At issue in these cases are HHS regulations promulgated under the Patient Protection and Affordable Care Act of 2010 (ACA). ACA generally requires employers with 50 or more full-time employees to offer "a group health plan or group health insurance coverage" that provides "minimum essential coverage." Any covered employer that does not provide such coverage must pay a substantial price. Specifically, if a covered employer provides group health insurance but its plan fails to comply with ACA's group-health-plan requirements, the employer may be required to pay $100 per day for each affected "individual." And if the employer decides to stop providing health insurance altogether and at least one full-time employee enrolls in a health plan and qualifies for a subsidy on one of the government-run ACA exchanges, the employer must pay $2,000 per year for each of its full-time employees.

> This is also known as the employer "pay or play" law, or "free rider" penalty, with both terms reflecting the fact that the ACA does not outright require employers to offer health insurance to their workers.

Unless an exception applies, ACA requires an employer's group health plan or group-health-insurance coverage to furnish "preventive care and screenings" for women without "any cost sharing requirements." Congress itself, however, did not specify what types of preventive care must be covered. Instead, Congress authorized the Health Resources and Services Administration (HRSA), a component of HHS, to make that important and sensitive decision. Ibid. The HRSA in turn consulted the Institute of Medicine, a nonprofit group of volunteer advisers, in determining which preventive services to require.

In August 2011, based on the Institute's recommendations, the HRSA promulgated the Women's Preventive Services Guidelines. The Guidelines provide that nonexempt employers are generally required to provide "coverage, without cost sharing" for "[a]ll Food and Drug Administration [(FDA)] approved contraceptive methods, sterilization procedures, and patient education and counseling." Although many of the required, FDA-approved methods of contraception work by preventing the fertilization of an egg, four of those methods (those specifically at issue in these cases) may have the effect of preventing an already fertilized egg from developing any further by inhibiting its attachment to the uterus.

HHS also authorized the HRSA to establish exemptions from the contraceptive mandate for "religious employers." That category encompasses "churches, their integrated auxiliaries, and conventions or associations of churches," as well as "the exclusively religious activities of any religious order." In its Guidelines, HRSA exempted these organizations from the requirement to cover contraceptive services.

In addition, HHS has effectively exempted certain religious nonprofit organizations, described under HHS regulations as "eligible organizations," from the contraceptive mandate. An "eligible organization" means a nonprofit organization that "holds itself out as a religious organization" and "opposes providing coverage for some or all of any contraceptive services required to be covered . . . on account of religious objections." To qualify for this accommodation, an employer must certify that it is such an organization. When a group-health-insurance issuer receives notice that one of its clients has invoked this provision, the issuer must then exclude contraceptive coverage from the employer's plan and provide separate payments for contraceptive services for plan participants without imposing any cost-sharing requirements on the eligible organization, its insurance plan, or its employee beneficiaries. Although this procedure requires the issuer to bear the cost of these services, HHS has determined that this obligation will not impose any net expense on issuers because its cost will be less than or equal to the cost savings resulting from the services.

. . . .

[Justice Alito concluded that secular for-profit corporations had standing to bring claims as a "person" under RFRA and that the HHS contraceptive mandate substantially burdens the exercise of religion for the plaintiffs. — EDS.]

V

Since the HHS contraceptive mandate imposes a substantial burden on the exercise of religion, we must move on and decide whether HHS has shown that the mandate both "(1) is in furtherance of a compelling governmental interest; and (2) is the least restrictive means of furthering that compelling governmental interest."

A

HHS asserts that the contraceptive mandate serves a variety of important interests, but many of these are couched in very broad terms, such as promoting "public health" and "gender equality." RFRA, however, contemplates a "more focused" inquiry: It "requires the Government to demonstrate that the compelling interest test is satisfied through application of the challenged law 'to the person' — the particular claimant whose sincere exercise of religion is being substantially burdened." . . .

We find it unnecessary to adjudicate this issue. We will assume that the interest in guaranteeing cost-free access to the four challenged contraceptive methods is compelling within the meaning of RFRA, and we will proceed to consider the final prong of the RFRA test, i.e., whether HHS has shown that the

This provision places the responsibility on the health plan, not the eligible employer, which could include a much broader range of non-church religious organizations. This provision was added in response to comments from the public.

contraceptive mandate is "the least restrictive means of furthering that compelling governmental interest."

B

The least-restrictive-means standard is exceptionally demanding, and it is not satisfied here. HHS has not shown that it lacks other means of achieving its desired goal without imposing a substantial burden on the exercise of religion by the objecting parties in these cases.

> The Court's acknowledgment that covering contraception is a compelling governmental interest was an important concession to a key goal of the ACA: getting more people more preventive care to improve the collective health of Americans. This policy goal arguably motivated the administrative agencies' decision to exempt as few employers as possible.

The most straightforward way of doing this would be for the Government to assume the cost of providing the four contraceptives at issue to any women who are unable to obtain them under their health-insurance policies due to their employers' religious objections. This would certainly be less restrictive of the plaintiffs' religious liberty, and HHS has not shown that this is not a viable alternative. HHS has not provided any estimate of the average cost per employee of providing access to these contraceptives, two of which, according to the FDA, are designed primarily for emergency use. Nor has HHS provided any statistics regarding the number of employees who might be affected because they work for corporations like Hobby Lobby, Conestoga, and Mardel. Nor has HHS told us that it is unable to provide such statistics. . . .

. . . HHS's view that RFRA can never require the Government to spend even a small amount reflects a judgment about the importance of religious liberty that was not shared by the Congress that enacted that law.

. . . HHS itself has demonstrated that it has at its disposal an approach that is less restrictive than requiring employers to fund contraceptive methods that violate their religious beliefs. As we explained above, HHS has already established an accommodation for nonprofit organizations with religious objections. Under that accommodation, the organization can self-certify that it opposes providing coverage for particular contraceptive services. If the organization makes such a certification, the organization's insurance issuer or third-party administrator must "[e]xpressly exclude contraceptive coverage from the group health insurance coverage provided in connection with the group health plan" and "[p]rovide separate payments for any contraceptive services required to be covered" without imposing "any cost-sharing requirements . . . on the eligible organization, the group health plan, or plan participants or beneficiaries."

> The Supreme Court refused to decide further questions posed by litigants in *Zubik v. Burwell*, instead asking lower federal courts to help negotiate a solution for religious entities dissatisfied with the existing exemptions.

We do not decide today whether an approach of this type complies with RFRA for purposes of all religious claims. At a minimum, however, it does not impinge on the plaintiffs' religious belief that providing insurance coverage for the contraceptives at issue here violates their religion, and it serves HHS's stated interests equally well. . . .

The contraceptive mandate, as applied to closely held corporations, violates RFRA. Our decision on that statutory question makes it unnecessary to reach the First Amendment claim. . . .

Justice GINSBURG, with whom Justice SOTOMAYOR joins, and with whom Justice BREYER and Justice KAGAN join as to all but Part III-C-1, dissenting.

In a decision of startling breadth, the Court holds that commercial enterprises, including corporations, along with partnerships and sole proprietorships, can opt out of any law (saving only tax laws) they judge incompatible with their sincerely held religious beliefs. Compelling governmental interests in uniform compliance with the law, and disadvantages that religion-based opt-outs impose on others, hold no sway, the Court decides, at least when there is a "less restrictive alternative." And such an alternative, the Court suggests, there always will be whenever, in lieu of tolling an enterprise claiming a religion-based exemption, the government, i.e., the general public, can pick up the tab.

The Court does not pretend that the First Amendment's Free Exercise Clause demands religion-based accommodations so extreme, for our decisions leave no doubt on that score. Instead, the Court holds that Congress, in the Religious Freedom Restoration Act of 1993 (RFRA), dictated the extraordinary religion-based exemptions today's decision endorses. In the Court's view, RFRA demands accommodation of a for-profit corporation's religious beliefs no matter the impact that accommodation may have on third parties who do not share the corporation owners' religious faith — in these cases, thousands of women employed by Hobby Lobby and Conestoga or dependents of persons those corporations employ. Persuaded that Congress enacted RFRA to serve a far less radical purpose, and mindful of the havoc the Court's judgment can introduce, I dissent.

I

"The ability of women to participate equally in the economic and social life of the Nation has been facilitated by their ability to control their reproductive lives." Congress acted on that understanding when, as part of a nationwide insurance program intended to be comprehensive, it called for coverage of preventive care responsive to women's needs. Carrying out Congress' direction, the Department of Health and Human Services (HHS), in consultation with public health experts, promulgated regulations requiring group health plans to cover all forms of contraception approved by the Food and Drug Administration (FDA). The genesis of this coverage should enlighten the Court's resolution of these cases.

A

The Affordable Care Act (ACA), in its initial form, specified three categories of preventive care that health plans must cover at no added cost to the plan participant or beneficiary. Particular services were to be recommended by the U.S. Preventive Services Task Force, an independent panel of experts. The scheme had a large gap, however; it left out preventive services that "many women's health advocates and medical professionals believe are critically important." To correct this oversight, Senator Barbara Mikulski introduced the Women's Health Amendment, which added to the ACA's minimum coverage requirements a new category of preventive services specific to women's health.

> Justice Ginsburg reviewed the administrative process leading up to the challenged regulation; many of these facts were recited in the Preamble to the February 2012 Final Regulation.

Women paid significantly more than men for preventive care, the amendment's proponents noted; in fact, cost barriers operated to block many women from obtaining needed care at all. . . .

As altered by the Women's Health Amendment's passage, the ACA requires new insurance plans to include coverage without cost sharing of "such additional preventive care and screenings . . . as provided for in comprehensive guidelines supported by the Health Resources and Services Administration [(HRSA)]," a unit of HHS. Thus charged, the HRSA developed recommendations in consultation with the Institute of Medicine (IOM). The IOM convened a group of independent experts, including "specialists in disease prevention [and] women's health"; those experts prepared a report evaluating the efficacy of a number of preventive services. Consistent with the findings of "[n]umerous health professional associations" and other organizations, the IOM experts determined that preventive coverage should include the "full range" of FDA-approved contraceptive methods.

In making that recommendation, the IOM's report expressed concerns similar to those voiced by congressional proponents of the Women's Health Amendment. The report noted the disproportionate burden women carried for comprehensive health services and the adverse health consequences of excluding contraception from preventive care available to employees without cost sharing. . . .

In line with the IOM's suggestions, the HRSA adopted guidelines recommending coverage of "[a]ll [FDA-]approved contraceptive methods, sterilization procedures, and patient education and counseling for all women with reproductive capacity." Thereafter, HHS, the Department of Labor, and the Department of Treasury promulgated regulations requiring group health plans to include coverage of the contraceptive services recommended in the HRSA guidelines, subject to certain exceptions, described infra. This opinion refers to these regulations as the contraceptive coverage requirement.

B

While the Women's Health Amendment succeeded, a countermove proved unavailing. The Senate voted down the so-called "conscience amendment," which would have enabled any employer or insurance provider to deny coverage based on its asserted "religious beliefs or moral convictions." That amendment, Senator Mikulski observed, would have "pu[t] the personal opinion of employers and insurers over the practice of medicine." Rejecting the "conscience amendment," Congress left health care decisions — including the choice among contraceptive methods — in the hands of women, with the aid of their health care providers. . . .

> Congress expressly rejected the religious exemption that the plaintiffs asked the Court to recognize.

The exemption sought by Hobby Lobby and Conestoga would override significant interests of the corporations' employees and covered dependents. It would deny legions of women who do not hold their employers' beliefs access to contraceptive coverage that the ACA would otherwise secure. . . .

4

After assuming the existence of compelling government interests, the Court holds that the contraceptive coverage requirement fails to satisfy RFRA's least restrictive means test. But the Government has shown that there is no less restrictive, equally effective means that would both (1) satisfy the challengers' religious objections to providing insurance coverage for certain contraceptives (which they believe cause abortions); and (2) carry out the objective of the ACA's contraceptive coverage requirement, to ensure that women employees receive, at no cost to them, the preventive care needed to safeguard their health and well being. A "least restrictive means" cannot require employees to relinquish benefits accorded them by federal law in order to ensure that their commercial employers can adhere unreservedly to their religious tenets. . . .

In sum, in view of what Congress sought to accomplish, i.e., comprehensive preventive care for women furnished through employer-based health plans, none of the proffered alternatives would satisfactorily serve the compelling interests to which Congress responded. . . .

For the reasons stated, I would reverse the judgment of the Court of Appeals for the Tenth Circuit and affirm the judgment of the Court of Appeals for the Third Circuit.

QUESTIONS

1. After *Hobby Lobby*, a business like the plaintiffs' might exclude insurance coverage for AIDS, substance use disorder, or smoking-related illnesses because they reflect lifestyles with which the company does not want to be associated. Could this position be protected under RFRA with the right set of facts?

2. What was the impact of the administrative law notice and comment process on the ultimate outcome of the contraception coverage requirement?

The *Hobby Lobby* decision effectively invalidated the narrow scope of eligible religious organizations under the July 2, 2013, final regulations, 78 Fed. Reg. 39,870. One month after the decision, affected agencies issued a notice of proposed rulemaking (NPRM) to amend the regulations. One issue was how to describe which for-profit companies were eligible for the new religious exemption. The agencies received and considered 75,000 public comments. *See* Coverage of Certain Preventive Services Under the Affordable Care Act, 80 Fed. Reg. 41,318 (July 14, 2015). One section of those regulations defined the types of organizations eligible for the *Hobby Lobby* exception, including for-profit closely held companies like Hobby Lobby. These regulations were again amended early in the Trump Administration, with a pair of Interim Final Rules issued October 6, 2017. The new regulations expanded the scope of the *Hobby Lobby* exception to additional religious and for-profit employers, including companies that are not closely held. Indeed, the regulations contemplate even publicly traded companies availing themselves of the *Hobby Lobby* exception, as a "person" entitled to protection of religious beliefs under RFRA. A coalition of state attorneys general challenged the regulations in federal court, and that case is still pending as of this writing. Commonwealth of Pennsylvania v. Trump et al., Civil Action No. 17-4540 (E.D. Pa., filed Oct. 11, 2017).

C. THE UNIQUE NATURE OF HEALTH CARE AND HEALTH CARE MARKETS

As the foregoing materials have demonstrated, health care law requires familiarity with a number of different related fields and subspecialties of law, including medicine, insurance, public health, constitutional law, and business law. Another, perhaps unfamiliar, domain for law students is health care economics. As the first section of this chapter noted, health care is big business in the United States. But

the key insight of health care economics is that health care does not operate according to standard microeconomic principles but rather is marred by a number of
market imperfections, many of which have led to rulemaking designed to level
the playing field between patients and health care providers and among health
care providers with differing levels of power.

The foundational text of health care economics is Kenneth Arrow's 1963 article,
which was perhaps the clearest description of how health care differs from other
goods and services. Arrow contended that health care faced difficult problems with
"information asymmetry," risk bearing, and trust. His observations have led to various
"social adjustments," including special legal rules for public provision or coverage of
health care. Arrow identified the issues that made health care economics a distinct
field, but to some degree he is a founder of health care law as well, given that his
observations have driven a great deal of health care policy making. As you read the
following excerpt, consider to what degree his description of medicine, which was
written in a very different medical environment, is still pertinent today.

Kenneth J. Arrow, Uncertainty and the Welfare Economics of Medical Care

53 Am. Econ. Rev. 941 (1963)

This section will list selectively some characteristics of medical care which distinguish it from the usual commodity of economics textbooks. The list is not exhaustive, and it is not claimed that the characteristics listed are individually unique to this
market. But, taken together, they do establish a special place for medical care in
economic analysis.

The Nature of Demand

The most obvious distinguishing characteristics of an individual's demand for
medical services is that it is not steady in origin as, for example, for food or clothing,
but irregular and unpredictable. Medical services, apart from preventive services,
afford satisfaction only in the event of illness, a departure from the normal state
of affairs. It is hard, indeed, to think of another commodity of significance in the
average budget of which this is true. . . .

In addition, the demand for medical services is associated, with a considerable
probability, with an assault on personal integrity. There is some risk of death and a
more considerable risk of impairment of full functioning. In particular, there is a major
potential for loss or reduction of earning ability. The risks are not by themselves
unique; food is also a necessity, but avoidance of deprivation of food can be guaranteed
with sufficient income, where the same cannot be said of avoidance of illness. Illness
is, thus, not only risky but a costly risk in itself, apart from the cost of medical care.

Expected Behavior of the Physician

It is clear from everyday observation that the behavior expected of sellers of
medical care is different from that of business [firms] in general. These expectations
are relevant because medical care belongs to the category of commodities for which
the product and the activity of production are identical. In all such cases, the customer cannot test the product before consuming it, and there is an element of trust
in the relation. But the ethically understood restrictions on the activities of a

physician are much more severe than on those of, say, a barber. His behavior is supposed to be governed by a concern for the customer's welfare which would not be expected of a sales [person]. In Talcott Parsons's terms, there is a "collectivity-orientation," which distinguishes medicine and other professions from business, where self-interest on the part of participants is the accepted norm.

A few illustrations will indicate the degree of difference between the behavior expected of physicians and that expected of the typical business [firm]. (1) Advertising and overt price competition are virtually eliminated among physicians. (2) Advice given by physicians as to further treatment by himself or others is supposed to be completely divorced from self-interest. (3) It is at least claimed that treatment is dictated by the objective needs of the case and not limited by financial considerations. While the ethical compulsion is surely not as absolute in fact as it is in theory, we can hardly suppose that it has no influence over resource allocation in this area. Charity treatment in one form or another does exist because of this tradition about human rights to adequate medical care. (4) The physician is relied on as an expert in certifying to the existence of illnesses and injuries for various legal and other purposes. It is socially expected that his concern for the correct conveying of information will, when appropriate, outweigh his desire to please his customers. . . .

> These four conditions are still applicable. While advertising is more common today in health care, real price competition is not.

Product Uncertainty

Uncertainty as to the quality of the product is perhaps more intense here than in any other important commodity. Recovery from disease is as unpredictable as is its incidence. In most commodities, the possibility of learning from one's own experience or that of others is strong because there is an adequate number of trials. In the case of severe illness, that is, in general, not true; the uncertainty due to inexperience is added to the intrinsic difficulty of prediction. Further, the amount of uncertainty, measured in terms of utility variability, is certainly much greater for medical care in severe cases than for, say, houses or automobiles, even though these are also expenditures sufficiently infrequent so that there may be considerable residual uncertainty.

Further, there is a special quality to the uncertainty; it is very different on the two sides of the transaction. Because medical knowledge is so complicated, the information possessed by the physician as to the consequences and possibilities of treatment is necessarily very much greater than that of the patient, or at least so it is believed by both parties. Further, both parties are aware of this informational inequality, and their relation is colored by this knowledge. . . .

Supply Conditions

In competitive theory, the supply of a commodity is governed by the net return from its production compared with the return derivable from the use of the same resources elsewhere. There are several significant departures from this theory in the case of medical care.

Most obviously, entry to the profession is restricted by licensing. Licensing, of course, restricts supply and therefore increases the cost of medical care. It is defended as guaranteeing a minimum of quality. . . .

One striking consequence of the control of quality is the restriction on the range offered. If many qualities of a commodity are possible, it would usually happen in a competitive market that many qualities will be offered on the market, at suitably varying prices, to appeal to different tastes and incomes. Both the licensing laws and the standards of medical-school training have limited the possibilities of alternative qualities of medical care. The declining ratio of physicians to total employees in the medical-care industry shows that substitution of less trained personnel, technicians, and the like, is not prevented completely, but the central role of the highly trained physician is not affected at all. . . .

[Licensing laws exclude] many imperfect substitutes for physicians. The licensing laws, though they do not effectively limit the number of physicians, do exclude all others from engaging in any one of the activities known as medical practice. As a result, costly physician time may be employed at specific tasks for which only a small fraction of their training is needed, and which could be performed by others less well trained and therefore less expensive. One might expect immunization centers, privately operated, but not necessarily requiring the services of doctors. . . .

Problems of Insurance

The moral hazard. The welfare case for insurance policies of all sorts is overwhelming. It follows that the government should undertake insurance in those cases where this market, for whatever reason, has failed to emerge. Nevertheless, there are a number of significant practical limitations on the use of insurance. It is important to understand them, though I do not believe that they alter the case for the creation of a much wider class of insurance policies than now exists.

The concepts in this section were key arguments during debates leading to the adoption of the ACA.

One of the limits which has been much stressed in insurance literature is the effect of insurance on incentives. What is desired in the case of insurance is that the event against which insurance is taken be out of the control of the individual. Unfortunately, in real life this separation can never be made perfectly. The outbreak of fire in one's house or business may be largely uncontrollable by the individual, but the probability of fire is somewhat influenced by carelessness, and of course arson is a possibility, if an extreme one. Similarly, in medical policies the cost of medical care is not completely determined by the illness suffered by the individual but depends on the choice of a doctor and his willingness to use medical services. It is frequently observed that widespread medical insurance increases the demand for medical care. Coinsurance provisions have been introduced into many major medical policies to meet this contingency as well as the risk aversion of the insurance companies.

To some extent the professional relationship between physician and patient limits the normal hazard in various forms of medical insurance. By certifying to the necessity of given treatment or the lack thereof, the physician acts as a controlling agent on behalf of the insurance companies. Needless to say, it is a far from perfect check; the physicians themselves are not under any control and it may be convenient for them or pleasing to their patients to prescribe more expensive medication, private nurses, more frequent treatments, and other marginal variations of care. . . .

Third-party control over payments. The moral hazard in physicians' control noted in paragraph 1 above shows itself in those insurance schemes where the physician has the greatest control, namely, major medical insurance. Here there has been a marked rise in expenditures over time.

In prepayment plans, where the insurance and medical service are supplied by the same group, the incentive to keep medical costs to a minimum is strongest.

In plans of the Blue Cross group, there has developed a conflict of interest between the insurance carrier and the medical-service supplier, in this case particularly the hospital.

The need for third-party control is reinforced by another aspect of the moral hazard. Insurance removes the incentive on the part of individuals, patients, and physicians to shop around for better prices for hospitalization and surgical care. The market forces, therefore, tend to be replaced by direct institutional control. . . .

Pooling of unequal risks. Hypothetically, insurance requires for its full social benefit a maximum possible discrimination of risks. Those in groups of higher incidences of illness should pay higher premiums. In fact, however, there is a tendency to equalize, rather than to differentiate, premiums, especially in the Blue Cross and similar widespread schemes. This constitutes, in effect, a redistribution of income from those with a low propensity to illness to those with a high propensity. The equalization, of course, could not in fact be carried through if the market were genuinely competitive. Under those circumstances, insurance plans could arise which charged lower premiums to preferred risks and draw them off, leaving the plan which does not discriminate among risks with only an adverse selection of them.

As we have already seen in the case of income redistribution, some of this may be thought of as insurance with a longer time perspective. If a plan guarantees to everybody a premium that corresponds to total experience but not to experience as it might be segregated by smaller subgroups, everybody is, in effect, insured against a change in his basic state of health which would lead to a reclassification. This corresponds precisely to the use of a level premium in life insurance instead of a premium varying by age, as would be the case for term insurance. . . .

Uncertainty of Effects of Treatment

There are really two major aspects of uncertainty for an individual already suffering from an illness. He is uncertain about the effectiveness of medical treatment, and his uncertainty may be quite different from that of his physician, based on the presumably quite different medical knowledges.

Ideal insurance. This will necessarily involve insurance against a failure to benefit from medical care, whether through recovery, relief of pain, or arrest of further deterioration. One form would be a system in which the payment to the physician is made in accordance with the degree of benefit. Since this would involve transferring the risks from the patient to the physician, who might certainly have an aversion to bearing them, there is room for insurance carriers to pool the risks, either by contract with physicians or by contract with the potential patients. Under ideal insurance, medical care will always be undertaken in any case in which the expected utility, taking account of the probabilities, exceeds the expected medical cost. This prescription would lead to an economic optimum. If we think of the failure to recover mainly in terms of lost working time, then this policy would, in fact, maximize economic welfare as ordinarily measured. . . .

> Many insurance reimbursement reforms, like paying for value rather than the number of services, follow this insight.

The concepts of trust and delegation. In the absence of ideal insurance, there arise institutions which offer some sort of substitute guarantees. Under ideal insurance the patient would actually have no concern with the informational inequality between himself and the physician, since he would only be paying by results anyway, and his utility position would in fact be thoroughly guaranteed.

In its absence he wants to have some guarantee that at least the physician is using his knowledge to the best advantage. This leads to the setting up of a relationship of trust and confidence, one which the physician has a social obligation to live up to. Since the patient does not, at least in his belief, know as much as the physician, he cannot completely enforce standards of care. In part, he replaces direct observation by generalized belief in the ability of the physician. To put it another way, the social obligation for best practice is part of the commodity the physician sells, even though it is a part that is not subject to thorough inspection by the buyer.

One consequence of such trust relations is that the physician cannot act, or at least appear to act, as if he is maximizing his income at every moment of time. As a signal to the buyer of his intentions to act as thoroughly in the buyer's behalf as possible, the physician avoids the obvious stigmata of profit-maximizing. Purely arms-length bargaining behavior would be incompatible, not logically, but surely psychologically, with the trust relations. From these special relations come the various forms of ethical behavior discussed above, and so also, I suggest, the relative unimportance of profit-making in hospitals. The very word, "profit," is a signal that denies the trust relations.

. . . As a second consequence of informational inequality between physician and patient and the lack of insurance of a suitable type, the patient must delegate to the physician much of his freedom of choice. He does not have the knowledge to make decisions on treatment, referral, or hospitalization. To justify this delegation, the physician finds himself somewhat limited, just as any agent would in similar circumstances. The safest course to take to avoid not being a true agent is to give the socially prescribed "best" treatment of the day. Compromise in quality, even for the purpose of saving the patient money, is to risk an imputation of failure to live up to the social bond. . . .

Licensing and educational standards. Delegation and trust are the social institutions designed to obviate the problem of informational inequality. The general uncertainty about the prospects of medical treatment is socially handled by rigid entry requirements. These are designed to reduce the uncertainty in the mind of the consumer as to the quality of product insofar as this is possible. I think this explanation, which is perhaps the naive one, is much more tenable than any idea of a monopoly seeking to increase incomes. No doubt restriction on entry is desirable from the point of view of the existing physicians, but the public pressure needed to achieve the restriction must come from deeper causes.

> Licensing of physicians and other providers establishes minimum quality standards and excludes competition. This is but one example of legal responses to the problems of trust, delegation, and information asymmetries.

The social demand for guaranteed quality can be met in more than one way, however. At least three attitudes can be taken by the state or other social institutions toward entry into an occupation or toward the production of commodities in general; examples of all three types exist. (1) The occupation can be licensed, nonqualified entrants being simply excluded. The licensing may be more complex than it is in medicine; individuals could be licensed for some, but not all, medical activities, for example. Indeed, the present all-or-none approach could be criticized as being insufficient with regard to complicated specialist treatment, as well as excessive with regard to minor medical skills. Graded licensing may, however, be much harder to enforce. Controls could be exercised analogous to those for foods; they can be excluded as being dangerous, or they can be permitted for animals but not for humans. (2) The state or other agency can certify or label, without compulsory exclusion. The category of Certified Psychologist is now under active discussion; canned goods are graded. Certification can be done by nongovernmental agencies, as in the medical-board examinations for specialists. (3) Nothing at all may be done; consumers make their own choices.

The choice among these alternatives in any given case depends on the degree of difficulty consumers have in making the choice unaided, and on the consequences of errors of judgment. It is the general social consensus, clearly, that the laissez-faire solution for medicine is intolerable. The certification proposal never seems to have been discussed seriously. It is beyond the scope of this paper to discuss these proposals in detail. I wish simply to point out that they should be judged in terms of the ability to relieve the uncertainty of the patient in regard to the quality of the commodity he is purchasing, and that entry restrictions are the consequences of an apparent inability to devise a system in which the risks of gaps in medical knowledge and skill are borne primarily by the patient, not the physician. . . .

Arrow wrote in a much earlier era of health care, at a time when health insurance was still a relatively rare commodity. We offer the following list of issues that health care economics has flagged over the years, topics and ideas that will appear throughout this book. Some of these issues also draw from bioethical principles, constitutional principles, and common law, reflecting the interdisciplinary nature of health care law. For example, the concept of autonomy is deeply embedded in common law, constitutional law, philosophy, and bioethics, revealing the many dimensions of analysis that are possible for any health care law problem related to autonomy.

- **Autonomy** is patients' right to control their own body, to know all of the relevant facts, and to make informed choices about their care. The legal tools include informed consent, bioethical principles, the common law and constitutional right to refuse treatment, and constitutionally protected personal control over reproduction.
- **Trust** is required when one person gives another authority over something important. In health care, we entrust our lives to physicians, hospitals, drug companies, and countless others. Ideally, health care providers would act entirely in the best interests of their patients, unaffected by rival considerations. But history and experience show that some providers violate this trust. Fiduciary duties are one prominent legal tool to address agency costs in health care.
- **Information** is a key to good health care decision making and treatment, but accurate information is expensive to obtain (examples include the expense of going to medical school and the costs of clinical trials for drugs). This expense means that in many health care settings, one party has much better information than the other, a condition called information asymmetry. The classic situation is a doctor talking with a patient: The doctor knows the medical research, the test results, and the risks of various treatment options; the patient knows his or her personal medical history, treatment preferences, religious or philosophical beliefs, and family circumstances. Information asymmetries create significant problems in health care and health insurance, threatening autonomy and putting more pressure on trust. Information about health is a very private matter; autonomy requires that you should have control

over how your health information is used. Health law regulates information in many ways, addressing issues of production, asymmetry, and privacy.

- **Insurance** has become the primary way that most people pay for health care in the United States, as opposed to paying out of pocket, the way that one would for home repairs and auto maintenance. Insurance is a financing and risk management mechanism for health care expenses, which can be larger than most individuals' or families' bank accounts. But health insurance can introduce problems such as adverse selection, wherein individuals may use knowledge of their personal health status to purchase insurance in the moment it is needed rather than in advance of a health problem. The primary goal of the ACA's requirement that most Americans obtain health insurance was to reduce adverse selection. Many other issues also arise from health insurance, including the temptation to spend more when someone else is paying the bills ("moral hazard") and discriminatory practices in health insurance underwriting, which raise prices for the sick. The ACA directly addressed these issues by guaranteeing the availability of affordable insurance without regard to medical history or preexisting conditions.

- **Market competition,** or the lack of it, is an entrenched, characteristic feature of the U.S. health care sector. Congress has repeatedly rejected proposals to remove health care from the private marketplace and provide it as a public service for the entire population, what some call "Medicare for all," as is done in many other countries' national health systems. Unlike when we shop for cars or phones, however, we generally do not and cannot comparison shop for health care services or items but instead rely on the judgments of others (doctors, hospitals, insurance companies, the FDA). Despite the critical nature of health care products and services, no comparison shopping site like Yelp, Trip Advisor, or their equivalent, exists for health care. Doctors and patients are often entirely ignorant of actual price. In many communities, especially rural areas, patients have very little choice between hospitals, physician groups, and health plans. Health care antitrust law is but one response to these problems in health care markets.

QUESTIONS

1. One example of information asymmetry is the doctor as expert. Why does that asymmetry pose a problem for patients?
2. Health insurance creates additional demand for covered care. Arrow calls this "moral hazard." Is this additional care intrinsically a bad thing?
3. If medical underwriting is prohibited, everyone pays the same amount for health insurance coverage, without regard to health status. Is that fair to healthy people?

D. HEALTH CARE AND DISTRIBUTIVE JUSTICE

Arrow's work offers one way to think about issues in U.S. health care. Another approach is distributive justice, based on the work of philosopher John Rawls. Distributive justice underlies some of the key choices made in the ACA, which will be discussed throughout this book.

Norman Daniels, Health-Care Needs and Distributive Justice

166-167 (1981)

Including health-care institutions among those which are to protect fair equality of opportunity is compatible with the central intuitions behind wanting to guarantee such opportunity in the first place. Rawls is primarily concerned with *the opportunity to pursue careers* — jobs and offices — that have various benefits attached to them. So equality of opportunity is *strategically* important: a person's well being will be measured for the most part by the primary goods that accompany placement in such jobs and offices. Rawls argues it is not enough simply to eliminate formal or legal barriers to persons seeking jobs — for example, race, class, ethnic, or sex barriers. Rather, positive steps should be taken to enhance the opportunity of those disadvantaged by such social factors as family background. The point is that none of us *deserves* the advantages conferred by the accidents of birth — either the genetic or social advantages. These advantages from the "natural lottery" are morally arbitrary, and to let them determine individual opportunity — and reward and success in life — is to confer arbitrariness on the outcomes. So positive steps, for example, through the educational system, are to be taken to provide fair equality of opportunity.

But if it is important to use resources to counter the advantages in opportunity some get in the natural lottery, it is equally important to use resources to counter the natural disadvantages induced by disease (and since class-differentiated social conditions contribute significantly to the etiology of disease, we are reminded disease is not just a product of the natural component of the lottery). But this does not mean we are committed to the futile goal of eliminating all natural differences between persons. Health care has as its goal normal functioning and so concentrates on a specific class of obvious disadvantages and tries to eliminate them. That is its *limited* contribution to guaranteeing fair equality of opportunity.

The approach taken here allows us to draw some interesting parallels between education and health care, for both are strategically important contributions to fair equality or opportunity. Both address needs which are not equally distributed between individuals. Various social factors, such as race, class, and family background, may produce special learning needs; so too many natural factors, such as the broad class of learning disabilities. To the extent that education is aimed at providing fair equality of opportunity, special provision must be made to meet these special needs, such as the need for food and clothing, which are more equally distributed between persons. The combination of unequal distribution and the great strategic importance of the opportunity to have health care and education puts these needs in a separate category from those basic needs we can expect people to purchase from their fair-income shares.

It is worth noting another point of fit between my analysis and Rawls' theory. In Rawls' contract situation, a "thick" veil of ignorance is imposed on contractors choosing basic principles of justice: they do not know their abilities, talents, place in society, or historical period. In selecting principles to govern health-care resource-allocation decisions, we need a thinner veil, for we must know about some features of the society, for example, its resource limitations.

CAPSTONE PROBLEM

How do Ken Arrow's and Norman Daniel's insights apply to *Jacobson, Hobby Lobby,* and *Redding*? Write a paragraph on each case, identifying the key connections.

PART I

HEALTH INSURANCE

Part I introduces the primary means by which Americans pay for medical care: health insurance. In the United States, health insurance is the gateway to accessing health care. Without health insurance, a person seeking health care can either attempt to pay out of pocket, which is too costly for most Americans, or seek medical attention in a hospital emergency department, which offers a point of rescue but not consistent care at an affordable price. Thus, we begin by thinking about health insurance because it both facilitates and regulates access to a vast majority of health care in the United States.

Chapter 2 discusses the two major public health insurance programs in the United States: Medicare and Medicaid. Although Medicare and Medicaid were once considered gap-fillers for private insurance, they now cover approximately one-third of the U.S. population, and they drive both health care and health insurance policy for the nation. **Chapter 3** covers private insurance, which most Americans historically have obtained as an employment benefit. The chapter covers basic concepts in private health insurance as well as the complications that arise from multiple insurance markets and the intermediary role of employers. These two chapters help to explain how the law shapes health care decision making in many settings.

CHAPTER 2

Public Provision of Health Insurance

A. INTRODUCTION

Health insurance in the United States historically has been financed by private sources — tied to employment, purchased through private health insurance companies or with individual funds, and dominated by privately contracted relationships (discussed further in Chapter 3). But today, direct and indirect public financing account for more than half of national health expenditures. A large part of that coverage derives from Medicare and Medicaid, the nation's two major public insurance programs. Broadly speaking, Medicare covers all of the nation's elderly, while Medicaid operates as a safety net program for the nation's poor. But the programs are significantly more complex than these simple descriptions indicate. In this chapter, we consider why Medicare and Medicaid are structured as they are, as well as their basic programmatic features and the aspects of the programs that have led to their ongoing growth and importance as mechanisms for both finance and delivery of care to more than a third of all Americans. Medicare and Medicaid are also powerful tools for the federal government to drive health policy, often through rules and regulations that reach far beyond these programs. By the end of this chapter, you will be able to describe basic features of each program, understand which parts of the American population benefit most from them, and consider major policy questions pertaining to each program standing alone and in the context of the U.S. health care industry.

B. MEDICARE

Medicare is a federal social insurance program that provides health insurance starting at age 65 to citizens and lawful permanent residents with sufficient work history. Medicare eligibility does not depend on health, wealth, or income. Medicare also covers people of any age who are deemed permanently disabled, as well as individuals with end-stage renal disease and those with amyotrophic lateral sclerosis (ALS, also called Lou Gehrig's disease). As of the end of calendar year 2017, Medicare accounts for about 20 percent of the nation's health care expenditures and covers approximately 58 million people, nearly 9 million of whom are non-elderly, permanently disabled beneficiaries. The vast majority of U.S. hospitals, physicians, and other health care providers participate in Medicare, giving them access to

Photo courtesy of LBJ Presidential Library (from SSA Web site).

insured Medicare patients, but also subjecting them to Medicare's "conditions of participation" and other rules.

1. HISTORY

Congress enacted Medicare in 1965 against a backdrop of widespread poverty among the elderly, one-third of whom qualified as impoverished and more than half of whom had no way to pay for needed medical expenses. Congress enacted Medicare as a major amendment to the Social Security Act, key New Deal legislation that provided governmental pensions to retirees and a lump-sum payment upon death. Even with that financial assistance, the elderly and their families suffered financial catastrophes when serious medical services were needed. Today, due in part to Medicare, only about 10 percent of the nation's elderly are living in poverty. Still, more than half of Medicare beneficiaries earn less than $24,000 per year, which is why some are enrolled in both Medicare and Medicaid.

President Truman, sitting on the right side of President Johnson in the picture above, was the first Medicare beneficiary to enroll in the program upon its enactment.

Prior to Medicare's passage, the elderly were assisted by states through locally run medical welfare programs and through federally funded medical vendor programs, which paid money to states to assist with the cost of medical care. While this meant that some government assistance was available to the elderly, funding was inconsistent and varied dramatically across states. When health care reform was being discussed by Congress during Lyndon Johnson's Administration, the elderly lobbied to have not only health insurance for all elderly but also a nationalized, rather than state-specific, program. They were successful on both counts. But the nation's major private insurance carriers at that time (mainly Blue Cross and Blue Shield companies) were concerned that social insurance would ruin private health insurance markets. So, after their successful lobbying, Medicare's nationally uniform, purely federal program was to be run by local insurers, called "contractors," who would help the federal government to implement and administer Medicare in various regions across the country.

Medicare echoed President Harry Truman's push for national health insurance after World War II. Some of the elderly who were to benefit from the program in the 1960s were veterans whose impoverishment was due to a lack of adequate finances to cover war-related injuries. The historical reliance on family to care for the elderly became inadequate, and some families were bankrupted taking care of their elderly relatives while others skimped on needed medical care. As President Truman stated, at the signing of Medicare:

> This is an important hour for the Nation, for those of our citizens who have completed their tour of duty and have moved to the sidelines. These are the days that we are trying to celebrate for them. These people are our prideful responsibility and they are entitled, among other benefits, to the best medical protection available.

On the heels of President Truman's remarks, President Johnson signed the bill into law, stating:

> No longer will older Americans be denied the healing miracle of modern medicine. No longer will illness crush and destroy the savings that they have so carefully put away over a lifetime so that they might enjoy dignity in their later years. No longer will young families see their own incomes, and their own hopes, eaten away simply because they are carrying out their deep moral obligations to their parents, and to their uncles, and their aunts. And no longer will this Nation refuse the hand of justice to those who have given a lifetime of service and wisdom and labor to the progress of this progressive country.

Physicians and other health care providers were concerned that Medicare would constitute a government takeover of the practice of medicine. In 1961, Ronald Reagan famously opposed a national health care program for the elderly, claiming that if it passed, "one of these days you and I are going to spend our sunset years telling our children and our children's children what it once was like in America when men were free." While Medicare became law, several provisions reflect these concerns. Thus, the first section of Medicare promised provider autonomy from federal bureaucracy:

42 U.S.C. §1395. Prohibition against any Federal interference

Nothing in this subchapter shall be construed to authorize any Federal officer or employee to exercise any supervision or control over the practice of medicine or the manner in which medical services are provided, or over the selection, tenure, or compensation of any officer or employee of any institution, agency, or person providing health services; or to exercise any supervision or control over the administration or operation of any such institution, agency, or person.

> Individuals earning less than the federal poverty level can have some or all of their Medicare premiums and cost sharing covered by Medicaid (discussed later in this chapter). People enrolled in both Medicare and Medicaid are called "dual eligibles."

A related concern was voiced by individuals who preferred private insurance and feared government interference in their free choice of health care provider. For them, the Medicare Act contained the following:

42 U.S.C. §1395b. Option to individuals to obtain other health insurance protection

Nothing contained in this title shall be construed to preclude any State from providing, or any individual from purchasing or otherwise securing, protection against the cost of any health services. ˙

A similar provision in §1395a guaranteed "free choice" of providers by patients. In short, the first three sections of Medicare promise that the law will not change the practice of medicine, patient choice of providers, or the ability to obtain other health insurance. As we move through the elements of the Medicare program, consider how Medicare shapes all three of these matters, despite this statutory language.

The Medicare Act also conditioned receipt of federal funds on the desegregation of hospitals, which was remarkably successful. Fearing opposition, Medicare did not require desegregation of physicians' offices. This lead to the creation of the Office for Civil Rights in the Department of Health, Education, and Welfare (now HHS).

Medicare does not cover all health expenditures but rather only "medically necessary" care within certain categories such as inpatient hospital stays and physician visits. Medicare did not originally cover expenditures common now, like prescription drugs or home health care. Even within covered categories, Medicare imposes various cost-sharing requirements, such as deductibles and copayments. A deductible is the amount that must be paid by the patient before an insurer covers an item or service. A copayment is a set payment amount, such as $10 per doctor visit, and coinsurance is a percentage of a bill that must be paid by the patient, such as 20 percent of a hospital bill. Because Medicare does not cover every health care service or device, many seniors purchase private insurance to supplement Medicare's coverage. That private insurance is called "Medicare Supplemental Insurance" or "Medigap," and it is a robust private market that exists alongside Medicare's public insurance.

QUESTION

Why is Medicare (and other insurance) structured in such a way that it does not completely cover the cost of medical care?

Medicare enrollment is handled by the Social Security Administration (SSA), but even though Medicare benefits and Social Security retirement benefits are linked, enrolling in Medicare is a separate process from claiming Social Security benefits. The Medicare program is otherwise administered and managed by the Department of Health and Human Services (HHS), primarily by the sub-agency called the Centers for Medicare & Medicaid Services (CMS). Much of this work is contracted out to private insurers, historically Blue Cross/Blue Shield health plans. The Office of the Inspector General for HHS (OIG) is responsible for programmatic oversight and compliance with the rules pertaining to participating in Medicare. The OIG often works with the Department of Justice and Medicaid Fraud Control Units in various states to prosecute health care fraud (discussed in Chapter 6).

2. ELIGIBILITY

As originally enacted in 1965, Medicare made all citizens and lawful permanent residents eligible for federal health insurance on their 65th birthday if they (or their spouse) had paid Social Security taxes for at least 40 calendar quarters (i.e., ten years). Just seven years later, Congress expanded Medicare eligibility to people who were permanently disabled (after a 24-month waiting period), which included people suffering with end-stage renal disease, who have no waiting period. In 2001, people with ALS were added to Medicare's eligibility, also with no waiting period.

> **42 U.S.C. §1395c. Description of program**
> The insurance program for which entitlement is established by sections 226 and 226A provides basic protection against the costs of hospital, related post-hospital, home health services, and hospice care in accordance with this part for (1) individuals who are age 65 or over and are eligible for retirement benefits under title II of this Act (or would be eligible for such benefits if certain government employment were covered employment under such title) or under the railroad retirement system, (2) individuals under age 65 who have been entitled for not less than 24 months to benefits under title II of this Act (or would have been so entitled to such benefits if certain government employment were covered employment under such title) or under the railroad retirement system on the basis of a disability, and (3) certain individuals who do not meet the conditions specified in either clause (1) or (2) but who are medically determined to have end stage renal disease.

Spouses can become eligible to enroll through the tax payments made by their partners, but Medicare has no spousal or partner benefits per se. In other words, if a wife turns 65 and has paid federal taxes for ten years, she becomes eligible for Medicare; if her husband is 62, he does not become eligible for Medicare simply because his wife has enrolled. He must wait until he becomes 65, and then he may qualify based either on her tax payments or his own, as applicable.

> After the Supreme Court's decision in United States v. Windsor, 133 S. Ct. 2675 (2013), Medicare eligibility includes same-sex spouses.

3. BENEFITS

Medicare offers a unique set of benefits that are called "Parts." Three of the Parts cover different types of medical care (Parts A, B, and D); the fourth is an alternative care delivery and financing mechanism (Part C), akin to managed care, a form of private health insurance that is discussed further in Chapter 3. The first two enacted parts of Medicare, or "original Medicare," were Part A, Hospital Insurance, and Part B, Supplementary Medical Insurance. Part A covers hospitals and other institutional care, and Part B covers physicians and other outpatient health care services. Later, Part C was added to facilitate a managed care system of delivery, now called "Medicare Advantage." Part C is misleadingly named, because it is not a separate insurance benefit in Medicare; instead, it provides a different method of delivering the coverage of Parts A and B to Medicare beneficiaries. The most recently enacted Part is the Medicare outpatient drug benefit, called Part D. Part D added outpatient prescription drug coverage to Medicare, an expensive yet important update to the program 40 years after enactment. Part D benefits can be, and generally are, also provided through Medicare Advantage. Additional benefits contribute to the increased cost of Medicare over time, though other factors such as the aging of the "baby boomer" generation, increased use of medical technologies, and expensive end-of-life care contribute to Medicare's cost curve as well.

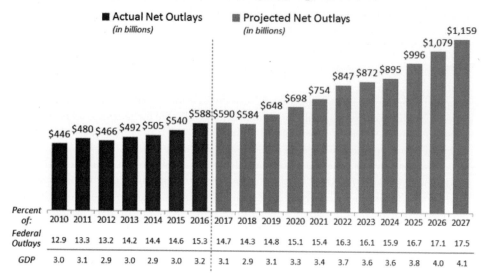

Actual and Projected Net Medicare Spending, 2010-2027

■ Actual Net Outlays *(in billions)*   ■ Projected Net Outlays *(in billions)*

Percent of:	2010	2011	2012	2013	2014	2015	2016	2017	2018	2019	2020	2021	2022	2023	2024	2025	2026	2027
	$446	$480	$466	$492	$505	$540	$588	$590	$584	$648	$698	$754	$847	$872	$895	$996	$1,079	$1,159
Federal Outlays	12.9	13.3	13.2	14.2	14.4	14.6	15.3	14.7	14.3	14.8	15.1	15.4	16.3	16.1	15.9	16.7	17.1	17.5
GDP	3.0	3.1	2.9	3.0	2.9	3.0	3.2	3.1	2.9	3.1	3.3	3.4	3.7	3.6	3.6	3.8	4.0	4.1

NOTE: All amounts are for federal fiscal years; amounts are in billions and consist of mandatory Medicare spending minus income from premiums and other offsetting receipts.
SOURCE: Congressional Budget Office, An Update to the Budget and Economic Outlook, 2017 to 2027 (June 2017).

a. Part A

At age 65, eligible individuals are enrolled automatically in Part A, which requires no premium for anyone who has paid into Social Security for 40 quarters or more. Those who reach 65 and have not paid sufficient Social Security taxes can buy into Part A for a relatively small monthly premium.

> Upon turning 65 and receiving Social Security benefits, enrollment in Part A is automatic and cannot be disclaimed. Hall v. Sebelius, 667 F.3d 1293 (D.C. Cir. 2012).

42 U.S.C. §1395d. Scope of benefits

(a) Entitlement to payment for inpatient hospital services, post-hospital extended care services, home health services, and hospice care.

The benefits provided to an individual by the insurance program under this part shall consist of entitlement to have payment made on his behalf or, in the case of payments referred to in section 1395f(d)(2) of this title to him (subject to the provisions of this part) for—

(1) inpatient hospital services or inpatient critical access hospital services for up to 150 days during any spell of illness minus 1 day for each day of such services in excess of 90 received during any preceding spell of illness (if such individual was entitled to have payment for such services made under this part unless he specifies in accordance with regulations of the Secretary that he does not desire to have such payment made);

(2)(A) post-hospital extended care services for up to 100 days during any spell of illness, and (B) to the extent provided in subsection (f) of this section, extended care services that are not post-hospital extended care services;

(3) in the case of individuals not enrolled in part B of this subchapter, home health services, and in the case of individuals so enrolled, post-institutional home health services furnished during a home health spell of illness for up to 100 visits during such spell of illness;

(4) in lieu of certain other benefits, hospice care with respect to the individual during up to two periods of 90 days each and an unlimited number of subsequent periods of 60 days each with respect to which the individual makes an election under subsection (d)(1) of this section; and

(5) for individuals who are terminally ill, have not made an election under subsection (d)(1) of this section, and have not previously received services under this paragraph, services that are furnished by a physician (as defined in section 1395x(r)(1) of this title) who is either the medical director or an employee of a hospice program and that —

(A) consist of —

(i) an evaluation of the individual's need for pain and symptom management, including the individual's need for hospice care; and

(ii) counseling the individual with respect to hospice care and other care options; and

(B) may include advising the individual regarding advanced care planning.

(b) Services not covered

Payment under this part for services furnished an individual during a spell of illness may not (subject to subsection (c) of this section) be made for —

(1) inpatient hospital services furnished to him during such spell after such services have been furnished to him for 150 days during such spell minus 1 day for each day of inpatient hospital services in excess of 90 received during any preceding spell of illness (if such individual was entitled to have payment for such services made under this part unless he specifies in accordance with regulations of the Secretary that he does not desire to have such payment made);

(2) post-hospital extended care services furnished to him during such spell after such services have been furnished to him for 100 days during such spell; or

(3) inpatient psychiatric hospital services furnished to him after such services have been furnished to him for a total of 190 days during his lifetime. . . .

42 U.S.C. §1395x. Definitions

For purposes of this subchapter —

(a) Spell of illness

The term "spell of illness" with respect to any individual means a period of consecutive days —

(1) beginning with the first day (not included in a previous spell of illness)

(A) on which such individual is furnished inpatient hospital services, inpatient critical access hospital services or extended care services, and

(B) which occurs in a month for which he is entitled to benefits under part A of this subchapter, and

(2) ending with the close of the first period of 60 consecutive days thereafter on each of which he is neither an inpatient of a hospital or critical access hospital nor an inpatient of a facility. . . .

PROBLEM

Your grandmother suffers a cardiac episode (minor heart attack) and stays in the hospital for 30 days due to complications. She leaves the hospital, only to return 45 days later for problems related to her arthritis that develop into additional cardiac and circulatory problems. She remains in the hospital for 40 days after being admitted the second time. Are these services covered by Medicare as a single spell of illness, based on the statutory excerpt immediately above? Will she have to pay any amount of money out of pocket for her hospital-based care? If so, how much? (Hint: This number changes yearly and requires minor Internet research.)

b. Part B

In addition to Part A, the Medicare Act provides coverage for physician services and other outpatient care.

42 U.S.C. §1395j. Establishment of supplementary medical insurance program for the aged and the disabled

There is hereby established a voluntary insurance program to provide medical insurance benefits in accordance with the provisions of this part for aged and disabled individuals who elect to enroll under such program, to be financed from premium payments by enrollees together with contributions from funds appropriated by the Federal Government.

42 U.S.C. §1395o. Eligible individuals

Every individual who—

(1) is entitled to hospital insurance benefits under part A, or

(2) has attained age 65 and is a resident of the United States, and is either

> Under current law, undocumented aliens are not eligible for Medicare, even if they have worked in the United States and have paid taxes into the Medicare trust fund for many years.

(A) a citizen or

(B) an alien lawfully admitted for permanent residence who has resided in the United States continuously during the 5 years immediately preceding the month in which he applies for enrollment under this part,

is eligible to enroll in the insurance program established by this part.

Medicare Part B requires premium payments for beneficiaries to enroll, unlike the automatic, premium-free enrollment in Part A. Part B premiums are low relative to private insurance and are calculated as a percentage of Part B costs. The original Part B premium was $3 per month. Part B premiums now equal 25 percent of the projected annual Part B expenditures per beneficiary aged 65 and older; this was approximately $134 per month in 2018 for the vast majority of enrollees. People with very low and very high incomes have slightly different rules: Those earning above $85,000 for individuals and $170,000 for couples have paid higher premiums for Medicare Part B (and Part D, discussed below) since 2007. The higher, income-dependent premiums are paid by about 5 percent of Medicare beneficiaries. For low-income Medicare beneficiaries, the Part B premium is covered by Medicaid.

Beneficiary premiums cover only 25 percent of the cost of Part B, and the remainder is funded by general revenues of the federal government. With the aging of a large segment of the U.S. population, policy-makers are concerned about the increasing cost of Medicare relative to the number of taxpayers providing revenue for the Medicare program. One suggestion that arises repeatedly is to change the Part B premium payment system so that beneficiaries who earn more pay more in premiums for Medicare. This already occurs for wealthier Medicare beneficiaries (those earning more than $85,000), as was noted above. Some policy-makers reject any further means-testing in Medicare, given that the program is social insurance designed to cover everyone equally; most elderly earn modest or low incomes (if any); and, means-testing could lead to a more stigmatized, welfare-like program. Other policy-makers find means-testing a fair path for a program that experiences rising cost pressures, with the idea that those who can afford to pay something for health insurance should. Yet another view holds that wealthier elderly who were successful in earning and saving throughout their lives should not be penalized by imposing means-testing on high earners.

QUESTION

What do you think of the idea of additional means-testing or increased cost sharing in Medicare? You may want to consider benefits and detriments for Medicare, its beneficiaries, and other federal programs that vie for federal tax dollars.

c. Part C

Managed care was an option for beneficiaries from the beginning of Medicare in 1965, with steady growth during the 1980s and especially after 1992. Medicare rules relating to managed care plans were codified under the Balanced Budget Act of 1997, which created Medicare Part C. Part C offered higher payments to managed care organizations to reward them for covering the senior risk pool. Over time, Congress has modified the payments for managed care companies under Part C, with predictable impact on enrollment. Despite adjustments in the Patient Protection and the passage of the Affordable Care Act (ACA), Medicare Advantage continues to cost more per beneficiary than traditional Medicare. Additional subsidies allow Medicare Advantage plans to offer more coverage than traditional Medicare. As a result, Medicare Advantage covered almost one-third of Medicare beneficiaries in 2015, especially the healthier members.

42 U.S.C. §1395w-21. Eligibility, election, and enrollment
    (a) Choice of Medicare benefits through Medicare+Choice plans
        (1) In general
        Subject to the provisions of this section, each Medicare+Choice eligible individual (as defined in paragraph (3)) is entitled to elect to receive

benefits (other than qualified prescription drug benefits) under this subchapter —

(A) through the original Medicare fee-for-service program under parts A and B of this subchapter, or

(B) through enrollment in a Medicare+Choice plan under this part, and may elect qualified prescription drug coverage in accordance with section 1395w-101 of this title.

(2) Types of Medicare+Choice plans that may be available

A Medicare+Choice plan may be any of the following types of plans of health insurance:

(A) Coordinated care plans (including regional plans)

(i) In general

Coordinated care plans which provide health care services, including but not limited to health maintenance organization plans (with or without point of service options), plans offered by provider-sponsored organizations, and regional or local preferred provider organization plans (including MA regional plans).

> Although now called Medicare Advantage, the Medicare Act still also uses the term "Medicare+Choice" for Part C. Pub. L. No. 108-173, §201 (the Medicare Modernization Act), specified the name change as a "note" in 42 U.S.C. §1395w-21.

(ii) Specialized MA plans for special needs individuals

Specialized MA plans for special needs individuals may be any type of coordinated care plan.

(B) Combination of MSA plan and contributions to Medicare+ Choice MSA

An MSA plan, as defined in section 1395w-28 (b)(3) of this title, and a contribution into a Medicare+Choice medical savings account (MSA).

(C) Private fee-for-service plans

A Medicare+Choice private fee-for-service plan, as defined in section 1395w-28(b)(2) of this title.

(3) Medicare+Choice eligible individual

(A) In general

In this subchapter, subject to subparagraph (B), the term "Medicare+ Choice eligible individual" means an individual who is entitled to benefits under part A of this subchapter and enrolled under part B of this subchapter.

(B) Special rule for end-stage renal disease

Such term shall not include an individual medically determined to have end-stage renal disease, except that —

(i) an individual who develops end-stage renal disease while enrolled in a Medicare+Choice plan may continue to be enrolled in that plan . . . [until the end of the plan year]. . . .

QUESTIONS

1. Which Medicare beneficiaries are eligible for Medicare Advantage?
2. Why would patients with end-stage renal disease be excluded from Medicare Advantage (Medicare+Choice)?

Congress has often modified how CMS pays Medicare managed care plans. In recent years, the payments have been more generous than traditional Medicare, which allows Medicare Advantage plans to offer coverage and services above and beyond traditional Medicare. (See 42 U.S.C. §1395w-23 for specifics on MA plans.) The payment methodologies are an important policy tool that drives enrollment and benefits. The following offers a glimpse of the methods CMS uses to contract with Medicare Advantage plans on behalf of Medicare beneficiaries. Medicare payments to Medicare Advantage plans vary depending on demographic characteristics of the beneficiaries and whether the contract is "risk-sharing" or not.

42 U.S.C. §1395mm. Payments to health maintenance organizations and competitive medical plans

(a) Rates and adjustments

(1)(A) The Secretary shall annually determine, and shall announce (in a manner intended to provide notice to interested parties) not later than September 7 before the calendar year concerned—

> (i) a per capita rate of payment for each class of individuals who are enrolled under this section with an eligible organization which has entered into a risk-sharing contract and who are entitled to benefits under part A of this subchapter and enrolled under part B of this subchapter, and

> (ii) a per capita rate of payment for each class of individuals who are so enrolled with such an organization and who are enrolled under part B of this subchapter only.

For purposes of this section, the term "risk-sharing contract" means a contract entered into under subsection (g) of this section and the term "reasonable cost reimbursement contract" means a contract entered into under subsection (h) of this section.

> (B) The Secretary shall define appropriate classes of members, based on age, disability status, and such other factors as the Secretary determines to be appropriate, so as to ensure actuarial equivalence. The Secretary may add to, modify, or substitute for such classes, if such changes will improve the determination of actuarial equivalence.

> (C) The annual per capita rate of payment for each such class shall be equal to 95 percent of the adjusted average per capita cost (as defined in paragraph (4)) for that class.

> (D) In the case of an eligible organization with a risk-sharing contract, the Secretary shall make monthly payments in advance and in accordance with the rate determined under subparagraph (C) and except as provided in subsection (g)(2) of this section, to the organization for each individual enrolled with the organization under this section.

> . . . .

(4) For purposes of this section, the term "adjusted average per capita cost" means the average per capita amount that the Secretary estimates in advance (on the basis of actual experience, or retrospective actuarial equivalent based upon an adequate sample and other

> "Actuarial equivalence" adjusts payments for differences in the health status (and therefore the likely costs) of different enrollees. A plan enrolling sicker than average enrollees would receive a higher payment, while a plan enrolling healthier beneficiaries would receive less. The goal is to reduce economic incentives for plans to enroll only the healthy.

"Adjusted average per capita cost" is a form of capitation, paying the Medicare Advantage plan based on the number and demographic characteristics of the people covered rather than the services ultimately rendered. With any capitation arrangement, some insurance risk has been shifted to the health care provider.

information and data, in a geographic area served by an eligible organization or in a similar area, with appropriate adjustments to assure actuarial equivalence) would be payable in any contract year for services covered under parts A and B of this subchapter, or part B only, and types of expenses otherwise reimbursable under parts A and B of this subchapter, or part B only (including administrative costs incurred by organizations . . .), if the services were to be furnished by other than an eligible organization. . . .

Medicare Advantage allows beneficiaries to receive the three parts of Medicare (Parts A, B, and D) in one centralized administrative mechanism. As more of the population that is familiar with managed care enters the Medicare program, Medicare Advantage is likely to continue to grow, and managed care entities will likely find this population more desirable and less financially risky to cover.

QUESTION

Why are payments to Medicare Advantage plans adjusted as described in the statutory excerpt immediately above?

d. Part D

In 2007, President George W. Bush signed a major expansion of Medicare to include outpatient prescription drugs, which are increasingly expensive. Medicare's drug benefit, called Part D, the Voluntary Prescription Drug Benefit Program, is quite

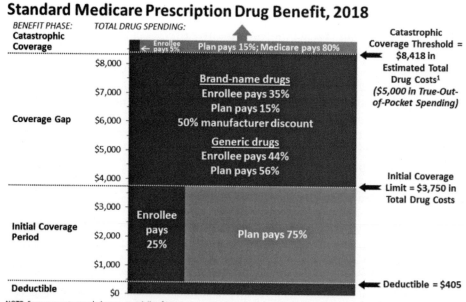

Standard Medicare Prescription Drug Benefit, 2018

NOTE: Some amounts rounded to nearest dollar. [1]Amount corresponds to the estimated catastrophic coverage limit for non-Low-Income Subsidy (LIS) enrollees ($7,509 for LIS enrollees), which corresponds to True Out-of-Pocket (TrOOP) spending of $5,000, the amount used to determine when an enrollee reaches the catastrophic coverage threshold in 2018.
SOURCE: Kaiser Family Foundation, based on Part D benefit parameters for 2018.

complex, even by Medicare standards. Part D has proven to be less expensive than originally estimated. To keep costs lower, the legislation contained an intricate cost-sharing scheme that involved premiums, copayments, and a coverage gap often called the "donut hole," which was subsequently phased down by the ACA and will be reduced to a flat 25 percent copayment by 2020.

The Part D benefit is not provided directly by Medicare but rather through stand-alone health insurance plans that cover pharmaceutical costs exclusively, called Prescription Drug Plans (PDPs) or Part D plans. To improve access to the benefit, low-income beneficiaries may qualify for subsidies for Part D. Medicare beneficiaries are given a choice upon initial enrollment: They can either obtain prescription drug coverage through a Part D plan or obtain it through a Medicare Advantage plan bundled with Part D coverage (called MA-PD). Alternatively, they can opt out of Medicare prescription drug coverage altogether. Anyone opting out upon their initial enrollment in Medicare cannot later join Part D unless they pay a 1 percent late enrollment penalty for each month that they refused Part D. This rule is designed to prevent adverse selection by relatively healthy Medicare enrollees. A similar rule governs late enrollment in Part B. The law also encourages HHS to educate consumers about Part D, nudging them toward enrollment.

> Insurance depends on healthy people joining the risk pool and paying premiums. If relatively healthy people can delay joining until they are sick, costs per enrollee will increase. Health economists call this tendency to wait to enroll until insurance coverage is needed "adverse selection."

42 U.S.C. §1395w-101. Eligibility, enrollment, and information

(a) Provision of qualified prescription drug coverage through enrollment in plans

(1) In general

Subject to the succeeding provisions of this part, each part D eligible individual (as defined in paragraph (3)(A)) is entitled to obtain qualified prescription drug coverage (described in section 1395w-102(a) of this title) as follows:

(A) Fee-for-service enrollees may receive coverage through a prescription drug plan

A part D eligible individual who is not enrolled in an MA plan may obtain qualified prescription drug coverage through enrollment in a prescription drug plan (as defined in section 1395w-151(a)(14) of this title).

(B) Medicare Advantage enrollees

(i) Enrollees in a plan providing qualified prescription drug coverage receive coverage through the plan

A part D eligible individual who is enrolled in an MA-PD plan obtains such coverage through such plan.

. . . .

(c) Providing information to beneficiaries. —

(1) Activities. —

The Secretary shall conduct activities that are designed to broadly disseminate information to part D eligible individuals (and prospective part D eligible individuals) regarding the coverage provided under this part. Such activities shall ensure that such information is first made available at least

30 days prior to the initial enrollment period described in subsection (b)(2)(A).

(2) Requirements. —

The activities described in paragraph (1) shall—

(A) be similar to the activities performed by the Secretary, including dissemination (including through the toll-free telephone number 1-800-MEDICARE) of comparative information for prescription drug plans and MA-PD plans; and

(B) be coordinated with the activities performed by the Secretary. . . .

(3) Comparative information. —

(A) In general. —

Subject to subparagraph (B), the comparative information referred to in paragraph (2)(A) shall include a comparison of the following with respect to qualified prescription drug coverage:

(i) Benefits. — The benefits provided under the plan.

(ii) Monthly beneficiary premium. — The monthly beneficiary premium under the plan.

(iii) Quality and performance. — The quality and performance under the plan.

(iv) Beneficiary cost-sharing. — The cost-sharing required of part D eligible individuals under the plan.

(v) Consumer satisfaction surveys. — The results of consumer satisfaction surveys regarding the plan. . . .

(B) Exception for unavailability of information. —

The Secretary is not required to provide comparative information under clauses (iii) and (v) of subparagraph (A) with respect to a plan —

(i) for the first plan year in which it is offered; and

(ii) for the next plan year if it is impracticable or the information is otherwise unavailable.

(4) Information on late enrollment penalty. —

The information disseminated under paragraph (1) shall include information concerning the methodology for determining the late enrollment penalty under section 1395w-113(b) of this title.

QUESTIONS

1. What kind of information must be delivered to Medicare beneficiaries about Part D?
2. Why did Congress mandate that this information be publicized, including the late enrollment penalty?

Prescription drug plans do not cover every drug, but only those in the "formulary." Congress did not specify precisely which drugs should be in the Part D "formulary" but also did not leave full discretion to the plans; only prescription drug coverage that meets certain standards receives payments under Part D. One important element in addition to the formulary is the degree of cost sharing by beneficiaries, whether through deductibles, copayments, or coinsurance. The following excerpt offers a sense of the complexity necessary to create legislation that designs a totally new benefit, like this Part D drug benefit, in a well-established public insurance program.

42 U.S.C. §1395w-102. Prescription drug benefits

. . . .

(b) Standard prescription drug coverage. — For purposes of this part and part C, the term "standard prescription drug coverage" means coverage of covered part D drugs that meets the following requirements:

(1) Deductible. —

(A) In general. — The coverage has an annual deductible —

(i) for 2006, that is equal to $250; or

(ii) for a subsequent year, that is equal to the amount specified under this paragraph for the previous year increased by the percentage specified in paragraph (6) for the year involved.

(B) Rounding. — Any amount determined under subparagraph (A)(ii) that is not a multiple of $5 shall be rounded to the nearest multiple of $5.

(2) Benefit structure. —

(A) 25 percent coinsurance. — The coverage has coinsurance (for costs above the annual deductible specified in paragraph (1) and up to the initial coverage limit under paragraph (3)) that is —

(i) equal to 25 percent; or

(ii) actuarially equivalent to an average expected payment of 25 percent of such costs.

. . . [The statute then describes the coverage gap or "donut hole."]

(4) Protection against high out-of-pocket expenditures. —

(A) In general. —

(i) In general. —

The coverage provides benefits, after the part D eligible individual has incurred costs (as described in subparagraph (C)) for covered part D drugs in a year equal to the annual out-of-pocket threshold specified in subparagraph (B), with cost-sharing that is equal to the greater of —

(I) a copayment of $2 for a generic drug or a preferred drug that is a multiple source drug and $5 for any other drug; or

(II) coinsurance that is equal to 5 percent.

(ii) Adjustment of amount. —

For a year after 2006, the dollar amounts specified in clause (i)(I) shall be equal to the dollar amounts specified in this subparagraph for the previous year, increased by the annual percentage increase described in paragraph (6) for the year involved. Any amount established under this clause that is not a multiple of a 5 cents shall be rounded to the nearest multiple of 5 cents.

(B) Annual out-of-pocket threshold. —

(i) In general. — For purposes of this part, the "annual out-of-pocket threshold" specified in this subparagraph —

(I) for 2006, is equal to $3,600; . . .

(5) Construction. — Nothing in this part shall be construed as preventing a PDP sponsor or an MA organization offering an MA-PD plan from reducing to 0 the cost-sharing otherwise applicable to preferred or generic drugs. . . .

QUESTION

After the annual out-of-pocket threshold has been met, a PDP covers a new drug at 50 percent coinsurance, but generic drugs are free (no copay or coinsurance). Does this satisfy the statutory definition of "standard prescription drug coverage"?

Part D was passed by a Republican Congress and signed by President Bush, with almost no Democratic support in Congress. One of the most politically controversial provisions promised "non-interference" with prescription drug prices. Social Security Act §1860D-11(i), 42 U.S.C. §1395w-111(i). Instead of using Medicare's buying power to negotiate lower prices, Congress blocked Medicare from collectively negotiating the prices of prescription drugs, effectively dividing the market among hundreds of competing drug plans. As this edition goes to press, a national conversation is ongoing regarding the ever-rising cost of pharmaceuticals, and some proposals attempt to ensure that the discounts insurers negotiate are passed on to patients, but with no apparent will to allow Medicare to negotiate drug prices.

4. PAYMENT: FEE FOR SERVICE, PROSPECTIVE PAYMENT SYSTEMS, AND ALTERNATIVES

In the 1960s, some private insurance plans paid physicians or hospitals directly, but most reimbursed patients for bills they had paid. Today, even though most health insurance payments are made directly to the health care provider, payment to the provider is generally called "reimbursement." Health plans did not make open-ended promises to pay every medical bill, but rather by contract they generally agreed to pay only for "medically necessary" care. As a result, health insurers (including Medicare) are closely involved in deciding whether care was medically necessary and therefore reimbursable. For example, in a typical labor and delivery without complications, a week-long hospital stay would exceed the medically necessary amount of time (two to three days is typical). Or consider the *Redding* case in the Introduction in Chapter 1: Heart surgery is not reimbursable unless adequate proof exists in the medical record that the patient's heart needed that surgery.

After a service has been determined to be medically necessary, insurance then calculates the amount of the fee. Physicians and hospitals have operated under different systems for many years. For physicians, payment was fee for service, much as a lawyer might bill by the hour. For hospitals, Blue Cross plans typically paid "reasonable costs" in a retrospective cost-based system, meaning that hospitals would receive interim payments during the year, which would be adjusted at year end based on the actual costs incurred at the hospital, as documented in a "cost report" filed each year. When Medicare was enacted in 1965, it copied these existing systems, with health insurance plans (often Blue Cross plans) serving as contractors for the federal government. Physicians essentially set their own prices, and hospitals were reimbursed based on their reasonable costs described in their Medicare Cost Reports. Not surprisingly, fee-for-service and cost-based reimbursement led to increases in the price, number, and intensity of services, as hospitals that spent more were paid more. Medicare costs continued to increase, both in absolute terms and as a percentage of the economy:

> A patient at a hospital will generally receive two sets of bills: one from treating physicians, called the "professional" fee, and a second from the hospital, called a "facility" or "technical" fee, for use of the room, equipment, and staffing such as nurses.

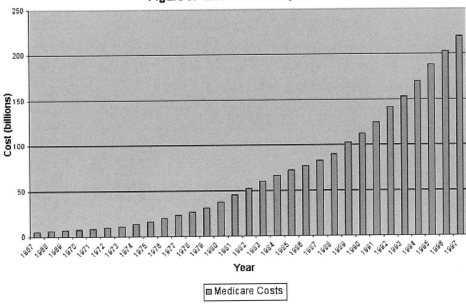

Figure 5: Medicare Costs, 1967-97

Source: http:// thomas. loc. gov/ medicare/ history.htm

In 1983, Congress dramatically altered Medicare's Part A payment system, adopting a system of bundled payments for most hospitals and other institutions, called the Prospective Payment System (PPS). 42 U.S.C. §1395ww(d). Instead of being paid for reasonable costs based on what they spent, hospitals were paid for a bundled episode of care, such as all of the care involved in a patient's coronary arterial bypass graft. These bundles are called diagnosis-related groups (DRGs). Under DRGs, hospitals experienced direct financial incentives to economize care; if the hospital could treat the patient more quickly or efficiently, profits increased.

The revolutionary change in physician reimbursement was passed in 1989, effective in 1992. In essence, Medicare sets a national physician budget, which is then allocated across specialties in a zero-sum game. Physicians are now paid based on specific codes for every imaginable service, called Current Procedural Terminology or CPT codes. Each year, CMS determines how much each CPT code (such as an office well-baby visit or setting a broken arm) is worth. That process involves comparing all CPT codes and comparing the "relative values" of each code, based on the relative amount of work and equipment required. This is called the resource-based relative value scale (RBRVS), which adjusted physician payments upward or downward based on the results. Billions of dollars of physician reimbursement are at risk whenever the RBRVS is updated. Physician professional societies control the process for assigning CPT codes and for allocating relative values, which shifts the zero-sum game to the advantage of procedure-based specialists as opposed to primary care doctors.

> The American Medical Association (AMA) owns and has trademarked Current Procedural Terminology (CPT), a significant money maker for the organization.

Both DRGs and CPTs fix the unit price for hospital and physician services in a given year, but they did not directly control the growth in the volume of services.

Annual Growth in Per-Beneficiary Spending in Parts A and B of Medicare, Fiscal Years 1980 to 2012

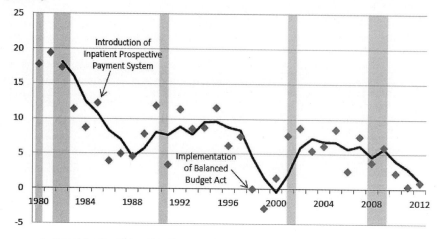

Source: Based on expenditure data provided by the Centers for Medicare and Medicaid Services, Office of the Actuary
Note: Shaded bars indicate recessions.

Faced with lower (or higher) reimbursement per unit of service, health care providers responded by billing more units. Some of this increased billing was appropriate; other episodes are explored in Chapter 6 on fraud and abuse. Nevertheless, prospective payment and related reforms seem to have slowed the growth in Medicare expenditures per beneficiary.

> The term "ambulatory" originally meant that the patient could walk out after a brief period of recovery. Today, the regulatory definition requires that such patients ordinarily do not stay in the hospital overnight (hence, they are "outpatients," not "inpatients"). A colloquial synonym is "same-day" surgery.

Today, the PPS in Medicare differs depending upon the type of institution. A few designated institutions, such as small rural "critical access" hospitals, remain under a modified version of the old Medicare cost report system, but over time most have been moved to prospective payment, often with individualized regulations and guidance. In other words, CMS uses separate PPS calculations to pay inpatient hospitals, home health agencies, hospices, hospital outpatient facilities, inpatient psychiatric facilities, inpatient rehabilitation facilities, long-term care hospitals, federally qualified health centers, and skilled nursing facilities. A related but distinct PPS applies to ambulatory surgical centers (ASCs). The ASC reimbursement system was specifically designed to encourage doctors to shift certain surgical procedures out of hospitals and into outpatient surgical centers that could deliver care more efficiently and without an overnight stay. This change in federal reimbursement dramatically shifted where surgical procedures occur in the United States, as many patients were moved to the ASC or outpatient setting in response to Medicare's economic incentives. Most hospitals responded by designating part of their hospital as an outpatient surgical center, even if located in the same building as the inpatient surgical areas. Many physicians who practiced such surgery chose to partner with either hospitals or national surgical companies and built many stand-alone ASCs, which generate additional income for the doctors, who profit from both the professional fee and the facility fee.

To gain a feel for PPS, consider the excerpt below from the Preamble to the 2015 update to the Inpatient Prospective Payment System (IPPS) Rule for hospitals. Under administrative law, the Preamble is not a regulation but is merely the agency's description of the process for creating a rule. Nevertheless, Preambles are read carefully for insight into an agency's understanding and interpretation of the law it is executing. Failure to follow the PPS rule may result in Medicare's refusing to pay for the care, or even a claim that the hospital engaged in Medicare fraud. The case that follows the IPPS Rule offers some historical background as well as a sense of the judiciary's uneasy role in Medicare payment disputes.

Hospital Inpatient Prospective Payment Systems for Acute Care Hospitals and the Long Term Care Hospital Prospective Payment System and Proposed Fiscal Year 2015 Rates

79 Fed. Reg. 27,978 (May 15, 2014)

I. Executive Summary and Background
A. Executive Summary
1. Purpose and Legal Authority

This proposed rule would make payment and policy changes under the Medicare inpatient prospective payment systems (IPPS) for operating and capital related costs of acute care hospitals as well as for certain hospitals and hospital units excluded from the IPPS. In addition, it would make payment and policy changes for inpatient hospital services provided by long-term care hospitals (LTCHs) under the long-term care hospital prospective payment system (LTCH PPS). It also would make policy changes to programs associated with Medicare IPPS hospitals, IPPS excluded hospitals, and LTCHs. Under various statutory authorities, we are proposing to make changes to the Medicare IPPS, to the LTCH PPS, and to other related payment methodologies and programs for FY 2015 and subsequent fiscal years. These statutory authorities include, but are not limited to, the following:

- Section 1886(d) of the Social Security Act (the Act), which sets forth a system of payment for the operating costs of acute care hospital inpatient stays under Medicare Part A (Hospital Insurance) based on prospectively set rates. Section 1886(g) of the Act requires that, instead of paying for capital-related costs of inpatient hospital services on a reasonable cost basis, the Secretary use a prospective payment system (PPS). . . .

B. Summary
1. Acute Care Hospital Inpatient Prospective Payment System (IPPS)

Section 1886(d) of the Social Security Act (the Act) sets forth a system of payment for the operating costs of acute care hospital inpatient stays under Medicare Part A (Hospital Insurance) based on prospectively set rates. Section 1886(g) of the Act requires the Secretary to use a prospective payment system (PPS) to pay for the capital-related costs of inpatient hospital services. . . . Under these PPSs, Medicare payment for hospital inpatient operating and capital-related costs is made at predetermined, specific rates for each hospital discharge. Discharges are classified according to a list of diagnosis-related groups (DRGs).

DRGs have been modified many times since 1983 as Medicare has fine-tuned this reimbursement system. One complaint was that some hospitals treated sicker patients than others, but these patients all received the same DRG reimbursement. The response has been to adjust DRGs for the severity of the case, resulting in MS-DRGs that are used today. Many such attempts to make the system fairer add to its complexity.

The base payment rate is comprised of a standardized amount that is divided into a labor-related share and a nonlabor-related share. The labor-related share is adjusted by the wage index applicable to the area where the hospital is located. If the hospital is located in Alaska or Hawaii, the nonlabor-related share is adjusted by a cost-of-living adjustment factor. This base payment rate is multiplied by the DRG relative weight. If the hospital treats a high percentage of certain low-income patients, it receives a percentage add-on payment applied to the DRG-adjusted base payment rate. This add-on payment, known as the disproportionate share hospital (DSH) adjustment, provides for a percentage increase in Medicare payments to hospitals that qualify under either of two statutory formulas designed to identify hospitals that serve a disproportionate share of low-income patients. For qualifying hospitals, the amount of this adjustment varies based on the outcome of the statutory calculations. The Affordable Care Act revised the Medicare DSH payment methodology and provides for a new additional Medicare payment that considers the amount of uncompensated care beginning on October 1, 2013.

If the hospital is an approved teaching hospital, it receives a percentage add-on payment for each case paid under the IPPS, known as the indirect medical education (IME) adjustment. This percentage varies, depending on the ratio of residents to beds. . . .

II. Proposed Changes to Medicare Severity Diagnosis-Related Group (MS-DRG) Classifications and Relative Weights

A. Background

Section 1886(d) of the Act specifies that the Secretary shall establish a classification system (referred to as diagnosis-related groups (DRGs)) for inpatient discharges and adjust payments under the IPPS based on appropriate weighting factors assigned to each DRG. Therefore, under the IPPS, Medicare pays for inpatient hospital services on a rate per discharge basis that varies according to the DRG to which a beneficiary's stay is assigned. The formula used to calculate payment for a specific case multiplies an individual hospital's payment rate per case by the weight of the DRG to which the case is assigned. Each DRG weight represents the average resources required to care for cases in that particular DRG, relative to the average resources used to treat cases in all DRGs.

Congress recognized that it would be necessary to recalculate the DRG relative weights periodically to account for changes in resource consumption. Accordingly, section 1886(d)(4)(C) of the Act requires that the Secretary adjust the DRG classifications and relative weights at least annually. These adjustments are made to reflect changes in treatment patterns, technology, and any other factors that may change the relative use of hospital resources. . . .

F. Proposed Adjustment to MS-DRGs for Preventable Hospital-Acquired Conditions (HACs), Including Infections for FY 2015

1. Background

Section 1886(d)(4)(D) of the Act addresses certain hospital-acquired conditions (HACs), including infections. This provision is part of an array of Medicare tools that we are using to promote increased quality and efficiency of care. Under the IPPS, hospitals are encouraged to treat patients efficiently because they receive the same DRG payment for stays that vary in length and in the services provided, which gives hospitals an incentive to avoid unnecessary costs in the delivery of care. In some cases, conditions acquired in the hospital do not generate higher payments than the hospital would otherwise receive for cases without these conditions. To this extent, the IPPS encourages hospitals to avoid complications.

However, the treatment of certain conditions can generate higher Medicare payments in two ways. First, if a hospital incurs exceptionally high costs treating a patient, the hospital stay may generate an outlier payment. Because the outlier payment methodology requires that hospitals experience large losses on outlier cases before outlier payments are made, hospitals have an incentive to prevent outliers. Second, under the MS-DRG system that took effect in FY 2008 and that has been refined through rulemaking in subsequent years, certain conditions can generate higher payments even if the outlier payment requirements are not met. Under the MS-DRG system, there are currently 261 sets of MS-DRGs that are split into 2 or 3 subgroups based on the presence or absence of a complication or comorbidity (CC) or a major complication or comorbidity (MCC). The presence of a CC or an MCC generally results in a higher payment.

Section 1886(d)(4)(D) of the Act specifies that, by October 1, 2007, the Secretary was required to select, in consultation with the Centers for Disease Control and Prevention (CDC), at least two conditions that: (a) Are high cost, high volume, or both; (b) are assigned to a higher paying MS-DRG when present as a secondary diagnosis (that is, conditions under the MS-DRG system that are CCs or MCCs); and (c) could reasonably have been prevented through the application of evidence based guidelines. Section 1886(d)(4)(D) of the Act also specifies that the list of conditions may be revised, again in consultation with the CDC, from time to time as long as the list contains at least two conditions.

Effective for discharges occurring on or after October 1, 2008, Medicare no longer assigns an inpatient hospital discharge to a higher paying MS-DRG if a selected condition is not present on admission (POA). Thus, if a selected condition that was not POA manifests during the hospital stay, it is considered a HAC and the case is paid as though the secondary diagnosis was not present. However, even if a HAC manifests during the hospital stay, if any nonselected CC or MCC appears on the claim, the claim will be paid at the higher MS-DRG rate. In addition,

Medicare continues to assign a discharge to a higher paying MS-DRG if a selected condition is POA. . . .

QUESTIONS

1. What kinds of factors does Medicare use to set prospective payment rates?
2. What is the purpose of the downward payment adjustments related to HACs?

Many hospitals look for areas where they are being under-reimbursed. Sometimes, providers cross legal and ethical boundaries when seeking higher reimbursement. Consider these business and legal problems as you read the next case, which exemplifies how interested parties can view the same Medicare reimbursement rules in disparate ways.

In a complex regulatory system, questions are sometimes left unanswered by statutory language, necessitating rulemaking by the relevant agency under the Administrative Procedure Act (APA). Medicare is a complex statute that has many interpretive and implementing regulations. In a federal spending program like Medicare, each regulatory decision can potentially shift billions of dollars, creating economic winners and losers. Some losers sue, claiming the regulation violates the APA. In the case that follows, several million dollars in Medicare reimbursement were at stake due to rival interpretations of the word "has." Read this case not solely for the narrow question at issue but also as an overview of Medicare reimbursement and as an example of the type of litigation that commonly follows a new Medicare regulation.

Transitional Hospitals Corp. of Louisiana, Inc. v. Shalala

222 F.3d 1019 (D.C. Cir. 2000)

The Medicare program reimburses certain categories of hospitals on a "reasonable cost" basis, rather than under the generally applicable, and less remunerative, "Prospective Payment System." Long-term care hospitals are one such category. Plaintiffs own two new facilities for which they sought classification as long-term care hospitals before they began admitting patients. The Department of Health and Human Services (HHS) rejected plaintiffs' request, citing regulations that require new hospitals to have six months of experience before they can qualify as "long-term." In enacting those regulations, the Secretary of HHS took the position that an initial data-collection period is statutorily required. Plaintiffs, challenging the regulations in the district court, took the opposite position: that the Medicare statute does not mandate an initial data-collection period and in fact manifestly requires HHS to reimburse them as long-term hospitals from the first day of operation. The district court agreed with plaintiffs and declared HHS' regulations invalid.

We do not find the statute as clear as either side suggests, but rather conclude that Congress intended the Secretary to exercise discretion in determining the manner in which a hospital qualifies as a long-term care facility. We therefore reverse the decision of the district court. However, because the Secretary mistakenly believed that she lacked such discretion, we remand the case to permit her to determine whether she wishes to retain the existing regulations knowing that other options are permissible.

I

Medicare is a federal health insurance program for the aged and disabled that is administered by the Health Care Financing Administration (HCFA) of HHS. Under Medicare Part A, institutional health care providers are reimbursed for their services to eligible patients. From its inception until 1983, Medicare reimbursed hospitals for the "reasonable cost" of providing inpatient care, subject to certain limitations.

By 1983, Congress had become concerned that hospitals reimbursed on a reasonable cost basis lacked incentives to operate efficiently. This concern led to the revision of the Medicare payment system in that year. In place of the reasonable cost method, Congress enacted the Prospective Payment System (PPS) as the principal method of compensating hospitals for inpatient care provided to eligible patients. Under PPS, hospitals are reimbursed according to flat rates established in advance for the various categories of patient diagnoses (known as "diagnosis-related groups" or "DRGs"). The rates reflect the average cost associated with treating a patient for a specific condition, and encourage hospitals to keep costs within the anticipated reimbursement levels. For the care of patients whose hospitalizations are extraordinarily costly or lengthy, the statute authorizes the Secretary to make "outlier payments" to supplement the standard PPS disbursement.

> Until June of 2001, Health Care Financing Administration (HCFA) was the name for the agency now called CMS. The HCFA acronym still appears in documents that pre-date that change, such as this decision.

Because PPS was "developed for short-term acute care general hospitals," Congress acknowledged that it did not "adequately take into account special circumstances of diagnoses requiring long stays." Thus, Congress altogether excluded from PPS certain types of hospitals that treat atypical patient populations. These hospitals instead receive reimbursement for inpatient care under the reasonable cost system. One type of hospital subject to the statutory exclusion is a long-term care hospital, which the statute describes as "a hospital which has an average inpatient length of stay (as determined by the Secretary) of greater than 25 days." The availability of this exclusion is the central issue in the case before us.

A

HHS implemented the new PPS reimbursement scheme by enacting regulations in 1984. In issuing its final rule, although not in the rule itself, HHS announced that it intended to apply the statutory exclusions prospectively only: any change in a hospital's status (i.e., whether it was subject to or excluded from PPS) that occurred during one cost reporting period would generally take effect only at the start of the next period, with each period typically lasting one year. Thus, a new hospital would not qualify for the exclusion at least until the initial reporting period was over. To accommodate new hospitals, HHS permitted an abbreviated initial cost reporting period of six months, rather than the usual one year.

In 1992, HHS formalized its prospective approach to exclusions by proposing and then adopting the following rule: For purposes of exclusion from the prospective payment systems . . . , the status of each currently participating hospital . . . is determined at the beginning of each cost reporting period and is effective for the entire cost reporting period. Any changes in the status of the hospital are made only at the start of a cost reporting period. 42 C.F.R. §412.22(d). Thus, a hospital that qualifies for the exclusion in the middle of a reporting period will not benefit until the next reporting period. By the same token, a hospital that ceases to qualify in the midst of a cost reporting period will nevertheless be compensated as though it were exempt for the entire period. For a new hospital, HHS' rule confirmed that the exclusion does not begin until the first six months of data collection have passed.

In response to the notice of proposed rulemaking, the National Association of Long Term Hospitals (NALTH) suggested that HHS permit new long-term care hospitals to self-certify their average length of stay from the start. HHS, however, concluded that it did not have the discretion to permit self-certification by long-term care hospitals. "We do not believe that the statute permits us," the Department said, "to extend the exclusion for long-term care hospitals to a hospital which has not demonstrated actual compliance with the statutory requirement." Medicare Program; Changes to the Hospital Inpatient Prospective Payment Systems and Fiscal Year 1993 Rates, 57 Fed. Reg. 39,746, 39,800–01 (1992) [hereinafter Final Rule]. The "criterion for exclusion as a long-term care hospital (average inpatient length of stay greater than 25 days) can be assessed only over a period of time. Thus, a hospital cannot qualify as a long-term care hospital until it has been in operation for some period of time."

B

Plaintiffs Transitional Hospitals Corporation of Louisiana and Transitional Hospitals Corporation of Texas (hereinafter "the THC plaintiffs") opened two new hospitals at the end of 1992. Both were intended to treat patients with medically complex conditions requiring extended inpatient stays, thereby qualifying for the long-term care hospital exclusion from PPS. Before commencing operations, the THC plaintiffs wrote HCFA stating that they "only expect to admit patients whose medical conditions will result in lengths of stay in excess of 25 days." They asked HCFA to exclude them from PPS from the starting date of their Medicare provider agreements, rather than reimburse them under PPS during their first six months of operation.

> Trade associations become involved in administrative decisions like this one, acting on behalf of their members. The government sometimes encourages their involvement, as it supplements other fact-finding during the administrative law process.

Kathleen Buto, the Director of HCFA's Bureau of Policy Development, wrote back denying plaintiffs' request. Buto said that the statute mandates exclusion only for "a hospital which *has* [emphasis added] an average length of stay (as determined by the Secretary) of greater than 25 days." Noting that HHS regulations implement that mandate by "examining [a hospital's] actual operating experience in a past period, rather than by relying on its admission criteria or other formalized statements of how the hospital is intended or expected to operate," Buto concluded that the THC plaintiffs could not qualify for the exclusion in advance.

Having had their request turned down, the THC plaintiffs proceeded with the six-month cost reporting period. During that time, they were reimbursed under PPS, supplemented by outlier payments. At the end of the six-month period, both hospitals demonstrated average inpatient lengths of stay exceeding 25 days, thereby qualifying for exclusion from PPS—and entitling them to payment for "reasonable costs"—during the next cost reporting period. Plaintiffs estimate that their PPS reimbursement during the initial six-month period was approximately $1.2 million per hospital less than it would have been under the reasonable cost standard.

The THC plaintiffs requested a hearing before the Provider Reimbursement Review Board, which is authorized by statute to hear the complaints of providers dissatisfied with the compensation they have received. Plaintiffs challenged the validity of the regulations that denied them compensation for reasonable costs during their first months of operation. The Board, however, concluded that it lacked authority to determine the validity of HHS regulations.

Plaintiffs then brought suit in the United States District Court for the District of Columbia. Ruling on the parties' cross motions for summary judgment, the court concluded that the Medicare statute was neither silent nor ambiguous on the question. Rather, the court concluded that the statute unambiguously requires HHS to provide a PPS exclusion from the beginning of a new long-term care hospital's participation in the Medicare program. The court further held that even if the statute were ambiguous, the Secretary's regulations did not constitute a permissible interpretation of the legislative language. The court therefore declared the regulations invalid insofar as they preclude new long-term care hospitals from securing immediate exclusion from PPS. This appeal by the Secretary followed.

> The plaintiffs had to exhaust administrative remedies before filing the federal lawsuit.

II

We review de novo the district court's ruling on the motions for summary judgment. In judging the validity of the Secretary's regulations, we apply the familiar two-step framework of Chevron U.S.A. Inc. v. Natural Resources Defense Council, Inc. We first ask "whether Congress has directly spoken to the precise question at issue," in which case we "must give effect to the unambiguously expressed intent of Congress." If the "statute is silent or ambiguous with respect to the specific issue," we move to the second step and defer to the agency's interpretation as long as it is "based on a permissible construction of the statute." However, deference is "only appropriate when the agency has exercised its own judgment." "When, instead, the agency's decision is based on an erroneous view of the law, its decision cannot stand."

A

We begin with *Chevron* step one, and with the Secretary's contention that Congress unambiguously expressed its intent to bar the relief plaintiffs request.

The statutory provision at issue is quite brief. It excludes from PPS any "hospital which has an average inpatient length of stay (as determined by the Secretary) of greater than 25 days." When the Secretary adopted her implementing regulations, she took the position that the statute does not permit her to certify a hospital as long-term in advance because the criterion for exclusion, an average inpatient length of stay greater than 25 days, "can be assessed only over a period of time." "Thus," she said, "a hospital cannot qualify as a long-term care hospital until it has been in operation for some period of time." Similarly, when HCFA turned down plaintiffs' request for self-certification, it stressed that, because under the statute only a hospital that "has" the requisite length of stay is eligible, a hospital cannot qualify until it makes the requisite showing that it "has" that average length of stay.

The statute seems neither so clear, nor so dictatorial, to us. Although it does establish a criterion based on average length of stay, the statute is silent as to how and when that length should be calculated. Nothing in the language precludes the Secretary from determining length of stay based on a prediction drawn, as plaintiffs suggest here, from a hospital's policy of admitting only "patients whose medical conditions will result in lengths of stay in excess of 25 days."

Nor does the statute's use of the present tense verb "has" definitively resolve the question. Although to qualify it must be true that a hospital "has" the requisite length of stay, that word does not tell us how to determine whether that state of being exists. The agency has implicitly recognized as much by adopting a policy of determining a hospital's status at the beginning of a cost reporting period, and then permitting it to retain that status for the entire period — even if conditions change in the interim. Under this policy, HHS excludes a hospital for the next period based on data derived from the prior period, regardless of whether the hospital actually "has" the requisite average on each day of the next period.

Moreover, nothing in the statutory language precludes an alternative form of relief requested by plaintiffs: retroactive reimbursement for reasonable costs incurred during the first six months if, at the end of that period, the hospital shows that it had a 25-day average during that period. Again, the word "has" does not unambiguously decide this question. Each of plaintiffs' hospitals could have accurately said on its six-month anniversary that today it "has" a greater than 25-day average — referring to the entire period from day one through and including day 180. It would therefore have been consistent with the literal language to reimburse the hospital on that day for all of its reasonable costs incurred to date.

Finally, and perhaps most important, this is not a statute as to which we can only infer, from Congress' silence, an implicit intent to delegate to the Secretary the authority to reasonably interpret the statutory terms. Rather, in this case the statute excludes a hospital that has an average length of stay of greater than 25 days, "as determined by the Secretary." Thus, Congress has provided "an express delegation of authority to the agency to elucidate a specific provision of the statute by regulation." This means that the Secretary has discretion to determine how to calculate the qualifying length of stay, and that we are bound to uphold her determination as long as she exercises that discretion in a reasonable way.

B

The THC plaintiffs also see the statute as clear and unambiguous — although in precisely the opposite way as that perceived by HHS. In their view, and in the view of the district court, the use of the present tense "has" requires that if during any given period the hospital "has" a 25-day average, it must be considered exempt for the entire period. The use of the present tense, plaintiffs contend, requires that the exclusion "be applied on a current basis," and "allows no alternative temporal reading." Or, as the district court put it, "the plain language of the statute indicates that a long-term care hospital may obtain an exemption from the Prospective Payment System whenever it 'has' an average inpatient length of stay greater than 25 days."

Again we disagree, this time for the mirror image of our reasoning with respect to HHS' interpretation. Because the statute does not tell us how to determine whether a hospital "has" the required average length of stay, it cannot be read as requiring the agency to make that determination constantly and instantaneously — any more than it can be read (as HHS would have it) as requiring the agency to make that determination prospectively only. . . .

But, plaintiffs argue, if Congress had intended the exclusion to apply prospectively, it could have drafted the statute to provide a PPS exclusion for a hospital that "had" an average inpatient length of stay greater than 25 days "during its most recent cost reporting period." Frankly, we do not see such a revised statute as particularly less ambiguous. Indeed, we do not see why HHS could not have proffered the same editorial suggestion and then made the opposite argument: If Congress had intended hospitals to receive retroactive reimbursement as plaintiffs contend, wouldn't it have defined the exclusion as covering hospitals that "had" the requisite average during their "most recent cost reporting period"? In any event, while positing a "clearer" way to write a statute may suggest that an existing statute is ambiguous, it surely does not establish that it is unambiguous. And if the statute is not unambiguous, *Chevron* requires us to defer to a reasonable reading by the Secretary.

We also must take care to read the word "has" in the context of the entire phrase of which it is a part. Two elements of that context are important here. First, the statutory exclusion is for a hospital that has "an average" inpatient length of stay of greater than 25 days. The criterion of "an average" strongly militates against plaintiffs' view that a hospital's status must be measured at every moment in time. As HHS correctly points out, an average is a criterion that can only be assessed over a period of time. Moreover, the statute refers not to an average "over" a period of 25 days, but to an average "of" 25 days — necessarily indicating that the period of measurement must be more than 25 days in order reasonably to determine whether the "average" during that period was at least 25 days. Hence, the use of the word "has" in conjunction with the word "average" would not preclude waiting until six months have passed to determine whether, at that point, the hospital "has" an average of 25 days over a 180-day period.

Indeed, were we to read the statute as literally as plaintiffs and the district court suggest, plaintiffs' own contention — that they "met the 25-day requirement at all times during their operation" and so were entitled to payment from the first day — would be plainly incorrect. On day one, the hospitals could not have had a 25-day average because 25 days had not yet passed. If a hospital must be, and may only be, paid for days on which it "has" a 25-day average, plaintiffs could not have qualified earlier than the 25th day. Even then, they could have done so only if every patient present on day one were still at the hospital 25 days later.

The second element of context that is important here is the statute's parenthetical phrase, "as determined by the Secretary." As we have discussed above, by employing this phrase Congress has made "an express delegation of authority to the agency to elucidate [the] specific provision of the statute by regulation." This further takes the case out of the realm of *Chevron* step one's de novo review, and into the realm of *Chevron* step two — which asks only whether the agency's interpretation is reasonable. And that gives the agency considerable leeway to determine how "has" is to be defined, and whether to require prospective, contemporaneous, or retrospective evaluation and payment.

Plaintiffs resist the conclusion that Congress has delegated definitional authority to HHS. They argue that the fact that the parenthetical "as determined by the Secretary" follows the phrase "an average inpatient length of stay," means that Congress has only given the agency "discretion to determine how the average length of stay will be calculated" — and not whether the hospital "has" that average. This is far too sophistic a reading. First, the concession that the agency has discretion to determine how to calculate the average necessarily means it has discretion to determine whether a hospital "has" that average — since a hospital cannot have a qualifying average unless it satisfies the agency's calculation methodology. Second, even if word placement were decisive, it is as true that the delegating parenthetical follows the phrase "has an average inpatient length of stay" as that it follows the phrase "an average inpatient length of stay." At most this renders the scope of Congress' delegation ambiguous, which again moves us to *Chevron*'s second step. . . .

III

Having concluded that the analysis of *Chevron* step one does not resolve the case, we would ordinarily move to step two and ask whether the Secretary's interpretation of the meaning of the statute is reasonable. Plaintiffs argue that the Secretary's interpretation is not reasonable, contending that HHS has no justification for not permitting self-certification, for not utilizing the alternative of retroactive reimbursement, and for denying both options to long-term care hospitals while making them available to another category of PPS-excluded institutions: rehabilitation hospitals.

HHS replies that it is perfectly reasonable to rely on actual data regarding length of stay rather than on a hospital's self-interested prediction. The Department explains that it permits self-certification by rehabilitation hospitals because the criteria for qualification of such hospitals are based on the "characteristics of the patients and the types of services that the facility furnishes," criteria which—unlike length of stay—a hospital can "virtually guarantee[ ]" from the first day of operations. With respect to the alternative of retroactive adjustment, HHS points out that no one suggested such an option until after the district court litigation began in this case. Moreover, HHS argues that retroactive adjustments are as likely to hurt hospitals that slip below the average during a period for which they have been prospectively qualified, as it is to help them by providing reimbursement for a prior period in which they became qualified along the way. By setting reimbursement rates "that are not later subject to retroactive correction," HHS contends, "the Secretary promotes certainty and predictability of payment for not only hospitals but the federal government."

Although we ordinarily would now proceed to evaluate these various arguments under the standards of *Chevron*'s second step, we cannot do so in this case. While the Secretary has discretion to establish a reasonable mechanism for determining whether a hospital has the requisite average length of inpatient stay, that discretion must be exercised through the eyes of one who realizes she possesses it. At several points, the Department's briefs suggest that the Secretary did realize that she had such discretion. At other points, the briefs suggest quite the opposite. Most relevant, however, is that the notice issued at the time the final rule was promulgated makes it quite clear the Secretary did not believe that she had the discretion to do what the plaintiffs request. . . .

As the Supreme Court has instructed, an agency "order may not stand if the agency has misconceived the law." Applying that principle, this court has held that "an agency regulation must be declared invalid, even though the agency might be able to adopt the regulation in the exercise of its discretion, if it was not based on the [agency's] own judgment but rather on the unjustified assumption that it was Congress' judgment that such [a regulation is] desirable" or required. Because the Secretary evaluated the various reimbursement alternatives on the assumption that "a hospital cannot qualify as a long-term care hospital until it has been in operation for some period of time," and because that assumption is incorrect, the Secretary must make a fresh determination as to whether she wishes to adopt the self-certification or retroactive adjustment options.

IV

For the foregoing reasons, the judgment of the district court is reversed. The case is remanded to that court with instructions to remand it to HHS for further consideration consistent with this opinion.

QUESTIONS

1. Why does the court both agree and disagree with each side in this case?
2. Who is the "winner" given the outcome?
3. Is the court's intervention a sound manner in which to administer a complex federal spending program? If you think not, what alternatives would you propose?

5. THE POWER OF GOVERNMENT REIMBURSEMENT TO CHANGE PROVIDER BEHAVIOR

Medicare influences provider behavior through its reimbursement policies in several ways. First, Medicare does not cover all medical services and items; for example, Medicare will pay for heart surgery but not for vacations to reduce stress or healthier food for a heart-healthy diet. Second, Medicare imposes minimum quality standards — called "conditions of participation" — on all providers seeking reimbursement. These standards change over time. For example, in 2016, CMS proposed to update Medicare conditions of participation to require all hospitals and long-term care facilities to operate an antibiotic stewardship program that would reduce unnecessary use of antibiotics to battle growing antibiotic resistance. This new condition of participation would influence how participating hospitals and long-term care facilities treat their patients. Third, while Medicare has historically paid on a fee-for-service basis, recent policy initiatives are beginning to shift the focus from quantity to value. CMS is trying to lead a quality revolution in U.S. health care by reimbursing for value (also called pay for performance or P4P).

Further, Medicare influences most U.S. health care spending, even spending by private insurance companies. The reason is that almost all U.S. hospitals participate in Medicare, with rare exceptions such as Shriners Hospitals that serve only children and never bill patients for any services. As a result, Medicare rules influence almost every hospital for all of their patients, whether or not Medicare covers the individual patient. No hospital wants to risk losing Medicare as a source of payment.

Physicians also are keenly interested in complying with Medicare rules. Federal law does not require physicians to become "participating providers," but a physician who does not contract with Medicare will be reimbursed at a lower rate. 42 U.S.C. §1395w-4, Incentives for participating physicians and suppliers, provides, in part:

> In . . . the case of a nonparticipating physician or a nonparticipating supplier or other person, the fee schedule amount shall be 95 percent of such amount otherwise applied under this subsection. . . . In the case of physicians' services . . . of a nonparticipating physician, supplier, or other person for which payment is made under this part on a basis other than the fee schedule amount, the payment shall be based on 95 percent of the payment basis for such services furnished by a participating physician, supplier, or other person.

While paying for value (or quality) can seem an attractive approach in theory, the practical aspects can be challenging. One source of added complexity is the fact that Medicare now has three primary payment models: traditional fee-for-service (FFS) Medicare (Parts A and B); Medicare Advantage, which uses a managed care model; and a new model, accountable care organizations (ACOs), which gives more power to manage health costs to providers, typically led by a hospital system. The Medicare

MedPAC is an independent advisory body created to give nonpartisan advice to Congress and CMS on the design and operation of the Medicare program.

Payment Advisory Commission (MedPAC) has studied Medicare payment methodologies, with some recommendations incorporated most recently into the ACA. The following report details some of the lessons learned in recent years.

Report to the Congress: Medicare and the Health Care Delivery System

(June 2014)

Chapter 3 Measuring Quality of Care in Medicare

Introduction

The Commission has been making quality measurement recommendations for Medicare since 2003. The Commission's initial work in this area was spurred in part by the publication of two reports by the Institute of Medicine in 1999 and 2001, which detailed poor quality of care across the U.S. health care system and proposed steps to improve it, including the development and use of evidence-based quality measures. The Commission also established a position that Medicare should no longer pay providers of care solely on the basis of the volume of services rendered, but also on the quality of the care delivered.

These two reports by the Institute of Medicine (now called the National Academy of Medicine) laid bare the quality problems endemic in the U.S. health care system.

The Commission's recommendations on quality have followed two paths. First, Medicare should use a set of process, outcome, and patient experience measures to evaluate the quality of care of Medicare Advantage (MA) plans and of providers in fee-for-service (FFS) Medicare (each provider type (hospitals, physicians, etc.) would be evaluated separately). The set of measures should be small to minimize the administrative burden on providers and CMS. Second, Medicare should base a small portion of payments to FFS providers or MA plans on their performance on the selected quality measures. The Commission has stated that outcome measures, such as mortality and health care–associated infection rates, should be weighted most heavily in Medicare's pay-for-performance programs.

Over the past 10 years, the Congress has enacted quality reporting programs for almost all of the major FFS provider types and MA plans and has gone further to mandate pay-for-performance programs (which Medicare refers to as value-based purchasing) for hospitals, dialysis facilities, MA plans, and physicians. Pay-for-performance is also a central component of Medicare policy for accountable care organizations (ACOs).

A decade ago, most quality measurement technology, . . . was designed to detect underuse of clinical services (e.g., preventive care and treatment of chronic diseases) in health plans. The Commission evaluated the feasibility of using these clinical process measures, as well as outcome measures such as inpatient mortality rates and patient experience, and made a number of recommendations about how to reliably assess quality in FFS by provider type and over time.

However, over the past few years the Commission has become increasingly concerned that Medicare's current quality measurement approach has gone off track in the following ways:

- It relies on too many clinical process measures that, at best, are weakly correlated with health outcomes and that reinforce undesirable payment incentives in FFS Medicare to increase volume of services.
- It is administratively burdensome due to its use of a large and growing number of clinical process measures.
- It creates an incentive for providers to focus resources on the exact care processes being measured, whether or not those processes address the most pressing quality concerns for that provider. As a result, providers have fewer resources available for crafting their own ways to improve the outcomes of care, such as reducing avoidable hospital admissions, emergency department visits, and readmissions and improving patients' experience of care.

In short, Medicare's quality measurement systems seem to be increasingly incompatible with the Commission's goal of promoting clinically appropriate, coordinated, and patient-centered care at a cost that is affordable to the program and beneficiaries. . . .

History of the Commission's work on quality in Medicare

In its June 2003 report to the Congress, the Commission recognized that Medicare payment systems were, at best, neutral toward quality: high-quality providers were paid no more than low-quality providers, and Medicare's payment policies could actually discourage the provision of high-quality care. For example, hospitals are paid more for treating readmissions for complications that resulted from low-quality care in the hospital, and if they took steps to decrease readmissions, their revenues would fall. In addition, because beneficiaries lacked information about quality differences across providers, they had difficulty identifying high-quality providers.

The Commission's June 2003 report considered a range of incentives to increase quality, including public reporting, quality-based payment differentials for providers and plans, cost-sharing differentials for beneficiaries, flexible oversight, shared savings, risk sharing, and capitation. Drawing on experiences in the private sector, available quality measures, and Medicare's administrative capabilities, the Commission recommended that Medicare pursue demonstrations of quality-based provider payment differentials and revise payment structures to reward quality improvements. The Commission concluded that Medicare managed care plans, dialysis providers, and certain post-acute care providers were promising areas for pay-for-performance programs. . . .

Growing concern about the proliferation of process measures

In May 2011, the Commission commented on CMS's proposed regulations for the Medicare inpatient hospital VBP program authorized in the Patient Protection and Affordable Care Act of 2010. Our letter noted that many of the proposed features of the program were consistent with the Commission's 2004 and 2005 pay-for-performance recommendations. However, we also raised concerns about the process measures that CMS proposed to use in the VBP program, noting that not only would the proposed measures impose costs on hospitals for the extraction of the needed data from medical charts, but, more significantly, there might be little or no gain in health outcomes in return for that expense.

> Value-based payment (VBP) is the name given to pay-for-performance initiatives in the ACA.

We cited the substantial body of published research that found little or no association between hospitals' performance on several of the clinical process measures Medicare proposed to use and hospitals' performance on the ostensibly related mortality or readmission rates for the same conditions.

The Commission suggested that Medicare should give the most weight to a hospital's performance on outcome measures, such as the proposed 30-day mortality rate measure for selected conditions, in calculating each hospital's VBP total performance score. We also noted it might be necessary to use broader measures (e.g., an all condition mortality rate) and assess hospital performance over longer performance periods (e.g., three to five years) to address "small numbers" concerns that can affect the statistical reliability of mortality rate measurements for individual hospitals. We underscored our preference for a limited number of outcomes-focused quality measures in our March 2012 report to the Congress, in which we recommended that CMS use quality data from ambulatory surgical centers (ASCs) to implement a VBP program for ASCs that would reward high-performing providers and penalize low-performing providers.

In 2012 and 2013 comment letters on CMS's proposed rules for the inpatient and outpatient hospital payment systems and the physician fee schedule, the Commission continued to raise concerns about the directions in which quality measurement was going for those provider types in FFS Medicare. The number of process measures in the inpatient and outpatient hospital quality reporting programs had grown rapidly since the programs' inceptions, and the Commission continued to point out that there was little evidence that performance on these measures was correlated with outcomes such as mortality rates. We also noted other literature suggesting that using process measures rather than outcome measures creates an incentive for providers to focus clinical resources on ensuring good performance on the process measures while diverting resources from areas of care not being assessed.

The Commission also commented in 2012 and 2013 on the physician value-based payment modifier that CMS is implementing under a statutory mandate. The value modifier will increase or decrease payments under the Medicare physician fee schedule, and it will be applied to physicians in groups of 100 or more eligible professionals (which includes physicians and other clinical professionals as defined by CMS) starting in 2015 and to all physicians starting in 2017. CMS is working to identify a sufficient number of quality measures (as of March 2014, the agency's "measure inventory" listed 290 separate measures for the value modifier), so that each specialty has at least some applicable measures. The Commission has expressed concern that many of these measures will not address significant gaps in the quality of care for beneficiaries, either because they measure marginally effective care or because they reflect basic standards of care. In any case, by being built on top of the Medicare physician fee schedule, the value-based payment modifier itself will reinforce existing incentives in FFS reimbursement to increase the volume of services.

Concept for a new approach to quality measurement

The Commission is considering a new approach to measuring and reporting on the quality of care within and across the three main payment models in Medicare: FFS Medicare, MA, and ACOs. This quality measurement approach would deploy a small set of population-based outcome measures (such as potentially preventable hospital admissions, potentially preventable ED visits, and patient experience measures) to assess the quality of care in each of the three payment models within a local area.

We also are examining the feasibility of applying one type of measure of potentially inappropriate use of certain services—specifically, overuse measures—to measure quality in each payment model. Most of the quality measurement activity in the U.S. health care system to date has been focused on detecting underuse ("stinting") of clinically appropriate services. Overuse, however, is also a quality concern because of the potential for harm to beneficiaries—both directly from the tests and procedures performed on them and indirectly from unnecessary treatments for false-positive diagnoses and for clinically insignificant findings. Overuse also contributes to unnecessary program spending.

The Commission's vision is that, over the next several years, Medicare will move away from publicly reporting on dozens of clinical process measures and toward reporting on a small set of population-based outcome measures for the beneficiary populations served by FFS Medicare, ACOs, and MA plans. For payment policy, Medicare also could use the same population-based outcome measures to compare the quality of care in the ACOs and MA plans in a local area with the quality of FFS Medicare in the same area and to determine quality-based payment adjustments for the ACOs and MA plans. However, population-based outcome measures would not be appropriate for making payment adjustments under FFS Medicare, so Medicare would have to continue to use other, provider-based quality measures to make FFS payment adjustments—but in a much more focused and parsimonious way than it does today.

QUESTION

What are the advantages and disadvantages of process and outcome measures of quality?

Medicare includes a variety of payment experiments that are designed to improve quality of care rather than paying for each procedure and rewarding quantity over quality, such as the Value-Based Purchasing Program (VBP), the Hospital Readmissions Reduction Program (HRR), and the Hospital-Acquired Condition Reduction Program (HAC).

The Medicare Shared Savings Program (MSSP) is a key innovation in the ACA (42 U.S.C. §1395jjj) that facilitates the creation of ACOs, which are designed to transform how health care is organized and delivered. ACOs are an example of Medicare's power to influence health care providers' relationships in the corporate and transactional realm, beyond payment rates. (Medicaid has its own version of ACOs, which have different structures and goals, discussed later in this chapter.) In the Preamble to the Notice of Proposed Rule Making (NPRM), HHS explained the ACA's statutory structure for ACOs. Because this regulatory scheme is complex, it may help to keep this graphic in mind as you read the excerpt, and to remember that ACOs are an attempt to create seamless care for Medicare beneficiaries.

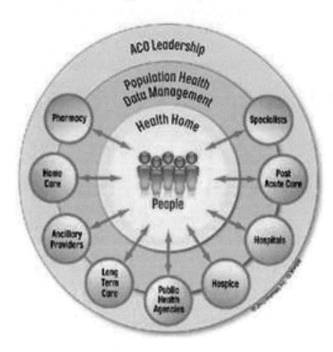

Medicare Program; Medicare Shared Savings Program: Accountable Care Organizations

76 Fed. Reg. 19,527 (Apr. 7, 2011)

. . . .

B. Statutory Basis for the Medicare Shared Savings Program

Section 3022 of the Affordable Care Act amended Title XVIII of the Social Security Act (the Act) (42 U.S.C. 1395 et seq.) by adding new section 1899 to the Act to establish a Shared Savings Program that promotes accountability for a patient population, coordinates items and services under Parts A and B, and encourages investment in infrastructure and redesigned care processes for high quality and efficient service delivery. Section 1899(a)(1) of the Act requires the Secretary to establish this program no later than January 1, 2012. Section 1899 (a)(1)(A) of the Act further provides that, "groups of providers of services and suppliers meeting criteria specified by the Secretary may work together to manage and coordinate care for Medicare fee-for-service beneficiaries through an [ACO]." Section 1899(a)(1)(B) of the Act also provides that ACOs that meet quality performance standards established by the Secretary are eligible to receive payments for "shared savings."

Section 1899(b)(1) of the Act establishes the types of groups of providers of services and suppliers, with established mechanisms for shared governance, that are eligible to participate as ACOs under the program, subject to the succeeding provisions of section 1899 of the Act, as determined appropriate by the Secretary.

Specifically, sections 1899(b)(1)(A) through (E) of the Act provide, respectively, that the following groups of providers of services and suppliers are eligible to participate:

- ACO professionals in group practice arrangements.
- Networks of individual practices of ACO professionals.
- Partnerships or joint venture arrangements between hospitals and ACO professionals.
- Hospitals employing ACO professionals.
- Such other groups of providers of services and suppliers as the Secretary determines appropriate.

> Physicians and hospitals are core participants in any Medicare ACO.

Section 1899(b)(2) of the Act establishes the requirements that such eligible groups must meet in order to participate in the program. Specifically, sections 1899(b)(2)(A) through (H) of the Act provide, respectively, that eligible groups of providers of services and suppliers must meet the following requirements to participate in the program as ACOs:

- The ACO shall be willing to become accountable for the quality, cost, and overall care of the Medicare fee-for-service (FFS) beneficiaries assigned to it.
- The ACO shall enter into an agreement with the Secretary to participate in the program for not less than a 3-year period.
- The ACO shall have a formal legal structure that would allow the organization to receive and distribute payments for shared savings to participating providers of services and suppliers.
- The ACO shall include primary care ACO professionals that are sufficient for the number of Medicare FFS beneficiaries assigned to the ACO. At a minimum, the ACO shall have at least 5,000 such beneficiaries assigned to it in order to be eligible to participate in the Shared Savings Program.
- The ACO shall provide the Secretary with such information regarding ACO professionals participating in the ACO as the Secretary determines necessary to support the assignment of Medicare fee-for-service beneficiaries to an ACO, the implementation of quality and other reporting requirements, and the determination of payments for shared savings.
- The ACO shall have in place a leadership and management structure that includes clinical and administrative systems.
- The ACO shall define processes to promote evidence-based medicine and patient engagement, report on quality and cost measures, and coordinate care, such as through the use of telehealth, remote patient monitoring, and other such enabling technologies.
- The ACO shall demonstrate to the Secretary that it meets patient-centeredness criteria specified by the Secretary, such as the use of patient and caregiver assessments or the use of individualized care plans.

Section 1899(b)(3) of the Act establishes the quality and other reporting requirements for the Shared Savings Program. For purposes of quality reporting, section 1899(b)(3)(A) of the Act provides that the Secretary shall determine appropriate measures to assess the quality of care furnished by the ACO, such as measures of clinical processes and outcomes, patient and, where practicable, caregiver experience of care, and utilization (such as rates of hospital admissions for ambulatory care sensitive conditions). Section 1899(b)(3)(B) of the Act requires an ACO to submit data in a form and manner specified by the Secretary on measures the Secretary determines necessary for the ACO to report in order to evaluate the quality of care furnished by the ACO. This provision further states that such data may include care transitions across health care settings, including hospital discharge planning and post-hospital discharge follow-up by ACO professionals, as determined to be appropriate by the Secretary. Section 1899(b)(3)(C) of the Act requires the Secretary to establish quality performance standards to assess the quality of care furnished by ACOs. That section also requires that the Secretary shall seek to improve the quality of care furnished by ACOs over time by specifying higher standards, new measures, or both for purposes of assessing such quality of care. Finally, section 1899(b)(3)(D) of the Act provides that the Secretary may, as the Secretary determines appropriate, incorporate reporting requirements and incentive payments related to the Physician Quality Reporting System under section 1848 of the Act, including such requirements and such payments related to electronic prescribing, electronic health records, and other similar initiatives under section 1848 of the Act, and may use alternative criteria than would otherwise apply under such section for determining whether to make such payments. CMS should not take the incentive payments described in the preceding sentence into consideration when calculating any payments otherwise made under of section 1899(d) the Act. . . .

> ACOs are attractive to providers for at least two reasons. First, the "shared savings" payment is additional revenue. Second, ACOs have the potential to shift market share, both initially when the ACOs are formed and over time as beneficiaries are assigned to new primary care physicians.

Section 1899(c) of the Act provides the Secretary with discretion to determine an appropriate method to assign Medicare FFS beneficiaries to an ACO participating in the Shared Savings Program. This discretion is limited, however, by the fact that under the Act, assignment must be based on beneficiaries' utilization of primary care services provided under Medicare by an ACO professional who is a physician as defined in section 1861(r)(1) of the Act.

Section 1899(d) of the Act establishes the principles and requirements for payments and treatment of savings under the Shared Savings Program. Specifically, section 1899(d)(1)(A) of the Act provides that, subject to the requirements concerning monitoring avoidance of at-risk patients, payments shall continue to be made to providers of services and suppliers participating in an ACO under the original Medicare FFS program under Parts A and B in the same manner as they would otherwise be made, except that a participating ACO is eligible to receive payment for shared savings if the following occur:

- The ACO meets quality performance standards established by the Secretary; and
- The ACO meets the requirements for realizing savings.

Section 1899(d)(1)(B) of the Act establishes the savings requirements and the method for establishing and updating the benchmark against which any savings would be determined. Specifically, section 1899(d)(1)(B)(i) of the Act establishes that, in each year of the agreement period, an ACO shall be eligible to receive payment for shared savings only if the estimated average per capita Medicare expenditures under the ACO for Medicare FFS beneficiaries for Parts A and B services, adjusted for beneficiary characteristics, is at least the percent specified by the Secretary below the applicable benchmark. The Secretary shall determine the appropriate percent of shared savings to account for normal variation in Medicare expenditures, based upon the number of Medicare FFS beneficiaries assigned to an ACO. Section 1899(d)(1)(B)(ii) of the Act, in turn, requires the Secretary to estimate a benchmark for each agreement period for each ACO using the most recent available 3 years of per beneficiary expenditures for Parts A and B services for Medicare FFS beneficiaries assigned to the ACO. This benchmark must be adjusted for beneficiary characteristics and such other factors as the Secretary determines appropriate and updated by the projected absolute amount of growth in national per capita expenditures for Parts A and B services under the original Medicare FFS program, as estimated by the Secretary. Furthermore, the benchmark must be reset at the start of each new agreement period.

Section 1899(d)(2) of the Act provides for the actual payments for shared savings under the Shared Savings Program. Specifically, if an ACO meets the quality performance standards established by the Secretary, and meets the savings requirements, a percent (as determined appropriate by the Secretary) of the difference between the estimated average per capita Medicare expenditures in the year, adjusted for beneficiary characteristics, and the benchmark for the ACO may be paid to the ACO as shared savings and the remainder of the difference shall be retained by the Medicare program. The Secretary is required to establish limits on the total amount of shared savings paid to an ACO.

Section 1899(d)(3) of the Act requires the Secretary to monitor ACOs for avoidance of at-risk patients. Specifically, if the Secretary determines that an ACO has taken steps to avoid patients at risk in order to reduce the likelihood of increasing costs to the ACO, the Secretary may impose an appropriate sanction on the ACO, including termination from the program. Section 1899(d)(4) of the Act, in turn, provides that the Secretary may terminate an agreement with an ACO if it does not meet the quality performance standards established by the Secretary. Section 1899(e) of the Act provides that chapter 35 of title 44 of the U.S. Code, which includes such provisions as the Paperwork Reduction Act (PRA), shall not apply to the Shared Savings Program. Section 1899(f) of the Act further provides the Secretary with the authority to waive such requirements of sections 1128A and 1128B of the Act and title XVIII of the Act as may be necessary to carry out the Shared Savings Program. Section 1899(g) of the Act establishes limitations on judicial and administrative review of the Shared Savings Program. This section provides that there shall be no administrative or judicial review under section 1869 of the Act, section 1878 of the Act, or otherwise of the following:

> CMS is concerned that ACOs may engage in adverse selection. If ACOs are rewarded for having healthy beneficiaries, they may try to boost payments by avoiding individuals who are chronically ill.

- The specification of criteria under 1899(a)(1)(B) of the Act.
- The assessment of the quality of care furnished by an ACO and the establishment of performance standards under 1899(b)(3) of the Act.
- The assignment of Medicare FFS beneficiaries to an ACO under 1899(c) of the Act.
- The determination of whether an ACO is eligible for shared savings under 1899(d)(2) of the Act and the amount of such shared savings, including the determination of the estimated average per capita Medicare expenditures under the ACO for Medicare FFS beneficiaries assigned to the ACO and the average benchmark for the ACO under 1899(d)(1)(B) of the Act.

- The percent of shared savings specified by the Secretary under 1899(d)(2) of the Act and any limit on the total amount of shared savings established by the Secretary under such subsection.
- The termination of an ACO under 1899(d)(4) of the Act for failure to meet the quality performance standards.

Section 1899(h) of the Act defines some basic terminology that applies to the Shared Savings Program. Specifically, section 1899(h)(1) of the Act defines the term "ACO professional" as a physician (as defined in section 1861(r)(1) of the Act) or a practitioner described in section 1842(b)(18)(C)(i) of the Act (that is, a physician assistant, nurse practitioner or clinical nurse specialist (as defined in section 1861(aa)(5) of the Act)). Section 1899(h)(2) of the Act defines the term "hospital" as a hospital (as defined in section 1886(d)(1)(B) of the Act[)].[ ] (A "subsection (d) hospital" is a hospital located in one of the fifty States or the District of Columbia, excluding hospitals and hospital units that are not paid under the inpatient prospective payment system under section 1886(d)(1)(B) of the Act, such as psychiatric, rehabilitation, long term care, children's, and cancer hospitals.) Section 1899(h)(3) of the Act defines the term "Medicare fee-for-service beneficiary" as an individual who is enrolled in the original Medicare FFS program under Medicare Parts A and B and is not enrolled in a Medicare Advantage (MA) plan under Medicare Part C, an eligible organization under section 1876 of the Act, or a Program of All-Inclusive Care for the Elderly (PACE) under section 1894 of the Act.

> The Shared Savings Program is designed to be budget neutral on a per beneficiary basis, unlike Medicare Advantage.

Section 1899(i) of the Act provides that the Secretary may use either a partial capitation model or other payment model, rather than the payment model described in section 1899(d) of the Act, for making payments under the Shared Savings Program. Sections 1899(i)(2)(B) and 1899(i)(3)(B) of the Act require that any such model maintain budget neutrality. Specifically, these sections require that any such model adopted by the Secretary, "does not result in spending more for such ACO for such beneficiaries than would otherwise be expended for such ACO for such beneficiaries for such year if the model were not implemented, as estimated by the Secretary."

QUESTIONS

1. From the perspective of Medicare beneficiaries, what are the advantages or disadvantages of ACOs?
2. Are ACOs consistent with the MedPAC payment recommendations?

The ACO initiative involves many different aspects of health care organizational principles and Medicare funding rules, all of which necessitated that federal agencies with differing tasks begin to work together to implement the ACA's design. Multiple joint agency statements have been issued to coordinate the regulatory compliance necessary to participate in the MSSP. For example, CMS drafted the primary Medicare ACO regulations, but CMS and the OIG issued a joint guidance waiving certain aspects of fraud and abuse laws. The Department of Justice and Federal Trade Commission also issued a joint guidance document explaining the antitrust implications of ACOs. The Internal Revenue Service issued a document explaining the implications of tax-exempt status for participants in ACOs. The quantity of guidance documents indicates the complexity of the program as well as the layers of regulation that health care providers face in everyday practice. ACOs are discussed further in the context of tax law in Chapter 5, fraud and abuse laws in Chapter 6, and antitrust laws in Chapter 7.

The Medicare Access and CHIP Reauthorization Act of 2015 (MACRA), Pub. L. No. 114-10 (April 16, 2015), also implemented payment reforms, under which health care providers are prompted to improve quality of care and enhance cost effectiveness through new VBP mechanisms. Under MACRA, providers' performance is used to adjust Part B payment rates that, as of 2019, will become known as the "Quality Payment Program," which includes the Merit-based Incentive Payment System (MIPS) and optional participation in Alternative Payment Models (APMs). Medicare providers choose how to participate based on their practice size, specialty, location, and patient population. CMS intends to phase in the new payment methodology with an eye toward compliance rather than punitive enforcement. Centers for Medicare and Medicaid Services, Quality Payment Program, https://www.cms.gov/Medicare/Quality-Payment-Program/Quality-Payment-Program.html.

6. MEDICARE APPEALS PROCESSES

Medicare is reputed to pay more reliably than other forms of health insurance, but claim denials and delays still occur. Private companies called Medicare Administrative Contractors (Contractors, or MACs) administer Medicare regionally for the federal government. Contractors deny care for the same reasons in Medicare that they do in the private insurance setting (within the parameters of the Medicare Act) on grounds such as lack of medical necessity or failure to obtain preapproval for a care path deemed experimental.

Medicare has administrative processes for payment appeals, one for providers who are denied payment or are paid less than they believe is appropriate, and one for beneficiaries. A five-level process for reviewing claims exists for Parts A and B. The Office of Medicare Hearings and Appeals (OMHA) employs Administrative Law Judges (ALJs) that hear appeals at Level 3. OMHA also educates the public about Medicare appeals and describes the five levels of appeal as follows:

> Level 1: Your Health Plan. If you disagree with a Medicare coverage decision, you may request your health plan to redetermine your claim.
> Level 2: An Independent Organization. If you disagree with the decision in Level 1, you may request a reconsideration by an independent organization.
> Level 3: Office of Medicare Hearings and Appeals (OMHA). If you disagree with the Level 2 decision, you may request that OMHA review your claim through an Administrative Law Judge.
> Level 4: The Medicare Appeals Council. If you disagree with the Administrative Law Judge's decision, you may request the Medicare Appeals Council review the decision.
> Level 5: Federal Court. If you disagree with the Medicare Appeals Council decision, you may seek a review of your claim in Federal District Court.

Appeal particulars depend upon which Part of Medicare is involved in the claim. Medicare Parts A and B are first appealed to a Medicare Contractor, then to the Qualified Independent Contractor (QIC), then to an ALJ at OMHA, then to the

HHS sometimes uses the same acronym for two different functions. Here, "MAC" means Medicare Appeals Council. "MAC" also is an acronym for Medicare Administrative Contractor, meaning private insurers who are administrators on behalf of HHS.

Medicare Appeals Council (MAC), and then to a federal district court. But an appeal of a Part C decision would first go to the Medicare Advantage Plan, then to an Independent Review entity, then to an ALJ, then to the MAC, then to federal court. The MAC must consider appeals that involve medical judgment and that contain statutory interpretation as well. Indeed, beneficiaries are almost always precluded from raising statutory, or even constitutional, challenges to Medicare rules or policies unless they present those arguments through the first four levels of appeals. The following MAC decision offers such an example.

In the Case of the Estate of W.D.

(Department of Health & Human Servs. Departmental
Appeals Bd., Decision of Medicare Appeals
Council 2009)

. . . .

BACKGROUND

Prior to the beneficiary's hospitalization for the dental surgery, he had undergone a coronary bypass with placement of 3 stents subsequent to having a myocardial infarction (MI). He also had a history of hypertension, cholesterol embolization to his legs and left arm, type II diabetes and congestive heart failure. Given the above conditions, the beneficiary's physicians determined that the dental surgery that he required to extract his mandibular and maxillary left two molars should be performed in *** Regional Medical Center rather than in a physician's office, so that his cardiac condition could be monitored during the procedure.

The beneficiary presented to the hospital's Same-Day Surgery area as an outpatient on April 25, 2007, for the dental surgery. As indicated below, the medical record indicates that the beneficiary was not admitted to the hospital an inpatient at any point in his hospital stay:

> The patient presented to Same-Day Surgery area and later he was taken to the operating room where the above surgery under general anesthesia was well tolerated. He was then taken to the recovery room and then back to the Same Day Surgical area where he was discharged later in satisfactory condition.

Initially and upon redetermination Cahaba GBA found the services were not covered. At reconsideration, the Qualified Independent Contractor (QIC) again denied coverage on the basis that Medicare does not cover dental services performed in a hospital setting on an outpatient basis. Both Cahaba GBA and the QIC found the beneficiary responsible for the non-covered services.

Following a November 12, 2008, telephone hearing, the ALJ found that the services provided to the beneficiary on April 25, 2007, were reimbursable under Medicare Part A. The ALJ concluded:

> [The] medical record and testimony clearly indicate [that] the services at issue were medically reasonable and necessary, if not imperative to treat the beneficiary. . . .
> [The] services at issue were not routine dental services that took place by chance in a

hospital setting. Rather, due to the beneficiary's underlying medical history and complications . . . it was medically necessary to extract teeth 15 and 18 in a hospital setting. The inpatient hospital services provided by the appellant to the beneficiary on April 25, 2007, are covered and payable under Part A of Title XVIII of the Social Security Act (Act), and were not otherwise excluded under Section 1862(a)(1) of the Act.

In its referral to the Council, CMS notes that the Medicare statute does not cover "services in connection with the care, treatment, filling, removal, or replacement of teeth" under §1862(a)(12) of the Act. CMS further notes that the statute provides that "'payment may be made under Part A in the case of inpatient hospital services in connection with the provision of such dental services' if the patient's underlying medical condition or the severity of the procedure is such that hospitalization is required." CMS does not dispute that the beneficiary's medical condition required that the extraction take place in a hospital setting. However, CMS contends that the ALJ erred in finding coverage for the services at issue because the beneficiary was not admitted as an inpatient, and, therefore, did not meet the conditions for payment of the hospital charges under §1862(a)(12) of the Act.

> The question is whether this dental surgery was an inpatient hospital stay (which is covered by Medicare) or dental surgery (which is not).

The appellant has responded to the agency referral. It argues that the beneficiary's medical condition warranted extraction of the teeth in a hospital setting, and that the prior denials of coverage, which analyzed whether the beneficiary was an inpatient, focused on "form over substance." The appellant summarizes its position by stating that the ALJ was "correct in examining in depth the nature of the services rendered and the intent of the doctors and patient."

As explained in detail below, the Council finds that the ALJ erred in finding that the hospital services were covered. The Council has reached this conclusion because the Medicare statute does not permit payment for outpatient hospital services provided in conjunction with outpatient dental surgery.

APPLICABLE LAW

Section 1862(a)(12) of the Social Security Act (Act) precludes Medicare coverage

> [w]here such expenses are for services in connection with the care, treatment, filling, removal or replacement of teeth or structures directly supporting teeth, except that payment may be made under part A in the case of inpatient hospital services in connection with the provision of such dental services if the individual, because of his underlying medical condition and clinical status or because of the severity of the dental procedure, requires hospitalization in connection with the provision of such services.

As noted above, payment may only be made for Medicare Part A inpatient hospital services provided in connection with the dental services, and not the dental services themselves. CMS has implemented the above exclusion in regulations found at 42 C.F.R. §411.15(i).

> The regulation provides that dental services are excluded from coverage — except for inpatient hospital services in connection with such dental procedures when the hospitalization is required because of —

(1) The individual's underlying medical condition or clinical status; or

(2) The severity of the dental procedures.

The Medicare Benefit Policy Manual (MBPM) defines an inpatient as a person admitted to a hospital for bed occupancy for purposes of receiving inpatient hospital services. Generally a person is considered an inpatient if formally admitted as an inpatient with the expectation that he will remain at least overnight and occupy a bed even though it later develops that he can be discharged or transferred to another hospital and does not actually use a hospital bed overnight.

In contrast, a hospital outpatient is defined as a person who has not been admitted by the hospital as an inpatient but is registered on the hospital records as an outpatient and receives services (rather than supplies alone) from the hospital.

When a patient is hospitalized for a dental procedure and the dentist's service is covered under Part B, the inpatient hospital services furnished are covered under Part A. . . . Regardless of whether the inpatient hospital services are covered, the medical services of physicians furnished in connection with noncovered dental services are not covered.

> The distinction between inpatient and outpatient care is key for many aspects of health care law, including reimbursement. Outpatient (or ambulatory) care by common standards requires less than 24 hours of care, meaning no overnight stay is anticipated. A patient would be transferred to a hospital if overnight care is required.

DISCUSSION

As explained above, the Medicare statute limits coverage of services related to the care of the teeth and related structures to coverage of inpatient hospital services that are provided, when necessary, when a beneficiary is hospitalized as an inpatient to undergo a dental procedure. However, in no circumstances does Medicare cover the Part B services for the dental procedure itself, nor does it cover the hospital charges if the beneficiary is admitted to the hospital as an outpatient.

The Council notes that CMS has not disputed that the beneficiary's medical status precluded dental surgery in an office setting, nor has it contended that it was inappropriate to admit him to the hospital to undergo the surgery. Rather, it contends that because he was admitted to the hospital as an outpatient, the statute does not allow coverage for the hospital services. As a result, the sole issue before the Council is whether the beneficiary was an "inpatient" or "outpatient" of the hospital during his dental surgery and subsequent period in the recovery room.

As discussed above, Medicare defines a hospital inpatient as a person admitted to a hospital for bed occupancy for purposes of receiving inpatient hospital services. An examination of the hospital record reveals that the ALJ erred in finding the hospital services were provided under Medicare Part A. Both the Operative Record and Medical/Surgical Sheet indicate that the beneficiary was discharged from the Same Day Surgical area without being admitted to the *** Regional Medical Center as an inpatient. Further, both the Medicare Part B Summary Notice and the hospital's itemized bill reflect that the hospital services were billed under Medicare Part B as outpatient services.

In summary, the Council does not disagree with the ALJ's general conclusion that the beneficiary had a medical condition that required that his teeth be extracted in a hospital setting. However, the ALJ erred in concluding that the beneficiary was admitted to the hospital as a Medicare Part A inpatient. Rather the beneficiary was admitted and received treatment as an outpatient. Therefore, the hospital services he received in connection with his dental surgery are excluded from coverage under section 1862(a)(12) of the Act.

This dispute is only over the Part A (hospital) expenses, not the Part B (physician) expenses.

LIABILITY

Finally, because the ALJ found coverage for the services at issue, the ALJ did not discuss liability for the services at issue. The Council finds that the beneficiary's estate is responsible for the hospital services because the services were excluded from coverage under section 1862(a)(12) of the Act, and, therefore, the estate's responsibility for the services may not be waived.

DECISION

Following a careful consideration of the record, it is the decision of the Medicare Appeals Council that the hospital services provided to the beneficiary on April 25, 2007, are not covered by Medicare and that the beneficiary's estate is responsible for the hospital charges. Accordingly, the ALJ's decision is reversed.

QUESTIONS

1. Why did the MAC refuse to pay this claim?
2. Was the MAC correct in refusing to allocate Medicare funds to this procedure?
3. Does the decision elevate form over substance?

The Social Security Act (SSA) contains specific rules regarding the power of federal courts in the realm of the SSA, including Medicare. By the time a federal court hears a case, the beneficiary has proceeded through four levels of appeal. The federal court will almost always lack subject matter jurisdiction unless the beneficiary has exhausted administrative remedies. The following excerpts provide a sense of the limitations courts face in appeals from Medicare coverage decisions. Note that these limitations also apply to provider challenges to sanctions by HHS, payment determinations, and other provider payment issues as well as beneficiary appeals.

42 U.S.C. §405(g). Judicial review

Any individual, after any final decision of the Commissioner of Social Security made after a hearing to which he was a party, irrespective of the amount in controversy, may obtain a review of such decision by a civil action commenced within sixty days after the mailing to him of notice of such decision or within such further time as the Commissioner of Social Security may allow. Such action shall be brought in the district court of the United States for the judicial district in which the plaintiff resides, or has his principal place of business, or, if he does not reside or have his principal place of business within any such judicial district, in the United States District Court for the District of Columbia. As part of the Commissioner's answer the Commissioner of Social Security shall file a certified copy of the transcript of the record including the evidence upon which the findings and decision complained of are based. The court shall have power to enter, upon the pleadings and transcript of the record, a judgment affirming, modifying, or reversing the decision of the Commissioner of Social Security, with or without remanding the cause for a rehearing. The findings of the Commissioner of Social Security as to any fact, if supported by substantial evidence, shall be conclusive, and where a claim has been denied by the Commissioner of Social Security or a decision is rendered under sub-section (b) of this section which is adverse to an individual who was a party to the hearing before the Commissioner of Social Security, because of failure of the claimant or such individual to submit proof in conformity with any regulation prescribed under subsection (a) of this section, the court shall review only the question of conformity with such regulations and the validity of such regulations. The court may, on motion of the Commissioner of Social Security made for good cause shown before the Commissioner files the Commissioner's answer, remand the case to the Commissioner of Social Security for further action by the Commissioner of Social Security, and it may at any time order additional evidence to be taken before the Commissioner of Social Security, but only upon a showing that there is new evidence which is material and that there is good cause for the failure to incorporate such evidence into the record in a prior proceeding; and the Commissioner of Social Security shall, after the case is remanded, and after hearing such additional evidence if so ordered, modify or affirm the Commissioner's findings of fact or the Commissioner's decision, or both, and shall file with the court any such additional and modified findings of fact and decision, and, in any case in which the Commissioner has not made a decision fully favorable to the individual, a transcript of the additional record and testimony upon which the Commissioner's action in modifying or affirming was based. Such additional or modified findings of fact and decision shall be reviewable only to the extent provided for review of the original findings of fact and decision. The judgment of the court shall be final except that it shall be subject to review in the same manner as a judgment in other civil actions. . . .

42 U.S.C. §405(h). Finality of Commissioner's decision

> This statute acts as a limitation on the federal question jurisdiction of district courts in Medicare payment matters.

The findings and decision of the Commissioner of Social Security after a hearing shall be binding upon all individuals who were parties to such hearing. No findings of fact or decision of the Commissioner of Social Security shall be reviewed by any person, tribunal, or governmental agency except as herein provided. No action against the United States, the Commissioner of Social Security, or any officer or employee thereof shall be brought under section 1331 or 1346 of Title 28 to recover on any claim arising under this subchapter.

Consider this excerpt from Justice Stevens's concurrence/dissent in Heckler v. Ringer, 466 U.S. 602 (1984), which highlights the conundrum presented by strict administrative processes:

> The complaint indicates that Ringer, "who is 68 years of age, suffers from severe, chronic obstructive airways disease (i.e., severe emphysema), *cor pulmonale* and right heart strain," and that he is eligible for Medicare benefits and needs the operation but cannot afford it unless the Secretary agrees to pay for it. The Secretary, however, has formally ruled that she will not pay for it, and has taken the position that Ringer cannot challenge her ruling, except in a proceeding seeking reimbursement for the cost of the surgery. Yet precisely because Ringer cannot afford the surgery, the Secretary will not permit him to file a claim for reimbursement, since he has incurred no expense that can be reimbursed. . . .

Thus, it would seem, Ringer both does and does not have a claim which arises under the Medicare Act. He cannot file a claim under the Medicare Act until after he has the operation; he cannot have the operation unless he can challenge the Secretary's ruling; and he cannot challenge that ruling except in an action seeking judicial review of the denial of a claim under the Medicare Act. This one-eyed procedural analysis frustrates the remedial intent of Congress as plainly as it frustrates this litigant's plea for a remedy. The cruel irony is that a statute designed to help the elderly in need of medical assistance is being construed to protect from administrative absolutism only those wealthy enough to be able to afford an operation and then seek reimbursement.

QUESTIONS

1. Based on §405(g) and (h), which tribunal is responsible for fact-finding, and are the facts reviewable?
2. What happens if the tribunal's decision is factually erroneous?
3. Why does the Medicare Act severely limit judicial review?
4. For which stakeholders do these jurisdictional limitations provide protection?

C. MEDICAID

Medicaid and the Children's Health Insurance Program (CHIP) cover about 74 million people, or about 24 percent of the U.S. population as of December 2017. That number is extraordinary given that Medicaid was not designed to be a permanent safety net program.

1. LEGISLATIVE HISTORY

Medicaid was enacted with the same pen stroke as Medicare, but the two programs are more like distant cousins than twins. While Medicare ushered in federal "compulsory" hospital insurance and optional physician insurance for all elderly, Medicaid continued a welfare-based approach to medical care for the poor, providing medical assistance only to certain designated "needy" individuals referred to as the "deserving poor." The Medicaid program was built on a federal foundation but allows for substantial influence by state policy choices within that federal statutory structure, creating a cooperative federalism scheme in which each state has its own version of Medicaid.

The idea of the "deserving poor" dates to Elizabethan Poor Laws, which only provided assistance to those deemed blameless for their poverty. This included children, pregnant women, the elderly, and people with permanent disabilities such as blindness. English exclusionary policies carried over to the American colonies and thus to American states, which were originally responsible for welfare programs. By the time of the Great Depression, medical welfare became too expensive for states, and they sought federal assistance in covering medical care for the poor—this state-requested federal funding eventually led to Medicaid.

Congress predicted in the legislative record: "The expanded medical assistance (Kerr-Mills) program is estimated to provide new or increased medical assistance to about 8 million needy persons during an early year of operation. States could, in the future, provide aid to as many as twice this." Congress greatly underestimated the need for medical assistance. Medicare's social insurance was limited only by prior worker status; otherwise, every elderly person is eligible. In contrast, Medicaid built on state efforts to address poverty through welfare, which contains an underlying assumption that everyone should become

"Medical assistance" indicates Medicaid is more than just money (despite the title of this chapter). Congress intended that participating states would be responsible for providing specified medical services to beneficiaries; in other words, states cannot agree to pay for care with Medicaid funds without ensuring beneficiaries receive promised care.

self-reliant. The program was not designed to offer long-term insurance coverage, because short-term coverage was the assumed paradigm.

This welfare-based perspective contributed to the limitations on Medicaid's eligibility to just the "deserving poor." Because welfare programs are perceived as government handouts, not "earned" in the way that social insurance is, they are also more politically vulnerable. Medicaid has long been treated as a political pariah, and it is the source of both ongoing cooperation and conflict between the federal government and the states. Further, thoughtful changes to the program have often been subsumed within larger efforts at health care reform, with the assumption being that Medicaid would eventually disappear. Yet Medicaid is poised to provide medical assistance to almost a quarter of the U.S. population. Medicaid pays for half of all U.S. births and more than a third of children's health care and is now the principal payer for long-term care and mental health services (both of which are benefits with more middle-class political support). It is essential to understand how the program works and what its strengths and limitations are.

2. STRUCTURE

Interest groups such as the AARP lobby to maintain a Medicare program that serves the needs of the elderly. In contrast, Medicaid beneficiaries have few resources and are often struggling with financial, housing, hunger, and other challenges, so they cannot lobby Congress or state legislatures to protect the Medicaid program in the same way.

42 U.S.C. §1396-1. Appropriations

For the purpose of enabling each State, as far as practicable under the conditions in such State, to furnish (1) medical assistance on behalf of families with dependent children and of aged, blind, or disabled individuals, whose income and resources are insufficient to meet the costs of necessary medical services, and (2) rehabilitation and other services to help such families and individuals attain or retain capability for independence or self-care, there is hereby authorized to be appropriated for each fiscal year a sum sufficient to carry out the purposes of this subchapter. The sums made available under this section shall be used for making payments to States which have submitted, and had approved by the Secretary, State plans for medical assistance.

42 U.S.C. §1396d. Definitions

For purposes of this subchapter —

(a) Medical assistance

The term "medical assistance" means payment of part or all of the cost of the following care and services or the care and services themselves, or both (if provided in or after the third month before the month in which the recipient makes application for assistance . . .). . . .

Consider how this introductory language for the "Medicaid Act" created an ongoing "contractual" connection between the federal government and the states. In order for states to enter that relationship to provide medical assistance to the poor, they must adhere to mandatory aspects of the Medicaid Act and decide which options they will exercise.

a. State Plans for Participating in Medicaid

The Medicaid Act states that federal payments will be made to states that have submitted "State plans for medical assistance." This statutory language indicates that each state must submit a state plan to HHS that demonstrates how the state will comply with the mandatory elements of Medicaid and which optional elements it would like to employ. The Medicaid Act contains numerous requirements for a state to receive federal funds for "medical assistance," and if the Medicaid Act is amended or modified, states submit state plan amendments (SPA) to indicate how they will comply. An SPA can be as simple as checking boxes on a form:

> The first question when researching a Medicaid issue, after reviewing federal law, should always be "which state"?

CMS   **Medicaid Eligibility**

OMB Control Number 0938-1148
OMB Expiration date: 10/31/2014

Eligibility Groups - Mandatory Coverage
Adult Group   S32

1902(a)(10)(A)(i)(VIII)
42 CFR 435.119

The state covers the Adult Group as described at 42 CFR 435.119.

◉ Yes   ○ No

▪ **Adult Group** - Non-pregnant individuals age 19 through 64, not otherwise mandatorily eligible, with income at or below 133% FPL.

  ☑ The state attests that it operates this eligibility group in accordance with the following provisions:

    ▪ Individuals qualifying under this eligibility group must meet the following criteria:

      ▪ Have attained age 19 but not age 65.

      ▪ Are not pregnant.

      ▪ Are not entitled to or enrolled for Part A or B Medicare benefits.

      ▪ Are not otherwise eligible for and enrolled for mandatory coverage under the state plan in accordance with 42 CFR 435, subpart B.

        Note: In 209(b) states, individuals receiving SSI or deemed to be receiving SSI who do not qualify for mandatory Medicaid eligibility due to more restrictive requirements may qualify for this eligibility group if otherwise eligible.

      ▪ Have household income at or below 133% FPL.

    ▪ MAGI-based income methodologies are used in calculating household income. Please refer as necessary to S10 MAGI-Based Income Methodologies, completed by the state.

    ▪ There is no resource test for this eligibility group.

    ▪ Parents or other caretaker relatives living with a child under the age specified below are not covered unless the child is receiving benefits under Medicaid, CHIP or through the Exchange, or otherwise enrolled in minimum essential coverage, as defined in 42 CFR 435.4.

      ○ Under age 19, or

      ◉ A higher age of children, if any, covered under 42 CFR 435.222 on March 23, 2010:

        ○ Under age 20

        ◉ Under age 21

  ▪ Presumptive Eligibility

    The state covers individuals under this group when determined presumptively eligible by a qualified entity. The state assures it also covers individuals under the Pregnant Women (42 CFR 435.116) and/or Infants and Children under Age 19 (42 CFR 435.118) eligibility groups when determined presumptively eligible.

    ○ Yes   ◉ No

TN No: MN-13-0027-MM1A   **Approval Date:** 12/13/13   **Effective Date:** January 1, 2014
Minnesota

Some amendments to the Act are mandatory, and some are options for states; states must comply with mandatory amendments to continue to receive the uncapped federal funding that the Medicaid Act offers.

    42 U.S.C. §1396b. Payment to States
      (a) Computation of amount
      From the sums appropriated therefor, the Secretary . . . shall pay to each State which has a plan approved under this subchapter, for each quarter. . . .

(1) an amount equal to the Federal medical assistance percentage (as defined in section 1396d(b) of this title, . . . of the total amount expended during such quarter as medical assistance under the State plan. . . .

(d) Estimates of State entitlement . . .

Federal payments to states for participating in Medicaid are not capped, in part because of the use of the word "entitled" in subsection (d). The federal government pays the federal medical assistant percentage (FMAP), without limit, depending on the relative poverty of a state's population.

(1) Prior to the beginning of each quarter, the Secretary shall estimate the amount to which a State will be entitled under subsections (a) and (b) of this section for such quarter, such estimates to be based on (A) a report filed by the State containing its estimate of the total sum to be expended in such quarter in accordance with the provisions of such subsections, and stating the amount appropriated or made available by the State and its political subdivisions for such expenditures in such quarter, and if such amount is less than the State's proportionate share of the total sum of such estimated expenditures, the source or sources from which the difference is expected to be derived, and (B) such other investigation as the Secretary may find necessary.

(2)(A) The Secretary shall then pay to the State, in such installments as he may determine, the amount so estimated, reduced or increased to the extent of any overpayment or underpayment which the Secretary determines was made under this section to such State for any prior quarter and with respect to which adjustment has not already been made under this subsection.

42 U.S.C. §1396d(b). Definitions

. . . [T]he term "Federal medical assistance percentage" for any State shall be 100 per centum less the State percentage; and the State percentage shall be that percentage which bears the same ratio to 45 per centum as the square of the per capita income of such State bears to the square of the per capita income of the continental United States (including Alaska) and Hawaii; except that (1) the Federal medical assistance percentage shall in no case be less than 50 per centum or more than 83 per centum, . . . (3) for purposes of this subchapter and subchapter XXI of this chapter, the Federal medical assistance percentage for the District of Columbia shall be 70 percent . . . and (5) in the case of a State that provides medical assistance for services and vaccines described in subparagraphs (A) and (B) of subsection (a)(13), and prohibits cost-sharing for such services and vaccines, the Federal medical assistance percentage, as determined under this subsection and subsection (y) (without regard to paragraph (1)(C) of such subsection), shall be increased by 1 percentage point with respect to medical assistance for such services and vaccines and for items and services described in subsection (a)(4)(D).

QUESTIONS

1. What is the most important factor for determining a state's "FMAP"?
2. What are the floor and ceiling for federal matching funds?
3. Certain services, such as family planning services and the Medicaid expansion under the ACA, receive higher federal matches than the state's usual FMAP. (See, e.g., 42 U.S.C. §1396b(a)(5).) Why do you think Congress made this funding decision?

b. State Medicaid Waivers and Medicaid Managed Care

States can request "waivers," which means HHS gives a state permission to not comply with, or to violate, some aspects of the Medicaid Act while exploring alternative means of providing medical assistance. Waivers historically were limited in scope, targeting one population of beneficiaries or type of service, but over time the scale of waivers has grown. HHS's waiver authority is linked to certain statutory provisions. For example, narrower "program waivers" fall under SSA section 1915. Section 1915(a) allows states to contract with managed care organizations, and 1915(b) waivers facilitate care delivery through managed care plans that, for example, may limit free choice of providers through networks (discussed further below). Section 1915(c) waivers for Home and Community Based Services (HCBS) allow beneficiaries with long-term services and supports (LTSS) to receive Medicaid-reimbursed care outside of an institutional setting. States can use applications supplied by HHS to request section 1915 waivers.

> The "Katie Beckett" option enables states to enroll certain children with disabilities living at home who need extensive care. Historically such non-institutionalized children would have been unable to qualify for Medicaid, because parental finances are measured differently for in-home and institutional care, which created a bias for institutional care that separated children from their families.

Broader "demonstration projects" fall under Section 1115 of the SSA. Under section 1115, states propose to create nonconforming Medicaid policies, which have become more popular in recent years and lead to wide variations in Medicaid across states. No application exists for Section 1115 demonstration projects because a state must provide more substantial information to HHS in its application.

> **42 U.S.C. §1315 (SSA §1115). Demonstration projects**
>
> (a) Waiver of State plan requirements; costs regarded as State plan expenditures; availability of appropriations
>
> In the case of any experimental, pilot, or demonstration project which, in the judgment of the Secretary, is likely to assist in promoting the objectives of subchapter . . . XIX of this chapter, . . . in a State or States —
>
> (1) the Secretary may waive compliance with any of the requirements of . . . section 1396a of this title . . . to the extent and for the period he finds necessary to enable such State or States to carry out such project, and
>
> (2)(A) costs of such project which would not otherwise be included as expenditures under section . . . 1396b of this title . . . and which are not included as part of the costs of projects under section 1310 of this title, shall, to the extent and for the period prescribed by the Secretary, be regarded as expenditures under the State plan or plans approved under such subchapter, or for administration of such State plan or plans, as may be appropriate, and
>
> (B) costs of such project which would not otherwise be a permissible use of funds under part A of subchapter IV of this chapter and which are not included as part of the costs of projects under section 1310 of this title, shall to the extent and for the period prescribed by the Secretary, be regarded as a permissible use of funds under such part. . . .
>
> (d) Regulations relating to applications for or renewals of demonstration projects

> Medicare and Medicaid are extensive statutory amendments to the Social Security Act (Medicaid is Part XIX), and their provisions often are cited as sections of the public law that is the SSA rather than using their U.S. Code citations.

(1) An application or renewal of any experimental, pilot, or demonstration project undertaken under subsection (a) to promote the objectives of subchapter XIX or XXI in a State that would result in an impact on eligibility, enrollment, benefits, cost-sharing, or financing with respect to a State program under subchapter XIX or XXI (in this subsection referred to as a "demonstration project") shall be considered by the Secretary in accordance with the regulations required to be promulgated under paragraph (2).

These provisions were drafted in response to sharp critiques that the waiver process was opaque and could not be monitored by interested parties because negotiations occurred behind closed doors with no input from stakeholders.

(2) . . . the Secretary shall promulgate regulations relating to applications for, and renewals of, a demonstration project that provide for —

(A) a process for public notice and comment at the State level, including public hearings, sufficient to ensure a meaningful level of public input;

(B) requirements relating to —

(i) the goals of the program to be implemented or renewed under the demonstration project;

(ii) the expected State and Federal costs and coverage projections of the demonstration project; and

(iii) the specific plans of the State to ensure that the demonstration project will be in compliance with subchapter XIX or XXI;

(C) a process for providing public notice and comment after the application is received by the Secretary, that is sufficient to ensure a meaningful level of public input;

(D) a process for the submission to the Secretary of periodic reports by the State concerning the implementation of the demonstration project; and

(E) a process for the periodic evaluation by the Secretary of the demonstration project.

(3) The Secretary shall annually report to Congress concerning actions taken by the Secretary with respect to applications for demonstration projects under this section. . . .

Prior to the ACA, the waiver process was conducted in a manner that was not transparent to the public. To address criticisms of the inaccessible process, as well as the seemingly standardless manner in which waivers were renewed, the ACA added state public notice and comment requirements for both initial waiver proposals and reporting for renewal applications. Notice and comment occurs at the federal level as well. 42 C.F.R. Part 431.

QUESTIONS

1. What is the statutory standard for a section 1115 waiver?
2. What section of the Medicaid Act is waivable for a state seeking to demonstrate a new way to promote the objectives of Medicaid under section 1115?
3. Will states or HHS experience greater accountability for the waiver of statutory requirements as a result of these statutory amendments?
4. What action must the Secretary of HHS take if evaluation of a demonstration project reveals that the demonstration is detrimental to the fiscal health of the Medicaid program? To the health of its beneficiaries?

Waivers are not automatically granted; new waiver requests are supposed to receive a hard look from CMS to ensure that the state is furthering the purposes of the Medicaid Act. The Government Accountability Office studied waivers and reported in 2018 that HHS is not properly reviewing the projects being demonstrated before renewing Medicaid waivers. *See* GAO 18-220, Medicaid Demonstrations: Evaluations Yielded Limited Results, Underscoring Need for Changes to Federal Policies and Procedures (Jan. 2018), at https://www.gao.gov/assets/690/689506.pdf. The following is an example of a failed waiver application, which illustrates the negotiations that occur between HHS and states:

March 1, 2013

Roderick Bremby
Commissioner
Connecticut Department of Social Services

Dear Commissioner Bremby:

This letter is in response to the state of Connecticut's August 20, 2012, request for a new section 1115 Medicaid demonstration, entitled the "Medicaid Low-Income Adult Coverage Demonstration." This proposal seeks to make changes to Connecticut's Medicaid for Low Income Adults program. The state currently covers individuals ages 19 to 64 years old with income at or below 55 percent of the federal poverty level (FPL) ($6,144 per year for a single individual) with no asset limitations. Under the section 1115 demonstration proposal, the state seeks to impose an asset limit of $10,000 and count parental assets and income above 185 percent of the FPL for individuals ages 19 through 25 who live with or are claimed by one or both parents as a tax dependent.

We are unable to approve the state's request because under section 1115 (a) of the Social Security Act, demonstrations must promote the objectives of title XIX. After carefully reviewing the information provided by the state in its August 20, 2012, proposal and the state's November 5, 2012, responses to the Federal Review Team questions and after further discussions with the state, we have determined that Connecticut's demonstration proposal is not likely to assist in promoting the objectives of title XIX and, therefore, cannot be approved. As described in the state's proposal, the demonstration would eliminate coverage for as many as 13,381 very low-income individuals for an approximate one year period, which is not consistent with the general statutory objective to extend coverage to low-income populations.

Although we are not able to approve this proposal, we appreciate the challenges the state faces with addressing its fiscal budget gap and we are happy to continue to work with you and members of your staff on other Medicaid initiatives.

Sincerely,
Marilyn Tavenner
Acting Administrator

Waivers can address various aspects of administering the Medicaid program. Some waivers are complex and allow states to vary from multiple statutory requirements relating to eligibility, such as those granted to several states creating their own version of the Medicaid expansion following *NFIB v. Sebelius* (excerpted below). Other waivers modify how care is delivered, such as those that facilitate contracting with private managed care organizations to deliver care to Medicaid beneficiaries. Today, a majority of Medicaid beneficiaries are enrolled in Medicaid managed care rather than fee-for-service Medicaid. Managed care is supposed to help states to control costs by allowing the state to pay a flat rate per beneficiary (capitation) to a private managed care company that contracts with the state to cover Medicaid populations. Managed care can also facilitate coordination of medical care between health care providers.

HHS wanted to improve delivery of care through Medicaid managed care and to improve coordination of rules between private and public insurance, as many beneficiaries move between the two kinds of insurance (a phenomenon called "churn"). The Medicaid managed care final rule was published in the May 6, 2016 *Federal Register*, and the Preamble to the NPRM provided useful background on Medicaid managed care, including statutory cites, history, demographics, and other valuable information:

Medicaid and Children's Health Insurance Program (CHIP) Programs; Medicaid Managed Care, CHIP Delivered in Managed Care, Medicaid and CHIP Comprehensive Quality Strategies, and Revisions Related to Third Party Liability

80 Fed. Reg. 31,097 (June 1, 2015)

Fee-for-service means that the state pays the health care provider for each service provided to a Medicaid beneficiary. Many believe this payment structure does not facilitate coordination of care for any patient needing treatment by more than one caregiver. Fee-for-service may also incentivize health care providers to provide too many services, which is why Medicare moved to an algorithmic payment method (discussed in the first part of this chapter). Chapter 3 discusses these ideas in greater depth.

Until the early 1990s, most Medicaid beneficiaries received Medicaid coverage through fee-for-service (FFS) arrangements. However, over time that practice has shifted and states are increasingly utilizing managed care arrangements to provide Medicaid coverage to beneficiaries. Under managed care, beneficiaries receive part or all of their Medicaid services from health care providers who are paid by an organization that is under contract with the state; the organization receives a monthly capitated payment for a specified benefit package. In 1992, 2.4 million Medicaid beneficiaries (or 8 percent of all Medicaid beneficiaries) accessed part or all of their Medicaid benefits through capitated health plans; by 1998, that number had increased fivefold to 12.6 million (or 41 percent of all Medicaid beneficiaries). In fiscal year (FY) 2011, at least 39 million (or 58 percent of all Medicaid beneficiaries) in 39 states and the District of Columbia accessed part or all of their Medicaid benefits through such capitated health plans.

In a Medicaid managed care delivery system, through contracts with health plans, states require that the plan provide or arrange for a specified package of Medicaid services for enrolled beneficiaries. Under these contracts, the organization offering the health plan is paid a fixed, prospective, monthly payment for each enrolled beneficiary. This payment approach is referred to as "capitation." Beneficiaries enrolled in capitated managed care organizations (MCOs) must access the Medicaid services covered under the state plan through the health plan. States may contract with managed care entities that offer comprehensive benefits, referred to as MCOs. Alternatively, managed care plans can receive a capitated payment for a limited array of services, such as behavioral health or dental services. Such entities that receive a capitated payment for a limited array of services are referred to as "prepaid inpatient health plans" (PIHPs) or "prepaid ambulatory health plans" (PAHPs) depending on the scope of services the health plan provides. Finally, applicable federal statute recognizes primary care case management as a type of managed care entity subject to some of the same standards as MCOs. States that do not pursue capitated arrangements but want to promote coordination and care management may contract with primary care providers or care management entities to support better health outcomes and increase the quality of care delivered to beneficiaries, but continue to pay for covered benefits on a FFS basis directly to the health care provider.

> The word capitation derives from Latin for "head," and capitation indicates a fixed payment per beneficiary for all covered services in a year. Capitation payments shift risk for the cost of delivering covered services from insurers to health care providers and are supposed to help control health care costs.

As Medicaid managed care grew in the 1990s, the Congress enacted specific standards for Medicaid managed care programs in sections 4701 through 4709 of the Balanced Budget Act of 1997 (BBA) (Pub. L. 105-33, enacted on August 5, 1997). The BBA represented the first comprehensive revision to federal statutes governing Medicaid managed care since the early 1980s. In general, the BBA modified the federal statute to: (1) Allow states to mandate the enrollment of certain Medicaid beneficiaries into MCOs without having to first seek a waiver of federal statutory standards. . . .

The predominant form of managed care in Medicaid is capitated risk-based arrangements—virtually identical in structure and payment to arrangements in the commercial marketplace. . . .

States may implement a managed care delivery system using four types of federal authorities. Under the authority of section 1915(a) of the Act, states can implement a voluntary managed care program by executing a contract with organizations that the state has procured using a competitive procurement process. To require beneficiaries to enroll in managed care to receive services, a state must obtain approval from CMS under two primary authorities:

(1) Through a state plan amendment that meets standards set forth in section 1932 of the Act, states can implement a mandatory managed care delivery system. This authority does not allow states to require beneficiaries who are dually eligible for Medicare and Medicaid (dually eligible), American Indians/Alaska Natives, or children with special health care needs to enroll in a managed care program. State plans, once approved, remain in effect until modified by the state.

Medicaid managed care can proceed under one or more of three different provisions: sections 1932, 1915(b), and 1115(a).

(2) CMS may grant a waiver under section 1915(b) of the Act, permitting a state to require all Medicaid beneficiaries to enroll in a managed care delivery system, including dually eligible beneficiaries, American Indians/Alaska Natives, or children with special health care needs. After approval, a state may operate a section 1915(b) waiver for a 2-year period (certain waivers can be operated for up to 5 years if they include dually eligible beneficiaries) before requesting a renewal for an additional 2 (or 5) year period.

CMS may also authorize managed care programs as part of demonstration projects under section 1115(a) of the Act that includes waivers permitting the state to require all Medicaid beneficiaries to enroll in a managed care delivery system, including dually eligible beneficiaries, American Indians/Alaska Natives, and children with special health care needs. Under this authority, states may seek additional flexibility to demonstrate and evaluate innovative policy approaches for delivering Medicaid benefits, as well as the option to provide services not typically covered by Medicaid. Such flexibility is approvable only if the objectives of the Medicaid statute are likely to be met, and is subject to evaluation.

These authorities may permit states to operate their programs without complying with the following standards of Medicaid law outlined in section of 1902 of the Act:

- Statewideness [section 1902(a)(1) of the Act]: States may implement a managed care delivery system in specific areas of the State (generally counties/parishes) rather than the whole state;
- Comparability of Services [section 1902(a)(10) of the Act]: States may provide different benefits to people enrolled in a managed care delivery system; and
- Freedom of Choice [section 1902(a)(23)(A) of the Act]: States may require people to receive their Medicaid services only from a managed care plan or primary care provider.

Laws passed since the Medicaid managed care regulations were promulgated in 2002 have altered the Medicaid program to such a degree that we believe our current regulatory framework for managed care is no longer the most appropriate. Such legislation includes . . . the Patient Protection and Affordable Care Act of 2010 (Affordable Care Act) (Pub. L. 111-148, enacted March 23, 2010). We note, in particular, that the Affordable Care Act provided states the option to expand Medicaid eligibility to most low-income adults, bringing millions of new beneficiaries into the Medicaid program, most of whom are likely to receive coverage through capitated managed care. In addition, the coverage provided under the Affordable Care Act has also made issues of coordination and alignment with the private insurance market increasingly important to improve operational efficiencies for health plans that operate in both public and private markets, and improve the experience of care for individuals moving between sources of health care coverage. Specifically, Medicaid beneficiaries who experience increases in income may move to receiving health insurance coverage through qualified health plans in the Marketplace. Greater alignment between Medicaid managed care plans and qualified health plans will help these individuals transition between sources of coverage.

> This movement between Medicaid and private insurance is called "churn." Churn might occur when a Medicaid beneficiary receives a new job with private health insurance benefits that disqualifies her from enrolling in the program. For some beneficiaries, this occurs more than once per year. Churn can cause discontinuity of care and loss of care, so coordination of the managed care markets is important in the universal coverage scheme of the ACA, discussed further in Chapter 3.

Because the health care delivery landscape has changed substantially, both within the Medicaid program and outside of it, and reflecting the significant role that managed care plays in the Medicaid program, this rule proposes to modernize the Medicaid managed care regulatory structure to facilitate and support delivery system reform initiatives to improve health care outcomes and the beneficiary experience while effectively managing costs. To that end, the proposed rule includes provisions that would strengthen the ability of states to use managed care to promote innovative and cost effective methods of delivering care to Medicaid and CHIP beneficiaries, to incent managed care plans to engage in state activities that promote certain performance targets, and to identify strategies for value-based purchasing models for provider reimbursement. The rule also includes provisions that strengthen the quality of care provided to Medicaid beneficiaries, including measuring and managing quality and improving coordination of care. The rule also promotes more effective use of data in overseeing managed care and promotes advances in health information exchange.

This proposed rule would revise the Medicaid managed care regulations to align with other statutory and regulatory provisions that pertain to other sources of coverage, strengthen actuarial soundness and other payment regulations to improve accountability of rates paid in the Medicaid managed care program, ensure beneficiary protections, and incorporate statutory provisions affecting Medicaid managed care passed since 2002. In addition, the rule promotes beneficiary access to care by strengthening provider networks. This proposed rule also recognizes that through managed care plans, state and federal taxpayer dollars are used to purchase covered services from providers on behalf of Medicaid enrollees, thus ensuring accountability and strengthening program integrity safeguards are necessary to ensure the appropriate stewardship of those funds.

We recognize that in addition to the changes the Affordable Care Act brought to the Medicaid program, it also included significant changes for private insurance and group health plans. Among the reforms of the private health care coverage market are the creation of minimum standards for the treatment of appeals by covered individuals, minimum medical loss ratios for health insurance, and certain minimum coverage standards for essential health benefits and preventive services. The Affordable Care Act created the Marketplaces (also known as "Exchanges") and qualified health plans (QHPs), which are private health plans that are certified as meeting minimum standards.

> The Exchanges are private health insurance markets regulated and supported by the federal government. They are a major feature of the ACA and are discussed in Chapter 3.

See 45 CFR 155.20. Only QHPs can be offered through Marketplaces and they are the only plans for which federal premium tax credits and cost-sharing reductions are available to assist many consumers with the cost of health care coverage. In developing these Medicaid managed care proposed regulations, we considered the market reforms, the standards established for QHPs, and our Medicare Advantage (MA) experience, which is the managed care component of the Medicare program that has also grown significantly since 2002.

Therefore, this proposed rule seeks to align Medicaid managed care rules with Marketplace or MA standards, where appropriate and feasible, to support administrative simplicity for states and health plans to manage health care delivery across different product lines, as well as to enhance beneficiary protections. In general, we believe that adopting standards for Medicaid managed care that parallel or align with those in the private health care and MA context where appropriate will benefit Medicaid programs and enrollees, both because those minimum standards would provide an appropriate level of protection for enrollees and because alignment would ease the administrative burden on issuers and regulators that work in all of those contexts and markets. By aligning Medicaid managed care with other programs when possible, we believe enrollees will experience smoother transitions and have fewer disruptions to care when they transition among sources of health care coverage. Improving beneficiary experience and alignment are important goals of this proposed rule, and the proposed changes would enable states and health plans to more successfully achieve these goals.

The final rule contains a number of modernizing and standardizing measures, three of which are likely to have immediate impact: the medical loss ratio (MLR), network adequacy, and quality rating requirements. The MLR rule compels Medicaid managed care contractors to spend at least 85 percent of revenue on medical expenses rather than administrative expenses and profit, which is consistent with the requirements imposed on Medicare Advantage plans. The network adequacy rule instructs states to create rules that will ensure plans have enough physicians and hospitals accessible to Medicaid populations, for example through "time and distance" limits, as well as regular updates to provider lists so that they accurately reflect provider availability. The third key change is the quality rating rule, which is intended to make plans' health results and customer experiences readily accessible.

PROBLEM

You represent the Commissioner of the State Department of Health and Human Services. If Medicaid managed care decreases the cost of care for Medicaid beneficiaries, what would your advice to the Commissioner be if special interest groups seek better coverage of their high-cost pharmaceutical needs? What if they have other requests that may increase costs to the state? What factors would influence your legal opinion on cost-increasing options?

3. ELIGIBILITY

Medicaid's insurance coverage was originally limited to the "deserving poor" until the ACA expanded eligibility to all non-elderly individuals who were not categorically eligible under the statute below.

> 42 U.S.C. §1396a(a)(10)(A). State plans for medical assistance
> A State plan for medical assistance must — provide — . . .
> (A) for making medical assistance available, including at least the care and services listed in . . . section 1396d (a) of this title, to —
> (i) all individuals —

> Subsection (I) reflects categories of welfare assistance, which historically have facilitated eligibility for Medicaid. We provided a simplified summary of the provision in brackets, but when researching you must be sure to follow the regulatory cross-reference.

> (I) who are receiving aid or assistance under any plan of the State approved under subchapter I [aged], X [blind], XIV [permanently disabled], or XVI [people receiving supplemental security income] of this chapter, or part A or part E of subchapter IV [families with children] . . . ,
> (II)(aa) with respect to whom supplemental security income benefits are being paid under subchapter XVI [people receiving supplemental security income] of this chapter . . . ,
> (bb) who are qualified severely impaired individuals (as defined in section 1396d(q) of this title), or
> (cc) who are under 21 years of age and with respect to whom supplemental security income benefits would be paid under subchapter XVI if subparagraphs (A) and (B) of section 1382(c)(7) of this title were applied without regard to the phrase "the first day of the month following,"
> (III) who are qualified pregnant women or children as defined in section 1396d(n) of this title,

(IV) who are described in subparagraph (A) or (B) of subsection (*l*) (1) of this section and whose family income does not exceed the minimum income level the State is required to establish under subsection (*l*)(2)(A) of this section for such a family;

(V) who are qualified family members as defined in section 1396d (m)(1) of this title,

(VI) who are described in subparagraph (C) of subsection (*l*)(1) of this section and whose family income does not exceed the income level the State is required to establish under subsection (*l*)(2)(B) of this section for such a family,

(VII) who are described in subparagraph (D) of subsection (*l*)(1) of this section and whose family income does not exceed the income level the State is required to establish under subsection (*l*)(2)(C) of this section for such a family;

(VIII) beginning January 1, 2014, who are under 65 years of age, not pregnant, not entitled to, or enrolled for, benefits under part A of subchapter XVIII, or enrolled for benefits under part B of subchapter XVIII, and are not described in a previous subclause of this clause, and whose income (as determined under subsection (e)(14)) does not exceed 133 percent of the poverty line (as defined in section 1397jj(c)(5) of this title) applicable to a family of the size involved, subject to subsection (k); or

> Subclause (VIII) is the ACA's addition — the expansion to everyone earning up to 133 percent of the FPL — which some call the "eighth category" of eligibility. With this statutory provision, low-income people became categorically eligible for Medicaid without regard to disability or reproductive status. A key issue in *NFIB v. Sebelius* is whether this expansion was too different from the historical concept of "deserving poor."

(IX) who —

(aa) are under 26 years of age;

(bb) are not described in or enrolled under any of subclauses (I) through (VII) of this clause or are described in any of such subclauses but have income that exceeds the level of income applicable under the State plan for eligibility to enroll for medical assistance under such subclause;

(cc) were in foster care under the responsibility of the State on the date of attaining 18 years of age or such higher age as the State has elected under section 675(8)(B)(iii) of this title; and

(dd) were enrolled in the State plan under this subchapter or under a waiver of the plan while in such foster care. . . .

Eligibility for Medicaid depends primarily upon income and secondarily upon category of eligibility, as delineated in 42 U.S.C. §1396a(a)(10)(A) above. To aid in eligibility and other programmatic determinations, the HHS Office of the Assistant Secretary for Planning and Evaluation (ASPE) issues "federal poverty guidelines," which are commonly called the "federal poverty level" (FPL). All Medicaid benefits hinge upon the FPL, so the annual update in the *Federal Register* is an important regular modification to the Medicaid program.

Annual Update of the HHS Poverty Guidelines

83 Fed. Reg. 2642 (Jan. 18, 2018)

Section 673(2) of the Omnibus Budget Reconciliation Act (OBRA) of 1981 (42 U.S.C. 9902(2)) requires the Secretary of the Department of Health and Human Services to update the poverty guidelines at least annually, adjusting them on the basis of the Consumer Price Index for All Urban Consumers (CPI-U). The poverty guidelines are used as an eligibility criterion by the Medicaid program and a number of other Federal programs. The poverty guidelines issued here are a simplified version of the poverty thresholds that the Census Bureau uses to prepare its estimates of the number of individuals and families in poverty.

As required by law, this update is accomplished by increasing the latest published Census Bureau poverty thresholds by the relevant percentage change in the Consumer Price Index for All Urban Consumers (CPI-U). The guidelines in this 2018 notice reflect the 2.1 percent price increase between calendar years 2016 and 2017. After this inflation adjustment, the guidelines are rounded and adjusted to standardize the differences between family sizes. . . . The following guideline figures represent annual income.

Persons in family/household	*Poverty guideline*
1	$12,140
2	16,460
3	20,780
4	25,100

For families/households with more than 8 persons, add $4,320 for each additional person.

QUESTION

How much does a person earning 133 percent of the FPL gross in one year? In one day?

The eighth category of eligibility for Medicaid created a mandatory element for states to adopt through SPAs, requiring states to cover not only the traditional categories of the "deserving poor" but also anyone earning up to 133 percent of the FPL as of January 1, 2014. (The ACA's companion legislation, the Health Care and Education Reconciliation Act, created a 5 percent income disregard, raising eligibility for the eighth category to 138 percent of FPL. Pub. L. No. 111-152, §1004(b), (e) (codified at 42 U.S.C. §1396a (2016)). The parties that challenged the constitutionality of the ACA attacked two of the pillars of the statute, the minimum coverage requirement ("individual mandate") and Medicaid expansion. As you read the next excerpt, consider how the Court characterized the markets being regulated; does the Court account for the complexity of the legislation in question? How does it matter for the outcome in this case?

National Federation of Independent Business v. Sebelius

567 U.S. 519 (2012)

Chief Justice ROBERTS announced the judgment of the Court and delivered the opinion of the Court with respect to Parts I, II, and III-C, an opinion with respect to Part IV, in which Justice BREYER and Justice KAGAN join, and an opinion with respect to Parts III-A, III-B, and III-D.

Today we resolve constitutional challenges to two provisions of the Patient Protection and Affordable Care Act of 2010: the individual mandate, which requires individuals to purchase a health insurance policy providing a minimum level of coverage; and the Medicaid expansion, which gives funds to the States on the condition that they provide specified health care to all citizens whose income falls below a certain threshold. We do not consider whether the Act embodies sound policies. That judgment is entrusted to the Nation's elected leaders. We ask only whether Congress has the power under the Constitution to enact the challenged provisions.

In our federal system, the National Government possesses only limited powers; the States and the people retain the remainder. Nearly two centuries ago, Chief Justice Marshall observed that "the question respecting the extent of the powers actually granted" to the Federal Government "is perpetually arising, and will probably continue to arise, as long as our system shall exist." *McCulloch v. Maryland*. In this case we must again determine whether the Constitution grants Congress powers it now asserts, but which many States and individuals believe it does not possess. Resolving this controversy requires us to examine both the limits of the Government's power, and our own limited role in policing those boundaries.

The Federal Government "is acknowledged by all to be one of enumerated powers." That is, rather than granting general authority to perform all the conceivable functions of government, the Constitution lists, or enumerates, the Federal Government's powers. . . . The enumeration of powers is also a limitation of powers, because "[t]he enumeration presupposes something not enumerated." *Gibbons v. Ogden*. The Constitution's express conferral of some powers makes clear that it does not grant others. And the Federal Government "can exercise only the powers granted to it."

. . . [W]hen the Bill of Rights was ratified, it made express what the enumeration of powers necessarily implied: "The powers not delegated to the United States by the Constitution . . . are reserved to the States respectively, or to the people." U.S. Const., Amdt. 10. The Federal Government has expanded dramatically over the past two centuries, but it still must show that a constitutional grant of power authorizes each of its actions.

> The Court's reasoning relies heavily on judicial enforcement of the Tenth Amendment to protect state sovereignty, but the provision is rarely cited throughout the various opinions.

The same does not apply to the States, because the Constitution is not the source of their power. The Constitution may restrict state governments — as it does, for example, by forbidding them to deny any person the equal protection of the laws. But where such prohibitions do not apply, state governments do not need constitutional authorization to act. . . . Our cases refer to this general power of governing, possessed by the States but not by the Federal Government, as the "police power."

The two primary issues were (1) whether the individual mandate exceeded Congress's Commerce Clause and Necessary and Proper Clause authority and (2) whether the Medicaid expansion to non-elderly individuals earning up to 133 percent FPL was an impermissibly coercive exercise of the Spending Power.

. . . This case concerns two powers that the Constitution does grant the Federal Government, but which must be read carefully to avoid creating a general federal authority akin to the police power. The Constitution authorizes Congress to "regulate Commerce with foreign Nations, and among the several States, and with the Indian Tribes." Art. I, §8, cl. 3. Our precedents read that to mean that Congress may regulate "the channels of interstate commerce," "persons or things in interstate commerce," and "those activities that substantially affect interstate commerce." The power over activities that substantially affect interstate commerce can be expansive. That power has been held to authorize federal regulation of such seemingly local matters as a farmer's decision to grow wheat for himself and his livestock, and a loan shark's extortionate collections from a neighborhood butcher shop.

Congress may also "lay and collect Taxes, Duties, Imposts and Excises, to pay the Debts and provide for the common Defence and general Welfare of the United States." U.S. Const., Art. I, §8, cl. 1. Put simply, Congress may tax and spend. This grant gives the Federal Government considerable influence even in areas where it cannot directly regulate. The Federal Government may enact a tax on an activity that it cannot authorize, forbid, or otherwise control. And in exercising its spending power, Congress may offer funds to the States, and may condition those offers on compliance with specified conditions. These offers may well induce the States to adopt policies that the Federal Government itself could not impose. See, e.g., *South Dakota v. Dole*.

The reach of the Federal Government's enumerated powers is broader still because the Constitution authorizes Congress to "make all Laws which shall be necessary and proper for carrying into Execution the foregoing Powers." Art. I, §8, cl. 18. We have long read this provision to give Congress great latitude in exercising its powers: "Let the end be legitimate, let it be within the scope of the constitution, and all means which are appropriate, which are plainly adapted to that end, which are not prohibited, but consist with the letter and spirit of the constitution, are constitutional." *McCulloch*.

. . . Our deference in matters of policy cannot, however, become abdication in matters of law. "The powers of the legislature are defined and limited; and that those limits may not be mistaken, or forgotten, the constitution is written." *Marbury v. Madison*. Our respect for Congress's policy judgments thus can never extend so far as to disavow restraints on federal power that the Constitution carefully constructed. "The peculiar circumstances of the moment may render a measure more or less wise, but cannot render it more or less constitutional." And there can be no question that it is the responsibility of this Court to enforce the limits on federal power by striking down acts of Congress that transgress those limits. *Marbury v. Madison*.

The questions before us must be considered against the background of these basic principles.

I.

In 2010, Congress enacted the Patient Protection and Affordable Care Act. The Act aims to increase the number of Americans covered by health insurance and decrease the cost of health care. The Act's 10 titles stretch over 900 pages and contain hundreds of provisions. This case concerns constitutional challenges to two key provisions, commonly referred to as the individual mandate and the Medicaid expansion.

The individual mandate requires most Americans to maintain "minimum essential" health insurance coverage. . . . Many individuals will receive the required coverage through their employer, or from a government program such as Medicaid or Medicare. But for individuals who are not exempt and do not receive health insurance through a third party, the means of satisfying the requirement is to purchase insurance from a private company.

Beginning in 2014, those who do not comply with the mandate must make a "[s]hared responsibility payment" to the Federal Government . . . .

The second provision of the Affordable Care Act directly challenged here is the Medicaid expansion. Enacted in 1965, Medicaid offers federal funding to States to assist pregnant women, children, needy families, the blind, the elderly, and the disabled in obtaining medical care. In order to receive that funding, States must comply with federal criteria governing matters such as who receives care and what services are provided at what cost. By 1982 every State had chosen to participate in Medicaid. Federal funds received through the Medicaid program have become a substantial part of state budgets, now constituting over 10 percent of most States' total revenue.

The Affordable Care Act expands the scope of the Medicaid program and increases the number of individuals the States must cover. For example, the Act requires state programs to provide Medicaid coverage to adults with incomes up to 133 percent of the federal poverty level, whereas many States now cover adults with children only if their income is considerably lower, and do not cover childless adults at all. *See* §1396a(a)(10)(A)(i)(VIII).

> HHS denied that it would ever do so (and has never done so), but the Secretary has power to terminate a state's funding for noncompliance with Medicaid's mandatory elements.

The Act increases federal funding to cover the States' costs in expanding Medicaid coverage, although States will bear a portion of the costs on their own. If a State does not comply with the Act's new coverage requirements, it may lose not only the federal funding for those requirements, but all of its federal Medicaid funds. *See* §1396c.

Along with their challenge to the individual mandate, the state plaintiffs in the Eleventh Circuit argued that the Medicaid expansion exceeds Congress's constitutional powers. . . . We granted certiorari to review the judgment of the Court of Appeals for the Eleventh Circuit with respect to both the individual mandate and the Medicaid expansion. . . .

III

The Government advances two theories for the proposition that Congress had constitutional authority to enact the individual mandate. First, the Government argues that Congress had the power to enact the mandate under the Commerce Clause. Under that theory, Congress may order individuals to buy health insurance because the failure to do so affects interstate commerce, and could undercut the Affordable Care Act's other reforms. Second, the Government argues that if the commerce power does not support the mandate, we should nonetheless uphold it as an exercise of Congress's power to tax. According to the Government, even if Congress lacks the power to direct individuals to buy insurance, the only effect of the individual mandate is to raise taxes on those who do not do so, and thus the law may be upheld as a tax.

A

The Government's first argument is that the individual mandate is a valid exercise of Congress's power under the Commerce Clause and the Necessary and Proper Clause. According to the Government, the health care market is characterized by a significant cost-shifting problem. Everyone will eventually need health care at a time and to an extent they cannot predict, but if they do not have insurance, they often will not be able to pay for it. Because state and federal laws nonetheless require hospitals to provide a certain degree of care to individuals without regard to their ability to pay, hospitals end up receiving compensation for only a portion of the services they provide. To recoup the losses, hospitals pass on the cost to insurers through higher rates, and insurers, in turn, pass on the cost to policy holders in the form of higher premiums. Congress estimated that the cost of uncompensated care raises family health insurance premiums, on average, by over $1,000 per year.

> Although the individual mandate was effectively repealed, the Court's discussion of Congress's authority to enact that provision remains an important, recent exposition on the scope of federal commerce power and an accurate description of various U.S. health care dynamics.

In the Affordable Care Act, Congress addressed the problem of those who cannot obtain insurance coverage because of preexisting conditions or other health issues. It did so through the Act's "guaranteed-issue" and "community-rating" provisions. These provisions together prohibit insurance companies from denying coverage to those with such conditions or charging unhealthy individuals higher premiums than healthy individuals.

> The federal requirement described here is found in the Emergency Medical Treatment and Labor Act, EMTALA, discussed in Chapter 8. This law requires hospitals to screen and treat medical emergencies, including labor and delivery, but not for free. Lack of insurance does not hinder access to emergency care, but a large bill may follow.

The guaranteed-issue and community-rating reforms do not, however, address the issue of healthy individuals who choose not to purchase insurance to cover potential health care needs. In fact, the reforms sharply exacerbate that problem, by providing an incentive for individuals to delay purchasing health insurance until they become sick, relying on the promise of guaranteed and affordable coverage. The reforms also threaten to impose massive new costs on insurers, who are required to accept unhealthy individuals but prohibited from charging them rates necessary to pay for their coverage. This will lead insurers to significantly increase premiums on everyone.

The individual mandate was Congress's solution to these problems. By requiring that individuals purchase health insurance, the mandate prevents cost-shifting by those who would otherwise go without it. In addition, the mandate forces into the insurance risk pool more healthy individuals, whose premiums on average will be higher than their health care expenses. This allows insurers to subsidize the costs of covering the unhealthy individuals the reforms require them to accept. The Government claims that Congress has power under the Commerce and Necessary and Proper Clauses to enact this solution.

1

The Government contends that the individual mandate is within Congress's power because the failure to purchase insurance "has a substantial and deleterious effect on interstate commerce" by creating the cost-shifting problem. The path of our

Commerce Clause decisions has not always run smooth, see *United States v. Lopez*, but it is now well established that Congress has broad authority under the Clause. We have recognized, for example, that "[t]he power of Congress over interstate commerce is not confined to the regulation of commerce among the states," but extends to activities that "have a substantial effect on interstate commerce." Congress's power, moreover, is not limited to regulation of an activity that by itself substantially affects interstate commerce, but also extends to activities that do so only when aggregated with similar activities of others.

. . . .

The individual mandate, however, does not regulate existing commercial activity. It instead compels individuals to become active in commerce by purchasing a product, on the ground that their failure to do so affects interstate commerce. Construing the Commerce Clause to permit Congress to regulate individuals precisely because they are doing nothing would open a new and potentially vast domain to congressional authority. . . .

The individual mandate's regulation of the uninsured as a class is, in fact, particularly divorced from any link to existing commercial activity. The mandate primarily affects healthy, often young adults who are less likely to need significant health care and have other priorities for spending their money. It is precisely because these individuals, as an actuarial class, incur relatively low health care costs that the mandate helps counter the effect of forcing insurance companies to cover others who impose greater costs than their premiums are allowed to reflect. If the individual mandate is targeted at a class, it is a class whose commercial inactivity rather than activity is its defining feature. . . .

Everyone will likely participate in the markets for food, clothing, transportation, shelter, or energy; that does not authorize Congress to direct them to purchase particular products in those or other markets today. The Commerce Clause is not a general license to regulate an individual from cradle to grave, simply because he will predictably engage in particular transactions. Any police power to regulate individuals as such, as opposed to their activities, remains vested in the States . . . .

The individual mandate forces individuals into commerce precisely because they elected to refrain from commercial activity. Such a law cannot be sustained under a clause authorizing Congress to "regulate Commerce."

> Massachusetts's universal health coverage was a model for the ACA. The Court appears to approve such state-based efforts.

2

The Government next contends that Congress has the power under the Necessary and Proper Clause to enact the individual mandate because the mandate is an "integral part of a comprehensive scheme of economic regulation"—the guaranteed-issue and community-rating insurance reforms. Under this argument, it is not necessary to consider the effect that an individual's inactivity may have on interstate commerce; it is enough that Congress regulate commercial activity in a way that requires regulation of inactivity to be effective.

The power to "make all Laws which shall be necessary and proper for carrying into Execution" the powers enumerated in the Constitution, Art. I, §8, cl. 18, vests Congress with authority to enact provisions "incidental to the [enumerated] power, and conducive to its beneficial exercise," *McCulloch*. Although the Clause gives Congress authority to "legislate on that vast mass of incidental powers which must be involved in the constitution," it does not license the exercise of any "great substantive and independent power[s]" beyond those specifically enumerated. Instead, the Clause is "'merely a declaration, for the removal of all uncertainty, that the means of carrying into execution those [powers] otherwise granted are included in the grant.'"

. . . [T]he individual mandate cannot be sustained under the Necessary and Proper Clause as an essential component of the insurance reforms. Each of our prior cases upholding laws under that Clause involved exercises of authority derivative of, and in service to, a granted power. . . . Even if the individual mandate is "necessary" to the Act's insurance reforms, such an expansion of federal power is not a "proper" means for making those reforms effective.

. . . .

Just as the individual mandate cannot be sustained as a law regulating the substantial effects of the failure to purchase health insurance, neither can it be upheld as a "necessary and proper" component of the insurance reforms. The commerce power thus does not authorize the mandate.

B

That is not the end of the matter. Because the Commerce Clause does not support the individual mandate, it is necessary to turn to the Government's second argument: that the mandate may be upheld as within Congress's enumerated power to "lay and collect Taxes." Art. I, §8, cl. 1.

Most of the briefing to the Court focused on the Commerce Clause issue, so it was something of a surprise that the government lost on the Commerce Clause but prevailed on the Taxing Power.

. . . [T]he Government asks us to read the mandate not as ordering individuals to buy insurance, but rather as imposing a tax on those who do not buy that product . . . .

Under the mandate, if an individual does not maintain health insurance, the only consequence is that he must make an additional payment to the IRS when he pays his taxes. That, according to the Government, means the mandate can be regarded as establishing a condition — not owning health insurance — that triggers a tax — the required payment to the IRS. Under that theory, the mandate is not a legal command to buy insurance. Rather, it makes going without insurance just another thing the Government taxes, like buying gasoline or earning income. And if the mandate is in effect just a tax hike on certain taxpayers who do not have health insurance, it may be within Congress's constitutional power to tax. . . .

C

The exaction the Affordable Care Act imposes on those without health insurance looks like a tax in many respects. The "[s]hared responsibility payment," as the statute entitles it, is paid into the Treasury by "tax-payer[s]" when they file their tax returns. It does not apply to individuals who do not pay federal income taxes because their household income is less than the filing threshold in the Internal Revenue Code. For taxpayers who do owe the payment, its amount is determined by such familiar factors as taxable income, number of dependents, and joint filing status. The requirement to pay is found in the Internal Revenue Code and enforced by the IRS, which — as we previously explained — must assess and collect it "in the same manner as taxes." This process yields the essential feature of any tax: it produces at least some revenue for the Government.

. . . .

None of this is to say that the payment is not intended to affect individual conduct. Although the payment will raise considerable revenue, it is plainly designed to expand health insurance coverage. But taxes that seek to influence conduct are nothing new. Some of our earliest federal taxes sought to deter the purchase of imported manufactured goods in order to foster the growth of domestic industry. . . .

Many taxes, such as those on cigarettes and alcohol, are designed to affect policy preferences to prevent unhealthy personal behaviors.

Our precedent demonstrates that Congress had the power to impose the exaction in §5000A under the taxing power, and that §5000A need not be read to do more than impose a tax. That is sufficient to sustain it. . . .

IV

A

The States also contend that the Medicaid expansion exceeds Congress's authority under the Spending Clause. They claim that Congress is coercing the States to adopt the changes it wants by threatening to withhold all of a State's Medicaid grants, unless the State accepts the new expanded funding and complies with the conditions that come with it. This, they argue, violates the basic principle that the "Federal Government may not compel the States to enact or administer a federal regulatory program."

There is no doubt that the Act dramatically increases state obligations under Medicaid. The current Medicaid program requires States to cover only certain discrete categories of needy individuals — pregnant women, children, needy families, the blind, the elderly, and the disabled. There is no mandatory coverage for most childless adults, and the States typically do not offer any such coverage. The States also enjoy considerable flex-

This part of the opinion surprised most experts by holding that the Medicaid expansion was an unconstitutionally coercive exercise of the Spending Power.

ibility with respect to the coverage levels for parents of needy families. On average States cover only those unemployed parents who make less than 37 percent of the federal poverty level, and only those employed parents who make less than 63 percent of the poverty line.

The Medicaid provisions of the Affordable Care Act, in contrast, require States to expand their Medicaid programs by 2014 to cover all individuals under the age of 65 with incomes below 133 percent of the federal poverty line. The Act also establishes a new "[e]ssential health benefits" package, which States must provide to all new Medicaid recipients — a level sufficient to satisfy a recipient's obligations under the individual mandate. The Affordable Care Act provides that the Federal Government will pay 100 percent of the costs of covering these newly eligible individuals through 2016. In the following years, the federal payment level gradually decreases, to a minimum of 90 percent. In light of the expansion in coverage mandated by the Act, the Federal Government estimates that its Medicaid spending will increase by approximately $100 billion per year, nearly 40 percent above current levels.

The Spending Clause grants Congress the power "to pay the Debts and provide for the . . . general Welfare of the United States." U.S. Const., Art. I, §8, cl. 1. We have long recognized that Congress may use this power to grant federal funds to the States, and may condition such a grant upon the States' "taking certain actions that Congress could not require them to take." Such measures "encourage a State to regulate in a particular way, [and] influenc[e] a State's policy choices." The conditions imposed by Congress ensure that the funds are used by the States to "provide for the . . . general Welfare" in the manner Congress intended.

At the same time, our cases have recognized limits on Congress's power under the Spending Clause to secure state compliance with federal objectives. "We have repeatedly characterized . . . Spending Clause legislation as 'much in the nature of a contract.'" The legitimacy of Congress's exercise of the spending power "thus rests on whether the State voluntarily and knowingly accepts the terms of the 'contract.'" *Pennhurst*. Respecting this limitation is critical to ensuring that Spending Clause legislation does not undermine the status of the States as independent sovereigns in our federal system. That system "rests on what might at first seem a counterintuitive insight, that 'freedom is enhanced by the creation of two governments, not one.'" For this reason, "the Constitution has never been understood to confer upon Congress the ability to require the States to govern according to Congress' instructions." Otherwise the two-government system established by the Framers would give way to a system that vests power in one central government, and individual liberty would suffer.

That insight has led this Court to strike down federal legislation that commandeers a State's legislative or administrative apparatus for federal purposes. *See, e.g., Printz; New York*. It has also led us to scrutinize Spending Clause legislation to ensure that Congress is not using financial inducements to exert a "power akin to undue influence." Steward Machine Co. v. Davis. Congress may use its spending power to create incentives for States to act in accordance with federal policies. But when "pressure turns into compulsion," the legislation runs contrary to our system of federalism. "[T]he Constitution simply does not give Congress the authority to require the States to regulate." That is true whether Congress directly commands a State to regulate or indirectly coerces a State to adopt a federal regulatory system as its own.

Permitting the Federal Government to force the States to implement a federal program would threaten the political accountability key to our federal system. . . . Spending Clause programs do not pose this danger when a State has a legitimate choice whether to accept the federal conditions in exchange for federal funds. In such a situation, state officials can fairly be held politically accountable for choosing to accept or refuse the federal offer. But when the State has no choice, the Federal Government can achieve its objectives without accountability, just as in *New York* and *Printz*. Indeed, this danger is heightened when Congress acts under the Spending Clause, because Congress can use that power to implement federal policy it could not impose directly under its enumerated powers. . . .

The States, however, argue that the Medicaid expansion is far from the typical case. They object that Congress has "crossed the line distinguishing encouragement from coercion," in the way it has structured the funding: Instead of simply refusing to grant the new funds to States that will not accept the new conditions, Congress has also threatened to withhold those States' existing Medicaid funds. The States claim that this threat serves no purpose other than to force unwilling States to sign up for the dramatic expansion in health care coverage effected by the Act.

Given the nature of the threat and the programs at issue here, we must agree. We have upheld Congress's authority to condition the receipt of funds on the States' complying with restrictions on the use of those funds, because that is the means by which Congress ensures that the funds are spent according to its view of the "general Welfare." Conditions that do not here govern the use of the funds, however, cannot be justified on that basis. When, for example, such conditions take the form of threats to terminate other significant independent grants, the conditions are properly viewed as a means of pressuring the States to accept policy changes.

In *South Dakota v. Dole*, we . . . asked whether "the financial inducement offered by Congress" was "so coercive as to pass the point at which 'pressure turns into compulsion.'" By "financial inducement" the Court meant the threat of losing five percent of highway funds; no new money was offered to the States to raise their drinking ages. We found that the inducement was not impermissibly coercive, because Congress was offering only "relatively mild encouragement to the States." . . .

In this case, the financial "inducement" Congress has chosen is much more than "relatively mild encouragement"—it is a gun to the head. Section 1396c of the Medicaid Act provides that if a State's Medicaid plan does not comply with the Act's require- ments, the Secretary of Health and Human Services may declare that "further payments will not be made to the State." A State that opts out of the Affordable Care Act's expansion in health care coverage thus stands to lose not merely "a relatively small percentage" of its existing Medicaid funding, but all of it. Medicaid spending accounts for over 20 percent of the average State's total budget, with federal funds covering 50 to 83 percent of those costs. The Federal Government estimates that it will pay out approximately $3.3 trillion between 2010 and 2019 in order to cover the costs of pre-expansion Medicaid. In addition, the States have developed intricate statutory and administrative regimes over the course of many decades to implement their objectives under existing Med- icaid. It is easy to see how the *Dole* Court could conclude that the threatened loss of less than half of one percent of South Dakota's budget left that State with a "pre- rogative" to reject Congress's desired policy, "not merely in theory but in fact." The threatened loss of over 10 percent of a State's overall budget, in contrast, is economic dragooning that leaves the States with no real option but to acquiesce in the Med- icaid expansion. . . .

> The so-called gun to the head provision has been in the Medicaid statute since inception in 1965. It was not added by the ACA.

Here, the Government claims that the Medicaid expansion is properly viewed merely as a modification of the existing program because the States agreed that Congress could change the terms of Medicaid when they signed on in the first place. The Government observes that the Social Security Act, which includes the original Medicaid provisions, contains a clause expressly reserving "[t]he right to alter, amend, or repeal any provision" of that statute. So it does. But "if Congress intends to impose a condition on the grant of federal moneys, it must do so unam- biguously." A State confronted with statutory language reserving the right to "alter" or "amend" the pertinent provisions of the Social Security Act might reasonably assume that Congress was entitled to make adjustments to the Medicaid program as it devel- oped. Congress has in fact done so, sometimes conditioning only the new funding, other times both old and new.

The Medicaid expansion, however, accomplishes a shift in kind, not merely degree. The original program was designed to cover medical services for four particular categories of the needy: the disabled, the blind, the elderly, and needy families with dependent children. Previous amendments to Medicaid eligibility merely altered and expanded the boundaries of these categories. Under the Afford- able Care Act, Medicaid is transformed into a program to meet the health care needs of the entire nonelderly population with income below 133 percent of the poverty level. It is no longer a program to care for the neediest among us, but rather an element of a comprehensive national plan to provide universal health insurance coverage. . . .

The Court in *Steward Machine* did not attempt to "fix the outermost line" where persuasion gives way to coercion. The Court found it "[e]nough for present purposes that wherever the line may be, this statute is within it." We have no need to fix a line either. It is enough for today that wherever that line may be, this statute is surely beyond it. Congress may not simply "conscript state [agencies] into the national bureaucratic army," and that is what it is attempting to do with the Medicaid expansion.

> The Court refuses to define coercion, leaving the door open to further litigation on this question.

B

Nothing in our opinion precludes Congress from offering funds under the Affordable Care Act to expand the availability of health care, and requiring that States accepting such funds comply with the conditions on their use. What Congress is not free to do is to penalize States that choose not to participate in that new program by taking away their existing Medicaid funding. Section 1396c gives the Secretary of Health and Human Services the authority to do just that. It allows her to withhold all "further [Medicaid] payments . . . to the State" if she determines that the State is out of compliance with any Medicaid requirement, including those contained in the expansion. In light of the Court's holding, the Secretary cannot apply §1396c to withdraw existing Medicaid funds for failure to comply with the requirements set out in the expansion.

That fully remedies the constitutional violation we have identified. The chapter of the United States Code that contains §1396c includes a severability clause confirming that we need go no further. That clause specifies that "[i]f any provision of this chapter, or the application thereof to any person or circumstance, is held invalid, the remainder of the chapter, and the application of such provision to other persons or circumstances shall not be affected thereby." §1303. Today's holding does not affect the continued application of §1396c to the existing Medicaid program. Nor does it affect the Secretary's ability to withdraw funds provided under the Affordable Care Act if a State that has chosen to participate in the expansion fails to comply with the requirements of that Act. . . .

We are confident that Congress would have wanted to preserve the rest of the Act. . . . The Court today limits the financial pressure the Secretary may apply to induce States to accept the terms of the Medicaid expansion. As a practical matter, that means States may now choose to reject the expansion; that is the whole point. But that does not mean all or even any will. Some States may indeed decline to participate, either because they are unsure they will be able to afford their share of the new funding obligations, or because they are unwilling to commit the administrative resources necessary to support the expansion. Other States, however, may voluntarily sign up, finding the idea of expanding Medicaid coverage attractive, particularly given the level of federal funding the Act offers at the outset. . . .

. . . .

The Affordable Care Act is constitutional in part and unconstitutional in part. The individual mandate cannot be upheld as an exercise of Congress's power under the Commerce Clause. That Clause authorizes Congress to regulate interstate commerce, not to order individuals to engage in it. In this case, however, it is reasonable to construe what Congress has done as increasing taxes on those who have a certain amount of income, but choose to go without health insurance. Such legislation is within Congress's power to tax.

As for the Medicaid expansion, that portion of the Affordable Care Act violates the Constitution by threatening existing Medicaid funding. Congress has no authority to order the States to regulate according to its instructions. Congress may offer the States grants and require the States to comply with accompanying conditions, but the States must have a genuine choice whether to accept the offer. The States are given no such choice in this case: They must either accept a basic change in the nature of Medicaid, or risk losing all Medicaid funding. The remedy for that constitutional violation is to preclude the Federal Government from imposing such a sanction. That remedy does not require striking down other portions of the Affordable Care Act . . . .

> In the aftermath of this decision, many state governments have struggled over whether and how Medicaid eligibility should be expanded.

The judgment of the Court of Appeals for the Eleventh Circuit is affirmed in part and reversed in part.

Justice GINSBURG, with whom Justice SOTOMAYOR joins, and with whom Justice BREYER and Justice KAGAN join as to Parts I, II, III, and IV, concurring in part, concurring in the judgment in part, and dissenting in part.

I

The provision of health care is today a concern of national dimension, just as the provision of old-age and survivors' benefits was in the 1930's. In the Social Security Act, Congress installed a federal system to provide monthly benefits to retired wage earners and, eventually, to their survivors. Beyond question, Congress could have adopted a similar scheme for health care. Congress chose, instead, to preserve a central role for private insurers and state governments. According to the Chief Justice, the Commerce Clause does not permit that preservation. This rigid reading of the Clause makes scant sense and is stunningly retrogressive.

Since 1937, our precedent has recognized Congress' large authority to set the Nation's course in the economic and social welfare realm. The Chief Justice's crabbed reading of the Commerce Clause harks back to the era in which the Court routinely thwarted Congress' efforts to regulate the national economy in the interest of those who labor to sustain it. It is a reading that should not have staying power.

A

In enacting the Patient Protection and Affordable Care Act (ACA), Congress comprehensively reformed the national market for health-care products and services. By any measure, that market is immense. Collectively, Americans spent $2.5 trillion on health care in 2009, accounting for 17.6% of our Nation's economy. Within the next decade, it is anticipated, spending on health care will nearly double.

The health-care market's size is not its only distinctive feature. Unlike the market for almost any other product or service, the market for medical care is one in which all individuals inevitably participate. Virtually every person residing in the United States, sooner or later, will visit a doctor or other health-care professional. Most people will do so repeatedly.

> Note how Justice Ginsburg explains the market being regulated differently from the Chief Justice. The opinions differ on both the relevant facts and the Constitution's application to those facts.

When individuals make those visits, they face another reality of the current market for medical care: its high cost. In 2010, on average, an individual in the United States incurred over $7,000 in health-care expenses. Over a lifetime, costs mount to hundreds of thousands of dollars. When a person requires nonroutine care, the cost will generally exceed what he or she can afford to pay. A single hospital stay, for instance, typically costs upwards of $10,000. Treatments for many serious, though not uncommon, conditions similarly cost a substantial sum.

Although every U.S. domiciliary will incur significant medical expenses during his or her lifetime, the time when care will be needed is often unpredictable. An accident, a heart attack, or a cancer diagnosis commonly occurs without warning. Inescapably, we are all at peril of needing medical care without a moment's notice.

To manage the risks associated with medical care — its high cost, its unpredictability, and its inevitability — most people in the United States obtain health insurance. Many (approximately 170 million in 2009) are insured by private insurance companies. Others, including those over 65 and certain poor and disabled persons, rely on government-funded insurance programs, notably Medicare and Medicaid. Combined, private health insurers and State and Federal Governments finance almost 85% of the medical care administered to U.S. residents.

Not all U.S. residents, however, have health insurance. In 2009, approximately 50 million people were uninsured, either by choice or, more likely, because they could not afford private insurance and did not qualify for government aid. As a group, uninsured individuals annually consume more than $100 billion in healthcare services, nearly 5% of the Nation's total. Over 60% of those without insurance visit a doctor's office or emergency room in a given year.

B

The large number of individuals without health insurance, Congress found, heavily burdens the national health-care market. As just noted, the cost of emergency care or treatment for a serious illness generally exceeds what an individual can afford to pay on her own. Unlike markets for most products, however, the inability to pay for care does not mean that an uninsured individual will receive no care. Federal and state law, as well as professional obligations and embedded social norms, require hospitals and physicians to provide care when it is most needed, regardless of the patient's ability to pay.

As a consequence, medical-care providers deliver significant amounts of care to the uninsured for which the providers receive no payment. In 2008, for example, hospitals, physicians, and other health-care professionals received no compensation for $43 billion worth of the $116 billion in care they administered to those without insurance.

Health-care providers do not absorb these bad debts. Instead, they raise their prices, passing along the cost of uncompensated care to those who do pay reliably: the government and private insurance companies. In response, private insurers increase their premiums, shifting the cost of the elevated bills from providers onto those who carry insurance. The net result: Those with health insurance subsidize the medical care of those without it. As economists would describe what happens, the uninsured "free ride" on those who pay for health insurance.

The size of this subsidy is considerable. Congress found that the cost-shifting just described "increases family [insurance] premiums by on average over $1,000 a year." Higher premiums, in turn, render health insurance less affordable, forcing more people to go without insurance and leading to further cost-shifting.

. . . [B]ecause any uninsured person may need medical care at any moment and because health-care companies must account for that risk, every uninsured person impacts the market price of medical care and medical insurance . . . .

C

States cannot resolve the problem of the uninsured on their own. Like Social Security benefits, a universal health-care system, if adopted by an individual State, would be "bait to the needy and dependent elsewhere, encouraging them to migrate and seek a haven of repose." *See also* Brief for Commonwealth of Massachusetts as Amicus Curiae in No. 11-398, p. 15 (noting that, in 2009, Massachusetts' emergency rooms served thousands of uninsured, out-of-state residents). An influx of unhealthy individuals into a State with universal health care would result in increased spending on medical services. To cover the increased costs, a State would have to raise taxes, and private health-insurance companies would have to increase premiums. Higher taxes and increased insurance costs would, in turn, encourage businesses and healthy individuals to leave the State.

States that undertake health-care reforms on their own thus risk "placing themselves in a position of economic disadvantage as compared with neighbors or competitors." Facing that risk, individual States are unlikely to take the initiative in addressing the problem of the uninsured, even though solving that problem is in all States' best interests. Congress' intervention was needed to overcome this collective-action impasse.

D

Aware that a national solution was required, Congress could have taken over the health-insurance market by establishing a tax-and-spend federal program like Social Security. Such a program, commonly referred to as a single-payer system (where the sole payer is the Federal Government), would have left little, if any, room for private enterprise or the States. Instead of going this route, Congress enacted the ACA, a solution that retains a robust role for private insurers and state governments. To make its chosen approach work, however, Congress had to use some new tools, including a requirement that most individuals obtain private health insurance coverage. . . .

A central aim of the ACA is to reduce the number of uninsured U.S. residents. The minimum coverage provision advances this objective by giving potential recipients of health care a financial incentive to acquire insurance. Per the minimum coverage provision, an individual must either obtain insurance or pay a toll constructed as a tax penalty. . . .

V

Through Medicaid, Congress has offered the States an opportunity to furnish health care to the poor with the aid of federal financing. To receive federal Medicaid funds, States must provide health benefits to specified categories of needy persons, including pregnant women, children, parents, and adults with disabilities. Guaranteed eligibility varies by category: for some it is tied to the federal poverty level (incomes up to 100% or 133%); for others it depends on criteria such as eligibility for designated state or federal assistance programs. The ACA enlarges the population of needy people States must cover to include adults under age 65 with incomes up to 133% of the federal poverty level. The spending power conferred by the Constitution, the Court has never doubted, permits Congress to define the contours of programs financed with federal funds. And to expand coverage, Congress could have recalled the existing legislation, and replaced it with a new law making Medicaid as embracive of the poor as Congress chose.

The question posed by the 2010 Medicaid expansion, then, is essentially this: To cover a notably larger population, must Congress take the repeal/reenact route, or may it achieve the same result by amending existing law? The answer should be that Congress may expand by amendment the classes of needy persons entitled to Medicaid benefits. . . .

Medicaid is a prototypical example of federal-state cooperation in serving the Nation's general welfare. Rather than authorizing a federal agency to administer a uniform national health-care system for the poor, Congress offered States the opportunity to tailor Medicaid grants to their particular needs, so long as they remain within bounds set by federal law. In shaping Medicaid, Congress did not endeavor to fix permanently the terms participating states must meet; instead, Congress reserved the "right to alter, amend, or repeal" any provision of the Medicaid Act. States, for their part, agreed to amend their own Medicaid plans consistent with changes from time to time made in the federal law. And from 1965 to the present, States have regularly conformed to Congress' alterations of the Medicaid Act.

The Chief Justice acknowledges that Congress may "condition the receipt of [federal] funds on the States' complying with restrictions on the use of those funds," but nevertheless concludes that the 2010 expansion is unduly coercive. His conclusion rests on three premises, each of them essential to his theory. First, the Medicaid expansion is, in the Chief Justice's view, a new grant program, not an addition to the Medicaid program existing before the ACA's enactment. Congress, the Chief Justice maintains, has threatened States with the loss of funds from an old program in an effort to get them to adopt a new one. Second, the expansion was unforeseeable by the States when they first signed on to Medicaid. Third, the threatened loss of funding is so large that the States have no real choice but to participate in the Medicaid expansion. The Chief Justice therefore — for the first time ever — finds an exercise of Congress' spending power unconstitutionally coercive.

> Congress has repeatedly modified Medicaid since 1965. This is the first time a modification has been held to be unconstitutionally coercive.

Medicaid, as amended by the ACA, however, is not two spending programs; it is a single program with a constant aim — to enable poor persons to receive basic health care when they need it. Given past expansions, plus express statutory warning that Congress may change the requirements participating States must meet, there can be no tenable claim that the ACA fails for lack of notice. Moreover, States have no entitlement to receive any Medicaid funds; they enjoy only the opportunity to accept funds on Congress' terms. Future Congresses are not bound by their predecessors' dispositions; they have authority to spend federal revenue as they see fit. The Federal Government, therefore, is not, as the Chief Justice charges, threatening States with the loss of "existing" funds from one spending program in order to induce them to opt into another program. Congress is simply requiring States to do what States have long been required to do to receive Medicaid funding: comply with the conditions Congress prescribes for participation.

A majority of the Court, however, buys the argument that prospective withholding of funds formerly available exceeds Congress' spending power. Given that holding, I entirely agree with the Chief Justice as to the appropriate remedy. It is to bar the withholding found impermissible — not, as the joint dissenters would have it, to scrap the expansion altogether. . . . Because the Chief Justice finds the withholding — not the granting — of federal funds incompatible with the Spending Clause, Congress' extension of Medicaid remains available to any State that affirms its willingness to participate.

A

. . . .

Since 1965, Congress has amended the Medicaid program on more than 50 occasions, sometimes quite sizably. Most relevant here, between 1988 and 1990, Congress required participating States to include among their beneficiaries pregnant women with family incomes up to 133% of the federal poverty level, children up to age 6 at the same income levels, and children ages 6 to 18 with family incomes up to 100% of the poverty level. These amendments added millions to the Medicaid-eligible population. . . .

Compared to past alterations, the ACA is notable for the extent to which the Federal Government will pick up the tab. Medicaid's 2010 expansion is financed largely by federal outlays. In 2014, federal funds will cover 100% of the costs for newly eligible beneficiaries; that rate will gradually decrease before settling at 90% in 2020. By comparison, federal contributions toward the care of beneficiaries eligible pre-ACA range from 50% to 83%, and averaged 57% between 2005 and 2008.

> The federal government pays for most of the Medicaid expansion through an exceptionally large match that remains greater than traditional federal matching in Medicaid, even after it is phased down.

Nor will the expansion exorbitantly increase state Medicaid spending. The Congressional Budget Office (CBO) projects that States will spend 0.8% more than they would have, absent the ACA. Whatever the increase in state obligations after the ACA, it will pale in comparison to the increase in federal funding.

Finally, any fair appraisal of Medicaid would require acknowledgment of the considerable autonomy States enjoy under the Act. Far from "conscript[ing] state agencies into the national bureaucratic army," Medicaid "is designed to advance cooperative federalism." Subject to its basic requirements, the Medicaid Act empowers States to "select dramatically different levels of funding and coverage, alter and experiment with different financing and delivery modes, and opt to cover (or not to cover) a range of particular procedures and therapies. States have leveraged this policy discretion to generate a myriad of dramatically different Medicaid programs over the past several decades." The ACA does not jettison this approach. States, as first-line administrators, will continue to guide the distribution of substantial resources among their needy populations.

The alternative to conditional federal spending, it bears emphasis, is not state autonomy but state marginalization. In 1965, Congress elected to nationalize health coverage for seniors through Medicare. It could similarly have established Medicaid as an exclusively federal program. Instead, Congress gave the States the opportunity to partner in the program's administration and development. Absent from the nationalized model, of course, is the state-level policy discretion and experimentation that is Medicaid's hallmark; undoubtedly the interests of federalism are better served when States retain a meaningful role in the implementation of a program of such importance.

. . . .

B

The Spending Clause authorizes Congress "to pay the Debts and provide for the . . . general Welfare of the United States." To ensure that federal funds granted to the States are spent "to 'provide for the . . . general Welfare' in the manner Congress intended," Congress must of course have authority to impose limitations on the States' use of the federal dollars. This Court, time and again, has respected Congress' prescription of spending conditions, and has required States to abide by them. In particular, we have recognized Congress' prerogative to condition a State's receipt of Medicaid funding on compliance with the terms Congress set for participation in the program.

Congress' authority to condition the use of federal funds is not confined to spending programs as first launched. The legislature may, and often does, amend the law, imposing new conditions grant recipients henceforth must meet in order to continue receiving funds.

Yes, there are federalism-based limits on the use of Congress' conditional spending power. In the leading decision in this area, *South Dakota v. Dole*, the Court identified four criteria. The conditions placed on federal grants to States must (a) promote the "general welfare," (b) "unambiguously" inform States what is demanded of them, (c) be germane "to the federal interest in particular national projects or programs," and (d) not "induce the States to engage in activities that would themselves be unconstitutional."

The Court in *Dole* mentioned, but did not adopt, a further limitation, one hypothetically raised a half-century earlier: In "some circumstances," Congress might be prohibited from offering a "financial inducement . . . so coercive as to pass the point at which 'pressure turns into compulsion.'" Prior to today's decision, however, the Court has never ruled that the terms of any grant crossed the indistinct line between temptation and coercion. . . .

The ACA, in contrast, relates solely to the federally funded Medicaid program; if States choose not to comply, Congress has not threatened to withhold funds earmarked for any other program. Nor does the ACA use Medicaid funding to induce States to take action Congress itself could not undertake. The Federal Government undoubtedly could operate its own health-care program for poor persons, just as it operates Medicare for seniors' health care.

. . . .

C

. . . .

1

The starting premise on which the Chief Justice's coercion analysis rests is that the ACA did not really "extend" Medicaid; instead, Congress created an entirely new program to co-exist with the old. The Chief Justice calls the ACA new, but in truth, it simply reaches more of America's poor than Congress originally covered.

> Was the Medicaid expansion an entirely new program?

Medicaid was created to enable States to provide medical assistance to "needy persons." By bringing health care within the reach of a larger population of Americans unable to afford it, the Medicaid expansion is an extension of that basic aim.

The Medicaid Act contains hundreds of provisions governing operation of the program. . . . The Medicaid expansion leaves unchanged the vast majority of these provisions; it adds beneficiaries to the existing program and specifies the rate at which States will be reimbursed for services provided to the added beneficiaries. The ACA does not describe operational aspects of the program for these newly eligible persons; for that information, one must read the existing Medicaid Act.

Congress styled and clearly viewed the Medicaid expansion as an amendment to the Medicaid Act, not as a "new" health-care program. To the four categories of beneficiaries for whom coverage became mandatory in 1965, and the three mandatory classes added in the late 1980's, the ACA adds an eighth: individuals under 65 with incomes not exceeding 133% of the federal poverty level. The expansion is effectuated by §2001 of the ACA, aptly titled: "Medicaid Coverage for the Lowest Income Populations." That section amends . . . the Medicaid Act. . . .

Consider also that Congress could have repealed Medicaid. Thereafter, Congress could have enacted Medicaid II, a new program combining the pre-2010 coverage with the expanded coverage required by the ACA. By what right does a court stop Congress from building up without first tearing down?

2

The Chief Justice finds the Medicaid expansion vulnerable because it took participating States by surprise. "A State could hardly anticipate that Congres[s]" would endeavor to "transform [the Medicaid program] so dramatically," he states. For the notion that States must be able to foresee, when they sign up, alterations Congress might make later on, The Chief Justice cites only one case: *Pennhurst State School and Hospital v. Halderman.* . . .

Pennhurst thus instructs that "if Congress intends to impose a condition on the grant of federal moneys, it must do so unambiguously." That requirement is met in this case. Section 2001 does not take effect until 2014. The ACA makes perfectly clear what will be required of States that accept Medicaid funding after that date: They must extend eligibility to adults with incomes no more than 133% of the federal poverty line.

The Chief Justice appears to find in *Pennhurst* a requirement that, when spending legislation is first passed, or when States first enlist in the federal program, Congress must provide clear notice of conditions it might later impose. If I understand his point correctly, it was incumbent on Congress, in 1965, to warn the States clearly of the size and shape potential changes to Medicaid might take. And absent such notice, sizable changes could not be made mandatory. Our decisions do not support such a requirement. . . .

In any event, from the start, the Medicaid Act put States on notice that the program could be changed: "The right to alter, amend, or repeal any provision of [Medicaid]," the statute has read since 1965, "is hereby reserved to the Congress." The "effect of these few simple words" has long been settled. By reserving the right to "alter, amend, [or] repeal" a spending program, Congress "has given special notice of its intention to retain . . . full and complete power to make such alterations and amendments . . . as come within the just scope of legislative power." . . .

The Chief Justice insists that the most recent expansion, in contrast to its predecessors, "accomplishes a shift in kind, not merely degree." But why was Medicaid altered only in degree, not in kind, when Congress required States to cover millions of children and pregnant women? Congress did not "merely alte[r] and expan[d] the boundaries of" the Aid to Families with Dependent Children program. Rather, Congress required participating States to provide coverage tied to the federal poverty level (as it later did in the ACA), rather than to the AFDC program. In short, given §1304, this Court's construction of §1304's language in *Bowen,* and the enlargement of Medicaid in the years since 1965, a State would be hard put to complain that it lacked fair notice when, in 2010, Congress altered Medicaid to embrace a larger portion of the Nation's poor.

3

The Chief Justice ultimately asks whether "the financial inducement offered by Congress . . . pass[ed] the point at which pressure turns into compulsion." The financial inducement Congress employed here, he concludes, crosses that threshold: The threatened withholding of "existing Medicaid funds" is "a gun to the head" that forces States to acquiesce.

The Chief Justice sees no need to "fix the outermost line," "where persuasion gives way to coercion." Neither do the joint dissenters. Notably, the decision on which they rely, *Steward Machine,* found the statute at issue inside the line, "wherever the line may be."

When future Spending Clause challenges arrive, as they likely will in the wake of today's decision, how will litigants and judges assess whether "a State has a legitimate choice whether to accept the federal conditions in exchange for federal funds"? Are courts to measure the number of dollars the Federal Government might withhold for noncompliance? The portion of the State's budget at stake? And which State's — or States' — budget is determinative: the lead plaintiff, all challenging States (26 in this case, many with quite different fiscal situations), or some national median? Does it matter that Florida, unlike most States, imposes no state income tax, and therefore might be able to replace foregone federal funds with new state revenue? Or that the coercion state officials in fact fear is punishment at the ballot box for turning down a politically popular federal grant? . . .

At bottom, my colleagues' position is that the States' reliance on federal funds limits Congress' authority to alter its spending programs. This gets things backwards: Congress, not the States, is tasked with spending federal money in service of the general welfare. And each successive Congress is empowered to appropriate funds as it sees fit. When the 110th Congress reached a conclusion about Medicaid funds that differed from its predecessors' view, it abridged no State's right to "existing," or "pre-existing," funds. For, in fact, there are no such funds. There is only money States anticipate receiving from future Congresses.

D

. . . .

But in view of the Chief Justice's disposition, I agree with him that the Medicaid Act's severability clause determines the appropriate remedy. That clause provides that "[i]f any provision of [the Medicaid Act], or the application thereof to any person or circumstance, is held invalid, the remainder of the chapter, and the application of such provision to other persons or circumstances shall not be affected thereby."

The Court does not strike down any provision of the ACA. It prohibits only the "application" of the Secretary's authority to withhold Medicaid funds from States that decline to conform their Medicaid plans to the ACA's requirements. Thus the ACA's authorization of funds to finance the expansion remains intact, and the Secretary's authority to withhold funds for reasons other than non-compliance with the expansion remains unaffected. . . .

For the reasons stated, I agree with the Chief Justice that, as to the validity of the minimum coverage provision, the judgment of the Court of Appeals for the Eleventh Circuit should be reversed. In my view, the provision encounters no constitutional obstruction. Further, I would uphold the Eleventh Circuit's decision that the Medicaid expansion is within Congress' spending power.

QUESTIONS

1. On which essential facts do Chief Justice Roberts and Justice Ginsburg agree or disagree?
2. What impact does each view have on the analysis of the ACA's constitutionality?
3. Why is it important that the Chief Justice sees the Medicaid expansion to be a new program?
4. Which features of the Medicaid Act lead Justice Ginsburg to dissent from the coercion analysis?
5. What impact does the Court's remedy for coercion have on Medicaid as a program and states' role in that program?

As this edition goes to press, 32 states and the District of Columbia have executed the ACA's Medicaid eligibility expansion. Millions of otherwise eligible people in non-expanding states have no ability to enroll in Medicaid. Those people have not been subject to tax penalties for failure to carry health insurance because they are low-income, but they also do not have health insurance coverage. The hold-out states are mostly located in the deep South, which already has higher rates of poverty and uninsurance. The question of expansion continues in these states, though; each legislative session and election cycle re-raises the question of expansion. For example, in November of 2017, Maine became the first state to expand Medicaid by voter referendum. The original Medicaid program was not immediately adopted by all states in 1965, but eventually all states accepted the program's terms in exchange for significant federal funding. The same is likely to occur here as well so long as the ACA remains the law of the land.

While *NFIB v. Sebelius* left the statutory language of the ACA intact, the decision has ongoing implications for Medicaid, the most important of which may be states' apparently increased bargaining power with HHS in expanding Medicaid eligibility. Waivers were discussed above in the context of general state participation in the Medicaid program and the structure of Medicaid delivery of care. Now we will consider the section 1115 waiver approval Arkansas received to expand Medicaid eligibility through the state's health insurance exchange. The Arkansas waiver became a model for the private insurance version of Medicaid eligibility expansion, a concept that was possible for years but that had no traction until *NFIB* was decided; this waiver also set off negotiations between states and the Obama Administration to obtain special terms for Medicaid expansion.

DEPARTMENT OF HEALTH & HUMAN SERVICES

Centers for Medicare & Medicaid Services

DEC 3 1 2014

Administrator
Washington, DC 20201

Mr. John Selig
Director
Arkansas Department of Human Services
700 Main Street
Little Rock, AR 72201

Dear Mr. Selig:

The Centers for Medicare & Medicaid Services (CMS) is approving Arkansas' request to amend its Medicaid demonstration entitled, Arkansas Health Care Independence Program (Private Option), Project Number 11-W-00287/6, originally approved by CMS on September 27, 2013.

This amendment provides a waiver of section 1902(a)(14) of the Social Security Act for Arkansas to establish Independence Accounts (IA) to collect monthly contributions from beneficiaries with incomes from 50 percent up to and including 133 percent of the Federal Poverty Level (FPL). With a few exceptions, beneficiaries with incomes starting from 50 percent up to 133 percent of the FPL will be asked to contribute a monthly amount based on income. Beneficiaries will not lose or be denied eligibility for the Private Option if they do not contribute to the IA. Beneficiaries who do not make monthly IA contributions will be charged cost sharing, in a manner consistent with federal regulations. This amendment will enable the state to test the impact of IA in smoothing beneficiary transitions out of the Private Option and into private market plans or Medicare.

CMS's approval of this amendment is conditioned upon compliance with the enclosed list of waiver and expenditure authorities and the Special Terms and Conditions (STCs) defining the nature, character, and extent of anticipated federal involvement in the project. The award is subject to our receiving your written acknowledgement of the award and acceptance of these STCs within 30 days of the date of this letter.

Your project officer for this demonstration is Mrs. Vanessa Sammy. She is available to answer any questions concerning your section 1115 demonstration Mrs. Sammy's contact information is as follows:

Centers for Medicare & Medicaid Services
Center for Medicaid & CHIP Services
Mail Stop: S2-01-16
7500 Security Boulevard
Baltimore, MD 21244-1850
Telephone: (410) 786-2613
Facsimile: (410) 786-5882

CENTERS FOR MEDICARE AND MEDICAID SERVICES
EXPENDITURE AUTHORITY
NUMBER: 11-W-00287/6
TITLE: Arkansas Health Care Independence Program (Private Option)
Section 1115 Demonstration
AWARDEE: Arkansas Department of Human Services

Note that HHS explicitly states it will match state funds spent on the waiver project, even though the state is not complying with the terms of the Medicaid Act. Then HHS gives the state permission to violate key sections of the Medicaid Act. This is typical language for a waiver approval.

Under the authority of section 1115(a)(2) of the Social Security Act (the Act), expenditures made by the state for the items identified below, which are not otherwise included as expenditure under section 1903 shall, for the period of this demonstration be regarded as expenditures under the state's Title XIX plan but are further limited by the Special Terms and Conditions (STCs) for the Arkansas Health Care Independence Program (Private Option) Section 1115 demonstration.

1. Premium Assistance and Cost Sharing Reduction Payments

Expenditures for part or all of the cost of private insurance premiums, and for payments to reduce cost sharing for certain individuals eligible under the approved state plan new adult group described in section 1902(a)(10)(A)(i)(XVIII) of the Act.

Requirements Not Applicable to the Expenditure Authority:

1. Cost Effectiveness   Section 1902(a)(4) and 42 CFR 435.1015(a)(4)

To the extent necessary to permit the state to offer premium assistance and cost sharing reduction payments that are determined to be cost effective using state developed tests of cost effectiveness that differ from otherwise permissible tests for cost effectiveness.

Approval Period: September 27, 2013 through December 31, 2016
Amended January 1, 2015

All requirements of the Medicaid program expressed in law, regulation, and policy statement, not expressly waived or identified as not applicable in accompanying expenditure authorities, shall apply to the demonstration project effective from September 27, 2013 through December 31, 2016. In addition, these waivers may only be implemented consistent with the approved Special Terms and Conditions (STCs).

Under the authority of section 1115(a)(1) of the Social Security Act (the Act), the following waivers of state plan requirements contained in section 1902 of the Act are granted subject to the STCs.

1. Freedom of Choice   Section 1902(a)(23)(A)

To the extent necessary to enable Arkansas to limit beneficiaries' freedom of choice among providers to the providers participating in the network of the Private Option beneficiary's Qualified Health Plan. No waiver of freedom of choice is authorized for family planning providers.

2. Payment to Providers   Section 1902(a)(13) and Section 1902(a)(30)

To the extent necessary to permit Arkansas to provide for payment to providers equal to the market-based rates determined by the Qualified Health Plan providing primary coverage for services under the Private Option.

3. Prior Authorization   Section 1902(a)(54) insofar as it incorporates Section 1927(d)(5)

To permit Arkansas to require that requests for prior authorization for drugs be addressed within 72 hours, rather than 24 hours as is currently required in their state policy. A 72-hour supply of the requested medication will be provided in the event of an emergency.

4. Independence Account Contributions   Section 1902(a)(14) insofar as it incorporates Sections 1916 and 1916A

Approval Period: September 27, 2013 through December 31, 2016
Amended January 1, 2015

To the extent necessary to enable the state to collect monthly contributions for individuals with incomes between 50 and 133 percent of the federal poverty level (FPL).

5. Comparability   Section 1902(a)(10)(B)

To the extent necessary to enable the state to impose targeted cost sharing on individuals in the eligibility group found at Section 1902(a)(10)(A)(i)(VIII) of the Act.

To the extent necessary to enable the state to impose targeted cost-sharing on individuals in the eligibility group found at Section 1902(a)(10)(A)(i)(VIII) of the Act who are not current with their Independence Account payments.

QUESTIONS

1. What is Arkansas permitted to do under this waiver that is different from "traditional" Medicaid?
2. Does the Arkansas waiver serve the federalism principles articulated by the Court in *NFIB v. Sebelius*?
3. What are the strengths and weaknesses of this privatized approach to expanding Medicaid?

In January of 2018, CMS approved a new condition of eligibility: work. No prior administration has approved work requirements in Medicaid, even though states have requested work requirements in their negotiations with HHS over Medicaid expansion. The following excerpt contains CMS's reasoning for the policy shift.

SMD: 18-002

RE: Opportunities to Promote Work and Community Engagement Among Medicaid Beneficiaries

January 11, 2018

Dear State Medicaid Director:

The Centers for Medicare & Medicaid Services (CMS) is announcing a new policy designed to assist states in their efforts to improve Medicaid enrollee health and well-being through incentivizing work and community engagement among non-elderly, non-pregnant adult Medicaid beneficiaries who are eligible for Medicaid on a basis other than disability. Subject to the full federal review process, CMS will support state efforts to test incentives that make participation in work or other community engagement a requirement for continued Medicaid eligibility or coverage for certain adult Medicaid beneficiaries in demonstration projects authorized under section 1115 of the Social Security Act (the Act). Such programs should be designed to promote better mental, physical, and emotional health in furtherance of Medicaid program objectives. Such programs may also, separately, be designed to help individuals and families rise out of poverty and attain independence, also in furtherance of Medicaid program objectives.

This guidance describes considerations for states that may be interested in pursuing demonstration projects under section 1115(a) of the Act that have the goal of creating incentives for Medicaid beneficiaries to participate in work and community engagement activities. It addresses the application of CMS' monitoring and evaluation protocols for this type of demonstration and identifies other programmatic and policy considerations for states, to help them design programs that meet the objectives of the Medicaid program, consistent with federal statutory requirements.

Health Benefits of Community Engagement, Including Work and Work Promotion

While high-quality health care is important for an individual's health and well-being, there are many other determinants of health. It is widely recognized that education, for example, can lead to improved health by increasing health knowledge and healthy behaviors. CMS recognizes that a broad range of social, economic, and behavioral factors can have a major impact on an individual's health and wellness, and a growing body of evidence suggests that targeting certain health determinants, including productive work and community engagement, may improve health outcomes. For example, higher earnings are positively correlated with longer lifespan. One comprehensive review of existing studies found strong evidence that unemployment is generally harmful to health, including higher mortality; poorer general health; poorer mental health; and higher medical consultation and hospital admission rates. Another academic analysis found strong evidence for a protective effect of employment on depression and general mental health. A 2013 Gallup poll found that unemployed Americans are more than twice as likely as those with full-time jobs to say they currently have or are being treated for depression. Other community engagement activities such as volunteering are also associated with improved health outcomes, and it can lead to paid employment.

> No study conclusively supports the idea that CMS is advocating — work causes good health. One of the studies cited here was performed in England, where the National Health Service exists to provide health care to everyone (the government provides true socialized medicine); no one could be excluded from health care for failure to work.

CMS, in accordance with principles supported by the Medicaid statute, has long assisted state efforts to promote work and community engagement and provide incentives to disabled beneficiaries to increase their sense of purpose, build a healthy lifestyle, and further the positive physical and mental health benefits associated with work. CMS supports state efforts to enable eligible individuals to gain and maintain employment. Optional Medicaid programs such as the Medicaid Buy-In, for example, allow workers with disabilities to have higher earnings and maintain their Medicaid coverage. For beneficiaries who are able to work but have been unable to find employment, some states encourage employment through concurrent enrollment in state sponsored job training and work referral, either automatically or at the option of the Medicaid beneficiary. A number of states have also initiated programs to connect non-disabled Medicaid beneficiaries to existing state workforce programs.

States also provide a range of employment supports to individuals receiving home and community based services under section 1915(c) waivers or section 1915(i) state plan services. These include habilitation services designed to "assist individuals in acquiring, retaining and improving the self-help, socialization, and adaptive skills necessary to reside successfully in home and community based settings." These activities have been historically focused on services and programs for individuals with disabilities and receipt of these supports is not a condition of eligibility or coverage.

The successes of all these programs suggest that a spectrum of additional work incentives, including those discussed in this letter, could yield similar outcomes while promoting these same objectives.

New Opportunity for Promoting Work and Other Community Engagement for Non-Elderly, Non-Pregnant Adult Beneficiaries Who Are Eligible for Medicaid on a Basis Other than Disability

This letter provided early insight into the Trump Administration's new approach to health policy.

On March 14, 2017, the Department of Health and Human Services (HHS) and CMS issued a letter to the nation's governors affirming the continued commitment to partner with states in the administration of the Medicaid program. In the letter, we noted that CMS will empower states to develop innovative proposals to improve their Medicaid programs. Demonstration projects under section 1115 of the Act give states more freedom to test and evaluate approaches to improving quality, accessibility, and health outcomes in the most cost-effective manner. CMS is committed to allowing states to test their approaches, provided that the Secretary determines that the demonstrations are likely to assist in promoting the objectives of the Medicaid program.

Some states are interested in pursuing demonstration projects to test the hypothesis that requiring work or community engagement as a condition of eligibility, as a condition of coverage, as a condition of receiving additional or enhanced benefits, or as a condition of paying reduced premiums or cost sharing, will result in more beneficiaries being employed or engaging in other productive community engagement, thus producing improved health and well-being. To determine whether this approach works as expected, states will need to link these community engagement requirements to those outcomes and ultimately assess the effectiveness of the demonstration in furthering the health and wellness objectives of the Medicaid program.

Today, CMS is committing to support state demonstrations that require eligible adult beneficiaries to engage in work or community engagement activities (e.g., skills training, education, job search, caregiving, volunteer service) in order to determine whether those requirements assist beneficiaries in obtaining sustainable employment or other productive community engagement and whether sustained employment or other productive community engagement leads to improved health outcomes. This is a shift from prior agency policy regarding work and other community engagement as a condition of Medicaid eligibility or coverage, but it is anchored in historic CMS principles that emphasize work to promote health and well-being.

Other federal laws such as Temporary Assistance for Needy Families (TANF) specifically promote work for enrollees. Medicaid's sole focus is "medical assistance" for impoverished individuals.

We look forward to working with states interested in testing innovative approaches to promote work and other community engagement, including approaches that make participation a condition of eligibility or coverage, among working-age, non-pregnant adult Medicaid beneficiaries who qualify for Medicaid on a basis other than a disability. Consistent with section1115(a) of the Act, demonstration applications will be reviewed on a case-by-case basis to determine whether the proposed approach is likely to promote the objectives of Medicaid. CMS is also committed to ensuring state accountability for the health outcomes produced by the program, and demonstration projects approved consistent with this guidance will be required to conduct outcomes-based evaluations, based on evaluation designs subject to CMS approval. We note that approved demonstration projects that promote positive health outcomes may also achieve the additional goal of the Medicaid program to promote independence. . . .

QUESTION

Revisit 42 U.S.C. §1396-1 and 42 U.S.C. §1315 (excerpted on page 93). Does "medical assistance" include work such that work would be deemed to "further the objectives" of Medicaid? What arguments can you make for or against this idea?

Kentucky was the first state to receive CMS approval, in January 2018, for a Section 1115 waiver that includes work requirements for the newly eligible enrollees. Shortly after CMS's approval, a lawsuit was filed challenging the agency's authority to approve work requirements and other features of Kentucky's waiver. Stewart v. Azar, Case 1:18-cv-00152 (D.D.C. April 6, 2018). Kentucky's waiver application predicted that as many as 100,000 people will be disenrolled due to work requirements, even though only about 7 percent of non-disabled, non-elderly beneficiaries will be affected by such pre-conditions on enrollment. (Studies in other safety net programs have shown that paperwork burdens alone lead to disenrollment, whether or not the beneficiaries at issue are complying with legal requirements.) The litigation is ongoing as this edition goes to print; meanwhile, Indiana and Arkansas also had waivers with work requirements approved by CMS within weeks of Kentucky's waiver approval, and New Hampshire's waiver was approved in May 2018.

PROBLEM

Some states have waivers that require Medicaid beneficiaries to engage in wellness programs, also called "healthy behavior incentives," to maintain their eligibility, to have lower cost sharing, or to have lower premiums. The healthy behavior incentive is becoming popular in states that resisted or that have not yet expanded Medicaid eligibility. For example: When Michigan expanded its Medicaid program under the ACA pursuant to a waiver approved at the end of 2013, the legislature required that the state seek an amended waiver by the end of 2015 to include wellness incentives for people earning more than 100 percent of the FPL. Michigan received that amendment at the end of 2015; if it did not, then the entire expansion would have expired. The "Healthy Michigan" waiver reduces premiums by half for beneficiaries earning between 100 and 133 percent of the FPL if beneficiaries complete tasks such as keeping an appointment with their primary care provider, receiving vaccines, and ceasing smoking. Beneficiaries who do not perform these tasks pay higher premiums. Indiana and Iowa had similar incentives approved in their expansion waivers. You are the Office of Legislative Counsel liaison for your state's Department of Health and Human Services, which administers Medicaid, and your state legislators are considering a wellness waiver as a condition of expanding Medicaid, which has not occurred yet in your state.

Analyze the legal steps required to obtain such a waiver, and then offer pros and cons for such a policy in the Medicaid program.

4. DELIVERY OF CARE AND BENEFITS

One of the goals in enacting Medicaid was to facilitate mainstream care for low-income Americans. To that end, Medicaid contains statutory provisions that require states to offer benefits across a state, on a nondiscriminatory basis, and with a baseline of coverage. States must provide the mandatory benefits and can offer optional benefits delineated in the Medicaid Act. For example, pharmaceuticals are an "optional" benefit, but every state covers them to some degree.

42 U.S.C. §1396a. State plans for medical assistance
  (a) Contents
  A State plan for medical assistance must—
      (1) provide that it shall be in effect in all political subdivisions of the State, and, if administered by them, be mandatory upon them; . . .

> This requirement is often called "statewideness."

      (10) . . . provide . . . (B) that the medical assistance made available to any individual described in subparagraph (A)—
          (i) shall not be less in amount, duration, or scope than the medical assistance made available to any other such individual. . . .

42 C.F.R. §440.230. Sufficiency of amount, duration, and scope
  (a) The plan must specify the amount, duration, and scope of each service that it provides for—
      (1) The categorically needy; and
      (2) Each covered group of medically needy.
  (b) Each service must be sufficient in amount, duration, and scope to reasonably achieve its purpose.
  (c) The Medicaid agency may not arbitrarily deny or reduce the amount, duration, or scope of a required service under §§440.210 and 440.220 to an otherwise eligible beneficiary solely because of the diagnosis, type of illness, or condition.

> This requirement is called "comparability."

      (d) The agency may place appropriate limits on a service based on such criteria as medical necessity or on utilization control procedures.

QUESTION

A state decides to contain Medicaid costs by the following means: (1) paying for no more than three prescriptions per month; (2) refusing to pay for sex reassignment surgery; (3) limiting payment to three primary care physician visits annually for adults; (4) limiting reimbursement to three pediatrician visits annually for children; (5) paying for dentures but not root canals. Are any of these cost-saving measures permissible?

One of the most important sets of benefits in Medicaid is called EPSDT (Early and Periodic Screening, Diagnostic, and Treatment benefits), which specifically delineates how children will be covered in the program. The next case is a classic explanation of Medicaid, its benefit structure, and beneficiaries' right to enforce the mandatory elements of Medicaid against a noncompliant state.

S.D. ex rel. Dickson v. Hood

391 F.3d 581 (5th Cir. 2004)[*]

The plaintiff, S.D., a sixteen-year-old Medicaid recipient, is afflicted with spina bifida, a congenital defect characterized by imperfect closure of the spinal column. Because of his birth defect, S.D. has total bowel and bladder incontinence and does not have sensation below his waist. Thus, he cannot sense potentially infectious skin irritations resulting from incontinence. S.D. also has two club feet and has trouble walking. He requires leg braces, forearm crutches, and a swing gate to move over short distances. He requires a wheelchair to move over long distances.

As an infant, S.D. was placed in foster care. He was adopted by his parents, and he receives Medicaid benefits pursuant to a federal policy to encourage the adoption of special needs children. He is a qualified recipient of Medicaid's EPSDT program, under which states provide, in accordance with federal law, screening, diagnosis and treatment services to individuals under age twenty-one. Before S.D. moved to Louisiana with his family, he was provided with disposable incontinence underwear by the Virginia Medicaid program.

In 2002, S.D.'s Louisiana physician, Dr. Ernest Edward Martin, Jr., Chairman of the Department of Family Medicine of the Ochsner Clinic, prescribed disposable incontinence underwear as health care that is necessary to ameliorate S.D.'s mental and physical conditions. Specifically, Dr. Martin concluded that the prescription of such underwear "was physically necessary because it draws moisture away from the skin which prevents chronic irritation and infection from urine wetness." According to Dr. Martin, "[t]his protection is especially important due to S.D.'s lack of sensation below the waist. Because of this lack of sensation, S.D. would not be aware if he developed an infection and an infection could then progress quickly." Finally, Dr. Martin determined that without such a prescription, S.D. would be home bound, isolated, and unable to attend school or engage in other age-appropriate activities. Thus, the prescription was necessary from a mental health standpoint as well. S.D. submitted a claim for medical assistance for the cost of the prescription to LDHH under the Louisiana State Medicaid Plan.

LDHH denied S.D.'s claim stating that "the appliance, equipment, supplies or service is available through another agency," "the item is not considered medically necessary" and that it was a "non-medical supply not covered by Medicaid." S.D. appealed administratively. The state administrative law judge ruled in favor of LDHH without referring to the Medicaid EPSDT provisions. Rather, the administrative law judge concluded that LDHH properly denied coverage because "diapers" are "specifically excluded from coverage" under the Louisiana State Medicaid Plan.

S.D. brought this action in the district court against LDHH under 42 U.S.C. §1983 seeking injunctive and declaratory relief. On cross motions for summary

---

[*]This case contains key cites for understanding Medicaid operations; therefore, many cites were retained for bibliographic purposes.

judgment, the district court granted S.D.'s motion and denied that of LDHH. The district court concluded that under the Medicaid Act's EPSDT program a qualified recipient is entitled to the health care, services, treatment and other measures described in §1396d(a) of the Act when such care or services are necessary for corrective or ameliorative purposes; the EPSDT provisions of the Medicaid Act create rights enforceable by §1983; and LDHH deprived S.D. of his federal right to EPSDT benefits in violation of the Medicaid Act. Accordingly, the district court rendered summary judgment declaring that S.D. is entitled to medical assistance for the prescribed disposable incontinence underwear under the EPSDT program and ordering LDHH to provide medical assistance to S.D. for that purpose. LDHH appealed. . . .

Medicaid is a cooperative federal-state program through which the federal government provides financial aid to states that furnish medical assistance to eligible low-income individuals. States electing to participate in the program must comply with certain requirements imposed by the Act and regulations of the Secretary of Health and Human Resources. The Secretary has delegated his federal administrative authority to the Centers for Medicare and Medicaid Services ("CMS"), an agency within the Department of Health and Human Services.

To qualify for federal assistance, a state must submit to the Secretary and have approved a "state plan" for "medical assistance," 42 U.S.C. §1396a(a), that contains a comprehensive statement describing the nature and scope of the state's Medicaid program. 42 C.F.R. §430.10 (1989). "The state plan is required to establish, among other things, a scheme for reimbursing health care providers for the medical assistance provided to eligible individuals." Wilder v. Virginia Hosp. Ass'n, 496 U.S. 498, 502 (1990).

The Medicaid Act defines "medical assistance" as "payment of part or all of the cost of . . . care and services" included in an enumerated list of twenty-seven general health care categories ("medical assistance categories"). 42 U.S.C. §1396d(a). Some of the categories must be included within state plans (mandatory categories) while others may be included at the option of the state (optional categories). 42 U.S.C. §1396a(a)(10)(A).

EPSDT is one of the most specific, protective benefits within the Medicaid program and exists in part because white doctors were inadequately treating African-American children who were covered by Medicaid. Today, a state that tries to modify or reduce EPSDT is likely to be challenged by beneficiaries and providers.

The Act requires that each state plan provide EPSDT health care and services as a mandatory category of medical assistance. The Act describes EPSDT as "early and periodic screening, diagnostic, and treatment services (as defined in subsection (r) of this section) for individuals who are eligible under the plan and are under the age of twenty-one." 42 U.S.C. §§1396a(a)10 (A), 1396d(4)(B). Subsection (r) further defines EPSDT services as, inter alia, "[s]uch other necessary health care, diagnostic services, treatment, and other measures described in [§1396d(a)] to correct or ameliorate defects and physical and mental illnesses and conditions discovered by the screening services, whether or not such services are covered under the State plan." 42 U.S.C. §1396d(r)(5).

Thus, EPSDT is a comprehensive child health program designed to assure the availability and accessibility of health care resources for the treatment, correction and amelioration of the unhealthful conditions of individual Medicaid recipients under the age of twenty-one. A principal goal of the program is to "[a]ssure that health problems found are diagnosed and treated early, before they become more complex and their treatment more costly."

Louisiana's State Medicaid Plan was approved by CMS. As part of its state plan, Louisiana proposed and CMS approved the provision of the optional medical assistance category of "home health care services" to Louisiana's general adult Medicaid population. Additionally, Louisiana proposed and CMS approved a "payment program" which excludes certain medical supplies from the "home health care services" made available to the general adult Medicaid population. The parties agree that the "payment program" exclusion implicitly disallows payment for disposable incontinence underwear for adult recipients over the age of twenty-one. The Louisiana state plan approved by CMS does not, however, explicitly or implicitly, exclude the prescription of incontinence supplies from the EPSDT benefits which must be provided to EPSDT children, i.e., recipients under the age of twenty-one qualified for the EPSDT program.

. . . [T]here is no factual or legal dispute as to the conclusions that S.D. is eligible to receive EPSDT services and that the medical assistance for the prescription of disposable incontinence underwear he seeks is necessary to ameliorate his unhealthful conditions discovered by screening within the terms of the EPSDT program.

LDHH contends, however, that, despite the necessity of the prescription of incontinence underwear to the amelioration of S.D.'s condition, the denial of S. D.'s claim should be reinstated because: (1) The district court overstated the scope of the EPSDT mandate by adopting the "convenient shorthand" or "erroneous assumption" that a state is required to provide EPSDT children with any service that could be provided for in a state plan, even if the service is not one that the state has elected to provide; . . . (3) Louisiana's State Medicaid Plan, as approved by CMS, excludes incontinence supplies from coverage under the EPSDT program; (4) LDHH had the implied authority or discretion to exclude this type of health care or service without the approval of CMS; and (5) Section 1983 of Title 42, which affords a cause of action for the "deprivation of any rights . . . secured by [federal] laws," does not provide S.D. with a right of action to sue LDHH because the provisions of the Medicaid Act upon which S.D. relies does [sic] not create an enforceable "right" within §1983's meaning. . . .

In determining the meaning of the Medicaid Act's EPSDT provisions, the starting point is the language of the statute itself. Section 1396a(a)(10) provides that a state plan for medical assistance must make available to all qualified individuals "the care and services listed in" §1396d(a)(4). Section 1396d(a)(4)(B) provides that "medical assistance" means payment of part or all of the "cost of the following care and services" for individuals: "early and periodic screening, diagnostic, and treatment [EPSDT] services (as defined in subsection (r) of this section) for individuals who are eligible under the plan and are under the age of twenty-one[.]" Section 1396d(r), in pertinent part, provides that "[t]he term 'early and periodic screening, diagnostic, and treatment services' means the following items and services: . . . (5) Such other necessary health care, diagnostic services, treatment, and other measures described in subsection (a) of this section to correct or ameliorate defects and physical and mental illnesses and conditions discovered by the screening services, whether or not such services are covered under the State plan."

The crucial phrases of §1396d(r)(5) provide that EPSDT care and services include: (1) "health care, diagnostic services, treatment, and other measures described in [§1396d(a)]" (2) "necessary . . . to correct or ameliorate . . . conditions discovered by the screening services" (3) "whether or not such services are covered under the State plan." The natural reading of §1396d(r)(5)'s phrases is that all of the health care, services, treatments and other measures described by §1396d(a) must be provided by state Medicaid agencies when necessary to correct or ameliorate unhealthful conditions discovered by screening, regardless of whether they are covered by the state plan. This reading is also required by the grammatical structure of §1396d(r)(5). The medical assistance made available to EPSDT children must be for health care described in the list of twenty-seven categories set forth in §1396d(a) — modified by the requirement that it must be necessary for corrective or ameliorative EPSDT purposes — further modified by the statutory mandate that it must be provided whether or not it is covered under the state plan. The language and structure Congress used cannot be read in any other way without rendering the crucial phrases meaningless.

The plain meaning of statutes is conclusive, except in the "rare cases [in which] the literal application of a statute will produce a result demonstrably at odds with the intentions of its drafters." This is not one of those rare cases because the Act, as literally applied, is fully consistent with the intent of its drafters. . . .

Congress therefore amended the Act in 1989 to mandate that a state agency must provide EPSDT-eligible children "[s]uch other necessary health care . . . described in [the Act's §1936d(a) definition of 'medical assistance'] to correct or ameliorate defects . . . illnesses and conditions discovered by the screening services, whether or not such services are covered under the State plan." Consequently, Congress in the 1989 amendment imposed a mandatory duty upon participating states to provide EPSDT-eligible children with all the health care, services, treatments and other measures described in §1396d(a) of the Act, when necessary to correct or ameliorate health problems discovered by screening, regardless of whether the applicable state plan covers such services.

Furthermore, the Senate Finance Committee noted that the 1989 amendments "require that states provide to children all treatment items and services that are allowed under federal law and that are determined to be necessary . . . even if such services are not otherwise included in the State's plan." Thus, the text of the statute and its legislative history demonstrate that states participating in the Medicaid program must provide all of the health care and services permitted under §1396d(a) when necessary to correct or ameliorate a defect or condition discovered by screening.

Accordingly, every Circuit which has examined the scope of the EPSDT program has recognized that states must cover every type of health care or service necessary for EPSDT corrective or ameliorative purposes that is allowable under §1396d(a).

CMS, the federal agency charged with the responsibility of administering the Medicaid Act, also recognizes that under the EPSDT mandate states are required to provide any service which can be provided under §1396d(a) if such service is necessary to correct or ameliorate a defect, illness or condition identified by screening. In the State Medicaid Manual, the "official medium by which [CMS] issues mandatory, advisory, and optional Medicaid policies and procedures to the Medicaid State agencies," CMS explains:

> . . . Under the EPSDT benefit . . . the Act requires that any service which you are permitted to cover under Medicaid that is necessary to treat or ameliorate a defect,

physical and mental illness, or a condition identified by a screen, must be provided to EPSDT participants regardless of whether the service or item is otherwise included in your Medicaid plan.

CMS State Medicaid Manual ("SMM") §5110 (1990). Thus, according to CMS "[t]he law requires the provision of the services needed by EPSDT clients if the services can be covered under the Medicaid program." . . .

On the contrary, appellate counsel for LDHH contend that the twenty-seven health care and service categories enumerated in §1396d(a) are only hollow forms that each state may fill with as few or as many types of health care, treatment, services and measures as it deems appropriate. . . .

The interpretation proffered by LDHH counsel conflicts sharply with the Congressional intent of the 1989 EPSDT amendment as expressed simply and clearly by its plain words, legislative history, CMS interpretations, and as recognized by the federal Circuits by which it has been considered. According to its words, a principal goal of the 1989 amendment is to correct or ameliorate the defects, illnesses and conditions of EPSDT children discovered by the screening services. The means to be used for this purpose are also clear: health care, diagnostic services, treatment, and other measures described in §1396d(a). Equally plain is the criterion for the application of these means: the health care requested must be necessary to "correct or ameliorate" an eligible EPSDT child's defect, illness or condition. Furthermore, the legislative history demonstrates Congress intended the health care and treatment available under the EPSDT program to be made more accessible and effective by: removing the Secretary's express authority to define the means and the standards for its operation; placing the goal, means and standards in the statute itself; and by imposing an obligatory, not discretionary, duty on states to effectuate this aspect of the EPSDT program "whether or not such services are covered under the State plan."

Thus the plain words of the statute and the legislative history make evident that Congress intended that the health care, services, treatment and other measures that must be provided under the EPSDT program be determined by reference to federal law, not state preferences. The 1989 amendment was clearly a response to the disappointing performance of the EPSDT treatment function as optional and within each state's discretion. We reject the notion of LDHH's counsel that Congress made the provision of such treatment mandatory on the states only to cede to the states complete discretion to decide upon the contents of the twenty-seven medical assistance categories purportedly made available to EPSDT eligible children. . . . For these reasons, we conclude that a state Medicaid agency must provide, under the EPSDT program, (1) any medical assistance that a state is permitted to cover under §1396d(a) of the Medicaid Act, that is (2) necessary to correct or ameliorate defects and physical and mental illnesses and conditions discovered by screening. . . .

> States repeatedly assert that state sovereignty should be protected by federal courts when their administration of the Medicaid Act is challenged as violating federal law.

Having concluded that the Medicaid Act's ESPDT mandate requires LDHH to provide S.D. with medical assistance for the prescribed disposable incontinence underwear because it is necessary to ameliorate S.D.'s conditions caused by his total bowel and bladder incontinence and spina bifida, we now confront LDHH's assertion that S.D. cannot enforce that requirement under 42 U.S.C. §1983.

Section 1983 provides a cause of action against state officials for "the deprivation of any rights, privileges, or immunities secured by the Constitution and laws" but does not provide a mechanism through which citizens can enforce federal law generally. Instead, it provides redress only for a plaintiff who asserts a "violation of a federal right, not merely a violation of federal law." Blessing v. Freestone, 520 U.S. 329, 340 (1997); *see also* Wilder v. Virginia Hosp. Ass'n.

In Blessing v. Freestone, the Supreme Court reiterated the three factors that it has traditionally considered when determining whether a particular federal statute gives rise to a right enforceable by §1983: (1) whether Congress intended for the provision to benefit the plaintiff; (2) whether the plaintiff can show that the right in question is not so "vague and amorphous" that its enforcement would "strain judicial competence"; and (3) whether the statute unambiguously imposes a binding obligation on the states.

As described below in *Armstrong v. Exceptional Child Center, Inc.*, private rights of action under Medicaid are currently more limited. We retained this discussion for historical context and because some §1983 rights of action remain valid.

In *Gonzaga University v. Doe*, the Supreme Court noted that some courts had misinterpreted the first *Blessing* factor as permitting a §1983 action whenever the plaintiff fell within the general zone of interests protected by the statute at issue. The Court clarified that nothing short of an unambiguously conferred right can support a cause of action under §1983. The appropriate inquiry, therefore, is "whether or not Congress intended to confer individual rights upon a class of beneficiaries." Critical to this inquiry is whether the pertinent statute contains "rights-creating" language such as that found in Title VI of the Civil Rights Act of 1964 and Title IX of the Education Amendments of 1972. Accordingly, we begin our analysis by returning to the text of the Medicaid Act.

The Medicaid Act provides that "[a] State Plan must provide for making medical assistance available, including at least the care and services listed in paragraphs (1) through (5), (17) and (21) of section 1396d(a) of this title, to all individuals" who meet certain eligibility criteria. EPSDT care and services are listed in paragraph 4 of §1396d(a) and, by reference to §1396d(r), include all the health care, treatment, services, and other measures described in §1396d(a) when necessary for corrective or ameliorative purposes. This is precisely the sort of "rights-creating" language identified in *Gonzaga* as critical to demonstrating a congressional intent to establish a new right. . . .

Moreover, the Medicaid Act confers the right to the health care, treatment, services and other measures described in §1396d(a) when necessary for EPSDT ameliorative purposes upon an identified class. The statute requires that participating states provide such care and services "to all individuals" who meet the plan eligibility requirements and are under the age of twenty-one. Thus, rather than having merely an aggregate focus, the EPSDT provisions are "concerned with whether the needs of [particular individuals] have been satisfied." Furthermore, the statutory provision at issue in the present case is not directed to the systemwide administration of the EPSDT program but, rather, requires that health care and services must be provided to all eligible recipients under the age of twenty-one. Thus, because it is undisputed that the plaintiff is an eligible recipient of EPSDT services, we conclude that the relevant provisions of the Medicaid Act satisfy the first *Blessing* factor, as clarified by *Gonzaga*, in that the Act evidences a congressional intent to confer a right to the health care, services, treatments and other measures described in §1396d(a), when necessary for EPSDT ameliorative purposes, upon the plaintiff.

Our conclusion is amply supported by the decisions of this court and other federal Circuits. Before the Supreme Court's decision in *Gonzaga*, numerous courts, including this court, had concluded that the Medicaid Act confers, upon eligible children, a federal right to the health care, treatment and measures mandated by the EPSDT program. Moreover, the district courts that have considered the enforceability of the EPSDT provisions after *Gonzaga* have concluded that the statute creates rights to treatment that are enforceable under §1983.

Finally, several post-*Gonzaga* circuit court decisions have held that provisions of the Medicaid Act containing language similar to §1396a(a)(10)(A), i.e. "[a] State Plan must provide for making medical assistance available, including [EPSDT benefits] to all individuals", are enforceable by §1983. . . .

Turning to the second *Blessing* factor, we conclude that the right asserted by S.D. is not so "vague and amorphous" that its enforcement would "strain judicial competence." S.D. asks the courts to interpret the EPSDT statutes to ascertain whether they require Louisiana to provide him with a specific benefit, namely, incontinence supplies medically necessary for EPSDT ameliorative purposes. That level of statutory analysis does not "strain judicial competence;" it is the sort of work in which courts engage every day. The EPSDT provisions at issue are no more "vague and amorphous" than other statutory terms that this court, as well as other courts, have found capable of judicial enforcement. In *Wilder v. Virginia Hosp. Ass'n*, the Supreme Court held enforceable under §1983 the Medicaid Act's requirement that states adopt Medicaid reimbursement rates that are "reasonable and adequate to meet the costs which must be incurred by efficiently and economically operated facilities." In *Evergreen Presbyterian Ministries*, 235 F.3d 908, 925 (5th Cir. 2000), this court followed the lead of "many other courts" and held that the "equal access" mandate of §1396(a)(30)(A) is not too vague to be enforceable. Other Circuits have found that the right to health care, services, treatment and other measures described in §1396d(a) when necessary for EPSDT ameliorative purposes is not too vague to be enforceable under §1983.

Finally, S.D. easily satisfies the third *Blessing* factor because the Medicaid statute unambiguously imposes EPSDT obligations on the participating states. Thus the statutory provisions at issue in the present case satisfy the *Blessing* test and are enforceable by §1983. . . .

QUESTIONS

1. Why does the Fifth Circuit interpret EPSDT to be a benefit that offers little discretion to states in their administration of Medicaid?
2. Can S.D. seek an injunction against the state for its violation of the Medicaid Act?
3. What are the benefits or detriments to allowing private rights of action in Medicaid?

A round of health care reform in 1997 extended coverage to some children who were not Medicaid eligible through a federal program called "CHIP," the Children's Health Insurance Program. 42 U.S.C. §§1397(a) et seq. CHIP does not offer unlimited funding like Medicaid does but instead offers block grants to states. CHIP can be operated separately from Medicaid, or the programs can be uniformly administered by a state, at the state's choosing.

42 U.S.C. §1397aa. Purpose; State child health plans

(a) Purpose

The purpose of this subchapter is to provide funds to States to enable them to initiate and expand the provision of child health assistance to uninsured, low-income children in an effective and efficient manner that is coordinated with other sources of health benefits coverage for children. Such assistance shall be provided primarily for obtaining health benefits coverage through —

(1) obtaining coverage that meets the requirements of section 1397cc of this title, or

(2) providing benefits under the State's medicaid plan under subchapter XIX of this chapter,

or a combination of both.

(b) State child health plan required

A State is not eligible for payment under section 1397ee of this title unless the State has submitted to the Secretary under section 1397ff of this title a plan that —

(1) sets forth how the State intends to use the funds provided under this subchapter to provide child health assistance to needy children consistent with the provisions of this subchapter, and

(2) has been approved under section 1397ff of this title . . . .

CHIP funding requires legislative action — in contrast to Medicaid — and that funding expired on October 1, 2017 during congressional debate about tying CHIP renewal to other health care program cuts and enactment of a tax bill (the one that ultimately repealed the monetary penalty associated with the individual mandate). CHIP was renewed on January 22, 2018, for six years, and that renewal was extended on February 7, 2018, for another four years. The CHIP program was scored by the Congressional Budget Office as saving the federal government money over time because CHIP is less costly than private insurance available through health insurance Exchanges (discussed in Chapter 3).

5. THE PROBLEM OF STATE NONCOMPLIANCE

Each state has wide latitude to abide by the mandatory elements of the Medicaid Act, which allows states to create individualized Medicaid programs; nevertheless, states can fail to comply with the Medicaid Act. The primary enforcement mechanism is CMS:

42 U.S.C. §1396c. Operation of State plans

If the Secretary, after reasonable notice and opportunity for hearing to the State agency administering or supervising the administration of the State plan approved under this subchapter, finds —

> This statute was the basis for the successful coercion claim in *NFIB v. Sebelius.*

(1) that the plan has been so changed that it no longer complies with the provisions of section 1396a of this title; or

(2) that in the administration of the plan there is a failure to comply substantially with any such provision;

the Secretary shall notify such State agency that further payments will not be made to the State (or, in his discretion, that payments will be limited to categories under or parts of the State plan not affected by such failure), until the Secretary is satisfied that there will no longer be any such failure to comply. Until he is so satisfied he shall make no further payments to such State (or shall limit payments to categories under or parts of the State plan not affected by such failure).

One area that has created great friction between states, Medicaid providers, HHS, federal courts, and the executive branch is the requirement for fair payment, called the "Equal Access" provision or simply "30(A)":

42 U.S.C. §1396a(a)(30)(A).
A State plan for medical assistance must— . . . provide such methods and procedures relating to the utilization of, and the payment for, care and services available under the plan . . . as may be necessary to safeguard against unnecessary utilization of such care and services and to assure that payments are consistent with efficiency, economy, and quality of care and are sufficient to enlist enough providers so that care and services are available under the plan at least to the extent that such care and services are available to the general population in the geographic area. . . .

Despite the requirement for "sufficient" payment, on average, Medicaid payment rates are 66 percent of what Medicare pays, and primary care payment rates are even lower, averaging 58 percent of Medicare rates. About half of states pay less than 75 percent of Medicare rates, and the states that serve about 40 percent of all enrollees have rates that are 10 percent below the national average. Medicaid payment rates are generally lower than private insurance payment rates, too. When states pay less than health care providers' costs for delivering care, health care providers are less likely to accept new Medicaid patients. Providers who do treat Medicaid patients may dump them in favor of higher-paying private insurance and Medicare patients, especially in primary care settings. Because of access problems caused by low payment rates, the ACA temporarily increased Medicaid rates to Medicare payment levels for primary care physicians in 2013 and 2014. This increase in payment rates was intended to encourage primary care physicians to treat Medicaid patients as the program's enrollment grew under the ACA, and early studies show that the payment increase achieved that goal.

Unlike Medicare's multilevel codified appeals process, Medicaid only addresses appeals of enrollment denial in its statutory structure. To fill the void, health care providers have initiated actions in federal courts against states to enforce the "Equal Access" provision, using §1983:

42 U.S.C. §1983. Civil action for deprivation of rights
Every person who, under color of any statute, ordinance, regulation, custom, or usage, of any State or Territory or the District of Columbia, subjects, or causes to be subjected, any citizen of the United States or other person within the jurisdiction thereof to the deprivation of any rights, privileges, or immunities secured by the Constitution and laws, shall be liable to the party injured in an action at law, suit in equity, or other proper proceeding for redress, except that in any action brought against a judicial officer for an act or omission taken in such officer's judicial capacity, injunctive relief shall not be granted unless a declaratory decree was violated or declaratory relief was unavailable. . . .

In 2002, the Supreme Court limited 42 U.S.C. §1983 actions as described above in *S.D. ex rel. Dickson v. Hood*. Health care providers and Medicaid advocates then turned to the Supremacy Clause, arguing that a federal suit could be brought alleging that the state official must be enjoined from violating federal law. The following case cut off that private enforcement possibility, but only after punting the question to HHS in another Supreme Court case decided just three years prior, Douglas v. Independent Living Center of Southern California, 565 U.S. 606 (2012).

Armstrong v. Exceptional Child Center, Inc.

135 S. Ct. 1378 (2015)

Justice SCALIA delivered the opinion of the Court, except as to Part IV.

We consider whether Medicaid providers can sue to enforce §(30)(A) of the Medicaid Act.

I

Medicaid is a federal program that subsidizes the States' provision of medical services to "families with dependent children and of aged, blind, or disabled individuals, whose income and resources are insufficient to meet the costs of necessary medical services." Like other Spending Clause legislation, Medicaid offers the States a bargain: Congress provides federal funds in exchange for the States' agreement to spend them in accordance with congressionally imposed conditions.

In order to qualify for Medicaid funding, the State of Idaho adopted, and the Federal Government approved, a Medicaid "plan," which Idaho administers through its Department of Health and Welfare. Idaho's plan includes "habilitation services"—in-home care for individuals who, "but for the provision of such services . . . would require the level of care provided in a hospital or a nursing facility or intermediate care facility for the mentally retarded the cost of which could be reimbursed under the State plan." Providers of these services are reimbursed by the Department of Health and Welfare. . . .

Respondents are providers of habilitation services to persons covered by Idaho's Medicaid plan. They sued petitioners—two officials in Idaho's Department of Health and Welfare—in the United States District Court for the District of Idaho, claiming that Idaho violates §30(A) by reimbursing providers of habilitation services at rates lower than §30(A) permits. They asked the court to enjoin petitioners to increase these rates.

The District Court entered summary judgment for the providers, holding that Idaho had not set rates in a manner consistent with §30(A). The Ninth Circuit affirmed. It said that the providers had "an implied right of action under the Supremacy Clause to seek injunctive relief against the enforcement or implementation of state legislation."

II

The Supremacy Clause, Art. VI, cl. 2, reads:

"This Constitution, and the Laws of the United States which shall be made in Pursuance thereof; and all Treaties made, or which shall be made, under the Authority of the United States, shall be the supreme Law of the Land; and the Judges in every State shall be bound thereby, any Thing in the Constitution or Laws of any State to the Contrary notwithstanding."

It is apparent that this Clause creates a rule of decision: Courts "shall" regard the "Constitution," and all laws "made in Pursuance thereof," as "the supreme Law of the Land." They must not give effect to state laws that conflict with federal laws. It is equally apparent that the Supremacy Clause is not the "'source of any federal rights,'" "and certainly does not create a cause of action. It instructs courts what to do when state and federal law clash, but is silent regarding who may enforce federal laws in court, and in what circumstances they may do so. . . .

To say that the Supremacy Clause does not confer a right of action is not to diminish the significant role that courts play in assuring the supremacy of federal law. For once a case or controversy properly comes before a court, judges are bound by federal law. . . .

Respondents contend that our preemption jurisprudence—specifically, the fact that we have regularly considered whether to enjoin the enforcement of state laws that are alleged to violate federal law—demonstrates that the Supremacy Clause creates a cause of action for its violation. They are incorrect. It is true enough that we have long held that federal courts may in some circumstances grant injunctive relief against state officers who are violating, or planning to violate, federal law. But that has been true not only with respect to violations of federal law by state officials, but also with respect to violations of federal law by federal officials. Thus, the Supremacy Clause need not be (and in light of our textual analysis above, cannot be) the explanation. What our cases demonstrate is that, "in a proper case, relief may be given in a court of equity . . . to prevent an injurious act by a public officer."

> This decision interprets a statute, not the Constitution, and therefore the decision could be, effectively, overturned by a congressional amendment to the Medicaid Act.

The ability to sue to enjoin unconstitutional actions by state and federal officers is the creation of courts of equity, and reflects a long history of judicial review of illegal executive action, tracing back to England. It is a judge-made remedy, and we have never held or even suggested that, in its application to state officers, it rests upon an implied right of action contained in the Supremacy Clause. That is because, as even the dissent implicitly acknowledges, it does not. The Ninth Circuit erred in holding otherwise.

III

A

We turn next to respondents' contention that, quite apart from any cause of action conferred by the Supremacy Clause, this suit can proceed against Idaho in equity.

The power of federal courts of equity to enjoin unlawful executive action is subject to express and implied statutory limitations. "'Courts of equity can no more disregard statutory and constitutional requirements and provisions than can courts of law.'" "In our view the Medicaid Act implicitly precludes private enforcement of §30(A), and respondents cannot, by invoking our equitable powers, circumvent Congress's exclusion of private enforcement. *See* Douglas v. Independent Living Center of Southern Cal., Inc. (Roberts, C.J., dissenting).

Two aspects of §30(A) establish Congress's "intent to foreclose" equitable relief. First, the sole remedy Congress provided for a State's failure to comply with Medicaid's requirements — for the State's "breach" of the Spending Clause contract — is the withholding of Medicaid funds by the Secretary of Health and Human Services. 42 U.S.C. §1396c. As we have elsewhere explained, the "express provision of one method of enforcing a substantive rule suggests that Congress intended to preclude others."

The provision for the Secretary's enforcement by withholding funds might not, by itself, preclude the availability of equitable relief. But it does so when combined with the judicially unadministrable nature of §30(A)'s text. It is difficult to imagine a requirement broader and less specific than §30(A)'s mandate that state plans provide for payments that are "consistent with efficiency, economy, and quality of care," all the while "safeguard[ing] against unnecessary utilization of . . . care and services." Explicitly conferring enforcement of this judgment-laden standard upon the Secretary alone establishes, we think, that Congress "wanted to make the agency remedy that it provided exclusive," thereby achieving "the expertise, uniformity, widespread consultation, and resulting administrative guidance that can accompany agency decisionmaking," and avoiding "the comparative risk of inconsistent interpretations and misincentives that can arise out of an occasional inappropriate application of the statute in a private action." Gonzaga Univ. v. Doe (Breyer, J., concurring in judgment). The sheer complexity associated with enforcing §30(A), coupled with the express provision of an administrative remedy, §1396c, shows that the Medicaid Act precludes private enforcement of §30(A) in the courts.

B

. . . The dissent insists that, "because Congress is undoubtedly aware of the federal courts' long-established practice of enjoining preempted state action, it should generally be presumed to contemplate such enforcement unless it affirmatively manifests a contrary intent." But a "long-established practice" does not justify a rule that denies statutory text its fairest reading. Section 30(A), fairly read in the context of the Medicaid Act, "display[s] a[n] intent to foreclose" the availability of equitable relief. We have no warrant to revise Congress's scheme simply because it did not "affirmatively" preclude the availability of a judge-made action at equity.

Equally unavailing is the dissent's reliance on §30(A)'s history. Section 30(A) was amended, on December 19, 1989, to include what the dissent calls the "equal access mandate," the requirement that reimbursement rates be "sufficient to enlist enough providers so that care and services are available under the plan at least to the extent that such care and services are available to the general population in the geographic area." There existed at the time another provision, known as the "Boren Amendment," that likewise imposed broad requirements on state Medicaid plans. Lower courts had interpreted the Boren Amendment to be privately enforceable under §1983. From this, the dissent infers that, when Congress amended §30(A), it could not "have failed to anticipate" that §30(A)'s broad language — or at least that of the equal access mandate — would be interpreted as enforceable in a private action. Thus, concludes the dissent, Congress's failure to expressly preclude the private enforcement of §30(A) suggests it intended not to preclude private enforcement.

This argument appears to rely on the prior-construction canon; the rule that, when "judicial interpretations have settled the meaning of an existing statutory provision, repetition of the same language in a new statute" is presumed to incorporate that interpretation. But that canon has no application here. The language of the two provisions is nowhere near identical; and even if it had been, the question whether the Boren Amendment permitted private actions was far from "settled." When Congress amended §30(A) in 1989, this Court had already granted certiorari to decide, but had not yet decided, whether the Boren Amendment could be enforced through a §1983 suit. Our decision permitting a §1983 action did not issue until June 14, 1990—almost six months after the amendment to §30(A). The existence of a granted petition for certiorari demonstrates quite clearly that the question whether the Boren Amendment could be privately enforced was unsettled at the time of §30(A)'s 1989 amendment—so that if Congress was aware of the parallel (which is highly doubtful) the course that awareness would have prompted (if any) would not have been legislative silence but rather express specification of the availability of private enforcement (if that was what Congress intended).

Finally, the dissent speaks as though we leave these plaintiffs with no resort. That is not the case. Their relief must be sought initially through the Secretary rather than through the courts. The dissent's complaint that the sanction available to the Secretary (the cut-off of funding) is too massive to be a realistic source of relief seems to us mistaken. We doubt that the Secretary's notice to a State that its compensation scheme is inadequate will be ignored.

> This reflects the coercion doctrine adopted in *NFIB*.

IV

The last possible source of a cause of action for respondents is the Medicaid Act itself. They do not claim that, and rightly so. Section 30(A) lacks the sort of rights-creating language needed to imply a private right of action. It is phrased as a directive to the federal agency charged with approving state Medicaid plans, not as a conferral of the right to sue upon the beneficiaries of the State's decision to participate in Medicaid. The Act says that the "Secretary shall approve any plan which fulfills the conditions specified in subsection (a)," the subsection that includes §30(A). We have held that such language "reveals no congressional intent to create a private right of action." And again, the explicitly conferred means of enforcing compliance with §30(A) by the Secretary's withholding funding, §1396c, suggests that other means of enforcement are precluded.

Spending Clause legislation like Medicaid "is much in the nature of a contract." Pennhurst State School and Hospital v. Halderman. The notion that respondents have a right to sue derives, perhaps, from the fact that they are beneficiaries of the federal-state Medicaid agreement, and that intended beneficiaries, in modern times at least, can sue to enforce the obligations of private contracting parties. We doubt, to begin with, that providers are intended beneficiaries (as opposed to mere incidental beneficiaries) of the Medicaid agreement, which was concluded for the benefit of the infirm whom the providers were to serve, rather than for the benefit of the providers themselves. More fundamentally, however, the modern jurisprudence permitting intended beneficiaries to sue does not generally apply to contracts between a private party and the government, much less to contracts between two governments. Our precedents establish that a private right of action under federal law is not created by mere implication, but

> Justice Breyer did not join Part IV, likely to limit the reach of this opinion. His concurrence does not address Part IV directly.

must be "unambiguously conferred". Nothing in the Medicaid Act suggests that Congress meant to change that for the commitments made under §30(A).

The judgment of the Ninth Circuit Court of Appeals is reversed.

Justice BREYER, concurring in part and concurring in the judgment.

. . . "[T]he statute books are too many, the laws too diverse, and their purposes too complex, for any single legal formula to offer" courts "more than general guidance." Rather, I believe that several characteristics of the federal statute before us, when taken together, make clear that Congress intended to foreclose respondents from bringing this particular action for injunctive relief.

For one thing, as the majority points out, §30(A) of the Medicaid Act sets forth a federal mandate that is broad and nonspecific. But, more than that, §30(A) applies its broad standards to the setting of rates. The history of ratemaking demonstrates that administrative agencies are far better suited to this task than judges. . . .

Reading §30(A) underscores the complexity and nonjudicial nature of the rate-setting task. . . . The methods that a state agency, such as Idaho's Department of Health and Welfare, uses to make this kind of determination may involve subsidiary determinations of, for example, the actual cost of providing quality services, including personnel and total operating expenses; changes in public expectations with respect to delivery of services; inflation; a comparison of rates paid in neighboring States for comparable services; and a comparison of any rates paid for comparable services in other public or private capacities.

At the same time, §30(A) applies broadly, covering reimbursements provided to approximately 1.36 million doctors, serving over 69 million patients across the Nation. And States engage in time-consuming efforts to obtain public input on proposed plan amendments.

I recognize that federal courts have long become accustomed to reviewing for reasonableness or constitutionality the rate-setting determinations made by agencies. But this is not such an action. Instead, the lower courts here, relying on the rate-setting standard articulated in *Orthopaedic Hospital v. Belshe*, required the State to set rates that "approximate the cost of quality care provided efficiently and economically." To find in the law a basis for courts to engage in such direct rate-setting could set a precedent for allowing other similar actions, potentially resulting in rates set by federal judges (of whom there are several hundred) outside the ordinary channel of federal judicial review of agency decisionmaking. The consequence, I fear, would be increased litigation, inconsistent results, and disorderly administration of highly complex federal programs that demand public consultation, administrative guidance and coherence for their success. . . .

For another thing, like the majority, I would ask why, in the complex rate-setting area, other forms of relief are inadequate. If the Secretary of Health and Human Services concludes that a State is failing to follow legally required federal rules, the Secretary can withhold federal funds. If withholding funds does not work, the federal agency may be able to sue a State to compel compliance with federal rules.

Moreover, why could respondents not ask the federal agency to interpret its rules to respondents' satisfaction, to modify those rules, to promulgate new rules or to enforce old ones? Normally, when such requests are denied, an injured party can seek judicial review of the agency's refusal on the grounds that it is "arbitrary, capricious, an abuse of discretion, or otherwise not in accordance with law." And an injured party can ask the court to "compel agency action unlawfully withheld or unreasonably delayed."

I recognize that the law may give the federal agency broad discretionary authority to decide when and how to exercise or to enforce statutes and rules. As a result, it may be difficult for respondents to prevail on an APA claim unless it stems from an agency's particularly egregious failure to act. But, if that is so, it is because Congress decided to vest broad discretion in the agency to interpret and to enforce §30(A). I see no reason for this Court to circumvent that congressional determination by allowing this action to proceed.

Justice SOTOMAYOR, with whom Justice KENNEDY, Justice GINSBURG, and Justice KAGAN join, dissenting.

Suits in federal court to restrain state officials from executing laws that assertedly conflict with the Constitution or with a federal statue are not novel. To the contrary, this Court has adjudicated such requests for equitable relief since the early days of the Republic. Nevertheless, today the Court holds that Congress has foreclosed private parties from invoking the equitable powers of the federal courts to require States to comply with §30(A) of the Medicaid Act. It does so without pointing to the sort of detailed remedial scheme we have previously deemed necessary to establish congressional intent to preclude resort to equity. Instead, the Court relies on Congress' provision for agency enforcement of §30(A) — an enforcement mechanism of the sort we have already definitively determined not to foreclose private actions — and on the mere fact that §30(A) contains relatively broad language. As I cannot agree that these statutory provisions demonstrate the requisite congressional intent to restrict the equitable authority of the federal courts, I respectfully dissent.

I

A

That parties may call upon the federal courts to enjoin unconstitutional government action is not subject to serious dispute. Perhaps the most famous exposition of this principle is our decision in *Ex parte Young*, from which the doctrine derives its usual name. . . .

A suit, like this one, that seeks relief against state officials acting pursuant to a state law allegedly preempted by a federal statute falls comfortably within this doctrine. A claim that a state law contravenes a federal statute is "basically constitutional in nature, deriving its force from the operation of the Supremacy Clause," and the application of preempted state law is therefore "unconstitutional." We have thus long entertained suits in which a party seeks prospective equitable protection from an injurious and preempted state law without regard to whether the federal statute at issue itself provided a right to bring an action. Indeed, for this reason, we have characterized "the availability of prospective relief of the sort awarded in *Ex parte Young*" as giving "life to the Supremacy Clause."

Thus, even though the Court is correct that it is somewhat misleading to speak of "an implied right of action contained in the Supremacy Clause," that does not mean that parties may not enforce the Supremacy Clause by bringing suit to enjoin preempted state action. As the Court also recognizes, we "have

> Unlike Medicare, Medicaid lacks a detailed remedial scheme for beneficiaries.

long held that federal courts may in some circumstances grant injunctive relief against state officers who are violating, or planning to violate, federal law."

B

. . . [B]ecause Congress is undoubtedly aware of the federal courts' long-established practice of enjoining preempted state action, it should generally be presumed to contemplate such enforcement unless it affirmatively manifests a contrary intent. . . .

In this respect, equitable preemption actions differ from suits brought by plaintiffs invoking 42 U.S.C. §1983 or an implied right of action to enforce a federal statute. Suits for "redress designed to halt or prevent the constitutional violation rather than the award of money damages" seek "traditional forms of relief." By contrast, a plaintiff invoking §1983 or an implied statutory cause of action may seek a variety of remedies — including damages — from a potentially broad range of parties. Rather than simply pointing to background equitable principles authorizing the action that Congress presumably has not overridden, such a plaintiff must demonstrate specific congressional intent to create a statutory right to these remedies. *See* Gonzaga Univ. v. Doe. For these reasons, the principles that we have developed to determine whether a statute creates an implied right of action, or is enforceable through §1983, are not transferable to the *Ex parte Young* context.

II

. . . What is the equivalent "carefully crafted and intricate remedial scheme" for enforcement of §30(A)? The Court relies on two aspects of the Medicaid Act, but, whether considered separately or in combination, neither suffices.

First, the Court cites 42 U.S.C. §1396c, which authorizes the Secretary of Health and Human Services (HHS) to withhold federal Medicaid payments to a State in whole or in part if the Secretary determines that the State has failed to comply with the obligations set out in §1396a, including §30(A). But . . . §1396c provides no specific procedure that parties actually affected by a State's violation of its statutory obligations may invoke in lieu of *Ex parte Young* — leaving them without any other avenue for seeking relief from the State. Nor will §1396c always provide a particularly effective means for redressing a State's violations: If the State has violated §30(A) by refusing to reimburse medical providers at a level "sufficient to enlist enough providers so that care and services are available" to Medicaid beneficiaries to the same extent as they are available to "the general population," agency action resulting in a reduced flow of federal funds to that State will often be self-defeating. Brief for Former HHS Officials as Amici Curiae (noting that HHS is often reluctant to initiate compliance actions because a "state's non-compliance creates a damned-if-you-do, damned-if-you-don't scenario where the withholding of state funds will lead to depriving the poor of essential medical assistance"). Far from rendering §1396c "superfluous," then, *Ex parte Young* actions would seem to be an anticipated and possibly necessary supplement to this limited agency-enforcement mechanism. . . .

Section 1396c also parallels other provisions scattered throughout the Social Security Act that likewise authorize the withholding of federal funds to States that fail to fulfill their obligations. Yet, we have consistently authorized judicial enforcement of the Act. . . .

Second, perhaps attempting to reconcile its treatment of §1396c with this long-standing precedent, the Court focuses on the particular language of §30(A), contending that this provision, at least, is so "judicially unadministrable" that Congress must have intended to preclude its enforcement in private suits. Admittedly, the standard set out in §30(A) is fairly broad. . . . But mere breadth of statutory language does not require the Court to give up all hope of judicial enforcement — or, more important, to infer that Congress must have done so.

In fact, the contention that §30(A)'s language was intended to foreclose private enforcement actions entirely is difficult to square with the provision's history. The specific equal access mandate invoked by the plaintiffs in this case — that reimbursement rates be "sufficient to enlist enough providers so that care and services are available under the plan at least to the extent that such care and services are available to the general population in the geographic area" — was added to §30(A) in 1989. At that time, multiple Federal Courts of Appeals had held that the so-called Boren Amendment to the Medicaid Act was enforceable pursuant to §1983 — as we soon thereafter concluded it was. The Boren Amendment employed language quite similar to that used in §30(A), requiring that a state plan:

> "provide . . . for payment . . . of the hospital services, nursing facility services, and services in an intermediate care facility for the mentally retarded provided under the plan through the use of rates . . . which the State finds, and makes assurances satisfactory to the Secretary, are reasonable and adequate to meet the costs which must be incurred by efficiently and economically operated facilities in order to provide care and services in conformity with applicable State and Federal laws, regulations, and quality and safety standards and to assure that individuals eligible for medical assistance have reasonable access . . . to in-patient hospital services of adequate quality."

It is hard to believe that the Congress that enacted the operative version of §30(A) could have failed to anticipate that it might be similarly enforceable. Even if, as the Court observes, the question whether the Boren Amendment was enforceable under §1983 was "unsettled at the time," surely Congress would have spoken with far more clarity had it actually intended to preclude private enforcement of §30(A) through not just §1983 but also *Ex parte Young*.

Of course, the broad scope of §30(A)'s language is not irrelevant. But rather than compelling the conclusion that the provision is wholly unenforceable by private parties, its breadth counsels in favor of interpreting §30(A) to provide substantial leeway to States, so that only in rare and extreme circumstances could a State actually be held to violate its mandate. The provision's scope may also often require a court to rely on HHS, which is "comparatively expert in the statute's subject matter." Douglas v. Independent Living Center of Southern Cal., Inc. When the agency has made a determination with respect to what legal standard should apply, or the validity of a State's procedures for implementing its Medicaid plan, that determination should be accorded the appropriate deference. And if faced with a question that presents a special demand for agency expertise, a court might call for the views of the agency, or refer the question to the agency under the doctrine of primary jurisdiction. Finally, because the authority invoked for enforcing §30(A) is equitable in nature, a plaintiff is not entitled to relief as of right, but only in the sound discretion of the court. Given the courts' ability to both respect States' legitimate choices and defer to the federal agency when necessary, I see no basis for presuming that Congress believed the Judiciary to be completely incapable of enforcing §30(A).

. . . .

. . . The Court's error today has very real consequences. Previously, a State that set reimbursement rates so low that providers were unwilling to furnish a covered service for those who need it could be compelled by those affected to respect the obligation imposed by §30(A). Now, it must suffice that a federal agency, with many programs to oversee, has authority to address such violations through the drastic and often counterproductive measure of withholding the funds that pay for such services. Because a faithful application of our precedents would have led to a contrary result, I respectfully dissent.

PROBLEM

Try to reconcile the *Armstrong* majority's analysis with the Summary of Argument from the Amicus Brief of Former HHS Officials filed in *Armstrong*:

Since the early days of the Medicaid program, federal courts have recognized that providers may sue to ensure that state Medicaid plans conform to the requirements of federal law. Congress intended for such enforcement, and HHS has understood — and come to rely upon — its existence. In *Wilder v. Virginia Hospital Ass'n*, the Court relied on this past practice and understanding in holding that a former provision of the Medicaid Act similar in structure to Section 30(A) could be enforced under 42 U. S.C. §1983. Although the issue here is whether a nonstatutory right of action under the Supremacy Cause should be recognized to enforce Section 30(A) (as opposed to a §1983 action), the reasoning of *Wilder* is still instructive. Applying *Wilder's* reasoning to the equal access provision reveals Section 30(A) imposes a mandate on states that, if violated in a manner that causes injury to providers and beneficiaries, can be enforced through the Supremacy Clause.

Not only has HHS historically understood and accepted that the Medicaid Act is privately enforceable, it has come to rely on that fact. Every aspect of the Department's administration of the Medicaid program — from its regulations to its annual budget — is premised on the understanding that private parties will shoulder much of the enforcement burden. CMS lacks the logistical and financial resources necessary to be the exclusive enforcer of the equal access mandate, and it is highly unlikely to receive the necessary resources in the future. Moreover, exclusive enforcement conflicts with the agency's regulatory priorities. Given that the Department's focus has always been to promote cost-savings and efficiency, charging HHS with the sole responsibility of ensuring the quality of care and availability of access — factors that increase the program's costs — makes little sense as a matter of practice or policy.

The Government also suggests Section 30(A) cannot be judicially administered because its standards are too vague and ambiguous. That argument is belied by the body of Section 30(A) caselaw. Judges have competently interpreted the provision for decades and will continue to do so, particularly if a state challenges the Secretary's decision to reject a plan for violating Section 30(A) — the very approach the Government argues for in lieu of private enforcement. Nor does private enforcement endanger HHS's expert role in administering Medicaid; should a court's interpretation of an ambiguous term in Section 30(A) conflict with the agency's, HHS will always prevail.

Finally, there is little merit to the Government's suggestion that the Medicaid Act's status as a Spending Clause statute militates against provider enforcement. Although Spending Clause laws are somewhat analogous to contracts, that does not mean only contractual principles are to be applied in interpreting such laws. And even under traditional principles of contract law, beneficiaries and providers can hardly be called "incidental" beneficiaries of the Medicaid Act.

The Former HHS Officials also filed an amicus brief in *Douglas v. Independent Living Center of Southern California, Inc.*, the earlier Supreme Court case mentioned before *Armstrong*, and made substantially similar arguments.

QUESTIONS

1. Would HHS be able to force the Idaho legislature to pay the rates determined to be sufficient by the state's Department of Health?
2. Are HHS's tools for setting payment rates more effective than a federal court's? What about their enforcement tools?
3. Is the majority correct that "sufficient" payment is not a judicially administrable concept?

In the wake of *Armstrong*, HHS issued final regulations interpreting 30(A) but only after members of Congress pleaded with the agency to complete a regulatory process begun in 2011. In the Preamble to the final rule, HHS wrote: "In this final rule with comment period, we are providing increased state flexibility within a framework to document measures supporting beneficiary access to services. This final rule with comment period implements methods for states to use in complying with section 1902(a)(30)(A) of the Act by requiring that states review data and trends to evaluate access to care for covered services and conduct public processes to obtain public input on the adequacy of access to covered services in the Medicaid program. This information will be updated and monitored regularly. Should the data reveal short-comings in Medicaid beneficiaries' access to care, states must take corrective actions. The final rule with comment period also recognizes electronic publication as an optional means of providing public notice of proposed changes in rates or ratesetting methodologies that the state intends to include in a Medicaid state plan amendment (SPA). . . . CMS will take a hard look at the state's proposed rate changes." 80 Fed. Reg. 67,576 (Nov. 2, 2015). The final rule attempts to provide a regulatory avenue for constituents to weigh in on state Medicaid ratemaking but falls well short of a judicial remedy.

Some §1983 actions remain for Medicaid beneficiaries and providers to force state compliance with the Medicaid Act, but not many. For example, the Medicaid Act's "freedom of choice" provision is still enforceable by beneficiaries and providers:

42 U.S.C. §1396a(a)(23)
A State plan for medical assistance must— . . . provide that (A) any individual eligible for medical assistance (including drugs) may obtain such assistance from any institution, agency, community pharmacy, or person, qualified to perform the service or services required (including an organization which pro-vides such services, or arranges for their availability, on a prepayment basis), who undertakes to provide him such services, and (B) an enrollment of an individual eligible for medical assistance in a primary care case-management system (described in section 1396n(b)(1) of this title), a medicaid managed

care organization, or a similar entity shall not restrict the choice of the qualified person from whom the individual may receive services. . . .

The free choice of provider provision has been invoked against states that have tried to exclude Planned Parenthood from Medicaid reimbursement. So far, federal courts have agreed with challengers that this provision prevents states from excluding Planned Parenthood clinics from Medicaid if their services would be covered in another setting.

QUESTION

Why is this provision enforceable through §1983 private actions when 30(A) is not?

Medicaid is the primary form of health insurance coverage for nearly one-quarter of Americans and was chosen by Congress as the platform for much of the insurance coverage expansion in the ACA. Including Medicare, Medicaid, and CHIP, the federal and state governments now spend more than $1 trillion per year on public health insurance programs. Without this coverage, more than a quarter of the U.S. population would not be able to afford health insurance coverage and would have limited access to health care.

CAPSTONE PROBLEM

Mario is a 59-year-old widower who lives in Arkansas and works independently as a massage therapist. Mario has been uninsured his entire adult life due to working for either himself or small businesses, but he also believed that clean living and exercise could stave off anyone's need for medical care. After a six-month battle with advanced thyroid cancer in 2013, Mario was anxious to enroll in some form of health insurance, but he was told when he sought individual insurance at the time that he had preexisting conditions that made him uninsurable. Mario needs to consistently fill his thyroid medication, because he relies on it to keep his body functioning; without this medicine, he will die in less than a month. His pharmacist told Mario that the company that makes his medication raised the per-pill price from $10 in 2014 to $90 in 2015. Mario told his pharmacist, "I'm down to 24 pills right now, so I'm counting them daily. If I have no insurance before I'm out of pills, I don't know what I'll do." In addition, to monitor his thyroid condition, Mario must have his blood tested at least twice every year. In the months following his thyroid cancer surgery, he could have the blood work done for $50 at the charitable hospital where his surgery occurred, but now that same service costs him $500. Mario also knows that at his age, he should have routine preventive procedures. It has been a year since Mario has seen the thyroid oncologist who treated his cancer, Dr. Trachelos, who strongly recommended twice yearly follow-up appointments. Dr. Trachelos charged $2,500 for a half-hour visit, and Mario could not afford to pay out of pocket anymore.

Mario has one daughter, Dina, who is 25, living in Texas, and getting her doctorate in physical therapy. Like her father, she could not afford to carry insurance, but she knows she should have a regular doctor to see, especially for her yearly well-woman exam. She does not have a consistent form of birth control and worries about accidentally getting pregnant while still a no-income student. She also worries about the stress of her doctoral program taking a toll on her health, as she has had a number of colds, headaches, fatigue, and other ailments since starting her degree;

she has also started smoking. She has taken care of her father during his cancer treatments and saw the strain of facing serious illness while also losing all of one's life savings. She worries that insurance will cost too much for a student, and she does not know if the various minor illnesses she has had will make it harder for her to obtain insurance coverage.

You are an associate in a local law firm, and Mario seeks your advice regarding his family's options. In a memorandum not to exceed 1,200 words, explain to Mario whether and how he and his daughter can obtain health insurance, including all of their current options and whether their options may change in the future.

Regulation of Private Health Insurance

A. INTRODUCTION

Chapter 2 emphasized the role of the government, both federal and state, in the financing and delivery of health care, primarily through large public insurance programs like Medicare and Medicaid. Beginning in 2014, under the Patient Protection and Affordable Care Act (ACA), almost all Americans are required to have health insurance, although the government does not have to provide it. Due to repeated rejection of proposals for a national health insurance system, the U.S. approach to health care finance and delivery remains fragmented, with some groups being eligible for public insurance and other groups being left to obtain health insurance on the private market. Over time, the government has taken on a more prominent role in regulating the private market, which includes a variety of employer-sponsored group insurance plans, other small-group plans, and individual plans. Historically, private health insurance was predominantly regulated by states, under their Tenth Amendment reserved police powers. Over time, the federal government has asserted a much stronger role, most dramatically in the ACA. This more prominent role provoked a strong political reaction.

1. COST SHARING IN PRIVATE HEALTH INSURANCE

Private health insurance often is purchased through an intermediary such as an employer. Employer-sponsored health insurance holds an important, but declining, share of the U.S. market. As a cost-saving move, most private health insurance requires various forms of cost sharing by the patient: *deductibles* are amounts the individual must pay before insurance begins for each term of the policy (typically a term runs for one year); *copayments* are fixed payments that accompany a good or service, such as a $5 copay for a generic prescription; *coinsurance* leaves a fixed percentage of a bill with the patient (e.g., 80 percent is covered by insurance, but 20 percent is the patient's responsibility). Collectively, these cost-sharing tools can be significant financial burdens to patients, so they are frequently subject to an *out-of-pocket* (OOP) cap that invokes 100 percent coverage once the full OOP amount has been reached (again, typically on an annual basis).

2. DUTY TO PROVIDE HEALTH CARE

As we discussed in Chapter 1, the United States has not recognized an affirmative right to health care, in contrast to most other developed countries. Absent special circumstances, including an established physician-patient relationship, generally no duty is imposed on the state or private actors to provide health care or health insurance. In Chapter 8, we consider some exceptions to the common law no-duty rule, including the emergency medical screening requirement under the federal Emergency Medical Treatment and Labor Act of 1986 (EMTALA). Even though EMTALA requires most Medicare-participating hospitals to screen and stabilize patients who present in their emergency departments, that is a far cry from a comprehensive, government-provided right to health care. The ACA includes a number of reforms designed to buttress the existing private market for health insurance, with the goal of increasing individuals' access to health insurance coverage and, thereby, health care.

3. MARKET FOR PRIVATELY PURCHASED HEALTH INSURANCE

It is important to recognize at the outset that the availability of private health insurance as a way to pay for health care is a relatively recent development. For much of the history of medicine, the limited interventions that were available often could be provided in the home. Patients and their families would simply pay the physician out of pocket, as they would for any other service. For individuals lacking resources or needing more extensive treatment, there were charitable almshouses, private sanatoriums, and "sliding scale" fees that varied according to the patient's ability to pay. As medical care became more advanced and expensive, paying out of pocket became less reliable.

The following excerpt, from an essential book, Paul Starr, *The Social Transformation of American Medicine* (1982), describes the origins of private health insurance in the United States.

> Before the 1930s, the only extensive private health plans offered direct services, usually to employees in an industry. Private health insurance had hardly developed because of what appeared to be unavoidably high expenses. The key obstacles were the difficulty in monitoring abuse, the high acquisition and collection costs because of the commissions paid to insurance agents, and the likelihood of "adverse selection"
>
> | Employer-based health insurance effectively started in the automotive industry. |
>
> (that is, the purchase of insurance by those most likely to become sick). One partial solution to these problems lay in group enrollment. By selling insurance via employers to large groups of workers, an insurer could restrict its policies to a predominantly healthy population. Getting employers to deduct the premium from payrolls could also greatly reduce the collection costs. In 1914 the Metropolitan Life Insurance Company introduced a disability insurance plan of this sort to cover its own home office employees. In 1919 the Illinois Insurance Commission noted the potential for group health insurance, but commented that unions were opposed because they believed it to be aimed at tying men to their jobs, weakening the union, and sorting out bad physical risks. The insurance companies were still treating it as "experimental" because of fear of "simulation and malingering." In the twenties, group disability insurance became more common; the major advance came in 1928 when General Motors signed a contract with Metropolitan to cover 180,000 workers. These policies were still mainly concerned with income protection rather than payment of

medical expenses. A study in 1930 concluded that benefits paid out for medical expenses amounted to only about 10 percent of benefits paid under health insurance. Some policies emphasizing medical expenses were available, but they were "in no sense important in insurance, very few being issued."

However, a new element in health insurance had developed quietly during the 1920s: the rising costs of hospital care and the new salience of such costs for middle-class families. This development had opened up a new market for health insurance, just as it had changed the politics of health insurance. It lay waiting for some organization to master the problems of adverse selection, acquisition costs, and provider acceptance when the Depression struck in 1929.

THE BIRTH OF THE BLUES, 1929-1945

The Emergence of Blue Cross

In 1932 the Committee on the Costs of Medical Care reviewed some twenty-five different plans and experiments in medical care and health insurance then in progress. Inconspicuous among these (number 19 to be exact) was insurance for hospital care, which the CCMC dismissed as failing to encourage preventive services or group practice and too limited even to cover most high-cost illness. The authors of the report, like others at the time, had no idea that "group hospitalization" would shortly become the gateway to health insurance in America.

The conventional account of the history of Blue Cross puts its origins in Dallas in late 1929, when the Baylor University Hospital agreed to provide 1,500 school teachers up to twenty-one days of hospital care a year for $6 per person. Soon Baylor extended the arrangement to other groups including several thousand people. Several other community hospitals in Dallas adopted similar plans. Dallas' Methodist Hospital used a private solicitation company, grandly called the National Hospitalization System, which charge $9 a year, retaining one third for expenses and profits. These early arrangements were all direct-service plans, set up by individual hospitals in competition with each other.

As these plans emerged, the Depression began to expose the financial insecurity of the nation's voluntary hospitals and encourage them to turn to insurance for a solution. In just one year after the crash, average hospital receipts per person fell from $236.12 to $59.26, and average hospital deficits rose from 15.2 to 20.6 percent of disbursements. In 1931, according to AMA data, only 62 percent of the beds in voluntary hospitals were occupied on an average day, compared to 89 percent in government hospitals. In late 1932 the president of the American Hospital Association said in a letter to its members that the AHA "would be unmindful of the members' interests if it did not recognize the possible breakdown of the voluntary hospital system in America. . . ." And in a book published that year called *The Crisis in Hospital Finance*, Michael Davis and C. Rufus Rorem warned that hospitals could not continue to rely on patients to pay all their bills when they were hospitalized; the costs had to be budgeted in advance through insurance. "The life of voluntary hospitals is threatened because of the instability and unevenness of this main source of income," they wrote, referring to payments by patients.

> In the United States, health insurance began as a way to stabilize income for hospitals and doctors.

Single-hospital plans, like those developing in Dallas, might well have brought more instability to the hospital industry because of the competition they would have promoted. But another response was already developing. In July 1932 the community hospitals of Sacramento jointly offered hospital service contracts to employed persons, and in January of the following year, hospitals in Essex County, New Jersey, authorized a similar joint plan. In February the AHA approved hospital insurance as "a practicable solution" to the problem of distributing the costs of hospital care, and that spring its Council on Community Relations and Administrative Practice adopted some guiding principles. The plans were to be nonprofit, to emphasize the public welfare, and to limit themselves to dignified promotion. They were only to cover hospital charges, thereby not infringing on the domain of private practitioners. And most important, they were to provide "free choice" of physician and hospital, a requirement that ruled out the single-hospital plan.

City-wide plans were organized in St. Paul that July, and the next year in Washington and Cleveland.

Unlike insurance companies, these plans were organized with hardly any starting capital. The Cleveland plan, for example, was launched with only $7,000 from a local welfare organization. This was possible because of "hospital underwriting." Instead of backing the promise of service with financial reserves, the plan had its member hospitals agree to provide service regardless of the remuneration they would receive. The hospital's guarantee of benefits took place of the capital funds that plans would have otherwise needed to protect subscribers' interests. "The drive and enthusiasm for the Blue Cross idea," writes Odin Anderson, "originated with the early pioneers, not the hospitals." But it was the hospitals that provided the underwriting: Other proposals, as we shall see, also had supporters with a lot of idealistic enthusiasm, but no resources — and that made the difference.

> Accountable care organizations (discussed later in this chapter) are the modern version of "hospital underwriting," encouraging the provider to accept risk.

The first few plans had been regarded as nothing more than the sale of hospital services on a prepaid basis and, therefore, within the voluntary hospitals' legal power. In New York, however, the state superintendent of insurance ruled that a hospital-service plan would be insurance and hence subject to all insurance regulations, including requirements for reserves. So hospital and medical leaders pressed for a special enabling act, which became law in New York in May 1934, exempting such plans from the reserve requirement. At the same time it provided that the insurance department regularly review the plan's rates and financial condition. The law also required that a majority of the directors of the plan be administrators or trustees of the hospitals that contracted to provide service. The hospitals were able to gain this authority since they were underwriting the plans. And in several plans that ran into trouble over the next decade, inducing New York's, the hospitals were obliged temporarily to accept reduced payments. This guarantee faded in importance, however, as the plans developed their own reserves, which were, in effect, contributed by subscribers. But the original hospital underwriting provided a basis of legal support for long-term control of Blue Cross by the voluntary hospitals.

The question of hospital control would not have been so important, except for the drift from competitive, single-hospital to community-wide plans that effectively became monopolies in hospital prepayment. Rorem, who became the AHA's chief expert on group hospitalization, ruefully recalled in 1944 that the early single-hospital plans had resulted in "competition among the hospitals, and interference with the subscribers' freedom of choice and the physicians' prerogatives in the care of private patients." It is unclear, however, why subscribers would have had less choice if they could choose from a variety of plans offered by hospitals in their community. The AHA did not encourage community-wide plans in addition to single-hospital plans, but instead of them. In this respect it denied consumers the choice of contracting with a single-hospital plan and possibly securing a more favorable price.

Whether because they were less attractive to consumers or because they were actively discouraged by the AHA and local hospital councils, the single-hospital plans grew more slowly than the community-wide ones. In July 1937 Rorem could report that while the single-hospital plans had 125,000 subscribers, about as many as a year before, the "free-choice" plans had grown from 200,000 to 800,000. The New York plan alone had 350,000 subscribers. . . .

By 1939 twenty-five states had passed special enabling acts for hospital service plans. Like the original New York law, these typically provided that a majority of the directors would represent hospitals, gave the insurance commissioners the power to review rates and financial operations, and declared the plans charitable and exempt from taxes. (In several other states, Blue Cross plans were allowed to operate under general incorporation statutes, which have no requirements for reserves.)

Blue Cross had started against the advice of professionals in the insurance industry. Actuaries did not believe adequate statistics were available to predict losses with confidence. Moreover, service benefits violated the concept of limited liability and the rule that insurance should never increase the hazard. "Insurance theory," writes Duncan MacIntyre, "says that the hazard insured against should be defined and measurable. In some respects service contracts were like blank checks for subscribers, physicians, and hospitals; they were open-ended and did not limit the plans' dollar liabilities." Their "first-day, first dollar" coverage would encourage hospitalization. Initially, one insurance expert later recalled, "a group of insurance men . . . told Mr. C. Rufus Rorem that the [hospital's financial problems] could not be solved by insurance." But when Blue Cross defied their expectations, the companies were, as C.A. Kulp describes it, "half-dragged, half-lured" into the field. In 1934 commercial carriers began offering indemnity coverage against hospital expenses on a group basis. Four years later they extended group coverage to surgical bills.

Since it enjoyed tax exemptions and privileged relations with hospitals, Blue Cross held an early advantage over its commercial competitors. However, the insurance companies had larger financial resources and long-established relations with employers. By 1940 the insurance companies had about 3.7 million subscribers, while the thirty-nine Blue Cross plans in operation had a total enrollment of more than 6 million.

> Community rating and nondiscrimination allow sicker patients to be subsidized by healthier people, spreading risk across society.

Health insurance solves several problems at once. For most people, paying premiums monthly is a more reliable financing mechanism than paying out of pocket. Insurance also spreads the risk of catastrophic medical bills, diffusing costs across the insured population. Blue Cross plans were "community rated," meaning that everyone in the community paid the same price, regardless of health status.

Over time, health insurance became a significant national business. Faced with competition from commercial for-profit health plans (including some that had formerly been Blue Cross plans), community ratings gave way to underwritten policies that varied in price based on the expected health and expenses of the group or individuals insured. For a small employer, if one employee suffered a catastrophic illness, premiums would rise dramatically for everyone the next year. Likewise, individuals found coverage to be very expensive, especially if they were older or had health problems. In one sense, this "discrimination" by health insurers was entirely rational and good business. Over time, state and federal law has restricted these practices, most dramatically in the ACA.

Blue Cross insurance plans started with premiums as low as $6 per year. Today, the average premium for a family plan in 2016 was over $16,800. As discussed below, individuals and families may receive employer or government assistance to pay a portion of their premiums.

QUESTIONS

1. Why did health insurance originate with hospital, rather than physician, coverage?
2. Which Part of Medicare (see Chapter 2) does Blue Cross resemble? As you read the remainder of this chapter, consider ways in which the post-ACA private insurance market departs from these early insurance products.

B. EXPANDING COVERAGE THROUGH THE PRIVATE MARKET

By the late 1960s, both the private market for health insurance and the major public insurance programs, Medicare and Medicaid (discussed in Chapter 2), were well established. Even as the need for some form of insurance to pay for health care became apparent, proposals for a national health plan were repeatedly rejected under the disparaging banner of "socialized medicine." Many Americans continue to resist government "handouts" to anyone other than the "deserving poor" and, therefore, still define health care mostly as a matter of individual, not government, responsibility.

The Paul Starr excerpt above described the historical origins of private health insurance. Implicit in that design is the notion of risk pooling. Under an employer-sponsored group plan, for example, all employees who are covered are in the same risk pool. To be financially sustainable, insurance requires a sufficient amount of premiums paid into the pool of funds to cover the costs of insurance claims paid out. Insurers, thus, manage the risk pool by both setting premiums and managing the risk profile of the pool. Recent developments, particularly in federal regulation of health insurance, limited both of these strategies—how insurers set premiums and whom they decide to cover.

1. INSURANCE RISK POOLING

As the private market for health insurance expanded, the nature of the product evolved. Insurance, in the most classical sense, exists to protect individuals from unknown, catastrophic risks. Risk-averse individuals choose to pay an amount-certain, in the form of a monthly premium, to protect themselves from unexpected financial loss due to events that are beyond their control. The health insurance company selling the plan takes a calculated risk that it will collect more in monthly premiums than it will have to pay out in medical claims. All the individual customers' premiums are collected together, with some (the healthy) paying in more than they take out and others (the sick) taking out more than they pay in. This arrangement is called "risk pooling." Risk pools can be established by defined groups, such as all benefits-eligible employees of the same employer, or more broadly, as all customers in a particular geographic market such as the "community rating" arrangements in traditional Blue Cross plans.

As just one example, given the extraordinary prices for curative drugs for Hepatitis C, a health plan will lose more than $100,000 if a Hepatitis C patient joins the plan.

To make the health insurance business work, insurers want to calculate their financial exposure as accurately as possible using actuarial methods. That means gathering as much information as possible about each customer's health risk profile, including age, gender, race, history of illness, family history, occupation, habits and activities, and a host of other factors bearing on health. Using that information, the insurance company can more accurately set each individual's premium rate. This practice of "experience rating" is similar to automobile insurers' offering lower rates to customers with good driving records and higher rates to those with multiple traffic citations. In addition, the insurance company may determine that there are certain risks or individual customers that they do not want to cover at all. Providing insurance coverage to someone who is already gravely ill, or very likely to become ill, is not a good risk from the insurance company's perspective. It would be like selling flood insurance to a coastal homeowner in the middle of a hurricane.

Over time, however, health insurance products evolved away from the traditional notion of providing financial protection against unknown risk into a way to prepay for health care, including annual checkups, prescription drugs, and a wide range of routine and preventive services other than costly inpatient hospital stays. Theoretically, it is in insurers' interest to keep patients healthy by covering those services and thereby potentially avoid more debilitating, costly health conditions. But in practice, since many people change health plans each year, the insurer may only focus on keeping its costs low *this year* and hope that an unhealthy individual selects another plan next year. Health plans continue to serve the risk-pooling function by allowing those who use less medical care effectively to subsidize those who use more medical care, but they may also emphasize preventive care and managing the use of health care services rather than simply paying for all services and items billed to the patient.

This more comprehensive model of health insurance is called "managed care." It exists in various forms, the most common of which are health maintenance organizations (HMOs), preferred provider organizations (PPOs), and point of service plans (POS). Managed care plans share a number of characteristic features, including restricted networks of providers; gatekeeping or preapproval before accessing some benefits of the plan; utilization review of provider-ordered medical care by plan administrators; case management and coordination of care, especially for customers with chronic conditions; and sometimes "capitated" or similar payment, whereby providers receive a pre-established amount per patient, rather than "fee-for-service" payment for each service they provide.

> Managed care plans frequently offer restricted provider networks, meaning that participants cannot see any doctor or hospital, just those that have agreed to accept the insurer's discounted rates and participate in utilization review, care coordination, and other plan requirements.

The following excerpt, from an opinion by (former) judge, scholar, and economist Richard Posner, describes the essential features of HMOs. The case involved an antitrust dispute under the Sherman Act (discussed in Chapter 7), filed by an insurance company and its subsidiary HMO against a physician-owned clinic and its HMO. In deciding whether physicians possessed unlawful monopoly power, the court first had to define the relevant market.

Blue Cross & Blue Shield United of Wisconsin v. Marshfield Clinic

65 F.3d 1406 (7th Cir. 1995)

. . . .

An HMO is basically a method of pricing medical services. Instead of having the patient pay separately for each medical procedure, the patient pays a fixed annual fee for all the services he needs and the HMO undertakes to provide those services with the physicians with whom it has contracts. The different method of pricing used by the HMO has, of course, consequences both for the practice of medicine and for the allocation of the risk of medical expenses. The method of pricing gives the HMO an incentive to minimize the procedures that it performs, since the marginal revenue it derives from each procedure is zero. Hence HMOs are thought to reduce "waste" and to encourage preventive care, although those hostile to the HMO concept believe that the principal effect is merely to reduce the amount of medical care that patients receive. The risk-shifting feature of the concept lies in the fact that if a subscriber incurs above-average medical expenses, the excess cost is borne by the HMO rather than by the subscriber (or by his insurer, or more likely by both because of copayment and deductible provisions in the insurance policy), while if he incurs below-average medical expense the difference enures to the benefit of the HMO rather than to him or his insurer (or, again, both). To control the upside risk that it incurs, the HMO provides medical services through physicians with whom it has contracts specifying their compensation, rather than merely reimbursing some per-

> Risk shifting happens several times in this example: first from the individual subscriber (patient) to the employer, then to the insurer or HMO, finally in some cases to the providers themselves through capitated or value-based reimbursement.

centage of whatever fee they might happen to charge for their services. This means that the HMO must be able to line up enough physicians with whom to contract to provide its subscribers with a more or less complete menu of medical services. Compcare complains that Security's contracts with physicians require them to refer their patients to the Clinic rather than to "independent" physicians. But that is of the essence of an HMO: the subscriber must take the service offered by the physicians whom the HMO has enlisted.

Compcare's principal argument is that Security has enlisted such a large fraction of the physicians in the 14-county north central region that Compcare cannot find enough "independent" physicians to be able to offer HMO services competitive with Security's—hence Security's huge market shares in 9 of the 14 counties. Supposing this is true—as seems unlikely since Security's almost 900 independent physicians are available to join other HMOs, along with an unknown number of physicians neither employed by the Marshfield Clinic nor retained by Security—it has monopolistic significance only if HMOs constitute a market separate from other contractual forms in which many of the same physicians sell their services. Of this we cannot find any evidence.

In defining a market, one must consider substitution both by buyers and by sellers, and let us start with buyers. The record shows, what is anyway well known, that

> Since this opinion was written in 1995, managed care has continued to grow in U.S. market share, currently accounting for the vast majority of private insurance, one-third of Medicare beneficiaries, and most of Medicaid's non-fragile beneficiaries.

individuals, and their employers, and medical insurers (the real "buyers" of medical services, according to the plaintiffs) regard HMOs as competitive not only with each other but also with the various types of fee-for-service provider, including "preferred provider" plans (generally referred to as "PPOs," for "preferred provider organization") under which the insurer offers more generous reimbursement if the insured patronizes physicians who have contracts with the insurer to provide service at low cost to its insureds. HMOs, though they have made great strides in recent years because of the widespread concern with skyrocketing medical costs, remain relative upstarts in the market for

physician services. Many people don't like them because of the restriction on the patient's choice of doctors or because they fear that HMOs skimp on service, since, as we said, the marginal revenue of a medical procedure to an HMO is zero. From a short-term financial standpoint — which we do not suggest is the only standpoint that an HMO is likely to have — the HMO's incentive is to keep you healthy if it can but if you get very sick, and are unlikely to recover to a healthy state involving few medical expenses, to let you die as quickly and cheaply as possible. HMOs compensate for these perceived drawbacks by charging a lower price than fee-for-service plans.

We do not wish to associate ourselves with the critics of HMOs. All that is important to our consideration of this appeal is that many people believe — whether rightly or wrongly is of no moment — that HMOs are not an unalloyed blessing; and this means that the price that an HMO can charge is constrained not only by competition from other HMOs but also by competition from forms of medical-services contracting that are free from the perceived perverse incentive effects of the HMO form. As far as we know or the record shows, even in areas where there is only one HMO most of the people in its service area do not subscribe to it even if its prices are lower than those of fee-for-service providers.

QUESTIONS

1. Does the HMO's desire to turn a profit create a conflict of interest with patients?
2. How can law regulate these conflicts of interest?

2. STATE REGULATION OF MANAGED CARE

Managed care is now the predominant model of health insurance, but it is not without its critics. Enrollees have long complained about coverage restrictions and exclusions, limited access to familiar providers, and plan administrators' review of providers' treatment recommendations. The following case provides an example of typical managed care coverage provisions and utilization review processes. As the case demonstrates, one way to regulate private insurance is by state contract law, applying common law doctrines.

Lubeznik v. HealthChicago, Inc.

644 N.E.2d 777 (Ill. App. Ct. 1994)

Opinion

Justice JOHNSON delivered the opinion of the court:

Plaintiff, Bonnie Lubeznik, filed this action in the circuit of Cook County seeking a permanent injunction requiring defendant, HealthChicago, Inc., to pre-certify her for certain medical treatment. Following a hearing, the trial court granted the injunction. Defendant appeals, contending the trial court improperly (1) determined that the requested treatment was a covered benefit under plaintiff's insurance policy; (2) interpreted portions of the Illinois Health Maintenance Organization Act; (3) admitted hearsay evidence; and (4) granted the injunction.

We affirm.

The record reveals that in November 1988 plaintiff was diagnosed with Stage III ovarian cancer. At the time of her diagnosis, the cancer had spread through plaintiff's abdomen and liver and she had a 20% survival rate over the next five years. Plaintiff underwent a surgical procedure known as debulking, during which cancerous tumors were removed to promote maximum results for chemotherapy. She then received chemotherapy and underwent additional surgery, which her doctors determined had failed. Plaintiff's doctors then unsuccessfully attempted several other treatment methods including intraperitoneal cisplatin therapy, which involves injecting chemotherapy agents directly into the abdomen.

In June 1991, plaintiff was referred to Dr. Patrick Stiff, the director of the bone marrow treatment program at Loyola University Medical Center (hereinafter Loyola). Dr. Stiff sought to determine the prospect of treating plaintiff with high dose chemotherapy with autologous bone marrow transplant (hereinafter HDCT/ABMT). HDCT/ABMT is a procedure where bone marrow stem cells are removed from the patient's body and frozen in storage until after the patient has been treated with high dose chemotherapy. Following chemotherapy, which destroys the cancer, the marrow previously extracted is reinfused to proliferate and replace marrow destroyed by the chemotherapy. HDCT/ABMT had been a state of the art treatment for leukemia and Hodgkin's disease for many years. It began to be used in the late 1980's for women who were in the late stages of breast cancer.

Autologous bone marrow transplant uses bone marrow from the patient rather than from a donor, which the patient's immune system is less likely to reject. The stem cells are removed before the patient receives high-dose chemotherapy and are returned to the patient after chemotherapy. ABMT is a form of organ transplant.

Dr. Stiff examined plaintiff but decided to forgo the HDCT/ABMT until an attempt was made to decrease the mass of tumors by using Carboplatin, an outpatient chemotherapy treatment. After plaintiff received three cycles of Carboplatin, Dr. Stiff observed very slight improvement in her condition. Plaintiff then sought treatment in a University of Chicago program, but was rejected for the program because of irregularities in her heartbeat. Thereafter, she returned to Dr. Stiff seeking inclusion in his HDCT/ABMT program.

On October 28, 1991, Dr. Stiff contacted defendant requesting that it pre-certify plaintiff for the HDCT/ABMT, i.e., agree in advance to pay for the treatment. Plaintiff's insurance policy required her to get pre-certified before receiving elective treatment, procedures and therapies. Dr. Wayne Mathy, defendant's medical director, received Dr. Stiff's pre-certification request and telephoned him shortly thereafter. During his conversation with Dr. Stiff, Dr. Mathy stated that the ABMT/HDCT was not a covered benefit under plaintiff's insurance policy because the treatment was considered experimental.

Pre-certification seeks the approval of the insurer before the care is provided. It is often required by contract, generally for more expensive treatments. Utilization review is a similar process, but it occurs after the care has been rendered.

On October 31, 1991, plaintiff filed a two-count complaint against defendant and Loyola. In count one, plaintiff sought a mandatory injunction against defendant to pre-certify her for the HDCT/ABMT. In her second count, plaintiff sought an injunction against Loyola to admit her for medical treatment without a deposit of $100,000. Both defendant and Loyola filed motions to dismiss plaintiff's complaint. Subsequently, plaintiff took a voluntary non-suit against Loyola.

Note that experimental treatments are excluded by contract. The issue, then, is determining what counts as "experimental."

Following a hearing, the trial court denied defendant's motion to dismiss and defendant filed its answer instanter. Thereafter, a hearing on the complaint was held at which Dr. Stiff testified that the HDCT/ABMT was an effective treatment for plaintiff given that all conventional treatments for her had been exhausted. He stated that he had performed 21 HDCT/ABMT procedures on patients with Stage III ovarian cancer and as a result, 75% of those patients were in complete remission.

During further testimony, Dr. Stiff opined that the HDCT/ABMT was not experimental and presented documents and literature in support of his testimony. Dr. Stiff also presented a letter from the American Medical Association indicating that autologous bone marrow was an appropriate method for managing bone marrow in patients undergoing treatment for cancer. He also opined that the HDCT/ABMT was accepted as a standard treatment for patients with ovarian cancer.

Dr. Mathy testified at the hearing that his responsibilities as defendant's medical director included determining whether a requested medical treatment is covered under an insurance policy issued by defendant. He stated that after he received plaintiff's request for pre-certification, a member of defendant's benefit analysis staff contacted the National Institute of Health, the National Cancer Institute, and Medicare seeking an assessment as to whether the requested treatment was experimental. According to Dr. Mathy, defendant determined that the HDCT/ABMT was experimental based on information received from those medical assessment bodies. Dr. Mathy also stated that he spoke with Dr. Harry Long of the Mayo Clinic concerning the HDCT/ABMT procedure. When defendant's counsel attempted to question Dr. Mathy concerning contents of his conversation with Dr. Long, plaintiff objected on the basis that the evidence was hearsay. The trial court sustained the objection.

During cross-examination, Dr. Mathy testified that he first learned on October 29, 1991, that Dr. Stiff was contemplating treating plaintiff with HDCT/ABMT. Dr. Mathy admitted that immediately upon learning of the proposed treatment, he decided that the HDCT/ABMT was experimental and that plaintiff's pre-certification request should be denied. Dr. Mathy stated that he did not consult with the National Institute of Health or the National Cancer Institute before making the decision to deny plaintiff's request.

> The insurance plan's medical director admitted that he determined that the requested treatment was experimental before consulting the various authorities that he cited at trial.

At the conclusion of the testimony, the parties presented final arguments to the trial court. Subsequently, the trial court issued an injunction against defendant ruling that the ABMT/HDCT is neither an experimental therapy for ovarian cancer, nor a transplant within the meaning of Illinois Health Maintenance Organization Act (hereinafter the Act). Defendant then filed this appeal.

Defendant initially argues that the trial court erroneously determined that the HDCT/ABMT procedure is a covered benefit under plaintiff's insurance policy. Defendant claims it supported its determination that the procedure is experimental with similar conclusions by appropriate medical technology boards as required by plaintiff's insurance contract. Plaintiff's insurance policy provides that "[e]xperimental medical, surgical, or other procedures as determined by the [Insurance] Plan in conjunction with appropriate medical technology assessment bodies," are excluded from coverage. Defendant contends that the trial court improperly disregarded the terms of the insurance contract, which, defendant argues, were clear and unambiguous.

At the outset, we note that coverage provisions in an insurance contract are to be liberally construed in favor of the insured to provide the broadest possible coverage. In determining whether a certain provision in an insurance contract is applicable, a trial court must first determine whether the specific provision is ambiguous.

However, where a provision is ambiguous, its language must be construed in favor of the insured.

Moreover, where an insurer seeks to deny insurance coverage based on an exclusionary clause contained in an insurance policy, the clause must be clear and free from doubt. This is so because all doubts with respect to coverage are resolved in favor of the insured. As this court held in *Economy Fire & Casualty Co. v. Kubik*, an exclusionary clause may be applied only where its terms are clear, definite and explicit.

After carefully reviewing the evidence, we cannot agree with defendant that the trial court improperly determined the HDCT/ABMT to be a covered benefit under plaintiff's insurance policy. First, we disagree with defendant that the exclusionary language was clear and unambiguous. We note that the plaintiff's insurance policy does not define the phrase "appropriate medical technology boards." The plain language of the policy does not indicate who will determine whether a certain medical board is appropriate. Further, the policy fails to outline any standards for determining how a medical board is deemed appropriate. Thus, the phrase, without more, gives rise to a genuine uncertainty about which medical boards are considered appropriate and how and by whom the determination is made.

Second, despite defendant's argument to the contrary, the exclusionary language in plaintiff's insurance contract varies significantly from the language in section 4-5 of the Act which provides as follows:

> "No contract or evidence of coverage issued by a health maintenance organization which provides coverage for health care services shall deny reimbursement for an otherwise covered expense incurred for any organ transplantation procedure solely on the basis that such procedure is deemed experimental or *investigational unless supported by the determination of the Office of Health Care Technology Assessment within the Agency for the Health Care Policy and Research within the federal Department of Health and Human Services that such a procedure is either experimental or investigational. . . .*" (Emphasis added.) (Ill. Rev. Stat. 1991, ch. 111 1/2, par. 1408.5.)

Unlike plaintiff's insurance contract, the Act specifically provides which agency has the authority to determine whether a procedure is experimental.

Third, we must note that even if the exclusionary language did apply, defendant failed to follow the terms of the insurance policy. Plaintiff's insurance policy excludes from coverage medical and surgical procedures that are considered experimental by defendant "in conjunction with appropriate technology assessment bodies." At the hearing, Dr. Mathy testified that upon learning of plaintiff's pre-certification request, he had already determined that the HDCT/ABMT was experimental prior to receiving or reviewing any information from the medical assessment boards. Given our careful review of the evidence, including defendant's admitted disregard for the terms of the insurance policy, we hold that the trial court did not err in ruling that the requested treatment was a covered benefit under the policy. . . .

> The injunction was granted because the plaintiff was fighting life-threatening cancer and might not have been able to obtain the treatment without insurance.

Lastly, defendant claims that the trial court improperly granted the mandatory injunction because plaintiff failed to meet the requirements for an injunction to issue. An injunction may be granted only after the plaintiff establishes that (1) a lawful right exists; (2) irreparable injury will result if the injunction is not granted; and (3) his or her remedy at law is inadequate. We recognize that injunctions are extraordinary remedies which lack judicial favor, and are granted when the trial court, in its discretion, determines that "the urgency of the situation necessitates such action." Unless the trial court abused its discretion and held contrary to the manifest weight of the evidence, a court of review should not set aside an injunction.

In the present case, defendant argues that plaintiff failed to meet the first two requirements for an injunction to issue. In support, it claims plaintiff failed to show she had a right to the treatment because she had not established that she met the eligibility requirements for inclusion in Dr. Stiff's HDCT/ABMT program. Also, defendant insists that plaintiff failed to prove that irreparable injury would occur if the injunction was not granted. Based on our review of the evidence, we disagree.

At the hearing, Dr. Stiff testified that given the steady development of plaintiff's disease, it was imperative to begin the HDCT/ABMT treatment as quickly as possible. He opined that delaying the HDCT/ABMT any further might have rendered plaintiff ineligible for such treatment due to further development of the disease. Based on our understanding of Dr. Stiff's testimony, we do not believe, as defendant now posits, that plaintiff was not eligible for the treatment.

Moreover, Dr. Stiff further testified that the HDCT/ABMT was an effective treatment for plaintiff and offered her a "very high chance of have [sic] a complete disappearance of her disease." In addition, when asked during direct examination to give a prognosis of plaintiff's condition, Dr. Stiff gave the following response:

> "[Plaintiff] has a fatal illness with a zero percent to one percent chance of being alive, in being alive at five years, let alone alive and disease free."

Given the evidence presented at the hearing, including Dr. Stiff's testimony, we do not agree with defendant that plaintiff failed to show she would suffer irreparable harm without the treatment. Therefore, we hold that the trial court did not abuse its discretion in granting the requested injunctive relief.

For the foregoing reasons, the judgment of the trial court is affirmed.

QUESTIONS

1. The treatment at issue in this case, HDCT/ABMT, was later determined to not be effective in treating several types of cancer. Are health plans required to cover ineffective medical treatments?
2. Should coverage be denied unless the clinical effectiveness of the desired treatment is well established?

The vast majority of privately insured U.S. residents are in employer-sponsored health plans, meaning that the employer negotiates the contract with the insurance company, on behalf of its employees and their dependents. How health plans are regulated at the state and federal levels turns to a remarkable degree on whether the health plan is employer-sponsored and how the employer pays for that health plan. These issues are explored in the following section.

3. FEDERALISM AND HEALTH INSURANCE REGULATION

As *Lubeznik* illustrates, common law canons of construction and other judge-made law provide some protection for insureds from coverage restrictions and other common managed care practices. In addition, states have long regulated various aspects of the private insurance market through executive-branch insurance agencies or commissions. State regulation has addressed business incorporation; licensure and examination of insurance companies for financial solvency; receivership of insolvent insurance companies (an exception to bankruptcy law, which is otherwise federal); and regulation of companies, brokers, and agents for consumer protection. Those matters historically had been understood to fall squarely within states' reserved police powers. While each state has regulated the business of insurance, states also have cooperated with each other by adopting model legislation and regulations promulgated by the National Association of Insurance Commissioners (NAIC), a private group that includes the insurance commissioner from each state and territory.

Federal assertion of authority over insurance was at issue in the U.S. Supreme Court's decision in United States v. South-Eastern Underwriters Ass'n, 322 U.S. 533 (1944). The Court held that federal commerce power — exercised in the Sherman Antitrust Act — could apply to the business of insurance. To restore the dominance of state authority, Congress subsequently enacted the McCarran-Ferguson Act of 1945, 15 U.S.C. §§1011-1015, which exempted the business of insurance from most federal regulation.

> **15 U.S.C. §1012. Regulation by State law; Federal law relating specifically to insurance; applicability of certain Federal laws after June 30, 1948**
>
> (a) State regulation
>
> The business of insurance, and every person engaged therein, shall be subject to the laws of the several States which relate to the regulation or taxation of such business.
>
> (b) Federal regulation
>
> No Act of Congress shall be construed to invalidate, impair, or supersede any law enacted by any State for the purpose of regulating the business of insurance, or which imposes a fee or tax upon such business, unless such Act specifically relates to the business of insurance. . . .
>
> Provided that [various federal antitrust laws] shall be applicable to the business of insurance to the extent that such business is not regulated by State law.

Within the federalism space protected by the McCarran-Ferguson Act, states have enacted a wide range of statutes regulating insurers, insurance policies, and managed care plans. These statutes are often based on NAIC Model Acts. For example, consider this state insurance law from Georgia:

> **Ga. Code Ann. §33-20A-9. Emergency services requirements; restrictive formulary requirements**
>
> Every managed care plan shall include provisions that:
>
> (1)(A) In the event that a patient seeks emergency services and if necessary in the opinion of the emergency health care provider responsible for the patient's emergency care and treatment and warranted by his or her evaluation, such emergency provider may initiate necessary intervention to stabilize the condition of the patient without seeking or receiving prospective authorization by the managed care entity or managed care plan. No managed care entity or private health benefit plan may subsequently deny payment for an evaluation, diagnostic testing, or treatment provided as part of such intervention for an

emergency condition. For purposes of this Code section, the term "emergency health care provider" includes without limitation an emergency services provider and a licensed ambulance service providing 911 emergency medical transportation.

(B) No managed care entity or private health benefit plan which has given prospective authorization after the stabilization of a person's condition for an evaluation, diagnostic testing, or treatment may subsequently deny payment for the provision of such evaluation, diagnostic testing, or treatment. An acknowledgment of an enrollee's eligibility for benefits by the managed care entity or private health benefit plan shall not, by itself, be construed as a prospective authorization for the purposes of this Code section.

(C) If in the opinion of the emergency health care provider, a patient's condition has stabilized and the emergency health care provider certifies that the patient can be transported to another facility without suffering detrimental consequences or aggravating the patient's condition, the patient may be relocated to another facility which will provide continued care and treatment as necessary; and

> A *formulary* is a list of approved drugs for a health plan or an institution. Drugs are placed on a formulary after both clinical and financial evaluations.

(2) When a managed care plan uses a restrictive formulary for prescription drugs, such use shall include a written procedure whereby patients can obtain, without penalty and in a timely fashion, specific drugs and medications not included in the formulary when:

(A) The formulary's equivalent has been ineffective in the treatment of the patient's disease or condition; or

(B) The formulary's drug causes or is reasonably expected to cause adverse or harmful reactions in the patient.

QUESTIONS

1. What is the purpose of state laws like this one if EMTALA already requires Medicare-participating hospitals to provide emergency medical treatment?
2. How might insurers respond to these sorts of coverage mandates?

In addition to complaints about managed care practices, public opinion became increasingly critical of health insurers' underwriting and ratemaking practices, namely, refusing to sell policies or charging exorbitant rates to individuals with preexisting conditions, canceling plans based on an enrollee's high utilization of covered services, and other practices that seemed to discriminate against the very people who most need health insurance — the sick. Although consistent with classical "actuarial fairness" models of insurance based on individual risk profiles, those practices undermined the "mutual aid" model of insurance whereby lower-risk members of the risk pool subsidize the cost of care for higher-risk individuals. Again, states responded with a variety of approaches, including community rating laws limiting the extent to which insurers can vary premiums based on individual risk profiles, state-subsidized high-risk pools, and guaranteed issue laws (applicable to all plans in a handful of states, and only to certain plans in a number of other states).

In 2006, Massachusetts Governor Mitt Romney signed one of the most comprehensive state health care reform laws, An Act Providing Access to Affordable, Quality, Accountable Health Care, which included many key features that later would be incorporated into the comprehensive federal health reform plan in 2010. The Massachusetts plan includes guaranteed issue and community rating but also additional features to guard against the risk of adverse selection destabilizing the new, more open commercial health insurance markets. One such reform is the Commonwealth Health Insurance Connector, a Web portal allowing residents to access subsidized and unsubsidized coverage that meets certain coverage and cost standards. Another new state law required most individuals to obtain health insurance, whether by qualifying for government health plans or purchasing commercial health insurance, on pain of a state tax penalty for failing to do so. Individuals below 150 percent of federal poverty level and with religious objections are exempt. In addition, employers in the state with 11 or more employees are required to contribute to the cost of employees' health insurance coverage or pay a "fair share" contribution of $295 per employee per year. Massachussets expanded coverage for low-income families and children through expansion of an existing 1115 Medicaid waiver.

The ACA departed from the trend of state primacy for health insurance regulation by imposing numerous federal requirements on health plans, many of which were modeled on Massachusetts' comprehensive plan. The ACA satisfies the McCarran-Ferguson Act because it "specifically relates to the business of insurance" and, therefore, preempts conflicting state law. But in areas that the ACA does not control, state law remains in place. As provisions of the ACA are eroded by congressional and administrative actions, such state laws take on renewed salience.

> The employer mandate, or "pay or play" provision, and similar versions adopted by Maryland and San Francisco raise ERISA preemption issues, discussed later in this chapter.

The ACA was by no means the first attempt to enact federal rules for health insurance. Indeed, various iterations were proposed over the decades, each time defeated by competing interest groups. As noted in Chapter 2, enactment of Medicare and Medicaid in 1965 under Lyndon B. Johnson's Great Society was a high-water mark for federal health reform. In 1993, President Bill Clinton (and First Lady Hillary Clinton) attempted to shepherd comprehensive health reform through Congress, but the effort was defeated, leaving a few legacies that we will discuss later. After that dramatic defeat, several attempts were made to respond to perceived abuses in managed care with a federal "Patients' Bill of Rights." *See, e.g.*, McCain-Edwards-Kennedy Patients' Bill of Rights, S. 1052, 107th Cong. (2001).

When President Barack Obama was elected in 2008, he vowed to enact comprehensive health care reform. As a symbolic down payment on that promise, one of the first bills that he signed into law as President was to reauthorize Children's Health Insurance Program (CHIP, discussed briefly in Chapter 2), which President George W. Bush had twice vetoed. Despite its popularity when enacted, CHIP's renewal became controversial because it provides public health insurance coverage to middle- or lower-middle-income families, generally not considered the "deserving" poor. Conservatives who favor greater reliance on market-based approaches and less government involvement in health care delivery favored a model of employment-based coverage or tax credits to support coverage.

Congressional debates culminating in the ACA never seriously broached the possibility of a single-payer, national health system. Rather, the proposals sought to build on the existing, patchwork non-system of health care. For example, some consideration was given to expanding Medicare to younger populations (say, age 55 and older) or to allow younger people to buy into Medicare early. These Medicare expansion proposals lacked sufficient support to end up in the ACA.

At the time of the ACA's enactment, roughly half of the insured population was covered by an employer-sponsored plan, as either an employee or dependent of an employee. Another 20 percent were insured through public programs. A relatively small 6 percent portion of the population obtained health insurance in the individual or small-group market. Finally, approximately 18 percent of the population was uninsured. The ACA promised to reduce the 18 percent gap by expanding or shoring up the other three pieces of the pie. Chapter 2 already discussed the ACA expansion of public programs, primarily Medicaid. This chapter discusses the operation and regulation of employer-sponsored health insurance and the individual and small-group markets.

Similar to the Massachusetts plan, the ACA included guaranteed issue and renewal, a modified version of community rating, an individual mandate, an employer mandate, and a Web portal for accessing government subsidies and purchasing standardized commercial health plans. Although the ACA's reforms were less dramatic than some might have hoped, many states resisted the intrusion of federal authority over health insurance, leading to litigation such as *NFIB v. Sebelius* (discussed in Chapter 2). The individual mandate was a particular target. A number of states enacted resolutions, legislation, and constitutional amendments providing that residents of their states could not be required to purchase health insurance. The Virginia Health Care Freedom Act, Va. Code §38.2-3430.1:1 (enacted in 2010), was representative:

> Although attacked by conservative circles, an individual mandate to purchase insurance was initially proposed by the Heritage Foundation, a think tank championing free enterprise, limited government, and individual freedom, as a counter-proposal to President Bill Clinton's failed 1993 comprehensive health care reform proposal.

> No resident of this Commonwealth, regardless of whether he has or is eligible for health insurance coverage under any policy or program provided by or through his employer, or a plan sponsored by the Commonwealth or the federal government, shall be required to obtain or maintain a policy of individual insurance coverage except as required by a court or the Department of Social Services where an individual is named a party in a judicial or administrative proceeding. No provision of this title shall render a resident of this Commonwealth liable for any penalty, assessment, fee, or fine as a result of his failure to procure or obtain health insurance coverage. . . .

The ACA enacted the goal of near-universal health insurance coverage by making most individuals responsible for obtaining their own health insurance and imposing a tax penalty if they fail to do so. The basic penalty for remaining uncovered started quite small ($95 per adult in 2014). By 2016 it is $695 per adult, with exceptions in the statute for taxpayers with lower incomes. "Repeal and replace" of the ACA was a top priority for President Donald Trump and the Republican-majority Congress elected in 2016. Despite repeated efforts, wholesale overhaul of federal health insurance reform did not garner enough votes to pass both houses of Congress. After those defeats, at the end of 2017, Republicans passed a major tax reform bill that included one critical item related to health reform. Namely, Congress repealed the tax penalty provision of the individual mandate, effective 2019, but left the substance of the requirement in place.

> To take advantage of the special legislative process called Budget Reconciliation, which requires only a majority of the Senate's votes to pass a bill, Congress focused on measures that involved only spending or revenues. This is why the tax penalty was repealed but not the substantive minimum essential coverage requirement.

26 U.S.C. §5000A. Requirement to maintain minimum essential coverage

(a) Requirement to maintain minimum essential coverage. — An applicable individual shall for each month beginning after 2013 ensure that the individual, and any dependent of the individual who is an applicable individual, is covered under minimum essential coverage for such month.

(b) Shared responsibility payment. —

Compliance is monitored through the annual income tax return individuals and families file with the IRS.

(1) In general. — If a taxpayer who is an applicable individual, or an applicable individual for whom the taxpayer is liable under paragraph (3), fails to meet the requirement of subsection (a) for 1 or more months, then, except as provided in subsection (e), there is hereby imposed on the taxpayer a penalty with respect to such failures in the amount determined under subsection (c).

(2) Inclusion with return. — Any penalty imposed by this section with respect to any month shall be included with a taxpayer's return under chapter 1 for the taxable year which includes such month. . . .

The following sections of the Internal Revenue Code, 26 U.S.C. §5000A, specify who is "an applicable individual" subject to the minimum essential coverage requirement excerpted above. The Code also specified who was exempt:

(d) Applicable individual. — For purposes of this section —

(1) In general. — The term "applicable individual" means, with respect to any month, an individual other than an individual described in paragraph (2), (3), or (4).

(2) Religious exemptions. —

(A) Religious conscience exemption. — Such term shall not include any individual for any month if such individual has in effect an exemption under section 1311(d)(4)(H) of the Patient Protection and Affordable Care Act which certifies that such individual is —

(i) a member of a recognized religious sect or division thereof which is described in section 1402(g)(1), and

(ii) an adherent of established tenets or teachings of such sect or division as described in such section.

(B) Health care sharing ministry. —

(i) In general. — Such term shall not include any individual for any month if such individual is a member of a health care sharing ministry for the month. . . .

> Health care sharing ministries rely on voluntary donations from other members to fund high-cost medical care; it is not considered to be insurance.

(3) Individuals not lawfully present. — Such term shall not include an individual for any month if for the month the individual is not a citizen or national of the United States or an alien lawfully present in the United States.

(4) Incarcerated individuals. — Such term shall not include an individual for any month if for the month the individual is incarcerated, other than incarceration pending the disposition of charges.

(e) Exemptions. — No penalty shall be imposed under subsection (a) with respect to —

(1) Individuals who cannot afford coverage. —

QUESTIONS

1. With repeal of the federal individual mandate tax penalty, how might states respond?
2. What is the effect of laws like the Virginia Health Care Freedom Act?

Although the tax penalty for failing to obtain minimum essential coverage no longer will be in effect starting in 2019, the substance of the law remains, including the ACA's various strategies for making coverage available. One way to obtain coverage is through public insurance programs, but, as noted in Chapter 2, only certain groups are eligible for those programs. Another option is an employer-sponsored health plan, which provides coverage for roughly half of all Americans, as employees or dependents. That avenue is discussed next, in Section C of this chapter. Barring those options, individual or group plans may be purchased on the private market. That third option, historically, has been challenging to navigate and fraught with various market failures. The ACA took several steps to rationalize the individual and small group market, discussed in more detail in Section D of this chapter. Repealing the individual mandate tax penalty, while leaving the other reforms in place, may challenge the stability of those markets and operation of those reforms, as we will discuss further below.

C. EMPLOYER-SPONSORED HEALTH INSURANCE

The majority of Americans not covered by public insurance programs receive health insurance as a benefit of employment, although at the time the ACA was enacted, only about 52 percent of all Americans received health insurance as an employment benefit, a percentage that has been decreasing since at least the early 2000s. Federal law, even after the ACA, does not require employers to provide health insurance to workers and their dependents, but strong tax incentives exist for doing so. First, any amounts spent on employee benefits are exempt from federal income tax, which means that offering more generous benefits is more tax efficient to employees than offering higher salaries. Second, certain employers that fail to offer insurance, or offer insurance that is not affordable or comprehensive, may face a tax penalty. Aside from those government incentives, rational business reasons exist for employers to offer benefits to encourage healthier, more productive workforces with lower absenteeism and to attract productive workers. Given the prevalence of employer-sponsored health insurance, workers in many industries have come to expect such coverage as an element of their compensation packages.

1. EMPLOYER SHARED RESPONSIBILITY

Prior to the ACA, several states and localities had tested employer "pay or play" mandates, requiring large employers to pay a penalty if they did not offer adequate and affordable health insurance to their employees. Some of those approaches were adjudged to be preempted by federal law. The Massachusetts pay-or-play law described above was never tested in federal court. But a law in Maryland, nicknamed the "Walmart Law," required employers with more than 10,000 employees in the state of Maryland (Walmart was the only employer that did) to spend 8 percent of their payroll toward employee health benefits or pay the difference to a state Medicaid fund. Federal courts struck down the Maryland law on ERISA preemption grounds. (ERISA is discussed in more detail below.)

Without the restrictions of federal preemption, the ACA adapted this pay-or-play idea and imposed it under federal law. The ACA's employer shared responsibility provision (§4980H of the Internal Revenue Code) penalizes applicable large employers that do not offer coverage that meets minimum value, minimum essential coverage (MEC), and affordability standards. An applicable large employer is defined as having 50 or more full-time equivalent employees. The penalty is triggered only if the employee receives federally subsidized coverage on the private marketplace Exchanges created by the ACA. Hence, this rule is dubbed the "free rider penalty": If the employee is receiving federally subsidized coverage, the employer is free riding on federal taxpayers rather than upholding its financial responsibility to its employees.

QUESTION

Large employers like Walmart and McDonalds employ large numbers of people receiving health coverage under CHIP, Medicaid, and Medicare. Is this free riding on the public fisc, or helping low-income and older Americans with valuable employment opportunities, or some other business strategy?

The following excerpt from the preamble to the final regulations implementing the ACA's employer shared responsibility provision explains the coverage requirement, penalty triggers, and penalties in greater detail.

Shared Responsibility for Employers Regarding Health Coverage

79 Fed. Reg. 8544-01 (Feb. 12, 2014)

**RULES and REGULATIONS
DEPARTMENT OF THE TREASURY
Internal Revenue Service
26 CFR Parts 1, 54, and 301**

Preambles are not formal regulations but are authoritative summaries of the agency's views; the final regulations are codified in the *Code of Federal Regulations* (C.F.R.) once the notice and comment process is complete. The Preambles remain an essential source of regulatory history and interpretation for health care lawyers.

AGENCY: Internal Revenue Service (IRS), Treasury.

ACTION: Final regulations.

SUMMARY: This document contains final regulations providing guidance to employers that are subject to the shared responsibility provisions regarding employee health coverage under section 4980H of the Internal Revenue Code (Code), enacted by the Affordable Care Act. These regulations affect employers referred to as applicable large employers (generally meaning, for each year, employers that had 50 or more full-time employees, including full-time equivalent employees, during the prior year). Generally, under section 4980H an applicable large employer that, for a calendar month, fails to offer to its full-time employees health coverage that is affordable and provides minimum value may be subject to an assessable payment if a full-time employee enrolls for that month in a qualified health plan for which the employee receives a premium tax credit.

DATES: Effective date: These regulations are effective February 12, 2014.

I. Shared Responsibility for Employers (Section 4980H)

A. In general

Section 4980H was added to the Code by section 1513 of the Patient Protection and Affordable Care Act, was amended by section 10106(e) and (f) of the Patient Protection and Affordable Care Act, was further amended by section 1003 of the Health Care and Education Reconciliation Act of 2010, and was further amended by the Department of Defense and Full-Year Continuing Appropriations Act, 2011 (collectively, the Affordable Care Act). Section 1513(d) of the Affordable Care Act provides that section 4980H applies to months beginning after December 31, 2013; however, Notice 2013-45 (2013-31 IRB 116), issued on July 9, 2013, provides transition relief for 2014 with respect to section 4980H.

> Note the many statutory and regulatory steps conducted before these rules took effect.

Section 4980H applies only to applicable large employers. An applicable large employer with respect to a calendar year is defined in section 4980H(c)(2) as an employer that employed an average of at least 50 full-time employees on business days during the preceding calendar year. For purposes of determining whether an employer is an applicable large employer, full-time equivalent employees (FTEs), as well as full-time employees, are taken into account. As set forth in section 4980H(c)(2)(E), the number of an employer's FTEs is determined based on the hours of service of employees who are not full-time employees. Under section 4980H(c)(2)(C), new employers, not in existence in the preceding calendar year, are deemed applicable larger employers based on the average number of employees that the employer reasonably expects to employ on business days in the current calendar year.

Section 4980H generally provides that an applicable large employer is subject to an assessable payment if either (1) the employer fails to offer to its full-time employees (and their dependents) the opportunity to enroll in minimum essential coverage (MEC) under an eligible employer-sponsored plan and any full-time employee is certified to the employer as having received an applicable premium tax credit or cost-sharing reduction (section 4980H(a) liability), or (2) the employer offers its full-time employees (and their dependents) the opportunity to enroll in MEC under an eligible employer-sponsored plan and one or more full-time employees is certified to the employer as having received an applicable premium tax credit or cost-sharing reduction (section 4980H(b) liability). Section 4980H(c)(4) provides that a full-time employee with respect to any month is an employee who is employed on average at least 30 hours of service per week. . . .

> Approximately 96 percent of employers are small businesses and have fewer than 50 FTEs. Of those employers subject to these requirements, only a fraction do not already offer qualifying coverage to full-time employees.

II. Minimum Essential Coverage, Minimum Value and Affordability (Sections 5000A and 36B)

MEC, MV and affordability are defined under Code provisions other than section 4980H, but all relate to the determination of liability under section 4980H, and accordingly are summarized briefly in this section of the preamble (but are more fully described in other cited guidance). Specifically, for purposes of section 4980H, an employer is not treated as having offered coverage to an employee unless the coverage is MEC. Moreover, under section 36B, an individual who is offered employer coverage but instead purchases coverage under a qualified health plan within the meaning of section 1301(a) of the Affordable Care Act on an Exchange may be eligible for a premium tax credit if the household income of the individual's family falls within certain thresholds and the coverage offered by the employer either does not provide MV or is not affordable. While an individual may purchase coverage under a qualified health plan on an Exchange without regard to whether the individual is eligible for a premium tax credit, an employer's potential liability under section 4980H is affected by the individual's purchase of coverage on an Exchange only if the individual receives a premium tax credit.

A. Minimum Essential Coverage (MEC)

MEC is defined in section 5000A(f) and the regulations under that section. Section 5000A(f)(1)(B) provides that MEC includes coverage under an eligible employer-sponsored plan. Under section 5000A(f)(2) and §1.5000A-2(c)(1), an eligible employer-sponsored plan is, with

> The ACA allows health plans in effect as of March 23, 2010, that have not been changed in ways that substantially increase costs or cut benefits for enrollees to retain "grandfathered" status and, therefore, exemption from a number of ACA requirements.

respect to any employee, (1) group health insurance coverage offered by, or on behalf of, an employer to the employee that is either (a) a governmental plan . . . , (b) any other plan or coverage offered in the small or large group market within a State, or (c) a grandfathered health plan . . . offered in a group market, or (2) a self-insured group health plan under which coverage is offered by, or on behalf of, an employer to the employee. Section 5000A(f)(3) and regulations thereunder provide that MEC does not include coverage consisting solely of excepted benefits described [in various sections of the] PHS Act [Public Health Service Act] or regulations issued under these provisions.

B. Minimum Value (MV)

If the coverage offered by an employer fails to provide MV, an employee may be eligible to receive coverage in a qualified health plan supported by the premium tax credit. Under section 36B(c)(2)(C)(ii), a plan fails to provide MV if the plan's share of the total allowed costs of benefits provided under the plan is less than 60 percent of those costs.

> An employer-sponsored health plan fails to provide MV if it fails to provide at least 60 percent actuarial value, the same standard as a bronze-level plan on the Exchanges. Actuarial value means, roughly, that the employer's contribution to the plan covers 60 percent of the allowed costs of medical care provided.

Section 1302(d)(2)(C) of the Affordable Care Act provides that, in determining the percentage of the total allowed costs of benefits provided under a group health plan, the regulations promulgated by the Secretary of Health and Human Services (HHS) under section 1302(d)(2) of the Affordable Care Act apply. HHS published final regulations under section 1302(d)(2) of the Affordable Care Act on February 25, 2013. On May 3, 2013, the Treasury Department and the IRS published a notice of proposed rulemaking that adopts the HHS rules and provides additional guidance on MV. The HHS regulations at 45 CFR 156.20 define the percentage of the total allowed costs of benefits provided under a group health plan as (1) the anticipated covered medical spending for essential health benefits (EHB) coverage (as defined in

45 CFR 156.110(a)) paid by a health plan for a standard population, (2) computed in accordance with the plan's cost sharing, and (3) divided by the total anticipated allowed charges for EHB coverage provided to the standard population. In addition, 45 CFR 156.145(c) provides that the standard population used to compute this percentage for MV (as developed by HHS for this purpose) reflects the population covered by typical self-insured group health plans. . . . Finally, 45 CFR 156.145(a)(4) provides that a plan in the small group market satisfies MV if it meets the requirements for any of the levels of metal coverage defined at 45 CFR 156.140(b) (bronze, silver, gold, or platinum).

C. Affordability

Under section 36B(c)(2)(B) and (C), an employee is not eligible for subsidized coverage for any month in which the employee is offered health coverage under an eligible employer-sponsored plan (as defined in section 5000A(f)(2)) that provides MV and that is affordable to the employee. Coverage for an employee under an eligible employer-sponsored plan is affordable if the employee's required contribution (within the meaning of section 5000A(e)(1)(B)) for self-only coverage does not exceed 9.5 percent of the taxpayer's household income for the taxable year. *See* section 36B (c)(2)(C)(i) and §1.36B-1(e).

> An employer-sponsored health plan is "unaffordable" if an employee's contribution for individual coverage, for herself only, exceeds 9.5 percent of the employee's annual household income.

QUESTIONS

1. Could an employer avoid the penalty by hiring workers for 29 or fewer hours per week and/or having fewer than 50 employees?
2. When might it make good business sense for an applicable large employer to pay the free rider penalty rather than offer health insurance to its workers?

Smaller employers face no penalty for failing to offer health insurance to their employees. Historically, small employers (generally, 50 or fewer employees) faced a difficult health insurance market. Even if premiums were community-rated across the group of employees, a single catastrophic claim (say, for cancer) would result in a dramatic increase in premiums across the board the following year. The ACA provides a couple of ways to assist small employers to provide insurance. First, employers with fewer than 25 full-time equivalent employees may be eligible for a Small Business Health Care Tax Credit to help cover the cost of providing coverage. 26 U.S.C. §45R. The credit is available for the first two consecutive taxable years in which the employer offers a qualified health plan to its employees. The provision is only available so long as the average annual wages of the eligible small employer are below a statutory cap, and the amount of the credit varies depending on whether the business is for profit or not for profit. Even if ineligible to receive tax credits, employers with 50 or fewer employees may be eligible to buy coverage through the Small Business Health Options Program (SHOP). SHOP is designed to make the market for small-group health insurance more efficient and transparent.

> The automatic enrollment default rule is a "nudge" suggested by behavioral economics rather than a mandatory rule, preserving an employee's right to dissent.

Starting in 2016, states had the option to expand SHOP to employers with 100 or fewer employees. Even if an employer offers a health plan to its employees, the employees are not required to enroll. Declining coverage, however, may make the employee ineligible for federal tax subsidies to purchase insurance on the Exchanges. As a further incentive for employees to accept employer-sponsored coverage, employers with 200 or more employees are required to automatically enroll new full-time employees in a coverage option and to automatically continue existing coverage for current full-time employees. In other words, enrollment is the default rule, and the employee must affirmatively elect otherwise. 29 U.S.C. §218a.

Coupling health insurance and employment is a historical anachronism and uniquely burdens U.S. employers, compared to their global competitors, many of which operate in countries with government-sponsored universal health care. Historically, the dominance of state regulation of health insurance in the United States also increased costs for companies that operate in more than one state because they would have to tailor their plans in myriad ways to comply with each state's laws. Consider, for example, Walmart, which operates across the country, being subject to a pay-or-play requirement in Maryland, a benefits mandate in Massachusetts, and myriad other state laws; it would have to tailor its health plans to each individual state. As a result, large employers and insurers selling plans to those companies generally would prefer uniform federal regulation of employee benefits, including health insurance. Since 1974, a federal statute called ERISA has provided that sort of preemptive protection from discordant state regulation.

2. ERISA PREEMPTION

The Employee Retirement Income Security Act of 1974 (ERISA) addressed the disuniformity-of-state-regulation concern, although employer-sponsored health plans were not the focus of the legislation. Congress was more concerned with a number of high-profile incidents of grossly underfunded employee pension plans and other financial malfeasance related to retirement plans. ERISA, accordingly, provides a fairly detailed set of regulations regarding employee pension and retirement plans. With respect to certain types of employer-sponsored health plans, ERISA's greatest impact is a sweeping preemption scheme that knocks out a host of state laws with which employers would otherwise have to comply while leaving little in the way of substantive federal regulation in their place. It is hard to overstate the scope and sweep of ERISA preemption over the decades leading up to the ACA.

The ACA imposes a number of federal requirements on employer-sponsored health plans. These reforms build on a prior federal statute, the Health Insurance Portability and Accountability Act of 1996 (HIPAA), a vestige of President Clinton's failed comprehensive health reform plan. But the essential ERISA preemption scheme is unchanged, and states remain mostly constrained in their ability to regulate most employer-sponsored health plans.

Two statutory provisions, commonly referred to as ERISA §514 and ERISA §502, are keys to ERISA preemption analysis. These relatively brief provisions have now resulted in dozens of full opinions from the U.S. Supreme Court. ERISA §514 determines which state laws are preempted:

29 U.S.C. §1144 (ERISA §514). Other laws
     (a) Supersedure; effective date

Federal Preemption

Federal preemption is the invalidation of U.S. state laws that conflict with federal law. The constitutional basis of the doctrine is the Supremacy Clause, U.S. Const. art. VI, para. 2. Congress may expressly preempt state laws with statutory language. Or preemption may be implied when compliance with both federal and state law would be impossible, or operation of state laws would be contrary to, frustrate the purpose of, or otherwise conflict with federal law. Also, when Congress has regulated expansively in a particular area, courts may conclude that federal law has "occupied the field," leaving no room for additional state regulation. Preemption analysis turns on close reading and interpretation of the applicable federal statute and implicated state laws.

Except as provided in subsection (b) of this section, the provisions of this subchapter and subchapter III of this chapter shall supersede any and all State laws insofar as they may now or hereafter relate to any employee benefit plan described in section 1003(a) of this title and not exempt under section 1003(b) of this title. This section shall take effect on January 1, 1975.

(b) Construction and application

(1) This section shall not apply with respect to any cause of action which arose, or any act or omission which occurred, before January 1, 1975.

(2)(A) Except as provided in subparagraph (B), nothing in this subchapter shall be construed to exempt or relieve any person from any law of any State which regulates insurance, banking, or securities.

> Section 514(b)(2)(A) is known as the "savings" clause, and section 514(b)(2)(B) is the "deemer" clause.

(B) Neither an employee benefit plan . . . nor any trust established under such a plan, shall be deemed to be an insurance company or other insurer, bank, trust company, or investment company or to be engaged in the business of insurance or banking for purposes of any law of any State purporting to regulate insurance companies, insurance contracts, banks, trust companies, or investment companies.

ERISA §502 describes the limited private right of action that may be brought alleging a violation of ERISA standards. This section has been interpreted as providing the exclusive remedy for ERISA plan coverage disputes, thereby impliedly preempting another body of state laws.

> The statute defines "employee benefit plan," in typical cross-referencing form, at 29 U.S. Code §1002, as "any plan, fund, or program . . . established or maintained by an employer or by an employee organization, or by both . . . for the purpose of providing for its participants or their beneficiaries, through the purchase of insurance or otherwise, (A) medical, surgical, or hospital care or benefits . . . ."

29 U.S.C. §1132 (ERISA §502). Civil enforcement

(a) Persons empowered to bring a civil action

A civil action may be brought —

(1) by a participant or beneficiary —

(A) for the relief provided for in subsection (c) of this section, or

(B) to recover benefits due to him under the terms of his plan, to enforce his rights under the terms of the plan, or to clarify his rights to future benefits under the terms of the plan;

(2) by the Secretary, or by a participant, beneficiary or fiduciary for appropriate relief under section 1109 of this title;

(3) by a participant, beneficiary, or fiduciary

(A) to enjoin any act or practice which violates any provision of this subchapter or the terms of the plan, or

(B) to obtain other appropriate equitable relief

(i) to redress such violations or

(ii) to enforce any provisions of this subchapter or the terms of the plan; . . . .

The following case is one of the many U.S. Supreme Court decisions interpreting ERISA. In the late 1990s, a number of states passed laws protecting consumers from some of the perceived abuses of managed care. Health plans and large employers with health plans covered by ERISA sought to avoid these laws, claiming they were preempted. Because federal law did not then contain similar substantive protections (the Clinton Health Plan had failed and the ACA was not yet law), a successful preemption claim under ERISA was a powerful deregulatory tool, striking down state law with very little federal law to replace it. In ERISA litigation, the Court frequently cites the *United States Code* (29 U.S.C. §1144) with or without the parallel citation to ERISA's Public Law sections (ERISA §514).

Rush Prudential HMO, Inc. v. Moran

536 U.S. 355 (2002)

Opinion

Justice SOUTER delivered the opinion of the Court.

Section 4-10 of Illinois's Health Maintenance Organization Act, 215 Ill. Comp. Stat., ch. 125, §4-10 (2000), provides recipients of health coverage by such organizations with a right to independent medical review of certain denials of benefits. The issue in this case is whether the statute, as applied to health benefits provided by a health maintenance organization under contract with an employee welfare benefit plan, is preempted by the Employee Retirement Income Security Act of 1974 (ERISA), 29 U.S.C. §1001 et seq. We hold it is not.

> The Court allows the Illinois independent medical review law to stand as not preempted by ERISA.

I

Petitioner, Rush Prudential HMO, Inc., is a health maintenance organization (HMO) that contracts to provide medical services for employee welfare benefit plans covered by ERISA. Respondent Debra Moran is a beneficiary under one such plan, sponsored by her husband's employer. Rush's "Certificate of Group Coverage," issued to employees who participate in employer-sponsored plans, promises that Rush will provide them with "medically necessary" services. The terms of the certificate give Rush the "broadest possible discretion" to determine whether a medical service claimed by a beneficiary is covered under the certificate. The certificate specifies that a service is covered as "medically necessary" if Rush finds:

"(a) [The service] is furnished or authorized by a Participating Doctor for the diagnosis or the treatment of a Sickness or Injury or for the maintenance of a person's good health.

"(b) The prevailing opinion within the appropriate specialty of the United States medical profession is that [the service] is safe and effective for its intended use, and that its omission would adversely affect the person's medical condition.

"(c) It is furnished by a provider with appropriate training, experience, staff and facilities to furnish that particular service or supply."

As the certificate explains, Rush contracts with physicians "to arrange for or provide services and supplies for medical care and treatment" of covered persons. Each covered person selects a primary care physician from those under contract to Rush, while Rush will pay for medical services by an unaffiliated physician only if the services have been "authorized" both by the primary care physician and Rush's medical director.

> This contract outlines key cost-saving features of HMOs: narrow networks of approved providers and preapproval of specialized services.

In 1996, when Moran began to have pain and numbness in her right shoulder, Dr. Arthur LaMarre, her primary care physician, unsuccessfully administered "conservative" treatments such as physiotherapy. In October 1997, Dr. LaMarre recommended that Rush approve surgery by an unaffiliated specialist, Dr. Julia Terzis, who had developed an unconventional treatment for Moran's condition. Although Dr. LaMarre said that Moran would be "best served" by that procedure, Rush denied the request and, after Moran's internal appeals, affirmed the denial on the ground that the procedure was not "medically necessary." Rush instead proposed that Moran undergo standard surgery, performed by a physician affiliated with Rush.

In January 1998, Moran made a written demand for an independent medical review of her claim, as guaranteed by §4-10 of Illinois's HMO Act, which provides:

"Each Health Maintenance Organization shall provide a mechanism for the timely review by a physician holding the same class of license as the primary care physician, who is unaffiliated with the Health Maintenance Organization, jointly selected by the patient . . . , primary care physician and the Health Maintenance Organization in the event of a dispute between the primary care physician and the Health Maintenance Organization regarding the medical necessity of a covered service proposed by a primary care physician. In the event that the reviewing physician determines the covered service to be medically necessary, the Health Maintenance Organization shall provide the covered service."

> The Illinois law required HMOs to establish external review mechanisms with a fair process; states impose similar requirements on other consumer services such as credit cards.

The Act defines a "Health Maintenance Organization" as

"any organization formed under the laws of this or another state to provide or arrange for one or more health care plans under a system which causes any part of the risk of health care delivery to be borne by the organization or its providers."

When Rush failed to provide the independent review, Moran sued in an Illinois state court to compel compliance with the state Act. Rush removed the suit to Federal District Court, arguing that the cause of action was "completely preempted" under ERISA.

While the suit was pending, Moran had surgery by Dr. Terzis at her own expense and submitted a $94,841.27 reimbursement claim to Rush. Rush treated the claim as a renewed request for benefits and began a new inquiry to determine coverage. The three doctors consulted by Rush said the surgery had been medically unnecessary.

> The dispute was essentially the same as *Lubeznik*: The parties disagreed as to whether the surgery was medically necessary and, therefore, covered.

Meanwhile, the federal court remanded the case back to state court on Moran's motion, concluding that because Moran's request for independent review under §4-10 would not require interpretation of the terms of an ERISA plan, the claim was not "completely preempted" so as to permit removal under 28 U.S.C. §1441. The state court enforced the state statute and ordered Rush to submit to review by an independent physician. The doctor selected was a reconstructive surgeon at Johns Hopkins Medical Center, Dr. A. Lee Dellon. Dr. Dellon decided that Dr. Terzis's treatment had been medically necessary, based on the definition of medical necessity in Rush's Certificate of Group Coverage, as well as his own medical judgment. Rush's medical director, however, refused to concede that the surgery had been medically necessary, and denied Moran's claim in January 1999.

Moran amended her complaint in state court to seek reimbursement for the surgery as "medically necessary" under Illinois's HMO Act, and Rush again removed to federal court, arguing that Moran's amended complaint stated a claim for ERISA benefits and was thus completely preempted by ERISA's civil enforcement provisions, 29 U.S.C. §1132(a), as construed by this Court in Metropolitan Life Ins. Co. v. Taylor, 481 U.S. 58 (1987). The District Court treated Moran's claim as a suit under ERISA, and denied the claim on the ground that ERISA preempted Illinois's independent review statute.

The Court of Appeals for the Seventh Circuit reversed. Although it found Moran's state-law reimbursement claim completely preempted by ERISA so as to place the case in federal court, the Seventh Circuit did not agree that the substantive provisions of Illinois's HMO Act were so preempted. The court noted that although ERISA broadly preempts any state laws that "relate to" employee benefit plans, 29 U.S.C. §1144(a), state laws that "regulat[e] insurance" are saved from preemption, §1144(b)(2)(A). The court held that the Illinois HMO Act was such a law, the independent review requirement being little different from a state-mandated contractual term of the sort this Court had held to survive ERISA preemption. The Seventh Circuit rejected the contention that Illinois's independent review requirement constituted a forbidden "alternative remedy" under this Court's holding in Pilot Life Ins. Co. v. Dedeaux, 481 U.S. 41 (1987), and emphasized that §4-10 does not authorize any particular form of relief in state courts; rather, with respect to any ERISA health plan, the judgment of the independent reviewer is only enforceable in an action brought under ERISA's civil enforcement scheme, 29 U.S.C. §1132(a).

> If the claim had been preempted, Moran would have lost, as no federal law gave any remedy for this issue.

Because the decision of the Court of Appeals conflicted with the Fifth Circuit's treatment of a similar provision of Texas law in Corporate Health Ins., Inc. v. Texas Dept. of Ins., 215 F.3d 526 (2000), we granted certiorari. We now affirm.

II

To "safeguar[d] . . . the establishment, operation, and administration" of employee benefit plans, ERISA sets "minimum standards . . . assuring the equitable character of such plans and their financial soundness," 29 U.S.C. §1001(a), and contains an express preemption provision that ERISA "shall supersede any and all State laws insofar as they may now or hereafter relate to any employee benefit plan. . . ." §1144(a). A saving clause then reclaims a substantial amount of ground with its provision that "nothing in this subchapter shall

> "The 'unhelpful' drafting of these antiphonal clauses . . . occupies a substantial share of this Court's time. . . ."

be construed to exempt or relieve any person from any law of any State which regulates insurance, banking, or securities." §1144(b)(2)(A). The "unhelpful" drafting of these antiphonal clauses, New York State Conference of Blue Cross & Blue Shield Plans v. Travelers Ins. Co., 514 U.S. 645 (1995), occupies a substantial share of this Court's time, *see, e.g.,* Egelhoff v. Egelhoff, 532 U.S. 141 (2001); UNUM Life Ins. Co. of America v. Ward, *supra*; California Div. of Labor Standards Enforcement v. Dillingham Constr., N.A., Inc., 519 U.S. 316 (1997); Metropolitan Life Ins. Co. v. Massachusetts, 471 U.S. 724 (1985). In trying to extrapolate congressional intent in a case like this, when congressional language seems simultaneously to preempt everything and hardly anything, we "have no choice" but to temper the assumption that "'the ordinary meaning . . . accurately expresses the legislative purpose,'" with the qualification "'that the historic police powers of the States were not [meant] to be superseded by the Federal Act unless that was the clear and manifest purpose of Congress.'"

It is beyond serious dispute that under existing precedent §4-10 of the Illinois HMO Act "relates to" employee benefit plans within the meaning of §1144(a). The state law bears "indirectly but substantially on all insured benefit plans," by requiring them to submit to an extra layer of review for certain benefit denials if they purchase medical coverage from any of the common types of health care organizations covered by the state law's definition of HMO. As a law that "relates to" ERISA plans under §1144(a), §4-10 is saved from preemption only if it also "regulates insurance" under §1144(b)(2)(A). Rush insists that the Act is not such a law.

A

[The Court then concluded that Illinois HMO Act §4-10 was "saved" from preemption under §1144(b)(2)(A), since the law clearly addressed health insurance. In reaching this conclusion, the Court used a test that has since been overruled. The test applied in *Moran* was based on three factors, borrowed from the McCarran-Ferguson Act for deciding whether federal antitrust laws apply. In the *Miller* case, decided a year after *Moran* and excerpted above, the Court defined a new two-part test. Presently, this two-part test identifies those laws saved from preemption under ERISA §504(b)(2)(A), so we briefly excerpt it here.]

III

Given that §4-10 regulates insurance, ERISA's mandate that "nothing in this subchapter shall be construed to exempt or relieve any person from any law of any State which regulates insurance," 29 U.S.C. §1144(b)(2)(A), ostensibly forecloses preemption. Rush, however, does not give up. It argues for preemption anyway, emphasizing that the question is ultimately one of congressional intent, which sometimes is so clear that it overrides a statutory provision designed to save state law from being preempted.

> A state law that is "saved" under ERISA §514 nevertheless may be preempted under ERISA §502(a) (29 U.S.C. §1132(a)).

In ERISA law, we have recognized one example of this sort of overpowering federal policy in the civil enforcement provisions, 29 U.S.C. §1132(a), authorizing civil actions for six specific types of relief. In Massachusetts Mut. Life Ins. Co. v. Russell, 473 U.S. 134 (1985), we said those provisions amounted to an "interlocking, interrelated, and interdependent remedial scheme," which *Pilot Life* described as "represent[ing] a careful balancing of the need for prompt and fair claims settlement procedures against the public interest in encouraging the

Kentucky Association of Health Plans v. Miller
538 U.S. 329 (2003)

Opinion

Justice SCALIA delivered the opinion of the Court.

Kentucky law provides that "[a] health insurer shall not discriminate against any provider who is located within the geographic coverage area of the health benefit plan and who is willing to meet the terms and conditions for participation established by the health insurer, including the Kentucky state Medicaid program and Medicaid partnerships." Ky. Rev. Stat. Ann. §304.17A-270 (West 2001). Moreover, any "health benefit plan that includes chiropractic benefits shall . . . [p]ermit any licensed chiropractor who agrees to abide by the terms, conditions, reimbursement rates, and standards of quality of the health benefit plan to serve as a participating primary chiropractic provider to any person covered by the plan." §304.17A171(2). We granted certiorari to decide whether the Employee Retirement Income Security Act of 1974 (ERISA) pre-empts either, or both, of these "Any Willing Provider" (AWP) statutes. . . .

Today we make a clean break from the McCarran-Ferguson factors and hold that for a state law to be deemed a "law . . . which regulates insurance" under §1144(b)(2)(A), it must satisfy two requirements. First, the state law must be specifically directed toward entities engaged in insurance. . . . Second, as explained above, the state law must substantially affect the risk pooling arrangement between the insurer and the insured. Kentucky's law satisfies each of these requirements. . . .

QUESTION

How does the Kentucky AWP law "substantially affect the risk pooling arrangement"?

formation of employee benefit plans." So, we have held, the civil enforcement provisions are of such extraordinarily preemptive power that they override even the "well-pleaded complaint" rule for establishing the conditions under which a cause of action may be removed to a federal forum.

A

Although we have yet to encounter a forced choice between the congressional policies of exclusively federal remedies and the "reservation of the business of insurance to the States," we have anticipated such a conflict, with the state insurance regulation losing out if it allows plan participants "to obtain remedies . . . that Congress rejected in ERISA," *Pilot Life,* 107 S. Ct. 1549.

In *Pilot Life,* an ERISA plan participant who had been denied benefits sued in a state court on state tort and contract claims. He sought not merely damages for breach of contract, but also damages for emotional distress and punitive damages, both of which we had held unavailable under relevant ERISA provisions. We not only rejected the notion that these common law contract claims "regulat[ed] insurance," *Pilot Life,* 481 U.S., at 50-51, but went on to say that, regardless, Congress intended a "federal common law of rights and obligations" to develop under ERISA, without embellishment by independent state remedies. As in *AT & T,* we said the saving clause had to stop short of subverting congressional intent, clearly expressed "through the structure and legislative history[,] that the federal remedy . . . displace state causes of action."

Rush says that the day has come to turn dictum into holding by declaring that the state insurance regulation, §4-10, is preempted for creating just the kind of "alternative remedy" we disparaged in *Pilot Life*. As Rush sees it, the independent review procedure is a form of binding arbitration that allows an ERISA beneficiary to submit claims to a new decisionmaker to examine Rush's determination de novo, supplanting judicial review under the "arbitrary and capricious" standard ordinarily applied when discretionary plan interpretations are challenged. Firestone Tire & Rubber Co. v. Bruch, 489 U.S. 101 (1989). Rush says that the beneficiary's option falls within *Pilot Life*'s notion of a remedy that "supplement[s] or supplant[s]" the remedies available under ERISA.

We think, however, that Rush overstates the rule expressed in *Pilot Life*. The enquiry into state processes alleged to "supplemen[t] or supplan[t]" the federal scheme by allowing beneficiaries "to obtain remedies under state law that Congress rejected in ERISA," has, up to now, been far more straightforward than it is here. The first case touching on the point did not involve preemption at all; it arose from an ERISA beneficiary's reliance on ERISA's own enforcement scheme to claim a private right of action for types of damages beyond those expressly provided. We concluded that Congress had not intended causes of action under ERISA itself beyond those specified in §1132(a). Two years later we determined in Metropolitan Life Ins. Co. v. Taylor, *supra*, that Congress had so completely preempted the field of benefits law that an ostensibly state cause of action for benefits was necessarily a "creature of federal law" removable to federal court. *Russell* and *Taylor* naturally led to the holding in *Pilot Life* that ERISA would not tolerate a diversity action seeking monetary damages for breach generally and for consequential emotional distress, neither of which Congress had authorized in §1132(a). These monetary awards were claimed as remedies to be provided at the ultimate step of plan enforcement, and even if they could have been characterized as products of "insurance regulation," they would have significantly expanded the potential scope of ultimate liability imposed upon employers by the ERISA scheme.

> The text of 29 U.S.C. §1132(a) (ERISA §502(a)) is reproduced above. The provision outlines ERISA's enforcement mechanisms. Rush claimed that these mechanisms are exclusive and preempt any additional rights under state law.

Since *Pilot Life*, we have found only one other state law to "conflict" with §1132(a) in providing a prohibited alternative remedy. In Ingersoll-Rand Co. v. McClendon, 498 U.S. 133 (1990), we had no trouble finding that Texas's tort of wrongful discharge, turning on an employer's motivation to avoid paying pension benefits, conflicted with ERISA enforcement; while state law duplicated the elements of a claim available under ERISA, it converted the remedy from an equitable one under §1132(a)(3) (available exclusively in federal district courts) into a legal one for money damages (available in a state tribunal). Thus, *Ingersoll-Rand* fit within the category of state laws *Pilot Life* had held to be incompatible with ERISA's enforcement scheme; the law provided a form of ultimate relief in a judicial forum that added to the judicial remedies provided by ERISA. Any such provision patently violates ERISA's policy of inducing employers to offer benefits by assuring a predictable set of liabilities, under uniform standards of primary conduct and a uniform regime of ultimate remedial orders and awards when a violation has occurred.

> The plaintiff received what ERISA requires, the health benefit. Additional remedies, including consequential and punitive damages, are not at issue here.

But this case addresses a state regulatory scheme that provides no new cause of action under state law and authorizes no new form of ultimate relief. While independent review under §4-10 may well settle the fate of a benefit claim under a particular contract, the state statute does not enlarge the claim beyond the benefits available in any action brought under §1132(a). And although the reviewer's determination would presumably replace that of the HMO as to what is "medically necessary" under this contract, the relief ultimately available would still be what ERISA authorizes in a suit for benefits under §1132(a). This case therefore does not involve the sort of additional claim or remedy exemplified in *Pilot Life, Russell,* and *Ingersoll-Rand,* but instead bears a resemblance to the claims-procedure rule that we sustained in UNUM Life Ins. Co. of America v. Ward, 526 U.S. 358 (1999), holding that a state law barring enforcement of a policy's time limitation on submitting claims did not conflict with §1132(a), even though the state "rule of decision," could mean the difference between success and failure for a beneficiary. The procedure provided by §4-10 does not fall within *Pilot Life*'s categorical preemption.

B

Rush still argues for going beyond *Pilot Life,* making the preemption issue here one of degree, whether the state procedural imposition interferes unreasonably with Congress's intention to provide a uniform federal regime of "rights and obligations" under ERISA. However, "[s]uch disuniformities . . . are the inevitable result of the congressional decision to 'save' local insurance regulation." *Metropolitan Life,* 471 U.S., at 747. Although we have recognized a limited exception from the saving clause for alternative causes of action and alternative remedies in the sense described above, we have never indicated that there might be additional justifications for qualifying the clause's application. Rush's arguments today convince us that further limits on insurance regulation preserved by ERISA are unlikely to deserve recognition.

To be sure, a State might provide for a type of "review" that would so resemble an adjudication as to fall within *Pilot Life*'s categorical bar. Rush, and the dissent, contend that §4-10 fills that bill by imposing an alternative scheme of arbitral adjudication at odds with the manifest congressional purpose to confine adjudication of disputes to the courts. It does not turn out to be this simple, however, and a closer look at the state law reveals a scheme significantly different from common arbitration as a way of construing and applying contract terms.

In the classic sense, arbitration occurs when "parties in dispute choose a judge to render a final and binding decision on the merits of the controversy and on the basis of proofs presented by the parties." 1 I. MacNeil, R. Speidel, & T. Stipanowich, Federal Arbitration Law §2.1.1 (1995) (internal quotation marks omitted). Arbitrators typically hold hearings at which parties may submit evidence and conduct cross-examinations and are often invested with many powers over the dispute and the parties, including the power to subpoena witnesses and administer oaths.

> The Court characterizes the Illinois independent medical review statute as more like a second medical opinion than binding arbitration.

Section 4-10 does resemble an arbitration provision, then, to the extent that the independent reviewer considers disputes about the meaning of the HMO contract and receives "evidence" in the form of medical records, statements from physicians, and the like. But this is as far as the resemblance to arbitration goes, for the other features of review under

§4-10 give the proceeding a different character, one not at all at odds with the policy behind §1132(a). The Act does not give the independent reviewer a free-ranging power to construe contract terms, but instead, confines review to a single term: the phrase "medical necessity," used to define the services covered under the contract. This limitation, in turn, implicates a feature of HMO benefit determinations that we described in Pegram v. Herdrich, 530 U.S. 211 (2000). We explained that when an HMO guarantees medically necessary care, determinations of coverage "cannot be untangled from physicians' judgments about reasonable medical treatment." This is just how the Illinois Act operates; the independent examiner must be a physician with credentials similar to those of the primary care physician and is expected to exercise independent medical judgment in deciding what medical necessity requires. Accordingly, the reviewer in this case did not hold the kind of conventional evidentiary hearing common in arbitration, but simply received medical records submitted by the parties, and ultimately came to a professional judgment of his own.

Once this process is set in motion, it does not resemble either contract interpretation or evidentiary litigation before a neutral arbiter, as much as it looks like a practice (having nothing to do with arbitration) of obtaining another medical opinion. The reference to an independent reviewer is similar to the submission to a second physician, which many health insurers are required by law to provide before denying coverage.

The practice of obtaining a second opinion, however, is far removed from any notion of an enforcement scheme, and once §4-10 is seen as something akin to a mandate for second-opinion practice in order to ensure sound medical judgments, the preemption argument that arbitration under §4-10 supplants judicial enforcement runs out of steam.

[The Court next considered Rush's argument that §4-10's independent medical review provision was preempted by ERISA's standard of review for ERISA §502 claims. Although the ERISA statute does not specify a standard of review, the courts developed one, borrowing from the National Labor Relations Act, on which ERISA was modeled. The *Moran* Court declined to give the *Bruch* standard of review, excerpted above, preemptive effect.]

In sum, §4-10 imposes no new obligation or remedy like the causes of action considered in *Russell*, *Pilot Life*, and *Ingersoll-Rand*. Even in its formal guise, the State Act bears a closer resemblance to second-opinion requirements than to arbitration schemes. Deferential review in the HMO context is not a settled given; §4-10 operates before the stage of judicial review; the independent reviewer's de novo examination of the benefit claim mirrors the general or default rule we have ourselves recognized; and its effect is no greater than that of mandated-benefit regulation.

In deciding what to make of these facts and conclusions, it helps to go back to where we started and recall the ways States regulate insurance in looking out for the welfare of their citizens. Illinois has chosen to regulate insurance as one way to regulate the practice of medicine, which we have previously held to be permissible under ERISA. While the statute designed to do this undeniably eliminates whatever may have remained of a plan sponsor's option to minimize scrutiny of benefit denials, this effect of eliminating an insurer's autonomy to guarantee terms congenial to its own interests is the stuff of garden variety insurance regulation through the imposition of standard policy terms. It is therefore hard to imagine a

"Garden variety insurance regulation" survives preemption here.

Firestone Tire & Rubber Co. v. Bruch
489 U.S. 101 (1989)

Justice O'CONNOR delivered the opinion of the Court.

. . . .

Consistent with established principles of trust law, we hold that a denial of benefits challenged under §1132(a)(1)(B) is to be reviewed under a de novo standard unless the benefit plan gives the administrator or fiduciary discretionary authority to determine eligibility for benefits or to construe the terms of the plan. Because we do not rest our decision on the concern for impartiality that guided the Court of Appeals, at 143-146, we need not distinguish between types of plans or focus on the motivations of plan administrators and fiduciaries. Thus, for purposes of actions under §1132(a)(1)(B), the de novo standard of review applies regardless of whether the plan at issue is funded or unfunded and regardless of whether the administrator or fiduciary is operating under a possible or actual conflict of interest. Of course, if a benefit plan gives discretion to an administrator or fiduciary who is operating under a conflict of interest, that conflict must be weighed as a "facto[r] in determining whether there is an abuse of discretion." Restatement (Second) of Trusts §187, Comment d (1959).

QUESTIONS

Why is the standard of review even a question in section 502 cases? That is, aren't federal district courts simply resolving contract disputes between insurers and insureds, as the state court did in *Lubeznik*? After the *Bruch* decision, why might ERISA plan administrators be sure to grant themselves discretion to determine eligibility or construe terms of the plans? When would plan administrators not have a conflict of interest?

---

reservation of state power to regulate insurance that would not be meant to cover restrictions of the insurer's advantage in this kind of way. And any lingering doubt about the reasonableness of §4-10 in affecting the application of §1132(a) may be put to rest by recalling that regulating insurance tied to what is medically necessary is probably inseparable from enforcing the quintessentially state-law standards of reasonable medical care. *See* Pegram v. Herdrich, 530 U.S., at 236. "[I]n the field of health care, a subject of traditional state regulation, there is no ERISA preemption without clear manifestation of congressional purpose." To the extent that benefit litigation in some federal courts may have to account for the effects of §4-10, it would be an exaggeration to hold that the objectives of §1132(a) are undermined. The saving clause is entitled to prevail here, and we affirm the judgment.

It is so ordered.

Justice THOMAS, with whom THE CHIEF JUSTICE, Justice SCALIA, and Justice KENNEDY join, dissenting.

This Court has repeatedly recognized that ERISA's civil enforcement provision, §502 of the Employee Retirement Income Security Act of 1974 (ERISA), 29 U.S.C. §1132, provides the exclusive vehicle for actions asserting a claim for benefits under health plans governed by ERISA, and therefore that state laws that create additional remedies are pre-empted. Such exclusivity of remedies is necessary to further Con-

This is the classic justification for ERISA preemption.

gress' interest in establishing a uniform federal law of employee benefits so that employers are encouraged to provide benefits to their employees: "To require plan providers to design their programs in an environment of differing state regulations would complicate the administration of nationwide plans, producing inefficiencies that employers might offset with decreased benefits."

Of course, the "expectations that a federal common law of rights and obligations under ERISA-regulated plans would develop . . . would make little sense if the remedies available to ERISA participants and beneficiaries under §502(a) could be supplemented or supplanted by varying state laws." *Pilot Life, supra,* at 56. Therefore, as the Court concedes, even a state law that "regulates insurance" may be pre-empted if it supplements the remedies provided by ERISA, despite ERISA's saving clause, §514(b)(2)(A). Today, however, the Court takes the unprecedented step of allowing respondent Debra Moran to short circuit ERISA's remedial scheme by allowing her claim for benefits to be determined in the first instance through an arbitral-like procedure provided under Illinois law, and by a decisionmaker other than a court. This decision not only conflicts with our precedents, it also eviscerates the uniformity of ERISA remedies Congress deemed integral to the "careful balancing of the need for prompt and fair claims settlement procedures against the public interest in encouraging the formation of employee benefit plans." I would reverse the Court of Appeals' judgment and remand for a determination whether Moran was entitled to reimbursement absent the independent review conducted under §4-10. . . .

II

Section 514(a)'s broad language provides that ERISA "shall supersede any and all State laws insofar as they . . . relate to any employee benefit plan," except as provided in §514(b). 29 U.S.C. §1144(a). This language demonstrates "Congress's intent to establish the regulation of employee welfare benefit plans 'as exclusively a federal concern.'" It was intended to "ensure that plans and plan sponsors would be subject to a uniform body of benefits law" so as to "minimize the administrative and financial burden of complying with conflicting directives among States or between States and the Federal Government" and to prevent "the potential for conflict in substantive law . . . requiring the tailoring of plans and employer conduct to the peculiarities of the law of each jurisdiction." . . .

Consequently, the Court until today had consistently held that state laws that seek to supplant or add to the exclusive remedies in §502(a) of ERISA, 29 U.S.C. §1132(a), are pre-empted because they conflict with Congress' objective that rights under ERISA plans are to be enforced under a uniform national system. The Court has explained that §502(a) creates an "interlocking, interrelated, and interdependent remedial scheme," and that a beneficiary who claims that he was wrongfully denied benefits has "a panoply of remedial devices" at his disposal. It is exactly this enforcement scheme that *Pilot Life* described as "represent[ing] a careful balancing of the need for prompt and fair claims settlement procedures against the public interest in encouraging the formation of employee benefit plans." Central to that balance is the development of "a federal common law of rights and obligations under ERISA-regulated plans."

The dissent concludes that the Illinois independent review provision upsets ERISA's uniformity goal by providing an alternative "arbitral-like" procedure.

In addressing the relationship between ERISA's remedies under §502(a) and a state law regulating insurance, the Court has observed that "[t]he policy choices reflected in the inclusion of certain remedies and the exclusion of others under the federal scheme would be completely undermined if ERISA-plan participants

The Deemer Clause and Self-Insured Plans

As the Court notes, ERISA §514 establishes a shifting, perplexing preemption scheme. The "relate to" preemption language in section 514(a) is interpreted broadly to preempt virtually all state laws touching on employee-benefit plans. At the same time, it is hard to identify laws not "saved" from preemption as state law regulating insurance under section 514(b)(2)(A). Section 514(b)(2)(B) adds another wrinkle to the analysis, the so-called "deemer bubble" in which certain employee benefit plans are shielded from application of otherwise "saved" state laws.

Broadly speaking, ERISA health plans are divided into two categories, based on whether the employer retains the insurance risk. If the employer bears the risk, this is called a "self-insured" or "self-funded" plan. The employer contracts with an insurance company to provide administrative services, including claims review, provider contracting and network development, payment, collections, and other administrative functions. The Court has interpreted the deemer clause to preempt state regulation of these self-insured plans. *See* FMC Corp. v. Holliday, 498 U.S. 52 (1990); Metropolitan Life Ins. Co. v. Massachusetts, 471 U.S. 742 (1985). In the second category, the employer contracts with a health insurer to accept the insurance risk, along with providing all of the plan administration. The deemer clause does not affect state laws that apply to these fully insured (or purchased) plans.

This creates a three-tiered structure of federal and state regulation: Non-ERISA plans (small employers and individuals) are fully regulated by the state; insured ERISA plans are subject to some state laws, as interpreted by the Court's ERISA preemption analysis; and self-funded ERISA plans receive the greatest level of preemption, due to the deemer clause. These distinctions are especially important when a state mandates certain benefits, such as a minimum level of mental health care. Because of the strong desire for uniform federal regulation and avoidance of expensive state coverage mandates, ERISA creates a strong incentive for companies to self-insure, to the extent they are financially able to do so.

QUESTION

How would *Moran* be decided if it had concerned a self-insured ERISA plan?

---

and beneficiaries were free to obtain remedies under state law that Congress rejected in ERISA." Thus, while the preeminent federal interest in the uniform administration of employee benefit plans yields in some instances to varying state regulation of the business of insurance, the exclusivity and uniformity of ERISA's enforcement scheme remains [*sic*] paramount. "Congress intended §502(a) to be the exclusive remedy for rights guaranteed under ERISA." In accordance with ordinary principles of conflict pre-emption, therefore, even a state law "regulating insurance" will be preempted if it provides a separate vehicle to assert a claim for benefits outside of, or in addition to, ERISA's remedial scheme....

Section 4-10 constitutes an arbitral-like state remedy through which plan members may seek to resolve conclusively a disputed right to benefits. Some 40 other States have similar laws, though these vary as to applicability, procedures, standards, deadlines, and consequences of independent review. Allowing disparate state laws that provide inconsistent external review requirements to govern a participant's or beneficiary's claim to benefits under an employee benefit plan is wholly destructive of Congress' expressly stated goal of uniformity in this area. Moreover, it is inimical to a scheme for furthering and protecting the "careful balancing of the need for prompt and fair claims settlement procedures against the public interest in encouraging the formation of employee benefit plans," given that the development of a federal common law under ERISA-regulated plans has consistently been deemed central to that balance. While it is true that disuniformity is the inevitable result of the congressional decision to save local insurance regulation, this does not answer the altogether different question before the Court today, which is whether a state law "regulating insurance" nonetheless provides a separate vehicle to assert a claim for benefits outside of, or in addition to, ERISA's remedial scheme. If it does, the exclusivity and uniformity of ERISA's enforcement scheme must remain paramount and the state law is pre-empted in accordance with ordinary principles of conflict pre-emption.

For the reasons noted by the Court, independent review provisions may sound very appealing. Efforts to expand the variety of remedies available to aggrieved beneficiaries beyond those set forth in ERISA are obviously designed to increase the chances that patients will be able to receive treatments they desire, and most of us are naturally sympathetic to those suffering from illness who seek further options. Nevertheless, the Court would do well to remember that no employer is required to provide any health benefit plan under ERISA and that the entire advent of managed care, and the genesis of HMOs, stemmed from spiraling health costs. To the extent that independent review provisions such as §4-10 make it more likely that HMOs will have to subsidize beneficiaries' treatments of choice, they undermine the ability of HMOs to control costs, which, in turn, undermines the ability of employers to provide health care coverage for employees. As a consequence, independent review provisions could create a disincentive to the formation of employee health benefit plans, a problem that Congress addressed by making ERISA's remedial scheme exclusive and uniform. While it may well be the case that the advantages of allowing States to implement independent review requirements as a supplement to the remedies currently provided under ERISA outweigh this drawback, this is a judgment that, pursuant to ERISA, must be made by Congress. I respectfully dissent.

In addition to laws requiring external review of medical necessity decisions, many states regulate aggressive provider contracting by health insurers. In order to drive down provider prices, health insurers would bargain with competing providers (such as hospitals, physicians, and pharmacies). Some providers were excluded from the resulting networks of preferred providers for particular companies. In a testament to the political power of providers, many states passed "any willing provider" laws, which prohibited health insurers from excluding from their network any willing provider who would sign the standard form contract. As excerpted above, the Supreme Court upheld these laws in *Kentucky Ass'n of Health Plans v. Miller*, finding that although they "relate to" employee benefits plans, they are state laws regulating insurance under the savings clause.

PROBLEM

After *Miller* and *Moran*, would state coverage mandates, like the Georgia statute above, requiring coverage for emergency room care and off-formulary drugs be preempted by federal law? Could a state enact a statute defining the term "medical necessity" for purposes of health insurance plan coverage disputes?

ERISA preemption can apply beyond state health insurance statutes. In the next case, the target for ERISA §502(a) preemption is Texas tort law, in a case focused on managed care practices by health plans.

Aetna Health Inc. v. Davila

542 U.S. 200 (2004)

Justice THOMAS delivered the opinion of the Court.

In these consolidated cases, two individuals sued their respective health maintenance organizations (HMOs) for alleged failures to exercise ordinary care in the handling of coverage decisions, in violation of a duty imposed by the Texas Health Care Liability Act (THCLA), Tex. Civ. Prac. & Rem. Code Ann. §§88.001-88.003 (West 2004 Supp. Pamphlet). We granted certiorari to decide whether the individuals' causes of action are completely pre-empted by the "interlocking, interrelated, and interdependent remedial scheme," found at §502(a) of the Employee Retirement Income Security Act of 1974 (ERISA). We hold that the causes of action are completely pre-empted and hence removable from state to federal court. The Court of Appeals, having reached a contrary conclusion, is reversed.

I

A

Respondent Juan Davila is a participant, and respondent Ruby Calad is a beneficiary, in ERISA-regulated employee benefit plans. Their respective plan sponsors had entered into agreements with petitioners, Aetna Health Inc. and CIGNA HealthCare of Texas, Inc., to administer the plans. Under Davila's plan, for instance, Aetna reviews requests for coverage and pays providers, such as doctors, hospitals, and nursing homes, which perform covered services for members; under Calad's plan sponsor's agreement, CIGNA is responsible for plan benefits and coverage decisions.

Respondents both suffered injuries allegedly arising from Aetna's and CIGNA's decisions not to provide coverage for certain treatment and services recommended by respondents' treating physicians. Davila's treating physician prescribed Vioxx to remedy Davila's arthritis pain, but Aetna refused to pay for it. Davila did not appeal or contest this decision, nor did he purchase Vioxx with his own resources and seek reimbursement. Instead, Davila began taking Naprosyn, from which he allegedly suffered a severe reaction that required extensive treatment and hospitalization. Calad underwent surgery, and although her treating physician recommended an extended hospital stay, a CIGNA discharge nurse determined that Calad did not meet the plan's criteria for a continued hospital stay. CIGNA consequently denied coverage for the extended hospital stay. Calad experienced postsurgery complications forcing her to return to the hospital. She alleges that these complications would not have occurred had CIGNA approved coverage for a longer hospital stay.

> A few months after this opinion, Vioxx was withdrawn from the market as dangerous.

Respondents brought separate suits in Texas state court against petitioners. Invoking THCLA §88.002(a), respondents argued that petitioners' refusal to cover the requested services violated their "duty to exercise ordinary care when making health care treatment decisions," and that these refusals "proximately caused" their injuries. Ibid. Petitioners removed the cases to Federal District Courts, arguing that respondents' causes of action fit within the scope of, and were therefore completely pre-empted by, ERISA §502(a). The respective District Courts agreed, and declined to remand the cases to state court. Because respondents refused to amend their complaints to bring explicit ERISA claims, the District Courts dismissed the complaints with prejudice.

B

Both Davila and Calad appealed the refusals to remand to state court. The United States Court of Appeals for the Fifth Circuit consolidated their cases with several others raising similar issues. The Court of Appeals recognized that state causes of action that "duplicat[e] or fal[l] within the scope of an ERISA §502(a) remedy" are completely pre-empted and hence removable to federal court. After examining the causes of action available under §502(a), the Court of Appeals determined that respondents' claims could possibly fall under only two: §502(a)(1)(B), which provides a cause of action for the recovery of wrongfully denied benefits, and §502(a)(2), which allows suit against a plan fiduciary for breaches of fiduciary duty to the plan.

> In Pegram v. Herdrich, 530 U.S. 211 (2000), the Court decided that state law medical malpractice and fraud claims were not preempted by ERISA, at least when brought as a breach of fiduciary duty claim against a treating physician who was also a plan administrator.

Analyzing §502(a)(2) first, the Court of Appeals concluded that, under Pegram v. Herdrich, 530 U.S. 211 (2000), the decisions for which petitioners were being sued were "mixed eligibility and treatment decisions" and hence were not fiduciary in nature.[1] The Court of Appeals next determined that respondents' claims did not fall within §502(a)(1)(B)'s scope. It found significant that respondents "assert tort claims," while §502(a)(1)(B) "creates a cause of action for breach of contract," and also that respondents "are not seeking reimbursement for benefits denied them," but rather request "tort damages" arising from "an external, statutorily imposed duty of 'ordinary care.'" From Rush Prudential HMO, Inc. v. Moran, 536 U.S. 355 (2002), the Court of Appeals derived the principle that complete pre-emption is limited to situations in which "States . . . duplicate the causes of action listed in ERISA §502 (a)," and concluded that "[b]ecause the THCLA does not provide an action for collecting benefits," it fell outside the scope of §502(a)(1)(B). . . .

II

B

Congress enacted ERISA to "protect . . . the interests of participants in employee benefit plans and their beneficiaries" by setting out substantive regulatory

---

1. In this Court, petitioners do not claim or argue that respondents' causes of action fall under ERISA §502(a)(2). Because petitioners do not argue this point, and since we can resolve these cases entirely by reference to ERISA §502(a)(1)(B), we do not address ERISA §502(a)(2).

requirements for employee benefit plans and to "provid[e] for appropriate remedies, sanctions, and ready access to the Federal courts." 29 U.S.C. §1001(b). The purpose of ERISA is to provide a uniform regulatory regime over employee benefit plans. To this end, ERISA includes expansive pre-emption provisions, *see* ERISA §514, which are intended to ensure that employee benefit plan regulation would be "exclusively a federal concern."

ERISA's "comprehensive legislative scheme" includes "an integrated system of procedures for enforcement." This integrated enforcement mechanism, ERISA §502(a), is a distinctive feature of ERISA, and essential to accomplish Congress' purpose of creating a comprehensive statute for the regulation of employee benefit plans. As the Court said in Pilot Life Ins. Co. v. Dedeaux, 481 U.S. 41 (1987):

> [T]he detailed provisions of §502(a) set forth a comprehensive civil enforcement scheme that represents a careful balancing of the need for prompt and fair claims settlement procedures against the public interest in encouraging the formation of employee benefit plans. The policy choices reflected in the inclusion of certain remedies and the exclusion of others under the federal scheme would be completely undermined if ERISA-plan participants and beneficiaries were free to obtain remedies under state law that Congress rejected in ERISA. "The six carefully integrated civil enforcement provisions found in §502(a) of the statute as finally enacted . . . provide strong evidence that Congress did not intend to authorize other remedies that it simply forgot to incorporate expressly."

Therefore, any state-law cause of action that duplicates, supplements, or supplants the ERISA civil enforcement remedy conflicts with the clear congressional intent to make the ERISA remedy exclusive and is therefore pre-empted.

The pre-emptive force of ERISA §502(a) is still stronger. In Metropolitan Life Ins. Co. v. Taylor, 481 U.S. 58, 65-66 (1987), the Court determined that the similarity of the language used in the Labor Management Relations Act, 1947 (LMRA), and ERISA, combined with the "clear intention" of Congress "to make §502(a)(1)(B) suits brought by participants or beneficiaries federal questions for the purposes of federal court jurisdiction in like manner as §301 of the LMRA," established that ERISA §502(a)(1)(B)'s pre-emptive force mirrored the pre-emptive force of LMRA §301. Since LMRA §301 converts state causes of action into federal ones for purposes of determining the propriety of removal, so too does ERISA §502(a)(1)(B). Thus, the ERISA civil enforcement mechanism is one of those provisions with such "extraordinary pre-emptive power" that it "converts an ordinary state common law complaint into one stating a federal claim for purposes of the well-pleaded complaint rule. Hence, "causes of action within the scope of the civil enforcement provisions of §502(a) [are] removable to federal court."

Note that under ERISA §502's "complete" preemption, the plaintiff is no longer the master of her complaint with respect to the legal claim asserted or choice of venue.

III

A

ERISA §502(a)(1)(B) provides:

"A civil action may be brought — (1) by a participant or beneficiary — . . . (B) to recover benefits due to him under the terms of his plan, to enforce his rights under the terms of the plan, or to clarify his rights to future benefits under the terms of the plan."

This provision is relatively straightforward. If a participant or beneficiary believes that benefits promised to him under the terms of the plan are not provided, he can bring suit seeking provision of those benefits. A participant or beneficiary can also bring suit generically to "enforce his rights" under the plan, or to clarify any of his rights to future benefits. Any dispute over the precise terms of the plan is resolved by a court under a de novo review standard, unless the terms of the plan "giv[e] the administrator or fiduciary discretionary authority to determine eligibility for benefits or to construe the terms of the plan." Firestone Tire & Rubber Co. v. Bruch, 489 U.S. 101, 115 (1989).

It follows that if an individual brings suit complaining of a denial of coverage for medical care, where the individual is entitled to such coverage only because of the terms of an ERISA-regulated employee benefit plan, and where no legal duty (state or federal) independent of ERISA or the plan terms is violated, then the suit falls "within the scope of" ERISA §502(a)(1)(B). In other words, if an individual, at some point in time, could have brought his claim under ERISA §502(a)(1)(B), and where there is no other independent legal duty that is implicated by a defendant's actions, then the individual's cause of action is completely pre-empted by ERISA §502(a)(1)(B).

To determine whether respondents' causes of action fall "within the scope" of ERISA §502(a)(1)(B), we must examine respondents' complaints, the statute on which their claims are based (the THCLA), and the various plan documents. Davila alleges that Aetna provides health coverage under his employer's health benefits plan. Davila also alleges that after his primary care physician prescribed Vioxx, Aetna refused to pay for it. The only action complained of was Aetna's refusal to approve payment for Davila's Vioxx prescription. Further, the only relationship Aetna had with Davila was its partial administration of Davila's employer's benefit plan.

Similarly, Calad alleges that she receives, as her husband's beneficiary under an ERISA-regulated benefit plan, health coverage from CIGNA. She alleges that she was informed by CIGNA, upon admittance into a hospital for major surgery, that she would be authorized to stay for only one day. She also alleges that CIGNA, acting through a discharge nurse, refused to authorize more than a single day despite the advice and recommendation of her treating physician. Calad contests only CIGNA's decision to refuse coverage for her hospital stay. And, as in Davila's case, the only connection between Calad and CIGNA is CIGNA's administration of portions of Calad's ERISA-regulated benefit plan.

It is clear, then, that respondents complain only about denials of coverage promised under the terms of ERISA-regulated employee benefit plans. Upon the denial of benefits, respondents could have paid for the treatment themselves and then sought reimbursement through a §502(a)(1)(B) action, or sought a preliminary injunction.

Respondents contend, however, that the complained-of actions violate legal duties that arise independently of ERISA or the terms of the employee benefit plans at issue in these cases. Both respondents brought suit specifically under the THCLA, alleging that petitioners "controlled, influenced, participated in and made decisions which affected the quality of the diagnosis, care, and treatment provided" in a manner that violated "the duty of ordinary care set forth in §§88.001 and

88.002." Respondents contend that this duty of ordinary care is an independent legal duty. . . . Because this duty of ordinary care arises independently of any duty imposed by ERISA or the plan terms, the argument goes, any civil action to enforce this duty is not within the scope of the ERISA civil enforcement mechanism.

The duties imposed by the THCLA in the context of these cases, however, do not arise independently of ERISA or the plan terms. The THCLA does impose a duty on managed care entities to "exercise ordinary care when making health care treatment decisions," and makes them liable for damages proximately caused by failures to abide by that duty. §88.002(a). However, if a managed care entity correctly concluded that, under the terms of the relevant plan, a particular treatment was not covered, the managed care entity's denial of coverage would not be a proximate cause of any injuries arising from the denial. Rather, the failure of the plan itself to cover the requested treatment would be the proximate cause.[2] More significantly, the THCLA clearly states that "[t]he standards in Subsections (a) and (b) create no obligation on the part of the health insurance carrier, health maintenance organization, or other managed care entity to provide to an insured or enrollee treatment which is not covered by the health care plan of the entity." §88.002(d). Hence, a managed care entity could not be subject to liability under the THCLA if it denied coverage for any treatment not covered by the health care plan that it was administering.

> A private health insurance plan has no obligation outside the terms of the plan contract to cover any particular medical treatment.

Thus, interpretation of the terms of respondents' benefit plans forms an essential part of their THCLA claim, and THCLA liability would exist here only because of petitioners' administration of ERISA-regulated benefit plans. Petitioners' potential liability under the THCLA in these cases, then, derives entirely from the particular rights and obligations established by the benefit plans. . . .

Hence, respondents bring suit only to rectify a wrongful denial of benefits promised under ERISA-regulated plans, and do not attempt to remedy any violation of a legal duty independent of ERISA. We hold that respondents' state causes of action fall "within the scope of" ERISA §502(a)(1)(B), *Metropolitan Life*, 481 U.S., at 66, 107 S. Ct. 1542, and are therefore completely pre-empted by ERISA §502 and removable to federal district court.

B

The Court of Appeals came to a contrary conclusion for several reasons, all of them erroneous. First, the Court of Appeals found significant that respondents "assert a tort claim for tort damages" rather than "a contract claim for contract damages," and that respondents "are not seeking reimbursement for benefits denied them." But, distinguishing between pre-empted and non-pre-empted claims based on the particular label affixed to them would "elevate form over substance and allow parties to evade" the preemptive scope of ERISA simply "by relabeling their contract

> The fact that the Texas statute provides additional remedies and requires different proof to establish a claim proves, rather than disproves, that it is preempted by section 502.

---

2. To take a clear example, if the terms of the health care plan specifically exclude from coverage the cost of an appendectomy, then any injuries caused by the refusal to cover the appendectomy are properly attributed to the terms of the plan itself, not the managed care entity that applied those terms.

claims as claims for tortious breach of contract." Nor can the mere fact that the state cause of action attempts to authorize remedies beyond those authorized by ERISA §502(a) put the cause of action outside the scope of the ERISA civil enforcement mechanism. . . . The limited remedies available under ERISA are an inherent part of the "careful balancing" between ensuring fair and prompt enforcement of rights under a plan and the encouragement of the creation of such plans.

Second, the Court of Appeals believed that "the wording of [respondents'] plans is immaterial" to their claims, as "they invoke an external, statutorily imposed duty of 'ordinary care.'" But as we have already discussed, the wording of the plans is certainly material to their state causes of action, and the duty of "ordinary care" that the THCLA creates is not external to their rights under their respective plans.

Ultimately, the Court of Appeals rested its decision on one line from *Rush Prudential.* There, we described our holding in *Ingersoll-Rand* as follows: "[W]hile state law duplicated the elements of a claim available under ERISA, it converted the remedy from an equitable one under §1132(a)(3) (available exclusively in federal district courts) into a legal one for money damages (available in a state tribunal)." The point of this sentence was to describe why the state cause of action in *Ingersoll-Rand* was pre-empted by ERISA §502(a): It was pre-empted because it attempted to convert an equitable remedy into a legal remedy. Nowhere in *Rush Prudential* did we suggest that the pre-emptive force of ERISA §502(a) is limited to the situation in which a state cause of action precisely duplicates a cause of action under ERISA §502(a).

Nor would it be consistent with our precedent to conclude that only strictly duplicative state causes of action are pre-empted. Frequently, in order to receive exemplary damages on a state claim, a plaintiff must prove facts beyond the bare minimum necessary to establish entitlement to an award. . . . Congress' intent to make the ERISA civil enforcement mechanism exclusive would be undermined if state causes of action that supplement the ERISA §502(a) remedies were permitted, even if the elements of the state cause of action did not precisely duplicate the elements of an ERISA claim.

C

[The Court next concluded that even if the Texas statute were saved as a state law regulating insurance under ERISA §514, the preemptive effect of §502's exclusive remedial scheme trumps the §514 savings clause, as noted similarly in *Moran.*]

IV

Respondents, their amici, and some Courts of Appeals have relied heavily upon Pegram v. Herdrich, 530 U.S. 211 (2000), in arguing that ERISA does not pre-empt or completely pre-empt state suits such as respondents'. They contend that *Pegram* makes it clear that causes of action such as respondents' do not "relate to [an] employee benefit plan," ERISA §514(a), and hence are not pre-empted.

Pegram cannot be read so broadly. In *Pegram,* the plaintiff sued her physician-owned-and-operated HMO (which provided medical coverage through plaintiff's employer pursuant to an ERISA-regulated benefit plan) and her treating physician, both for medical malpractice and for a breach of an ERISA fiduciary duty. The plaintiff's treating physician was also the person charged with administering plaintiff's benefits; it was she who decided whether certain treatments were covered. We reasoned that the physician's "eligibility decision and the treatment decision were inextricably mixed." We concluded that "Congress did not intend [the defendant HMO] or any other HMO to be treated as a fiduciary to the extent that it makes mixed eligibility decisions acting through its physicians."

A benefit determination under ERISA, though, is generally a fiduciary act. "At common law, fiduciary duties characteristically attach to decisions about managing assets and distributing property to beneficiaries." Hence, a benefit determination is part and parcel of the ordinary fiduciary responsibilities connected to the administration of a plan. The fact that a benefits determination is infused with medical judgments does not alter this result.

Pegram itself recognized this principle. Pegram, in highlighting its conclusion that "mixed eligibility decisions" were not fiduciary in nature, contrasted the operation of "[t]raditional trustees administer[ing] a medical trust" and "physicians through whom HMOs act." A traditional medical trust is administered by "paying out money to buy medical care, whereas physicians making mixed eligibility decisions consume the money as well." And, significantly, the Court stated that "[p]rivate trustees do not make treatment judgments." But a trustee managing a medical trust undoubtedly must make administrative decisions that require the exercise of medical judgment. Petitioners are not the employers of respondents' treating physicians and are therefore in a somewhat analogous position to that of a trustee for a traditional medical trust. . . .

Classifying any entity with discretionary authority over benefits determinations as anything but a plan fiduciary would thus conflict with ERISA's statutory and regulatory scheme.

> For a time, the decision in *Pegram*, allowing a state law medical malpractice claim to go forward, free from ERISA preemption, appeared to open the door to tort-like claims, such as the one provided in the Texas statute. The *Davila* Court, however, severely clipped *Pegram*'s wings, limiting the holding to a special breed of physician-owned and - operated HMO.

Since administrators making benefits determinations, even determinations based extensively on medical judgments, are ordinarily acting as plan fiduciaries, it was essential to *Pegram*'s conclusion that the decisions challenged there were truly "mixed eligibility and treatment decisions," 530 U.S., at 229, 120 S. Ct. 2143, i.e., medical necessity decisions made by the plaintiff's treating physician qua treating physician and qua benefits administrator. Put another way, the reasoning of *Pegram* "only make[s] sense where the underlying negligence also plausibly constitutes medical maltreatment by a party who can be deemed to be a treating physician or such a physician's employer." Here, however, petitioners are neither respondents' treating physicians nor the employers of respondents' treating physicians. Petitioners' coverage decisions, then, are pure eligibility decisions, and *Pegram* is not implicated.

V

We hold that respondents' causes of action, brought to remedy only the denial of benefits under ERISA-regulated benefit plans, fall within the scope of, and are completely pre-empted by, ERISA §502(a)(1)(B), and thus removable to federal district court. The judgment of the Court of Appeals is reversed, and the cases are remanded for further proceedings consistent with this opinion.

It is so ordered.

[Justice Ginsburg and Justice Breyer concurred, writing separately to emphasize that the "equitable relief" allowable under section 502(a)(3) could be construed more broadly to allow some forms of "make-whole" relief, in light of the general availability of such relief in equity and under "core principles of trust remedy law."]

PROBLEM

Consider how the claim in *Davila* might proceed under state common law, if the Texas tort statute had not been enacted. Would there be a medical malpractice claim against the plan administrator? A breach of contract claim? Would denial of coverage constitute fraud? Do plan administrators owe fiduciary duties to plan participants with respect to benefits? What damages would be available to a successful plaintiff in any of those cases?

3. SUBSTANTIVE FEDERAL REGULATION OF EMPLOYER-SPONSORED HEALTH PLANS

After more than two dozen Supreme Court decisions on ERISA, the substantive regulation of health insurance was a patchwork quilt of federal rules applying to some aspects of health insurance in addition to existing state insurance laws, some of which were preempted. Even within states, the availability of substantive consumer and provider protections varied dramatically with the plan's status under ERISA. Under the ACA, many of these issues have now been resolved as a matter of federal law. While ERISA was not modified, and specific ERISA cases were not overruled, many of the substantive rules for private health insurance markets have now changed under federal law, effectively bypassing many of the ERISA preemption rulings.

One of the most important packages of new substantive regulation of the health insurance market effectively homogenized the national risk pool, moving decisively away from pricing health insurance based on the individual's risks and toward pricing based on the average risk to all Americans. Unlike auto insurance, where driving record alters an individual's premium, the ACA in many ways insulates individuals from the cost of having been unhealthy. Under the guaranteed issue rule, health insurers cannot turn an individual down due to his or her age or health status. The impact of those reforms is most dramatic in the individual health insurance market, discussed in the next part of this chapter. Some of those protections, however, already existed in the employer-based group insurance market since 1996, when HIPAA was passed.

Better known for its privacy provisions (discussed in Chapter 10), HIPAA also contained important protections for employees insured through group health plans. In particular, HIPAA sought to address concerns over "job lock," meaning that employees, especially those with serious or chronic health conditions, would be reluctant to take advantage of new job opportunities out of fear of losing health insurance coverage. HIPAA, operating effectively as an amendment to ERISA, imposed a number of specific requirements on group health insurers, some of which are discussed after the following principal case.

The case pre-dates HIPAA and the ACA, and arises under a different ERISA provision, but offers perspective on the types of common discriminatory practices that prompted congressional response.

McGann v. H & H Music Co.

946 F.2d 401 (5th Cir. 1991)

Opinion

GARWOOD, Circuit Judge:

Plaintiff-appellant John McGann (McGann) filed this suit under section 510 of the Employee Retirement Income Security Act of 1974 (ERISA), against defendants-appellees H & H Music Company (H & H Music), Brook Mays Music Company (Brook Mays) and General American Life Insurance Company (General American) (collectively defendants) claiming that they discriminated against McGann, an employee of H & H Music, by reducing benefits available to H & H Music's group medical plan beneficiaries for treatment for acquired immune deficiency syndrome (AIDS) and related illnesses. The district court granted defendants' motion for summary judgment on the ground that an employer has an absolute right to alter the terms of medical coverage available to plan beneficiaries. We affirm.

FACTS AND PROCEEDINGS BELOW

McGann, an employee of H & H Music, discovered that he was afflicted with AIDS in December 1987. Soon thereafter, McGann submitted his first claims for reimbursement under H & H Music's group medical plan, provided through Brook Mays, the plan administrator, and issued by General American, the plan insurer, and informed his employer that he had AIDS. McGann met with officials of H & H Music in March 1988, at which time they discussed McGann's illness. Before the change in the terms of the plan, it provided for lifetime medical benefits of up to $1,000,000 to all employees.

In July 1988, H & H Music informed its employees that, effective August 1, 1988, changes would be made in their medical coverage. These changes included, but were not limited to, limitation of benefits payable for AIDS-related claims to a lifetime maximum of $5,000. No limitation was placed on any other catastrophic illness. H & H Music became self-insured under the new plan and General American became the plan's administrator. By January 1990, McGann had exhausted the $5,000 limit on coverage for his illness.

> A lifetime benefit cap reduces plan expenses for the entire group, but leaves employees exposed to financial ruin if the cap is exceeded. Here, the company reduced the cap from $1,000,000 to $5,000 for AIDS.

In August 1989, McGann sued H & H Music, Brook Mays and General American under section 510 of ERISA, which provides, in part, as follows:

"It shall be unlawful for any person to discharge, fine, suspend, expel, discipline, or discriminate against a participant or beneficiary for exercising any right to which he is entitled under the provisions of an employee benefit plan, . . . or for the purpose of interfering with the attainment of any right to which such participant may become entitled under the plan. . . ." 29 U.S.C. §1140.

McGann claimed that defendants discriminated against him in violation of both prohibitions of section 510. He claimed that the provision limiting coverage for

AIDS-related expenses was directed specifically at him in retaliation for exercising his rights under the medical plan and for the purpose of interfering with his attainment of a right to which he may become entitled under the plan.

Defendants, conceding the factual allegations of McGann's complaint, moved for summary judgment. These factual allegations include no assertion that the reduction of AIDS benefits was intended to deny benefits to McGann for any reason which would not be applicable to other beneficiaries who might then or thereafter have AIDS, but rather that the reduction was prompted by the knowledge of McGann's illness, and that McGann was the only beneficiary then known to have AIDS. On June 26, 1990, the district court granted defendants' motion on the ground that they had an absolute right to alter the terms of the plan, regardless of their intent in making the alterations. The district court also held that even if the issue of discriminatory motive were relevant, summary judgment would still be proper because the defendants' motive was to ensure the future existence of the plan and not specifically to retaliate against McGann or to interfere with his exercise of future rights under the plan.

DISCUSSION

McGann contends that defendants violated both clauses of section 510 by discriminating against him for two purposes: (1) "for exercising any right to which [the beneficiary] is entitled," and (2) "for the purpose of interfering with the attainment of any right to which such participant may become entitled." In order to preclude summary judgment in defendants' favor, McGann must make a showing sufficient to establish the existence of a genuine issue of material fact with respect to each material element on which he would carry the burden of proof at trial. . . .

> Since ERISA preempts contrary state law, the plaintiff proceeded solely under ERISA.

Although we assume there was a connection between the benefits reduction and either McGann's filing of claims or his revelations about his illness, there is nothing in the record to suggest that defendants' motivation was other than as they asserted, namely to avoid the expense of paying for AIDS treatment (if not, indeed, also for other treatment), no more for McGann than for any other present or future plan beneficiary who might suffer from AIDS. McGann concedes that the reduction in AIDS benefits will apply equally to all employees filing AIDS-related claims and that the effect of the reduction will not necessarily be felt only by him. He fails to allege that the coverage reduction was otherwise specifically intended to deny him particularly medical coverage except "in effect." He does not challenge defendants' assertion that their purpose in reducing AIDS benefits was to reduce costs.

Furthermore, McGann has failed to adduce evidence of the existence of "any right to which [he] may become entitled under the plan." The right referred to in the second clause of section 510 is not simply any right to which an employee may conceivably become entitled, but rather any right to which an employee may become entitled pursuant to an existing, enforceable obligation assumed by the employer. "Congress viewed [section 510] as a crucial part of ERISA because, without it, employers would be able to circumvent the provision of promised benefits."

McGann's allegations show no promised benefit, for there is nothing to indicate that defendants ever promised that the $1,000,000 coverage limit was permanent. The H & H Music plan expressly provides: "Termination or Amendment of Plan: The Plan Sponsor may terminate or amend the Plan at any time or terminate any benefit under the Plan at any time." There is no allegation or evidence that any oral or written representations were made to McGann that the $1,000,000 coverage limit would never be lowered. Defendants broke no promise to McGann. The continued availability of the $1,000,000 limit was not a right to which McGann may have become entitled for the purposes of section 510. To adopt McGann's contrary construction of this portion of section 510 would mean that an employer could not effectively reserve the right to amend a medical plan to reduce benefits respecting subsequently incurred medical expenses, as H & H Music did here, because such an amendment would obviously have as a purpose preventing participants from attaining the right to such future benefits as they otherwise might do under the existing plan absent the amendment. But this is plainly not the law, and ERISA does not require such "vesting" of the right to a continued level of the same medical benefits once those are ever included in a welfare plan.

McGann appears to contend that the reduction in AIDS benefits alone supports an inference of specific intent to retaliate against him or to interfere with his future exercise of rights under the plan. McGann characterizes as evidence of an individualized intent to discriminate the fact that AIDS was the only catastrophic illness to which the $5,000 limit was applied and the fact that McGann was the only employee known to have AIDS. He contends that if defendants reduced AIDS coverage because they learned of McGann's illness through his exercising of his rights under the plan by filing claims, the coverage reduction therefore could be "retaliation" for McGann's filing of the claims. Under McGann's theory, any reduction in employee benefits would be impermissibly discriminatory if motivated by a desire to avoid the anticipated costs of continuing to provide coverage for a particular beneficiary. McGann would find an implied promise not to discriminate for this purpose; it is the breaking of this promise that McGann appears to contend constitutes interference with a future entitlement. . . .

> Despite the employer's clear intent to exclude McGann, ERISA did not provide a remedy.

The Supreme Court has observed in dictum: "ERISA does not mandate that employers provide any particular benefits, and does not itself proscribe discrimination in the provision of employee benefits." Shaw v. Delta Air Lines, Inc., 463 U.S. 85, 103 S. Ct. 2890, 2897, 77 L. Ed. 2d 490 (1983) [additional citations to various circuit court opinions omitted]. To interpret "discrimination" broadly to include defendants' conduct would clearly conflict with Congress's intent that employers remain free to create, modify and terminate the terms and conditions of employee benefits plans without governmental interference. . . .

McGann's claim cannot be reconciled with the well-settled principle that Congress did not intend that ERISA circumscribe employers' control over the content of benefits plans they offered to their employees. McGann interprets section 510 to prevent an employer from reducing or eliminating coverage for a particular illness in response to the escalating costs of covering an employee suffering from that illness. Such an interpretation would, in effect, change the terms of H & H Music's plan. Instead of making the $1,000,000 limit available for medical expenses on an as-incurred basis only as long as the limit remained in effect, the policy would make the limit permanently available for all medical expenses as they might thereafter be incurred because of a single event, such as the contracting of AIDS. Under McGann's theory, defendants would be effectively proscribed from reducing coverage for AIDS once McGann had contracted that illness and filed claims for AIDS-related expenses. If a federal court could prevent an employer from reducing an employee's coverage limits for AIDS treatment once that employee contracted AIDS, the boundaries of judicial involvement in the creation, alteration or termination of ERISA plans would be sorely tested.

As noted, McGann has failed to adduce any evidence of defendants' specific intent to engage in conduct proscribed by section 510. A party against whom summary judgment is ordered cannot raise a fact issue simply by stating a cause of action where defendants' state of mind is a material element. "'There must be some indication that he can produce the requisite quantum of evidence to enable him to reach the jury with his claim.'"

Proof of defendants' specific intent to discriminate among plan beneficiaries on grounds not proscribed by section 510 does not enable McGann to avoid summary judgment. ERISA does not broadly prevent an employer from "discriminating" in the creation, alteration or termination of employee benefits plans; thus, evidence of such intentional discrimination cannot alone sustain a claim under section 510. That section does not prohibit welfare plan discrimination between or among categories of diseases. Section 510 does not mandate that if some, or most, or virtually all catastrophic illnesses are covered, AIDS (or any other particular catastrophic illness) must be among them. It does not prohibit an employer from electing not to cover or continue to cover AIDS, while covering or continuing to cover other catastrophic illnesses, even though the employer's decision in this respect may stem from some "prejudice" against AIDS or its victims generally. The same, of course, is true of any other disease and its victims. That sort of "discrimination" is simply not addressed by section 510. Under section 510, the asserted discrimination is illegal only if it is motivated by a desire to retaliate against an employee or to deprive an employee of an existing right to which he may become entitled. The district court's decision to grant summary judgment to defendants therefore was proper. Its judgment is accordingly

AFFIRMED.

> "ERISA does not broadly prevent an employer from 'discriminating' in the creation, alteration or termination of employee benefits plans; thus, evidence of such intentional discrimination cannot alone sustain a claim under section 510."

PROBLEM

As you read the 1996 HIPAA provisions below, consider the following variation on the facts of *McGann*: Suppose that McGann left employment with H&H Music and took a new, full-time position with Amazon's music department in 2018. Amazon also offers employer-sponsored health insurance. Could Amazon deny coverage to McGann based on his preexisting condition? Could Amazon exclude all employees with AIDS from health insurance coverage? Could it impose a $5,000 lifetime cap on expenses for employees diagnosed with AIDS?

29 U.S.C. §1181. Increased portability through limitation on preexisting condition exclusions

(a) Limitation on preexisting condition exclusion period; crediting for periods of previous coverage

Subject to subsection (d) of this section, a group health plan, and a health insurance issuer offering group health

> HIPAA defines various forms of "creditable coverage" for purposes of the waiting period on new coverage.

insurance coverage, may, with respect to a participant or beneficiary, impose a preexisting condition exclusion only if —

(1) such exclusion relates to a condition (whether physical or mental), regardless of the cause of the condition, for which medical advice, diagnosis, care, or treatment was recommended or received within the 6-month period ending on the enrollment date;

(2) such exclusion extends for a period of not more than 12 months (or 18 months in the case of a late enrollee) after the enrollment date; and

(3) the period of any such preexisting condition exclusion is reduced by the aggregate of the periods of creditable coverage (if any, as defined in subsection (c)(1) of this section) applicable to the participant or beneficiary as of the enrollment date.

(b) Definitions

For purposes of this part —

(1) Preexisting condition exclusion

(A) In general

The term "preexisting condition exclusion" means, with respect to coverage, a limitation or exclusion of benefits relating to a condition based on the fact that the condition was present before the date of enrollment for such coverage, whether or not any medical advice, diagnosis, care, or treatment was recommended or received before such date.

QUESTION

What is the effect of a preexisting condition that dates more than six months before coverage is sought?

29 U.S.C. §1182. Prohibiting discrimination against individual participants and beneficiaries based on health status

(a) In eligibility to enroll

(1) In general

Subject to paragraph (2), a group health plan, and a health insurance issuer offering group health insurance coverage in connection with a group health plan, may not establish rules for eligibility (including continued eligibility) of any individual to enroll under the terms of the plan based on any of the following health status-related factors in relation to the individual or a dependent of the individual:

(A) Health status.

(B) Medical condition (including both physical and mental illnesses).

(C) Claims experience.

(D) Receipt of health care.

(E) Medical history.

(F) Genetic information.

(G) Evidence of insurability (including conditions arising out of acts of domestic violence).

(H) Disability.

(2) No application to benefits or exclusions

Under this provision, an insurer may still consider the overall risk profile of the group when pricing the plan but may not charge higher rates to any individual members of the group based on these factors.

To the extent consistent with section 1181 of this title, paragraph (1) shall not be construed—

    (A) to require a group health plan, or group health insurance coverage, to provide particular benefits other than those provided under the terms of such plan or coverage, or

    (B) to prevent such a plan or coverage from establishing limitations or restrictions on the amount, level, extent, or nature of the benefits or coverage for similarly situated individuals enrolled in the plan or coverage.

(3) Construction

For purposes of paragraph (1), rules for eligibility to enroll under a plan include rules defining any applicable waiting periods for such enrollment.

(b) In premium contributions

    (1) In general

A group health plan, and a health insurance issuer offering health insurance coverage in connection with a group health plan, may not require any individual (as a condition of enrollment or continued enrollment under the plan) to pay a premium or contribution which is greater than such premium or contribution for a similarly situated individual enrolled in the plan on the basis of any health status-related factor in relation to the individual or to an individual enrolled under the plan as a dependent of the individual.

HIPAA did not squarely address the problem at issue in *H&H Music*, namely, lifetime monetary caps on the dollar-value of coverage. The later-enacted ACA prohibits both lifetime and annual caps on benefits on almost all private health plans, including employer-sponsored plans.

29 C.F.R. §2590.715-2711. No lifetime or annual limits

(a) Prohibition—

    (1) Lifetime limits. Except as provided in paragraph (b) of this section, a group health plan, or a health insurance issuer offering group health insurance coverage, may not establish any lifetime limit on the dollar amount of benefits for any individual.

    (2) Annual limits—

        (i) General rule. Except as provided in paragraphs (a)(2)(ii), (b), and (d) of this section, a group health plan, or a health insurance issuer offering group health insurance coverage, may not establish any annual limit on the dollar amount of benefits for any individual. . . .

(b) Construction—

    (1) Permissible limits on specific covered benefits. The rules of this section do not prevent a group health plan, or a health insurance issuer offering group health insurance coverage, from placing annual or lifetime dollar limits with respect to any individual on specific covered benefits that are not essential health benefits to the extent that such limits are otherwise permitted under applicable Federal or State law. (The scope of essential health benefits is addressed in paragraph (c) of this section). . . .

(c) Definition of essential health benefits. The term "essential health benefits" means essential health benefits under section 1302(b) [discussed in the next part of this chapter] of the Patient Protection and Affordable Care Act and applicable regulations.

The ACA's prohibition on lifetime and annual limits is just one of many federal regulations applicable to both employer-sponsored and individual, private market health plans. With the passage of the ACA, Congress largely filled the regulatory void left by ERISA preemption of state law with a comprehensive body of federal laws applicable to employer-sponsored as well as other private insurance plans. It is fair to say that primary authority for regulating the health insurance market shifted from the states to the federal government. Despite the federal power, the ACA, by design, relies heavily on state expertise and infrastructure in insurance market regulation and seeks, through various strategies, to enlist states as partners in implementing the broad federal scheme. As you have already learned with respect to Medicaid expansion, states' willingness to assist in implementing comprehensive federal health care reform is by no means consistent.

PROBLEM

On October 12, 2017, President Trump issued Executive Order 13813, encouraging federal authorities to expand access to various alternative health insurance options, including short-term plans, health reimbursement arrangements, and association health plans (AHPs). Association health plans typically are formed by business and employer trade associations, such as chambers of commerce, farm bureaus, or trade groups. With respect to AHPs, the Department of Labor responded to the Executive Order with a proposed rule expanding ERISA's definition of "employer" to allow more AHPs to fall under it. Using your knowledge of ERISA and employer-sponsored plan regulation, write a 600-word comment to the proposed rulemaking, supporting or opposing the proposed definition change, explaining the effects that you anticipate it would have on health plans.

D. INDIVIDUAL AND SMALL-GROUP MARKETS

The ACA's private insurance market reforms most dramatically impacted the individual and small-group markets. ERISA preemption and HIPAA portability rules both protected employer-sponsored health plans from state regulation and provided substantive rules, such as requiring community rating within the group and limiting the duration of preexisting condition exclusions. The ACA extended, expanded, and harmonized those consumer protections across all types of health insurance markets: First, the statute outright prohibits exclusions based on preexisting conditions. Second, it largely prohibits experience rating (meaning premium rates based on individual risk profiles), subject to a few limited exceptions, discussed below.

In addition to those nationwide underwriting and ratemaking reforms, the ACA attempted to address a number of flaws in the individual and small-group health insurance market. One of the reforms, also modeled on the Massachusetts state health care reform plan, was the creation of health insurance Exchanges (also called Marketplaces, due to the difficulty of translating the word Exchanges into Spanish). Exchanges are highly regulated online portals for individual consumers to shop for health insurance. Plans sold on the Exchanges must comply with a number of federal requirements intended to protect and inform consumers. The

Exchanges also operate as application sites and data hubs to verify income and employment, citizenship status, and other eligibility criteria for public health insurance programs and federal financial assistance.

Under the ACA, plans sold on the private health insurance Exchanges are labelled according to four "metallic" tiers: bronze, silver, gold, and platinum. Each tier signifies a different ratio of expenses that the insurer covers compared to costs that the insured pays out of pocket in terms of deductibles, copayments, and coinsurance. Premium assistance tax credits are available regardless which tier of coverage the customer chooses, but the amount of the credit is calculated based on the silver plan costs.

More precisely, Exchange plans are graded based on "actuarial value," which refers to the percentage of total average costs for covered benefits that a plan will cover. For example, if a plan has an actuarial value of 70 percent, on average, the insured will be responsible for 30 percent of the costs of all covered benefits. Bronze plans have 60 percent actuarial value; silver plans have 70 percent actuarial value; gold plans have 80 percent; and platinum plans have 90 percent. Higher actuarial value plans have higher premiums and lower out-of-pocket costs. Because actuarial value is based on average costs, any one customer's actual experience may vary from those percentages. The purpose of the metallic tiers is to help consumers compare plans sold on the Exchanges, recognizing consumer difficulty in understanding actuarial equivalence.

1. COVERAGE THROUGH THE EXCHANGES

The following case discusses how several critical provisions of the ACA fit together with the overall statutory design for near-universal coverage, especially in the non-group, private market. The plaintiffs brought this case hoping to unravel a key component of the ACA. If they had been successful, millions of Americans would have found that health insurance was unaffordable because they would have lost federal tax credit subsidies for purchasing private insurance.

King v. Burwell

135 S. Ct. 2480 (2015)

Chief Justice ROBERTS delivered the opinion of the Court.

The Patient Protection and Affordable Care Act adopts a series of interlocking reforms designed to expand coverage in the individual health insurance market. First, the Act bars insurers from taking a person's health into account when deciding whether to sell health insurance or how much to charge. Second, the Act generally requires each person to maintain insurance coverage or make a payment to the Internal Revenue Service. And third, the Act gives tax credits to certain people to make insurance more affordable.

In addition to those reforms, the Act requires the creation of an "Exchange" in each State—basically, a marketplace that allows people to compare and purchase insurance plans. The Act gives each State the opportunity to establish its own Exchange, but provides that the Federal Government will establish the Exchange if the State does not.

This case is about whether the Act's interlocking reforms apply equally in each State no matter who establishes the State's Exchange. Specifically, the question presented is whether the Act's tax credits are available in States that have a Federal Exchange.

I

A

The Patient Protection and Affordable Care Act grew out of a long history of failed health insurance reform. In the 1990s, several States began experimenting with ways to expand people's access to coverage. One common approach was to impose a pair of insurance market regulations—a "guaranteed issue" requirement, which barred insurers from denying coverage to any person because of his health, and a "community rating" requirement, which barred insurers from charging a person higher premiums for the same reason. Together, those requirements were designed to ensure that anyone who wanted to buy health insurance could do so.

The guaranteed issue and community rating requirements achieved that goal, but they had an unintended consequence: They encouraged people to wait until they got sick to buy insurance. Why buy insurance coverage when you are healthy, if you can buy the same coverage for the same price when you become ill? This consequence—known as "adverse selection"—led to a second: Insurers were forced to increase premiums to account for the fact that, more and more, it was the sick rather than the healthy who were buying insurance. And that consequence fed back into the first: As the cost of insurance rose, even more people waited until they became ill to buy it.

This led to an economic "death spiral." As premiums rose higher and higher, and the number of people buying insurance sank lower and lower, insurers began to leave the market entirely. As a result, the number of people without insurance increased dramatically.

This cycle happened repeatedly during the 1990s. For example, in 1993, the State of Washington reformed its individual insurance market by adopting the guaranteed issue and community rating requirements. Over the next three years, premiums rose by 78 percent and the number of people enrolled fell by 25 percent. By 1999, 17 of the State's 19 private insurers had left the market, and the remaining two had announced their intention to do so.

> As discussed in Chapter 1, adverse selection and the death spiral were concepts pioneered by Kenneth Arrow in 1963.

For another example, also in 1993, New York adopted the guaranteed issue and community rating requirements. Over the next few years, some major insurers in the individual market raised premiums by roughly 40 percent. By 1996, these reforms had "effectively eliminated the commercial individual indemnity market in New York with the largest individual health insurer exiting the market."

In 1996, Massachusetts adopted the guaranteed issue and community rating requirements and experienced similar results. But in 2006, Massachusetts added two more reforms: The Commonwealth required individuals to buy insurance or pay a penalty, and it gave tax credits to certain individuals to ensure that they could afford the insurance they were required to buy. The combination of these three reforms—insurance market regulations, a coverage mandate, and tax credits—reduced the uninsured rate in Massachusetts to 2.6 percent, by far the lowest in the Nation.

B

The Affordable Care Act adopts a version of the three key reforms that made the Massachusetts system successful. First, the Act adopts the guaranteed issue and community rating requirements. The Act provides that "each health insurance issuer that offers health insurance coverage in the individual . . . market in a State must accept every . . . individual in the State that applies for such coverage." The Act also bars insurers from charging higher premiums on the basis of a person's health.

Second, the Act generally requires individuals to maintain health insurance coverage or make a payment to the IRS. Congress recognized that, without an incentive, "many individuals would wait to purchase health insurance until they needed care." So Congress adopted a coverage requirement to "minimize this adverse selection and broaden the health insurance risk pool to include healthy individuals, which will lower health insurance premiums." In Congress's view, that coverage requirement was "essential to creating effective health insurance markets." Congress also provided an exemption from the coverage requirement for anyone who has to spend more than eight percent of his income on health insurance.

Third, the Act seeks to make insurance more affordable by giving refundable tax credits to individuals with household incomes between 100 percent and 400 percent of the federal poverty line. §36B. Individuals who meet the Act's requirements may purchase insurance with the tax credits, which are provided in advance directly to the individual's insurer.

These three reforms are closely intertwined. As noted, Congress found that the guaranteed issue and community rating requirements would not work without the coverage requirement. And the coverage requirement would not work without the tax credits. The reason is that, without the tax credits, the cost of buying insurance would exceed eight percent of income for a large number of individuals, which would exempt them from the coverage requirement. Given the relationship between these three reforms, the Act provided that they should take effect on the same day—January 1, 2014.

> The *King* opinion accurately describes the key components of the ACA's strategy for expanding coverage in the individual and small-group market, the so-called "three-legged stool," suggesting that removal of any one of the components would cause the whole thing to collapse.

C

In addition to those three reforms, the Act requires the creation of an "Exchange" in each State where people can shop for insurance, usually online. 42 U.S.C. §18031(b)(1). An Exchange may be created in one of two ways. First, the Act provides that "[e]ach State shall . . . establish an American Health Benefit Exchange . . . for the State." Ibid. Second, if a State nonetheless chooses not to establish its own Exchange, the Act provides that the Secretary of Health and Human Services "shall . . . establish and operate such Exchange within the State." §18041(c)(1).

The issue in this case is whether the Act's tax credits are available in States that have a Federal Exchange rather than a State Exchange. The Act initially provides that tax credits "shall be allowed" for any "applicable taxpayer." 26 U.S.C. §36B(a). The Act then provides that the amount of the tax credit depends in part on whether the taxpayer has enrolled in an insurance plan through "an Exchange *established by the State* under section 1311 of the Patient Protection and Affordable Care Act [hereinafter 42 U.S.C. §18031]." 26 U.S.C. §§36B(b)-(c) (emphasis added).

The IRS addressed the availability of tax credits by promulgating a rule that made them available on both State and Federal Exchanges. As relevant here, the IRS Rule provides that a taxpayer is eligible for a tax credit if he enrolled in an insurance plan through "an Exchange," which is defined as "an Exchange serving the individual market . . . regardless of whether the Exchange is established and operated by a State . . . or by HHS." At this point, 16 States and the District of Columbia have established their own Exchanges; the other 34 States have elected to have HHS do so.

D

Petitioners are four individuals who live in Virginia, which has a Federal Exchange. They do not wish to purchase health insurance. In their view, Virginia's Exchange does not qualify as "an Exchange established by the State under [42 U.S. C. §18031]," so they should not receive any tax credits. That would make the cost of buying insurance more than eight percent of their income, which would exempt them from the Act's coverage requirement.

Under the IRS Rule, however, Virginia's Exchange would qualify as "an Exchange established by the State under [42 U.S.C. §18031]," so petitioners would receive tax credits. That would make the cost of buying insurance less than eight percent of petitioners' income, which would subject them to the Act's coverage requirement. The IRS Rule therefore requires petitioners to either buy health insurance they do not want, or make a payment to the IRS.

> The case turns on the Court's interpretation of five key words: "Exchange established by the State."

Petitioners challenged the IRS Rule in Federal District Court. The District Court dismissed the suit, holding that the Act unambiguously made tax credits available to individuals enrolled through a Federal Exchange. The Court of Appeals for the Fourth Circuit affirmed. The Fourth Circuit viewed the Act as "ambiguous and subject to at least two different interpretations." The court therefore deferred to the IR's interpretation under Chevron U.S.A. Inc. v. Natural Resources Defense Council, Inc., 467 U.S. 837 (1984).

The same day that the Fourth Circuit issued its decision, the Court of Appeals for the District of Columbia Circuit vacated the IRS Rule in a different case, holding that the Act "unambiguously restricts" the tax credits to State Exchanges. We granted certiorari in the present case.

II

The Affordable Care Act addresses tax credits in what is now Section 36B of the Internal Revenue Code. That section provides: "In the case of an applicable taxpayer, there shall be allowed as a credit against the tax imposed by this subtitle . . . an amount equal to the premium assistance credit amount." 26 U.S.C. §36B(a). Section 36B then defines the term "premium assistance credit amount" as "the sum of the *premium assistance amounts* determined under paragraph (2) with respect to all *coverage months* of the taxpayer occurring during the taxable year." §36B(b)(1) (emphasis added). Section 36B goes on to define the two italicized terms — "premium assistance amount" and "coverage month" — in part by referring to an insurance plan that is enrolled in through "an Exchange established by the State under [42 U.S.C. §18031]." 26 U.S.C. §§36B(b)(2)(A), (c)(2)(A)(i).

The parties dispute whether Section 36B authorizes tax credits for individuals who enroll in an insurance plan through a Federal Exchange. Petitioners argue that a

Federal Exchange is not "an Exchange established by the State under [42 U.S.C. §18031]," and that the IRS Rule therefore contradicts Section 36B. The Government responds that the IRS Rule is lawful because the phrase "an Exchange established by the State under [42 U.S.C. §18031]" should be read to include Federal Exchanges.

When analyzing an agency's interpretation of a statute, we often apply the two-step framework announced in *Chevron*. Under that framework, we ask whether the statute is ambiguous and, if so, whether the agency's interpretation is reasonable. This approach "is premised on the theory that a statute's ambiguity constitutes an implicit delegation from Congress to the agency to fill in the statutory gaps." FDA v. Brown & Williamson Tobacco Corp., 529 U.S. 120 (2000). "In extraordinary cases, however, there may be reason to hesitate before concluding that Congress has intended such an implicit delegation."

> In *Brown & Williamson*, the Court concluded that Congress had not delegated to the FDA the authority to regulate tobacco products as drugs or devices.

This is one of those cases. The tax credits are among the Act's key reforms, involving billions of dollars in spending each year and affecting the price of health insurance for millions of people. Whether those credits are available on Federal Exchanges is thus a question of deep "economic and political significance" that is central to this statutory scheme; had Congress wished to assign that question to an agency, it surely would have done so expressly. It is especially unlikely that Congress would have delegated this decision to the IRS, which has no expertise in crafting health insurance policy of this sort. This is not a case for the IRS.

It is instead our task to determine the correct reading of Section 36B. If the statutory language is plain, we must enforce it according to its terms. But oftentimes the "meaning — or ambiguity — of certain words or phrases may only become evident when placed in context." So when deciding whether the language is plain, we must read the words "in their context and with a view to their place in the overall statutory scheme." Our duty, after all, is "to construe statutes, not isolated provisions."

> The Court interpreted the statute and did not reach the *Chevron* analysis, which means that a subsequent presidential administration cannot change the IRS's position on section 36B. Overturning *King's* interpretation of the ACA would require congressional action.

A

We begin with the text of Section 36B. As relevant here, Section 36B allows an individual to receive tax credits only if the individual enrolls in an insurance plan through "an Exchange established by the State under [42 U.S.C. §18031]." In other words, three things must be true: First, the individual must enroll in an insurance plan through "an Exchange." Second, that Exchange must be "established by the State." And third, that Exchange must be established "under [42 U.S.C. §18031]." We address each requirement in turn.

First, all parties agree that a Federal Exchange qualifies as "an Exchange" for purposes of Section 36B. Section 18031 provides that "[e]ach State shall . . . establish an American Health Benefit Exchange . . . for the State." §18031(b)(1). Although phrased as a requirement, the Act gives the States "flexibility" by allowing them to "elect" whether they want to establish an Exchange. §18041(b). If the State chooses not to do so, Section 18041 provides that the Secretary "shall . . . establish and operate *such Exchange* within the State." §18041(c)(1) (emphasis added).

By using the phrase "such Exchange," Section 18041 instructs the Secretary to establish and operate the same Exchange that the State was directed to establish under Section 18031. *See* Black's Law Dictionary 1661 (10th ed. 2014) (defining "such" as "That or those; having just been mentioned"). In other words, State Exchanges and Federal Exchanges are equivalent—they must meet the same requirements, perform the same functions, and serve the same purposes. Although State and Federal Exchanges are established by different sovereigns, Sections 18031 and 18041 do not suggest that they differ in any meaningful way. A Federal Exchange therefore counts as "an Exchange" under Section 36B.

Second, we must determine whether a Federal Exchange is "established by the State" for purposes of Section 36B. At the outset, it might seem that a Federal Exchange cannot fulfill this requirement. After all, the Act defines "State" to mean "each of the 50 States and the District of Columbia"—a definition that does not include the Federal Government. 42 U.S.C. §18024(d). But when read in context, "with a view to [its] place in the overall statutory scheme," the meaning of the phrase "established by the State" is not so clear.

After telling each State to establish an Exchange, Section 18031 provides that all Exchanges "shall make available qualified health plans to qualified individuals." 42 U.S.C. §18031(d)(2)(A). Section 18032 then defines the term "qualified individual" in part as an individual who "resides in the State that established the Exchange." §18032(f)(1)(A). And that's a problem: If we give the phrase "the State that established the Exchange" its most natural meaning, there would be no "qualified individuals" on Federal Exchanges. But the Act clearly contemplates that there will be qualified individuals on every Exchange. As we just mentioned, the Act requires all Exchanges to "make available qualified health plans to qualified individuals"—something an Exchange could not do if there were no such individuals. §18031(d)(2)(A). And the Act tells the Exchange, in deciding which health plans to offer, to consider "the interests of qualified individuals . . . in the State or States in which such Exchange operates"—again, something the Exchange could not do if qualified individuals did not exist. §18031(e)(1)(B). This problem arises repeatedly throughout the Act. *See, e.g.,* §18031(b)(2) (allowing a State to create "one Exchange . . . for providing . . . services to both qualified individuals and qualified small employers," rather than creating separate Exchanges for those two groups).

These provisions suggest that the Act may not always use the phrase "established by the State" in its most natural sense. Thus, the meaning of that phrase may not be as clear as it appears when read out of context.

Third, we must determine whether a Federal Exchange is established "under [42 U.S.C. §18031]." This too might seem a requirement that a Federal Exchange cannot fulfill, because it is Section 18041 that tells the Secretary when to "establish and operate such Exchange." But here again, the way different provisions in the statute interact suggests otherwise.

The Act defines the term "Exchange" to mean "an American Health Benefit Exchange established under section 18031." §300gg-91(d)(21). If we import that definition into Section 18041, the Act tells the Secretary to "establish and operate such 'American Health Benefit Exchange established under section 18031.'" That suggests that Section 18041 authorizes the Secretary to establish an Exchange under Section 18031, not (or not only) under Section 18041. Otherwise, the Federal Exchange, by definition, would not be an "Exchange" at all.

This interpretation of "under [42 U.S.C. §18031]" fits best with the statutory context. All of the requirements that an Exchange must meet are in Section 18031, so it is sensible to regard all Exchanges as established under that provision. In addition, every time the Act uses the word "Exchange," the definitional provision requires that we substitute the phrase "Exchange established under section 18031." If Federal Exchanges were not established under Section 18031, therefore, literally none of the Act's requirements would apply to them. Finally, the Act repeatedly uses the phrase "established under [42 U.S.C. §18031]" in situations where it would make no sense to distinguish between State and Federal Exchanges. *See, e.g.,* 26 U.S.C. §125(f)(3)(A) (2012 ed., Supp. I) ("The term 'qualified benefit' shall not include any qualified health plan . . . offered through an Exchange established under [42 U.S.C. §18031]"); 26 U.S.C. §6055(b)(1)(B)(iii)(I) (2012 ed.) (requiring insurers to report whether each insurance plan they provided "is a qualified health plan offered through an Exchange established under [42 U.S.C. §18031]"). A Federal Exchange may therefore be considered one established "under [42 U.S.C. §18031]."

The upshot of all this is that the phrase "an Exchange established by the State under [42 U.S.C. §18031]" is properly viewed as ambiguous. The phrase may be limited in its reach to State Exchanges. But it is also possible that the phrase refers to all Exchanges — both State and Federal — at least for purposes of the tax credits. If a State chooses not to follow the directive in Section 18031 that it establish an Exchange, the Act tells the Secretary to establish "such Exchange." §18041. And by using the words "such Exchange," the Act indicates that State and Federal Exchanges should be the same. But State and Federal Exchanges would differ in a fundamental way if tax credits were available only on State Exchanges — one type of Exchange would help make insurance more affordable by providing billions of dollars to the States' citizens; the other type of Exchange would not. . . .

Petitioners and the dissent respond that the words "established by the State" would be unnecessary if Congress meant to extend tax credits to both State and Federal Exchanges. But "our preference for avoiding surplusage constructions is not absolute." And specifically with respect to this Act, rigorous application of the canon does not seem a particularly useful guide to a fair construction of the statute.

The Affordable Care Act contains more than a few examples of inartful drafting. (To cite just one, the Act creates three separate Section 1563s. *See* 124 Stat. 270, 911, 912.) Several features of the Act's passage contributed to that unfortunate reality. Congress wrote key parts of the Act behind closed doors, rather than through "the traditional legislative process." And Congress passed much of the Act using a complicated budgetary procedure known as "reconciliation," which limited opportunities for debate and amendment, and bypassed the Senate's normal 60-vote filibuster requirement. As a result, the Act does not reflect the type of care and deliberation that one might expect of such significant legislation. *Cf.* Frankfurter, Some Reflections on the Reading of Statutes, 47 Colum. L. Rev. 527, 545 (1947) (describing a cartoon "in which a senator tells his colleagues 'I admit this new bill is too complicated to understand. We'll just have to pass it to find out what it means.'").

Anyway, we "must do our best, bearing in mind the fundamental canon of statutory construction that the words of a statute must be read in their context and with a view to their place in the overall statutory scheme." After reading Section 36B along with other related provisions in the Act, we cannot conclude that the phrase "an Exchange established by the State under [Section 18031]" is unambiguous.

B

Given that the text is ambiguous, we must turn to the broader structure of the Act to determine the meaning of Section 36B. "A provision that may seem ambiguous in isolation is often clarified by the remainder of the statutory scheme . . . because only one of the permissible meanings produces a substantive effect that is compatible with the rest of the law." Here, the statutory scheme compels us to reject petitioners' interpretation because it would destabilize the individual insurance market in any State with a Federal Exchange, and likely create the very "death spirals" that Congress designed the Act to avoid.

As discussed above, Congress based the Affordable Care Act on three major reforms: first, the guaranteed issue and community rating requirements; second, a requirement that individuals maintain health insurance coverage or make a payment to the IRS; and third, the tax credits for individuals with household incomes between 100 percent and 400 percent of the federal poverty line. In a State that establishes its own Exchange, these three reforms work together to expand insurance coverage. The guaranteed issue and community rating requirements ensure that anyone can buy insurance; the coverage requirement creates an incentive for people to do so before they get sick; and the tax credits — it is hoped — make insurance more affordable. Together, those reforms "minimize . . . adverse selection and broaden the health insurance risk pool to include healthy individuals, which will lower health insurance premiums." 42 U.S.C. §18091(2)(I).

Under petitioners' reading, however, the Act would operate quite differently in a State with a Federal Exchange. As they see it, one of the Act's three major reforms — the tax credits — would not apply. And a second major reform — the coverage requirement — would not apply in a meaningful way. As explained earlier, the coverage requirement applies only when the cost of buying health insurance (minus the amount of the tax credits) is less than eight percent of an individual's income. So without the tax credits, the coverage requirement would apply to fewer individuals. And it would be a lot fewer. In 2014, approximately 87 percent of people who bought insurance on a Federal Exchange did so with tax credits, and virtually all of those people would become exempt. If petitioners are right, therefore, only one of the Act's three major reforms would apply in States with a Federal Exchange.

The combination of no tax credits and an ineffective coverage requirement could well push a State's individual insurance market into a death spiral. One study predicts that premiums would increase by 47 percent and enrollment would decrease by 70 percent. Another study predicts that premiums would increase by 35 percent and enrollment would decrease by 69 percent. And those effects would not be limited to individuals who purchase insurance on the Exchanges. Because the Act requires insurers to treat the entire individual market as a single risk pool, 42 U.S.C. §18032(c)(1), premiums outside the Exchange would rise along with those inside the Exchange.

It is implausible that Congress meant the Act to operate in this manner. *See* National Federation of Independent Business v. Sebelius, 132 S. Ct. 2566, 2674 (2012) (Scalia, Kennedy, Thomas, and Alito, JJ., dissenting) ("Without the federal subsidies . . . the exchanges would not operate as Congress intended and may not operate at all."). Congress made the guaranteed issue and community rating requirements applicable in every State in the Nation. But those requirements only work when combined with the coverage requirement and the tax credits. So it stands to reason that Congress meant for those provisions to apply in every State as well.

Petitioners respond that Congress was not worried about the effects of withholding tax credits from States with Federal Exchanges because "Congress evidently believed it was offering states a deal they would not refuse." Congress may have been wrong about the States' willingness to establish their own Exchanges, petitioners continue, but that does not allow this Court to rewrite the Act to fix that problem. That is particularly true, petitioners conclude, because the States likely would have created their own Exchanges in the absence of the IRS Rule, which eliminated any incentive that the States had to do so.

Section 18041 refutes the argument that Congress believed it was offering the States a deal they would not refuse. That section provides that, if a State elects not to establish an Exchange, the Secretary "shall . . . establish and operate such Exchange within the State." 42 U.S.C. §18041(c)(1)(A). The whole point of that provision is to create a federal fallback in case a State chooses not to establish its own Exchange. Contrary to petitioners' argument, Congress did not believe it was offering States a deal they would not refuse — it expressly addressed what would happen if a State did refuse the deal. . . .

> Consider other constitutional objections to Congress's offering states a deal they could not refuse, recalling the "coercion" argument in *NFIB v. Sebelius*, in Chapter 2.

We have held that Congress "does not alter the fundamental details of a regulatory scheme in vague terms or ancillary provisions." But in petitioners' view, Congress made the viability of the entire Affordable Care Act turn on the ultimate ancillary provision: a sub-sub-sub section of the Tax Code. We doubt that is what Congress meant to do. Had Congress meant to limit tax credits to State Exchanges, it likely would have done so in the definition of "applicable taxpayer" or in some other prominent manner. It would not have used such a winding path of connect-the-dots provisions about the amount of the credit.

D

Petitioners' arguments about the plain meaning of Section 36B are strong. But while the meaning of the phrase "an Exchange established by the State under [42 U.S.C. §18031]" may seem plain "when viewed in isolation," such a reading turns out to be "untenable in light of [the statute] as a whole." In this instance, the context and structure of the Act compel us to depart from what would otherwise be the most natural reading of the pertinent statutory phrase.

Reliance on context and structure in statutory interpretation is a "subtle business, calling for great wariness lest what professes to be mere rendering becomes creation and attempted interpretation of legislation becomes legislation itself." For the reasons we have given, however, such reliance is appropriate in this case, and leads us to conclude that Section 36B allows tax credits for insurance purchased on any Exchange created under the Act. Those credits are necessary for the Federal Exchanges to function like their State Exchange counterparts, and to avoid the type of calamitous result that Congress plainly meant to avoid.

. . . .

In a democracy, the power to make the law rests with those chosen by the people. Our role is more confined — "to say what the law is." Marbury v. Madison, 1 Cranch 137 (1803). That is easier in some cases than in others. But in every case we must respect the role of the Legislature, and take care not to undo what it has done. A fair reading of legislation demands a fair understanding of the legislative plan.

Congress passed the Affordable Care Act to improve health insurance markets, not to destroy them. If at all possible, we must interpret the Act in a way that is consistent with the former, and avoids the latter. Section 36B can fairly be read consistent with what we see as Congress's plan, and that is the reading we adopt.

The judgment of the United States Court of Appeals for the Fourth Circuit is Affirmed.

Justice SCALIA, with whom Justice THOMAS and Justice ALITO join, dissenting.

The Court holds that when the Patient Protection and Affordable Care Act says "Exchange established by the State" it means "Exchange established by the State or the Federal Government." That is of course quite absurd, and the Court's 21 pages of explanation make it no less so.

I

. . . .

Words no longer have meaning if an Exchange that is not established by a State is "established by the State." It is hard to come up with a clearer way to limit tax credits to state Exchanges than to use the words "established by the State." And it is hard to come up with a reason to include the words "by the State" other than the purpose of limiting credits to state Exchanges. "[T]he plain, obvious, and rational meaning of a statute is always to be preferred to any curious, narrow, hidden sense that nothing but the exigency of a hard case and the ingenuity and study of an acute and powerful intellect would discover." Under all the usual rules of interpretation, in short, the Government should lose this case. But normal rules of interpretation seem always to yield to the overriding principle of the present Court: The Affordable Care Act must be saved.

II

The Court interprets §36B to award tax credits on both federal and state Exchanges. It accepts that the "most natural sense" of the phrase "Exchange established by the State" is an Exchange established by a State. (Understatement, thy name is an opinion on the Affordable Care Act!) Yet the opinion continues, with no semblance of shame, that "it is also possible that the phrase refers to all Exchanges—both State and Federal." (Impossible possibility, thy name is an opinion on the Affordable Care Act!) The Court claims that "the context and structure of the Act compel [it] to depart from what would otherwise be the most natural reading of the pertinent statutory phrase."

I wholeheartedly agree with the Court that sound interpretation requires paying attention to the whole law, not homing in on isolated words or even isolated sections. Context always matters. Let us not forget, however, why context matters: It is a tool for understanding the terms of the law, not an excuse for rewriting them.

Any effort to understand rather than to rewrite a law must accept and apply the presumption that lawmakers use words in "their natural and ordinary signification." Ordinary connotation does not always prevail, but the more unnatural the proposed interpretation of a law, the more compelling the contextual evidence must be to show that it is correct. Today's interpretation is not merely unnatural; it is unheard of. Who would ever have dreamt that "Exchange established by the State" means

"Exchange established by the State or the Federal Government"? Little short of an express statutory definition could justify adopting this singular reading. Yet the only pertinent definition here provides that "State" means "each of the 50 States and the District of Columbia." 42 U.S.C. §18024(d). Because the Secretary is neither one of the 50 States nor the District of Columbia, that definition positively contradicts the eccentric theory that an Exchange established by the Secretary has been established by the State. . . .

Worst of all for the repute of today's decision, the Court's reasoning is largely self-defeating. The Court predicts that making tax credits unavailable in States that do not set up their own Exchanges would cause disastrous economic consequences there. If that is so, however, wouldn't one expect States to react by setting up their own Exchanges? And wouldn't that outcome satisfy two of the Act's goals rather than just one: enabling the Act's reforms to work and promoting state involvement in the Act's implementation? The Court protests that the very existence of a federal fallback shows that Congress expected that some States might fail to set up their own Exchanges. So it does. It does not show, however, that Congress expected the number of recalcitrant States to be particularly large. The more accurate the Court's dire economic predictions, the smaller that number is likely to be. That reality destroys the Court's pretense that applying the law as written would imperil "the viability of the entire Affordable Care Act." All in all, the Court's arguments about the law's purpose and design are no more convincing than its arguments about context. . . .

Today's opinion changes the usual rules of statutory interpretation for the sake of the Affordable Care Act. That, alas, is not a novelty. In National Federation of Independent Business v. Sebelius, 567 U.S. ___, 132 S. Ct. 2566, 183 L. Ed. 2d 450, this Court revised major components of the statute in order to save them from unconstitutionality. The Act that Congress passed provides that every individual "shall" maintain insurance or else pay a "penalty." This Court, however, saw that the Commerce Clause does not authorize a federal mandate to buy health insurance. So it rewrote the mandate-cum-penalty as a tax. The Act that Congress passed also requires every State to accept an expansion of its Medicaid program, or else risk losing all Medicaid funding. This Court, however, saw that the Spending Clause does not authorize this coercive condition. So it rewrote the law to withhold only the incremental funds associated with the Medicaid expansion. Having trans-formed two major parts of the law, the Court today has turned its attention to a third. The Act that Congress passed makes tax credits available only on an "Exchange established by the State." This Court, however, concludes that this limitation would prevent the rest of the Act from working as well as hoped. So it rewrites the law to make tax credits available everywhere. We should start calling this law SCOTUScare.

Perhaps the Patient Protection and Affordable Care Act will attain the enduring status of the Social Security Act or the Taft-Hartley Act; perhaps not. But this Court's two decisions on the Act will surely be remembered through the years. The somersaults of statutory interpretation they have performed ("penalty" means tax, "further [Medicaid] payments to the State" means only incremental Medicaid payments to the State, "established by the State" means not established by the State) will be cited by litigants endlessly, to the confusion of honest jurisprudence. And the cases will publish forever the discouraging truth that the Supreme Court of the

United States favors some laws over others, and is prepared to do whatever it takes to uphold and assist its favorites.

I dissent.

QUESTIONS

1. What would have been the effect if the Court had held that premium assistance tax credits were unavailable in states with federally facilitated Exchanges? Consider, in particular, the spillover effects on the employer free rider penalty and states' Medicaid expansion decisions.
2. What rationale does the dissent suggest for that possible outcome?

In *King*, the Court discussed the anticipated effect of removing the premium assistance tax credits from the three-legged stool. But consider the effect of removing the individual mandate leg: Will the experiences of Washington and New York be replicated at the national level? That was a major question when Congress repealed the individual mandate tax penalty as part of the 2017 tax bill. In November 2017, the Congressional Budget Office (CBO) and Joint Committee on Taxation (JCT) estimated that repealing the individual mandate would have the following effects:

Congressional Budget Office Repealing the Individual Health Insurance Mandate: An Updated Estimate

November 2017

. . . .

The Results of CBO and JCT's Analysis

CBO and JCT estimate that repealing that mandate starting in 2019 — and making no other changes to current law — would have the following effects:

- Federal budget deficits would be reduced by about $338 billion between 2018 and 2027.
- The number of people with health insurance would decrease by 4 million in 2019 and 13 million in 2027.
- Nongroup insurance markets would continue to be stable in almost all areas of the country throughout the coming decade.
- Average premiums in the nongroup market would increase by about 10 percent in most years of the decade (with no changes in the ages of people purchasing insurance accounted for) relative to CBO's baseline projections.

Those effects would occur mainly because healthier people would be less likely to obtain insurance and because, especially in the nongroup market, the resulting increases in premiums would cause more people to not purchase insurance.

If the individual mandate penalty was eliminated but the mandate itself was not repealed, the results would be very similar to those presented in this report. In CBO and JCT's estimation, with no penalty at all, only a small number of people who enroll in insurance because of the mandate under current law would continue to do so solely because of a willingness to comply with the law. If eliminating the mandate was accompanied by changes to tax rates or premium tax credits or by other significant changes, then the policy analyzed here would interact with those changes and have different effects.

Table 2.

Effects of Repealing the Individual Mandate on Health Insurance Coverage for People Under Age 65

Millions of People, by Calendar Year

	2018	2019	2020	2021	2022	2023	2024	2025	2026	2027
Change in Coverage Under the Policy										
Medicaid[a]	0	-1	-2	-4	-4	-4	-4	-5	-5	-5
Nongroup coverage, including marketplaces	0	-3	-4	-5	-5	-5	-5	-5	-5	-5
Employment-based coverage	0	*	-1	-2	-2	-3	-3	-3	-2	-2
Other coverage[b]	0	*	*	*	*	*	*	*	*	*
Uninsured	0	4	7	12	12	12	12	13	13	13

Sources: Congressional Budget Office; staff of the Joint Committee on Taxation.

Estimates are based on CBO's summer 2017 baseline. They reflect average enrollment over the course of a year among noninstitutionalized civilian residents of the 50 states and the District of Columbia who are under age 65, and they include spouses and dependents covered under family policies.

For these estimates, CBO and the staff of the Joint Committee on Taxation consider individuals to be uninsured if they would not be enrolled in a policy that provides financial protection from major medical risks.

Numbers may not add up to totals because of rounding.

* = between -500,000 and zero.

a. Includes noninstitutionalized enrollees with full Medicaid benefits.

b. Includes coverage under the Basic Health Program, which allows states to establish a coverage program primarily for people whose income is between 138 percent and 200 percent of the federal poverty level. To subsidize that coverage, the federal government provides states with funding that is equal to 95 percent of the subsidies for which those people would otherwise have been eligible.

PROBLEM

Research health insurance premium averages and trends for your state, taking note of the large-group, small-group, and individual market differences, as compared to the rest of the country. Are premiums increasing or decreasing? What explains the variation from state to state?

2. GOVERNMENT SUBSIDIES FOR PRIVATE HEALTH INSURANCE PURCHASE

The premium assistance tax credits, upheld in *King* above and excerpted below, fit within the ACA's overall strategy to extend health insurance coverage to more people. A large group of Americans receive employer-sponsored coverage, as discussed above. In expansion states, Medicaid covers up to 133 percent of the FPL, as discussed in Chapter 2. Exchange subsidies kick in at 100 percent of the FPL, providing some overlap between Medicaid and subsidy eligibility. People eligible for Medicaid must enroll in it; they cannot opt for private insurance purchased through an Exchange instead. This is financially a better bet for the beneficiary, as Medicaid premiums and copayments are nonexistent or minimal compared with private insurance. The overlap also covers some lawfully present immigrants who are ineligible for Medicaid but eligible for federal subsidies on the Exchanges.

Premium assistance tax credits are aimed at lower-income individuals who are not eligible for public insurance coverage and do not obtain affordable or adequate employer-sponsored coverage. The tax credits, which are calculated on a monthly basis and payable directly to the insurer, are available for taxpayers earning between 100 and 400 percent of the FPL. The amount of federal assistance is provided on a sliding scale, based on income, and will increase over time to keep pace with rising health insurance premiums. To access the subsidies, individuals must purchase a plan through their state Exchange, which may be federally or state operated.

26 U.S.C. §36B. Refundable credit for coverage under a qualified health plan

(a) In general

In the case of an applicable taxpayer, there shall be allowed as a credit against the tax imposed by this subtitle for any taxable year an amount equal to the premium assistance credit amount of the taxpayer for the taxable year.

(b) Premium assistance credit amount

For purposes of this section —

(1) In general

The term "premium assistance credit amount" means, with respect to any taxable year, the sum of the premium assistance amounts determined under paragraph (2) with respect to all coverage months of the taxpayer occurring during the taxable year.

(2) Premium assistance amount

The premium assistance amount determined under this subsection with respect to any coverage month is the amount equal to the lesser of —

(A) the monthly premiums for such month for 1 or more qualified health plans offered in the individual market within a State which cover the taxpayer, the taxpayer's spouse, or any dependent (as defined in section 152) of the taxpayer and which were enrolled in through an Exchange established by the State under 1311[1] of the Patient Protection and Affordable Care Act, or

(B) the excess (if any) of —

(i) the adjusted monthly premium for such month for the applicable second lowest cost silver plan with respect to the taxpayer, over

(ii) an amount equal to 1/12 of the product of the applicable percentage and the taxpayer's household income for the taxable year.

(3) Other terms and rules relating to premium assistance amounts

For purposes of paragraph (2) —

(A) Applicable percentage

(i) In general

Except as provided in clause (ii), the applicable percentage for any taxable year shall be the percentage such that the applicable percentage for any taxpayer whose household income is within an income tier specified in the following table shall increase, on a sliding scale in a linear manner, from the initial premium percentage to the final premium percentage specified in such table for such income tier:

In the case of household income (expressed as a percent of poverty line) within the following income tier:	The initial premium percentage is—	The final premium percentage is—
Up to 133%	2.0%	2.0%
133% up to 150%	3.0%	4.0%
150% up to 200%	4.0%	6.3%
200% up to 250%	6.3%	8.05%
250% up to 300%	8.05%	9.5%
300% up to 400%	9.5%	9.5% . . .

QUESTIONS

1. Why aren't premium assistance tax credits available to individuals below 100 percent of the FPL or people above 400 percent of the FPL?
2. How much would a family earning 200 percent of the FPL have to pay out of pocket to purchase private insurance on an Exchange?

As the statutory excerpt provides, the availability of premium assistance tax credits is tied to the cost of the second lowest-cost "silver" plans purchased on the health insurance Exchanges. Individuals may purchase other levels of Exchange plans, applying the subsidy toward those plans. If applied toward a bronze plan, premiums might be "free," but the individual might still be subject to a high deductible or other OOP costs before coverage kicks in.

In addition to premium assistance tax credits and precious metals tiers, the ACA provides two other protections for consumers' out-of-pocket costs. First, the law includes an overall annual OOP limit. For 2018, the OOP limit is $7,350 for an individual (self-only) coverage and $14,700 for a family plan; however, the self-only limit applies to each individual. Therefore, OOP costs for any member of the family could not exceed $7,350. These OOP limits apply to non-grandfathered individual market, small-group, large-group, and self-insured group coverage.

Second, the ACA provided another form of financial assistance for individuals shopping for health insurance on the Exchanges. As enacted, individuals at a slightly lower income level, between 100 and 250 percent of the FPL, may be eligible for cost-sharing reduction (CSR) payments. CSR payments are another federal tax credit payable directly to insurance companies on behalf of eligible individuals. The CSR payments are available only for individuals or families who purchase silver plans on the Exchanges. Like the premium assistance tax credits, cost-sharing reduction payments apply on a sliding scale, based on income. They effectively increase the actuarial value of the plans for lower-income individuals.

Like other ACA individual and small-group market reforms, CSR payments also have been a source of controversy. HHS began making these payments to insurers in January 2014, as scheduled under the statute, at the same time the Exchanges opened and the individual mandate first applied. Congress, however, did not specifically appropriate funds for the payments. Accordingly, in November 2014, Republican members of Congress filed a lawsuit, *House v. Burwell*. The federal district court for the District of Columbia initially enjoined HHS from making the CSR payments but stayed the injunction pending appeal. The Obama Administration appealed, but the House was granted multiple delays, holding the decision in abeyance even after the 2016 election of President Trump. Ultimately, 17 states and the District of Columbia were allowed to intervene, claiming that the states would be injured if the payments were not made. The parties settled in December 2017 (*House v. Hargan*, after Deputy Secretary of HHS, Eric Hargan), and, as of this writing, HHS has ceased making CSR payments to insurers. The CSR provision of the ACA remains in place without amendment, and Congress has not passed a specific appropriation. Meanwhile, a number of other lawsuits challenging the Administration's non-payment policy are pending, including *Maine Community Health Options v. United States*, filed by a nonprofit insurer in Maine.

Just as repeal of the individual mandate penalty risks upsetting the three-legged stool, denying CSR payments to insurers injects considerable uncertainty into the individual insurance market. Insurers still are required under the ACA to offer silver plans with reduced cost-sharing obligations to individuals between 100 and 250 percent of FPL. But without the infusion of federal dollars to make up the shortfall, insurers may respond, as authorized by state law, by increasing premium rates across the board, for all ACA-compliant plans inside and outside the Exchanges; increasing premiums for silver-level plans inside and outside the Exchanges; or increasing premiums for silver-level Exchange plans only (on the logic that CSR payments would have applied only to those). A few states prohibited premium rate increases to offset the CSR loss, or allow rate increases only during annual open enrollment periods, thus limiting insurers' abilities to respond.

Under the ACA's original design, the availability of federal financial assistance and other consumer protections creates strong incentives for individuals to purchase health insurance through the Exchanges. Although insurers are left scrambling to deal with the loss of the CSR payments, the consumer incentives to purchase on-Exchange remain. Moreover, all plans sold on the Exchanges are considered qualified health plans (QHPs) that satisfy the individual health insurance mandate, which now lacks the bite of a tax penalty. Private health insurance remains available outside those special marketplaces and could become more attractive, depending on how these various market uncertainties shake out. In 2018, the Trump Administration also shortened the annual open enrollment period and put fewer resources toward marketing the Exchanges to consumers, but enrollment remained robust. Even so, insurer and consumer participation in the Exchanges remains uncertain. Without the mandate, individuals — especially young, healthy, low-risk individuals — may opt out of coverage at a higher rate, thus decreasing the number of customers for those markets. At the same time, insurers may find the remaining customers' higher risk profiles and uncertainty regarding the future of CSR payments make those markets unattractive and, thus, may decline to offer products there. Under the ACA, all plans, whether sold on or off the Exchanges, must cover the ten essential health benefits (EHB), discussed below. Off-Exchange plans also may offer more choices in terms of deductibles and provider networks, and may be especially appealing to higher-income individuals who would not qualify for government subsidies. In addition, tailored health insurance products, like short-term coverage, long-term care coverage, or prescription-drug-only plans may be available off the Exchanges.

The ACA also allowed catastrophic-only coverage for individuals who are under age 30 or qualified for a hardship exemption (meaning that they were unable to find coverage that cost less than 8 percent of their income). Catastrophic plans have very low monthly premiums but very high OOP costs, which is to say that their actuarial value may be lower than 60 percent. Catastrophic plans still must cover all ten categories of EHB, including preventive and primary care, and are subject to the same annual OOP limits noted above. Federal premium assistance tax credits and cost-sharing reduction payments are not available for these plans. In 2017, less than 1 percent of Exchange enrollees eligible for catastrophic plans took that option.

Finally, the ACA requires health plans to extend dependent child coverage until age 26, meaning that young adults may remain on their parents' employer-sponsored or other health plan. The child need not be financially dependent on or living with the parent. Plans may not charge higher rates to the adult dependents than other family members. This requirement also applies to grandfathered health plans.

PROBLEM

Seema Student is 25 years old and recently graduated with a Master's in Business Administration (MBA) from her home-state public university. She has student loans to repay and does not yet have a job. Therefore, as of now, her annual income is zero. During school, Seema's parents covered her as a dependent on their employer-sponsored health insurance plan. But, upon completion of her MBA, they will no longer provide that assistance. Seema comes to you as an expert on health care law with a few questions:

1. She understands that federal law requires her to have health insurance. True or false. Explain your answer.
2. Even if federal law does not require her to have health insurance, Seema wonders how she might pay for medical care when and if she needs it. For example, she wears glasses for corrective vision, takes birth control pills, and has seasonal allergies for which she sometimes takes prescription drugs. She recognizes, of course, that she also could experience unexpected medical problems. Please list five options available to Seema to address her concerns.

3. PROHIBITION ON HEALTH STATUS DISCRIMINATION

As noted above, the ACA effectively extended and expanded the HIPAA portability protections for employer-sponsored health plans into the individual and small-group market for plans sold both on and off the Exchanges. To varying degrees, states had regulated health insurance underwriting and ratemaking, but the ACA enacted nationwide, standardized rules. Those provisions—the ban on preexisting condition exclusions and experience rating—were and remain among the law's most popular reforms. In addition, section 1557 of the ACA, for the first time, expressly prohibits discrimination in health insurance and government-operated and funded health care programs. By largely disallowing individual health status to be considered, the ACA signals a shift in public perception about the role of health insurance as offering not merely individual protection against financial risk. Instead, it operates as a mechanism for extending access to insurance—and thereby care—to more Americans.

42 U.S.C. §300gg. Fair health insurance premiums
(a) Prohibiting discriminatory premium rates
(1) In general
With respect to the premium rate charged by a health insurance issuer for health insurance coverage offered in the individual or small group market—
(A) such rate shall vary with respect to the particular plan or coverage involved only by—
(i) whether such plan or coverage covers an individual or family;
(ii) rating area, as established in accordance with paragraph (2);
(iii) age, except that such rate shall not vary by more than 3 to 1 for adults (consistent with section 300gg-6(c) of this title); and
(iv) tobacco use, except that such rate shall not vary by more than 1.5 to 1; and
(B) such rate shall not vary with respect to the particular plan or coverage involved by any other factor not described in subparagraph (A). . . .

QUESTIONS

1. Why does the ACA allow variations in premium rates based on age and tobacco use? Do those exceptions represent a return to an "actuarial fairness" model?
2. What is the effect of the 3:1 and 1.5:1 rating bands?

42 U.S.C. §300gg-1. Guaranteed availability of coverage
(a) Guaranteed issuance of coverage in the individual and group market
Subject to subsections (b) through (e), each health insurance issuer that offers health insurance coverage in the individual or group market in a State must accept every employer and individual in the State that applies for such coverage. . . .

42 U.S.C. §300gg-2. Guaranteed renewability of coverage
(a) In general
Except as provided in this section, if a health insurance issuer offers health insurance coverage in the individual or group market, the issuer must renew or continue in force such coverage at the option of the plan sponsor or the individual, as applicable.
(b) General exceptions
A health insurance issuer may nonrenew or discontinue health insurance coverage offered in connection with a health insurance coverage offered in the group or individual market based only on one or more of the following:
(1) Nonpayment of premiums
The plan sponsor, or individual, as applicable, has failed to pay premiums or contributions in accordance with the terms of the health insurance coverage or the issuer has not received timely premium payments.
(2) Fraud
The plan sponsor, or individual, as applicable, has performed an act or practice that constitutes fraud or made an intentional misrepresentation of material fact under the terms of the coverage.
(3) Violation of participation or contribution rates

In the case of a group health plan, the plan sponsor has failed to comply with a material plan provision relating to employer contribution or group participation rules, pursuant to applicable State law.

(4) Termination of coverage

The issuer is ceasing to offer coverage in such market in accordance with subsection (c) of this section and applicable State law.

. . . .

QUESTIONS

1. May a health plan cancel coverage if it later discovers that an enrollee failed to disclose a history of treatment for alcohol abuse six years prior to the coverage term?
2. If an insurer decides to exit the Exchange market in a particular geographic area, may it decline to renew policyholders' coverage?

42 U.S.C. §300gg-3. Prohibition of preexisting condition exclusions or other discrimination based on health status

(a) In general

A group health plan and a health insurance issuer offering group or individual health insurance coverage may not impose any preexisting condition exclusion with respect to such plan or coverage.

(b) Definitions

For purposes of this part —

(1) Preexisting condition exclusion

(A) In general

The term "preexisting condition exclusion" means, with respect to coverage, a limitation or exclusion of benefits relating to a condition based on the fact that the condition was present before the date of enrollment for such coverage, whether or not any medical advice, diagnosis, care, or treatment was recommended or received before such date.

(B) Treatment of genetic information

Genetic information shall not be treated as a condition described in subsection (a)(1) of this section in the absence of a diagnosis of the condition related to such information. . . .

QUESTION

Compare this ACA provision on preexisting conditions to the HIPAA portability provisions excerpted above. Which statute is more protective of insureds?

42 U.S.C. §300gg-4. Prohibiting discrimination against individual participants and beneficiaries based on health status

(a) In general

A group health plan and a health insurance issuer offering group or individual health insurance coverage may not establish rules for eligibility (including continued eligibility) of any individual to enroll under the terms of the plan or coverage based on any of the following health status-related factors in relation to the individual or a dependent of the individual:

(1) Health status.

(2) Medical condition (including both physical and mental illnesses).

(3) Claims experience.

(4) Receipt of health care.

(5) Medical history.

(6) Genetic information.

(7) Evidence of insurability (including conditions arising out of acts of domestic violence).

(8) Disability.

(9) Any other health status-related factor determined appropriate by the Secretary.

> The ACA provides stronger protection for mental health coverage than the prior federal Mental Health Parity Act.

(b) In premium contributions

(1) In general

A group health plan, and a health insurance issuer offering group or individual health insurance coverage, may not require any individual (as a condition of enrollment or continued enrollment under the plan) to pay a premium or contribution which is greater than such premium or contribution for a similarly situated individual enrolled in the plan on the basis of any health status-related factor in relation to the individual or to an individual enrolled under the plan as a dependent of the individual.

(2) Construction

Nothing in paragraph (1) shall be construed —

(A) to restrict the amount that an employer or individual may be charged for coverage under a group health plan except as provided in paragraph (3) or individual health coverage, as the case may be; or

(B) to prevent a group health plan, and a health insurance issuer offering group health insurance coverage, from establishing premium discounts or rebates or modifying otherwise applicable copayments or deductibles in return for adherence to programs of health promotion and disease prevention.

The prohibition on health status discrimination in health insurance premiums contains another notable exception (in addition to age and tobacco, noted above), which is that plans may offer discounts, rebates, or reduced cost sharing for participation in "Programs of Health Promotion or Disease Prevention" (more popularly known as "wellness programs") that comply with statutory and regulatory requirements. These programs have been particularly popular in corporate settings as a way to encourage a healthier workforce and thereby reduce overall group plan insurance premiums, reduce absenteeism, and improve morale, among other benefits. Generally speaking, programs that offer incentives merely for participating are subject to fewer federal requirements than programs that require achievement of certain health statuses or biometric indicators, such as body-mass index.

> Wellness programs are an exception to the general ACA trend toward community-rated risk pooling.

For example, an employer may offer discounts on employees' premium contributions for receiving annual checkups or medically recommended and appropriate immunizations, or for participating in a health screening or smoking cessation class, as long as the program is available to all similarly situated individuals. On the other hand, incentives based on achieving a certain weight, blood pressure level, or body-mass index, or successfully completing a smoking cessation class, will be subject to additional requirements. The additional requirements are intended to protect employees whose individual health conditions may make those goals difficult or impossible to achieve. *See generally* 42 U.S.C. §300gg-4(j). For example, JetBlue Airways Corporation offered financial incentives for a range of activities, from teeth cleaning ($25) to completing an Ironman triathlon ($400). Employees of the City of Houston were required to complete certain tasks, such as filling out a health risk assessment, undergoing a biometric screening, signing up for Weight Watchers, and getting other types of screening, such as a mammogram, to avoid a $25 monthly paycheck surcharge.

QUESTION

Wellness programs, by their terms, treat individual employees differently based on their health status, or at least their health-related conduct and activities. Does that differentiation contradict the ACA's overarching policy of decoupling health status from insurance availability and pricing?

4. ESSENTIAL HEALTH BENEFITS

Prior to enactment of the ACA, federal law contained very few requirements regarding the content of health insurance plans. States, by contrast, had long required coverage of a wide array of benefits, including emergency room care, off-formulary drugs, clinical trials, mental health care, cancer screenings, contraceptives, infertility treatment, childhood vaccinations, newborn hearing screenings, and autism treatment, to name just a few. But ERISA's preemption scheme sharply limited the reach of those state coverage mandates. Prior to the ACA, a few coverage mandates were enacted into federal law, bypassing ERISA preemption, including laws requiring insurers to cover breast reconstruction following mastectomy; minimum hospital stays following vaginal or cesarean births (the prohibition on so-called "drive-by deliveries"); and mental health benefits to the same extent as physical health benefits (mental health parity legislation).

> Which ERISA preemption path, §514 express or §502 implied, applies to state coverage mandates?

The ACA signifies a dramatic expansion of federal regulation of the content of health insurance plans. The law added several new federal coverage mandates, including routine patient care costs for approved clinical trials for cancer and other life-threatening conditions and emergency room care without prior authorization and out-of-network charges. The ACA also requires insurers offering coverage in the individual and small-group market to cover a defined package of "essential health benefits" (EHB). The EHB requirement does not apply to large-group, self-insured, or grandfathered health plans but does apply to plans sold inside and outside the Exchanges, including catastrophic-only plans.

    42 U.S.C. §18022. Essential health benefits requirements
      (b) Essential health benefits
        (1) In general
        Subject to paragraph (2), the Secretary shall define the essential health benefits, except that such benefits shall include at least the following general categories and the items and services covered within the categories:
          (A) Ambulatory patient services.

(B) Emergency services.

(C) Hospitalization.

(D) Maternity and newborn care.

(E) Mental health and substance use disorder services, including behavioral health treatment.

(F) Prescription drugs.

(G) Rehabilitative and habilitative services and devices.

(H) Laboratory services.

(I) Preventive and wellness services and chronic disease management.

(J) Pediatric services, including oral and vision care.

(2) Limitation

(A) In general

> Note that the EHB package is defined by reference to a typical employer plan, but large-group and self-insured plans are not required to provide EHB. The presumption is that they will anyway, due to market forces.

The Secretary shall ensure that the scope of the essential health benefits under paragraph (1) is equal to the scope of benefits provided under a typical employer plan, as determined by the Secretary. . . .

As the statutory excerpt states, Congress left to administrative agency rulemaking the task of defining the precise content of the EHB package. Under that delegated authority, HHS initially implemented the provision by asking each state to designate a "benchmark" plan, among a list of approved plans, which list includes certain commercial plans, state employee plans, and federal employee plans, as long as the selected benchmark plan covers the ten broad categories of EHB. These benchmark plans are standards against which other health plans offered in the state are measured. To assist states and insurers in complying with the standards, a summary of each state's benchmark plan, supporting documents, and other state coverage mandates is available on the HHS Web site.

Plans may offer benefits in excess of EHB, but federal premium assistance and cost-sharing reduction subsidies apply only to EHB. States also may mandate coverage of additional benefits to be covered but must pay for the costs of those benefits for any insureds enrolled in QHPs sold on the Exchanges. *See* 42 U.S.C. §18031(d)(3)(B)(ii).

QUESTIONS

1. Recall the discussion in the Introduction (Chapter 1) regarding the rejection of an affirmative right to health care under U.S. law. Does EHB constitute a right to health care?

2. Do the ten categories include what you would consider to be the essence of a health care right?

3. Which of the listed categories might you exclude, or which additional categories might you include, in defining the content of such a right?

4. Return to the Problem at the end of Section C above, page 202, regarding extending ERISA's reach to include more AHPs. Would those plans have to cover EHB?

The list of EHB includes "preventive and wellness services." An additional, related provision of the ACA requires coverage of preventive services without cost-sharing, meaning that insureds access those services without having to pay a copayment or coinsurance or having to meet their plan's deductible. This requirement applies to all private plans, including individual and small-group plans, on and off the Exchanges, as well as large-group and self-insured plans. Catastrophic-only plans also must cover three primary care physician visits annually as well as other preventive services, without regard to otherwise applicable cost-sharing requirements. Grandfathered plans are exempt from the preventive care coverage requirement.

42 U.S.C. §300gg-13. Coverage of preventive health services

(a) In general

A group health plan and a health insurance issuer offering group or individual health insurance coverage shall, at a minimum provide coverage for and shall not impose any cost sharing requirements for —

> Congress delegated the task of creating these evidence-based lists to various groups. An updated recommendation from these groups automatically changes what preventive care must be provided in EHB.

(1) evidence-based items or services that have in effect a rating of "A" or "B" in the current recommendations of the United States Preventive Services Task Force;

(2) immunizations that have in effect a recommendation from the Advisory Committee on Immunization Practices of the Centers for Disease Control and Prevention with respect to the individual involved; and

(3) with respect to infants, children, and adolescents, evidence-informed preventive care and screenings provided for in the comprehensive guidelines supported by the Health Resources and Services Administration.

(4) with respect to women, such additional preventive care and screenings not described in paragraph (1) as provided for in comprehensive guidelines supported by the Health Resources and Services Administration for purposes of this paragraph.

(5) for the purposes of this chapter, and for the purposes of any other provision of law, the current recommendations of the United States Preventive Service Task Force regarding breast cancer screening, mammography, and prevention shall be considered the most current other than those issued in or around November 2009.

Nothing in this subsection shall be construed to prohibit a plan or issuer from providing coverage for services in addition to those recommended by [the] United States Preventive Services Task Force or to deny coverage for services that are not recommended by such Task Force.

The statute refers to the U.S. Preventive Services Task Force (Task Force) recommendations to define the content of the preventive services mandate. The Task Force is not a governmental agency or official body but rather an independent, volunteer panel of national experts in prevention and evidence-based medicine. It is notable that Congress delegated this essential definitional work to an expert yet nongovernmental entity.

The Task Force's definition of preventive care for women includes 20 FDA-approved contraceptive methods. The so-called federal "contraceptive mandate" generated considerable controversy. First, some individuals objected on moral and public policy grounds to the government's provision of "free" birth control, although, to be accurate, covered individuals still pay for these services through their health insurance premiums.

Second, certain religious employers claimed that the law violated the Religious Freedom Restoration Act of 1993 (RFRA) because it included coverage for four forms of contraception that have the effect of terminating a fertilized egg. According to those employers, requiring them to pay a portion of the premium for those forms of contraception substantially burdened their sincerely held religious belief that life begins at conception. By statute, religious employers, such as churches, were exempt from the requirement. By regulation, HHS provided an accommodation to nonprofit religious organizations, such as religiously affiliated hospitals and universities. But certain for-profit religious employers objected that the law also violated their religious freedom under RFRA.

> One of the more high-profile attacks on the contraceptive mandate was conservative pundit Rush Limbaugh's rant in his weekly radio show against a Georgetown law student, Sandra Fluke, who had testified before a congressional committee about the importance of requiring universities to provide coverage for birth control.

This ACA issue also reached the U.S. Supreme Court, first in *Burwell v. Hobby Lobby Stores, Inc.*, excerpted in Chapter 1, holding that Congress had not established that the contraceptive mandate was the least restrictive means of furthering the compelling government interest. The Court reasoned that the government had not shown why the accommodation for nonprofit religious organizations could not be extended to closely held for-profit employers. Subsequently, that very accommodation was challenged as violating RFRA. The U.S. Supreme Court ultimately avoided the issue in Zubik v. Burwell, 578 U.S. (2016), vacating the circuit court opinions on which it had granted certoriari and remanding those for further consideration. In essence, the Court came to understand, through supplemental briefing, that the government was already crafting an alternative that better accommodated the employer's religious objections. Ultimately, in October 2017, the Trump Administration issued regulations — interim final rules, bypassing the notice and comment rulemaking process — greatly expanding religious and moral exemptions from the contraception mandate. Pennsylvania Attorney General Josh Shapiro, supported by 19 other state attorneys general, challenged the "moral" exemption in federal court. As of this writing, that case is still pending in a federal district court. Commonwealth of Pennsylvania v. Trump et al., Civil Action No. 17-4540 (E.D. Pa., filed Oct. 11, 2017). If those rules stand, only employers with no religious or moral objection, and publicly traded for-profit companies with no religious objection, will be required to cover contraception for their employees.

Prior to the ACA, 29 states had contraceptive coverage mandates, but the ACA disallowed charging employees for the cost of that coverage, treating contraception as preventive care. The ACA dramatically reduced the percentage of women who had to pay some portion of their contraception, from 20 percent to 3.6 percent. It is unclear as of this writing how many employers will avail themselves of the exemptions, but conceivably thousands of women would again have to pay more for contraception on their own or forgo using it.

5. STATE INNOVATION WAIVERS

Starting January 1, 2017, the ACA offers one further approach to expanding health insurance coverage: section 1332 waivers (codified at 42 U.S.C. §18052). This provision allows states to apply to the Secretary of HHS for a waiver of any or all requirements for major components of the ACA's strategy, including Exchanges, QHPs, premium assistance tax credits, cost-sharing reduction payments, small-employer tax credits, and individual and employer responsibility provisions. Section 1332 waivers can pertain solely to the private insurance market, or may be combined with the Medicaid waivers described in Chapter 2. States operating under approved waivers receive the equivalent federal funding that would be available under federal subsidies and the federal medical assistance percentage (FMAP), as applicable. Waiver requests are subject to a number of substantive and procedural requirements. The procedural requirements concern opportunities for public input. The substantive requirements are detailed in the regulations below.

31 C.F.R. §33.100. Basis and purpose

(a) Statutory basis. This part implements provisions of section 1332 of the Patient Protection and Affordable Care Act (Affordable Care Act), Public Law 111-148, relating to Waivers for State Innovation, which the Secretary may authorize for plan years beginning on or after January 1, 2017. . . .

> These waivers were to begin no earlier than January 1, 2017.

31 C.F.R. §33.102. Coordinated waiver process

(a) Coordination with applications for waivers under other Federal laws. A State may submit a single application to the Secretary of Health and Human Services for a waiver under section 1332 of the Affordable Care Act and a waiver under one or more of the existing waiver processes applicable under titles XVIII, XIX, and XXI of the Social Security Act, or under any other Federal law relating to the provision of health care items or services, provided that such application is consistent with the procedures described in this part, the procedures for demonstrations under section 1115 of the Social Security Act, if applicable, and the procedures under any other applicable Federal law under which the State seeks a waiver.

(b) Coordinated process for section 1332 waivers. A State seeking a section 1332 waiver must submit a waiver application to the Secretary of Health and Human Services. Any application submitted to the Secretary of Health and Human Services that requests to waive sections 36B, 4980H, or 5000A of the Internal Revenue Code, in accordance with section 1332(a)(2)(D) of the Affordable Care Act, shall upon receipt be transmitted by the Secretary of Health and Human Services to the Secretary to be reviewed in accordance with this part.

The Secretaries of HHS and the Treasury issued guidance regarding the waiver process, including the four substantive requirements of coverage, affordability, comprehensiveness, and deficit neutrality.

Waivers for State Innovation

80 Fed. Reg. 78,131 (Dec. 16, 2015)

DEPARTMENT OF THE TREASURY
31 CFR Part 33
DEPARTMENT OF HEALTH AND HUMAN SERVICES
45 CFR Part 155

AGENCY: Centers for Medicare & Medicaid Services (CMS), HHS; Department of the Treasury.

ACTION: Guidance.

SUMMARY: This guidance relates to Section 1332 of the Patient Protection and Affordable Care Act (ACA) and its implementing regulations. Section 1332 provides the Secretary of Health and Human Services and the Secretary of the Treasury with the discretion to approve a state's proposal to waive specific provisions of the ACA (a State Innovation Waiver), provided the proposal meets certain requirements. In particular, the Secretaries can only exercise their discretion to approve a waiver if they find that the waiver would provide coverage to a comparable number of residents of the state as would be provided coverage absent the waiver, would provide coverage that is at least as comprehensive and affordable as would be provided absent the waiver, and would not increase the Federal deficit. If the waiver is approved, the state may receive funding equal to the amount of forgone Federal financial assistance that would have been provided to its residents pursuant to specified ACA programs, known as pass-through funding. State Innovation Waivers are available for effective dates beginning on or after January 1, 2017. They may be approved for periods up to 5 years and can be renewed. The Departments promulgated implementing regulations in 2012. This document provides additional information about the requirements that must be met, the Secretaries' application review procedures, the amount of pass-through funding, certain analytical requirements, and operational considerations. . . .

> The guidance offers four "guardrails" for state-innovation waivers: (1) coverage must be comprehensive; (2) coverage must be affordable; (3) the waiver must cover a comparable number of state residents; and (4) the waiver must not increase the federal deficit.

A. Coverage

To meet the coverage requirement, a comparable number of state residents must be forecast to have coverage under the waiver as would have coverage absent the waiver.

Coverage refers to minimum essential coverage (or, if the individual shared responsibility provision is waived under a State Innovation Waiver, to something that would qualify as minimum essential coverage but for the waiver). For this purpose, "comparable" means that the forecast of the number of covered individuals is no less than the forecast of the number of covered individuals absent the waiver. This condition generally must be forecast to be met in each year that the waiver would be in effect.

The impact on all state residents is considered, regardless of the type of coverage they would have absent the waiver. (For example, while a State Innovation Waiver may not change the terms of a state's Medicaid coverage or change existing Medicaid demonstration authority, changes in Medicaid enrollment that result from a State Innovation Waiver, holding the state's Medicaid policies constant, are considered in evaluating the number of residents with coverage under a waiver.)

Assessment of whether the proposal covers a comparable number of individuals also takes into account the effects across different groups of state residents, and, in particular, vulnerable residents, including low-income individuals, elderly individuals, and those with serious health issues or who have a greater risk of developing serious health issues. Reducing coverage for these types of vulnerable groups would cause a waiver application to fail this requirement, even if the waiver would provide coverage to a comparable number of residents overall. Finally, analysis under the coverage requirement takes into account whether the proposal sufficiently prevents gaps in or discontinuations of coverage. . . .

B. Affordability

To meet the affordability requirement, health care coverage under the waiver must be forecast to be as affordable overall for state residents as coverage absent the waiver.

Affordability refers to state residents' ability to pay for health care and may generally be measured by comparing residents' net out-of-pocket spending for health coverage and services to their incomes. Out-of-pocket expenses include both premium contributions (or equivalent costs for enrolling in coverage), and any cost sharing, such as deductibles, co-pays, and co-insurance, associated with the coverage. Spending on health care services that are not covered by a plan may also be taken into account if they are affected by the waiver proposal. The impact on all state residents is considered, regardless of the type of coverage they would have absent the waiver. This condition generally must be forecast to be met in each year that the waiver would be in effect.

Waivers are evaluated not only based on how they affect affordability on average, but also on how they affect the number of individuals with large health care spending burdens relative to their incomes. Increasing the number of state residents with large health care spending burdens would cause a waiver to fail the affordability requirement, even if the waiver would increase affordability for many other state residents. Assessment of whether the proposal meets the affordability requirement also takes into account the effects across different groups of state residents, and, in particular, vulnerable residents, including low-income individuals, elderly individuals, and those with serious health issues or who have a greater risk of developing serious health issues. Reducing affordability for these types of vulnerable groups would cause a waiver to fail this requirement, even if the waiver maintained affordability in the aggregate.

In addition, a waiver would fail the affordability requirement if it would reduce the number of individuals with coverage that provides a minimal level of protection against excessive cost sharing. In particular, waivers that reduce the number of people with insurance coverage that provides both an actuarial value equal to or greater than 60 percent and an out-of-pocket maximum that complies with section 1302(c)(1) of the ACA, would fail this requirement. So too would waivers that reduce the number of people with coverage that meets the affordability requirements set forth in sections 1916 and 1916A of the Social Security Act, as codified in 42 CFR part 447, subpart A, while holding the state's Medicaid policies constant. . . .

C. Comprehensiveness

To meet the comprehensiveness requirement, health care coverage under the waiver must be forecast to be at least as comprehensive overall for residents of the state as coverage absent the waiver.

Comprehensiveness refers to the scope of benefits provided by the coverage as measured by the extent to which coverage meets the requirements for essential health benefits (EHBs) as defined in section 1302(b) of the ACA, or, as appropriate, Medicaid and/or CHIP standards. The impact on all state residents is considered, regardless of the type of coverage they would have absent the waiver.

Comprehensiveness is evaluated by comparing coverage under the waiver to the state's EHB benchmark, selected by the state (or if the state does not select a benchmark, the default base-benchmark plan) pursuant to 45 CFR 156.100, as well as to, in certain cases, the coverage provided under the state's Medicaid and/or CHIP programs. A waiver cannot satisfy the comprehensiveness requirement if the waiver decreases: (1) The number of residents with coverage that is at least as comprehensive as the benchmark in all ten EHB categories; (2) for any of the ten EHB categories, the number of residents with coverage that is at least as comprehensive as the benchmark in that category; or (3) the number of residents whose coverage includes the full set of services that would be covered under the state's Medicaid and/or CHIP programs, holding the state's Medicaid and CHIP policies constant. That is, the waiver must not decrease the number of individuals with coverage that satisfies EHB requirements, the number of individuals with coverage of any particular category of EHB, or the number of individuals with coverage that includes the services covered under the state's Medicaid and/or CHIP programs.

Assessment of whether the proposal meets the comprehensiveness requirement also takes into account the effects across different groups of state residents, and, in particular, vulnerable residents, including low-income individuals, elderly individuals, and those with serious health issues or who have a greater risk of developing serious health issues. A waiver would fail the comprehensiveness requirement if it would reduce the comprehensiveness of coverage provided to these types of vulnerable groups, even if the waiver maintained comprehensiveness in the aggregate. This condition generally must be forecast to be met in each year that the waiver would be in effect. . . .

D. Deficit Neutrality

Under the deficit neutrality requirement, the projected Federal spending net of Federal revenues under the State Innovation Waiver must be equal to or lower than projected Federal spending net of Federal revenues in the absence of the waiver.

The estimated effect on Federal revenue includes all changes in income, payroll, or excise tax revenue, as well as any other forms of revenue (including user fees), that would result from the proposed waiver. Estimated effects would include, for example, changes in: The premium tax credit and health coverage tax credit, individual shared responsibility payments, employer shared responsibility payments, the excise tax on high-cost employer-sponsored plans, the credit for small businesses offering health insurance, and changes in income and payroll taxes resulting from changes in tax exclusions for employer-sponsored insurance and in deductions for medical expenses.

The effect on Federal spending includes all changes in Exchange financial assistance and other direct spending, such as changes in Medicaid spending (while holding the state's Medicaid policies constant) that result from the changes made through the State Innovation Waiver. Projected Federal spending under the waiver proposal also includes all administrative costs to the Federal government, including any changes in Internal Revenue Service administrative costs, Federal Exchange administrative costs, or other administrative costs associated with the waiver.

Waivers must not increase the Federal deficit over the period of the waiver (which may not exceed 5 years unless renewed) or in total over the ten-year budget plan submitted by the state as part of the State Innovation Waiver application. The ten-year budget plan must describe for both the period of the waiver and for the ten-year budget the projected Federal spending net of Federal revenues under the State Innovation Waiver and the projected Federal spending net of Federal revenues in the absence of the waiver.

The ten-year budget plan should assume the waiver would continue permanently, but should not include Federal spending or savings attributable to any period outside of the ten-year budget window. A variety of factors, including the likelihood and accuracy of projected spending and revenue effects and the timing of these effects, are considered when evaluating the effect of the waiver on the Federal deficit. A waiver that increases the deficit in any given year is less likely to meet the deficit neutrality requirement.

The state should also provide a description of the model used to produce these estimates, including data sources and quality, key assumptions, and parameters. The state may be required to provide micro data and other information to inform the Secretaries' analysis. . . .

CAPSTONE PROBLEM

Although Congress declined to consider any sort of national health system, or single-payer approach to universal coverage, could an individual state design such a program for its population under section 1332? How would that approach differ from the ACA? What challenges or obstacles would a state face implementing such a plan covering its entire population?

THE BUSINESS OF HEALTH CARE

Part II covers a range of topics typically included in a course on Corporations or Business Organizations, although tailored to the unique challenges of the health care sector. Health care is different from most regulated businesses, calling for a range of unique approaches and considerations that build upon traditional business, tax, and antitrust law.

In the chapters that follow, we examine regulation of the business of health care. **Chapter 4** discusses how health care providers are governed, with examples mainly drawn from nonprofit hospitals. **Chapter 5** covers special tax rules imposed on tax-exempt health care organizations, which include the majority of U.S. hospitals. **Chapter 6** tackles the complex world of federal and state management of financial conflicts of interest in health care, especially the body of law called "health care fraud and abuse" and related compliance obligations. Finally, competition is foundational for the capitalist U.S. economy, but in health care competition is fraught with many problems, including lopsided provider market power in many regions and lack of consumer information that undermines the ability to comparison shop. **Chapter 7** examines these topics through the lens of antitrust law and health care competition. These four chapters are core practice areas for many health care lawyers.

CHAPTER 4

Structure and Governance
of Health Care Entities

A. OVERVIEW OF HEALTH CARE BUSINESS ENTITIES

Health care is a big business, and so we should expect a variety of business entities to be active in the sector. If you are not already familiar with business organizations or corporations, the following summary will introduce you to the major corporate entities relevant to health care law.

When starting a business, the most fundamental legal choice is whether to organize the business as a for-profit business or instead as a nonprofit business. For-profit businesses have shareholders who can receive dividends. Nonprofit businesses cannot have shareholders and are forbidden to pay dividends. Tax rules are also different for nonprofits. If they meet Internal Revenue Service (IRS) and state law standards, they may be exempt from income and property taxes.

For-profit businesses can choose a number of legal forms under state law. The most common business entities in health care include corporations, limited liability companies (LLCs), and limited liability partnerships (LLPs). Each state has statutes enabling the formation of these entities. Lawyers can choose to organize businesses under any state law, even a state where the client does not have an office or other operations. Delaware is a popular choice for larger businesses due to Delaware's reputation for predictable and favorable corporate law. However, most nonprofit hospitals are incorporated under their local state law.

If physicians own 100 percent of a for-profit physician practice, most state laws allow the corporation, LLC, or LLP to be designated as a "professional" corporation (PC), professional LLC (PLLC), or professional LLP (PLLP). All of these owners must hold the appropriate license to practice medicine. Other professions can also form their own version of a PC, PLLC, or PLLP, including lawyers, accountants, and engineers.

For all of these for-profit business forms, an official filing must be accepted by the state where the business was formed as well as every state where it does business. These businesses pay taxes under both state and federal law.

Nonprofit corporations are organized under a different set of state statutes. In health care, nonprofits can be very large businesses, as are the majority of U.S. hospitals and health systems. The terms "nonprofit," "non-profit," and "not for profit" mean the same thing; the terms vary by state statute. Importantly, nonprofit organizations can turn a profit, but that profit cannot be disbursed to shareholders (there are none) and instead the profits must be directed to the charitable or other nonprofit purposes for which the nonprofit was formed. If physicians are not directly employed by a health system, or their own professional organizations, they occasionally practice in nonprofit associated entities sometimes called "foundations." Nonprofits can also be organized as charitable trusts.

Nonprofit status under state law is generally necessary but not sufficient for qualifying as a tax-exempt charitable organization under federal income tax law under §501(c)(3) of the Internal Revenue Code (26 U.S.C. or I.R.C.). Most of the hospital systems in the United States qualify as tax-exempt charitable organizations and are run on professional business principles, despite the "charitable" designation. But tax law imposes a host of unique fiduciary duties on charitable health care organizations, a major focus in Chapter 5.

Nonprofit health care organizations will also want to qualify as charitable for other purposes, including state income tax law and local property tax law. These tax statuses are separately determined, although the criteria may overlap. Additional complexity arises when exempt organizations such as hospitals collaborate with taxable businesses such as private physician groups. These joint ventures and other arrangements are subject to additional scrutiny by the IRS. These tax issues are discussed in Chapter 5.

Health insurance companies, whether for profit or nonprofit, are organized and regulated traditionally by state insurance law. If an insurance company becomes insolvent, federal bankruptcy law does not apply and state insurance insolvency law controls. Blue Cross Blue Shield plans and other nonprofit health insurers also are covered by unique federal tax rules, which are described in I.R.C. §833.

B. THE ROLE OF THE HOSPITAL MEDICAL STAFF

The board of directors is the ultimate governing authority in a hospital (if nonprofit, the directors are occasionally called trustees, with similar functions). State law and common practice also require hospitals to assist in the organization of the physicians and other providers who have been given admitting or clinical privileges to practice in the hospital. Admitting privileges allow physicians to admit patients to a hospital, but they may not treat patients once they are admitted. Clinical privileges are more complete and allow physicians to both admit and treat patients at the privileging hospital. Collectively, the providers that hold admitting and clinical privileges are called the medical staff.

A license to practice medicine is sufficient to open an office practice, but if a physician wants to admit patients to a hospital or needs to perform clinical procedures in a hospital, a second step is necessary: obtaining permission from the hospital itself by joining the medical staff with "admitting privileges" and/or "clinical privileges." The medical staff bylaws typically govern this process.

The medical staff are governed by the medical staff bylaws, which is a separate document from the bylaws that govern the corporate entity of the hospital. For reasons related to their professional autonomy (discussed more fully below), the medical staff does not fit squarely under the typical corporate hierarchy, subject to direct control and supervision of corporate officers and directors. Ongoing tension occurs between the corporation's need to manage its operations and the medical staff's preference to operate as a self-governing unit. The staff bylaws define the rights of the members of the medical staff, which include processes for both admittance to the staff ("credentialing") and processes for removal from the staff. The medical staff bylaws processes are a form of common law due process.

While many of these relationships are amicable, sometimes they sour. In the case that follows, the hospital unilaterally amended the medical staff bylaws, raising the key question of who is in charge of the medical staff: the hospital's board or the medical staff themselves.

> Medicare conditions of participation require hospitals receiving Medicare reimbursement to ensure that their medical staff bylaws follow certain quality and fair process rules. 42 C.F.R. §482.22.

Medical Staff of Avera Marshall Regional Medical Center v. Avera Marshall

857 N.W.2d 695 (Minn. 2014)

In 2012, the governing board of respondent Avera Marshall Regional Medical Center, a nonprofit hospital in Marshall, Minnesota, announced a plan to repeal the hospital's medical staff bylaws and replace them with revised bylaws. Avera Marshall's Medical Staff, its Chief of Staff, and Chief of Staff-elect eventually commenced an action seeking, as relevant here, a declaration that the Medical Staff has standing to sue Avera Marshall and that the medical staff bylaws are an enforceable contract between Avera Marshall and the Medical Staff. The district court entered judgment for Avera Marshall and dismissed the case after concluding both that the Medical Staff lacked the capacity to sue Avera Marshall and that the medical staff bylaws do not constitute an enforceable contract between Avera Marshall and the Medical Staff. The court of appeals affirmed the district court. For the reasons discussed below, we reverse the court of appeals and remand to the district court for further proceedings.

Avera Marshall is owned and operated by Avera Health and is incorporated under the Minnesota Nonprofit Corporation Act, Minn. Stat. ch. 317A (2012). Under Avera Marshall's articles of incorporation and corporate bylaws, Avera Marshall's board of directors (the board) is vested with the general responsibility for management of Avera Marshall. The corporate bylaws require the board to "organize the physicians and appropriate other persons granted practice privileges in the hospital . . . into a medical-dental staff under medical-dental staff bylaws approved by the [board]."

Appellants include two individual physicians and Avera Marshall's Medical Staff. The medical staff is composed of practitioners, primarily physicians with admitting and clinical privileges to care for patients at the hospital. The Medical Staff is subject to medical staff bylaws originally enacted by the board in 1995. When this case commenced, appellant Dr. Steven Meister was the Chief of Staff of the Medical Staff and appellant Dr. Jane Willett was the Medical Staff's Chief of Staff-elect. Dr. Meister was the chair of the Medical Executive Committee (the MEC), a medical staff committee that acts on the Medical Staff's behalf, and Dr. Willett was a member of the MEC.

> Hospitals restrict doctors' ability to practice in their facilities for both quality control and competitive reasons. The process of joining the medical staff and receiving admitting privileges is called credentialing, as it includes a quality control check on the physician's medical credentials and any prior issues with errors or malpractice.

Before May 1, 2012, the medical staff bylaws provided that, in order to admit patients, a practitioner was required to be a member of the medical staff. To serve on the medical staff, a physician was required to agree to be bound by the medical staff bylaws. One of the "enumerated purposes" for the medical staff set out in the bylaws was "[t]o initiate and maintain rules, regulations and policies for the internal governance of the Medical Staff." Another enumerated purpose was "[t]o provide a means whereby issues concerning the Medical Staff and the Medical Center [could] be directly discussed by the Medical Staff with the Board of Directors and the Administration, with the understanding that the Medical Staff [was] subject to the ultimate authority of the Board of Directors."

The bylaws also gave the Medical Staff authority, "[s]ubject to the authority and approval of [the board]," to "exercise such power as is reasonably necessary to discharge its responsibilities under these bylaws and under the corporate bylaws of the Medical Center." The Medical Staff was also afforded "prerogatives," such as attending and voting on matters presented at medical staff and committee meetings and holding medical staff office. The bylaws described these prerogatives as "general in nature" and possibly "subject to limitations by special conditions . . . , by other sections of these Medical Staff Bylaws and by the Medical Staff Rules and Regulations, subject to approval by [the board]."

Under the bylaws, the Chief of Staff, the MEC, the board, or one-third of active medical staff members could propose amendments to or repeal of medical staff bylaws. The bylaws further provided for review of proposed amendments to the bylaws, either by the MEC itself or by special committee. Section 17.2 of the bylaws specifically provided that, "for the purposes of enacting a bylaws change, the change shall require an affirmative vote of . . . two-thirds of the Members eligible to vote." Bylaws changes recommended by the Medical Staff would not become effective until approved by the board. The bylaws were silent with respect to bylaws changes proposed by the board but not recommended for approval by the Medical Staff. However, the amendment and repeal process was "subject to approval by a majority vote of [the board]" and could not "supersede the general authority of [the board] as set forth in its corporate bylaws or applicable common law or statutes."

In January 2012, the board notified the Medical Staff that the board had approved the repeal of the medical staff bylaws and that a set of revised medical staff bylaws had been approved. The notice solicited the Medical Staff's input but explained that the revised bylaws would take effect on April 1, 2012. At a medical staff meeting on January 24, 2012, Avera Marshall's CEO and President announced that, while individual members of the Medical Staff could comment on the changes, the board would not accept comments from the Medical Staff as an organized body, and the proposed changes would not be submitted to the Medical Staff for a vote.

After review, the MEC concluded that the proposed revisions to the bylaws restricted the rights of the Medical Staff, the functioning of medical-staff committees, and the Medical Staff's ability to ensure the quality of patient care. On that basis, MEC recommended that the board reject the changes. Notwithstanding the board's decision that the repeal and revision of the bylaws would not be submitted to the Medical Staff for a vote, on March 20, 2012, relying on section 17.2 of the former bylaws, the Medical Staff voted on the proposed changes and rejected both the repeal of the former bylaws and the enactment of the revised bylaws. Ultimately, the revised bylaws took effect on May 1, 2012. . . .

With respect to whether the former bylaws create a contract, the district court and court of appeals agreed with Avera Marshall, concluding that the former medical staff bylaws are not an enforceable contract because of a lack of consideration. Both courts reasoned that the bylaws lacked consideration because the bylaws simply memorialized Avera Marshall's preexisting duty under Minnesota Rules to adopt medical staff bylaws.[3]

. . . .

The record in this case indicates that Avera Marshall formed a contractual relationship with each member of the Medical Staff upon appointment.[5] Avera Marshall offered privileges to each member of the Medical Staff, so long as the Medical Staff member agreed to be bound by the medical staff bylaws as a condition of appointment. Each member of the Medical Staff who accepted Avera Marshall's offer of appointment agreed to be bound by the bylaws. Thus, there was a bargained-for exchange of promises and mutual consent to the exchange. Importantly, there was also consideration. Both Avera Marshall and the members of its Medical Staff voluntarily assumed obligations on the condition of an act or forbearance on the part of the other.

The district court and court of appeals both concluded that the Medical Staff did not have the capacity to sue Avera Marshall and that the medical staff bylaws did not constitute an enforceable contract between Avera Marshall and the Medical Staff. As a result, appellants' claims were dismissed. Because we conclude that the Medical Staff has the capacity to sue and be sued under Minn. Stat. §540.151, and that the medical staff bylaws constitute an enforceable contract between Avera Marshall and the individual members of the Medical Staff, we reverse the decision of the court of appeals and remand to the district court for further proceedings consistent with this opinion.

Reversed and remanded.

---

3. Minn. R. 4640.0700 provides in part:

The governing body or the person or persons designated as the governing authority in each institution shall be responsible for its management, control, and operation. It shall appoint a hospital administrator and the medical staff. It shall formulate the administrative policies for the hospital.

Minn. R. 4640.0700, subp. 2 (2013).
Minn. R. 4640.0800 provides in part:

The medical staff shall be responsible to the governing body of the hospital for the clinical and scientific work of the hospital. It shall be called upon to advise regarding professional problems and policies.

In any hospital used by two or more practitioners, the medical staff shall be an organized group which shall formulate and, with the approval of the governing body, adopt bylaws, rules, regulations, and policies for the proper conduct of its work. The medical staff shall: designate one of its members as chief of staff; hold regular meetings for which minutes and records of attendance shall be kept; and review and analyze at regular intervals the clinical experience in the hospital.

Minn. R. 4640.0800, subps. 1-2 (2013).
5. Other courts have similarly held that medical staff bylaws may be an enforceable contract, or an enforceable part of a contract, between a hospital and members of its medical staff. *See, e.g.,* Williams v. Univ. Med. Ctr. of S. Nev., 688 F. Supp. 2d 1134, 1142-43 (D. Nev. 2010); Gianetti v. Norwalk Hosp., 211 Conn. 51, 557 A.2d 1249, 1255 (1989); Lo v. Provena Covenant Med. Ctr., 356 Ill. App. 3d 538, 292 Ill. Dec. 451, 826 N.E.2d 592, 598-99 (2005); Terre Haute Reg'l Hosp., Inc. v. El-Issa, 470 N.E.2d 1371, 1376-77 (Ind. Ct. App. 1984); Virmani v. Presbyterian Health Serv. Corp., 127 N.C. App. 71, 488 S.E.2d 284, 287-88 (1997); St. John's Hosp. Med. Staff v. St. John Reg'l Med. Ctr., Inc., 90 S.D. 674, 245 N.W.2d 472, 474-75 (1976); Lewisburg Cmty. Hosp., Inc. v. Alfredson, 805 S.W.2d 756, 759 (Tenn. 1991); Bass v. Ambrosius, 185 Wis. 2d 879, 520 N.W.2d 625, 628 (App. 1994).

ANDERSON, Justice (dissenting).

I respectfully dissent. At its heart, this case is about who has ultimate control of Avera Marshall Regional Medical Center — Avera Marshall's Medical Staff or Avera Marshall's board of directors. As a matter of contract law, and under the terms of Avera Marshall's corporate bylaws and the medical staff bylaws, the answer to that question is Avera Marshall's board of directors. Consequently, I would affirm summary judgment in favor of respondents Avera Marshall, et al.

I

I agree with the majority's recitation of the facts, but think it important to first address why Avera Marshall's board of directors unilaterally amended the medical staff bylaws, which gets to the heart of the dispute in this case. In 2009, Avera Health Systems assumed control of Weiner Memorial Medical Center, which had previously been owned and operated by the City of Marshall, and the hospital was incorporated as a nonprofit under the name Avera Marshall Regional Medical Center. Shortly thereafter, tension and conflict arose between members of the Medical Staff employed by Affiliated Community Medical Centers, P.A. (ACMC), who held privileges at Avera Marshall, and Avera Marshall's governing body. According to the President and CEO of Avera Marshall, the board of directors subsequently amended the medical staff bylaws to address the "dysfunction" of the Medical Staff, particularly its Medical Executive Committee (MEC), "which [wa]s obvious and ha[d] gone on for almost sixteen months." The adoption of the new bylaws "was also a result of [board of directors'] growing concerns about Dr. Meister's leadership" as he "conducted himself in a manner designed to exploit and harm [Avera Marshall], as opposed to being an effective leader of the entire medical staff." Moreover, the problems within the MEC "resulted in dysfunctional quality review and credentialing processes at the Hospital"; the MEC had failed to carry out its functions under the old medical staff bylaws, including its credentialing and peer review functions; and the new bylaws were meant to "better promote quality review and patient safety free from bias." . . .

> Failures of quality review and credentialing could hurt patient safety.

II

I am skeptical that appellant Medical Staff has standing to sue under Minn. Stat. §540.151 (2012), but I need not decide this issue, because even if the Medical Staff has standing to sue, the Medical Staff and its members do not have the rights they claim to have under the medical staff bylaws because those bylaws do not create an enforceable contract. There is a split of authority regarding whether medical staff bylaws constitute a contract between a hospital's medical staff or its members and the hospital. *See* 1 Karen S. Rieger et al., Health Law Practice Guide §2:16 (2014) (listing cases in which courts recognized medical staff bylaws as a contract, and those in which they did not). Those courts holding that medical staff bylaws do not constitute a contract often do so on the ground that a necessary component of contract formation is missing in medical staff bylaws — namely, consideration.

. . . This is not to say that medical staff bylaws can never constitute a contract between a medical staff and a hospital. A medical staff could bargain with a hospital's governing body to secure language in the medical staff bylaws expressly declaring the medical staff's rights under the bylaws. If the medical staff bylaws are written to give the medical staff and its members the rights to sue and recover for breach of the medical staff bylaws, such an agreement arguably would be enforceable against the hospital. But here, there is no language in the medical staff bylaws stating that the provisions of the bylaws are enforceable against the hospital, and so I would conclude that the bylaws do not constitute an enforceable contract. Because there is no contract, I would affirm summary judgment in favor of the respondents on count two of the complaint.

III

Having determined that the medical staff bylaws do not constitute a contract between the medical staff or its members and Avera Marshall, I turn to the final issue in this appeal: whether Avera Marshall's board of directors was authorized to unilaterally amend the medical staff bylaws. The appellants, representing the interests of the medical staff, argue that Avera Marshall breached the medical staff bylaws by unilaterally changing the bylaws over the objection of the majority of medical staff members. Essentially, they argue that the medical staff bylaws outline a specific process for amending the bylaws, which includes obtaining an affirmative vote of two-thirds of the medical staff members eligible to vote, and that Avera Marshall breached this process by amending the medical staff bylaws without obtaining two-thirds approval. I disagree. In my view, under the terms of Avera Marshall's corporate bylaws and the medical staff bylaws, the board of directors was authorized to unilaterally amend the medical staff bylaws.

> The rule in a majority of states reaches the dissent's result, but with diverse approaches.

A

I first turn to Avera Marshall's corporate bylaws for guidance as to the process required for amending the medical staff bylaws. Avera Marshall's articles of incorporation vest management and control of the hospital in its board of directors. Any powers supposedly granted to the medical staff under the medical staff bylaws "must originate from, and be authorized by, the Board pursuant to the Corporate Bylaws." Mahan v. Avera St. Luke's, 621 N.W.2d 150, 155 (S.D. 2001). Although not binding on this court, *Mahan* is helpful in articulating the relationship between medical staff bylaws and a hospital's corporate bylaws:

> Their legal relationship is similar to that between statutes and a constitution. They are not separate and equal sovereigns. The former derives its power and authority from the latter. Hence, to determine whether the staff was granted the power that it now claims to possess, any judicial analysis must begin with an examination of the Corporate Bylaws.

Put simply, the corporate bylaws are a superior source of authority as compared to the medical staff bylaws when determining what process is required for amending the medical staff bylaws.

To determine what rights the medical staff and its individual members have, therefore, it is necessary to analyze Avera Marshall's corporate bylaws. The corporate bylaws provide that "[t]he Board of Directors shall organize the physicians and appropriate other persons granted practice privileges in the hospital owned and operated by the Corporation into a medical-dental staff under medical-dental staff bylaws." Under this provision, Avera Marshall's board of directors was required not only to organize a medical staff, but also to adopt medical staff bylaws that would govern the medical staff. The corporate bylaws further provide that:

There shall be bylaws, rules and regulations, or amendments thereto, for the medical-dental staff that set forth its organization and government. Proposed bylaws, rules and regulations, or amendments thereto, *may be recommended by the medical-dental staff or the Board of Directors.*

Importantly, Avera Marshall's corporate bylaws grant to the medical staff the right to recommend medical staff bylaws. The corporate bylaws say nothing, however, about requiring a two-thirds vote from voting members of the medical staff in order to amend the bylaws. . . .

[T]he corporate bylaws only grant to the medical staff the limited power to propose amendments. Under the terms of its corporate bylaws, therefore, Avera Marshall retained the authority to unilaterally amend the medical staff bylaws. . . .

C

Finally, the appellants argue that the standards promulgated by the Joint Commission on Accreditation of Hospitals (Joint Commission) preclude a hospital from unilaterally amending medical staff bylaws, providing evidence that Avera Marshall could not unilaterally amend the medical staff bylaws. The appellants are wrong. Hospitals licensed in Minnesota may choose either to be inspected by the Commissioner of Health or alternatively be accredited by "an approved accrediting organization." One such approved accrediting organization is the Joint Commission, which has historically "played a defining role in developing, implementing and enforcing minimum standards of conduct by which hospitals and their stakeholders function." Under Minnesota law, it is recommended, but not required, that a hospital adopt the Joint Commission standards. Across the nation, 88 percent of hospitals are accredited by the Joint Commission. Prior to 2012, Avera Marshall was accredited by the Joint Commission.

> The Joint Commission is an influential private accreditation organization. Many states and the federal government delegate accreditation of health care facilities to private organizations like the Joint Commission. Without this accreditation, hospitals and other entities cannot participate in public insurance programs like Medicare and Medicaid, as well as some private insurance plans.

One of the Joint Commission's standards provides that "[n]either the organized medical staff nor the governing body may unilaterally amend the medical staff bylaws or rules and regulations." JCAH Comprehensive Accreditation Manual for Hospitals, 2010, Standard MS.01.01.03. If this provision applied to Avera Marshall, it is arguable that Avera Marshall violated the provision when it amended the medical staff bylaws without obtaining the approval of the medical staff. Notably, however, the bylaws in effect at the time Avera Marshall amended the medical staff bylaws did not contain Standard MS.01.01.03, or language similar to that standard. More importantly, even if Avera Marshall was subject to the standard by reason of its decision to be accredited by the Joint Commission, it withdrew from Joint Commission accreditation on January 19, 2012, effective as of January 30, 2012. The amended medical staff bylaws did not take effect until May 1, 2012. Consequently, Standard MS.01.01.03—and its prohibition on unilaterally amending medical staff bylaws—did not apply to Avera Marshall.

IV

I am concerned that today's majority opinion will encourage conflict between medical staffs and a hospital's board of directors. Ultimately, in my view, a hospital's board of directors must be allowed to amend medical staff bylaws when it has expressly reserved ultimate authority over the medical staff and determines that doing so is in the best interest of the hospital and patient care. This does not mean, of course, that a hospital board of directors will make the correct decision or that members of the medical staff should not provide advice, guidance, and, where necessary, criticism of board decisions. But, in the end, the board must have the power to take steps to resolve problems and end conflict by amending the medical staff bylaws, without fear of prolonged litigation.

For the foregoing reasons, I would affirm the decision of the court of appeals, and so I respectfully dissent.

QUESTIONS

1. Could a hospital amend the medical staff bylaws to fire the entire radiology department and hire an outside firm to provide the services?
2. If a hospital has unilateral authority to amend medical staff bylaws, why does it matter whether the relationship was strained, according to the dissent?
3. What is the legal reasoning behind specially protecting a medical staff through separate governance and special legal procedures?

An important source of the conflict in the *Avera Marshall* case was the hospital's acquisition of physician practices, effectively transitioning many in the medical staff from independent practice owners to employed, hospital-controlled physicians. Nationally, the number of physicians who own their practice is declining, especially among younger physicians. The American Medical Association's Physician Practice Benchmark Survey has tracked this trend for many years.

QUESTIONS

1. From the hospital's perspective, what are the advantages and disadvantages of organizing the medical staff as employees rather than independent contractors?
2. Why would physicians find employment by hospitals to be desirable or undesirable?

C. PROHIBITION ON THE CORPORATE PRACTICE OF MEDICINE

Being an employed physician raises questions about financial conflicts of interest, particularly when the employer is not a physician or any other kind of health care provider. One example of efforts to curb such conflicts of interest is the so-called "corporate practice of medicine" doctrine, an older rule that prohibits physicians from being employed by a corporation. The reasoning of the doctrine, that a corporation is not human and literally cannot practice medicine, has remained surprisingly robust in some states, even though many physicians and other health care providers are employed by corporate entities in the modern era. State laws allowing physicians to practice in professional groups owned exclusively by physicians typically bypass the doctrine. Potential problems arise, however, when some of the owners of an entity that employs physicians are not physicians, even if they are health care providers with a different scope of practice, such as a hospital.

The prohibition on the corporate practice of medicine is often implied from state physician licensure laws; therefore, the doctrine varies across states. In some states, the doctrine has been repealed. In others, it has been restricted through exceptions for various types of employers, such as nonprofit hospitals. In many states, the doctrine is not found in statutes at all but is only found in judicial decisions. The doctrine can threaten economic relationships that are commonplace in other sectors and puts a premium on understanding the precise contours of the doctrine's relationship to licensure law in the particular state at issue. The following case represents well the type of arguments deployed under the corporate practice of medicine doctrine, but the law varies widely on these points from state to state.

> In the late nineteenth and early twentieth centuries, the corporate practice of medicine doctrine thwarted large companies who wanted to hire doctors to care for workers in factories. Today, the doctrine is most often applied against hospitals and health systems that employ physicians.

Berlin v. Sarah Bush Lincoln Health Center

688 N.E.2d 106 (Ill. 1997)

Plaintiff, Richard Berlin, Jr., M.D., filed a complaint for declaratory judgment and a motion for summary judgment seeking to have a restrictive covenant contained in an employment agreement with defendant, Sara Bush Lincoln Health Center (the Health Center), declared unenforceable. The circuit court of Coles County, finding the entire employment agreement unenforceable, granted summary judgment in favor of Dr. Berlin. The circuit court reasoned that the Health Center, as a nonprofit corporation employing a physician, was practicing medicine in violation of the prohibition on the corporate practice of medicine. A divided appellate court affirmed, and this court granted the Health Center's petition for leave to appeal.

The central issue involved in this appeal is whether the "corporate practice doctrine" prohibits corporations which are licensed hospitals from employing physicians to provide medical services.

We find the doctrine inapplicable to licensed hospitals and accordingly reverse.

BACKGROUND

The facts are not in dispute. The Health Center is a nonprofit corporation duly licensed under the Hospital Licensing Act to operate a hospital. In December 1992, Dr. Berlin and the Health Center entered into a written agreement whereby the Health Center employed Dr. Berlin to practice medicine for the hospital for five years. The agreement provided that Dr. Berlin could terminate the employment relationship for any reason prior to the end of the five-year term by furnishing the Health Center with 180 days['] advance written notice of such termination. The agreement also contained a restrictive covenant which prohibited Dr. Berlin from competing with the hospital by providing health services within a 50-mile radius of the Health Center for two years after the end of the employment agreement.

> Note that Dr. Berlin is trying to use the doctrine to break an otherwise valid contract he signed in order to work at a competitor.

On February 4, 1994, Dr. Berlin informed the Health Center by letter that he was resigning effective February 7, 1994, and accepting employment with the Carle Clinic Association. After his resignation, Dr. Berlin immediately began working at a Carle Clinic facility located approximately one mile from the Health Center. Shortly thereafter, the Health Center sought a preliminary injunction to prohibit Dr. Berlin from practicing at the Carle Clinic based on the restrictive covenant contained in the aforesaid employment agreement. . . .

This court granted the Health Center's petition for leave to appeal. We granted the County of Cook, the Illinois Hospital and Health Systems Association, the Metropolitan Chicago Healthcare Council, the American Hospital Association, and OSF HealthCare System leave to file amicus curiae briefs in support of the Health Center. We granted leave to the American Medical Association, the Illinois State Medical Society, the Illinois State Dental Society, and several regional medical societies to file amicus curiae briefs in support of Dr. Berlin's position. . . .

Hospital Employment of Physicians

The Health Center and its supporting amici curiae contend that no judicial determination exists which prohibits hospitals from employing physicians. In support of this contention, the Health Center argues that this court has acknowledged the legitimacy of such employment practices in past decisions. In the alternative, the Health Center contends that if a judicial prohibition on hospital employment of physicians does exist, it should be overruled. In support of this contention, the Health Center argues that the public policies behind such a prohibition are inapplicable to licensed hospitals, particularly nonprofit hospitals.

The Health Center also contends that there is no statutory prohibition on the corporate employment of physicians. The Health Center notes that no statute has ever expressly stated that physicians cannot be employed by corporations. To the contrary, the Health Center argues that other legislative actions recognize that hospitals can indeed employ physicians.

Dr. Berlin and supporting amici curiae contend that this court, in *Kerner*, adopted the corporate practice of medicine doctrine, which prohibits corporations from employing physicians. Dr. Berlin concludes that the Health Center, as a nonprofit corporation, is prohibited by the *Kerner* rule from entering into employment agreements with physicians.

Dr. Berlin also disputes the Health Center's contention that public policy supports creating an exception to the *Kerner* rule for hospitals. He argues that, because no legislative enactment subsequent to the *Kerner* case expressly grants hospitals the authority to employ physicians, the legislature has ratified the corporate practice of medicine doctrine as the public policy of Illinois. At this point, a review of the corporate practice of medicine doctrine is appropriate.

> In Illinois, the corporate practice of medicine doctrine was not statutory but rather implied from a 1936 Illinois Supreme Court decision. It would have been difficult to know this from a search of the Illinois Code.

Corporate Practice of Medicine Doctrine

The corporate practice of medicine doctrine prohibits corporations from providing professional medical services. Although a few states have codified the doctrine, the prohibition is primarily inferred from state medical licensure acts, which regulate the profession of medicine and forbid its practice by unlicensed individuals. The rationale behind the doctrine is that a corporation cannot be licensed to practice medicine because only a human being can sustain the education, training, and character-screening which are prerequisites to receiving a professional license. Since a corporation cannot receive a medical license, it follows that a corporation cannot legally practice the profession.

The rationale of the doctrine concludes that the employment of physicians by corporations is illegal because the acts of the physicians are attributable to the corporate employer, which cannot obtain a medical license. The prohibition on the corporate employment of physicians is invariably supported by several public policy arguments which espouse the dangers of lay control over professional judgment, the division of the physician's loyalty between his patient and his profit-making employer, and the commercialization of the profession. . . .

> Consider whether the legal profession would permit nonlawyers to exercise "lay control over professional judgment."

Application of Doctrine in Illinois

. . . *People ex rel. Kerner v. United Medical Service, Inc.* involved a corporation which operated a low-cost health clinic in which all medical services were rendered by duly-licensed physicians. The State brought a *quo warranto* action against the corporation, alleging it was illegally engaged in the practice of medicine in violation of the Medical Practice Act. The lower court found the corporation guilty and rendered the judgment of ouster against it.

In affirming, this court rejected defendant's contention that the practice of medicine does not encompass the corporate ownership of a health clinic where treatment is rendered solely by licensed physician employees. The court observed that section 24 of the Medical Practice Act specifically prohibits the performance of certain acts without a medical license, including the diagnosis and treatment of human ailments and the maintenance of an office for the examination and treatment of human ailments. The court stated that "[t]he legislative intent manifest from a view of the entire [Medical Practice Act] is that only individuals may obtain a license thereunder. No corporation can meet the requirements of the statute essential to the issuance of a license."

Prior to the instant action, apparently no Illinois court has applied the corporate practice of medicine rule set out in *Kerner*, or specifically addressed the issue of whether licensed hospitals are prohibited from employing physicians. We therefore look to other jurisdictions with reference to the application of the corporate practice of medicine doctrine to hospitals.

Applicability of Doctrine to Hospitals in Other Jurisdictions

Although the corporate practice of medicine doctrine has long been recognized by a number of jurisdictions, the important role hospitals serve in the health care field has also been increasingly recognized. Accordingly, numerous jurisdictions have recognized either judicial or statutory exceptions to the corporate practice of medicine doctrine which allow hospitals to employ physicians and other health care professionals. *See, e.g.,* Cal. Bus. & Prof. Code §2400 (West 1990) (exception for charitable hospitals); Colo. Rev. Stat. §25-3-103.7(2) (West Supp. 1997) (hospitals may employ physicians); Rush v. City of St. Petersburg, 205 So. 2d 11 (Fla. App. 1967); St. Francis Regional Medical Center, Inc. v. Weiss, 254 Kan. 728, 869 P.2d 606 (1994); People v. John H. Woodbury Dermatological Institute, 192 N.Y. 454, 85 N.E. 697 (1908). A review of this authority reveals that there are primarily three approaches utilized in determining that the corporate practice of medicine doctrine is inapplicable to hospitals.

First, some states refused to adopt the corporate practice of medicine doctrine altogether when initially interpreting their respective medical practice act. These states generally determined that a hospital corporation which employs a physician is not practicing medicine, but rather is merely making medical treatment available. . . .

Under the second approach, the courts of some jurisdictions determined that the corporate practice doctrine is inapplicable to nonprofit hospitals and health associations. These courts reasoned that the public policy arguments supporting the corporate practice doctrine do not apply to physicians employed by charitable institutions.

In the third approach, the courts of several states have determined that the corporate practice doctrine is not applicable to hospitals which employ physicians because hospitals are authorized by other laws to provide medical treatment to patients.

We find the rationale of the latter two approaches persuasive. We decline to apply the corporate practice of medicine doctrine to licensed hospitals. The instant cause is distinguishable from *Kerner, Allison,* and *Winberry.* None of those cases specifically involved the employment of physicians by a hospital. More important, none of those cases involved a corporation licensed to provide health care services to the general public. Accordingly, we decline to extend the *Kerner* corporate practice rule to licensed hospitals.

> Which of these three approaches is most protective of the patient?

The corporate practice of medicine doctrine set forth in *Kerner* was not an interpretation of the plain language of the Medical Practice Act. The Medical Practice Act contains no express prohibition on the corporate employment of physicians. Rather, the corporate practice of medicine doctrine was inferred from the general policies behind the Medical Practice Act. Such a prohibition is entirely appropriate to a general corporation possessing no licensed authority to offer medical services to the public, such as the appellant in *Kerner.* However, when a corporation has been sanctioned by the laws of this state to operate a hospital, such a prohibition is inapplicable. . . .

We further see no justification for distinguishing between nonprofit and for-profit hospitals in this regard. The authorities and duties of licensed hospitals are conferred equally upon both entities.

In addition, we find the public policy concerns which support the corporate practice doctrine inapplicable to a licensed hospital in the modern health care industry. The concern for lay control over professional judgment is alleviated in a licensed hospital, where generally a separate professional medical staff is responsible for the quality of medical services rendered in the facility.

Furthermore, we believe that extensive changes in the health care industry since the time of the *Kerner* decision, including the emergence of corporate health maintenance organizations (Health Maintenance Organization Act), have greatly altered the concern over the commercialization of health care. In addition, such concerns are relieved when a licensed hospital is the physician's employer. Hospitals have an independent duty to provide for the patient's health and welfare. . . .

CONCLUSION

For the reasons stated, the judgment of the appellate court affirming the circuit court's award of summary judgment for plaintiff is reversed. The judgment of the circuit court is reversed and the cause is remanded to the circuit court for further proceedings not inconsistent with this opinion.

Appellate court judgment reversed; circuit court judgment reversed; cause remanded.

Justice HARRISON, dissenting:

In *Kerner*, this court held that a corporation cannot employ physicians and collect fees for their services because such conduct constitutes the practice of medicine and the practice of medicine by corporations is prohibited. The court based its conclusion on the Medical Practice Act, reasoning that under the statute, a license is required to practice medicine and "[t]he legislative intent manifest from a view of the entire law is that only individuals may obtain a license thereunder. No corporation can meet the requirements of the statute essential to the issuance of a license."

More than 60 years have passed since *Kerner* was decided. If the legislature believed that our construction of the Act was erroneous or that the rule announced in *Kerner* should be changed, it could have amended the law to authorize the practice of medicine by entities other than individuals. With limited exceptions not applicable here, it has not done so. To the contrary, it has continued to adhere to the requirements that medicine can only be practiced by those who hold valid licenses from the state and that only individuals can obtain such licenses.

The legislature is presumed to know the construction the courts have placed upon a statute. When it amends a statute but does not alter a previous interpretation by this court, we assume that the legislature intended for the amendment to have the same interpretation previously given. . . .

[T]he General Assembly has expressly authorized the employment of physicians by Health Maintenance Organizations (HMOs) under the Health Maintenance Organization Act. If the General Assembly had intended to grant the same authority to hospitals, I believe that it would have been similarly straightforward and unambiguous in doing so.

In addition to creating special rules for HMOs, the General Assembly has also decided to allow physicians to employ various forms of business organizations in practicing their profession. Physicians may incorporate in accordance with the Professional Service Corporation Act, they may form corporations to provide medical services under the Medical Corporation Act, they have the right to practice in a professional association organized pursuant to the Professional Association Act, and they can organize and operate limited liability companies to practice medicine under the recently amended Limited Liability Company Act. Again, however, none of these provisions pertains to hospitals, and no inference can be drawn from any of them that the General Assembly intended to alter the prohibition against the corporate practice of medicine by hospitals.

For the foregoing reasons, I agree with the appellate court that the corporate practice doctrine prohibited defendant, Sarah Bush Lincoln Health Center, from entering into an employment agreement with Dr. Berlin. That agreement, including its restrictive covenant, was void and unenforceable. Dr. Berlin's motion for summary judgment was therefore properly granted, and the judgment of the appellate court should be affirmed.

QUESTIONS

1. Why did the Sarah Bush Lincoln Health Center want a restrictive covenant in the contract with its physicians?
2. Was the restrictive covenant reasonable in scope and duration?
3. Was *Kerner* overruled? What is the current state of the law in Illinois?

In other states, statutes and regulations have been amended to address this question. For example, consider the careful hierarchies and organizational forms permitted in New Jersey:

N.J. Admin. Code §13:35-6.16. Professional practice structure

(f) Acceptable professional practice forms are as follows:

1. Solo: A practitioner may practice solo and/or may employ or otherwise remunerate other licensed practitioners to render professional services within the scope of practice of each employee's license, but which scope shall not exceed that of the employer's license. The practitioner may employ ancillary non-licensed staff in accordance with Board rules, if any, and accepted standards of practice.

2. Partnership, professional association or limited liability company: A practitioner may practice in a partnership, professional association, or limited liability company, but such entity shall be composed solely of health care professionals, each of whom is duly licensed or otherwise authorized to render the same or closely allied professional service within this State. . . . A practitioner who is a member, employee, agent, or representative of the limited liability company shall remain personally responsible for his or her own negligence, wrongful acts, or misconduct, and that of any person under his or her direct supervision and control while rendering professional services on behalf of the limited liability company in this State to the person for whom such professional service was being rendered. The professional services offered by each practitioner, whether a partner, member or shareholder, shall be the same or in a closely allied medical or professional health care field. . . .

> An essential feature of corporations and LLCs is limited liability, which shields professionally licensed owners from legal liability from the entity's wrongdoing, though not necessarily from professional misdeeds.

3. Associational relationship with other practitioner or professional entity: For the purpose of this rule, the term "employment" shall include an ongoing associational relationship between a licensee and professional practitioner(s) or entity on the professional practice premises for the provision of professional services, whether the licensee is denominated as an employee or independent contractor, for any form of remuneration.

i. A practitioner may be employed, as so defined, within the scope of the practitioner's licensed practice and in circumstances where quality control of the employee's professional practice can be and is lawfully supervised and evaluated by the employing practitioner. Thus, a practitioner with a plenary license shall not be employed by a practitioner with a limited scope of license, nor shall a practitioner with a limited license be employed by a practitioner with a more limited form of limited

> Note that these restrictions are hierarchical; those holding a more limited license cannot employ providers with a broader license or control their practice.

license. By way of example, a physician with a plenary license may be employed by another plenary licensed physician, but an M.D. or D.O. may not be employed by a podiatrist (D.P.M.) or chiropractor (D.C.) or midwife or certified nurse midwife (R.M., C.N.M.). A podiatrist may not employ a chiropractor. This section shall not preclude any licensee from employing licensed personnel such as nurses, x-ray technologists, physical therapists, ophthalmic dispensers and ophthalmic technicians, etc., as appropriate to the primary practice of the employer.

4. Shareholder or employee of a general business corporation: A licensee may offer health care services as an employee of a general business corporation in this State only in one or more of the following settings. Any such setting shall have a designated medical director licensed in this State who is regularly on the premises and who (alone or with other persons authorized by the State Department of Health and Senior Services, if applicable) is responsible for licensure credentialing and provision of medical services.

i. The corporation is licensed by the New Jersey Department of Health and Senior Services as a health maintenance organization, hospital, long- or short-term care facility, ambulatory care facility or other type of health care facility or health care provider, such as a diagnostic imaging facility. The above may include a licensed facility, which is a component part of a for-profit corporation employing or otherwise remunerating licensed physicians.

ii. The corporation is not in the business of offering treatment services but maintains a medical clinic for the purpose of providing first aid to customers or employees and/or for monitoring the health environment of employees. The provisions of N.J.A.C. 13:35-6.5 regarding preparation, maintenance and release of treatment and health monitoring records shall apply to persons receiving care or evaluation in this setting.

iii. The corporation is a non-profit corporation sponsored by a union, social or religious or fraternal-type organization providing health care services to members only.

iv. The corporation is an accredited educational institution which maintains a medical clinic for health care service to students and faculty.

v. The corporation is licensed by the State Department of Insurance as an insurance carrier offering coverage for medical treatment and the licensee is employed to perform quality assurance services for the insurance carrier. . . .

(h) In addition to the practice forms set forth above, a licensee may participate in organized managed health care plans including, but not limited to, those involving wholly or partially pre-paid medical services. By way of example, this includes plans commonly described as health maintenance organizations, preferred provider organizations, competitive medical plans, individual practice associations, or other similar designations. Such plans typically cover certain types of health care services but only when the services are rendered by licensees who are provider-members of the plan; or the patient has been referred to a specialist or admitted to a hospital by a provider-member and has secured the advance approval of the plan administration. Such plans usually permit coverage for referrals in situations of emergency or other special conditions. A licensee may participate in any such plan which complies with the following professional requirements:

    1. The licensee retains authority at all times to exercise professional judgment within accepted standards of practice regarding care, skill and diligence in examinations, diagnosis and treatment of each patient.

    2. The licensee retains authority at all times to inform the patient of appropriate referrals to any other health care providers:

        i. Whether or not those persons are provider-members of the plan; and

        ii. Whether or not the plan covers the cost of service by such non-member providers to the patient.

    3. Plan patients are informed that they may be personally responsible for the cost of treatment by a provider who is not a member-provider within the plan, or for treatment not having the approval of the plan administration. . . .

> Reimbursement models in health insurance have increasingly called for providers to accept some of the financial risk of patient care. These rules are designed to retain professional autonomy to practice medicine while also informing and protecting patients.

QUESTIONS

1. How would *Berlin v. Sarah Lincoln Bush Health Center* be decided in New Jersey?
2. Why does the New Jersey statute only allow broader licensees to supervise lesser licensees?
3. Under what circumstances can a health care institution employ physicians in New Jersey?
4. Which communications between a physician and a patient are protected by the New Jersey statute and why?

The corporate practice of medicine doctrine is aimed at a particular type of financial conflict of interest: whether corporate managers will improperly influence the practice of medicine, harming patients. But by no means does this exhaust the list of potential financial conflicts of interest in medicine. A growing literature of peer-reviewed research has found many other examples. For example, physicians who are more generously reimbursed prescribe more expensive chemotherapy drugs for cancer;[1] physicians who own private ambulatory surgery centers are more likely to keep their privately insured patients but to send less well reimbursed patients to the local hospital;[2] and the rates for some orthopedic surgeries are significantly higher when the surgeon owns a financial interest in the hospital or facility.[3] State and

---

1. Mireille Jacobson et al., *Does Reimbursement Influence Chemotherapy Treatment for Cancer Patients?*, 25 Health Aff. 347-443 (2006).

2. Jon R. Gabel et al., *Where Do I Send Thee? Does Physician-Ownership Affect Referral Patterns to Ambulatory Surgery Centers?*, 27 Health Aff. w165-w174 (2008).

3. Jean M. Mitchell, *Effect of Physician Ownership of Specialty Hospitals and Ambulatory Surgery Centers on Frequency of Use of Outpatient Orthopedic Surgery*, 145 Archives Surgery 732-738 (2010).

federal authorities are well aware of these problems. In 2007, a special commission in Massachusetts found:

> Physicians who have an ownership stake in medical diagnostic services face a potential conflict of interest when referring their patients to use those services. Self-referral arrangements tend to result in increased utilization of services, some of which may not be medically necessary. This is a significant concern because increased utilization is a major driver of escalating health insurance premiums and rising health care expenditures. . . . Massachusetts does not have a set of safeguards similar to the federal rules or these other states.[4]

Many more examples could be given, and these financial conflicts of interest are a core motivation for the fraud and abuse rules found in Chapter 6, especially the Stark II rules prohibiting certain forms of physician self-referral and the Anti-Kickback Statute, prohibiting referrals in exchange for remuneration.

QUESTIONS

1. If the patient receives excellent care, who is harmed by financial conflicts of interest?
2. Does hospital employment of a physician negate all concerns about financial conflicts of interest?

D. SPECIAL GOVERNANCE ISSUES FOR NONPROFIT HEALTH CARE ORGANIZATIONS

Nonprofit organizations can be very substantial businesses. The majority of U.S. hospitals are organized as nonprofit corporations under state law. These hospitals may employ thousands of people, own assets worth more than a billion dollars, and earn annual revenues of several hundred million dollars or more. Frequently a hospital is one of the largest employers in the county in which it sits, especially in rural areas. The special rules that apply to health care institutions that are organized as nonprofit entities influence both day-to-day operations as well as big-picture planning.

Corporations are governed by a board of directors, and members of the board are required to fulfill fiduciary duties owed to the corporation, namely, the duty of care and the duty of loyalty. In the for-profit corporate world, the shareholders elect the board. This annual election is a safeguard in preventing the board from mishandling the assets of the company. If the board performs poorly, shareholders can vote to replace it, for example, at the annual shareholders' meeting. If the members of a board violate fiduciary duties, shareholders can bring a derivative suit for damages or an injunction. Shareholders can also sell their shares if they are unhappy with a company's performance.

But nonprofit entities do not have shareholders or owners in the traditional corporate mold. The company holds assets for a charitable purpose defined by state law, such as educational, religious, or charitable purposes, which includes providing health care to the community in which a hospital sits. When a nonprofit board

---

4. Commonwealth of Massachusetts, Report of the Special Commission on Ambulatory Surgical Centers & Medical Diagnostic Services 33 (July 1, 2007).

member violates fiduciary duties, who has standing to intervene? In almost every state, courts or the state attorney general retains supervisory powers over charitable and nonprofit entities, either under the common law doctrine of *parens patriae* or under a statutory scheme or state constitutional provision. We will examine two examples of the special rules that apply to nonprofit organizations: The first is a court opinion requiring adherence to the hospital's charitable mission; the second considers self-dealing by the board of a hospital.

1. OBEDIENCE TO THE CHARITABLE MISSION

The Manhattan Eye, Ear & Throat Hospital (MEETH) enjoyed a long, distinguished history as a specialty hospital for ophthalmology, otolaryngology, and plastic surgery. In the Certificate of Incorporation, the corporate purpose was

> to establish, provide, conduct, operate and maintain a hospital in the City, County and State of New York for the general treatment of persons suffering from acute short-term illnesses; performing general plastic surgery; treating persons suffering from diseases of the eye, ear, nose or throat; and maintaining a school for post graduate instruction in the treatment of such illnesses, performing such surgery, and the treatment of such diseases, and conducting associated and basic research.

In the late 1990s, facing financial pressure, MEETH's board of directors explored strategic options and ultimately decided to sell the hospital at an auction. Pursuant to the New York Not-For-Profit Corporation Law section 511, the Board filed a petition with the court seeking approval to sell substantially all of its assets. The New York Attorney General, Eliot Spitzer, intervened to oppose the petition. The MEETH case illustrates failures by board members to conduct a reasonable process before making substantial structural changes and to recognize and isolate financial conflicts of interest. Pay attention to the sequence of events leading up to the proposed sale as well as the role of New York's regulations in the court's recognizing what is called the "duty of obedience," meaning obedience to the charitable mission of the organization as stated in its certificate of incorporation.

In re Manhattan Eye, Ear & Throat Hospital v. Spitzer

715 N.Y.S.2d 575 (Sup. Ct. 1999)

. . . [T]he conclusion is inescapable, based upon all the credible evidence, that the Board, recognizing MEETH's financial problems, . . . chose not to seek a solution that would preserve the Hospital, either itself, or in some sort of affiliation with a major medical institution that would be willing to try and preserve MEETH's historic purposes. Rather, the Board decided on a course of action which would lead to the sale and closure of the hospital, and then provide the Board with a substantial sum of money to allow it to take MEETH down the path to new, unstudied and unevaluated charitable purposes [opening free-standing diagnostic and treatment (D&T) centers for the poor]. . . .

Attorney General Becomes Involved

Since as a Type B, i.e., charitable, corporation, MEETH does not have shareholders, the Attorney General, acting as *parens patriae*, is statutorily involved whenever such a charity seeks to dispose of all, or substantially all, of its assets, as MEETH resolved to do. Upon learning from the NY Times article of the decision to sell, Paula Gellman, Esq., Assistant Attorney General, Division of Public Advocacy, wrote to Dr. Sarkar on April 27, 1999, and explained that it was "common practice" for the AG to become involved "before a formal submission is made to the Supreme Court so that we may review the papers and raise any questions or concerns we have in advance." This led to a meeting at the AG's office. . . .

On June 23, 1999, Dietrich L. Snell, Esq., Deputy Attorney General, Division of Public Advocacy, wrote to MEETH's counsel, complaining that there were other "bona fide offerors" and that "[w]e are not aware of . . . one single shred of evidence that MEETH is actively exploring in good faith all or even any of these expressions of interest [which would preserve MEETH]." This statement proved to be accurate.

Thereafter, the AG's representatives were ultimately invited to attend the July 26, 1999 Board meeting, both the full meeting attended by several doctors from the medical staff, and the Executive Session. At both of these meetings, Mr. Scibetta evaluated various offers, and reiterated that it was the opinion of [financial advisor] Shattuck Hammond that the Hospital's "business had negative value." At the end of the Executive Session, Mr. Herkness said that "[i]t was the sense of the Board of Directors to monetize the real estate. . . ." The decision to go forward with the sale to MSKCC and Downtown was unchanged.

Representatives of the AG continued to meet with MEETH, [Department of Health (DOH)] officials, and others, over the additional concern that MEETH was engaging in a de facto closure of the Hospital, since its closure plan had not received DOH approval. The AG also continued to insist that MEETH must negotiate in good faith with other potential bidders. When MEETH filed this petition, the AG opposed it on the ground that other offers had been submitted, which would have preserved MEETH, and that there had been no genuine effort to negotiate with these bidders in good faith. . . .

> Why is the AG's Office concerned about the bidding process for the sale of this hospital?

CONCLUSIONS OF LAW

At issue is whether, as required under section 511(d) of the Not-For-Profit Corporation Law, MEETH has shown "to the satisfaction of the court," both that the "consideration and the terms of the transaction are fair and reasonable" and that "the purposes of the corporation . . . will be promoted" by the sale of all or substantially all of the hospital's assets to Downtown and MSKCC. . . .

> Section 511 is the law in New York, but the process and standards in other states are different and should be separately researched.

Given my Findings of Fact, I conclude that MEETH has not satisfied either prong of section 511. Therefore I deny MEETH's petition to approve the proposed sale.

Before turning to section 511, there are several areas that warrant brief discussion. Not-for-profit corporations operate under legal regimes designed for traditional for-profit corporations. However, fundamental structural differences between not-for-profit corporations and for-profit corporations render this approach incapable of providing effective internal mechanisms to guard against directors' improvident use of charitable assets. For example, in the for-profit context, shareholder power ensures that Boards make provident decisions, while in the not-for-profit context, this internal check does not exist. To put it another way, a nonprofit corporation has no "owners" or private parties with a pecuniary stake to monitor and scrutinize actions by the directors. This distinction is even more significant in the case of charitable corporations, such as MEETH, where there are no members, because the board is essentially self-perpetuating.

The Not-for-Profit Corporation Law addresses this lack of accountability by requiring court approval of fundamental changes in the life of a Type B charitable corporation, such as a disposition of all or substantially all assets, since there are no shareholders whose approval can be sought. The Attorney General is made a statutory party to such petitions, and his "active participation" is presumed. This is to ensure that the interests of the ultimate beneficiaries of the corporation, the public, are adequately represented and protected from improvident transactions. It is pursuant to this mandate that this court is called upon to review the sale of substantially all of MEETH's assets. . . .

> Some charitable organizations have members who elect the board. Some religious and civil organizations operate in this fashion. But if a charitable organization does not have official members, the board is self-perpetuating—they elect their own replacements. Self-perpetuating boards are common in not-for-profit hospitals and are not inherently problematic for charitable organizations.

A charitable Board is essentially a caretaker of the not-for-profit corporation and its assets. As caretaker, the Board "ha[s] the fiduciary obligation to act on behalf of the corporation . . . and advance its interests" in "good faith and with that degree of diligence, care and skill which ordinarily prudent men would exercise under similar circumstances in like positions." This formulation of the Board's duty of care is an "expansion" of the comparable section of the Business Corporation Law which does not contain the words "care" and "skill" and firmly establishes the appropriate standard of care for directors of a not-for-profit corporation.

It is axiomatic that the Board of Directors is charged with the duty to ensure that the mission of the charitable corporation is carried out. This duty has been referred to as the "duty of obedience." It requires the director of a not-for-profit corporation to "be faithful to the purposes and goals of the organization," since "[u]nlike business corporations, whose ultimate objective is to make money, nonprofit corporations are defined by their specific objectives: perpetuation of particular activities are central to the raison d'être of the organization." . . . But the duty of obedience, perforce, must inform the question of whether a proposed transaction to sell all or substantially all of a charity's assets promotes the purposes of the charitable corporation when analyzed under section 511.

In recent years, across the United States, there have been a series of transactions that, although certainly different from this petition, nevertheless resemble, in certain basics, MEETH's proposal. I am referring to the nationwide spate of conversions of nonprofit hospitals into for-profit hospitals which has caused a substantial output of commentary. It has also resulted in some twenty states enacting or considering legislation regulating such conversions. However, there has been no similar activity and little discussion in New York where such conversions are not permitted.

Nonetheless, the conversion analogy is analytically useful. This is because, absent the for-profit component, which of course is absent in a section 511 petition, a conversion is conceptually similar to MEETH's petition, inasmuch as in both there is a charitable organization which alleges that it is incapable of continuing its primary mission of operating a hospital, seeks approval of the sale of all its assets, and plans to apply the sale proceeds towards a newly revised mission. As is relevant to the analysis, for example, legislation in one state requires that the attorney general examine the transaction to determine "(2) Whether the nonprofit hospital exercised due diligence in deciding to sell, selecting the purchaser, and negotiating the terms and conditions of the sale; (3) Whether the procedures used by the seller in making its decision, including whether appropriate expert assistance was used (were fair); (4) Whether conflict of interest was disclosed, including, but not limited to, conflicts of interest [of] board members . . . and experts retained by the seller[;] [and] (5) Whether the seller will receive reasonably fair value for its assets." I believe this to be a clear and concise statement of factors which a court should be concerned with in evaluating a transaction under section 511 to sell all the assets. Indeed, they are in many respects mirrored in the AG's June 3, 1999 letter to MEETH, in essence agreed to by MEETH's counsel, in which the AG wrote "Elementary principles of corporate and fiduciary law require the Board, after it has decided to sell the hospital, to entertain all responsible proposals, not to favor any bidder over another in the process, and to treat all bidders and potential bidders identically and fairly." . . .

Under the second prong of section 511, which requires that "the purposes of the corporation . . . will be promoted," MEETH's petition fares no better. Unfortunately, there is lacking judicial precedent concerning a proposal of this magnitude. While MEETH has argued that the proposal to abandon the acute care, teaching and research hospital component of its mission and to pursue the D&T centers does not require an amendment, this argument is belied by the Board's own action on April 29th, authorizing submission of an Amendment to its Certificate of Incorporation (although never submitted) expressly providing for the D&T centers. This is behavioral evidence that the Board knew that it was proposing a fundamental change in the corporation's mission, which indeed it was doing. For generations MEETH's mission, as stated in its Certificate of Incorporation, was understood to be the operation of an acute care, specialty teaching and research hospital dedicated to "plastic surgery" and to the treatment of "persons suffering from diseases of the eye, ear, nose or throat." While it is certainly correct that the definition of "hospital" contained in section 2801(1) of the Public Health Law includes a diagnostic and treatment center, as MEETH now argues, it is sophistry to contend that this means that MEETH is not seeking a new and fundamentally different purpose, in light of the overwhelming evidence which demonstrates this is exactly what it is doing. The conclusion is inescapable that the proposed use of the assets involves a new and fundamentally different corporate purpose. . . .

> If the Articles of Incorporation had been properly amended, would this case have been litigated?

The [first offer to buy MEETH] drove the decision to retain a strategic advisor, Shattuck Hammond, which had a direct and substantial interest in a sale of the real estate, i.e., the 1% transaction fee. This arrangement, regardless of whether it was traditional in investment banking, as Mr. Hammond testified, resulted in a situation where the Board put its reliance upon a strategic advisor which had an actual interest in the recommendations of its strategic study. It is not necessary for me to conclude that this conflict of interest compromised the result; the fee arrangement certainly gives the appearance that the integrity of the process was flawed and that the Board had not obtained the assistance of a truly independent expert. Moreover, there does not appear to have been full disclosure to the Board of the potential for a conflict of interest in the expert. The evidence showed that two Board members were unaware of the percentage fee which was a part of Shattuck Hammond's retention.

Additionally, there was no discussion or deliberation by the Board over the fact that its strategic advisor had a direct, and perhaps disabling, financial interest in the outcome of the strategic option it was recommending. Nor was there a decision by the Board to retain and rely upon Shattuck Hammond, notwithstanding this issue. The issue simply was never raised. As a result, it cannot be concluded with confidence that the Board received wholly disinterested advice. This becomes more troubling in view of the manner in which Shattuck Hammond dealt with bidders such as Continuum and Lenox Hill, which were not interested in purchasing the real estate, by providing misleading information concerning their offers, often omitting crucial details, and by asserting that the only realistic option was the sale of the real estate. . . .

Moreover, the record also demonstrates that the Board failed to properly consider the various alternatives submitted which would have preserved MEETH's mission. The Board had concluded that these alternatives were the equivalent of "giving the keys away," and summarily rejected them. However, the Board has no independent vitality. It appears that the Board confused preservation of the Hospital with pre-servation of the Board, when the appropriate calculus should be what is good for the Hospital is good for the Board. . . .

In sum, it is evident that this petition fails to meet the two pronged test of section 511. The terms of the transaction are not fair and reasonable to the corporation, inasmuch as no consideration was given to the value of MEETH as a going concern; rather, this value was disregarded. Moreover, evaluating the transaction at the time of the petition, it is clear that there has not been a showing that the sale will promote the purposes of the corporation. To the contrary, MEETH decided to sell, and then evolved its new or "reprioritized mission." There has been no reasoned determination that MEETH cannot continue to operate an acute care, specialty research and teaching hospital, as other medical institutions are proposing to do, and are willing to invest substantial sums to accomplish. MEETH instead chose to sell its real estate, to seek DOH approval to close its hospital, and then apply for judicial imprimatur of this plan. I conclude that this sales transaction should be disapproved.

QUESTIONS

1. Did the court find any evidence that the sales price was too low?
2. Why does the state of New York, acting as *parens patriae*, need to intervene?

PROBLEM

You are counsel to MEETH in 1998. In 500 words or less, how would you advise the board so they could sell the hospital's property and open D&T centers?

In 2000, MEETH affiliated with Lenox Hill Hospital. MEETH now operates as a division of Lenox Hill, and it is still in the original location on East 64th Street. In 2010, Lenox Hill (including MEETH) became part of the North Shore–Long Island Jewish Health System. This chain of mergers, acquisitions, and sales is common in hospital markets over the past few decades (discussed further in Chapter 7).

2. SELF-DEALING BY DIRECTORS AND OFFICERS

The following case was brought as a class action alleging self-dealing among the hospital trustees: the members of the hospital board of directors. Given that the members of the class did not stand to gain monetarily from this action, the reader senses that the members of the board must have been behaving egregiously. Consider whether the district court's resolution addresses the problem of self-dealing adequately, given that you now know that nonprofit boards can be self-perpetuating.

Stern v. Lucy Webb Hayes National Training School for Deaconesses & Missionaries

381 F. Supp. 1003 (D.D.C. 1974)

. . . The two principal contentions in the complaint are that the defendant trustees conspired to enrich themselves and certain financial institutions with which they were affiliated by favoring those institutions in financial dealings with the Hospital, and that they breached their fiduciary duties of care and loyalty in the management of Sibley's funds. The defendant financial institutions are said to have joined in the alleged conspiracy and to have knowingly benefited from the alleged breaches of duty. The Hospital is named as a nominal defendant for the purpose of facilitating relief.

I. Corporate History

The Lucy Webb Hayes National Training School for Deaconesses and Missionaries was established in 1891 by the Methodist Women's Home Missionary Society for the purpose, in part, of providing health care services to the poor of the Washington area. The School was incorporated under the laws of the District of Columbia as a charitable, benevolent and educational institution by instrument dated August 8, 1894. During the following year, the School built the Sibley Memorial Hospital on North Capitol Street to facilitate its charitable work. Over the years, operation of the Hospital has become the School's principal concern, so that the two institutions have been referred to synonymously by all parties and will be so treated in this Opinion. As increasing demands were made upon Sibley's facilities, the Hospital was renovated several times. Finally, in the mid-1950's, it was decided to move the Hospital to a new location on Loughboro Road in Northwest Washington. The nearby Hahnemann Hospital, another Methodist charity, was merged with Sibley in 1956 in anticipation of this move. The new Sibley Memorial Hospital was dedicated on June 17, 1962.

In 1960, shortly after ground was broken for the new building, the Sibley Board of Trustees revised the corporate by-laws in preparation for an expected increase in the volume and complexity of Hospital business following the move. Under the new by-laws, the Board was to consist of from 25 to 35 trustees, who were to meet at least twice each year. Between such meetings, an Executive Committee was to represent the Board, and was authorized, inter alia, to open checking and savings accounts, approve the Hospital budget, renew mortgages, and enter into contracts. A Finance Committee was created to review the budget and to report regularly on the amount of cash available for investment. Management of those investments was to be supervised by an Investment Committee, which was to work closely with the Finance Committee in such matters.

In fact, management of the Hospital from the early 1950's until 1968 was handled almost exclusively by two trustee officers: Dr. Orem, the Hospital Administrator, and Mr. Ernst, the Treasurer. Unlike most of their fellow trustees, to whom membership on the Sibley Board was a charitable service incidental to their principal vocations, Orem and Ernst were continuously involved on almost a daily basis in the affairs of Sibley. They dominated the Board and its Executive Committee, which routinely accepted their recommendations and ratified their actions. Even more significantly, neither the Finance Committee nor the Investment Committee ever met or conducted business from the date of their creation until 1971, three years after the death of Dr. Orem. As a result, budgetary and investment decisions during this period, like most other management decisions affecting the Hospital's finances, were handled by Orem and Ernst, receiving only cursory supervision from the Executive Committee and the full Board.

Dr. Orem's death on April 5, 1968, obliged some of the other trustees to play a more active role in running the Hospital. The Executive Committee, and particularly defendant Stacy Reed (as Chairman of the Board, President of the Hospital, and ex officio member of the Executive Committee), became more deeply involved in the day-to-day management of the Hospital while efforts were made to find a new Administrator. The man who was eventually selected for that office, Dr. Jarvis, had little managerial experience and his performance was not entirely satisfactory. Mr. Ernst still made most of the financial and investment decisions for Sibley, but his actions and failures to act came slowly under increasing scrutiny by several of the other trustees, particularly after a series of disagreements between Ernst and the Hospital Comptroller which led to the discharge of the latter early in 1971.

Prompted by these difficulties, Mr. Reed decided to activate the Finance and Investment Committee in the Fall of 1971. However, as Chairman of the Finance Committee and member of the Investment Committee as well as Treasurer, Mr. Ernst continued to exercise dominant control over investment decisions and, on several occasions, discouraged and flatly refused to respond to inquiries by other trustees into such matters. It has only been since the death of Mr. Ernst on October 30, 1972, that the other trustees appear to have assumed an identifiable supervisory role over investment policy and Hospital fiscal management in general.

> Interlocking directorates are somewhat common among charitable organizations in certain communities, and they are not inherently illegal.

Against this background, the basic claims will be examined.

II. Conspiracy

Plaintiffs first contend that the five defendant trustees and the five defendant financial institutions were involved in a conspiracy to enrich themselves at the expense of the Hospital. They point to the fact that each named trustee held positions of responsibility with one or more of the defendant institutions as evidence that the trustees had both motive and opportunity to carry out such a conspiracy. The extent of these interlocking duties and interests is revealed by the following table:

Plaintiffs further contend that the defendants accomplished the alleged conspiracy by arranging to have Sibley maintain unnecessarily large amounts of money on deposit with the defendant banks and savings and loan associations, drawing inadequate or no interest. As shown by table II, below, the Hospital in fact maintained much of its liquid assets in savings and checking accounts rather than in Treasury bonds or investment securities, at least until the investment review instituted by

TABLE I

Hospital Responsibilities	Defendant Trustees	Financial Institution Responsibilities
SIBLEY Trustee (1956–) Executive Com. (1961–) Finance Com. (1961–) Investment Com. (1961–) Board Chairman (1960–) President (1968–72; 1973–)	STACY M. REED	SECURITY NATIONAL BANK Director (1930–) Executive Com. (1937–) Minor stockholder
SIBLEY Trustee (1956–) Investment Com. (1960–73)	LANIER P. McLACHLEN	McLACHLEN NATIONAL BANK Director (1974–) Board Chairman (1953–73) President (1922–54) Principal stockholder (8.1%)
SIBLEY Trustee (1956–) Finance Com. (1973–) Investment Com. (1962–70) Acting Treas. (1972–73)	GEORGE M. FERRIS	FERRIS & CO. Senior Partner (–1971) Board Chairman (1971–) Principal stockholder (42%)
SIBLEY Trustee (1959–) Executive Com. (1959–) Finance Com. (1960–73) Investment Com. (1971–73)	EDWARD K. JONES	INTERSTATE BUILDING ASSOC. Director (1932–) Executive Com. (1932–) Board Chairman (1969–) President (1954–69) Minor stockholder RIGGS NATIONAL BANK Director (1967–) Executive Com. (1967–74) Minor stockholder
SIBLEY Trustee (1964–) Executive Com. (1964–) Investment Com. (1967–73)	FRED W. SMITH	RIGGS NATIONAL BANK Advisory Director (1964–) Minor stockholder JEFFERSON FEDERAL S. & L. Director (1954–) Executive Com. (1957–) President (1959–)

Mr. Reed late in 1971. In that year, for example, more than one-third of the nearly four million dollars available for investment was deposited in checking accounts, as compared to only about $135,000 in securities and $311,000 in Treasury bills. Although substantial sums were used to purchase certificates of deposit, which produce at least a moderate amount of income, the Hospital occasionally purchased a certificate yielding lower interest rates than were available at other institutions.

It is also undisputed that most of these funds were deposited in the defendant financial institutions. A single checking account, drawing no interest whatever and maintained alternately at Riggs National Bank and Security National Bank, usually contained more than $250,000 and on one occasion grew to nearly $1,000,000.

Defendants were able to offer no adequate justification for this utilization of the Hospital's liquid assets. By the same token, however, plaintiffs failed to establish that it was the result of a conscious direction on the part of the named defendants. As mentioned above, it was Mr. Ernst alone rather than any of the defendant trustees who maintained almost exclusive control over the Hospital's investments until his death in 1972. As Treasurer, he could shift money between banks or accounts within banks and purchase or sell securities without consulting any other trustee. Since the Investment and Finance Committees never met, only Dr. Orem and a few of the other officers apparently were aware of Mr. Ernst's investment policies. While it is true that a yearly audit was made available to the Board and that the Executive Committee had to approve the opening of new accounts, these matters were treated as mere formalities. All of the defendant trustees testified that they approved Ernst's recommendations as a matter of course, rarely if ever read the relevant details of audits critically, and generally left investment decisions to the presumed expertise of Mr. Ernst. Several also commented that the Treasurer regarded their suggestions as "interference" in these matters and none forced the issue.

TABLE II

SUMMARY OF SIBLEY FINANCIAL ASSETS

1967–1972, as of December 31st

Type of Accounts	1972	1971	1970	1969	1968	1967
Sibley checking	$ 501,333	1,148,769	1,265,288	588,735	522,174	655,084
Sibley savings	2,015,448	826,435	588,979	866,374	774,661	646,649
Sibley certificates	2,043,435	2,029,211	1,325,000	900,000	900,000	900,000
Sibley U.S. Treasuries	310,764	310,436	383,786	220,000	220,000	———
Sibley securities (at cost)	135,749	135,646	140,446	71,621	71,621	70,052
All Hahnemann net financial assets	413,152	588,464	538,755	505,046	687,909	427,638
TOTAL	$5,419,881	5,038,961	4,242,254	3,151,776	3,176,365	2,699,423

Mr. Ernst's own reasons for pursuing this conservative investment policy are not altogether clear. It has been suggested that his experience in the Depression was an important contributing factor. That same experience undoubtedly helps explain his belief that Sibley should maintain close relationships with a few local banks and his evident decision to favor those banks which held a mortgage on the Hospital and which had interlocking directorships with the Sibley Board.

There is no evidence that the defendant trustees reached a mutual agreement to direct or even to encourage Ernst in such favoritism. It is true that the trustees frequently approved transactions which benefited institutions with which they were affiliated and that occasionally a particular trustee would even seek out such an arrangement, but plaintiffs have not shown that any of these decisions derived from a conspiratorial agreement. Moreover, when the Board's own investigations brought the inadequacy of Mr. Ernst's policies home to the Board, the trustees moved toward a more realistic investment program in a manner that negates existence of a prior agreement. Significant reductions in bank deposits have been made, and the newly elected Treasurer is attempting—with mixed success—to hold demand deposits below $500,000, a level which he deems adequate for the operation of the Hospital.

Plaintiffs also attempted to bolster the conspiracy theory by pointing to two other Hospital transactions: the continuation of a mortgage with the defendant financial institutions and the signing of an investment advisory agreement with Ferris & Co. The mortgage in question dates back to the late 1950's, when the Sibley Board began negotiations with various local banks to obtain a loan to finance construction of the new hospital building. When these negotiations fell through, the Board obtained an adequate loan commitment from a Texas bank. Although local banks had earlier refused to assist the Hospital, several of the trustees then organized a syndicate of Washington banks willing to provide the loan on equally favorable terms to the Texas proposal and persuaded the Board to accept the local offer. As a result, the syndicate agreed in 1959 to lend Sibley $3,000,000, secured by a mortgage on the hospital. This sum was increased to $3,500,000 in 1961.

The loan was renewed in 1969 and is still partially outstanding. Although Sibley probably had sufficient funds to pay off the loan without totally impairing its ability to meet obligations as they become due, the Executive Committee voted instead for renewal. The cash flow would have put operations on a tight basis and the trustees had in mind that available money might well be needed for the renovation of certain property owned by Sibley.

The terms of this loan were entirely fair to Sibley at all times. There is no indication that the Board could have received better terms elsewhere or that it failed diligently to seek an optimum arrangement at the time of the original loan. The renewal in 1969 also appears to have been a reasonable, good-faith business decision. There is no indication that either decision was motivated by a desire to benefit the banks involved at the Hospital's expense.

The idea of employing an investment service was raised by Mr. Jones at the meeting of Sibley's Investment Committee. It was decided that Mr. Ferris, a member of that committee, should present a proposal from Ferris & Co., of which Mr. Ferris was Chairman of the Board and principal stockholder, for the provision of continuing investment advisory services to Sibley. Mr. Ferris presented such a proposal on April 12, 1971, and the committee voted to recommend approval. Mr. Ferris urged and may have voted in favor of that recommendation at an informal session of the Investment Committee, but thereafter he resigned from the Investment Committee to avoid further possible conflicts of interest. For a short time he then served as Acting Treasurer over the objection of some trustees. Upon formal approval by the Hospital's counsel and the Executive Committee, of which Ferris was not a member, Sibley entered into the "Investment Advisory Agreement" with Ferris & Co., which written contract is still in effect today. Plaintiffs concede, and the Court finds, that Ferris & Co.'s fee for investment service was fair and equitable. Plaintiffs concede that Ferris & Co. did a good job, although shifts in market prices resulted in some losses in the account which, incidentally, would not have occurred if the Hospital had kept the money in certificates of deposit. . . .

Self-dealing

Under District of Columbia Law, neither trustees nor corporate directors are absolutely barred from placing funds under their control into a bank having an interlocking directorship with their own institution. In both cases, however, such transactions will be subjected to the closest scrutiny to determine whether or not the duty of loyalty has been violated. A deliberate conspiracy among trustees or Board members to enrich the interlocking bank at the expense of the trust or corporation would, for example, constitute such a breach and render the conspirators liable for any losses. In the absence of clear evidence of wrongdoing, however, the courts appear to have used different standards to determine whether or not relief is appropriate, depending again on the legal relationship involved. Trustees may be found guilty of a breach of trust even for mere negligence in the maintenance of accounts in banks with which they are associated, while corporate directors are generally only required to show "entire fairness" to the corporation and "full disclosure" of the potential conflict of interest to the Board.

Most courts apply the less stringent corporate rule to charitable corporations in this area as well. It is, however, occasionally added that a director should not only disclose his interlocking responsibilities but also refrain from voting on or otherwise influencing a corporate decision to transact business with a company in which he has a significant interest or control. Although defendants have argued against the imposition of even these limitations on self-dealing by the Sibley trustees, the Hospital Board recently adopted a new by-law, based upon guidelines issued by the American Hospital Association, which essentially imposes the modified corporate rule described above:

> In many charitable hospitals, the board members are called "trustees" even though they are technically directors of a corporation. Stricter standards apply in trust law to actual trustees.

Article XXVIII, Conflicts of Interests

Section 1. Any duality of interest or possible conflict of interest on the part of any governing board member shall be disclosed to the other members of the board and made a matter of record through an annual procedure and also when the interest becomes a matter of board action.

Section 2. Any governing board member having a duality of interest or possible conflict of interest on any matter shall not vote or use his personal influence on the matter, and he shall not be counted in determining the quorum for the meeting, even where permitted by law. The minutes of the meeting shall reflect that a disclosure was made, the abstention from voting, and the quorum situation.

Section 3. The foregoing requirements shall not be construed as preventing the governing board member from briefly stating his position in the matter, nor from answering pertinent questions of other board members since his knowledge may be of great assistance.

Section 4. Any new member of the board will be advised of this policy upon entering on the duties of his office.

Having surveyed the authorities as outlined above and weighed the briefs, arguments and evidence submitted by counsel, the Court holds that a director or so-called trustee of a charitable hospital organized under the Non-Profit Corporation Act of the District of Columbia (D.C. Code §29-1001 et seq.) is in default of his fiduciary duty to manage the fiscal and investment affairs of the hospital if it has been shown by a preponderance of the evidence that:

(1) while assigned to a particular committee of the Board having general financial or investment responsibility under the by-laws of the corporation, he has failed to use due diligence in supervising the actions of those officers, employees or outside experts to whom the responsibility for making day-to-day financial or investment decisions has been delegated; or

(2) he knowingly permitted the hospital to enter into a business transaction with himself or with any corporation, partnership or association in which he then had a substantial interest or held a position as trustee, director, general manager or principal officer without having previously informed the persons charged with approving that transaction of his interest or position and of any significant reasons,

unknown to or not fully appreciated by such persons, why the transaction might not be in the best interests of the hospital; or

(3) except as required by the preceding paragraph, he actively participated in or voted in favor of a decision by the Board or any committee or subcommittee thereof to transact business with himself or with any corporation, partnership or association in which he then had a substantial interest or held a position as trustee, director, general manager or principal officer; or

(4) he otherwise failed to perform his duties honestly, in good faith, and with a reasonable amount of diligence and care.

Applying these standards to the facts in the record, the Court finds that each of the defendant trustees has breached his fiduciary duty to supervise the management of Sibley's investments. All except Mr. Jones were duly and repeatedly elected to the Investment Committee without ever bothering to object when no meetings were called for more than ten years. Mr. Jones was a member of the equally inactive Finance Committee, the failure of which to report on the existence of investable funds was cited by several other defendants as a reason for not convening the Investment Committee. In addition, Reed, Jones and Smith were, for varying periods of time, also members of the Executive Committee, which was charged with acquiring at least enough information to vote intelligently on the opening of new bank accounts. By their own testimony, it is clear that they failed to do so. And all of the individual defendants ignored the investment sections of the yearly audits which were made available to them as members of the Board. In short, these men have in the past failed to exercise even the most cursory supervision over the handling of Hospital funds and failed to establish and carry out a defined policy.

> The defendants breached their fiduciary duties.

The record is unclear on the degree to which full disclosure preceded the frequent self-dealing which occurred during the period under consideration. It is reasonable to assume that the Board was generally aware of the various bank affiliations of the defendant trustees, but there is no indication that these conflicting interests were brought home to the relevant committees when they voted to approve particular transactions. Similarly, while plaintiffs have shown no active misrepresentation on defendants' part, they have established instances in which an interested trustee failed to alert the responsible officials to better terms known to be available elsewhere.

It is clear that all of the defendant trustees have, at one time or another, affirmatively approved self-dealing transactions. Most of these incidents were of relatively minor significance: one interested trustee would join a dozen disinterested fellow members of the Executive Committee in unanimously approving the opening of a bank account; two or three interested trustees would support a similarly large group in voting to give or renew the mortgage. Others cannot be so easily disregarded. Defendant Ferris' advice and vote in the relatively small Investment Committee to recommend approval of the investment contract with Ferris & Co. may have been crucial to that transaction. Defendant Reed assumed principal responsibility for account levels between 1969 and 1971, during which period the [Bank] checking account grew to more than a million dollars. And defendant Smith, in his capacity as President of Jefferson Federal, personally negotiated the interest rates on a $230,000 certificate account with the Hospital.

> Why is the court concerned in the absence of fiscal or other harm?

That the Hospital has suffered no measurable injury from many of these transactions — including the mortgage and the investment contract — and that the excessive deposits which were the real source of harm were caused primarily by the uniform failure to supervise rather than the occasional self-dealing vote are both facts that the Court must take into account in fashioning relief, but they do not alter the principle that the trustee of a charitable hospital should always avoid active participation in a transaction in which he or a corporation with which he is associated has a significant interest. . . .

IV. Relief

. . . [P]laintiffs press for injunctive relief. Among other things, they urge that defendant trustees be removed and disqualified, that the Hospital be barred from transacting business with any firm if an officer, director, partner or substantial shareholder of that firm is a Hospital trustee, that an accounting be ordered, and that damages be assessed against the defendant trustees. In short, plaintiffs approach this matter as though each trustee of the Hospital were individually responsible for an abuse of fiduciary duty under an express trust which has made the Hospital's patients beneficiaries. Were such the case, application of very strict sanctions would be necessary. However, the trustees here stand in a different status, as the Court's analysis shows, and the proof does not in any way necessitate sanctions as harsh as those suggested.

The function of equity is not to punish but merely to take such action as the Court in its discretion deems necessary to prevent the recurrence of improper conduct. Where voluntary action has been taken in good faith to minimize such recurrence, even though under the pressure of litigation, this is a factor which the Court can take into account in formulating relief.

In attempting to balance the equities under the circumstances shown by the record, there are a number of factors which lead the Court to feel that intervention by injunction should be limited. First, the defendant trustees in this case constitute but a small minority of the full Sibley Board. Yet, in several respects, the responsibility for past failures adequately to supervise the handling of Hospital funds rests equally on all Board members. Second, it is clear that the practices criticized by plaintiffs have, to a considerable extent, been corrected and that the employees and trustees who were principally responsible for lax handling of funds have died or have been dismissed. Third, there is no indication that any of the named trustees were involved in fraudulent practices or profited personally by lapses in proper fiscal supervision, and, indeed, the overall operation of the Hospital in terms of low costs, efficient services and quality patient care has been superior. Finally, this case is in a sense one of first impression, since it brings into judicial focus for the first time in this jurisdiction the nature and scope of trustee obligations in a nonprofit, non-member charitable institution incorporated under D.C. Code §29-1001 et seq.

The Court is well aware that it must take proper steps to insure a clean break between the past and the future. Personnel changes and a recent greater awareness of past laxity are encouraging, as is the addition of Article XXVIII to the Hospital's by-laws, but good intentions expressed post-litem must be accompanied by concrete action. Accordingly, it is desirable to require by injunction that the appropriate committees and officers of the Hospital present to the full Board a written policy statement governing investments and the use of idle cash in the Hospital's bank accounts and other funds, and establish a procedure for the periodic reexamination of existing investments and other financial arrangements to insure compliance with Board policies. No existing financial relationships should be continued unless consistent with established policy and found by disinterested members of the Board to be in the Hospital's best interests. In addition, each trustee should fully disclose his affiliation with banks, savings and loan associations and investment firms now doing business with the Hospital.

Removal of the defendant trustees from the Sibley Board would be unduly harsh, and this will not be ordered. These trustees are now completing long years of service and they will soon become less active in the day-to-day affairs of the Hospital because of age or illness. It would unduly disrupt the affairs of the Hospital abruptly to terminate their relationship with that institution. Others must soon take over their roles in carrying forward the Hospital's affairs, and it is therefore unnecessary to interfere by order of removal or disqualification with a transition that is necessarily already taking place due to other immutable factors.

> The problematic trustees were not removed from the Sibley Board.

The management of a non-profit charitable hospital imposes a severe obligation upon its trustees. A hospital such as Sibley is not closely regulated by any public authority, it has no responsibility to file financial reports, and its Board is self-perpetuating. The interests of its patients are funneled primarily through large group insurers who pay the patients' bills, and the patients lack meaningful participation in the Hospital's affairs. It is obvious that, in due course, new trustees must come to the Board of this Hospital, some of whom will be affiliated with banks, savings and loan associations and other financial institutions. The tendency of representatives of such institutions is often to seek business in return for advice and assistance rendered as trustees. It must be made absolutely clear that Board membership carries no right to preferential treatment in the placement or handling of the Hospital's investments and business accounts. The Hospital would be well advised to restrict membership on its Board to the representatives of financial institutions which have no substantial business relationship with the Hospital. The best way to avoid potential conflicts of interest and to be assured of objective advice is to avoid the possibility of such conflicts at the time new trustees are selected. . . .

ORDER

This action came on for trial before the Court and the Court having considered the briefs, arguments and evidence presented by all parties and having set forth its findings of fact and conclusions of law in a Memorandum Opinion filed herewith, it is hereby

Declared that each director or trustee of a charitable hospital organized under the Non-Profit Corporation Act of the District of Columbia, D.C. Code §29-1001 et seq., has a continuing fiduciary duty of loyalty and care in the management of the hospital's fiscal and investment affairs and acts in violation of that duty if:

> This order gives unusually detailed instructions on board conduct.

(1) he fails, while assigned to a particular committee of the Board having stated financial or investment responsibilities under the by-laws of the corporation, to use diligence in supervising and periodically inquiring into the actions of those officers, employees and outside experts to whom any duty to make day-to-day financial or investment decisions within such committee's responsibility has been assigned or delegated; or

(2) he knowingly permits the hospital to enter into a business transaction with himself or with any corporation, partnership or association in which he holds a position as trustee, director, partner, general manager, principal officer or substantial shareholder without previously having informed all persons charged with approving that transaction of his interest or position and of any significant facts known to him indicating that the transaction might not be in the best interests of the hospital; or

(3) he actively participates in, except as required by the preceding paragraph, or votes in favor of a decision by the board or any committee or subcommittee thereof to transact business with himself or with any corporation, partnership or association in which he holds a position as trustee, director, partner, general manager, principal officer, or substantial shareholder; or

(4) he fails to perform his duties honestly, in good faith, and with reasonable diligence and care; and it is hereby

Ordered that the appropriate officers and/or trustee committees of Sibley Memorial Hospital shall, prior to the next regularly scheduled meeting of the full Board of Trustees, draft and submit to the full Board, and the Board shall modify as it deems appropriate and adopt at said meeting, a written policy statement governing the utilization and investment of the Hospital's liquid assets, including cash on hand, savings and checking accounts, certificates of deposit, Treasury bonds, and investment securities; and it is further

Ordered that the Board and its appropriate committees shall, promptly after adoption of said policy statement and periodically thereafter, review all of the Hospital's liquid assets to insure that they conform to the guidelines set forth in said policy statement; and it is further

Ordered that each trustee of Sibley Memorial Hospital shall disclose to the full Board of Trustees prior to its next regularly scheduled meeting, in writing, his or her affiliations, if any, with any bank, savings and loan association, investment firm or other financial institution presently doing business with the Hospital and shall thereafter quarterly amend such writing to reflect any changes; and it is further

Ordered that the Treasurer of Sibley Memorial Hospital shall, at least one week prior to each regularly scheduled meeting of the Board of Trustees for a period of five years from the date of this Order, prepare and transmit to each trustee a written statement setting forth in detail all business conducted since the last Board meeting between the Hospital and any bank, savings and loan association, investment firm or other financial institution with which any Sibley officer or trustee is affiliated as a trustee, director, partner, general manager, principal officer, or substantial shareholder; and it is further

Ordered that the auditors of Sibley Memorial Hospital shall, for a period of five years from the date of this Order, Incorporate into each annual audit a written summary of all business conducted during the preceding fiscal year between the Hospital and any bank, savings and loan association, investment firm or other financial institution with which any Sibley officer or trustee is affiliated as a trustee, director, partner, general manager, principal officer or substantial stockholder, and shall make a copy of said audit available on request for inspection by any patient of the Hospital at the Hospital's offices during business hours; and it is further

Ordered that each present trustee of Sibley Memorial Hospital and each future trustee selected during the next five years shall, within two weeks of this Order or promptly after election to the Board, read this Order and the attached Memorandum

Opinion and shall signify in writing or by notation in the minutes of a Board meeting that he or she has done so. . . .

QUESTIONS

1. Does the court forbid all self-dealing by the board?
2. What would be required before this court would order removal of a director?
3. Is it better for the hospital to retain negligent directors than to remove them and start fresh?
4. Why are patients the only ones who get access to the audit report?

Under state corporate law, the duty of care and the duty of loyalty are not treated with similar deference. Self-dealing and other violations of the duty of loyalty by directors and officers are treated as inherently suspect and are not afforded deference. On the other hand, when considering whether directors have adhered to their duty of care, a powerful presumption of board independence exists in the "business judgment rule," which defers to the decision making of boards so long as a reasonable process was followed.

For the duty of loyalty, most states follow a "safe harbor" rule that requires self-dealing to be fully disclosed to the board in advance of a vote, followed by a vote involving only disinterested board members. If these procedures are followed, the duty of loyalty generally is deemed not to be breached. Del. Gen. Corp. Law §144; Rev. Model Bus. Corp. Act §8.62. As we will see in Chapter 5, the federal government has adopted a similar approach for health care charities that have acted against the interest of their tax-exempt status. *See* I.R.C. §4958.

3. CONFLICTS OF INTEREST WITH DIRECTORS AND OFFICERS

The following document is a letter sent by the Massachusetts Office of the Attorney General, after the board of the Beth Israel Deaconess Medical Center in Boston requested a review of an investigation regarding a personal relationship between a hospital employee and the chief executive officer (CEO) of the hospital. While the attorney general had the power to independently initiate this investigation, in this case the request came from the board, partially in response to significant press coverage of the allegations.

The Commonwealth of Massachusetts
Office of the Attorney General
One Ashburton Place
Boston, Massachusetts 02108

September 1, 2010
Stephen Kay, Chair
Beth Israel Deaconess Medical Center
330 Brookline Avenue
Boston, MA 02215

Dear Chairman Kay:

By letter dated May 13, 2010, the Board of Directors (the "Board") of Beth Israel Deaconess Medical Center ("BIDMC" or the "Medical Center") requested that the

Office of the Attorney General (the "Office") conduct a review of the "appropriateness of the Board's governance process and conclusions" in connection with the Board's investigation and disposition of an anonymous complaint (the "Complaint") made against Paul Levy, the Chief Executive Officer ("CEO") of BIDMC with respect to his personal relationship with an employee (the "Employee"). In response, the Office, through its Non-Profit Organizations/Public Charities Division (the "Division"), initiated a review (the "Review") under its authority to *enforce the due application of funds given or appropriated to public charities within the commonwealth and prevent breaches of trust in the administration thereof*." *See* M.G.L. c. 12, s. 8. BIDMC is a public charity and subject to the jurisdiction of the Division. This letter sets forth the results of the Review.

This Review does not constitute a *de novo* investigation of the Complaint or the personal relationship between Paul Levy and the Employee. The primary responsibility for providing oversight of the Commonwealth's more than 22,000 registered and operating public charities lies squarely with their respective governing bodies, which have the greatest familiarity with institutional operations, personnel and challenges. The Division generally does not substitute its judgments for these boards and will intervene in these situations only when a board has a fiduciary duty to act and fails to. As a result, while

> States have limited resources to investigate charities and therefore must rely on most boards to fulfill their fiduciary duties.

by necessity the Division evaluated and took into account underlying facts pertinent to the Complaint, the Review was primarily directed at the Board's actions with respect to the Complaint and whether those actions were consistent with its fiduciary obligations to BIDMC and the public BIDMC serves.

Executive Summary

On the basis of the Review and for the reasons set forth in the body of this letter, the Division has made the following primary findings.

(1) The Division found no basis to conclude that the Employee was not qualified for the positions she held at the Medical Center or its affiliate, Beth Israel Deaconess Medical Center Needham ("BI-Needham"). Her personnel record and the Division's interviews reflect that she received satisfactory performance reviews, was compensated in amounts within the range set for her job grade, and upon termination received a severance payment consistent with Medical Center severance policies. The Division therefore found no evidence of misuse or abuse of charitable funds.

Nevertheless, the predictable and unfortunate result of combining personal and professional relationships within a workplace environment means decisions made regarding the Employee's hiring, transfer, pay, bonuses, and performance reviews will always be subject to the perception they may have been influenced as much by the personal relationship with Levy as by her own professional performance.

(2) The outstanding reputation of an organization and its CEO are valuable assets of any charitable organization. The personal relationship between the CEO and the Employee, which continued throughout her tenure despite repeated expressions of concern by senior staff and certain Board members, clearly damaged his reputation and, of greater concern, endangered the reputation of the institution and its management. As such his continued, repeated and acknowledged failure to appreciate and address the situation merited, if not compelled, disciplinary action by the Board.

(3) Once the Complaint was received, the full Board acted in a manner consistent with its fiduciary obligations. While reasonable people, including some Board members, may and did differ on whether the Board action was too harsh or not harsh enough, the action was the result of an investigation done in the framework of an organized and thoughtful process, included a vigorous exchange of differing opinions and views, and left open the possibility of further action if merited.

Notwithstanding the foregoing conclusion, had the entire Board been informed and taken definitive action when concerns regarding the relationship were first expressed to Levy, much, if not all, of the damage would have been averted. The Board members who communicated their concerns to the CEO or management, but then failed to convey them to the full Board, may well have felt such direct communications were sufficient. Others may have heard rumors, but failed to follow-up. With the acknowledged aid of hindsight, it is now clear the entire Board should have been informed and taken action years before the lodging of the Complaint. Accordingly, the Division cannot conclude that neither the Board nor senior management of the Medical Center is without some level of responsibility for these events. Had Levy been called on his failure to act, or had his failure to act been reported to the entire Board, this acknowledged "lapse of judgment" might never have occurred. For senior managers who reported to Levy, demanding a response was likely difficult. For Board members, it was their job. Respect for Mr. Levy and his accomplishments may have created among some Board members a level of deference to management that was, and is, inconsistent with the level of vigorous and fully independent Board oversight that would have compelled definitive action far earlier. Oversight of management is a primary duty and responsibility of a governing body and this unfortunate and preventable situation should serve as a stark reminder to all our boards of the importance of diligent and independent management oversight.

> This paragraph and the discussion that follows illustrate this board's failures and, by negative example, how the law expects boards to act.

Scope of Inquiry; Review Process

The Review focused primarily on two areas of inquiry.

- Did any aspect of hiring, transfer, promotion, or severance decisions regarding the Employee, or other benefits provided to the Employee during her tenure, constitute a breach of trust in the administration of charitable funds?
- Did the Board exercise "due care" in its investigation and disposition of the allegations regarding the CEO?

The Division reviewed numerous records provided by BIDMC including records and information relating to the Board's investigation of the allegation(s), employment records pertaining to the Employee, and relevant Medical Center employee policies and procedures. In addition, Division staff conducted lengthy and detailed interviews with eleven individuals including BIDMC counsel, current and former Board members, members of senior management and the CEO. . . .

Discussion

Use of Charitable Funds

Payment of excessive amounts for work performed, or payment for work not performed, constitutes a breach of trust in the administration of charitable funds.

On that basis, both the BIDMC Board and the Division reviewed the employment and compensation history of the Employee to determine whether there were any irregularities in the manner or amount of her compensation, including the terms of her severance. During the course of the Board's investigation and the Review, no information has been presented that Levy was directly involved in any compensation decisions pertaining to the Employee, although he did participate in her evaluation when she was working in the Office of the President. As previously noted, the Division was advised that compensation levels for employees are determined through a Compensation Unit and not by hospital executives, and that such a process was followed with respect to the Employee's compensation.

The Review found that during her time at BIDMC and BI-Needham, the Employee's salary was within the range of her job grade. For example, for her highest salary year, 2009 (annual salary of $104,000), a grade 10 employee could earn a minimum of $63,960, a maximum of $122,720 with the median being $93,340. From 2002 through 2009, her salary, while subject to annual increases and performance bonuses, was within established ranges for each of those years. Similarly, her severance of approximately $29,000 was consistent with Medical Center policy and represents six month[s'] salary, offset by salary earned in her new job that commenced in February of 2010.

Two aspects of her compensation and employment history do merit discussion. First, while her overall salary was within the range of her job grade, she was the only non-physician director who received a bonus in all four of the years reviewed. Second, both positions that the Employee held at BIDMC and BI-Needham were newly created and not maintained after she left. In the context of the widely known personal relationship between the CEO and the Employee, each is inevitably subject to the perception that it was influenced by the personal relationship. Nevertheless, the record before the Division evidences excellent academic credentials, a good work history, positive performance reviews, and total compensation within the ranges for her job grade including bonuses approved by BI-Needham CEO Jeff Liebman. Based on evidence available to it, the Division has no basis to conclude that charitable funds were misused through excessive compensation or payment for work not performed.

> The hospital did not overpay the employee.

The CEO's Actions

Emphasizing again that the Review was not a *de novo* investigation of the Complaint, certain conclusions can be clearly drawn regarding the CEO's conduct which are relevant to our review of the Board's actions.

Neither the record nor Mr. Levy dispute that he (i) failed to separate a professional and personal relationship with an employee of the Medical Center and BI-Needham that spanned many years and was known throughout these institutions; (ii) was alerted on numerous occasions by staff and Board chairs that he needed to take action to end either the personal relationship or the employment relationship; and (iii) failed to heed those warnings.

> The relationship affected senior management throughout the hospital.

While the Division cannot measure the impact of these failures, the public attention, exposure and criticism which inevitably took place most certainly had a negative impact on the institution. Internally such actions may also have negative repercussions. Lines of authority and responsibility can become blurred. Decisions may become suspect and subject to differing interpretations. Considered against the power of the CEO, which most certainly reached beyond the President's Office to the rest of the Medical Center and to BI-Needham, no decision regarding the Employee was immune from his influence. The existence of a personal relationship between a CEO and a subordinate inevitably causes other employees, including managers, to factor that relationship into their decision making regarding the subordinate. No explicit direction from the CEO is required. Perhaps more troublesome, attitudes, real or perceived, may be fostered within the workforce that personal relationships trump professional qualifications. The Employee may well have succeeded entirely on her own professional qualifications and performance, however her relationship with Levy will always foster doubts in the minds of some.

The Board Investigation

In Massachusetts, corporate fiduciaries of charitable organizations must act prudently, in good faith and exercise reasonable judgment. Faced with an anonymous, racist, and sexist complaint concerning a former employee that, without corroboration, would have likely been disregarded, the Board addressed the Complaint seriously and moved swiftly. Chairman Kay established a process for review and action, retained the services of outside counsel Robert Sherman, and established a diverse ad-hoc committee to take primary responsibility for fact finding, including interviewing Mr. Levy and making preliminary recommendations to the Board. The Board's review of this matter spanned approximately two weeks and involved three specially scheduled meetings that were attended in person or over the phone by a majority of the Board members able to participate. BIDMC management fully cooperated with the Board's investigation.

The Board's deliberations were wide ranging and were geared to determining what was in the best long-term interest of the Medical Center. There were a wide range of opinions on whether to review the Complaint and ultimately how to address it. The Board was not constrained and was specifically advised it had the authority to consider options ranging from disregarding the Complaint to terminating the CEO. It carefully considered the facts that were available to it and engaged in back and forth discussion as to what those facts were, what weight they should be given and how they should be applied to a decision. The process was inclusive and Chairman Kay made every attempt to ensure minority opinions were heard. The Division considers differing views and vigorous debate as a clear sign of a healthy board that takes its responsibilities seriously. Similarly, the Division views the resignation of a Board member, not as a failure, but as another indication of diverse opinions that were debated and discussed but ultimately could not be reconciled to everyone's satisfaction. The resigning Board member played a valuable role throughout this process.

Two aspects of the Board's review merit discussion: (1) the scope of the review, and (2) the existing relationship between Robert Sherman and the Medical Center. As to the scope of the review, any investigation, including this one conducted by the Board, must ultimately determine how extensive the scope should be. That determination is shaped by the nature of the issue, the need for speed, the results of initial interviews and document reviews, and the cost of any additional inquiry against its likely return. In this case, the Board applied that criteria and determined that it had sufficient information to appropriately respond. The Division has no basis to conclude a greater scope was called for. Moreover, if additional information arises that is relevant to the Board's oversight of management, it is clearly obligated to consider that information and, if merited, act on it.

The hiring of Attorney Robert Sherman, a non-fiduciary trustee of BIDMC, to lead the investigation was recognized as a potential conflict of interest by Chairman Kay. As we have repeatedly stated, conflicts of interest are not per se illegal or inappropriate, but do require disclosure and findings that the arrangement is in the best interests of the organization. This issue was considered by Chairman Kay and BIDMC counsel. Ultimately, they decided that Mr. Sherman's familiarity with BIDMC would allow him to move much more quickly than other outside investigators who were less familiar with BIDMC. Because this issue was disclosed and considered, the Division has no basis to conclude that the retention of Mr. Sherman to undertake the investigation was inappropriate.

Disciplining its CEO is a difficult action for a Board. While Board members, BIDMC staff and employees, and members of the public may all have differing views about the adequacy or propriety of the sanctions imposed, the Division has no basis to second guess this action or its scope.

Board Independence

The Division, however, cannot conclude that neither the Board nor senior management of the Medical Center is without some level of responsibility for these events. Clearly members of senior management, two former Board chairs and at least one non-officer Board member were aware of the relationship and had directly and indirectly alerted Mr. Levy to the problems it was creating. Had he been called on his failure to act, or had his failure to act been reported to the entire Board, this acknowledged "lapse of judgment" might never have occurred. For senior managers who reported to Levy, demanding a response was likely difficult. For Board members, it was their job.

We state this with a level of conviction clearly aided by hindsight and with the knowledge that some past and current Board members are still unconvinced that the investigation should have taken place or, having taken place, that sanctions were warranted. Nevertheless, we believe that at some level deference to a successful CEO, widely perceived as having rescued the Medical Center, may have impaired Board independence. As the charitable sector strives to improve and enhance effective governance, this unfortunate outcome serves as a stark and compelling reminder to all our charitable boards of the critical importance of board independence in all aspects of management oversight.

On a going forward basis, we note that the Board recently added provisions to the BIDMC human resources policies requiring disclosure of certain personal relationships within the workplace, commonly referred to as "anti-fraternization policies." Additionally, the Board Chair has emphasized that the Board will continue to monitor and review the impact of this situation on BIDMC and the CEO's ability to lead. We expect that the Board will keep the Division informed of any significant developments in this area. The Division believes both actions are entirely appropriate and consistent with the Board's obligations.

In closing, the Division notes that the need for Board independence of management, whether it relate to conflicts of interest, executive compensation, dual office

The CEO resigned in January 2011 after continued public pressure. Today, he writes about health care in his blog: *Not Running a Hospital*.

holding or diligent management oversight, remains a high priority for the Division's oversight activities of all public charities.

Thank you for your attention and cooperation throughout the Review.

Sincerely,

Jed M. Nosal
Assistant Attorney General
Chief, Business and Labor Bureau

PROBLEM

Draft a 300-word policy to prevent this type of conflict of interest.

E. THE BOARD'S DUTY TO OVERSEE COMPANY OPERATIONS TO ENSURE COMPLIANCE WITH STATE AND FEDERAL LAWS

The Beth Israel board eventually conducted a thorough investigation. Boards cannot be passive but must take actions that ensure that the board is properly informed and that the company complies with applicable laws. These systems are known as compliance programs. The Delaware Chancery Court issued the foundational compliance case in 1996, which has had profound influence in succeeding decades on the fiduciary duty that must be exercised by a board to understand a company's operations.

In re Caremark International Inc. Derivative Litigation

698 A.2d 959 (Del. Ch. 1996)

ALLEN, Chancellor.

. . . The suit involves claims that the members of Caremark's board of directors (the "Board") breached their fiduciary duty of care to Caremark in connection with alleged violations by Caremark employees of federal and state laws and regulations applicable to health care providers. As a result of the alleged violations, Caremark was subject to an extensive four year investigation by the United States Department of Health and Human Services and the Department of Justice. In 1994 Caremark was charged in an indictment with multiple felonies. It thereafter entered into a number of agreements with the Department of Justice and others. Those agreements included a plea agreement in which Caremark pleaded guilty to a single felony of mail fraud and agreed to pay civil and criminal fines. Subsequently, Caremark agreed to make reimbursements to various private and public parties. In all, the payments that Caremark has been required to make total approximately $250 million. . . .

During the relevant period Caremark was involved in two main health care business segments, providing patient care and managed care services. As part of its patient care business, which accounted for the majority of Caremark's revenues, Caremark provided alternative site health care services, including infusion therapy, growth hormone therapy, HIV/AIDS-related treatments and hemophilia therapy. Caremark's managed care services included prescription drug programs and the operation of multi-specialty group practices.

A. Events Prior to the Government Investigation

A substantial part of the revenues generated by Caremark's businesses is derived from third party payments, insurers, and Medicare and Medicaid reimbursement programs. The latter source of payments [is] subject to the terms of the Anti-Referral Payments Law ("ARPL") which prohibits health care providers from paying any form of remuneration to induce the referral of Medicare or Medicaid patients. From its inception, Caremark entered into a variety of agreements with hospitals, physicians, and health care providers for advice and services, as well as distribution agreements with drug manufacturers, as had its predecessor prior to 1992. Specifically, Caremark did have a practice of entering into contracts for services (e.g., consultation agreements and research grants) with physicians at least some of whom prescribed or recommended services or products that Caremark provided to Medicare recipients and other patients. Such contracts were not prohibited by the ARPL but they obviously raised a possibility of unlawful "kickbacks."

> There is no law commonly called the "Anti-Referral Payments Law." The correct name is the Anti-Kickback Statute, and it is discussed in Chapter 6.

As early as 1989, Caremark's predecessor issued an internal "Guide to Contractual Relationships" ("Guide") to govern its employees in entering into contracts with physicians and hospitals. The Guide tended to be reviewed annually by lawyers and updated. Each version of the Guide stated as Caremark's and its predecessor's policy that no payments would be made in exchange for or to induce patient referrals. But what one might deem a prohibited quid pro quo was not always clear. Due to a scarcity of court decisions interpreting the ARPL, however, Caremark repeatedly publicly stated that there was uncertainty concerning Caremark's interpretation of the law.

To clarify the scope of the ARPL, the United States Department of Health and Human Services ("HHS") issued "safe harbor" regulations in July 1991 stating conditions under which financial relationships between health care service providers and patient referral sources, such as physicians, would not violate the ARPL. Caremark contends that the narrowly drawn regulations gave limited guidance as to the legality of many of the agreements used by Caremark that did not fall within the safe-harbor. Caremark's predecessor, however, amended many of its standard forms of agreement with health care providers and revised the Guide in an apparent attempt to comply with the new regulations.

B. Government Investigation and Related Litigation

In August 1991, the HHS Office of the Inspector General ("OIG") initiated an investigation of Caremark's predecessor. Caremark's predecessor was served with a subpoena requiring the production of documents, including contracts between Caremark's predecessor and physicians (Quality Service Agreements ("QSAs")). Under the QSAs, Caremark's predecessor appears to have paid physicians fees for monitoring patients under Caremark's predecessor's care, including Medicare and Medicaid recipients. Sometimes apparently those monitoring patients were referring physicians, which raised ARPL concerns.

> The allegation was that the payments were not for legitimate services but were rewards to induce referrals of Medicare patients.

In March 1992, the Department of Justice ("DOJ") joined the OIG investigation and separate investigations were commenced by several additional federal and state agencies.

C. Caremark's Response to the Investigation

During the relevant period, Caremark had approximately 7,000 employees and ninety branch operations. It had a decentralized management structure. By May 1991, however, Caremark asserts that it had begun making attempts to centralize its management structure in order to increase supervision over its branch operations.

The first action taken by management, as a result of the initiation of the OIG investigation, was an announcement that as of October 1, 1991, Caremark's predecessor would no longer pay management fees to physicians for services to Medicare and Medicaid patients. Despite this decision, Caremark asserts that its management, pursuant to advice, did not believe that such payments were illegal under the existing laws and regulations.

> These types of payments were once common practice by drug company representatives who wanted physicians to select their drugs as much as possible.

During this period, Caremark's Board took several additional steps consistent with an effort to assure compliance with company policies concerning the ARPL and the contractual forms in the Guide. In April 1992, Caremark published a fourth revised version of its Guide apparently designed to assure that its agreements either complied with the ARPL and regulations or excluded Medicare and Medicaid patients altogether. In addition, in September 1992, Caremark instituted a policy requiring its regional officers, Zone Presidents, to approve each contractual relationship entered into by Caremark with a physician.

Although there is evidence that inside and outside counsel had advised Caremark's directors that their contracts were in accord with the law, Caremark recognized that some uncertainty respecting the correct interpretation of the law existed. In its 1992 annual report, Caremark disclosed the ongoing government investigations, acknowledged that if penalties were imposed on the company they could have a material adverse effect on Caremark's business, and stated that no assurance could be given that its interpretation of the ARPL would prevail if challenged.

Throughout the period of the government investigations, Caremark had an internal audit plan designed to assure compliance with business and ethics policies. In addition, Caremark employed Price Waterhouse as its outside auditor. On February 8, 1993, the Ethics Committee of Caremark's Board received and reviewed an outside auditors report by Price Waterhouse which concluded that there were no material weaknesses in Caremark's control structure. Despite the positive findings of Price Waterhouse, however, on April 20, 1993, the Audit & Ethics Committee adopted a new internal audit charter requiring a comprehensive review of compliance policies and the compilation of an employee ethics handbook concerning such policies.

The Board appears to have been informed about this project and other efforts to assure compliance with the law. For example, Caremark's management reported to the Board that Caremark's sales force was receiving an ongoing education regarding the ARPL and the proper use of Caremark's form contracts which had been approved by in-house counsel. On July 27, 1993, the new ethics manual, expressly prohibiting payments in exchange for referrals and requiring employees to report all illegal conduct to a toll free confidential ethics hotline, was approved and allegedly disseminated. The record suggests that Caremark continued these policies in subsequent years, causing employees to be given revised versions of

> These are common features in health care compliance programs.

the ethics manual and requiring them to participate in training sessions concerning compliance with the law.

During 1993, Caremark took several additional steps which appear to have been aimed at increasing management supervision. These steps included new policies requiring local branch managers to secure home office approval for all disbursements under agreements with health care providers and to certify compliance with the ethics program. In addition, the chief financial officer was appointed to serve as Caremark's compliance officer. In 1994, a fifth revised Guide was published.

> Today, chief compliance officers at major firms are generally in that role full time, with a direct line of reporting to the board.

D. Federal Indictments Against Caremark and Officers

On August 4, 1994, a federal grand jury in Minnesota issued a 47 page indictment charging Caremark, two of its officers (not the firm's chief officer), an individual who had been a sales employee of Genentech, Inc., and David R. Brown, a physician practicing in Minneapolis, with violating the ARPL over a lengthy period. According to the indictment, over $1.1 million had been paid to Brown to induce him to distribute Protropin, a human growth hormone drug marketed by Caremark. The substantial payments involved started, according to the allegations of the indictment, in 1986 and continued through 1993. Some payments were "in the guise of research grants" and others were "consulting agreements". The indictment charged, for example, that Dr. Brown performed virtually none of the consulting functions described in his 1991 agreement with Caremark, but was nevertheless neither required to return the money he had received nor precluded from receiving future funding from Caremark. In addition the indictment charged that Brown received from Caremark payments of staff and office expenses, including telephone answering services and fax rental expenses.

In reaction to the Minnesota Indictment and the subsequent filing of this and other derivative actions in 1994, the Board met and was informed by management that the investigation had resulted in an indictment; Caremark denied any wrongdoing relating to the indictment and believed that the OIG investigation would have a favorable outcome. Management reiterated the grounds for its view that the contracts were in compliance with law. . . .

2. Liability for failure to monitor: The second class of cases[*] in which director liability for inattention is theoretically possible entail circumstances in which a loss eventuates not from a decision but, from unconsidered inaction. Most of the decisions that a corporation, acting through its human agents, makes are, of course, not the subject of director attention. Legally, the board itself will be required only to authorize the most significant corporate acts or transactions: mergers, changes in capital structure, fundamental changes in business, appointment and compensation of the CEO, etc. As the facts of this case graphically demonstrate, ordinary business decisions that are made by officers and employees deeper in the interior of the organization can, however, vitally affect the welfare of the corporation and its ability to achieve its various strategic and financial goals. If this case did not prove the point itself, recent business history would. Recall for example the displacement of senior

---

*Chancellor Allen began the legal analysis with board decisions that were not made in good faith.

management and much of the board of Salomon, Inc.; the replacement of senior management of Kidder, Peabody following the discovery of large trading losses resulting from phantom trades by a highly compensated trader; or the extensive financial loss and reputational injury suffered by Prudential Insurance as a result its junior officers['] misrepresentations in connection with the distribution of limited partnership interests. Financial and organizational disasters such as these raise the question, what is the board's responsibility with respect to the organization and monitoring of the enterprise to assure that the corporation functions within the law to achieve its purposes?

Modernly this question has been given special importance by an increasing tendency, especially under federal law, to employ the criminal law to assure corporate compliance with external legal requirements, including environmental, financial, employee and product safety as well as assorted other health and safety regulations. In 1991, pursuant to the Sentencing Reform Act of 1984, the United States Sentencing Commission adopted Organizational Sentencing Guidelines which impact importantly on the prospective effect these criminal sanctions might have on business corporations. The Guidelines set forth a uniform sentencing structure for organizations to be sentenced for violation of federal criminal statutes and provide for penalties that equal or often massively exceed those previously imposed on corporations. The Guidelines offer powerful incentives for corporations today to have in place compliance programs to detect violations of law, promptly to report violations to appropriate public officials when discovered, and to take prompt, voluntary remedial efforts. . . .

Obviously the level of detail that is appropriate for such an information system is a question of business judgment. And obviously too, no rationally designed information and reporting system will remove the possibility that the corporation will violate laws or regulations, or that senior officers or directors may nevertheless sometimes be misled or otherwise fail reasonably to detect acts material to the corporation's compliance with the law. But it is important that the board exercise a good faith judgment that the corporation's information and reporting system is in concept and design adequate to assure the board that appropriate information will come to its attention in a timely manner as a matter of ordinary operations, so that it may satisfy its responsibility.

Thus, I am of the view that a director's obligation includes a duty to attempt in good faith to assure that a corporate information and reporting system, which the board concludes is adequate, exists, and that failure to do so under some circumstances may, in theory at least, render a director liable for losses caused by noncompliance with applicable legal standards. I now turn to an analysis of the claims asserted with this concept of the directors duty of care, as a duty satisfied in part by assurance of adequate information flows to the board, in mind. . . .

These board obligations are now known as "Caremark duties."

Here the record supplies essentially no evidence that the director defendants were guilty of a sustained failure to exercise their oversight function. To the contrary, insofar as I am able to tell on this record, the corporation's information systems appear to have represented a good faith attempt to be informed of relevant facts. If the directors did not know the specifics of the activities that lead to the indictments, they cannot be faulted.

QUESTIONS

1. Should it have been obvious to the board of directors that employees' payments to influence a physician's purchasing decision were illegal?
2. Is the court's remedy of creating new lines of communication and expected information sharing appropriate given that the court otherwise appears to defer to the board's judgment?

While this decision is couched in the language of the duty of care, later Delaware decisions have shifted *Caremark* duties to a form of the duty of loyalty. The primary substantive effect of this change is that *Caremark* duties cannot be routinely waived in the corporate charter. Del. Gen. Corp. Law §102(b)(7).

CAPSTONE PROBLEM

You are the chief compliance officer of a regional hospital, organized as a nonprofit corporation in your state. An anonymous call was made to the compliance hotline, alleging preferential treatment had been given to the Chief of Surgery and other key doctors at the hospital, including below-market-rate rent on physician office space, free preferential parking, and an all-expenses-paid medical staff leadership and hospital board retreat in Costa Rica with spouses and guests. During your investigation, you also discover that one of the spouses at that retreat (the spouse of the board chair) does business with the hospital through their construction firm. Write a 1,000-word memorandum on the possible exposures for the hospital, with recommendations for action.

CHAPTER 5

Tax-Exempt Health Care Charitable Organizations

A. INTRODUCTION

Tax law is an effective and common tool for influencing health policy and for regulating health care providers. This chapter studies the principal federal and state tax rules that impact how charitable health care organizations operate. We noted in Chapter 4 that a majority of hospitals in the United States are charitable organizations under state law, and those hospitals also maintain tax-exempt status under federal law. The benefits of tax-exempt status under federal and state law include exemption from federal and state income taxes, opportunities to sell tax-exempt bonds at lower interest rates, access to tax-advantaged pension plans, lower postage costs, and exemptions from state and local property taxes. For most tax-exempt health care providers, these are very valuable benefits. The Internal Revenue Service (IRS) has articulated important standards for the operation of tax-exempt entities and their boards of directors. Foremost among the IRS's goals is to ensure devotion to the charitable mission of the organization.

B. HEALTH CARE AS A CHARITABLE PURPOSE

IRS involvement with health care corporate governance expanded greatly in the years following the enactment of Medicare and Medicaid. A significant early example is Revenue Ruling 69-545, an administrative pronouncement by the IRS in 1969 that elaborated rules based upon §501(c)(3) of the Internal Revenue Code and related regulations.

> 26 U.S.C. §501. Exemption from tax on corporations, certain trusts, etc.
> . . . (c) List of exempt organizations
> . . . (3) Corporations, and any community chest, fund, or foundation, organized and operated exclusively for religious, charitable, scientific, testing for public safety, literary, or educational purposes, or to foster national or international amateur sports competition (but only if no part of its activities involve the provision of athletic facilities or equipment), or for the prevention of cruelty to children or animals, no part of the net earnings of which inures to the benefit of any private shareholder or individual, no substantial part of the activities of which is carrying on propaganda,

or otherwise attempting, to influence legislation (except as otherwise provided in subsection (h)), and which does not participate in, or intervene in (including the publishing or distributing of statements), any political campaign on behalf of (or in opposition to) any candidate for public office.

Revenue Rulings are not regulations under the Administrative Procedure Act but represent the published views of the IRS on pending audits and litigation issues. Nevertheless, they are important examples of tax guidance, offer insight into the current thinking of the IRS, and are frequently cited by courts. The style you see below is common for Revenue Rulings, with the IRS offering both positive and negative examples.

Revenue Ruling 69-545

1969-2 C.B. 117

Examples illustrate whether a nonprofit hospital claiming exemption under section 501(c)(3) of the Code is operated to serve a public rather than a private interest; Revenue Ruling 56-185 modified.

Advice has been requested whether the two nonprofit hospitals described below qualify for exemption from Federal income tax under section 501(c)(3) of the Internal Revenue Code of 1954. The articles of organization of both hospitals meet the organizational requirements of section 1.501(c)(3)-1(b) of the Income Tax Regulations, including the limitation of the organizations' purposes to those described in section 501(c)(3) of the Code and the dedication of their assets to such purposes.

Situation 1. Hospital A is a 250-bed community hospital. Its board of trustees is composed of prominent citizens in the community. Medical staff privileges in the hospital are available to all qualified physicians in the area, consistent with the size and nature of its facilities. The hospital has 150 doctors on its active staff and 200 doctors on its courtesy staff. It also owns a medical office building on its premises with space for 60 doctors. Any member of its active medical staff has the privilege of leasing available office space. Rents are set at rates comparable to those of other commercial buildings in the area.

The hospital operates a full time emergency room and no one requiring emergency care is denied treatment. The hospital otherwise ordinarily limits admissions to those who can pay the cost of their hospitalization, either themselves, or through private health insurance, or with the aid of public programs such as Medicare. Patients who cannot meet the financial requirements for admission are ordinarily referred to another hospital in the community that does serve indigent patients.

The hospital usually ends each year with an excess of operating receipts over operating disbursements from its hospital operations. Excess funds are generally applied to expansion and replacement of existing facilities and equipment, amortization of indebtedness, improvement in patient care, and medical training, education, and research.

> The hospital turns a profit but reinvests the money in the charitable mission.

Situation 2. Hospital B is a 60-bed general hospital which was originally owned by five doctors. The owners formed a nonprofit organization and sold their interests in the hospital to the organization at fair market value. The board of trustees of the organization consists of the five doctors, their accountant, and their lawyer. The five doctors also comprise the hospital's medical committee and thereby control the selection and the admission of other doctors to the medical staff. During its first five years of operations, only four other doctors have been granted staff privileges at the hospital. The applications of a number of qualified doctors in the community have been rejected.

Hospital admission is restricted to patients of doctors holding staff privileges. Patients of the five original physicians have accounted for a large majority of all hospital admissions over the years. The hospital maintains an emergency room, but on a relatively inactive basis, and primarily for the convenience of the patients of the staff doctors. The local ambulance services have been instructed by the hospital to take emergency cases to other hospitals in the area. The hospital follows the policy of ordinarily limiting admissions to those who can pay the cost of the services rendered. The five doctors comprising the original medical staff have continued to maintain their offices in the hospital since its sale to the nonprofit organization. The rental paid is less than that of comparable office space in the vicinity. No office space is available for any of the other staff members.

Section 501(c)(3) of the Code provides for exemption from Federal income tax or organizations organized and operated exclusively for charitable, scientific, or educational purposes, no part of the net earnings of which inures to the benefit of any private shareholder or individual.

> These are the core statutes and regulations for tax-exempt institutions. Health care is not on the list but may qualify as "charitable" if the conditions articulated below are met. The entity must be: (1) *organized* and (2) *operated* exclusively for charitable purposes, without *private benefit or private inurement.*

Section 1.501(c)(3)-1(d)(1)(ii) of the regulations provides that an organization is not organized or operated exclusively for any purpose set forth in section 501(c)(3) of the Code unless it serves a public rather than a private interest.

Section 1.501(c)(3)-1(d)(2) of the regulations states that the term "charitable" is used in section 501(c)(3) of the Code in its generally accepted legal sense.

To qualify for exemption from Federal income tax under section 501(c)(3) of the Code, a nonprofit hospital must be organized and operated exclusively in furtherance of some purpose considered "charitable" in the generally accepted legal sense of that term, and the hospital may not be operated, directly or indirectly, for the benefit of private interests.

In the general law of charity, the promotion of health is considered to be a charitable purpose. Restatement (Second), Trusts, sec. 368 and sec. 372; IV Scott on Trusts (3rd ed. 1967), sec. 368 and sec. 372. A nonprofit organization whose purpose and activity are providing hospital care is promoting health and may, therefore, qualify as organized and operated in furtherance of a charitable purpose. If it meets the other requirements of section 501(c)(3) of the Code, it will qualify for exemption from Federal income tax under section 501(a).

Since the purpose and activity of Hospital [A], apart from its related educational and research activities and purposes, are providing hospital care on a nonprofit basis for members of its community, it is organized and operated in furtherance of a purpose considered "charitable" in the generally accepted legal sense of that term. The promotion of health, like the relief of poverty and the advancement of education and religion, is one of the purposes in the general law of charity that is deemed beneficial to the community as a whole even though the class of beneficiaries eligible to receive a direct benefit from its activities does not include all members of the community, such as indigent members of the community, provided that the class is not so small that its relief is not of

> Community benefit must be demonstrated, here through an emergency department that is open to all without regard to the ability to pay.

benefit to the community. Restatement (Second), Trusts, sec. 368, comment (b) and sec. 372, comments (b) and (c); IV Scott on Trusts (3rd ed. 1967), sec. 368 and sec. 372.2. By operating an emergency room open to all persons and by providing hospital care for all those persons in the community able to pay the cost thereof either directly or through third party reimbursement, Hospital A is promoting the health of a class of persons that is broad enough to benefit the community.

The fact that Hospital A operates at an annual surplus of receipts over disbursements does not preclude its exemption. By using its surplus funds to improve the quality of patient care, expand its facilities, and advance its medical training, education, and research programs, the hospital is operating in furtherance of its exempt purposes.

Furthermore, Hospital A is operated to serve a public rather than a private interest. Control of the hospital rests with its board of trustees, which is composed of independent civic leaders. The hospital maintains an open medical staff, with privileges available to all qualified physicians. Members of its active medical staff have the privilege of leasing available space in its medical building. It operates an active and generally accessible emergency room. These factors indicate that the use and control of Hospital A are for the benefit of the public and that no part of the income of the organization is inuring to the benefit of any private individual nor is any private interest being served.

Accordingly, it is held that Hospital A is exempt from Federal income tax under section 501(c)(3) of the Code.

Hospital B is also providing hospital care. However, in order to qualify under section 501(c)(3) of the Code, an organization must be organized and operated exclusively for one or more of the purposes set forth in that section. Hospital B was initially established as a proprietary institution operated for the benefit of its owners. Although its ownership has been transferred to a nonprofit organization, the hospital has continued to operate for the private benefit of its original owners who exercise control over the hospital through the board of trustees and the medical committee. They have used their control to restrict the number of doctors admitted to the medical staff, to enter into favorable rental agreements with the hospital, and to limit emergency room care and hospital admission substantially to their own patients. These facts indicate that the hospital is operated for the private benefit of its original owners, rather than for the exclusive benefit of the public.

Accordingly, it is held that Hospital B does not qualify for exemption from Federal income tax under section 501(c)(3) of the Code. In considering whether a nonprofit hospital claiming such exemption is operated to serve a private benefit, the Service will weigh all of the relevant facts and circumstances in each case. The absence of particular factors set forth above or the presence of other factors will not necessar[ily] be determinative.

Even though an organization considers itself within the scope of Situation 1 of this Revenue Ruling, it must file an application on Form 1023, Exemption Application, in order to be recognized by the Service as exempt under

> Form 1023 is still used today to apply for exemption under §501(c)(3).

section 501(c)(3) of the Code. The application should be filed with the District Director of Internal Revenue for the district in which is located the principal place of business or principal office of the organization. See section 1.501(a)-1 of the regulations.

Ruling 56-185, C.B. 1956-1, 202, sets forth requirements for exemption of hospitals under section 501(c)(3) more restrictive than those contained in this Revenue

Ruling with respect to caring for patients without charge or at rates below cost. In addition, the fourth requirement of Revenue Ruling 56-185 is ambiguous in that it can be read as implying that the possibility of "shareholders" or "members" sharing in the assets of a hospital upon its dissolution will not preclude exemption of the hospital as a charity described in section 501(c)(3) of the Code. Section 1.501(c)(3)-1(b)(4) of the regulations promulgated subsequent to Revenue Ruling 56-185 makes it clear, however, that an absolute dedication of assets to charity is a precondition to exemption under section 501(c)(3) of the Code. Revenue Ruling 56-185 is hereby modified to remove therefrom the requirements relating to caring for patients without charge or at rates below cost. Furthermore, requirement four has been modified by section 1.501(c)(3)-1(b)(4) of the regulations.

QUESTIONS

1. Why is running an emergency department important to the determination of charitable status in this Revenue Ruling?
2. Why did the original ownership of Hospital B doom its tax-exempt status?

To qualify as a tax-exempt hospital, two key tests must be met. Hospitals must be both organized and operated exclusively for "charitable" purposes, which includes providing health care that benefits the community. These are the "organizational" and "operational" tests for charitable purpose.

The **organizational test** is met by properly structuring corporate documents, especially the Articles of Incorporation. Typically, the hospital is organized as a nonprofit under state law, which was discussed in Chapter 4. The legal purpose of the hospital must be exclusively charitable, as recorded in the Articles of Incorporation. The IRS suggests the following language in Form 1023:

> The corporation is organized exclusively for charitable, religious, educational, and scientific purposes, including, for such purposes, the making of distributions to organizations that qualify as exempt organizations under section 501(c)(3) of the Internal Revenue Code, or the corresponding section of any future federal tax code.

The IRS also requires a provision in the Articles of Incorporation or under applicable state law ensuring that the assets are irrevocably devoted to a charitable purpose, even after dissolution of the corporation. The IRS suggests language in Publication 557:

> Upon the dissolution of the corporation, assets shall be distributed for one or more exempt purposes within the meaning of section 501(c)(3) of the Internal Revenue Code, or the corresponding section of any future federal tax code, or shall be distributed to the federal government, or to a state or local government, for a public purpose. Any such assets not so disposed of shall be disposed of by a Court of Competent Jurisdiction of the county in which the principal office of the corporation is then located, exclusively for such purposes or to such organization or organizations, as said Court shall determine, which are organized and operated exclusively for such purposes.

Form 1023 requires proof that both of these elements of the organizational test are met before the IRS will approve the application for exemption.

While the organizational test focuses on the Articles of Incorporation when the entity is formed, the **operational test** examines how the charity is actually operated over time. Tax-exempt entities generally must file Form 990 each year, which includes many questions relating to the operational test. The operational test includes two key elements of particular importance for hospitals, one positive requirement and one negative prohibition.

First, the hospital must be operated exclusively for charitable purposes. Private benefits must be merely incidental to this charitable purpose. Promotion of health to the community counts as a charitable public benefit, as we saw in Revenue Ruling 69-545, especially through an emergency department open to all without regard to ability to pay. Other qualifying purposes include medical education and research, and providing charitable care to indigent people unable to pay for health care. The Patient Protection and Affordable Care Act (ACA) added a new provision to the Internal Revenue Code that requires hospitals to report their community benefits to the public, under I.R.C. §501(r), which we will consider in more detail below.

Second, charities cannot permit any part of their net earnings to "inure to the benefit" of any insider (i.e., there can be no "private inurement"). Charities do not have shareholders, so dividends — or anything based on net earnings that looks like dividends — cannot be paid to influential insiders.

But in hospitals, most people receive compensation for their work, from the highest-paid physician to part-time workers in the cafeteria. Charities are allowed to pay employees and others for work actually performed, but payments cannot exceed fair market value, nor can any transaction proceed that in substance allows some of the net earnings of the charity to "inure" to private interests through self-dealing or giving inappropriate control over charitable assets to for-profit companies. The suggested language from IRS Publication 557 covers these issues and also includes other charitable restrictions on political activity:

> No part of the net earnings of the corporation shall inure to the benefit of, or be distributable to its members, trustees, officers, or other private persons, except that the corporation shall be authorized and empowered to pay reasonable compensation for services rendered and to make payments and distributions in furtherance of the purposes set forth in Article Third hereof. No substantial part of the activities of the corporation shall be the carrying on of propaganda, or otherwise attempting to influence legislation, and the corporation shall not participate in, or intervene in (including the publishing or distribution of statements) any political campaign on behalf of or in opposition to any candidate for public office. Notwithstanding any other provision of these articles, the corporation shall not carry on any other activities not permitted to be carried on (a) by a corporation exempt from federal income tax under section 501(c)(3) of the Internal Revenue Code, or the corresponding section of any future federal tax code, or (b) by a corporation, contributions to which are deductible under section 170(c)(2) of the Internal Revenue Code, or the corresponding section of any future federal tax code.

We examine the organizational and operational tests below in the *St. David's* case, in the context of a hospital joint venture with a for-profit entity.

PROBLEM

You represent Hospital B in Revenue Ruling 69-545. Write a 600-word memo describing changes that will need to occur in order to qualify under §501(c)(3).

C. FEDERAL REQUIREMENTS FOR TAX-EXEMPT HOSPITALS

Federal tax law is a complicated subject in its own right. The IRS devotes a specialized division to "exempt organizations," which includes hospitals, but also many other charities such as universities, religious institutions, and disaster relief organizations such as the Red Cross. At the risk of oversimplifying a complex area, we offer three important examples of federal tax rules that impact the governance of charitable hospitals: community health needs assessments (CHNAs) under §501(r) of the Code; joint ventures with for-profit entities; and the "intermediate sanctions" rules that prescribe governance procedures for boards to manage financial conflicts of interest and self-dealing.

1. COMMUNITY HEALTH NEEDS ASSESSMENTS AND OTHER REQUIRE- MENTS UNDER SECTION 501(r)

In the years running up to the adoption of the ACA, news reports and congressional testimony highlighted aggressive bill collection practices of some tax-exempt hospitals. Yale-New Haven Hospital was the subject of one such story, profiled in the *Wall Street Journal*:

Lucette Lagnado, Jeanette White Is Long Dead but Her Hospital Bill Lives On

Wall St. J., Mar. 13, 2003

Quinton White lies in bed at his home in Bridgeport, Conn., suffering from kidney ailments and the aftereffects of a heart attack and dreaming of a trip to Paris, which he has seen only in the movies.

But for Mr. White, a retired dry-cleaning worker, seeing Europe is probably as likely as a trip to the moon. In addition to his health troubles, the 77-year-old is strapped with nearly $40,000 of debt.

He owes the money to Yale-New Haven Hospital, a distinguished not-for-profit facility where his wife, Jeanette, was treated 20 years ago. Mrs. White died in 1993, but her debt lives on, growing like her cancer because of the 10% interest charged on her original $18,740 bill. Back in 1983, the hospital's lawyer got a lien on the Whites' house, and in 1996 nearly cleaned out Mr. White's bank account.

Mr. White figures he will be stuck paying the hospital until his own dying day, though he adds, with a mischievous glint in his eye, "They will never get the whole amount. I am not gonna live that long."

Mr. White isn't alone in his predicament. Many hospitals besides Yale-New Haven have adopted aggressive collection practices aimed at their uninsured and underinsured patients as they seek extra income to stay afloat. Collection dollars are one of the ways hospitals are compensating for the squeeze on HMO and government reimbursements and countering their losses from caring for the uninsured.

Recently patient advocates from Connecticut to California have begun to criticize the way hospitals pursue patients who owe them money. As part of a national campaign by the Service Employees International Union, the New England health-care local has been researching Yale-New Haven's collection practices. Grace Rollins spent months looking up court cases the hospital has brought and interviewing some of the patients involved. Some of these people "are living hand to mouth," Ms. Rollins says. "These debts are literally crippling them."

Indeed, medical bills are now the second biggest cause of personal bankruptcies, according to a study by Elizabeth Warren, who heads Harvard University's Consumer Bankruptcy Project. Along with the astronomical cost of even routine hospital procedures, she blames hospitals' aggressive collection tactics.

> Medical debt was the number one cause of personal bankruptcy in the years leading up to enactment of the ACA.

The patients who suffer the most aren't necessarily indigent. The very poor can get Medicaid, the government health plan that pays hospital tabs for those who qualify, while most middle-class families have health coverage that picks up the bulk of their medical bills. It is working-class families like the Whites, with some assets but no insurance coverage, who are penalized the most by the system.

Yale-New Haven, the primary teaching hospital for Yale University's medical school, defends its collection practices. The hospital, whose board includes the university's president and the medical school's dean, says prudent business practices mean that the hospital must at least try to get back money for care rendered. "I can attest vehemently to the ethics, the goodwill, and the intent of this organization," says Marna Borgstrom, Yale-New Haven's chief operating officer.

Mr. White seems more resigned to his fate than resentful. Leaning back on his mattress, his skinny limbs covered by a worn blanket, he points to desk drawers stuffed with stacks of canceled checks. Many are made out to Yale-New Haven Hospital, tangible proof, he says, of how month after month he faithfully attempted to repay the institution for its care.

Over the years, Mr. White has paid Yale $16,000 — close to the amount the hospital originally billed for his wife's stays. But interest on the bill now exceeds $33,000. Indeed, between the principal Mr. White has paid off, the principal that remains to be paid, and the interest and fees owed to the hospital's attorneys and others, the total bill for Mrs. White's treatment has ballooned to around $55,000. The hospital confirms that Mr. White still owes $39,000. "I accept it. That's the way it is," Mr. White says with a shrug. "How are you gonna fight them?"

But E. Richard Brown, a professor at the UCLA School of Public Health who studies the uninsured, argues that a hospital's tax-exempt status should require it to steer clear of hard-nosed tactics, including lawsuits, wage garnishing, liens and unrelenting claims for payment. "If we are going to give them that status," Professor Brown says of hospitals, including Yale-New Haven, "they should be responsible for fulfilling the intent. The intent is to create a community benefit, a public good, and not simply act like a for-profit hospital but with a taxpayer subsidy."

. . . [I]n 1982, Mrs. White was diagnosed with throat cancer and admitted to Yale-New Haven, first in March and again in May. In return for her care, she signed a note agreeing to pay the hospital "regular charges" and late fees. A couple of months later, her husband signed a similar note agreeing to guarantee payment. . . .

The hospital says it held frequent discussions with the Whites over how its bill would be paid. Early on, Mrs. White applied for Medicaid but was turned down. She offered to pay $25 a month, but the hospital considered that unacceptable. In August 1982, Yale-New Haven's lawyer, Joseph Tobin, was brought in, and several months later he got a court order for a lien on the Whites' house, guaranteeing that the hospital's debt would be repaid in the event of any sale.

Numerous motions were filed with the court in late 1982 and early 1983, culminating the following May in a summary judgment and an order for payment that included the original debt, Mr. Tobin's $2,811 in legal fees, $192 in court costs and $153 in late charges, for a total of nearly $22,000. The judge then signed off on a payment schedule of $5 a week.

In 1993, Mrs. White succumbed to her cancer, but her husband continued to send the hospital checks. In January 1996, hospital lawyers sought a higher monthly payment, and a judge agreed, tripling the amount Mr. White had to pay to $15 a week.

That same year, the attorneys upped the ante again, moving to seize Mr. White's savings to pay down his debt. He responded that he had been making regular installment payments and that the funds the hospital sought amounted to his entire savings. He also pointed out that some of the money came from Social Security payments deposited directly to his bank account but protected by law from seizure by creditors. As a result, the court agreed to allow Mr. White to keep $5,416.87 and let attorneys for Yale-New Haven seize $9,627.49.

Even after Mr. White retired from his job at the dry cleaner's, he continued to make payments on his wife's bill. But last year, he became seriously ill himself, suffering from heart and kidney conditions. Though his niece and his son were supposed to pay his bills while he was hospitalized at St. Vincent's Medical Hospital in Bridgeport, Conn., his son concedes that he missed some hospital installments. (Yale-New Haven says that Mr. White has missed 17 payments over the past 20 years, the bulk of them in 2002.)

The hospital's attorneys quickly went back to court, seeking to seize whatever was left in Mr. White's bank account. A June 25, 2002, letter from the hospital's attorneys to the state marshal offers crisp instructions on what to do: "Go immediately to the main branch of the below named bank and make demand on the defendant's checking and/or savings account." The letter adds that, "in addition to the judgment debt, bank fees, and your service fees, you are hereby instructed to collect legal interest at a rate of 10% from the date of judgment on the unpaid principal. Collect interest in the amount of $32,119.37 from May 17, 1982, to June 25, 2002." When the $491 in Mr. White's account turned out to be Social Security money, however, the hospital halted its effort.

At Yale-New Haven, Ms. Borgstrom defends the hospital's approach. "In this business you deal with a lot of sad stories," she says. "The reality is they came to the hospital, they were given service and to the best I know it was the very best service." A senior hospital official adds that hospital policy is to try to work out payment arrangements with patients before resorting to collection actions. Officials also stress that the hospital doesn't charge interest when it bills patients directly.

But lawyers retained by the hospital to collect debts are permitted to charge interest under Connecticut law. The law firm that has pursued Mr. White these many years is Yale-New Haven's most highly paid outside consultant, Tobin & Melien, which received more than $2 million from the hospital in 2000, according to Internal Revenue Service filings. (The firm declined to comment on its role, referring questions about collection practices to the hospital's public-relations office. A hospital spokesman, Mark D'Antonio, verified the history of the hospital's debt-collection efforts and the sums involved, as did Ms. Borgstrom.)

Yale-New Haven has operated in the black in recent years, says Ms. Borgstrom, but margins are "very thin." In 2002, the hospital had to deal with $52 million in bad debt and uncompensated care.

"Are there areas where a mistake has been made? Undoubtedly," Ms. Borgstrom says. In Mr. White's case, the hospital might even be willing to forego interest payments, she says. "I read his file; he is not a wealthy man."

But Ms. Borgstrom denies that Mr. White's case indicates a need to rethink the hospital's debt-collection methods. "You would not be surprised I am sure to know there are a lot of people who have perhaps many more means than this individual who go to great lengths to avoid obligations," she says. She adds that the hospital is mindful of its responsibilities to the poor and indigent of New Haven. "We live as a mission-driven organization."

Note use of the term "mission"; it relates directly to the special fiduciary duties discussed in Chapter 4 and is key to understanding tax-exempt status.

Nancy Kane, a professor of health finances at Harvard University, is skeptical. "There is always tension, of course, between charitable mission and bottom line," she says, "but to pursue these people the way they are pursuing them is highly uncharitable."

The hospital's practices are indeed legal, says Peter Looney, the state senate majority leader whose district includes New Haven, but he suggests that legislation could change that. Noting that "no one incurs a hospital bill by choice," he argues that debt-collection laws should be amended to make hospital charges "a special area of debt." After all, he says, "it is very different from people who purchase a car and then default on that obligation."

Another issue is Yale-New-Haven's receipt of $2.5 million in federal funds for construction projects from the 1950s to the 1970s under the Hill-Burton Act. In return for such funding, hospitals were supposed to perform public service and provide either free or subsidized care to patients who couldn't afford to pay. UCLA's Prof. Brown suggests that Yale-New Haven had a responsibility under Hill-Burton to help the Whites.

Ms. Borgstrom says no, because Yale-New Haven long ago met its obligation to provide $12.8 million in free care. In addition, she says, to be eligible under Hill-Burton rules, a family's income wasn't supposed to exceed 185% of the poverty level, and the Whites were $4,000 over the limit.

But Prof. Brown responds that while the hospital may have met the letter of the law, it appears to have ignored its larger intent: "The obligation is about more than specific dollars," he says. "It is an orientation to helping people in the community, and this was a man who clearly needed help."

In California, Tenet Healthcare Corp., a for-profit hospital system based in Santa Barbara, was recently targeted by a group of Hispanic patients who alleged they were the victims of overly aggressive billing and collection efforts. In a sharp turnaround, Tenet unveiled a "Compact With Uninsured Patients" in late January, announcing that it would change the way it bills and collects money from the poor.

In the wake of the Tenet scandals, says Jan Emerson, the spokeswoman for the California Healthcare Association, "We as an industry need to take ownership and need to put some restrictions on ourselves." The association supports legislative measures that would place "restrictions on hospital collection processes," she says, adding, "No one's goal is to drive the uninsured into bankruptcy or to have their house taken."

These days, Mr. White spends his days watching TV in the cramped bedroom he used to share with his wife. His son, who works as a mechanic nearby, says he does his best to care for his dad, but the two are clearly having trouble coping. Mr. White, though 6 feet tall, weighs barely 135 pounds.

What would he do with the money the hospital has taken over the years, he is asked. Mr. White flashes a wistful smile. He says he has never traveled farther than Canada, but if he had some of that money back, he would muster the energy to travel to Paris.

His son confirms that he has often heard his dad speak of his longing to visit France. "He will probably never get there," he says sadly.

QUESTION

Is Yale-New Haven Hospital a business or a charity, and which facts lead you to your conclusion?

Many other examples could be given that question whether tax-exempt hospitals were providing sufficient community benefits to justify their tax exemptions. In partial response, the ACA included a new requirement that tax-exempt hospitals create CHNAs, designed in part to improve the delivery of community benefits from these hospitals. Final regulations for 501(r) were promulgated in early 2015, after an extensive notice and comment period. The penalty exposure for failure to comply with 501(r) requirements is enormous: Hospitals can lose their federal tax exemption, unless they self-disclose and remedy the failure in a timely fashion.

> Revocation of tax-exempt status would be a financial disaster for most charitable hospitals.

26 C.F.R. §1.501(r)-2. Failures to satisfy section 501(r)

(a) *Revocation of section 501(c)(3) status.* Except as otherwise provided in paragraphs (b) and (c) of this section, a hospital organization failing to meet one or more of the requirements of section 501(r) separately with respect to one or more hospital facilities it operates may have its section 501(c)(3) status revoked as of the first day of the taxable year in which the failure occurs. In determining whether to continue to recognize the section 501(c)(3) status of a hospital organization that fails to meet one or more of the requirements of section 501(r) with respect to one or more hospital facilities, the Commissioner will consider all relevant facts and circumstances including, but not limited to, the following:

(1) Whether the organization has previously failed to meet the requirements of section 501(r), and, if so, whether the same type of failure previously occurred.

(2) The size, scope, nature, and significance of the organization's failure(s).

(3) In the case of an organization that operates more than one hospital facility, the number, size, and significance of the facilities that have failed to meet the section 501(r) requirements relative to those that have complied with these requirements.

(4) The reason for the failure(s).

(5) Whether the organization had, prior to the failure(s), established practices or procedures (formal or informal) reasonably designed to promote and facilitate overall compliance with the section 501(r) requirements.

(6) Whether the practices or procedures had been routinely followed and the failure(s) occurred through an oversight or mistake in applying them.

(7) Whether the organization has implemented safeguards that are reasonably calculated to prevent similar failures from occurring in the future.

(8) Whether the organization corrected the failure(s) as promptly after discovery as is reasonable given the nature of the failure(s).

(9) Whether the organization took the measures described in paragraphs (a)(7) and (a)(8) of this section before the Commissioner discovered the failure(s). . . .

(c) *Excusing certain failures if hospital facility corrects and discloses.* A hospital facility's failure to meet one or more of the requirements described in §§1.501(r)-3 through 1.501(r)-6 that is neither willful nor egregious shall be excused for purposes of this section if the hospital facility corrects and makes disclosure in accordance with rules set forth by revenue procedure, notice, or other guidance published in the Internal Revenue Bulletin. For purposes of this paragraph (c), a "willful" failure includes a failure due to gross negligence, reckless disregard, or willful neglect, and an "egregious" failure includes only a very serious failure, taking into account the severity of the impact and the number of affected persons. Whether a failure is willful or egregious will be determined based on all of the facts and circumstances. A hospital facility's correction and disclosure of a failure in accordance with the relevant guidance is a factor tending to show that the failure was not willful.

> Subsection (c) rewards an effective compliance program. The most common penalty for failure to have a CNHA is a $50,000 excise tax, but willful failure to comply can result in loss of tax-exempt status.

QUESTION

You are the compliance officer of a tax-exempt health system. How do you revise the compliance program in light of §1.501(r)-2?

The substantive provisions of the 501(r) regulations require all charitable hospitals to create and implement CHNAs, financial assistance policies (FAPs), and emergency medical care policies. Excerpts from the regulations are below, with some examples:

26 C.F.R. §1.501(r)-3. Community health needs assessments

(a) In general. With respect to any taxable year, a hospital organization meets the requirements of section 501(r)(3) with respect to a hospital facility it operates only if —

(1) The hospital facility has conducted a community health needs assessment (CHNA) that meets the requirements of paragraph (b) of this section in such taxable year or in either of the two taxable years immediately preceding such taxable year (except as provided in paragraph (d) of this section); and

(2) An authorized body of the hospital facility (as defined in §1.501(r)-1(b)(4)) has adopted an implementation strategy to meet the community health needs identified through the CHNA, as described in paragraph (c) of this section, on or before the 15th day of the fifth month after the end of such taxable year.

> The "authorized body" is generally the board of directors.

(b) Conducting a CHNA—(1) In general. To conduct a CHNA for purposes of paragraph (a) of this section, a hospital facility must complete all of the following steps:

(i) Define the community it serves.

(ii) Assess the health needs of that community.

(iii) In assessing the health needs of the community, solicit and take into account input received from persons who represent the broad interests of that community, including those with special knowledge of or expertise in public health.

(iv) Document the CHNA in a written report (CHNA report) that is adopted for the hospital facility by an authorized body of the hospital facility.

(v) Make the CHNA report widely available to the public. . . .

(3) Community served by a hospital facility. In defining the community it serves for purposes of paragraph (b)(1)(i) of this section, a hospital facility may take into account all of the relevant facts and circumstances, including the geographic area served by the hospital facility, target population(s) served (for example, children, women, or the aged), and principal functions (for example, focus on a particular specialty area or targeted disease). However, a hospital facility may not define its community to exclude medically underserved, low-income, or minority populations who live in the geographic areas from which the hospital facility draws its patients (unless such populations are not part of the hospital facility's target patient population(s) or affected by its principal functions) or otherwise should be included based on the method the hospital facility uses to define its community. In addition, in determining its patient populations for purposes of defining its community, a hospital facility must take into account all patients without regard to whether (or how much) they or their insurers pay for the care received or whether they are eligible for assistance under the hospital facility's financial assistance policy. In the case of a hospital facility consisting of multiple buildings that operate under a single state license and serve different geographic areas or populations, the community served by the hospital facility is the aggregate of such areas or populations. . . .

> This definition of "community" is designed to increase the benefits flowing from a charitable hospital, especially to people unable to pay for services.

(5) Persons representing the broad interests of the community—(i) In general. For purposes of paragraph (b)(1)(iii) of this section, a hospital facility must solicit and take into account input received from all of the following sources in identifying and prioritizing significant health needs and in identifying resources potentially available to address those health needs:

(A) At least one state, local, tribal, or regional governmental public health department (or equivalent department or agency), or a State Office of Rural Health described in section 338J of the Public Health Service Act (42 U.S.C. 254r), with knowledge, information, or expertise relevant to the health needs of that community.

(B) Members of medically underserved, low-income, and minority populations in the

> The regulation does not require that community representatives be on the hospital board but nevertheless gives them a voice in the CHNA process, which will end with board action.

community served by the hospital facility, or individuals or organizations serving or representing the interests of such populations. For purposes of this paragraph (b), medically underserved populations include populations experiencing health disparities or at risk of not receiving adequate medical care as a result of being uninsured or underinsured or due to geographic, language, financial, or other barriers.

(C) Written comments received on the hospital facility's most recently conducted CHNA and most recently adopted implementation strategy. . . .

Example. M is a hospital facility that last conducted a CHNA and adopted an implementation strategy in Year 1. In Year 3, M defines the community it serves, assesses the significant health needs of that community, and solicits and takes into account input received from persons who represent the broad interests of that community. In Year 4, M documents its CHNA in a CHNA report that is adopted by an authorized body of M, makes the CHNA report widely available on a Web site, and makes paper copies of the CHNA report available for public inspection. To meet the requirements of paragraph (a)(2) of this section, an authorized body of M must adopt an implementation strategy to meet the health needs identified through the CHNA completed in Year 4 by the 15th day of the fifth month of Year 5. . . .

26 C.F.R. §1.501(r)-4. Financial assistance policy and emergency medical care policy

(a) In general. A hospital organization meets the requirements of section 501(r)(4) with respect to a hospital facility it operates only if the hospital organization establishes for that hospital facility —

(1) A written financial assistance policy (FAP) that meets the requirements of paragraph (b) of this section; and

(2) A written emergency medical care policy that meets the requirements of paragraph (c) of this section.

(b) Financial assistance policy — (1) In general. To satisfy paragraph (a)(1) of this section, a hospital facility's FAP must —

(i) Apply to all emergency and other medically necessary care provided by the hospital facility, including all such care provided in the hospital facility by a substantially-related entity (as defined in §1.501(r)-1(b)(28));

(ii) Be widely publicized as described in paragraph (b)(5) of this section; and

(iii) Include —

(A) The eligibility criteria for financial assistance and whether such assistance includes free or discounted care;

(B) The basis for calculating amounts charged to patients;

(C) The method for applying for financial assistance;

(D) In the case of a hospital facility that does not have a separate billing and collections policy, the actions that may be taken in the event of nonpayment;

(E) If applicable, any information obtained from sources other than an individual seeking financial assistance that the hospital facility uses, and whether and under what circumstances it uses prior FAP-eligibility determinations, to presumptively determine that the individual is FAP-eligible, as described in §1.501(r)-6(c)(2); and

(F) A list of any providers, other than the hospital facility itself, delivering emergency or other medically necessary care in the hospital facility that specifies which providers are covered by the hospital facility's FAP and which are not. . . .

(v) Examples. The following examples illustrate [these provisions]:

Example 1. (i) Z is a hospital facility. The home page and main billing page of Z's Web site conspicuously display the following message: "Need help paying your bill? You may be eligible for financial assistance. Click here for more information." When readers click on the link, they are taken to a Web page that explains the various discounts available under Z's FAP and the specific eligibility criteria for each such discount. This Web page also provides all of the other information required to be included in a plain language summary of the FAP (as defined in §1.501(r)-1(b)(24)), including a telephone number of Z that individuals can call and a room number of Z that individuals can visit for more information about the FAP and assistance with FAP applications. In addition, the Web page contains prominently-displayed links that allow readers to download PDF files of the FAP and the FAP application form, free of charge and without being required to create an account or provide personally identifiable information. Z provides any individual who asks how to access a copy of the FAP, FAP application form, or plain language summary of the FAP online with the URL of this Web page. By implementing these measures, Z has made its FAP widely available on a Web site within the meaning of paragraph (b)(5)(i)(A) of this section. . . .

Example 2. Assume the same facts as Example 1, except that Z serves a community in which 6% of the members speak Spanish and have limited proficiency in English. Z translates its FAP, FAP application form, and FAP brochure (which constitutes a plain language summary of the FAP) into Spanish, and displays and distributes both Spanish and English versions of these documents in its hospital facility using all of the measures described in Example 1. Z also distributes Spanish versions of its FAP application form and FAP brochure to organizations serving Spanish-speaking members of its community. Moreover, the home page and main billing page of Z's Web site conspicuously display an "¿Habla Español?" link that takes readers to a Web page that summarizes the FAP in Spanish and contains links that allow readers to download PDF files of the Spanish versions of the FAP and FAP application form, free of charge and without being required to create an account or provide personally identifiable information. Z meets the requirement to widely publicize its FAP under paragraph (b)(1)(ii) of this section. . . .

> Limited English proficiency is a judicially protected class under Title VI, 42 U.S.C. §§2000d et seq., which prohibits discrimination in certain federal programs, including Medicare and Medicaid. This regulation duplicates some of those protections, but as a condition of tax-exemption under §501(c)(3).

(c) Emergency medical care policy — (1) In general. To satisfy paragraph (a)(2) of this section, a hospital organization must establish a written policy for a hospital facility that requires the hospital facility to provide, without discrimination, care for emergency medical conditions to individuals regardless of whether they are FAP-eligible.

(2) Interference with provision of emergency medical care. A hospital facility's emergency medical care policy will not be described in paragraph (c)(1) of this section unless it prohibits the hospital facility from engaging in actions that discourage individuals from seeking emergency medical care, such as by demanding that emergency department patients pay before receiving treatment for emergency medical conditions or by permitting debt collection activities that interfere with the provision, without discrimination, of emergency medical care.

(3) Relation to federal law governing emergency medical care. Subject to paragraph (c)(2) of this section, a hospital facility's emergency medical care policy will be described in paragraph (c)(1) of this section if it requires the hospital facility to provide the care for emergency medical conditions that the hospital facility is required to provide under Subchapter G of Chapter IV of Title 42 of the Code of Federal Regulations (or any successor regulations).

(4) Examples. The following examples illustrate this paragraph (c):

Example 1. F is a hospital facility with a dedicated emergency department that is subject to the Emergency Medical Treatment and Labor Act (EMTALA) and is not a critical access hospital. F establishes a written emergency medical care policy requiring F to comply with EMTALA by providing medical screening examinations and stabilizing treatment and referring or transferring an individual to another facility, when appropriate, and providing emergency services in accordance with 42 CFR 482.55 (or any successor regulation). F's emergency medical care policy also states that F prohibits any actions that would discourage individuals from seeking emergency medical care, such as by demanding that emergency department patients pay before receiving treatment for emergency medical conditions or permitting debt collection activities that interfere with the provision, without discrimination, of emergency medical care. F's emergency medical care policy is described in paragraph (c)(1) of this section. . . .

> Discussed in Chapter 8, EMTALA requires a hospital to render treatment for emergencies without regard to the patient's ability to pay. This regulation is satisfied under subsection (c)(3) if the hospital does what EMTALA already requires. The difference is that the IRS can enforce this requirement in addition to any action taken by HHS.

(d) Establishing the FAP and other policies — (1) In general. A hospital organization has established a FAP, a billing and collections policy, or an emergency medical care policy for a hospital facility only if an authorized body of the hospital facility (as defined in § 1.501(r)-1(b)(4)) has adopted the policy for the hospital facility and the hospital facility has implemented the policy. . . .

QUESTION

Would the new 501(r) regulations have helped Mr. Quentin White with his bill payments to Yale-New Haven Hospital?

The 501(r) regulations also forbid "extraordinary collection activities" against patients and limit how much uninsured patients may be charged. 26 C.F.R. §1.501(r)-6. The rules force hospital boards to directly address issues of providing charitable care and benefits to an expanded definition of the community served by the hospital. Other rules and regulations in the ACA limit various billing practices in Medicare, Medicaid, and insurance plans sold through the Exchanges, including prohibitions on "balance billing" patients for amounts not covered by insurance and billing higher charges for out-of-network care. Several states have enacted state laws also regulating out-of-network charges and billing practices, many of which are preempted by ERISA for employer plans.

Since 2016, the IRS has stepped up enforcement activity under section 501(r). In the Tax Exempt and Government Entities FY 2017 Work Plan, the IRS reported it had completed 968 reviews of hospital tax filings under section 501(r) and had referred 363 hospitals for a field examination by IRS agents on these issues. On February 14, 2017, the IRS issued its first notice of revocation of tax-exempt status to a hospital for violation of section 501(r).

2. JOINT VENTURES WITH FOR-PROFIT ENTITIES

Given the financial pressure that many nonprofit hospitals have faced, the fiscal opportunities and administrative efficiencies of joint ventures have acted as a siren call. The ACA's promotion of accountable care organizations likewise encourages joint ventures, mergers, and other financial and administrative alignments between health care providers. But tax-exempt entities face special limits in such joint ventures with for-profit companies, classically explained in the following case.

St. David's Health Care System v. United States

349 F.3d 232 (5th Cir. 2003)

St. David's Health Care System, Inc. ("St. David's") brought suit in federal court to recover taxes that it paid under protest. St. David's argued that it was a charitable hospital, and therefore tax-exempt under 26 U.S.C. §501(c)(3). The Government responded that St. David's was not entitled to a tax exemption because it had formed a partnership with a for-profit company and ceded control over its operations to the for-profit entity. Both St. David's and the Government filed motions for summary judgment. The district court granted St. David's motion, and ordered the Government to refund the taxes paid by St. David's for the 1996 tax year. The district court also ordered the Government to pay $951,569.83 in attorney's fees and litigation costs. The Government filed the instant appeal. We conclude that this case raises genuine issues of material fact, and that the district court thus erred in granting St. David's motion for summary judgment. We therefore vacate the district court's decision, and remand for further proceedings.

I

For many years, St. David's owned and operated a hospital and other health care facilities in Austin, Texas. For most of its existence, St. David's was recognized as a charitable organization entitled to tax-exempt status under §501(c)(3).

HCA remains the largest for-profit hospital chain, providing 4 to 5 percent of all inpatient care in the United States. HCA was founded by Dr. Thomas Frist, Sr. At the time the court issued this opinion, the founder's son, Dr. Bill Frist (R-TN), was the Senate Majority Leader.

In the 1990s, due to financial difficulties in the health care industry, St. David's concluded that it should consolidate with another health care organization. Ultimately, in 1996, St. David's decided to form a partnership with Columbia/HCA Healthcare Corporation ("HCA"), a for-profit company that operates 180 hospitals nationwide. HCA already owned several facilities in the suburbs of Austin, and was interested in entering the central Austin market. A partnership with St. David's would allow HCA to expand into that urban market.

St. David's contributed all of its hospital facilities to the partnership. HCA, in turn, contributed its Austin-area facilities. The partnership hired Galen Health Care, Inc. ("Galen"), a subsidiary of HCA, to manage the day-to-day operations of the partnership medical facilities.

In 1998, the IRS audited St. David's and concluded that, due to its partnership with HCA, St. David's no longer qualified as a charitable (and, thus, tax-exempt) hospital. The IRS ordered St. David's to pay taxes. St. David's paid the requisite amount under protest, and subsequently filed the instant action, requesting a refund. . . .

The Government claims that the district court erred in concluding that St. David's was entitled to §501(c)(3) tax-exempt status. The burden was on St. David's to prove that it qualified for a tax exemption. *See* Nationalist Movement v. Commissioner, 37 F.3d 216, 219 (5th Cir. 1994) ("It is the burden of the party claiming the exemption . . . to prove entitlement to it.").

Tax cases are frequently heard in the federal Tax Court, which does not require prepayment of the tax. In order to sue in the federal district court or the U.S. Court of Federal Claims, typically taxpayers must first pay the tax in full and sue for a refund.

In order to qualify for tax-exempt status, St. David's was required to show that it was "organized and operated exclusively" for a charitable purpose. 26 C.F.R. §1.501(c)(3)-1(a). The "organizational test" required St. David's to demonstrate that its founding documents: (1) limit its purpose to "one or more exempt purposes"; and (2) do not expressly empower St. David's to engage more than "an insubstantial part of its activities" in conduct that fails to further its charitable goals. *Id.* §1.501(c)(3)-1(b). The parties agree that St. David's articles of incorporation satisfy the organizational test.

To pass the "operational test," St. David's was required to show: (1) that it "engage[s] primarily in activities which accomplish" its exempt purpose; (2) that its net earnings do not "inure to the benefit of private shareholders or individuals"; (3) that it does "not expend a substantial part of its resources attempting to influence legislation or political campaigns"; and (4) that it "serve[s] a valid purpose and confer[s] a public benefit." The parties appear to agree that, because St. David's contributed all of its medical facilities to the partnership, we must look to the activities of the partnership to determine if St. David's satisfies the operational test.

The Government argues that St. David's cannot demonstrate the first element of the operational test. The Government asserts that, because of its partnership with HCA, St. David's cannot show that it engages "primarily" in activities that accomplish its charitable purpose. The Government does not contend that a non-profit organization should automatically lose its tax-exempt status when it forms a partnership with a for-profit entity. Instead, the Government argues that a non-profit organization must sacrifice its tax exemption if it cedes control over the partnership to the for-profit entity. The Government asserts that, when a non-profit cedes control, it can no longer ensure that its activities via the partnership primarily further its charitable purpose. In this case, the Government contends that St. David's forfeited its exemption because it ceded control over its operations to HCA.

St. David's responds in part that the central issue in determining its tax-exempt status is not which entity controls the partnership. Instead, St. David's appears to assert, the pivotal question is one of function: whether the partnership engages in activities that further its exempt purpose. St. David's argues that it passes the "operational test" because its activities via the partnership further its charitable purpose of providing health care to all persons.

St. David's relies in particular on a revenue ruling issued by the IRS, which provides guidelines for hospitals seeking a §501(c)(3) exemption. Revenue Ruling 69-545 sets forth what has come to be known as the "community benefit standard." The IRS generally accords tax-exempt status to independent non-profit hospitals that satisfy this standard.

Under the "community benefit standard," a non-profit hospital can qualify for a tax exemption if it: (1) provides an emergency room open to all persons, regardless of their ability to pay; (2) is willing to hire any qualified physician; (3) is run by an independent board of trustees composed of representatives of the community ("community board"); and (4) uses all excess revenues to improve facilities, provide educational services, and/or conduct medical research. *See* Rev. Rul. 69-545, 1969-2 C.B. 117, 1969 WL 19168 (1969) (outlining the community benefit standard); *see also IHC Health Plans*, 325 F.3d at 1197 n. 16 (noting several relevant factors for determining whether a hospital confers a significant community benefit, including the provision of free or below-cost care; the treatment of individuals eligible for Medicare or Medicaid; the use of extra funds for research and educational programs; and the composition of the board of trustees). A hospital need not demonstrate all of these factors in order to qualify for §501(c)(3) tax-exempt status. *See Geisinger*, 985 F.2d at 1219; Rev. Rul. 69-545, 1969-2 C.B. 117 (1969) (stating that "[t]he absence of particular factors" will not necessarily prevent a hospital from obtaining an exemption); *see also* Rev. Rul. 83-157, 1983-2 C.B. 94 (1983) (noting that, under certain circumstances, a hospital can satisfy the community benefit standard even if it does not provide free emergency room care). Instead, the hospital must show, based on the "totality of the circumstances," that it is entitled to a tax exemption. *Geisinger*, 985 F.2d at 1219.

> This paragraph's cites offer key authorities for understanding the standards for maintaining tax-exempt status.

St. David's contends that its activities via the partnership more than satisfy the community benefit standard. St. David's notes that the partnership hospitals perform a number of charitable functions in the Austin community. According to St. David's, the partnership not only provides free emergency room care, but also has opened the rest of its facilities to all persons, regardless of their ability to pay. In addition, St. David's asserts, the partnership hospitals maintain open medical staffs. Finally, St. David's states that it uses the profits that it receives from the partnership revenues to fund research grants and other health-related initiatives.

We have no doubt that St. David's via the partnership provides important medical services to the Austin community. Indeed, if the issue in this case were whether the partnership performed any charitable functions, we would be inclined to affirm the district court's grant of summary judgment in favor of St. David's.

However, we cannot agree with St. David's suggestion that the central issue in this case is whether the partnership provides some (or even an extensive amount of) charitable services. It is important to keep in mind that §501(c)(3) confers tax-exempt status only on those organizations that operate exclusively in furtherance of exempt purposes. As a result, in determining whether an organization satisfies the operational test, we do not simply consider whether the organization's activities further its charitable purposes. We must also ensure that those activities do not substantially further other (non-charitable) purposes. If more than an "insubstantial" amount of the partnership's activities further non-charitable interests, then St. David's can no longer be deemed to operate exclusively for charitable purposes. *See Nationalist Movement*, 37 F.3d at 220 ("'An organization will not be . . . regarded [as operated exclusively for an exempt purpose] if more than an insubstantial part of its activities is not in furtherance of an exempt purpose.'") (quoting 26 C.F.R. §1.501(c)(3)-1(c)(1)).

Therefore, even if St. David's performs important charitable functions, St. David's cannot qualify for tax-exempt status under §501(c)(3) if its activities via the partnership substantially further the private, profit-seeking interests of HCA. *See id.* at 220 ("'[T]he presence of a single [nonexempt] purpose, if substantial in nature, will destroy the exemption regardless of the number or importance of truly [exempt] purposes.'").

In order to ascertain whether an organization furthers non-charitable interests, we can examine the structure and management of the organization. In other words, we look to which individuals or entities control the organization. If private individuals or for-profit entities have either formal or effective control, we presume that the organization furthers the profit-seeking motivations of those private individuals or entities. That is true, even when the organization is a partnership between a non-profit and a for-profit entity. When the non-profit organization cedes control over the partnership to the for-profit entity, we assume that the partnership's activities substantially further the for-profit's interests. As a result, we conclude that the non-profit's activities via the partnership are not exclusively or primarily in furtherance of its charitable purposes. Thus, the non-profit is not entitled to a tax exemption. *See* Rev. Rul. 98-15, 1998-1 C.B. 718, 1998 WL 89783 (1998) ("[I]f a private party is allowed to control or use the non-profit organization's activities or assets for the benefit of the private party, and the benefit is not incidental to the accomplishment of exempt purposes, the organization will fail to be organized and operated exclusively for exempt purposes.").

> Charities must not cede control to for-profit entities, which was clearly spelled out in Revenue Ruling 98-15.

Conversely, if the non-profit organization enters into a partnership agreement with a for-profit entity, and retains control, we presume that the non-profit's activities via the partnership primarily further exempt purposes. Therefore, we can conclude that the non-profit organization should retain its tax-exempt status.

The present case illustrates why, when a non-profit organization forms a partnership with a for-profit entity, courts should be concerned about the relinquishment of control. St. David's, by its own account, entered the partnership with HCA out of financial necessity (to obtain the revenues needed for it to stay afloat). HCA, by contrast, entered the partnership for reasons of financial convenience (to enter a new market). The starkly different financial positions of these two parties at the beginning of their partnership negotiations undoubtedly affected their relative bargaining strength. Because St. David's "needed" this partnership more than HCA, St. David's may have been willing to acquiesce to many (if not most) of HCA's demands for the final Partnership Agreement. In the process, of course, St. David's may not have been able to give a high priority to its charitable objectives. As a result, St.

David's may not have been able to ensure that its partnership with HCA would continually provide a "public benefit" as opposed to a private benefit for HCA.

These precedents and policy concerns indicate that, when a non-profit organization forms a partnership with a for-profit entity, the non-profit should lose its tax-exempt status if it cedes control to the for-profit entity. Therefore, in our review of the district court's summary judgment ruling, we examine whether St. David's has shown that there is no genuine issue of material fact regarding whether St. David's ceded control to HCA.

A recent IRS revenue ruling provides a starting point for our analysis. In Revenue Ruling 98-15, the IRS indicated how a non-profit organization that forms a partnership with a for-profit entity can establish that it has retained control over the partnership's activities. The revenue ruling states that a non-profit can demonstrate control by showing some or all of the following: (1) that the founding documents of the partnership expressly state that it has a charitable purpose and that the charitable purpose will take priority over all other concerns; (2) that the partnership agreement gives the non-profit organization a majority vote in the partnership's board of directors; and (3) that the partnership is managed by an independent company (an organization that is not affiliated with the for-profit entity).

The partnership documents in the present case, examined in light of the above factors, leave us uncertain as to whether St. David's has ceded control to HCA. St. David's did manage to secure some protections for its charitable mission. First of all, Section 3.2 of the Partnership Agreement expressly states that the manager of the partnership "shall" operate the partnership facilities in a manner that complies with the community benefit standard. This provision appears to comport with the first factor in Revenue Ruling 98-15, which indicates that the partnership's founding documents should contain a statement of the partnership's charitable purpose. St. David's asserts that if Galen, the manager of the partnership facilities, fails to adhere to this requirement, St. David's can sue in Texas state court for specific performance of the Partnership Agreement.

The Management Services Agreement between Galen and the Partnership further provides that, if Galen takes any action with a "material probability of adversely affecting" St. David's tax-exempt status, that action will be considered an "[e]vent of [d]efault." Management Services Agreement, section 7(d). The Management Services Agreement authorizes St. David's to unilaterally terminate the contract with Galen if it commits such a "default." See Management Services Agreement, section 7 ("If any Event of Default shall occur and be continuing, the non-defaulting party may terminate this Agreement. . . . Any action to be taken by the Partnership under this paragraph may be taken by the [St. David's] representatives on the Governing Board[.]").

In addition, St. David's can exercise a certain degree of control over the partnership via its membership on the partnership's Board of Governors. St. David's and HCA each appoint half of the Board. No measure can pass the Board without the support of a majority of the representatives of both St. David's and HCA. See Partnership Agreement, section 1.8 (noting that Board approval "means approval of not less than a majority of a quorum of [HCA] Governors and not less than a majority of a quorum of [St. David's] Governors"). Thus, through its voting power, St. David's can effectively veto any proposed action of the Board of Governors.

St. David's also contends that the Partnership Agreement gives it authority over the partnership's Chief Executive Officer ("CEO"). The agreement permitted St. David's to appoint the initial CEO, subject to the approval of the HCA members of the Board of Governors. *See* Partnership Agreement, section 8.2. The agreement further provides that either HCA or St. David's can unilaterally remove the CEO. St. David's suggests that this termination power enables it to ensure that the CEO will promote charitable objectives.

Finally, St. David's argues that its power to dissolve the partnership provides it with a significant amount of control over partnership operations. The Partnership Agreement states that, if St. David's receives legal advice (from an attorney that has been deemed acceptable by both HCA and St. David's) that its participation in the partnership will hinder its tax-exempt status, St. David's can request dissolution. *See* Partnership Agreement, section 15.1(f). St. David's asserts that it can use the threat of dissolution to force the partnership to give priority to charitable concerns.

According to St. David's, the above protections in the partnership documents (the purpose statement in the Partnership Agreement; St. David's power to terminate the Management Services Agreement and the CEO; its ability to block proposed action of the Board of Governors; and its power of dissolution) provide it with a large measure of control over partnership operations.

However, as the Government argues, there are reasons to doubt that the partnership documents provide St. David's with sufficient control. First of all, St. David's authority within the Board of Governors is limited. St. David's does not control a majority of the Board. As a result, although St. David's can veto board actions, it does not appear that it can initiate action without the support of HCA. Thus, at best, St. David's can prevent the partnership from taking action that might undermine its charitable goals; St. David's cannot necessarily ensure that the partnership will take new action that furthers its charitable purposes.

Second, Galen, which manages the operations of the partnership on a day-to-day basis, is a for-profit subsidiary of HCA. As a result, it is not apparent that Galen would be inclined to serve charitable interests. It seems more likely that Galen would prioritize the (presumably non-charitable) interests of its parent organization, HCA.

Galen's apparent conflict of interest is only partly mitigated by the fact that Section 3.2 of the Partnership Agreement requires the manager to abide by the community benefit standard. As the Government points out, that requirement is useful only to the extent that the governing documents of the partnership empower St. David's to enforce the provision. St. David's appears to assert that the primary means through which it can force Galen to comply with Section 3.2 is by taking legal action. Given the time and expense of judicial proceedings, we doubt that St. David's will resort to litigation every time Galen makes a single decision that appears to conflict with the community benefit standard.

St. David's also asserts that it can control the management of the partnership via its position on the Board of Governors. However, the power of the Board is limited in scope. The Board of Governors is empowered to deal with only major decisions, not the day-to-day operation of the partnership hospitals. Thus, St. David's could not, via its position on the Board, overrule a management decision that fell outside the range of the Board's authority.

The Management Services Agreement does appear to provide St. David's with a certain degree of control over Galen. The agreement permits St. David's to unilaterally cancel the contract with Galen if the manager takes action that has a "material probability" of undermining St. David's tax-exempt status. It is not entirely clear whether St. David's would be willing to exercise this termination option without the consent of HCA. Nor is it clear whether St. David's could ensure that Galen was replaced by a manager that would prioritize charitable purposes. Nonetheless, the Management Services Agreement does appear to give St. David's some authority over Galen, and therefore seems to provide St. David's with a degree of control over partnership operations.

We are also uncertain about the amount of control that St. David's exercises over the partnership's CEO. St. David's appears to assert that its authority to appoint the initial CEO, and its power to terminate the officer, demonstrate its control within the partnership. The Government has created a general issue of material fact, however, regarding St. David's by pointing to instances in which the CEO failed to comply with the Partnership Agreement. Although the Partnership Agreement states that the CEO "shall" provide the Board of Governors with annual reports of the amount of charity care, *see* Partnership Agreement, section 8.4(f), it seems that no such report was prepared for 1996 (the first year of the partnership and the tax year at issue in this case). Indeed, it does not appear that any annual report on charity care was prepared until after the IRS began auditing the partnership. Despite St. David's assertions about its power over the CEO, the non-profit does not claim to have taken any punitive action against the CEO for failing to prepare these reports. If St. David's was in fact unable to enforce a provision of the Partnership Agreement dealing specifically with charity care, that raises serious doubts about St. David's capacity to ensure that the partnership's operations further charitable purposes.

Finally, we question the degree to which St. David's has the power to control the partnership by threatening dissolution. First of all, the Partnership Agreement appears to permit St. David's to request dissolution only when there is a change in the law, not simply when the partnership fails to perform a few charitable functions. *See* Partnership Agreement, section 15.1(f) (indicating that the partnership "shall" be dissolved upon "[t]he request of [St. David's] for dissolution . . . in the event [St. David's] receives an opinion of counsel, from counsel reasonably acceptable to [St. David's] and the [HCA] Governors, that as a result of a rule, regulation, statute, Internal Revenue Service government pronouncement, or court decision . . . enacted or issued subsequent to the date hereof which would cause the participation of [St. David's] or the [St. David's] Affiliates in the Partnership to be inconsistent with [their] Status . . . as organizations described in Section 501(c)(3) of the Code"). Second, HCA may not take seriously any threat of dissolution made by St. David's. HCA must be aware that St. David's has a strong incentive not to exercise its power to dissolve the corporation. The partnership documents include a non-compete clause, which provides that, in the event of dissolution, neither partner can compete in the Austin area for two years. *See* Contribution Agreement, section 11.1. That result might be slightly unpleasant for HCA, but would not destroy the entity; HCA would still have its nationwide health care business. For St. David's, by contrast, dissolution would be disastrous. St. David's serves only the Austin community. If it were forbidden from competing in that area, St. David's would (in effect) cease to exist. In light of the realities of the situation, it seems unlikely that St. David's would exercise its option to dissolve the partnership even if the partnership strayed from St. David's charitable mission.

The evidence presented by the parties demonstrates that there remain genuine issues of material fact regarding whether St. David's ceded control to HCA. Therefore, we vacate the district court's grant of summary judgment in favor of St. David's.

For the above reasons, we VACATE the district court's summary judgment ruling and its award of attorney's fees and costs and REMAND for further proceedings.

QUESTIONS

1. Which elements of the Partnership Agreement, Management Services Agreement, or Contribution Agreement serve to either support or undermine tax-exempt status?
2. Does the power held by the board of directors or officers offer support for finding tax-exempt status should be continued? Why or why not?

PROBLEM

You represent St. David's. What one provision of the agreement with HCA would you renegotiate after this opinion in order to best preserve tax-exempt status?

After remand from the Fifth Circuit, a jury trial was held, reaching a verdict in favor of St. David's on these facts. Nevertheless, for whole-hospital joint ventures, *St. David's* remains an important case. In addition, charitable hospitals engage in many smaller joint ventures with for-profit entities to operate specific service lines such as diagnostic imaging, ambulatory surgery, the emergency department, and pathology. Many of these transactions involve physicians who admit patients to the hospital and therefore also raise fraud and abuse questions under Stark II and the Anti-Kickback Statute, discussed in Chapter 6.

3. INTERMEDIATE SANCTIONS FOR EXCESS BENEFIT TRANSACTIONS

While most tax restrictions on charitable hospitals are found in §501(c)(3), another important provision is an excise tax on self-dealing. Section 4958 regulates "excess benefit transactions," largely replicating the state corporate duty of loyalty owed to shareholders but mapping it into a nonprofit context where there are no shareholders and expanding the impact of the rule by holding key managers personally liable.

The "excess benefit transaction" regulations are also known as "intermediate sanctions." The IRS always had the legal authority to revoke federal tax exemption for an entity that engaged in egregious self-dealing, but for a large institution like a hospital, this so-called "nuclear option" was so damaging to the community that it was not a credible threat. Section 4958 and related sections were enacted to give the IRS some more flexible and less cataclysmic tools to police self-dealing by charitable insiders. The tool is an excise tax calibrated to the amount of self-dealing identified. The tax is only triggered when certain insiders (known as "disqualified persons") receive something in excess of fair market value from the charity. From the Code:

> **26 U.S.C. §4958. Taxes on excess benefit transactions**
> (a) Initial taxes. —
> (1) On the disqualified person. — There is hereby imposed on each excess benefit transaction a tax equal to 25 percent of the excess benefit. The tax imposed by this paragraph shall be paid by any disqualified person referred to in subsection (f)(1) with respect to such transaction.
> (2) On the management. — In any case in which a tax is imposed by paragraph (1), there is hereby imposed on the participation of any organization manager in the excess benefit transaction, knowing that it is such a transaction, a tax

It is extraordinarily rare under state corporate law for penalties like these to be imposed on managers. The penalties imposed by §4958 increase dramatically unless the excess benefits are promptly corrected.

equal to 10 percent of the excess benefit, unless such participation is not willful and is due to reasonable cause. The tax imposed by this paragraph shall be paid by any organization manager who participated in the excess benefit transaction.

(b) Additional tax on the disqualified person. — In any case in which an initial tax is imposed by subsection (a)(1) on an excess benefit transaction and the excess benefit involved in such transaction is not corrected within the taxable period, there is hereby imposed a tax equal to 200 percent of the excess benefit involved. The tax imposed by this subsection shall be paid by any disqualified person referred to in subsection (f)(1) with respect to such transaction.

(c) Excess benefit transaction; excess benefit. — For purposes of this section —

(1) Excess benefit transaction. —

(A) In general. — The term "excess benefit transaction" means any transaction in which an economic benefit is provided by an applicable tax-exempt organization directly or indirectly to or for the use of any disqualified person if the value of the economic benefit provided exceeds the value of the consideration (including the performance of services) received for providing such benefit. For purposes of the preceding sentence, an economic benefit shall not be treated as consideration for the performance of services unless such organization clearly indicated its intent to so treat such benefit. . . .

(4) Authority to include certain other private inurement. — To the extent provided in regulations prescribed by the Secretary, the term "excess benefit transaction" includes any transaction in which the amount of any economic benefit provided to or for the use of a disqualified person is determined in whole or in part by the revenues of 1 or more activities of the organization but only if such transaction results in inurement not permitted under paragraph (3) or (4) of section 501(c), as the case may be. In the case of any such transaction, the excess benefit shall be the amount of the inurement not so permitted.

> Private inurement can trigger both tax-exempt status revocation and an excess benefit transaction penalty.

(d) Special rules. — For purposes of this section —

(1) Joint and several liability. — If more than 1 person is liable for any tax imposed by subsection (a) or subsection (b), all such persons shall be jointly and severally liable for such tax.

(2) Limit for management. — With respect to any 1 excess benefit transaction, the maximum amount of the tax imposed by subsection (a)(2) shall not exceed $20,000. . . .

(f) Other definitions. — For purposes of this section —

(1) Disqualified person. — The term "disqualified person" means, with respect to any transaction —

(A) any person who was, at any time during the 5-year period ending on the date of such transaction, in a position to exercise substantial influence over the affairs of the organization.

(B) a member of the family of an individual described in subparagraph (A),

(C) a 35-percent controlled entity,

(D) any person who is described in subparagraph (A), (B), or (C) with respect to an organization described in section 509(a)(3) and organized and operated exclusively for the benefit of, to perform the functions of, or to carry out the purposes of the applicable tax-exempt organization.

(E) which involves a donor advised fund (as defined in section 4966(d)(2)), any person who is described in paragraph (7) with respect to such donor advised fund (as so defined), and

(F) which involves a sponsoring organization (as defined in section 4966(d)(1)), any person who is described in paragraph (8) with respect to such sponsoring organization (as so defined).

(2) Organization manager. — The term "organization manager" means, with respect to any applicable tax-exempt organization, any officer, director, or trustee of such organization (or any individual having powers or responsibilities similar to those of officers, directors, or trustees of the organization).

(3) 35-percent controlled entity. —

(A) In general. — The term "35-percent controlled entity" means —

(i) a corporation in which persons described in subparagraph (A) or (B) of paragraph (1) own more than 35 percent of the total combined voting power,

(ii) a partnership in which such persons own more than 35 percent of the profits interest, and

(iii) a trust or estate in which such persons own more than 35 percent of the beneficial interest.

(B) Constructive ownership rules. — Rules similar to the rules of paragraphs (3) and (4) of section 4946(a) shall apply for purposes of this paragraph.

(4) Family members. — The members of an individual's family shall be determined under section 4946(d); except that such members also shall include the brothers and sisters (whether by the whole or half blood) of the individual and their spouses. . . .

(6) Correction. — The terms "correction" and "correct" mean, with respect to any excess benefit transaction, undoing the excess benefit to the extent possible, and taking any additional measures necessary to place the organization in a financial position not worse than that in which it would be if the disqualified person were dealing under the highest fiduciary standards, except that in the case of any correction of an excess benefit transaction described in subsection (c)(2), no amount repaid in a manner prescribed by the Secretary may be held in any donor advised fund. . . .

QUESTIONS

1. You represent a tax-exempt hospital subject to §4958. A member of the board is also a partner at an accounting firm that performs consulting services for the hospital. How should this relationship be reviewed in light of §4958?
2. Who are the potentially liable parties?

D. RELATED ISSUE...

In general, state incom... ...l path. But an important distinction arises ... ...hich for a hospital can
amount to millions ... ...s have been deemed to
qualify, but in rece... ...f fiscal difficulties, have
challenged whethe... ...spital should be subject to
property taxes du... ...cific locations. Other state
statutes require ... ...and some state courts are
looking more c... ...ing the hospital. Note that
these hospital... ...ions under federal and state
income tax la... ...e charitable nature of hospitals
as never bef...

The foll... ...emption under Illinois statutory
and consti... ...hat the property was owned and
used excl... ...ts are very typical for a nonprofit
hospital, ...rising.

...dical Center v.
...Revenue

...8 (2010)

...tes six hospitals, including Provena Cove-
...vice hospital located in the City of Urbana.
...of Burnham City Hospital and Mercy Hos-
...hospitals in Champaign/Urbana and serves a
...s. The services it provides include a 24-hour
...enter; intensive care, neonatal intensive care,
...iac care, cancer treatment, rehabilitation and
...ne health care, including hospice. It offers case
...der persons to remain in their homes and runs
...n-related classes. It also provides smoking cessation
...for high cholesterol and blood pressure as well as

...n 260 and 268 licensed beds. Each year it admits
...ents and 100,000 outpatients." Some 60% of its inpa-
...rough the hospital's emergency room, which treats some

...ergency department because it is required to do so by the
Hospital Em... ...vice Act. Where emergency room services are offered, a
certain level of heal... ...are is required to be provided to every person who seeks
treatment there. That is so as a matter of both state and federal law.

Staffing PCMC are approximately 1,000 employees, 400 volunteers and 200
physicians. The physicians are not employed or paid by the hospital. They are merely
credentialed to provide services there in exchange for paying $50 per year in dues to
the hospital's library fund, and agreeing to serve on hospital committees and to be on
call to attend patients without their own physicians. With respect to the emergency
department, PCMC contracts with a for-profit private company to provide the

necessary physicians. The company, not the hospital, bills patients and any third-party payors directly for emergency room services. The company likewise pursues payment of those bills independently from PCMC.

Just as PCMC relies on private physicians to fill its medical staff, it utilizes numerous third-party providers to furnish other services at the hospital. Among these are pharmacy, laundry, MRI/CT and lab services, and staffing for the rehabilitation and cardiovascular surgery programs. The company providing lab services is one of the businesses owned by Provena Enterprises, a Provena Health subsidiary. It is operated for profit.

Provena Hospitals' employees do not work gratuitously. Everyone employed by the corporation, including those with religious affiliations, are paid for their services. Compensation rates for senior executives are reviewed annually and compared against national surveys. Provena Health "has targeted the 75th percentile of the market for senior executive total cash compensation."

According to the record, PCMC's inpatient admissions encompass three broad categories of patients: those who have private health insurance, those who are on Medicare or Medicaid, and those who are "self pay (uninsured)." PCMC has agreements with some private third-party payers which provide for payment at rates different from "its established rates." The payment amounts under these agreements cover the actual costs of care. The amounts PCMC receives from Medicare and Medicaid are not sufficient to cover the costs of care. Although PCMC has the right to collect a certain portion of the charges directly from Medicare and Medicaid patients and has exercised that right, there is still a gap between the amount of payments received and the costs of care for such patients. For 2002, PCMC calculated the difference to be $7,418,150 in the case of Medicare patients and $3,105,217 for Medicaid patients.

> Most U.S. hospitals claim that they lose money on Medicaid, and on Medicare to a lesser degree.

PCMC was not required to participate in the Medicare and Medicaid programs, but did so because it believed participation was "consistent with its mission." Participation was also necessary in order for Provena Hospitals to qualify for tax exemption under federal law. In addition, it provided the institution with a steady revenue stream.

During 2002, Provena Hospitals' "net patient service revenue" was $713,911,000, representing approximately 96.5% of the corporation's total revenue. No findings were made regarding the precise source of the remainder of its revenue. Provena Hospitals' "expenses and losses" exceeded its "revenue and gains" during this period by $4,869,000. In other words, the corporation was in the red. The following year, this changed. The corporation's revenue and gains exceeded its expenses and losses by $10,548,000.

Of Provena Hospitals' "net patient service revenue" for 2002, $113,494,000, or approximately 16%, was generated by PCMC. Unlike its parent, PCMC realized a net gain of income over "expenses and losses" of $2,165,388 for that year. This surplus existed even after provision for uncollectible accounts receivable (i.e., bad debt) in the amount of $7,101,000. Virtually none of PCMC's income was derived from charitable contributions. The dollar amount of "unrestricted donations" received by PCMC for the year ending December 31, 2002, was a mere $6,938.

> PCMC is one of six hospitals in the Provena system, with 2002 net patient service revenues of $113,494,000. The property tax liability in this case was $1.1 million per year.

PCMC experienced a modest net loss in 2003. The record discloses, however, that Provena Hospitals' auditors showed accrued property tax liabilities in the amount of $1.1 million per year for both 2002 and 2003 in the accounts payable and accrued expenses portions of the 2003 balance sheet. Had only the 2003 property tax been posted against the revenue and gains for 2003, that year would also have shown a net gain for PCMC.

In years when PCMC realizes a net gain, the gain is "reinvested in order to sustain and further [the corporation's] charitable mission and ministry." No findings were made regarding how much of the reinvestment occurs at PCMC and how much is allocated to other aspects of Provena Hospitals' operations. Nor were specific findings made regarding the particular purposes to which the reinvested funds were put. The record indicates, however, that PCMC "generally needs approximately two to four million dollars in margin each year to replace broken items and fix non-operating equipment."

In 2002, PCMC budgeted $813,694 for advertising and advertised in newspapers, phone directories, event playbills, and Chamber of Commerce publications; on television and radio; and through public signage. It also advertised using "booths, tables, and/or tents at community health or nonprofit fundraising events; sponsorship of sports teams and other community events; and banner advertisements at sponsored community events." The ads taken out by PCMC in 2002 covered a variety of matters, including employee want ads. None of its ads that year mentioned free or discounted medical care.

While not mentioned in PCMC's advertisements, a charity care policy was in place at the hospital, and the parties stipulated that PCMC's staff made "outreach efforts to communicate the availability of charity care and other assistance to patients." The charity care policy, which was shared with at least one other hospital under Provena Hospitals' auspices, provided that the institution would "offer, to the extent that it is financially able, admission for care or treatment, and the use of the hospital facilities and services regardless of race, color, creed, sex, national origin, ancestry or ability to pay for these services."

> PCMC's charity care policy predated and presaged the 501(r) rules under the ACA.

The charity policy was not self-executing. An application was required. Whether an application would be granted was determined by PCMC on a case-by-case basis using eligibility criteria based on federal poverty guidelines. A sliding scale was employed. Persons whose income was below the guidelines were eligible for "a 100% reduction from the patient portion of the billed charges." Persons whose income was not more than 125% of the guidelines could qualify for a 75% reduction. With an income level not more than 150% of the guidelines the discount fell to 50%. At an income level not more than 200% of the guidelines, the potential reduction was 25%. Eligibility was also affected by the value of an applicant's assets. Patients who qualified based on low income might nevertheless be rendered ineligible if the equity in their principal residence exceeded $10,000 or they held other assets valued at more than $5,000.

PCMC's policy specified that the hospital would give a charity care application to anyone who requested one, but it was the patient's responsibility to provide all the information necessary to verify income level and other requested information. To verify income, a patient was required to present documentation "such as check stubs, income tax returns, and bank statements."

PCMC believed that its charity care program should be the payer of last resort. It encouraged patients to apply for charity care before receiving services, and if a patient failed to obtain an advance determination of eligibility under the program, normal collection practices were followed. PCMC would look first to private insurance, if there was any, then pursue any possible sources of reimbursement from the government. Failing that, the hospital would seek payment from the patient directly.

Short-term collection matters were handled by Provena Hospitals' "Extended Business Office." Staffed by a small group of employees in Joliet, the Extended Business Office would typically make three or four phone calls and send three or four statements to patients owing outstanding balances. If a balance remained unpaid following such efforts, which typically did not extend beyond three months, Provena Hospitals would treat the account as "bad debt" and refer it to a collection agency. From time to time, the collection agencies would seek and were given authorization to pursue legal action against an account "on which, over the course of several months, the agency had not received any response, cooperation or payment from the patient." Provena Hospitals' decision as to whether to pursue legal action against a patient depended on review of the particular account. During 2002, it did not have a blanket policy requiring referral to a collection attorney in every case.

The fact that a patient's account had been referred to collection did not disqualify the patient from applying to the charity care program. Applications would be considered "[a]t any time during the collection process." PCMC had financial counselors to assist patients with paying outstanding balances and review all payment options with them. The counselors helped patients seek and qualify for financial assistance from other sources. Where a patient was given an application for charity care but failed to return it, the counselors would send letters and call the patients to remind them to do so.

During 2002, the amount of aid provided by Provena Hospitals to PCMC patients under the facility's charity care program was modest. The hospital waived $1,758,940 in charges, representing an actual cost to it of only $831,724. This was equivalent to only 0.723% of PCMC's revenues for that year and was $268,276 less than the $1.1 million in tax benefits which Provena stood to receive if its claim for a property tax exemption were granted.[6]

The number of patients benefitting from the charitable care program was similarly small. During 2002, only 302 of PCMC's 10,000 inpatient and 100,000 outpatient admissions were granted reductions in their bills under the charitable care program. That figure is equivalent to just 0.27% of the hospital's total annual patient census. . . .

> The property tax benefit exceeded the charitable care expense.

Under Illinois law, taxation is the rule. Tax exemption is the exception. All property is subject to taxation, unless exempt by statute, in conformity with the constitutional provisions relating thereto. Statutes granting tax exemptions must be strictly

---

6. The disparity between the amount of free or discounted care dispensed and the amount of property tax that would be saved through receipt of a charitable exemption is in no way unique to the case before us here. Excluding bad debt, "the amount of uncompensated care provided by as many as three-quarters of nonprofit hospitals is less than their tax benefits." J. Colombo, *Federal & State Tax Exemption Policy, Medical Debt & Healthcare for the Poor*, 51 St. Louis L.J. 433, 433 n. 2 (2007).

construed in favor of taxation and courts have no power to create exemption from taxation by judicial construction.

The burden of establishing entitlement to a tax exemption rests upon the person seeking it. The burden is a very heavy one. The party claiming an exemption must prove by clear and convincing evidence that the property in question falls within both the constitutional authorization and the terms of the statute under which the exemption is claimed. A basis for exemption may not be inferred when none has been demonstrated. To the contrary, all facts are to be construed and all debatable questions resolved in favor of taxation, and every presumption is against the intention of the state to exempt property from taxation. If there is any doubt as to applicability of an exemption, it must be resolved in favor of requiring that tax be paid.

As noted earlier in this opinion, Provena Hospitals has been granted a tax exemption by the federal government. There is no dispute, however, that tax exemption under federal law is not dispositive of whether real property is exempt from property tax under Illinois law. Similarly, the fact that Provena Hospitals is exempt from state retailers' occupation, service occupation, use and service use taxes does not mean that the corporation must likewise be granted an exemption from paying tax on the real property it owns.

> Each form of federal and state tax exemption is determined under similar, but distinct rules.

Authority to exempt certain real property from taxation emanates from article IX, section 6, of the 1970 Illinois Constitution. Section 6 provides that the General Assembly may, by law, exempt from taxation property owned by "the State, units of local government and school districts" and property "used exclusively for agricultural and horticultural societies, and for school, religious, cemetery and charitable purposes."

Section 6 is not self-executing. It merely authorizes the General Assembly to enact legislation exempting certain property from taxation. The General Assembly is not required to exercise that authority. Where it does elect to recognize an exemption, it must remain within the limitations imposed by the constitution. No other subjects of property tax exemption are permitted. The legislature cannot add to or broaden the exemptions specified in section 6.

While the General Assembly has no authority to grant exemptions beyond those authorized by section 6, it "may place restrictions, limitations, and conditions on [property tax] exemptions as may be proper by general law." In accordance with this power, the legislature has elected to impose additional restrictions with respect to section 6's charitable exemption. Pursuant to section 15-65 of the Property Tax Code, eligibility for a charitable exemption requires not only that the property be "actually and exclusively used for charitable or beneficent purposes, and not leased or otherwise used with a view to profit," but also that it be owned by an institution of public charity or certain other entities, including "old people's homes," qualifying not-for-profit health maintenance organizations, free public libraries and historical societies.

In Methodist Old Peoples Home v. Korzen, 39 Ill. 2d 149, 156-57, 233 N.E.2d 537 (1968), we identified the distinctive characteristics of a charitable institution as follows: (1) it has no capital, capital stock, or shareholders; (2) it earns no profits or dividends but rather derives its funds mainly from private and public charity and holds them in trust for the purposes expressed in the charter; (3) it dispenses charity to all who need it and apply for it; (4) it does not provide gain or profit in a private sense to any person connected with it; and (5) it does not appear to place any obstacles in the way of those who need and would avail themselves of the charitable benefits it dispenses. For purposes of applying these criteria, we defined charity as "a gift to be applied * * * for the benefit of an indefinite number of persons, persuading them to an educational or religious conviction, for their general welfare—or in some way reducing the burdens of government."

This court has held, on several occasions, that a "hospital not owned by the State or any other municipal corporation, but which is open to all persons, regardless of race, creed or financial ability," qualifies as a charitable institution under Illinois law provided certain conditions are satisfied. There is, however, no blanket exemption under the law for hospitals or health-care providers. Whether a particular institution qualifies as a charitable institution and is exempt from property tax is a question which must be determined on a case-by-case basis.

Provena Hospitals clearly satisfies the first of the factors identified by this court in *Methodist Old Peoples Home v. Korzen* for determining whether an organization can be considered a charitable institution: it has no capital, capital stock, or shareholders. Provena Hospitals also meets the fourth *Korzen* factor. It does not provide gain or profit in a private sense to any person connected with it. While the record focused on PCMC rather than Provena Hospitals, it was assumed by all parties during the administrative proceedings that Provena Hospitals' policies in this regard were the same as those of PCMC, and it was stipulated that PCMC diverted no profits or funds to individuals or entities for their own interests or private benefit . . . .

While *Korzen* factors one and four thus tilt in favor of characterizing Provena Hospitals as a charitable institution, application of the remaining factors demonstrates that the characterization will not hold. Provena Hospitals plainly fails to meet the second criterion: its funds are not derived mainly from private and public charity and held in trust for the purposes expressed in the charter. They are generated, overwhelmingly, by providing medical services for a fee. While the corporation's consolidated statement of operations for 2002 ascribes $25,282,000 of Provena Hospitals' $739,293,000 in total revenue to "other revenue," that sum represents a mere 3.4% of Provena's income, and no showing was made as to how much, if any, of it was derived from charitable contributions. The only charitable donations documented in this case were those made to PCMC, one of Provena Hospitals' subsidiary institutions, and they were so small, a mere $6,938, that they barely warrant mention.

Provena Hospitals likewise failed to show by clear and convincing evidence that it satisfied factors three or five, namely, that it dispensed charity to all who needed it and applied for it and did not appear to place any obstacles in the way of those who needed and would have availed themselves of the charitable benefits it dispenses. . . .

As detailed earlier in this opinion, eligibility for a charitable exemption under section 15-65 of the Property Tax Code requires not only charitable ownership, but charitable use. Specifically, an organization seeking an exemption under section 15-65 must establish that the subject property is "actually and exclusively used for charitable or beneficent purposes, and not leased or otherwise used with a view to profit." When the law says that property must be "exclusively used" for charitable or beneficent purposes, it means that charitable or beneficent purposes are the primary ones for which the property is utilized. Secondary or incidental charitable benefits will not suffice, nor will it be enough that the institution professes a charitable purpose or aspires to using its property to confer charity on others. "[S]tatements of the agents of an institution and the wording of its governing legal documents evidencing an intention to use its property exclusively for charitable purposes will not relieve such institution of the burden of proving that its property actually and factually is so used."

> Both ownership and use must be charitable, meaning that if a charity leased office space from a for-profit business, the office would remain taxable. Many states have similar rules.

In rejecting Provena Hospitals' claim for exemption, the Department determined that the corporation also failed to satisfy this charitable use requirement. As with the issue of charitable ownership, the appellate court concluded that this aspect of the Department's decision was not clearly erroneous. Again we agree.

In explaining what constitutes charity, *Methodist Old Peoples Home v. Korzen* applied the definition adopted by our court more than a century ago in *Crerar v. Williams.* We held there that

> "'charity, in a legal sense, may be more fully defined as a gift, to be applied consistently with existing laws, for the benefit of an indefinite number of persons, either by bringing their hearts under the influence of education or religion, by relieving their bodies from disease, suffering or constraint, by assisting them to establish themselves for life, or by erecting or maintaining public buildings or works, or otherwise lessening the burdens of government.'"

Following *Crerar*, we explained that "[t]he reason for exemptions in favor of charitable institutions is the benefit conferred upon the public by them, and a consequent relief, to some extent, of the burden upon the State to care for and advance the interests of its citizens." Our court continues to apply this rationale.

Conditioning charitable status on whether an activity helps relieve the burdens on government is appropriate. After all, each tax dollar lost to a charitable exemption is one less dollar affected governmental bodies will have to meet their obligations directly. If a charitable institution wishes to avail itself of funds which would otherwise flow into a public treasury, it is only fitting that the institution provide some compensatory benefit in exchange. While Illinois law has never required that there be a direct, dollar-for-dollar correlation between the value of the tax exemption and the value of the goods or services provided by the charity, it is a sine qua non of charitable status that those seeking a charitable exemption be able to demonstrate that their activities will help alleviate some financial burden incurred by the affected taxing bodies in performing their governmental functions. . . .

> Illinois also requires the hospital to "relieve the burdens on government," a line of reasoning that supports the idea that tax-exempt status is essentially a government subsidy that supports privatized supply of goods that otherwise would be publicly provided.

We further note that even if there were evidence that Provena Hospitals used the PCMC property to provide the type of services which the local taxing bodies might find helpful in meeting their obligations to the citizenry of Champaign County, that still would not suffice, in itself, to meet this requirement. The terms of the service also make a difference. As the appellate court correctly recognized, "'services extended * * * for value received * * * do not relieve the [s]tate of its burden.'"

The situation before us here stands in contrast to People ex rel. Cannon v. Southern Illinois Hospital Corp., 404 Ill. 66, 88 N.E.2d 20 (1949). In that case, the hospital seeking the charitable exemption adduced evidence showing that the county in question did undertake to provide treatment for indigent residents. The hospital charged the county deeply discounted rates to treat those patients. Moreover, because the hospital was the only one in the area, the court reasoned that its acceptance of relief patients relieved the government from having to transport and pay for the treatment of those patients elsewhere. As a result, the hospital's operations could be said to reduce a burden on the local taxing body. No such conclusion was made or could be made based on the record in this case.

Even if Provena Hospitals were able to clear this hurdle, there was ample support for the Department of Revenue's conclusion that Provena failed to meet its burden of showing that it used the parcels in the PCMC complex actually and exclusively for charitable purposes. As our review of the undisputed evidence demonstrated, both the number of uninsured patients receiving free or discounted care and the dollar value of the care they received were de minimus. With very limited exception, the property was devoted to the care and treatment of patients in exchange for compensation through private insurance, Medicare and Medicaid, or direct payment from the patient or the patient's family.

To be sure, Provena Hospitals did not condition the receipt of care on a patient's financial circumstances. Treatment was offered to all who requested it, and no one was turned away by PCMC based on their inability to demonstrate how the costs of their care would be covered. The record showed, however, that during the period in question here, Provena Hospitals did not advertise the availability of charitable care at PCMC. Patients were billed as a matter of course, and unpaid bills were automatically referred to collection agencies. Hospital charges were discounted or waived only after it was determined that a patient had no insurance coverage, was not eligible for Medicare or Medicaid, lacked the resources to pay the bill directly, and could document that he or she qualified for participation in the institution's charitable care program. As a practical matter, there was little to distinguish the way in which Provena Hospitals dispensed its "charity" from the way in which a for-profit institution would write off bad debt. Under similar circumstances, our appellate court has consistently refused to recognize a medical facility's actions as the bestowal of charity within the meaning of section 15-65 of the Property Tax. The appellate court's decision in the present case is in accord with this line of precedent.

The minimal amount of charitable care dispensed by Provena Hospitals at the PCMC complex cannot be rationalized on the grounds that the area's residents did not require additional services. For one thing, the argument that there really was no demand for additional charitable care in Champaign County is one that Provena Hospitals cannot comfortably make. That is so because such a contention, if true, would bring into question the veracity of the corporation's claim that it is committed to the values of the Catholic health-care ministry PCMC was purportedly obligated to advance. One of those values was that the institution was to

> "distinguish itself by service to and advocacy for those people whose social condition puts them at the margins of our society and makes them vulnerable to discrimination: the poor[,] the uninsured and the underinsured."

If the number of poor, uninsured and underinsured residents of Champaign County was as insignificant as PCMC's charitable care program reflects, the opportunities for Provena Hospitals to further its mission there would be virtually non-existent. And if the opportunities were so limited, it is difficult to understand why Provena Hospitals would continue to devote its resources to serving that community.

The only plausible explanation would be that its princip[al] purposes in operating PCMC were, in reality, more temporal than it professes.

The argument is problematic for other reasons as well. Federal census figure[s] show that approximately 13.4% of Champaign County's more than 185,000 residents have incomes below the federal poverty guidelines. That amounts to nearly 25,000 people. In addition, nearly 20,000 county residents are estimated to be without any health-care coverage. There is no reason to believe that these groups of indigent and/or uninsured citizens are any healthier than the population at large. To the contrary, experience teaches that such individuals are likely to have significant unmet health-care needs. If Provena Hospitals were truly using the PCMC complex exclusively for charitable purposes, one would therefore expect to see a significant portion of its annual admissions served by Provena Hospitals' charitable care policy. Instead, as we have noted, a mere 302 of its 110,000 admissions received reductions in their bills based on charitable considerations.

Further undermining Provena Hospitals' claims of charity is that even where it did offer discounted charges, the charity was often illusory. As described earlier in this opinion, uninsured patients were charged PCMC's "established" rates, which were more than double the actual costs of care. When patients were granted discounts at the 25% and 50% levels, the hospital was therefore still able to generate a surplus. In at least one instance, the discount was not applied until after the patient had died, producing no benefit to that patient at all. Moreover, it appears that in every case when a "charitable" discount was granted or full payment for a bill was otherwise not received, the corporation expected the shortfall to be offset by surpluses generated by the higher amounts it was able to charge other users of its facilities and services. Such "cross-subsidies" are a pricing policy any fiscally sound business enterprise might employ. We cannot fault Provena Hospitals for following this strategy, and there is no question that an institution is not ineligible for a charitable exemption simply because those patients who are able to pay are required to do so. We note merely that such conduct is in no way indicative of any form of charitable purpose or use of the subject property.[11]

The minimal amount of free and discounted care provided at the PCMC cannot be excused under the theory that aid to indigent persons is not a prerequisite to charity. In the context of municipal taxation, we recently reaffirmed that, under Illinois law, charity "is not confined to the relief of poverty or distress or to mere almsgiving" but may also include gifts to the general public use from which the rich as well as the poor may benefit. It is a fundamental principle of law, however, that a gift is "a voluntary, gratuitous transfer of property by one to another," and that "[i]t is essential to a gift that it should be without consideration." When patients are treated for a fee, consideration is passed. The treatment therefore would not qualify as a gift. If it were not a gift, it could not be charitable.

Provena Hospitals argues that the amount of free and discounted care it provides to self-pay patients at the PCMC complex is not an accurate reflection of the scope

---

11. Some commentators have been more pointed in assessing the charitable nature of this practice. *See* M. Bloche, *Health Policy Below the Waterline: Medical Care & the Charitable Exemption,* 80 Minn. L. Rev. 299, 355 (1995) ("the imagery of charity rings hollow when it comes to hospitals" because, most obviously, "the free care provided by nonprofit hospitals is financed largely by private payers, who are hardly inspired by donative benevolence").

of its charitable use of the property. In its view, its treatment of Medicare and Medicaid patients should also be taken into account because the payments it receives for treating such patients do not cover the full costs of care. As noted earlier in this opinion, however, participation in Medicare and Medicaid is not mandatory. Accepting Medicare and Medicaid patients is optional. While it is consistent with Provena Hospitals' mission, it also serves the organization's financial interests. In exchange for agreeing to accept less than its "established" rate, the corporation receives a reliable stream of revenue and is able to generate income from hospital resources that might otherwise be underutilized. Participation in the programs also enables the institution to qualify for favorable treatment under federal tax law, which is governed by different standards.

Mindful of such considerations, our appellate court has held that discounted care provided to Medicare and Medicaid patients is not considered charity for purposes of assessing eligibility for a property tax exemption. Similarly, the Catholic Health Association of the United States, one of the signatories to a friend of the court brief filed in this case in support of Provena Hospitals, does not include shortfalls from Medicaid and Medicare payments in its definition of charity. Provena Health itself adopted this view. The consolidated financial statements and supplementary information it prepared for itself and its affiliates for 2001 and 2002 did not identify any costs or charges incurred by PCMC in connection with subsidizing Medicaid or Medicare patients in its explanation of "charity care." That being so, it can scarcely complain that such costs and charges should have been included by the Department in evaluating Provena Hospitals' charitable contributions.[12]

Community benefit is a key standard for federal income tax exemption for hospitals but is not relevant to Illinois property tax exemption.

Provena Hospitals asserts that assessment of its charitable endeavors should also take into account subsidies it provides for ambulance service, its support of the crisis nursery, donations made to other not-for-profit entities, volunteer initiatives it undertakes, and support it provides for graduate medical education, behavioral health services, and emergency services training.

This contention is problematic for several reasons. First, while all of these activities unquestionably benefit the community, community benefit is not the test. Under Illinois law, the issue is whether the property at issue is used exclusively for a charitable purpose.[13]

---

12. It would, in fact, be anomalous to characterize services provided to Medicare and Medicaid patients as charity. That is so because, as the Department correctly points out, charity is, by definition, a type of gift and gifts, as we have explained, must, by definition, be gratuitous. Hospitals do not serve Medicare and Medicaid patients gratuitously. They are paid to do so.

13. Illinois' charity requirements distinguish our property tax exemption standards from the requirements a hospital must meet in order to qualify for tax-exempt status under the Internal Revenue Code. When the Medicare and Medicaid programs were being established in the late 1960s, there was concern that many hospitals would lose their federal tax-exempt status because there would no longer be sufficient demand for charity care to satisfy IRS requirements. In response, the IRS loosened its previous standards, under which hospitals were required to provide financial assistance to those who could not afford to pay for services, and began to measure a hospital's eligibility for tax exemption by utilizing other "community benefit" factors. Adoption of this community benefit standard "abandoned charity care as the touchstone of exemption at the federal level." Illinois has not adopted this approach. Although our General Assembly now requires certain hospitals in Illinois to file annual "community benefits plans" with the Illinois Attorney General's office that requirement is not part of the Property Tax Code and does not purport to alter Illinois law with respect to property tax exemptions.

Provena Hospitals' decision to make charitable contributions to other not-for-profit entities does not demonstrate an exclusively charitable use of the PCMC complex. Indeed, it tells us nothing about the use of the property at all. It is relevant only with respect to the question of how Provena Hospitals elected to disburse funds generated by the facility. That, however, is not dispositive. The critical issue is the use to which the property itself is devoted, not the use to which income derived from the property is employed. . . .

In this case, the record clearly established that the primary purpose for which the PCMC property was used was providing medical care to patients for a fee. Although the provision of such medical services may have provided an opportunity for various individuals affiliated with the hospital to express and to share their Catholic principles and beliefs, medical care, while potentially miraculous, is not intrinsically, necessarily, or even normally religious in nature. We note, moreover, that no claim has been made that operation of a fee-based medical center is in any way essential to the practice or observance of the Catholic faith.

Provena Hospitals argues that religious institutions alone have the right to assess the religious nature of their activities and that courts may not second-guess those assessments without violating constitutional guarantees regarding the free exercise of religion. If Provena Hospitals' argument were valid, it would mean that the church rather than the judiciary is the ultimate arbiter of when and under what circumstances church property is exempt from taxation under the constitution and statutes of the State of Illinois. Provena Hospitals has not cited any authority to support such a claim, nor was it raised by Provena Hospitals in its petition for leave to appeal. It is therefore not properly before us.

> The hospital also does not qualify as a religious charity, which is true for most nonprofit hospitals.

CONCLUSION

For the foregoing reasons, the Department of Revenue properly denied the charitable and religious property tax exemptions requested by Provena Hospitals in this case. The judgment of the appellate court reversing the circuit court and upholding the Department's decision is therefore affirmed.

QUESTIONS

1. How does the state court's analysis differ from the federal tax-exemption standards we have read thus far?
2. Why do states have a different set of concerns than the federal government in tax-exemption matters?

Following *Provena*, the Illinois Hospital Association successfully sponsored legislation that became effective June 14, 2012:

Illinois Income Tax Act §223. Hospital credit

(a) For tax years ending on or after December 31, 2012, a taxpayer that is the owner of a hospital licensed under the Hospital Licensing Act, but not including an organization that is exempt from federal income taxes under the Internal Revenue Code, is entitled to a credit against the taxes imposed under subsections (a) and (b) of Section 201 of this Act in an amount equal to the lesser of the amount of real property taxes paid during the tax year on real property used for hospital purposes during the prior tax year or the cost of free or discounted services provided during the tax year pursuant to the hospital's charitable financial assistance policy, measured at cost.

In 2016, an Illinois Appellate Court held section 223 to be unconstitutional, reasoning that it exceeded the authority granted to the state under the Illinois Constitution. Carle Foundation v. Cunningham Twp., 2016 IL App (4th) 140795 (Jan. 6, 2016). The Illinois Supreme Court vacated and remanded on other grounds, leaving the state constitutional question unresolved. Carle Foundation v. Cunningham Twp., 2017 IL 120427 (March 23, 2017).

CAPSTONE PROBLEM

You are general counsel to PCMC in 2018. List the key changes in hospital operations, policy, and governance that are required in order to receive both state and federal tax exemption.

CHAPTER 6

Health Care Fraud and Abuse

A. INTRODUCTION

The early chapters of this book highlight a number of unique features of health care as an industry and a market, including the highly personal, essential nature of medical products and services; the extent of government involvement in funding and arranging health care delivery; and the potential for third-party insurance to skew patients' and providers' incentives. We go to doctors because they are experts in medical care, but when doctors and other health care providers have strong financial incentives that might affect their clinical choices, health care law steps in to attempt to protect both the patient and the insurer. This important subtopic is called "health care fraud and abuse," and it involves billions of dollars in penalties and repayments each year.

The reach of these laws goes well beyond blatant fraud, such as billing for services never rendered. Many practices that are legal in other sectors are federal and state crimes in health care, particularly when dealing with public insurance (discussed in Chapter 2). Problematic practices can involve employment agreements, real estate leases, rebates, customer loyalty programs, donations, and referrals of patients to health care businesses in which a provider has a financial interest. Even well-meaning providers can find themselves ensnared in violations of these laws and facing very steep criminal and civil sanctions. Knowledge of this area of the law is essential for health care lawyers, as it is key to both structuring transactions to avoid liability and to representing clients facing government enforcement actions and private litigation.

Health care fraud and abuse is a high-stakes business and a core practice area for many health care lawyers. The following Press Release evidences the federal government's strong commitment to increased enforcement in this area.

FOR IMMEDIATE RELEASE
July 13, 2017
Department of Justice, Office of Public Affairs

NATIONAL HEALTH CARE FRAUD TAKEDOWN RESULTS IN CHARGES AGAINST OVER 412 INDIVIDUALS RESPONSIBLE FOR $1.3 BILLION IN FRAUD LOSSES

LARGEST HEALTH CARE FRAUD ENFORCEMENT ACTION IN DEPARTMENT OF JUSTICE HISTORY

Attorney General Jeff Sessions and Department of Health and Human Services (HHS) Secretary Tom Price, M.D., announced today the largest ever health care fraud enforcement action by the Medicare Fraud Strike Force, involving 412 charged defendants across 41 federal districts, including 115 doctors, nurses and other licensed medical professionals, for their alleged participation in health care fraud schemes involving approximately $1.3 billion in false billings. Of those charged, over 120 defendants, including doctors, were charged for their roles in prescribing and distributing opioids and other dangerous narcotics. Thirty state Medicaid Fraud Control Units also participated in today's arrests. In addition, HHS has initiated suspension actions against 295 providers, including doctors, nurses and pharmacists. . . .

Today's enforcement actions were led and coordinated by the Criminal Division, Fraud Section's Health Care Fraud Unit in conjunction with its Medicare Fraud Strike Force (MFSF) partners, a partnership between the Criminal Division, U.S. Attorney's Offices, the FBI and HHS-OIG. In addition, the operation includes the participation of the DEA, DCIS, and State Medicaid Fraud Control Units.

The charges announced today aggressively target schemes billing Medicare, Medicaid, and TRICARE (a health insurance program for members and veterans of the armed forces and their families) for medically unnecessary prescription drugs and compounded medications that often were never even purchased and/or distributed to beneficiaries. The charges also involve individuals contributing to the opioid epidemic, with a particular focus on medical professionals involved in the unlawful distribution of opioids and other prescription narcotics, a particular focus for the Department. According to the CDC, approximately 91 Americans die every day of an opioid related overdose.

"Too many trusted medical professionals like doctors, nurses, and pharmacists have chosen to violate their oaths and put greed ahead of their patients," said Attorney General Sessions. "Amazingly, some have made their practices into multimillion dollar criminal enterprises. They seem oblivious to the disastrous consequences of their greed. Their actions not only enrich themselves often at the expense of taxpayers but also feed addictions and cause addictions to start. The consequences are real: emergency rooms, jail cells, futures lost, and graveyards. While today is a historic day, the Department's work is not finished. In fact, it is just beginning. We will continue to find, arrest, prosecute, convict, and incarcerate fraudsters and drug dealers wherever they are."

"Healthcare fraud is not only a criminal act that costs billions of taxpayer dollars — it is an affront to all Americans who rely on our national healthcare programs for access to critical healthcare services and a violation of trust," said Secretary Price. "The United States is home to the world's best medical professionals, but their ability to provide affordable, high-quality care to their patients is jeopardized every time a criminal commits healthcare fraud. That is why this Administration is committed to bringing these criminals to justice, as President Trump demonstrated in his

2017 budget request calling for a new $70 million investment in the Health Care Fraud and Abuse Control Program. The historic results of this year's national take-down represent significant progress toward protecting the integrity and sustainability of Medicare and Medicaid, which we will continue to build upon in the years to come."

According to court documents, the defendants allegedly participated in schemes to submit claims to Medicare, Medicaid and TRICARE for treatments that were medically unnecessary and often never provided. In many cases, patient recruiters, beneficiaries and other co-conspirators were allegedly paid cash kickbacks in return for supplying beneficiary information to providers, so that the providers could then submit fraudulent bills to Medicare for services that were medically unnecessary or never performed. The number of medical professionals charged is particularly significant, because virtually every health care fraud scheme requires a corrupt medical professional to be involved in order for Medicare or Medicaid to pay the fraudulent claims. Aggressively pursuing corrupt medical professionals not only has a deterrent effect on other medical professionals, but also ensures that their licenses can no longer be used to bilk the system. . . .

In addition to the broad reach of fraud and abuse laws, the range of parties responsible for enforcing the laws is extensive. You already have learned that both federal and state governments are involved in health care delivery and insurance regulation; the same is true of fraud and abuse enforcement. Various private parties are engaged in fraud enforcement as well, including companies hired by the government to conduct audits ferreting out abusive billing practices, and individuals who come forward as whistleblowers, called "*qui tam* relators." Criminal, civil, and administrative enforcement may be pursued in conjunction, and violation of one law may suffice as violation of another law, thus exposing the provider to even greater liability. The Patient Protection and Affordable Care Act (ACA) also expanded the fraud and abuse laws in a number of key respects.

The following statement from the head of the Criminal Division of the U.S. Department of Justice announces as official policy a long-standing practice of reviewing all civil whistleblower complaints for potential criminal involvement. This commitment to pursue "parallel proceedings" increases liability exposure significantly.

Remarks by Assistant Attorney General for the Criminal Division Leslie R. Caldwell at the Taxpayers Against Fraud Education Fund Conference

Wednesday, September 17, 2014

. . . It has been my privilege, over the past several months, to serve as Assistant Attorney General for the Criminal Division of the Department of Justice.

The Criminal Division handles a wide range of cases: from sophisticated financial fraud to global narcotics trafficking, from cybercrime to corruption, and many other matters in between.

We have more than 600 smart, hard-working prosecutors who operate at the cutting edge of criminal law enforcement. When a new fraud scheme evolves from an old scheme, we often are the first to see it, and we often are the first to investigate and prosecute it. When criminals adapt their techniques, we see it, and we too adapt.

Together with our partners in the 94 U.S. Attorney's Offices around the country, as well as our law enforcement partners in the United States and across the globe, we in the Criminal Division are committed to investigating and prosecuting the most challenging types of criminal cases as they arise.

In bringing those cases, we use all of the many tools available to us. Today, I want to announce that we will be stepping up our use of one tool, and that is the fine work done by all of you in investigating and filing cases under the False Claims Act.

Through our Fraud Section, we will be committing more resources to this vital area, so that we can move swiftly and effectively to combat major fraud involving government programs.

To that end, when you are thinking of filing a qui tam case that alleges conduct that potentially could be criminal, I encourage you to consider reaching out to criminal authorities, just as you now do with our civil counterparts in the department and the U.S. Attorney's Offices.

We in the Criminal Division have unparalleled experience prosecuting health care fraud, procurement fraud, and financial fraud. We can and we will bring that expertise to bear by increasing our commitment to criminal investigations and prosecutions that stem from allegations in False Claims Act lawsuits. . . .

New Qui Tam Process

The courageous efforts by relators to bring criminal and civil misconduct to light have driven many of the largest and most important health care fraud investigations over the last several decades. And that is thanks to the work of many in this room.

I am here to tell you that the Criminal Division will redouble our efforts to work alongside you. Qui tam cases are a vital part of the Criminal Division's future efforts.

. . . We in the Criminal Division have recently implemented a procedure so that all new qui tam complaints are shared by the Civil Division with the Criminal Division as soon as the cases are filed. Experienced prosecutors in the Fraud Section are immediately reviewing the qui tam cases when we receive them to determine whether to open a parallel criminal investigation. . . .

The following sections explore the intricacies of health care fraud and abuse laws under which individual health care providers or entities may face civil or criminal investigation or charges. The final section of the chapter highlights the important role of administrative audits, compliance, and enforcement as well as parallel state laws and regulation.

B. FEDERAL FALSE CLAIMS ACT

One of the most powerful weapons for attacking health care waste, fraud, and abuse is not a health care law at all. The federal False Claims Act (FCA) is a Civil War–era statute enacted to address the problem of unscrupulous contractors selling faulty munitions and supplies to the Union Army. In modern times, the law applies broadly to all government contractors, meaning anyone who submits claims to the federal government for reimbursement for their services. But the largest category of prosecutions and financial recoupments relates to health care providers that participate in federal health care programs, such as Medicare and Medicaid. Federal law also encourages states to enact parallel laws, reaching nonfederally funded behaviors within the states. Most providers receive payment from at least one of these sources and, therefore, strive to comply with the entire package of laws.

1. CIVIL LIABILITY AND PENALTIES

The FCA, 31 U.S.C. §3729, in subsection (a)(1) establishes civil liability for any person who:

> (A) knowingly presents, or causes to be presented, a false or fraudulent claim for payment or approval;
> (B) knowingly makes, uses, or causes to be made or used, a false record or statement material to a false or fraudulent claim;
> (C) conspires to commit a violation of [this statute];
> . . . ; or
> (G) knowingly makes, uses, or causes to be made or used, a false record or statement material to an obligation to pay or transmit money or property to the Government, or knowingly conceals or knowingly and improperly avoids or decreases an obligation to pay or transmit money or property to the Government.

Violators of the Act are:

> liable to the United States Government for a civil penalty of not less than $5,000 and not more than $10,000, as adjusted by the Federal Civil Penalties Inflation Adjustment Act of 1990, plus 3 times the amount of damages which the Government sustains because of the act of that person.

In 2017, the U.S. Department of Justice issued a long overdue inflation adjustment to the statutory penalty. As a result, the range of DOJ penalties for FCA violations issued after January 29, 2018, is from $11,181 minimum to $22,363 maximum. 28 C.F.R. §85.5.

These civil monetary penalties (CMPs) can add up quickly. For health care providers, a "claim" may refer to each separate request for payment or line of code on a billing statement. For example, a health care provider that submits 10,000 false claims for even as little as $1 each may be liable for triple the damages ($30,000), plus CMPs of $5,500 to $11,000 for each false claim. In this example, the maximum CMP could be $110,000,000. The *Krizek* case below addresses the extraordinary liability CMPs can impose under the FCA.

2. REVERSE FALSE CLAIMS

In addition to liability for knowingly presenting a false claim or bill to the government, providers may also be liable under subsection (G), the "reverse false claims" provision, for knowingly retaining an overpayment from the government. The ACA gave new force to this provision by specifying that knowing retention of identified overpayments for more than 60 days constitutes a false claim, subject to civil liability. The statute, however, did not define the point at which a claim is considered to be "identified" for purposes of triggering the 60-day rule. On February 16, 2012, CMS issued proposed rules regarding the 60-day rule. The rules were not finalized until four years later, on February 12, 2016. The following case involves one court's judicial interpretation of key terms in the rule in the interim. An excerpt from the 2016 final rules follows.

Kane ex rel. United States v. Healthfirst, Inc.

120 F. Supp. 3d 370 (S.D.N.Y. 2015)

Relator Robert P. Kane ("Kane" or the "Relator") filed this case in 2011 as a qui tam action under the False Claims Act ("FCA"), 31 U.S.C. §§3729 et seq., and related state laws. In 2014, after investigating Kane's allegations, the United States Government (the "United States" or "Government") and the State of New York ("New York") elected to intervene as plaintiffs against three of the defendants named in Kane's Complaint. Presently before the Court are those defendants' motions to dismiss the United States' and New York's Complaints-in-Intervention, pursuant to Rules 9(b) and 12(b)(6) of the Federal Rules of Civil Procedure. For the following reasons, both motions are DENIED.

> "Relator" means *"qui tam relator,"* a person who acts as a whistleblower to bring false claims to the attention of the government under the FCA.

I. BACKGROUND

A. Factual Background

This action stems from a software glitch on the part of Healthfirst, Inc. ("Healthfirst"), a private, non-profit insurance program, which caused three New York City hospitals to submit improper claims seeking reimbursement from Medicaid for services rendered to beneficiaries of a managed care program administered by Healthfirst. The hospitals—Beth Israel Medical Center d/b/a Mount Sinai Beth Israel ("Beth Israel"), St. Luke's–Roosevelt Hospital Center d/b/a Mount Sinai St. Luke's and Mount Sinai Roosevelt ("SLR"), and Long Island College Hospital ("LICH" and, collectively, the "Hospitals")—all belonged to a network of non-profit hospitals operated and coordinated by Continuum Health Partners, Inc. ("Continuum"). All three Hospitals were also members of the Healthfirst hospital network and provided care to numerous patients enrolled in Healthfirst's Medicaid managed-care plan.

Pursuant to a contract entered into by Healthfirst and the New York State Department of Health ("DOH") on October 1, 2005, Healthfirst provides certain "Covered Services," including hospital and physician services, to its Medicaid-eligible enrollees in exchange for a monthly payment from DOH. Healthfirst's reimbursement for the Covered Services is limited to that monthly fee; it may not otherwise bill DOH on a "fee-for service" or other basis. All doctors, hospitals, and providers that participate in the Healthfirst network must agree that the payment they receive from Healthfirst for Covered Services rendered to Healthfirst's Medicaid enrollees will constitute payment in full for those services, except for co-payments that may be collected from enrollees where applicable. Healthfirst contracts with such providers ("Participating Providers") and pays them for the Covered Services they render to Healthfirst's Medicaid-eligible enrollees; in turn, Healthfirst is compensated through DOH's monthly payments.

The error giving rise to the instant controversy relates to electronic remittances, issued by Healthfirst to its Participating Providers, which indicated the amount of any payment due for services rendered by the provider. These remittance statements also contained "codes" that signaled whether a provider could seek additional payment from secondary payors in addition to Healthfirst, such as Medicaid, other insurance carriers, or patients themselves. The remittances submitted by Healthfirst for Covered Services rendered to its Medicaid-eligible enrollees should have contained codes informing providers that they could not seek secondary payment for such services, with the limited exception of co-payments from certain patients.

Beginning in 2009, however, due to a software glitch, Healthfirst's remittances to Participating Providers erroneously indicated that they could seek additional payment for Covered Services from secondary payors. Consequently, electronic billing programs used by numerous Participating Providers automatically generated and submitted bills to secondary payors, including Medicaid. Starting in or around January 2009, Continuum submitted claims to DOH on behalf of the Hospitals seeking additional payment for Covered Services rendered to Healthfirst enrollees, and DOH mistakenly paid the Hospitals for many of those improper claims.

> A software glitch, not intent to defraud the government, caused hundreds of false claims to be submitted.

In September 2010, auditors from the New York State Comptroller's office (the "Comptroller") approached Continuum with questions regarding the incorrect billing. Eventually, discussions among the Comptroller, Continuum, and the software vendor revealed that the problem occurred when the codes used in Healthfirst's billing software were "translated" to codes used in Continuum's billing software. On December 13, 2010, approximately two years after the problem first arose, the vendor provided a corrective software patch designed to prevent Continuum and other providers from improperly billing secondary payors like Medicaid for services provided to Healthfirst enrollees, along with an explanatory memorandum. After the problem was discovered, Continuum tasked its employee, Relator Kane, with ascertaining which claims had been improperly billed to Medicaid. In late 2010 and early 2011, Kane and other Continuum employees reviewed Continuum's billing data in an effort to comprehensively "identify" all claims potentially affected by the software glitch. In January 2011, the Comptroller alerted Continuum to several additional claims for which Continuum had billed Medicaid as a secondary payor.

On February 4, 2011, approximately five months after the Comptroller first informed Continuum about the glitch, Kane sent an email to several members of Continuum's management, attaching a spreadsheet that contained more than 900 Beth Israel, SLR, and LICH claims — totaling over $1 million — that Kane had identified as containing the erroneous billing code. His email indicated that further analysis would be needed to confirm his findings and stated that the spreadsheet gave "some insight to the magnitude of the issue." There is no dispute that Kane's spreadsheet was overly inclusive, in that approximately half of the claims listed therein were never actually overpaid; nor is there any dispute that the spreadsheet correctly included "the vast majority of the claims that had been erroneously billed." On February 8, 2011, four days after sending his email and spreadsheet, Kane was terminated.

According to the United States and New York, Continuum "did nothing further" with Kane's analysis or the universe of claims he identified. In February 2011, Continuum reimbursed DOH for only five improperly submitted claims. Meanwhile, the

Comptroller conducted further analysis and identified several additional tranches of wrongful claims, which it brought to Continuum's attention starting in March 2011 and continuing through February 2012. The United States and New York allege that although Continuum began to reimburse DOH for improperly billed claims in April 2011, it did not conclude until March 2013, "fraudulently delaying its repayments for up to two years after Continuum knew of the extent of the overpayments." In addition, it was not until the Government issued a Civil Investigative Demand ("CID") in June 2012, seeking additional information about the overpayments, that Continuum finally reimbursed DOH for more than 300 of the affected claims. They further allege that "Continuum never brought Kane's analysis to the attention of the Comptroller despite many communications with the Comptroller concerning additional claims to be repaid."

By "intentionally or recklessly" failing to take necessary steps to timely identify claims affected by the Healthfirst software glitch or timely reimburse DOH for the overbilling, the United States and New York allege, Defendants violated the False Claims Act and its New York corollary.

B. Procedural Background

... The United States asserts that Defendants violated the FCA's "reverse false claims" provision, 31 U.S.C. §3729(a)(1)(G). New York asserts that Defendants violated State Financial Law §189(1)(h), a similar "reverse false claims" provision contained in the NYFCA. Both attached two exhibits to their Complaints: (1) a list of the erroneous claims submitted by Beth Israel, SLR, and LICH as a result of the software glitch, and their subsequent histories; and (2) Kane's February 4, 2011 email and approximately 900-claim spreadsheet of potential overpayments. The United States seeks treble damages, plus an $11,000 penalty for each improperly retained overpayment. New York also seeks treble damages, along with a $12,000 penalty for each overpayment. On September 22, 2014, Defendants filed motions to dismiss both Intervenor-Complaints.

C. Statutory Framework

1. The False Claims Act and the Fraud Enforcement and Recovery Act

Congress enacted the FCA, also known as the "Informer's Act" or the "Lincoln Law," in 1863 in order "to combat rampant fraud in Civil War defense contracts."

More than a century after the FCA was initially signed into law, Congress determined that the "growing pervasiveness of fraud necessitate[d] modernization of the Government's primary litigative tool for combatting fraud. In 1986, Congress amended the FCA "to enhance the Government's ability to recover losses sustained as a result of fraud against the Government." The so-called "reverse false claims" provision at issue in this litigation was added at that time. As enacted, the reverse false claims provision imposed liability on any person who "knowingly makes, uses, or causes to be made or used, a false record or statement to conceal, avoid, or decrease an obligation to pay or transmit money or property to the Government." 31 U.S.C. §3729(a)(7). It is described as the "reverse false claims" provision "because the financial obligation that is the subject of the fraud flows in the opposite of the usual direction."

The 1986 amendments also raised the fixed statutory penalty for FCA violations, which had not been altered since the Act's initial passage, such that a party found to have violated the Act, including the reverse false claims provision, is liable to the United States Government for a civil penalty of not less than $5,000 and not more than $10,000, to be adjusted for inflation. In so doing, Congress "reaffirm[ed] the apparent belief of the act's initial drafters that defrauding the Government is serious enough to warrant an automatic forfeiture rather than leaving fine determinations with district courts, possibly resulting in discretionary nominal payments." Additionally, the 1986 amendments increased the Government's recoverable damages in FCA cases from double to treble. Finally, among the other 1986 changes was the adoption of a provision granting "Civil Investigative Demand" or CID authority to the Civil Division of the United States Department of Justice.

Twenty-three years later, in 2009, Congress passed the Fraud Enforcement and Recovery Act ("FERA"), which further amended the FCA and its reverse false claims provision. Prior to the 2009 amendments, the reverse false claims provision left a "loophole" that excused from liability the concealment, avoidance, or decreasing of an obligation to return to the Government "money or property that is knowingly retained by a person even though they have no right to it." As amended by the FERA, the reverse false claims provision now imposes liability for any person who "knowingly makes, uses, or causes to be made or used, a false record or statement material to an obligation to pay or transmit money or property to the Government, or knowingly conceals or *knowingly and improperly avoids or decreases an obligation* to pay or transmit money or property to the Government." 31 U.S.C. §3729(a)(1)(G) (emphasis added). As defined in the FCA, the terms "knowing" and "knowingly" encompass "actual knowledge," as well as situations in which a person "acts in deliberate ignorance" or "reckless disregard" of the truth or falsity of information. This knowledge standard expressly requires no proof of specific intent to defraud.

In addition, the FERA aimed to address a "confusion" that had arisen among several courts that had "developed conflicting definitions of the term 'obligation,'" which previously was not defined in the FCA. In direct response to those conflicting court decisions, the FERA amended the FCA by defining an "obligation" as "an established duty, whether or not fixed, arising from an express or implied contractual, grantor-grantee, or licensor-licensee relationship, from a fee-based or similar relationship, from statute or regulation, or from the retention of an overpayment."

2. The Patient Protection and Affordable Care Act

In 2010, less than a year after the FERA was signed into law, Congress passed the Patient Protection and Affordable Care Act of 2010 ("ACA"), a broad healthcare reform statute that, as relevant to these proceedings, included a provision prohibiting retention of Government overpayments in the healthcare context. Specifically, the ACA requires a person who receives an overpayment of Medicare or Medicaid funds to "report and return" the overpayment to HHS, the State, or another party if appropriate. 42 U.S.C. §1320a-7k(d)(1). The statute sets a deadline for such reporting and returning: An overpayment must be reported and returned within sixty days of the "date on which the overpayment was identified" (the "sixty-day rule" or "report and return" provision), and any overpayment retained beyond that point constitutes an "obligation" carrying liability under the FCA. More simply stated, the ACA provides that any person who has received an overpayment from Medicare or Medicaid and knowingly fails to report and return it within sixty days after the date on which it was identified has violated the FCA. *Id.* §1320a-7k(d).

The report and return provision does not actually deploy the terms "knowing" or "knowingly," but the provision contains its own succinct "Definitions" section, which states that provides that "knowing" and "knowingly" should "have the meaning given those terms in [the FCA]." *Id.* §1320a-7k(d)(4)(A). However, Congress did not define the pivotal word "identified," which triggers the sixty-day report and return clock, in the text of the ACA. Its meaning governs the outcome of the motions before the Court.

3. *The New York False Claims Act*

The NYFCA, "closely modeled on the federal FCA," was enacted on April 1, 2007. It has a similar penalty scheme as well: Under the NYFCA, the State of New York is entitled to recover three times the amount of each improper claim and, for each claim or overpayment, a civil penalty of not less than $6,000 and not more than $12,000. When interpreting the NYFCA, New York courts rely on federal FCA precedent.

Section 189(1)(h) of the NYFCA, which New York contends Defendants violated, provides that a person violates the NYFCA if he or she "knowingly conceals or knowingly and improperly avoids or decreases an obligation to pay or transmit money or property to the state or a local government, or conspires to do the same[.]" It is identical to the second clause of the FCA's reverse false claims provision but applies to obligations to pay the State government or a local government rather than the federal government. Like the FCA, the NYFCA defines an "obligation" to include "retention of an overpayment," and defines "knowing" to include reckless disregard or deliberate ignorance to the truth or falsity of information.

The reverse false claims provision was not included in the statute as initially enacted in 2007. Rather, the New York State Legislature amended the NYFCA in March 2013 to include it, thereby incorporating into the Act those provisions of the federal FCA implemented by the FERA. . . .

III. DISCUSSION

A. The United States' Complaint

Defendants argue that the United States' Complaint-in-Intervention is insufficient to meet the high bar set by Rule 9(b) because it fails to allege: (1) that Defendants had an "obligation," (2) that Defendants knowingly concealed or knowingly and improperly avoided or decreased an obligation, and (3) that Defendants had an obligation to pay or transmit money to the federal "Government." The Court rejects each of these propositions.

1. *The United States Properly Pleads an "Obligation"*

Kane's February 4, 2011 email and spreadsheet, which he sent to Continuum managers, isolated approximately 900 claims that he recognized as containing the erroneous billing code and, therefore, as being potential overpayments. Approximately half of the items listed did, in fact, constitute overpayments. The Government argues that Kane's email and spreadsheet properly "identified" overpayments within the meaning of the ACA, and that these overpayments matured into "obligations" in violation of the FCA when they were not reported and returned by Defendants within sixty days. Defendants, on the other hand, argue that Kane's email only provided notice of potential overpayments and did not identify actual overpayments so as to trigger the ACA's sixty-day report and return clock.

In essence, Defendants urge the Court to adopt a definition of "identified" that means "classified with certainty," whereas the Government urges a definition of "identified" that would be satisfied where, as here, a person is put on notice that a certain claim may have been overpaid. The Government's proposal — that "an entity 'has identified an overpayment' when it 'has determined, or should have determined through the exercise of reasonable diligence, that [it] has received an overpayment' to identify," — treats "identified" as synonymous with "known" as it is defined in the FCA. Congress did not define the term "identified" in the ACA, and no other court has weighed in on its meaning or on the application of the ACA sixty-day rule. This case thus presents a novel question of statutory interpretation. . . .

—————————————————————

The court ultimately rejected the defendants' position that an overpayment is "identified" only when it can be "classified with certainty" or "conclusively ascertained." Instead, the court accepted the government's broader definition that an overpayment has been "identified" whenever a provider is put "on notice" that a certain claim or claims may have been overpaid. According to the court, that interpretation was consistent with the purpose behind the statute and the legislative history of the FCA. Allowing the defendants to escape liability because Kane's e-mail did not conclusively identify improperly submitted claims by an exact amount would be counter to the goal of establishing "robust" anti-fraud measures.

The court suggested that the harshness of its interpretation of the rule was mitigated by prosecutorial discretion, which should prevent diligent and reasonable providers from being targeted by the government. The court further suggested that if providers could show that they had taken good-faith steps to investigate and ascertain the overpayments, and continued to do so, past the 60-day window, the government may not be able to prove a separate element of an FCA claim — that is, that the provider "knowingly concealed" or "knowingly and improperly avoided or decreased" an obligation.

QUESTIONS

1. How did Continuum's mistake lead to the alleged false claims?
2. When does the obligation to self-report begin?

The Centers for Medicare & Medicaid Services (CMS) final rule adopted a somewhat more defendant-friendly standard, providing that "[a] person has identified an overpayment when the person has, or should have through the exercise of reasonable diligence, determined that the person has received an overpayment and quantified the amount of the overpayment. A person should have determined that the person received an overpayment and quantified the amount of the overpayment if the person fails to exercise reasonable diligence and the person in fact received an overpayment." 42 C.F.R. §401.305(a)(2). The preamble to the final rule further explains the standard.

Medicare Program; Reporting and Returning of Overpayments

81 Fed. Reg. 7654 (Feb. 12, 2016)

RULES and REGULATIONS
DEPARTMENT OF HEALTH AND HUMAN SERVICES
Centers for Medicare & Medicaid Services
42 CFR Parts 401 and 405

AGENCY: Centers for Medicare & Medicaid Services (CMS), HHS.

ACTION: Final rule.

SUMMARY: This final rule requires providers and suppliers receiving funds under the Medicare program to report and return overpayments by the later of the date that is 60 days after the date on which the overpayment was identified; or the date any corresponding cost report is due, if applicable. The requirements in this rule are meant to ensure compliance with applicable statutes, promote the furnishing of high quality care, and to protect the Medicare Trust Funds against fraud and improper payments. This rule provides needed clarity and consistency in the reporting and returning of self-identified overpayments.

DATES: These regulations are effective on March 14, 2016.

. . . .

The final rule states that a person has identified an overpayment when the person has, or should have through the exercise of reasonable diligence, determined that the person has received an overpayment and quantified the amount of the overpayment. A person should have determined that the person received an overpayment if the person fails to exercise reasonable diligence and the person in fact received an overpayment. "Reasonable diligence" includes both proactive compliance activities conducted in good faith by qualified individuals to monitor for the receipt of overpayments and investigations conducted in good faith and in a timely manner by qualified individuals in response to obtaining credible information of a potential overpayment.

The regulation uses a single term — reasonable diligence — to cover both proactive compliance activities to monitor claims and reactive investigative activities undertaken in response to receiving credible information about a potential overpayment. We believe that compliance with the statutory obligation to report and return received overpayments requires both proactive and reactive activities. In addition, we also clarify that the quantification of the amount of the overpayment may be determined using statistical sampling, extrapolation methodologies, and other methodologies as appropriate.

As to the circumstances that give rise to a duty to exercise reasonable diligence, we are not able to identify all factual scenarios in this rulemaking. Providers and suppliers are responsible for ensuring their Medicare claims are accurate and proper and are encouraged to have effective compliance programs as a way to avoid receiving or retaining overpayments. Indeed, many commenters told us that they have active compliance programs and that we should recognize these compliance efforts in the final rule. It was also apparent from some commenters that they do not currently engage in compliance efforts to ensure that the claims they submitted to Medicare were accurate and proper and that payments received are appropriate. We advise those

> The 60-day rule increases the incentive for providers to put in place effective compliance programs, discussed in more detail below.

providers and suppliers to undertake such efforts to ensure they fulfill their obligations under section 1128J(d) of the Act. We believe that undertaking no or minimal compliance activities to monitor the accuracy and appropriateness of a provider or supplier's Medicare claims would expose a provider or supplier to liability under the identified standard articulated in this rule based on the failure to exercise reasonable diligence if the provider or supplier received an overpayment. We also recognize that compliance programs are not uniform in size and scope and that compliance activities in a smaller setting, such as a solo practitioner's office, may look very different than those in larger setting, such as a multi-specialty group. Compliance activities may also appropriately vary based on the type of provider.

We note that in discussing the standard term "reasonable diligence" in the preamble, we are interpreting the obligation to "report and return the overpayment" that is contained in section 1128J(d) of the Social Security Act. We are not seeking to interpret the terms "knowing" and "knowingly," which are defined in the Civil False Claims Act and have been interpreted by a body of False Claims Act case law.

Comment: Several commenters stated that they interpreted the preamble to the proposed rule as permitting providers and suppliers time to conduct a reasonable inquiry before the 60-day time period begins to run. These commenters noted that the preamble provides that providers and suppliers may receive information concerning a potential overpayment that creates a duty to conduct a reasonable inquiry to determine whether an overpayment exists. If the reasonable inquiry reveals an overpayment, then the provider has 60 days to report and return the overpayment. On the other hand, failure to make a reasonable inquiry, including failure to conduct such inquiry with all deliberate speed after obtaining the information, could result in the provider or supplier knowingly retaining an overpayment because it acted in reckless disregard or deliberate ignorance of whether it received such an overpayment. Commenters stated that this explanation and the examples in the preamble together suggested that once a provider is placed on notice of a potential overpayment, it must conduct a reasonably diligent inquiry under the circumstances and the 60-day period does not start until either the inquiry reveals an overpayment or the provider or supplier is reckless or deliberately ignorant because it failed to conduct the reasonable inquiry. Commenters requested that we clarify whether this interpretation was accurate.

Response: We agree with the commenters' interpretation of the proposed rule and have revised §401.305(a) and (b) in this final rule to clarify the duty to investigate through a reasonable diligence standard. When a person obtains credible information concerning a potential overpayment, the person needs to undertake reasonable diligence to determine whether an overpayment has been received and to quantify the amount. The 60-day time period begins when either the reasonable diligence is completed or on the day the person received credible information of a potential overpayment if the person failed to conduct reasonable diligence and the person in fact received an overpayment.

. . . .

Comment: A number of commenters requested clarification on the meaning of "all deliberate speed" a phrase used in the preamble to the proposed rule. Commenters stated that we effectively established a time limit for preliminary action before the 60-day clock began to toll, yet did not clearly state what this time limit is or what a person must do to meet it. Commenters stated that the proposed rule was not clear about how to determine whether an ongoing investigation occurred with "all deliberate speed." Commenters noted that in many circumstances, multiple people will be involved in determining whether an overpayment exists and in what amount, such as auditors, billing personnel, and legal counsel. Commenters believed we should issue additional guidance in the final rule, particularly what documentation we expect providers and suppliers to maintain to show compliance with the rule. Some commenters suggested that we adopt an approach that would allow for a "reasonable period of time to investigate" a potential overpayment. . . .

> Under the final rule, providers effectively have eight months to investigate and return overpayments.

Response: The preamble to this final rule does not include the phrase "all deliberate speed" as the benchmark of compliance. Instead, we adopt the standard of reasonable diligence and establish that this is demonstrated through the timely, good faith investigation of credible information, which is at most 6 months from receipt of the credible information, except in extraordinary circumstances. We considered but rejected adopting a "reasonable period of time to investigate" standard because we concluded that an open-ended timeframe would likely be viewed as no more clear than "all deliberate speed" and establishing a time frame would better respond to commenters' concerns on this issue. We choose 6 months as the benchmark for timely investigation because we believe that providers and suppliers should prioritize these investigations and also to recognize that completing these investigations may require the devotion of resources and time. Receiving overpayments from Medicare is sufficiently important that providers and suppliers should devote appropriate attention to resolving these matters. A total of 8 months (6 months for timely investigation and 2 months for reporting and returning) is a reasonable amount of time, absent extraordinary circumstances affecting the provider, supplier, or their community. What constitutes extraordinary circumstances is a fact-specific question. Extraordinary circumstances may include unusually complex investigations that the provider or supplier reasonably anticipates will require more than six months to investigate, such as physician self-referral law violations that are referred to the CMS Voluntary Self-Referral Disclosure Protocol (SRDP). Specific examples of other types of extraordinary circumstances include natural disasters or a state of emergency.

. . . .

In order to assist providers and suppliers with understanding when an overpayment has been identified, we provided the following examples, which were intended to be illustrative and not an exhaustive list of circumstances:

- A provider of services or supplier reviews billing or payment records and learns that it incorrectly coded certain services, resulting in increased reimbursement.
- A provider of services or supplier learns that a patient death occurred prior to the service date on a claim that has been submitted for payment.
- A provider of services or supplier learns that services were provided by an unlicensed or excluded individual on its behalf.
- A provider of services or supplier performs an internal audit and discovers that overpayments exist.
- A provider of services or supplier is informed by a government agency of an audit that discovered a potential overpayment, and the provider or supplier fails to make a reasonable inquiry. (When a government agency informs a provider or supplier of a potential overpayment, the provider or supplier has a

duty to accept the finding or make a reasonable inquiry. If the provider's or supplier's inquiry verifies the audit results, then it has identified an overpayment and, assuming there is no applicable cost report, has 60 days to report and return the overpayment. As noted previously, failure to make a reasonable inquiry, including failure to conduct such inquiry with all deliberate speed after obtaining the information, could result in the provider or supplier knowingly retaining an overpayment because it acted in reckless disregard or deliberate ignorance of whether it received such an overpayment).

- A provider of services or supplier experiences a significant increase in Medicare revenue and there is no apparent reason — such as a new partner added to a group practice or a new focus on a particular area of medicine — for the increase. However, the provider or supplier fails to make a reasonable inquiry into whether an overpayment exists. (When there is reason to suspect an overpayment, but a provider or supplier fails to make a reasonable inquiry into whether an overpayment exists, it may be found to have acted in reckless disregard or deliberate ignorance of any overpayment.)

. . . .

QUESTIONS

1. How does the regulation's "reasonable diligence" standard differ from the *Healthfirst* court's "notice" standard for identifying an overpayment?
2. How should the defendants have proceeded had the final regulations been in place at the time of the activities in question?

3. SCIENTER REQUIREMENT

The False Claims Act is a civil statute that requires "knowing" violation of the law. The statute specifies as follows:

31 U.S.C. §3729(b). Definitions
For purposes of this section —
    (1) the terms "knowing" and "knowingly" —
        (A) mean that a person, with respect to information —
            (i) has actual knowledge of the information;
            (ii) acts in deliberate ignorance of the truth or falsity of the information; or
            (iii) acts in reckless disregard of the truth or falsity of the information; and
        (B) require no proof of specific intent to defraud; . . . .

The following opinion applies the "knowingly" standard, considering whether a defendant can be liable for mere negligence or inadvertent errors. As the opinion highlights, CMPs in health care cases can be staggeringly high because they are assessed on a per-claim basis, which the government argued should mean each line of billing code on each patient claim form. In many cases, the government's actual damages (even when trebled under the statute) may be relatively insignificant; in fact, the government need not suffer any harm in order for liability to attach under the FCA. Also note Judge Sporkin's sympathy for a small business run by a well-intentioned physician who became ensnared in the government's labyrinthine billing rules.

United States v. Krizek

859 F. Supp. 5 (D.D.C. 1994)

SPORKIN, District Judge.

On January 11, 1993, the United States filed this civil suit against George O. Krizek, M.D. and Blanka H. Krizek under the False Claims Act and at common law. The government brought the action against the Krizeks alleging false billing for Medicare and Medicaid patients. The five counts include claims for (1) "Knowingly Presenting a False or Fraudulent Claim," 31 U.S.C. §3729(a)(1); (2) "Knowingly Presenting a False or Fraudulent Record," 31 U.S.C. §3729(a)(2); (3) "Conspiracy to Defraud the Government"; (4) "Payment under Mistake of Fact;" and (5) "Unjust Enrichment." In its claim for relief, the government asks for triple the alleged actual damages of $245,392 and civil penalties of $10,000 for each of the 8,002 allegedly false reimbursement claims pursuant to 31 U.S.C. §3729.

> At the time of this case, the maximum CMP for a false claim was $10,000. It has since been adjusted upward for inflation.

The government alleges two types of misconduct related to the submission of bills to Medicare and Medicaid. The first category of misconduct relates to the use of billing codes found in the American Medical Association's "Current Procedural Terminology" ("CPT"), a manual that lists terms and codes for reporting procedures performed by physicians. The government alleges that Dr. Krizek "up-coded" the bills for a large percentage of his patients by submitting bills coded for a service with a higher level of reimbursement than that which Dr. Krizek provided. As a second type of misconduct, the government alleges Dr. Krizek "performed services that should not have been performed at all in that they were not medically necessary." . . .

Findings of Fact

Dr. Krizek is a psychiatrist. Dr. Krizek's wife, Blanka Krizek was responsible for overseeing Dr. Krizek's billing operation for a part of the period in question. Dr. Krizek's Washington, D.C. psychiatric practice consists in large part in the treatment of Medicare and Medicaid patients. Much of Doctor Krizek's work involves the provision of psychotherapy and other psychiatric care to patients at the Washington Hospital Center.

Under the Medicare and Medicaid systems, claims for reimbursement are submitted on documents known as Health Care Financing Administration ("HCFA") 1500 Forms. These forms are supposed to contain the patient's identifying information, the provider's Medicaid or Medicare identification number, and a description of the provided procedures for which reimbursement is sought. These procedures are identified by a standard, uniform code number as set out in the American Medical Association's "Current Procedural Terminology" ("CPT") manual, a book that lists the terms and codes for reporting procedures performed by physicians. . . .

> The certification from the current version of this billing form is printed after this case.

The government in its complaint alleges both improper billing for services provided and the provision of medically unnecessary services. The latter of these two claims will be addressed first.

Medical Necessity

The record discloses that Dr. Krizek is a capable and competent physician. Dr. Krizek was originally trained in Prague, in what was then Czechoslovakia, at the Charles University School of Medicine. Dr. Krizek also received a medical degree from Rudolf's University, in Vienna, Austria. Dr. Krizek came to the United States in 1968, where he did a residency at Beth Israel Hospital in New York City. He arrived in the Washington, D.C. area in the early 1970's where he has been engaged in the practice of psychiatry for approximately 21 years. The trial testimony of Dr. Krizek, his colleagues at the Washington Hospital Center, as well as the testimony of a former patient, established that Dr. Krizek was providing valuable medical and psychiatric care during the period covered by the complaint. The testimony was undisputed that Dr. Krizek worked long hours on behalf of his patients, most of whom were elderly and poor.

Many of Dr. Krizek's patients were afflicted with horribly severe psychiatric disorders and often suffered simultaneously from other serious medical conditions. For example, one of the seven representative patients had paranoid psychosis and organic brain dementia, coupled with a series of other medical problems including colon cancer, diabetes, herpes, and viral encephalitis. Another patient suffered from chronic depression and had accompanying delusions. A third had a history of repeated psychiatric hospitalizations, was in an acute schizophrenic state, and also suffered from epilepsy. A fourth patient suffered from suicidal and assaultive behavior, hallucinations, paralysis of the left side of the body, and was an intravenous cocaine and heroin user.

The government takes issue with Dr. Krizek's method of treatment of his patients, arguing that some patients should have been discharged from the hospital sooner, and that others suffered from conditions which could not be ameliorated through psychotherapy sessions, or that the length of the psychotherapy sessions should have been abbreviated. The government's expert witness's opinions on this subject came from a cold review of Dr. Krizek's notes for each patient. The government witness did not examine or interview any of the patients, or speak with any other doctors or nurses who had actually served these patients to learn whether the course of treatment prescribed by Dr. Krizek exceeded that which was medically necessary.

Dr. Krizek testified credibly and persuasively as to the basis for the course of treatment for each of the representative patients. The medical necessity of treating Dr. Krizek's patients through psychotherapy and hospitalization was confirmed via the testimony of other defense witnesses. The Court credits Dr. Krizek's testimony on this question as well as his interpretation of his own notes regarding the seriousness of each patients' condition and the medical necessity for the procedures and length of hospital stay required. The Court finds that the government was unable to prove that Dr. Krizek rendered services that were medically unnecessary.

> In some FCA cases with a large number of claims, the government and the defendant will agree to litigate a much smaller number of "representative" patients or claims, with the results of the sample binding the full set of claims at issue in the case.

Improper Billing

On the question of improper billing or "up-coding," the government contends that for approximately 24 percent of the bills submitted, Dr. Krizek used the CPT Code for a 45-50 minute psychotherapy session (CPT Code 90844) when he should have billed for a 20-30 minute session (CPT Code 90843). The government also contends that for at least 33 percent of his patients, Dr. Krizek billed for a full 45-50 minute psychotherapy session, again by using CPT code 90844, when he should have billed for a "minimal psychotherapy" session (CPT 90862). These two latter procedures are reimbursed at a lower level than 90844, the 45-50 minute psychotherapy session, which the government has referred to as "the Cadillac" of psychiatric reimbursement codes.

The primary thrust of the government's case revolves around the question whether Dr. Krizek's use of the 90844 CPT code was appropriate. For the most part, the government does not allege that Dr. Krizek did not see the patients for whom he submitted bills. Instead, the government posits that the services provided during his visits either did not fall within the accepted definition of "individual medical psychotherapy" or, if the services provided did fit within this definition, the reimbursable service provided was not as extensive as that which was billed for. In sum, the government claims that whenever Dr. Krizek would see a patient, regardless of whether he simply checked a chart, spoke with nurses, or merely prescribed additional medication, his wife or his employee, a Mrs. Anderson, would, on the vast majority of occasions, submit a bill for CPT code 90844 — 45-50 minutes of individual psychotherapy.

In presenting its case that Dr. Krizek did not provide the billed-for services as required by the CPT, the government contends that the definition of the 90844 code requires 45-50 minutes of "face-to-face" contact with the patient. By example, if a doctor were to spend 10 minutes reviewing a patient's file and talking to nurses about the patient's condition, then spend 20 minutes in a face-to-face psychiatry session with the patient, and finally take an additional fifteen minutes after the session to consult with the patient's spouse or prescribe medication, this would, according to the government, count only as a 20-30 minute individual psychotherapy session, to be billed as code 90843. Under the government's interpretation of the code, even if as much as an hour of a physician's time is devoted to a patient's case, with half that time spent in a face-to-face psychotherapy session and the rest spent on related services, the doctor is only permitted reimbursement under the 90800 series of codes for the 30 minutes spent face-to-face.

The government's witnesses testified that as initially conceived, the definition of the CPT codes is designed to incorporate the extra time spent in its level of reimbursement. It was expected by the authors of the codes that for a 45-50 minute 90844 session a doctor would spend additional time away from the patient reviewing or dictating records, speaking with nurses, or prescribing medication. The government's witnesses testified that the reimbursement rate for 90844 took into account the fact that on a 45-50 minute session the doctor would likely spend twenty additional minutes away from the patient. As such, the doctor is limited to billing for time actually spent "face-to-face" with the patient.

Dr. and Mrs. Krizek freely admit that when a 90844 code bill was submitted on the doctor's behalf, it did not always reflect 45-50 minutes of face-to-face psychotherapy with the patient. Instead, the 45-50 minutes billed captured generally the total amount of time spent on the patient's case, including the "face-to-face" psychotherapy session, discussions with medical staff about the patient's treatment/progress, medication management, and other related services. Dr. Krizek referred to this as "bundling" of services, all of which, Dr. and Mrs. Krizek testified, they reasonably believed were reimbursable under the 90844 "individual medical psychotherapy" code.

Defendant's witnesses testified that it was a common and proper practice among psychiatrists nationally, and in the Washington, D.C. area, to "bundle" a variety of services, including prescription management, review of the patient file, consultations with nurses or the patients' relatives into a bill for individual psychotherapy, whether or not these services took place literally in view of the patient. Under the defense theory, if a doctor spent 20 minutes in a session with a patient and ten minutes before that in a different room discussing the patient's symptoms with a nurse, and fifteen minutes afterwards outlining a course of treatment to the medical staff, it would be entirely appropriate, under their reading and interpretation of the CPT, to bill the 45 minutes spent on that patients' care by using CPT code 90844.

The testimony of the defense witnesses on this point was credible and persuasive. . . . The CPT codes which the government insists require face-to-face rendition of services never used the term "face-to-face" in its code description during the time period covered by this litigation. The relevant language describing the code is ambiguous.

The Court finds that the government's position on this issue is not rational and has been applied in an unfair manner to the medical community, which for the most part is made up of honorable and dedicated professionals. One government witness testified that a 15 minute telephone call made to a consulting physician in the patient's presence would be reimbursable, while if the doctor needed to go outside the patient's room to use the telephone — in order to make the same telephone call — the time would not be reimbursable. . . .

> The provider is expected to know the detailed rules surrounding CPT codes and reimbursement, but he cannot be expected to know what the government intended with coding or guidance that is unclear.

The Court will not impose False Claims Act liability based on such a strained interpretation of the CPT codes. The government's theory of liability is plainly unfair and unjustified. Medical doctors should be appropriately reimbursed for services legitimately provided. They should be given clear guidance as to what services are reimbursable. The system should be fair. The system cannot be so arbitrary, so perverse, as to subject a doctor whose annual income during the relevant period averaged between $100,000 and $120,000, to potential liability in excess of 80 million dollars[3] because telephone calls were made in one room rather than another.

The Court finds that Doctor Krizek did not submit false claims when he submitted a bill under CPT Code 90844 after spending 45-50 minutes working on a

---

3. The government alleges in the complaint that overbills amounted to $245,392 during the six-year period covered by the lawsuit. Trebling this damage amount, and adding the $10,000 statutory maximum penalty requested by the government for each of the 8,002 alleged false claims, results in a total potential liability under the complaint of more than $80,750,000. Dr. Krizek is not public enemy number one. He is at worst, a psychiatrist with a small practice who keeps poor records. For the government to sue for more than eighty million dollars in damages against an elderly doctor and his wife is unseemly and not justified. During this period, a psychiatrist in most instances would be reimbursed between $48 and $60 for a 45-50 minute session and $40 or less for a 20-30 minute session. This is hardly enough for any professional to get rich.

patient's case, even though not all of that time was spent in direct face-to-face contact with the patient. . . . The Court finds that the defendants' "bundled" services interpretation of the CPT code 90844 is not inconsistent with the plain, common-sense reading of the "description of services" listed by [the Medicare contractor for Dr. Krizek's area] in its published Procedure Terminology Manual.

Billing Irregularities

While Dr. Krizek was a dedicated and competent doctor and cannot be faulted for his interpretation of the 90844 code, his billing practices, or at a minimum his oversight of his wife's and Mrs. Anderson's billing system, was seriously deficient. Dr. Krizek knew little or nothing of the details of how the bills were submitted by his wife and Mrs. Anderson. Mrs. Krizek was responsible for submitting to Medicare/Medicaid claims for reimbursement for the patients who were admitted to Dr. Krizek's service at the Washington Hospital Center and for those few Medicare/Medicaid outpatients Dr. Krizek saw in his home. Mrs. Anderson was responsible for submitting bills when Dr. Krizek saw as "consults" Medicare/Medicaid patients who were admitted to another physician's service at Washington Hospital Center, and when Dr. Krizek was "covering" for other physicians.

> Mrs. Anderson would contact a hospital to gather information and would submit claims to Medicare or Medicaid without communicating with Dr. or Mrs. Krizek about the claims she was submitting. Dr. Krizek, conversely, never asked to see the claims she submitted, conduct the appellate court called "struthious."

The basic method of billing by Mrs. Krizek and Mrs. Anderson was to determine which patients Dr. Krizek had seen, and then to assume what had taken place was a 50-minute psychotherapy session, unless told specifically by Dr. Krizek that the visit was for a shorter duration. Mrs. Krizek frequently made this assumption without any input from her husband. Mrs. Krizek acknowledged at trial that she never made any specific effort to determine exactly how much time was spent with each patient. Mrs. Krizek felt it was fair and appropriate to use the 90844 code as a rough approximation of the time spent, because on some days, an examination would last up to two hours and Mrs. Krizek would still bill 90844.

Mrs. Anderson also would prepare and submit claims to Medicare/Medicaid with no input from Dr. Krizek. Routinely, Mrs. Anderson would simply contact the hospital to determine what patients were admitted to various psychiatrists' services, and would then prepare and submit claims to Medicare/Medicaid without communicating with Dr. or Mrs. Krizek about the claims she was submitting and certifying on Dr. Krizek's behalf. . . .

The net result of this system, or more accurately "nonsystem," of billing was that on a number of occasions, Mrs. Krizek and Mrs. Anderson submitted bills for 45-50 minute psychotherapy sessions on Dr. Krizek's behalf when Dr. Krizek could not have spent the requisite time providing services, face-to-face, or otherwise. For example, on March 9, 1985 Dr. Krizek submitted to Medicare and Medicaid 23 claims for 90844 (45-50 minutes of individual medical psychotherapy) and 5 claims for 90843 (25-30 minutes of individual medical psychotherapy). These 29 claims totaled 21.5 hours of services provided during one 24 hour period. In August 31, 1985, thirty 90844's and one 90843 were submitted. At minimum, this is the equivalent of 23 hours in patient services in a 24 hour period. While Dr. Krizek may have been a tireless worker, it is difficult for the Court to comprehend how he could have spent more than even ten hours in a single day serving patients. . . . The defendants do not deny that these unsubstantiated reimbursement claims occurred or that billing practices which led to such inaccurate billings continued through March of 1992.

While the Court does not find that Dr. Krizek submitted bills for patients he did not see, the Court does find that because of Mrs. Krizek's and Mrs. Anderson's presumption that whenever Dr. Krizek saw a patient he worked at least 45 minutes on the matter, bills were improperly submitted for time that was not spent providing patient services. Again, the defendants admit this occurred. . . .

Nature of Liability

While the parties have agreed as to the presumptive number of excess submissions for which Dr. and Mrs. Krizek may be found liable, they do not agree on the character of the liability. The government submits that the Krizeks should be held liable under the False Claims Act, 31 U.S.C. §3729, et seq. By contrast, defendants posit that while the United States may be entitled to reimbursement for any unjust enrichment attributable to the excess billings, the Krizeks' conduct with regard to submission of excess bills to Medicare/Medicaid was at most negligent, and not "knowing" within the definition of the statute. In their defense, defendants emphasize the "Ma and Pa" nature of Dr. Krizek's medical practice, the fact that Mrs. Krizek did attend some Medicare billing seminars in an effort to educate herself, and the fact that Mrs. Krizek consulted hospital records and relied on information provided by her husband in preparing bills. . . .

The mental state required to find liability under the False Claims Act is also defined by the statute:

For the purposes of this section, the terms "knowing" and "knowingly" mean that a person, with respect to information —

> (1) has actual knowledge of the information;
> (2) acts in deliberate ignorance of the truth or falsity of the information; or
> (3) acts in reckless disregard of the truth or falsity of the information, and no proof
> of specific intent is required.

31 U.S.C. §3729(b). The provision allowing for a finding of liability without proof of specific intent to defraud was a feature of the 1986 amendments to the Act. As explained by one of the 1986 Act's sponsors:

> While the Act was not intended to apply to mere negligence, it is intended to apply in situations that could be considered gross negligence where the submitted claims to the government are prepared in such a sloppy or unsupervised fashion that [it] resulted in overcharges to the government.

. . . .

The Court finds that, at times, Dr. Krizek was submitting claims for 90844 when he did not provide patient services for the requisite 45 minutes. The testimony makes clear that these submissions were made by Mrs. Krizek or Mrs. Anderson with little, if any, factual basis. Mrs. Krizek made no effort to establish how much time Dr. Krizek spent on a particular matter. Mrs. Krizek and Mrs. Anderson simply presumed that 45-50 minutes had been spent. There was no justification for making that assumption. In addition, Dr. Krizek failed utterly in supervising these agents in their submissions of claims on his behalf. As a result of his failure to supervise, Dr. Krizek received reimbursement for services which he did not provide.

These were not "mistakes" nor merely negligent conduct. Under the statutory definition of "knowing" conduct, the Court is compelled to conclude that the defendants acted with reckless disregard as to the truth or falsity of the submissions. As such, they will be deemed to have violated the False Claims Act.

Note that Dr. Krizek is liable even though he did not actually submit the claims to the government himself. He is liable — as are all health care providers — for his failure to supervise those submitting the claims on his behalf.

Conclusion

Dr. Krizek must be held accountable for his billing system along with those who carried it out. Dr. Krizek was not justified in seeing patients and later not verifying the claims submitted for the services provided to these patients. Doctors must be held strictly accountable for requests filed for insurance reimbursement.

The Court believes that the Krizeks' billing practices must be corrected before they are permitted to further participate in the Medicare or Medicaid programs. Therefore an injunction will issue, enjoining the defendants from participating in these systems until such time as they can show the Court that they can abide by the relevant rules.

The Court also will hold the defendants liable under the False Claims Act on those days where claims were submitted in excess of the equivalent of twelve (12) 90844 claims (nine patient-treatment hours) in a single day and where the defendants cannot establish that Dr. Krizek legitimately devoted the claimed amount of time to patient care on the day in question. The government also will be entitled to introduce proof that the defendants submitted incorrect bills when Dr. Krizek submitted bills for less than nine (9) hours in a single day. The assessment of the amount of overpayment and penalty will await these future proceedings.

Other Observations

While the Court does not discount the seriousness of the Krizeks' conduct here, this case demonstrates several flaws in this country's government health insurance program. The government was right in bringing this action, because it could not countenance the reckless nature of the reimbursement systems in this case. . . .

Nonetheless, the Court found rather troubling some of the government's procedures that control reimbursements paid to providers of services. Here are some of these practices:

1) The government makes no distinction in reimbursement as to the status or professional attainment or education of the provider. Thus, a non-technical person rendering a coded service will be reimbursed the same amount as a board-certified physician.

2) The sums that the Medicare and Medicaid systems reimburse physicians for services rendered seem to be so far below the norm for charges reimbursed by non-governmental insurance carriers. Indeed, the amount could hardly support a medical practice. As the evidence shows in this case, Board certified physicians in most instances were paid at a rate less than $60 per hour and less than $35 per hour. The government must certainly review these charges because if providers are not adequately compensated, they may not provide the level of care that our elderly and underprivileged citizens require. What is more, the best physicians will simply not come into the system or will refuse to take on senior citizens or the poor as patients.

3) The unrealistic billing concept of requiring doctors to bill only for face-to-face time is not consistent with effective use of a doctor's time or with the provision of good medical services. Doctors must be able to study, research, and discuss a patient's case and be reimbursed for such time.

4) When Medicare dictates that a physician must report each service rendered as a separate code item, the physician is entitled to believe that he will be reimbursed for each of the services rendered. In actuality, the system pays for only one of the multitude of services provided. If this were done by a private sector entity, it would be considered deceitful. Because the government engages in such a deceitful practice does not make it right.

When a provider bills federal health care programs, she signs the following certification on the CMS 1500 (formerly, HCFA 1500) Form:

SIGNATURE OF PHYSICIAN OR SUPPLIER (MEDICARE, CHAMPUS, FECA AND BLACK LUNG)

I certify that the services shown on this form were medically indicated and necessary for the health of the patient and were personally furnished by me or were furnished incident to my professional service by my employee under my immediate personal supervision, except as otherwise expressly permitted by Medicare or CHAMPUS regulations.

For services to be considered as "incident" to a physician's professional service, 1) they must be rendered under the physician's immediate personal supervision by his/her employee, 2) they must be an integral, although incidental part of a covered physician's service, 3) they must be of kinds commonly furnished in physician's offices, and 4) the services of nonphysicians must be included on the physician's bills.

NOTICE: Any one who misrepresents or falsifies essential information to receive payment from Federal funds requested by this form may upon conviction be subject to fine and imprisonment under applicable Federal laws.

QUESTIONS

1. Did Dr. Krizek know that his billing practices were deemed illegal? Do they appear inherently wrong to you?
2. What is the legal or policy relevance of Judge Sporkin's "other observations"?
3. Consider the certification that each physician is deemed to have signed when submitting the Form 1500; do you think doctors read and think about this language and relevant laws each time a claim form is submitted? What is the reason for including this language on each Form 1500?

4. MATERIALITY

For purposes of FCA liability, 31 U.S.C. §3729(b)(2) defines a "claim" as "any request or demand, whether under a contract or otherwise, for money or property and whether or not the United States has title to the money or property, that is presented to an officer, employee, or agent of the United States." For a time, federal circuit courts were split over whether the false claim must be "material," that is, whether it must actually motivate the government's payment under the contract. Now, the statute, at subpart (b)(4), expressly defines materiality as "having a natural tendency to influence, or be capable of influencing, the payment or receipt of money or property."

The FCA's materiality element is akin to the causation element for common law negligence. It is not enough that the defendant breached the standard of care and that the plaintiff suffered injury; the breach must also *cause* the injury. Likewise, the FCA's materiality element suggests that the false claim or statement must "cause"— or motivate or have the tendency to motivate—the government's improper payment.

A further circuit split existed over the recognition of the so-called "implied false certification" theory. As noted above, the CMS billing form contains an express certification of medical necessity and personal performance of services. But lower courts also had allowed claims based on implied certification. The scope of the theory varied: By submitting claims to the government, are providers and suppliers impliedly certifying compliance with all relevant federal laws, or merely laws that are conditions of payment?

The following Supreme Court opinion involved a Massachusetts mental health facility that submitted claims to Medicaid, some of which were for services provided by mental health professionals not properly licensed under state law. The federal district court held that professional licensure was not an express condition of payment; therefore, the plaintiffs had no FCA claim. The First Circuit reversed, holding that licensure was a material precondition of payment; therefore, the plaintiffs had stated a claim. The Supreme Court disagreed with both opinions and elucidated the implied false certification theory and materiality elements of the FCA.

Universal Health Services, Inc. v. United States ex rel. Julio Escobar

136 S. Ct. 1989 (2016)

THOMAS, Justice:

The False Claims Act, 31 U.S.C. §3729 et seq., imposes significant penalties on those who defraud the Government. This case concerns a theory of False Claims Act liability commonly referred to as "implied false certification." According to this theory, when a defendant submits a claim, it impliedly certifies compliance with all conditions of payment. But if that claim fails to disclose the defendant's violation of a material statutory, regulatory, or contractual requirement, so the theory goes, the defendant has made a misrepresentation that renders the claim "false or fraudulent" under §3729(a)(1)(A). This case requires us to consider this theory of liability and to clarify some of the circumstances in which the False Claims Act imposes liability.

We first hold that, at least in certain circumstances, the implied false certification theory can be a basis for liability. Specifically, liability can attach when the defendant submits a claim for payment that makes specific representations about the goods or services provided, but knowingly fails to disclose the defendant's noncompliance with a statutory, regulatory, or contractual requirement. In these circumstances, liability may attach if the omission renders those representations misleading.

We further hold that False Claims Act liability for failing to disclose violations of legal requirements does not turn upon whether those requirements were expressly designated as conditions of payment. Defendants can be liable for violating requirements even if they were not expressly designated as conditions of payment.

Conversely, even when a requirement is expressly designated a condition of payment, not every violation of such a requirement gives rise to liability. What matters is not the label the Government attaches to a requirement, but whether the defendant knowingly violated a requirement that the defendant knows is material to the Government's payment decision.

A misrepresentation about compliance with a statutory, regulatory, or contractual requirement must be material to the Government's payment decision in order to be actionable under the False Claims Act. We clarify below how that rigorous materiality requirement should be enforced.

Because the courts below interpreted §3729(a)(1)(A) differently, we vacate the judgment and remand so that those courts may apply the approach set out in this opinion.

I

A

Enacted in 1863, the False Claims Act "was originally aimed principally at stopping the massive frauds perpetrated by large contractors during the Civil War." "[A] series of sensational congressional investigations" prompted hearings where witnesses "painted a sordid picture of how the United States had been billed for non-existent or worthless goods, charged exorbitant prices for goods delivered, and generally robbed in purchasing the necessities of war." Congress responded by imposing civil and criminal liability for 10 types of fraud on the Government, subjecting violators to double damages, forfeiture, and up to five years' imprisonment.

Since then, Congress has repeatedly amended the Act, but its focus remains on those who present or directly induce the submission of false or fraudulent claims. A "claim" now includes direct requests to the Government for payment as well as reimbursement requests made to the recipients of federal funds under federal benefits programs. The Act's scienter requirement defines "knowing" and "knowingly" to mean that a person has "actual knowledge of the information," "acts in deliberate ignorance of the truth or falsity of the information," or "acts in reckless disregard of the truth or falsity of the information." And the Act defines "material" to mean "having a natural tendency to influence, or be capable of influencing, the payment or receipt of money or property."

Congress also has increased the Act's civil penalties so that liability is "essentially punitive in nature." Defendants are subjected to treble damages plus civil penalties of up to $10,000 per false claim.

B

The alleged False Claims Act violations here arose within the Medicaid program, a joint state-federal program in which healthcare providers serve poor or disabled patients and submit claims for government reimbursement. The facts recited in the complaint, which we take as true at this stage, are as follows. For five years, Yarushka Rivera, a teenage beneficiary of Massachusetts' Medicaid program, received counseling services at Arbour Counseling Services, a satellite mental health facility in Lawrence, Massachusetts, owned and operated by a subsidiary of petitioner Universal Health Services. Beginning in 2004, when Yarushka started having behavioral problems, five medical

> The patient's psychologist's degree was from an unaccredited Internet university, and his medications were prescribed by a nurse who claimed to be a physician.

professionals at Arbour intermittently treated her. In May 2009, Yarushka had an adverse reaction to a medication that a purported doctor at Arbour prescribed after diagnosing her with bipolar disorder. Her condition worsened; she suffered a seizure that required hospitalization. In October 2009, she suffered another seizure and died. She was 17 years old.

Thereafter, an Arbour counselor revealed to respondents Carmen Correa and Julio Escobar—Yarushka's mother and stepfather—that few Arbour employees were actually licensed to provide mental health counseling and that supervision of them was minimal. Respondents discovered that, of the five professionals who had treated Yarushka, only one was properly licensed. The practitioner who diagnosed Yarushka as bipolar identified herself as a psychologist with a Ph.D., but failed to mention that her degree came from an unaccredited Internet college and that Massachusetts had rejected her application to be licensed as a psychologist. Likewise, the practitioner who prescribed medicine to Yarushka, and who was held out as a psychiatrist, was in fact a nurse who lacked authority to prescribe medications absent supervision. Rather than ensuring supervision of unlicensed staff, the clinic's director helped to misrepresent the staff's qualifications. And the problem went beyond those who treated Yarushka. Some 23 Arbour employees lacked licenses to provide mental health services, yet—despite regulatory requirements to the contrary—they counseled patients and prescribed drugs without supervision.

When submitting reimbursement claims, Arbour used payment codes corresponding to different services that its staff provided to Yarushka, such as "Individual Therapy" and "family therapy." Staff members also misrepresented their qualifications and licensing status to the Federal Government to obtain individual National Provider Identification numbers, which are submitted in connection with Medicaid reimbursement claims and correspond to specific job titles. For instance, one Arbour staff member who treated Yarushka registered for a number associated with "'Social Worker, Clinical,'" despite lacking the credentials and licensing required for social workers engaged in mental health counseling. . . .

In 2011, respondents filed a qui tam suit in federal court, alleging that Universal Health had violated the False Claims Act under an implied false certification theory of liability. The operative complaint asserts that Universal Health (acting through Arbour) submitted reimbursement claims that made representations about the specific services provided by specific types of professionals, but that failed to disclose serious violations of regulations pertaining to staff qualifications and licensing requirements for these services. Specifically, the Massachusetts Medicaid program requires satellite facilities to have specific types of clinicians on staff, delineates licensing requirements for particular positions (like psychiatrists, social workers, and nurses), and details supervision requirements for other staff. Universal Health allegedly flouted these regulations because Arbour employed unqualified, unlicensed, and unsupervised staff. The Massachusetts Medicaid program, unaware of these deficiencies, paid the claims. Universal Health thus allegedly defrauded the program, which would not have reimbursed the claims had it known that it was billed for mental health services that were performed by unlicensed and unsupervised staff. The United States declined to intervene.

The District Court granted Universal Health's motion to dismiss the complaint. Circuit precedent had previously embraced the implied false certification theory of liability. But the District Court held that respondents had failed to state a claim under that theory because, with one exception not relevant here, none of the regulations that Arbour violated was a condition of payment.

The United States Court of Appeals for the First Circuit reversed in relevant part and remanded. The court observed that each time a billing party submits a claim, it "implicitly communicate[s] that it conformed to the relevant program requirements, such that it was entitled to payment." To determine whether a claim is "false or fraudulent" based on such implicit communications, the court explained, it "asks simply whether the defendant, in submitting a claim for reimbursement, knowingly misrepresented compliance with a material precondition of payment." In the court's view, a statutory, regulatory, or contractual requirement can be a condition of payment either by expressly identifying itself as such or by implication. The court then held that Universal Health had violated Massachusetts Medicaid regulations that "clearly impose conditions of payment." The court further held that the regulations themselves "constitute[d] dispositive evidence of materiality," because they identified adequate supervision as an "express and absolute" condition of payment and "repeated[ly] reference[d]" supervision.

We granted certiorari to resolve the disagreement among the Courts of Appeals over the validity and scope of the implied false certification theory of liability. The Seventh Circuit has rejected this theory, reasoning that only express (or affirmative) falsehoods can render a claim "false or fraudulent" under 31 U.S.C. §3729(a)(1)(A). Other courts have accepted the theory, but limit its application to cases where defendants fail to disclose violations of expressly designated conditions of payment. Yet others hold that conditions of payment need not be expressly designated as such to be a basis for False Claims Act liability.

II

We first hold that the implied false certification theory can, at least in some circumstances, provide a basis for liability. By punishing defendants who submit "false or fraudulent claims," the False Claims Act encompasses claims that make fraudulent misrepresentations, which include certain misleading omissions. When, as here, a defendant makes representations in submitting a claim but omits its violations of statutory, regulatory, or contractual requirements, those omissions can be a basis for liability if they render the defendant's representations misleading with respect to the goods or services provided.

To reach this conclusion, "[w]e start, as always, with the language of the statute." The False Claims Act imposes civil liability on "any person who . . . knowingly presents, or causes to be presented, a false or fraudulent claim for payment or approval." Congress did not define what makes a claim "false" or "fraudulent." But "[i]t is a settled principle of interpretation that, absent other indication, Congress intends to incorporate the well-settled meaning of the common-law terms it uses." And the term "fraudulent" is a paradigmatic example of a statutory term that incorporates the common-law meaning of fraud.[1]

---

1. The False Claims Act abrogates the common law in certain respects. For instance, the Act's scienter requirement "require[s] no proof of specific intent to defraud." 31 U.S.C. §3729(b)(1)(B). But we presume that Congress retained all other elements of common-law fraud that are consistent with the statutory text because there are no textual indicia to the contrary.

Because common-law fraud has long encompassed certain misrepresentations by omission, "false or fraudulent claims" include more than just claims containing express falsehoods. The parties and the Government agree that misrepresentations by omission can give rise to liability.

The parties instead dispute whether submitting a claim without disclosing violations of statutory, regulatory, or contractual requirements constitutes such an actionable misrepresentation. Respondents and the Government invoke the common-law rule that, while nondisclosure alone ordinarily is not actionable, "[a] representation stating the truth so far as it goes but which the maker knows or believes to be materially misleading because of his failure to state additional or qualifying matter" is actionable. They contend that every submission of a claim for payment implicitly represents that the claimant is legally entitled to payment, and that failing to disclose violations of material legal requirements renders the claim misleading. Universal Health, on the other hand, argues that submitting a claim involves no representations, and that a different common-law rule thus governs: nondisclosure of legal violations is not actionable absent a special "'duty . . . to exercise reasonable care to disclose the matter in question,'" which it says is lacking in Government contracting.

We need not resolve whether all claims for payment implicitly represent that the billing party is legally entitled to payment. The claims in this case do more than merely demand payment. They fall squarely within the rule that half-truths — representations that state the truth only so far as it goes, while omitting critical qualifying information — can be actionable misrepresentations.[2] A classic example of an actionable half-truth in contract law is the seller who reveals that there may be two new roads near a property he is selling, but fails to disclose that a third potential road might bisect the property. "The enumeration of two streets, described as unopened but projected, was a tacit representation that the land to be conveyed was subject to no others, and certainly subject to no others materially affecting the value of the purchase." Likewise, an applicant for an adjunct position at a local college makes an actionable misrepresentation when his resume lists prior jobs and then retirement, but fails to disclose that his "retirement" was a prison stint for perpetrating a $12 million bank fraud.

So too here, by submitting claims for payment using payment codes that corresponded to specific counseling services, Universal Health represented that it had provided individual therapy, family therapy, preventive medication counseling, and other types of treatment. Moreover, Arbour staff members allegedly made further representations in submitting Medicaid reimbursement claims by using National Provider Identification numbers corresponding to specific job titles. And these representations were clearly misleading in context. Anyone informed that a social worker at a Massachusetts mental health clinic provided a teenage patient with individual counseling services would probably — but wrongly — conclude that the clinic had complied with core Massachusetts Medicaid requirements (1) that a counselor "treating children [is] required to have specialized training and experience in children's services," and also (2) that, at a minimum, the social worker

---

2. This rule recurs throughout the common law. In tort law, for example, "if the defendant does speak, he must disclose enough to prevent his words from being misleading." W. Keeton, D. Dobbs, R. Keeton, & D. Owen, Prosser and Keeton on Law of Torts §106, p. 738 (5th ed. 1984). Contract law also embraces this principle. See, *e.g.*, Restatement (Second) of Contracts §161, Comment *a*, p. 432 (1979). . . .

possesses the prescribed qualifications for the job. By using payment and other codes that conveyed this information without disclosing Arbour's many violations of basic staff and licensing requirements for mental health facilities, Universal Health's claims constituted misrepresentations.

Accordingly, we hold that the implied certification theory can be a basis for liability, at least where two conditions are satisfied: first, the claim does not merely request payment, but also makes specific representations about the goods or services provided; and second, the defendant's failure to disclose noncompliance with material statutory, regulatory, or contractual requirements makes those representations misleading half-truths.

> The Court resolved the circuit split, recognizing the theory of implied false certification.

III

The second question presented is whether, as Universal Health urges, a defendant should face False Claims Act liability only if it fails to disclose the violation of a contractual, statutory, or regulatory provision that the Government expressly designated a condition of payment. We conclude that the Act does not impose this limit on liability. But we also conclude that not every undisclosed violation of an express condition of payment automatically triggers liability. Whether a provision is labeled a condition of payment is relevant to but not dispositive of the materiality inquiry.

> Implied false certification claims are not limited to express conditions of payment.

A

Nothing in the text of the False Claims Act supports Universal Health's proposed restriction. Section 3729(a)(1)(A) imposes liability on those who present "false or fraudulent claims" but does not limit such claims to misrepresentations about express conditions of payment. Nor does the common-law meaning of fraud tether liability to violating an express condition of payment. A statement that misleadingly omits critical facts is a misrepresentation irrespective of whether the other party has expressly signaled the importance of the qualifying information.

The False Claims Act's materiality requirement also does not support Universal Health. Under the Act, the misrepresentation must be material to the other party's course of action. But, as discussed below, statutory, regulatory, and contractual requirements are not automatically material, even if they are labeled conditions of payment.

Nor does the Act's scienter requirement, support Universal Health's position. A defendant can have "actual knowledge" that a condition is material without the Government expressly calling it a condition of payment. If the Government failed to specify that guns it orders must actually shoot, but the defendant knows that the Government routinely rescinds contracts if the guns do not shoot, the defendant has "actual knowledge." Likewise, because a reasonable person would realize the imperative of a functioning firearm, a defendant's failure to appreciate the materiality of that condition would amount to "deliberate ignorance" or "reckless disregard" of the "truth or falsity of the information" even if the Government did not spell this out.

Universal Health nonetheless contends that False Claims Act liability should be limited to undisclosed violations of expressly designated conditions of payment to provide defendants with fair notice and to cabin liability. But policy arguments cannot supersede the clear statutory text. In any event, Universal Health's approach risks undercutting these policy goals. The Government might respond by designating every legal requirement an express condition of payment. But billing parties are often subject to thousands of complex statutory and regulatory provisions. Facing False Claims Act liability for violating any of them would hardly help would-be defendants anticipate and prioritize compliance obligations. And forcing the Government to expressly designate a provision as a condition of payment would create further arbitrariness. Under Universal Health's view, misrepresenting compliance with a requirement that the Government expressly identified as a condition of payment could expose a defendant to liability. Yet, under this theory, misrepresenting compliance with a condition of eligibility to even participate in a federal program when submitting a claim would not.

> The Court responded to providers' concerns about sweeping liability for implied false certification with every imaginable statutory and regulatory requirement by strictly enforcing the materiality and scienter requirements.

Moreover, other parts of the False Claims Act allay Universal Health's concerns. "[I]nstead of adopting a circumscribed view of what it means for a claim to be false or fraudulent," concerns about fair notice and open-ended liability "can be effectively addressed through strict enforcement of the Act's materiality and scienter requirements." Those requirements are rigorous.

B

As noted, a misrepresentation about compliance with a statutory, regulatory, or contractual requirement must be material to the Government's payment decision in order to be actionable under the False Claims Act. We now clarify how that materiality requirement should be enforced.

Section 3729(b)(4) defines materiality using language that we have employed to define materiality in other federal fraud statutes: "[T]he term 'material' means having a natural tendency to influence, or be capable of influencing, the payment or receipt of money or property." This materiality requirement descends from "common-law antecedents." Indeed, "the common law could not have conceived of 'fraud' without proof of materiality."

We need not decide whether §3729(a)(1)(A)'s materiality requirement is governed by §3729(b)(4) or derived directly from the common law. Under any understanding of the concept, materiality "look[s] to the effect on the likely or actual behavior of the recipient of the alleged misrepresentation." In tort law, for instance, a "matter is material" in only two circumstances: (1) "[if] a reasonable man would attach importance to [it] in determining his choice of action in the transaction"; or (2) if the defendant knew or had reason to know that the recipient of the representation attaches importance to the specific matter "in determining his choice of action," even though a reasonable person would not. Materiality in contract law is substantially similar.[3]

The materiality standard is demanding. The False Claims Act is not "an all-purpose antifraud statute," or a vehicle for punishing garden-variety breaches of contract or regulatory violations. A misrepresentation cannot be deemed material

---

3. Accord, Williston §69:12, pp. 549-550 ("most popular" understanding is "that a misrepresentation is material if it concerns a matter to which a reasonable person would attach importance in determining his or her choice of action with respect to the transaction involved: which will induce action by a complaining party[,] knowledge of which would have induced the recipient to act differently". . . .

merely because the Government designates compliance with a particular statutory, regulatory, or contractual requirement as a condition of payment. Nor is it sufficient for a finding of materiality that the Government would have the option to decline to pay if it knew of the defendant's noncompliance. Materiality, in addition, cannot be found where noncompliance is minor or insubstantial.

In sum, when evaluating materiality under the False Claims Act, the Government's decision to expressly identify a provision as a condition of payment is relevant, but not automatically dispositive. Likewise, proof of materiality can include, but is not necessarily limited to, evidence that the defendant knows that the Government consistently refuses to pay claims in the mine run of cases based on noncompliance with the particular statutory, regulatory, or contractual requirement. Conversely, if the Government pays a particular claim in full despite its actual knowledge that certain requirements were violated, that is very strong evidence that those requirements are not material. Or, if the Government regularly pays a particular type of claim in full despite actual knowledge that certain requirements were violated, and has signaled no change in position, that is strong evidence that the requirements are not material.

These rules lead us to disagree with the Government's and First Circuit's view of materiality: that any statutory, regulatory, or contractual violation is material so long as the defendant knows that the Government would be entitled to refuse payment were it aware of the violation. At oral argument, the United States explained the implications of its position: If the Government contracts for health services and adds a requirement that contractors buy American-made staplers, anyone who submits a claim for those services but fails to disclose its use of foreign staplers violates the False Claims Act. To the Government, liability would attach if the defendant's use of foreign staplers would entitle the Government not to pay the claim in whole or part — irrespective of whether the Government routinely pays claims despite knowing that foreign staplers were used. Likewise, if the Government required contractors to aver their compliance with the entire U.S. Code and Code of Federal Regulations, then under this view, failing to mention noncompliance with any of those requirements would always be material. The False Claims Act does not adopt such an extraordinarily expansive view of liability. . . .

Because both opinions below assessed respondents' complaint based on interpretations of §3729(a)(1)(A) that differ from ours, we vacate the First Circuit's judgment and remand the case for reconsideration of whether respondents have sufficiently pleaded a False Claims Act violation. We emphasize, however, that the False Claims Act is not a means of imposing treble damages and other | Federal Rule of Civil Procedure Rule 9(b), requiring allegations of fraud to be pled with particularity, applies to the False Claims Act.

penalties for insignificant regulatory or contractual violations. This case centers on allegations of fraud, not medical malpractice. Respondents have alleged that Universal Health misrepresented its compliance with mental health facility requirements that are so central to the provision of mental health counseling that the Medicaid program would not have paid these claims had it known of these violations. Respondents may well have adequately pleaded a violation of §3729(a)(1)(A). But we leave it to the courts below to resolve this in the first instance.

The judgment of the Court of Appeals is vacated, and the case is remanded for further proceedings consistent with this opinion.

It is so ordered.

QUESTIONS

1. Is the *Escobar* opinion a victory for the government and *qui tam* relators?
2. Do you anticipate that the opinion will expand or limit the availability of implied false certification claims in lower courts?
3. Suppose a provider, facing FCA liability, has reason to know that the government is aware of the provider's noncompliance with the regulations at issue and has continued to make payments. What defenses might the provider assert?

5. *QUI TAM* ACTIONS

As the foregoing materials have illustrated, a great number of FCA cases are initiated by whistleblowers, or *qui tam* relators, as authorized under 31 U.S.C. §3730. The threat of FCA liability is greatly increased by the very active role of whistleblowers and the attorneys representing them. Relators often are disgruntled former or current employees or other insiders who become aware of potential wrongdoing through their positions. "*Qui tam*" is an abbreviation of the Latin phrase, "*qui tam pro domino rege quam pro se ipso in hac parte sequitur,*" meaning "[he] who sues in this matter for the king as well as for himself." Relators must first present their complaints in secret to the government, offering the option to intervene and take over the case. If the government declines, the relator may proceed to litigate the case on his own. Either way, successful relators are entitled to a share of any awards assessed against the defendants, and their attorneys are entitled to attorney's fees.

> 31 U.S.C. §3730(b). **Actions by private persons**
>
> (1) A person may bring a civil action for a violation of section 3729 [the FCA] for the person and for the United States Government. The action shall be brought in the name of the Government. The action may be dismissed only if the court and the Attorney General give written consent to the dismissal and their reasons for consenting.
>
> (2) A copy of the complaint and written disclosure of substantially all material evidence and information the person possesses shall be served on the Government pursuant to Rule 4(d)(4) of the Federal Rules of Civil Procedure. The complaint shall be filed in camera, shall remain under seal for at least 60 days, and shall not be served on the defendant until the court so orders. The Government may elect to intervene and proceed with the action within 60 days after it receives both the complaint and the material evidence and information.
>
> (3) The Government may, for good cause shown, move the court for extensions of the time during which the complaint remains under seal under paragraph (2). . . .
>
> (4) Before the expiration of the 60-day period or any extensions obtained under paragraph (3), the Government shall —
>
>   (A) proceed with the action, in which case the action shall be conducted by the Government; or
>
>   (B) notify the court that it declines to take over the action, in which case the person bringing the action shall have the right to conduct the action.
>
> (5) When a person brings an action under this subsection, no person other than the Government may intervene or bring a related action based on the facts underlying the pending action.

If the government intervenes, the relator's portion of the damages is 15 to 25 percent of the proceeds of the action or settlement of the claim. If the government declines to intervene, the relator may recover between 25 and 30 percent. In either case, the court may award reasonable expenses, fees, and costs against the defendant. 31 U.S.C. §3730(d).

Under the FCA, the *qui tam* relator must be the "original source" of the allegations or transactions on which the complaint is based. That means that information that had already been publicly disclosed through the media, congressional or other federal report, audit, hearing, or investigation, or government criminal, civil, or administrative litigation cannot support a *qui tam* action. 31 U.S.C. §3730(e)(4).

In addition to the "public disclosure" bar, the FCA *qui tam* provisions contain a "first to file" bar, at 31 U.S.C. §3731(b)(5), at issue in the following 2015 U.S. Supreme Court decision. To understand why health lawyers should care about a decision involving a U.S. military contractor for the war in Iraq, keep in mind that the defendant's "once filed, always barred" interpretation would have blocked all related FCA cases, as long as the complaint was ever filed, and even if it was subsequently dismissed voluntarily or without prejudice.

Kellogg Brown & Root Services, Inc. v. United States ex rel. Carter

135 S. Ct. 1970 (2015)

Justice ALITO delivered the opinion of the Court.

Wars have often provided "exceptional opportunities" for fraud on the United States Government. "The False Claims Act was adopted in 1863 and signed into law by President Abraham Lincoln in order to combat rampant fraud in Civil War defense contracts." S. Rep. No. 99-345, p. 8 (1986). Predecessors of the Wartime Suspension of Limitations Act were enacted to address similar problems that arose during the First and Second World Wars.

In this case, we must decide two questions regarding those laws: first, whether the Wartime Suspension of Limitations Act applies only to criminal charges or also to civil claims; second, whether the False Claims Act's first-to-file bar keeps new claims out of court only while related claims are still alive or whether it may bar those claims in perpetuity.

I

A

The False Claims Act (FCA) imposes liability on any person who "knowingly presents . . . a false or fraudulent claim for payment or approval," 31 U.S.C. §3729(a)(1)(A), "to an officer or employee of the United States," 3729(b)(2)(A)(i). The FCA may be enforced not just through litigation brought by the Government itself, but also through civil *qui tam* actions that are filed by private parties, called relators, "in the name of the Government." §3730(b).

In a *qui tam* suit under the FCA, the relator files a complaint under seal and serves the United States with a copy of the complaint and a disclosure of all material evidence. After reviewing these materials, the United States may "proceed with the action, in which case the action shall be conducted by the Government," or it may "notify the court that it declines to take over the action, in which case the person bringing the action shall have the right to conduct the action." Regardless of the option that the United States selects, it retains the right at any time to dismiss the action entirely, or to settle the case.

> The complaint is filed "under seal," meaning that it is not served on the defendant and remains entirely secret. If the government accepts the case, it can remain under seal for years while the investigation proceeds.

The FCA imposes two restrictions on *qui tam* suits that are relevant here. One, the "first-to-file" bar, precludes a *qui tam* suit "based on the facts underlying [a] pending action." The other, the FCA's statute of limitations provision, states that a *qui tam* action must be brought within six years of a violation or within three years of the date by which the United States should have known about a violation. In no circumstances, however, may a suit be brought more than 10 years after the date of a violation.

II

Petitioners are defense contractors and related entities that provided logistical services to the United States military during the armed conflict in Iraq. From January to April 2005, respondent worked in Iraq for one of the petitioners as a water purification operator. He subsequently filed a *qui tam* complaint against petitioners (*Carter I*), alleging that they had fraudulently billed the Government for water purification services that were not performed or not performed properly. The Government declined to intervene.

In 2010, shortly before trial, the Government informed the parties about an earlier filed *qui tam* lawsuit, *United States ex rel. Thorpe v. Halliburton Co.*, that arguably contained similar claims. This initiated a remarkable sequence of dismissals and filings.

The District Court held that respondent's suit was related to *Thorpe* and thus dismissed his case without prejudice under the first-to-file bar. Respondent appealed, and while his appeal was pending, *Thorpe* was dismissed for failure to prosecute. Respondent quickly filed a new complaint (*Carter II*), but the District Court dismissed this second complaint under the first-to-file rule because respondent's own earlier case was still pending on appeal. Respondent then voluntarily dismissed this appeal, and in June 2011, more than six years after the alleged fraud, he filed yet another complaint (*Carter III*), and it is this complaint that is now at issue.

Petitioners sought dismissal of this third complaint under the first-to-file rule, pointing to two allegedly related cases, one in Maryland and one in Texas, that had been filed in the interim between the filing of *Carter I* and *Carter III*. This time, the court dismissed respondent's complaint with prejudice. The court held that the latest complaint was barred under the first-to-file rule because the Maryland suit was already pending when that complaint was filed. . . .

The Fourth Circuit reversed, rejecting the District Court's analysis of both the [statute of limitations under the Wartime Suspensions of Limitations Act (WSLA)] and first-to-file issues. Concluding that the WSLA applies to civil claims based on fraud committed during the conflict in Iraq, the Court of Appeals held that respondent's claims had been filed on time. The Court of Appeals also held that the first-to-file bar ceases to apply once a related action is dismissed. Since the Maryland and Texas cases had been dismissed by the time of the Fourth Circuit's decision, the court held that respondent had the right to refile his case. The Court of Appeals thus remanded *Carter III* with instructions to dismiss without prejudice.

After this was done, respondent filed *Carter IV*, but the District Court dismissed *Carter IV* on the ground that the petition for a writ of certiorari in *Carter III* (the case now before us) was still pending.

We granted that petition, and we now reverse in part and affirm in part.

[The Court's decision regarding the applicability of the WSLA to civil claims is omitted.]

IV

Petitioners acknowledge that respondent has raised other arguments that, if successful, could render at least one claim timely on remand. We therefore consider whether respondent's claims must be dismissed with prejudice under the first-to-file rule. We conclude that dismissal with prejudice was not called for.

The first-to-file bar provides that "[w]hen a person brings an action . . . no person other than the Government may intervene or bring a related action based on the facts underlying the *pending* action." 31 U.S.C. §3730(b)(5) (emphasis added). The term "pending" means "[r]emaining undecided; awaiting decision." Black's 1314 (10th ed. 2014). If the reference to a "pending" action in the FCA is interpreted in this way, an earlier suit bars a later suit while the earlier suit remains undecided but ceases to bar that suit once it is dismissed. We see no reason not to interpret the term "pending" in the FCA in accordance with its ordinary meaning.

Petitioners argue that Congress used the term "pending" in a very different — and very peculiar — way. In the FCA, according to petitioners, the term "pending" "is 'used as a short-hand for the first filed action.'" Thus, as petitioners see things, the first-filed action remains "pending" even after it has been dismissed, and it forever bars any subsequent related action.

This interpretation does not comport with any known usage of the term "pending." Under this interpretation, *Marbury v. Madison* is still "pending." So is the trial of Socrates.

. . . .

Not only does petitioners' argument push the term "pending" far beyond the breaking point, but it would lead to strange results that Congress is unlikely to have wanted. Under petitioners' interpretation, a first-filed suit would bar all subsequent related suits even if that earlier suit was dismissed for a reason having nothing to do with the merits. Here, for example, the *Thorpe* suit, which provided the ground for the initial invocation of the first-to-file rule, was dismissed for failure to prosecute. Why would Congress want the abandonment of an earlier suit to bar a later potentially successful suit that might result in a large recovery for the Government?

> Petitioners' argument would transform the first-to-file bar into a "get out of jail free" card, as long as the action is dismissed, for any reason.

Petitioners contend that interpreting "pending" to mean pending would produce practical problems, and there is some merit to their arguments. In particular, as petitioners note, if the first-to-file bar is lifted once the first-filed action ends, defendants may be reluctant to settle such actions for the full amount that they would accept if there were no prospect of subsequent suits asserting the same claims. Respondent and the United States argue that the doctrine of claim preclusion may protect defendants if the first-filed action is decided on the merits, but that issue is not before us in this case. The False Claims Act's *qui tam* provisions present many interpretive challenges, and it is beyond our ability in this case to make them operate together smoothly like a finely tuned machine. We hold that a *qui tam* suit under the FCA ceases to be "pending" once it is dismissed. We therefore agree with the Fourth Circuit that the dismissal with prejudice of respondent's one live claim was error.

_____

QUESTION

Is Justice Alito's interpretation consistent with the goals of the FCA?

6. CRIMINAL SANCTIONS FOR FALSE CLAIMS

The FCA addresses a wide range of billing practices and errors, including upcoding, unbundling, billing for services not rendered, billing for medically unnecessary or otherwise noncovered services, billing for services without proper documentation or physician certification, billing for worthless services, falsely certifying compliance with conditions of payments, submitting false records or documents in support of payment requests, and retaining overpayments. In addition to treble damages and CMPs discussed above, these practices may support criminal liability under a generally applicable federal statute and a statute specific to federal health care programs.

The general federal statute, 18 U.S.C. §287, provides:

> Whoever makes or presents to any person or officer in the civil, military, or naval service of the United States, or to any department or agency thereof, any claim upon or against the United States, or any department or agency thereof, knowing such claim to be false, fictitious, or fraudulent, shall be imprisoned not more than five years and shall be subject to a fine in the amount provided in this title.

18 U.S.C. §3571 provides the schedule of fines, including up to $250,000 for an individual, or $500,000 for an organization, convicted of a felony.

Also, the Social Security Act (SSA), which contains the Medicare and Medicaid statutes, imposes criminal liability for some of the same acts covered by the FCA, as well as other acts specific to federal health care programs. 42 U.S.C. §1320a-7b, titled "Criminal penalties for acts involving Federal health care programs," prohibits:

> **(a) Making or causing to be made false statements or representations**
> Whoever —
> (1) knowingly and willfully makes or causes to be made any false statement or representation of a material fact in any application for any benefit or payment under a Federal health care program,
> (2) at any time knowingly and willfully makes or causes to be made any false statement or representation of a material fact for use in determining rights to such benefit or payment,
> (3) having knowledge of the occurrence of any event affecting
> (A) his initial or continued right to any such benefit or payment, or
> (B) the initial or continued right to any such benefit or payment of any other individual in whose behalf he has applied for or is receiving such benefit or payment, conceals or fails to disclose such event with an intent fraudulently to secure such benefit or payment either in a greater

[handwritten margin note: Always ask if there are any parallel proceedings when your client has a civil case — there may also be criminal proceedings]

amount or quantity than is due or when no such benefit or payment is authorized,

(4) having made application to receive any such benefit or payment for the use and benefit of another and having received it, knowingly and willfully converts such benefit or payment or any part thereof to a use other than for the use and benefit of such other person,

(5) presents or causes to be presented a claim for a physician's service for which payment may be made under a Federal health care program and knows that the individual who furnished the service was not licensed as a physician, or

(6) for a fee knowingly and willfully counsels or assists an individual to dispose of assets (including by any transfer in trust) in order for the individual to become eligible for medical assistance under a State plan under subchapter XIX of this chapter, if disposing of the assets results in the imposition of a period of ineligibility for such assistance under section 1396p(c) of this title,

. . . .

Violators of the SSA's criminal penalties provisions are subject to felony prosecution and fines up to $25,000 or imprisonment for up to five years, or both. Those who counsel or assist others with violation of the SSA may be guilty of a misdemeanor and, upon conviction, fined up to $10,000 or imprisoned for up to one year, or both.

Despite the availability of criminal sanctions and health care–specific nature of the SSA provisions, the general civil FCA remains prosecutors' go-to statute for policing health care fraud and abuse because of its relatively easy-to-satisfy scienter requirement and potential for exponentially high CMPs and treble damages. In addition, *qui tam* relators and their attorneys file a high number of FCA cases. Moreover, as the following sections explain, violation of other health care fraud and abuse statutes may also constitute a false claim under the FCA.

C. ANTI-KICKBACK STATUTE

Offering gifts or rewards for past or future business referrals, such as loyalty programs like frequent-flyer miles, is commonplace in other industries. But in health care, those offers or payments may be criminal. The SSA's provisions on "Criminal penalties for acts involving Federal health care programs," discussed briefly above, also prohibit "illegal remunerations." This is also known as the "Anti-Kickback Statute," 42 U.S.C. §1320a-7b(b).

The Anti-Kickback Statute prohibits "quid pro quo" arrangements, such as bestowing a benefit or favor or anything of value in exchange for referral of patients covered under government health care programs. Payments or inducements offered directly to patients, such as coupons, discounts, fee waivers, and giveaways, are also prohibited under the Anti-Kickback Statute.

The rationale for the Anti-Kickback Statute is concern that patients and providers will be improperly influenced by factors other than best medical judgment if rewards are offered. Related to that overarching concern is the belief that providers and patients will seek out more services and supplies than they would absent the inducement, thereby increasing utilization and government program costs. Moreover, providers that are able to afford such payments and rewards would compete unfairly with less well-resourced providers. Finally, the federal government can simply place limitations on the use of federal funds, regardless of the common practices in other industries.

1. CRIMINAL STATUTE

Although the civil sanctions available under the False Claims Act can be very steep, the Anti-Kickback Statute exposes potential defendants to criminal sanctions, including fines and incarceration. Health care providers that contract with the government under Medicare and Medicaid as well as other businesses or services that may do business with health care providers may be liable. The DOJ's 2015 policy statement regarding "Individual Accountability for Corporate Wrongdoing" (known as the "Yates Memo," for Deputy Attorney General Sally Quillian Yates, who issued the policy), further raises the stakes for individuals involved in health care fraud and abuse. *See* https://www.justice.gov/dag/file/769036/download.

> It is essential to correctly cite all of the sections and subsections of the Anti-Kickback Statute; otherwise, you will be citing a different law with different standards.

42 U.S.C. §1320a-7b(b). Illegal remunerations

(1) Whoever knowingly and willfully solicits or receives any remuneration (including any kickback, bribe, or rebate) directly or indirectly, overtly or covertly, in cash or in kind—

    (A) in return for referring an individual to a person for the furnishing or arranging for the furnishing of any item or service for which payment may be made in whole or in part under a Federal health care program, or

    (B) in return for purchasing, leasing, ordering, or arranging for or recommending purchasing, leasing, or ordering any good, facility, service, or item for which payment may be made in whole or in part under a Federal health care program, shall be guilty of a felony and upon conviction thereof, shall be fined not more than $25,000 or imprisoned for not more than five years, or both.

(2) Whoever knowingly and willfully offers or pays any remuneration (including any kickback, bribe, or rebate) directly or indirectly, overtly or covertly, in cash or in kind to any person to induce such person—

    (A) to refer an individual to a person for the furnishing or arranging for the furnishing of any item or service for which payment may be made in whole or in part under a Federal health care program, or

    (B) to purchase, lease, order, or arrange for or recommend purchasing, leasing, or ordering any good, facility, service, or item for which payment may be made in whole or in part under a Federal health care program. . . .

The Anti-Kickback Statute imposes criminal liability for both sides of the transaction—both soliciting and receiving, as well as offering or paying illegal remuneration. It is possible, however, for the state-of-mind requirement to be met with respect to one party but not the other. "Remuneration" is defined broadly and may include cash, free or below-market rates, swapping, cross-referrals, payments for "sham" services, discounts, absorbing costs the referral source otherwise would pay, among other direct, indirect, cash, in-kind exchanges. A wide array of activities have been analyzed as potential violations of the Anti-Kickback Statute, including restocking ambulances with hospital supplies after delivering a patient; installing computer equipment in physician offices that links to a hospital's electronic medical records system; giving physicians free lunches and parking; and offering hotels for patients' families who travel long distances to the hospital.

The Office of Inspector General of the U.S. Department of Health and Human Services also has authority to impose administrative sanctions, including CMPs up to $50,000 per violation, civil damages up to three times the amount of the kickback, and exclusion from federal health care program participation. *See* 42 U.S.C. §§1320a-7a(a) (CMPs), 1320a-7 (mandatory program exclusion).

In addition to those criminal and civil sanctions, Anti-Kickback Statute violations may also support FCA civil liability, which cases may be initiated by either the government or *qui tam* relators. The theory is that filing a claim for reimbursement becomes a false claim when the arrangement also violated the Anti-Kickback Statute. Those "bootstrapped" cases are common and important.

The following Department of Justice settlement announcement provides a prime example of Anti-Kickback Statute and related charges, brought initially by a *qui tam* relator under the FCA. Note the remuneration at issue included free trips to resorts and free drug samples that doctors sold to patients. The company also remunerated physicians by selling the drug to physicians with secret discounts, then physicians billed the full price to the Medicare program, a then-popular practice known as "marketing the spread."

> For details and other examples, see the advisory opinions issued by the Office of Inspector General (OIG), http://oig.hhs.gov/compliance/advisory-opinions/.

FOR IMMEDIATE RELEASE
WEDNESDAY, OCTOBER 3, 2001
WWW.USDOJ.GOV

TAP PHARMACEUTICAL PRODUCTS INC. AND SEVEN OTHERS CHARGED WITH HEALTH CARE CRIMES; COMPANY AGREES TO PAY $875 MILLION TO SETTLE CHARGES

Boston, MA... United States Attorney Michael J. Sullivan, Department of Health and Human Services Inspector General Janet Rehnquist, Assistant Inspector General for Investigations and Director of the Department of Defense Criminal Investigation Service Carol Levy, and Special Agent in Charge of the Federal Bureau of Investigation in New England Charles S. Prouty, announced today that:

(1) TAP Pharmaceutical Products Inc. ("TAP"), a major American pharmaceutical manufacturer, has agreed to pay $875,000,000 to resolve criminal charges and civil liabilities in connection with its fraudulent drug pricing and marketing conduct with regard to Lupron, a drug sold by TAP primarily for treatment of advanced prostate cancer in men. The global agreement includes:

(a) TAP has agreed to plead guilty to a conspiracy to violate the Prescription Drug Marketing Act and to pay a $290,000,000 criminal fine, the largest criminal fine ever in a health care fraud prosecution. The plea agreement between the United States and TAP specifically states that TAP's criminal conduct caused losses of $145,000,000.

> The largest health care fraud settlement to date was the GlaxoSmithKline $3 billion settlement in 2012, which included a $1 billion criminal fine.

(b) TAP has agreed to settle its federal civil False Claims Act liabilities and to pay the U.S. Government $559,483,560 for filing false and fraudulent claims with the Medicare and Medicaid programs as a result of TAP's fraudulent drug pricing schemes and sales and marketing misconduct.

(c) TAP has agreed to settle its civil liabilities to the fifty states and the District of Columbia and to pay them $25,516,440 for filing false and fraudulent claims with the states, as a result of TAP's drug pricing and marketing misconduct, and from TAP's failure to provide the state Medicaid programs TAP's best price for those drugs as required by law.

(d) TAP has agreed to comply with the terms of a sweeping corporate integrity agreement which, among other things, significantly changes the manner in which TAP supervises its marketing and sales staff, and ensures that TAP will report to the Medicare and Medicaid programs the true average sale price for drugs reimbursed by those programs.

Corporate Integrity Agreements, also known as CIAs, are a feature of almost every settlement agreement, designed to reform internal corporate governance and compliance with laws. They typically have five-year terms and are published on the HHS Web site, http://oig.hhs.gov/compliance/corporate-integrity-agreements/cia-documents.asp.

(2) A federal grand jury returned an indictment unsealed today, charging one physician and six TAP managers with conspiracy to pay kickbacks to doctors and other customers, conspiracy to defraud the state Medicaid programs on TAP's obligation to sell products to those programs at its best price, and conspiracy to violate the Prescription Drug Marketing Act by causing free samples to be illegally billed to the Medicare program. The indictment charges that the TAP defendants offered to give things of value, including free drugs, so-called educational grants, trips to resorts, free consulting services, medical equipment, and forgiveness of debt, to physicians and other customers to obtain their referrals of prescriptions for Lupron to Medicare program beneficiaries, in violation of the anti-kickback statute. The indictment also charges that the TAP defendants aided and abetted, and caused the billings to hundreds of elderly Medicare program beneficiaries and to the Medicare program directly, for thousands of free samples of Lupron, used in the treatment of prostate cancer, in violation of the Prescription Drug Marketing Act. . . .

Prior to yesterday's indictment, four other physicians have been charged and have pleaded guilty in this investigation. . . .

AWP offers just one example of the potential for "gaming" the Medicare reimbursement methodology, a problem that is especially acute when providers' costs or charges are the basis for payment. Consider that potential in reference to Medicare's shift to prospective payment systems and fee schedules, discussed in Chapter 2.

Lupron is marketed by TAP primarily for the treatment of prostate cancer. Lupron is identical in effectiveness to the drug Zolodex, produced by a competitor, which was also available for prescription in the 1990s. While Medicare does not pay for most drugs needed by Medicare beneficiaries, Medicare does cover drugs, such as Lupron, that must be injected under the supervision of a physician. Medicare paid for 80% of either the urologist's charge for Lupron or the average wholesale price reported by TAP, whichever was lower, and the patient was responsible for the remaining 20% as a copayment.

As part of its civil allegations, the Government alleged that throughout the 1990s, TAP set and controlled the price at which the Medicare program reimbursed physicians for the prescription of Lupron by reporting its average wholesale price ("AWP"). The

AWP reported by TAP was significantly higher than the average sales price TAP offered physicians and other customers for the drug. The Government alleged that TAP marketed the spread between its discounted prices paid by physicians and the significantly higher Medicare reimbursement based on AWP as an inducement to physicians to obtain their Lupron business. The Government further alleged that TAP concealed the true discounted prices paid by physicians from Medicare, and falsely advised physicians to report the higher AWP rather than their real discounted price for the drug. The Government further alleged that TAP set its AWPs of Lupron at levels far higher than the price for which wholesalers or distributors actually sold the drug, resulting in falsely inflated prices that were neither the physician's actual cost nor the true wholesaler's average price.

"The Medicare and Medicaid drug programs are bulwarks against the financial hardship that can be caused by the need for life-saving medical treatments," said Robert D. McCallum, Jr., Assistant Attorney General for the Justice Department's Civil Division. "These programs cannot afford abuses that enrich doctors or drug companies at the expense of taxpayers and patients. This settlement agreement and the compliance steps that TAP has agreed to take will reinforce the government's long-standing objective of paying Medicare and Medicaid providers for the reasonable costs of the drugs they administer."

"The urologists and the TAP employees who knowingly participated in this broad conspiracy took advantage of older Americans suffering from prostate cancer. The indictment unsealed today alleges that TAP employees sought to influence the doctors' decisions about what drug to prescribe to patients by giving them kickbacks and bribes, from free samples to free consulting services to expensive trips to golf and ski resorts to so-called educational grants," said U.S. Attorney Sullivan. "In all instances where the kickbacks worked to ensure the prescription of TAP's product Lupron, the Medicare Program and the elderly Americans suffering from prostate cancer paid more for their care than if the doctor had prescribed the competitor's product."

"Medicare beneficiaries and all American patients need to get the right pharmaceuticals, based on medical criteria, and at a fair price. This is crucial both to ensure good quality health care and to use our resources effectively. Today's settlement is a clear message that the federal government will protect the best interests of beneficiaries and taxpayers," said HHS Secretary Tommy G. Thompson.

"This prosecution has resulted in the largest criminal and civil recoveries in any health care fraud case in the country. The fraud schemes used by TAP Pharmaceuticals and others impact[ ] significantly on the integrity of TRICARE, the Department of Defense's healthcare system," stated DCIS Special Agent in Charge Edward Bradley. "Healthcare fraud increases patients' costs and negatively [a]ffects the delivery of health care services to over 8 million military members, retirees, and their dependents."

> Proof of actual harm to a patient or the government is not necessary to establish a violation of the Anti-Kickback Statute.

The indictment unsealed today against the seven individuals alleges that inducements to physicians included free products; free consulting services; trips to expensive golf and ski resorts; money disguised as "educational grants," but in fact was used and intended to be used for many purposes, including cocktail party bar tabs, office Christmas parties, medical equipment, travel expenses for urologists and their staff to attend conferences; and discounts on Lupron sold to treat endometriosis in women to effect a lower price on Lupron used in the treatment of men with prostate cancer.

The investigation commenced in the District of Massachusetts in 1997 after a urologist employed by Tufts Associated Health Maintenance Organization ("Tufts HMO") in Waltham, Dr. Joseph Gerstein, reported to law enforcement authorities that he had been offered an educational grant if he would reverse a decision he had made on behalf of Tufts that it would only cover the less expensive drug Zoladex. As charged in the indictment, SWIRSKI and CHASE met with Dr. Gerstein after he began working with the FBI and the Office of Inspector General, and during those meetings, offered him $65,000 in educational grants that he could use for any purpose "whatever," together with discounts on other products, if he would reverse Tufts' decision not to include Lupron on its formulary for treating patients that it insured who were suffering from prostate cancer. The investigation was also triggered by a civil False Claims Act suit filed in 1996 by Douglas Durand, after he had quit his employment at TAP as Vice President of Sales, after just one year because of his concerns about the illegal marketing conduct of some of TAP's employees.

Qui tam relators may be awarded close to one-third of the judgment, amounting to a hefty "bounty."

The civil False Claims Act provides that where persons submit, cause others to submit, or conspire to submit, false or fraudulent claims to the United States Government, including its federal health care programs, the Government is entitled to recover treble damages and $5,500 to $11,000 for each false or fraudulent claim submitted. Private individuals, like Dr. Gerstein and Douglas Durand, are allowed to file whistleblower suits under the False Claims Act to bring the government information about wrongdoing, and if the government is successful in resolving or litigating their claims, to share in the recovery by receiving generally 15% to 25% of the amount recovered. As a part of today's resolution, those two individuals together with Tufts Associated HMO will share as whistleblowers, pursuant to the Congressional directive in the False Claims Act, 17% of the civil recovery, or an amount of approximately $95 million.

"The payment by TAP of nearly $900 million including the highest criminal fine ever imposed on any health care company, and the indictment of the six TAP employees sends a very strong signal to the pharmaceutical industry that it best police its employees' conduct and deal strongly with those who would gain sales at the expense of the health care programs for the poor and the elderly and the persons insured by those programs," said U.S. Attorney Sullivan.

As part of a condition for doing business in the future with providers who are members of the Medicare and Medicaid programs, TAP agreed to enter into an extensive Corporate Integrity Agreement. That agreement provides for significant training of TAP's sales and marketing employees and changes in supervision and controls. It also requires TAP to report to the Medicare and Medicaid programs accurate pricing information showing TAP's true average sales price.

"In recent years, the pharmaceutical industry has come under increasing scrutiny for its pricing, sales, and marketing practices. The OIG, together with other government agencies, will use all available enforcement authorities, where appropriate, to address these practices," said HHS Inspector General Janet Rehnquist.

2. SCIENTER REQUIREMENT UNDER THE ANTI-KICKBACK STATUTE

The Anti-Kickback Statute, as a criminal statute, requires that the person act "knowingly and willfully." The ACA legislatively overrules prior case law interpreting the intent standard to require both intent to induce referrals and knowledge that the arrangement was unlawful. *See, e.g.,* Hanlester Network v. Shalala, 51 F.3d 1390, 1400 (9th Cir. 1995) (holding that the Anti-Kickback Statute is not violated unless the defendant knew the AKS prohibited the giving or receiving of remuneration in return for referrals and acted with specific intent to disobey the law). The ACA added 42 U.S.C. §1320a-7b(h), which relaxes the scienter requirement under the Anti-Kickback Statute: "With respect to violations of this section, a person need not have actual knowledge of this section or specific intent to commit a violation of this section."

That amendment expands the risk of criminal liability for illegal remuneration. The following Seventh Circuit decision further discusses the Anti-Kickback Statute's scienter requirement.

United States v. Borrasi

639 F.3d 774 (7th Cir. 2011)

Roland Borrasi, a medical doctor, was convicted of Medicare fraud after he accepted a salary from a hospital in exchange for continually referring patients to the facility, a violation of 42 U.S.C. §1320a-7b. In this appeal, Borrasi attacks both his conviction and his sentence. We find that the district court did not err by admitting minutes from hospital committee meetings to prove attendance records while excluding discussion of reports to which the minutes refer, as the latter constituted inadmissible hearsay. Because the Medicare fraud statute criminalizes payments when induction of referrals is among the purposes for the payments, we also find that the district court did not err in instructing the jury. Accordingly, we affirm his conviction. In addition, we find that the district court did not err in sentencing Borrasi. It reasonably estimated the loss amount in determining his offense level, it properly assessed a leadership enhancement to his offense level, and it expressed adequate reasons to sentence Borrasi to a longer term than his co-defendant. Accordingly, we affirm his sentence as well.

I. Background

Dr. Borrasi owned Integrated Health Centers, S.C. ("Integrated"), a corporate group of healthcare providers in Romeoville, Illinois. He worked primarily at nursing homes and hospitals. Through this work, he became acquainted with Chief Executive Officer Wendy Mamoon, Director of Operations Mahmood Baig, and other officers and directors of Rock Creek Center, L.P., a licensed inpatient psychiatric hospital in Lemont, Illinois. Reimbursements from the Medicare federal health care program constituted the vast majority of payments received by Rock Creek.

At some time between 1999 and 2002, Borrasi, Mamoon, Baig, and others conspired to pay bribes to Borrasi and other individuals at

> Rock Creek is an acute inpatient psychiatric hospital. Dr. Borrasi was convicted for sending 484 of his patients there. Note that the Anti-Kickback Statute may be violated even if the level of treatment was entirely appropriate for the patients' conditions.

Integrated in exchange for an increasing stream of Medicare patient referrals. Doctors Zafer Jawich, Bruce Roper, and Abhin Singla, as well as psychologist Agnes Jonas, were among those employed at Integrated at that time. Over that period, a sum of $647,204 in potential bribes was paid to Borrasi and Integrated physicians by Rock Creek. In 2001 alone, Borrasi referred approximately 484 Medicare patients to Rock Creek.

In order to conceal these bribes, Borrasi and other Integrated employees were placed on the Rock Creek payroll, given false titles and faux job descriptions, and asked to submit false time sheets. Borrasi, for example, was named "Service Medical Director" and was allegedly required to be available at all times; Baig later testified that Borrasi was not expected to perform any of the duties listed in his job description. According to minutes of Rock Creek's various committee meetings, Borrasi and some Integrated physicians occasionally attended meetings and submitted reports of their work. But they attended only a very small percentage of the actual meetings, and multiple witnesses testified to rarely seeing them in the Rock Creek facility for meetings or other duties. Jonas, Jawich, and Roper each testified that the Integrated physicians did not perform their assigned administrative duties, their reports and time sheets notwithstanding. Baig testified that he, Borrasi, and Mamoon did not expect the Integrated physicians to perform any actual administrative duties.

Many of these patients were discharged from the Rock Creek hospital back to the nursing homes that Borrasi controlled, another violation of the Anti-Kickback Statute.

In addition, Rock Creek paid the salary for Integrated's secretary, as well as lease payments for one of Integrated's offices. This arrangement purportedly gave Rock Creek an outpatient clinic at Borrasi's building and certainly supplemented Borrasi's rent. Further, Baig was paid both to oversee the admission and stays of Integrated's referrals to Rock Creek and also to ensure the referred patients were returned to nursing homes and facilities that Borrasi could access and control. These methods enabled Rock Creek and Borrasi to maximize their Medicare reimbursement claims.

In December 2006, a grand jury returned an indictment against Borrasi, Mamoon, and Baig, charging them with one count of conspiracy to defraud the United States government, in violation of 18 U.S.C. §371, and six counts each of Medicare-related bribery, in violation of 42 U.S.C. §1320a-7b et seq. Baig pled guilty to all seven counts, but Mamoon and Borrasi proceeded to trial. The three-week trial included testimony from Integrated and Rock Creek employees; documentary evidence comprising time sheets, attendance records from meeting minutes, and Medicare reimbursement claims; and recordings of Borrasi's conversations with Integrated physicians recorded by Singla, including one in which Borrasi admitted to referring patients in exchange for "free money" from Rock Creek. The jury returned verdicts of guilty on each count against Borrasi and Mamoon.

The district court then held a joint, two-day sentencing hearing for Borrasi and Mamoon. . . . The court sentenced Borrasi to seventy-two months' imprisonment and two years' supervised release. Mamoon was sentenced to six months' imprisonment, one year of home confinement, and five years' supervised release. Each defendant was required to pay $497,204 in restitution.

Borrasi then moved the district court to reconsider his sentence, arguing that it should be significantly lower to comport with Mamoon's. After holding a hearing on the matter, the district court denied his motion, concluding that the disparate sentences were justified by the facts of the case and the individual defendants' characteristics. Borrasi then timely appealed.

II. Analysis

Borrasi challenges both his conviction and his sentence in this appeal. He first argues that two errors during the guilt phase of his trial require a new trial. He then argues that, even if his conviction stands, we must remand for resentencing because of three errors during the sentencing phase. The government argues that the decisions about which Borrasi complains were not erroneous. We will consider each of Borrasi's five issues in turn, beginning with the alleged infirmities in his conviction.

A. Challenges to Conviction

At the conclusion of his trial, Borrasi moved for a new trial or, in the alternative, a judgment of acquittal, alleging twelve separate grounds for relief that included alleged evidentiary, procedural, and instructional errors. On appeal, he wisely limits his attack on his conviction to two allegations of error. His first allegation of error involves an evidentiary ruling, and the second focuses on the government's commentary during closing arguments regarding the statute he was charged with violating. We find neither argument persuasive.

[Discussion of evidentiary ruling regarding exclusion of hearsay omitted.]

2. Interpretation of 42 U.S.C. §1320a-7b

Borrasi's second challenge to his conviction turns on the interpretation of the criminal statute he was charged with violating and conspiring to violate. Because medical services for the patients Borrasi referred to Rock Creek were paid for by Medicare, his referrals and conduct were subject to certain statutory restrictions. Borrasi was charged, for example, with violating one statute designed to help combat health care fraud:

> [W]hoever knowingly and willfully solicits or receives any remuneration (including any kickback, bribe, or rebate) . . . in return for referring an individual to a person for the furnishing or arranging for the furnishing of any item or service for which payment may be made in whole or in part under a Federal health care program . . . shall be guilty of a felony and upon conviction thereof, shall be fined not more than $25,000 or imprisoned for not more than five years, or both.

42 U.S.C. §1320a-7b(b)(1). The government theorized that Borrasi and the other Integrated physicians received payments—in the guise of salaries—from Rock Creek for their referrals of Medicare patients.

Borrasi points out, however, that the statute exempts some behavior from its coverage. It does not criminalize "any amount paid by an employer to an employee (who has a bona fide employment relationship with such employer) for employment in the provision of covered items or services." 42 U.S.C. §1320a-7b(b)(3). Seizing this language, Borrasi argues that the prosecution prejudicially misstated the law in its closing argument by suggesting that it did not matter if any portion of Rock Creek's payments to him or other Integrated physicians was pursuant to legitimate employment relationships because the statute was violated if any portion of the payments was for patient referrals. He contends that the government's argument to the jury nullified his theory of defense and that the district court did not cure the misconduct by striking the argument and by giving an adequate curative instruction.

> Dr. Borrasi argued that the payments fit within the bona fide employment relationships safe harbor.

Because Borrasi's challenge to the district court's jury instructions necessarily implicates a question of law—the scope of §1320a-7b(b)(3)'s exemption—we review the district court's instructions de novo. We also review de novo whether a particular instruction was appropriate as a matter of law. We will affirm Borrasi's conviction if the jury instructions fairly and accurately summarized the law, and we will reverse only if the instructions misled the jury and prejudiced his defense.

Borrasi urges us to adopt a "primary motivation" doctrine, under which the trier of fact would determine the defendants' intent in any given case and find them not guilty if the primary motivation behind the remuneration was to compensate for bona fide services provided. Under the primary motivation doctrine, the district court's instructions in this case would have been both inaccurate as to the law and inadequate to cure any prejudice from the government's statements during its closing arguments. He contends that such a construction is necessary both to avoid the possibility of conviction based on innocent or de minimis conduct and also to give effect to the rule of lenity in the face of statutory ambiguity.

> This string-cite provides a "who's who" of major Anti-Kickback Statute decisions. In particular, *Greber*'s "one purpose" test is widely accepted.

Persuasive authority weighs heavily against Borrasi's proposal. He relies on United States v. Bay State Ambulance and Hosp. Rental Serv., Inc., 874 F.2d 20 (1st Cir. 1989), where the First Circuit affirmed the appellants' convictions after "the district court instructed that the defendants could only be found guilty if the payments were made primarily as [referral] inducements."

But contrary to his allegation, there does not appear to be a circuit split regarding the appropriate interpretation of §1320a-7b(b). The First Circuit did not decide in *Bay State* "whether the government must show that such payments were made primarily or solely with a corrupt intent." Rather, it held that the district court's instruction at least "comport[ed] with congressional intent." Each circuit to actually reach the issue has rejected the primary motivation theory Borrasi advocates. *See* United States v. Greber, 760 F.2d 68, 71 (3d Cir. 1985) ("The text refers to 'any remuneration.' That includes not only sums for which no actual service was performed but also those amounts for which some professional time was expended."); United States v. Davis, 132 F.3d 1092, 1094 (5th Cir. 1998) (holding that §1320a-7b(b)(2) is violated whenever the benefits extended were partially to induce patient referrals); United States v. Kats, 871 F.2d 105, 108 (9th Cir. 1989) ("[T]he Medicare fraud statute is violated if 'one purpose of the payment was to induce future referrals.'" (quoting *Greber*, 760 F.2d at 69)); United States v. McClatchey, 217 F.3d 823, 835 (10th Cir. 2000) ("[A] person who offers or pays remuneration to another person violates the Act so long as one purpose of the offer or payment is to induce Medicare or Medicaid patient referrals.").

We find the reasoning of the Third, Fifth, Ninth, and Tenth Circuits convincing, and we decline Borrasi's invitation to create a circuit split. Nothing in the Medicare fraud statute implies that only the primary motivation of remuneration is to be considered in assessing Borrasi's conduct. We join our sister circuits in holding that if part of the payment compensated past referrals or induced future referrals, that portion of the payment violates 42 U.S.C. §1320a-7b(b)(1).

The district court's instructions comported with this common-sense holding. The instruction tracked the language of §1320a-7b(b)(1), combining it with a definition of remuneration. To convict Borrasi, the instruction required the jury to find—beyond a reasonable doubt—that some amount was paid not pursuant to a bona fide employment relationship. The trial court did not err in instructing the jury, and the government's comments during its closing arguments did not entitle Borrasi to a curative instruction. Because at least part of the payments to Borrasi was "intended to induce" him to refer patients to Rock Creek, "the statute was violated, even if the payments were also intended to compensate for professional services." *Greber*, 760 F.2d at 72. . . .

QUESTIONS

1. Did Borrasi's patients receive high quality care at Rock Creek?
2. Was the government financially harmed by the referrals? If not, why is the conduct nevertheless criminal?
3. If Borrasi actually had provided legitimate services as "Service Medical Director," would the arrangement have been proper?

3. SAFE HARBORS

As *Borrasi* illustrates, as long as one purpose of paying or receiving remuneration is to induce referrals of federal health care program business, then the statute has been violated. Accordingly, a host of typical and necessary arrangements, including employment contracts, medical directorships, physician recruitment packages, consulting relationships, integrated delivery systems (including accountable care organizations), waivers of copayments or other cost-sharing obligations, group purchasing agreements, space and equipment rentals, would all be subject to Anti-Kickback Statute criminal liability as long as "one purpose" was to induce referrals.

Because it would be impossible to operate a health care business without certain types of seemingly prohibited referrals, the Anti-Kickback Statute as well as regulations implementing it provide a number of exceptions, called "safe harbors." If all of the requirements of an applicable safe harbor are met, the arrangement will not be subject to prosecution under the Anti-Kickback Statute. The AKS safe harbors are voluntary, meaning that failure to fit within one is not fatal; there may be other arrangements that do not fall strictly into the safe harbors but nevertheless will not subject the parties to criminal liability.

> Health care practice in this area revolves around the safe harbors. Some AKS safe harbors are statutory, but most arise under administrative regulations. HHS solicits input for new safe harbors in the *Federal Register* each year.

Statutory safe harbors, including the bona fide employment relationship exception on which Borrasi attempted to rely, are listed at 42 U.S.C. §1320a-7b(b)(3). The following is a selected list:

(A) a discount or other reduction in price obtained by a provider of services or other entity under a Federal health care program if the reduction in price is properly disclosed and appropriately reflected in the costs claimed or charges made by the provider or entity under a Federal health care program;

(B) any amount paid by an employer to an employee (who has a bona fide employment relationship with such employer) for employment in the provision of covered items or services;

(C) any amount paid by a vendor of goods or services to a person authorized to act as a purchasing agent for a group of individuals or entities who are furnishing services reimbursed under a Federal health care program . . . ;

(D) a waiver of any coinsurance under part B . . . of this chapter by a Federally qualified health care center with respect to an individual who qualifies for subsidized services under a provision of the Public Health Service Act; . . .

(J) a discount in the price of an applicable drug of a manufacturer that is furnished to an applicable beneficiary under the Medicare coverage gap discount program. . . .

Regulations at 42 C.F.R. §1001.952 contain a number of additional safe harbors. A few examples are excerpted below for illustrative purposes. Even attorneys experienced in this area of practice are well advised to review the specific requirements of any applicable safe harbor before advising a client. As you read the examples, note a number of common elements of the safe harbors, including fair market value, arms-length transactions, legitimate services (i.e., reasonable and necessary and actually provided), not conditioned on the volume or value of referrals, and properly documented transactions.

> Can a hospital lease medical equipment to a physician who refers patients to the hospital? Is it easier for General Electric to lease medical equipment to that same physician?

(c) Equipment rental. As used in section 1128B [42 U.S.C. §1320a-7b] of the Act, "remuneration" does not include any payment made by a lessee of equipment to the lessor of the equipment for the use of the equipment, as long as all of the following six standards are met—

(1) The lease agreement is set out in writing and signed by the parties.

(2) The lease covers all of the equipment leased between the parties for the term of the lease and specifies the equipment covered by the lease.

(3) If the lease is intended to provide the lessee with use of the equipment for periodic intervals of time, rather than on a full-time basis for the term of the lease, the lease specifies exactly the schedule of such intervals, their precise length, and the exact rent for such interval.

(4) The term of the lease is for not less than one year.

(5) The aggregate rental charge is set in advance, is consistent with fair market value in arms-length transactions and is not determined in a manner that takes into account the volume or value of any referrals or business otherwise generated between the parties for which payment may be made in whole or in part under Medicare, Medicaid or all other Federal health care programs.

(6) The aggregate equipment rental does not exceed that which is reasonably necessary to accomplish the commercially reasonable business purpose of the rental. Note that for purposes of paragraph (c) of this section, the term *fair market value* means the value of the equipment when obtained from a manufacturer or professional distributor, but shall not be adjusted to reflect the additional value one party (either the prospective lessee or lessor) would attribute to the equipment as a result of its proximity or convenience to sources of referrals or business otherwise generated for which payment may be made in whole or in part under Medicare, Medicaid or other Federal health care programs.

(d) Personal services and management contracts. As used in section 1128B [42 U.S.C. 1320a-7b] of the Act, "remuneration" does not include any payment made by a principal to an agent as compensation for the services of the agent, as long as all of the following seven standards are met—

(1) The agency agreement is set out in writing and signed by the parties.

(2) The agency agreement covers all of the services the agent provides to the principal for the term of the agreement and specifies the services to be provided by the agent.

(3) If the agency agreement is intended to provide for the services of the agent on a periodic, sporadic or part-time basis, rather than on a full-time basis for the term of the agreement, the agreement specifies exactly the schedule of such intervals, their precise length, and the exact charge for such intervals.

> Why does the government insist on agreements lasting longer than one year, with fair market value compensation set in advance?

(4) The term of the agreement is for not less than one year.

(5) The aggregate compensation paid to the agent over the term of the agreement is set in advance, is consistent with fair market value in arms-length transactions and is not determined in a manner that takes into account the volume or value of any referrals or business otherwise generated between the parties for which payment may be made in whole or in part under Medicare, Medicaid or other Federal health care programs.

(6) The services performed under the agreement do not involve the counselling or promotion of a business arrangement or other activity that violates any State or Federal law.

(7) The aggregate services contracted for do not exceed those which are reasonably necessary to accomplish the commercially reasonable business purpose of the services.

For purposes of paragraph (d) of this section, an agent of a principal is any person, other than a bona fide employee of the principal, who has an agreement to perform services for, or on behalf of, the principal.

. . . .

(n) Practitioner recruitment. As used in section 1128B [42 U.S.C. 1320a-7b] of the Act, "remuneration" does not include any payment or exchange of anything of value by an entity in order to induce a practitioner who has been practicing within his or her current specialty for less than one year to locate, or to induce any other practitioner to relocate, his or her primary place of practice into a HPSA for his or her specialty area, as defined in Departmental regulations, that is served by the entity, as long as all of the following nine standards are met —

(1) The arrangement is set forth in a written agreement signed by the parties that specifies the benefits provided by the entity, the terms under which the benefits are to be provided, and the obligations of each party.

> Physicians are frequently recruited to join existing practices and health systems. Why does this safe harbor apply only to new physicians in provider shortage areas?

(2) If a practitioner is leaving an established practice, at least 75 percent of the revenues of the new practice must be generated from new patients not previously seen by the practitioner at his or her former practice.

(3) The benefits are provided by the entity for a period not in excess of 3 years, and the terms of the agreement are not renegotiated during this 3-year period in any substantial aspect; provided, however, that if the HPSA to which the practitioner was recruited ceases to be a HPSA during the term of the written agreement, the payments made

under the written agreement will continue to satisfy this paragraph for the duration of the written agreement (not to exceed 3 years).

(4) There is no requirement that the practitioner make referrals to, be in a position to make or influence referrals to, or otherwise generate business for the entity as a condition for receiving the benefits; provided, however, that for purposes of this paragraph, the entity may require as a condition for receiving benefits that the practitioner maintain staff privileges at the entity.

(5) The practitioner is not restricted from establishing staff privileges at, referring any service to, or otherwise generating any business for any other entity of his or her choosing.

(6) The amount or value of the benefits provided by the entity may not vary (or be adjusted or renegotiated) in any manner based on the volume or value of any expected referrals to or business otherwise generated for the entity by the practitioner for which payment may be made in whole or in part under Medicare, Medicaid or any other Federal health care programs.

(7) The practitioner agrees to treat patients receiving medical benefits or assistance under any Federal health care program in a nondiscriminatory manner.

(8) At least 75 percent of the revenues of the new practice must be generated from patients residing in a HPSA or a Medically Underserved Area (MUA) or who are part of a Medically Underserved Population (MUP), all as defined in paragraph (a) of this section.

(9) The payment or exchange of anything of value may not directly or indirectly benefit any person (other than the practitioner being recruited) or entity in a position to make or influence referrals to the entity providing the recruitment payments or benefits of items or services payable by a Federal health care program.

QUESTIONS

1. Identify the features that are common to most or all of the safe harbors. What is the reasoning that required their inclusion in the safe harbor?
2. What happens if a provider meets almost all of these elements of the safe harbor, failing only one by a small margin?

4. ADVISORY OPINIONS

Although arrangements outside the statutory and regulatory safe harbors are not per se illegal, providers are understandably wary of venturing into potentially dangerous waters. To provide guidance regarding arrangements that do not clearly fall within safe harbors, the OIG occasionally issues Special Fraud Alerts that advise the public about the OIG's views on fraud topics. The OIG also provides an administrative process for requesting advisory opinions addressing particular areas of concern for requestor-proposed transactions. Advisory opinions are binding for the specific party requesting them, but they are not binding on other parties or the government. Nevertheless, they are closely followed by health care lawyers as good evidence of the positions currently being taken by the government. The following example concerns an arrangement between local pharmacies and a pharmaceutical-dispensing company.

Department of Health and Human Services Office of Inspector General Re: OIG Advisory Opinion No. 14-06

Issued: August 7, 2014
Posted: August 15, 2014

[Name and address redacted]

[We redact certain identifying information and certain potentially privileged, confidential, or proprietary information associated with the individual or entity, unless otherwise approved by the requestor.]

We are writing in response to your request for an advisory opinion regarding a specialty pharmacy's proposal to pay local retail pharmacies a fee for support services they provide in connection with patient referrals to the specialty pharmacy (the "Proposed Arrangement"). Specifically, you have inquired whether the Proposed Arrangement would constitute grounds for the imposition of sanctions under the exclusion authority, or the civil monetary penalty provision, as those sections relate to the commission of acts described in the Federal anti-kickback statute.

You have certified that all of the information provided in your request, including all supplemental submissions, is true and correct and constitutes a complete description of the relevant facts and agreements among the parties.

In issuing this opinion, we have relied solely on the facts and information presented to us. We have not undertaken an independent investigation of such information. This opinion is limited to the facts presented. If material facts have not been disclosed or have been misrepresented, this opinion is without force and effect.

Based on the facts certified in your request for an advisory opinion and supplemental submissions, we conclude that the Proposed Arrangement could potentially generate prohibited remuneration under the anti-kickback statute and that the Office of Inspector General ("OIG") could potentially impose administrative sanctions on [name redacted] under sections 1128(b)(7) or 1128A(a)(7) of the Act (as those sections relate to the commission of acts described in section 1128B(b) of the Act) in connection with the Proposed Arrangement. Any definitive conclusion regarding the existence of an anti-kickback violation requires a determination of the parties' intent, which determination is beyond the scope of the advisory opinion process.

> The government's conclusion is based on the facts certified by the applicant. Any deviation can negate the advisory opinion's conclusions.

This opinion may not be relied on by any persons other than [name redacted], the requestor of this opinion, and is further qualified as set out in Part IV below and in 42 C.F.R. Part 1008.

I. FACTUAL BACKGROUND

[Name redacted] ("Requestor") dispenses specialty pharmaceuticals, which may be unavailable at local retail pharmacies for various reasons. Requestor states, for example, that some manufacturers limit distribution of their specialty drugs to a small network of pharmacies to dispense to patients. Some managed care payors designate certain pharmacies to dispense specialty drugs to their members. Additionally, local retail pharmacies may be prohibited or restricted from dispensing specialty drugs due to challenges associated with special handling requirements and inventory management.

Requestor dispenses specialty pharmaceuticals prescribed for patients with a wide variety of chronic and life-threatening diseases, including various forms of cancer, HIV/AIDS, multiple sclerosis, and hemophilia (the "Specialty Drugs"). The Specialty Drugs include pharmaceuticals payable by Federal health care programs. Requestor dispenses the Specialty Drugs directly to patients through its nationwide distribution channel for prescriptions received by licensed physicians. Requestor also operates eight free-standing pharmacies in locations across the country. When Requestor fills prescriptions through its distribution channel or at one of its locations, it also provides the following services to the patient: (1) counseling by a team of health professionals consisting of a patient care coordinator and a pharmacist or nurse; (2) proactive renewal reminders as well as utilization and adherence assessments tailored to the patient's day supply versus dispensed quantity; and (3) support finding financial assistance through third-party foundations for financially needy patients.

In some instances, a patient who is prescribed a Specialty Drug may present the prescription at a local pharmacy that is unable to fill it for reasons that may include any of those described above. Requestor states that the local pharmacy may not have the information necessary to direct the patient to a pharmacy that has the ability to dispense the Specialty Drug. Under the Proposed Arrangement, Requestor would enter into contracts with various local pharmacies and pharmacy networks (the "Local Pharmacies") to help these patients obtain their Specialty Drugs from Requestor. The Local Pharmacy would be required to provide various support services, including: (1) accepting new Specialty Drug prescriptions from patients or their prescribers; (2) gathering patient and prescriber demographic information; (3) recording patient-specific medication history and use, including drug names, strength, and directions; (4) counseling patients on appropriate use of their medications; (5) informing the patients about Specialty Drug access and services generally provided by specialty pharmacies; (6) obtaining patient consent to forward the Specialty Drug prescription to Requestor; (7) transferring the Specialty Drug prescription information to Requestor; and (8) providing ongoing assessments for subsequent refills, including transmitting information on any changes in the patients' medication regimens to Requestor (the "Support Services").

Requestor certified that it would compensate the Local Pharmacy for the fair market value of the Support Services performed on a per-fill basis, i.e., upon Requestor's receipt of the initial prescription for the Specialty Drug and upon each subsequent refill throughout the course of the patient's therapy (the "Per-Fill Fees").

II. LEGAL ANALYSIS

A. Law

Note that the OIG cites the same key cases as the *Borrasi* court did. The "Law" section is virtually identical in all of the OIG's Anti-Kickback Statute advisory opinions and provides a good, brief summary of the law.

The anti-kickback statute makes it a criminal offense to knowingly and willfully offer, pay, solicit, or receive any remuneration to induce or reward referrals of items or services reimbursable by a Federal health care program. *See* section 1128B(b) of the Act. Where remuneration is paid purposefully to induce or reward referrals of items or services payable by a Federal health care program, the anti-kickback statute is violated. By its terms, the statute ascribes criminal liability to parties on both sides of an impermissible "kickback" transaction. For purposes of the anti-kickback statute, "remuneration" includes the transfer of anything of value, directly or indirectly, overtly or covertly, in cash or in kind.

The statute has been interpreted to cover any arrangement where one purpose of the remuneration was to obtain money for the referral of services or to induce further referrals. *See, e.g.,* United States v. Borrasi, 639 F.3d 774 (7th Cir. 2011); United States v. McClatchey, 217 F.3d 823 (10th Cir. 2000); United States v. Davis, 132 F.3d 1092 (5th Cir. 1998); United States v. Kats, 871 F.2d 105 (9th Cir. 1989); United States v. Greber, 760 F.2d 68 (3d Cir. 1985), *cert. denied,* 474 U.S. 988 (1985). Violation of the statute constitutes a felony punishable by a maximum fine of $25,000, imprisonment up to five years, or both. Conviction will also lead to automatic exclusion from Federal health care programs, including Medicare and Medicaid. Where a party commits an act described in section 1128B(b) of the Act, the OIG may initiate administrative proceedings to impose civil monetary penalties on such party under section 1128A(a)(7) of the Act. The OIG may also initiate administrative proceedings to exclude such party from the Federal health care programs under section 1128(b)(7) of the Act.

One Purpose Rule

B. Analysis

The Proposed Arrangement would implicate the anti-kickback statute because Requestor would pay Local Pharmacies a fee for Support Services each time the services result in a referral to Requestor to dispense a Specialty Drug, including those payable by Federal health care programs. We therefore must determine whether, given all of the relevant facts, the Proposed Arrangement would pose no more than a minimal risk of fraud and abuse under the anti-kickback statute. For the following reasons, we conclude that the Proposed Arrangement would pose more than a minimal risk of fraud and abuse.

The Per-Fill Fees, which Requestor would pay on the basis of orders for Specialty Drugs, are inherently subject to abuse because they would be directly linked to business generated by the Local Pharmacies for Requestor. Specifically, the amount of Per-Fill Fees the Local Pharmacy would receive would be directly tied to the number of patients with Specialty Drug prescriptions that the Local Pharmacy would refer to Requestor. While we recognize that the Support Services to be provided by the Local Pharmacies would include certain patient care coordination services that could benefit patients, the Local Pharmacy would receive compensation under the Proposed Arrangement only when the Support Services result in referrals of patients to Requestor to fill prescriptions for Specialty Drugs. Requestor does not propose to pay Local Pharmacies for such services for patients who are not referred to it by the Local Pharmacies. The anti-kickback statute is violated if one purpose of the remuneration is to induce referrals of Federal health care program business. There is significant risk that the Per-Fill Fees would represent compensation for the Local Pharmacies generating business, including Federal health care program business, rather than solely compensation for bona fide, commercially reasonable services.

> The OIG suggests concern that the per-fill fees are tied to the volume or value of referrals, a key element of many of the safe harbors and exceptions.

Because the Proposed Arrangement would include potentially problematic financial incentives that could influence the Local Pharmacies' referral decisions in a material way, we cannot conclude that the Proposed Arrangement would pose no more than a minimal risk of fraud and abuse under the anti-kickback statute.

III. CONCLUSION

Based on the facts certified in your request for an advisory opinion and supplemental submissions, we conclude that the Proposed Arrangement could potentially generate prohibited remuneration under the anti-kickback statute and that the OIG could potentially impose administrative sanctions on [name redacted] under sections 1128(b)(7) or 1128A(a)(7) of the Act (as those sections relate to the commission of acts described in section 1128B(b) of the Act) in connection with the Proposed Arrangement. Any definitive conclusion regarding the existence of an anti-kickback violation requires a determination of the parties' intent, which determination is beyond the scope of the advisory opinion process.

IV. LIMITATIONS

The limitations applicable to this opinion include the following:

- This advisory opinion is issued only to [name redacted], the requestor of this opinion. This advisory opinion has no application to, and cannot be relied upon by, any other individual or entity.
- This advisory opinion may not be introduced into evidence by a person or entity other than [name redacted] to prove that the person or entity did not violate the provisions of sections 1128, 1128A, or 1128B of the Act or any other law.
- This advisory opinion is applicable only to the statutory provisions specifically noted above. No opinion is expressed or implied herein with respect to the application of any other Federal, state, or local statute, rule, regulation, ordinance, or other law that may be applicable to the Proposed Arrangement, including, without limitation, the physician self-referral law, section 1877 of the Act (or that provision's application to the Medicaid program at section 1903(s) of the Act).
- This advisory opinion will not bind or obligate any agency other than the U.S. Department of Health and Human Services.
- This advisory opinion is limited in scope to the specific arrangement described in this letter and has no applicability to other arrangements, even those which appear similar in nature or scope.
- No opinion is expressed herein regarding the liability of any party under the False Claims Act or other legal authorities for any improper billing, claims submission, cost reporting, or related conduct.

This opinion is also subject to any additional limitations set forth at 42 C.F.R. Part 1008. The OIG reserves the right to reconsider the questions and issues raised in this advisory opinion and, where the public interest requires, to rescind, modify, or terminate this opinion.

Sincerely,
Gregory E. Demske
Chief Counsel to the Inspector General

PROBLEM

Revise the per-fill fee to address the government's concern while still providing a financial relationship between the local pharmacies and the sponsor. Draft this contractual language in 100 words or less.

5. FRAUD ALERTS AND OTHER GUIDANCE

OIG advisory opinions, while not binding precedent, do provide guidance to other parties besides the requestor regarding the types of arrangements that may raise questions under the Anti-Kickback Statute. Repeated requests for advisory opinions regarding similar arrangements may result in the issuance of new regulatory exceptions, as occurred with arrangements between ambulance companies and hospitals to replenish supplies and medications used during patient transport. *See, e.g.,* OIG Adv. Ops. 98-7, 98-13, 98-14, 00-09, 02-02, and 02-03 (approving restocking arrangements). *But see* OIG Adv. Op. 97-6 (concluding that restocking could violate the Anti-Kickback Statute). Over time, the OIG builds expertise in particular areas and may eventually decide to issue guidance to reduce the number of duplicative requests. This guidance can be informal (a Fraud Alert or Special Fraud Alert) or a formal regulation. The regulatory safe harbor for ambulance replenishing, 42 C.F.R. §1001.952(v), became effective January 3, 2002, after a host of advisory opinions on the issue.

An example of informal guidance follows, addressing physician compensation arrangements.

Department of Health and Human Services
Office of Inspector General
Washington, DC 20201

Fraud Alert: Physician Compensation Arrangements May Result in Significant Liability

June 9, 2015

Physicians who enter into compensation arrangements such as medical directorships must ensure that those arrangements reflect fair market value for bona fide services the physicians actually provide. Although many compensation arrangements are legitimate, a compensation arrangement may violate the anti-kickback statute if even one purpose of the arrangement is to compensate a physician for his or her past or future referrals of Federal health care program business. OIG encourages physicians to carefully consider the terms and conditions of medical directorships and other compensation arrangements before entering into them.

> Doesn't a hospital need well-trained physicians? Why then is paying for continuing medical education illegal?

OIG recently reached settlements with 12 individual physicians who entered into questionable medical directorship and office staff arrangements. OIG alleged that the compensation paid to these physicians under the medical directorship arrangements constituted improper remuneration under the anti-kickback statute for a number of reasons, including that the payments took into account the physicians' volume or value of referrals and did not reflect fair market value for the services to be performed, and because the physicians did not actually provide the services called for under the agreements. OIG also alleged that some of the 12 physicians had entered into arrangements under which an affiliated health care entity paid the salaries of the physicians' front office staff. Because these arrangements relieved the physicians of a financial burden they otherwise would have incurred, OIG alleged that the salaries paid under these arrangements constituted improper remuneration to the physicians. OIG determined that the physicians were an integral part of the scheme and subject to liability under the Civil Monetary Penalties Law.

Those who commit fraud involving Federal health care programs are subject to possible criminal, civil, and administrative sanctions.

. . . .

Key guidance on Anti-Kickback Statute compliance appears in a December 1994 *Federal Register* Notice. The Notice included five previously issued Special Fraud Alerts, published since 1988, addressing (1) joint venture arrangements, (2) routine waiver of Medicare Part D copayments and deductibles, (3) hospital incentives to referring physicians, (4) prescription drug marketing practices, and (5) arrangements for the provision of clinical laboratory services. The Notice was published in the *Federal Register*, but it has not become a formal regulation under the Administrative Procedure Act. The Notice on hospital incentives, describing a number of practices that might not at first blush seem to be criminal in nature, is excerpted below:

Department of Health and Human Services Publication of OIG Special Fraud Alerts

59 Fed. Reg. 65,372 (Dec. 19, 1994)

Why Do Hospitals Provide Economic Incentives to Physicians?

As many hospitals have become more aggressive in their attempts to recruit and retain physicians and increase patient referrals, physician incentives (sometimes referred to as "practice enhancements") are becoming increasingly common. Some physicians actively solicit such incentives. These incentives may result in reductions in the physician's professional expenses or an increase in his or her revenues. In exchange, the physician is aware that he or she is often expected to refer the majority, if not all, of his or her patients to the hospital providing the incentives.

> OIG alleged that the salaries paid under these arrangements constituted improper remuneration to the physicians.

Why Is It Illegal for Hospitals to Provide Financial Incentives to Physicians for Their Referrals?

The Office of Inspector General has become aware of a variety of hospital incentive programs used to compensate physicians (directly or indirectly) for referring patients to the hospital. These arrangements are implicated by the anti-kickback statute because they can constitute remuneration offered to induce, or in return for, the referral of business paid for by Medicare or Medicaid. In addition, they are not protected under the existing "safe harbor" regulations. These incentive programs can interfere with the physician's judgment of what is the most appropriate care for a patient. They can inflate costs to the Medicare program by causing physicians to overuse inappropriately the services of a particular hospital. The incentives may result in the delivery of inappropriate care to Medicare beneficiaries and Medicaid recipients by inducing the physician to refer patients to the hospital providing financial incentives rather than to another hospital (or non-acute care facility) offering the best or most appropriate care for that patient.

Suspect Hospital Incentive Arrangements — What to Look For

To help identify suspect incentive arrangements, examples of practices which are often questionable are listed [below]. Please note that this list is not intended to be exhaustive but, rather, to suggest some indicators of potentially unlawful activity.

- Payment of any sort of incentive by the hospital each time a physician refers a patient to the hospital.
- The use of free or significantly discounted office space or equipment (in facilities usually located close to the hospital).
- Provision of free or significantly discounted billing, nursing or other staff services.
- Free training for a physician's office staff in such areas as management techniques, CPT coding and laboratory techniques.
- Guarantees which provide that, if the physician's income fails to reach a predetermined level, the hospital will supplement the remainder up to a certain amount.
- Low-interest or interest-free loans, or loans which may be "forgiven" if a physician refers patients (or some number of patients) to the hospital.
- Payment of the cost of a physician's travel and expenses for conferences.
- Payment for a physician's continuing education courses.
- Coverage on hospitals' group health insurance plans at an inappropriately low cost to the physician.
- Payment for services (which may include consultations at the hospital) which require few, if any, substantive duties by the physician, or payment for services in excess of the fair market value of services rendered.

Financial incentive packages which incorporate these or similar features may be subject to prosecution under the Medicare and Medicaid anti-kickback statute, if one of the purposes of the incentive is to influence the physician's medical decision as to where to refer his or her patients for treatment.

. . . .

The Anti-Kickback Statute's statutory and regulatory safe harbors, if met, shield an arrangement from criminal and civil liability. As the advisory opinions and Fraud Alerts suggest, however, providers may also structure arrangements outside the specific safe harbors that nevertheless will not be subject to Anti-Kickback Statute liability. In actual practice, many arrangements fail to fully comply with an AKS safe harbor but still are approved by companies under the guidance of careful legal counsel. In these cases, perhaps the violation of the safe harbor is merely technical, or counsel has determined that controls are in place such that no one intends to induce or reward a referral. As a result, many health care providers operate in a grey zone slightly outside the safe harbors. Further, given the statute's mens rea requirement, keep in mind the government must always prove its case under the Anti-Kickback Statute.

D. STARK LAW

The Ethics in Patient Referrals Act, 42 U.S.C. §1395nn, commonly known as the Stark Law (eponymously named for its sponsor, Representative Fortney "Pete" Stark of California), or Physician Self-Referral Law, prohibits a physician from referring (and a provider from billing) Medicare and Medicaid patients for certain services (called "Designated Health Services" or "DHS") in which the physician (or an immediate family member) has a financial relationship, unless an exception applies. The Stark Law is an "exceptions law," meaning that it broadly prohibits certain arrangements, and the only way to avoid liability is to fit squarely within an express exception. Unlike the Anti-Kickback Statute, no leeway exists for "close enough" arrangements. That approach yields a very technical statutory and regulatory regime with severe consequences for violations of any kind. The essential prohibition is relatively straightforward; the law's complexity lies in the myriad, detailed statutory and regulatory exceptions.

> If a financial relationship exists, a referral cannot be made or billed for DHS. A financial relationship is any ownership or investment interest or any compensation arrangement, unless an exception applies.

(a) Prohibition of certain referrals

(1) In general

Except as provided in subsection (b) of this section, if a physician (or an immediate family member of such physician) has a financial relationship with an entity specified in paragraph (2), then —

(A) the physician may not make a referral to the entity for the furnishing of designated health services for which payment otherwise may be made under this subchapter, and

(B) the entity may not present or cause to be presented a claim under this subchapter or bill to any individual, third-party payor, or other entity for designated health services furnished pursuant to a referral prohibited under subparagraph (A).

(2) Financial relationship specified

For purposes of this section, a financial relationship of a physician (or an immediate family member of such physician) with an entity specified in this paragraph is —

(A) except as provided in subsections (c) and (d) of this section, an ownership or investment interest in the entity, or

(B) except as provided in subsection (e) of this section, a compensation arrangement (as defined in subsection (h)(1) of this section) between the physician (or an immediate family member of such physician) and the entity.

An ownership or investment interest described in subparagraph (A) may be through equity, debt, or other means and includes an interest in an entity that holds an ownership or investment interest in any entity providing the designated health service.

Services provided in violation of the statute cannot be billed to the government. Stark contains no scienter requirement; a physician may be liable even if he or she was entirely unaware of the law, the prohibited referral, or the failure to fit within an exception. For the other party (often a hospital), Stark II (the statute as amended in 1993) forbids the entity from billing for any DHS provided under a referral that violates Stark II. For example, if a hospital and a physician have a financial relationship that does not meet an exception, the physician may not refer patients to the hospital and the hospital may not bill for any DHS rendered to that patient. If a local physician group is subsequently found to have a Stark violation, then not only are the physicians liable, but also the hospital has violated Stark every time it billed on those patients for any DHS. Further, an FCA case can be bootstrapped from an underlying Stark violation, just as from an underlying Anti-Kickback Statute violation.

In addition to payment being denied for any services provided in violation of the Stark Law, sanctions for violating Stark can be extensive. "Any person" may be liable for CMPs up to $15,000 per service if he submits claims for payment for services that he knew or should have known were from prohibited referrals. The statute also provides for CMPs up to $100,000 for "circumvention schemes," which the physician or another entity "knows or should know has a principal purpose of assuring referrals" that, if made directly by the physician, would be prohibited.

> Claims for government payment for services provided under a Stark Law–prohibited arrangement are "false" for purposed of the FCA.

Finally, providers may be excluded from Medicare and Medicaid administratively, in addition to the other penalties described above. Exclusion and other administrative remedies are discussed below.

1. FINANCIAL RELATIONSHIP

If a financial relationship exists, a referral cannot be made or billed for DHS. A financial relationship is any ownership or investment interest or any compensation arrangement, unless an exception applies as described in the statute and regulations.

Ownership or investment interests can include all manner of investments held by physicians (or an immediate family member), including debt, equity, and indirect arrangements using other entities. An example of a prohibited ownership or investment interest would be a physician's part ownership of a pharmacy, an imaging center, a hospital, or a supplier of durable medical equipment. Exceptions are described below; they are dependent on the category of financial relationship — ownership, investment, or compensation — which makes understanding the nature of the relationship very important in structuring any deal between physicians and other health care providers.

A "compensation arrangement" is virtually any contractual or informal arrangement that results in any "remuneration" passing to the physician making the referral (or an immediate family member). Remuneration is defined broadly, as under the Anti-Kickback Statute, to include anything of value whether "directly or indirectly, overtly or covertly, in cash or in kind." 42 U.S.C. §1395nn(h)(1)(B).

The extension of Stark to compensation arrangements includes a host of common and necessary business arrangements among health care providers. For example, as you learned in earlier chapters, physicians quite often form multispecialty group practices, bill services to a single group number, divide expenses and revenues, and refer to other members of the same group. Group practices may be formed as a legal entity (e.g., corporation, professional corporation, partnership), even if the physicians do not share all or any physical office space. Nevertheless, if physicians in the same group refer to other group members for DHS, potential for Stark liability exists unless the group complies with every element of an exception. The following DOJ settlement announcement was one of the first cases charging physicians with Stark violations based on the compensation arrangement among members of a group practice.

Department of Justice
U.S. Attorney's Office
Northern District of New York
FOR IMMEDIATE RELEASE
Thursday, August 14, 2014

NEW YORK HEART CENTER TO PAY MORE THAN $1.33 MILLION TO SETTLE ALLEGATIONS OF FALSE CLAIMS ACT AND STARK LAW VIOLATIONS

Cardiology Practice Allegedly Compensated Physicians for Improper Referrals

ALBANY, NEW YORK:—Cardiovascular Specialists, P.C., d/b/a New York Heart Center (NYHC), a group practice of cardiologists with offices throughout central and northern New York—has agreed to pay the United States $1,336,636.98 plus interest to resolve allegations that it violated the False Claims Act and the Physician Self-Referral Law (commonly known as the Stark Law) by knowingly compensating its physicians in a manner that violated federal law, announced United States Attorney Richard S. Hartunian.

The Stark Law is intended to ensure that a physician's medical judgment is not compromised by improper financial incentives that encourage referrals for unnecessary services, which drive up health care costs for Medicare beneficiaries and the Medicare program. The law prohibits physicians from referring Medicare beneficiaries to health care providers, including providers in their own group medical practices, for certain services if their financial relationships with the provider do not fall within an exception to the Stark Law. In the case of financial relationships between a medical practice and its physicians, the exceptions do not permit practices to compensate physicians in a manner that directly takes into account the volume or value of the physician's referrals for services that are not personally performed by the ordering physician. If a group's financial relationship with a physician does not satisfy an exception, the group cannot bill Medicare for the physician's prohibited referrals.

The settlement announced today resolves allegations that, from September 2007 through August 2008, compensation for each NYHC partner-physician was determined using a formula that took into account the volume or value of that physician's referrals for nuclear scans and CT scans, in violation of the Stark Law and the False Claims Act. The government's investigation revealed that NYHC adopted this formula with knowledge that it could violate the Stark Law.

United States Attorney Hartunian said: "Today's settlement is another example of this office's commitment to ensure that services paid for by federal health care programs are based on the best interests of patients rather than the financial interests of referring physicians. The United States Department of Health and Human Services' Office of Inspector General should be commended for bringing this issue to light and for its outstanding investigation."

> Which DHS was implicated here?

"Medical decisions should always be made on the basis on what's best for the patient's health, not the physician's finances. The compensation system in place in this case had the potential to influence medical judgment, which would be unacceptable," said Special Agent in Charge Thomas O'Donnell of the Department of

Health and Human Services Office of Inspector General (HHS-OIG), New York region. . . .

PROBLEM

You are counsel to the New York Heart Center after this settlement. How do you advise the Center to pay physicians for nuclear scans and CT (computerized tomography) scans?

2. DESIGNATED HEALTH SERVICES

Congress enacted the Stark Law in response to studies showing an increase in referrals by physicians to entities in which they had a financial interest. As originally enacted in 1989 ("Stark I"), the law applied only to referrals of Medicare patients for clinical laboratory services. In 1993, the statute was amended (hence, "Stark II") to include referrals for eleven designated health services (DHS) and extended the prohibition to Medicaid. DHS are defined in subsection (h)(6) to include much of modern medical practice:

> (6) Designated health services
> The term "designated health services" means any of the following items or services:
>> (A) Clinical laboratory services.
>> (B) Physical therapy services.
>> (C) Occupational therapy services.
>> (D) Radiology services, including magnetic resonance imaging, computerized axial tomography scans, and ultrasound services.
>> (E) Radiation therapy services and supplies.
>> (F) Durable medical equipment and supplies.
>> (G) Parenteral and enteral nutrients, equipment, and supplies.
>> (H) Prosthetics, orthotics, and prosthetic devices and supplies.
>> (I) Home health services.
>> (J) Outpatient prescription drugs.
>> (K) Inpatient and outpatient hospital services.
>> (L) Outpatient speech-language pathology services.

QUESTION

Recall the *Health Affairs* article regarding increased referrals to (presumptively) physician-owned ambulatory surgery centers (ASCs) included in the Introduction, Chapter 1. What DHS is implicated with those services? Does that study support the need for the Stark Law?

3. EXCEPTIONS

The Stark Law has many exceptions. Some apply only to ownership or investment interests; others apply only to compensation arrangements; some exceptions apply to both. The core exceptions are found in the statute, but extensive regulations have been issued with very detailed descriptions of the statutory exceptions and additional regulatory exceptions.

One of the most important general exceptions is for "in-office ancillary" services, protecting both ownership interests and compensation arrangements. Absent the in-office ancillary exception, a group practice could not use an imaging machine (such as an x-ray or MRI (magnetic resonance imaging)) or diagnostic device (such as a rapid strep test) that was owned or leased by the practice. Instead, physicians in that group would have to send the patient to another provider that had no financial relationship with the group practice.

Returning to the New York Heart Center settlement announcement above, one problem for the physicians is the lack of a blanket exception for group practices. Referrals for DHS among members of a group practice are prohibited unless the group meets all of the terms of a safe harbor. Members of the cardiovascular group had relevant financial relationships: a compensation arrangement that paid a bonus based on the volume or value of the referred scans. (They also had an ownership interest in the group practice, but that interest qualified for an exception.) Because of the compensation arrangement, they cannot refer or bill for DHS, including radiology services (CT scans and nuclear scans). Groups like this would most likely try to come within the exception for in-office ancillary services, codified at 42 U.S.C. §1395nn(b)(2):

> (2) In-office ancillary services
>
> In the case of services (other than durable medical equipment (excluding infusion pumps) and parenteral and enteral nutrients, equipment, and supplies)—
>
> (A) that are furnished—
>
> (i) personally by the referring physician, personally by a physician who is a member of the same group practice as the referring physician, or personally by individuals who are directly supervised by the physician or by another physician in the group practice, and
>
> (ii)
>
> (I) in a building in which the referring physician (or another physician who is a member of the same group practice) furnishes physicians' services unrelated to the furnishing of designated health services, or
>
> (II) in the case of a referring physician who is a member of a group practice, in another building which is used by the group practice—
>
> (aa) for the provision of some or all of the group's clinical laboratory services, or
>
> (bb) for the centralized provision of the group's designated health services (other than clinical laboratory services), unless the Secretary determines other terms and conditions under which the provision of such services does not present a risk of program or patient abuse, and
>
> (B) that are billed by the physician performing or supervising the services, by a group practice of which such physician is a member under a billing number assigned to the group practice, or by an entity that is wholly owned by such physician or such group practice, if the ownership or investment interest

Why do these rules restrict the location where these services are provided?

in such services meets such other requirements as the Secretary may impose by regulation as needed to protect against program or patient abuse.

To meet this safe harbor a physician group would have to ensure that the scans were provided by proper personnel, performed in a proper location, and billed under a proper individual or group number. But, as a threshold matter, the group must satisfy the statute's definition of "group practice," at 42 U.S.C. §1395nn(h)(4):

> (4) Group practice
> (A) Definition of group practice
> The term "group practice" means a group of 2 or more physicians legally organized as a partnership, professional corporation, foundation, not-for-profit corporation, faculty practice plan, or similar association—
>> (i) in which each physician who is a member of the group provides substantially the full range of services which the physician routinely provides, including medical care, consultation, diagnosis, or treatment, through the joint use of shared office space, facilities, equipment and personnel,
>> (ii) for which substantially all of the services of the physicians who are members of the group are provided through the group and are billed under a billing number assigned to the group and amounts so received are treated as receipts of the group,
>> (iii) in which the overhead expenses of and the income from the practice are distributed in accordance with methods previously determined,
>> (iv) except as provided in subparagraph (B)(i), in which no physician who is a member of the group directly or indirectly receives compensation based on the volume or value of referrals by the physician,

Can a physician join more than one group practice?

>> (v) in which members of the group personally conduct no less than 75 percent of the physician-patient encounters of the group practice, and
>> (vi) which meets such other standards as the Secretary may impose by regulation.
> (B) Special rules
>> (i) Profits and productivity bonuses. A physician in a group practice may be paid a share of overall profits of the group, or a productivity bonus based on services personally performed or services incident to such personally performed services, so long as the share or bonus is not determined in any manner which is directly related to the volume or value of referrals by such physician.

Cardiovascular Specialists, P.C., d/b/a New York Heart Center (NYHC), the entity charged in the settlement announcement excerpted above, was legally organized as a professional corporation under New York law but ran awry of other requirements, namely subsection (A)(iv), as compensation was based on a formula that took into account the individual group members' volume or value of referrals for DHS. Accordingly, the referrals violated the Stark Law, and any claims for Medicare payment submitted to the government were false under the FCA.

Note that 42 U.S.C. §1395nn(b)(2)(B) above delegates authority to the Secretary of HHS to impose additional requirements by regulation. Accordingly, in addition to the statutory language excerpted above, the Secretary has promulgated detailed regulations for the in-office ancillary services exception at 42 C.F.R. §411.355(b), which requirements the physician group would also have to meet.

42 C.F.R. §411.355(b). In-office ancillary services

(b) In-office ancillary services. Services (including certain items of durable medical equipment (DME), as defined in paragraph (b)(4) of this section, and infusion pumps that are DME (including external ambulatory infusion pumps), but excluding all other DME and parenteral and enteral nutrients, equipment, and supplies (such as infusion pumps used for PEN)), that meet the following conditions:

(1) They are furnished personally by one of the following individuals:

(i) The referring physician.

(ii) A physician who is a member of the same group practice as the referring physician.

(iii) An individual who is supervised by the referring physician or, if the referring physician is in a group practice, by another physician in the group practice, provided that the supervision complies with all other applicable Medicare payment and coverage rules for the services.

(2) They are furnished in one of the following locations:

(i) The same building (as defined at §411.351), but not necessarily in the same space or part of the building, in which all of the conditions of paragraph (b)(2)(i)(A), (b)(2)(i)(B), or (b)(2)(i)(C) of this section are satisfied:

(A)(1) The referring physician or his or her group practice (if any) has an office that is normally open to the physician's or group's patients for medical services at least 35 hours per week; and

> What is the purpose of the strict limits on hours?

(2) The referring physician or one or more members of the referring physician's group practice regularly practices medicine and furnishes physician services to patients at least 30 hours per week. The 30 hours must include some physician services that are unrelated to the furnishing of DHS payable by Medicare, any other Federal health care payer, or a private payer, even though the physician services may lead to the ordering of DHS; or

(B)(1) The patient receiving the DHS usually receives physician services from the referring physician or members of the referring physician's group practice (if any);

(2) The referring physician or the referring physician's group practice owns or rents an office that is normally open to the physician's or group's patients for medical services at least 8 hours per week; and

(3) The referring physician regularly practices medicine and furnishes physician services to patients at least 6 hours per week. The 6 hours must include some physician services that are unrelated to the furnishing of DHS payable by Medicare, any other Federal health care payer, or a private payer, even though the physician services may lead to the ordering of DHS; or

(C)(1) The referring physician is present and orders the DHS during a patient visit on the premises as set forth in paragraph (b)(2)(i)(C)(2) of this section or the referring physician or a member of the referring physician's group practice (if any) is present while the DHS is furnished during occupancy of the premises as set forth in paragraph (b)(2)(i)(C)(2) of this section;

(2) The referring physician or the referring physician's group practice owns or rents an office that is normally open to the physician's or group's patients for medical services at least 8 hours per week; and

(3) The referring physician or one or more members of the referring physician's group practice regularly practices medicine and furnishes physician services to patients at least 6 hours per week. The 6 hours must include some physician services that are unrelated to the furnishing of DHS payable by Medicare, any other Federal health care payer, or a private payer, even though the physician services may lead to the ordering of DHS.

(ii) A centralized building (as defined at §411.351) that is used by the group practice for the provision of some or all of the group practice's clinical laboratory services.

(iii) A centralized building (as defined at §411.351) that is used by the group practice for the provision of some or all of the group practice's DHS (other than clinical laboratory services).

(3) They are billed by one of the following:

(i) The physician performing or supervising the service.

(ii) The group practice of which the performing or supervising physician is a member under a billing number assigned to the group practice.

(iii) The group practice if the supervising physician is a "physician in the group practice" (as defined at §411.351) under a billing number assigned to the group practice.

(iv) An entity that is wholly owned by the performing or supervising physician or by that physician's group practice under the entity's own billing number or under a billing number assigned to the physician or group practice.

(v) An independent third party billing company acting as an agent of the physician, group practice, or entity specified in paragraphs (b)(3)(i) through (b)(3)(iv) of this section under a billing number assigned to the physician, group practice, or entity, provided that the billing arrangement meets the requirements of §424.80(b)(5) of this chapter. For purposes of this paragraph (b)(3), a group practice may have, and bill under, more than one Medicare billing number, subject to any applicable Medicare program restrictions.

(4) For purposes of paragraph (b) of this section, DME covered by the in-office ancillary services exception means canes, crutches, walkers and folding manual wheelchairs, and blood glucose monitors. . . .

> DME is generally excluded from the in-office ancillary exception, except as permitted here in (b)(4). Why do the regulations permit physicians to sell those particular types of DME in their offices?

(5) A designated health service is "furnished" for purposes of paragraph (b) of this section in the location where the service is actually performed upon a patient or where an item is dispensed to a patient in a manner that is sufficient to meet the applicable Medicare payment and coverage rules.

The regulations also separately define "member of a group practice," applicable to the in-office ancillary services exception.

42 C.F.R. §411.351. Definitions

Member of the group or member of a group practice means, for purposes of this subpart, a direct or indirect physician owner of a group practice (including a physician whose interest is held by his or her individual professional corporation or by another entity), a physician employee of the group practice (including a physician employed by his or her individual professional corporation that has an equity interest in the group practice), a locum tenens physician (as defined in this section), or an on-call physician while the physician is providing on-call services for members of the group practice. A physician is a member of the group during the time he or she furnishes "patient care services" to the group as defined in this section. An independent contractor or a leased employee is not a member of the group (unless the leased employee meets the definition of an "employee" under this §411.351).

QUESTIONS

1. After seeing these regulations, how would you advise your client, the New York Heart Center?
2. Can its compensation system be changed to comply?

We include these detailed in-office ancillary regulations and definitions here not because you are expected to become an expert in this important exception, but rather to give you a flavor for the challenges of practicing in this area of the law. Other common exceptions, each with similar statutory and regulatory complexity, include rental of office space or equipment, bona fide employment arrangements, personal service arrangements, physician recruitment, personally performed physician services, academic medical centers, ownership interests in rural hospitals, publicly traded securities, and more.

The ACA effectively eliminated one long-standing Stark Law exception that was one of the drivers of a controversial trend of physician-owned specialty hospitals. Under the Stark Law's "Whole Hospital" exception, physicians may refer Medicare or Medicaid patients for the provision of DHS to a hospital in which the referring physician has an ownership interest, as long as the referring physician is authorized to perform services at the hospital and the physician's ownership is in the entire hospital, not merely a department or subdivision of the hospital. Under the ACA, the Whole Hospital exception applies only to grandfathered hospitals, that is, those that had existing physician investment and existing provider agreements with CMS in place as of December 31, 2010. 42 U.S.C. §1395(i)(1). Specialty physician-owned hospitals were widely criticized for driving up health care costs by overutilization and threatening the viability of general acute care hospitals by cherry-picking high reimbursement cases, as discussed in Chapter 4.

Because of the regulatory complexity and strict liability nature of the Stark Law, the best practice is to consult the federal and state statutes, regulations, and agency interpretations each time a question arises regarding compliance or potential liability. There are, however, certain common elements in the exceptions. With respect to compensation arrangements, they generally must be in writing, signed by the parties, for fair market value, commercially reasonable, for specified services and a specified term, and not based on volume or value of referrals.

The Secretary's interpretive guidance suggests that all of the elements of each exception must be met at the time of the referral in question, creating the potential for various technical violations based on missing signatures, expiration of contract dates, incomplete or unwritten agreements, amendments to contracts with no written addendum, missing effective dates, or other scriveners' errors. Attorneys advising clients, accordingly, must be vigilant in drafting and updating contracts as necessary.

Also, providers must be aware of the possibility of "mistaken" or "accidental" payments outside the exceptions. Even if most of the financial relationships met an exception, a single payment that did not could result in denial of reimbursement for all referred DHS and, once identified, could trigger the 60-day rule, discussed above.

QUESTIONS

1. The Community Hospital cafeteria routinely does not charge surgeons, who have only a short break for lunch and cannot wait in the checkout line. Would that constitute a "financial relationship" between the physician and the hospital?
2. Are the surgeons at risk of CMPs and program exclusion?
3. Are all of the inpatient and outpatient services performed by the hospital for those surgeons' patients non-reimbursable under Medicare?

As the following opinion illustrates, the Secretary's delegated authority to promulgate regulations under the Stark Law is not without limits. The court struck down a long-standing regulatory prohibition on "per click" arrangements between hospitals and physician-owned equipment-leasing companies. (A per-click (meaning per-use) lease on an imaging machine like an MRI incurs a charge every time the machine is used.)

Council for Urological Interests v. Burwell

790 F.3d 212 (D.C. Cir. 2015)

I

The Secretary of Health and Human Services issued regulations that effectively prohibit physicians who lease medical equipment to hospitals from referring their Medicare patients to these same hospitals for outpatient care involving that equipment. The regulations accomplish this through two separate provisions. The first prohibits physicians from charging hospitals for leased equipment on a per-use basis when the physicians also refer patients to the hospital for procedures using that equipment. The second interprets the relevant statute to apply to physician-groups that perform procedures rather than only the entities that bill Medicare. Challenging the regulations here is an association of physicians who participate in leasing agreements with hospitals, under which they charge hospitals for equipment on a per-use basis and perform the procedures using the equipment. The association argues that the regulations exceed the Secretary's statutory authority and violate both the Administrative Procedure Act and the Regulatory Flexibility Act. The district court granted the Secretary's motion for summary judgment. Although one majority agrees with the district court that the statute is ambiguous as to the regulation of leases that charge on a per-use basis (Part II.A), a different majority concludes that the Secretary's explanation for prohibiting these leases is unreasonable (Part II.B). The court unanimously concludes that the Secretary's interpretation of the statute to apply to the physician-groups performing the procedures is reasonable (Part III), and that the Secretary complied with the Regulatory Flexibility Act (Part IV). We therefore affirm in part, reverse in part, and remand to the district court with instructions to remand the regulation relating to leases charging by use to the Secretary for further proceedings.

> Urologists sometimes treat kidney stones with a procedure called lithotripsy, which uses ultrasonic sound waves that break up the stones. Lithotripsy is reimbursed more generously if performed in hospital outpatient departments. But urologists, seeking additional income from the technical fee, prefer to own the machine and lease it to the hospital. Urologists fought CMS for more than a decade to permit per-click leases of these machines.

A

This case involves the interplay between complicated statutory provisions and regulations. Resolving the questions before us requires that we undertake a sometimes arduous journey through the tangled regime. We begin our slog with a look at the Medicare program.

Medicare provides federally funded health insurance to disabled persons and those aged 65 or older for various services, including the outpatient hospital procedures at issue here. In addition to paying the performing physician a fee that covers her services for the outpatient care, Medicare also pays the hospital a fee that covers charges for space, equipment, supplies, diagnostic testing, and the services of any non-physician personnel. Typically a hospital will have an employee perform the outpatient procedures using its own equipment, but Medicare also permits hospitals to contract with third parties to provide such outpatient services. Under these agreements, the third party provides equipment and technicians for a procedure while the hospital provides space and support services, pays for the lease of the equipment, and bills Medicare.

The members of the association challenging the regulations here have just this kind of relationship with hospitals. These arrangements are attractive to them because Medicare reimburses outpatient procedures that take place in hospitals at higher rates than if they were performed elsewhere.

This disparity creates a financial incentive for physicians to make referrals based more on maximizing their income than on maximizing the Medicare patient's well-being. For example, suppose a physician has an ownership interest in a hospital laboratory that diagnoses various illnesses. The physician profits by sending his Medicare patient to that hospital to undergo the diagnostic tests. The patient, by contrast, has little financial incentive to limit the cost of the tests, as Medicare covers most of the costs. This imbalance in interests can lead to a physician ordering a battery of unnecessary tests. In fact, a 1991 study showed this very outcome where Florida physicians had ownership interests in diagnostic clinics. To address this problem, Congress enacted the Stark Law (named for former Representative Pete Stark of California). The Stark Law places restrictions on both the referring physicians and the hospitals. It prohibits a physician who has a "financial relationship" with a hospital from referring Medicare patients to that hospital. It also bars hospitals from receiving Medicare payments based on these prohibited referrals. For the Stark Law's purposes, a physician has a "financial relationship" with a hospital if she owns or invests in it, or if she has a compensation agreement with the hospital covering services, equipment, and the like. *Id.* §1395nn(a)(2)(A)-(B), (h)(1).

Despite the general prohibition on potentially self-interested referrals, the Stark Law permits referrals by physicians to entities in which they have a financial interest in certain limited circumstances. It does so by excluding some forms of compensation agreements and ownership interests from the definition of "financial relationship," thus allowing both the relationships and the referrals. The provision at issue here is the equipment rental exception, under which physicians may both lease equipment to a hospital and refer their Medicare patients to that hospital for procedures using the equipment so long as the leasing agreement meets certain conditions. The lease must (1) be in writing; (2) assign use of the equipment exclusively to the hospital; (3) last for a term of at least one year; (4) set rental charges in advance that are consistent with fair market value and "not determined in a manner that takes into account the volume or value of any referrals or other business generated between the parties"; (5) satisfy the standard of commercial reasonableness even absent any referrals; and (6) meet "such other requirements as the Secretary may impose by regulation as needed to protect against program or patient abuse." 42 U.S.C. §1395(e)(1)(B)(i)-(vi).

> The key regulation in this case is the equipment rental exception.

In 1998, the Secretary proposed a rule that would prevent a physician with an ownership interest in a group that leased equipment and performed procedures under contract with a hospital from referring Medicare patients to the hospital for those procedures. The proposed rule accomplished this by adopting a broader interpretation of the statutory language that prevents physicians from referring Medicare patients to an entity "for the furnishing of designated health services" when the physician and the entity have a financial relationship. 42 U.S.C. §1395nn(a)(1)(A). Specifically, the proposed rule expanded the definition of an entity "furnishing" such services. The previous definition included only the party billing Medicare, usually the hospital where the procedures were performed. The new rule would extend to the party performing the procedures, including the third parties that contracted to perform outpatient procedures in hospital facilities. The proposed rule also altered the equipment rental exception by banning leases that charged the hospital for each use of the equipment — also referred to as leases with "per-click" payments — for patients referred by the physician-lessor.

To give an example of the regulatory scheme at work, prior to the proposed regulations, a single doctor could own laser equipment that she leased to a hospital, refer patients to that hospital for laser procedures, and profit each time the laser equipment was used. Because Medicare gives greater reimbursements for procedures performed at hospitals than for those same procedures performed in physicians' offices, it would be more profitable for a doctor to enter into such arrangements with a hospital than it would be for the doctor to purchase the laser for use in her own office. The Secretary's proposal forbade this practice. While a doctor could still own laser equipment and lease it to the hospital to which she referred her patients, she would only be permitted to receive time-based payments from the hospital, such as yearly or monthly charges. The frequency of laser usage would have no bearing on the doctor's profit, so she would no longer have a financial incentive to refer patients to the hospital for laser procedures. By the same token, a physician with an ownership interest in a group that leased laser equipment and performed laser procedures under contract with a hospital could no longer refer patients to the hospital for such procedures.

After considering comments, the Secretary decided against including either of these proposed alterations in the rule promulgated in 2001. Instead, the final rule provided that an entity is "furnishing designated health services" only if it is the entity that actually bills Medicare for the services. Physicians with an ownership interest in a group that contracted with a hospital could continue to refer patients to the hospital because any such groups performing the procedures and supplying the equipment were not billing Medicare. The 2001 rule also continued to allow leases with per-click payment terms. Even so, the preamble to the regulation explained that the Secretary continued to be concerned that contractual arrangements between physician-owned groups and hospitals "could be used to circumvent" the Stark Law, and also recognized the "obvious potential for abuse" in per-click payments. In both cases, the Secretary advised that she would monitor the arrangements and reconsider the decision if necessary.

> Before the amendment to this "furnishing" rule, technically the physician was referring only to the hospital and the physicians were not billing Medicare for the technical services. Meeting an exception was not necessary.

That reconsideration came in 2007 with another notice of proposed rulemaking. The Secretary again proposed banning per-click leases and forbidding physicians from making referrals to hospitals for procedures to be performed by a group practice in which the physician has an ownership interest. This time, the Secretary adopted both proposed regulations with minimal changes in 2008. According to the new rule, an entity that either performs or bills for designated health services is considered to be "furnishing" such services, meaning that physicians with ownership interests in groups that perform outpatient services in hospitals cannot refer patients for the procedures. With respect to the equipment rental exception, the rule states that the lease may not use per-click rates. 42 C.F.R. §411.357(b)(4)(ii)(B). Thus, under the regulations challenged here, a physician-owned group that contracts to lease equipment to a hospital cannot do so on a per-click basis while referring patients to that hospital for procedures using the equipment. Nor can a physician with an ownership interest in the group refer patients for outpatient procedures in a hospital where the group performs the procedures, unless she qualifies for one of the narrow ownership exceptions.

B

The Council for Urological Interests is made up of a group of joint ventures principally owned by urologists. These joint ventures lease laser technology to hospitals. Urologists generally prefer to furnish their services in a hospital because of the higher reimbursement rate available there. The Council contends that the lower rate paid for its members' services outside a hospital is insufficient to cover the cost of the equipment. Thus, to make the purchase of laser equipment economically viable, the urologists enter into agreements with a hospital, where the hospital pays the joint venture for the equipment on a per-click basis. The new regulation the Council challenges prohibits these arrangements.

> In 2015, urologists were among the better-paid physicians in the United States, averaging $344,000 per year. Family medicine doctors averaged $195,000.

C

The Council filed this action in March 2009, alleging that the 2008 rule exceeded the Secretary's authority under the Administrative Procedure Act (APA) and violated the procedural requirements of the Regulatory Flexibility Act (RFA). [Following resolution of a jurisdictional dispute,] the parties filed cross-motions for summary judgment. The district court granted the government's motion, concluding that the agency regulations were entitled to *Chevron* deference and that the agency's construction of the statute was a reasonable one. The district court also rejected the Council's claims under the RFA, finding that the Council had conceded a crucial portion of the Secretary's argument by failing to provide a response. The Council timely appealed both the APA and RFA claims. On appeal, the Council argues that the text and legislative history of the Stark Law preclude the Secretary from banning physicians who refer patients to a hospital from leasing equipment to that hospital on a per-click basis. The Council also argues that the Secretary unreasonably interpreted the statute to forbid physicians from referring patients to a hospital for procedures performed by a group in which the physician has an ownership interest. Finally, the Council argues that the Secretary failed to complete the requisite regulatory flexibility analysis called for by the RFA.

II

When Congress gives an agency authority to interpret a statute, we review the agency's interpretation under the deferential two-step test set forth in *Chevron U.S. A. Inc. v. Natural Resources Defense Council, Inc.* At step one, to determine whether Congress has directly spoken to the precise question at issue, we use "the traditional tools of statutory interpretation." If it is clear that Congress has addressed the issue, we give effect to congressional intent. If the statute is silent or ambiguous on the matter, we move to second step that asks whether the agency's interpretation is "based on a permissible construction of the statute." An interpretation is permissible if it is a "reasonable explanation of how an agency's interpretation serves the statute's objectives." If the agency's construction is reasonable, we defer.

A

"We begin, as always, with the plain language of the statute in question." The Council argues that the Stark Law expressly permits per-click rates for equipment rentals and that the Secretary thus lacked authority to ban per-click leases. The Council points to language in a clause of the equipment rental exception that permits equipment lease arrangements when "rental charges over the term of the lease are set in advance, are consistent with fair market value, and are not determined in a manner that takes into account the volume or value of any referrals or other business generated between the parties." This rental-charge clause, the Council argues, means that per-click rates are necessarily permissible so long as they meet these requirements. Per-click charges pass muster, according to the Council, because a charge based on use can be set in advance and be consistent with fair market value, and the charge would not take into account volume or value of referrals when the per-use charge is stable across the leasing period, rather than increasing after a certain number of uses. The Council is wrong. Its argument ignores the

> Prior to this case, most observers thought that per-click leases failed the exception because, under those arrangements, physicians were paid more if the machine was used more; therefore, payment was based on the volume or value of referrals.

remaining requirements of the equipment rental exception. Importantly, the final clause states that the lease must also "meet[ ] such other requirements as the Secretary may impose by regulation as needed to protect against program or patient abuse." 42 U.S.C. §1395nn(e)(1)(B)(vi). The Secretary explicitly relied on this authority in promulgating the regulation forbidding per-click payments. *See* 42 C.F.R. §411.357(b)(4)(ii)(B). Because any lease must comply with the listed rental charge requirements and any further requirements the Secretary adds, the fact that per-click leases comply with the rental charge requirements alone is insufficient. The text of the statute does not unambiguously preclude the Secretary from using her authority to add a requirement that bans per-click leases. *See* 42 U.S.C. §1395nn(e)(1)(B). To the contrary, the statutory text of the exception clearly provides the Secretary with the discretion to impose any additional requirements that she deems necessary "to protect against program or patient abuse." *See id.* §1395nn(e)(1)(B)(vi).

Nevertheless, the Council argues that because the statute's text already lists specific requirements for rental charges, the Secretary cannot add further requirements related to rental charges because these cannot properly qualify as "other" requirements under the final clause of the exception. . . . The Stark Law gives the Secretary power to add requirements "as needed to protect against program or patient abuse," even if Congress did not anticipate such abuses at the time of enactment. While Congress may not have originally intended the ban of per-click leases, it empowered the Secretary to make her own assessment of the needs of the Medicare program and regulate accordingly. And, as distinct from the statute in *Financial Planning*, the text of the Stark Law makes no reference to per-click rates. In other words, the statute explicitly permits the Secretary to impose additional conditions on equipment rental agreements and nowhere expressly states that per-click rates are permitted. Thus, the Secretary's regulation can properly be classified as an "other" requirement.

The Secretary's freedom to ban per-click leases is all the more clear when the equipment rental exception is compared to other provisions within the Stark Law. For example, the statute elsewhere expressly permits charging per-click fees in other contexts, showing that Congress knew how to authorize such payment terms when it wanted to. In 42 U.S.C. §1395nn(e)(7)(A) Congress created an exception to the Stark Law that allows the continuation of certain group practice arrangements with a hospital. Under the Law, a group practice is defined to include a group of physicians who join together to perform the full range of medical services in one office, billing Medicare under one provider number. *See* 42 U.S.C. §1395nn(h)(4). The provision states that "[a]n arrangement between a hospital and a group under which designated health services are provided by the group but are billed by the hospital" is excepted from the ban on referrals if, among other things, "the compensation paid over the term of the agreement is consistent with fair market value and the compensation *per unit of services* is fixed in advance and is not determined in a manner that takes into account the volume or value of any referrals or other business generated between the parties." *Id.* §1395nn(e)(7)(A)(v) (emphasis added). Comparing this provision to the equipment rental exception shows that Congress knew how to permit per-click payments explicitly, suggesting that the omission in this particular context was deliberate. In other words, Congress's decision not to include similar language in the equipment rental exception supports our conclusion that the statute is silent regarding the permissibility of per-click leases for equipment rentals.

Yet another provision of the Stark Law shows that Congress knew how to limit the Secretary's authority to impose additional requirements to the various exceptions. In 42 U.S.C. §1395nn(e)(2), Congress excludes bona fide employment relationships from the definition of compensation arrangements. This provision states that the employment relationship must comply with various requirements, including that the pay not be determined "in a manner that takes into account (directly or indirectly) the volume or value of any referrals by the referring physician." This employment exception also allows the Secretary to impose "other requirements," just as the equipment rental exception. *Id.* But the statute then goes on to say that the listed requirements "shall not prohibit the payment of remuneration in the form of a productivity bonus based on services performed personally by the physician." This language shows that Congress knew how to cabin the Secretary's authority to impose "other" requirements and that it knew how to further clarify what it meant by compensation that does not take into account the volume of business generated between parties. That Congress employed neither of these tools with reference to the equipment rental exception again supports reading the statute as giving the Secretary broad discretion as she regulates in this area.

We conclude that the statute does not unambiguously forbid the Secretary from banning per-click leases as she evaluates the needs of the Medicare system and its patients.

B

The per-click ban falters, however, at *Chevron* step two. Although *Chevron's* second step largely "overlaps" with arbitrary-and-capricious review under the APA, the overlap is not complete. We primarily assess the agency's statutory interpretation to determine whether it is a "permissible" and "reasonable" view of the Congress's intent. In making this assessment, we look to what the agency said at the time of the rulemaking—not to its lawyers' post-hoc rationalizations.

In the preamble to the per-click ban, the Secretary identified the 1993 Conference Report as an important locus of statutory interpretation. This is unsurprising as the Secretary felt completely bound by the Conference Report in 2001. The Secretary now believes the Conference Report is ambiguous but her explanation in the 2008 rulemaking borders on the incomprehensible. According to the Secretary:

> Where the *total amount of rent* (that is, the rental charges) over the term of the lease is directly affected by the number of patients referred by one party to the other, those rental charges can arguably be said to . . . "fluctuate during the contract period based on" the volume or value of referrals between the parties. Thus, . . . the Conference Report can reasonably be interpreted to exclude from the space and lease exceptions leases that include per-click payments for services provided to patients referred from one party to the other.

This jargon is plainly not a reasonable attempt to grapple with the Conference Report; it belongs instead to the cross-your-fingers-and-hope-it-goes-away school of statutory interpretation. The Conference Report makes clear that the "units of service *rates*" are what cannot "fluctuate during the contract period," not the lessor's total rental *income*. The Secretary's interpretation reads the word "rates" out of the Conference Report entirely. If a "reasonable" explanation is "the stuff of which a 'permissible' construction is made," the Secretary's tortured reading of the Conference Report is the stuff of caprice.

On appeal, counsel for the Secretary minimizes the Conference Report, noting that its language does not appear in the statutory text and does not limit the Secretary's "other requirements" authority. We cannot consider this argument, however, because the Secretary did not articulate it during the 2008 rulemaking and, in fact, contradicted it by treating the Conference Report as a key interpretive roadblock. What is left is the Secretary's bewildering statutory exegesis — one we cannot affirm even under *Chevron*'s deferential standard of review.

> The court's analysis puts a premium on how regulatory Preambles are written. Although not legally binding, Preambles to proposed and final rulemaking offer essential interpretive guidance.

On this record, the per-click ban fails at *Chevron* step two. We remand 42 C.F.R. §411.357(b)(4)(ii)(B) to the district court with instructions to remand to the Secretary for further proceedings consistent with this opinion. On remand, the Secretary should consider — with more care than she exercised here — whether a per-click ban on equipment leases is consistent with the 1993 Conference Report.

. . . .

KAREN LECRAFT HENDERSON, Circuit Judge, dissenting in part:

In my view, the Congress unambiguously intended to authorize per-click equipment leases. I therefore do not believe the per-click ban satisfies the first step of *Chevron* and respectfully dissent from Part II.A of the majority opinion.

The Stark Law broadly prohibits self-referrals: if a doctor has a financial interest in an entity, he cannot refer patients to that entity for designated health services. Nevertheless, the Stark Law contains multiple exceptions. This case involves the equipment exception. A physician can lease equipment to an entity — and refer patients to it — if:

> (i) the lease is set out in writing, signed by the parties, and specifies the equipment covered by the lease,
>
> (ii) the equipment rented or leased does not exceed that which is reasonable and necessary for the legitimate business purposes of the lease or rental and is used exclusively by the lessee when being used by the lessee,
>
> (iii) the lease provides for a term of rental or lease of at least 1 year,
>
> (iv) the *rental charges* over the term of the lease are set in advance, are consistent with fair market value, and *are not determined in a manner that takes into account the volume* or value *of any referrals* or other business generated between the parties,
>
> (v) the lease would be commercially reasonable even if no referrals were made between the parties, and
>
> (vi) the lease meets such *other requirements* as the Secretary may impose by regulation as needed to protect against program or patient abuse.

The Centers for Medicare and Medicaid Services (CMS or Agency) relied on subsection (vi) to enact the per-click ban, which ban specifies that an equipment lease can no longer utilize "[p]er-unit of service rental charges." 42 C.F.R. §411.357(b)(4)(ii)(B) (emphasis added). The question is whether the CMS can use its "other requirements" authority to ban per-click leases. I think not.

An agency cannot use its delegated authority in a way that contradicts the Congress's unambiguous intent. An agency crosses an impermissible line when it moves from interpreting a statute to *rewriting* it. Even if the Congress wanted to authorize agency rewrites, the Constitution would stand in its way. . . .

Mathematically, a per-click lease can be expressed as $Y = R \bullet X$, with Y as the physician's total rental income, R as the charge per patient and X as the number of patients served. The term "rental charges" in subsection (iv) can have two meanings. On the one hand, "rental charges" may refer to the variable Y. If "rental charges" means "rental income," then per-click leases do not qualify for the equipment exception. A per-click lease would "take[ ] into account the volume" of referrals because the physician's rental income would depend directly on the number of patients he refers. On the other hand, "rental charges" may refer to the variable R in the equation above (i.e., the per-patient rate). If a per-click lease charges a flat per-patient rate over the term of the lease, it does not "take into account the volume" of referrals and is therefore eligible for the equipment exception. But if a per-click lease adopts a tiered system — e.g., $1,000 for the first 20 patients, $2,000 for the next 20 patients, $3,000 for the next 20 patients, and so on — it would not qualify. Because the text of the equipment exception is "reasonably susceptible" to either of these interpretations, it is ambiguous. . . .

The Conference Report on the 1993 amendments to the Stark Law resolves the textual ambiguity in the equipment exception. According to the Conference Report:

> The conferees intend that charges for . . . equipment leases may be based on daily, monthly, or other time-based rates, or *rates based on units of service furnished*, so long as the amount of the time-based or units of service *rates* does not fluctuate during the contract period based on the volume or value of referrals between the parties to the lease or arrangement.

H.R. Rep. No. 103-213, at 814 (1993) (Conf. Rep.) (emphases added). This legislative history makes clear that the term "rental charges" in subsection (iv) refers to rental "rates," not total rental income. Thus, so long as the per-patient rate is fixed over the course of the lease, a per-click lease qualifies for the equipment exception. The Conference Report could not have been clearer on this point and the CMS has identified nothing to controvert it. Conference reports, moreover, are the gold standard when it comes to legislative history.

In short, the Conference Report demonstrates that the "rental charges" in a per-click equipment lease do not "take[ ] into account the volume . . . of any referrals . . . between the parties." Per-click leases are therefore eligible for the equipment exception and the CMS lacks the authority to say otherwise. . . .

The CMS's ban on per-click equipment leases therefore fails at *Chevron* Step One. Because my colleagues hold otherwise, I respectfully dissent on this issue.

QUESTIONS

1. How do per-click arrangements allegedly violate the Stark Law?
2. Why did the court strike down the agency's regulation?
3. After this opinion, how would you advise a group of physicians interested in purchasing an MRI unit?
4. Does a per-click lease give a urologist a financial incentive to use the machine more?
5. Why does Congress expressly authorize physician productivity bonuses?

To date, the government has initiated relatively few Stark Law investigations; most allegations have been initiated by *qui tam* relators under the FCA. As noted above, relators may build an FCA case from an alleged Stark violation on the theory that any claims for payment for DHS for Medicare patients that resulted from prohibited self-referrals are considered "false." Moreover, under the ACA's 60-day rule, knowing retention of identified payments based on prohibited referrals constitutes a "reverse" false claim.

The vast majority of Stark and FCA cases are resolved by settlement. Most providers opt not to take the risk of a jury verdict when the stakes are so high and the legal questions so complex. The following opinion offers a cautionary tale about the risks of litigation to other providers facing similar allegations.

United States ex rel. Drakeford v. Tuomey

792 F.3d 364 (4th Cir. 2015)

> Tuomey is a mid-sized community hospital in South Carolina. Damages of this magnitude could force the hospital to close or merge.

In a qui tam action in which the government intervened, a jury determined that Tuomey Healthcare System, Inc., did not violate the False Claims Act ("FCA"). The district court, however, vacated the jury's verdict and granted the government a new trial after concluding that it had erroneously excluded excerpts of a Tuomey executive's deposition testimony. The jury in the second trial found that Tuomey knowingly submitted 21,730 false claims to Medicare for reimbursement. The district court then entered final judgment for the government and awarded damages and civil penalties totaling $237,454,195.

Tuomey contends that the district court erred in granting the government's motion for a new trial. Tuomey also lodges numerous other challenges to the judgment entered against it following the second trial. It argues that it is entitled to judgment as a matter of law (or, in the alternative, yet another new trial) because it did not violate the FCA. In the alternative, Tuomey asks for a new trial because the district court failed to properly instruct the jury. Finally, Tuomey asks us to strike the damages and civil penalties award as either improperly calculated or unconstitutional.

We conclude that the district court correctly granted the government's motion for a new trial, albeit for a reason different than that relied upon by the district court. We also reject Tuomey's claims of error following the second trial. Accordingly, we affirm the district court's judgment. . . .

Tuomey is a nonprofit hospital located in Sumter, South Carolina, a small, largely rural community that is a federally-designated medically underserved area. At the time of the events leading up to this lawsuit, most of the physicians that practiced at Tuomey were not directly employed by the hospital, but instead were members of independent specialty practices.

> The physicians self-referred to their offices or ASCs. The hospital responded by trying to regain the lost business.

Beginning around 2000, doctors who previously performed outpatient surgery at Tuomey began doing so in their own offices or at off-site surgery centers. The loss of this revenue stream was a source of grave concern for Tuomey because it collected substantial facility fees from patients who underwent surgery at the hospital's outpatient center. Tuomey estimated that it stood to lose $8 to $12 million over a thirteen-year period from the loss of fees associated with gastrointestinal procedures alone. To stem this loss, Tuomey sought to negotiate part-time employment contracts with a number of local physicians.

In drafting the contracts, Tuomey was well aware of the constraints imposed by the Stark Law. While we discuss the provisions of that law in greater detail below, in broad terms, the statute, 42 U.S.C. §1395nn, prohibits physicians from making referrals to entities where "[t]he referring physician . . . receives aggregate compensation . . . that varies with, or takes into account, the volume or value of referrals or other business generated by the referring physician for the entity furnishing" the designated health services. Pursuant to the Stark Law, "[a] hospital may not submit for payment a Medicare claim for services rendered pursuant to a prohibited referral." United States ex rel. Drakeford v. Tuomey Healthcare Sys., Inc., 675 F.3d 394, 397-98 (4th Cir. 2012).

Beginning in 2003, Tuomey sought the advice of its longtime counsel, Nexsen Pruet, on the Stark Law implications arising from the proposed employment contracts. Nexsen Pruet in turn engaged Cejka Consulting, a national consulting firm that specialized in physician compensation, to provide an opinion concerning the commercial reasonableness and fair market value of the contracts. Tuomey also conferred with Richard Kusserow, a former Inspector General for the United States Department of Health and Human Services, and later, with Steve Pratt, an attorney at Hall Render, a prominent healthcare law firm.

The part-time employment contracts had substantially similar terms. Each physician was paid an annual guaranteed base salary. That salary was adjusted from year to year based on the amount the physician collected from all services rendered the previous year. The bulk of the physicians' compensation was earned in the form of a productivity bonus, which paid the physicians eighty percent of the amount of their collections for that year. The physicians were also eligible for an incentive bonus of up to seven percent of their earned productivity bonus. In addition, Tuomey agreed to pay for the physicians' medical malpractice liability insurance as well as their practice group's share of employment taxes. The physicians were also allowed to participate in Tuomey's health insurance plan. Finally, Tuomey agreed to absorb each practice group's billing and collections costs.

The contracts had ten-year terms, during which physicians could maintain their private practices, but were required to perform outpatient surgical procedures exclusively at the hospital. Physicians could not own any interest in a facility located in Sumter that provided ambulatory surgery services, save for a less-than-two-percent interest in a publicly traded company that provided such services. The physicians also agreed not to perform outpatient surgical procedures within a thirty-mile radius of the hospital for two years after the expiration or termination of the contracts.

> These agreements essentially tied these physicians to Tuomey for outpatient surgical procedures.

Tuomey ultimately entered into part-time employment contracts with nineteen physicians. Tuomey, however, was unable to reach an agreement with Dr. Michael Drakeford, an orthopedic surgeon. Drakeford believed that the proposed contracts violated the Stark Law because the physicians were being paid in excess of their collections. He contended that the compensation package did not reflect fair market value, and thus the government would view it as an unlawful payment for the doctor's facility-fee-generating referrals.

To address Drakeford's concerns, Tuomey suggested a joint venture as an alternative business arrangement, whereby doctors would become investors . . .

in . . . a management company that would provide day-to-day management of the outpatient surgery center, and both Tuomey and its co-investors would receive payments based on that management [structure]. Drakeford, however, declined that option.

Unable to break the stalemate in their negotiations, in May 2005, Tuomey and Drakeford sought the advice of Kevin McAnaney, an attorney in private practice with expertise in the Stark Law. McAnaney had formerly served as the Chief of the Industry Guidance Branch of the United States Department of Health and Human Services Office of Counsel to the Inspector General. In that position, McAnaney wrote a substantial portion of the regulations implementing the Stark Law.

> After this decision, some attorneys thought that Tuomey was actually put at a disadvantage for having sought out advice from several experts.

McAnaney advised the parties that the proposed employment contracts raised significant "red flags" under the Stark Law. In particular, Tuomey would have serious difficulty persuading the government that the contracts did not compensate the physicians in excess of fair market value. Such a contention, said McAnaney, would not pass the red face test. McAnaney also warned Tuomey that the contracts presented an easy case to prosecute for the government.

Drakeford ultimately declined to enter into a contract with Tuomey. He later sued the hospital under the qui tam provisions of the FCA, alleging that because the part-time employment contracts violated the Stark Law, Tuomey had knowingly submitted false claims for payment to Medicare. As was its right, the government intervened in the action and filed additional claims seeking equitable relief for payments made under mistake of fact and unjust enrichment theories. . . .

While the case was on appeal, the presiding judge passed away. At the second trial, the new presiding judge allowed the government to introduce the previously excluded Martin deposition testimony, and also allowed McAnaney to testify. The jury found that Tuomey violated both the Stark Law and the FCA. It further found that Tuomey had submitted 21,730 false claims to Medicare with a total value of $39,313,065. The district court trebled the actual damages and assessed an additional civil penalty, both actions required by the FCA. From the resulting judgment of $237,454,195, Tuomey appeals. . . .

Tuomey's appeal presents these issues: First, did the district court err in granting the government's motion for a new trial on the FCA claim? If not, did the district court err in (1) denying Tuomey's motion for judgment as a matter of law (or, in the alternative, for yet another new trial) following the second trial; and (2) awarding damages and penalties against Tuomey based on the jury's finding of an FCA violation? We address each issue in turn, but first provide a general overview of the Stark Law. . . .

The Stark Law is intended to prevent overutilization of services by physicians who stand to profit from referring patients to facilities or entities in which they have a financial interest. The statute prohibits a physician from making a referral to an entity, such as a hospital, with which he or she has a financial relationship, for the furnishing of designated health services. If the physician makes such a referral, the hospital may not submit a bill for reimbursement to Medicare. Similarly, the government may not make any payment for a designated health service provided in violation of the Stark Law. If a person collects any payment for a service billed in violation of the Stark Law, the person shall be liable to the individual for, and shall refund on a timely basis to the individual, any amounts so collected.

Inpatient and outpatient hospital services are considered designated health services under the law. A referral includes the request by a physician for the item or service. A referral does not include any designated health service personally performed or provided by the referring physician. However, there is a referral when the hospital bills a "facility fee" (also known as a "facility component" or "technical component") in connection with the personally performed service.

A financial relationship constitutes a prohibited "indirect compensation arrangement," if (1) "there exists an unbroken chain of any number . . . of persons or entities that have financial relationships . . . between them," (2) "[t]he referring physician . . . receives aggregate compensation . . . that varies with, or takes into account, the volume or value of referrals or other business generated by the referring physician for the entity furnishing" the designated health services, and (3) the entity has knowledge that the compensation so varies. The statute, however, does not bar indirect compensation arrangements where: (1) the referring physician is compensated at fair market value for "services and items actually provided"; (2) the compensation arrangement is "not determined in any manner that takes into account the volume or value of referrals"; (3) the compensation arrangement is "commercially reasonable"; and (4) the compensation arrangement does not run afoul of any other federal or state law.

Once a relator or the government has established the elements of a Stark Law violation, it becomes the defendant's burden to show that the indirect compensation arrangement exception shields it from liability. . . .

[The court first concluded that the district court judge did not commit reversible error by excluding certain testimony.]

Nonetheless, we affirm the district court's order granting a new trial on the alternative ground urged by the government—that it was prejudiced by the exclusion of McAnaney's testimony and other related evidence of his warnings to Tuomey regarding the legal peril that the employment contracts posed. To make its case that Tuomey "knowingly" submitted false claims under the FCA, the government needed to show that Tuomey knew that there was a substantial risk that the contracts violated the Stark Law, and was nonetheless deliberately ignorant of, or recklessly disregarded that risk. In our view, McAnaney's testimony was a relevant, and indeed essential, component of the government's evidence on that element, and Tuomey offered no good reason why the jury should not hear it.

The district court has now presided over two trials in this case, with strikingly disparate results. In the first trial, the jury did not hear from McAnaney and found for Tuomey on the FCA claim. When the case was retried, McAnaney was allowed to testify and the jury found for the government. Coincidence? We think not. Rather, we believe that these results bespeak the importance of what the jury in the first trial was not allowed to consider.

And this is so even while acknowledging that McAnaney was a looming presence throughout the first trial. For example, the jury heard audio of a Tuomey board meeting, where a board member mentioned that McAnaney had voiced concerns with the part-time employment contracts. Left unsaid, however, was the precise nature of those concerns or the weight and seriousness that McAnaney attached to them. The jury also knew that Hewson (Tuomey's counsel at Nexson Pruet) was generally aware of McAnaney's views on the employment contracts, but that he dismissed them as not credible because, in his view, Drakeford was deliberately seeking to cherry pick a legal opinion that would undermine the entire deal.

The jury was also aware that Drakeford wrote to Tuomey's board summarizing McAnaney's opinions. The district court, however, excluded Drakeford's letter, although it did allow the jury to consider the board's response wherein it summarily rejected Drakeford's unspecified objections. Finally, the jury heard that Tuomey refused to allow McAnaney to prepare a written opinion discussing his concerns regarding the contracts, and subsequently terminated McAnaney's engagement altogether on September 2, 2005.

While certainly not insubstantial, the sum of the evidence at the first trial regarding McAnaney was that Tuomey (1) was aware that McAnaney had unspecified concerns about the employment contracts; (2) refused to allow McAnaney to relay his concerns in writing; and (3) later terminated McAnaney's joint representation. Yet, under the FCA, the government had to prove that Tuomey knew of, was deliberately ignorant of, or recklessly disregarded the falsity of its claims (i.e. that its claims violated the Stark Law). We think that McAnaney's specific warnings to Tuomey regarding the dangers posed by the contracts were critical to making this showing.

McAnaney warned Tuomey that procuring fair market valuations, by itself, was not conclusive of the accuracy of the valuation. He emphasized that it would be very hard to convince the government that a contract that paid physicians substantially above even their collections, much less their collections minus expenses, would constitute fair market value. According to McAnaney, compensation arrangements under which the contracting physicians are paid in excess of their collections were "basically a red flag to the government." He noted that similar cases had previously been prosecuted before, although all of them ultimately settled.

> From his perspective as a regulatory agency insider, McAnaney warned that contracts that paid substantially above physicians' collections, "much less their collections minus expenses," raised red flags to the government.

McAnaney also pointed out that the ten-year term of the contracts, combined with the thirty-mile, two-year noncompete provision would reinforce the government's view that Tuomey was paying the physicians above fair market value for referrals. He concluded that the contracts did not pass the "red face test," and warned that the government would find this an easy case to prosecute.

We think the importance of McAnaney's testimony to the government's case is self-evident. Indeed, it is difficult to imagine any more probative and compelling evidence regarding Tuomey's intent than the testimony of a lawyer hired by Tuomey, who was an undisputed subject matter expert on the intricacies of the Stark Law, and who warned Tuomey in graphic detail of the thin legal ice on which it was treading with respect to the employment contracts. . . .

In sum, Tuomey has offered no good reason why the jury in the first trial was not allowed to hear from McAnaney. And we agree with the government that this evidence was critical to its ability to satisfy its burden to prove that Tuomey acted with the requisite intent under the FCA. We therefore affirm the district court's order granting a new trial on the FCA claim. . . .

We turn now to Tuomey's challenges to the judgment entered following the second trial. Tuomey asks for judgment as a matter of law because a reasonable jury could not have found that (1) the part-time employment contracts violated the Stark Law, or (2) Tuomey knowingly submitted false claims. Alternatively, Tuomey asks for a new trial because of the district court's refusal to tender certain jury instructions. . . .

Tuomey argues that it is entitled to judgment as a matter of law because the contracts between it and the physicians did not run afoul of the Stark Law. As we explain, however, a reasonable jury could find that Tuomey violated the Stark Law when it paid aggregate compensation to physicians that varied with or took into account the volume or value of actual or anticipated referrals to Tuomey.

To begin with, we note that the Stark Law's "volume or value" standard can be implicated when aggregate compensation varies with the volume or value of referrals, or otherwise takes into account the volume or value of referrals. That is precisely what the district court directed the jury in the second trial to assess. Tuomey insists, however, that our earlier opinion in this case foreclosed the jury's consideration of whether the contracts varied with the volume or value of referrals. Instead, says Tuomey, the only question that should have been put to the jury was "whether the contracts, on their face, took into account the value or volume of anticipated referrals."

We disagree. The district court properly understood that the jury was entitled to pass on the contracts as they were actually implemented by the parties. We said as much in our earlier opinion, where

> This position appears to be inconsistent with some of the per-click language in *Council for Urological Interests*.

> we emphasize[d] that our holding . . . [was] limited to the issues we specifically address[ed]. On remand, a jury must determine, in light of our holding, whether the aggregate compensation received by the physicians under the contracts varied with, or took into account, the volume or value of the facility component referrals.

A reasonable jury could have found that Tuomey's contracts in fact compensated the physicians in a manner that varied with the volume or value of referrals. There are two different components of the physicians' compensation that we believe so varied. First, each year, the physicians were paid a base salary that was adjusted upward or downward depending on their collections from the prior year. In addition, the physicians received the bulk of their compensation in the form of a productivity bonus, pegged at eighty percent of the amount of their collections.

As Tuomey concedes, the aggregate compensation received by the physicians under the Contracts was based solely on collections for personally performed professional services. And as we noted in our earlier opinion, there are referrals here, "consisting of the facility component of the physicians' personally performed services, and the resulting facility fee billed by Tuomey based upon that component." In sum, the more procedures the physicians performed at the hospital, the more facility fees Tuomey collected, and the more compensation the physicians received in the form of increased base salaries and productivity bonuses.

The nature of this arrangement was confirmed by Tuomey's former Chief Financial Officer, William Paul Johnson, who admitted "that every time one of the 19 physicians . . . did a legitimate procedure on a Medicare patient at the hospital pursuant to the part-time agreement[,] the doctor [got] more money," and "the hospital also got more money." We thus think it plain that a reasonable jury could find that the physicians' compensation varied with the volume or value of actual referrals. The district court did not err in denying Tuomey's motion for judgment as a matter of law on this ground. . . .

Tuomey next argues that the district court erred in not granting its motion for judgment as a matter of law because it did not knowingly violate the FCA. Specifically, Tuomey claims that because it reasonably relied on the advice of counsel, no reasonable jury could find that Tuomey possessed the requisite intent to violate the FCA. Because the record here is replete with evidence indicating that Tuomey shopped for legal opinions approving of the employment contracts, while ignoring negative assessments, we disagree.

The FCA imposes civil liability on any person who "knowingly presents, or causes to be presented, a false or fraudulent claim for payment or approval" to an officer or employee of the United States Government. 31 U.S.C. §3729(a)(1)(A), (b)(2)(A)(i). Under the Act, the term "knowingly" means that a person, with respect to information contained in a claim, (1) "has actual knowledge of the information"; (2) "acts in deliberate ignorance of the truth or falsity of the information;" or (3) "acts in reckless disregard of the truth or falsity of the information." *Id.* §3729(b)(1). The purpose of the FCA's scienter requirement is to avoid punishing honest mistakes or incorrect claims submitted through mere negligence.

The record evidence provides ample support for the jury's verdict as to Tuomey's intent. Indeed, McAnaney's testimony, summarized above, is alone sufficient to sweep aside Tuomey's claim of error. We agree with the district court's conclusion that a reasonable jury could have found that Tuomey possessed the requisite scienter once it determined to disregard McAnaney's remarks. A reasonable jury could indeed be troubled by Tuomey's seeming inaction in the face of McAnaney's warnings, particularly given Tuomey's aggressive efforts to avoid hearing precisely what McAnaney had to say regarding the contracts.

Nonetheless, a defendant may avoid liability under the FCA if it can show that it acted in good faith on the advice of counsel. However, consultation with a lawyer confers no automatic immunity from the legal consequences of conscious fraud. Rather, to establish the advice-of-counsel defense, the defendant must show the (a) full disclosure of all pertinent facts to counsel, and (b) good faith reliance on counsel's advice.

Tuomey contends that it provided full and accurate information regarding the proposed employment contracts to Hewson, who in turn advised Tuomey that the contracts did not run afoul of the Stark Law. But as the government aptly notes, in determining whether Tuomey reasonably relied on the advice of its counsel, the jury was entitled to consider all the advice given to it by any source.

In denying Tuomey's post-trial motions, the district court noted — and we agree — that a reasonable jury could have concluded that Tuomey was, after September 2005, no longer acting in good faith reliance on the advice of its counsel when it refused to give full consideration to McAnaney's negative assessment of the part-time employment contracts and terminated his representation. Tuomey defends its dismissal of McAnaney's warnings by claiming that his opinion was tainted by undue influence exerted by Drakeford and his counsel. But there was evidence before the jury suggesting that Tuomey also tried to procure a favorable opinion from McAnaney. Indeed, Tuomey's counsel admitted that he was trying to steer McAnaney towards Tuomey's desired outcome and that Tuomey needed to continue playing along and influence the outcome of the game as best we can. Thus, a reasonable jury could conclude that Tuomey ignored McAnaney because it simply did not like what he had to say.

> The hospital would lose $1.5 to $2 million per year but would more than make that up with the additional facility fees. These numbers suggest that Tuomey was splitting the facility fees with the physicians.

Tuomey points to the fact that it retained Steve Pratt, a prominent healthcare lawyer, and Richard Kusserow, former Inspector General at the United States

Department of Health and Human Services, as further evidence that it acted in good faith and did not ignore McAnaney's warnings. Pratt rendered two opinions that generally approved of the employment contracts. But he did so without being told of McAnaney's unfavorable assessment, even though Tuomey had that information available to it at the time. In addition, Pratt reviewed and relied on the view of Tuomey's fair-market-value consultant that the employment contracts would compensate the physicians at fair market value, but he did not consider how the consultant arrived at its opinion. Nor did he know how much the doctors earned prior to entering into the contracts, or that the hospital stood to lose $1.5–2 million a year, not taking into account facility fees, by compensating the physicians above their collections. We thus think it entirely reasonable for a jury to look skeptically on Pratt's favorable advice regarding the contracts.

The same can be said of the Kusserow's advice. Kusserow — who was called by the government to rebut Tuomey's advice-of-counsel defense — advised Tuomey regarding the employment contracts about eighteen months before the parties retained McAnaney. As was the case with Pratt, he received no information regarding the fair market value of the employment contracts, information that Kusserow considered vital to be able to do a full Stark analysis of the proposed contracts. And although Kusserow did say in a letter to Tuomey's counsel that he did not believe the contracts presented significant Stark issues, he hedged considerably on that view because of potentially troubling issues related to the productivity and incentive bonus provisions in the contracts that have not been fully addressed.

The $237 million verdict against Tuomey is believed to be the largest ever levied against a community hospital and exceeded the hospital's annual revenue. Subsequent to the Fourth Circuit Court's affirming the district court verdict, the DOJ resolved the judgment. Under the terms of the settlement, the government received $72.4 million, and Tuomey Health System was sold to Palmetto Health, a multi-hospital system based in Columbia, South Carolina. http://www.justice.gov/opa/pr/ united-states-resolves-237- million-false-claims-act- judgment-against-south- carolina-hospital.

As the district court observed, "the jury evidently rejected Tuomey's advice of counsel defense" as of the date that Tuomey received McAnaney's warnings, "grounded on the fact that the jury excluded damages from [before the termination of McAnaney's engagement] in making its determination" of the civil penalty and damages. Thus, while Kusserow's advice was certainly relevant to Tuomey's advice-of-counsel defense, a reasonable jury could have determined that McAnaney's warnings (and Tuomey's subsequent inaction) were far more probative on the issue.

In sum, viewing the evidence in the light most favorable to the government, we have no cause to upset the jury's reasoned verdict that Tuomey violated the FCA.

. . . .

PROBLEM

You are the general counsel to Tuomey in 2003. How do you proceed to meet your client's business goals, without risking a huge monetary loss?

The Stark Law is the third principal federal law for policing health care fraud and abuse that we have discussed thus far in this chapter. As the foregoing discussion illustrates, providers may find themselves ensnared in these laws even when they believe they are acting appropriately and otherwise providing quality health care. The final section of this chapter suggests some additional areas of attention for providers seeking to maintain compliance with fraud and abuse laws.

E. OTHER SANCTIONS, COMPLIANCE PROGRAMS, AND STATE LAWS

As the preceding materials have highlighted, the U.S. Department of Justice and U.S. Attorney's Offices, both civil and criminal divisions, are the lead prosecutors of health care fraud and abuse. Many of those actions are initiated or independently litigated by private *qui tam* relators.

In addition to those parties, health care lawyers need to be familiar with the "alphabet soup" of other authorities responsible for regulating fraud and abuse. In addition to HHS, which houses the Medicare and Medicaid programs, other federal agencies concerned with health care fraud include the Department of Veterans Affairs, Department of Labor, Food and Drug Administration, and Federal Trade Commission.

1. ADMINISTRATIVE SANCTIONS

The OIG within HHS is specifically charged with ensuring the integrity of Medicare, Medicaid, and other programs within HHS's authority, as well as the health and welfare of program beneficiaries. The OIG may conduct investigations, studies, and audits and has authority to impose administrative sanctions, including CMPs and exclusion from participation in Medicare, Medicaid, and other government health care programs. 42 U.S.C. §1320a-7(a) lists the circumstances in which the Secretary must exercise exclusion authority.

(a) Mandatory exclusion

The Secretary shall exclude the following individuals and entities from participation in any Federal health care program:

(1) Conviction of program-related crimes

Any individual or entity that has been convicted of a criminal offense related to the delivery of an item or service under subchapter XVIII of this chapter or under any State health care program.

(2) Conviction relating to patient abuse

Any individual or entity that has been convicted, under Federal or State law, of a criminal offense relating to neglect or abuse of patients in connection with the delivery of a health care item or service.

(3) Felony conviction relating to health care fraud

Any individual or entity that has been convicted for an offense which occurred after August 21, 1996, under Federal or State law, in connection with the delivery of a health care item or service or with respect to any act or omission in a health care program (other than those specifically described in paragraph (1)) operated by or financed in whole or in part by any Federal, State, or local government agency, of a criminal offense consisting of a felony relating to fraud, theft, embezzlement, breach of fiduciary responsibility, or other financial misconduct.

(4) Felony conviction relating to controlled substance

Any individual or entity that has been convicted for an offense which occurred after August 21, 1996, under Federal or State law, of a criminal offense consisting of a felony relating to the unlawful manufacture, distribution, prescription, or dispensing of a controlled substance.

Subsection (b) also lists a number of circumstances in which the Secretary may exercise exclusion authority, including:

(1) Conviction relating to fraud
(2) Conviction relating to obstruction of an investigation or audit
(3) Misdemeanor conviction relating to controlled substance
(4) License revocation or suspension
(5) Exclusion or suspension under Federal or State health care program
(6) Claims for excessive charges or unnecessary services and failure of certain organizations to furnish medically necessary services
(7) Fraud, kickbacks, and other prohibited activities
(8) Entities controlled by a sanctioned individual
(9) Failure to disclose required information
(10) Failure to supply requested information on subcontractors and suppliers
(11) Failure to supply payment information
(12) Failure to grant immediate access
(13) Failure to take corrective action
(14) Default on health education loan or scholarship obligations
(15) Individuals controlling a sanctioned entity
(16) Making false statements or misrepresentation of material facts

Program exclusion is a particularly serious sanction, often operating as the "death penalty" for providers, which derive a substantial portion of their revenue from government programs. Moreover, private insurers may refuse to contract with excluded providers, and non-penalized health care providers cannot use any federal funds to pay excluded providers.

2. PRIVATE CONTRACTORS

HHS also employs a number of private contractors to assist its fraud enforcement efforts. First, Medicare Administrative Contractors (MACs), which generally make coverage determinations and process providers' claims for reimbursement, also play a role in policing fraud and abuse. MACs may deny or recoup improper payment for various reasons, including improper coding, upcoding, improper documentation, lack of medical necessity, and lack of physician certification. MACs also may conduct audits, educate providers, and screen beneficiary allegations of provider fraud.

Second, Recovery Audit Contractors (RACs), another type of private entity, were permanently established in 2006 under the Tax Relief and Healthcare Act, after a multiyear demonstration project. RACs are expressly hired by the government to identify improper payments to Medicare. RACs are paid "bounty hunters," retaining a percentage of the amounts they recover for the program. Providers may appeal MAC and RAC determinations through several steps of administrative adjudication and, under some circumstances, to federal district court. If the RAC determination is overturned on appeal, the RAC must return the contingency fee it received but faces no other financial penalty. Accordingly, RACs have been increasingly zealous in their pursuit of improper payments, and providers have been correspondingly active in appealing the denials.

3. COMPLIANCE AND SELF-DISCLOSURE

In addition to the various sanctions already described, providers may agree, during settlement negotiations, to institute Corporate Integrity Agreements (CIAs) to prevent further wrongdoing. CIAs effectively mandate detailed compliance programs and may be even more onerous than monetary fines. Common elements include external monitors, paid by the subject provider, to strengthen the compliance program and independently report infractions to the government.

Proof of an effective compliance program may be a mitigating factor in criminal sentencing.

Health care providers have for many years operated internal compliance programs, developed in accordance with standards established through guidance for each type of health care provider by the OIG; consistent with U.S. Sentencing Guidelines; and consonant with fiduciary duties imposed on boards of directors and other organizational leaders. Beginning 2010, with the passage of the ACA compliance programs are mandatory for all providers as a condition of Medicare, Medicaid, or Children's Health Insurance Program (CHIP) participation. Implementing regulations have not yet been promulgated for these compliance programs, and it remains to be seen how the requirement will change existing health care compliance activities.

In some cases, lawyers may advise their clients to notify the government of known noncompliance, rather than waiting for the government, a whistleblower, or a contractor to discover it. The ACA's 60-day rule increases the pressure to self-disclose by deeming knowing retention of identified overpayments, including payments for referrals prohibited by the Stark Law, as reverse false claims. As discussed above in the final regulations implementing the 60-day rule, a provider is considered to have "identified" an overpayment when the provider has, or should have through the exercise of reasonable diligence, determined that it has received an overpayment and quantified the amount of the overpayment. That definition means that providers cannot simply claim ignorance but must undertake proactive compliance efforts, including self-audits and other research to inform themselves of potential payment issues.

Routine self-disclosures and accompanying refunds are administered through the provider's MAC. The OIG also provides two protocols for self-disclosure, one general and one specific to Stark issues. The Provider Self-Disclosure Protocol (PSDP) provides a well-established, detailed process for all health care providers, suppliers, and other individuals subject to CMPs, premised on FCA or AKS violations. The Self-Referral Disclosure Protocol (SRDP) is much less utilized and provides a lengthier process. In either case, the advantage of self-disclosure is potentially to cut off *qui tam* actions and the running of the 60-day clock. In addition, providers gain certain advantages in settlement negotiations, including a presumption against CIAs, release from permissive exclusion, demonstration of an effective compliance program (and associated sentencing mitigation), reduction in the damages multiplier, and ability to control the disclosure, narrative, and media attention.

4. STATE FRAUD AND ABUSE LAWS

State fraud and abuse laws frequently differ in important aspects from their federal counterparts.

States have enacted local versions of the federal fraud and abuse laws. Many of these state laws mirror the federal statutes, but with significant modifications. These state laws frequently feature different exceptions and lack the extensive regulatory guidance provided under federal law. For example, the Georgia Patient Self-Referral Act of 1993 generally mirrors the Stark Law, but with elements that are both broader and narrower than the federal law. As of 2016, Georgia had not yet issued any regulations under its Act. Absent regulations, legal counsel frequently are constrained in their ability to offer an opinion on state fraud and abuse laws. It is possible that an arrangement that qualifies as legal under Stark nevertheless could run afoul of the corresponding state self-referral prohibition, or vice versa. If a state law criminalized conduct permitted by federal law, a defendant might successfully claim federal preemption. *See* State v. Harden, 938 So. 2d 480 (Fla. 2006).

Providers may be subject to investigations and prosecution by state authorities, including specialized Medicaid Fraud Control Units (MFCUs). MFCUs are usually housed under the state attorney general's office and are certified annually by HHS to investigate violations of state laws pertaining to Medicaid fraud.

In 2005, Congress enacted 42 U.S.C. §1396h, which creates a financial incentive for states to enact legislation that establishes state liability for false and fraudulent claims under their state Medicaid programs. Generally, if a state receives a recovery under state law for false or fraudulent claims submitted to the state Medicaid program, it must share a portion of the recovery with the federal government. The federal government's share is the same proportion as the federal medical assistance percentage (FMAP). Thus, if the state's FMAP is 60 percent, it may retain 40 percent of the recovery while returning the remaining 60 percent to the federal government. Under this Medicaid provision, however, states that enact false claims acts embodying key elements parallel to the federal law are entitled to retain an additional 10 percent of any recovery.

42 U.S.C. §1396h. State false claims act requirements for increased State share of recoveries

(a) In general. Notwithstanding section 1396d(b) of this title [regarding FMAP], if a State has in effect a law relating to false or fraudulent claims that meets the requirements of subsection (b), the Federal medical assistance percentage with respect to any amounts recovered under a State action brought under such law, shall be decreased by 10 percentage points.

(b) Requirements. For purposes of subsection (a), the requirements of this subsection are that the Inspector General of the Department of Health and Human Services, in consultation with the Attorney General, determines that the State has in effect a law that meets the following requirements:

(1) The law establishes liability to the State for false or fraudulent claims described in section 3729 of title 31 with respect to any expenditure described in section 1396b (a) of this title.

(2) The law contains provisions that are at least as effective in rewarding and facilitating qui tam actions for false or fraudulent claims as those described in sections 3730 through 3732 of title 31.

(3) The law contains a requirement for filing an action under seal for 60 days with review by the State Attorney General.

(4) The law contains a civil penalty that is not less than the amount of the civil penalty authorized under section 3729 of title 31.

In March 2013, the OIG published updated Guidelines for Evaluating State False Claims Acts. As of October 2015, the OIG had evaluated laws in 29 states, finding that 19 state laws meet the federal standards and therefore qualify for the

FMAP bonus on Medicaid fraud claims. More surprising are the 10 state laws that were reviewed but found to be noncompliant. As of October 2015, those states were Florida, Louisiana, Michigan, Nevada, New Hampshire, New Jersey, New Mexico, North Carolina, Oklahoma, and Wisconsin. Those state laws are valid but decrease the financial reward available for pursuing Medicaid fraud. The denial letters, such as the New Mexico letter below, offer insight into how states' law fell short of federal standards:

> **Office of Inspector General**
> **U.S. Department of Health & Human Services**
> July 24, 2008
> Elizabeth Staley
> Director Medicaid Fraud and Elder Abuse Division
> State of New Mexico Attorney General's Office
> 111 Lomas Boulevard, NW, Suite 300
> Albuquerque, New Mexico 87102
> Dear Ms. Staley:

The Office of Inspector General (OIG) of the U.S. Department of Health and Human Services (HHS) has received your request to review the New Mexico Fraud Against Taxpayers Act, N.M. Stat. §§44-9-1 through 44-9-14, under the requirements of section 6031(b) of the Deficit Reduction Act (DRA). Section 6031 of the DRA provides a financial incentive for states to enact laws that establish liability to the state for individuals and entities that submit false or fraudulent claims to the state Medicaid program. For a state to qualify for this incentive, the state law must meet certain requirements enumerated under section 6031(b) of the DRA, as determined by the Inspector General of HHS in consultation with the Department of Justice (DOJ). Based on our review of the law and consultation with DOJ, we have determined that the New Mexico Fraud Against Taxpayers Act does not meet the requirements of section 6031(b) of the DRA.

Section 6031(b)(2) of the DRA requires the state law to contain provisions that are at least as effective in rewarding and facilitating qui tam actions for false and fraudulent claims as those described in sections 3730 through 3732 of the Federal False Claims Act. The Federal False Claims Act provides that no court shall have jurisdiction over an action that is based upon a public disclosure unless the action is brought by the Attorney General or by a relator who is an "original source" of the information. *See* 31 U.S.C. §3730(e)(4). In contrast, the New Mexico Fraud Against Taxpayers Act, which provides that the court may dismiss an action if the elements of the alleged false or fraudulent claim have been publicly disclosed in the news media or in a publicly disseminated governmental report at the time the complaint is filed, does not provide an exception for a relator who is an "original source." *See* N.M. Stat. Ann. §44-9-9(D). Because the New Mexico Fraud Against Taxpayers Act public disclosure provision does not include an original source exception, it is not at least as effective in facilitating and rewarding qui tam actions as the Federal False Claims Act.

If the New Mexico Fraud Against Taxpayers Act is amended to address the issue noted above, please notify OIG for further consideration of the New Mexico Fraud Against Taxpayers Act. If you have any questions regarding this review, please contact me, or your staff may contact Karla Hampton at (202) 205-3158 or karla.hampton@oig.hhs.gov.

Sincerely,
/s/
Daniel R. Levinson
Inspector General

A number of states significantly revised existing state laws to obtain the enhanced FMAP under 42 U.S.C. §1396h. For example, the Georgia Taxpayer Protection False Claims Act was enacted on April 16, 2012, in response to an OIG letter concluding that Georgia's existing Medicaid False Claims Act was not rigorous enough to merit the extra 10 percent recovery. Georgia has now received a letter certifying compliance. Notably, the new Georgia law greatly expands liability beyond false claims for Medicaid-related services to every industry doing business with state or local governments in Georgia.

Ga. Code Ann. §23-3-121. Civil penalties

(a) Any person, firm, corporation, or other legal entity that:

(1) Knowingly presents or causes to be presented a false or fraudulent claim for payment or approval;

(2) Knowingly makes, uses, or causes to be made or used a false record or statement material to a false or fraudulent claim;

(3) Conspires to commit a violation of paragraph (1), (2), (4), (5), (6), or (7) of this subsection;

(4) Has possession, custody, or control of property or money used, or to be used, by the state or local government and knowingly delivers, or causes to be delivered, less than all of that money or property;

(5) Being authorized to make or deliver a document certifying receipt of property used, or to be used, by the state or local government and, intending to defraud the state or local government, makes or delivers the receipt without completely knowing that the information on the receipt is true;

(6) Knowingly buys, or receives as a pledge of an obligation or debt, public property from an officer or employee of the state or local government who lawfully may not sell or pledge the property; or

(7) Knowingly makes, uses, or causes to be made or used a false record or statement material to an obligation to pay or transmit money or property to the state or local government, or knowingly conceals, knowingly and improperly avoids, or decreases an obligation to pay or transmit money or property to the state or a local government shall be liable to the State of Georgia for a civil penalty of not less than $5,500.00 and not more than $11,000.00 for each false or fraudulent claim, plus three times the amount of damages which the state or local government sustains because of the act of such person.

> The ongoing effort to bring state laws into compliance with §1396h is but one example of the federal spending power being used to encourage state laws that the federal government cannot mandate directly.

Most providers accept payment from many payers, including Medicare, Medicaid, state employee insurance plans, and private health insurers and find it difficult to segregate any financial relationships by payer class. As a result, practically speaking, providers aim to comply with all of these federal and state fraud and abuse laws for all of their patients, even those not covered by the particular program.

CAPSTONE PROBLEM

Your client (Hipster, Inc.) manufactures and sells total hip replacement joints to surgeons. In order to improve the product, Hipster recruits leading surgeons as key opinion leaders and pays them for design improvement ideas. These surgeons also lead educational sessions for other surgeons. For these and other services, Hipster offers consulting fees and occasionally stock in the company. For some surgeons, their ideas on improvements are rewarded through a royalty, approximately 5 percent of the sales price of the device, with a higher royalty rate for sales to the physicians themselves. In a 500-word memo, outline the likely issues under the fraud and abuse statutes and rules discussed in this chapter.

CHAPTER 7

Competition in Health Care Markets

A. INTRODUCTION

Health care is a big business. A fault line in American health care policy is to what degree health care should be treated as an ordinary market good. Conservatives and libertarians generally argue for a market-based competitive approach with less governmental interference. Liberals and progressives generally claim that market failures necessitate more government regulation. Both major parties currently support public financing of care to the elderly in Medicare but disagree on such issues as Medicaid expansion and government subsidies in the Exchanges.

A major change in the Patient Protection and Affordable Care Act (ACA) was the effective consolidation of risk pools across most private health plans, encouraging health insurance companies to stop medical underwriting. Some conservative policy experts continue to oppose this consolidation, calling for individuals with unhealthy lifestyles to bear more of their own risk. Some see this consolidation of risk pools as an interim step on the road to single-payer health insurance.

These political forces have been at odds in American health care markets for decades, resulting in a system with a remarkable array of complex public and private markets in both the finance and delivery of health care, under layers of pervasive federal and state regulation. Health insurance (studied in Chapters 2 and 3) is a prime example of this dense regulatory mix. In this chapter, we consider competition in health care markets, particularly how antitrust law applies to many business and professional relationships in health care.

In this chapter, we first review the threshold question of why competition may not function well in health care, together with providing a basic introduction to antitrust law. We then explore five important categories of health care competition legal issues: (1) hospital mergers; (2) collaborative arrangements with provider networks, including accountable care organizations (ACOs); (3) medical licensing laws and certificate of need requirements as devices to hinder market entry by competitors; (4) the role of states in health care antitrust law; and (5) laws that seek to improve health care competition through access to better information.

In addition to antitrust doctrine, it is important to see how major parts of the health care system interact with each other. The goal is to understand both the business context as well as the legal doctrine.

B. HEALTH CARE MARKET IMPERFECTIONS

As discussed in Chapter 1, the economist Kenneth Arrow observed several distinctive features in health care that impede normal market functioning:

- **Information asymmetries** — The customer buying health care services often has much less information about quality or value. Buyers have a good sense of what a smartphone or sandwich is worth; patients often have little information about the price or value of a prescribed test, pill, or procedure. Consumers face significant product and service uncertainty and lack transparent pricing. Instead, patients rely on experts (physicians and health plans) to tell them what to buy.
- **Unpredictable demand** — Outside routine prevention, our need for medical care is relatively unpredictable. No one knows when an accident, infection, or chronic condition will occur. The typical market solution to unpredictable risk is insurance, which leads to the next problem.
- **Third-party payment** — Most of what we buy in health care is covered by insurance, so "someone else" is paying. If all transportation was covered in a "major transportation policy," then everyone might drive fancier cars. The incentive to be careful shoppers is diminished with third-party payment. People may consume more care when it is free at the point of care or nearly so. If all restaurants were "all you can eat" buffets, consumption would increase. Copays and deductibles are designed to partially offset these incentives.
- **Licensing** — While many professions require licensing, health care is particularly rife with licensing and certifications. These are a response to information asymmetries, protecting consumers by establishing minimum quality standards across the board, such as minimum educational standards for becoming a physician or nurse anesthetist, or minimum quality standards before opening a hospital. But licensing also restricts competition and raises costs.
- **Pooling of unequal risks** — In a system approximating a single risk pool (such as Medicare, traditional Blue Cross policies, or most private health insurance after the ACA), the currently sick are being subsidized by the currently healthy. Of course, that is the purpose of health insurance — to help pay for needed care when illness strikes. But in the absence of a regulatory mechanism to consolidate the risk pool, the market would offer cheaper policies to the healthy and force the sick to pay much more.
- **Failure to pay for value** — Arrow called this a lack of "ideal insurance," where providers would be rewarded only if the patient recovered, but not if the treatment failed. Imagine if we had "smartphone insurance" that promised unlimited access to smartphones but said nothing about whether the phones worked at all. Some data indicates that many medical treatments do not benefit the patient, and yet payments follow. One area of health policy that enjoys bipartisan support is revising Medicare to "pay for performance" (P4P), also known as value-based reimbursement (discussed in Chapter 2).

In this chapter, we examine two approaches to imperfections in health care markets: restoring competition and addressing information asymmetries. The first approach is to regulate the market with the primary goal of restoring competition. That is the realm of antitrust law. The application of antitrust law to health care is relatively recent but offers a number of complex and thought-provoking issues to consider. Despite the size of the health care sector, many areas of health care are remarkably uncompetitive in practice. Most health care is delivered locally; and through consolidation and attrition, in many markets little choice of provider networks remains.

Second, information asymmetries in health care markets have led to both restrictive and permissive regulatory projects. For a restrictive example, every state has limited patients' choice in the name of safety and quality control. Licensing creates minimum standards, below which the market is not legally permitted to offer medical services: For example, surgery is only available from a licensed physician in an accredited facility. The alternative, more permissive, strategy is to provide higher-quality information to the market, helping patients make better choices. We examine both approaches.

C. INTRODUCTION TO ANTITRUST LAW

At the federal level, antitrust law is founded on the Sherman Antitrust Act of 1890, the Clayton Antitrust Act, and the Federal Trade Commission Act (FTC Act):

15 U.S.C. §1 [section 1 of the Sherman Act]. Trusts, etc., in restraint of trade illegal; penalty

Every contract, combination in the form of trust or otherwise, or conspiracy, in restraint of trade or commerce among the several States, or with foreign nations, is declared to be illegal. Every person who shall make any contract or engage in any combination or conspiracy hereby declared to be illegal shall be deemed guilty of a felony. . . .

15 U.S.C. §2 [section 2 of the Sherman Act]. Monopolizing trade a felony; penalty

Every person who shall monopolize, or attempt to monopolize, or combine or conspire with any other person or persons, to monopolize any part of the trade or commerce among the several States, or with foreign nations, shall be deemed guilty of a felony. . . .

15 U.S.C. §18 [section 7 of the Clayton Act]. Acquisition by one corporation of stock of another

No person engaged in commerce or in any activity affecting commerce shall acquire, directly or indirectly, the whole or any part of the stock or other share capital and no person subject to the jurisdiction of the Federal Trade Commission shall acquire the whole or any part of the assets of another person engaged also in commerce or in any activity affecting commerce, where in any line of commerce or in any activity affecting commerce in any section of the country, the effect of such acquisition may be substantially to lessen competition, or to tend to create a monopoly . . . .

15 U.S.C. §45(a) [section 5 of the FTC Act]. Unfair methods of competition unlawful; prevention by Commission

(1) Unfair methods of competition in or affecting commerce, and unfair or deceptive acts or practices in or affecting commerce, are hereby declared unlawful.

(2) The Commission is hereby empowered and directed to prevent persons, partnerships, or corporations . . . from using unfair methods of competition in or affecting commerce and unfair or deceptive acts or practices in or affecting commerce.

Section 1 of the Sherman Act reaches agreements in restraint of trade, which could include many agreements in health care such as provider networks and hospital merger agreements. Because almost every agreement could be seen to restrain trade, the Supreme Court has limited section 1 to "unreasonable" restraints on trade.

Section 2 of the Sherman Act covers unilateral conduct by a monopolist. Proscribed conduct includes possession of market power combined with willful steps to expand and use market power. For example, if a sole hospital raised prices and blocked competition by controlling doctors, that conduct might violate section 2, even in the absence of an agreement necessary under section 1.

Section 7 of the Clayton Act also governs mergers and other acquisitions that may substantially lessen competition or tend to create a monopoly. Under section 7, courts examine evidence about the competitive effects of a proposed merger on the ability to raise prices, a common issue in hospital mergers.

Section 5 of the FTC Act covers all violations of the Sherman and Clayton Acts (as "unfair methods of competition") in addition to unfair or deceptive acts or practices. While the FTC Act is limited to for-profit enterprises, section 5 can apply if a nonprofit engages in substantial economic activity for their members.

Several parties have standing to initiate an antitrust action. The Federal Trade Commission enforces the FTC Act, with administrative power to conduct hearings and to file civil suits. The U.S. Department of Justice enforces the Sherman Act and the Clayton Act in federal court. Many states have local versions of these acts, which may be enforced by the state attorney general. Finally, private parties harmed by anticompetitive conduct may file private antitrust lawsuits.

In the early decades, antitrust laws did not apply to much of the health care sector, including health insurance and health care providers. In 1948, Congress passed the McCarran-Ferguson Act, 15 U.S.C. §1012, which for the first time applied the Sherman, Clayton, and FTC Acts to the business of insurance, but only to the extent not regulated by state law.

Until the Supreme Court's decision in Goldfarb v. Virginia State Bar, 421 U.S. 773 (1975), "learned professions" like law and medicine also enjoyed partial exemption from the antitrust laws. In *Goldfarb*, the county bar association enforced a minimum fee schedule for legal services. Courts below had ruled that learned professions like law and medicine were not "trade or commerce" under the Sherman Act. The Supreme Court held that learned professions are indeed subject to the Sherman Act. In the four decades since *Goldfarb*, health care antitrust law has probed many aspects of health care markets. We turn to some of those cases now.

D. INCREASING MARKET POWER THROUGH MERGER

1. HOSPITAL MERGERS

After decades of consolidations and mergers, hospital markets across the United States are increasingly concentrated. In the next case, two of the four hospitals in Toledo, Ohio, proposed a merger, leading to fears that the combined hospital would be able to raise prices for private insurers. The case contains rich facts, which have been retained to display the full context of the business implications of this merger. Mergers between competitors are called "horizontal" mergers in antitrust law.

ProMedica Health System, Inc. v. Federal Trade Commission

749 F.3d 559 (6th Cir. 2014)

This is an antitrust case involving a proposed merger between two of the four hospital systems in Lucas County, Ohio. The parties to the merger were ProMedica, by far the county's dominant hospital provider, and St. Luke's, an independent community hospital. The two merged in August 2010, leaving ProMedica with a market share above 50% in one relevant product market (for so-called primary and secondary services) and above 80% in another (for obstetrical services). Five months later, the Federal Trade Commission challenged the merger under §7 of the Clayton Act, 15 U.S.C. §18. After extensive hearings, an Administrative Law Judge and later the Commission found that the merger would adversely affect competition in violation of §7. The Commission therefore ordered ProMedica to divest St. Luke's. ProMedica now petitions for review of the Commission's order, arguing that the Commission was wrong on both the law and the facts in its analysis of the merger's competitive effects. We think the Commission was right on both counts, and deny the petition.

Lucas County is located in the northwestern corner of Ohio, with approximately 440,000 residents. Toledo lies near the county's center; more affluent suburbs lie to the southwest. Two-thirds of the county's patients have government-provided health insurance, such as Medicare or Medicaid. Twenty-nine percent of the county's patients have private health insurance, which pays significantly higher rates to hospitals than government-provided insurance does. (Medicare and Medicaid reimbursements generally do not cover the providers' actual cost of services.) A relatively large proportion of the county's privately insured patients reside in the county's southwestern corner.

This case concerns the market—or markets, depending on how one defines them—for "general acute-care" (GAC) inpatient services in Lucas County. GAC comprises four basic categories of services. The most basic are "primary services," such as hernia surgeries, radiology services, and most kinds of inpatient obstetrical (OB) services. "Secondary services," such as hip replacements and bariatric surgery, require the hospital to have more specialized resources. "Tertiary services," such as brain surgery and treatments for severe burns, require even more specialized resources. And "quaternary services," such as major organ transplants, require the most specialized resources of all.

Different hospitals offer different levels of these services. There are four hospital providers in Lucas County. The most dominant is ProMedica, with 46.8% of the GAC market in Lucas County in 2009. ProMedica operates three hospitals in the county, which together provide primary (including OB), secondary, and tertiary services. The county's second-largest provider is Mercy Health Partners, with 28.7% of the GAC market in 2009. Mercy likewise operates three hospitals in the county, which together provide primary (including OB), secondary, and tertiary services. The University of Toledo Medical Center (UTMC) is the county's

> In the proposed merger, the largest local system (ProMedica) acquires the smallest (St. Luke's).

third-largest provider, with 13% of the GAC market. UTMC operates a single teaching and research hospital, just south of downtown Toledo, and focuses on tertiary and quaternary services. It does not offer OB services. The remaining provider is St. Luke's Hospital, which before the merger was an independent, not-for-profit hospital with 11.5% of the GAC market. St. Luke's offers primary (including OB) and secondary services, and is located in southwest Lucas County.

With respect to privately insured patients, hospital providers do not all receive the same rates for the same services. Far from it: each hospital negotiates its rates with private insurers (known as Managed Care Organizations, or MCOs); and the rates themselves are determined by each party's bargaining power.

The parties' bargaining power depends on a variety of factors. An MCO's bargaining power depends primarily on the number of patients it can offer a hospital provider. Hospitals need patients like stores need customers; and hence the greater the number of patients that an MCO can offer a provider, the greater the MCO's leverage in negotiating the hospital's rates. But MCOs compete with each other just as hospitals do. And to attract patients, an MCO's health-care plan must offer a comprehensive range of services—primary, secondary, tertiary, and quaternary—within a geographic range that patients are willing to travel for each of those services. (The range is greater for some services than others.) These criteria in turn create leverage for hospitals to raise rates: to the extent patients view a hospital's services as desirable or even essential—say, because of the hospital's location or its reputation for quality—the hospital's bargaining power increases.

But another important criterion for a plan's competitiveness is its cost. Thus, if a hospital demands rates above a certain level—the so-called "walk-away" point—the MCO will try to assemble a network without that provider. For example, rather than include all four hospital providers in its network, the MCO might include only three. If a provider becomes so dominant in a particular market that no MCO can walk away from it and remain competitive, however, then that provider can demand—and more to the point receive—monopoly rates (*i.e.*, prices significantly higher than what the MCOs would pay in a competitive market).

Here, before the merger, MCOs in Lucas County had sometimes offered networks that included all four hospital providers, but sometimes offered networks that included only three. From 2001 until 2008, for example, Lucas County's largest MCO, Medical Mutual of Ohio, successfully marketed a network of Mercy, UTMC, and St. Luke's. Since 2000, however, no MCO has offered a network that did not include either ProMedica or St. Luke's—the parties to the merger here.

> After this merger, Medical Mutual of Ohio will probably not be able to assemble a network that excludes ProMedica.

The likely reason MCOs have historically found it necessary to include either ProMedica or St. Luke's in their networks is that those providers are dominant in southwest Lucas County, where St. Luke's is located. In that part of the county—relatively affluent, and with a high proportion of privately insured patients—ProMedica and St. Luke's were direct competitors before the merger at issue here. Indeed, St. Luke's viewed ProMedica as its "most significant competitor," while ProMedica viewed St. Luke's as a "[s]trong competitor"—strong enough, in fact, that ProMedica offered to discount its rates by 2.5% for MCOs who excluded St. Luke's from their networks. But in this competition ProMedica had the upper hand. It is harder for an MCO to exclude the county's most dominant hospital system than it is for the MCO to exclude a single hospital that services just one corner of the county—a corner, moreover, that the dominant system also services. And that means the MCOs' walk-away point for the dominant system is higher—perhaps much higher—than it is for the single hospital. Here, the record bears out that conclusion: ProMedica's rates before the merger were among the highest in the State, while St. Luke's rates did not even cover its cost of patient care. That was true even though St. Luke's quality ratings on the whole were better than ProMedica's.

As a result, St. Luke's struggled in the years before the merger, losing more than $25 million between 2007 and 2009. To improve matters, St. Luke's hired Daniel Wakeman, a hospital-turnaround specialist, as its CEO. Wakeman implemented a three-year plan to reduce costs, increase revenues, and regain patient volume from ProMedica. Eventually St. Luke's fortunes began to improve: by August 2010, St. Luke's was out of the red (albeit barely), and Wakeman reported that "this positive margin confirms that we can run in the black if activity stays high."

By then, however, St. Luke's was contemplating other options. In August 2009, Wakeman presented three options to St. Luke's Board. The first was for St. Luke's to "[r]emain independent" by "cut[ting] major services" until an "accepted margin is realized." The second was for St. Luke's to "[p]ush the [MCOs] . . . to raise St. Luke's reimbursement rates to an acceptable margin." Under this option, Wakeman noted, "the message [to MCOs] would be [to] pay us now (a little bit more) or pay us later (at the other hospital system contractual rates)." The third option was for St. Luke's to join one of the three other providers in Lucas County—ProMedica, Mercy, or UTMC.

Of all these options, Wakeman believed that a merger with ProMedica "ha[d] the greatest potential for higher hospital rates. A ProMedica-[St. Luke's] partnership would have a lot of negotiating clout." Wakeman also recognized, however, that an affiliation with ProMedica could "[h]arm the community by forcing higher hospital rates on them."

Three months later, Wakeman recommended to St. Luke's Board that it pursue a merger with ProMedica. The Board accepted the recommendation the same day. Six months later, on May 25, 2010, ProMedica and St. Luke's signed a merger agreement.

In July 2010—less than two months after the agreement was signed—the FTC opened an investigation into the merger's competitive effects. A month later, the FTC and ProMedica entered into a "Hold Separate Agreement" that allowed ProMedica to close the deal, but that, during the pendency of the FTC investigation, barred ProMedica from terminating St. Luke's contracts with MCOs, eliminating or transferring St. Luke's clinical services, or terminating St. Luke's employees without cause. With these restrictions in place, ProMedica and St. Luke's closed the merger deal on August 31, 2010.

In January 2011, the FTC filed an administrative complaint against ProMedica. Later that month, the FTC and the state of Ohio filed a separate complaint in federal district court in Toledo, seeking a preliminary injunction that would extend the Hold Separate Agreement pending the outcome of the FTC's administrative complaint. The district court granted the injunction.

Meanwhile, in the administrative proceeding, an ALJ held a hearing that lasted over 30 days and produced more than 8,000 pages of trial testimony and over 2,600 exhibits. In December 2011, the ALJ issued a lengthy written decision. The ALJ found that the merger would "result[ ] in a tremendous increase in concentration in a

Note the parallel proceedings: The FTC first filed an administrative complaint within the FTC, heard by an administrative law judge (ALJ). The FTC then sued in federal district court, joined by Ohio, which has independent authority in antitrust matters. The U.S. Department of Justice also has authority to enforce federal antitrust laws. Some private parties would also have standing to sue, including rival hospitals and health plans hurt by the merger.

market that already was highly concentrated"; that the merger would eliminate competition between ProMedica and St. Luke's, thereby increasing ProMedica's bargaining power with MCOs; and that ProMedica would be particularly dominant in southwest Lucas County — an area with a relatively high proportion of privately insured patients. Thus, the ALJ found that the merger would allow ProMedica unilaterally to increase its prices above a competitive level. The ALJ also found that the merger did not create any efficiencies sufficient to offset its anticompetitive effects. Consequently, the ALJ concluded that the merger likely would substantially lessen competition in violation of §7 of the Clayton Act. As a remedy, the ALJ ordered ProMedica to divest St. Luke's.

ProMedica appealed the ALJ's decision to the Commission, which found that the merger increased ProMedica's market share far above the threshold required to create a presumption that the merger would lessen competition. The Commission also found that a large body of other evidence — including documents and testimony from the merging parties themselves, testimony from the MCOs, and expert testimony — confirmed that the merger would have a substantial anticompetitive effect. The Commission therefore affirmed the ALJ's decision and ordered ProMedica to divest St. Luke's.

. . . Section 7 of the Clayton Act prohibits mergers "where in any line of commerce . . . the effect of such acquisition may be substantially to lessen competition, or to tend to create a monopoly." As its language suggests, Section 7 deals in "probabilities, not certainties."

"Merger enforcement, like other areas of antitrust, is directed at market power." Market power is itself a term of art that the Department of Justice's Horizontal Merger Guidelines (which we consider useful but not binding upon us here) define as the power of "one or more firms to raise price, reduce output, diminish innovation, or otherwise harm consumers as a result of diminished competitive constraints or incentives." *Horizontal Merger Guidelines* (2010) ("Merger Guidelines") §1 at 2.

These guidelines are informal administrative guidance from the federal agencies enforcing antitrust laws. They are discussed in almost every horizontal merger case.

Often, the first steps in analyzing a merger's competitive effects are to define the geographic and product markets affected by it. Here, the parties agree that the relevant geographic market is Lucas County. The relevant product market or markets, however, are more difficult. The first principle of market definition is substitutability: a relevant product market must "identify a set of products that are reasonably interchangeable[.]" Horizontal Merger Guidelines §4.1. Chevrolets and Fords might be interchangeable in this sense, but Chevrolets and Lamborghinis are probably not. "The general question is whether two products can be used for the same purpose, and if so, whether and to what extent purchasers are willing to substitute one for the other."

By this measure, each individual medical procedure could give rise to a separate market: "[i]f you need your hip replaced, you can't decide to have chemotherapy instead." But nobody advocates that we analyze the effects of this merger upon hundreds if not thousands of markets for individual procedures; instead, the parties agree that we should "cluster" these markets somehow. The parties disagree, however, on the principles that should govern which services are clustered and which are not. . . .

The competitive conditions for hospital services include the barriers to entry for a particular service — *e.g.*, how difficult it might be for a new competitor to buy the equipment and sign up the professionals necessary to offer the service — as well as the hospitals' respective market shares for the service and the geographic market for the service. If these conditions are similar for a range of services, then the antitrust analysis should be similar for each of them. Thus, if the competitive conditions for, say, secondary inpatient procedures are all reasonably similar, then we can cluster those services when analyzing a merger's competitive effects.

Here, the Commission applied this theory to cluster both primary services (but excluding OB, for reasons discussed below) and secondary services for purposes of analyzing the merger's competitive effects. Substantial evidence supports that demarcation. The respective market shares for each of Lucas County's four hospital systems (ProMedica, Mercy, UTMC, St. Luke's) are similar across the range of primary and secondary services. A hospital's market share for shoulder surgery, for example, is similar to its market share for knee replacements. Barriers to entry are likewise similar across primary and secondary services. So are the services' respective geographic markets. Thus, the competitive conditions across the markets for primary and secondary services are similar enough to justify clustering those markets when analyzing the merger's competitive effects.

But the same is not true for OB services, whose competitive conditions differ in at least two respects from those for other services. First, before the merger, ProMedica's market share for OB services (71.2%) was more than half-again greater than its market share for primary and secondary services (46.8%). And the merger would drive ProMedica's share for OB services even higher, to 80.5% — no small number in this area of the law. Second, and relatedly, before the merger there were only three hospital systems that provided OB services in Lucas County (ProMedica, Mercy, St. Luke's) rather than four; after the merger, there would be only two. (One might also suspect that the geographic market for OB services is smaller than it is for other primary services — one can drive only so far when the baby is on the way — but the record is not clear on that point.) The Commission therefore flagged OB as a separate relevant market for purposes of analyzing the merger's competitive effects. For the reasons just stated, substantial evidence supports that decision. . . .

[T]he record makes plain that the MCOs do not demand from each hospital a package of services that includes tertiary and OB. For example, St. Luke's offers virtually no tertiary services, and yet the MCOs still contract for the services that St. Luke's does offer. Likewise, UTMC does not offer OB services, and yet the MCOs still contract with UTMC. And as for the hospital systems that do provide all those services — *i.e.*, ProMedica and Mercy — there is no evidence that MCOs are willing to pay a premium to have all of those services delivered by either of those providers in a single package. It is true that MCOs must offer their *members* (*i.e.*, patients) a network that provides a complete package of hospital services. But the record shows that the MCOs do not need to obtain all of those services from a single provider. There are no market forces that bind primary, secondary, tertiary, and OB services together like a single plywood sheet.

In summary, even ProMedica conceded in its answer to the FTC's complaint that the "more sophisticated and specialized tertiary and quaternary services, such as major surgeries and organ transplants, also are properly excluded from the relevant market[.]" ProMedica was correct to make that concession then, and incorrect to seek to retract it now. The relevant markets, for purposes of analyzing the merger's competitive effects, are what the Commission says they are: (1) a cluster market of primary (but not OB) and secondary inpatient services (hereafter, the "GAC market"), and (2) a separate market for OB services. . . .

ProMedica's next argument is that the Commission relied too heavily on market-concentration data to establish a presumption of anticompetitive harm. Agencies typically use the Herfindahl–Hirschman Index (HHI) to measure market concentration. "The HHI is calculated by summing the squares of the individual firms' market shares, and thus gives proportionately greater weight to the larger market shares." *Merger Guidelines* §5.3 at 18. Agencies use HHI data to classify markets into three types: "unconcentrated markets," which have an HHI below 1500; "moderately concentrated markets," which have an HHI between 1500 and 2500; and "highly concentrated markets," which have an HHI above 2500. *Id.* at 19. The Guidelines further provide that "[m]ergers resulting in highly concentrated markets that involve an increase in the HHI of more than 200 points will be presumed to be likely to enhance market power." Thus, as a general matter, a merger that increases HHI by more than 200 points, to a total number exceeding 2500, is presumptively anticompetitive.

The merger here blew through those barriers in spectacular fashion. In the GAC market, the merger would increase the HHI by 1,078 (more than five times the increase necessary to trigger the presumption of illegality) to a total number of 4,391 (almost double the 2,500 threshold for a highly concentrated market). The OB numbers are even worse: the merger would increase HHI by 1,323 points (almost seven times the increase necessary for the presumption of illegality) to a total number of 6,854 (almost triple the threshold for a highly concentrated market). The Commission therefore found the merger to be presumptively illegal . . . [but ProMedica] argues that the Commission was wrong to presume the merger illegal based upon HHI data alone.

The argument is one to be taken seriously. The Guidelines themselves state that "[a]gencies rely much more on the value of diverted sales [*i.e.*, in rough terms, the extent to which the products of the merging firms are close substitutes] than on the level of HHI for diagnosing unilateral price effects in markets with differentiated products." *Id.* But this case is exceptional in two respects. First, even without conducting a substitutability analysis, the record already shows a strong correlation between ProMedica's prices—*i.e.*, its ability to impose unilateral price increases—and its market share. Before the merger, ProMedica's share of the GAC market was 46.8%, followed by Mercy with 28.7%, UTMC with 13%, and St. Luke's with 11.5%. And ProMedica's prices were on average 32% higher than Mercy's, 51% higher than UTMC's, and 74% higher than St. Luke's. Thus, in this market, the higher a provider's market share, the higher its prices. In ProMedica's case, that fact is not explained by the quality of ProMedica's services or by its underlying costs. Instead, ProMedica's prices—already among the highest in the State—are explained by *bargaining power*. As the Commission explained: "the hospital provider's bargaining leverage will depend upon how the MCO would fare if its network did not include the hospital provider (and therefore became less attractive to potential members who prefer that provider's services)." Here, the record makes clear that a network which does not include a hospital provider that services almost half the county's patients in one relevant market, and more than 70% of the county's patients in another relevant market, would be unattractive to a huge swath of potential members. Thus, the Commission had every reason to conclude that, as ProMedica's dominance in the relevant markets increases, so does the need for MCOs to include ProMedica in their networks—and thus so too does ProMedica's leverage in demanding higher rates.

The second respect in which this case is exceptional is simply the HHI numbers themselves. Even in unilateral-effects cases, at some point the Commission is entitled to take seriously the alarm sounded by a merger's HHI data. And here the numbers are in every respect multiples of the numbers necessary for the presumption of illegality. Before the merger, ProMedica already held dominant market shares in the relevant markets, which were themselves already highly concentrated. The merger would drive those numbers even higher—ProMedica's share of the OB market would top 80%—which makes it extremely likely, as matter of simple mathematics, that a "significant fraction" of St. Luke's patients viewed ProMedica as a close substitute for services in the relevant markets. On this record, the Commission was entitled to put significant weight upon the market-concentration data standing alone.

These two aspects of this case—the strong correlation between market share and price, and the degree to which this merger would further concentrate markets that are already highly concentrated—converge in a manner that fully supports the Commission's application of a presumption of illegality. What ProMedica overlooks is that the "ultimate inquiry in merger analysis" is not substitutability, but "'whether the merger is likely to create or enhance *market power* or facilitate its exercise.'" Here, as shown above, the correlation between market share and price reflects a correlation between market share and market power; and the HHI data strongly suggest that this merger would enhance ProMedica's market power even more, to levels rarely tolerated in antitrust law. In the context of this record, therefore, the HHI data speak to our "ultimate inquiry" as directly as an analysis of substitutability would. The Commission was correct to presume the merger substantially anticompetitive.

The remaining question is whether ProMedica has rebutted that presumption. ProMedica argues on several grounds that it has; but more remarkable is what Pro-Medica does not argue. By way of background, the goal of antitrust law is to enhance consumer welfare. And the Merger Guidelines themselves recognize that "a primary benefit of mergers to the economy is their potential to generate significant efficiencies and thus enhance the merged firm's ability and incentive to compete, which may result in lower prices, improved quality, enhanced service, or new products." Thus, the parties to a merger often seek to overcome a presumption of illegality by arguing that the merger would create efficiencies that enhance consumer welfare. But ProMedica did not even attempt to argue before the Commission, and does not attempt to argue here, that this merger would benefit consumers (as opposed to only the merging parties themselves) in any way. To the contrary, St. Luke's CEO admitted that a merger with ProMedica might "[h]arm the community by forcing higher rates on them." The record with respect to the merger's effect on consumer welfare, therefore, only diminishes ProMedica's prospects here.

> Most merging hospitals will try to offer stronger evidence of pro-competitive effects of the merger.

That the Commission did not merely rest upon the presumption, but instead discussed a wide range of evidence that buttresses it, makes ProMedica's task more difficult still. On that score the Commission's best witnesses were the merging parties themselves. Those witnesses established that ProMedica and St. Luke's are direct competitors: St. Luke's CEO testified that ProMedica was St. Luke's "most significant competitor," while a ProMedica witness testified that ProMedica viewed St. Luke's as a "[s]trong competitor"—strong enough that ProMedica offered at least one MCO a 2.5% discount off its rates if the MCO excluded St. Luke's from its network. St. Luke's management was also candid about the merger's potential impacts on its prices: its CEO stated that a merger with ProMedica "has the greatest potential for higher hospital rates" and would bring "a lot of negotiating clout." The parties' own statements, therefore, tend to confirm the presumption rather than rebut it.

The same is true of testimony from the MCO witnesses. Those witnesses testified that a network comprising only Mercy and UTMC—the only other providers who would remain after the merger—would not be commercially viable because it would leave them with a "hole" in the suburbs of southwest Lucas County. (That no MCO has offered such a network during the past decade corroborates the point.) Consequently, the MCO witnesses explained, they would have no walk-away option in post-merger negotiations with ProMedica—and thus little ability to resist ProMedica's demands for even higher rates. ProMedica responds that this testimony is self-serving, which might well be true (though one might construe ProMedica's response as an implicit admission of the MCOs' point). But ProMedica otherwise offers no reason to think the MCOs' predictions are wrong—and the record offers plenty of reason to think they are right.

> Testimony from MCOs is important because they are the primary payers for services from the hospitals.

ProMedica's task, then, is to overcome not merely the presumption of anticompetitive effects, but also the statements of the merging parties themselves, and the MCOs' testimony, and ProMedica's failure to cite any efficiencies that would result from this merger. To that end, ProMedica argues that Mercy, rather than St. Luke's, is ProMedica's closest substitute—because Mercy, like ProMedica, offers tertiary services, whereas St. Luke's does not. But any argument about substitutes must begin with a definition of the relevant market; and ProMedica's argument is based upon a market definition that we have already rejected. That Mercy offers tertiary services, and St. Luke's for the most part does not, matters only if the relevant market is one for a primary, secondary, and tertiary services wrapped together *in a single package*. That is not the relevant market here. Instead, the relevant markets are those for GAC services and OB services, respectively—markets in which the merging parties' own statements show that ProMedica and St. Luke's are direct competitors. ProMedica's argument is meritless.

ProMedica also argues that MCOs, rather than patients, are the relevant consumers here, and that the Commission therefore erred by "assess[ing] substitutability from the patients' perspective." But this is an argument about semantics. MCOs assemble networks based primarily upon patients' preferences, not their own; and thus the extent to which an MCO regards ProMedica and St. Luke's as close substitutes depends upon the extent to which the MCO's members do.

Finally, ProMedica argues that St. Luke's was in such dire financial straits before the merger that it "was not a meaningful competitive constraint on ProMedica." This argument is known as a "weakened competitor" one, and is itself "probably the weakest ground of all for justifying a merger." Courts "credit such a defense only in rare cases, when the [acquiring firm] makes a substantial showing that the acquired

> This is also known as the failing- or flailing-firm defense.

firm's weakness, which cannot be resolved by any competitive means, would cause that firm's market share to reduce to a level that would undermine the government's *prima facie* case." In other words, this argument is the Hail-Mary pass of presumptively doomed mergers — in this case thrown from ProMedica's own end zone. The record demonstrates that St. Luke's market share was increasing prior to the merger; that St. Luke's had sufficient cash reserves to pay all of its obligations and meet its capital needs without any additional borrowing; and that, according to St. Luke's CEO, "we can run in the black if activity stays high." St. Luke's difficulties before the merger provide no basis to reject the Commission's findings about the merger's anticompetitive effects.

ProMedica has failed to rebut the presumption that its merger with St. Luke's would reduce competition in violation of the Clayton Act. We therefore need not address ProMedica's remaining criticisms of various other evidence that merely buttressed that presumption.

. . . Once a merger is found illegal, "an undoing of the acquisition is a natural remedy." Here, the Commission found that divestiture would be the best means to preserve competition in the relevant markets. The Commission also found that ProMedica's suggested "conduct remedy" — which would establish, among other things, separate negotiation teams for ProMedica and St. Luke's — was disfavored because "there are usually greater long term costs associated with monitoring the efficacy of a conduct remedy than with imposing a structural solution." And the Commission found no circumstances warranting such a remedy here. We have no basis to dispute any of those findings. The Commission did not abuse its discretion in choosing divestiture as a remedy.

The Commission's analysis of this merger was comprehensive, carefully reasoned, and supported by substantial evidence in the record. The petition is denied.

PROBLEM

After a case like this in the City of Bostonia, assume that several leading physicians from St. Theoden's become disenchanted and begin to discuss their options. The largest hospital system (SuperMedica) meets with these physicians and recruits them to join the SuperMedica medical staff. After a short period, most of the former St. Theoden's physicians have relocated their offices to the SuperMedica physician office building and now admit patients exclusively to SuperMedica. St. Theoden's closes in bankruptcy. You work at the FTC. In a 500-word memorandum, evaluate whether SuperMedica has violated federal antitrust laws.

2. REMEDIES

Anticompetitive effects may be more apparent several years after a merger. *Evanston Northwestern Healthcare* involved a hospital merger on Chicago's North Shore. The FTC did not block the original merger but brought this administrative enforcement action four years later with evidence that the merger had allowed the hospitals to raise prices. The following document is an opinion from the Federal Trade Commission. The ruling is most significant for the uncommon remedy it chose: Instead of unwinding the merger (a "structural" remedy), the FTC ordered the parties to conduct their negotiations with health plans in a more competitive fashion (a "conduct" remedy).

In the Matter of Evanston Northwestern Healthcare Corp.

FTC Docket No. 9315 (Aug. 6, 2007)

By MAJORAS, Chairman.

I. INTRODUCTION

In 2000, Evanston Northwestern Healthcare Corporation ("Evanston") merged with Highland Park Hospital ("Highland Park"). Prior to the merger, Evanston owned Evanston Hospital and Glenbrook Hospital.

The Commission issued an administrative complaint challenging Evanston's acquisition of Highland Park under Section 7 of the Clayton Act four years after the transaction closed. Given that the merger was consummated well before the Commission commenced this case, we were able to examine not only pre-merger evidence, but also evidence about what happened after the merger.

There is no dispute that ENH substantially raised its prices shortly after the merging parties consummated the transaction. There is disagreement about the cause of those price increases, however. Complaint counsel maintains that the merger eliminated significant competition between Evanston and Highland Park, which allowed ENH to exercise market power against health care insurance companies. Respondent argues that, during the due diligence process for the merger, ENH obtained information about Highland Park's prices that showed that Evanston had been charging rates that were below competitive levels for a number of years. Respondent contends that most of ENH's merger-related price increases simply reflect its efforts to raise Evanston Hospital's prices to competitive rates. Respondent also maintains that some portion of the merger-related price increases reflects increased demand for Highland Park's services due to post-merger improvements at the hospital.

Chief Administrative Law Judge Stephen J. McGuire ("ALJ") found in his Initial Decision that the transaction violated Section 7 of the Clayton Act and ordered ENH to divest Highland Park. We affirm the ALJ's decision that the transaction violated Section 7 of the Clayton Act. Considered as a whole, the evidence demonstrates that the transaction enabled the merged firm to exercise market power and that the resulting anticompetitive effects were not offset by merger-specific efficiencies. The record shows that senior officials at Evanston and Highland Park anticipated that the merger would give them greater leverage to raise prices, that the merged firm did raise its prices immediately and substantially after completion of the transaction, and that the same senior officials attributed the price increases in part to increased bargaining leverage produced by the merger.

The econometric analyses performed by both complaint counsel's and respondent's economists also strongly support the conclusion that the merger gave the combined entity the ability to raise prices through the exercise of market power. The economists determined that there were substantial merger-coincident price increases and ran regressions using different data sets and a variety of control groups that ruled out the most likely competitively-benign explanations for substantial portions of these increases. The record does not support respondent's position that the merger-coincident price increases reflect ENH's attempts to correct a multi-year failure by Evanston's senior officials to charge market rates to many of its customers, or increased demand for Highland Park's services due to post-merger improvements.

We do not agree with the ALJ, however, that a divestiture is warranted. The potentially high costs inherent in the separation of hospitals that have functioned as a merged entity for seven years instead warrant a remedy that restores the lost competition through injunctive relief. . . .

FINDINGS OF FACT

[The FTC discusses the relevant markets for hospital services. On Chicago's North Shore, preferred provider organizations (PPOs) have recently grown to dominate through broader provider networks but more beneficiary cost sharing than under health maintenance organizations (HMOs).]

Depending on the type of insurance plan, when consumers receive services from an in-network hospital, they pay a deductible and/or a co-payment, which usually constitutes a small portion of the total price for the services that the patient receives. PPOs generally are more expensive than HMOs because they provide coverage or reimbursement for a larger set of providers. In the Chicago area, the use of HMOs has declined substantially in favor of PPOs.

Competition Among Hospitals for MCO Contracts

MCOs enter into two basic types of contracts with hospitals — "per diem" and "discount off charges." In per diem contracts, there is an all-inclusive per day charge, based on the class of services, for each day that the patient is in the hospital, regardless of the amount or the total cost of the services that the patient receives. Under discount off charges contracts, the MCO agrees to pay the hospital a rate for each service performed. The paid rate is equal to the hospital's list price of the service, discounted by an agreed upon percentage. The list prices are contained in the hospital's "chargemaster." Thus, the prices paid by MCOs increase as a hospital increases the prices in its chargemaster. All else being equal, MCOs usually prefer per diem contracts because they allow for greater certainty about MCOs' costs.

> Chargemaster rates vary widely and have no clear relationship to either actual costs to provide the service or net final prices to purchase them. The chargemaster is simply the administrative, and often proprietary, basis from which hospital charges are calculated.

MCOs do not typically select every hospital in a geographic region for their HMO networks, and they do not designate every provider as preferred for their PPOs. Rather, physicians and hospitals compete to be included in HMO and PPO networks. The central terms of competition are price, quality of service, and geographic proximity to the MCO's members. The use of a business model that potentially excludes some providers allows MCOs to leverage competing providers against each other to negotiate lower prices. Through this competitive process, MCOs seek to assemble high-quality networks at competitive rates that include a sufficient number of hospitals and physicians to attract employers and their employees.

Competition Among MCOs to Be Selected by Employers

As stated, a majority of people in the United States who have private health insurance obtain it through their employers. Typically, the employer selects which MCOs and plans to offer its employees. Because employees sometimes consider the quality of health care benefits when they decide where to accept employment, many employers try to provide health care plans that are attractive to their employees. Thus, employer demand for MCO services is a partially derived demand from employee preferences. As a general matter, employees prefer health plans that offer a broad choice of hospitals (and physicians) that are geographically convenient for them and their families. At the same time, employees (and employers) want to limit the amount of money that they spend on employee health benefits.

Consequently, MCOs compete to have employers offer their plans based on price, quality, the geographic convenience of the hospitals and physicians in their networks, and other factors relevant to employees and employers. Similarly, because some employers offer their employees several plans from which to choose, an MCO needs to offer an attractive network to convince employees to enroll in its plan as opposed to a plan from one of its competitors.

Consumer Harm from Increases in Hospital Prices

Consumers are harmed when hospital prices increase due to the exercise of market power, even though they usually do not pay directly the full price of a hospital visit. When a hospital succeeds in raising its prices to an MCO, the MCO generally passes on those costs to the employers, which in turn pass them on to the employees. Similarly, self-insured employers often pass on higher hospital costs to their employees. Thus, if a hospital can increase its market power by merging with a close competitor, the resulting price increases harm consumers....

Evanston's consultants also expressed confidence, prior to the closing, that the merger would give the combined company greater bargaining leverage with MCO customers. Evanston engaged the Bain consulting firm in the fall of 1999 to assist in strategic planning related to the merger. In an August 30, 1999 proposal letter from Bain to Neaman, Bain wrote: "As a consequence of the merger, ENH will have broad geographic coverage on the North Shore, with three hospitals and an extensive physician network. The merger provides the opportunity to reduce costs, refocus activities at the three hospitals, shift activity from the overcrowded Evanston Hospital, and negotiate contracts with payors from a stronger position." In October 1999, in a document entitled "Growth Opportunities from the Highland Park Merger," Bain wrote that "[b]etter integration with the ENH Medical Group and the addition of Highland Park will substantially improve ENH's leverage."

In October and November of 1999, Bain reviewed and analyzed Evanston's and Highland Park's contracts. Bain concluded that the merger would enable Evanston to grow net income by increasing revenue, due in part to higher prices and greater market share, and to reduce costs through economies of scale, elimination of duplicate costs, and capital investment savings. Bain also determined that the combined Evanston and Highland Park Hospitals would have "significant leverage with payors as [it has] the largest [number of] admissions" among other Chicago area hospitals. An Evanston senior official testified at trial that he felt that Bain's analyses were accurate and helpful.

ENH's Post-Merger Price Increases

After the merger closed, ENH rapidly increased the prices that it charged to most of its MCO customers to the higher of Evanston's or Highland Park's pre-merger rate for a particular service. ENH then set about negotiating a single contract for all three of its hospitals with each MCO. ENH did not offer the MCOs the option to enter into separate contracts for the hospitals, or to decline to use one or more of the three hospitals. In addition, ENH sought to raise its prices through the conversion of portions of some of its contracts from per diem to discount off charges payment structures.

The record reflects that ENH's post-merger negotiation strategy was highly successful. ENH negotiated with its MCO customers a single contract for all three of its hospitals with substantial price increases, and converted a number of its contracts from per diem to discount off charges structures. In addition, from 2002 to 2003, ENH increased its chargemaster rates four times.

As we describe in detail below in our findings about the econometrics, the actual amount of ENH's price increases depends on the calculation method. Using data that included all patients in Illinois, complaint counsel's economist, Deborah Haas-Wilson, computed that from 1998 through 2002, ENH increased its *per day* average net prices by 48% for all patients; 46% for the commercial and self-pay patients; and 46% for commercial, self-pay, self-administered, and HMO patients. On a *per case* basis, the corresponding average net price increases from 1998 to 2002 were 30%, 27%, and 26%, respectively. . . .

To summarize, we find that the documentary evidence and testimony support the conclusion that senior officials at Evanston and Highland Park anticipated that the merger would give them greater leverage to raise prices to MCOs, the merged firm did raise its prices to MCOs immediately and substantially after consummation of the transaction, and the same senior officials attributed the price increase in part to increased bargaining leverage with payors produced by the merger. . . .

REMEDY

Having found that Evanston's acquisition of Highland Park violated Section 7 of the Clayton Act, we turn to fashioning the appropriate remedy. The ALJ determined that ENH should divest Highland Park. The ALJ also proposed a variety of other requirements intended to ensure that Highland Park would remain a viable hospital after divestiture and retain certain improvements that were implemented after the merger. Complaint counsel argues that the Commission should affirm the ALJ's order, but also cross-appeals and urges the Commission to add provisions that would require ENH to assist Highland Park in the continuation of its cardiac surgery program, provide incentives for ENH's employees to accept job offers from Highland Park, and indemnify any monitor or trustee charged with overseeing the divestiture. Respondent argues that, if we find liability, we should forgo ordering divestiture and instead should restore competition by requiring ENH to negotiate and maintain separate MCO contracts on behalf of Evanston on the one hand and Highland Park on the other. In conjunction, or in the alternative, respondent also suggests that we could require ENH to give the Commission advance notification of any future acquisition or joint venture that ENH proposes to undertake.

The goal of a remedy for a Section 7 violation is to impose relief that is "necessary and appropriate in the public interest to eliminate the effects of the acquisition offensive to the statute." United States v. E.I. du Pont de Nemours & Co., 353 U.S. 586, 607 (1957). Thus, we attempt to craft a remedy that will create a competitive environment that would have existed in the absence of the violations. "The antitrust laws would deserve little respect if they permitted those who violated them to escape with the fruits of their misconduct on the grounds that imposition of an effective remedy would incidentally result in even a substantial monetary loss."

Structural remedies are preferred for Section 7 violations. *See* United States v. E. I. du Pont de Nemours & Co. (calling divestiture "a natural remedy" when a merger violates the antitrust laws). As we recently said, "[m]uch of the case law has . . . found divestiture the most appropriate means for restoring competition lost as a consequence of a merger or acquisition." In re Chicago Bridge & Iron Co., at 93. Divestiture is desirable because, in general, a remedy is more likely to restore competition if the firms that engaged in pre-merger competition are not under common ownership. There are also usually greater long-term costs associated with monitoring the efficacy of a conduct remedy than with imposing a structural solution.

In this case, the transaction eliminated the pre-merger price competition between Evanston and Highland Park, as well as the MCOs' option of contracting with one hospital but not the other. We can seek to remedy this competitive harm by requiring ENH to divest Highland Park or through injunctive restraints. After careful review of the record, we have determined that this is the highly unusual case in which a conduct remedy, rather than divestiture, is more appropriate.

> "Structural remedies" prevent mergers or require divestiture. "Conduct remedies" allow the merger to stand but prescribe the way the firm operates going forward.

A long time has elapsed between the closing of the merger and the conclusion of the litigation. This does not preclude the Commission from ordering divestiture, but it would make a divestiture much more difficult, with a greater risk of unforeseen costs and failure. ENH has integrated the operations of Evanston, Glenbrook, and Highland Park Hospitals, and has made improvements at Highland Park since the merger. The large majority of these improvements could have occurred without the merger, and therefore do not bear on whether the transaction violated Section 7. Nonetheless, while the improvements do not vindicate the merger under the antitrust laws, they are relevant to determining whether divestiture is appropriate because divestiture may reduce or eliminate the resulting benefits for a material period of time.

Thus, we need to consider whether certain improvements would not survive the divestiture *and* would take Highland Park a significant time to implement on its own after a divestiture. Two significant improvements meet these conditions—the development and implementation of the cardiac surgery program and the implementation at Highland Park of the state-of-the-art medical record computer system.

The record reflects that a divestiture may have a substantial negative effect on Highland Park's cardiac surgery programs. Complaint counsel's expert, Dr. Romano, testified that it was not clear whether, without Evanston, Highland Park would have the volume that it needed to maintain the cardiac surgery program. If Highland Park lost its cardiac surgery program, or if the quality of its surgical program diminished, then the quality of patient care to the community would suffer. Highland Park would need to transport some or all of its patients needing emergency cardiac surgery to other hospitals, potentially creating life threatening risks. The possibility of a delay in reestablishing cardiac surgery services at Highland Park is a significant factor that we must weigh in considering a remedy.

A delay in reestablishing Highland Park's cardiac surgery program also could put at risk Highland Park's interventional cardiology services. An interventional cardiology program involves procedures that may be scheduled in advance. To provide interventional cardiology services, however, it is necessary to have a cardiac surgery program as a back-up for the interventional program if complications occur.

We are also concerned about the effect of divestiture on Highland Park's ability to use EPIC. Although the implementation of the EPIC system at Highland Park was not a merger specific efficiency, it likely would take Highland Park significant time to install EPIC (or a comparable record keeping system) independently, at a cost of millions of dollars if we ordered divestiture. ENH spent approximately $14 million on EPIC and took more than one year to deploy the system fully. We could order ENH to continue to make EPIC available to Highland Park for some time, but we are concerned about the potential effects on patient care from the inevitable glitches involved in Highland Park's swapping out complex software systems.

> EPIC is a well-known electronic medical records system.

Accordingly, we reject divestiture as a remedy and will impose an injunctive remedy that requires respondent to establish separate and independent negotiating teams—one for Evanston and Glenbrook Hospitals ("E&G"), and another for Highland Park. While not ideal, this remedy will allow MCOs to negotiate separately again for these competing hospitals, thus re-injecting competition between them for the business of MCOs. Further, ENH should be able to implement the required modifications to its contract negotiating procedures in a very short time. In contrast, divesting Highland Park after seven years of integration would be a complex, lengthy, and expensive process.

We note that our rationale for not requiring a divestiture in this case is likely to have little applicability to our consideration of the proper remedy in a future challenge to an unconsummated merger, including a hospital merger. For example, had we challenged this transaction prior to consummation, Evanston's intention to implement a cardiac surgery program and install EPIC at Highland Park likely would not have carried much weight in our analysis of the proper remedy because, at that time, Highland Park probably could have produced both improvements on its own in a comparable period, and thus neither improvement would have been merger-specific.

Nor will our reasoning here necessarily apply to consideration of the appropriate remedy in a future challenge to a consummated merger, including a consummated hospital merger. Divestiture is the preferred remedy for challenges to unlawful mergers, regardless of whether the challenge occurs before or after consummation. Thus, where it is relatively clear that the unwinding of a hospital merger would be unlikely to involve substantial costs, all else being equal, the Commission likely would select divestiture as the remedy.

Although we have decided on the nature of the relief that is appropriate for this case, we lack sufficiently detailed information about the personnel involved in ENH's contract negotiation operations, or ENH's overall business operations, to craft the remedial order with the necessary precision. Accordingly, we order that, within thirty (30) calendar days, respondent must submit a detailed proposal to the Commission for implementing the type of injunctive relief that we have selected. Specifically, the proposal must identify and describe the mechanisms that respondent will use, and the steps that respondent will take, to implement the following requirements:

1. Respondent must allow all payors to negotiate separate contracts for E&G on the one hand and for Highland Park on the other hand;
2. Respondent must establish separate negotiating teams (and other relevant personnel) for E&G and Highland Park that will compete with each other, and other hospitals, for payors' business;
3. Respondent must establish a firewall-type mechanism that prevents the E&G and Highland Park contract negotiating teams (and other relevant personnel) from sharing any information that would inhibit them from competing with each other and with other hospitals;
4. Respondent may not make any contract for E&G or Highland Park contingent on entering into a contract for the other, and may not make the availability of any price or term for a contract for E&G contingent on entering into a contract for Highland Park, or *vice-versa*; and
5. Respondent shall promptly offer all payors with which it currently has contracts the option of reopening and renegotiating their contracts under the terms of this order.

Respondent's proposal should also describe, where appropriate, mechanisms for the Commission to monitor the establishment of the organizational structure needed to implement the terms of the order, as well as respondent's compliance with the order throughout its term. Respondent's proposal shall also recommend mechanisms for resolving disputes between payors and respondent with respect to respondent's compliance with the terms of the order, including a discussion of the potential value of some form of dispute resolution mechanism.

QUESTION

What are the strengths and weaknesses of these two types of remedies in hospital merger cases?

E. COLLABORATIONS WITH COMPETITORS

While a few hospital mergers occur each year, a much larger number of contractual arrangements are signed between health care providers that fall short of a full merger. These collaborative arrangements might be precisely the type of coordination that the fragmented U.S. health care system needs. They are also potentially illegal contracts that could forestall competition and raise prices. The ACA placed significant emphasis on a particular form of provider collaboration, known as an accountable care organization (ACO). The government hopes that ACOs can deliver higher-quality care at lower prices through collaboration and exposure to both upside and downside financial risk of performance. But some forms of collaboration run afoul of the Sherman Act, including price fixing, which is a *per se* violation of section 1 of the Sherman Act. Other arrangements are analyzed under the *rule of reason*:

Federal Antitrust Analysis of Collaborative Arrangements Among Health Care Providers That Are Actual or Potential Competitors

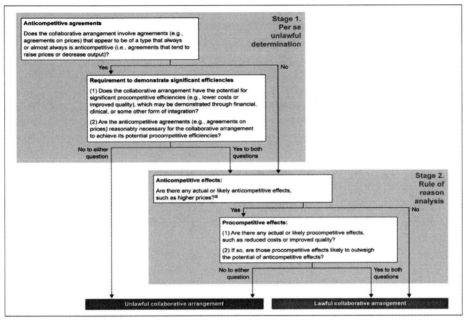

Source: GAO, Federal Antitrust Policy: Stakeholders' Perspectives Differed on the Adequacy of Guidance for Collaboration Among Health Care Providers (Mar. 16, 2012).

1. PHYSICIAN PRICE FIXING

Arizona v. Maricopa County Medical Society

457 U.S. 332 (1982)

Justice STEVENS delivered the opinion of the Court.

The question presented is whether §1 of the Sherman Act has been violated by agreements among competing physicians setting, by majority vote, the maximum fees that they may claim in full payment for health services provided to policyholders of specified insurance plans. The United States Court of Appeals for the Ninth Circuit held that the question could not be answered without evaluating the actual purpose and effect of the agreements at a full trial. Because the undisputed facts disclose a violation of the statute, we granted certiorari, and now reverse. . . .

The Maricopa Foundation for Medical Care is a nonprofit Arizona corporation composed of licensed doctors of medicine, osteopathy, and podiatry engaged in private practice. Approximately 1,750 doctors, representing about 70% of the practitioners in Maricopa County, are members. . . .

At the time this lawsuit was filed, [the] foundation made use of "relative values" and "conversion factors" in compiling its fee schedule. The conversion factor is the dollar amount used to determine fees for a particular medical specialty. Thus, for example, the conversion factors for "medicine" and "laboratory" were $8 and $5.50, respectively, in 1972, and $10 and $6.50 in 1974. The relative value schedule provides a numerical weight for each different medical service—thus, an office consultation has a lesser value than a home visit. The relative value was multiplied by the conversion factor to determine the maximum fee. The fee schedule has been revised periodically. The foundation board of trustees would solicit advice from various medical societies about the need for change in either relative values or conversion factors in their respective specialties. The board would then formulate the new fee schedule and submit it to the vote of the entire membership.

> In 1992, Medicare adopted a similar basis for paying physicians, the resource-based relative value scale or RBRVS.

The fee schedules limit the amount that the member doctors may recover for services performed for patients insured under plans approved by the foundations. To obtain this approval the insurers—including self-insured employers as well as insurance companies—agree to pay the doctors' charges up to the scheduled amounts, and in exchange the doctors agree to accept those amounts as payment in full for their services. The doctors are free to charge higher fees to uninsured patients, and they also may charge any patient less than the scheduled maxima. A patient who is insured by a foundation-endorsed plan is guaranteed complete coverage for the full amount of his medical bills only if he is treated by a foundation member. He is free to go to a nonmember physician and is still covered for charges that do not exceed the maximum-fee schedule, but he must pay any excess that the nonmember physician may charge. . . .

The respondents recognize that our decisions establish that price-fixing agreements are unlawful on their face. But they argue that the *per se* rule does not govern this case because the agreements at issue are horizontal and fix maximum prices, are among members of a profession, are in an industry with which the judiciary has little antitrust experience, and are alleged to have procompetitive justifications. . . .

We have not wavered in our enforcement of the *per se* rule against price fixing. Indeed, in our most recent price-fixing case we summarily reversed the decision of another Ninth Circuit panel that a horizontal agreement among competitors to fix credit terms does not necessarily contravene the antitrust laws. . . .

The respondents' principal argument is that the *per se* rule is inapplicable because their agreements are alleged to have procompetitive justifications. The argument indicates a misunderstanding of the *per se* concept. The anticompetitive potential inherent in all price-fixing agreements justifies their facial invalidation even if procompetitive justifications are offered for some. Those claims of enhanced competition are so unlikely to prove significant in any particular case that we adhere to the rule of law that is justified in its general application. Even when the respondents are given every benefit of the doubt, the limited record in this case is not inconsistent with the presumption that the respondents' agreements will not significantly enhance competition.

The respondents contend that their fee schedules are procompetitive because they make it possible to provide consumers of health care with a uniquely desirable form of insurance coverage that could not otherwise exist. The features of the foundation-endorsed insurance plans that they stress are a choice of doctors, complete insurance coverage, and lower premiums. The first two characteristics, however, are hardly unique to these plans. Since only about 70% of the doctors in the relevant market are members of either foundation, the guarantee of complete coverage only applies when an insured chooses a physician in that 70%. If he elects to go to a nonfoundation doctor, he may be required to pay a portion of the doctor's fee. It is fair to presume, however, that at least 70% of the doctors in other markets charge no more than the "usual, customary, and reasonable" fee that typical insurers are willing to reimburse in full. Thus, in Maricopa and Pima Counties as well as in most parts of the country, if an insured asks his doctor if the insurance coverage is complete, presumably in about 70% of the cases the doctor will say "Yes" and in about 30% of the cases he will say "No."

It is true that a binding assurance of complete insurance coverage — as well as most of the respondents' potential for lower insurance premiums — can be obtained only if the insurer and the doctor agree in advance on the maximum fee that the doctor will accept as full payment for a particular service. Even if a fee schedule is therefore desirable, it is not necessary that the doctors do the price fixing. The record indicates that the Arizona Comprehensive Medical/Dental Program for Foster Children is administered by the Maricopa Foundation pursuant to a contract under which the maximum-fee schedule is prescribed by a state agency rather than by the doctors. This program and the Blue Shield plan challenged in *Group Life & Health Insurance Co. v. Royal Drug Co.* indicate that insurers are capable not only of fixing maximum reimbursable prices but also of obtaining binding agreements with providers guaranteeing the insured full reimbursement of a participating provider's fee. In light of these examples, it is not surprising that nothing in the record even arguably supports the conclusion that this type of insurance program could not function if the fee schedules were set in a different way.

The most that can be said for having doctors fix the maximum prices is that doctors may be able to do it more efficiently than insurers. The validity of that assumption is far from obvious,[28] but in any event there is no reason to believe that any savings that might accrue from this arrangement would be sufficiently great to affect the competitiveness of these kinds of insurance plans. It is entirely possible that the potential or actual power of the foundations to dictate the terms of such insurance plans may more than offset the theoretical efficiencies upon which the respondents' defense ultimately rests.[29] . . .

---

28. In order to create an insurance plan under which the doctor would agree to accept as full payment a fee prescribed in a fixed schedule, someone must canvass the doctors to determine what maximum prices would be high enough to attract sufficient numbers of individual doctors to sign up but low enough to make the insurance plan competitive. In this case that canvassing function is performed by the foundation; the foundation then deals with the insurer. It would seem that an insurer could simply bypass the foundation by performing the canvassing function and dealing with the doctors itself. Under the foundation plan, each doctor must look at the maximum-fee schedule fixed by his competitors and vote for or against approval of the plan (and, if the plan is approved by majority vote, he must continue or revoke his foundation membership). A similar, if to some extent more protracted, process would occur if it were each insurer that offered the maximum-fee schedule to each doctor.

29. In this case it appears that the fees are set by a group with substantial power in the market for medical services, and that there is competition among insurance companies in the sale of medical insurance. Under these circumstances the insurance companies are not likely to have significantly greater bargaining power against a monopoly of doctors than would individual consumers of medical services.

Having declined the respondents' invitation to cut back on the *per se* rule against price fixing, we are left with the respondents' argument that their fee schedules involve price fixing in only a literal sense. For this argument, the respondents rely upon *Broadcast Music, Inc. v. Columbia Broadcasting System, Inc.*

In *Broadcast Music* we were confronted with an antitrust challenge to the marketing of the right to use copyrighted compositions derived from the entire membership of the American Society of Composers, Authors and Publishers (ASCAP). The so-called "blanket license" was entirely different from the product that any one composer was able to sell by himself. Although there was little competition among individual composers for their separate compositions, the blanket-license arrangement did not place any restraint on the right of any individual copyright owner to sell his own compositions separately to any buyer at any price. But a "necessary consequence" of the creation of the blanket license was that its price had to be established. We held that the delegation by the composers to ASCAP of the power to fix the price for the blanket license was not a species of the price-fixing agreements categorically forbidden by the Sherman Act. The record disclosed price fixing only in a "literal sense."

This case is fundamentally different. Each of the foundations is composed of individual practitioners who compete with one another for patients. Neither the foundations nor the doctors sell insurance, and they derive no profits from the sale of health insurance policies. The members of the foundations sell medical services. Their combination in the form of the foundation does not permit them to sell any different product.[33] Their combination has merely permitted them to sell their services to certain customers at fixed prices and arguably to affect the prevailing market price of medical care.

The foundations are not analogous to partnerships or other joint arrangements in which persons who would otherwise be competitors pool their capital and share the risks of loss as well as the opportunities for profit. In such joint ventures, the partnership is regarded as a single firm competing with other sellers in the market. The agreement under attack is an agreement among hundreds of competing doctors concerning the price at which each will offer his own services to a substantial number of consumers. It is true that some are surgeons, some anesthesiologists, and some psychiatrists, but the doctors do not sell a package of three kinds of services. If a clinic offered complete medical coverage for a flat fee, the cooperating doctors would have the type of partnership arrangement in which a price-fixing agreement among the doctors would be perfectly proper. But the fee agreements disclosed by the record in this case are among independent competing entrepreneurs. They fit squarely into the horizontal price-fixing mold.

The judgment of the Court of Appeals is reversed.

---

33. It may be true that by becoming a member of the foundation the individual practitioner obtains a competitive advantage in the market for medical services that he could not unilaterally obtain. That competitive advantage is the ability to attract as customers people who value both the guarantee of full health coverage and a choice of doctors. But, as we have indicated, the setting of the price *by doctors* is not a "necessary consequence" of an arrangement with an insurer in which the doctor agrees not to charge certain insured customers more than a fixed price.

QUESTIONS

1. How is the arrangement distinct from the "blanket license" agreement in *Broadcast Music*?

2. If the foundations were full partnerships, can they set prices for their doctors?

2. PRO-COMPETITIVE PHYSICIAN COLLABORATIONS

In response to *Maricopa County Medical Society*, physicians tested other collaboration efforts, including so-called "messenger model" individual practice associations (IPAs) and physician joint ventures. In the two readings that follow, the federal antitrust enforcement agencies found that these efforts can be pro-competitive under proper circumstances. The next two readings are taken from the influential *Joint Statements of Antitrust Enforcement Policy in Health Care* by the Department of Justice and the Federal Trade Commission, the federal agencies that enforce antitrust law. The Health Care Statements do not have the legal force of a regulation under the Administrative Procedure Act but are an important example of sub-regulatory guidance from an agency. Lawyers consider them significant because they describe the internal positions taken by the enforcement agencies when they evaluate bringing a health care antitrust case.

> Anyone beginning a practice in health care antitrust will need to study all nine Health Care Statements in full.

Statement 5 deals primarily with jointly providing information about fees. Statement 8 addresses joint ventures to integrate providers.

Department of Justice & Federal Trade Commission, Statements of Antitrust Enforcement Policy in Health Care

Statement 5: Enforcement Policy on Providers' Collective Provision of Fee-Related Information to Purchasers of Health Care Services

(rev. 1996)

. . . This statement sets forth an antitrust safety zone that describes collective provision of fee-related information that will not be challenged by the Agencies under the antitrust laws, absent extraordinary circumstances. It also describes types of conduct that are expressly excluded from the antitrust safety zone, some clearly unlawful, and others that may be lawful depending on the circumstances.

A. *Antitrust Safety Zone*: Providers' Collective Provision of Fee-Related Information That Will Not Be Challenged, Absent Extraordinary Circumstances, by the Agencies

Providers' collective provision to purchasers of health care services of factual information concerning the providers' current or historical fees or other aspects of reimbursement, such as discounts or alternative reimbursement methods accepted (including capitation arrangements, risk-withhold fee arrangements, or use of all-inclusive fees), is unlikely to raise significant antitrust concern and will not be challenged by the Agencies, absent extraordinary circumstances. Such factual information can help purchasers efficiently develop reimbursement terms to be offered to providers and may be useful to a purchaser when provided in response to a request from the purchaser or at the initiative of providers.

In assembling information to be collectively provided to purchasers, providers need to be aware of the potential antitrust consequences of information exchanges among competitors. The principles expressed in the Agencies' statement on provider participation in exchanges of price and cost information are applicable in this context. Accordingly, in order to qualify for this safety zone, the collection of information to be provided to purchasers must satisfy the following conditions:

The third party is the "messenger."

1. The collection is managed by a third party (*e.g.*, a purchaser, government agency, health care consultant, academic institution, or trade association);

2. Although current fee-related information may be provided to purchasers, any information that is shared among or is available to the competing providers furnishing the data must be more than three months old; and

3. For any information that is available to the providers furnishing data, there are at least five providers reporting data upon which each disseminated statistic is based, no individual provider's data may represent more than 25 percent on a weighted basis of that statistic, and any information disseminated must be sufficiently aggregated such that it would not allow recipients to identify the prices charged by any individual provider.

The conditions that must be met for an information exchange among providers to fall within the antitrust safety zone are intended to ensure that an exchange of price or cost data is not used by competing providers for discussion or coordination of provider prices or costs. They represent a careful balancing of a provider's individual interest in obtaining information useful in adjusting the prices it charges or the wages it pays in response to changing market conditions against the risk that the exchange of such information may permit competing providers to communicate with each other regarding a mutually acceptable level of prices for health care services or compensation for employees.

B. The Agencies' Analysis of Providers' Collective Provision of Fee-Related Information That Falls Outside the Antitrust Safety Zone

The safety zone set forth in this policy statement does not apply to collective negotiations between unintegrated providers and purchasers in contemplation or in furtherance of any agreement among the providers on fees or other terms or aspects of reimbursement, or to any agreement among unintegrated providers to deal with purchasers only on agreed terms. Providers also may not collectively threaten, implicitly or explicitly, to engage in a boycott or similar conduct, or actually undertake such a boycott or conduct, to coerce any purchaser to accept collectively-determined fees or other terms or aspects of reimbursement. These types of conduct likely would violate the antitrust laws and, in many instances, might be per se illegal. . . .

Competing providers who are considering collectively providing fee-related information to purchasers, and are unsure of the legality of their conduct under the antitrust laws, can take advantage of the Department of Justice's expedited business review procedure announced on December 1, 1992 (58 Fed. Reg. 6132 (1993)) or the Federal Trade Commission's advisory opinion procedure contained at 16 C.F.R.

§§1.1-1.4 (1993). The Agencies will respond to a business review or advisory opinion request on behalf of providers who are considering collectively providing fee-related information within 90 days after all necessary information is submitted. The Department's December 1, 1992 announcement contains specific guidance as to the information that should be submitted.

> Advisory opinions and business review letters are important sources of guidance but are binding only on the parties.

QUESTION

Could the Maricopa County physicians achieve their primary business objectives within this safety zone by slightly modifying their conduct?

Department of Justice & Federal Trade Commission, Statements of Antitrust Enforcement Policy in Health Care

Statement 8: Enforcement Policy on Physician Network Joint Ventures

(rev. 1996)

Introduction

In recent years, health plans and other purchasers of health care services have developed a variety of managed care programs that seek to reduce the costs and assure the quality of health care services. Many physicians and physician groups have organized physician network joint ventures, such as individual practice associations ("IPAs"), preferred provider organizations ("PPOs"), and other arrangements to market their services to these plans. Typically, such networks contract with the plans to provide physician services to plan subscribers at predetermined prices, and the physician participants in the networks agree to controls aimed at containing costs and assuring the appropriate and efficient provision of high quality physician services. By developing and implementing mechanisms that encourage physicians to collaborate in practicing efficiently as part of the network, many physician network joint ventures promise significant procompetitive benefits for consumers of health care services. . . .

Experience indicates that, in general, more significant efficiencies are likely to result from a physician network joint venture's substantial financial risk sharing or substantial clinical integration. However, the Agencies will consider a broad range of possible cost savings, including improved cost controls, case management and quality assurance, economies of scale, and reduced administrative or transaction costs.

QUESTION

Why do the Agencies prize "substantial financial risk sharing" or "substantial clinical integration" as hallmarks of a pro-competitive joint venture?

3. ACCOUNTABLE CARE ORGANIZATIONS

Many health policy experts have lamented the fragmented nature of the U.S. health care sector. Patients with complex conditions regularly see many physicians in completely independent medical practices and who may have admitting privileges at different hospitals. Sharing of information across providers is a major goal of U.S. health policy, as we will discuss in Chapter 10. But the ACA also sparked more intense contractual collaborations between legally independent providers, with explicit goals of improvements in quality and reductions in cost. One model in Medicare is called "accountable care organizations" or ACOs (introduced above in this chapter and discussed in Chapter 2). ACOs generally share some financial risk and pursue clinical integration, though the participants may remain distinct legal entities. It is hoped (but not yet proven) that ACOs will deliver high quality care more cheaply. Following enactment of the ACA, the DOJ and FTC issued antitrust guidance for ACOs in 2011:

Federal Trade Commission & Department of Justice, Statement of Antitrust Enforcement Policy Regarding Accountable Care Organizations Participating in the Medicare Shared Savings Program

I. Introduction

The Patient Protection and Affordable Care Act and the Health Care and Education Reconciliation Act of 2010 (collectively, the "Affordable Care Act") seek to improve the quality and reduce the costs of health care services in the United States by, among other things, encouraging physicians, hospitals, and other health care providers to become accountable for a patient population through integrated health care delivery systems. One delivery system reform is the Affordable Care Act's Medicare Shared Savings Program (the "Shared Savings Program"), which promotes the formation and operation of Accountable Care Organizations ("ACOs") to serve Medicare fee-for-service beneficiaries. Under this provision, "groups of providers of services and suppliers meeting criteria specified by the [Department of Health and Human Services] Secretary may work together to manage and coordinate care for Medicare fee-for-service beneficiaries through an [ACO]." An ACO may share in some portion of any savings it creates if the ACO meets certain quality performance standards established by the Secretary of Health and Human Services through the Centers for Medicare and Medicaid Services ("CMS"). The Affordable Care Act requires an ACO that wishes to participate in the Shared Savings Program to enter into an agreement with CMS for not less than three years. Recent commentary suggests that some health care providers are likely to create and participate in ACOs that serve both Medicare beneficiaries and commercially insured patients. The Federal Trade Commission and the Antitrust Division of the Department of Justice (the "Agencies") recognize that ACOs may generate opportunities for health care providers to innovate in both the Medicare and commercial markets and achieve for many other consumers the benefits Congress intended for Medicare beneficiaries through the Shared Savings Program. Therefore, to maximize and foster opportunities for ACO innovation and better health for patients, the Agencies wish to clarify their antitrust enforcement policy regarding collaborations among independent providers that seek to become ACOs in the Shared Savings Program. The Agencies recognize that not all such ACOs are likely to benefit consumers, and under certain conditions ACOs could reduce competition and harm consumers through higher prices or lower quality of care. Thus, the antitrust analysis of ACO applicants to the Shared Savings Program seeks to protect both Medicare beneficiaries and commercially insured patients from potential anticompetitive harm while allowing ACOs the opportunity to achieve significant efficiencies. . . .

III. The Agencies Will Apply Rule of Reason Analysis to ACOs That Meet Certain Conditions

The antitrust laws treat naked price-fixing and market-allocation agreements among competitors as per se illegal. Joint price agreements among competing health care providers are evaluated under the rule of reason, however, if the providers are financially or clinically integrated and the agreement is reasonably necessary to accomplish the procompetitive benefits of the integration.

A rule of reason analysis evaluates whether the collaboration is likely to have anticompetitive effects and, if so, whether the collaboration's potential procompetitive efficiencies are likely to outweigh those effects. The greater the likely anticompetitive effects, the greater the likely efficiencies must be for the collaboration to pass muster under the antitrust laws. The Agencies have articulated the standards for both financial and clinical integration in various policy statements, speeches, business reviews, and advisory opinions. For example, the Agencies' *Statements of Antitrust Enforcement Policy in Health Care* (the "Health Care Statements") explain that where participants in physician or multiprovider joint ventures have agreed to share substantial financial risk as defined in the Health Care Statements, their risk-sharing arrangement generally establishes both an overall efficiency goal for the venture and the incentives for the participants to meet that goal. Accordingly, the setting of price is integral to the venture's use of such an arrangement and therefore warrants evaluation under the rule of reason. The Health Care Statements provide examples of financial risk-sharing arrangements that can satisfy this standard, but also recognize that other acceptable financial risk-sharing arrangements might develop.

> Price setting with financial risk sharing or clinical integration is evaluated under the rule of reason.

The Health Care Statements further explain that provider joint ventures also may involve clinical integration sufficient to ensure that the venture is likely to produce significant efficiencies. Clinical integration can be evidenced by the joint venture implementing an active and ongoing program to evaluate and modify practice patterns by the venture's providers and to create a high degree of interdependence and cooperation among the providers to control costs and ensure quality. Federal Trade Commission staff advisory opinions discuss evidence that appears sufficient to demonstrate clinical integration in specific factual circumstances.

The Affordable Care Act provides that CMS may approve ACOs that meet certain eligibility criteria, including (1) a formal legal structure that allows the ACO to receive and distribute payments for shared savings; (2) a leadership and management structure that includes clinical and administrative processes; (3) processes to promote evidence-based medicine and patient engagement; (4) reporting on quality and cost measures; and (5) coordinated care for beneficiaries. CMS has further defined these eligibility criteria through regulations.

By contrast, the Agencies have not previously listed specific criteria required to establish clinical integration, but instead have responded to detailed proposals from health care providers who have decided on specific ways to integrate their health care delivery systems to improve quality and lower costs. The Agencies have chosen to avoid prescribing how clinical integration should take place. Nonetheless, the Agencies recognize that health care providers seeking to create ACOs in the context of the Shared Savings Program could benefit from additional antitrust guidance in evaluating whether an ACO that satisfies the CMS eligibility criteria could be subject to an antitrust investigation and potential challenge as engaging in per se illegal conduct.

The Agencies have determined that CMS's eligibility criteria are broadly consistent with the indicia of clinical integration that the Agencies previously set forth in the Health Care Statements and identified in the context of specific proposals for clinical integration from health care providers. The Agencies also have determined that organizations meeting the eligibility requirements for the Shared Savings Program are reasonably likely to be bona fide arrangements intended to improve the quality, and reduce the costs, of providing medical and other health care services through their participants' joint efforts.

To assess whether an ACO has improved quality and reduced costs to Medicare, CMS will collect and evaluate cost, utilization, and quality metrics relating to each ACO's performance in the Shared Savings Program. The results of this monitoring will help the Agencies determine whether the CMS eligibility criteria have required a sufficient level of clinical integration to produce cost savings and quality improvements, and may help inform the Agencies' future analysis of ACOs and other provider organizations.

In light of CMS's eligibility criteria, and its monitoring of each ACO's results, the Agencies will treat joint negotiations with private payers as reasonably necessary to an ACO's primary purpose of improving health care delivery, and will afford rule of reason treatment to an ACO that meets CMS's eligibility requirements for, and participates in, the Shared Savings Program and uses the same governance and leadership structures and clinical and administrative processes it uses in the Shared Savings Program to serve patients in commercial markets. The Agencies further note that CMS's regulations allow an ACO to propose alternative ways to establish clinical management and oversight of the ACO, and the Agencies are willing to consider other proposals for clinical integration as well.

> ACOs can serve both Medicare and private health plans. This guidance protects ACOs that negotiate jointly outside Medicare.

IV. The Agencies' Antitrust Analysis of ACOs That Meet CMS Eligibility Criteria

The following Sections provide additional antitrust guidance for ACOs that are eligible and intend, or have been approved, to participate in the Shared Savings Program, including those ACOs that also plan to operate in the commercial market. Section A sets forth a safety zone for certain ACOs that are highly unlikely to raise significant competitive concerns and, therefore, will not be challenged by the Agencies under the antitrust laws, absent extraordinary circumstances.

The Agencies emphasize that ACOs outside the safety zone may be procompetitive and legal. An ACO that does not impede the functioning of a competitive market will not raise competitive concerns. The creation of a safety zone reflects the view that ACOs that fall within the safety zone are highly unlikely to raise significant competitive concerns; it does not imply that ACOs outside the safety zone necessarily present competitive concerns.

Section B offers options for ACOs that seek additional antitrust guidance. It describes certain conduct all ACOs generally should avoid, other conduct that ACOs with high Primary Service Area ("PSA") shares or other possible indicia of market power may wish to avoid, and the process by which a newly formed ACO may obtain a voluntary expedited antitrust review.

A. The Antitrust Safety Zone for ACOs in the Shared Savings Program

This Section sets forth an antitrust safety zone for ACOs that meet the CMS eligibility criteria for and intend, or have been approved, to participate in the Shared Savings Program and are highly unlikely to raise significant competitive concerns. The Agencies will not challenge ACOs that fall within the safety zone, absent extraordinary circumstances.

To determine whether it falls within the safety zone, an ACO should evaluate the ACO's share of services in each ACO participant's PSA. Although a PSA does not necessarily constitute a relevant antitrust geographic market, it nonetheless serves as a useful screen for evaluating potential competitive effects.

The Policy Statement focuses on PSA shares for three major categories of services: physician specialties, major diagnostic categories ("MDCs") for inpatient facilities, and outpatient categories, as defined by CMS, for outpatient facilities. Although these services are useful in evaluating potential anticompetitive effects, they do not necessarily constitute relevant antitrust product markets. The Appendix to the Policy Statement describes how to calculate an ACO's shares of these services in the relevant PSAs, identifies data sources available for these calculations, and provides illustrative examples.

For an ACO to fall within the safety zone, independent ACO participants that provide the same service (a "common service") must have a combined share of 30 percent or less of each common service in each participant's PSA, wherever two or more ACO participants provide that service to patients from that PSA. As noted above, a service is defined as a primary specialty for physicians, an MDC for inpatient facilities, or an outpatient category for outpatient facilities. The PSA for each participant is defined as "the lowest number of postal zip codes from which the [ACO participant] draws at least 75 percent of its [patients]," separately for all physician, inpatient, or outpatient services. Thus, for purposes of determining whether the ACO is eligible for the safety zone, each independent physician solo practice, each fully integrated physician group practice, each inpatient facility (even if part of a hospital system), and each outpatient facility will have its own PSA. In addition, each inpatient facility hospital will have separate PSAs for its (1) inpatient services, (2) outpatient services, and (3) physician services provided by its physician employees, if any.

> The combined PSA market share must be 30 percent or less for each common service.

As described below, the availability of the PSA safety zone differs in some cases depending on whether an ACO participant is exclusive or non-exclusive to the ACO. To participate in an ACO on a non-exclusive basis, a participant must be allowed to contract with private payers through entities other than the ACO, including contracting individually or through other ACOs or analogous collaborations. The ACO must be non-exclusive in fact and not just in name. Exclusivity may be present explicitly or implicitly, formally or informally, through a written or de facto agreement as shown by conduct.

Non-exclusive contracting is favored as less threatening to competition.

Hospitals and Ambulatory Surgical Centers. Any hospital or ambulatory surgery center ("ASC") participating in an ACO must be non-exclusive to the ACO to fall within the safety zone, regardless of its PSA share.

Physicians. The safety zone for physicians (regardless of whether the physicians are hospital employees) does not differ based on whether the physicians are exclusive or non-exclusive to the ACO, unless they fall within the rural exception or dominant participant limitation described below.

1. Rural Exception

An ACO that exceeds the 30 percent PSA share may still fall within the safety zone if it qualifies for this rural exception. The rural exception allows such an ACO to include one physician or physician group practice per specialty from each rural area *on a non-exclusive basis* and still fall within the safety zone, provided the physician's or physician group practice's primary office is in a zip code that is classified as "isolated rural" or "other small rural." Thus, an ACO may qualify for the safety zone as long as it includes only one physician or physician group practice per specialty for each county that contains at least one "isolated rural" or "other small rural" zip code, even if the inclusion of these physicians causes the ACO's share of any common service to exceed 30 percent in any ACO participant's PSA.

Likewise, an ACO may include Rural Hospitals *on a non-exclusive basis* and qualify for the safety zone, even if the inclusion of a Rural Hospital causes the ACO's share of any common service to exceed 30 percent in any ACO participant's PSA.

2. Dominant Participant Limitation

The dominant participant limitation applies to any ACO that includes a participant with a greater than 50 percent share in its PSA of any service that no other ACO participant provides to patients in that PSA. Under these conditions, the ACO participant must be *non-exclusive* to the ACO for the ACO to fall within the safety zone. In addition, to fall within the safety zone, an ACO with a dominant participant cannot require a private payer to contract exclusively with the ACO or otherwise restrict a private payer's ability to contract or deal with other ACOs or provider networks.

. . . .

The safety zone will remain in effect for the duration of an ACO's agreement with CMS, provided the ACO continues to meet the safety zone's requirements. An ACO will not lose its safety zone status solely because it attracts more patients.

B. ACOs Outside the Safety Zone

ACOs that fall outside the safety zone may be procompetitive and lawful. An ACO that does not impede the functioning of a competitive market will not raise competitive concerns.

Nonetheless, there may be circumstances in which an ACO would raise competitive concerns. This section describes some types of conduct by an ACO that, under certain circumstances, may raise competitive concerns and outlines how an ACO may obtain further antitrust guidance from the Agencies.

1. Conduct to Avoid

a. Improper Sharing of Competitively Sensitive Information

Regardless of an ACO's PSA shares or other indicia of market power, significant competitive concerns can arise when an ACO's operations lead to price-fixing or other collusion among ACO participants in their sale of competing services outside the ACO. For example, improper exchanges of prices or other competitively sensitive information among competing participants could facilitate collusion and reduce competition in the provision of services outside the ACO, leading to increased prices or reduced quality or availability of health care services. ACOs should refrain from, and implement appropriate firewalls or other safeguards against, conduct that may facilitate collusion among ACO participants in the sale of competing services outside the ACO.

b. Conduct by ACOs with High PSA Shares or Other Possible Indicia of Market Power That May Raise Competitive Concerns

For ACOs with high PSA shares or other possible indicia of market power, the Agencies identify four types of conduct that may raise competitive concerns. The Agencies recognize that some of the conduct described in (1) through (4) below may be competitively neutral or even procompetitive, depending on the circumstances, including whether the ACO has market power. For example, an ACO that requires its participants to contract exclusively through the ACO to increase the ACO's efficiency is generally less likely to raise competitive concerns the greater the number of competing ACOs or independent providers available to contract with private payers or to participate in competing ACOs or other analogous collaborations.

An ACO with high PSA shares or other possible indicia of market power may wish to avoid the conduct set forth in (1) through (4) below. Depending on the circumstances, the conduct identified below may prevent private payers from obtaining lower prices and better quality service for their enrollees:

1. Preventing or discouraging private payers from directing or incentivizing patients to choose certain providers, including providers that do not participate in the ACO, through "anti-steering," "anti-tiering," "guaranteed inclusion," "most favored-nation," or similar contractual clauses or provisions
2. Tying sales (either explicitly or implicitly through pricing policies) of the ACO's services to the private payer's purchase of other services from providers outside the ACO (and vice versa), including providers affiliated with an ACO participant (e.g., an ACO should not require a purchaser to contract with *all* of the hospitals under common ownership with a hospital that participates in the ACO)
3. Contracting on an exclusive basis with ACO physicians, hospitals, ASCs, or other providers, thereby preventing or discouraging those providers from contracting with private payers outside the ACO, either individually or through other ACOs or analogous collaborations
4. Restricting a private payer's ability to make available to its health plan enrollees cost, quality, efficiency, and performance information to aid enrollees in evaluating and selecting providers in the health plan, if that information is similar to the cost, quality, efficiency, and performance measures used in the Shared Savings Program.

> The early evidence on ACOs does not indicate clearly superior quality or lower costs, but nevertheless hundreds of ACOs have been formed across the country.

2. Availability of Expedited Voluntary Antitrust Review

Any newly formed ACO that desires further antitrust guidance regarding its formation and planned operation can seek expedited 90 day review from the Agencies. . . .

PROBLEM

A college town (Sparta) has ten OB/GYNs, each of whom has always practiced independently in a separate office. The physicians are unhappy with declining reimbursement but are unwilling to form a medical partnership with full financial sharing of risk. After meeting with a consultant, they intend to pursue clinical integration with electronic health records (EHR) so they can jointly negotiate prices with private insurance companies. Projections suggest they can raise prices by 25 percent, more than offsetting the cost of the consultant and the EHR system. You are counsel to the physicians. What do you advise? Write a 300-word letter to the client.

F. LAWS LIMITING COMPETITIVE MARKET ENTRY

While antitrust law wields government power to facilitate or restore market competition, other state and federal laws limit competition by restricting market entry. For example, licensing laws limit the market for health care services by setting minimum standards for the practice of medicine or the operation of a hospital. Licensing laws set minimum quality standards, in part because consumers are unable to accurately judge cost/quality tradeoffs in health care.

A second example is state "certificate of need" or CON laws, originally put in place after federal legislative encouragement in 1974. CON laws manage major capital expenditures in local health care markets by requiring prior approval by an administrative tribunal before the project can proceed. In a CON state, a health system might need prior approval before building a new hospital wing or adding an ambulatory surgery center. The theory behind CONs was to avoid wasteful spending by local rivals. In practice, CON laws have often been used by politically powerful health care entities to block entry by competitors. After the 1974 federal law was repealed in 1987, many states repealed their CON laws, but a significant number retained them, with modifications that have tended to narrow the scope of coverage over time. Licensing and CON laws are inherently anticompetitive but are intended to address market imperfections inherent in the health care sector.

1. SCOPE OF PRACTICE

State law licenses the medical professions as a minimum standard of quality. State law also regulates the appropriate scope of practice for each licensed group of health professionals, such as doctors, nurses, and pharmacists, including practice from other states using telemedicine. In many states, power to issue these rules has been delegated by the legislature to the relevant professional board, which might have a conflict of interest in trying to defend turf from a competitor. In the following letter, the FTC recommends that Alabama reject a proposed rule from the medical board (dominated by physicians) that would have restricted the scope of practice for certified registered nurse anesthetists (CRNAs). In this letter, the federal government addresses an area historically regulated by states.

Letter from the Staff of the FTC to the Alabama State Board of Medical Examiners

(Nov. 3, 2010)

The staffs of the Federal Trade Commission's Office of Policy Planning, Bureau of Economics, and Bureau of Competition appreciate this opportunity to comment on the proposed regulation of interventional pain management services (Proposed Rule) issued by the Alabama State Board of Medical Examiners. The Proposed Rule restricts the "interventional treatment of pain" to "qualified, licensed medical doctors and doctors of osteopathy," who "may not delegate to non-physician personnel the authority to utilize such procedures to diagnosis [sic], manage or treat chronic pain patients." The rule appears to prohibit certified registered nurse anesthetists (CRNAs) from performing, under the supervision of a physician, pain management procedures that the Board of Nursing considers within the scope of CRNA practice. Absent evidence that the proposed restrictions are necessary to protect the public, there appears to be no reason to sacrifice the benefits of CRNA pain management services as currently available under Alabama law.

> The Alabama Board of Nursing and the Board of Medical Examiners are fighting over scope of practice state licensure matters when the FTC steps in.

Unnecessary restrictions on the ability of physicians to provide pain management services in collaboration with CRNAs are likely to reduce the availability, and raise the prices, of pain management services in Alabama. In particular, the Proposed Rule may burden cancer patients and others with chronic pain, rural Alabamans and others whose access to health care, or ability to pay for it, is limited, and hospice patients. We therefore urge the Board to consider carefully the impact of the Proposed Rule and to avoid adopting provisions that would limit the role of CRNAs in pain management more strictly than patient protection requires. The Proposed Rule provides no evidence that the current practice has harmed patients. Further, studies that have examined CRNA provision of anesthesia services have not found safety or quality defects in CRNA practice.

Interest and Experience of the Federal Trade Commission

The FTC is charged under the FTC Act with preventing unfair methods of competition and unfair or deceptive acts or practices in or affecting commerce. Competition is at the core of America's economy, and vigorous competition among sellers in an open marketplace gives consumers the benefits of lower prices, higher quality products and services, more choices, and greater innovation. Because of the importance of health care competition to the economy and consumer welfare, anticompetitive conduct in health care markets has long been a key target of FTC law enforcement, research, and advocacy, such as this letter. Recently, FTC staff have urged several states to reject or narrow restrictions that limit health care access and raise prices to consumers by limiting competition among health care providers and professionals. . . .

Because the proposed rule effectively prohibits non-physicians from providing interventional pain treatment, and physicians from delegating authority to provide such treatment to other licensed health care professionals, the Proposed Rule appears to prevent CRNAs from performing many of the pain management procedures that the Board of Nursing considers to be within the scope of CRNA practice in Alabama, subject to physician supervision. For example, the scope of CRNA practice includes "intradermal, subcutaneous, or intramuscular administration of a local anesthetic agent in a specified amount designated by order of a licensed physician or dentist," and "the monitoring and adjustment of local anesthetic agent(s) and analgesic agent(s) infusing via an epidural, brachial plexus, or femoral catheter placed by a qualified [CRNA] or qualified licensed physician may be performed by a registered nurse . . . as ordered by a licensed prescriber."

Consumer Protection Concerns and the Scope of Practice

Patient safety or consumer protection concerns can justify licensure requirements and scope of practice restrictions. FTC staff recognize that particular pain management procedures may require the specific training and experience of a board certified anesthesiologist and that other particular interventions may require the special skills of a certified surgical sub-specialist. Staff notes, however, that the Proposed Rule applies broadly and does not identify such particular procedures.

Available evidence indicates that CRNAs operating within the scope of their licensure provide pain management services safely. Published data tend to indicate that the baseline risk of anesthesia is extremely low across all providers, and provider settings, with several studies indicating that recent decades have seen "a remarkably abrupt decrease in anesthetic related death rates, morbidity, and risk of perioperative deaths." In publishing its final rule regarding the provision of hospital anesthesia services under the Medicare and Medicaid programs, the U.S. Department of Health and Human Services (HHS) concluded that, "the anesthesia-related death rate is extremely low, and that the administration of anesthesia in the United States is safe relative to surgical risk." Moreover, HHS found no "need for Federal intervention in State professional practice laws governing CRNA practice . . . [and] no reason to require a Federal rule in these conditions of participation mandating that physicians supervise the practice of [state-licensed CRNAs]."

Likely Effects on Alabama Health Care Consumers

The Proposed Rule's restrictions on the ability of physicians to direct and supervise CRNA provision of interventional pain treatments to chronic pain patients practice may increase prices for pain management services and decrease access to such services. By limiting the number of health care professionals licensed to provide pain management services, the Proposed Rule would reduce price competition. Further, prices may rise to the extent that physician services are substituted for lower-cost CRNA services. Finally, the Proposed Rule may thwart innovation in health care delivery by limiting the ability of health care providers to develop, test, and implement the most efficient teams of pain management professionals.

Moreover, the burdens imposed by the Proposed Rule may be felt especially by some of the most vulnerable citizens of Alabama. For example, CRNA practices disproportionately serve smaller, rural hospitals. In addition, hospice providers and patients may face both increased prices and reduced access to care if only physicians can provide palliative care for chronic pain.

It is possible that the Proposed Rule may, on balance, reduce patient safety. As noted, economic or geographic access problems may place some Alabamans at risk of inadequate care. Also, if CRNA pain management specialists are sometimes replaced not by board certified anesthesiologists, but by physicians and osteopaths who do not specialize in pain management, the average quality of interventional pain management in Alabama, or certain parts of Alabama, could be reduced.

Conclusion

If particular interventional pain treatment services demonstrably require more specialized training and experience than CRNAs working under physician supervision posses[s], then the Board should tailor the rule to address those particular services. To the extent that there is no evidence that CRNA practice harms patients, staff recommend that the Board reject the Proposed Rule outright.

PROBLEM

You represent the Alabama State Board of Medical Examiners. How do you respond to the FTC Letter? What type of evidence do you need to support your case?

2. CERTIFICATE OF NEED LAWS

"Certificate of need" (CON) laws are another approach to restricting market entry by competitors. CONs were originally designed as a cost-saving measure under the Nixon and Ford Administrations. The identified problem was a race by hospitals to build new buildings and purchase expensive equipment in order to attract patients, partially in response to generous reimbursement in the early years after the introduction of Medicare. In most industries, competitors are entirely free to build nicer hotels or restaurants in order to attract customers. But in health care it was thought that excessive competition by hospitals was wasteful, especially when a large part of the bill was paid by government in the Medicare and Medicaid program.

Under the federal law (the National Health Planning and Resources Development Act of 1974), the country was divided into 205 health service areas with a state agency in each area designated to create a plan for hospital construction and investment in new equipment. If a hospital wanted to build a new wing or add an expensive new diagnostic machine, they had to ask the state agency for permission, based on whether there was a "need" for the new services according to a state plan. If so, the state would issue the "certificate of need" and construction could begin, with licensure to follow when the project was complete. Even after the repeal of this federal law, state versions remain. Take, for example, Georgia's CON statute:

> As discussed in Chapter 2, in 1974 Medicare reimbursed hospitals based on their reasonable costs, so (almost) no matter what the hospital spent, Medicare paid for it. That system was changed in 1983.

> **Ga. Code Ann. §31-6-40. Certificate of need required for new institutional health services; exemption**
>
> (a) On and after July 1, 2008, any new institutional health service shall be required to obtain a certificate of need pursuant to this chapter. New institutional health services include:
>
> (1) The construction, development, or other establishment of a new health care facility;

(2) Any expenditure by or on behalf of a health care facility in excess of $2.5 million which, under generally accepted accounting principles consistently applied, is a capital expenditure, except expenditures for acquisition of an existing health care facility not owned or operated by or on behalf of a political subdivision of this state, or any combination of such political subdivisions, or by or on behalf of a hospital authority, as defined in Article 4 of Chapter 7 of this title, or certificate of need owned by such facility in connection with its acquisition. The dollar amounts specified in this paragraph and in subparagraph (A) of paragraph (14) of Code Section 31-6-2 shall be adjusted annually by an amount calculated by multiplying such dollar amounts (as adjusted for the preceding year) by the annual percentage of change in the composite index of construction material prices, or its successor or appropriate replacement index, if any, published by the United States Department of Commerce for the preceding calendar year, commencing on July 1, 2009, and on each anniversary thereafter of publication of the index. The department shall immediately institute rulemaking procedures to adopt such adjusted dollar amounts. In calculating the dollar amounts of a proposed project for purposes of this paragraph and subparagraph (A) of paragraph (14) of Code Section 31-6-2, the costs of all items subject to review by this chapter and items not subject to review by this chapter associated with and simultaneously developed or proposed with the project shall be counted, except for the expenditure or commitment of or incurring an obligation for the expenditure of funds to develop certificate of need applications, studies, reports, schematics, preliminary plans and specifications or working drawings, or to acquire sites;

(3) The purchase or lease by or on behalf of a health care facility or a diagnostic, treatment, or rehabilitation center of diagnostic or therapeutic equipment with a value in excess of $1 million; provided, however, that diagnostic or other imaging services that are not offered in a hospital or in the offices of an individual private physician or single group practice of physicians exclusively for use on patients of that physician or group practice shall be deemed to be a new institutional health service regardless of the cost of equipment; and provided, further, that this shall not include build out costs, as defined by the department, but shall include all functionally related equipment, software, and any warranty and services contract costs for the first five years. The acquisition of one or more items of functionally related diagnostic or therapeutic equipment shall be considered as one project. The dollar amount specified in this paragraph, in subparagraph (B) of paragraph (14) of Code Section 31-6-2, and in paragraph (10) of subsection (a) of Code Section 31-6-47 shall be adjusted annually by an amount calculated by multiplying such dollar amounts (as adjusted for the preceding year) by the annual percentage of change in the consumer price index, or its successor or appropriate replacement index, if any, published by the United States Department of Labor for the preceding calendar year, commencing on July 1, 2010;

(4) Any increase in the bed capacity of a health care facility except as provided in Code Section 31-6-47;

(5) Clinical health services which are offered in or through a health care facility, which were not offered on a regular basis in or through such health

care facility within the 12 month period prior to the time such services would be offered;

(6) Any conversion or upgrading of any general acute care hospital to a specialty hospital or of a facility such that it is converted from a type of facility not covered by this chapter to any of the types of health care facilities which are covered by this chapter; and

(7) Clinical health services which are offered in or through a diagnostic, treatment, or rehabilitation center which were not offered on a regular basis in or through that center within the 12 month period prior to the time such services would be offered, but only if the clinical health services are any of the following:

(A) Radiation therapy;

(B) Biliary lithotripsy;

(C) Surgery in an operating room environment, including but not limited to ambulatory surgery; and

(D) Cardiac catheterization.

(b) Any person proposing to develop or offer a new institutional health service or health care facility shall, before commencing such activity, submit a letter of intent and an application to the department and obtain a certificate of need in the manner provided in this chapter unless such activity is excluded from the scope of this chapter.

PROBLEM

You represent a group of physicians in Atlanta who want to offer a new type of cancer treatment using proton beam therapy. Will a CON be required?

The DOJ views CON laws as a dangerous relic and occasionally testifies at the state level to encourage repeal of the laws, as in the following excerpt:

Competition in Healthcare and Certificates of Need
Statement of the Antitrust Division, U.S. Department of Justice
Before the Florida Senate Committee on Health
and Human Services
Appropriations
JOSEPH M. MILLER
Assistant Chief, Litigation I Section

March 25, 2008

The Antitrust Division's experience and expertise has [sic] taught us that Certificate of Need laws pose a substantial threat to the efficient performance of healthcare markets. By their very nature, CON laws create barriers to entry and expansion and thus restrict free and open competition. They undercut consumer choice, weaken markets' ability to contain healthcare costs, and stifle innovation.

We have examined historical and current arguments for CON laws, and conclude that these arguments provide no economic justification for depriving consumers of the benefits of free markets. To the extent that CONs are used to further noneconomic goals, those goals can be more efficiently achieved through other means that do not impose the substantial (perhaps unintended) costs on consumers that restrictive CON laws impose. We hope you will carefully consider those significant costs as you evaluate whether to eliminate those laws in Florida. . . .

Our concerns about the harm from CON laws are informed by one fundamental principle: market forces improve the quality and lower the costs of healthcare services. They drive innovation and ultimately lead to the delivery of better healthcare. Government intervention can undermine market forces to the detriment of healthcare consumers.

In our antitrust investigations we often hear the argument that healthcare is "different" and that competition principles do not apply to the provision of healthcare services. The proposition that competition cannot work in healthcare is simply not true. Similar arguments made by engineers and lawyers that competition fundamentally does not work[,] and[] is in fact harmful to public policy goals, have been rejected by the courts and private restraints on competition have long been condemned. Indeed, at least since the Supreme Court's seminal 1943 decision in a case brought by the Department of Justice against the American Medical Association, competition has played a critical role in shaping the delivery of healthcare in this country. The Antitrust Division and the Federal Trade Commission have worked diligently to make sure that private barriers to that competition do not arise.

During our extensive healthcare hearings in 2003, we obtained substantial evidence generally about the role of competition in our healthcare delivery system and reached the conclusion that vigorous competition among healthcare providers "promotes the delivery of high-quality, cost-effective healthcare." Specifically, competition results in lower prices and broader access to health care and health insurance, while nonprice competition can promote higher quality.

> In AMA v. United States, 317 U.S. 519 (1943), the Court upheld a Sherman Act indictment for conspiracy in restraint of trade under section 3 of the Sherman Act against the AMA, which had tried to block physician participation in a prepaid group health plan.

This finding is not new. We saw in the 1990s the growth of managed care and the impact it had on the cost and availability of insurance. Competition among and between hospitals and physicians intensified with the development of managed care organizations. In addition to putting pressure on costs, managed care plans have caused providers to use shorter hospital stays and to offer alternative outpatient treatments. This evolution in health care purchasing led to lower costs and increased choice without sacrificing quality. Moreover, lower costs and improved efficiency made more affordable and available health insurance.

Competition also helped bring to consumers important innovations in healthcare technology. For example, health plan demand for lower costs and "patient demand for a non-institutional, friendly, convenient setting for their surgical care" drove the growth of Ambulatory Surgery Centers (ASCs). Ambulatory surgery centers offered patients more "convenient locations, shorter wait time, and lower coinsurance than a hospital department." Important to the success of these competitive forces in improving the delivery of care to consumers was the availability of technological advances, such as endoscopic surgery and advanced anesthetic agents.

Competition harnessed this new technology and brought it to consumers in the lower cost, more convenient setting of ambulatory surgery centers. Also important to the success of innovative forms of healthcare delivery has been the ability for hospitals and other healthcare facilities to provide specialized services, reaping the benefits of specialization and economies of scale, without being encumbered by unnecessary regulatory requirements that these facilities provide the full spectrum of services available at general hospitals. The impact of innovation by competitors on traditional general acute care hospitals led to those hospitals responding to the competition by delivering more care, in a better manner, in an outpatient setting, both at their own campuses and at ambulatory surgery centers in which they invested.

Laser eye surgery is comparatively competitive, perhaps because it is rarely covered by insurance and patients can compare costs of this discrete, elective service relatively easily.

This type of competitive success story has occurred again and again in healthcare in the area of pharmaceuticals, urgent care centers, and elective surgeries such as Lasik procedures, to name just a few. Without private or governmental impediments to their performance, we can expect healthcare markets to continue to deliver these benefits.

CON Laws Create Barriers to Beneficial Competition

CON laws are a classic government-erected barrier to entry, and by their nature are an impediment to the proper functioning of the market process. Accordingly, in *A Dose of Competition*, the Federal Trade Commission and we urged the states to rethink their CON laws.

Original Cost-Control Reasons for CON Laws No Longer Apply

We made that recommendation in part because the original reason for the adoption of CON laws is no longer valid. Many CON programs trace their origin to a repealed federal mandate, the National Health Planning and Resources Development Act of 1974, which offered incentives for states to implement CON programs. At the time, the federal government and private insurance reimbursed healthcare charges predominantly on a "cost-plus" basis, which provided incentives for overinvestment. The hope was that CON laws would provide a counterweight against that skewed incentive.

In considering this historical justification for CON laws, we need to keep clear that a number of other arguments made today in support of CON laws were not part of the rationale for their original adoption:

- CON laws were not adopted as a means of cross-subsidizing care;
- CON laws were not adopted in order to have centralized planning of the location and nature of healthcare facilities; and
- CON laws were not adopted to protect the health and safety of the population from poor quality medicine.

Instead, CON laws were adopted because excessive capital investments, spurred by the then-current cost-plus method of reimbursement, were driving up healthcare costs. There was concern that, because patients are usually not price-sensitive, providers engaged in a "medical arms race" by unnecessarily expanding their services to offer the perceived highest quality services.

CON laws appear to have failed in their intended purpose of containing costs. Several studies have examined the effectiveness of CONs in controlling costs. The empirical evidence on the economic effects of CON programs demonstrated near-universal agreement among health economists that CON laws were unsuccessful in containing healthcare costs.

In addition, the reimbursement methodologies that in theory may have justified the adoption of CON laws in the 1970s have changed significantly. The federal

Despite the FTC's opposition, many states retain CON laws.

government no longer reimburses on a cost-plus basis. In 1986, Congress repealed the National Health Planning and Resources Development Act of 1974. And, health plans and other purchasers routinely bargain with healthcare providers over prices. In sum, changed government regulation has eliminated the original justification for CON programs, leaving us with CON laws that now only serve to impede competition we rely on to spur innovation and contain costs.

Protecting Revenues of Incumbents Does Not Justify CON Laws and Other Regulations

In lobbying for CON laws, incumbent hospitals often argue that they should be protected against additional competition so that they can continue to cross-subsidize care provided to uninsured or under-insured patients. In essence, they argue that they cannot provide care to needy patients unless they can continue to charge high prices to patients more able to pay without fear of losing them to more attractive healthcare alternatives. In other words, those patients from whom the higher prices are obtained need to be kept "captive" through the lack of alternative healthcare choices.

As discussed below, however, the premise of the argument is false: a recent study shows that competition does not undercut the ability of community hospitals to fulfill their charitable mission. In addition, CON laws actually do more harm than good by restricting the output of healthcare services, keeping prices high, and reducing innovation, quality and choice. The government pays more for less care delivered to those in need while consumers more able to pay also pay too much for less.

While we wholeheartedly appreciate the laudatory goal of providing healthcare services to those who cannot afford them, we want to make clear our belief that limiting competition in order to achieve this goal is the wrong way to go. CON laws unnecessarily impose significant costs on all healthcare consumers, including the needy, by restricting the output of healthcare services and diminishing incentives to pursue innovation and cost containment. There are more efficient ways to accomplish the goal of providing healthcare to the uninsured citizens of Florida that will better ensure that an optimal amount of healthcare is actually delivered to those persons in need without impeding the proper functioning of health care markets. Put more starkly, by protecting incumbent hospitals from competition, CON laws allow[ ] dominant hospitals to tax consumers through the exercise of market power in order to pursue the charitable goal of providing care to other, less fortunate consumers. In using that funding mechanism, however, the CON laws may do more harm than good.

First, CON laws harm consumers who would have chosen lower priced, higher quality, or more convenient sources of care if they were permitted the choice. This includes all consumers, including the uninsured.

Second, CON laws impose that cost without any clear evidence that other desired social goals are advanced. The evidence to date indicates that new competition does *not* undercut community hospitals' ability to fulfill their charitable mission. In 2006 the Medicare Payment Advisory Commission (MedPAC) studied just this issue in connection with the emergence of single-specialty hospitals around the country. The MedPAC study found that, for several reasons, specialty hospitals did not undercut the financial viability of rival community hospitals. One reason for this was that specialty hospitals generally locate in areas that have above average population growth. Thus, they are competing for a new and growing patient population, not just siphoning off the existing customer base of the community hospitals.

Third, new competition can force community hospitals to improve their performance. In studying the effect of single-specialty hospitals, MedPAC found that the community hospitals responded to the competition by improving efficiency, adjusting their pricing, and expanding profitable lines of business. Community hospitals encouraged physicians to perform procedures on the hospital campus by developing centers of excellence and building physician offices on campus. Overall, community hospitals affected by specialty hospital entry maintained profit margins in line with national averages. Rather than undercutting community hospitals, new entry drives them to do a better job. Thus, in addition to the harm to the consumers who would have chosen the new healthcare provider, CON laws harm society in general by depriving it of the increased efficiency that competition would have brought to the health care market. We accordingly urge you to consider going further in the reform of your law by eliminating CON requirements that currently apply to all healthcare facilities, which will directly benefit Florida's healthcare consumers, and also provide incentives to general hospitals to improve quality and lower costs.

CON Laws Impose Other Costs and May Facilitate Anti-Competitive Behavior

CON laws appear to raise a particularly substantial barrier to entry and expansion of competitors because they create an opportunity for existing competitors to exploit procedural opportunities to thwart or delay new competition. Such behavior, commonly called "rent seeking" conduct, is a well-recognized consequence of regulatory intervention in the market. Essentially, an existing competitor uses the hearing and appeals process to cause substantial delays, leading both the existing competitor and the new entrant to divert significant funds away from delivering healthcare and to spend them on legal fees, consulting fees, and lobbying efforts. Moreover, much of this conduct, even if exclusionary and anticompetitive, is unlikely to be subject to legal challenge as a violation of the antitrust laws because it involves petitioning of the state government by the existing competitor. Indeed, during our hearings, we received evidence of the widespread recognition that existing competitors use the CON process "to forestall competitors from entering an incumbent's market."

We have found that existing competitors, at times with the encouragement or acquiescence of state officials, go further and enter into agreements not required by the CON laws but nonetheless facilitated by them. Two examples arise from West Virginia, and a third comes from Vermont.

In the first West Virginia case, we found that a Charleston, West Virginia hospital used the threat of objection during the CON process, and the potential ensuing delay and cost, to induce a hospital seeking a certificate of need for an open heart surgery program not to apply for it at the location that would have well served Charleston consumers and provided greater competition for their business. Instead, the Charleston hospital successfully prevented the possibility of this competing open heart program. The state authorities never had the opportunity to decide whether under the CON laws that second program would have been approved because of the unlawful agreement among the hospitals.

In 2016, West Virginia passed a law (S. 597) that exempted state board-approved hospital mergers from federal antitrust review under the state action doctrine, discussed later in this chapter.

In the second West Virginia case, two closely competing hospitals decided to allocate healthcare services between themselves. The informal urging of state CON officials led them to agree unlawfully that only the one hospital would apply for an open heart program and only the other would apply to provide cancer services. Again, the state took no official action and consumers were deprived of the potential competition between these hospitals.

A third example comes from the State of Vermont. There, home health agencies entered into territorial market allocations, again under cover of the state regulatory program, to give each other exclusive geographic markets. That state's CON laws prevented competitive entry, which normally might have disciplined such cartel behavior. We found that Vermont consumers were paying higher prices than were consumers in states where home health agencies competed against each other.

We have learned from these matters and others that CON laws have the potential to impede competition in ways well beyond what is intended by their supporters.

Conclusion

My remarks are intended to convey to you our belief that CON laws impose substantial costs on consumers and healthcare markets. In light of these costs, the Antitrust Division believes that Florida should carefully consider whether on balance its CON laws and other requirements applied to healthcare facilities as part of the licensing process do more harm than good. Let me close by encouraging you not to accept without careful scrutiny claims that elimination of CON laws will visit significant harm on your state.

Thank you again for the opportunity to discuss our views on how CON laws affect competition and consumers in healthcare.

Florida did not repeal its CON laws after this testimony. As of 2016, 36 states plus the District of Columbia and Puerto Rico still have CON laws on the books. While 14 states have repealed CON laws, most still retain some regulations to restrain duplication of services. Even after a CON is granted, it is risky to begin construction until all appeals are final. Since these appeals can take many years, competition can be delayed through litigation. In an epic battle in Jackson, Mississippi, Methodist Medical Center was forced to close a new $30 million hospital after it lost a CON appeal. St. Dominic-Jackson Mem'l Hosp. v. Mississippi State Dep't of Health, 728 So. 2d 81 (Miss. 1999).

One issue that Joseph Miller from the Antitrust Division of the Department of Justice did not focus on is corruption. CON cases can be very political. The next case provides a flavor for the rough-and-tumble political world of state CON boards. A governor and the CEO of a large publicly traded health care company both ended up in federal prison for bribery relating to appointments to the Alabama CON board.

United States v. Siegelman

640 F.3d 1159 (11th Cir. 2011)

PER CURIAM

This case is before us on remand from the Supreme Court of the United States for reconsideration in light of Skilling v. United States, 561 U.S. ——, 130 S. Ct.

2896 (2010). The parties were ordered to re-brief the case; oral argument was heard.

I.

Don Eugene Siegelman is the former Governor of Alabama. Richard Scrushy is the founder and former Chief Executive Officer of HealthSouth Corporation ("HealthSouth"), a major hospital corporation with operations throughout Alabama. The defendants were convicted of federal funds bribery, in violation of 18 U.S.C. §666(a)(1)(B), and five counts of honest services mail fraud and conspiracy, in violation of 18 U.S.C. §§1341, 1346, and 18 U.S.C. §371. Siegelman was also convicted of obstruction of justice, in violation of 18 U.S.C. §1512(b)(3).

At the time, HealthSouth was a major publicly traded health care company with vast operations in all 50 states. It was one of the most successful health care companies in the 1990s. Richard Scrushy was the founder and CEO. He was also the first corporate executive prosecuted under the Sarbanes-Oxley Act for an accounting scandal.

The bribery convictions were based on allegations that the defendants made and executed a corrupt agreement whereby Scrushy gave Siegelman $500,000 in exchange for Siegelman's appointing him to Alabama's Certificate of Need Review Board (the "CON" Board). The honest services mail fraud convictions were also based in part upon these bribery allegations, but two of the counts also alleged that Scrushy used the CON Board seat to obtain favorable treatment for HealthSouth's applications. The conspiracy count alleged that Scrushy and Siegelman conspired to violate the honest services statute. Siegelman's obstruction of justice conviction is based on allegations that he corruptly influenced another to create a series of sham check transactions to cover up a separate "pay-to-play" payment to him.

This is an extraordinary case. It involves allegations of corruption at the highest levels of Alabama state government. Its resolution has strained the resources of both Alabama and the federal government. . . .

II.

Don Siegelman was elected Governor of Alabama in 1998 on a campaign platform that advocated the establishment of a state lottery to help fund education in Alabama. After his election, he established the Alabama Education Lottery Foundation (the "Foundation") to raise money to campaign for voter approval of a ballot initiative to establish a state lottery. Darren Cline, the Foundation's fundraising director, testified that Siegelman "called the shots" on the lottery campaign. The lottery initiative was eventually defeated in a referendum held in October of 1999.

On March 9, 2000, the Foundation borrowed $730,789.29 from an Alabama bank in order to pay down debt incurred by the Alabama Democratic Party for get-out-the-vote expenses during the lottery campaign. This note was personally and unconditionally guaranteed by Siegelman.

Richard Scrushy, the CEO of HealthSouth[,] had served on the CON Board under three previous governors of Alabama. The CON Board is an arm of the State Health Planning and Development Agency and exists to prevent unnecessary duplication of healthcare services in Alabama. The Board determines the number of healthcare facilities in Alabama through a process that requires healthcare providers to apply for and obtain a certificate of a healthcare need before opening a new facility or offering a special healthcare service. The CON Board decides which healthcare applications will be approved for an announced healthcare need, choosing between competing applications and ruling on objections filed by an applicant's competitor. The Governor of Alabama has sole discretion to appoint the members of the CON Board, who serve at his pleasure. Scrushy had supported Siegelman's opponent in the just prior election.

Nick Bailey was one of Siegelman's closest associates and had worked on Siegelman's campaign for governor. Cline testified that "whatever [Bailey] told me that the Governor wanted was what the Governor said." Cline also testified that "if the Governor wanted to get something done, then [Bailey] went ahead—blindly went ahead and did it."

Bailey testified that, after Siegelman's election in 1998, Siegelman met with Eric Hanson, an outside lobbyist for HealthSouth, and told Hanson that because Scrushy had contributed at least $350,000 to Siegelman's opponent in the election, Scrushy needed to "do" at least $500,000 in order to "make it right" with the Siegelman campaign. Bailey testified that Siegelman was referring to the campaign for the lottery initiative, and that Hanson was to relay this conversation to Scrushy. Bailey also testified that, in another conversation, Hanson told Bailey that Scrushy wanted control of the CON Board.

Mike Martin is the former Chief Financial Officer of HealthSouth. He testified that having influence over the CON Board was important to Scrushy and HealthSouth because it determined the number of healthcare facilities in the state, thereby affecting HealthSouth's ability to grow. He testified that Scrushy told him that to "have some influence or a spot on the CON Board," they had to help Siegelman raise money for the lottery campaign. Scrushy said that if they did so, "[they] would be assured a seat on the CON Board." Martin testified, "[W]e were making a contribution . . . in exchange for a spot on the CON Board."

Bailey testified that lobbyist Hanson "made it clear to him that if Mr. Scrushy gave the $500,000 to the lottery campaign that we could not let him down" with respect to the CON Board seat. Bailey also testified that he "reminded the Governor periodically of the conversations that [Bailey] had with Eric Hanson and the conversations that the Governor had with Eric Hanson about what Mr. Scrushy wanted for his contributions, and that was the CON Board."

Martin also testified that Scrushy told him that HealthSouth could not make the payment to the lottery campaign, nor could he do it personally because "we [HealthSouth] had not supported that and that his wife, Leslie, was against the lottery, and it would just look bad if HealthSouth made a direct contribution to the lottery, so we needed to ask—he instructed me in particular to ask our investment banker, Bill McGahan, from [the Swiss bank] UBS, to make the contribution."

Bill McGahan did not want to make such an "out of the norm" donation and hoped the matter would "go away." Over the next two weeks, Martin called McGahan at least once a day to ask him about the status of the UBS donation, and told McGahan that Scrushy was going to fire UBS if it did not make the contribution. Finally, Martin testified, Scrushy himself called McGahan to "put more pressure" on him to make the contribution.

> The donation from Scrushy was routed through HealthSouth's investment banker, UBS, and one of their clients, IHS.

McGahan testified that he did not want UBS to make such a large contribution directly, so he told Martin that he would get Integrated Health Services ("IHS") of Maryland to make the donation to the lottery campaign in exchange for UBS reducing an outstanding fee that IHS owed UBS. IHS agreed to this arrangement and donated $250,000 to the Foundation in exchange for a reduction of $267,000 in the fee it owed UBS.

The IHS "donation" was in the form of a check dated July 19, 1999, made payable from itself to the Foundation. Martin testified that Scrushy told him it was important that he, Scrushy, hand deliver the IHS check to Siegelman, so Martin delivered the check to Scrushy so that he could do so.

Some time later, Siegelman and Scrushy met in Siegelman's office. Bailey testified that after Scrushy left, Siegelman showed the IHS check to Bailey and told him that Scrushy was "halfway there." Bailey asked, "what in the world is he [Scrushy] going to want for that?" Siegelman replied, "the CON Board." Bailey then asked, "I wouldn't think that would be a problem, would it?" Siegelman responded, "I wouldn't think so."

Siegelman appointed Scrushy to the CON Board on July 26, 1999—one week after the date on the IHS check. Siegelman directed Bailey to contact the Board chair-designee to tell her that Siegelman wanted Scrushy to be vice-chair of the CON Board, and the Board so chose. Bailey testified that Siegelman made Scrushy vice-chair "[b]ecause [Scrushy] asked for it." Scrushy stayed on the Board until January of 2001, at which time Siegelman appointed Thom Carman, HealthSouth's vice-president, to the remainder of Scrushy's term. Siegelman subsequently reappointed Carman to a full term. While Carman was on the Board, HealthSouth successfully applied for and received Certificates of Need for a mobile PET scanner and a rehabilitation hospital. . . .

In May, Siegelman and Bailey traveled to HealthSouth's headquarters in Birmingham, where Siegelman met privately with Scrushy in Scrushy's office. At that meeting, Scrushy gave Siegelman a check issued by HealthSouth for $250,000 payable to the Foundation. On May 23, 2000, the $250,000 check was applied directly against the Foundation's loan balance.

The Foundation was required to disclose contributions received and expenditures made in statements filed with the Alabama Secretary of State. It failed to file timely any disclosure regarding any funds received until July of 2002, after Alabama newspapers questioned whether the financial dealings between the Foundation and the Alabama Democratic Party had been properly reported and the Secretary of State's Office had written a letter to the state Attorney General's Office about the Foundation's non-disclosure of the payoff of the Democratic Party's campaign loan. All funds received were then reported.

. . . .

On December 12, 2005, a grand jury returned a second superseding indictment against Siegelman and Scrushy and two other defendants. Both Siegelman and Scrushy were charged with federal funds bribery, honest services conspiracy and honest services mail fraud. Siegelman was also charged with multiple counts of racketeering conspiracy, racketeering, honest services wire fraud, obstruction of justice and extortion.

Trial on the indictment began on May 1, 2006. On June 29, 2006, the jury convicted Siegelman and Scrushy on the bribery, conspiracy and honest services mail fraud counts, and Siegelman was convicted of one count of obstruction of justice. The jury acquitted Siegelman on the remaining twenty-two counts. The other two defendants were acquitted on all counts against them. . . .

Siegelman and Scrushy were each sentenced to approximately seven years in federal prison. Scrushy served his time and was granted supervised release in 2012, after nearly six years in a federal prison. In separate trials, he was acquitted of violations of federal securities laws but was found liable for $2.8 billion in related civil suits. Siegelman was released from federal prison on February 8, 2017.

QUESTION

Why was a seat on the Alabama CON board worth $500,000 to Richard Scrushy?

G. THE ROLE OF STATES IN ANTITRUST ENFORCEMENT

The FTC and Department of Justice enforce federal antitrust laws, and some market participants may have standing to bring a private antitrust suit. But another important source of antitrust enforcement power resides with the state attorney general, under state law analogues to the Sherman and Clayton Acts. The state can also act as a preemptive shield, even from federal enforcement, under the "state action doctrine."

1. STATE ATTORNEY GENERAL ACTIONS

We first look at an example of a state attorney general trying to improve price transparency in Massachusetts hospital pricing, before turning to a recent U.S. Supreme Court decision on the state action doctrine, *Phoebe Putney*.

Office of Attorney General Martha Coakley
 Examination of Health Care Cost Trends and Cost Drivers
 Pursuant to G.L. c. 118G, §61/2(b)
 REPORT FOR ANNUAL PUBLIC HEARING UNDER
 G.L. c. 118G, §61/2

March 16, 2010

Summary of Findings

[The attorney general issued subpoenas to hospitals and health insurers in Massachusetts to obtain comprehensive information about pricing.] Our examination identified several factors that we believe should be considered when analyzing cost drivers and pursuing cost containment. We found:

A. Prices paid by health insurers to hospitals and physician groups vary significantly within the same geographic area and amongst providers offering similar levels of service.

B. Price variations are not correlated to (1) quality of care, (2) the sickness of the population served or complexity of the services provided, (3) the extent to which a provider cares for a large portion of patients on Medicare or Medicaid, or (4) whether a provider is an academic teaching or research facility. Moreover, (5) price variations are not adequately explained by differences in hospital costs of delivering similar services at similar facilities.

C. Price variations are correlated to market leverage as measured by the relative market position of the hospital or provider group compared with other hospitals or provider groups within a geographic region or within a group of academic medical centers.

D. Variation in total medical expenses on a per member per month basis is not correlated to the methodology used to pay for health care, with total medical expenses sometimes higher for risk-sharing providers than for providers paid on a fee-for-service basis.

E. Price increases, not increases in utilization, caused most of the increases in health care costs during the past few years in Massachusetts.

F. Higher priced hospitals are gaining market share at the expense of lower priced hospitals, which are losing volume.

G. The commercial health care marketplace has been distorted by contracting practices that reinforce and perpetuate disparities in pricing.

The Massachusetts AG's work was primarily building a factual record as opposed to a legal proceeding. The Legislature responded with a series of reforms to address hospital pricing in the Commonwealth.

Each of these findings is detailed in the report.

Implications of These Findings for Cost Containment

These findings have meaningful implications for efforts to control health care costs. One threshold question is whether we can expect the existing health care market in Massachusetts to successfully contain health care costs. To date, the answer is an unequivocal "no." The market players—whether insurers, providers, or the businesses and consumers who pay for health insurance—have not effectively controlled costs in recent years. If we accept that our health care system can be improved by better aligning payment incentives and controlling cost growth, then we must begin to shift how we purchase health care to align payments with "value," measured by those factors the health care market should justly reward, such as better quality.

Until now, only insurers have been privy to information on price differences and total medical expenses across their entire network. Insurers are in the best position to align price with quality, complexity, or other rational values.

Health care providers have much less information on a network-wide basis and naturally focus on their own delivery of health care services. Although hospitals in Massachusetts are predominantly not-for-profit, because they are mission-driven to provide high quality health care, they seek to increase their volume and prices to increase their resources to provide those services.

Those who purchase health insurance—the businesses and individuals subject to ever-increasing premiums—should care deeply about controlling costs. But the current market is not well aligned to promote cost containment. Insurance buyers have little information on prices paid and the reasons behind price disparities; nor do consumers generally have sufficient information, insurance product options, or incentives to make value-based health care decisions. The increased transparency about pricing and health care cost drivers reflected in this report is an important starting point to empower consumers in cost containment efforts. Such informational tools can only make a difference, however, if health insurance buyers seriously engage in the process of cost

Paying for value is a major health policy initiative, attempting to correct for market imperfections and information asymmetries.

containment. We as health care consumers cannot demand that costs stabilize without recognizing our role in the health care market. It is essential that businesses and consumers be engaged in efforts to promote a value-based health care market. Without the participation of all market players, the goal of cost containment is unlikely to be attained.

Moving Forward on Cost Containment

The market dynamics and distortions reflected in this report should be considered as the Commonwealth and market participants pursue strategies to contain health care costs. Based on our review and analysis, we recommend:

1. Increasing transparency and standardization in both health care payment and health care quality to promote market effectiveness and value-based purchasing by employers and consumers, including:

- Tracking and publishing total medical expenses (TME) for all providers;
- Promoting uniform quality measurement and reporting; and
- Promoting standardization of units of payment and other administrative processes;

2. Consideration of steps to improve market function, including:

- Adopting payment reform measures that account for and do not exacerbate existing market dynamics and distortions;
- Developing legislative or regulatory proposals to mitigate health care market dysfunction and price disparities;

3. Engaging all participants in the development of a value-based health care market by promoting creation of insurance products and decision-making tools that allow and encourage employers and consumers to make prudent health care decisions;

4. Prompt consideration of legislative or administrative action to discourage or prohibit insurer-provider contract provisions that perpetuate market disparities and inhibit product innovation.

The Legislature responded by establishing the Massachusetts Health Policy Commission, which has taken up the work of transforming provider reimbursement to account for value.

The Office of the Attorney General looks forward to collaborating with the Legislature, policymakers, insurers, hospitals, all other health care providers, businesses, municipalities, and consumers in promoting a value-based health care market that controls future health care cost growth while maintaining quality and access. We will strive to illuminate facts about the Massachusetts health care market that should be considered as those efforts proceed.

In addition to the ability to enforce state antitrust laws, attorneys general in most states retain powers to supervise the management of charitable assets. This power is frequently called *cy pres* and is potentially important since most U.S. hospitals are charitable corporations formed under state law. The *MEETH v. Spitzer* case, discussed in Chapter 4, is an example of the exercise of this supervisory power.

2. STATE ACTION DOCTRINE

The next case illustrates a state government's power to authoritatively foreclose competition, known as the *state action doctrine*. Unlike most areas of law, in this situation the state can effectively bypass federal law by preventing all antitrust enforcement. Here, the question was whether Georgia had clearly expressed a desire to foreclose competition.

Federal Trade Commission v. Phoebe Putney Health System, Inc.

133 S. Ct. 1003 (2013)

Justice SOTOMAYOR delivered the opinion of the Court.

Under this Court's state-action immunity doctrine, when a local governmental entity acts pursuant to a clearly articulated and affirmatively expressed state policy to displace competition, it is exempt from scrutiny under the federal antitrust laws. In this case, we must decide whether a Georgia law that creates special-purpose public entities called hospital authorities and gives those entities general corporate powers, including the power to acquire hospitals, clearly articulates and affirmatively expresses a state policy to permit acquisitions that substantially lessen competition. Because Georgia's grant of general corporate powers to hospital authorities does not include permission to use those powers anticompetitively, we hold that the clear-articulation test is not satisfied and state-action immunity does not apply.

I

A

In 1941, the State of Georgia amended its Constitution to allow political subdivisions to provide health care services. The State concurrently enacted the Hospital Authorities Law (Law), "to provide a mechanism for the operation and maintenance of needed health care facilities in the several counties and municipalities of th[e] state." "The purpose of the constitutional provision and the statute based thereon was to . . . create an organization which could carry out and make more workable the duty which the State owed to its indigent sick." DeJarnette v. Hospital Auth. of Albany, 195 Ga. 189, 200, 23 S.E.2d 716, 723 (1942). As amended, the Law authorizes each county and municipality, and certain combinations of counties or municipalities, to create "a public body corporate and politic" called a "hospital authority." Hospital authorities are governed by 5- to 9-member boards that are appointed by the governing body of the county or municipality in their area of operation.

> Many states have state- and county-level hospital authorities with various powers and responsibilities.

Under the Law, a hospital authority "exercise[s] public and essential governmental functions" and is delegated "all the powers necessary or convenient to carry out and effectuate" the Law's purposes. Giving more content to that general delegation, the Law enumerates 27 powers conferred upon hospital authorities, including the power "[t]o acquire by purchase, lease, or otherwise and to operate projects," which are defined to include hospitals and other public health facilities; "[t]o construct, reconstruct, improve, alter, and repair projects"; "[t]o lease . . . for operation by others any project" provided certain conditions are satisfied; and "[t]o establish rates and charges for the services and use of the facilities of the authority." Hospital authorities may not operate or construct any project for profit, and accordingly they must set rates so as only to cover operating expenses and create reasonable reserves.

B

In the same year that the Law was adopted, the city of Albany and Dougherty County established the Hospital Authority of Albany-Dougherty County (Authority) and the Authority promptly acquired Phoebe Putney Memorial Hospital (Memorial), which has been in operation in Albany since 1911. In 1990, the Authority restructured its operations by forming two private nonprofit corporations to manage Memorial: Phoebe Putney Health System, Inc. (PPHS), and its subsidiary, Phoebe Putney Memorial Hospital, Inc. (PPMH). The Authority leased Memorial to PPMH for $1 per year for 40 years. Under the lease, PPMH has exclusive authority over the operation of Memorial, including the ability to set rates for services. Consistent with §31-7-75(7), PPMH is subject to lease conditions that require provision of care to the indigent sick and limit its rate of return.

Memorial is one of two hospitals in Dougherty County. The second, Palmyra Medical Center (Palmyra), was established in Albany in 1971 and is located just two miles from Memorial. At the time suit was brought in this case, Palmyra was operated by a national for-profit hospital network, HCA, Inc. (HCA). Together, Memorial and Palmyra account for 86 percent of the market for acute-care hospital services provided to commercial health care plans and their customers in the six counties surrounding Albany. Memorial accounts for 75 percent of that market on its own.

> HCA is the largest national operator of for-profit hospitals, with more than 160 hospitals and more than 110 freestanding ASCs in 2016.

In 2010, PPHS began discussions with HCA about acquiring Palmyra. Following negotiations, PPHS presented the Authority with a plan under which the Authority would purchase Palmyra with PPHS controlled funds and then lease Palmyra to a PPHS subsidiary for $1 per year under the Memorial lease agreement. The Authority unanimously approved the transaction.

The Federal Trade Commission (FTC) shortly thereafter issued an administrative complaint alleging that the proposed purchase-and-lease transaction would create a virtual monopoly and would substantially reduce competition in the market for acute-care hospital services, in violation of §5 of the Federal Trade Commission Act, and §7 of the Clayton Act. The FTC, along with the State of Georgia, subsequently filed suit against the Authority, HCA, Palmyra, PPHS, PPMH, and the new PPHS subsidiary created to manage Palmyra (collectively respondents), seeking to enjoin the transaction pending administrative proceedings.

The United States District Court for the Middle District of Georgia denied the request for a preliminary injunction and granted respondents' motion to dismiss. The District Court held that respondents are immune from antitrust liability under the state-action doctrine.

The United States Court of Appeals for the Eleventh Circuit affirmed. As an initial matter, the court "agree[d] with the [FTC] that, on the facts alleged, the joint operation of Memorial and Palmyra would substantially lessen competition or tend to create, if not create, a monopoly." But the court concluded that the transaction was immune from antitrust liability. The Court of Appeals explained that as a local governmental entity, the Authority was entitled to state-action immunity if the challenged anticompetitive conduct was a "foreseeable result" of Georgia's legislation. According to the court, anticompetitive conduct is foreseeable if it could have been "reasonably anticipated" by the state legislature; it is not necessary, the court reasoned, for an anticompetitive effect to "be 'one that ordinarily occurs, routinely occurs, or is inherently likely to occur as a result of the empowering legislation." Applying that standard, the Court of Appeals concluded that the Law contemplated the anticompetitive conduct challenged by the FTC. The court noted the "impressive breadth" of the powers given to hospital authorities, which include traditional powers of private corporations and a few additional capabilities, such as the power to exercise eminent domain. More specifically, the court reasoned that the Georgia Legislature must have anticipated that the grant of power to hospital authorities to acquire and lease projects would produce anticompetitive effects because "[f]ore-seeably, acquisitions could consolidate ownership of competing hospitals, eliminating competition between them."

The Court of Appeals also rejected the FTC's alternative argument that state-action immunity did not apply because the transaction in substance involved a transfer of control over Palmyra from one private entity to another, with the Authority acting as a mere conduit for the sale to evade antitrust liability.

We granted certiorari on two questions: whether the Georgia Legislature, through the powers it vested in hospital authorities, clearly articulated and affirmatively expressed a state policy to displace competition in the market for hospital services; and if so, whether state-action immunity is nonetheless inapplicable as a result of the Authority's minimal participation in negotiating the terms of the sale of Palmyra and the Authority's limited supervision of the two hospitals' operations. Concluding that the answer to the first question is "no," we reverse without reaching the second question.

II

In Parker v. Brown, 317 U.S. 341 (1943), this Court held that because "nothing in the language of the Sherman Act or in its history" suggested that Congress intended to restrict the sovereign capacity of the States to regulate their economies, the Act should not be read to bar States from imposing market restraints "as an act of government." Following *Parker*, we have held that under certain circumstances, immunity from the federal antitrust laws may extend to nonstate actors carrying out the State's regulatory program.

> State law does not preempt federal law, but the Sherman Act has been interpreted to not reach anticompetitive actions specifically undertaken or approved by states.

But given the fundamental national values of free enterprise and economic competition that are embodied in the federal antitrust laws, "state-action immunity is disfavored, much as are repeals by implication." Consistent with this preference, we recognize state-action immunity only when it is clear that the challenged anticompetitive conduct is undertaken pursuant to a regulatory scheme that "is the State's own." Accordingly, "[c]loser analysis is required when the activity at issue is not directly that of" the State itself, but rather "is carried out by others pursuant to state authorization." When determining whether the anticompetitive acts of private parties are entitled to immunity, we employ a two-part test, requiring first that "the challenged restraint . . . be one clearly articulated and affirmatively expressed as state policy," and second that "the policy . . . be actively supervised by the State."

This case involves allegedly anticompetitive conduct undertaken by a substate governmental entity. Because municipalities and other political subdivisions are not themselves sovereign, state-action immunity under *Parker* does not apply to them directly. At the same time, however, substate governmental entities do receive immunity from antitrust scrutiny when they act "pursuant to state policy to displace competition with regulation or monopoly public service." This rule "preserves to the States their freedom . . . to use their municipalities to administer state regulatory policies free of the inhibitions of the federal antitrust laws without at the same time permitting purely parochial interests to disrupt the Nation's free-market goals."

As with private parties, immunity will only attach to the activities of local governmental entities if they are undertaken pursuant to a "clearly articulated and affirmatively expressed" state policy to displace competition. But unlike private parties, such entities are not subject to the "active state supervision requirement" because they have less of an incentive to pursue their own self-interest under the guise of implementing state policies.

"[T]o pass the 'clear articulation' test," a state legislature need not "expressly state in a statute or its legislative history that the legislature intends for the delegated action to have anticompetitive effects." Rather, we explained in *Hallie* that state-action immunity applies if the anticompetitive effect was the "foreseeable result" of what the State authorized. We applied that principle in *Omni*, where we concluded that the clear-articulation test was satisfied because the suppression of competition in the billboard market was the foreseeable result of a state statute authorizing municipalities to adopt zoning ordinances regulating the construction of buildings and other structures.

> State action requires "clear articulation."

III

A

Applying the clear-articulation test to the Law before us, we conclude that respondents' claim for state-action immunity fails because there is no evidence the State affirmatively contemplated that hospital authorities would displace competition by consolidating hospital ownership. The acquisition and leasing powers exercised by the Authority in the challenged transaction, which were the principal powers relied upon by the Court of Appeals in finding state-action immunity, mirror general powers routinely conferred by state law upon private corporations. Other powers possessed by hospital authorities that the Court of Appeals characterized as having "impressive breadth" also fit this pattern, including the ability to make and execute contracts, to set rates for services, to sue and be sued, to borrow money, and the residual authority to exercise any or all powers possessed by private corporations.

Our case law makes clear that state-law authority to act is insufficient to establish state-action immunity; the substate governmental entity must also show that it has been delegated authority to act or regulate anticompetitively. In *Boulder*, we held that Colorado's Home Rule Amendment allowing municipalities to govern local affairs did not satisfy the clear-articulation test. There was no doubt in that case that the city had authority as a matter of state law to pass an ordinance imposing a moratorium on a cable provider's expansion of service. But we rejected the proposition that "the general grant of power to enact ordinances necessarily implies state authorization to enact specific anticompetitive ordinances" because such an approach "would wholly eviscerate the concepts of 'clear articulation and affirmative expression' that our precedents require." We explained that when a State's position "is one of mere *neutrality* respecting the municipal actions challenged as anticompetitive," the State cannot be said to have "'contemplated'" those anticompetitive actions.

The principle articulated in *Boulder* controls this case. Grants of general corporate power that allow substate governmental entities to participate in a competitive marketplace should be, can be, and typically are used in ways that raise no federal antitrust concerns. As a result, a State that has delegated such general powers "can hardly be said to have 'contemplated'" that they will be used anticompetitively. Thus, while the Law does allow the Authority to acquire hospitals, it does not clearly articulate and affirmatively express a state policy empowering the Authority to make acquisitions of existing hospitals that will substantially lessen competition.

B

In concluding otherwise, and specifically in reasoning that the Georgia Legislature "must have anticipated" that acquisitions by hospital authorities "would produce anticompetitive effects," the Court of Appeals applied the concept of "foreseeability" from our clear-articulation test too loosely.

. . . .

We have no doubt that Georgia's hospital authorities differ materially from private corporations that offer hospital services. But nothing in the Law or any other provision of Georgia law clearly articulates a state policy to allow authorities to exercise their general corporate powers, including their acquisition power, without regard to negative effects on competition. The state legislature's objective of improving access to affordable health care does not logically suggest that the State intended that hospital authorities pursue that end through mergers that create monopolies. Nor do the restrictions imposed on hospital authorities, including the requirement that they operate on a nonprofit basis, reveal such a policy. Particularly in light of our national policy favoring competition, these restrictions should be read to reflect more modest aims. The legislature may have viewed profit generation as incompatible with its goal of providing care for the indigent sick. In addition, the legislature may have believed that some hospital authorities would operate in markets with characteristics of natural monopolies, in which case the legislature could not rely on competition to control prices.

We recognize that Georgia, particularly through its certificate of need requirement, does limit competition in the market for hospital services in some respects. But regulation of an industry, and even the authorization of discrete forms of anticompetitive conduct pursuant to a regulatory structure, does not establish that the State has affirmatively contemplated other forms of anticompetitive conduct that are only tangentially related. Thus, in Goldfarb v. Virginia State Bar, we rejected a state-action defense to price-fixing claims where a state bar adopted a compulsory minimum fee schedule. Although the State heavily regulated the practice of law, we found no evidence that it had adopted a policy to displace price competition among lawyers. And in *Cantor*, we concluded that a state commission's regulation of rates for electricity charged by a public utility did not confer state-action immunity for a claim that the utility's free distribution of light bulbs restrained trade in the light-bulb market.

In this case, the fact that Georgia imposes limits on entry into the market for medical services, which apply to both hospital authorities and private corporations, does not clearly articulate a policy favoring the consolidation of existing hospitals that are engaged in active competition. As to the Authority's eminent domain power, it was not exercised here and we do not find it relevant to the question whether the State authorized hospital authorities to consolidate market power through potentially anticompetitive acquisitions of existing hospitals.

. . . .

We hold that Georgia has not clearly articulated and affirmatively expressed a policy to allow hospital authorities to make acquisitions that substantially lessen competition. The judgment of the Court of Appeals is reversed, and the case is remanded for further proceedings consistent with this opinion.

It is so ordered.

Antitrust is taking a more prominent role in this era of heightened concern about health care competition. Many health care transactions, collaborations, and regulations require antitrust analysis, and the larger mergers require advance pre-merger notice to the federal government under the Hart-Scott-Rodino Antitrust Improvements Act, 15 U.S.C. §18a. The ACA has accelerated preexisting trends toward provider consolidation, which will keep these issues in the forefront of health law practice for many years to come.

CAPSTONE PROBLEM

Conduct brief research to find out whether your home jurisdiction:

1. Requires any CON for hospital beds or ambulatory surgery centers; or
2. Permits CRNAs to practice without the supervision of a physician.

PART III

PATIENT PROTECTIONS

Parts I and **II** largely involve laws and policies governing the relationships between health care providers and payors, including both private insurers and government health care programs, as well as a host of laws regulating the business of health care. **Part III** focuses more directly on patients and their encounters with medical care and treatment. This part is dedicated to exploring the divergent areas of the law that, read together, protect patients in the health care (non)system and the decisions that they make related to medical care. More than **Parts I** and **II**, **Part III**'s seemingly disparate subjects reflect the development of health law over time, which has been incremental and often in response to medical imperatives and emerging issues. Yet, the common themes outlined in **Chapter 1** remain as important to understanding this material as the chapters that came before; the role of individual rights is particularly important in this part.

 Chapter 8 explores the sources and contents of duties that health care professionals, entities, and insurers owe to patients in providing medical care. **Chapter 9** addresses the law that has developed surrounding the complex medical questions that arise in the beginning and at the end of life. This chapter takes a pragmatic approach, focusing on the way that courts, statutes, and regulations treat the medical profession and patients, so that a lawyer providing a client advice would know what the law is (notwithstanding societal debates). **Chapter 10** covers various laws aimed at protecting the privacy, confidentiality, and security of patients' medical information. **Chapter 11** provides historical context for and an overview of the protections for individuals who participate in clinical research, which differs from medical care. Taken together, these chapters build a picture of a complex web of laws that protects patients encountering medical care but also leaves many spaces where law does not reach.

CHAPTER 8

Duties Related to Patient Care

A. INTRODUCTION

Parts I and II of this book emphasize the modern, integrated delivery of health care through sophisticated entities of various forms. But this is not the way that medical care has always been delivered; historically, the physician-patient relationship was at the center of medicine's universe. Today, most patients' experience with health care is a far cry from the *Marcus Welby, M.D.* era of medicine, where one kindly doctor would see a patient, diagnose injury or illness, treat it, and be done. Family doctors and other primary care physicians, such as internists, pediatricians, and geriatricians, serve now as gatekeepers and a central referral point for a wide range of specialty and subspecialty care. Under cost-containment pressures, as well as primary care physician shortages, patients may receive much of their direct care from "mid-level" providers, also called physician extenders, which include nurses, physician assistants, and other technicians, all of whom act under the supervision of a physician.

> *Marcus Welby, M.D.* was a popular 1970s television medical drama about a benevolent family physician who employed sometimes unconventional approaches to treat his patients, often by making house calls.

In addition, third-party payment and other organizational pressures influence physicians' professional judgment and discretion in ways not associated with the traditional physician-patient relationship. The Patient Protection and Affordable Care Act (ACA) formalized a number of the trends in health care delivery toward greater coordination and financial risk-sharing among providers, with initiatives such as accountable care organizations (ACOs), discussed in Chapter 2, and patient-centered medical homes, a new, patient-centered, comprehensive, team-based, coordinated model of health care delivery organized around primary care physicians. As a result, patients' experience with health care has changed significantly.

That said, a number of essential legal issues continue to build on the physician-patient relationship, which this chapter discusses. In the modern era of health care, patients also have relationships with other types of providers and with the insurance companies that pay for their care. The chapter is organized around two themes: first, whether any duty is owed to a patient, and, second, what the content of any such duty might be. Thematically, these materials suggest various approaches to ensuring appropriate standards and quality of care. Sources of authority bearing on these questions include contract and commercial law, common law, and statutory and regulatory law. The chapter concludes by considering the ever-present alternative of market-based or contractual approaches to ensuring quality of care.

B. DUTY TO TREAT

Most health care providers in the United States are private individuals and entities that remain free, absent contractual obligations, to choose which patients they will or will not treat. No doubt you are familiar with basic freedom of contract and tort no-duty rules from first-year law school classes. Some states have adopted Good Samaritan laws, which typically do not impose affirmative duties on health care providers to respond to individuals in need of medical care, although they may grant immunity from liability if they elect to render assistance.

> The Medicaid Act specifies that the program is not simply a method of payment, but of rather an obligation on states to ensure medical care for beneficiaries. Nevertheless, the program still relies on private health care providers and follows general health insurance principles.

The absence of an affirmative duty to treat, or any other right or entitlement to health care remains even as the number of Americans enrolled in government health care programs, like Medicare and Medicaid, increases. Rather than providing care through government-owned and staffed facilities (as is done in the United Kingdom's National Health Service), our federal health care programs operate as public insurance, providing beneficiaries with access to participating providers on roughly the same terms as privately insured individuals. With a few exceptions, providers are not compelled to treat government program patients, unless they contractually agree to participate and thus to comply with statutory and regulatory requirements as conditions of participation. Even then, physicians often have a mix of privately insured and publicly insured patients, and they can make choices to cap the number of publicly insured patients they will accept. Notably, a regulatory requirement for Medicare, discussed below, abrogates the common law no-duty rule, compelling some providers to provide treatment under specific circumstances.

1. HEALTH CARE PROVIDERS

The following case, although an older opinion, accurately states the common law rule that physicians have no affirmative duty to treat patients, even when death or serious injury could result. The rule is supported by policies favoring professional autonomy and freedom of contract but is sometimes hard to square against competing ethical and social justice concerns. Although courts and legislatures have recognized common law and statutory exceptions to the otherwise draconian no-duty rule, none applied in the following case.

a. Common Law

Hurley v. Eddingfield

---

59 N.E. 1058 (Ind. 1901)

BAKER, J.

The appellant sued appellee for $10,000 damages for wrongfully causing the death of his intestate. The court sustained appellee's demurrer to the complaint, and this ruling is assigned as error.

The material facts alleged may be summarized thus: At and for years before decedent's death appellee was a practicing physician at Mace, in Montgomery county, duly licensed under the laws of the state. He held himself out to the public as a general practitioner of medicine. He had been decedent's family physician. Decedent became dangerously ill, and sent for appellee. The messenger informed appellee of decedent's violent sickness, tendered him his fee for his services, and stated to him that no other physician was procurable in time, and that decedent relied on him for attention. No other physician was procurable in time to be of any use, and decedent did rely on appellee for medical assistance. Without any reason whatever, appellee refused to render aid to decedent. No other patients were requiring appellee's immediate service, and he could have gone to the relief of decedent if he had been willing to do so. Death ensued, without decedent's fault, and wholly from appellee's wrongful act. The alleged wrongful act was appellee's refusal to enter into a contract of employment. Counsel do not contend that, before the enactment of the law regulating the practice of medicine, physicians were bound to render professional service to every one who applied. The act regulating the practice of medicine provides for a board of examiners, standards of qualification, examinations, licenses to those found qualified, and penalties for practicing without license. The act is a preventive, not a compulsive, measure. In obtaining the state's license (permission) to practice medicine, the state does not require, and the licensee does not engage, that he will practice at all or on other terms than he may choose to accept. Counsel's analogies, drawn from the obligations to the public on the part of innkeepers, common carriers, and the like, are beside the mark. Judgment affirmed.

> The decedent in the case experienced complications during childbirth. Her husband sent for Dr. Eddingfield. Both the mother and the baby died.

QUESTIONS

1. Why doesn't the physician have a duty to treat based on the history of being the patient's family physician?
2. Why aren't physicians analogous to innkeepers and common carriers?
3. Does this opinion value freedom of contract over human health?

b. Statutory Exceptions: EMTALA

In July 2007, not quite three years before the ACA was enacted under President Barack Obama, his predecessor, President George W. Bush, remarked to a crowd in Cleveland, Ohio:

> Let me talk about health care, since it's fresh on my mind. The objective has got to be to make sure America is the best place in the world to get health care, that we're the most innovative country, that we encourage doctors to stay in practice, that we are robust in the funding of research, and that patients get good, quality care at a reasonable cost.
>
> The immediate goal is to make sure there are more people on private insurance plans. I mean, people have access to health care in America. After all, you just go to an emergency room.

The statute that President Bush had in mind is the Emergency Medical Treatment and Labor Act of 1986 (EMTALA), popularly referred to as the "anti-dumping statute," which was briefly considered in Chapter 3 in the context of whether a right to health care exists in the United States. As you read the longer excerpt below, evaluate the accuracy of the suggestion that universal access to health care already existed in the United States, pre-ACA, because anyone could go to the emergency room for medical care.

Emergency Medical Treatment and Labor Act
42 U.S.C. §1395dd. Examination and treatment for emergency medical conditions and women in labor

(a) Medical screening requirement. In the case of a hospital that has a hospital emergency department, if any individual (whether or not eligible for benefits under this subchapter [Medicare]) comes to the emergency department and a request is made on the individual's behalf for examination or treatment for a medical condition, the hospital must provide for an appropriate medical screening examination within the capability of the hospital's emergency department, including ancillary services routinely available to the emergency department, to determine whether or not an emergency medical condition (within the meaning of subsection (e)(1) of this section) exists.

(b) Necessary stabilizing treatment for emergency medical conditions and labor

(1) In general

(a) If any individual (whether or not eligible for benefits under this subchapter) comes to a hospital and the hospital determines that the individual has an emergency medical condition, the hospital must provide either—

> The EMTALA duty is measured by a subjective standard; the hospital is required only to provide the same, "non-disparate" screening to all patients, regardless of ability to pay or insurance status, within the actual capabilities of the hospital. The key to compliance is that the exam does not treat EMTALA patients differently, not that it necessarily meets professional standards of care.

(A) within the staff and facilities available at the hospital, for such further medical examination and such treatment as may be required to stabilize the medical condition, or

(B) for transfer of the individual to another medical facility in accordance with subsection (c).

. . . .

(c) Restricting transfers until individual stabilized.

(1) Rule. If an individual at a hospital has an emergency medical condition which has not been stabilized (within the meaning of subsection (e)(3)(B) of this section), the hospital may not transfer the individual unless—

(A)(i) the individual (or a legally responsible person acting on the individual's behalf) after being informed of the hospital's obligations under this section and of the risk of transfer, in writing requests transfer to another medical facility,

(ii) a physician . . . has signed a certification that[,] based upon the information available at the time of transfer, the medical benefits reasonably expected from the provision of appropriate medical treatment at another medical facility outweigh the increased risks to the individual and, in the case of labor, to the unborn child from effecting the transfer.

(iii) if a physician is not physically present in the emergency department at the time an individual is transferred, a qualified medical person . . . has signed a certification described in clause (ii) after a physician . . . , in consultation with the person, has made the determination described in such clause, and subsequently countersigns the certification; and

(B) the transfer is an appropriate transfer (within the meaning of paragraph (2)) to that facility.

(2) Appropriate Transfer. An appropriate transfer to a medical facility is a transfer

(A) in which the transferring hospital provides the medical treatment within its capacity which minimizes the risks to the individual's health and, in the case of a woman in labor, the health of the unborn child;

> If a patient is evaluated and stabilized, she may be discharged without further treatment rather than transferred to another medical facility.

(B) in which the receiving facility —

(i) has available space and qualified personnel for the treatment of the individual, and

(ii) has agreed to accept transfer of the individual and to provide appropriate medical treatment;

(C) in which the transferring hospital sends to the receiving facility all medical records (or copies thereof) related to the emergency condition for which the individual has presented, available at the time of the transfer . . . , [and]

(D) in which the transfer is effected through qualified personnel and transportation equipment. . . .

(d) Enforcement.

(1) Civil monetary penalties.

(A) A participating hospital that negligently violates a requirement of this section is subject to a civil money penalty of not more than $50,000 for each such violation. . . .

(B) [A]ny physician who is responsible for the examination, treatment, or transfer of an individual in a participating hospital, including a physician on-call for the care of such an individual, and who negligently violates a requirement of this section, including on-call for the care of such individual, is subject to a civil money penalty of not more than $50,000 for each such violation and, if the violation is gross and flagrant or is repeated, to exclusion from participation in [Medicare and Medicaid]. . . .

(2) Civil enforcement.

(A) Personal harm. Any individual who suffers personal harm as a direct result of a participating hospital's violation of a requirement of this section may, in a civil action against the participating hospital, obtain those damages available for personal injury under the law of the State in which the hospital is located, and such equitable relief as is appropriate. (B) Financial loss to other medical facility. Any medical facility that suffers a financial loss as a direct result of a participating hospital's violation of a requirement of this section may, in a civil action against the participating hospital, obtain those damages available for financial loss, under the law of the State in which the hospital is located, and such equitable relief as is appropriate. . . .

(e) Definitions. In this section:

(1) The term "emergency medical condition" means —

(A) a medical condition manifesting itself by acute symptoms of sufficient severity (including severe pain) such that the absence of immediate medical attention could reasonably be expected to result in—

    (i) placing the health of the individual (or, with respect to a pregnant woman, the health of the woman or her unborn child) in serious jeopardy,

    (ii) serious impairment to bodily functions, or

    (iii) serious dysfunction of any bodily organ or part; or

(B) with respect to a pregnant woman who is having contractions—

    (i) that there is inadequate time to effect a safe transfer to another hospital before delivery, or

    (ii) that transfer may pose a threat to the health or safety of the woman or the unborn child.

(2) The term "participating hospital" means a hospital that has entered into a provider agreement under [the Medicare Act]

(3)(A) The term "to stabilize" means, with respect to an emergency medical condition described in paragraph (1)(A), to provide such medical treatment of the condition as may be necessary to assure, within reasonable medical probability, that no material deterioration of the condition is likely to result from or occur during the transfer of the individual from a facility or, with respect to an emergency medical condition described in paragraph (1)(B), to deliver (including the placenta).

    (B) The term "stabilized" means, with respect to an emergency medical condition described in paragraph (1)(A), that no material deterioration of the condition is likely, within reasonable medical probability, to result from or occur during the transfer of the individual from a facility, or, with respect to an emergency medical condition described in paragraph (1)(B), that the woman has delivered (including the placenta). . . .

(h) No delay in examination or treatment. A participating hospital may not delay provision of an appropriate medical screening examination required under subsection (a) of this section or further medical examination and treatment required under subsection (b) of this section in order to inquire about the individual's method of payment or insurance status.

QUESTIONS

1. Would this statute change the outcome in the *Hurley* case above?
2. If a patient who has been admitted to the hospital for further stabilization elects to sign out against medical advice, does EMTALA impose any duty on the hospital at that point?
3. Does EMTALA prohibit hospitals from billing patients for emergency room care after it has been provided? What happens if a patient has no insurance coverage?

EMTALA is a condition of participation under the Medicare Act. Thus, EMTALA's requirements apply only to hospitals that have agreed to accept Medicare patients, but that includes the vast majority of general acute-care hospitals because Medicare offers a reliable and significant revenue stream. Although EMTALA is a Medicare condition of participation, the duty extends to all patients who come to the emergency department, regardless of their insurer or lack thereof. Some specialty hospitals may be able to avoid EMTALA obligations by refusing to accept Medicare patients or by not maintaining an emergency department. Since 2007, however, the Centers for Medicare and Medicaid Services (CMS) has specified that even hospitals without dedicated emergency departments must be capable of providing initial treatment in emergencies and arranging for appropriate referral or transfer to more comprehensive facilities.

The ACA does not amend the EMTALA duty, although the ACA's insurance coverage expansion is anticipated to reduce the amount of uncompensated care that hospitals provide in their emergency departments (EDs). Even if President Bush's suggestion that EMTALA operates as universal access to care for all Americans were accurate, EDs are an extremely expensive, inefficient, and sub-quality approach to meeting most people's regular health care needs. For example, a child who suffers severe asthma may receive treatment for respiratory distress in an ED. But what she needs is consistent primary care to control the asthmatic symptoms before they require emergency treatment; that type of consistent care is not the job of an ED.

Note that EMTALA can be civilly enforced against the "dumping" hospital by both patients and "dumpee" hospitals harmed by the violation, though physicians working for the hospital are not subject to private actions. The government, through CMS and the Office of Inspector General (OIG), also may enforce the statute against hospitals and physicians, as specified in the statute.

PROBLEM

An ED physician, after performing an initial evaluation of a patient presenting to the emergency room with abdominal pain, believes that the patient may have intestinal obstruction. The ED physician consults the gastroenterologist on-call that day, asking him to examine the patient. The on-call gastroenterologist declines to come in to examine the patient, offering no reason for the refusal. The patient's intestines rupture, causing life-threatening infection and other serious injuries. Would either physician be liable under EMTALA? What about the hospital? How could the hospital ensure that on-call specialists actually respond to emergency room requests for consultation? What fraud and abuse implications might there be with any of the strategies you propose?

c. Federal Nondiscrimination Statutes

Other federal statutes, including Title VI of the Civil Rights Act of 1964 (Title VI), the Americans with Disabilities Act (ADA), and section 1557 of the ACA also limit providers' common law freedom of contract to refuse treatment to some patients. These and other federal and state laws bear on many aspects of health care, including employment, access to care, public and private contracting, insurance, and charity or other financial assistance. Health care attorneys should keep these various discrimination claims in mind as they advise their clients.

Title VI, 42 U.S.C. §2000d, prohibits any program receiving federal financial assistance from discriminating on the basis of race, color, or national origin. Title VI has been interpreted to apply to hospitals and other providers receiving Medicare, Medicaid, or other grants, including the Hill-Burton Act, a federal program started in 1946 to fund hospital construction and modernization in exchange for those facilities providing services to the local community and free or reduced cost care to patients unable to pay.

HHS regulations implementing Title VI are at 42 C.F.R. Part 80 and provide, in part:

§80.3 Discrimination prohibited

(a) General. No person in the United States shall, on the ground of race, color, or national origin be excluded from participation in, be denied the benefits of, or be otherwise subjected to discrimination under any program to which this part applies.

(b) Specific discriminatory actions prohibited. (1) A recipient under any program to which this part applies may not, directly or through contractual or other arrangements, on ground of race, color, or national origin:

(i) Deny an individual any service, financial aid, or other benefit provided under the program;

(ii) Provide any service, financial aid, or other benefit to an individual which is different, or is provided in a different manner, from that provided to others under the program;

(iii) Subject an individual to segregation or separate treatment in any matter related to his receipt of any service, financial aid, or other benefit under the program;

(iv) Restrict an individual in any way in the enjoyment of any advantage or privilege enjoyed by others receiving any service, financial aid, or other benefit under the program;

(v) Treat an individual differently from others in determining whether he satisfies any admission, enrollment, quota, eligibility, membership or other requirement or condition which individuals must meet in order to be provided any service, financial aid, or other benefit provided under the program;

(vi) Deny an individual an opportunity to participate in the program through the provision of services or otherwise or afford him an opportunity to do so which is different from that afforded others under the program (including the opportunity to participate in the program as an employee but only to the extent set forth in paragraph (c) of this section).

(vii) Deny a person the opportunity to participate as a member of a planning or advisory body which is an integral part of the program. . . .

Despite the clear prohibition, Title VI implementation and enforcement has been relatively weak. For one reason, the prohibition has been interpreted to apply to hospitals but not individual physicians, even if they receive reimbursement under Medicare Part B. Also, the Supreme Court in Alexander v. Sandoval, 532 U.S. 275 (2001), established that private enforcement actions under Title VI are limited to those involving intentional discrimination — that is, disparate treatment claims. Only the federal government may enforce disparate impact claims.

Another federal law, the ADA, prohibits discrimination against persons who have a "disability," within the statutory definition. The ADA applies to both public and private actors, including places of employment; state and local government services; places of public accommodation; and, to some extent, insurance, as discussed below. The provision most relevant to the issue of duties owed by health care providers is the public accommodations provision, which requires a wide range of private facilities open to the public to provide nondiscriminatory treatment. For purposes of the ADA, it is not necessary that the health care provider receive federal funding (although the vast majority do).

42 U.S.C. §12182. Prohibition of discrimination by public accommodations

(a) General rule

No individual shall be discriminated against on the basis of disability in the full and equal enjoyment of the goods, services, facilities, privileges, advantages, or accommodations of any place of public accommodation by any person who owns, leases (or leases to), or operates a place of public accommodation.

(b) Construction

(1) General prohibition

(A) Activities

(i) Denial of participation

It shall be discriminatory to subject an individual or class of individuals on the basis of a disability or disabilities of such individual or class, directly, or through contractual, licensing, or other arrangements, to a denial of the opportunity of the individual or class to participate in or benefit from the goods, services, facilities, privileges, advantages, or accommodations of an entity.

(ii) Participation in unequal benefit

It shall be discriminatory to afford an individual or class of individuals, on the basis of a disability or disabilities of such individual or class, directly, or through contractual, licensing, or other arrangements with the opportunity to participate in or benefit from a good, service, facility, privilege, advantage, or accommodation that is not equal to that afforded to other individuals.

(iii) Separate benefit

It shall be discriminatory to provide an individual or class of individuals, on the basis of a disability or disabilities of such individual or class, directly, or through contractual, licensing, or other arrangements with a good, service, facility, privilege, advantage, or accommodation that is different or separate from that provided to other individuals, unless such action is necessary to provide the individual or class of individuals with a good, service, facility, privilege, advantage, or accommodation, or other opportunity that is as effective as that provided to others.

(iv) Individual or class of individuals

For purposes of clauses (i) through (iii) of this subparagraph, the term "individual or class of individuals" refers to the clients or customers of the covered public accommodation that enters into the contractual, licensing or other arrangement.

(2) Specific prohibitions

(A) Discrimination

For purposes of subsection (a) of this section, discrimination includes—

(i) the imposition or application of eligibility criteria that screen out or tend to screen out an individual with a disability or any class of individuals with disabilities from fully and equally enjoying any goods, services, facilities, privileges, advantages, or accommodations, unless such criteria can be shown to be necessary for the provision of the goods, services, facilities, privileges, advantages, or accommodations being offered;

(ii) a failure to make reasonable modifications in policies, practices, or procedures, when such modifications are necessary to afford such goods, services, facilities, privileges, advantages, or accommodations to individuals with disabilities, unless the entity can demonstrate that making such modifications would fundamentally alter the nature of such goods, services, facilities, privileges, advantages, or accommodations;

(iii) a failure to take such steps as may be necessary to ensure that no individual with a disability is excluded, denied services, segregated or otherwise treated differently than other individuals because of the absence of auxiliary aids and services, unless the entity can demonstrate that taking such steps would fundamentally alter the nature of the good, service, facility, privilege, advantage, or accommodation being offered or would result in an undue burden;

(iv) a failure to remove architectural barriers, and communication barriers that are structural in nature, in existing facilities, and transportation barriers in existing vehicles and rail passenger cars used by an establishment for transporting individuals (not including barriers that can only be removed through the retrofitting of vehicles or rail passenger cars by the installation of a hydraulic or other lift), where such removal is readily achievable; and

(v) where an entity can demonstrate that the removal of a barrier under clause (iv) is not readily achievable, a failure to make such goods, services, facilities, privileges, advantages, or accommodations available through alternative methods if such methods are readily achievable.

There are a number of ways that disabled individuals may face discrimination in access to medical care. First, the architecture of health care facilities and medical equipment, including beds, wheelchairs, examination tables, and imaging devices, such as mammography, may be inaccessible to patients with mobility impairments and other disabilities. Second, individuals with disabilities tend to have lower than average income and employment, higher poverty rates, and other obstacles to obtaining adequate health insurance or otherwise paying for health care. With pressure from disability rights advocates, health care providers have made strides in making their facilities and equipment more accessible.

With respect to discrimination in health insurance, whether employer-sponsored or privately sold, the ADA provides relatively little protection.

In the employment context, courts have held that the ADA does not require employers to offer any particular form of coverage, but they must offer the same terms and conditions of coverage to both disabled and nondisabled workers. With respect to insurance sold on the private market, the ADA's "public accommodations" provision requires physical access to insurance offices but has not been interpreted to extend to the terms and conditions of the policies sold. Private insurance policies, compared to government health care programs, tend to have more limited coverage for durable medical equipment, such as wheelchairs and walkers, prostheses, and assistive technology, such as hearing aids.

Given the ADA's relatively limited protections, the ACA included a specific civil rights provision that attaches to private insurance subsidized by the federal government and public insurance. The provision is called section 1557. Patient Protection and Affordable Care Act, Pub. L. No. 111-148, §1557 (codified at 42 U.S.C. §18116). Section 1557 is the first federal law to prohibit gender discrimination in health care and is enforced by HHS's Office of Civil Rights. Section 1557, along with the Health Insurance Portability and Accountability Act (HIPAA), sharply restrict entrenched discrimination in health insurance.

42 U.S.C. §18116. Nondiscrimination

(a) [A]n individual shall not, on the ground prohibited under title VI of the Civil Rights Act of 1964 (42 U.S.C. 2000d et seq.), title IX of the Education Amendments of 1972 (U.S.C. 1681 et seq.), the Age Discrimination Act of 1975 (42 U.S.C. 6101 et seq.), or section 504 of the Rehabilitation Act of 1973 (29 U.S.C. 794), be excluded from participation in, be denied the benefits of, or be subjected to discrimination under, any health program or activity, any part of which is receiving Federal financial assistance, including credits, subsidies, or contracts of insurance, or under any program or activity that is administered by an Executive Agency or any entity established under this title (or amendments).

2. INSURERS

Although health insurers do not "treat" patients in the same way that a physician or hospital does, they are intimately involved in access to and the provision of medical care for most patients. The prevailing managed care model of health insurance, applicable to virtually all private, most Medicaid, and an increasing number of Medicare enrollees, is defined by a fusion of health care delivery and financing. As a practical matter, a health care provider participating in a managed care plan may decline to treat patients not enrolled in that plan (or another private or government plan in which the provider participates). Thus, as a parallel to the foregoing discussion of health care providers' duty to treat, we also consider health insurers' duty to cover individuals.

The *King v. Burwell* decision, excerpted in Chapter 3, provides a good discussion of the ACA's restrictions on private insurers' freedom of contract. Namely, one leg of the "three-legged stool" is the ACA's guaranteed issue and community rating provisions. Even though the tax penalty associated with the individual mandate leg of the stool was knocked out by statutory amendment, those provisions remain by federal law, as they existed piecemeal under state law pre-ACA. Guaranteed issue and community rating rules restrict insurers' choices regarding whom to cover and under what terms. Guaranteed issue, combined with the ACA's rules regarding guaranteed renewal and restrictions on rescission, essentially constitutes a robust duty to cover the treatment of most Americans.

The ACA's guaranteed issue provision, 29 U.S.C. §1182 (see Chapter 3), prohibits health insurers from establishing eligibility rules that discriminate against health plan participants and beneficiaries based on health status, medical condition (including mental illness), claims experience, receipt of health care, medical history, genetic information, evidence of insurability, disability, and any other health status-related factor determined appropriate by HHS regulations—the same list of health-status protections as HIPAA. The following regulations promulgated under the ACA provide that once a policy is issued, insurers further must renew the policy and may not rescind coverage, absent exceptional circumstances.

45 C.F.R. §148.122. Guaranteed renewability of individual health insurance coverage

(a) Applicability. This section applies to non-grandfathered and grandfathered health plans . . . that are individual health insurance coverage. . . .

(b) General rules.

The ACA's policy on coverage rescission was prompted by a common practice of "post-claims underwriting," by which insurers would issue a policy but then find grounds for cancellation, including technical omissions or errors in the application, after coverage was invoked (especially for costly treatments). As a result, a patient might find herself without coverage at the very time she needed it most, after experiencing a catastrophic injury or being diagnosed with a serious medical condition.

(1) Except as provided in paragraph (c) of this section, an issuer must renew or continue in force the coverage at the option of the individual.

(2) Medicare eligibility or entitlement is not a basis for nonrenewal or termination of an individual's health insurance coverage in the individual market.

(c) Exceptions to renewing coverage. An issuer may non-renew or discontinue health insurance coverage of an individual in the individual market based only on one or more of the following:

(1) Nonpayment of premiums. The individual has failed to pay premiums or contributions in accordance with the terms of the health insurance coverage, including any timeliness requirements.

(2) Fraud. The individual has performed an act or practice that constitutes fraud or made an intentional misrepresentation of material fact under the terms of the coverage.

(3) Termination of product. The issuer is ceasing to offer coverage in the market in accordance with paragraph (d) or (e) of this section and applicable State law.

(4) Movement outside the service area. For network plans, the individual no longer resides, lives, or works in the service area of the issuer, or area for which the issuer is authorized to do business, but only if coverage is terminated uniformly without regard to any health status-related factor of covered individuals.

. . . .

(d) Discontinuing a particular type of coverage. An issuer may discontinue offering a particular type of health insurance coverage offered in the individual market only if it meets the following requirements:

(1) Provides notice in writing, in a form and manner specified by the Secretary, to each individual provided coverage of that type of health insurance at least 90 calendar days before the date the coverage will be discontinued.

(2) Offers to each covered individual, on a guaranteed issue basis, the option to purchase any other individual health insurance coverage currently being offered by the issuer for individuals in that market.

(3) Acts uniformly without regard to any health status-related factor of covered individuals or dependents of covered individuals who may become eligible for coverage.

(e) Discontinuing all coverage. An issuer may discontinue offering all health insurance coverage in the individual market in a State only if it meets the following requirements.

(1) Provides notice in writing to the applicable State authority and to each individual of the discontinuation at least 180 days before the date the coverage will expire.

(2) Discontinues and does not renew all health insurance policies it issues or delivers for issuance in the State in the individual market.

(3) Acts uniformly without regard to any health status-related factor of covered individuals or dependents of covered individuals who may become eligible for coverage.

QUESTIONS

1. If an insurance policyholder failed to disclose that she had an abnormal pap smear (a routine test for detecting cervical cancer) five years before applying for insurance coverage, could the plan cancel her coverage?
2. May an insurance company cancel a grandfathered plan (one that was in existence prior to the ACA's enactment and is excused from compliance with a number of ACA requirements)?

PROBLEM

You are a staffer for a state legislator. Representatives of a patient protection advocacy group are concerned about patients' inability to access primary care, even after the changes to public and private insurance under the ACA. The group asks you to sponsor legislation that would require all primary care physicians licensed in the state to include within their overall patient mix at least 5 percent uninsured or Medicaid patients. They explain that this would be akin to a pro bono service requirement on licensed attorneys. Write a brief memo to your boss recommending how she might vote and what further questions she might ask the advocacy group.

C. CONTENT OF THE DUTY TO TREAT

This part of the chapter considers the duty to provide a certain level of care to patients and various legal mechanisms for ensuring quality of care. These include tort standards, contractual agreements, regulatory requirements, and market-based influences.

1. IN TORT: MEDICAL MALPRACTICE AND INFORMED CONSENT

In most health care contexts, the question whether the provider has a duty to treat a particular patient is not in issue. There is ample case law discussing formation of the physician-patient relationship as a matter of contract. But, generally speaking, once the physician has examined the patient and recommended a course of treatment, the duty attaches. The next question then becomes the content of that duty.

For medical professionals, like most professionals, the tort law duty requires treatment consistent with prevailing customary standards — the standard of the profession. In a medical negligence case, a jury generally may not decide for itself whether a physician acted reasonably with respect to a patient. Rather, they must accept expert testimony establishing the applicable professional standard and explaining how the physician has breached it. Tort law also imposes an affirmative duty of informed consent, requiring physicians to disclose to the patient certain risks, benefits, and alternatives of the proposed course of treatment. The informed consent duty may be judged according to a professional standard or, more commonly, a reasonable patient standard.

a. Duty of Informed Consent

In addition to being potentially liable for breaching the applicable professional standard of care or for basic negligence, physicians have an affirmative duty imposed by common law to disclose material information related to the recommended course of treatment, including available alternatives to treatment. Traditionally, tort liability may not be imposed for failing to act (nonfeasance) but can be imposed for acting and doing so negligently (misfeasance). The informed consent duty, an exception to tort law's general resistance to impose liability for nonfeasance, can be justified by physicians' ethical duty to respect patients' autonomy as well as the common law tort doctrine of battery, which prevents unpermitted touching. Further, physicians typically are in a better position to provide information about the available medical care than patients would be, which was discussed in the Kenneth Arrow excerpt in Chapter 1. Accepting the existence of the duty, questions have arisen regarding the scope of the duty and what must be disclosed, as considered in the following case.

Hidding v. Williams

578 So. 2d 1192 (La. Ct. App. 1991)

The issue before us in this medical malpractice case is whether the district judge was correct in finding that the defendant doctor failed to obtain his patient's informed consent to surgery. We affirm.

On December 17, 1984, fifty-nine year old Paul Hidding underwent a decompressive central laminectomy, L-3 to the sacrum, at the hands of orthopaedic surgeon Randall A. Williams, M.D. Mr. Hidding immediately suffered a loss of bowel and bladder control. His excretory systems were rendered non-functional and he remained incontinent until his death from an unrelated cause in January, 1990.

Paul Hidding and his wife Rubinell filed suit against Dr. Williams and his insurer, The Hartford Fire Insurance Company, contending that the doctor was negligent in performing the lumbar surgery and in failing to adequately advise Mr. Hidding of the risks associated with the surgery. After a two day bench trial the district judge found in favor of plaintiff and against the defendant doctor; he awarded Mrs. Hidding $307,006.50 in medical and general damages.

> In a lumbar laminectomy, the surgeon makes an incision in the lower back, pulling the muscles aside to expose the spine. Then the surgeon removes bone and bone spurs that are pressing onto nerves in the area and cuts away thickened ligaments to decompress swelling in the area.

. . . .

Appellants urge that the district judge committed reversible error in finding that Dr. Williams did not obtain Mr. Hidding's informed consent to undergo the lumbar laminectomy. They contend that the fact-finder was clearly wrong in concluding that: (1) Dr. Williams failed to disclose to the patient the fact that nerve damage is a known risk of this surgery, and (2) Dr. Williams was suffering from alcohol abuse at the time of the surgery and should have made this condition known to the patient. We disagree.

The informed consent doctrine is based on the principle that every human being of adult years and sound mind has a right to determine what shall be done to his own body. A doctor is required to provide his patient with sufficient information to permit the patient himself to make an informed and intelligent decision on whether to submit to a proposed course of treatment. Where circumstances permit, the patient should be told the nature of the pertinent ailment or condition, the general nature of the proposed treatment or procedure, the risks involved in the proposed treatment or procedure, the prospects of success, the risks of failing to undergo any treatment or procedure at all, and the risks of any alternative method of treatment.

In a trial on the merits of a suit for inadequate disclosure of risk information by a physician, the patient must provide evidence to establish, prima facie, the essential elements of the cause of action. The plaintiff patient bears the burden of persuasion on these elements: (1) the existence of a material risk unknown to the patient; (2) a failure to disclose the risk on the part of the physician; (3) that disclosure of the risk would have led a reasonable patient in plaintiff's position to reject the medical procedure or choose a different course of treatment; (4) injury. It is clear from the record evidence that plaintiff Rubinell Hidding proved the elements of her claim at trial. The district judge was correct in finding a violation of the informed consent doctrine and granting judgment in her favor.

The inquiry of whether the procedure to be performed involves a material risk is conducted, initially, by examination of the "incidence of injury/degree of harm" ratio. On this aspect of materiality some expert testimony is necessary because only a physician or other qualified expert is capable of judging what risk exists and the likelihood of its occurrence. Once the probability of harm is defined and the parameters of the risk are established, the question of materiality becomes one for the trier of fact who must then determine whether a reasonable person in the patient's position would attach significance to the specific risk.

The physician is required to advise a patient of any material consequence that would influence the decision of a reasonable person in the patient's condition. Thus the second inquiry is whether Dr. Williams failed to disclose this material risk to Mr. Hidding.

LSA-R.S. 40:1299.40 requires that the nature and purpose, together with the known risks, of a medical or surgical procedure be disclosed to the patient who must then be afforded the opportunity to ask questions and must acknowledge in writing his consent to the treatment. When the form is signed the patient is presumed to have understood and agreed to encounter whatever risk a reasonable person, in what the doctor knows or should have known to be the patient's position, would have apprehended from the written form. The statutory presumption of "consent" to encounter risks adequately described in the form is rebuttable, by showing that the consent was induced by misrepresentation, that is, that it was uninformed.

> Under the Louisiana statute, the patient's signature on an informed consent form establishes a rebuttable presumption that the physician satisfied his duty. Should it matter if the patient testifies that he did not read or understand the form? Such forms sometimes are presented in less than ideal circumstances, such as just before surgery, when a patient is under stress.

With respect to the third and fourth elements of proof, there must be a causal relationship between the doctor's failure to disclose material information and a material risk of damage to the patient. The courts have adopted an objective standard of causation: whether a reasonable patient in plaintiff's position would have consented to the treatment or procedure had the material information and risks been disclosed.

Applying these legal precepts to the facts of the instant case, we find that the record supports the conclusion that Dr. Williams failed to adequately advise Mr. and Mrs. Hidding that bowel and bladder dysfunction was a risk of lumbar surgery.

Paul Hidding had undergone a prior laminectomy in 1972. Thereafter he had only intermittent back complaints, stiffness and soreness. In 1984 while on a fishing trip with his son, Mr. Hidding experienced a flare-up. According to Mrs. Hidding, he was suffering excruciating pain when he visited Dr. Williams for an examination on December 10, 1984. After conducting x-rays and a CT scan Dr. Williams diagnosed Mr. Hidding's condition as spinal stenosis: a narrowing of the spinal processes. He admitted Mr. Hidding to the hospital for surgery on December 13, 1984. Dr. Williams told Mr. Hidding that he had no choice but to undergo surgery or he would end up in a wheelchair.

At trial orthopaedic surgeon Dr. Russell Levy testified that the loss of bowel and bladder function as a result of lumbar laminectomy occurs once in 200,000 cases. While it is not the most common complication associated with back surgery it is certainly, excluding death, the most feared. Dr. Williams himself admitted the loss of excretory functioning is a known complication of spinal surgery. Dr. Levy testified that considering the generic consent form commonly in use at that time, Dr. Williams should have specifically discussed the potential for loss of bowel and bladder control with Mr. Hidding prior to surgery. The materiality of the risk is clearly established. The consequent issue is whether this risk was adequately disclosed and consented to.

The hospital records contain a surgical consent form signed on December 16, 1984 by Paul Hidding consenting to a decompressive lumbar laminectomy the purpose of which is "to attempt to relieve nerve pressure and pain." The form states that no guarantees of treatment have been made; alternative methods of treatment and the possibility of complications have been fully explained and contains the following disclaimer:

> I understand and acknowledge that the following known risks are associated with this procedure including anesthesia: death; brain damage; disfiguring scars; paralysis; the loss of or loss of function of body organs; and the loss or loss of function of any arm or leg. I further acknowledge that all questions I have asked about the procedure have been answered in a satisfactory manner.

At trial Dr. Williams testified that both in office and at the hospital he explained the serious nature of the injury to Mr. Hidding and emphasized that if he did not have surgery he would lose lower body control. The progress note for December 16, 1984 states: "For decompression lam. in a.m. The procedure, alt. and possible complications discussed. No guarantee given."

On direct examination Mrs. Hidding testified that her husband had only a 6th grade education; his reading skills were minimal. At his request she accompanied him on doctors visits to insure that he understood the doctor's orders and instructions; Mr. Hidding was afraid he would miss something.

. . . Mrs. Hidding interpreted the phrase "loss of function of body organs" to mean "you can't get up and walk around or that when you do, you may stumble or fall or be very weak or wobbly on your feet."

To establish consent to a risk it must be shown both that the patient was aware of the risk and that he agreed to encounter it. The physician is required to disclose material risks in such terms as a reasonable doctor would believe a reasonable patient would understand. In order for a reasonable patient to have awareness of a risk he should be told in lay language the nature and severity of the risk and the likelihood of its occurrence. A bland statement as to a risk of "loss of function of body organs" when not accompanied by any estimate of its frequency does not amount to understandable communication of any specific real risk. "An ordinary lay person would not gather from a warning that surgery involves a risk of loss of function of body organs that he or she is asked to encounter the specific material risk of being rendered permanently incontinent through loss of bladder control."

Trial testimony supports the conclusion that Dr. Williams did not disclose to Paul Hidding the risk that the laminectomy could result in impairment of his bowel and bladder functioning. Mrs. Hidding has successfully rebutted the presumption attached to the signed consent form. There was no "informed consent" to surgery.

Of equal if not more importance, the district judge found that Dr. Williams' failure to disclose his chronic alcohol abuse to Mr. and Mrs. Hidding vitiated their consent to surgery. Because this condition creates a material risk associated with the surgeon's ability to perform, which if disclosed would have obliged the patient to have elected another course of treatment, the fact-finder's conclusion that non-disclosure is a violation of the informed consent doctrine is entirely correct.

In October, 1986 the Louisiana State Board of Medical Examiners suspended Dr. Williams' medical license on charges of "[h]abitual or recurring drunkenness," LSA-R.S. 37:1285(4); "[p]rofessional or medical incompetency," 37:1285(12); "[u]nprofessional conduct," 37:1285(13); "[c]ontinuing or recurring medical practice which fails to satisfy the prevailing and usually accepted standards of medical practice in this state," 37:1285(14); and "[i]nability to practice medicine with reasonable skill or safety to patients because of mental illness or deficiency; physical illness, including but not limited to deterioration through the aging process or loss of motor skills; and/or, excessive use or abuse of drugs, including alcohol." 37:1285(25).

Dr. Patrick McClain testified as an expert in the field of addictive medicine. He stated that alcoholism is a gradual disease that progresses over a lengthy period. By the time it develops to the stage where an individual's professional life is affected, it is in a chronic state. At that point, compensatory mechanisms can no longer disguise the problem and the individual becomes florid and outwardly manifests the illness.

At trial Dr. Russell Levy testified that it was the opinion of the medical review panel that, if Dr. Williams were under the influence of a foreign substance, it would have been a breach of the standard of care for him to have performed the surgery. When asked whether a doctor suffering from alcohol or drug dependency has an affirmative obligation to relay this to the patient, he answered, "I certainly think that if a physician or anybody in a position of life and death over someone knows that they're suffering from this condition, they should at least let this person know that they have these problems." . . .

The district judge found as a matter of fact that Dr. Williams abused alcohol at the time of Paul Hidding's surgery. Based on both fact and expert testimony the court concluded that this condition presented a material risk to the patient, the increased potential for injury during surgery, that was not disclosed. Had the risk been disclosed, Mr. and Mrs. Hidding would have selected another course of treatment. Thus by failing to disclose his chronic alcohol abuse Dr. Williams violated the informed consent doctrine. These factual findings are based on a determination of witnesses' credibility and are entitled to great deference; they are not clearly wrong.

The district court with the benefit of lay and expert evidence found that Dr. Williams had breached the applicable standard of care in failing to inform Mr. Hidding of the risk of injury associated with surgery, and of the doctor's own prolonged alcohol abuse. . . . Our review of the evidence shows no manifest error in the district court ruling. The trier of fact was justified in his conclusion that Dr. Williams breached the informed consent doctrine.

For the foregoing reasons, the district judgment in favor of plaintiff Rubinell Hidding is affirmed. Costs are to be borne by Appellants.

QUESTIONS

1. Why wasn't the surgical consent form signed by Hidding enforced in this case?
2. If Dr. Williams had performed only two prior laminectomies, would that information be material to informed consent?

b. Vicarious Liability of Managed Care Organizations

Medical malpractice claims most often are brought against physicians. But in some instances, hospitals or other persons or entities for which physicians work may be held liable. Under one theory, those other defendants may be vicariously liable by virtue of their status as employers or principals of the physician employee or agent. Vicarious liability is a form of strict liability, which does not require proof of fault by the employer. Under other theories, those defendants may be directly liable for their negligent failure to supervise, hire, or discipline a physician, or for the conditions of the facility or other staff. Breach of contract or warranty claims may also be available. The following case considers the liability of a managed care company for the malpractice of a physician in its network. As you read, consider what it takes for a plaintiff to prove vicarious liability and whether every networked physician will create expanded liability exposure for a managed care organization.

Petrovich v. Share Health Plan of Illinois, Inc.

188 Ill. 2d 17 (1999)

The plaintiff brought this medical malpractice action against a physician and others for their alleged negligence in failing to diagnose her oral cancer in a timely manner. The plaintiff also named her health maintenance organization (HMO) as a defendant. The central issue here is whether the plaintiff's HMO may be held vicariously liable for the negligence of its independent-contractor physicians under agency law. The plaintiff contends that the HMO is vicariously liable under both the doctrines of apparent authority and implied authority. . . .

FACTS

In 1989, plaintiff's employer, the Chicago Federation of Musicians, provided health care coverage to all of its employees by selecting Share and enrolling its employees therein. Share is an HMO and pays only for medical care that is obtained within its network of physicians. In order to qualify for benefits, a Share member must select from the network a primary care physician who will provide that member's overall care and authorize referrals when necessary. Share gives its members a list of participating physicians from which to choose. Share has about 500 primary care physicians covering Share's service area, which includes the counties of Cook, Du Page, Lake, McHenry and Will. Plaintiff selected Dr. Marie Kowalski from Share's list, and began seeing Dr. Kowalski as her primary care physician in August of 1989. Dr. Kowalski was employed at a satellite facility of Illinois Masonic Medical Center (Illinois Masonic), which had a contract with Share to provide medical services to Share members.

> The plaintiff did not choose Share HMO; it was selected by her employer.

In September of 1990, plaintiff saw Dr. Kowalski because she was experiencing persistent pain in the right sides of her mouth, tongue, throat and face. Plaintiff also complained of a foul mucus in her mouth. Dr. Kowalski referred plaintiff to two other physicians who had contracts with Share: Dr. Slavick, a neurologist, and Dr. Friedman, an ear, nose and throat specialist.

Plaintiff informed Dr. Friedman of her pain. Dr. Friedman observed redness or marked erythema alongside plaintiff's gums on the right side of her mouth. He recommended that plaintiff have a magnetic resonance imaging (MRI) test or a computed tomography (CT) scan performed on the base of her skull. According to plaintiff's testimony at her evidence deposition, Dr. Kowalski informed her that Share would not allow new tests as recommended by Dr. Friedman. Plaintiff did not consult with Share about the test refusals because she was not aware of Share's grievance procedure. Dr. Kowalski gave Dr. Friedman a copy of an old MRI test result at that time. The record offers no further information about this old MRI test.

Nonetheless, Dr. Kowalski later ordered an updated MRI of plaintiff's brain, which was performed on October 31, 1990. Inconsistent with Dr. Friedman's directions, however, this MRI failed to image the right base of the tongue area where redness existed. Plaintiff and Dr. Kowalski discussed the results of this MRI test on November 19, 1990, during a follow-up visit. Plaintiff testified that Dr. Kowalski told her that the MRI revealed no abnormality.

Plaintiff's pain persisted. In April or May of 1991, Dr. Kowalski again referred plaintiff to Dr. Friedman. This was plaintiff's third visit to Dr. Friedman. Dr. Friedman examined plaintiff and observed that plaintiff's tongue was tender. Also, plaintiff reported that she had a foul odor in her mouth and was experiencing discomfort. On June 7, 1991, Dr. Friedman performed multiple biopsies on the right side of the base of plaintiff's tongue and surrounding tissues. The biopsy results revealed squamous cell carcinoma, a cancer, in the base of plaintiff's tongue and the surrounding tissues of the pharynx. Later that month, Dr. Friedman operated on plaintiff to remove the cancer. He removed part of the base of plaintiff's tongue, and portions of her palate, pharynx and jaw bone. After the surgery, plaintiff underwent radiation treatments and rehabilitation.

Plaintiff subsequently brought this medical malpractice action against Share, Dr. Kowalski and others. Dr. Friedman was not named a party defendant. Plaintiff's complaint, though, alleges that both Drs. Kowalski and Friedman were negligent in failing to diagnose plaintiff's cancer in a timely manner, and that Share is vicariously liable for their negligence under agency principles. Share filed a motion for summary judgment, arguing that it cannot be held liable for the negligence of Dr. Kowalski or Friedman because they were acting as independent contractors in their treatment of plaintiff, not as Share's agents. Plaintiff countered that Share is not entitled to summary judgment because Drs. Kowalski and Friedman were Share's agents. The parties submitted various depositions, affidavits and exhibits in support of their respective positions.

Share is a for-profit corporation. At all relevant times, Share was organized as an "independent practice association-model" HMO under the Illinois Health Maintenance Organization Act. This means that Share is a financing entity that arranges and pays for health care by contracting with independent medical groups and practitioners. Share does not employ physicians directly, nor does it own, operate, maintain or supervise the offices where medical care is provided to its members. Rather, Share contracts with independent medical groups and physicians that have the facilities, equipment and professional skills necessary to render medical care. Physicians desiring to join Share's network are required to complete an application procedure and meet with Share's approval.

Share utilizes a method of compensation called "capitation" to pay its medical groups. Share also maintains a "quality assurance program." Share's capitation method of compensation and "quality assurance program" are more fully described later in this opinion.

Share provides a member handbook to each of its members, including plaintiff. The handbook states to its members that Share will provide "all your healthcare needs" and "comprehensive high quality services." The handbook also states that the primary care physician is "your health care manager" and "makes the decisions" about the member's care. The handbook further states that Share is a "good partner in sickness and in health." Unlike the master agreements and benefits contract discussed below, the member handbook which plaintiff received does not contain any provision that identifies Share physicians as independent contractors or nonemployees of Share. Rather, the handbook describes the physicians as "your Share physician," "Share physicians" and "our staff." Furthermore, Share refers to the physicians' offices as "Your Share physician's office" and states: "All of the Share staff and Medical Offices look forward to serving you * * *."

> This kind of promotional language is common in health insurance contractual literature. Do you think it could mislead covered individuals in their understanding of the insurer's role?

Plaintiff confirmed that she received the member handbook. Plaintiff did not read the handbook in its entirety, but read portions of it as she needed the information. She relied on the information contained in the handbook while Drs. Kowalski and Friedman treated her.

The record also contains a "Health Care Services Master Agreement," entered into by Share and Illinois Masonic. Dr. Kowalski is a signatory of this agreement. The agreement states, "It is understood and agreed that [Illinois Masonic] and [primary care physicians] are independent contractors and not employees or agents of SHARE." A separate agreement between Share and Dr. Friedman contains similar language. Plaintiff did not receive these agreements.

Share's primary care physicians, under their agreements with Share, are required to approve patients' medical requests and make referrals to specialists. These physicians use Share's standard referral forms to indicate their approval of the referral. Dr. Kowalski testified at an evidence deposition that she did not feel constrained by Share in making medical decisions regarding her patients, including whether to order tests or make referrals to specialists.

Another document in the record is Share's benefits contract. The benefits contract contains a subscriber certificate. The subscriber certificate sets forth a member's rights and obligations with respect to Share. Additionally, the subscriber certificate states that Share's physicians are independent contractors and that "SHARE Plan Providers and Enrolling Groups are not agents or employees of SHARE nor is SHARE or any employee of SHARE an agent or employee of SHARE Plan Providers or Enrolling Groups." The certificate elaborates: "The relationship between a SHARE Plan Provider and any Member is that of provider and patient. The SHARE Plan Physician is solely responsible for the medical services provided to any Member. The SHARE Plan Hospital is solely responsible for the Hospital services provided to any Member."

> Share repeatedly attempted in writing to disavow an agency relationship with the plan providers and physicians.

Plaintiff testified that she did not recall receiving the subscriber certificate. In response, Share stated that Share customarily provides members with this information. Share does not claim to know whether Share actually provided plaintiff with this information. Plaintiff acknowledged that she received a "whole stack" of information from Share upon her enrollment.

Plaintiff was not aware of the type of relationship that her physicians had with Share. At the time she received treatment, plaintiff believed that her physicians were employees of Share.

In the circuit court, Share argued that it was entitled to summary judgment because the independent-contractor provision in the benefits contract established, as a matter of law, that Drs. Kowalski and Friedman were not acting as Share's agents in their treatment of plaintiff. The circuit court agreed and entered summary judgment for Share.

The appellate court reversed, holding that a genuine issue of material fact is presented as to whether plaintiff's treating physicians are Share's apparent agents. The appellate court stated that a number of factors support plaintiff's apparent agency claim, including plaintiff's testimony, Share's member handbook, Share's quality assessment program and Share's capitation method of compensation. The appellate court therefore remanded the cause for trial. The appellate court did not address the theory of implied authority.

ANALYSIS

This appeal comes before us amidst great changes to the relationships among physicians, patients and those entities paying for medical care. Traditionally, physicians treated patients on demand, while insurers merely paid the physicians their fee for the services provided. Today, managed care organizations (MCOs) have stepped into the insurer's shoes, and often attempt to reduce the price and quantity of health care services provided to patients through a system of health care cost containment. MCOs may, for example, use prearranged fee structures for compensating physicians. MCOs may also use utilization-review procedures, which are procedures designed to determine whether the use and volume of particular health care services are appropriate. MCOs have developed in response to rapid increases in health care costs.

HMOs, i.e., health maintenance organizations, are a type of MCO. HMOs are subject to both state and federal laws. Under Illinois law, an HMO is defined as "any organization formed under the laws of this or another state to provide or arrange for one or more health care plans under a system which causes any part of the risk of health care delivery to be borne by the organization or its providers." Because HMOs may differ in their structures and the cost-containment practices that they employ, a court must discern the nature of the organization before it, where relevant to the issues. As earlier noted, Share is organized as an independent practice association (IPA)-model HMO. IPA-model HMOs are financing entities that arrange and pay for health care by contracting with independent medical groups and practitioners.

This court has never addressed a question of whether an HMO may be held liable for medical malpractice. Share asserts that holding HMOs liable for medical malpractice will cause health care costs to increase and make health care inaccessible to large numbers of people. Share suggests that, with this consideration in mind, this court should impose only narrow, or limited, forms of liability on HMOs. We disagree with Share that the cost-containment role of HMOs entitles them to special consideration. The principle that organizations are accountable for their tortious actions and those of their agents is fundamental to our justice system. There is no exception to this principle for HMOs. Moreover, HMO accountability is essential to counterbalance the HMO goal of cost-containment. To the extent that HMOs are profit-making entities, accountability is also needed to counterbalance the inherent drive to achieve a large and ever-increasing profit margin. Market forces alone "are insufficient to cure the deleterious [e]ffects of managed care on the health care industry." Courts, therefore, should not be hesitant to apply well-settled legal theories of liability to HMOs where the facts so warrant and where justice so requires.

> The issue of an HMO's vicarious liability for a plan physician was a question of first impression for this court.

Indeed, the national trend of courts is to hold HMOs accountable for medical malpractice under a variety of legal theories, including vicarious liability on the basis of apparent authority, vicarious liability on the basis of respondeat superior, direct corporate negligence, breach of contract and breach of warranty. Share concedes that HMOs may be held liable for medical malpractice under these five theories.

This appeal concerns whether Share may be held vicariously liable under agency law for the negligence of its independent-contractor physicians. We must determine whether Share was properly awarded summary judgment on the ground that Drs. Kowalski and Friedman were not acting as Share's agents in their treatment of plaintiff. Plaintiff argues that Share is not entitled to summary judgment on this record. Plaintiff asserts that genuine issues of material fact exist as to whether Drs. Kowalski and Friedman were acting within Share's apparent authority, implied authority or both.

As a general rule, no vicarious liability exists for the actions of independent contractors. Vicarious liability may nevertheless be imposed for the actions of independent contractors where an agency relationship is established under either the doctrine of apparent authority or the doctrine of implied authority.

I. Apparent Authority

Apparent authority, also known as ostensible authority, has been a part of Illinois jurisprudence for more than 140 years. Under the doctrine, a principal will be bound not only by the authority that it actually gives to another, but also by the authority that it appears to give. Where the principal creates the appearance of authority, a court will not hear the principal's denials of agency to the prejudice of an innocent third party, who has been led to reasonably rely upon the agency and is harmed as a result. . . .

We now hold that the apparent authority doctrine may also be used to impose vicarious liability on HMOs. . . .

To establish apparent authority against an HMO for physician malpractice, the patient must prove (1) that the HMO held itself out as the provider of health care, without informing the patient that the care is given by independent contractors, and (2) that the patient justifiably relied upon the conduct of the HMO by looking to the HMO to provide health care services, rather than to a specific physician. Apparent agency is a question of fact.

A. Holding Out

The element of "holding out" means that the HMO, or its agent, acted in a manner that would lead a reasonable person to conclude that the physician who was alleged to be negligent was an agent or employee of the HMO. Where the acts of the agent create the appearance of authority, a plaintiff must also prove that the HMO had knowledge of and acquiesced in those acts. Significantly, the holding-out element does not require the HMO to make an express representation that the physician alleged to be negligent is its agent or employee. Rather, this element is met where the HMO holds itself out as the provider of health care without informing the patient that the care is given by independent contractors. Vicarious liability under the apparent authority doctrine will not attach, however, if the patient knew or should have known that the physician providing treatment is an independent contractor.

Here, Share contends that the independent-contractor provisions in the two master agreements and the benefits contract conclusively establish, as a matter of law, that Share did not hold out Drs. Kowalski and Friedman to be Share's agents. Although all three of these contracts clearly express that the physicians are independent contractors and not agents of Share, we disagree with Share's contention for the reasons explained below.

First, the two master agreements at issue are private contractual agreements between Share and Illinois Masonic, with Dr. Kowalski as a signatory, and between Share and Dr. Friedman. The record contains no indication that plaintiff knew or should have known of these private contractual agreements between Share and its physicians. *Gilbert* expressly rejected the notion that such private contractual agreements can control a claim of apparent agency. We hold that this same rationale applies to private contractual agreements between physicians and an HMO. Because there is no dispute that the master agreements at bar were unknown to plaintiff, they cannot be used to defeat her apparent agency claim.

Share also relies on the benefits contract. Plaintiff was not a party or a signatory to this contract. The benefits contract contains a subscriber certificate, which states that Share physicians are independent contractors. Share claims that this language alone conclusively overcomes plaintiff's apparent agency claim. We do not agree.

Whether a person has notice of a physician's status as an independent contractor, or is put on notice by the circumstances, is a question of fact. In this case, plaintiff testified at her evidence deposition that she did not recall receiving the subscriber certificate. Share responded only that it customarily provides members with this information. Share has never claimed to know whether Share actually provided plaintiff with this information. Thus, a question of fact exists as to whether Share gave this information to plaintiff. If this information was not provided to plaintiff, it cannot be used to defeat her apparent agency claim.

Share nonetheless maintains that plaintiff's testimony that she received a "whole stack" of information from Share upon her enrollment proves that plaintiff received the subscriber certificate. Share is not entitled to summary judgment on the basis of this testimony. Even if Share did send this single disclaimer of an agency relationship to plaintiff within a "whole stack" of information, this fact would not conclusively resolve plaintiff's claim. As we discuss below, the record contains evidence that Share held itself out as the provider of health care without informing plaintiff that the care was given by independent contractors. A trier of fact must therefore be permitted to weigh the conflicting evidence and decide this issue based on the totality of the circumstances.

> Would the "holding out" element be met if a hospital's independent contractor physicians were required to wear white lab coats bearing the hospital's logo?

Only a trier of fact can properly determine whether plaintiff had notice of the physicians' status as independent contractors, or was put on notice by the circumstances.

Evidence in the record supports plaintiff's contentions that Share held itself out to its members as the provider of health care, and that plaintiff was not aware that her physicians were independent contractors. Notably, plaintiff stated that, at the time that she received treatment, plaintiff believed that Drs. Kowalski and Friedman were Share employees. Plaintiff was not aware of the type of relationship that her physicians had with Share.

Moreover, Share's member handbook contains evidence that Share held itself out to plaintiff as the provider of her health care. The handbook stated to Share members that Share will provide "all your healthcare needs" and "comprehensive high quality services." The handbook did not contain any provision that identified Share physicians as independent contractors or nonemployees of Share. Instead, the handbook referred to the physicians as "your Share physician," "Share physicians" and "our staff." Share also referred to the physicians' offices as "Your Share physician's office." The record shows that Share provided this handbook to each of its enrolled members, including plaintiff. Representations made in the handbook are thus directly attributable to Share and were intended by Share to be communicated to its members. . . .

We hold that the above testimony by plaintiff and Share's member handbook support the conclusion that Share held itself out to plaintiff as the provider of her health care, without informing her that the care was actually provided by independent contractors. Therefore, a triable issue of fact exists as to the holding-out element. We need not resolve whether any other evidence in the record also supports plaintiff's claim. Our task here is to review whether Share is entitled to summary judgment on this element. We hold that Share is not.

B. Justifiable Reliance

A plaintiff must also prove the element of "justifiable reliance" to establish apparent authority against an HMO for physician malpractice. This means that the plaintiff acted in reliance upon the conduct of the HMO or its agent, consistent with ordinary care and prudence.

The element of justifiable reliance is met where the plaintiff relies upon the HMO to provide health care services, and does not rely upon a specific physician. This element is not met if the plaintiff selects his or her own personal physician and merely looks to the HMO as a conduit through which the plaintiff receives medical care.

Concerning the element of justifiable reliance in the hospital context, *Gilbert* explained that the critical distinction is whether the plaintiff sought care from the hospital itself or from a personal physician. . . . This rationale applies even more forcefully in the context of an HMO that restricts its members to the HMO's chosen physicians. Accordingly, unless a person seeks care from a personal physician, that person is seeking care from the HMO itself. A person who seeks care from the HMO itself accepts that care in reliance upon the HMO's holding itself out as the provider of care.

Share maintains that plaintiff cannot establish the justifiable reliance element because she did not select Share. Share argues that, unless the plaintiff actually selects the HMO, there is no reliance upon the HMO and thus no nexus between the HMO's alleged wrongful conduct and the plaintiff's injury. Share takes the position that, if a person did not select the HMO, then that person can never claim apparent agency, regardless of what the HMO does, says or leads the person to believe.

We reject Share's argument. It is true that, where a person selects the HMO and does not rely upon a specific physician, then that person is relying upon the HMO to provide health care. This principle, derived directly from *Gilbert,* is set forth above. Equally true, however, is that where a person has no choice but to enroll with a single HMO and does not rely upon a specific physician, then that person is likewise relying upon the HMO to provide health care.

In the present case, the record discloses that plaintiff did not select Share. Plaintiff's employer selected Share for her. Plaintiff had no choice of health plans whatsoever. Once Share became plaintiff's health plan, Share required plaintiff to obtain her primary medical care from one of its primary care physicians. If plaintiff did not do so, Share did not cover plaintiff's medical costs. In accordance with Share's requirement, plaintiff selected Dr. Kowalski from a list of physicians that Share provided to her. Plaintiff had no prior relationship with Dr. Kowalski. As to Dr. Kowalski's selection of Dr. Friedman for plaintiff, Share required Dr. Kowalski to make referrals only to physicians approved by Share. Plaintiff had no prior relationship with Dr. Friedman. We hold that these facts are sufficient to raise the reasonable inference that plaintiff relied upon Share to provide her health care services.

Were we to conclude that plaintiff was not relying upon Share for health care, we would be denying the true nature of the relationship among plaintiff, her HMO and the physicians. Share, like many HMOs, contracted with plaintiff's employer to become plaintiff's sole provider of health care, to the exclusion of all other providers. Share then restricted plaintiff to its chosen physicians. Under these facts, plaintiff's reliance on Share as the provider of her health care is shown not only to be compelling, but literally compelled. Plaintiff's reliance upon Share was inherent in Share's method of operation. . . .

In conclusion, as set forth above, plaintiff has presented sufficient evidence to support justifiable reliance, as well as a holding out by Share. Share, therefore, is not entitled to summary judgment against plaintiff's claim of apparent authority.

II. Implied Authority

Implied authority is actual authority, circumstantially proved. One context in which implied authority arises is where the facts and circumstances show that the defendant exerted sufficient control over the alleged agent so as to negate that person's status as an independent contractor, at least with respect to third parties. The cardinal consideration for determining the existence of implied authority is whether the alleged agent retains the right to control the manner of doing the work. Where a person's status as an independent contractor is negated, liability may result under the doctrine of respondeat superior.

Plaintiff contends that the facts and circumstances of this case show that Share exerted sufficient control over Drs. Kowalski and Friedman so as to negate their status as independent contractors. Share responds that the act of providing medical care is peculiarly within a physician's domain because it requires the exercise of independent medical judgment. Share thus maintains that, because it cannot control a physician's exercise of medical judgment, it cannot be subject to vicarious liability under the doctrine of implied authority. . . .

> Even if formally the arrangement involves an independent contractor, facts and circumstances may give rise to vicarious liability.

We now address whether the implied authority doctrine may be used against HMOs to negate a physician's status as an independent contractor. Our appellate court in *Raglin* suggested that it can. Case law from other jurisdictions lends support to this view as well. . . .

We do not find the above decisions rendered in the hospital context to be dispositive of whether an HMO may exert such control over its physicians so as to negate their status as independent contractors. We can readily discern that the relationships between physicians and HMOs are often much different than the traditional relationships between physicians and hospitals. This reality is underscored by the amicus brief filed by the physicians group. Therein, the [Illinois State Medical] Society describes in concrete terms how many physicians in Illinois perceive their current relationships with HMOs. The Society's description of that relationship does not resemble the traditional relationship between physicians and hospitals. We reject Share's claim that, for purposes of the implied authority doctrine, the exercise of medical judgment by physicians can never be subject to control by an HMO.

Physicians, of course, should not allow the exercise of their medical judgment to be corrupted or controlled. Physicians have professional ethical, moral and legal obligations to provide appropriate medical care to their patients. These obligations on physicians, however, will not act to relieve an HMO of its own legal responsibilities. Where an HMO effectively controls a physician's exercise of medical judgment, and that judgment is exercised negligently, the HMO cannot be allowed to claim that the physician is solely responsible for the harm that results. In such a circumstance, both the physician and the HMO are liable for the harm that results. We therefore hold that the implied authority doctrine may be used against an HMO to negate a physician's status as an independent contractor. An implied agency exists where the facts and circumstances show that an HMO exerted such sufficient control over a participating physician so as to negate that physician's status as an independent contractor, at least with respect to third parties.

No precise formula exists for deciding when a person's status as an independent contractor is negated. Rather, the determination of whether a person is an agent or an independent contractor rests upon the facts and circumstances of each case. As noted, the cardinal consideration is whether that person retains the right to control the manner of doing the work. Facts bearing on the question of whether a person is an agent or an independent contractor include "the question of the hiring, the right to discharge, the manner of direction of the servant, the right to terminate the relationship, and the character of the supervision of the work done." The presence of contractual provisions subjecting the person to control over the manner of doing the work is a traditional indicia that a person's status as an independent contractor should be negated. The presence of one or more of the above facts and indicia are not necessarily conclusive of the issue. They merely serve as guides to resolving the primary question of whether the alleged agent is truly an independent contractor or is subject to control.

With these established principles in mind, we turn to the present case. Plaintiff contends that her physicians' status as independent contractors should be negated. Plaintiff asserts that Share actively interfered with her physicians' medical decision-making by designing and executing its capitation method of compensation and "quality assurance" programs. Plaintiff also points to Share's referral system as evidence of control.

Plaintiff submits that Share's capitation method of compensating its medical groups is a form of control because it financially punishes physicians for ordering certain medical treatment. The record discloses that Share utilizes a method of compensation called "capitation." Under capitation, Share prepays contracting medical groups a fixed amount of money for each member who enrolls with that group. In exchange, the medical groups agree to render health care to their enrolled Share members in accordance with the Share plan. Each medical group contracting with Share has its own capitation account. Deducted from that capitation account are the costs of any services provided by the primary care physician, the costs of medical procedures and tests, and the fees of all consulting physicians. The medical group then retains the surplus left in the capitation account. The costs for hospitalizations and other services are charged against a separate account. Reinsurance is provided for the capitation account and the separate account for certain high cost claims. Share pays Illinois Masonic in accordance with its capitation method of compensation. Dr. Kowalski testified that Illinois Masonic pays her the same salary every month. Plaintiff maintains that a reasonable inference to be drawn from Share's capitation method of compensation is that Share provides financial disincentives to its primary care physicians in order to discourage them from ordering the medical care that they deem appropriate. Plaintiff argues that this is an example of Share's influence and control over the medical judgment of its physicians.

> Capitation is a common payment methodology in physician-HMO contracts. The court allows that arrangement as evidence of plan control over the physician.

Share counters that its capitation method of compensation cannot be used as evidence of control here because Dr. Kowalski is paid the same salary every month. We disagree with Share that this fact makes Share's capitation system irrelevant to our inquiry. Whether control was actually exercised is not dispositive in this context. Rather, the right to control the alleged agent is the proper query, even where that right is not exercised. . . .

[The court's discussion of Share's "quality assurance program" is omitted. The court rejected the existence of that program as evidence of control because it was done primarily under state Department of Public Health requirements. The court did allow evidence of chart review, control over referrals to specialists, and gatekeeping by primary care physicians to evidence control by Share.]

We conclude that plaintiff has presented adequate evidence to entitle her to a trial on the issue of implied authority. All the facts and circumstances before us, if proven at trial, raise the reasonable inference that Share exerted such sufficient control over Drs. Kowalski and Friedman so as to negate their status as independent contractors. As discussed above, plaintiff presents relevant evidence of Share's capitation method of compensation, . . . Share's referral system and Share's requirement that its primary care physicians act as gatekeepers for Share. These facts support plaintiff's argument that Share subjected its physicians to control over the manner in which they did their work. The facts surrounding treatment also support plaintiff's argument. According to plaintiff's evidence, Dr. Kowalski referred plaintiff to Dr. Friedman. Dr. Friedman evaluated plaintiff and recommended that plaintiff have either an MRI test or a CT scan performed on the base of her skull. Dr. Friedman, however, did not order the test that he recommended for plaintiff. Rather, he reported this information back to Dr. Kowalski in her role as plaintiff's primary care physician. Dr. Kowalski initially sent Dr. Friedman a copy of an old MRI test. Dr. Kowalski later ordered that an updated MRI be taken. In doing so, she directed that the MRI be taken of plaintiff's "brain." Hence, that MRI failed to image the base of plaintiff's skull as recommended by Dr. Friedman. Dr. Kowalski then reviewed the MRI test results herself and informed plaintiff that the results revealed no abnormality. From all the above facts and circumstances, a trier of fact could reasonably infer that Share promulgated such a system of control over its physicians that Share effectively negated the exercise of their independent medical judgment, to plaintiff's detriment.

We note that Dr. Kowalski testified at an evidence deposition that she did not feel constrained by Share in making medical decisions regarding her patients, including whether to order tests or make referrals to specialists. This testimony is not controlling at the summary judgment stage. The trier of fact is entitled to weigh all the conflicting evidence above against Dr. Kowalski's testimony.

In conclusion, plaintiff has presented adequate evidence to support a finding that Share exerted such sufficient control over its participating physicians so as to negate their status as independent contractors. Share, therefore, is not entitled to summary judgment against plaintiff's claim of implied authority.

. . . .

CONCLUSION

An HMO may be held vicariously liable for the negligence of its independent-contractor physicians under both the doctrines of apparent authority and implied authority. Plaintiff here is entitled to a trial on both doctrines. The circuit court therefore erred in awarding summary judgment to Share. The appellate court's judgment, which reversed the circuit court's judgment and remanded the cause to the circuit court for further proceedings, is affirmed.

QUESTIONS

1. Which theory—apparent authority or implied authority—looks most promising for the plaintiff on remand at trial?

2. What steps would you advise Share to take to avoid vicarious liability claims in the future?
3. If an emergency room posts signs in the patient registration and waiting areas, explaining that the emergency room physicians are independent contractors and not employees of the hospital, will that negate any vicarious liability claims for negligence by the emergency room doctors?

2. IN CONTRACT: WAIVERS AND WARRANTIES

The two cases above demonstrate the limits of freedom of contract, with courts imposing tort duties on defendants despite the presence of written contracts between the parties. Similarly, courts are reluctant to enforce exculpatory clauses in contracts for health care. In the leading case, Tunkl v. Regents of University of California, 383 P.2d 441 (Cal. 1963), the California Supreme Court declined to enforce an otherwise validly executed contract that included, as a condition of admission to a charitable hospital, a release of liability for negligence occurring during the admission.

But allowing health care contracts that permit parties to agree how to allocate losses among themselves may have benefits. Contractual agreements respect the personal and professional autonomy of both parties. Health care contracts also may result in a more economically efficient allocation of resources, for example, patients who prefer to bear the risk of injury may be able to access more affordable health care. Providers who contractually limit their liability exposure can more ably predict costs and conduct operations accordingly. Nevertheless, significant questions remain regarding the desirability of contracts limiting recovery in the health care context given the significant power imbalance between patients and health care providers.

a. Waivers

Although complete waivers of liability for negligence or other mistreatment by health care providers may not be enforceable, courts have been willing to enforce contracts limiting the remedies available or the forum for resolving disputes. In particular, arbitration clauses, which are common but controversial in various consumer products, may be enforceable.

Laizure v. Avante at Leesburg, Inc.

109 So. 3d 752 (Fla. 2013)

A nursing home patient, Harry Lee Stewart, signed an agreement providing for arbitration of disputes arising out of treatment and care at the nursing home. Stewart subsequently died, allegedly as a result of the nursing home's negligence. Through the personal representative, Debra Laizure, his survivors brought a cause of action in circuit court for deprivation of rights under the applicable nursing home statute and, alternatively, a wrongful death action. The issue in this case presented through the Fifth District's opinion in Laizure v. Avante at Leesburg, Inc., 44 So. 3d 1254 (Fla. 5th DCA 2010), is whether an arbitration agreement signed by the decedent requires his estate and heirs to arbitrate their wrongful death claims. In its decision, the Fifth District Court of Appeal concluded that the estate and heirs were bound by the arbitration agreement signed by the patient, but certified the following question to be of great public importance:

> DOES THE EXECUTION OF A NURSING HOME ARBITRATION AGREE-
> MENT BY A PARTY WITH THE CAPACITY TO CONTRACT, BIND THE
> PATIENT'S ESTATE AND STATUTORY HEIRS IN A SUBSEQUENT WRONG-
> FUL DEATH ACTION ARISING FROM AN ALLEGED TORT WITHIN THE
> SCOPE OF AN OTHERWISE VALID ARBITRATION AGREEMENT[?]

. . . .

This case requires us to examine the nature of wrongful death actions under Florida law and is not about the quality of care provided by nursing homes or other related policy issues. The question presented is whether an arbitration provision in an otherwise valid contract binds the signing party's estate and heirs in a subsequent wrongful death case. For the reasons more fully explained below, we hold that it does.[1] Our decision flows from the nature of wrongful death actions in Florida, which we conclude is derivative for purposes of the issue presented in this case. Because the signing party's estate and heirs are bound by defenses that could be raised in a personal injury suit brought by the decedent, as well as by releases signed by the decedent, it would be anomalous to conclude that they are not also bound by a choice of forum agreement signed by the decedent in a wrongful death action arising out of the treatment and care of the decedent. Accordingly, we answer the certified question in the affirmative and approve the Fifth District's decision.

FACTS AND BACKGROUND

Harry Lee Stewart died several days after he was admitted to Avante at Leesburg (AVL) in May 2006 for rehabilitation after surgery. Debra Laizure, as personal representative of Stewart's estate, filed a complaint in circuit court seeking damages in excess of $15,000 against AVL, Avante Ancillary Services, Inc., and Avante Group, Inc. (together "Avante"). Laizure asserted against each of the defendants a claim for deprivation or infringement of Stewart's statutory nursing home residents' rights pursuant to the Florida Nursing Home Residents' Rights Act (NHRRA), embodied in chapter 400, Florida Statutes (2008). Laizure pled in the alternative a claim against each of the defendants for wrongful death based on negligence.

The patient signed his own admissions paperwork, which included the arbitration clause.

The defendants filed a motion to compel arbitration predicated on an arbitration agreement that Stewart signed on May 15, the day after his admission to AVL. The arbitration agreement was presented to Stewart as part of a packet of admissions paperwork and was entitled "ADDENDUM TO ADMISSION AGREEMENT." It provided in relevant part as follows:

> The Facility and the Resident and/or Resident's Authorized Representative (herein-
> after referred to collectively as the "Parties") understand and agree that any legal

---

1. Laizure also argues that the arbitration agreement in this case is unconscionable, and the Respondents argue that the arbitration agreement binds the estate and statutory heirs because they are third-party beneficiaries to the agreement. We decline to address both of these arguments because they are outside the scope of, and unrelated to, the certified question before this Court.

dispute, controversy, demand, or claim where the damages or other amount in controversy is/are alleged to exceed ten thousand dollars ($10,000.00), and that arises out of or relates to the Resident Admission Agreement or is in any way connected to the Resident's stay at the Facility shall be resolved exclusively by binding Arbitration; and not by a lawsuit or resort to other court process. The parties understand that arbitration is a process in which a neutral third person or persons ("arbitrator(s)") consider[ ] the facts and arguments presented by the parties and render[ ] a binding decision.

This agreement to arbitrate shall include, but is not limited to, any claim based on . . . breach of contract, breach of fiduciary duty, fraud or misrepresentation, common law or statutory negligence, gross negligence, malpractice or a claim based on any departure from accepted standards of medical or nursing care (collectively "Disputes"), where the damages or other amount in controversy is/are alleged to exceed ten thousand dollars ($10,000.00). This shall expressly include, without limitation, claims based on Chapter 400, Florida Statutes, which allege damages in excess of ten thousand dollars ($10,000.00).

This agreement shall be binding upon, and shall include any claims brought by or against the Parties' representatives, agents, heirs, assigns, employees, managers, directors, shareholders, management companies, parent companies, subsidiary companies or related or affiliated business entities.

. . . .

THE PARTIES UNDERSTAND AND AGREE THAT BY ENTERING THIS ARBITRATION AGREEMENT THEY ARE GIVING UP AND WAIVING THEIR CONSTITUTIONAL RIGHT TO HAVE ANY CLAIM OR DISPUTE THAT FALLS WITHIN THE SCOPE OF THIS AGREEMENT DECIDED IN A COURT OF LAW BEFORE A JUDGE AND JURY. IN THE EVENT A COURT OF COMPETENT JURISDICTION SHALL RULE THAT A DISPUTE BETWEEN THE PARTIES IS NOT SUBJECT TO ARBITRATION THEN RESIDENT AND FACILITY ACKNOWLEDGE AND AGREE TO WAIVE ALL RIGHTS TO A TRIAL BY JURY AND TO HAVE THEIR DISPUTE DECIDED ONLY BY A JUDGE OF A COURT OF COMPETENT JURISDICTION IN THE COUNTY AND STATE IN WHICH THE FACILITY IS LOCATED.

Finally, the Resident or his/her Authorized Representative understands that: (1) he/she has the right to seek legal counsel concerning this agreement; (2) he/she is not required to use the Facility for his/her healthcare needs and that there are numerous other health care providers in the State where Facility is located that are qualified to provide such care; and (3) this Arbitration Agreement may be rescinded by written notice to the Facility from the Resident or Authorized Representative within three (3) business days of signing the Agreement. If not rescinded within three (3) business days of signing, this Arbitration shall remain in effect for all care and services rendered at Facility subsequent to the date the agreement was signed, even if such care and services are rendered during a subsequent admission (i.e. following the Resident's discharge from and readmission to the Facility).

Laizure opposed arbitration, contending that the arbitration agreement was procedurally and substantively unconscionable and that the wrongful death claims were not arbitrable. The trial court found that the arbitration agreement was valid, that the claims brought by Laizure were arbitrable issues, and that the beneficiaries of the estate were intended third-party beneficiaries of the agreement.

On appeal, the Fifth District affirmed the trial court's order. The Fifth District focused primarily on Laizure's argument that the arbitration agreement did not, and could not, encompass a wrongful death claim because the claim did not belong to

Stewart, but rather was an independent claim belonging to the estate and the statutory heirs. The Fifth District observed that no Florida decision appears to have directly addressed the issue of whether a nursing home arbitration agreement executed by a patient is binding on his estate and heirs in a wrongful death action. . . .

ANALYSIS

In Florida, "there are three elements for courts to consider in ruling on a motion to compel arbitration of a given dispute: (1) whether a valid written agreement to arbitrate exists; (2) whether an arbitrable issue exists; and (3) whether the right to arbitration was waived." The certified question in this case — whether the arbitration agreement requires arbitration of the wrongful death claims brought by Laizure on behalf of Stewart's estate and heirs — relates to the first two elements. The question presented is a pure question of law, and this Court's review is de novo.

We begin our analysis by addressing Laizure's argument that the wrongful death claims are not within the scope of the arbitration agreement. Then, we analyze the issue of whether a nursing home arbitration agreement signed by a nursing home resident, or his or her representative, can bind the resident's estate and statutory heirs to arbitration. To analyze this issue, we first review Florida's Wrongful Death Act. Next we discuss the Florida Nursing Home Residents' Rights Act (NHRRA). Finally, we analyze the nature of wrongful death claims in Florida and answer the certified question in the affirmative.

I. The Scope of the Arbitration Agreement

There is no question that the wrongful death claims under chapter 400 of the Florida Statutes fall within the language of the arbitration agreement in this case. In *Seifert v. U.S. Home Corp.*, this Court held that an arbitration provision in a sales agreement for a home did not require arbitration of a wrongful death claim based on negligence where the contract did not mention any of the parties' rights in the event of personal injuries or death but rather referred only to the sale and purchase of the home and the tort action did not bear a significant relationship to the contract. Here, unlike the contract and claim in *Seifert*, there is a "significant relationship," between the contract and the allegations in the complaint. Further, unlike *Seifert*, the terms of the arbitration agreement in this case specifically "contemplated the existence and arbitration of future tort claims for personal injuries based on a party's common law negligence." The agreement expressly encompasses claims arising out of or relating to Stewart's stay at the facility, including negligence and malpractice, and is expressly binding upon and includes claims brought by Stewart's "heirs." As reflected in the terms of the arbitration agreement, it is clear that the contracting parties intended to include wrongful death claims such as those brought in this case.

Laizure nevertheless contends that the wrongful death claims are not arbitrable because a wrongful death claim is an independent cause of action belonging to the survivors under Florida's Wrongful Death Act. We now turn to an examination of the Act.

II. Florida's Wrongful Death Act

"A court's purpose in construing a statute is to give effect to legislative intent, which is the polestar that guides the court in statutory construction." The Legislature has expressly provided in the wrongful death statute that it is "the public policy of the state to shift the losses resulting when wrongful death occurs from the survivors of the decedent to the wrongdoer."

The Act provides for a cause of action that may be brought by a decedent's personal representative when the decedent's death is caused by the wrongful act, negligence, default, or breach of contract or warranty of any person:

> When the death of a person is caused by the wrongful act, negligence, default, or breach of contract or warranty of any person, including those occurring on navigable waters, and the event would have entitled the person injured to maintain an action and recover damages if death had not ensued, the person or watercraft that would have been liable in damages if death had not ensued shall be liable for damages as specified in this act notwithstanding the death of the person injured, although death was caused under circumstances constituting a felony.

The next section further provides:

> The action shall be brought by the decedent's personal representative, who shall recover for the benefit of the decedent's survivors and estate all damages, as specified in this act, caused by the injury resulting in death. When a personal injury to the decedent results in death, no action for the personal injury shall survive, and any such action pending at the time of death shall abate. . . . A defense that would bar or reduce a survivor's recovery if she or he were the plaintiff may be asserted against the survivor, but shall not affect the recovery of any other survivor.

The Act also provides for damages that may be recovered by the survivors and requires that "[t]he amounts awarded to each survivor and to the estate shall be stated separately in the verdict."

Because this case also involves the Florida Nursing Home Residents' Rights Act, we briefly discuss that statutory scheme next.

III. Florida Nursing Home Residents' Rights Act

The purpose of the NHRRA is to provide for the "development, establishment, and enforcement of basic standards for: (1) the health, care, and treatment of persons in nursing homes and related health care facilities; and (2) the maintenance and operation of such institutions that will ensure safe, adequate, and appropriate care, treatment, and health of persons in such facilities." The NHRRA sets forth the statutory rights of nursing home residents. The NHRRA includes a provision for civil enforcement that provides for a cause of action for negligence or a violation of the rights set forth in section 400.022. The action may be brought by the resident or his or her guardian, by a person or organization acting on behalf of a resident, or by the personal representative of the estate of a deceased resident regardless of the cause of death. The NHRRA provides that the action may be brought in any court of competent jurisdiction and that the claimant may recover actual and punitive damages.

> By statute, Florida has provided a private cause of action for claims brought against nursing homes.

If the action alleges that negligence or a violation of the resident's rights caused the resident's death, the claimant is "required to elect either survival damages pursuant to s. 46.021 or wrongful death damages pursuant to s. 768.21."[2] Section 46.021 provides that "[n]o cause of action dies with the person. All causes of action

---

2. This provision was added in 2001. At the same time, the Legislature amended section 400.023 to provide that "[s]ections 400.023-400.0238 provide the exclusive remedy for a cause of action for recovery of damages for the personal injury or death of a nursing home resident arising out of negligence or a violation of

survive and may be commenced, prosecuted, and defended in the name of the person prescribed by law." Section 768.21 is part of Florida's Wrongful Death Act and provides for the damages that may be claimed by the decedent's estate and statutory heirs.

The ability of a claimant to elect between a survival action and a wrongful death action emanates from the NHRRA. When the NHRRA does not apply, the personal injury cause of action abates upon the death of the injured party under the Wrongful Death Act, and the wrongful death cause of action becomes the only avenue for recovery.

IV. Answering the Certified Question

Although Florida's Wrongful Death Act has "long [been] characterized . . . as creating a new and distinct right of action from the right of action the decedent had prior to death," courts have also characterized wrongful death actions as derivative because they are dependent on a wrong committed against the decedent. This Court has explained that "[w]hile the Wrongful Death Act creates independent claims for the survivors, these claims are also derivative in the sense that they are dependent upon a wrong committed upon another person. No Florida decision has allowed a survivor to recover under the wrongful death statute where the decedent could not have recovered."

The right of the survivors to recover is predicated in the Act on the decedent's right to recover. In other words, recovery is precluded if the decedent could not have maintained an action and recovered damages if death had not ensued. Section 768.19, Florida Statutes (2008), provides for a cause of action "[w]hen the death of a person is caused by the wrongful act, negligence, default, or breach of contract or warranty of any person, . . . *and the event would have entitled the person injured to maintain an action and recover damages if death had not ensued.*" (Emphasis added.) . . .

More recently, in *Toombs*, this Court barred recovery for a wrongful death claim predicated upon the dangerous instrumentality doctrine where the decedent had no right of action because she was a co-bailee of the vehicle. This Court held that "no right of action originated in the decedent to which a wrongful death cause of action could attach" and concluded as follows:

> Although we have long emphasized that an action for wrongful death is distinct from the decedent's action for personal injuries had he or she survived because it involves different rights of recovery and damages, the language of the Act makes clear a cause of action for wrongful death that is predicated on the decedent's entitlement to "maintain an action and recover damages if death had not ensued." Accordingly, . . . we hold that no cause of action for wrongful death survived the decedent in the instant case because she had no right of action at her death.

Similarly, Florida cases have held that a general release executed by the decedent in resolution of a personal injury action bars any subsequent wrongful death action.

The above cases illustrate that in wrongful death actions in Florida, the defendant's liability flows from actions toward the decedent, and the ability of the estate

rights specified in s. 400.022. This section does not preclude theories of recovery not arising out of negligence or s. 400.022 which are available to a resident or to the agency."

and heirs to recover is predicated on the decedent's entitlement to maintain an action and recover damages if death had not ensued. As the Fifth District observed in this case:

> While we agree that a wrongful death action belongs to the survivors of the decedent, by statute, such an action is predicated on the "wrongful act, negligence, default or breach of contract or warranty" committed by the defendant which, as the result of the decedent's death, transformed a personal injury claim into one for wrongful death. *See* §768.19, Fla. Stat. (2009). Consequently, *courts generally agree that wrongful death claims are derivative in nature, at least in the sense that they are dependent on a wrong committed against the decedent.*

We acknowledge that courts in other states are split when considering the question of whether the estate and heirs are bound by an arbitration agreement signed by the decedent, even in states with provisions similar to Florida that predicate a wrongful death claim on the ability of the decedent to have brought suit and recover damages had he or she lived. We also acknowledge that the measure of damages for a wrongful death cause of action under Florida law is different than for a personal injury claim that could have been brought by the decedent.

> Under this reasoning, would the estate's or heirs' wrongful death recovery be reduced by any contributory negligence by the decedent?

Principled arguments exist on both sides of this issue. However, we ultimately conclude that the nature of a wrongful death cause of action in Florida is derivative in the context of determining whether a decedent's estate and heirs are bound by the decedent's agreement to arbitrate. The estate and heirs stand in the shoes of the decedent for purposes of whether the defendant is liable and are bound by the decedent's actions and contracts with respect to defenses and releases. For example, if a decedent signs a release of liability in resolution of a personal injury action, the estate and heirs would be precluded from bringing a wrongful death cause of action based on the same conduct. We see no reason that a different result is compelled for the decedent's choice of forum, and it would be anomalous to give greater rights to the estate and heirs than to the decedent. Finally, we note that holding otherwise in the nursing home context would give the personal representative of an estate the strategic choice under the NHRRA to elect to pursue a wrongful death claim, rather than a survivor action on behalf of the decedent, simply to avoid arbitration that was agreed to by the decedent.

In sum, the wrongful death claims in this case are clearly within the scope of the arbitration agreement. With respect to whether they are arbitrable, we conclude that the estate and statutory heirs are bound by the arbitration agreement to the same extent that Stewart would have been bound. Therefore, they are required to arbitrate their wrongful death claims under the arbitration agreement signed by Stewart.

CONCLUSION

For the foregoing reasons, we answer the certified question in the affirmative and hold that the execution of a nursing home arbitration agreement by a party with the capacity to contract binds the decedent's estate and statutory heirs in a subsequent wrongful death action arising from an alleged tort within the scope of an otherwise valid arbitration agreement. Accordingly, we approve the Fifth District's decision.

Not all courts follow Florida in holding a resident's agreement to arbitrate binds the heirs in a wrongful death action. Generally speaking, however, nursing home arbitration clauses are enforceable. In 2012, in Marmet Health Care Center v. Brown, 132 S. Ct. 1201 (2012), the U.S. Supreme Court rejected West Virginia's categorical decision that nursing home pre-dispute arbitration clauses were unenforceable as violating public policy. The West Virginia holding violated the Federal Arbitration Act, according to *Marmet*.

QUESTIONS

1. *Marmet* notwithstanding, what other arguments might a plaintiff's lawyer assert against enforcement of arbitration clauses?
2. Should arbitration clauses be allowed in settings other than nursing homes?

b. Warranties

In addition to contractually limiting their liability exposure, health care providers may contractually guarantee or warranty their services, promising certain outcomes and money back if not achieved, or offering to pay for any follow-up treatment costs. Payers may also require health care providers to warranty a certain level of care, with the understanding that payment will be denied if the standard is not met.

Francois de Brantes, Guy D'Andrea, & Meredith B. Rosenthal, *Should Health Care Come with a Warranty?*

28 Health Aff. no. 4, at w678-w687 (July/Aug. 2009)

An Imperfect Market

There is a rich economic literature on the performance of markets in which there is imperfect information about product quality. When information gathering is costly and consumers cannot fully observe product quality until after a purchase, the usual notions about competition and market outcomes fail. Many goods and services, including automobiles, consumer electronics, and legal counsel, fall into this category of so-called experience goods. Warranties (and secondary warranties that are available in some cases) can signal the manufacturer's (and market's) valuation of product quality and the risk of product failure.

Health care markets offer perhaps the most extreme example of costly search and imperfect product information. Imagine, for example, trying to identify systematically the best-value primary care physician in a major metropolitan area. In this light one can easily see, on a conceptual level, how warranties might increase the efficiency of market outcomes.

The key to making warranties viable is defining which failures are the supplier's fault and which are not. After all, suppliers offer warranties only if they think they can anticipate or control the associated risk, and they prefer to cover failures they know are largely preventable. In health care, the primary sources of uncontrollable "product failure" are patient factors, including clinical risks, comorbidities, and behavioral risks (such as failure to adhere to discharge instructions). Other sources of failure are controllable by the service providers. These might result from poorly coordinated care, errors of omission and commission, and other actions that harm patients or fail to optimize outcomes.

Some experimentation with warranties in health care has occurred where providers were confident that they had developed reliable systems and processes. More than a decade ago Lanny Johnson, a surgeon, approached one of his largest payers to conduct a two-year pilot. His idea was to create a medical episode-of-care payment for knee and shoulder arthroscopic surgery, to prove their relative effectiveness over more prevalent surgical methods. Johnson posted a $20,000 bond to release patients, payer, and hospital from liability for any unexpected charges above the negotiated case rate, thus effectively creating a warranty.

The published results of the pilot were encouraging. Price per case was in fact lower than in the comparable FFS environment. Profit margins for the surgeon and the hospital increased, while potentially avoidable complications and the number of reoperations decreased. (Johnson had to absorb the cost of four "redos," but his overall margin rose anyway.) And the patients were generally satisfied with their treatment. To balance the provider's incentive to increase the volume of knee surgeries, the payer instituted a prior authorization process but did not observe any measurable increase of unnecessary procedures.

Since then, the warranty concept has filtered into the self-pay portion of health care, such as corrective eye surgery, general cosmetic surgery, and dental care, which are often based on a global fee that includes any necessary rework by the provider. But it has taken much longer for warranties to appear in the third-party payer system. In mid-2007 the Geisinger Health System in Pennsylvania introduced a global episode price for elective cardiac bypass surgery that included a ninety-day warranty, although Geisinger did not use that term. Under its ProvenCare model, Geisinger charges a global episode price for bypass surgery, covering any preoperative, operative, and postoperative expenses up to ninety days after the surgery. Geisinger took this step after a major effort to improve its care processes based on a forty-item best-practice checklist. Geisinger has since expanded its fixed-price model to include a number of other types of episodes.

Johnson and Geisinger were driven mainly by the conviction that better surgical and patient management techniques could reduce potentially avoidable complications. They believed that delivering more reliable care would yield lower and less-variable total costs. And they believed that fixing a price at or slightly below the current average cost (which was inflated by potentially avoidable complications) could generate sufficient margins to cover the financial risk inherent in offering a warranty and reward them for high-quality care.

Such examples are intriguing, but their widespread applicability remains in question. Could warranties be used in arm's-length provider payment arrangements generally? What—exactly—would these warranties cover? How would such a payment model affect providers' profitability and behavior? What would providers need to consider before accepting a warranty approach? And what must payers consider before deciding what they are willing to pay? . . .

As the excerpt indicates, warranties have become more common, especially within some medical specialties. For example, ophthalmologists may offer "lifetime guarantees" for refractive surgery, such as LASIK, a procedure that uses lasers to shape the cornea in order to cure nearsightedness. One provider's Web site, for example, touts:

> [W]e are so confident in our laser eye surgeons and the high quality of vision that our patients achieve that we offer you the Lifetime Assurance Plan.
>
> If at any time you experience visual changes, you will receive a same-technology procedure free of charge when deemed medically appropriate by the surgeon. While perfection cannot be guaranteed, with the Lifetime Assurance Plan, we'll help you maintain your personal best vision throughout your life.

Guarantees are also common in fertility treatment. Patients with certain clinical profiles may be offered a money-back guarantee of pregnancy after a specified number of treatment cycles. Hospitals and health systems, like Geisinger, may also offer warranties on some procedures, such hip and knee replacements, with the hospital agreeing to cover the costs of avoidable, surgery-related complications.

PROBLEM

Draft a warranty for an anterior cruciate ligament (ACL) repair, in 300 words or less.

c. Reimbursement Policy

Payers, including government health care programs, have also required providers to effectively warranty the care that they provide by denying payment for egregious mistakes or complications. These "never event" policies are part of a larger movement to align payment with performance and quality. Inasmuch as providers agree to certain reimbursement rules as a condition of participating in government health care programs or managed care networks, the policies effectively operate as contractual agreements to provide a certain standard of care.

The ACA included several initiatives designed to link Medicare payment with quality of care. One that has drawn considerable attention is the Medicare Shared Savings Program (MSSP), which rewards providers that create or participate in ACOs (discussed in Chapter 2). The Hospital Readmissions Reduction Program reduces payments to acute care hospitals with high rates of readmission for certain conditions within 30 days of discharge. The Value-Based Purchasing Program provides payment enhancements based on certain performance measures. Finally, the Hospital-Acquired Condition (HAC) Reduction Program reduces payment to hospitals that perform the worst in terms of a list of 14 common HACs, including falls and trauma, foreign object retained after surgery, blood incompatibility, surgical site infection, and catheter-associated urinary tract infections. The following press release predates these ACA pay-for-performance innovations but offers a clear policy statement regarding quality of care warranties in government health care program reimbursement.

Eliminating Serious, Preventable, and Costly Medical Errors — Never Events

Date: 2006-05-18
Title: ELIMINATING SERIOUS, PREVENTABLE, AND COSTLY MEDICAL ERRORS — NEVER EVENTS
For Immediate Release: Thursday, May 18, 2006

Contact: press@cms.hhs.gov

OVERVIEW

As part of its ongoing effort to pay for better care, not just more services and higher costs, the Centers for Medicare & Medicaid Services (CMS) today announced that it is investigating ways that Medicare can help to reduce or eliminate the occurrence of "never events" — serious and costly errors in the provision of health care services that should never happen. "Never events," like surgery on the wrong body part or mismatched blood transfusion, cause serious injury or death to beneficiaries, and result in increased costs to the Medicare program to treat the consequences of the error.

BACKGROUND

According to the National Quality Forum (NQF), "never events" are errors in medical care that are clearly identifiable, preventable, and serious in their consequences for patients, and that indicate a real problem in the safety and credibility of a health care facility. The criteria for "never events" are listed in Appendix 1. Examples of "never events" include surgery on the wrong body part; foreign body left in a patient after surgery; mismatched blood transfusion; major medication error; severe "pressure ulcer" acquired in the hospital; and preventable post-operative deaths. NQF's full list is included in Appendix 2. NQF developed this list with support from CMS.

While the exact number of "never events" is not known, they result in many deaths and additional health care costs. In 1999, the Institute of Medicine (IOM) estimated that as many as 98,000 deaths a year were attributable to medical errors, and recommended that error-related deaths be decreased by 50 percent over five years. A second study concluded that "never events" add significantly to Medicare hospital payments, ranging from an average of an additional $700 per case to treat decubitus ulcers to $9,000 per case to treat postoperative sepsis. Another study, reviewing 18 types of medical events, concluded that medical errors may account for 2.4 million extra hospital days, $9.3 billion in excess charges (for all payers), and 32,600 deaths.

Some states have enacted legislation requiring reporting of incidents on the NQF list. . . .

Questions have been raised about whether such mandatory reporting leads to accurate estimates, because of the continued potential for underreporting of "never events." Even with incomplete estimates, it is clear that, while there has been improvement in some areas of quality and safety since the IOM report, our health care system still has not reached the IOM's goal of a 50 percent reduction in the number of deaths due to medical errors. Consequently, working with provider associations and other public and private groups, the Centers for Medicare & Medicaid Services is taking further steps to prevent "never events."

NEXT STEPS

From its beginning, the Medicare program has generally paid for services under fee-for-service payment systems, without regard to quality, outcomes, or overall costs of care. In the past several years, CMS has been working with provider groups to identify quality standards that can be a basis for public reporting and payment. This includes the efforts of the Hospital Quality Alliance, which has developed an expanding set of quality measures. As a result of the Medicare Modernization Act and the Deficit Reduction Act, hospitals that publicly report these quality measures receive higher Medicare payment updates. In addition, CMS has launched a number of demonstrations aimed at improving quality of care, including by tying payment to quality. These include the Physician Group Practice Demonstration, the Premier Hospital Quality Incentive Demonstration, the Health Care Quality Demonstration, and the Care Management Performance Demonstration. As the results of these demonstrations become available, CMS expects to work with Congress on legislation that would support adjusting payments based on quality and efficiency of care.

> Medicare fee-for-service reimbursement creates a perverse incentive to treat more in order to get paid more. Accordingly, poor-quality treatment may even be incentivized so that more treatment is necessary. The never-event policy fights that impulse.

Clearly, paying for "never events" is not consistent with the goals of these Medicare payment reforms. Reducing or eliminating payments for "never events" means more resources can be directed toward preventing these events rather than paying more when they occur. The Deficit Reduction Act represents a first step in this direction, allowing CMS, beginning in FY 2008, to begin to adjust payments for hospital-acquired infections. CMS is interested in working with our partners and Congress to build on this initial step to more broadly address the persistence of "never events."

In particular, CMS is reviewing its administrative authority to reduce payments for "never events," and to provide more reliable information to the public about when they occur. CMS will also work with Congress on further legislative steps to reduce or eliminate these payments. CMS intends to partner with hospitals and other healthcare organizations in these efforts.

APPENDIX 1

CRITERIA FOR INCLUSION ON THE NEVER EVENT LIST

To be included on NQF's list of "never events," an event had to have been characterized as:

- Unambiguous — clearly identifiable and measurable, and thus feasible to include in a reporting system;
- Usually preventable — recognizing that some events are not always avoidable, given the complexity of health care;
- Serious — resulting in death or loss of a body part, disability, or more than transient loss of a body function; and
- Any of the following:

Adverse and/or,
Indicative of a problem in a health care facility's safety systems and/or,
Important for public credibility or public accountability.

APPENDIX 2

CURRENT NATIONAL QUALITY FORUM LIST OF "NEVER EVENTS"
Surgical Events

- Surgery performed on the wrong body part
- Surgery performed on the wrong patient
- Wrong surgical procedure on a patient
- Retention of a foreign object in a patient after surgery or other procedure

- Intraoperative or immediately post-operative death in a normal health patient (defined as a Class 1 patient for purposes of the American Society of Anesthesiologists patient safety initiative)

Product or Device Events

- Patient death or serious disability associated with the use of contaminated drugs, devices, or biologics provided by the healthcare facility
- Patient death or serious disability associated with the use or function of a device in patient care in which the device is used or functions other than as intended
- Patient death or serious disability associated with intravascular air embolism that occurs while being cared for in a healthcare facility

Patient Protection Events

- Infant discharged to the wrong person
- Patient death or serious disability associated with patient elopement (disappearance) for more than four hours
- Patient suicide, or attempted suicide resulting in serious disability, while being cared for in a healthcare facility

Care Management Events

- Patient death or serious disability associated with a medication error (e.g., error involving the wrong drug, wrong dose, wrong patient, wrong time, wrong rate, wrong preparation, or wrong route of administration)
- Patient death or serious disability associated with a hemolytic reaction due to the administration of ABO-incompatible blood or blood products
- Maternal death or serious disability associated with labor or delivery on a low-risk pregnancy while being cared for in a healthcare facility
- Patient death or serious disability associated with hypoglycemia, the onset of which occurs while the patient is being cared for in a healthcare facility
- Death or serious disability (kernicterus) associated with failure to identify and treat hyperbilirubinemia in neonates
- Stage 3 or 4 pressure ulcers acquired after admission to a healthcare facility
- Patient death or serious disability due to spinal manipulative therapy

Environmental Events

- Patient death or serious disability associated with an electric shock while being cared for in a healthcare facility
- Any incident in which a line designated for oxygen or other gas to be delivered to a patient contains the wrong gas or is contaminated by toxic substances
- Patient death or serious disability associated with a burn incurred from any source while being cared for in a healthcare facility
- Patient death associated with a fall while being cared for in a healthcare facility
- Patient death or serious disability associated with the use of restraints or bedrails while being cared for in a healthcare facility

Criminal Events

- Any instance of care ordered by or provided by someone impersonating a physician, nurse, pharmacist, or other licensed healthcare provider

- Abduction of a patient of any age
- Sexual assault on a patient within or on the grounds of a healthcare facility
- Death or significant injury of a patient or staff member resulting from a physical assault (i.e., battery) that occurs within or on the grounds of a healthcare facility

---

QUESTIONS

1. Should courts be more willing to enforce contractual limits on financial liability between payers and providers, as compared to similar agreements between providers and patients?
2. Which operates as a better incentive for safety: potential tort liability or potential denial of payment?

3. DIRECT GOVERNMENT REGULATION OF QUALITY

A third approach to enforcing certain standards of care by health care providers is through government regulation. This part of the chapter considers ways in which regulatory regimes, rather than common law, may protect patients and ensure quality of care.

a. State Licensure

One regulatory approach to regulating standards for quality of care is through professional and facility licensure, which every state requires. The effect of those laws is to prohibit patients and providers from entering contracts with respect to certain services unless the provider has been licensed by the state according to specified standards designed to ensure safe medical care. Licensure is often justified by the information asymmetrics problem, which we described in Chapter 1 and implicitly revisit throughout this chapter. That is, patients are unable to judge the quality of care offered by providers and should be prevented from exposing themselves to the risk of care by unlicensed providers.

Licensure for the practice of medicine and related professions is the norm. The following Virginia Board of Medicine regulations provide an example of the requirements for licensure under state law.

Regulations Governing the Practice of Medicine, Osteopathy, Podiatry and Chiropractic

Virginia Board of Medicine
Title of Regulations: 18 VAC 85-20-10 et seq.
Statutory Authority: §54.1-2400 and Chapter 29 of
Title 54.1 of the Code of Virginia
(Revised Date: January 27, 2016)

18VAC85-20-120. Prerequisites to licensure
Every applicant for licensure shall:

1. Meet the educational requirements specified in 18VAC85-20-121 or 18VAC85-20-122 and the examination requirements as specified for each profession in 18VAC85-20-140;

2. File the complete application and appropriate fee as specified in 18VAC85-20-22 with the executive director of the board; and

3. File the required credentials with the executive director as specified below:

    a. Graduates of an approved institution shall file:

        (1) Documentary evidence that he received a degree from the institution; and

        (2) A complete chronological record of all professional activities since graduation from professional school, giving location, dates, and types of services performed.

    b. Graduates of an institution not approved by an accrediting agency recognized by the board shall file:

        (1) Documentary evidence of education as required by 18VAC85-20-122;

        (2) A translation made and endorsed by a consul or by a professional translating service of all such documents not in the English language; and

        (3) A complete chronological record of all professional activities since graduation from professional school, giving location, dates, and types of services performed.

18VAC85-20-121. Educational requirements: Graduates of approved institutions

A. Such an applicant shall be a graduate of an institution that meets the criteria appropriate to the profession in which he seeks to be licensed, which are as follows:

    1. For licensure in medicine. The institution shall be approved or accredited by the Liaison Committee on Medical Education or other official accrediting body recognized by the American Medical Association, or by the Committee for the Accreditation of Canadian Medical Schools or its appropriate subsidiary agencies or any other organization approved by the board.

    . . . .

    [The regulations further specify educational requirements for podiatry, osteopathy, and chiropractic.]

18VAC85-20-140. Examinations, general

A. The Executive Director of the Board of Medicine or his designee shall review each application for licensure and in no case shall an applicant be licensed unless there is evidence that the applicant has passed an examination equivalent to the Virginia Board of Medicine examination required at the time he was examined and meets all requirements of Part III (18VAC85-20-120 et seq.) of this chapter. If the executive director or his designee is not fully satisfied that the applicant meets all applicable requirements of Part III of this chapter and this part, he shall refer the application to the Credentials Committee for a determination on licensure.

B. A Doctor of Medicine or Osteopathic Medicine who has passed the examination of the National Board of Medical Examiners or of the National Board of Osteopathic Medical Examiners, Federation Licensing Examination, or the United States Medical Licensing Examination, or the examination of the Licensing Medical Council of Canada or other such examinations as prescribed in §54.1-2913.1 of the Code of Virginia may be accepted for licensure. . . .

QUESTIONS

1. Are the various requirements for licensure reasonable as measures to protect public health and safety?
2. Could the same information be made available to patients, while leaving them the choice regarding which provider to see? How does your answer fit with the Kenneth Arrow excerpt in Chapter 1?

b. Report Cards and Databases

In addition to requirements for licensure, Virginia, like many states, further requires licensed doctors to disclose certain information, which may be made publicly available. Disclosure is another way of addressing the information asymmetries in health care and addressing quality of care concerns.

Va. Code §54.1-2910.1. Certain data required

A. The Board of Medicine shall require all doctors of medicine, osteopathy and podiatry to report and shall make available the following information:

1. The names of the schools of medicine, osteopathy, or podiatry and the years of graduation;

2. Any graduate medical, osteopathic, or podiatric education at any institution approved by the Accreditation Council for Graduation Medical Education, the American Osteopathic Association or the Council on Podiatric Medical Education;

3. Any specialty board certification as approved by the American Board of Medical Specialties, the Bureau of Osteopathic Specialists of the American Osteopathic Association, the American Board of Multiple Specialties in Podiatry, or the Council on Podiatric Medical Education of the American Podiatric Medical Association;

4. The number of years in active, clinical practice as specified by regulations of the Board;

5. Any hospital affiliations;

6. Any appointments, within the most recent 10-year period, of the doctor to the faculty of a school of medicine, osteopathy or podiatry and any publications in peer-reviewed literature within the most recent five-year period and as specified by regulations of the Board;

7. The location and telephone number of any primary and secondary practice settings and the approximate percentage of the doctor's time spent practicing in each setting. For the sole purpose of expedited dissemination of information about a public health emergency, the doctor shall also provide to the Board any e-mail address or facsimile number; however, such e-mail address or facsimile number shall not be published on the profile database and shall not be released or made available for any other purpose;

8. The access to any translating service provided to the primary and secondary practice settings of the doctor;

9. The status of the doctor's participation in the Virginia Medicaid Program;

10. Any final disciplinary or other action required to be reported to the Board by health care institutions, other practitioners, insurance companies, health maintenance organizations, and professional organizations pursuant to 54.1-2400.6, 54.1-2908, and 54.1-2909 that results in a suspension or revocation of privileges or the termination of employment or a final order of the Board relating to disciplinary action;

11. Conviction of any felony; and

12. Other information related to the competency of doctors of medicine, osteopathy, and podiatry, as specified in the regulations of the Board.

B. In addition, the Board shall provide for voluntary reporting of insurance plans accepted and managed care plans in which the doctor participates.

QUESTIONS

1. What other information might you, as a patient, like to have disclosed regarding your health care providers? How likely are you to use that information when deciding which primary care physician, specialist, or hospital to go to?
2. Recall the discussion of the Stark Law in Chapter 6 and other topics regarding physicians' conflicts of interest in Chapter 5; would simple disclosure regarding those conflicts be adequate to protect patients?

Virtually all states have established some quality reporting system to assess health care providers. Some states' health care provider report cards contain detailed information, including physicians' mortality rates or other outcome data, which may provoke physicians to avoid higher-risk, less-healthy patients who may decrease their quality ratings. Patients may not use report card data, which arguably would be more useful than seeking referrals from friends or other providers. New York recently considered shutting its program down as too expensive, especially given that most of the information is readily available from other sources, including privately maintained health grading Web sites: http://takingnote.blogs.nytimes.com/2015/02/24/report-card-for-doctors/.

The trend of state health care report cards is more recent. But since 1986, HHS has maintained a National Practitioner Data Bank (NPDB). The NPDB was a key component of the Health Care Quality Improvement Act (HCQIA). The NPDB operates as an electronic repository, containing information on medical malpractice payments and certain adverse actions related to health care practitioners, entities, providers, and suppliers. The data are not available to the public, and organizations must be authorized by federal law to report to or query the NPDB. The following regulations outline duties to report and query.

45 C.F.R. §60.5. When information must be reported

Information required under §§60.7, 60.8, and 60.12 must be submitted to the NPDB within 30 days following the action to be reported, beginning with actions occurring on or after September 1, 1990; information required under §60.11 must be submitted to the NPDB within 30 days following the action to be reported, beginning with actions occurring on or after January 1, 1992; and information required under §§60.9, 60.10, 60.13, 60.14, 60.15, and 60.16 must be submitted to the NPDB within 30 days following the action to be reported, beginning with actions occurring on or after August 21, 1996.

Persons or entities responsible for submitting reports of malpractice payments (§60.7), negative actions or findings (§60.11), or adverse actions (§60.12) must additionally provide to their respective state authorities a copy of the report they submit to the NPDB. Following is the list of reportable actions:

(a) Malpractice payments (§60.7);

(b) Licensure and certification actions (§§60.8, 60.9, and 60.10);

(c) Negative actions or findings (§60.11);

(d) Adverse actions (§60.12);

(e) Health Care-related Criminal Convictions (§60.13);

(f) Health Care-related Civil Judgments (§60.14);

(g) Exclusions from Federal or state health care programs (§60.15); and

(h) Other adjudicated actions of decisions (§60.16).

45 C.F.R. §60.17. Information which hospitals must request from the National Practitioner Data Bank

(a) When information must be requested. Each hospital, either directly or through an authorized agent, must request information from the NPDB concerning a health care practitioner, as follows:

(1) At the time a health care practitioner applies for a position on its medical staff (courtesy or otherwise) or for clinical privileges at the hospital; and

(2) Every 2 years for any health care practitioner who is on its medical staff (courtesy or otherwise) or has clinical privileges at the hospital.

(b) Failure to request information. Any hospital which does not request the information as required in paragraph (a) of this section is presumed to have knowledge of any information reported to the NPDB concerning this health care practitioner.

(c) Reliance on the obtained information. Each hospital may rely upon the information provided by the NPDB to the hospital. A hospital shall not be held liable for this reliance unless the hospital has knowledge that the information provided was false.

The NPDB is aimed primarily at physicians with medical staff privileges at hospitals. It operates as a national clearinghouse of information so that physicians who are disciplined in one locale cannot simply move elsewhere and establish privileges there, while exposing patients to the same risk of poor quality or negligent treatment. Despite its mandatory duties, underreporting has plagued the NPDB, making it a less than fully effective tool for ensuring that incompetent physicians do not continue treating patients.

c. Peer Review

Staff, or clinical, privileges refer to authority granted to a physician by a hospital governing board to provide patient care in the hospital. Until relatively recently, most physicians were not employed by hospitals but instead were independent contractors with "privileges" at one or more hospitals. The scope of the privileges varies; some physicians merely have rights to admit their patients to the hospital or to provide consultations, while others have privileges to treat their patients by performing surgeries or other interventions.

To obtain privileges, physicians undergo "peer review," conducted by a committee of physicians, who are ultimately overseen by the hospital board of directors. Although the board of directors has the final say on privileging decisions, the physician peer review committee operates largely autonomously and with considerable influence. The criteria for granting privileges are promulgated under medical staff bylaws and traditionally focus on quality of care (e.g., education, experience, training, board certification, other appointments or affiliations, and references). More recent judicial decisions have also allowed hospitals to take economic considerations into account, including efficiency and potential for competition with the hospital, when granting or denying privileges. The following case further illustrates the challenges of relying on voluntary disclosure within the peer review context, specifically, and as a way of regulating quality of health care, more generally.

> Chapter 4 discusses the role of the medical staff from a corporate governance perspective; here, we consider how medical staff privileges can act as a quality control device in hospitals.

Kadlec Medical Center v. Lakeview Anesthesia Associates

527 F.3d 412 (5th Cir. 2008)

. . . .

I. Factual Background

Dr. Berry was a licensed anesthesiologist in Louisiana and practiced with Drs. William Preau, Mark Dennis, David Baldone, and Allan Parr at LAA. From November 2000 until his termination on March 13, 2001, Dr. Berry was a shareholder of LAA, the exclusive provider of anesthesia services to Lakeview Medical (a Louisiana hospital).

In November 2000, a small management team at Lakeview Medical investigated Dr. Berry after nurses expressed concern about his undocumented and suspicious withdrawals of Demerol. The investigative team found excessive Demerol withdrawals by Dr. Berry and a lack of documentation for the withdrawals.

Lakeview Medical CEO Max Lauderdale discussed the team's findings with Dr. Berry and Dr. Dennis. Dr. Dennis then discussed Dr. Berry's situation with his partners. They all agreed that Dr. Berry's use of Demerol had to be controlled and monitored. But Dr. Berry did not follow the agreement or account for his continued Demerol withdrawals. Three months later, Dr. Berry failed to answer a page while on-duty at Lakeview Medical. He was discovered in the call-room, asleep, groggy, and unfit to work. Personnel immediately called Dr. Dennis, who found Dr. Berry not communicating well and unable to work. Dr. Dennis had Dr. Berry taken away after Dr. Berry said that he had taken prescription medications.

Lauderdale, Lakeview Medical's CEO, decided that it was in the best interest of patient safety that Dr. Berry not practice at the hospital. Dr. Dennis and his three partners at LAA fired Dr. Berry and signed his termination letter on March 27, 2001, which explained that he was fired "for cause":

> [You have been fired for cause because] you have reported to work in an impaired physical, mental, and emotional state. Your impaired condition has prevented you from properly performing your duties and puts our patients at significant risk. . . .
> [P]lease consider your termination effective March 13, 2001.

At Lakeview Medical, Lauderdale ordered the Chief Nursing Officer to notify the administration if Dr. Berry returned.

Despite recognizing Dr. Berry's drug problem and the danger he posed to patients, neither Dr. Dennis nor Lauderdale reported Dr. Berry's impairment to the hospital's Medical Executive Committee, eventually noting only that Dr. Berry was "no longer employed by LAA." Neither one reported Dr. Berry's impairment to Lakeview Medical's Board of Trustees, and no one on behalf of Lakeview Medical reported Dr. Berry's impairment or discipline to the Louisiana Board of Medical Examiners or to the National Practitioner's Data Bank. In fact, at some point Lauderdale took the unusual step of locking away in his office all files, audits, plans, and notes concerning Dr. Berry and the investigation.

> The medical profession has long been characterized by a "conspiracy of silence." Does that explain the defendants' actions here?

After leaving LAA and Lakeview Medical, Dr. Berry briefly obtained work as a locum tenens (traveling physician) at a hospital in Shreveport, Louisiana. In October 2001, he applied through Staff Care, a leading locum tenens staffing firm, for locum tenens privileges at Kadlec Medical Center in Washington State. After receiving his application, Kadlec began its credentialing process. Kadlec examined a variety of materials, including referral letters from LAA and Lakeview Medical.

LAA's Dr. Preau and Dr. Dennis, two months after firing Dr. Berry for his on-the-job drug use, submitted referral letters for Dr. Berry to Staff Care, with the intention that they be provided to future employers. The letter from Dr. Dennis stated that he had worked with Dr. Berry for four years, that he was an excellent clinician, and that he would be an asset to any anesthesia service. Dr. Preau's letter said that he worked with Berry at Lakeview Medical and that he recommended him highly as an anesthesiologist. Dr. Preau's and Dr. Dennis's letters were submitted on June 3, 2001, only sixty-eight days after they fired him for using narcotics while on-duty and stating in his termination letter that Dr. Berry's behavior put "patients at significant risk."

On October 17, 2001, Kadlec sent Lakeview Medical a request for credentialing information about Berry. The request included a detailed confidential questionnaire, a delineation of privileges, and a signed consent for release of information. The interrogatories on the questionnaire asked whether "[Dr. Berry] has been subject to any disciplinary action," if "[Dr. Berry has] the ability (health status) to perform the privileges requested," whether "[Dr. Berry has] shown any signs of behavior/personality problems or impairments," and whether Dr. Berry has satisfactory "judgement."

Nine days later, Lakeview Medical responded to the requests for credentialing information about fourteen different physicians. In thirteen cases, it responded fully and completely to the request, filling out forms with all the information asked for by the requesting health care provider. The fourteenth request, from Kadlec concerning Berry, was handled differently. Instead of completing the multi-part forms, Lakeview Medical staff drafted a short letter. In its entirety, it read:

> This letter is written in response to your inquiry regarding [Dr. Berry]. Due to the large volume of inquiries received in this office, the following information is provided.
>
> Our records indicate that Dr. Robert L. Berry was on the Active Medical Staff of Lakeview Regional Medical Center in the field of Anesthesiology from March 04, 1997 through September 04, 2001.
>
> If I can be of further assistance, you may contact me at (504) 867-4076.

The letter did not disclose LAA's termination of Dr. Berry; his on-duty drug use; the investigation into Dr. Berry's undocumented and suspicious withdrawals of

Demerol that "violated the standard of care"; or any other negative information. The employee who drafted the letter said at trial that she just followed a form letter, which is one of many that Lakeview Medical used.

Kadlec then credentialed Dr. Berry, and he began working there. After working at Kadlec without incident for a number of months, he moved temporarily to Montana where he worked at Benefis Hospital. During his stay in Montana, he was in a car accident and suffered a back injury. Kadlec's head of anesthesiology and the credentialing department all knew of Dr. Berry's accident and back injury, but they did not investigate whether it would impair his work.

After Dr. Berry returned to Kadlec, some nurses thought that he appeared sick and exhibited mood swings. One nurse thought that Dr. Berry's entire demeanor had changed and that he should be watched closely. In mid-September 2002, Dr. Berry gave a patient too much morphine during surgery, and she had to be revived using Narcan. The neurosurgeon was irate about the incident.

On November 12, 2002, Dr. Berry was assigned to the operating room beginning at 6:30 a.m. He worked with three different surgeons and multiple nurses well into the afternoon. According to one nurse, Dr. Berry was "screwing up all day" and several of his patients suffered adverse effects from not being properly anesthetized. He had a hacking cough and multiple nurses thought he looked sick. During one procedure, he apparently almost passed out.

Kimberley Jones was Dr. Berry's fifth patient that morning. She was in for what should have been a routine, fifteen minute tubal ligation. When they moved her into the recovery room, one nurse noticed that her fingernails were blue, and she was not breathing. Dr. Berry failed to resuscitate her, and she is now in a permanent vegetative state.

Dr. Berry's nurse went directly to her supervisor the next morning and expressed concern that Dr. Berry had a narcotics problem. Dr. Berry later admitted to Kadlec staff that he had been diverting and using Demerol since his June car accident in Montana and that he had become addicted to Demerol. Dr. Berry wrote a confession, and he immediately admitted himself into a drug rehabilitation program.

Jones's family sued Dr. Berry and Kadlec in Washington. Dr. Berry's insurer settled the claim against him. After the Washington court ruled that Kadlec would be responsible for Dr. Berry's conduct under respondeat superior, Western, Kadlec's insurer, settled the claim against Kadlec.

II. Procedural History

Kadlec and Western filed this suit in Louisiana district court against LAA, Dr. Dennis, Dr. Preau, Dr. Baldone, Dr. Parr, and Lakeview Medical, asserting Louisiana state law claims for intentional misrepresentation, negligent misrepresentation, strict responsibility misrepresentation, and general negligence. Plaintiffs alleged that defendants' tortious activity led to Kadlec's hiring of Dr. Berry and the resulting millions of dollars it had to expend settling the Jones lawsuit. Plaintiffs' claim against LAA for negligence, based on a negligent monitoring and investigation theory, was dismissed before trial.

Plaintiffs' surviving claims for intentional and negligent misrepresentation arise out of the alleged misrepresentations in, and omissions from, the defendants' referral letters for Dr. Berry. These claims were tried to a jury, which returned a verdict in favor of the plaintiffs on both claims. The jury awarded plaintiffs $8.24 million, which is approximately equivalent to the amount Western spent settling the Jones lawsuit ($7.5 million) plus the amount it spent on attorneys' fees, costs, and expenses (approximately $744,000) associated with the Jones lawsuit. The jury also found Kadlec and Dr. Berry negligent. The jury apportioned fault as follows: Dr. Dennis 20%; Dr. Preau 5%; Lakeview Medical 25%; Kadlec 17%; and Dr. Berry 33%. The judgments against Dr. Dennis and Dr. Preau were in solido with LAA. Because defendants were found liable for intentional misrepresentation, plaintiffs' recovery was not reduced by the percentage of fault ascribed to Kadlec. But the amount was reduced to $5.52 million to account for Dr. Berry's 33% of the fault. The district court entered judgment against Lakeview Medical and LAA.

III. Discussion

A. The Intentional and Negligent Misrepresentation Claims

The plaintiffs allege that the defendants committed two torts: intentional misrepresentation and negligent misrepresentation. The elements of a claim for intentional misrepresentation in Louisiana are: (1) a misrepresentation of a material fact; (2) made with intent to deceive; and (3) causing justifiable reliance with resultant injury. To establish a claim for intentional misrepresentation when it is by silence or inaction, plaintiffs also must show that the defendant owed a duty to the plaintiff to disclose the information. To make out a negligent misrepresentation claim in Louisiana: (1) there must be a legal duty on the part of the defendant to supply correct information; (2) there must be a breach of that duty, which can occur by omission as well as by affirmative misrepresentation; and (3) the breach must have caused damages to the plaintiff based on the plaintiff's reasonable reliance on the misrepresentation.

The defendants argue that any representations in, or omissions from, the referral letters cannot establish liability. We begin our analysis below by holding that after choosing to write referral letters, the defendants assumed a duty not to make affirmative misrepresentations in the letters. We next analyze whether the letters were misleading, and we conclude that the LAA defendants' letters were misleading, but the letter from Lakeview Medical was not. We also examine whether the defendants had an affirmative duty to disclose negative information about Dr. Berry in their referral letters, and we conclude that there was not an affirmative duty to disclose. Based on these holdings, Lakeview Medical did not breach any duty owed to Kadlec, and therefore the judgment against it is reversed. Finally, we examine other challenges to the LAA defendants' liability, and we conclude that they are without merit.

> The court finds that the defendants assumed a duty to disclose non-negligently by undertaking to write the referral letter.

1. The Affirmative Misrepresentations

The defendants owed a duty to Kadlec to avoid affirmative misrepresentations in the referral letters. In Louisiana, "[a]lthough a party may keep absolute silence and violate no rule of law or equity, . . . if he volunteers to speak and to convey information which may influence the conduct of the other party, he is bound to [disclose] the whole truth." In negligent misrepresentation cases, Louisiana courts have held that even when there is no initial duty to disclose information, "once [a party] volunteer[s] information, it assume[s] a duty to insure that the information volunteered [is] correct."

Consistent with these cases, the defendants had a legal duty not to make affirmative misrepresentations in their referral letters. A party does not incur liability every time it casually makes an incorrect statement. But if an employer makes a misleading statement in a referral letter about the performance of its former employee, the former employer may be liable for its statements if the facts and circumstances warrant. Here, defendants were recommending an anesthesiologist, who held the lives of patients in his hands every day. Policy considerations dictate that the defendants had a duty to avoid misrepresentations in their referral letters if they misled plaintiffs into thinking that Dr. Berry was an "excellent" anesthesiologist, when they had information that he was a drug addict. Indeed, if defendants' statements created a misapprehension about Dr. Berry's suitability to work as an anesthesiologist, then by "volunteer[ing] to speak and to convey information which . . . influence[d] the conduct of [Kadlec], [they were] bound to [disclose] the whole truth." In other words, if they created a misapprehension about Dr. Berry due to their own statements, they incurred a duty to disclose information about his drug use and for-cause firing to complete the whole picture.

We now review whether there is evidence that the defendants' letters were misleading. We start with the LAA defendants. The letter from Dr. Preau stated that Dr. Berry was an "excellent anesthesiologist" and that he "recommend[ed] him highly." Dr. Dennis's letter said that Dr. Berry was "an excellent physician" who "he is sure will be an asset to [his future employer's] anesthesia service." These letters are false on their face and materially misleading. Notably, these letters came only sixty-eight days after Drs. Dennis and Preau, on behalf of LAA, signed a letter terminating Dr. Berry for using narcotics while on-duty and stating that Dr. Berry's behavior put "patients at significant risk." Furthermore, because of the misleading statements in the letters, Dr. Dennis and Dr. Preau incurred a duty to cure these misleading statements by disclosing to Kadlec that Dr. Berry had been fired for on-the-job drug use.

The question as to whether Lakeview Medical's letter was misleading is more difficult. The letter does not comment on Dr. Berry's proficiency as an anesthesiologist, and it does not recommend him to Kadlec. Kadlec says that the letter is misleading because Lakeview Medical stated that it could not reply to Kadlec's detailed inquiry in full "[d]ue to the large volume of inquiries received." But whatever the real reason that Lakeview Medical did not respond in full to Kadlec's inquiry, Kadlec did not present evidence that this could have affirmatively misled it into thinking that Dr. Berry had an uncheckered history at Lakeview Medical.

Kadlec also says that the letter was misleading because it erroneously reported that Dr. Berry was on Lakeview Medical's active medical staff until September 4, 2001. Kadlec presented testimony that had it known that Dr. Berry never returned to Lakeview Medical after March 13, 2001, it would have been suspicious about the apparently large gap in his employment. While it is true that Dr. Berry did not return to Lakeview Medical after March 13, this did not terminate his privileges at the hospital, or mean that he was not on "active medical staff." In fact, it appears that Dr. Berry submitted a formal resignation letter on October 1, 2001, weeks after September 4. Therefore, while the September 4 date does not accurately reflect when Dr. Berry was no longer on Lakeview Medical's active medical staff, it did not mislead Kadlec into thinking that he had less of a gap in employment than he actually had.

In sum, we hold that the letters from the LAA defendants were affirmatively misleading, but the letter from Lakeview Medical was not. Therefore, Lakeview Medical cannot be held liable based on its alleged affirmative misrepresentations. It can only be liable if it had an affirmative duty to disclose information about Dr. Berry. We now examine the theory that, even assuming that there were no misleading statements in the referral letters, the defendants had an affirmative duty to disclose. We discuss this theory with regard to both defendants for reasons that will be clear by the end of the opinion.

2. *The Duty to Disclose*

In Louisiana, a duty to disclose does not exist absent special circumstances, such as a fiduciary or confidential relationship between the parties, which, under the circumstances, justifies the imposition of the duty. Louisiana cases suggest that before a duty to disclose is imposed the defendant must have had a pecuniary interest in the transaction. . . .

Plaintiffs assert that Lakeview Medical and the LAA doctors had a pecuniary interest in the referral letters supplied to Kadlec. The plaintiffs rely on the pecuniary interest definition in the Second Restatement of Torts. Section 552, comment d of the Restatement, provides (with emphasis added):

> The defendant's pecuniary interest in supplying the information will normally lie in a consideration paid to him for it or paid in a transaction in the course of and as a part of which it is supplied. It may, however, be of a more indirect character. . . .
>
> *The fact that the information is given in the course of the defendant's business, profession or employment is a sufficient indication that he has a pecuniary interest in it, even though he receives no consideration for it at the time.* It is not, however, conclusive. . . .

The "course of business" definition of pecuniary interest has been endorsed by Louisiana appellate courts. In *Anderson v. Heck*, the court defined the "pecuniary interest" of the defendant by directly quoting and applying the portion of the Restatement comment highlighted above. The court in *Dousson v. South Central Bell* held that the fact that information is given in the course of a party's business or profession is a sufficient indication of pecuniary interest even though the party receives no consideration for it at the time.

The defendants argue that, even assuming the Restatement governs, they did not have a pecuniary interest in providing reference information. They contend that any information provided to future employers about Dr. Berry was gratuitous, and they point out that the Restatement's comments say that a party will not be considered to have a pecuniary interest in a transaction where the information is given "purely gratuitously."

The defendants have the better argument on the lack of pecuniary interest and, in addition, the requisite "special relationship" between the defendants and Kadlec, necessary to impose a duty to disclose, is lacking.

The court found no exception to the general rule that there is no affirmative duty to disclose.

Plaintiffs argue that policy considerations weigh in favor of recognizing a duty to disclose. They contend that imposing a duty on health care employers to disclose that a physician's drug dependence could pose a serious threat to patient safety promotes important policy goals recognized by Louisiana courts. . . .

Despite these compelling policy arguments, we do not predict that courts in Louisiana — absent misleading statements such as those made by the LAA defendants — would impose an affirmative duty to disclose. The defendants did not have a fiduciary or contractual duty to disclose what it knew to Kadlec. And although the defendants might have had an ethical obligation to disclose their knowledge of Dr. Berry's drug problems, they were also rightly concerned about a possible defamation claim if they communicated negative information about Dr. Berry. As a general policy matter, even if an employer believes that its disclosure is protected because of the truth of the matter communicated, it would be burdensome to impose a duty on employers, upon receipt of an employment referral request, to investigate whether the negative information it has about an employee fits within the courts' description of which negative information must be disclosed to the future employer. Finally, concerns about protecting employee privacy weigh in favor of not mandating a potentially broad duty to disclose.

The Louisiana court in *Louviere* recognized that no court in Louisiana has imposed on an employer a duty to disclose information about a former employee to a future employer. Furthermore, we have not found a single case outside of Louisiana where a court imposed an affirmative duty on an employer to disclose negative information about a former employee. Some courts have held that employers have a legal duty to disclose negative information about former employees who later cause foreseeable physical harm in their new jobs, at least when there are misleading statements made by the former employer. But each of these cases based its conclusion on the fact that the former employer had made affirmative misrepresentations in its referral, and none imposed a duty based on the employer's mere nondisclosure. These cases reinforce our conclusion that the defendants had a duty to avoid misleading statements in their referral letters, but they do not support plaintiffs' duty to disclose theory. In fact, one court explicitly held that a hospital did not have an affirmative duty to disclose a nurse's past sexual misconduct toward patients when asked for an evaluation by a prospective employer, but that "[the defendant did] not challenge the proposition that, in undertaking to provide . . . a reference, and in volunteering information about [the employee's] qualities as a nurse, it incurred a duty to use reasonable care to avoid disclosing factually misleading information."

3. *Legal Cause*

LAA contends that even if it breached a legal duty to Kadlec, the plaintiffs' claims fail for lack of legal causation. LAA argues that legal cause is not met here because Kadlec's and Dr. Berry's intervening negligence precludes concluding that it is a legal cause of plaintiffs' injuries. . . .

The LAA defendants' argument that the intervening negligence of Dr. Berry and Kadlec absolves them of liability is not accepted. Roberts held that "[i]t is well settled in Louisiana law that an intervening act does not automatically absolve a prior negligent party from liability." Whether an intervening act absolves a prior negligent actor from liability depends on the foreseeability of the act from the perspective of the original tortfeasor and whether the intervening act is "easily associated" with the risk of harm brought about by the breach of the original duty. Dr. Berry's hiring and his subsequent negligent use of narcotics while on-duty was foreseeable and "easily associated" with the LAA defendants' actions. He had

> Under Louisiana law, "legal," or proximate, cause is analyzed under the predominant "scope of the risk" or foreseeability approach.

used narcotics while on-duty in the past, and the LAA defendants could foresee that he would do so again if they misled a future employer about his drug problem.

The LAA defendants focus on Kadlec's negligence and claim that it was a superseding cause of plaintiffs' injuries. They argue that Kadlec had multiple warning signs that Dr. Berry was using drugs, and had it responded with an investigation, plaintiffs' injuries would have been avoided. The LAA defendants focus on Dr. Berry's erratic behavior after his return from Montana, his over-anesthetization of a patient in September 2002, and the signs that he was ill on the day of Jones's surgery. The jury found that Kadlec's own negligence was a cause of plaintiffs' financial injury. But this does not relieve the defendants of liability. The jury also reasonably concluded that the LAA defendants negligently and intentionally misled Kadlec about Dr. Berry's drug addiction. By intentionally covering up Dr. Berry's drug addiction in communications with a future employer, they should have foreseen that the future employer might miss the warning signs of Dr. Berry's addiction. This was within the scope of the risk they took.

Indeed, both plaintiffs' and defendants' witnesses agreed at trial that narcotics addiction is a disease, that addicts try to hide their disease from their co-workers, and that particularly in the case of narcotics-addicted anesthesiologists, for whom livelihood and drug supply are in the same place, colleagues may be the last to know about their addiction and impairment. This is not a case where a future tortious act is so unforeseeable that it should relieve the earlier tortfeasor of liability. In fact, this case illustrates why the comparative fault system was developed — so, as here, multiple actors can share fault for an injury based on their respective degrees of responsibility.

. . . .

E. Summary and Remand Instructions

The district court properly instructed the jury to find for the plaintiffs on their intentional and negligent misrepresentation claims if the jury concluded that the defendants' letters to Kadlec were intentionally and negligently misleading in a manner that caused injury to the plaintiffs. But the district court's instructions also improperly enabled the jury to find for the plaintiffs on these claims if the defendants intentionally and negligently did not disclose their knowledge of Dr. Berry's drug problems, irrespective of whether the letters to Kadlec were false or misleading. Because the verdict form only inquired as to whether the plaintiffs' claims for intentional and negligent misrepresentation, in separate interrogatories, were met as to each defendant, but did not request special findings of fact as to each of the separate possible theories, we cannot know whether the jury's verdict was based on the proper or improper theory. But the fact that the jury instructions stated both a valid and invalid theory of recovery for plaintiffs' claims does not require a new trial because the error here was harmless. The letters from Dr. Dennis and Dr. Preau were false on their face and patently misleading. There is no question about the purpose or effect of the letters. Because no reasonable juror could find otherwise, we uphold the finding of liability against Dr. Dennis and Dr. Preau. But because Lakeview Medical's letter was not materially misleading, and because the hospital did not have a legal duty to disclose its investigation of Dr. Berry and its knowledge of his drug problems, the judgment against Lakeview Medical must be reversed.

The district court entered judgment consistent with how the jury allocated fault among the entities it found to be legally responsible for the plaintiffs' injuries. The jury's allocation was as follows: Dr. Dennis 20%; Dr. Preau 5%; Lakeview Medical 25%; Kadlec 17%; and Dr. Berry 33%. We have affirmed the liability finding of the jury against the LAA defendants. But now that we have reversed the judgment against Lakeview Medical, the question arises whether there must be a reapportionment of fault with a corresponding change to damages assessed against the LAA defendants. It is possible that this is unnecessary, if under Louisiana law we can simply compare the fault percentages of the remaining parties. But Louisiana law might also require a reapportionment of fault and, therefore, a fresh determination of damages. Because there was no briefing on this issue, we vacate the judgment against the LAA defendants and remand the case to the district court to determine what, if anything, needs to be redone on the apportionment and damages issues, and then to enter judgment against the LAA defendants accordingly. . . .

The *Kadlec* district court opinion attracted considerable attention from hospital administrators and their peer review committees. Although decided under Louisiana law, the case stood for the proposition that hospitals and other health care providers have an affirmative duty, under common law, to disclose to one another certain information relevant to credentialing. The Fifth Circuit's opinion scaled that decision back, rejecting the affirmative duty but holding that a provider may be liable for negligent disclosure if it voluntarily assumes a duty to disclose.

QUESTIONS

1. As general counsel for a hospital, what advice would you give following the *Kadlec* opinion?
2. Would a form letter, like the one that Lakeview Medical provided, be the best approach to reference requests?
3. Would you advise your client simply to ignore reference requests and provide no information?
4. What implications does this decision have for the quality of medical care?

For most physicians, staff privileges are essential components of their practice. It is not enough merely to be licensed and maintain an office practice. Imagine, for example, how a cardiologist, obstetrician, gastroenterologist, or any other specialist who necessarily performs surgeries and other procedures could practice without access to a hospital. Accordingly, for physicians, the stakes are high in denial or revocation of privileges. If NPDB reporting is accurate and complete, an adverse credentialing decision at one hospital could prevent a physician from fully practicing anywhere else.

Accordingly, some measure of due process is required for peer review decisions that occur after privileges have been granted. There is no affirmative right to staff privileges at any hospital, including public hospitals. Hospitals are not "public utilities," giving all doctors a right of access. But once a physician has been granted privileges, the hospital generally cannot revoke or reduce them without some procedural protections. Most courts defer to the peer review committee on the substance of the decision to terminate or restrict privileges but will review the procedural adequacy of the process, sometimes applying the common law doctrine of "fundamental fairness." Generally, no right to due process exists if the hospital changes administrative policies or makes a business decision to reorganize its medical staff, even if those changes have the effect of reducing or eliminating physicians' privileges. The peer review due process right may derive from various sources, including medical staff bylaws, accrediting agencies' standards for peer review, state regulations, state common law, or contract.

The predominant private accrediting organization is the Joint Commission, described on its Web site as follows:

> An independent, not-for-profit organization, The Joint Commission accredits and certifies nearly 21,000 health care organizations and programs in the United States. Joint Commission accreditation and certification is recognized nationwide as a symbol of quality that reflects an organization's commitment to meeting certain performance standards.
>
> **Our Mission:** To continuously improve health care for the public, in collaboration with other stakeholders, by evaluating health care organizations and inspiring them to excel in providing safe and effective care of the highest quality and value.
>
> **Vision Statement:** All people always experience the safest, highest quality, best-value health care across all settings.

Accreditation is voluntary; however, health care organizations that achieve accreditation through a Joint Commission survey are granted "deemed status" for purposes of Medicare and Medicaid conditions of participation. CMS conducts oversight of Joint Commission accredited and deemed organizations to ensure that the private standards are met and continue to meet or exceed federal requirements.

PROBLEM

Even if accorded due process protections, physicians aggrieved by privileging decisions still may seek recovery on various common law theories. Brainstorm a list of possible tort, contract, and other claims that a physician might bring if aggrieved by a privileging decision.

Although the claims you suggest may not always be strong or viable under the relevant facts and applicable law, the threat of a lawsuit sometimes deters physicians from agreeing to serve on peer review committees. HCQIA was enacted in response to a rise in medical malpractice lawsuits in the 1970s and 1980s. One of the explanations for that trend was physicians' reluctance to engage in peer review activities. Accordingly, HCQIA contains a "stick," the requirement to report and query the NPDB, discussed above, as well as a "carrot," immunity from civil liability, as follows.

42 U.S.C. §11112. Standards for professional review actions
    (a) In general
    For purposes of the protection set forth in section 11111(a) of this title, a professional review action must be taken —
        (1) in the reasonable belief that the action was in the furtherance of quality health care,
        (2) after a reasonable effort to obtain the facts of the matter,

(3) after adequate notice and hearing procedures are afforded to the physician involved or after such other procedures as are fair to the physician under the circumstances, and

(4) in the reasonable belief that the action was warranted by the facts known after such reasonable effort to obtain facts and after meeting the requirement of paragraph (3).

A professional review action shall be presumed to have met the preceding standards necessary for the protection set out in section 11111(a) of this title unless the presumption is rebutted by a preponderance of the evidence.

HCQIA does not create a cause of action for a physician aggrieved by a credentialing decision but provides immunity from liability for peer review committee members and the hospital itself as long as the "four reasonables" are met. The defendants enjoy a presumption that the peer review action meets the standards, and it is the plaintiff/physician's burden to rebut that presumption. Reasonableness is an objective standard; therefore, even evidence of the defendants' subjective bad faith in the credentialing process will not rebut HCQIA immunity. HCQIA also contains a fee-shifting provision, awarding the defendants costs and fees under certain circumstances. The statute thus erects a high bar, deterring physicians from challenging peer review actions and resulting in their often losing at the summary judgment stage, even if they do bring a lawsuit.

Sithian v. Staten Island University Hospital

189 Misc. 2d 410 (N.Y. Sup. Ct. 2001)

Facts

The actions arise out of a peer review of Nedunchezian Sithian, M.D., (Dr. Sithian), a vascular surgeon by Staten Island University Hospital (SIUH). In November of 1993 Dr. Worth, the Director of Surgery at SIUH, sought an independent outside review of Dr. Sithian's surgical cases due to a high incidence of morbidity and mortality (M & M) amongst Dr. Sithian's patients. Dr. Anthony Imparato was appointed to review Dr. Sithian's cases and he found serious quality of care issues present. Dr. Worth retired in 1995 and was replaced by Dr. Richard Spence who became the Director of Surgery and Chief of Vascular Surgery. After a review of all vascular surgeons and departmental M & M conferences, and after reading Dr. Imparato's outside report, Dr. Sithian was suspended from performing complex (index) vascular surgery procedures (aortic, carotid and peripheral arteries) by Staten Island University Hospital.

> Does a physician's high rate of M & M necessarily indicate poor-quality care?

Following SIUH's suspension of privileges, Dr. Chang was retained to conduct a peer review of Dr. Sithian's cases. Dr. Chang who is a vascular surgeon was employed by the Albany Medical Center Hospital.

After a three day hearing before an ad hoc Committee of the Medical Staff of SIUH, at the request of Dr. Sithian, the committee was requested to rule without the report of Dr. Chang. The committee recommended that Dr. Sithian be permitted to perform vascular surgery only with a mandatory pre-operative consultation with another vascular surgeon and with another vascular surgeon in the operating room.

Six days later, the hospital received Dr. Chang's review on July 8, 1996. After a review of the records and reports of SIUH, Dr. Chang concluded that Dr. Sithian had failed to provide surgical treatment commensurate with accepted medical and surgical standards and that he should not be permitted to perform index (complex) vascular procedures. The Medical Executive Committee of SIUH then voted unanimously to recommend to their Board of Trustees that the suspension be upheld until Dr. Sithian obtained retraining through an approved vascular surgery fellowship program. That meeting was also attended by Rick Varone in his capacity as Chief Executive Officer of the hospital, but he did not have the right to vote. Dr. Spence, as Director of Surgery with voting rights, was also present.

> For purposes of a defamation claim, reporting an adverse credentialing decision to the NPDB may constitute a "publication." Truth, however, is an absolute defense to defamation.

On April 25, 1997, while the matter was still under consideration by the Board of Trustees, Dr. Sithian commenced a lawsuit against Dr. Spence. A separate action against Dr. Chang and the Medical Executive Committee was thereafter commenced for inter alia libel, slander and economic interference.

Dr. Sithian also filed an administrative complaint with the New York State Public Health Council. The New York State Public Health Council found no cause to Dr. Sithian's complaint and determined that the hospital's decision to suspend him was based upon principles of patient care, patient welfare, the practitioner's character, competence and the objectives of the institution.

The defendants asserted immunity under New York State Public Health Law §2805-m(3)3, New York State Education Law §6527(5)4 and the Health Care Quality Improvement Act (42 USC §11101 et seq.) ("HCQIA").

Justice Peter P. Cusick in his decision of January 19, 2000 held:

> that all defendants established their rights to immunity from the plaintiff's suit as a matter of law. The retaliatory lawsuits of this nature are precisely what the HCQIA and the State immunity statutes were intended to discourage in order to encourage frank, open, and meaningful medical peer review to monitor the quality of care rendered to patients.

As a result of Justice Cusick's decision the defendants moved for costs and attorney fees under the HCQIA, and Judge Cusick calendared the case for that purpose. However, due to the death of Justice Cusick, the motion was reassigned to Justice Gerard H. Rosenberg who held that the defendants were "substantially prevailing parties" under the HCQIA, but denied the motion pending the appeal of Justice Cusick's decision to the Supreme Court, Appellate Division, Second Department.

The Appellate Division, Second Department unanimously affirmed Justice Cusick and held that "the Supreme Court properly determined that the plaintiff failed to raise an issue of fact as to whether the defendants were immune from liability for their participation in the professional peer review of the plaintiff."

After the appeal, the motion was renewed to this court, for a determination of costs and attorney fees.

Discussion

No New York State Court has yet awarded attorney fees under the Health Care Quality Improvement Act (HCQIA) (42 USC §11113), which states, in part:

In any suit brought against a defendant, to the extent that a defendant has met the standards set forth under section 412(a) [42 USCS §11112(a)] and the defendant substantially prevails, the court *shall*, at the conclusion of the action, award to a substantially prevailing party defending against any such claim the cost of the suit attributable to such claim, including a reasonable attorney's fee, if the claim, or the claimant's conduct during the litigation of the claim, was frivolous, unreasonable, without foundation, or in bad faith. For the purposes of this section, a defendant shall not be considered to have substantially prevailed when the plaintiff obtains an award for damages or permanent injunctive or declaratory relief. (emphasis added)

The HCQIA was purposely designed to prevent the chilling effect which this type of lawsuit could have upon the participants in the peer review process. The public is protected when there is a full and frank discussion of a physician's abilities. The purpose of this statute is to deter groundless suits against participants in the medical peer review process. In passing the HCQIA in 1986, the United States Congress made the following findings:

(1) The increasing occurrence of medical malpractice and the need to improve the quality of medical care have become nationwide problems that warrant greater efforts than those that can be undertaken by any individual State.

(2) There is a national need to restrict the ability of incompetent physicians to move from State to State without disclosure or discovery of the physician's previous damaging or incompetent performance.

(3) This nationwide problem can be remedied through effective professional peer review.

(4) The threat of private money damage liability under Federal laws, including treble damage liability under Federal antitrust law, unreasonably discourages physicians from participating in effective professional peer review.

(5) There is an overriding national need to provide incentive and protection for physicians engaging in effective professional peer review.

The purpose of the legislation "is to improve the quality of medical care by encouraging physicians to identify and discipline other physicians who are incompetent or who engage in unprofessional behavior" (H.R.99-903, 99TH Cong. 2nd Sess. 2 (1986) U.S. Code Cong. & Admin. News 1986 at pp. 6384, 6384).

Clearly the defendants have proven that they were engaged in a legitimate endeavor—to conduct a peer review of Dr. Sithian. Both prior judges have held that the defendants have satisfied all of the requirements for immunity under the HCQIA. The only issue before this court is whether Dr. Sithian's "claim, or the claimant's conduct during the litigation of the claim, was frivolous, unreasonable, without foundation, or in bad faith." Justice Cusick's decision held that "there was no evidence that any defendant acted with malice or in bad faith, and the plaintiff's conclusory allegations of malice and speculation that such proof might develop in the future is not sufficient." Whether a party's conduct is frivolous or without foundation is left to the of the trial court.

In order to have commenced his action against Dr. Chang the plaintiff should have had proof of actual malice—to do otherwise was to bring a frivolous law. In bringing a frivolous lawsuit, the defendants are entitled to reasonable attorney fees and costs.

Additionally, it was bad faith to sue the Medical Executive Committee of SIUH and Dr. Chang while the matter was still under consideration by the Board of Trustees. Such a lawsuit sends a chilling effect to the Board of Trustee[s] that any adverse action will result in personal litigation. "Doctors who are sufficiently fearful of the threat of litigation will simply not do meaningful peer review. The result would be to continue the possibilities for abuse by bad doctors" (H.R.99-903, 99TH Cong. 2nd Sess. 3 (1986) U.S. Code Cong. & Admin. News 1986 at pp. 6384, 6385).

Dr. Chang agreed to participate in the peer review to assist the quality of care in his field. He had no contact with Dr. Sithian, and was independent from the hospital. Dr. Chang was not a member of the SIUH Board and practices in the Albany area. His defense of this action has resulted in legal fees of $21,796. The costs of the instant motion have been $1,440. After an examination of the attorney billing records, this court finds the fees charged to be reasonable. Accordingly, the defendant, Dr. Chang's motion for a judgment for attorney fees and costs in the amount of $23,236.00 is granted.

The defense of SIUH and the members of the Board of Directors of SIUH have resulted in legal fees in the amount $256,034.33 in attorney fees and cost. After an examination of the attorney billing records, this court finds the fees charged to be reasonable. The hospital law firm clearly was lead defense and as a result has larger fees than the counsel for Dr. Chang. However, a line by line review of the billing records shows instances of billing for the same work, numerous bills for review of prior work, and some billing items redacted so that the court cannot determine what they are for. Accordingly, the court will reduce the bills . . . the fees will be reduced by $40,347.50 for a total billing owed of $215,686.83

4. COMPARATIVE EFFECTIVENESS RESEARCH

This chapter has surveyed various approaches to regulating the standard of care, whether by tort liability, contractual agreement, or various forms of government regulation. Comparative effectiveness research (CER) is another health care reform initiative, designed to determine which treatments, diagnostic tests, public health strategies, and other health care services are the most effective for people in general, or for particular groups within the population. Perhaps surprisingly, little scientific evidence supports much of the health care provided in the United States. As the Introduction in Chapter 1 explained, we spend a great deal on health care but may not be getting very much for it. CER attempts to address that problem, arming providers with evidence-based research to choose among various treatment alternatives.

> 42 U.S.C. §1320e. Comparative clinical effectiveness research
> (a) Definitions
> In this section:
> . . . .
>> (2) Comparative clinical effectiveness research; research
>> (A) In general
>> The terms "comparative clinical effectiveness research" and "research" mean research evaluating and comparing health outcomes and the clinical effectiveness, risks, and benefits of 2 or more medical treatments, services, and items described in subparagraph (B).
>> (B) Medical treatments, services, and items described
>> The medical treatments, services, and items described in this subparagraph are health care interventions, protocols for treatment, care

management, and delivery, procedures, medical devices, diagnostic tools, pharmaceuticals (including drugs and biologicals), integrative health practices, and any other strategies or items being used in the treatment, management, and diagnosis of, or prevention of illness or injury in, individuals.

. . . .

(b) Patient-Centered Outcomes Research Institute

(1) Establishment

There is authorized to be established a nonprofit corporation, to be known as the "Patient-Centered Outcomes Research Institute" (referred to in this section as the "Institute") which is neither an agency nor establishment of the United States Government.

(2) Application of provisions

The Institute shall be subject to the provisions of this section, and, to the extent consistent with this section, to the District of Columbia Nonprofit Corporation Act.

(3) Funding of comparative clinical effectiveness research

For fiscal year 2010 and each subsequent fiscal year, amounts in the Patient-Centered Outcomes Research Trust Fund (referred to in this section as the "PCORTF") under section 9511 of the Internal Revenue Code of 1986 shall be available, without further appropriation, to the Institute to carry out this section.

(c) Purpose

The purpose of the Institute is to assist patients, clinicians, purchasers, and policy-makers in making informed health decisions by advancing the quality and relevance of evidence concerning the manner in which diseases, disorders, and other health conditions can effectively and appropriately be prevented, diagnosed, treated, monitored, and managed through research and evidence synthesis that considers variations in patient subpopulations, and the dissemination of research findings with respect to the relative health outcomes, clinical effectiveness, and appropriateness of the medical treatments, services, and items described in subsection (a)(2)(B). . . .

The ACA limits the use of CER, in various respects, especially under the Medicare program.

42 U.S.C. §1320e-1. Limitations on certain uses of comparative clinical effectiveness research

. . . .

(b) Nothing in section 1320e of this title shall be construed as—

(1) superceding or modifying the coverage of items or services under [the Medicare Act] that the Secretary determines are reasonable and necessary . . . ; or

(2) authorizing the Secretary to deny coverage of items or services under such subchapter solely on the basis of comparative clinical effectiveness research.

(c)(1) The Secretary shall not use evidence or findings from comparative clinical effectiveness research conducted under section 1320e of this title in determining coverage, reimbursement, or incentive programs under [the Medicare Act] in a manner that treats extending the life of an elderly, disabled, or terminally ill individual as of lower value than extending the life of an individual who is younger, nondisabled, or not terminally ill.

. . . .

(d)(1) The Secretary shall not use evidence or findings from comparative clinical effectiveness research conducted under section 1320e of this title in determining coverage, reimbursement, or incentive programs under [the Medicare Act] in a manner that precludes, or with the intent to discourage, an individual from choosing a health care treatment based on how the individual values the tradeoff between extending the length of their life and the risk of disability.

. . . .

(e) The Patient-Centered Outcomes Research Institute [PCORI] established under section 1320e(b)(1) of this title shall not develop or employ a dollars-per-quality adjusted life year (or similar measure that discounts the value of a life because of an individual's disability) as a threshold to establish what type of health care is cost effective or recommended. The Secretary shall not utilize such an adjusted life year (or such a similar measure) as a threshold to determine coverage, reimbursement, or incentive programs under subchapter XVIII of this chapter.

CAPSTONE PROBLEM

At the time the ACA was being debated, Sarah Palin, Governor of Alaska and Republican Vice Presidential candidate, posted a statement on her Facebook page (Aug. 7, 2009) that included the following:

> The Democrats promise that a government health care system will reduce the cost of health care, but as the economist Thomas Sowell has pointed out, government health care will not reduce the cost; it will simply refuse to pay the cost. And who will suffer the most when they ration care? The sick, the elderly, and the disabled, of course. The America I know and love is not one in which my parents or my baby with Down Syndrome will have to stand in front of Obama's "death panel" so his bureaucrats can decide, based on a subjective judgment of their "level of productivity in society," whether they are worthy of health care. Such a system is downright evil.

In leveling a charge against the so-called "death panels," Palin had in mind the CER and PCORI provisions of the proposed health reform legislation. The charge, while almost entirely without basis, resonated deeply with voters. Explain how the excerpted provisions of 42 U.S.C. §1320e-1 address the concerns that Palin raised in the public's mind, which involves many aspects of the physician-patient relationship.

CHAPTER **9**

Regulation of the Beginning and End of Life

A. INTRODUCTION

Issues related to health care at the beginning and end of life are policy hot potatoes. Despite the political, sociological, cultural, and ethical questions raised by these issues, practically speaking, they involve important medical care that has complex legal dimensions. A health care lawyer will quickly learn that doctors, hospitals, and other institutions such as nursing homes struggle to understand the constitutional law, state statutes, and other regulations pertaining to patient care at the beginning and end of life. Even if never summoned to a patient's bedside to advise whether life support can be terminated, health care lawyers need to know the status of the law to effectively represent health care clients on a host of daily medical and operational concerns.

Therefore, our goal for this chapter is to form a baseline for understanding how governments may (or may not) regulate health care at the beginning of life, meaning regulation pertaining to reproductive medicine, and at the end of life, a time when studies indicate that health care spending is disproportionately high relative to the value of interventions. We will develop a working understanding of the Supreme Court's framework for protecting individual privacy and autonomy while balancing these rights against the state interest in protecting life. As with other federalism discussions in this book, federal law answers only some of the questions that arise in this context, leaving states with room to regulate. In these decisions, the facts are key; they are where the Court grapples with medical questions raised by state regulation of the patient and the care provider.

The state is tasked with protecting the health, safety, and welfare of citizens, yet citizens often desire freedom from government interference. This tension between liberty and security has persisted for more than 100 years, as reflected by the Supreme Court's decision in *Jacobson v. Massachusetts* (Chapter 1). In *Jacobson*, the Court interpreted the U.S. Constitution to permit states to protect public health when disease outbreak or other widespread health threats require collective action. State power, however, is checked by constitutional protection for individuals' liberty, privacy, property, and other interests, with which federal and state law may not interfere.

U.S. Const. amend. V

No person shall be . . . deprived of life, liberty, or property, without due process of law. . . .

U.S. Const. amend. XIV, §1

. . . nor shall any State deprive any person of life, liberty, or property, without due process of law; nor deny to any person within its jurisdiction the equal protection of the laws.

No right is absolute, and the rights protected by these clauses are no different. The Supreme Court historically applies particular frameworks for evaluating whether state action improperly infringes individual rights, and "strict scrutiny" typically is used when evaluating whether the state has infringed fundamental rights. This test requires that the government provide a compelling reason for acting in a manner that infringes the right and that the law be narrowly tailored to that compelling interest. Legal analysis requires, first, identifying whether the right in question is "fundamental"; second, whether the government's interest in regulating is "compelling"; and, third, whether the means chosen to regulate are narrowly tailored to that interest. This rigorous test is usually fatal for the government action in question. Less exacting standards apply to those rights not deemed fundamental.

As you will see below, rights applicable at the beginning of life and the end of life are treated differently, despite being rooted in the same constitutional doctrines. We start with the opinions that create a web of rights related to the "beginning of life"—meaning procreation, contraception, and abortion—all of which relate to liberty interests protected within the right to privacy.

B. REGULATION OF REPRODUCTION

Viewing the issues through a statistical lens helps to illuminate the practical import of cases pertaining to reproductive medicine and health. Our point is to illustrate that beginning-of-life questions are much more than rarified questions of legal theory but rather are central to the operation of U.S. health care. According to the U.S. Census Bureau, as of 2014, 57.6 percent of all American females of reproductive age (15 to 44) have children; 71.1 percent of women aged 30 to 34 have children; and 83.3 percent of all women aged 45 to 50 have children. In other words, most American women of childbearing age eventually have children, which means most American families include children. But the average American family wants no more than two children, which means a woman of childbearing age must use contraceptives for roughly 30 years to avoid an unintended pregnancy. Accordingly, about 62 percent of women of reproductive age use at least one method of contraception regularly, and 99 percent have used a form of contraception at some point.

> Contraceptives are used for more than just prevention of pregnancy; depending on the device or medication, they can protect against sexually transmitted diseases, suppress hormonally activated acne, help to control painful or irregular menstruation, and prevent endometriosis, among other health benefits.

Despite the prevalence of contraception, Americans are relatively inconsistent in their use of it; therefore, it is not surprising that 45 percent of all pregnancies in the United States are unintended, which is among the highest rates for industrialized nations. About 40 percent of unintended pregnancies end through abortion. Approximately 15 to 33 percent of conceptions end with miscarriage (difficult to measure, as women may miscarry before realizing that they are pregnant, especially given how many pregnancies are unintended). Among all females of reproductive age (15 to 44), one-third will have an abortion during her reproductive years.

Corresponding to the high percentage of families with children, obstetrics/gynecology is the specialty with the fourth largest number of active physicians (pediatrics has the third largest number of active physicians). Half of all births and two-thirds of unintended births are paid for by public insurance (primarily Medicaid, discussed in Chapter 2). Medicaid covers approximately 40 percent of U.S. children aged 0 to 18. Most health care services and items related to the beginning of life such as contraception, pregnancy care, labor and delivery, and postpartum care are reimbursed by private and public health insurance, but abortion is largely excluded from public insurance coverage (discussed further below). The federal government also funds family planning for a substantial portion of the population through Title X of the Public Health Service Act, Pub. L. No. 91-572 (1970).

None of these health care services would be possible without the line of Supreme Court precedents protecting civil rights surrounding reproduction. That line begins with the following case.

Skinner v. Oklahoma

316 U.S. 535 (1942)

. . . We are dealing here with legislation which involves one of the basic civil rights of man. Marriage and procreation are fundamental to the very existence and survival of the race. The power to sterilize, if exercised, may have subtle, far-reaching and devastating effects. In evil or reckless hands, it can cause races or types which are inimical to the dominant group to wither and disappear. There is no redemption for the individual whom the law touches. Any experiment which the State conducts is to his irreparable injury. He is forever deprived of a basic liberty. We mention these matters not to reexamine the scope of the police power of the States. We advert to them merely in emphasis of our view that strict scrutiny of the classification which a State makes in a sterilization law is essential, lest unwittingly, or otherwise, invidious discriminations are made against groups or types of individuals in violation of the constitutional guaranty of just and equal laws. The guaranty of "equal protection of the laws is a pledge of the protection of equal laws." When the law lays an unequal hand on those who have committed intrinsically the same quality of offense and sterilizes one and not the other, it has made as invidious a discrimination as if it had selected a particular race or nationality for oppressive treatment. . . .

> Prisoners were sterilized for committing two or more crimes of moral turpitude, a result of the eugenics movement, which believed that criminal behavior, poverty, and "imbecilism" were heritable traits that should be eradicated through restricting reproduction by undesirable populations. This "scientific" and political movement ended when Nazis adopted and expanded the policies of eugenicists and took them to extreme and tragic ends.

States also sterilized non-prisoners during this period, which the Supreme Court infamously upheld in Buck v. Bell, 274 U.S. 200 (1927). Recognition of the constitutionally protected right to procreate likely saved thousands of Americans from forced sterilization. The scope of the right to procreate has grown. Though it took 20 years to develop, the next inquiry would be whether the Court would recognize a right *not* to procreate.

Griswold v. Connecticut

381 U.S. 479 (1965)

Mr. Justice Douglas delivered the opinion of the Court.

Estelle Griswold saw that women, especially poor women, struggled to control their own reproductive capacity. She purposefully challenged Connecticut's law prohibiting prescription or use of contraceptives by transporting women across state lines to purchase contraception and later opening a birth control clinic with the help of a Yale physician.

Appellant Griswold is Executive Director of the Planned Parenthood League of Connecticut. Appellant Buxton is a licensed physician and a professor at the Yale Medical School who served as Medical Director for the League at its Center in New Haven—a center open and operating from November 1 to November 10, 1961, when appellants were arrested.

They gave information, instruction, and medical advice to married persons as to the means of preventing conception. They examined the wife and prescribed the best contraceptive device or material for her use. Fees were usually charged, although some couples were serviced free.

The statutes whose constitutionality is involved in this appeal are §§53-32 and 54-196 of the General Statutes of Connecticut (1958 rev.). The former provides:

"Any person who uses any drug, medicinal article or instrument for the purpose of preventing conception shall be fined not less than fifty dollars or imprisoned not less than sixty days nor more than one year or be both fined and imprisoned."

Section 54-196 provides:

"Any person who assists, abets, counsels, causes, hires or commands another to commit any offense may be prosecuted and punished as if he were the principal offender."

The appellants were found guilty as accessories and fined $100 each, against the claim that the accessory statute as so applied violated the Fourteenth Amendment. The Appellate Division of the Circuit Court affirmed. The Supreme Court of Errors affirmed that judgment. . . . We think that appellants have standing to raise the constitutional rights of the married people with whom they had a professional relationship. . . .

Coming to the merits, we are met with a wide range of questions that implicate the Due Process Clause of the Fourteenth Amendment. . . . We do not sit as a super-legislature to determine the wisdom, need, and propriety of laws that touch economic problems, business affairs, or social conditions. This law, however, operates directly on an intimate relation of husband and wife and their physician's role in one aspect of that relation.

. . . [S]pecific guarantees in the Bill of Rights have penumbras, formed by emanations from those guarantees that help give them life and substance. Various guarantees create zones of privacy. The right of association contained in the penumbra of the First Amendment is one, as we have seen. The Third Amendment in its prohibition against the quartering of soldiers "in any house" in time of peace without the consent of the owner is another facet of that privacy. The Fourth Amendment explicitly affirms the "right of the people to be secure in their persons, houses, papers, and effects, against unreasonable searches and seizures." The Fifth Amendment in its Self-Incrimination Clause enables the citizen to create a zone

Doctors attempted to have the Court declare these laws unconstitutional in Poe v. Ullman, 367 U.S. 497 (1961), but the Court refused to hear the case, declaring that the claims were not ripe until contraceptives were prescribed.

of privacy which government may not force him to surrender to his detriment. The Ninth Amendment provides: "The enumeration in the Constitution, of certain rights, shall not be construed to deny or disparage others retained by the people." . . .

We have had many controversies over these penumbral rights of "privacy and repose." These cases bear witness that the right of privacy which presses for recognition here is a legitimate one.

The present case, then, concerns a relationship lying within the zone of privacy created by several fundamental constitutional guarantees. And it concerns a law which, in forbidding the use of contraceptives rather than regulating their manufacture or sale, seeks to achieve its goals by means having a maximum destructive impact upon that relationship. Such a law cannot stand in light of the familiar principle, so often applied by this Court, that a "governmental purpose to control or prevent activities constitutionally subject to state regulation may not be achieved by means which sweep unnecessarily broadly and thereby invade the area of protected freedoms." Would we allow the police to search the sacred precincts of marital bedrooms for telltale signs of the use of contraceptives? The very idea is repulsive to the notions of privacy surrounding the marriage relationship.

> Connecticut outlawed contraception as part of the "Comstock Laws" that rose to prominence in state legislatures during the late 1800s and were designed to stimulate morality, discourage adultery, and encourage reproduction within marriage.

We deal with a right of privacy older than the Bill of Rights — older than our political parties, older than our school system. Marriage is a coming together for better or for worse, hopefully enduring, and intimate to the degree of being sacred. It is an association that promotes a way of life, not causes; a harmony in living, not political faiths; a bilateral loyalty, not commercial or social projects. Yet it is an association for as noble a purpose as any involved in our prior decisions. Reversed.

QUESTIONS

1. What is the nature of the privacy right as articulated in *Griswold*?
2. Which relationship is protected by the "penumbras" and "emanations" of the Bill of Rights?
3. Are physicians directly or indirectly protected by the decision?

Many states had laws like Connecticut's that outlawed the use of contraceptives for all people, married or unmarried. The next case addressed such laws outside marriage and completed U.S. access to contraceptives. Without these two cases, the Patient Protection and Affordable Care Act (ACA) would not have extended no-cost health insurance coverage to contraceptives (discussed in Chapters 1 and 3).

Eisenstadt v. Baird

---

405 U.S. 438 (1972)

Mr. Justice BRENNAN delivered the opinion of the Court.

Appellee William Baird was convicted at a bench trial in the Massachusetts Superior Court first, for exhibiting contraceptive articles in the course of delivering a lecture on contraception to a group of students at Boston University and, second, for giving a young woman a package of Emko vaginal foam at the close of his address.

The Massachusetts Supreme Judicial Court unanimously set aside the conviction for exhibiting contraceptives on the ground that it violated Baird's First Amendment rights, but by a four-to-three vote sustained the conviction for giving away the foam. . . .

Massachusetts General Laws Ann., c. 272, §21, under which Baird was convicted, provides a maximum five-year term of imprisonment for "whoever . . . gives away . . . any drug, medicine, instrument or article whatever for the prevention of conception," except as authorized in §21A. Under §21A, "(a) registered physician may administer to or prescribe for any married person drugs or articles intended for the prevention of pregnancy or conception. (And a) registered pharmacist actually engaged in the business of pharmacy may furnish such drugs or articles to any married person presenting a prescription from a registered physician." . . .

> The state's claim of protecting health, when contraceptives were not dangerous in any known way, is echoed in the justifications states now use for restricting access to abortion through Targeted Regulation of Abortion Provider laws (TRAP laws), discussed below.

The legislative purposes that the statute is meant to serve are not altogether clear. . . . The Court of Appeals, for reasons that will appear, did not consider the promotion of health or the protection of morals through the deterrence of fornication to be the legislative aim. Instead, the court concluded that the statutory goal was to limit contraception in and of itself — a purpose that the court held conflicted "with fundamental human rights" under *Griswold v. Connecticut*, where this Court struck down Connecticut's prohibition against the use of contraceptives as an unconstitutional infringement of the right of marital privacy.

We agree that the goals of deterring premarital sex and regulating the distribution of potentially harmful articles cannot reasonably be regarded as legislative aims of §§21 and 21A. And we hold that the statute, viewed as a prohibition on contraception per se, violates the rights of single persons under the Equal Protection Clause of the Fourteenth Amendment. . . .

. . . The question for our determination in this case is whether there is some ground of difference that rationally explains the different treatment accorded married and unmarried persons under Massachusetts General Laws Ann., c. 272, §§21 and 21A. For the reasons that follow, we conclude that no such ground exists. . . .

Second. Section 21A was added to the Massachusetts General Laws by Stat. 1966, c. 265, §1. The Supreme Judicial Court in *Commonwealth v. Baird* held that the purpose of the amendment was to serve the health needs of the community by regulating the distribution of potentially harmful articles. It is plain that Massachusetts had no such purpose in mind before the enactment of §21A. As the Court of Appeals remarked, "Consistent with the fact that the statute was contained in a chapter dealing with 'Crimes Against Chastity, Morality, Decency and Good Order,' it was cast only in terms of morals. A physician was forbidden to prescribe contraceptives even when needed for the protection of health. . . ." Nor did the Court of Appeals "believe that the legislature (in enacting §21A) suddenly reversed its field and developed an interest in health. Rather, it merely made what it thought to be the precise accommodation necessary to escape the *Griswold* ruling."

Again, we must agree with the Court of Appeals. If health were the rationale of §21A, the statute would be both discriminatory and overbroad. Dissenting in *Commonwealth v. Baird*, Justices Whittemore and Cutter stated that they saw "in §21 and §21A, read together, no public health purpose. If there is need to have physician prescribe (and a pharmacist dispense) contraceptives, that need is as great for unmarried persons as for married persons." The Court of Appeals added:

"If the prohibition (on distribution to unmarried persons) . . . is to be taken to mean that the same physician who can prescribe for married patients does not have sufficient skill to protect the health of patients who lack a marriage certificate, or who may be currently divorced, it is illogical to the point of irrationality." Furthermore, we must join the Court of Appeals in noting that not all contraceptives are potentially dangerous. As a result, if the Massachusetts statute were a health measure, it would not only invidiously discriminate against the unmarried, but also be overbroad with respect to the married, a fact that the Supreme Judicial Court itself seems to have conceded. . . .

> Public health is often a justification for state action in fields as diverse as health, criminal justice, and the environment. The field has wide reach, but the rationale can also be misused.

Third. If the Massachusetts statute cannot be upheld as a deterrent to fornication or as a health measure, may it, nevertheless, be sustained simply as a prohibition on contraception? The Court of Appeals analysis "led inevitably to the conclusion that, so far as morals are concerned, it is contraceptives per se that are considered immoral — to the extent that *Griswold* will permit such a declaration." The Court of Appeals went on to hold:

> "To say that contraceptives are immoral as such, and are to be forbidden to unmarried persons who will nevertheless persist in having intercourse, means that such persons must risk for themselves an unwanted pregnancy, for the child, illegitimacy, and for society, a possible obligation of support. Such a view of morality is not only the very mirror image of sensible legislation; we consider that it conflicts with fundamental human rights. In the absence of demonstrated harm, we hold it is beyond the competency of the state."

We need not and do not, however, decide that important question in this case because, whatever the rights of the individual to access to contraceptives may be, the rights must be the same for the unmarried and the married alike.

If under *Griswold* the distribution of contraceptives to married persons cannot be prohibited, a ban on distribution to unmarried persons would be equally impermissible. It is true that in *Griswold* the right of privacy in question inhered in the marital relationship. Yet the marital couple is not an independent entity with a mind and heart of its own, but an association of two individuals each with a separate intellectual and emotional makeup. If the right of privacy means anything, it is the right of the individual, married or single, to be free from unwarranted governmental intrusion into matters so fundamentally affecting a person as the decision whether to bear or beget a child. *See also Skinner v. Oklahoma*; *Jacobson v. Massachusetts*. . . .

QUESTIONS

1. Can states prohibit either prescribing or using contraceptive devices or medications?
2. Whose rights are protected and how in these cases?
3. What do states learn about regulating medicine to protect health when the proscribed product is not actually dangerous?

Once the right to privacy was established, and access to contraception was secured both as a matter of personal privacy and as a health matter, the next step to improving reproductive care was challenging state criminal laws that outlawed abortion. *Roe v. Wade* certainly did not invent abortion, but it did formally legalize the medical procedure. As you read, consider how the Court draws on *Griswold* and *Eisenstadt* as well as medical history and expertise in extending the right to privacy to protect this medical procedure.

Roe v. Wade

410 U.S. 113 (1973)

Mr. Justice BLACKMUN delivered the opinion of the Court.

This Texas federal appeal and its Georgia companion, *Doe v. Bolton*, present constitutional challenges to state criminal abortion legislation. The Texas statutes under attack here are typical of those that have been in effect in many States for approximately a century. The Georgia statutes, in contrast, have a modern cast and are a legislative product that, to an extent at least, obviously reflects the influences of recent attitudinal change, of advancing medical knowledge and techniques, and of new thinking about an old issue.

We forthwith acknowledge our awareness of the sensitive and emotional nature of the abortion controversy, of the vigorous opposing views, even among physicians, and of the deep and seemingly absolute convictions that the subject inspires. One's philosophy, one's experiences, one's exposure to the raw edges of human existence, one's religious training, one's attitudes toward life and family and their values, and the moral standards one establishes and seeks to observe, are all likely to influence and to color one's thinking and conclusions about abortion.

In addition, population growth, pollution, poverty, and racial overtones tend to complicate and not to simplify the problem.

Our task, of course, is to resolve the issue by constitutional measurement, free of emotion and of predilection. We seek earnestly to do this, and, because we do, we have inquired into, and in this opinion place some emphasis upon, medical and medical-legal history and what that history reveals about man's attitudes toward the abortion procedure over the centuries. We bear in mind, too, Mr. Justice Holmes' admonition in his now-vindicated dissent in *Lochner v. New York*:

> Justice Blackmun was General Counsel to the Mayo Clinic, which helps to explain the majority's sensitivity to the health care provider's perspective.

"[The Constitution] is made for people of fundamentally differing views, and the accident of our finding certain opinions natural and familiar, or novel, and even shocking, ought not to conclude our judgment upon the question whether statutes embodying them conflict with the Constitution of the United States."

I

The Texas statutes that concern us here . . . make it a crime to "procure an abortion," as therein defined, or to attempt one, except with respect to "an abortion procured or attempted by medical advice for the purpose of saving the life of the mother." Similar statutes are in existence in a majority of the States.

Texas first enacted a criminal abortion statute in 1854. This was soon modified into language that has remained substantially unchanged to the present time. The final article in each of these compilations provided the same exception, as does the present Article 1196, for an abortion by "medical advice for the purpose of saving the life of the mother."

II

Jane Roe, a single woman who was residing in Dallas County, Texas, instituted this federal action in March 1970 against the District Attorney of the county. She sought a declaratory judgment that the Texas criminal abortion statutes were unconstitutional on their face, and an injunction restraining the defendant from enforcing the statutes.

Roe alleged that she was unmarried and pregnant; that she wished to terminate her pregnancy by an abortion "performed by a competent, licensed physician, under safe, clinical conditions"; that she was unable to get a "legal" abortion in Texas because her life did not appear to be threatened by the continuation of her pregnancy; and that she could not afford to travel to another jurisdiction in order to secure a legal abortion under safe conditions. She claimed that the Texas statutes were unconstitutionally vague and that they abridged her right of personal privacy, protected by the First, Fourth, Fifth, Ninth, and Fourteenth Amendments. By an amendment to her complaint Roe purported to sue "on behalf of herself and all other women" similarly situated.

James Hubert Hallford, a licensed physician, sought and was granted leave to intervene in Roe's action. In his complaint he alleged that he had been arrested previously for violations of the Texas abortion statutes and that two such prosecutions were pending against him. He described conditions of patients who came to him seeking abortions, and he claimed that for many cases he, as a physician, was unable to determine whether they fell within or outside the exception recognized by Article 1196. He alleged that, as a consequence, the statutes were vague and uncertain, in violation of the Fourteenth Amendment, and that they violated his own and his patients' rights to privacy in the doctor-patient relationship and his own right to practice medicine, rights he claimed were guaranteed by the First, Fourth, Fifth, Ninth, and Fourteenth Amendments. . . .

> By the time the Court decided this case, "Jane Roe" gave birth and her child was adopted by another family.

V

The principal thrust of appellant's attack on the Texas statutes is that they improperly invade a right, said to be possessed by the pregnant woman, to choose to terminate her pregnancy. Appellant would discover this right in the concept of personal "liberty" embodied in the Fourteenth Amendment's Due Process Clause; or in personal marital, familial, and sexual privacy said to be protected by the Bill of Rights or its penumbras, *see* Griswold v. Connecticut; Eisenstadt v. Baird; or among those rights reserved to the people by the Ninth Amendment, Griswold v. Connecticut (Goldberg, J., concurring). Before addressing this claim, we feel it desirable briefly to survey, in several aspects, the history of abortion, for such insight as that history may afford us, and then to examine the state purposes and interests behind the criminal abortion laws.

VI

It perhaps is not generally appreciated that the restrictive criminal abortion laws in effect in a majority of States today are of relatively recent vintage. Those laws, generally proscribing abortion or its attempt at any time during pregnancy except when necessary to preserve the pregnant woman's life, are not of ancient or even of common-law origin. Instead, they derive from statutory changes effected, for the most part, in the latter half of the 19th century. . . .

[Author note: The opinion traces at length the history of abortion-related laws from ancient civilizations through modern laws and medical attitudes.]

5. The American law. In this country, the law in effect in all but a few States until mid-19th century was the pre-existing English common law. Connecticut, the first State to enact abortion legislation, adopted in 1821 that part of Lord Ellenborough's Act that related to a woman "quick with child." The death penalty was not imposed. Abortion before quickening was made a crime in that State only in 1860. In 1828, New York enacted legislation that, in two respects, was to serve as a model for early anti-abortion statutes. First, while barring destruction of an unquickened fetus as well as a quick fetus, it made the former only a misdemeanor, but the latter second-degree manslaughter. Second, it incorporated a concept of therapeutic abortion by providing that an abortion was excused if it "shall have been necessary to preserve the life of such mother, or shall have been advised by two physicians to be necessary for such purpose." By 1840, when Texas had received the common law, only eight American States had statutes dealing with abortion. It was not until after the War Between the States that legislation began generally to replace the common law. Most of these initial statutes dealt severely with abortion after quickening but were lenient with it before quickening. Most punished attempts equally with completed abortions. While many statutes included the exception for an abortion thought by one or more physicians to be necessary to save the mother's life, that provision soon disappeared and the typical law required that the procedure actually be necessary for that purpose.

"Quickening" describes the moment when a pregnant woman can feel the movement of a fetus in her uterus, generally around 20 weeks of gestation.

Gradually, in the middle and late 19th century the quickening distinction disappeared from the statutory law of most States and the degree of the offense and the penalties were increased. By the end of the 1950's a large majority of the jurisdictions banned abortion, however and whenever performed, unless done to save or preserve the life of the mother. The exceptions, Alabama and the District of Columbia, permitted abortion to preserve the mother's health. Three States permitted abortions that were not "unlawfully" performed or that were not "without lawful justification," leaving interpretation of those standards to the courts. In the past several years, however, a trend toward liberalization of abortion statutes has resulted in adoption, by about one-third of the States, of less stringent laws, most of them patterned after the ALI Model Penal Code.

It is thus apparent that at common law, at the time of the adoption of our Constitution, and throughout the major portion of the 19th century, abortion was viewed with less disfavor than under most American statutes currently in effect. Phrasing it another way, a woman enjoyed a substantially broader right to terminate a pregnancy than she does in most States today. At least with respect to the early stage of pregnancy, and very possibly without such a limitation, the opportunity to make this choice was present in this country well into the 19th century. Even later, the law continued for some time to treat less punitively an abortion procured in early pregnancy.

6. The position of the American Medical Association. The anti-abortion mood prevalent in this country in the late 19th century was shared by the medical

profession. Indeed, the attitude of the profession may have played a significant role in the enactment of stringent criminal abortion legislation during that period. . . .

In 1970, after the introduction of a variety of proposed resolutions, and of a report from its Board of Trustees, a reference committee noted "polarization of the medical profession on this controversial issue"; division among those who had testified; a difference of opinion among AMA councils and committees; "the remarkable shift in testimony" in six months, felt to be influenced "by the rapid changes in state laws and by the judicial decisions which tend to make abortion more freely available"; and a feeling "that this trend will continue." On June 25, 1970, the House of Delegates adopted preambles and most of the resolutions proposed by the reference committee. The preambles emphasized "the best interests of the patient," "sound clinical judgment," and "informed patient consent," in contrast to "mere acquiescence to the patient's demand." The resolutions asserted that abortion is a medical procedure that should be performed by a licensed physician in an accredited hospital only after consultation with two other physicians and in conformity with state law, and that no party to the procedure should be required to violate personally held moral principles. The AMA Judicial Council rendered a complementary opinion.

> Physicians desired to distinguish themselves as the exclusive legitimate providers of medical care in the late nineteenth century, and one method they employed was discrediting other health care providers. Until that point, midwives provided reproductive care, and outlawing abortion was a method for discrediting and outlawing midwifery.

7. The position of the American Public Health Association. In October 1970, the Executive Board of the APHA adopted Standards for Abortion Services. These were five in number:

> "a. Rapid and simple abortion referral must be readily available through state and local public health departments, medical societies, or other non-profit organizations.
>
> b. An important function of counseling should be to simplify and expedite the provision of abortion services; it should not delay the obtaining of these services.
>
> c. Psychiatric consultation should not be mandatory. As in the case of other specialized medical services, psychiatric consultation should be sought for definite indications and not on a routine basis.
>
> d. A wide range of individuals from appropriately trained, sympathetic volunteers to highly skilled physicians may qualify as abortion counselors.
>
> e. Contraception and/or sterilization should be discussed with each abortion patient."

Among factors pertinent to life and health risks associated with abortion were three that "are recognized as important":

> "a. the skill of the physician,
>
> b. the environment in which the abortion is performed, and above all
>
> c. The duration of pregnancy, as determined by uterine size and confirmed by menstrual history."

It was said that "a well-equipped hospital" offers more protection "to cope with unforeseen difficulties than an office or clinic without such resources. . . . The factor of gestational age is of overriding importance." . . .

VII

Three reasons have been advanced to explain historically the enactment of criminal abortion laws in the 19th century and to justify their continued existence.

It has been argued occasionally that these laws were the product of a Victorian social concern to discourage illicit sexual conduct. Texas, however, does not advance this justification. . . .

A second reason is concerned with abortion as a medical procedure. When most criminal abortion laws were first enacted, the procedure was a hazardous one for the woman. This was particularly true prior to the development of antisepsis. Antiseptic techniques, of course, were based on discoveries by Lister, Pasteur, and others first announced in 1867, but were not generally accepted and employed until about the turn of the century. Abortion mortality was high. Even after 1900, and perhaps until as late as the development of antibiotics in the 1940's, standard modern techniques such as dilation and curettage were not nearly so safe as they are today. Thus, it has been argued that a State's real concern in enacting a criminal abortion law was to protect the pregnant woman, that is, to restrain her from submitting to a procedure that placed her life in serious jeopardy.

Modern medical techniques have altered this situation. Appellants and various amici refer to medical data indicating that abortion in early pregnancy, that is, prior to the end of the first trimester, although not without its risk, is now relatively safe. Mortality rates for women undergoing early abortions, where the procedure is legal, appear to be as low as or lower than the rates for normal childbirth. Consequently, any interest of the State in protecting the woman from an inherently hazardous procedure, except when it would be equally dangerous for her to forgo it, has largely disappeared. Of course, important state interests in the areas of health and medical standards do remain. The State has a legitimate interest in seeing to it that abortion, like any other medical procedure, is performed under circumstances that insure maximum safety for the patient. This interest obviously extends at least to the performing physician and his staff, to the facilities involved, to the availability of after-care, and to adequate provision for any complication or emergency that might arise. The prevalence of high mortality rates at illegal "abortion mills" strengthens, rather than weakens, the State's interest in regulating the conditions under which abortions are performed. Moreover, the risk to the woman increases as her pregnancy continues. Thus, the State retains a definite interest in protecting the woman's own health and safety when an abortion is proposed at a late stage of pregnancy.

The third reason is the State's interest—some phrase it in terms of duty—in protecting prenatal life. Some of the argument for this justification rests on the theory that a new human life is present from the moment of conception. The State's interest and general obligation to protect life then extends, it is argued, to prenatal life. Only when the life of the pregnant mother herself is at stake, balanced against the life she carries within her, should the interest of the embryo or fetus not prevail. Logically, of course, a legitimate state interest in this area need not stand or fall on acceptance of the belief that life begins at conception or at some other point prior to live birth. In assessing the State's interest, recognition may be given to the less rigid claim that as long as at least potential life is involved, the State may assert interests beyond the protection of the pregnant woman alone.

. . . .

VIII

The Constitution does not explicitly mention any right of privacy. In a line of decisions, however, going back perhaps as far as *Union Pacific R. Co. v. Botsford*

(1891), the Court has recognized that a right of personal privacy, or a guarantee of certain areas or zones of privacy, does exist under the Constitution. In varying contexts, the Court or individual Justices have, indeed, found at least the roots of that right in the First Amendment; in the Fourth and Fifth Amendments; in the penumbras of the Bill of Rights, *Griswold v. Connecticut*; in the Ninth Amendment, *id.*, at 486 (Goldberg, J., concurring); or in the concept of liberty guaranteed by the first section of the Fourteenth Amendment, *see* Meyer v. Nebraska. These decisions make it clear that only personal rights that can be deemed "fundamental" or "implicit in the concept of ordered liberty" are included in this guarantee of personal privacy. They also make it clear that the right has some extension to activities relating to marriage, *Loving v. Virginia*; procreation, *Skinner v. Oklahoma*; contraception, *Eisenstadt v. Baird*; family relationships, *Prince v. Massachusetts*; and child rearing and education, *Pierce v. Society of Sisters, Meyer v. Nebraska.*

This right of privacy, whether it be founded in the Fourteenth Amendment's concept of personal liberty and restrictions upon state action, as we feel it is, or, as the District Court determined, in the Ninth Amendment's reservation of rights to the people, is broad enough to encompass a woman's decision whether or not to terminate her pregnancy. The detriment that the State would impose upon the pregnant woman by denying this choice altogether is apparent. Specific and direct harm medically diagnosable even in early pregnancy may be involved. Maternity, or additional offspring, may force upon the woman a distressful life and future. Psychological harm may be imminent. Mental and physical health may be taxed by child care. There is also the distress, for all concerned, associated with the unwanted child, and there is the problem of bringing a child into a family already unable, psychologically and otherwise, to care for it. In other cases, as in this one, the additional difficulties and continuing stigma of unwed motherhood may be involved. All these are factors the woman and her responsible physician necessarily will consider in consultation.

On the basis of elements such as these, appellant and some amici argue that the woman's right is absolute and that she is entitled to terminate her pregnancy at whatever time, in whatever way, and for whatever reason she alone chooses. With this we do not agree. Appellant's arguments that Texas either has no valid interest at all in regulating the abortion decision, or no interest strong enough to support any limitation upon the woman's sole determination, are unpersuasive. The Court's decisions recognizing a right of privacy also acknowledge that some state regulation in areas protected by that right is appropriate. As noted above, a State may properly assert important interests in safeguarding health, in maintaining medical standards, and in protecting potential life. At some point in pregnancy, these respective interests become sufficiently compelling to sustain regulation of the factors that govern the abortion decision. The privacy right involved, therefore, cannot be said to be absolute. In fact, it is not clear to us that the claim asserted by some amici that one has an unlimited right to do with one's body as one pleases bears a close relationship to the right of privacy previously articulated in the Court's decisions. The Court has refused to recognize an unlimited right of this kind in the past.

> This articulation of a state's interests often appears in subsequent cases.

We, therefore, conclude that the right of personal privacy includes the abortion decision, but that this right is not unqualified and must be considered against important state interests in regulation. . . .

Where certain "fundamental rights" are involved, the Court has held that regulation limiting these rights may be justified only by a "compelling state interest," and that legislative enactments must be narrowly drawn to express only the legitimate state interests at stake . . . .

IX

. . . .

A. . . . The Constitution does not define "person" in so many words. Section 1 of the Fourteenth Amendment contains three references to "person." The first, in defining "citizens," speaks of "persons born or naturalized in the United States." The word also appears both in the Due Process Clause and in the Equal Protection Clause. "Person" is used in other places in the Constitution. . . . But in nearly all these instances, the use of the word is such that it has application only postnatally. None indicates, with any assurance, that it has any possible prenatal application.

All this, together with our observation that throughout the major portion of the 19th century prevailing legal abortion practices were far freer than they are today, persuades us that the word "person," as used in the Fourteenth Amendment, does not include the unborn. This is in accord with the results reached in those few cases where the issue has been squarely presented. . . .

This conclusion, however, does not of itself fully answer the contentions raised by Texas, and we pass on to other considerations.

B. The pregnant woman cannot be isolated in her privacy. She carries an embryo and, later, a fetus, if one accepts the medical definitions of the developing young in the human uterus. The situation therefore is inherently different from marital intimacy, or bedroom possession of obscene material, or marriage, or procreation, or education, with which *Eisenstadt* and *Griswold*, *Stanley*, *Loving*, *Skinner* and *Pierce* and *Meyer* were respectively concerned. As we have intimated above, it is reasonable and appropriate for a State to decide that at some point in time another interest, that of health of the mother or that of potential human life, becomes significantly involved. The woman's privacy is no longer sole and any right of privacy she possesses must be measured accordingly.

Texas urges that, apart from the Fourteenth Amendment, life begins at conception and is present throughout pregnancy, and that, therefore, the State has a compelling interest in protecting that life from and after conception. We need not resolve the difficult question of when life begins. When those trained in the respective disciplines of medicine, philosophy, and theology are unable to arrive at any consensus, the judiciary, at this point in the development of man's knowledge, is not in a position to speculate as to the answer. . . . In short, the unborn have never been recognized in the law as persons in the whole sense.

X

In view of all this, we do not agree that, by adopting one theory of life, Texas may override the rights of the pregnant woman that are at stake. We repeat, however, that the State does have an important and legitimate interest in preserving and protecting the health of the pregnant woman, whether she be a resident of the State or a nonresident who seeks medical consultation and treatment there, and that it has still another important and legitimate interest in protecting the potentiality of human life. These interests are separate and distinct. Each grows in substantiality as the woman approaches term and, at a point during pregnancy, each becomes "compelling."

With respect to the State's important and legitimate interest in the health of the mother, the "compelling" point, in the light of present medical knowledge, is at approximately the end of the first trimester. This is so because of the now-established medical fact that until the end of the first trimester mortality in abortion may be less than mortality in normal childbirth. It follows that, from and after this point, a State may regulate the abortion procedure to the extent that the regulation reasonably relates to the preservation and protection of maternal health. Examples of permissible state regulation in this area are requirements as to the qualifications of the person who is to perform the abortion; as to the licensure of that person; as to the facility in which the procedure is to be performed, that is, whether it must be a hospital or may be a clinic or some other place of less-than-hospital status; as to the licensing of the facility; and the like.

This means, on the other hand, that, for the period of pregnancy prior to this "compelling" point, the attending physician, in consultation with his patient, is free to determine, without regulation by the State, that, in his medical judgment, the patient's pregnancy should be terminated. If that decision is reached, the judgment may be effectuated by an abortion free of interference by the State.

> Note the Court's deference to physicians' medical judgment within the physician-patient relationship (discussed in Chapters 8 and 10).

With respect to the State's important and legitimate interest in potential life, the "compelling" point is at viability. This is so because the fetus then presumably has the capability of meaningful life outside the mother's womb. State regulation protective of fetal life after viability thus has both logical and biological justifications. If the State is interested in protecting fetal life after viability, it may go so far as to proscribe abortion during that period, except when it is necessary to preserve the life or health of the mother.

Measured against these standards, Art. 1196 of the Texas Penal Code, in restricting legal abortions to those "procured or attempted by medical advice for the purpose of saving the life of the mother," sweeps too broadly. The statute makes no distinction between abortions performed early in pregnancy and those performed later, and it limits to a single reason, "saving" the mother's life, the legal justification for the procedure. The statute, therefore, cannot survive the constitutional attack made upon it here. . . .

This holding, we feel, is consistent with the relative weights of the respective interests involved, with the lessons and examples of medical and legal history, with the lenity of the common law, and with the demands of the profound problems of the present day. The decision leaves the State free to place increasing restrictions on abortion as the period of pregnancy lengthens, so long as those restrictions are tailored to the recognized state interests. The decision vindicates the right of the physician to administer medical treatment according to his professional judgment up to the points where important state interests provide compelling justifications for intervention. Up to those points, the abortion decision in all its aspects is inherently, and primarily, a medical decision, and basic responsibility for it must rest with the physician. If an individual practitioner abuses the privilege of exercising proper medical judgment, the usual remedies, judicial and intra-professional, are available.

. . . Affirmed in part and reversed in part.

QUESTIONS

1. When and why does a pregnant woman have a privacy right under this decision?
2. Is there a point at which the state's interest in potential life of the fetus out-weighs a woman's fundamental right?
3. 3. What are the state's interests, and are they limited in any way?
4. Under *Roe*, could a state outlaw abortion in all circumstances after fetal viability?

After *Roe v. Wade*, the legality of abortion was settled, but the extent to which governments could limit physicians' services and women's access to abortion were not. Politicians introduced legislation that would limit governmental support for abortion, either by banning the procedure in state facilities, or prohibiting use of state funds for abortions, or by creating regulatory regimes limiting physicians' ability to provide abortions. In 1976, Representative Henry Hyde stated on the floor of the House of Representatives: "I certainly would like to prevent, if I could legally, any-body having an abortion, a rich woman, a middle-class woman, or a poor woman. Unfortunately, the only vehicle available is the HEW Medicaid bill." The "Hyde Amendment" has attached to Medicaid's funding bill every year since, preventing public funding of abortion except to save the life of the woman or in instances of rape or incest. The following case resolves the constitutionality of the Hyde Amendment and articulates states' obligation to pay for health care beyond federal requirements in Medicaid (discussed in Chapter 2).

Harris v. McRae

448 U.S. 297 (1980)

Mr. Justice STEWART delivered the opinion of the Court.

This case presents statutory and constitutional questions concerning the public funding of abortions under Title XIX of the Social Security Act, commonly known as the "Medicaid" Act, and recent annual Appropriations Acts containing the so-called "Hyde Amendment." The statutory question is whether Title XIX requires a State that participates in the Medicaid program to fund the cost of medically necessary abortions for which federal reimbursement is unavailable under the Hyde Amend-ment. The constitutional question, which arises only if Title XIX imposes no such requirement, is whether the Hyde Amendment, by denying public funding for certain medically necessary abortions, contravenes the liberty or equal protection guarantees of the Due Process Clause of the Fifth Amendment, or either of the Religion Clauses of the First Amendment.

I

The Medicaid program was created in 1965 . . . for the purpose of providing federal financial assistance to States that choose to reimburse certain costs of med-ical treatment for needy persons. Although participation in the Medicaid program is entirely optional, once a State elects to participate, it must comply with the require-ments of Title XIX.

One such requirement is that a participating State agree to provide financial assistance to the "categorically needy" with respect to five general areas of medical treatment: (1) inpatient hospital services, (2) outpatient hospital services, (3) other laboratory and X-ray services, (4) skilled nursing facilities services, periodic screening and diagnosis of children, and family planning services, and (5) services of physicians. Although a participating State need not "provide funding for all medical treatment falling within the five general categories, [Title XIX] does require that [a] state Medicaid pla[n] establish 'reasonable standards . . . for determining . . . the extent of medical assistance under the plan which . . . are consistent with the objectives of [Title XIX.].'" Beal v. Doe.

Since September, 1976, Congress has prohibited — either by an amendment to the annual appropriations bill for the Department of Health, Education, and Welfare or by a joint resolution — the use of any federal funds to reimburse the cost of abortions under the Medicaid program except under certain specified circumstances. This funding restriction is commonly known as the "Hyde Amendment," after its original congressional sponsor, Representative Hyde. The current version of the Hyde Amendment, applicable for fiscal year 1980, provides:

> "[N]one of the funds provided by this joint resolution shall be used to perform abortions except where the life of the mother would be endangered if the fetus were carried to term; or except for such medical procedures necessary for the victims of rape or incest when such rape or incest has been reported promptly to a law enforcement agency or public health service."

The Department of Health, Education, and Welfare was divided into the Department of Education and the Department of Health and Human Services in 1980. It is the same agency that regulated Medicaid when this case was decided as today, using a different name.

Pub. L. 96-123, 109, 93 Stat. 926. This version of the Hyde Amendment is broader than that applicable for fiscal year 1977, which did not include the "rape or incest" exception, but narrower than that applicable for most of fiscal year 1978, and all of fiscal year 1979, which had an additional exception for "instances where severe and long-lasting physical health damage to the mother would result if the pregnancy were carried to term when so determined by two physicians."

On September 30, 1976, the day on which Congress enacted the initial version of the Hyde Amendment, these consolidated cases were filed in the District Court for the Eastern District of New York. The plaintiffs — Cora McRae, a New York Medicaid recipient then in the first trimester of a pregnancy that she wished to terminate, the New York City Health and Hospitals Corp., a public benefit corporation that operates 16 hospitals, 12 of which provide abortion services, and others — sought to enjoin the enforcement of the funding restriction on abortions. They alleged that the Hyde Amendment violated the First, Fourth, Fifth, and Ninth Amendments of the Constitution insofar as it limited the funding of abortions to those necessary to save the life of the mother, while permitting the funding of costs associated with childbirth. . . .

II

. . . [W]e turn first to the question whether Title XIX requires a State that participates in the Medicaid program to continue to fund those medically necessary abortions for which federal reimbursement is unavailable under the Hyde Amendment. If a participating State is under such an obligation, the constitutionality of the Hyde Amendment need not be drawn into question in the present case, for the availability of medically necessary abortions under Medicaid would continue, with the participating State shouldering the total cost of funding such abortions.

The appellees assert that a participating State has an independent funding obligation under Title XIX because (1) the Hyde Amendment is, by its own terms, only a limitation on federal reimbursement for certain medically necessary abortions, and (2) Title XIX does not permit a participating State to exclude from its Medicaid plan any medically necessary service solely on the basis of diagnosis or condition, even if federal reimbursement is unavailable for that service. It is thus the appellees' view that the effect of the Hyde Amendment is to withhold federal reimbursement for certain medically necessary abortions, but not to relieve a participating State of its duty under Title XIX to provide for such abortions in its Medicaid plan . . . .

> Even if federal law prohibits federal funding for certain Medicaid services, states may provide them if funded entirely with state dollars. For example, some states pay for Medicaid beneficiaries' abortions outside the Hyde Amendment restrictions (but a majority do not).

Since the Congress that enacted Title XIX did not intend a participating State to assume a unilateral funding obligation for any health service in an approved Medicaid plan, it follows that Title XIX does not require a participating State to include in its plan any services for which a subsequent Congress has withheld federal funding. Title XIX was designed as a cooperative program of shared financial responsibility, not as a device for the Federal Government to compel a State to provide services that Congress itself is unwilling to fund. Thus, if Congress chooses to withdraw federal funding for a particular service, a State is not obliged to continue to pay for that service as a condition of continued federal financial support of other services. . . . Title XIX does not obligate a participating State to pay for those medical services for which federal reimbursement is unavailable. . . .

III

. . . It is well settled that, quite apart from the guarantee of equal protection, if a law "impinges upon a fundamental right explicitly or implicitly secured by the Constitution, [it] is presumptively unconstitutional." Accordingly, before turning to the equal protection issue in this case, we examine whether the Hyde Amendment violates any substantive rights secured by the Constitution.

A

We address first the appellees' argument that the Hyde Amendment, by restricting the availability of certain medically necessary abortions under Medicaid, impinges on the "liberty" protected by the Due Process Clause as recognized in *Roe v. Wade*, and its progeny. . . .

[The Court described *Roe v. Wade* in detail.]

In *Maher v. Roe*, the Court was presented with the question whether the scope of personal constitutional freedom recognized in *Roe v. Wade* included an entitlement to Medicaid payments for abortions that are not medically necessary. At issue in *Maher* was a Connecticut welfare regulation under which Medicaid recipients received payments for medical services incident to childbirth, but not for medical services incident to nontherapeutic abortions. . . .

The doctrine of *Roe v. Wade*, the Court held in *Maher*, "protects the woman from unduly burdensome interference with her freedom to decide whether to terminate her pregnancy," such as the severe criminal sanctions at issue in *Roe v. Wade*, or the absolute requirement of spousal consent for an abortion challenged in *Planned Parenthood of Central Missouri v. Danforth*.

But the constitutional freedom recognized in *Wade* and its progeny, the *Maher* Court explained, did not prevent Connecticut from making "a value judgment favoring childbirth over abortion, and . . . implement[ing] that judgment by the allocation of public funds." . . .

The Court in *Maher* noted that its description of the doctrine recognized in *Wade* and its progeny signaled "no retreat" from those decisions. In explaining why the constitutional principle recognized in *Wade* and later cases — protecting a woman's freedom of choice — did not translate into a constitutional obligation of Connecticut to subsidize abortions, the Court cited the "basic difference between direct state interference with a protected activity and state encouragement of an alternative activity consonant with legislative policy. Constitutional concerns are greatest when the State attempts to impose its will by force of law; the State's power to encourage actions deemed to be in the public interest is necessarily far broader." Thus, even though the Connecticut regulation favored childbirth over abortion by means of subsidization of one and not the other, the Court in *Maher* concluded that the regulation did not impinge on the constitutional freedom recognized in *Wade* because it imposed no governmental restriction on access to abortions.

> The U.S. Constitution instructs government to refrain from infringing rights but articulates almost no positive rights, and the lack of positive rights makes it hard for the law's challengers to argue for a right to government payment for any medical care, let alone a fraught procedure.

The Hyde Amendment, like the Connecticut welfare regulation at issue in *Maher*, places no governmental obstacle in the path of a woman who chooses to terminate her pregnancy, but rather, by means of unequal subsidization of abortion and other medical services, encourages alternative activity deemed in the public interest. The present case does differ factually from *Maher* insofar as that case involved a failure to fund nontherapeutic abortions, whereas the Hyde Amendment withholds funding of certain medically necessary abortions. Accordingly, the appellees argue that, because the Hyde Amendment affects a significant interest not present or asserted in *Maher* — the interest of a woman in protecting her health during pregnancy — and because that interest lies at the core of the personal constitutional freedom recognized in *Wade*, the present case is constitutionally different from *Maher*. It is the appellees' view that, to the extent that the Hyde Amendment withholds funding for certain medically necessary abortions, it clearly impinges on the constitutional principle recognized in *Wade*.

It is evident that a woman's interest in protecting her health was an important theme in *Wade*. . . . But, regardless of whether the freedom of a woman to choose to terminate her pregnancy for health reasons lies at the core or the periphery of the due process liberty recognized in *Wade*, it simply does not follow that a woman's freedom of choice carries with it a constitutional entitlement to the financial resources to avail herself of the full range of protected choices. The reason why was explained in *Maher*: although government may not place obstacles in the path of a woman's exercise of her freedom of choice, it need not remove those not of its own creation. Indigency falls in the latter category. The financial constraints that restrict an indigent woman's ability to enjoy the full range of constitutionally protected freedom of choice are the product not of governmental restrictions on access to abortions, but rather of her indigency. Although Congress has opted to subsidize medically necessary services generally, but not certain medically necessary abortions, the fact remains that the Hyde Amendment leaves an indigent woman with at least the same range of choice in deciding whether to obtain a medically

> Mandatory and optional elements of Medicaid require covering outpatient hospital services and physician services, which would cover an outpatient surgical procedure such as abortion but for the Hyde Amendment's limitations.

necessary abortion as she would have had if Congress had chosen to subsidize no health care costs at all. We are thus not persuaded that the Hyde Amendment impinges on the constitutionally protected freedom of choice recognized in *Wade*.

Although the liberty protected by the Due Process Clause affords protection against unwarranted government interference with freedom of choice in the context of certain personal decisions, it does not confer an entitlement to such funds as may be necessary to realize all the advantages of that freedom. To hold otherwise would mark a drastic change in our understanding of the Constitution. It cannot be that, because government may not prohibit the use of contraceptives or prevent parents from sending their child to a private school, government therefore has an affirmative constitutional obligation to ensure that all persons have the financial resources to obtain contraceptives or send their children to private schools. . . . Accordingly, we conclude that the Hyde Amendment does not impinge on the due process liberty recognized in *Wade*. . . .

C

It remains to be determined whether the Hyde Amendment violates the equal protection component of the Fifth Amendment. This challenge is premised on the fact that, although federal reimbursement is available under Medicaid for medically necessary services generally, the Hyde Amendment does not permit federal reimbursement of all medically necessary abortions. The District Court held, and the appellees argue here, that this selective subsidization violates the constitutional guarantee of equal protection[.]

The guarantee of equal protection under the Fifth Amendment is not a source of substantive rights or liberties, but rather a right to be free from invidious discrimination in statutory classifications and other governmental activity. It is well settled that where a statutory classification does not itself impinge on a right or liberty protected by the Constitution, the validity of classification must be sustained unless "the classification rests on grounds wholly irrelevant to the achievement of [any legitimate governmental] objective." This presumption of constitutional validity, however, disappears if a statutory classification is predicated on criteria that are, in a constitutional sense, "suspect," the principal example of which is a classification based on race, *e.g.*, Brown v. Board of Education.

1

For the reasons stated above, we have already concluded that the Hyde Amendment violates no constitutionally protected substantive rights. We now conclude as well that it is not predicated on a constitutionally suspect classification. In reaching this conclusion, we again draw guidance from the Court's decision in *Maher v. Roe*. As to whether the Connecticut welfare regulation providing funds for childbirth but not for nontherapeutic abortions discriminated against a suspect class, the Court in *Maher* observed: "An indigent woman desiring an abortion does not come within the limited category of disadvantaged classes so recognized by our cases. Nor does the fact that the impact of the regulation falls upon those who cannot pay lead to a different conclusion. In a sense, every denial of welfare to an indigent creates a wealth classification as compared to nonindigents who are able to pay for the desired goods or services. But this Court has never held that financial need alone identifies a suspect class for purposes of equal protection analysis." Thus, the Court in *Maher* found no basis for concluding that the Connecticut regulation was predicated on a suspect classification.

It is our view that the present case is indistinguishable from *Maher* in this respect. Here, as in *Maher*, the principal impact of the Hyde Amendment falls on the indigent. But that fact does not itself render the funding restriction constitutionally invalid, for this Court has held repeatedly that poverty, standing alone, is not a suspect classification. . . .

The remaining question then is whether the Hyde Amendment is rationally related to a legitimate governmental objective. It is the Government's position that the Hyde Amendment bears a rational relationship to its legitimate interest in protecting the potential life of the fetus. We agree.

. . . [T]he Hyde Amendment, by encouraging childbirth except in the most urgent circumstances, is rationally related to the legitimate governmental objective of protecting potential life. By subsidizing the medical expenses of indigent women who carry their pregnancies to term while not subsidizing the comparable expenses of women who undergo abortions (except those whose lives are threatened), Congress has established incentives that make childbirth a more attractive alternative than abortion for persons eligible for Medicaid. These incentives bear a direct relationship to the legitimate congressional interest in protecting potential life. Nor is it irrational that Congress has authorized federal reimbursement for medically necessary services generally, but not for certain medically necessary abortions. Abortion is inherently different from other medical procedures, because no other procedure involves the purposeful termination of a potential life. . . .

Where, as here, the Congress has neither invaded a substantive constitutional right or freedom nor enacted legislation that purposefully operates to the detriment of a suspect class, the only requirement of equal protection is that congressional action be rationally related to a legitimate governmental interest. The Hyde Amendment satisfies that standard. . . .

> This is consistent with the lack of a right to health care as well as the negative rights view of the U.S. Constitution described above: The government may not unduly interfere with a woman's right to abortion but has no affirmative obligation to help her obtain one.

IV

For the reasons stated in this opinion, we hold that a State that participates in the Medicaid program is not obligated under Title XIX to continue to fund those medically necessary abortions for which federal reimbursement is unavailable under the Hyde Amendment. . . . Accordingly, the judgment of the District Court is reversed, and the case is remanded to that court for further proceedings consistent with this opinion.

Mr. Justice MARSHALL, dissenting.

. . . Under the Hyde Amendment, federal funding is denied for abortions that are medically necessary and that are necessary to avert severe and permanent damage to the health of the mother. The Court's opinion studiously avoids recognizing the undeniable fact that for women eligible for Medicaid — poor women — denial of a Medicaid-funded abortion is equivalent to denial of legal abortion altogether. By definition, these women do not have the money to pay for an abortion themselves. If abortion is medically necessary and a funded abortion is unavailable, they must resort to back-alley butchers, attempt to induce an abortion themselves by crude and dangerous methods, or suffer the serious medical consequences of attempting to carry the fetus to term. Because legal abortion is not a realistic option for such women, the predictable result of the Hyde Amendment will be a significant increase in the number of poor women who will die or suffer significant health damage because of an inability to procure necessary medical services.

Justice Marshall's dissent was the only opinion to directly account for the fact that — by definition — women in the Medicaid program cannot afford to pay for any kind of medical care.

The legislation before us is the product of an effort to deny to the poor the constitutional right recognized in *Roe v. Wade*, even though the cost may be serious and long-lasting health damage. As my Brother Stevens has demonstrated, the premise underlying the Hyde Amendment was repudiated in *Roe v. Wade*, where the Court made clear that the state interest in protecting fetal life cannot justify jeopardizing the life or health of the mother. The denial of Medicaid benefits to individuals who meet all the statutory criteria for eligibility, solely because the treatment that is medically necessary involves the exercise of the fundamental right to choose abortion, is a form of discrimination repugnant to the equal protection of the laws guaranteed by the Constitution. The Court's decision today marks a retreat from *Roe v. Wade* and represents a cruel blow to the most powerless members of our society. I dissent. . . .

QUESTIONS

1. Under what circumstances must a state pay for Medicaid beneficiaries' abortions?
2. When may a state pay?
3. Could a state totally refuse to pay for abortions while participating in Medicaid?

The ACA extended the Hyde Amendment's limitations on abortion coverage to private insurance (discussed in Chapter 3). The ACA requires most private, individual, and small-group insurance plans sold on and off the Exchanges to cover a federal package of essential health benefits (EHB), defined by reference to a state benchmark plan. States also may impose additional coverage mandates, beyond the federal EHB.

42 U.S.C. §18023. Special rules

(a) State opt-out of abortion coverage

(1) In general

A State may elect to prohibit abortion coverage in qualified health plans offered through an Exchange in such State if such State enacts a law to provide for such prohibition.

(2) Termination of opt out

A State may repeal a law described in paragraph (1) and provide for the offering of such services through the Exchange.

(b) Special rules relating to coverage of abortion services

(1) Voluntary choice of coverage of abortion services

(A) In general

Notwithstanding any other provision of this title —

(i) nothing in this title shall be construed to require a qualified health plan to provide coverage of services described in subparagraph (B)(i) or (B)(ii) as part of its essential health benefits for any plan year; and

(ii) subject to subsection (a), the issuer of a qualified health plan shall determine whether or not the plan provides coverage of services described in subparagraph (B)(i) or (B)(ii) as part of such benefits for the plan year.

(B) Abortion services

(i) Abortions for which public funding is prohibited

The services described in this clause are abortions for which the expenditure of Federal funds appropriated for the Department of Health and Human Services is not permitted, based on the law as in effect as of the date that is 6 months before the beginning of the plan year involved.

This provision imports the Hyde Amendment into private insurance.

(ii) Abortions for which public funding is allowed

The services described in this clause are abortions for which the expenditure of Federal funds appropriated for the Department of Health and Human Services is permitted, based on the law as in effect as of the date that is 6 months before the beginning of the plan year involved.

(2) Prohibition on the use of Federal funds

(A) In general

If a qualified health plan provides coverage of services described in paragraph (1)(B)(i), the issuer of the plan shall not use any amount attributable to any of the following for purposes of paying for such services:

(i) The credit under section 36B of Title 26. . . .

(ii) Any cost-sharing reduction under section 18071 of this title. . . .

(B) Establishment of allocation accounts

In the case of a plan to which subparagraph (A) applies, the issuer of the plan shall—

(i) collect from each enrollee in the plan (without regard to the enrollee's age, sex, or family status) a separate payment for each of the following:

(I) an amount equal to the portion of the premium to be paid directly by the enrollee for coverage under the plan of services other than services described in paragraph (1)(B)(i) (after reduction for credits and cost-sharing reductions described in subparagraph (A)); and

(II) an amount equal to the actuarial value of the coverage of services described in paragraph (1)(B)(i), and

(ii) shall deposit all such separate payments into separate allocation accounts as provided in subparagraph (C). . . .

(C) Segregation of funds

(i) In general

The issuer of a plan to which subparagraph (A) applies shall establish allocation accounts described in clause (ii) for enrollees receiving amounts described in subparagraph (A). . . .

(E) Ensuring compliance with segregation requirements
(i) In general
Subject to clause (ii), State health insurance commissioners shall ensure that health plans comply with the segregation requirements in this subsection through the segregation of plan funds in accordance with applicable provisions of generally accepted accounting requirements, circulars on funds management of the Office of Management and Budget, and guidance on accounting of the Government Accountability Office. . . .

. . . .

(4) No discrimination on basis of provision of abortion
No qualified health plan offered through an Exchange may discriminate against any individual health care provider or health care facility because of its unwillingness to provide, pay for, provide coverage of, or refer for abortions[.]
(c) Application of State and Federal laws regarding abortion
(1) No preemption of State laws regarding abortion
Nothing in this Act shall be construed to preempt or otherwise have any effect on State laws regarding the prohibition of (or requirement of) coverage, funding, or procedural requirements on abortions, including parental notification or consent for the performance of an abortion on a minor.
(2) No effect on Federal laws regarding abortion
(A) In general
Nothing in this Act shall be construed to have any effect on Federal laws regarding—
(i) conscience protection;
(ii) willingness or refusal to provide abortion; and
(iii) discrimination on the basis of the willingness or refusal to provide, pay for, cover, or refer for abortion or to provide or participate in training to provide abortion. . . .
(d) Application of emergency services laws
Nothing in this Act shall be construed to relieve any health care provider from providing emergency services as required by State or Federal law, including . . . "EMTALA."

The contrast is notable; on one hand, under the ACA, health insurers must cover all contraceptives approved by the Food and Drug Administration (FDA) for women. On the other hand, no abortions will be covered by Medicaid or federal tax subsidies for purchasing private health insurance through the Exchanges, and an elaborate opt-out scheme is created by the statutory provisions above (26 states restrict abortion coverage in plans offered through the Exchanges as of March 2018). Poor women are the most likely to seek an abortion and the least likely to be able to pay for one, which often delays the point at which the abortion is performed, making an abortion more expensive and more medically involved. The support for contraceptive coverage enacted by the ACA may reverse this long-standing trend, although administrative actions taken by the Trump Administration may weaken the universal coverage enacted by the ACA (such as allowing employers' "moral objections" to contraceptive coverage, as discussed in Chapter 3).

QUESTIONS

1. Can one medical service be assigned a valid actuarial value for insurance under-writing purposes?
2. In states that require this type of separate insurance for abortions, evidence indicates that insurers do not offer riders that would pay for abortion separately because individuals do not purchase them (and may not even be aware of them). Why might this be the experience so far?

Roe's highly structured approach to decriminalizing and regulating abortion services did not sit well with state politicians and advocacy groups that oppose abortion. After 20 years of passing state laws designed to challenge the *Roe* framework, a test case was granted certiorari by the Court.

Planned Parenthood of Southeastern Pennsylvania v. Casey

505 U.S. 833 (1992)

Justice O'CONNOR, Justice KENNEDY, and Justice SOUTER announced the judgment of the Court and delivered the opinion of the Court with respect to Parts I, II, III, V-A, V-C, and VI, an opinion with respect to Part V-E, in which Justice STEVENS joins, and an opinion with respect to Parts IV, V-B, and V-D.

I

Liberty finds no refuge in a jurisprudence of doubt. . . .

At issue in these cases are five provisions of the Pennsylvania Abortion Control Act of 1982. . . . The Act requires that a woman seeking an abortion give her informed consent prior to the abortion procedure, and specifies that she be provided with certain information at least 24 hours before the abortion is performed. For a minor to obtain an abortion, the Act requires the informed consent of one of her parents, but provides for a judicial bypass option if the minor does not wish to or cannot obtain a parent's consent. Another provision of the Act requires that, unless certain exceptions apply, a married woman seeking an abortion must sign a statement indicating that she has notified her husband of her intended abortion. The Act exempts compliance with these three requirements in the event of a "medical emergency," which is defined in the Act. In addition to the above provisions regulating the performance of abortions, the Act imposes certain reporting requirements on facilities that provide abortion services. . . .

After considering the fundamental constitutional questions resolved by *Roe*, principles of institutional integrity, and the rule of stare decisis, we are led to conclude this: the essential holding of *Roe v. Wade* should be retained and once again reaffirmed.

It must be stated at the outset and with clarity that *Roe*'s essential holding, the holding we reaffirm, has three parts. First is a recognition of the right of the woman to choose to have an abortion before viability and to obtain it without undue interference from the State. Before viability, the State's interests are not strong enough to support a prohibition of abortion or the imposition of a substantial obstacle to the woman's effective right to elect the procedure. Second is a confirmation of

> The Court explicitly reaffirmed *Roe* because the case experienced many challenges since 1973. At the same time, this decision opened the door to more state regulation of abortion by introducing the more flexible "undue burden" standard.

the State's power to restrict abortions after fetal viability, if the law contains exceptions for pregnancies which endanger the woman's life or health. And third is the principle that the State has legitimate interests from the outset of the pregnancy in protecting the health of the woman and the life of the fetus that may become a child. These principles do not contradict one another; and we adhere to each....

II

....

It should be recognized, moreover, that in some critical respects the abortion decision is of the same character as the decision to use contraception, to which *Griswold v. Connecticut, Eisenstadt v. Baird,* and *Carey v. Population Services International* afford constitutional protection. We have no doubt as to the correctness of those decisions. They support the reasoning in *Roe* relating to the woman's liberty because they involve personal decisions concerning not only the meaning of procreation but also human responsibility and respect for it....

While we appreciate the weight of the arguments made on behalf of the State in the cases before us, arguments which in their ultimate formulation conclude that *Roe* should be overruled, the reservations any of us may have in reaffirming the central holding of *Roe* are outweighed by the explication of individual liberty we have given combined with the force of stare decisis. We turn now to that doctrine....

IV

From what we have said so far it follows that it is a constitutional liberty of the woman to have some freedom to terminate her pregnancy. We conclude that the basic decision in *Roe* was based on a constitutional analysis which we cannot now repudiate. The woman's liberty is not so unlimited, however, that from the outset the State cannot show its concern for the life of the unborn, and at a later point in fetal development the State's interest in life has sufficient force so that the right of the woman to terminate the pregnancy can be restricted.

That brings us, of course, to the point where much criticism has been directed at *Roe,* a criticism that always inheres when the Court draws a specific rule from what in the Constitution is but a general standard. We conclude, however, that the urgent claims of the woman to retain the ultimate control over her destiny and her body, claims implicit in the meaning of liberty, require us to perform that function. Liberty must not be extinguished for want of a line that is clear. And it falls to us to give some real substance to the woman's liberty to determine whether to carry her pregnancy to full term.

We conclude the line should be drawn at viability, so that before that time the woman has a right to choose to terminate her pregnancy. We adhere to this principle for two reasons. First, as we have said, is the doctrine of stare decisis....

The second reason is that the concept of viability, as we noted in *Roe,* is the time at which there is a realistic possibility of maintaining and nourishing a life outside the womb, so that the independent existence of the second life can in reason and all fairness be the object of state protection that now overrides the rights of the woman. Consistent with other constitutional norms, legislatures may draw lines which appear arbitrary without the necessity of offering a justification. But courts may not. We must justify the lines we draw. And there is no line other than viability which is more workable. To be sure, as we have said, there may be some medical developments that affect the precise point of viability, but this is an imprecision within tolerable limits given that the medical community and all those who must apply its discoveries will continue to explore the matter. The viability line also has, as a practical matter, an element of fairness. In some broad sense it might be said that a woman who fails to act before viability has consented to the State's intervention on behalf of the developing child.

The woman's right to terminate her pregnancy before viability is the most central principle of *Roe v. Wade*. It is a rule of law and a component of liberty we cannot renounce. . . .

Yet it must be remembered that *Roe v. Wade* speaks with clarity in establishing not only the woman's liberty but also the State's "important and legitimate interest in potential life." That portion of the decision in *Roe* has been given too little acknowledgment and implementation by the Court in its subsequent cases. . . .

Though the woman has a right to choose to terminate or continue her pregnancy before viability, it does not at all follow that the State is prohibited from taking steps to ensure that this choice is thoughtful and informed. Even in the earliest stages of pregnancy, the State may enact rules and regulations designed to encourage her to know that there are philosophic and social arguments of great weight that can be brought to bear in favor of continuing the pregnancy to full term and that there are procedures and institutions to allow adoption of unwanted children as well as a certain degree of state assistance if the mother chooses to raise the child herself. "'[T]he Constitution does not forbid a State or city, pursuant to democratic processes, from expressing a preference for normal childbirth.'" It follows that States are free to enact laws to provide a reasonable framework for a woman to make a decision that has such profound and lasting meaning. This, too, we find consistent with *Roe*'s central premises, and indeed the inevitable consequence of our holding that the State has an interest in protecting the life of the unborn.

> Full-term delivery occurs at 40 weeks of pregnancy, and full-term delivery begins at 38 weeks. Birth before that time period is deemed premature, but "viability" is a challenging concept, even for physicians that specialize in neonatal care. Studies show that infants born before 25 weeks' gestation will most likely die in the neonatal period. But survival is not the sole factor for care of an extremely preterm infant; they often experience lifelong neurological and organ function complications and may require heroic interventions in a hospital neonatal intensive care unit (NICU).

We reject the trimester framework, which we do not consider to be part of the essential holding of *Roe*. Measures aimed at ensuring that a woman's choice contemplates the consequences for the fetus do not necessarily interfere with the right recognized in *Roe*, although those measures have been found to be inconsistent with the rigid trimester framework announced in that case. A logical reading of the central holding in *Roe* itself, and a necessary reconciliation of the liberty of the woman and the interest of the State in promoting prenatal life, require, in our view, that we abandon the trimester framework as a rigid prohibition on all previability regulation aimed at the protection of fetal life. The trimester framework suffers from these basic flaws: in its formulation it misconceives the nature of the pregnant woman's interest; and in practice it undervalues the State's interest in potential life, as recognized in *Roe*.

. . . Numerous forms of state regulation might have the incidental effect of increasing the cost or decreasing the availability of medical care, whether for abortion or any other medical procedure. The fact that a law which serves a valid purpose, one not designed to strike at the right itself, has the incidental effect of making it more difficult or more expensive to procure an abortion cannot be enough to invalidate it. Only where state regulation imposes an undue burden on a woman's ability to make this decision does the power of the State reach into the heart of the liberty protected by the Due Process Clause. . . .

The very notion that the State has a substantial interest in potential life leads to the conclusion that not all regulations must be deemed unwarranted. Not all burdens on the right to decide whether to terminate a pregnancy will be undue. In our view, the undue burden standard is the appropriate means of reconciling the State's interest with the woman's constitutionally protected liberty. . . .

A finding of an undue burden is a shorthand for the conclusion that a state

This begins the articulation of the new "undue burden" standard.	regulation has the purpose or effect of placing a substantial obstacle in the path of a woman seeking an abortion of a nonviable fetus. A statute with this purpose is invalid because the means chosen by the State to further the interest in potential life

must be calculated to inform the woman's free choice, not hinder it. And a statute which, while furthering the interest in potential life or some other valid state interest, has the effect of placing a substantial obstacle in the path of a woman's choice cannot be considered a permissible means of serving its legitimate ends. . . .

Some guiding principles should emerge. What is at stake is the woman's right to make the ultimate decision, not a right to be insulated from all others in doing so. Regulations which do no more than create a structural mechanism by which the State, or the parent or guardian of a minor, may express profound respect for the life of the unborn are permitted, if they are not a substantial obstacle to the woman's exercise of the right to choose. Unless it has that effect on her right of choice, a state measure designed to persuade her to choose childbirth over abortion will be upheld if reasonably related to that goal. Regulations designed to foster the health of a woman seeking an abortion are valid if they do not constitute an undue burden.

. . . We give this summary:

(a) To protect the central right recognized by *Roe v. Wade* while at the same time accommodating the State's profound interest in potential life, we will employ the undue burden analysis as explained in this opinion. An undue burden exists, and therefore a provision of law is invalid, if its purpose or effect is to place a substantial obstacle in the path of a woman seeking an abortion before the fetus attains viability.

(b) We reject the rigid trimester framework of *Roe v. Wade*. To promote the State's profound interest in potential life, throughout pregnancy the State may take measures to ensure that the woman's choice is informed, and measures

States have long regulated medicine to protect the public's health and safety, but recently they have used this summary of *Casey's* analytical structure to create abortion-limiting laws that are justified as promoting the "health" of women. Regulation in the name of health is explored below in the context of "TRAP laws."	designed to advance this interest will not be invalidated as long as their purpose is to persuade the woman to choose childbirth over abortion. These measures must not be an undue burden on the right. (c) As with any medical procedure, the State may enact regulations to further the health or safety of a woman seeking an abortion. Unnecessary health regulations that have the purpose or effect of presenting a substantial obstacle to a woman seeking an abortion impose an undue burden on the right. (d) Our adoption of the undue burden analysis does not disturb the central holding of *Roe v. Wade*, and we reaffirm that holding. Regardless of whether exceptions are made for

particular circumstances, a State may not prohibit any woman from making the ultimate decision to terminate her pregnancy before viability.

(e) We also reaffirm *Roe*'s holding that "subsequent to viability, the State in promoting its interest in the potentiality of human life may, if it chooses, regulate, and even proscribe, abortion except where it is necessary, in appropriate medical judgment, for the preservation of the life or health of the mother."

These principles control our assessment of the Pennsylvania statute, and we now turn to the issue of the validity of its challenged provisions.

V

. . . .

A

Because it is central to the operation of various other requirements, we begin with the statute's definition of medical emergency. Under the statute, a medical emergency is

> "[t]hat condition which, on the basis of the physician's good faith clinical judgment, so complicates the medical condition of a pregnant woman as to necessitate the immediate abortion of her pregnancy to avert her death or for which a delay will create serious risk of substantial and irreversible impairment of a major bodily function."

Petitioners argue that the definition is too narrow, contending that it forecloses the possibility of an immediate abortion despite some significant health risks. If the contention were correct, we would be required to invalidate the restrictive operation of the provision, for the essential holding of *Roe* forbids a State to interfere with a woman's choice to undergo an abortion procedure if continuing her pregnancy would constitute a threat to her health.

. . . While the definition could be interpreted in an unconstitutional manner, the Court of Appeals construed the phrase "serious risk" to include those circumstances. It stated: "[W]e read the medical emergency exception as intended by the Pennsylvania legislature to assure that compliance with its abortion regulations would not in any way pose a significant threat to the life or health of a woman." . . . We adhere to that course today, and conclude that, as construed by the Court of Appeals, the medical emergency definition imposes no undue burden on a woman's abortion right.

B

We next consider the informed consent requirement. Except in a medical emergency, the statute requires that at least 24 hours before performing an abortion a physician inform the woman of the nature of the procedure, the health risks of the abortion and of childbirth, and the "probable gestational age of the unborn child." The physician or a qualified nonphysician must inform the woman of the availability of printed materials published by the State describing the fetus and providing information about medical assistance for childbirth, information about child support from the father, and a list of agencies which provide adoption and other services as alternatives to abortion. An abortion may not be performed unless the woman certifies in writing that she has been informed of the availability of these printed materials and has been provided them if she chooses to view them.

Our prior decisions establish that as with any medical procedure, the State may require a woman to give her written informed consent to an abortion. In this respect, the statute is unexceptional. Petitioners challenge the statute's definition of informed consent because it includes the provision of specific information by the doctor and the mandatory 24-hour waiting period. . . .

. . . In attempting to ensure that a woman apprehend the full consequences of her decision, the State furthers the legitimate purpose of reducing the risk that a woman may elect an abortion, only to discover later, with devastating psychological consequences, that her decision was not fully informed. If the information the State requires to be made available to the woman is truthful and not misleading, the requirement may be permissible.

We also see no reason why the State may not require doctors to inform a woman seeking an abortion of the availability of materials relating to the consequences to the fetus, even when those consequences have no direct relation to her health. . . . In short, requiring that the woman be informed of the availability of information relating to fetal development and the assistance available should she decide to carry the pregnancy to full term is a reasonable measure to ensure an informed choice, one which might cause the woman to choose childbirth over abortion. This requirement cannot be considered a substantial obstacle to obtaining an abortion, and, it follows, there is no undue burden.

> The Court's upholding the provision that forces doctors to deliver state-scripted information that may not be medically accurate (or even further women's health) is a notable move away from the physician-centric prose in *Roe*. State-scripted information is an ongoing issue that is before the Court in the 2017-2018 term, discussed further below.

Our prior cases also suggest that the "straitjacket" of particular information which must be given in each case interferes with a constitutional right of privacy between a pregnant woman and her physician. As a preliminary matter, it is worth noting that the statute now before us does not require a physician to comply with the informed consent provisions "if he or she can demonstrate by a preponderance of the evidence, that he or she reasonably believed that furnishing the information would have resulted in a severely adverse effect on the physical or mental health of the patient." In this respect, the statute does not prevent the physician from exercising his or her medical judgment.

. . . All that is left of petitioners' argument is an asserted First Amendment right of a physician not to provide information about the risks of abortion, and childbirth, in a manner mandated by the State. To be sure, the physician's First Amendment rights not to speak are implicated, *see* Wooley v. Maynard, but only as part of the practice of medicine, subject to reasonable licensing and regulation by the State. We see no constitutional infirmity in the requirement that the physician provide the information mandated by the State here.

The Pennsylvania statute also requires us to reconsider the holding in *Akron I* that the State may not require that a physician, as opposed to a qualified assistant, provide information relevant to a woman's informed consent. Since there is no evidence on this record that requiring a doctor to give the information as provided by the statute would amount in practical terms to a substantial obstacle to a woman seeking an abortion, we conclude that it is not an undue burden. . . .

Whether the mandatory 24-hour waiting period is nonetheless invalid because in practice it is a substantial obstacle to a woman's choice to terminate her pregnancy is a closer question. The findings of fact by the District Court indicate that because of the distances many women must travel to reach an abortion provider, the practical effect will often be a delay of much more than a day because the waiting period requires that a woman seeking an abortion make at least two visits to the doctor. . . . As a result, the District Court found that for those women who have the fewest financial resources, those who must travel long distances, and those who have difficulty explaining their whereabouts to husbands, employers, or others, the 24-hour waiting period will be "particularly burdensome."

> The Court's rejection of the district court's findings and conclusion echoes *Harris v. McRae* and the Court's reluctance to recognize the medical access difficulties of low-income women.

These findings are troubling in some respects, but they do not demonstrate that the waiting period constitutes an undue burden. We do not doubt that, as the District Court held, the waiting period has the effect of "increasing the cost and risk of delay of abortions," but the District Court did not conclude that the increased costs and potential delays amount to substantial obstacles. . . . [A]s we have stated, under the undue burden standard a State is permitted to enact persuasive measures which favor childbirth over abortion, even if those measures do not further a health interest. And while the waiting period does limit a physician's discretion, that is not, standing alone, a reason to invalidate it. In light of the construction given the statute's definition of medical emergency by the Court of Appeals, and the District Court's findings, we cannot say that the waiting period imposes a real health risk.

We also disagree with the District Court's conclusion that the "particularly burdensome" effects of the waiting period on some women require its invalidation. A particular burden is not of necessity a substantial obstacle. Whether a burden falls on a particular group is a distinct inquiry from whether it is a substantial obstacle even as to the women in that group. And the District Court did not conclude that the waiting period is such an obstacle even for the women who are most burdened by it. Hence, on the record before us, and in the context of this facial challenge, we are not convinced that the 24-hour waiting period constitutes an undue burden.

. . . .

C

Section 3209 of Pennsylvania's abortion law provides, except in cases of medical emergency, that no physician shall perform an abortion on a married woman without receiving a signed statement from the woman that she has notified her spouse that she is about to undergo an abortion. The woman has the option of providing an alternative signed statement certifying that her husband is not the man who impregnated her; that her husband could not be located; that the pregnancy is the result of spousal sexual assault which she has reported; or that the woman believes that notifying her husband will cause him or someone else to inflict bodily injury upon her. A physician who performs an abortion on a married woman without receiving the appropriate signed statement will have his or her license revoked, and is liable to the husband for damages. . . .

In well-functioning marriages, spouses discuss important intimate decisions such as whether to bear a child. But there are millions of women in this country who are the victims of regular physical and psychological abuse at the hands of their husbands. Should these women become pregnant, they may have very good reasons for not wishing to inform their husbands of their decision to obtain an abortion. Many may have justifiable fears of physical abuse, but may be no less fearful of the consequences of reporting prior abuse to the Commonwealth of Pennsylvania. Many may have a reasonable fear that notifying their husbands will provoke further instances of child abuse; these women are not exempt from §3209's notification requirement. Many may fear devastating forms of psychological abuse from their husbands, including verbal harassment, threats of future violence, the destruction of possessions, physical confinement to the home, the withdrawal of financial support, or the disclosure of the abortion to family and friends. These methods of psychological abuse may act as even more of a deterrent to notification than the possibility of physical violence, but women who are the victims of the abuse are not exempt from §3209's notification requirement. And many women who are pregnant as a result of sexual assaults by their husbands will be unable to avail themselves of the exception for spousal sexual assault, §3209 (b)(3), because the exception requires that the woman have notified law enforcement authorities within 90 days of the assault, and her husband will be notified of her report once an investigation begins, §3128(c). If anything in this field is certain, it is that victims of spousal sexual assault are extremely reluctant to report the abuse to the government; hence, a great many spousal rape victims will not be exempt from the notification requirement imposed by §3209.

> The Court's evaluation of the five statutory provisions at issue in *Casey* became a blueprint for states interested in restricting access to abortions. States have also pushed the boundaries of this analysis, for example, by requiring 48-hour waiting periods rather than 24-hour waiting periods. Thus, lower federal courts frequently have had to follow this analysis as the model for evaluating regulation of abortion providers and services.

The spousal notification requirement is thus likely to prevent a significant number of women from obtaining an abortion. It does not merely make abortions a little more difficult or expensive to obtain; for many women, it will impose a substantial obstacle. We must not blind ourselves to the fact that the significant number of women who fear for their safety and the safety of their children are likely to be deterred from procuring an abortion as surely as if the Commonwealth had outlawed abortion in all cases. . . . It is an undue burden, and therefore invalid. . . .

D

We next consider the parental consent provision. Except in a medical emergency, an unemancipated young woman under 18 may not obtain an abortion unless she and one of her parents (or guardian) provides informed consent as defined above. If neither a parent nor a guardian provides consent, a court may authorize the performance of an abortion upon a determination that the young woman is mature and capable of giving informed consent and has in fact given her informed consent, or that an abortion would be in her best interests.

> Judicial bypass produces a possible paradox: If a judge were to decide that a minor is not mature enough to have an abortion, she would have a child to raise (if adoption does not occur). The minor parent will make medical decisions for her child, yet she was not permitted to make such decisions for herself.

We have been over most of this ground before. Our cases establish, and we reaffirm today, that a State may require a minor seeking an abortion to obtain the consent of a parent or guardian, provided that there is an adequate judicial bypass procedure. . . .

E

Under the recordkeeping and reporting requirements of the statute, every facility which performs abortions is required to file a report stating its name and address as well as the name and address of any related entity, such as a controlling or subsidiary organization. In the case of state-funded institutions, the information becomes public.

. . . In *Danforth*, we held that recordkeeping and reporting provisions "that are reasonably directed to the preservation of maternal health and that properly respect a patient's confidentiality and privacy are permissible." We think that under this standard, all the provisions at issue here, except that relating to spousal notice, are constitutional. . . .

Subsection (12) of the reporting provision requires the reporting of, among other things, a married woman's "reason for failure to provide notice" to her husband. §3214(a)(12). This provision in effect requires women, as a condition of obtaining an abortion, to provide the Commonwealth with the precise information we have already recognized that many women have pressing reasons not to reveal. Like the spousal notice requirement itself, this provision places an undue burden on a woman's choice, and must be invalidated for that reason.

QUESTIONS

1. What kind of state action constitutes an undue burden?
2. What can a state do in the name of regulating for health?
3. Are reproductive care questions still treated by the Court as a deeply private matter between the physician and the patient, or may the state play a role under the *Casey* analysis?

The right to procreate articulated in *Skinner* has been extended in two directions, to a right not to procreate, which we have just explored, and seeking assistance in reproduction. Assisted reproductive technologies (ART) remain remarkably unregulated in the United States, and so the leading Supreme Court cases are often used as a baseline to help state courts to decide cases of first impression regarding ART. For example, in an early ART case, Davis v. Davis, 842 S.W.2d 588 (Tenn. 1992), the Tennessee Supreme Court had to decide whose demands should control when a divorced couple disagreed whether cryogenically preserved (frozen) gametes from in vitro fertilization procedures could be used by the ex-wife, against the ex-husband's wishes. Relying on *Skinner*, *Griswold*, *Roe*, and related cases, the court constructed a balancing test to determine whether the right to procreate was stronger than the right not to procreate (and found for the latter position, as the ex-husband's desire not to procreate was given primacy without second-guessing his decision, unlike the extra scrutiny states apply to an abortion decision).

In 2007, the Supreme Court decided *Gonzales v. Carhart*, which upheld the federal Partial Birth Abortion Ban Act, 18 U.S.C. §1531. 550 U.S. 124 (2007). Though the Court struck down a similar Nebraska statute in 2000, Justice O'Connor's retirement and replacement by Justice Samuel Alito shifted the voting balance away from reaffirming or expanding *Casey* and *Roe*. *Gonzales v. Carhart* was remarkable for allowing federal law to ban certain abortion procedures without an exception for the health of the pregnant woman (required in prior decisions) and without considering the treating physician's opinion on the best course of treatment. Both were meaningful steps away from the *Roe* and *Casey* architecture.

"Partial birth abortion" is not a medical or scientific term. In medicine, the procedure is known as "dilation and extraction" (D&X) or "intact dilation and evacuation" (intact D&E).

States enacted a variety of new laws in the wake of *Gonzales v. Carhart*. Some banned "partial birth abortion." Others created a new kind of law to limit access to abortion dubbed Targeted Regulation of Abortion Provider laws (TRAP laws). These laws attach special regulations to doctors and clinics that provide abortions, while similar health care providers are subject to less rigorous regulation. Examples include more frequent licensure and inspection for abortion providers; requiring abortions to be performed only in a setting that meets licensure standards for ambulatory surgery centers, which are larger and more complex than the usual doctor's office setting; requiring women seeking medical abortion (rather than surgical) to take the medication in an outpatient surgical setting; or requiring physicians who provide surgical abortions to have admitting privileges at a hospital within a short distance of the doctor's office (many hospitals refuse to grant such privileges, or no hospital is within

> Medical abortions (rather than surgical) have become more common, especially for rural women who have a harder time accessing all medical care, including reproductive health care. The FDA requires that the prescription and ingestion of the first drug — mifepristone, followed by misoprostol within 24 to 48 hours — be taken in a clinic, doctor's office, or hospital.

range). The American Medical Association and the American College of Obstetricians and Gynecologists oppose such laws as jeopardizing women's health, because they tend to close abortion providers; therefore, women seeking an abortion must travel great distances to access safe abortion services.

Texas's TRAP laws were struck down by the Supreme Court in 2016. This was first time the Court evaluated how the undue burden test applies to state laws enacted under the guise of protecting the health of women seeking abortions but that have the intended effect of limiting access to care. TRAP laws are known to close women's health clinics, forcing women to travel great distances (150 miles or more) to access reproductive services. This incongruity made the Court reconsider what constitutes legitimate state regulation for protecting the "health" of citizenry; as noted above, courts often defer to state action to protect public health, but TRAP laws gave the Court reason to be skeptical.

Whole Women's Health v. Hellerstedt

136 S. Ct. 2922 (2016)

Justice BREYER delivered the opinion of the Court.

In *Planned Parenthood of Southeastern Pa. v. Casey*, a plurality of the Court concluded that there "exists" an "undue burden" on a woman's right to decide to have an abortion, and consequently a provision of law is constitutionally invalid, if the "*purpose or effect*" of the provision "*is to place a substantial obstacle* in the path of a woman seeking an abortion before the fetus attains viability." (Emphasis added.) The plurality added that "[u]nnecessary health regulations that have the purpose or effect of presenting a substantial obstacle to a woman seeking an abortion impose an undue burden on the right."

We must here decide whether two provisions of Texas' House Bill 2 violate the Federal Constitution as interpreted in *Casey*. The first provision, which we shall call the "admitting-privileges requirement," says that

> "[a] physician performing or inducing an abortion . . . must, on the date the abortion is performed or induced, have active admitting privileges at a hospital that . . . is located not further than 30 miles from the location at which the abortion is performed

or induced." Tex. Health & Safety Code Ann. §171.0031(a) (West Cum. Supp. 2015).

This provision amended Texas law that had previously required an abortion facility to maintain a written protocol "for managing medical emergencies and the transfer of patients requiring further emergency care to a hospital." 38 Tex. Reg. 6546 (2013).

The second provision, which we shall call the "surgical-center requirement," says that

"the minimum standards for an abortion facility must be equivalent to the minimum standards adopted under [the Texas Health and Safety Code section] for ambulatory surgical centers." Tex. Health & Safety Code Ann. §245.010(a).

We conclude that neither of these provisions confers medical benefits sufficient to justify the burdens upon access that each imposes. Each places a substantial obstacle in the path of women seeking a previability abortion, each constitutes an undue burden on abortion access, *Casey*, and each violates the Federal Constitution. Amdt. 14, §1.

I

A

In July 2013, the Texas Legislature enacted House Bill 2 (H.B. 2 or Act). In September (before the new law took effect), a group of Texas abortion providers filed an action in Federal District Court seeking facial invalidation of the law's admitting-privileges provision. In late October, the District Court granted the injunction. But three days later, the Fifth Circuit vacated the injunction, thereby permitting the provision to take effect. Planned Parenthood of Greater Tex. Surgical Health Servs. v. Abbott, 734 F.3d 406 (2013).

The Fifth Circuit subsequently upheld the provision, and set forth its reasons in an opinion released late the following March. In that opinion, the Fifth Circuit pointed to evidence introduced in the District Court the previous October. It noted that Texas had offered evidence designed to show that the admitting-privileges requirement "will reduce the delay in treatment and decrease health risk for abortion patients with critical complications," and that it would "'screen out' untrained or incompetent abortion providers." The opinion also explained that the plaintiffs had not provided sufficient evidence "that abortion practitioners will likely be unable to comply with the privileges requirement." The court said that all "of the major Texas cities, including Austin, Corpus Christi, Dallas, El Paso, Houston, and San Antonio," would "continue to have multiple clinics where many physicians will have or obtain hospital admitting privileges." The *Abbott* plaintiffs did not file a petition for certiorari in this Court.

B

On April 6, one week after the Fifth Circuit's decision, petitioners, a group of abortion providers (many of whom were plaintiffs in the previous lawsuit), filed the present lawsuit in Federal District Court. They sought an injunction preventing enforcement of the admitting-privileges provision as applied to physicians at two abortion facilities, one operated by Whole Woman's Health in McAllen and the other operated by Nova Health Systems in El Paso. They also sought an injunction prohibiting enforcement of the surgical-center provision anywhere in Texas. They claimed that the admitting-privileges provision and the surgical-center provision violated the Constitution's Fourteenth Amendment, as interpreted in *Casey*....

The District Court determined that the surgical-center requirement "imposes an undue burden on the right of women throughout Texas to seek a previability abortion," and that the "admitting-privileges requirement, ... in conjunction with the ambulatory-surgical-center requirement, imposes an undue burden on the right of women in the Rio Grande Valley, El Paso, and West Texas to seek a previability abortion." The District Court concluded that the "two provisions" would cause "the closing of almost all abortion clinics in Texas that were operating legally in the fall of 2013," and thereby create a constitutionally "impermissible obstacle as applied to all women seeking a previability abortion" by "restricting access to previously available legal facilities." On August 29, 2014, the court enjoined the enforcement of the two provisions.

C

... On June 9, 2015, the Court of Appeals reversed the District Court on the merits. With minor exceptions, it found both provisions constitutional and allowed them to take effect. ...

II

Before turning to the constitutional question, we must consider the Court of Appeals' procedural grounds for holding that (but for the challenge to the provisions of H.B. 2 as applied to McAllen and El Paso) petitioners were barred from bringing their constitutional challenges. [The Court held that res judicata did not bar the claims.]

III

Undue Burden—Legal Standard

We begin with the standard, as described in *Casey*. We recognize that the "State has a legitimate interest in seeing to it that abortion, like any other medical procedure, is performed under circumstances that insure maximum safety for the patient." Roe v. Wade. But, we added, "a statute which, while furthering [a] valid state interest, has the effect of placing a substantial obstacle in the path of a woman's choice cannot be considered a permissible means of serving its legitimate ends." *Casey*. Moreover, "[u]nnecessary health regulations that have the purpose or effect of presenting a substantial obstacle to a woman seeking an abortion impose an undue burden on the right." Id.

> The Supreme Court upheld the federal Partial Birth Abortion Ban Act in *Gonzales v. Carhart* after applying rational basis review, which many interpreted to weaken *Casey* (until this case).

The Court of Appeals wrote that a state law is "constitutional if: (1) it does not have the purpose or effect of placing a substantial obstacle in the path of a woman seeking an abortion of a nonviable fetus; and (2) it is reasonably related to (or designed to further) a legitimate state interest." The Court of Appeals went on to hold that "the district court erred by substituting its own judgment for that of the legislature" when it conducted its "undue burden inquiry," in part because "medical uncertainty underlying a statute is for resolution by legislatures, not the courts."

The Court of Appeals' articulation of the relevant standard is incorrect. The first part of the Court of Appeals' test may be read to imply that a district court should not consider the existence or nonexistence of medical benefits when considering whether a regulation of abortion constitutes an undue burden. The rule announced in *Casey*, however, requires that courts consider the burdens a law imposes on abortion access together with the benefits those laws confer. And the second part of the test is wrong to equate the judicial review applicable to the regulation of a constitutionally protected personal liberty with the less strict review applicable where, for example, economic legislation is at issue. The Court of Appeals' approach simply does not match the standard that this Court laid out in *Casey*, which asks courts to consider whether any burden imposed on abortion access is "undue."

The statement that legislatures, and not courts, must resolve questions of medical uncertainty is also inconsistent with this Court's case law. Instead, the Court, when determining the constitutionality of laws regulating abortion procedures, has placed considerable weight upon evidence and argument presented in judicial proceedings. In *Casey*, for example, we relied heavily on the District Court's factual findings and the research-based submissions of amici in declaring a portion of the law at issue unconstitutional. And, in *Gonzales* the Court, while pointing out that we must review legislative "factfinding under a deferential standard," added that we must not "place dispositive weight" on those "findings." *Gonzales* went on to point out that the "Court retains an independent constitutional duty to review factual findings where constitutional rights are at stake." Although there we upheld a statute regulating abortion, we did not do so solely on the basis of legislative findings explicitly set forth in the statute, noting that "evidence presented in the District Courts contradicts" some of the legislative findings. In these circumstances, we said, "[u]ncritical deference to Congress' factual findings . . . is inappropriate."

Unlike in *Gonzales*, the relevant statute here does not set forth any legislative findings. Rather, one is left to infer that the legislature sought to further a constitutionally acceptable objective (namely, protecting women's health). For a district court to give significant weight to evidence in the judicial record in these circumstances is consistent with this Court's case law. . . .

IV

Undue Burden — Admitting-Privileges Requirement

Turning to the lower courts' evaluation of the evidence, we first consider the admitting-privileges requirement. Before the enactment of H.B. 2, doctors who provided abortions were required to "have admitting privileges or have a working arrangement with a physician(s) who has admitting privileges at a local hospital in order to ensure the necessary back up for medical complications." Tex. Admin. Code, tit. 25, §139.56 (2009). The new law changed this requirement by requiring that a "physician performing or inducing an abortion . . . must, on the date the abortion is performed or induced, have active admitting privileges at a hospital that . . . is located not further than 30 miles from the location at which the abortion is performed or induced." Tex. Health & Safety Code Ann. §171.0031(a). The District Court held that the legislative change imposed an "undue burden" on a woman's right to have an abortion. We conclude that there is adequate legal and factual support for the District Court's conclusion.

The purpose of the admitting-privileges requirement is to help ensure that women have easy access to a hospital should complications arise during an abortion procedure. But the District Court found that it brought about no such health-related benefit. The court found that "[t]he great weight of evidence demonstrates that, before the act's passage, abortion in Texas was extremely safe with particularly low rates of serious complications and virtually no deaths occurring on account of the procedure." Thus, there was no significant health-related problem that the new law helped to cure.

The evidence upon which the court based this conclusion included, among other things:

- A collection of at least five peer-reviewed studies on abortion complications in the first trimester, showing that the highest rate of major complications — including those complications requiring hospital admission — was less than one-quarter of 1%.
- Figures in three peer-reviewed studies showing that the highest complication rate found for the much rarer second trimester abortion was less than one-half of 1% (0.45% or about 1 out of about 200).
- Expert testimony to the effect that complications rarely require hospital admission, much less immediate transfer to a hospital from an outpatient clinic. . . .
- Expert testimony stating that "it is extremely unlikely that a patient will experience a serious complication at the clinic that requires emergent hospitalization" and "in the rare case in which [one does], the quality of care that the patient receives is not affected by whether the abortion provider has admitting privileges at the hospital."
- Expert testimony stating that in respect to surgical abortion patients who do suffer complications requiring hospitalization, most of these complications occur in the days after the abortion, not on the spot.
- Expert testimony stating that a delay before the onset of complications is also expected for medical abortions, as "abortifacient drugs take time to exert their effects, and thus the abortion itself almost always occurs after the patient has left the abortion facility."
- Some experts added that, if a patient needs a hospital in the day or week following her abortion, she will likely seek medical attention at the hospital nearest her home.

We have found nothing in Texas' record evidence that shows that, compared to prior law (which required a "working arrangement" with a doctor with admitting privileges), the new law advanced Texas' legitimate interest in protecting women's health.

We add that, when directly asked at oral argument whether Texas knew of a single instance in which the new requirement would have helped even one woman obtain better treatment, Texas admitted that there was no evidence in the record of such a case. This answer is consistent with the findings of the other Federal District Courts that have considered the health benefits of other States' similar admitting-privileges laws.

After H.B. 2 passed, Texas's lieutenant governor tweeted a state map showing the clinics that would close as a result of the state's new TRAP laws.

At the same time, the record evidence indicates that the admitting-privileges requirement places a "substantial obstacle in the path of a woman's choice." The District Court found, as of the time the admitting-privileges requirement began to be enforced, the number of facilities providing abortions dropped in half, from about 40 to about 20. Eight abortion clinics closed in the months leading up to the requirement's effective date. Eleven more closed on the day the admitting-privileges requirement took effect.

Other evidence helps to explain why the new requirement led to the closure of clinics. We read that other evidence in light of a brief filed in this Court by the Society of Hospital Medicine. That brief describes the undisputed general fact that "hospitals often condition admitting privileges on reaching a certain number of admissions per year." Returning to the District Court record, we note that, in direct testimony, the president of Nova Health Systems, implicitly relying on this general fact, pointed out that it would be difficult for doctors regularly performing abortions at the El Paso clinic to obtain admitting privileges at nearby hospitals because "[d]uring the past 10 years, over 17,000 abortion procedures were performed at the El Paso clinic [and n]ot a single one of those patients had to be transferred to a hospital for emergency treatment, much less admitted to the hospital." In a word, doctors would be unable to maintain admitting privileges or obtain those privileges for the future, because the fact that abortions are so safe meant that providers were unlikely to have any patients to admit.

. . . .

In our view, the record contains sufficient evidence that the admitting-privileges requirement led to the closure of half of Texas' clinics, or thereabouts. Those closures meant fewer doctors, longer waiting times, and increased crowding. Record evidence also supports the finding that after the admitting-privileges provision went into effect, the "number of women of reproductive age living in a county . . . more than 150 miles from a provider increased from approximately 86,000 to 400,000 . . . and the number of women living in a county more than 200 miles from a provider from approximately 10,000 to 290,000." We recognize that increased driving distances do not always constitute an "undue burden." But here, those increases are but one additional burden, which, when taken together with others that the closings brought about, and when viewed in light of the virtual absence of any health benefit, lead us to conclude that the record adequately supports the District Court's "undue burden" conclusion.

> This is the first time the Court took a hard look at state legislation enacted to "protect" women's health when, contrary to the state's assertion, the law will foreseeably harm women's health by significantly increasing driving distances to access safe services.

The dissent's only argument why these clinic closures, as well as the ones discussed in Part V, may not have imposed an undue burden is this: Although "H.B. 2 caused the closure of some clinics," other clinics may have closed for other reasons (so we should not "actually count" the burdens resulting from those closures against H.B. 2). But petitioners satisfied their burden to present evidence of causation by presenting direct testimony as well as plausible inferences to be drawn from the timing of the clinic closures. The District Court credited that evidence and concluded from it that H.B. 2 in fact led to the clinic closures. The dissent's speculation that perhaps other evidence, not presented at trial or credited by the District Court, might have shown that some clinics closed for unrelated reasons does not provide sufficient ground to disturb the District Court's factual finding on that issue.

In the same breath, the dissent suggests that one benefit of H.B. 2's requirements would be that they might "force unsafe facilities to shut down." To support that assertion, the dissent points to the Kermit Gosnell scandal. Gosnell, a physician in Pennsylvania, was convicted of first-degree murder and manslaughter. He "staffed his facility with unlicensed and indifferent workers, and then let them practice medicine unsupervised" and had "[d]irty facilities; unsanitary instruments; an absence of functioning monitoring and resuscitation equipment; the use of cheap, but dangerous, drugs; illegal procedures; and inadequate emergency access for when things inevitably went wrong." Gosnell's behavior was terribly wrong. But there is no reason to believe that an extra layer of regulation would have affected that behavior. Determined wrongdoers, already ignoring existing statutes and safety measures, are unlikely to be convinced to adopt safe practices by a new overlay of regulations. Regardless, Gosnell's deplorable crimes could escape detection only because his facility went uninspected for more than 15 years. Pre-existing Texas law already contained numerous detailed regulations covering abortion facilities, including a requirement that facilities be inspected at least annually. The record contains nothing to suggest that H.B. 2 would be more effective than pre-existing Texas law at deterring wrongdoers like Gosnell from criminal behavior.

V

Undue Burden — Surgical-Center Requirement

The second challenged provision of Texas' new law sets forth the surgical-center requirement. Prior to enactment of the new requirement, Texas law required abortion facilities to meet a host of health and safety requirements. Under those pre-existing laws, facilities were subject to annual reporting and recordkeeping requirements; a quality assurance program; personnel policies and staffing requirements; physical and environmental requirements; infection control standards; disclosure requirements; patient-rights standards; and medical- and clinical-services standards, including anesthesia standards.

> These Texas laws are of the kind approved by the Court in *Casey*, as they are considered within traditional state police power to regulate medicine to protect the public.

These requirements are policed by random and announced inspections, at least annually, as well as administrative penalties, injunctions, civil penalties, and criminal penalties for certain violations.

H.B. 2 added the requirement that an "abortion facility" meet the "minimum standards . . . for ambulatory surgical centers" under Texas law. The surgical-center regulations include, among other things, detailed specifications relating to the size of the nursing staff, building dimensions, and other building requirements. The nursing staff must comprise at least "an adequate number of [registered nurses] on duty to meet the following minimum staff requirements: director of the department (or designee), and supervisory and staff personnel for each service area to assure the immediate availability of [a registered nurse] for emergency care or for any patient when needed," as well as "a second individual on duty on the premises who is trained and currently certified in basic cardiac life support until all patients have been discharged from the facility" for facilities that provide moderate sedation, such as most abortion facilities. Facilities must include a full surgical suite with an operating room that has "a clear floor area of at least 240 square feet" in which "[t]he minimum clear dimension between built-in cabinets, counters, and shelves shall be 14 feet." There must be a preoperative patient holding room and a postoperative recovery suite. The former "shall be provided and arranged in a one-way traffic pattern so that patients entering from outside the surgical suite can change, gown, and move directly into the restricted corridor of the surgical suite," and the latter "shall be arranged to provide a one-way traffic pattern from the restricted surgical corridor to the postoperative recovery suite, and then to the extended observation rooms or discharge." Surgical centers must meet numerous other spatial requirements, including specific corridor widths.

Surgical centers must also have an advanced heating, ventilation, and air conditioning system and must satisfy particular piping system and plumbing requirements. Dozens of other sections list additional requirements that apply to surgical centers.

There is considerable evidence in the record supporting the District Court's findings indicating that the statutory provision requiring all abortion facilities to meet all surgical-center standards does not benefit patients and is not necessary. The District Court found that "risks are not appreciably lowered for patients who undergo abortions at ambulatory surgical centers as compared to nonsurgical-center facilities." The court added that women "will not obtain better care or experience more frequent positive outcomes at an ambulatory surgical center as compared to a previously licensed facility." And these findings are well supported.

The record makes clear that the surgical-center requirement provides no benefit when complications arise in the context of an abortion produced through medication. That is because, in such a case, complications would almost always arise only after the patient has left the facility. The record also contains evidence indicating that abortions taking place in an abortion facility are safe — indeed, safer than numerous procedures that take place outside hospitals and to which Texas does not apply its surgical-center requirements. The total number of deaths in Texas from abortions was five in the period from 2001 to 2012, or about one every two years (that is to say, one out of about 120,000 to 144,000 abortions). Nationwide, childbirth is 14 times more likely than abortion to result in death, but Texas law allows a midwife to oversee childbirth in the patient's own home. Colonoscopy, a procedure that typically takes place outside a hospital (or surgical center) setting, has a mortality rate 10 times higher than an abortion. Medical treatment after an incomplete miscarriage often involves a procedure identical to that involved in a nonmedical abortion, but it often takes place outside a hospital or surgical center. And Texas partly or wholly grandfathers (or waives in whole or in part the surgical-center requirement for) about two-thirds of the facilities to which the surgical-center standards apply. But it neither grandfathers nor provides waivers for any of the facilities that perform abortions. These facts indicate that the surgical-center provision imposes "a requirement that simply is not based on differences" between abortion and other surgical procedures "that are reasonably related to" preserving women's health, the asserted "purpos[e] of the Act in which it is found."

Moreover, many surgical-center requirements are inappropriate as applied to surgical abortions. Requiring scrub facilities; maintaining a one-way traffic pattern through the facility; having ceiling, wall, and floor finishes; separating soiled utility and sterilization rooms; and regulating air pressure, filtration, and humidity control can help reduce infection where doctors conduct procedures that penetrate the skin. But abortions typically involve either the administration of medicines or procedures performed through the natural opening of the birth canal, which is itself not sterile. Nor do provisions designed to safeguard heavily sedated patients (unable to help themselves) during fire emergencies, provide any help to abortion patients, as abortion facilities do not use general anesthesia or deep sedation. Further, since the few instances in which serious complications do arise following an abortion almost always require hospitalization, not treatment at a surgical center, surgical-center standards will not help in those instances either.

"Surgical abortion" is a misnomer because no surgery is performed (no cutting occurs).

The upshot is that this record evidence, along with the absence of any evidence to the contrary, provides ample support for the District Court's conclusion that "[m]any of the building standards mandated by the act and its implementing rules have such a tangential relationship to patient safety in the context of abortion as to be nearly arbitrary." That conclusion, along with the supporting evidence, provides sufficient support for the more general conclusion that the surgical-center requirement "will not [provide] better care or . . . more frequent positive outcomes." The record evidence thus supports the ultimate legal conclusion that the surgical-center requirement is not necessary.

At the same time, the record provides adequate evidentiary support for the District Court's conclusion that the surgical-center requirement places a substantial obstacle in the path of women seeking an abortion. The parties stipulated that the requirement would further reduce the number of abortion facilities available to seven or eight facilities, located in Houston, Austin, San Antonio, and Dallas/Fort Worth. In the District Court's view, the proposition that these "seven or eight providers could meet the demand of the entire State stretches credulity." We take this statement as a finding that these few facilities could not "meet" that "demand."

. . . .

For one thing, the record contains charts and oral testimony by Dr. Grossman, who said that, as a result of the surgical-center requirement, the number of abortions that the clinics would have to provide would rise from "'14,000 abortions annually'" to "'60,000 to 70,000'"—an increase by a factor of about five. The District Court credited Dr. Grossman as an expert witness. . . . In this case Dr. Grossman's opinion rested upon his participation, along with other university researchers, in research that tracked "the number of open facilities providing abortion care in the state by . . . requesting information from the Texas Department of State Health Services . . . [, t]hrough interviews with clinic staff[,] and review of publicly available information." The District Court acted within its legal authority in determining that Dr. Grossman's testimony was admissible.

. . . .

Texas suggests that the seven or eight remaining clinics could expand sufficiently to provide abortions for the 60,000 to 72,000 Texas women who sought them each year. Because petitioners had satisfied their burden, the obligation was on Texas, if it could, to present evidence rebutting that issue to the District Court. Texas admitted that it presented no such evidence. Instead, Texas argued before this Court that one new clinic now serves 9,000 women annually. In addition to being outside the record, that example is not representative. The clinic to which Texas referred apparently cost $26 million to construct—a fact that even more clearly demonstrates that requiring seven or eight clinics to serve five times their usual number of patients does indeed represent an undue burden on abortion access.

. . . .

More fundamentally, in the face of no threat to women's health, Texas seeks to force women to travel long distances to get abortions in crammed-to-capacity super-facilities. Patients seeking these services are less likely to get the kind of individualized attention, serious conversation, and emotional support that doctors at less taxed facilities may have offered. Healthcare facilities and medical professionals are not fungible commodities. Surgical centers attempting to accommodate sudden, vastly increased demand may find that quality of care declines. Another commonsense inference that the District Court made is that these effects would be harmful to, not supportive of, women's health.

Finally, the District Court found that the costs that a currently licensed abortion facility would have to incur to meet the surgical-center requirements were considerable, ranging from $1 million per facility (for facilities with adequate space) to $3 million per facility (where additional land must be purchased). This evidence supports the conclusion that more surgical centers will not soon fill the gap when licensed facilities are forced to close.

We agree with the District Court that the surgical-center requirement, like the admitting-privileges requirement, provides few, if any, health benefits for women, poses a substantial obstacle to women seeking abortions, and constitutes an "undue burden" on their constitutional right to do so.

* * *

For these reasons the judgment of the Court of Appeals is reversed, and the case is remanded for further proceedings consistent with this opinion.

QUESTIONS

1. How far would a woman have to travel for distance to be deemed an undue burden?
2. What features of TRAP laws rendered them an undue burden in the majority's view?
3. Would these constitutional infirmities exist if hospitals did not engage in economic credentialing but rather allowed any safe provider to have admitting privileges (consider the discussion of privileges in Chapter 4)?

Women's health advocates argued for many years that travel distance constitutes an undue burden, but the Court had not accepted that argument until *Whole Women's Health*. Other state laws continue to involve federal courts in evaluating the balance between individual rights and state regulation protecting life. For example, in March of 2018, Mississippi passed a bill that bans most abortions after 15 weeks of pregnancy, limiting abortion before viability and containing no exemptions for pregnancies that result from rape or incest. This bill tests the limits set in *Casey*. The state has one abortion clinic, which will likely challenge the constitutionality of this law. Likewise, in Kentucky the governor blocked licensure of the one remaining abortion clinic, raising the question of whether a state can force women to seek medical care in other states; this question arose in *Whole Women's Health* but did not need to be decided.

PROBLEM

Kentucky has enacted laws that create the following statutory landscape:

- A pregnant woman considering abortion must receive state-directed counseling that includes information designed to discourage her from having an abortion and then wait 24 hours before a physician performs the procedure or prescribes medication;
- Rape victims may not receive abortion counseling in emergency rooms;
- Private insurance policies only cover abortion in cases of life endangerment, unless an insurance rider is separately purchased (this law predated the ACA);
- Qualified health plans in the state's health Exchange only cover abortion when the woman's life is endangered, unless a rider is purchased separately;

- Insurance policies for public employees do not cover abortions;
- Public funding through Medicaid or otherwise is available for abortion only in cases of life endangerment, rape, or incest;
- No state funds may be used to obtain or perform an abortion on behalf of state employees or their dependents;
- A woman may not obtain an abortion at a publicly owned hospital or other publicly owned health care facility unless the procedure is necessary to preserve her life;
- No abortion may be performed after "viability" unless necessary to preserve the woman's life or health, and an attending physician must take all steps consistent with reasonable medical practices to preserve the life of the fetus;
- A minor must obtain parental consent before an abortion can be provided, or obtain the permission of a court; and
- A living will that directs health care providers to remove "life support" becomes ineffective if a woman is pregnant and the fetus can be kept alive with no harm to the woman's body.

Are these laws constitutional? Is the answer unclear for any of these provisions? If you were writing a law designed to limit access to abortions, how would you do it within the current Supreme Court framework and still offer adequate guidance to health care providers? Keep the last law in mind as you move into the end-of-life materials in the next section.

C. AUTONOMY AND DECISION MAKING AT THE END OF LIFE

Many Americans face a prolonged death and experience various forms of medical treatment, welcome and unwelcome, in that process. Yet decisions about care when death is imminent have remained an uncomfortable topic for many health care providers and their patients. Even when a patient is aware that she is dying, her family may not be able to accept that reality. These tensions are heightened by politicians who have intervened in patients' care to impose a so-called "culture of life" on intimate, often family-based medical decision making. These tensions, and uncertainty in state laws generally, have led to a slow but steady stream of cases involving the asserted right to refuse treatment before both state and federal courts.

1. JUDICIALLY RECOGNIZED PROTECTIONS AT THE END OF LIFE

We begin with the constitutional baseline for a right to refuse medical treatment, and then we consider the related question of assistance in dying. *Cruzan* was the first case in which the U.S. Supreme Court considered the rights that attach to the common law understanding of autonomy and informed consent as it applies to withdrawal of treatment. As many courts do when facing a novel health care question, the Court surveyed prior decisions in the states to discern a pattern to the law pertaining to the withdrawal of treatment. Additionally, note the overlapping concepts of constitutionally protected privacy and autonomy at the heart of these cases.

Cruzan v. Director, Missouri Department of Health

497 U.S. 261 (1990)

Chief Justice REHNQUIST delivered the opinion of the Court.

Petitioner Nancy Beth Cruzan was rendered incompetent as a result of severe injuries sustained during an automobile accident. Copetitioners Lester and Joyce Cruzan, Nancy's parents and coguardians, sought a court order directing the withdrawal of their daughter's artificial feeding and hydration equipment after it became apparent that she had virtually no chance of recovering her cognitive faculties. The Supreme Court of Missouri held that because there was no clear and convincing evidence of Nancy's desire to have life-sustaining treatment withdrawn under such circumstances, her parents lacked authority to effectuate such a request. We granted certiorari and now affirm.

On the night of January 11, 1983, Nancy Cruzan lost control of her car as she traveled down Elm Road in Jasper County, Missouri. The vehicle overturned, and Cruzan was discovered lying face down in a ditch without detectable respiratory or cardiac function. Paramedics were able to restore her breathing and heartbeat at the accident site, and she was transported to a hospital in an unconscious state. An attending neurosurgeon diagnosed her as having sustained probable cerebral contusions compounded by significant anoxia (lack of oxygen). The Missouri trial court in this case found that permanent brain damage generally results after 6 minutes in an anoxic state; it was estimated that Cruzan was deprived of oxygen from 12 to 14 minutes. She remained in a coma for approximately three weeks and then progressed to an unconscious state in which she was able to orally ingest some nutrition. In order to ease feeding and further the recovery, surgeons implanted a gastrostomy feeding and hydration tube in Cruzan with the consent of her then husband. Subsequent rehabilitative efforts proved unavailing. She now lies in a Missouri state hospital in what is commonly referred to as a persistent vegetative state: generally, a condition in which a person exhibits motor reflexes but evinces no indications of significant cognitive function. The State of Missouri is bearing the cost of her care.

> An individual in persistent vegetative state (PVS) would qualify for Medicaid as being permanently disabled, which is why Missouri paid for Nancy Cruzan's care. PVS is a diagnosis that indicates total brain death except for the brain stem, which is responsible for involuntary bodily functions.

After it had become apparent that Nancy Cruzan had virtually no chance of regaining her mental faculties, her parents asked hospital employees to terminate the artificial nutrition and hydration procedures. All agree that such a removal would cause her death. The employees refused to honor the request without court approval. The parents then sought and received authorization from the state trial court for termination. The court found that a person in Nancy's condition had a fundamental right under the State and Federal Constitutions to refuse or direct the withdrawal of "death prolonging procedures." The court also found that Nancy's "expressed thoughts at age twenty-five in somewhat serious conversation with a housemate friend that if sick or injured she would not wish to continue her life unless she could live at least halfway normally suggests that given her present condition she would not wish to continue on with her nutrition and hydration."

The Supreme Court of Missouri reversed by a divided vote. The court recognized a right to refuse treatment embodied in the common-law doctrine of informed consent, but expressed skepticism about the application of that doctrine in the circumstances of this case. The court also declined to read a broad right of privacy into the State Constitution which would "support the right of a person to refuse medical treatment in every circumstance," and expressed doubt as to whether such a right existed under the United States Constitution. . . . The court found that Cruzan's statements to her roommate regarding her desire to live or die under certain conditions were "unreliable for the purpose of determining her intent, and thus insufficient to support the co-guardians['] claim to exercise substituted judgment on Nancy's behalf." It rejected the argument that Cruzan's parents were entitled to order the termination of her medical treatment, concluding that "no person can assume that choice for an incompetent in the absence of the formalities required under Missouri's Living Will statutes or the clear and convincing, inherently reliable evidence absent here." . . .

We granted certiorari to consider the question whether Cruzan has a right under the United States Constitution which would require the hospital to withdraw life-sustaining treatment from her under these circumstances.

At common law, even the touching of one person by another without consent and without legal justification was a battery. Before the turn of the century, this Court observed that "[n]o right is held more sacred, or is more carefully guarded, by the common law, than the right of every individual to the possession and control of his own person, free from all restraint or interference of others, unless by clear and unquestionable authority of law." This notion of bodily integrity has been embodied in the requirement that informed consent is generally required for medical treatment. Justice Cardozo, while on the Court of Appeals of New York, aptly described this doctrine: "Every human being of adult years and sound mind has a right to determine what shall be done with his own body; and a surgeon who performs an operation without his patient's consent commits an assault, for which he is liable in damages." The informed consent doctrine has become firmly entrenched in American tort law.

Note the importance of common law in the Court's analysis. The common law doctrine of informed consent is rooted in the tort theories of battery and negligence, meaning that the touching is unpermitted and the physician does not meet modern standards if adequate information is not given to a patient. A patient has a right to consent but also not to consent to treatment.

The logical corollary of the doctrine of informed consent is that the patient generally possesses the right not to consent, that is, to refuse treatment. Until about 15 years ago and the seminal decision in In re Quinlan, 70 N.J. 10 (1976), the number of right-to-refuse-treatment decisions was relatively few. Most of the earlier cases involved patients who refused medical treatment forbidden by their religious beliefs, thus implicating First Amendment rights as well as common-law rights of self-determination. More recently, however, with the advance of medical technology capable of sustaining life well past the point where natural forces would have brought certain death in earlier times, cases involving the right to refuse life-sustaining treatment have burgeoned.

In the *Quinlan* case, young Karen Quinlan suffered severe brain damage as the result of anoxia and entered a persistent vegetative state. Karen's father sought judicial approval to disconnect his daughter's respirator. The New Jersey Supreme Court granted the relief, holding that Karen had a right of privacy grounded in the Federal Constitution to terminate treatment. Recognizing that this right was not absolute, however, the court balanced it against asserted state interests. Noting that the State's interest "weakens and the individual's right to privacy grows as the degree of bodily invasion increases and the prognosis dims," the court concluded that the state interests had to give way in that case. The court also concluded that the "only practical way" to prevent the loss of Karen's privacy right due to her incompetence was to allow her guardian and family to decide "whether she would exercise it in these circumstances."

After *Quinlan*, however, most courts have based a right to refuse treatment either solely on the common-law right to informed consent or on both the common-law right and a constitutional privacy right. In Superintendent of Belchertown State School v. Saikewicz, 373 Mass. 728 (1977), the Supreme Judicial Court of Massachusetts relied on both the right of privacy and the right of informed consent to permit the withholding of chemotherapy from a profoundly retarded 67-year-old man suffering from leukemia. Reasoning that an incompetent person retains the same rights as a competent individual "because the value of human dignity extends to both," the court adopted a "substituted judgment" standard whereby courts were to determine what an incompetent individual's decision would have been under the circumstances. Distilling certain state interests from prior case law-the preservation of life, the protection of the interests of innocent third parties, the prevention of suicide, and the maintenance of the ethical integrity of the medical profession — the court recognized the first interest as paramount and noted it was greatest when an affliction was curable, "as opposed to the State interest where, as here, the issue is not whether, but when, for how long, and at what cost to the individual [a] life may be briefly extended."

In In re Storar, 52 N.Y.2d 363 (1981), the New York Court of Appeals declined to base a right to refuse treatment on a constitutional privacy right. Instead, it found such a right "adequately supported" by the informed consent doctrine. In In re Eichner (decided with In re Storar), an 83-year-old man who had suffered brain damage from anoxia entered a vegetative state and was thus incompetent to consent to the removal of his respirator. The court, however, found it unnecessary to reach the question whether his rights could be exercised by others since it found the evidence clear and convincing from statements made by the patient when competent that he "did not want to be maintained in a vegetative coma by use of a respirator." In the companion *Storar* case, a 52-year-old man suffering from bladder cancer had been profoundly retarded during most of his life. Implicitly rejecting the approach taken in *Saikewicz*, the court reasoned that due to such life-long incompetency, "it is unrealistic to attempt to determine whether he would want to continue potentially life prolonging treatment if he were competent." As the evidence showed that the patient's required blood transfusions did not involve excessive pain and without them his mental and physical abilities would deteriorate, the court concluded that it should not "allow an incompetent patient to bleed to death because someone, even someone as close as a parent or sibling, feels that this is best for one with an incurable disease."

These paragraphs offer a nice rundown of the key state court decisions in this area, so the full cites are included for future reference. The state courts' precedents demonstrate that a common law right to refuse treatment existed for all patients, not just the terminally ill, before *Cruzan* was decided.

Many of the later cases build on the principles established in *Quinlan*, *Saikewicz*, and *Storar/Eichner*. For instance, in In re Conroy, 98 N.J. 321 (1985), the same court that decided *Quinlan* considered whether a nasogastric feeding tube could be removed from an 84-year-old incompetent nursing-home resident suffering irreversible mental and physical ailments. While recognizing that a federal right of privacy might apply in the case, the court, contrary to its approach in *Quinlan*, decided to base its decision on the common-law right to self-determination and informed consent. "On balance, the right to self-determination ordinarily outweighs any coun-tervailing state interests, and competent persons generally are permitted to refuse medical treatment, even at the risk of death. Most of the cases that have held otherwise, unless they involved the interest in protecting innocent third parties, have concerned the patient's competency to make a rational and considered choice."

Reasoning that the right of self-determination should not be lost merely because an individual is unable to sense a violation of it, the court held that incompetent individuals retain a right to refuse treatment. It also held that such a right could be exercised by a surrogate decisionmaker using a "subjective" standard when there was clear evidence that the incompetent person would have exercised it. Where such evidence was lacking, the court held that an individual's right could still be invoked in certain circumstances under objective "best interest" standards. Thus, if some trustworthy evidence existed that the individual would have wanted to terminate treatment, but not enough to clearly establish a person's wishes for purposes of the subjective standard, and the burden of a prolonged life from the experience of pain and suffering markedly outweighed its satisfactions, treatment could be ter-minated under a "limited-objective" standard. Where no trustworthy evidence existed, and a person's suffering would make the administration of life-sustaining treatment inhumane, a "pure-objective" standard could be used to terminate treat-ment. If none of these conditions obtained, the court held it was best to err in favor of preserving life.

The court also rejected certain categorical distinctions that had been drawn in prior refusal-of-treatment cases as lacking substance for decision purposes: the dis-tinction between actively hastening death by terminating treatment and passively allowing a person to die of a disease; between treating individuals as an initial matter versus withdrawing treatment afterwards; between ordinary versus extraordinary treatment; and between treatment by artificial feeding versus other forms of life-sustaining medical procedures. As to the last item, the court acknowledged the "emotional significance" of food, but noted that feeding by implanted tubes is a "medical procedur[e] with inherent risks and possible side effects, instituted by skilled health-care providers to compensate for impaired physical functioning" which analytically was equivalent to artificial breathing using a respirator.

In contrast to *Conroy*, the Court of Appeals of New York recently refused to accept less than the clearly expressed wishes of a patient before permitting the exercise of her right to refuse treatment by a surrogate decisionmaker. In re Westchester County Medical Center on behalf of O'Connor, 72 N.Y.2d 517 (1988). There, the court, over the objection of the patient's family members, granted an order to insert a feeding tube into a 77-year-old woman rendered incompetent as a result of several strokes. While continuing to recognize a common-law right to refuse treatment, the court rejected the substituted judgment approach for asserting it "because it is inconsistent with our fundamental commitment to the notion that no person or court should substitute its judgment as to what would be an acceptable quality of life for another. Consequently, we adhere to the view that, despite its pitfalls and inevitable uncertainties, the inquiry must always be narrowed to the patient's expressed intent, with every effort made to minimize the opportunity for error." The court held that the record lacked the requisite clear and convincing evidence of the patient's expressed intent to withhold life-sustaining treatment.

. . . As these cases demonstrate, the common-law doctrine of informed consent is viewed as generally encompassing the right of a competent individual to refuse medical treatment. Beyond that, these cases demonstrate both similarity and diversity in their approaches to decision of what all agree is a perplexing question with unusually strong moral and ethical overtones. State courts have available to them for decision a number of sources — state constitutions, statutes, and common law — which are not available to us. In this Court, the question is simply and starkly whether the United States Constitution prohibits Missouri from choosing the rule of decision which it did. This is the first case in which we have been squarely presented with the issue whether the United States Constitution grants what is in common parlance referred to as a "right to die." We follow the judicious counsel of our decision in *Twin City Bank v. Nebeker*, where we said that in deciding "a question of such magnitude and importance . . . it is the [better] part of wisdom not to attempt, by any general statement, to cover every possible phase of the subject."

The Fourteenth Amendment provides that no State shall "deprive any person of life, liberty, or property, without due process of law." The principle that a competent person has a constitutionally protected liberty interest in refusing unwanted medical treatment may be inferred from our prior decisions. In *Jacobson v. Massachusetts*, for instance, the Court balanced an individual's liberty interest in declining an unwanted smallpox vaccine against the State's interest in preventing disease. . . .

> This is a very specific reformulation of the question in the case: Can the state constitutionally require clear and convincing evidence of an incompetent patient's wishes before treatment is refused on her behalf?

But determining that a person has a "liberty interest" under the Due Process Clause does not end the inquiry; "whether respondent's constitutional rights have been violated must be determined by balancing his liberty interests against the relevant state interests."

Petitioners insist that under the general holdings of our cases, the forced administration of life-sustaining medical treatment, and even of artificially delivered food and water essential to life, would implicate a competent person's liberty interest. Although we think the logic of the cases discussed above would embrace such a liberty interest, the dramatic consequences involved in refusal of such treatment would inform the inquiry as to whether the deprivation of that interest is constitutionally permissible. But for purposes of this case, we assume that the United States Constitution would grant a competent person a constitutionally protected right to refuse lifesaving hydration and nutrition.

Petitioners go on to assert that an incompetent person should possess the same right in this respect as is possessed by a competent person. . . .

The difficulty with petitioners' claim is that in a sense it begs the question: An incompetent person is not able to make an informed and voluntary choice to exercise a hypothetical right to refuse treatment or any other right. Such a "right" must be exercised for her, if at all, by some sort of surrogate. Here, Missouri has in effect recognized that under certain circumstances a surrogate may act for the patient in electing to have hydration and nutrition withdrawn in such a way as to cause death, but it has established a procedural safeguard to assure that the action of the surrogate conforms as best it may to the wishes expressed by the patient while competent. Missouri requires that evidence of the incompetent's wishes as to the withdrawal of treatment be proved by clear and convincing evidence. The question, then, is whether the United States Constitution forbids the establishment of this procedural requirement by the State. We hold that it does not.

Whether or not Missouri's clear and convincing evidence requirement comports with the United States Constitution depends in part on what interests the State may properly seek to protect in this situation. Missouri relies on its interest in the protection and preservation of human life, and there can be no gainsaying this interest. As a general matter, the States — indeed, all civilized nations — demonstrate their commitment to life by treating homicide as a serious crime. Moreover, the majority of States in this country have laws imposing criminal penalties on one who assists another to commit suicide. We do not think a State is required to remain neutral in the face of an informed and voluntary decision by a physically able adult to starve to death.

But in the context presented here, a State has more particular interests at stake. The choice between life and death is a deeply personal decision of obvious and overwhelming finality. We believe Missouri may legitimately seek to safeguard the personal element of this choice through the imposition of heightened evidentiary requirements. It cannot be disputed that the Due Process Clause protects an interest in life as well as an interest in refusing life-sustaining medical treatment. Not all incompetent patients will have loved ones available to serve as surrogate decision-makers. And even where family members are present, "[t]here will, of course, be some unfortunate situations in which family members will not act to protect a patient." A State is entitled to guard against potential abuses in such situations. Similarly, a State is entitled to consider that a judicial proceeding to make a determination regarding an incompetent's wishes may very well not be an adversarial one, with the added guarantee of accurate fact finding that the adversary process brings with it. Finally, we think a State may properly decline to make judgments about the "quality" of life that a particular individual may enjoy, and simply assert an unqualified interest in the preservation of human life to be weighed against the constitutionally protected interests of the individual.

In our view, Missouri has permissibly sought to advance these interests through the adoption of a "clear and convincing" standard of proof to govern such proceedings. "The function of a standard of proof, as that concept is embodied in the Due Process Clause and in the realm of factfinding, is to 'instruct the factfinder concerning the degree of confidence our society thinks he should have in the correctness of factual conclusions for a particular type of adjudication.'" "This Court has mandated an intermediate standard of proof — 'clear and convincing evidence' — when the individual interests at stake in a state proceeding are both 'particularly important' and 'more substantial than mere loss of money.'" . . .

. . . We believe that Missouri may permissibly place an increased risk of an erroneous decision on those seeking to terminate an incompetent individual's life-sustaining treatment. An erroneous decision not to terminate results in a maintenance of the status quo; the possibility of subsequent developments such as advancements in medical science, the discovery of new evidence regarding the patient's intent, changes in the law, or simply the unexpected death of the patient despite the administration of life-sustaining treatment at least create the potential that a wrong decision will eventually be corrected or its impact mitigated. An erroneous decision to withdraw life-sustaining treatment, however, is not susceptible of correction. In *Santosky*, one of the factors which led the Court to require proof by clear and convincing evidence in a proceeding to terminate parental rights was that a decision in such a case was final and irrevocable. The same must surely be said of the decision to discontinue hydration and nutrition of a patient such as Nancy Cruzan, which all agree will result in her death.

. . . In sum, we conclude that a State may apply a clear and convincing evidence standard in proceedings where a guardian seeks to discontinue nutrition and hydration of a person diagnosed to be in a persistent vegetative state. We note that many courts which have adopted some sort of substituted judgment procedure in situations like this, whether they limit consideration of evidence to the prior expressed wishes of the incompetent individual, or whether they allow more general proof of what the individual's decision would have been, require a clear and convincing standard of proof for such evidence.

> The clear and convincing evidence standard falls somewhere between the criminal beyond a reasonable doubt standard and the civil preponderance of the evidence standard.

The Supreme Court of Missouri held that in this case the testimony adduced at trial did not amount to clear and convincing proof of the patient's desire to have hydration and nutrition withdrawn. In so doing, it reversed a decision of the Missouri trial court which had found that the evidence "suggest[ed]" Nancy Cruzan would not have desired to continue such measures, but which had not adopted the standard of "clear and convincing evidence" enunciated by the Supreme Court. The testimony adduced at trial consisted primarily of Nancy Cruzan's statements made to a housemate about a year before her accident that she would not want to live should she face life as a "vegetable," and other observations to the same effect. The observations did not deal in terms with withdrawal of medical treatment or of hydration and nutrition. We cannot say that the Supreme Court of Missouri committed constitutional error in reaching the conclusion that it did.

Petitioners alternatively contend that Missouri must accept the "substituted judgment" of close family members even in the absence of substantial proof that their views reflect the views of the patient. . . .

No doubt is engendered by anything in this record but that Nancy Cruzan's mother and father are loving and caring parents. If the State were required by the United States Constitution to repose a right of "substituted judgment" with anyone, the Cruzans would surely qualify. But we do not think the Due Process Clause requires the State to repose judgment on these matters with anyone but the patient herself. Close family members may have a strong feeling—a feeling not at all ignoble or unworthy, but not entirely disinterested, either—that they do not wish to witness the continuation of the life of a loved one which they regard as hopeless, meaningless, and even degrading. But there is no automatic assurance that the view of close family members will necessarily be the same as the patient's would have been had she been confronted with the prospect of her situation while competent. All of the reasons previously discussed for allowing Missouri to require clear and convincing evidence of the patient's wishes lead us to conclude that the State may choose to defer only to those wishes, rather than confide the decision to close family members.

The judgment of the Supreme Court of Missouri is Affirmed.

Justice O'CONNOR, concurring.

I agree that a protected liberty interest in refusing unwanted medical treatment may be inferred from our prior decisions and that the refusal of artificially delivered food and water is encompassed within that liberty interest. I write separately to clarify why I believe this to be so.

As the Court notes, the liberty interest in refusing medical treatment flows from decisions involving the State's invasions into the body. Because our notions of liberty are inextricably entwined with our idea of physical freedom and self-determination, the Court has often deemed state incursions into the body repugnant to the interests protected by the Due Process Clause. . . .

I also write separately to emphasize that the Court does not today decide the issue whether a State must also give effect to the decisions of a surrogate decision-maker. In my view, such a duty may well be constitutionally required to protect the patient's liberty interest in refusing medical treatment. Few individuals provide explicit oral or written instructions regarding their intent to refuse medical treatment should they become incompetent. States which decline to consider any evidence other than such instructions may frequently fail to honor a patient's intent. Such failures might be avoided if the State considered an equally probative source of evidence: the patient's appointment of a proxy to make health care decisions on her behalf. Delegating the authority to make medical decisions to a family member or friend is becoming a common method of planning for the future. Several States have recognized the practical wisdom of such a procedure by enacting durable power of attorney statutes that specifically authorize an individual to appoint a surrogate to make medical treatment decisions. Some state courts have suggested that an agent appointed pursuant to a general durable power of attorney statute would also be empowered to make health care decisions on behalf of the patient. Other States allow an individual to designate a proxy to carry out the intent of a living will. These procedures for surrogate decisionmaking, which appear to be rapidly gaining in acceptance, may be a valuable additional safeguard of the patient's interest in directing his medical care. Moreover, as patients are likely to select a family member as a surrogate, giving effect to a proxy's decisions may also protect the "freedom of personal choice in matters of . . . family life."

> Note the emphasis on substituted judgment and honoring the proxy's decision on behalf of a patient. Patient advocates rely on this concurrence for its strong articulation of a health care proxy's role.

Today's decision, holding only that the Constitution permits a State to require clear and convincing evidence of Nancy Cruzan's desire to have artificial hydration and nutrition withdrawn, does not preclude a future determination that the Constitution requires the States to implement the decisions of a patient's duly appointed surrogate. Nor does it prevent States from developing other approaches for protecting an incompetent individual's liberty interest in refusing medical treatment. . . . Today we decide only that one State's practice does not violate the Constitution; the more challenging task of crafting appropriate procedures for safeguarding incompetents' liberty interests is entrusted to the "laboratory" of the States, New State Ice Co. v. Liebmann, 285 U.S. 262 (1932) (Brandeis, J., dissenting), in the first instance.

QUESTIONS

1. Must states enact one particular standard of evidence for a patient's surrogate to refuse treatment?
2. If you were writing a policy for a hospital, what information would you instruct health care providers to seek from patients?

3. Would you allow anything less than clear and convincing evidence of the patient's desires if you were a state legislator? What would it be, and why?

The right to refuse treatment feels more like a theory than a reality to the terminally ill who are not being kept alive by medical technology. The next cases reflect their effort to argue that a constitutional right to assistance in dying should be recognized by the Supreme Court.

Washington v. Glucksberg

521 U.S. 702 (1997)

Chief Justice REHNQUIST delivered the opinion of the Court.

The question presented in this case is whether Washington's prohibition against "caus[ing]" or "aid[ing]" a suicide offends the Fourteenth Amendment to the United States Constitution. We hold that it does not.

It has always been a crime to assist a suicide in the State of Washington. In 1854, Washington's first Territorial Legislature outlawed "assisting another in the commission of self-murder." Today, Washington law provides: "A person is guilty of promoting a suicide attempt when he knowingly causes or aids another person to attempt suicide." "Promoting a suicide attempt" is a felony, punishable by up to five years' imprisonment and up to a $10,000 fine. At the same time, Washington's Natural Death Act, enacted in 1979, states that the "withholding or withdrawal of life-sustaining treatment" at a patient's direction "shall not, for any purpose, constitute a suicide."

Petitioners in this case are the State of Washington and its Attorney General. Respondents Harold Glucksberg, M.D., Abigail Halperin, M.D., Thomas A. Preston, M.D., and Peter Shalit, M.D., are physicians who practice in Washington. These doctors occasionally treat terminally ill, suffering patients, and declare that they would assist these patients in ending their lives if not for Washington's assisted-suicide ban. In January 1994, respondents, along with three gravely ill, pseudonymous plaintiffs who have since died and Compassion in Dying, a nonprofit organization that counsels people considering physician-assisted suicide, sued in the United States District Court, seeking a declaration that Wash. Rev. Code §9A.36.060(1) (1994) is, on its face, unconstitutional.

The plaintiffs asserted "the existence of a liberty interest protected by the Fourteenth Amendment which extends to a personal choice by a mentally competent, terminally ill adult to commit physician-assisted suicide." Relying primarily on *Planned Parenthood of Southeastern Pa. v. Casey*, and *Cruzan v. Director, Mo. Dept. of Health*, the District Court agreed and concluded that Washington's assisted-suicide ban is unconstitutional because it "places an undue burden on the exercise of [that] constitutionally protected liberty interest." The District Court also decided that the Washington statute violated the Equal Protection Clause's requirement that "'all persons similarly situated . . . be treated alike.'"

. . . Like the District Court, the en banc Court of Appeals emphasized our *Casey* and *Cruzan* decisions. The court also discussed what it described as "historical" and "current societal attitudes" toward suicide and assisted suicide and concluded that "the Constitution encompasses a due process liberty interest in controlling the time and manner of one's death — that there is, in short, a constitutionally-recognized 'right to die.'" After "[w]eighing and then balancing" this interest against

Richard Sheinwald / AP Photo

Dr. Jack Kevorkian and his suicide device, pictured here, may have been in the Justices' minds as they decided these cases. Dr. Kevorkian supported physician assistance in dying and designed this "machine" to help patients seeking to control their own exit. He was ultimately convicted of second-degree murder for his administration of deadly medications.

Washington's various interests, the court held that the State's assisted-suicide ban was unconstitutional "as applied to terminally ill competent adults who wish to hasten their deaths with medication prescribed by their physicians." The court did not reach the District Court's equal protection holding. We granted certiorari, and now reverse.

I

We begin, as we do in all due process cases, by examining our Nation's history, legal traditions, and practices. In almost every State—indeed, in almost every western democracy—it is a crime to assist a suicide. The States' assisted-suicide bans are not innovations. Rather, they are longstanding expressions of the States' commitment to the protection and preservation of all human life. Indeed, opposition to and condemnation of suicide—and, therefore, of assisting suicide—are consistent and enduring themes of our philosophical, legal, and cultural heritages.

. . . Though deeply rooted, the States' assisted-suicide bans have in recent years been reexamined and, generally, reaffirmed. Because of advances in medicine and technology, Americans today are increasingly likely to die in institutions, from chronic illnesses. Public concern and democratic action are therefore sharply focused on how best to protect dignity and independence at the end of life, with the result that there have been many significant changes in state laws and in the attitudes these laws reflect. Many States, for example, now permit "living wills," surrogate health-care decisionmaking, and the withdrawal or refusal of life-sustaining medical treatment. Vacco v. Quill, 521 U.S. 793. At the same time, however, voters and legislators continue for the most part to reaffirm their States' prohibitions on assisting suicide.

The Washington statute at issue in this case, Wash. Rev. Code §9A.36.060 (1994), was enacted in 1975 as part of a revision of that State's criminal code. Four years later, Washington passed its Natural Death Act, which specifically stated that the "withholding or withdrawal of life-sustaining treatment . . . shall not, for any purpose, constitute a suicide" and that "[n]othing in this chapter shall be construed to condone, authorize, or approve mercy killing. . . ." In 1991, Washington voters rejected a ballot initiative which, had it passed, would have permitted a form of physician-assisted suicide. Washington then added a provision to the Natural Death Act expressly excluding physician-assisted suicide.

California voters rejected an assisted-suicide initiative similar to Washington's in 1993. On the other hand, in 1994, voters in Oregon enacted, also through ballot initiative, that State's "Death With Dignity Act," which legalized physician-assisted suicide for competent, terminally ill adults. Since the Oregon vote, many proposals to legalize assisted-suicide have been and continue to be introduced in the States' legislatures, but none has been enacted. And just last year, Iowa and Rhode Island joined the overwhelming majority of States explicitly prohibiting assisted suicide. Also, on April 30, 1997, President Clinton signed the Federal Assisted Suicide Funding Restriction Act of 1997, which prohibits the use of federal funds in support of physician-assisted suicide.

> The diversity of states' legal responses to physician-assisted suicide is a good example of the "states as laboratories" value of federalism.

Thus, the States are currently engaged in serious, thoughtful examinations of physician-assisted suicide and other similar issues. For example, New York State's Task Force on Life and the Law — an ongoing, blue-ribbon commission composed of doctors, ethicists, lawyers, religious leaders, and interested laymen — was convened in 1984 and commissioned with "a broad mandate to recommend public policy on issues raised by medical advances." Over the past decade, the Task Force has recommended laws relating to end-of-life decisions, surrogate pregnancy, and organ donation. After studying physician-assisted suicide, however, the Task Force unanimously concluded that "[l]egalizing assisted suicide and euthanasia would pose profound risks to many individuals who are ill and vulnerable. . . . [T]he potential dangers of this dramatic change in public policy would outweigh any benefit that might be achieved." . . .

II

The Due Process Clause guarantees more than fair process, and the "liberty" it protects includes more than the absence of physical restraint. The Clause also provides heightened protection against government interference with certain fundamental rights and liberty interests. In a long line of cases, we have held that, in addition to the specific freedoms protected by the Bill of Rights, the "liberty" specially protected by the Due Process Clause includes the rights to marry; to have children; to direct the education and upbringing of one's children; to marital privacy; to use contraception; to bodily integrity, and to abortion. We have also assumed, and strongly suggested, that the Due Process Clause protects the traditional right to refuse unwanted lifesaving medical treatment. *Cruzan.*

But we "ha[ve] always been reluctant to expand the concept of substantive due process because guideposts for responsible decisionmaking in this unchartered area are scarce and open-ended." By extending constitutional protection to an asserted right or liberty interest, we, to a great extent, place the matter outside the arena of public debate and legislative action. We must therefore "exercise the utmost care whenever we are asked to break new ground in this field," lest the liberty protected by the Due Process Clause be subtly transformed into the policy preferences of the Members of this Court.

. . . .

Turning to the claim at issue here, the Court of Appeals stated that "[p]roperly analyzed, the first issue to be resolved is whether there is a liberty interest in determining the time and manner of one's death," or, in other words, "[i]s there a right to die?" Similarly, respondents assert a "liberty to choose how to die" and a right to "control of one's final days," and describe the asserted liberty as "the right to choose a humane, dignified death," and "the liberty to shape death." As noted above, we have a tradition of carefully formulating the interest at stake in substantive-due-process cases. For example, although *Cruzan* is often described as a "right to die" case, we were, in fact, more precise: We assumed that the Constitution granted competent persons a "constitutionally protected right to refuse lifesaving hydration and nutrition." The Washington statute at issue in this case prohibits "aid[ing] another person to attempt suicide," and, thus, the question before us is whether the "liberty" specially protected by the Due Process Clause includes a right to commit suicide which itself includes a right to assistance in doing so.

> The Court minimized the right to refuse life-sustaining treatment, clarifying that it did not recognize a "right to die" in *Cruzan*. Here, the Court takes pains to frame the asserted right to assistance in committing suicide as quite distinct from the right at the heart of *Cruzan*.

We now inquire whether this asserted right has any place in our Nation's traditions. Here, as discussed, we are confronted with a consistent and almost universal tradition that has long rejected the asserted right, and continues explicitly to reject it today, even for terminally ill, mentally competent adults. To hold for respondents, we would have to reverse centuries of legal doctrine and practice, and strike down the considered policy choice of almost every State.

Respondents contend, however, that the liberty interest they assert is consistent with this Court's substantive-due-process line of cases, if not with this Nation's history and practice. Pointing to *Casey* and *Cruzan,* respondents read our jurisprudence in this area as reflecting a general tradition of "self-sovereignty," and as teaching that the "liberty" protected by the Due Process Clause includes "basic and intimate exercises of personal autonomy." According to respondents, our liberty jurisprudence, and the broad, individualistic principles it reflects, protects the "liberty of competent, terminally ill adults to make end-of-life decisions free of undue government interference." The question presented in this case, however, is whether the protections of the Due Process Clause include a right to commit suicide with another's assistance. With this "careful description" of respondents' claim in mind, we turn to *Casey* and *Cruzan*.

. . . .

The history of the law's treatment of assisted suicide in this country has been and continues to be one of the rejection of nearly all efforts to permit it. That being the case, our decisions lead us to conclude that the asserted "right" to assistance in committing suicide is not a fundamental liberty interest protected by the Due

Process Clause. The Constitution also requires, however, that Washington's assisted-suicide ban be rationally related to legitimate government interests. This requirement is unquestionably met here. As the court below recognized, Washington's assisted-suicide ban implicates a number of state interests.

First, Washington has an "unqualified interest in the preservation of human life." *Cruzan.* The State's prohibition on assisted suicide, like all homicide laws, both reflects and advances its commitment to this interest. This interest is symbolic and aspirational as well as practical: "While suicide is no longer prohibited or penalized, the ban against assisted suicide and euthanasia shores up the notion of limits in human relationships. It reflects the gravity with which we view the decision to take one's own life or the life of another, and our reluctance to encourage or promote these decisions."

Respondents admit that "[t]he State has a real interest in preserving the lives of those who can still contribute to society and have the potential to enjoy life." The Court of Appeals also recognized Washington's interest in protecting life, but held that the "weight" of this interest depends on the "medical condition and the wishes of the person whose life is at stake." Washington, however, has rejected this sliding-scale approach and, through its assisted-suicide ban, insists that all persons' lives, from beginning to end, regardless of physical or mental condition, are under the full protection of the law. As we have previously affirmed, the States "may properly decline to make judgments about the 'quality' of life that a particular individual may enjoy." This remains true, as *Cruzan* makes clear, even for those who are near death.

Relatedly, all admit that suicide is a serious public-health problem, especially among persons in otherwise vulnerable groups. The State has an interest in preventing suicide, and in studying, identifying, and treating its causes.

Those who attempt suicide — terminally ill or not — often suffer from depression or other mental disorders. Research indicates, however, that many people who request physician-assisted suicide withdraw that request if their depression and pain are treated. The New York Task Force, however, expressed its concern that, because depression is difficult to diagnose, physicians and medical professionals often fail to respond adequately to seriously ill patients' needs. Thus, legal physician-assisted suicide could make it more difficult for the State to protect depressed or mentally ill persons, or those who are suffering from untreated pain, from suicidal impulses.

The State also has an interest in protecting the integrity and ethics of the medical profession. In contrast to the Court of Appeals' conclusion that "the integrity of the medical profession would [not] be threatened in any way by [physician-assisted suicide]," the American Medical Association, like many other medical and physicians' groups, has concluded that "[p]hysician-assisted suicide is fundamentally incompatible with the physician's role as healer." And physician-assisted suicide could, it is argued, undermine the trust that is essential to the doctor-patient relationship by blurring the time-honored line between healing and harming.

Next, the State has an interest in protecting vulnerable groups — including the poor, the elderly, and disabled persons — from abuse, neglect, and mistakes. The Court of Appeals dismissed the State's concern that disadvantaged persons might be pressured into physician-assisted suicide as "ludicrous on its face." We have recognized, however, the real risk of subtle coercion and undue influence in end-of-life situations. Similarly, the New York Task Force warned that "[l]egalizing physician-assisted suicide would pose profound risks to many individuals who are ill and vulnerable. . . . The risk of harm is greatest for the many individuals in our society whose autonomy and well-being are already compromised by poverty, lack of access to good medical care, advanced age, or membership in a stigmatized social group." If physician-assisted suicide were permitted, many might resort to it to spare their families the substantial financial burden of end-of-life health-care costs.

The State's interest here goes beyond protecting the vulnerable from coercion; it extends to protecting disabled and terminally ill people from prejudice, negative and inaccurate stereotypes, and "societal indifference." The State's assisted-suicide ban reflects and reinforces its policy that the lives of terminally ill, disabled, and elderly people must be no less valued than the lives of the young and healthy, and that a seriously disabled person's suicidal impulses should be interpreted and treated the same way as anyone else's.

Finally, the State may fear that permitting assisted suicide will start it down the path to voluntary and perhaps even involuntary euthanasia. The Court of Appeals struck down Washington's assisted-suicide ban only "as applied to competent, terminally ill adults who wish to hasten their deaths by obtaining medication prescribed by their doctors." Washington insists, however, that the impact of the court's decision will not and cannot be so limited. If suicide is protected as a matter of constitutional right, it is argued, "every man and woman in the United States must enjoy it." The Court of Appeals' decision, and its expansive reasoning, provide ample support for the State's concerns. The court noted, for example, that the "decision of a duly appointed surrogate decision maker is for all legal purposes the decision of the patient himself"; that "in some instances, the patient may be unable to self-administer the drugs and . . . administration by the physician . . . may be the only way the patient may be able to receive them"; and that not only physicians, but also family members and loved ones, will inevitably participate in assisting suicide. Thus, it turns out that what is couched as a limited right to "physician-assisted suicide" is likely, in effect, a much broader license, which could prove extremely difficult to police and contain. Washington's ban on assisting suicide prevents such erosion.

    . . . .

We need not weigh exactly the relative strengths of these various interests. They are unquestionably important and legitimate, and Washington's ban on assisted suicide is at least reasonably related to their promotion and protection. We therefore hold that Wash. Rev. Code §9A.36.060(1) (1994) does not violate the Fourteenth Amendment, either on its face or "as applied to competent, terminally ill adults who wish to hasten their deaths by obtaining medication prescribed by their doctors."

Throughout the Nation, Americans are engaged in an earnest and profound debate about the morality, legality, and practicality of physician-assisted suicide. Our holding permits this debate to continue, as it should in a democratic society. The decision of the en banc Court of Appeals is reversed, and the case is remanded for further proceedings consistent with this opinion.

QUESTIONS

1. What are the recognized state interests? Must states outlaw physician-assisted death in pursuit of those interests?

2. How does the Court weigh state interests against the individual's liberty interest in refusing unwanted treatment?
3. Is refusing treatment equivalent to seeking assistance in dying when the underlying disease is terminal?
4. Part of the Court's rationale is concern for vulnerable populations; is the decision over-inclusive to the extent it applies equally to fully rational, fully functional (i.e., "competent") adults, who otherwise must give consent to every medical procedure?

Consider the companion case to *Glucksberg*:

Vacco v. Quill

521 U.S. 793 (1997)

In New York, as in most States, it is a crime to aid another to commit or attempt suicide, but patients may refuse even lifesaving medical treatment. The question presented by this case is whether New York's prohibition on assisting suicide therefore violates the Equal Protection Clause of the Fourteenth Amendment. We hold that it does not.

. . . .

New York's statutes outlawing assisting suicide affect and address matters of profound significance to all New Yorkers alike. They neither infringe fundamental rights nor involve suspect classifications. Washington v. Glucksberg. These laws are therefore entitled to a "strong presumption of validity."

On their faces, neither New York's ban on assisting suicide nor its statutes permitting patients to refuse medical treatment treat anyone differently from anyone else or draw any distinctions between persons. Everyone, regardless of physical condition, is entitled, if competent, to refuse unwanted lifesaving medical treatment; no one is permitted to assist a suicide. Generally speaking, laws that apply even-handedly to all "unquestionably comply" with the Equal Protection Clause.

. . . Unlike the Court of Appeals, we think the distinction between assisting suicide and withdrawing life-sustaining treatment, a distinction widely recognized and endorsed in the medical profession and in our legal traditions, is both important and logical; it is certainly rational.

The distinction comports with fundamental legal principles of causation and intent. First, when a patient refuses life-sustaining medical treatment, he dies from an underlying fatal disease or pathology; but if a patient ingests lethal medication prescribed by a physician, he is killed by that medication.

Furthermore, a physician who withdraws, or honors a patient's refusal to begin, life-sustaining medical treatment purposefully intends, or may so intend, only to respect his patient's wishes and "to cease doing useless and futile or degrading things to the patient when [the patient] no longer stands to benefit from them." The same is true when a doctor provides aggressive palliative care; in some cases, painkilling drugs may hasten a patient's death, but the physician's purpose and intent is, or may be, only to ease his patient's pain. A doctor who assists a suicide, however, "must, necessarily and indubitably, intend primarily that the patient be made dead." Similarly, a patient who commits suicide with a doctor's aid necessarily has the specific intent to end his or her own life, while a patient who refuses or discontinues treatment might not.

The law has long used actors' intent or purpose to distinguish between two acts that may have the same result. Put differently, the law distinguishes actions taken "because of" a given end from actions taken "in spite of" their unintended but foreseen consequences.

> The ethical principle of "double effect," with origins in Roman Catholic theology, allows prescription of high doses of sedatives and opioids to relieve pain, even if hastening death is foreseen.

Given these general principles, it is not surprising that many courts, including New York courts, have carefully distinguished refusing life-sustaining treatment from suicide. In fact, the first state-court decision explicitly to authorize withdrawing lifesaving treatment noted the "real distinction between the self-infliction of deadly harm and a self-determination against artificial life support." And recently, the Michigan Supreme Court also rejected the argument that the distinction "between acts that artificially sustain life and acts that artificially curtail life" is merely a "distinction without constitutional significance — a meaningless exercise in semantic gymnastics," insisting that "the *Cruzan* majority disagreed and so do we."

Similarly, the overwhelming majority of state legislatures have drawn a clear line between assisting suicide and withdrawing or permitting the refusal of unwanted lifesaving medical treatment by prohibiting the former and permitting the latter. And "nearly all states expressly disapprove of suicide and assisted suicide either in statutes dealing with durable powers of attorney in health-care situations, or in 'living will' statutes." Thus, even as the States move to protect and promote patients' dignity at the end of life, they remain opposed to physician-assisted suicide. . . .

This Court has also recognized, at least implicitly, the distinction between letting a patient die and making that patient die. In *Cruzan v. Director, Mo. Dept. of Health*, we concluded that "[t]he principle that a competent person has a constitutionally protected liberty interest in refusing unwanted medical treatment may be inferred from our prior decisions," and we assumed the existence of such a right for purposes of that case. But our assumption of a right to refuse treatment was grounded not, as the Court of Appeals supposed, on the proposition that patients have a general and abstract "right to hasten death," but on well-established, traditional rights to bodily integrity and freedom from unwanted touching, *Cruzan* (O'Connor, J., concurring). In fact, we observed that "the majority of States in this country have laws imposing criminal penalties on one who assists another to commit suicide." *Cruzan* therefore provides no support for the notion that refusing life-sustaining medical treatment is "nothing more nor less than suicide."

For all these reasons, we disagree with respondents' claim that the distinction between refusing lifesaving medical treatment and assisted suicide is "arbitrary" and "irrational." Granted, in some cases, the line between the two may not be clear, but certainty is not required, even were it possible. Logic and contemporary practice support New York's judgment that the two acts are different, and New York may therefore, consistent with the Constitution, treat them differently. By permitting everyone to refuse unwanted medical treatment while prohibiting anyone from assisting a suicide, New York law follows a longstanding and rational distinction.

QUESTION

Why does the Court deny petitioners' claim when the patients correctly assert that the state is treating them differently from other patients who are also terminally ill?

PROBLEM

How would you advise state legislators who want to facilitate physician-assisted death given the Court's analysis in *Washington v. Glucksberg* and *Vacco v. Quill*? Draft a statute that comports with but does not challenge existing case law.

A handful of states have acted on the federalism-oriented dicta allowing states to determine whether physician assistance in death is desirable as a policy matter. As of this printing, Oregon, Washington, Vermont, California, Colorado, and the District of Columbia have laws permitting physician assistance in dying in proscribed circumstances. Montana's supreme court held that physician compliance with a competent patient's request for assistance is permitted. Consider provisions from Oregon's Death with Dignity Act (ODWDA), first approved by state voters in 1994, which has been the model for other states that have passed or attempted to pass "death with dignity" laws. The ODWDA is lengthy, but the following excerpt offers a sense of the rights and responsibilities the law conveys:

Or. Rev. Stat. §127.805 §2.01. Written request for medication to end one's life

(1) An adult who is capable, is a resident of Oregon, and has been determined by the attending physician and consulting physician to be suffering from a terminal disease, and who has voluntarily expressed his or her wish to die, may make a written request for medication for the purpose of ending his or her life in a humane and dignified manner in accordance with ORS 127.800 to 127.897.

(2) No person shall qualify under the provisions of ORS 127.800 to 127.897 solely because of age or disability.

Or. Rev. Stat. §127.810 §2.02. Form of the written request

(1) A valid request for medication under ORS 127.800 to 127.897 shall be in substantially the form described in ORS 127.897, signed and dated by the patient and witnessed by at least two individuals who, in the presence of the patient, attest that to the best of their knowledge and belief the patient is capable, acting voluntarily, and is not being coerced to sign the request.

(2) One of the witnesses shall be a person who is not:

(a) A relative of the patient by blood, marriage or adoption;

(b) A person who at the time the request is signed would be entitled to any portion of the estate of the qualified patient upon death under any will or by operation of law; or

(c) An owner, operator or employee of a health care facility where the qualified patient is receiving medical treatment or is a resident.

(3) The patient's attending physician at the time the request is signed shall not be a witness.

(4) If the patient is a patient in a long term care facility at the time the written request is made, one of the witnesses shall be an individual designated

by the facility and having the qualifications specified by the Department of Human Services by rule.

Or. Rev. Stat. §127.815. §3.01. Responsibilities of the attending physician
(1) The attending physician shall:

(a) Make the initial determination of whether a patient has a terminal disease, is capable, and has made the request voluntarily;

(b) Request that the patient demonstrate Oregon residency pursuant to ORS 127.860;

(c) To ensure that the patient is making an informed decision, inform the patient of:

(A) His or her medical diagnosis;

(B) His or her prognosis;

(C) The potential risks associated with taking the medication to be prescribed;

(D) The probable result of taking the medication to be prescribed; and

(E) The feasible alternatives, including, but not limited to, comfort care, hospice care and pain control;

(d) Refer the patient to a consulting physician for medical confirmation of the diagnosis, and for a determination that the patient is capable and acting voluntarily;

(e) Refer the patient for counseling if appropriate pursuant to ORS 127.825;

(f) Recommend that the patient notify next of kin;

(g) Counsel the patient about the importance of having another person present when the patient takes the medication prescribed pursuant to ORS 127.800 to 127.897 and of not taking the medication in a public place;

(h) Inform the patient that he or she has an opportunity to rescind the request at any time and in any manner, and offer the patient an opportunity to rescind at the end of the 15-day waiting period pursuant to ORS 127.840;

(i) Verify, immediately prior to writing the prescription for medication under ORS 127.800 to 127.897, that the patient is making an informed decision;

(j) Fulfill the medical record documentation requirements of ORS 127.855;

(k) Ensure that all appropriate steps are carried out in accordance with ORS 127.800 to 127.897 prior to writing a prescription for medication to enable a qualified patient to end his or her life in a humane and dignified manner; and

(l)(A) Dispense medications directly, including ancillary medications intended to facilitate the desired effect to minimize the patient's discomfort, provided the attending physician is registered as a dispensing physician with the Oregon Medical Board, has a current Drug Enforcement Administration certificate and complies with any applicable administrative rule; or

(B) With the patient's written consent:

(i) Contact a pharmacist and inform the pharmacist of the pre-scription; and

(ii) Deliver the written prescription personally or by mail to the pharmacist, who will dispense the medications to either the patient, the attending physician or an expressly identified agent of the patient.

(2) Notwithstanding any other provision of law, the attending physician may sign the patient's report of death.

QUESTIONS

The Oregon Health Authority keeps annual records of the implementation of this law and publishes them for the public each year. Does it surprise you to learn that the vast majority of patients that avail themselves of the law are in the educated, white, middle- to upper-class demographic? People of color and people with disabilities as well as low-income individuals are significantly less likely to use the ODWDA. What do you make of this divide?

2. STATUTORY FACILITATION OF END-OF-LIFE DECISION MAKING

Influenced by end-of-life case law, both the states and the federal government have encouraged patients to create living wills, which provide instructions for care when a patient becomes incompetent for medical purposes. Sometimes this document is called an advance directive, though advance directive is a slightly broader term that can encompass designating a medical proxy (health care decision-maker) for the patient in addition to setting forth medical care instructions. Since 1991, Medicare and Medicaid have required participating providers to inform all patients of their rights regarding end-of-life decisions. In addition, the Joint Commission (discussed in Chapters 4 and 8) requires hospitals to maintain bioethics committees that address issues not easily answered by physicians at the patient's bedside. First, we study the federal standards that encourage use of advance directives and the patient's right to refuse medical care, and then we explore related state law.

a. Federal Law and End-of-Life Decisions

Medicare Hospice Conditions of Participation
42 C.F.R. §418.52. Condition of participation: Patient's rights

The patient has the right to be informed of his or her rights, and the hospice must protect and promote the exercise of these rights.

(a) Standard: Notice of rights and responsibilities. (1) During the initial assessment visit in advance of furnishing care the hospice must provide the patient or representative with verbal (meaning spoken) and written notice of the patient's rights and responsibilities in a language and manner that the patient understands.

(2) The hospice must comply with the requirements of subpart I of part 489 of this chapter regarding advance directives. The hospice must inform and distribute written information to the patient concerning its policies on

> A statute or regulation cannot be fully understood without following its cross-references. Here, the Hospice Conditions of Participation in Medicare specifically reference the Advance Directive standards for all Medicare participating providers (Part 489, included below).

advance directives, including a description of applicable State law.

(3) The hospice must obtain the patient's or representative's signature confirming that he or she has received a copy of the notice of rights and responsibilities. . . .

(c) Standard: Rights of the patient. The patient has a right to the following:

(1) Receive effective pain management and symptom control from the hospice for conditions related to the terminal illness;

(2) Be involved in developing his or her hospice plan of care;

(3) Refuse care or treatment; . . .

42 C.F.R. §489.100. Definition

For purposes of this part, advance directive means a written instruction, such as a living will or durable power of attorney for health care, recognized under State law (whether statutory or as recognized by the courts of the State), relating to the provision of health care when the individual is incapacitated.

42 C.F.R. §489.102. Requirements for providers

(a) Hospitals, critical access hospitals, skilled nursing facilities, nursing facilities, home health agencies, providers of home health care (and for Medicaid purposes, providers of personal care services), hospices, and religious non-medical health care institutions must maintain written policies and procedures concerning advance directives with respect to all adult individuals receiving medical care, or patient care in the case of a patient in a religious nonmedical health care institution, by or through the provider and are required to:

(1) Provide written information to such individuals concerning—

(i) An individual's rights under State law (whether statutory or recognized by the courts of the State) to make decisions concerning such

> Note the incorporation of state law into the federal standards. An advising attorney's research is not complete until the pertinent state law has been examined.

medical care, including the right to accept or refuse medical or surgical treatment and the right to formulate, at the individual's option, advance directives. Providers are permitted to contract with other entities to furnish this information but are still legally responsible for ensuring that the requirements of this section are met. Providers are to update and disseminate amended information as soon as possible, but no later than 90 days from the effective date of the changes to State law; and

(ii) The written policies of the provider or organization respecting the implementation of such rights, including a clear and precise statement of limitation if the provider cannot implement an advance directive on the basis of conscience. At a minimum, a provider's statement of limitation should:

(A) Clarify any differences between institution-wide conscience objections and those that may be raised by individual physicians;

(B) Identify the state legal authority permitting such objection; and

(C) Describe the range of medical conditions or procedures affected by the conscience objection.

(2) Document in a prominent part of the individual's current medical record, or patient care record in the case of an individual in a religious

nonmedical health care institution, whether or not the individual has executed an advance directive;

(3) Not condition the provision of care or otherwise discriminate against an individual based on whether or not the individual has executed an advance directive;

(4) Ensure compliance with requirements of State law (whether statutory or recognized by the courts of the State) regarding advance directives. The provider must inform individuals that complaints concerning the advance directive requirements may be filed with the State survey and certification agency;

(5) Provide for education of staff concerning its policies and procedures on advance directives; and

(6) Provide for community education regarding issues concerning advance directives that may include material required in paragraph (a) (1) of this section, either directly or in concert with other providers and organizations. Separate community education materials may be developed and used, at the discretion of providers. The same written materials do not have to be provided in all settings, but the material should define what constitutes an advance directive, emphasizing that an advance directive is designed to enhance an incapacitated individual's control over medical treatment, and describe applicable State law concerning advance directives. A provider must be able to document its community education efforts.

(b) The information specified in paragraph (a) of this section is furnished:

(1) In the case of a hospital, at the time of the individual's admission as an inpatient.

(2) In the case of a skilled nursing facility at the time of the individual's admission as a resident.

(3)(i) In the case of a home health agency, in advance of the individual coming under the care of the agency. The HHA may furnish advance directives information to a patient at the time of the first home visit, as long as the information is furnished before care is provided.

(ii) In the case of personal care services, in advance of the individual coming under the care of the personal care services provider. The personal care provider may furnish advance directives information to a patient at the time of the first home visit, as long as the information is furnished before care is provided.

(4) In the case of a hospice program, at the time of initial receipt of hospice care by the individual from the program.

(c) The providers listed in paragraph (a) of this section—

(1) Are not required to provide care that conflicts with an advance directive.

(2) Are not required to implement an advance directive if, as a matter of conscience, the provider cannot implement an advance directive and State law allows any health care provider or any agent of such provider to conscientiously object.

(d) Prepaid or eligible organizations must meet the requirements specified in §417.436 of this chapter.

(e) If an adult individual is incapacitated at the time of admission or at the start of care and is unable to receive information (due to the incapacitating conditions or a mental disorder) or articulate whether or not he or she has executed an advance directive, then the provider may give advance directive information to the individual's family or surrogate in the same manner that it issues other materials about policies and procedures to the family of the inca-pacitated individual or to a surrogate or other concerned persons in accordance with State law. The provider is not relieved of its obligation to provide this information to the individual once he or she is no longer incapacitated or unable to receive such information. Follow-up procedures must be in place to provide the information to the individual directly at the appropriate time.

QUESTIONS

1. A provision of the bill that became the ACA, later deleted, would have paid physicians to discuss with their Medicare patients, on an annual basis, end-of-life planning. The proposal got caught up in the "death panels" controversy. Why did the public react so negatively to the idea of the government paying for those conversations?
2. What are the policy considerations behind reimbursing physicians for the time spent engaging in those conversations, which Medicare now does?

b. State Law Facilitating Substituted Judgment

With the federal standards in mind, and the long history of state common law per-taining to refusal of treatment (well summarized in *Cruzan*), it should be unsurpris-ing that every state has some form of law addressing end-of-life care. To cover the greatest number of medical possibilities, state laws generally include instructions regarding the state's expectations for a living will, designation of a health care surrogate or proxy, and a list of individuals to consult in the absence of a designation by the patient, but laws vary greatly from state to state. As you read the following example of one of the more thorough state statutes, consider whether this law protects patient autonomy and self-determination and effectively facilitates substituted judgment. The issue of patient capacity or competence is a specific evalua-tion in health care that is unrelated to other issues (such as abil-ity to execute a will or contract) and that tends to be slightly more flexible in a medical setting than other legal contexts. In other words, if a patient can display an ability to speak for herself, health care providers will generally take that expression into consideration. Also consider whether this statute facilitates decision making that would be meaningful to the patient, the patient's surrogate, and health care providers treating a termin-ally ill patient.

In 2005, Florida was the locus of the infamous Terri Schiavo case, in which the husband and guardian of a woman in PVS sought to remove her feeding tube, believing that to be her desire, after ten years of futile treatment. Her parents tried to prevent him from exercising his power as guardian and involved right-to-life politicians in their effort, including then-Governor Jeb Bush. The family's dispute bounced between state courts and federal courts several times. The statute excerpted here existed largely in the same form at the time.

Fla. Stat. ch. 765. Health Care Advance Directives
Part I. General Provisions

. . . .

765.102. Legislative findings and intent

(1)   The Legislature finds that every competent adult has the fundamental right of self-determination regarding decisions pertaining to his or her own health, including the right to choose or refuse medical treatment. This right is subject to certain interests of society, such as the protection of human life and the preservation of ethical standards in the medical profession.

(2)   To ensure that such right is not lost or diminished by virtue of later physical or mental incapacity, the Legislature intends that a procedure be established to allow a person to plan for incapacity by executing a document or orally designating another person to direct the course of his or her health care or receive his or her health information, or both, upon his or her incapacity. Such procedure should be less expensive and less restrictive than guardianship and permit a previously incapacitated person to exercise his or her full right to make health care decisions as soon as the capacity to make such decisions has been regained.

(3)   The Legislature also recognizes that some competent adults may want to receive immediate assistance in making health care decisions or accessing health information, or both, without a determination of incapacity. The Legislature intends that a procedure be established to allow a person to designate a surrogate to make health care decisions or receive health information, or both, without the necessity for a determination of incapacity under this chapter.

Legislative findings such as these do not have direct legal effect but help those interpreting the law to understand its history and intent.

(4)   The Legislature recognizes that for some the administration of life-prolonging medical procedures may result in only a precarious and burdensome existence. In order to ensure that the rights and intentions of a person may be respected even after he or she is no longer able to participate actively in decisions concerning himself or herself, and to encourage communication among such patient, his or her family, and his or her physician, the Legislature declares that the laws of this state recognize the right of a competent adult to make an advance directive instructing his or her physician to provide, withhold, or withdraw life-prolonging procedures or to designate another to make the health care decision for him or her in the event that such person should become incapacitated and unable to personally direct his or her health care.

(5)   The Legislature recognizes the need for all health care professionals to rapidly increase their understanding of end-of-life and palliative care. Therefore, the Legislature encourages the professional regulatory boards to adopt appropriate standards and guidelines regarding end-of-life care and pain management and encourages educational institutions established to train health care professionals and allied health professionals to implement curricula to train such professionals to provide end-of-life care, including pain management and palliative care.

(6)   For purposes of this chapter:

(a)   Palliative care is the comprehensive management of the physical, psychological, social, spiritual, and existential needs of patients. Palliative care is especially suited to the care of persons who have incurable, progressive illnesses.

(b)   Palliative care must include:

1.   An opportunity to discuss and plan for end-of-life care.

2.   Assurance that physical and mental suffering will be carefully attended to.

3.   Assurance that preferences for withholding and withdrawing life-sustaining interventions will be honored.

4.   Assurance that the personal goals of the dying person will be addressed.

5.   Assurance that the dignity of the dying person will be a priority.

6.   Assurance that health care providers will not abandon the dying person.

7.   Assurance that the burden to family and others will be addressed.

8.   Assurance that advance directives for care will be respected regardless of the location of care.

9.   Assurance that organizational mechanisms are in place to evaluate the availability and quality of end-of-life, palliative, and hospice care services, including the evaluation of administrative and regulatory barriers.

10.   Assurance that necessary health care services will be provided and that relevant reimbursement policies are available.

11.   Assurance that the goals expressed in subparagraphs 1.-10. will be accomplished in a culturally appropriate manner.

. . . .

765.104. Amendment or revocation

(1)   An advance directive may be amended or revoked at any time by a competent principal:

(a)   By means of a signed, dated writing;

(b)   By means of the physical cancellation or destruction of the advance directive by the principal or by another in the principal's presence and at the principal's direction;

(c)   By means of an oral expression of intent to amend or revoke; or

(d)   By means of a subsequently executed advance directive that is materially different from a previously executed advance directive.

(2)   Unless otherwise provided in the advance directive or in an order of dissolution or annulment of marriage, the dissolution or annulment of marriage of the principal revokes the designation of the principal's former spouse as a surrogate.

(3)   Any such amendment or revocation will be effective when it is communicated to the surrogate, health care provider, or health care facility. No civil or criminal liability shall be imposed upon any person for a failure to act upon an amendment or revocation unless that person has actual knowledge of such amendment or revocation. . . .

765.105. Review of surrogate or proxy's decision

(1)   The patient's family, the health care facility, or the primary physician, or any other interested person who may reasonably be expected to be directly affected by the surrogate or proxy's decision concerning any health care

decision may seek expedited judicial intervention pursuant to rule 5.900 of the Florida Probate Rules, if that person believes:

(a)   The surrogate or proxy's decision is not in accord with the patient's known desires or this chapter;

(b)   The advance directive is ambiguous, or the patient has changed his or her mind after execution of the advance directive;

(c)   The surrogate or proxy was improperly designated or appointed, or the designation of the surrogate is no longer effective or has been revoked;

(d)   The surrogate or proxy has failed to discharge duties, or incapacity or illness renders the surrogate or proxy incapable of discharging duties;

(e)   The surrogate or proxy has abused his or her powers; or

(f)   The patient has sufficient capacity to make his or her own health care decisions.

(2)   This section does not apply to a patient who is not incapacitated and who has designated a surrogate who has immediate authority to make health care decisions or receive health information, or both, on behalf of the patient.

. . . .

765.107. Construction

. . . .

(2)   Procedures provided in this chapter permitting the withholding or withdrawal of life-prolonging procedures do not apply to a person who never had capacity to designate a health care surrogate or execute a living will.

765.108. Effect with respect to insurance

The making of an advance directive pursuant to the provisions of this chapter shall not affect the sale, procurement, or issuance of any policy of life insurance, nor shall such making of an advance directive be deemed to modify the terms of an existing policy of life insurance. . . .

765.109. Immunity from liability; weight of proof; presumption

(1)   A health care facility, provider, or other person who acts under the direction of a health care facility or provider is not subject to criminal prosecution or civil liability, and will not be deemed to have engaged in unprofessional conduct, as a result of carrying out a health care decision made in accordance with the provisions of this chapter. The surrogate or proxy who makes a health care decision on a patient's behalf, pursuant to this chapter, is not subject to criminal prosecution or civil liability for such action.

In the first "right-to-die case," In re Quinlan, 70 N.J. 10, 355 A.2d 647 (1976), the New Jersey Supreme Court had to determine whether withdrawal of treatment would subject health care providers to criminal liability. State statutes since then have included this kind of immunity provision.

(2)   The provisions of this section shall apply unless it is shown by a preponderance of the evidence that the person authorizing or effectuating a health care decision did not, in good faith, comply with the provisions of this chapter.

765.110. Health care facilities and providers; discipline

(1)   A health care facility . . . shall provide to each patient written information concerning the individual's rights concerning advance directives and the health care facility's policies respecting the implementation of such rights,

and shall document in the patient's medical records whether or not the individual has executed an advance directive.

(2)   A health care provider or health care facility may not require a patient to execute an advance directive or to execute a new advance directive using the facility's or provider's forms. The patient's advance directives shall travel with the patient as part of the patient's medical record.

(3)   A health care provider or health care facility shall be subject to professional discipline and revocation of license or certification, and a fine of not more than $1,000 per incident, or both, if the health care provider or health care facility, as a condition of treatment or admission, requires an individual to execute or waive an advance directive.

. . . .

765.1105. Transfer of a patient

(1)   A health care provider or facility that refuses to comply with a patient's advance directive, or the treatment decision of his or her surrogate or proxy, shall make reasonable efforts to transfer the patient to another health care provider or facility that will comply with the directive or treatment decision. This chapter does not require a health care provider or facility to commit any act which is contrary to the provider's or facility's moral or ethical beliefs, if the patient:

(a)   Is not in an emergency condition; and

(b)   Has received written information upon admission informing the patient of the policies of the health care provider or facility regarding such moral or ethical beliefs.

(2)   A health care provider or facility that is unwilling to carry out the wishes of the patient or the treatment decision of his or her surrogate or proxy because of moral or ethical beliefs must within 7 days either:

(a)   Transfer the patient to another health care provider or facility. The health care provider or facility shall pay the costs for transporting the patient to another health care provider or facility; or

(b)   If the patient has not been transferred, carry out the wishes of the patient or the patient's surrogate or proxy, unless s. 765.105 applies.

765.1115. Falsification, forgery, or willful concealment, cancellation, or destruction of directive or revocation or amendment; penalties

(1)   Any person who willfully conceals, cancels, defaces, obliterates, or damages an advance directive without the principal's consent or who falsifies or forges the revocation or amendment of an advance directive of another, and who thereby causes life-prolonging procedures to be utilized in contravention of the previously expressed intent of the principal, commits a felony of the third degree. . . .

> More than half of states prohibit withdrawal of life support from a pregnant woman, regardless of whether the woman's living will directs otherwise, and some states do not draw the line at viability.

765.112. Recognition of advance directive executed in another state

An advance directive executed in another state in compliance with the law of that state or of this state is validly executed for the purposes of this chapter.

765.113. Restrictions on providing consent

Unless the principal expressly delegates such authority to the surrogate in writing, or a surrogate or proxy has sought and received court approval . . . , a surrogate or proxy may not provide consent for:

(1) Abortion, sterilization, electroshock therapy, psychosurgery, experimental treatments that have not been approved by a federally approved institutional review board . . . or voluntary admission to a mental health facility.

(2) Withholding or withdrawing life-prolonging procedures from a pregnant patient prior to viability as defined in s. 390.0111(4).

Part II. Health Care Surrogate

. . . .

765.202. Designation of a health care surrogate

(1) A written document designating a surrogate to make health care decisions for a principal or receive health information on behalf of a principal, or both, shall be signed by the principal in the presence of two subscribing adult witnesses. A principal unable to sign the instrument may, in the presence of witnesses, direct that another person sign the principal's name as required herein. An exact copy of the instrument shall be provided to the surrogate.

(2) The person designated as surrogate shall not act as witness to the execution of the document designating the health care surrogate. At least one person who acts as a witness shall be neither the principal's spouse nor blood relative.

(3) A document designating a health care surrogate may also designate an alternate surrogate provided the designation is explicit. The alternate surrogate may assume his or her duties as surrogate for the principal if the original surrogate is not willing, able, or reasonably available to perform his or her duties. The principal's failure to designate an alternate surrogate shall not invalidate the designation of a surrogate.

(4) If neither the designated surrogate nor the designated alternate surrogate is willing, able, or reasonably available to make health care decisions on behalf of the principal and in accordance with the principal's instructions, the health care facility may seek the appointment of a proxy pursuant to part IV.

. . . .

(7) Unless the document states a time of termination, the designation shall remain in effect until revoked by the principal.

(8) A written designation of a health care surrogate executed pursuant to this section establishes a rebuttable presumption of clear and convincing evidence of the principal's designation of the surrogate.

> Note the evidentiary standard articulated specifically by the statute.

765.203. Suggested form of designation

A written designation of a health care surrogate executed pursuant to this chapter may, but need not be, in the following form:

DESIGNATION OF HEALTH CARE SURROGATE

I, (name), designate as my health care surrogate under s. 765.202, Florida Statutes:

Name: (name of health care surrogate)

Address: (address)
Phone: (telephone)
If my health care surrogate is not willing, able, or reasonably available to perform his or her duties, I designate as my alternate health care surrogate:
Name: (name of alternate health care surrogate)
Address: (address)
Phone: (telephone)

INSTRUCTIONS FOR HEALTH CARE
I authorize my health care surrogate to:
(Initial here) Receive any of my health information, whether oral or recorded in any form or medium, that:
1. Is created or received by a health care provider, health care facility, health plan, public health authority, employer, life insurer, school or university, or health care clearinghouse; and
2. Relates to my past, present, or future physical or mental health or condition; the provision of health care to me; or the past, present, or future payment for the provision of health care to me.
I further authorize my health care surrogate to:
(Initial here) Make all health care decisions for me, which means he or she has the authority to:
1. Provide informed consent, refusal of consent, or withdrawal of consent to any and all of my health care, including life-prolonging procedures.
2. Apply on my behalf for private, public, government, or veterans' benefits to defray the cost of health care.
3. Access my health information reasonably necessary for the health care surrogate to make decisions involving my health care and to apply for benefits for me.
4. Decide to make an anatomical gift pursuant to part V of chapter 765, Florida Statutes.
(Initial here) Specific instructions and restrictions:

While I have decisionmaking capacity, my wishes are controlling and my physicians and health care providers must clearly communicate to me the treatment plan or any change to the treatment plan prior to its implementation.

To the extent I am capable of understanding, my health care surrogate shall keep me reasonably informed of all decisions that he or she has made on my behalf and matters concerning me.
THIS HEALTH CARE SURROGATE DESIGNATION IS NOT AFFECTED BY MY SUBSEQUENT INCAPACITY EXCEPT AS PROVIDED IN CHAPTER 765, FLORIDA STATUTES.
PURSUANT TO SECTION 765.104, FLORIDA STATUTES, I UNDERSTAND THAT I MAY, AT ANY TIME WHILE I RETAIN MY CAPACITY, REVOKE OR AMEND THIS DESIGNATION BY:
(1) SIGNING A WRITTEN AND DATED INSTRUMENT WHICH EXPRESSES MY INTENT TO AMEND OR REVOKE THIS DESIGNATION;
(2) PHYSICALLY DESTROYING THIS DESIGNATION THROUGH MY OWN ACTION OR BY THAT OF ANOTHER PERSON IN MY PRESENCE AND UNDER MY DIRECTION;
(3) VERBALLY EXPRESSING MY INTENTION TO AMEND OR REVOKE THIS DESIGNATION; OR

(4) SIGNING A NEW DESIGNATION THAT IS MATERIALLY DIFFERENT FROM THIS DESIGNATION.

MY HEALTH CARE SURROGATE'S AUTHORITY BECOMES EFFECTIVE WHEN MY PRIMARY PHYSICIAN DETERMINES THAT I AM UNABLE TO MAKE MY OWN HEALTH CARE DECISIONS UNLESS I INITIAL EITHER OR BOTH OF THE FOLLOWING BOXES:

IF I INITIAL THIS BOX [ ], MY HEALTH CARE SURROGATE'S AUTHORITY TO RECEIVE MY HEALTH INFORMATION TAKES EFFECT IMMEDIATELY.

IF I INITIAL THIS BOX [ ], MY HEALTH CARE SURROGATE'S AUTHORITY TO MAKE HEALTH CARE DECISIONS FOR ME TAKES EFFECT IMMEDIATELY. PURSUANT TO SECTION 765.204(3), FLORIDA STATUTES, ANY INSTRUCTIONS OR HEALTH CARE DECISIONS I MAKE, EITHER VERBALLY OR IN WRITING, WHILE I POSSESS CAPACITY SHALL SUPERSEDE ANY INSTRUCTIONS OR HEALTH CARE DECISIONS MADE BY MY SURROGATE THAT ARE IN MATERIAL CONFLICT WITH THOSE MADE BY ME.

SIGNATURES: Sign and date the form here:

(date)   (sign your name)
(address)   (print your name)
(city)   (state)

SIGNATURES OF WITNESSES:

First witness   Second witness
(print name)   (print name)
(address)   (address)
(city) (state)   (city) (state)
(signature of witness)   (signature of witness)
(date)   (date)

. . . .

765.204. Capacity of principal; procedure

(1) A principal is presumed to be capable of making health care decisions for herself or himself unless she or he is determined to be incapacitated. While a principal has decisionmaking capacity, the principal's wishes are controlling. Each physician or health care provider must clearly communicate to a principal with decisionmaking capacity the treatment plan and any change to the treatment plan prior to implementation of the plan or the change to the plan. Incapacity may not be inferred from the person's voluntary or involuntary hospitalization for mental illness or from her or his intellectual disability.

Pay close attention to the definition of capacity and take note of the line drawing between capacity and incapacity. What should happen if health care providers are uncertain how much capacity a "principal" retains?

(2) If a principal's capacity to make health care decisions for herself or himself or provide informed consent is in question, the primary or attending physician shall evaluate the principal's capacity and, if the evaluating physician concludes that the principal lacks capacity, enter that evaluation in the principal's medical record. If the evaluating physician has a question as to whether the principal lacks capacity, another physician shall also evaluate the principal's capacity, and if the second physician agrees that the

principal lacks the capacity to make health care decisions or provide informed consent, the health care facility shall enter both physician's evaluations in the principal's medical record. If the principal has designated a health care surrogate or has delegated authority to make health care decisions to an attorney in fact under a durable power of attorney, the health care facility shall notify such surrogate or attorney in fact in writing that her or his authority under the instrument has commenced, as provided in chapter 709 or s. 765.203. If an attending physician determines that the principal lacks capacity, the hospital in which the attending physician made such a determination shall notify the principal's primary physician of the determination.

(3)   The surrogate's authority commences either upon a determination under subsection (2) that the principal lacks capacity or upon a stipulation of such authority pursuant to s. 765.101(21). Such authority remains in effect until a determination that the principal has regained such capacity, if the authority commenced as a result of incapacity, or until the authority is revoked, if the authority commenced immediately pursuant to s. 765.101(21). Upon commencement of the surrogate's authority, a surrogate who is not the principal's spouse shall notify the principal's spouse or adult children of the principal's designation of the surrogate. Except if the principal provided immediately exercisable authority to the surrogate pursuant to s. 765.101(21), in the event that the primary or attending physician determines that the principal has regained capacity, the authority of the surrogate shall cease, but recommences if the principal subsequently loses capacity as determined pursuant to this section. A health care provider is not liable for relying upon health care decisions made by a surrogate while the principal lacks capacity. . . .

(5)   A determination made pursuant to this section that a principal lacks capacity to make health care decisions shall not be construed as a finding that a principal lacks capacity for any other purpose.

(6)   If the surrogate is required to consent to withholding or withdrawing life-prolonging procedures, part III applies.

765.205. Responsibility of the surrogate

(1)   The surrogate, in accordance with the principal's instructions, unless such authority has been expressly limited by the principal, shall:

(a)   Have authority to act for the principal and to make all health care decisions for the principal during the principal's incapacity.

(b)   Consult expeditiously with appropriate health care providers to provide informed consent, and make only health care decisions for the principal which he or she believes the principal would have made under the circumstances if the principal were capable of making such decisions. If there is no indication of what the principal would have chosen, the surrogate may consider the patient's best interest in deciding that proposed treatments are to be withheld or that treatments currently in effect are to be withdrawn.

(c)   Provide written consent using an appropriate form whenever consent is required, including a physician's order not to resuscitate.

(d)   Be provided access to the appropriate health information of the principal.

(e)   Apply for public benefits, such as Medicare and Medicaid, for the principal and have access to information regarding the principal's income and assets and banking and financial records to the extent required to make application. A health care provider or facility may not, however, make such application a condition of continued care if the principal, if capable, would have refused to apply.

(2)   The surrogate may authorize the release of health information to appropriate persons to ensure the continuity of the principal's health care and may authorize the admission, discharge, or transfer of the principal to or from a health care facility or other facility or program licensed under chapter 400 or chapter 429.

(3)   If, after the appointment of a surrogate, a court appoints a guardian, the surrogate shall continue to make health care decisions for the principal, unless the court has modified or revoked the authority of the surrogate pursuant to s. 744.3115. The surrogate may be directed by the court to report the principal's health care status to the guardian.

Part III. Life-Prolonging Procedures

. . . .

765.302. Procedure for making a living will; notice to physician

(1)   Any competent adult may, at any time, make a living will or written declaration and direct the providing, withholding, or withdrawal of life-prolonging procedures in the event that such person has a terminal condition, has an end-stage condition, or is in a persistent vegetative state. A living will must be signed by the principal in the presence of two subscribing witnesses, one of whom is neither a spouse nor a blood relative of the principal. If the principal is physically unable to sign the living will, one of the witnesses must subscribe the principal's signature in the principal's presence and at the principal's direction.

(2)   It is the responsibility of the principal to provide for notification to her or his primary physician that the living will has been made. In the event the principal is physically or mentally incapacitated at the time the principal is admitted to a health care facility, any other person may notify the physician or health care facility of the existence of the living will. A primary physician or health care facility which is so notified shall promptly make the living will or a copy thereof a part of the principal's medical records.

(3)   A living will, executed pursuant to this section, establishes a rebuttable presumption of clear and convincing evidence of the principal's wishes.

765.303. Suggested form of a living will

(1)   A living will may, BUT NEED NOT, be in the following form:
Living Will

Declaration made this __ day of ___, ___ (year), I, ____, willfully and voluntarily make known my desire that my dying not be artificially prolonged under the circumstances set forth below, and I do hereby declare that, if at any time I am incapacitated and

__ (initial) I have a terminal condition

or __ (initial) I have an end-stage condition

or __ (initial) I am in a persistent vegetative state

and if my primary physician and another consulting physician have determined that there is no reasonable medical probability of my recovery from such condition, I direct that life-prolonging procedures be withheld or withdrawn when the application of such procedures would serve only to prolong artificially the process of dying, and that I be permitted to die naturally with only the administration of medication or the performance of any medical procedure deemed necessary to provide me with comfort care or to alleviate pain.

It is my intention that this declaration be honored by my family and physician as the final expression of my legal right to refuse medical or surgical treatment and to accept the consequences for such refusal.

In the event that I have been determined to be unable to provide express and informed consent regarding the withholding, withdrawal, or continuation of life-prolonging procedures, I wish to designate, as my surrogate to carry out the provisions of this declaration:

Name:
Address:
Zip Code:
Phone:

I understand the full import of this declaration, and I am emotionally and mentally competent to make this declaration.

Additional Instructions (optional):

(Signed)

Witness
Address
Phone

Witness
Address
Phone

(2)   The principal's failure to designate a surrogate shall not invalidate the living will.

765.304. Procedure for living will

(1)   If a person has made a living will expressing his or her desires concerning life-prolonging procedures, but has not designated a surrogate to execute his or her wishes concerning life-prolonging procedures or designated a surrogate under part II, the person's primary physician may proceed as directed by the principal in the living will. In the event of a dispute or disagreement concerning the primary physician's decision to withhold or withdraw life-prolonging procedures, the primary physician shall not withhold or withdraw life-prolonging procedures pending review under s. 765.105. If a review of a disputed decision is not sought within 7 days following the primary physician's decision to withhold or withdraw life-prolonging procedures, the primary physician may proceed in accordance with the principal's instructions.

(2)   Before proceeding in accordance with the principal's living will, it must be determined that:

(a)   The principal does not have a reasonable medical probability of recovering capacity so that the right could be exercised directly by the principal.

(b)   The principal has a terminal condition, has an end-stage condition, or is in a persistent vegetative state.

(c)   Any limitations or conditions expressed orally or in a written declaration have been carefully considered and satisfied.

765.305. Procedure in absence of a living will

(1)   In the absence of a living will, the decision to withhold or withdraw life-prolonging procedures from a patient may be made by a health care surrogate designated by the patient pursuant to part II unless the designation limits the surrogate's authority to consent to the withholding or withdrawal of life-prolonging procedures.

> Because many patients do not execute advance directives, a hierarchy of decision-makers is a key mechanism for keeping these decisions out of the courts.

(2)   Before exercising the incompetent patient's right to forego treatment, the surrogate must be satisfied that:

(a)   The patient does not have a reasonable medical probability of recovering capacity so that the right could be exercised by the patient.

(b)   The patient has an end-stage condition, the patient is in a persistent vegetative state, or the patient's physical condition is terminal.

765.306. Determination of patient condition

In determining whether the patient has a terminal condition, has an end-stage condition, or is in a persistent vegetative state or may recover capacity, or whether a medical condition or limitation referred to in an advance directive exists, the patient's primary physician and at least one other consulting physician must separately examine the patient. The findings of each such examination must be documented in the patient's medical record and signed by each examining physician before life-prolonging procedures may be withheld or withdrawn.

765.309. Mercy killing or euthanasia not authorized; suicide distinguished

(1)   Nothing in this chapter shall be construed to condone, authorize, or approve mercy killing or euthanasia, or to permit any affirmative or deliberate act or omission to end life other than to permit the natural process of dying.

(2)   The withholding or withdrawal of life-prolonging procedures from a patient in accordance with any provision of this chapter does not, for any purpose, constitute a suicide.

Part IV. Absence of Advance Directive

765.401. The proxy

(1)   If an incapacitated or developmentally disabled patient has not executed an advance directive, or designated a surrogate to execute an advance directive, or the designated or alternate surrogate is no longer available to make health care decisions, health care decisions may be made for the patient by any of the following individuals, in the following order of priority, if no individual in a prior class is reasonably available, willing, or competent to act:

(a) The judicially appointed guardian of the patient or the guardian advocate of the person having a developmental disability as defined in s. 393.063, who has been authorized to consent to medical treatment, if such guardian has previously been appointed; however, this paragraph shall not be construed to require such appointment before a treatment decision can be made under this subsection;

(b) The patient's spouse;

(c) An adult child of the patient, or if the patient has more than one adult child, a majority of the adult children who are reasonably available for consultation;

(d) A parent of the patient;

(e) The adult sibling of the patient or, if the patient has more than one sibling, a majority of the adult siblings who are reasonably available for consultation;

(f) An adult relative of the patient who has exhibited special care and concern for the patient and who has maintained regular contact with the patient and who is familiar with the patient's activities, health, and religious or moral beliefs; or

(g) A close friend of the patient.

(h) A clinical social worker. . . .

> A lawyer who drafts living wills, health care proxies, or related documents must encourage clients to distribute these documents to health care providers and family members alike. The documents should be widely shared to encourage understanding of individual wishes, not hidden away with a will to be found after death. Otherwise, the state's law pertaining to incapacitated individuals without expressed end-of-life desires will apply.

(2) Any health care decision made under this part must be based on the proxy's informed consent and on the decision the proxy reasonably believes the patient would have made under the circumstances. If there is no indication of what the patient would have chosen, the proxy may consider the patient's best interest in deciding that proposed treatments are to be withheld or that treatments currently in effect are to be withdrawn.

(3) Before exercising the incapacitated patient's rights to select or decline health care, the proxy must comply with the provisions of ss. 765.205 and 765.305, except that a proxy's decision to withhold or withdraw life-prolonging procedures must be supported by clear and convincing evidence that the decision would have been the one the patient would have chosen had the patient been competent or, if there is no indication of what the patient would have chosen, that the decision is in the patient's best interest.

. . . .

765.404. Persistent vegetative state

For persons in a persistent vegetative state, as determined by the person's primary physician in accordance with currently accepted medical standards, who have no advance directive and for whom there is no evidence indicating what the person would have wanted under such conditions, and for whom, after a reasonably diligent inquiry, no family or friends are available or willing to serve as a proxy to make health care decisions for them, life-prolonging procedures may be withheld or withdrawn under the following conditions:

(1) The person has a judicially appointed guardian representing his or her best interest with authority to consent to medical treatment; and

(2) The guardian and the person's primary physician, in consultation with the medical ethics committee of the facility where the patient is located, conclude that the condition is permanent and that there is no reasonable medical

probability for recovery and that withholding or withdrawing life-prolonging procedures is in the best interest of the patient. If there is no medical ethics committee at the facility, the facility must have an arrangement with the medical ethics committee of another facility or with a community-based ethics committee approved by the Florida Bioethics Network. The ethics committee shall review the case with the guardian, in consultation with the person's primary physician, to determine whether the condition is permanent and there is no reasonable medical probability for recovery. The individual committee members and the facility associated with an ethics committee shall not be held liable in any civil action related to the performance of any duties required in this subsection. . . .

QUESTIONS

1. What is the standard of evidence that the statute indicates is necessary for withdrawal of treatment?
2. Who may effectuate withdrawal of treatment, and under what circumstances?
3. Complete the model forms in the statute for yourself. Do you think the forms provided are adequate? If not, how would you change the forms?
4. Does this law help health care providers or proxies to make decisions when health care would be futile (meaning there is no therapeutic benefit to medical care)? How should futility be defined for purposes of advance directives?

Patients' failure to execute an advance directive, living will, or health care proxy seems to be an intractable problem, even though state and federal governments have encouraged the creation of these documents for many years. Some states have gotten more creative in attempting to facilitate the creation and use of these documents. For example, some states, such as Nevada, Washington, and Vermont, created advance directive registries. Some states also encourage the use of Physician or Medical Orders for Life-Sustaining Treatment (POLST or MOLST) forms. Physicians complete a MOLST or POLST with their patients and then insert the document in the patient's medical record. The document is executed by a physician and added to the medical record. The purpose is to facilitate consistent treatment for patients receiving care at the end of life; it is not a substitute for a proxy or living will. The MOLST that Massachusetts requires health care providers to use offers an example.

MASSACHUSETTS MEDICAL ORDERS for LIFE-SUSTAINING TREATMENT (MOLST) www.molst-ma.org		Patient's Name _____ Date of Birth _____ Medical Record Number if applicable: _____

INSTRUCTIONS: *Every patient should receive full attention to comfort.*

→ This form should be signed based on goals of care discussions between the patient (or patient's representative signing below) and the signing clinician.
→ Sections A–C are valid orders only if Sections D and E are complete. Section F is valid only if Sections G and H are complete.
→ If any section is not completed, there is no limitation on the treatment indicated in that section.
→ The form is effective immediately upon signature. Photocopy, fax or electronic copies of properly signed MOLST forms are valid.

A Mark one circle →	**CARDIOPULMONARY RESUSCITATION: for a patient in cardiac or respiratory arrest** O Do Not Resuscitate O Attempt Resuscitation
B Mark one circle → Mark one circle →	**VENTILATION: for a patient in respiratory distress** O Do Not Intubate and Ventilate O Intubate and Ventilate O Do Not Use Non-invasive Ventilation (e.g. CPAP) O Use Non-invasive Ventilation (e.g. CPAP)
C Mark one circle →	**TRANSFER TO HOSPITAL** O Do Not Transfer to Hospital (*unless needed for comfort*) O Transfer to Hospital
PATIENT or patient's representative signature **D** *Required* Mark one circle and fill in every line for valid Page 1.	**Mark one circle below to indicate who is signing Section D:** o Patient o Health Care Agent o Guardian* o Parent/Guardian* of minor Signature of patient confirms this form was signed of patient's own free will and reflects his/her wishes and goals of care as expressed to the Section E signer. Signature by the patient's representative (indicated above) confirms that this form reflects his/her assessment of the patient's wishes and goals of care, or if those wishes are unknown, his/her assessment of the patient's best interests. *A guardian can sign only to the extent permitted by MA law. Consult legal counsel with questions about a guardian's authority.* **✗**_____ _____ Signature of Patient (or Person Representing the Patient) Date of Signature _____ _____ Legible Printed Name of Signer Telephone Number of Signer
CLINICIAN signature **E** *Required* Fill in every line for valid Page 1.	Signature of physician, nurse practitioner or physician assistant confirms that this form accurately reflects his/her discussion(s) with the signer in Section D. **✗**_____ _____ Signature of Physician, Nurse Practitioner, or Physician Assistant Date and Time of Signature _____ _____ Legible Printed Name of Signer Telephone Number of Signer
Optional Expiration date (if any) and other information	This form does not expire unless expressly stated. *Expiration date (if any) of this form:* _____ Health Care Agent Printed Name _____ Telephone Number _____ Primary Care Provider Printed Name _____ Telephone Number _____

SEND THIS FORM WITH THE PATIENT AT ALL TIMES.
HIPAA permits disclosure of MOLST to health care providers as necessary for treatment.

Approved by DPH   August 10, 2013   MOLST Form Page 1 of 2

Patient's Name: _____ Patient's DOB _____ Medical Record # if applicable_____

F	Statement of Patient Preferences for Other Medically-Indicated Treatments		
	INTUBATION AND VENTILATION		
Mark one circle →	○ Refer to Section B on Page 1	○ Use intubation and ventilation as marked in Section B, but short term only	○ Undecided ○ Did not discuss
	NON-INVASIVE VENTILATION (e.g. Continuous Positive Airway Pressure - CPAP)		
Mark one circle →	○ Refer to Section B on Page 1	○ Use non-invasive ventilation as marked in Section B, but short term only	○ Undecided ○ Did not discuss
	DIALYSIS		
Mark one circle →	○ No dialysis	○ Use dialysis ○ Use dialysis, but short term only	○ Undecided ○ Did not discuss
	ARTIFICIAL NUTRITION		
Mark one circle →	○ No artificial nutrition	○ Use artificial nutrition ○ Use artificial nutrition, but short term only	○ Undecided ○ Did not discuss
	ARTIFICIAL HYDRATION		
Mark one circle →	○ No artificial hydration	○ Use artificial hydration ○ Use artificial hydration, but short term only	○ Undecided ○ Did not discuss
	Other treatment preferences specific to the patient's medical condition and care _____ _____ _____		

PATIENT or patient's representative signature **G** *Required* Mark one circle and fill in every line for valid Page 2.	**Mark one circle below to indicate who is signing Section G:** ○ Patient ○ Health Care Agent ○ Guardian* ○ Parent/Guardian* of minor Signature of patient confirms this form was signed of patient's own free will and reflects his/her wishes and goals of care as expressed to the Section H signer. Signature by the patient's representative (indicated above) confirms that this form reflects his/her assessment of the patient's wishes and goals of care, or if those wishes are unknown, his/her assessment of the patient's best interests. *A guardian can sign only to the extent permitted by MA law. Consult legal counsel with questions about a guardian's authority.*
	Signature of Patient (or Person Representing the Patient) _____ Date of Signature _____
	Legible Printed Name of Signer _____ Telephone Number of Signer _____
CLINICIAN signature **H** *Required* Fill in every line for valid Page 2.	Signature of physician, nurse practitioner or physician assistant confirms that this form accurately reflects his/her discussion(s) with the signer in Section G.
	Signature of Physician, Nurse Practitioner, or Physician Assistant _____ Date and Time of Signature _____
	Legible Printed Name of Signer _____ Telephone Number of Signer _____

Additional Instructions For Health Care Professionals
→ Follow orders listed in A, B and C and honor preferences listed in F until there is an opportunity for a clinician to review as described below.
→ Any change to this form requires the form to be voided and a new form to be signed. To void the form, write VOID in large letters across both sides of the form. *If no new form is completed, no limitations on treatment are documented and full treatment may be provided.*
→ Re-discuss the patient's goals for care and treatment preferences as clinically appropriate to disease progression, at transfer to a new care setting or level of care, or if preferences change. Revise the form when needed to accurately reflect treatment preferences.
→ The patient or health care agent (if the patient lacks capacity), guardian*, or parent/guardian* of a minor can revoke the MOLST form at any time and/or request and receive previously refused medically-indicated treatment. *A guardian can sign only to the extent permitted by MA law. Consult legal counsel with questions about a guardian's authority.*

Approved by DPH   August 10, 2013   MOLST Form Page 2 of 2

QUESTIONS

1. How could this form clarify or confuse a patient's care?
2. Does the MOLST form hold potential to improve care at the end of life, such that states should adopt such forms into hospital regulations or other statutory schemes?

CAPSTONE PROBLEM

Arlene is a 32-year-old nurse who lives in Alabama. She has two children under the age of ten, who have been removed to state care by child protective services. Arlene has one son, John, who is 20 years old and lives at home. John does not work or attend college; he has mild mental retardation that resulted from Arlene's drug abuse when John was in utero. Arlene has said to her friends that she would abort if she became pregnant again, as she has been in and out of rehab and has not been able to beat her addiction to opiates. She specifically told her friends that she "does not want to harm any more babies," and that she does not want any more children. Arlene is not married and has no connections to living family members.

Arlene was in a car accident and suffered severe head trauma, and she was rushed to the regional medical center 75 miles away. There, she was declared to be in persistent vegetative state (PVS). During a period when she was clean of all drugs, she wrote a living will declaring her desire not to be kept alive if she should become terminally ill or otherwise dependent on medical technology such as a ventilator or feeding tube. Although John has not read his mother's living will, he knew his mother would not have wanted to live like "a vegetable," and he requested that life-sustaining treatment be withdrawn because he believed that would be Arlene's desire. Unbeknownst to both John and Arlene, Arlene was six weeks' pregnant at the time of the accident.

Alabama law declares: "The advance directive for health care of a declarant who is known by the attending physician to be pregnant shall have no effect during the course of the declarant's pregnancy." Ala. Code §22-8A-4. Despite John's correct understanding of Arlene's desires, Arlene's living will was deemed ineffective because she was a pregnant woman. As a result, her attending physicians refused to remove the feeding tube keeping Arlene's body alive. When her breathing ceased, the medical team put her on a ventilator and then weaned her off of it again. She also suffered pneumonia and other illnesses typical of a person in PVS, all of which were treated. She remained in this state for 30 more weeks so that the fetus could be brought to term, at which point the feeding tube, ventilator, and other medical interventions ceased. Medicaid paid for the care Arlene received. Her baby was born with low birth weight and developmental delay, and is now in state care because John is not able to raise his brother.

Alabama is one of many states with laws facilitating advance directives that also prohibit the advance directive from applying to a pregnant woman if her wish is to have life support removed. The laws vary, with some states obstructing a living will for every pregnant woman; some barring the living will if a fetus is viable; some requiring continued treatment unless it would not facilitate live birth, would be physically harmful to the woman, or would prolong severe pain; and some imposing a rebuttable presumption that a patient would not want life-sustaining treatment withdrawn were she found to be pregnant. Evaluate and outline the constitutionality of state laws that block implementation of living wills for pregnant women, considering all of the rights discussed in this chapter.

CHAPTER **10**

Health Privacy in the Digital Age

A. INTRODUCTION

Americans enjoy having access to the latest medical technology, and health care providers regularly use data, information, and treatment technologies in all aspects of the curative setting. The federal government has established support for medical technologies through multiple laws; and states regularly rely on medical technology to achieve many tasks, such as enrolling Medicaid-eligible individuals in a timely manner and gathering data to understand health care costs. Medical technology encompasses many forms of both low and high technology, and so it helps to consider what the most prominent forms of medical information technology are at a given moment. That list could include telemedicine; electronic medical records (EMR), electronic health records (EHR), and other health information technology (HIT); health insurance exchanges (discussed in Chapter 3); collection and use of big data; new health tracking tools (such as "wearables"); clinical research trials; and diagnostic and therapeutic technologies, including innovations in medical devices, biologics, cell therapies, and other alterations to the human body or its components.

As we will see, technologies have the ability to increase efficiency and quality of care in medicine by, for example, improving communication among health care providers, or by making a patient's medical history more readily available and searchable. The advantages of medical technologies must be balanced against risks, especially to patient privacy and the security and confidentiality of patient information. As with all forms of technology, both intentional and unintentional breaches of security inevitably occur. For example, in January 2015, Anthem (Blue Cross), the nation's second-largest health insurance company, reported an external cyber-attack affecting 80 million customers.

In medicine, security breaches involve a person's most intimate, private, and potentially perilous information. Data hackers and identity thieves will pay more for medical records than for many other forms of personal information because such records contain data useful not only for individual identity theft but also for defrauding government health care programs. But it does not take a hacker to initiate a security breach or other privacy violation. The following press release shines a light on the ease with which electronic data is stolen.

U.S. Department of Health and Human Services
For Immediate Release: HIPAA Settlement Reinforces Lessons
for Users of Medical Devices (Nov. 25, 2015)

Lahey Hospital and Medical Center (Lahey) has agreed to settle potential violations of the Health Insurance Portability and Accountability Act of 1996 (HIPAA) Privacy and Security Rules with the U.S. Department of Health and Human Services (HHS), Office for Civil Rights (OCR). Lahey will pay $850,000 and will adopt a robust corrective action plan to correct deficiencies in its HIPAA compliance program.

> HIPAA is a major federal statute that protects confidentiality of patient records through the HIPAA Privacy Rule, discussed below.

Lahey is a nonprofit teaching hospital affiliated with Tufts Medical School, providing primary and specialty care in Burlington, Massachusetts. Lahey notified OCR that a laptop was stolen from an unlocked treatment room during the overnight hours on August 11, 2011. The laptop was on a stand that accompanied a portable CT scanner; the laptop operated the scanner and produced images for viewing through Lahey's Radiology Information System and Picture Archiving and Communication System. The laptop hard drive contained the protected health information (PHI) of 599 individuals. Evidence obtained through OCR's subsequent investigation indicated widespread non-compliance with the HIPAA rules, including:

- Failure to conduct a thorough risk analysis of all of its ePHI;
- Failure to physically safeguard a workstation that accessed ePHI;
- Failure to implement and maintain policies and procedures regarding the safeguarding of ePHI maintained on workstations utilized in connection with diagnostic/laboratory equipment;

> ePHI is electronic Protected Health Information, a category within the HIPAA Privacy Rule.

- Lack of a unique user name for identifying and tracking user identity with respect to the workstation at issue in this incident;
- Failure to implement procedures that recorded and examined activity in the workstation at issue in this incident; and
- Impermissible disclosure of 599 individuals' PHI.

"It is essential that covered entities apply appropriate protections to workstations associated with medical devices such as diagnostic or laboratory equipment," said OCR Director Jocelyn Samuels. "Because these workstations often contain ePHI and are highly portable, such ePHI must be considered during an entity's risk analysis, and entities must ensure that necessary safeguards that conform to HIPAA's standards are in place."

In addition to the $850,000 settlement, Lahey must address its history of non-compliance with the HIPAA Rules by providing OCR with a comprehensive, enterprise-wide risk analysis and corresponding risk management plan, as well as reporting certain events and providing evidence of compliance.

The Resolution Agreement and Corrective Action Plan can be found on the OCR website at: http://www.hhs.gov/ocr/privacy/hipaa/enforcement/examples/Lahey .html.

Such errors are common. In 2015, a laptop containing patient information was stolen from a member of UCLA's medical faculty. In 2011, a laptop containing patient medical records, including patients with HIV-positive status, was left on a commuter train in Boston and never recovered. In March of 2016, cyber-attackers hacked into the MedStar hospital chain's technology infrastructure and uploaded a virus that took over the information technology (IT), forcing the hospitals to shut down their EMR and other medical technologies until the virus was resolved. Cyber-attackers also uploaded a virus into the IT of Hollywood Presbyterian Medical Center in early 2016, demanding a ransom and receiving about $17,000 to resolve the invading ransomware.

Adding a layer of difficulty, patients use personal mobile devices to communicate confidential medical information and regularly lose them; and yet mobile health holds promise for those who cannot otherwise easily access the Internet. These incidents are the tip of the iceberg. Not only do health care providers and patients fail to secure the electronic devices that contain sensitive, private, and confidential information, but they also do not realize how far their data travels as it is used to collect insurance payments and for other medical business purposes. And business associates may not know that they are responsible for medical information that must be treated with special care.

In this chapter, we study the legal structure surrounding some common medical information technologies. These technologies trigger federal and state rules that attempt to protect privacy, confidentiality, and security. We study the structure of the statutes and regulations as they apply to health care providers and their business associates. This area of the law still contains room for states to build on the federal scheme, but the rapid growth of health IT is an uneasy fit for traditional, slow moving regulatory and licensure schemes. Yet principles of federalism and the historical rules concerning protecting patients remain common themes.

B. FEDERAL PROTECTIONS FOR PRIVACY, CONFIDENTIALITY, AND SECURITY

Almost everyone who has received medical care is familiar with "HIPAA privacy." Health care providers are required to advise patients of their privacy practices, and patients must acknowledge receipt of those notices. The Health Insurance Portability and Accountability Act of 1996 (HIPAA), however, is an oft-misunderstood statute. The preamble to Public Law 104-191 stated that HIPAA was

> The acronym is "HIPAA" *not* "HIPPA," and "P" does not stand for "privacy."

[a]n Act to amend the Internal Revenue Code of 1986 to improve portability and continuity of health insurance coverage in the group and individual markets, to combat waste, fraud, and abuse in health insurance and health care delivery, to promote the use of medical savings accounts, to improve access to long-term care services and coverage, to simplify the administration of health insurance, and for other purposes.

The major health care access achievement of the law was to facilitate portability of health insurance coverage, meaning a person who had coverage would get credit for that coverage by the next insurer and could not be excluded on the basis of preexisting conditions. (Much of this aspect of the law became obsolete after enactment of the ACA, as discussed in Chapter 3.) In creating portability, Congress also decided to facilitate administrative efficiency through the electronic tools then available.

Subtitle F—Administrative Simplification
Sec. 261. Purpose
It is the purpose of this subtitle to improve the Medicare program under title XVIII of the Social Security Act, the Medicaid program under title XIX of such Act, and the efficiency and effectiveness of the health care system, by encouraging the development of a health information system through the establishment of standards and requirements for the electronic transmission of certain health information.

The Office for Civil Rights of HHS (OCR), which is responsible for HIPAA interpretation, compliance, and enforcement, explains the law this way:

> To improve the efficiency and effectiveness of the health care system, [HIPAA] included Administrative Simplification provisions that required HHS to adopt national standards for electronic health care transactions and code sets, unique health identifiers, and security. At the same time, Congress recognized that advances in electronic technology could erode the privacy of health information. Consequently, Congress incorporated into HIPAA provisions that mandated the adoption of Federal privacy protections for individually identifiable health information.
>
> HHS published a final Privacy Rule in December 2000, which was later modified in August 2002. This Rule set national standards for the protection of individually identifiable health information by three types of covered entities: health plans, health care clearinghouses, and health care providers who conduct the standard health care transactions electronically. Compliance with the Privacy Rule was required as of April 14, 2003 (April 14, 2004, for small health plans).
>
> HHS published a final Security Rule in February 2003. This Rule sets national standards for protecting the confidentiality, integrity, and availability of electronic protected health information. Compliance with the Security Rule was required as of April 20, 2005 (April 20, 2006 for small health plans).

http://www.hhs.gov/ocr.

1. STRUCTURE OF HEALTH PRIVACY AND CONFIDENTIALITY

HIPAA guards the PHI of patients and imposes rules regarding PHI on health care providers, health insurers, and health care clearinghouses, as well as their business associates. The HIPAA privacy regulations are fairly straightforward; for example, they set forth a regulatory standard followed immediately by implementation specifications. Further, the OCR Web site is a good resource. The Privacy Rules are extensive, so we can provide only an introduction to their full scope.

Administrative Data Standards and Related Requirements
45 C.F.R. §160.103. Definitions
Business associate:
    (1) Except as provided in paragraph (4) of this definition, business associate means, with respect to a covered entity, a person who:
        (i) On behalf of such covered entity or of an organized health care arrangement (as defined in this section) in which the covered entity

participates, but other than in the capacity of a member of the workforce of such covered entity or arrangement, creates, receives, maintains, or transmits protected health information for a function or activity regulated by this subchapter, including claims processing or administration, data analysis, processing or administration, utilization review, quality assurance, patient safety activities listed at 42 C.F.R. §3.20, billing, benefit management, practice management, and repricing; or

(ii) Provides, other than in the capacity of a member of the workforce of such covered entity, legal, actuarial, accounting, consulting, data aggregation (as defined in §164.501 of this subchapter), management, administrative, accreditation, or financial services to or for such covered entity, or to or for an organized health care arrangement in which the covered entity participates, where the provision of the service involves the disclosure of protected health information from such covered entity or arrangement, or from another business associate of such covered entity or arrangement, to the person.

(2) A covered entity may be a business associate of another covered entity.

(3) Business associate includes:

(i) A Health Information Organization, E-prescribing Gateway, or other person that provides data transmission services with respect to protected health information to a covered entity and that requires access on a routine basis to such protected health information.

(ii) A person that offers a personal health record to one or more individuals on behalf of a covered entity.

(iii) A subcontractor that creates, receives, maintains, or transmits protected health information on behalf of the business associate.

(4) Business associate does not include:

(i) A health care provider, with respect to disclosures by a covered entity to the health care provider concerning the treatment of the individual.

(ii) A plan sponsor, with respect to disclosures by a group health plan (or by a health insurance issuer or HMO with respect to a group health plan) to the plan sponsor, to the extent that the requirements of §164.504(f) of this subchapter apply and are met.

(iii) A government agency, with respect to determining eligibility for, or enrollment in, a government health plan that provides public benefits and is administered by another government agency, or collecting protected health information for such purposes, to the extent such activities are authorized by law. . . .

Privacy of Individually Identifiable Health Information
45 C.F.R. §164.500. Applicability

(a) Except as otherwise provided herein, the standards, requirements, and implementation specifications of this subpart apply to covered entities with respect to protected health information.

. . . .

(c) Where provided, the standards, requirements, and implementation specifications adopted under this subpart apply to a business associate with respect to the protected health information of a covered entity. . . .

Privacy and confidentiality are supported by the ethical principles of "respect for persons" and "beneficence," which were articulated in the Belmont Report and are key principles for treatment of and research on patients (discussed in Chapter 11).

It may be tempting to skip definitions, but they are the key to understanding regulatory schemes where every subsection contains defined words or phrases. The other important set of HIPAA definitions is found in 45 C.F.R. Part 160.

45 C.F.R. §164.501. Definitions

As used in this subpart, the following terms have the following meanings: . . .

Data aggregation means, with respect to protected health information created or received by a business associate in its capacity as the business associate of a covered entity, the combining of such protected health information by the business associate with the protected health information received by the business associate in its capacity as a business associate of another covered entity, to permit data analyses that relate to the health care operations of the respective covered entities.

Designated record set means:

(1) A group of records maintained by or for a covered entity that is:

(i) The medical records and billing records about individuals maintained by or for a covered health care provider;

(ii) The enrollment, payment, claims adjudication, and case or medical management record systems maintained by or for a health plan; or

(iii) Used, in whole or in part, by or for the covered entity to make decisions about individuals.

(2) For purposes of this paragraph, the term record means any item, collection, or grouping of information that includes protected health information and is maintained, collected, used, or disseminated by or for a covered entity.

. . . .

Health care operations means any of the following activities of the covered entity to the extent that the activities are related to covered functions:

(1) Conducting quality assessment and improvement activities, including outcomes evaluation and development of clinical guidelines, provided that the obtaining of generalizable knowledge is not the primary purpose of any studies resulting from such activities; patient safety activities (as defined in 42 CFR 3.20); population-based activities relating to improving health or reducing health care costs, protocol development, case management and care coordination, contacting of health care providers and patients with information about treatment alternatives; and related functions that do not include treatment;

(2) Reviewing the competence or qualifications of health care professionals, evaluating practitioner and provider performance, health plan performance, conducting training programs in which students, trainees, or practitioners in areas of health care learn under supervision to practice or improve their skills as health care providers, training of non-health care professionals, accreditation, certification, licensing, or credentialing activities;

(3) Except as prohibited under §164.502(a)(5)(i), underwriting, enrollment, premium rating, and other activities related to the creation, renewal, or replacement of a contract of health insurance or health benefits . . . ;

(4) Conducting or arranging for medical review, legal services, and auditing functions, including fraud and abuse detection and compliance programs;

(5) Business planning and development, such as conducting cost-management and planning-related analyses related to managing and operating the entity, including formulary development and administration, development or improvement of methods of payment or coverage policies; and

(6) Business management and general administrative activities of the entity, including, but not limited to:

(i) Management activities relating to implementation of and compliance with the requirements of this subchapter;

(ii) Customer service, including the provision of data analyses for policy holders, plan sponsors, or other customers, provided that protected health information is not disclosed to such policy holder, plan sponsor, or customer;

(iii) Resolution of internal grievances;

(iv) The sale, transfer, merger, or consolidation of all or part of the covered entity with another covered entity, or an entity that following such activity will become a covered entity and due diligence related to such activity; and

(v) Consistent with the applicable requirements of §164.514, creating de-identified health information or a limited data set, and fundraising for the benefit of the covered entity.

. . . .

Research means a systematic investigation, including research development, testing, and evaluation, designed to develop or contribute to generalizable knowledge.

> This definition of research is consistent with the Common Rule, which regulates how individuals involved in biomedical research are treated, as discussed in Chapter 11.

Treatment means the provision, coordination, or management of health care and related services by one or more health care providers, including the coordination or management of health care by a health care provider with a third party; consultation between health care providers relating to a patient; or the referral of a patient for health care from one health care provider to another.

45 C.F.R. §164.502. Uses and disclosures of protected health information: General rules

(a) Standard. A covered entity or business associate may not use or disclose protected health information, except as permitted or required by this subpart or by subpart C of part 160 of this subchapter.

(1) Covered entities: Permitted uses and disclosures. A covered entity is permitted to use or disclose protected health information as follows:

(i) To the individual;

(ii) For treatment, payment, or health care operations, as permitted by and in compliance with §164.506;

(iii) Incident to a use or disclosure . . . ;

(iv) Except for uses and disclosures prohibited under §164.502(a)(5)(i), pursuant to and in compliance with a valid authorization under §164.508;

(v) Pursuant to an agreement under, or as otherwise permitted by, §164.510; . . . . . .

(2) Covered entities: Required disclosures. A covered entity is required to disclose protected health information:

(i) To an individual, when requested under, and required by §164.524 or §164.528; and

(ii) When required by the Secretary . . . to investigate or determine the covered entity's compliance with this subchapter.

(3) Business associates: Permitted uses and disclosures. A business associate may use or disclose protected health information only as permitted or required by its business associate contract or other arrangement pursuant to §164.504(e) or as required by law. The business associate may not use or disclose protected health information in a manner that would violate the requirements of this subpart, if done by the covered entity. . . .

The Genetic Information Nondiscrimination Act (GINA) added specific protections for genetic information to the HIPAA privacy scheme.

(4) Business associates: Required uses and disclosures. A business associate is required to disclose protected health information:

(i) When required by the Secretary . . . to investigate or determine the business associate's compliance with this subchapter.

(ii) To the covered entity, individual, or individual's designee, as necessary to satisfy a covered entity's obligations. . . .

(5) Prohibited uses and disclosures.

(i) Use and disclosure of genetic information for underwriting purposes: Notwithstanding any other provision of this subpart, a health plan, excluding an issuer of a long-term care policy falling within paragraph (1)(viii) of the definition of health plan, shall not use or disclose protected health information that is genetic information for underwriting purposes. . . .

(ii) Sale of protected health information:

(A) Except pursuant to and in compliance with §164.508(a)(4), a covered entity or business associate may not sell protected health information. . . .

Adults up to age 26 can be covered on their parents' health plans under the ACA, which led to an uptick in adult patients' confidential medical information being revealed to family members through Explanation of Benefits forms, in which insurers describe which items or services are covered. HIPAA's "minimum necessary" standard does not apply to "uses and disclosures made to the individual," which the insurer (a covered entity) could reasonably assume to be the policyholder. Five states now have laws permitting insurers to send the EOB to the patient rather than the policyholder. Such laws also protect those in sensitive family situations, such as domestic violence or divorce.

(b) Standard: Minimum necessary—

(1) Minimum necessary applies. When using or disclosing protected health information or when requesting protected health information from another covered entity or business associate, a covered entity or business associate must make reasonable efforts to limit protected health information to the minimum necessary to accomplish the intended purpose of the use, disclosure, or request.

(2) Minimum necessary does not apply. This requirement does not apply to:

(i) Disclosures to or requests by a health care provider for treatment;

(ii) Uses or disclosures made to the individual . . . ;

(iii) Uses or disclosures made pursuant to an authorization under §164.508;

(iv) Disclosures made to the Secretary in accordance with subpart C of part 160 of this subchapter;

(v) Uses or disclosures that are required by law . . . ; and

(vi) Uses or disclosures that are required for compliance with applicable requirements of this subchapter.

. . . .

(d) Standard: Uses and disclosures of de-identified protected health information—

(1) Uses and disclosures to create de-identified information. A covered entity may use protected health information to create information that is not individually identifiable health information or disclose protected health information only to a business associate for such purpose, whether or not the de-identified information is to be used by the covered entity.

(2) Uses and disclosures of de-identified information. Health information that meets the standard and implementation specifications for de-identification under §164.514(a) and (b) is considered not to be individually identifiable health information, i.e., de-identified. . . .

(e)(1) Standard: Disclosures to business associates.

(i) A covered entity may disclose protected health information to a business associate and may allow a business associate to create, receive, maintain, or transmit protected health information on its behalf, if the covered entity obtains satisfactory assurance that the business associate will appropriately safeguard the information. A covered entity is not required to obtain such satisfactory assurances from a business associate that is a subcontractor.

(ii) A business associate may disclose protected health information to a business associate that is a subcontractor and may allow the subcontractor to create, receive, maintain, or transmit protected health information on its behalf, if the business associate obtains satisfactory assurances, in accordance with §164.504(e)(1)(i), that the subcontractor will appropriately safeguard the information.

(2) Implementation specification: Documentation. The satisfactory assurances required by paragraph (e)(1) of this section must be documented through a written contract or other written agreement. . . .

> "Individually identifiable health information" is defined in 45 C.F.R. §160.103 as "information that is a subset of health information, including demographic information collected from an individual, and: (1) Is created or received by a health care provider, health plan, employer, or health care clearinghouse; and (2) Relates to the past, present, or future physical or mental health or condition of an individual; the provision of health care to an individual; or the past, present, or future payment for the provision of health care to an individual; and (i) That identifies the individual; or (ii) With respect to which there is a reasonable basis to believe the information can be used to identify the individual."

(f) Standard: Deceased individuals. A covered entity must comply with the requirements of this subpart with respect to the protected health information of a deceased individual for a period of 50 years following the death of the individual.

(g)(1) Standard: Personal representatives. As specified in this paragraph, a covered entity must, except as provided in paragraphs (g)(3) and (g)(5) of this section, treat a personal representative as the individual for purposes of this subchapter. . . .

Once HIPAA regulations describe PHI and what can be done with it, health care providers still need to know whether and how they can share patients' information with people or organizations that perform health care and health care–related services, such as billing companies. This is where the business associate rules fit.

45 C.F.R. §164.504. Uses and disclosures: Organizational requirements

. . .

(e)(1) Standard: Business associate contracts.

(i) The contract or other arrangement required by §164.502(e)(2) must meet the requirements of paragraph (e)(2), (e)(3), or (e)(5) of this section, as applicable.

(ii) A covered entity is not in compliance with the standards in §164.502(e) and this paragraph, if the covered entity knew of a pattern of activity or practice of the business associate that constituted a material breach or violation of the business associate's obligation under the contract or other arrangement, unless the covered entity took reasonable steps to cure the breach or end the violation, as applicable, and, if such steps were unsuccessful, terminated the contract or arrangement, if feasible. . . .

(2) Implementation specifications: Business associate contracts. A contract between the covered entity and a business associate must:

> The subcontractor rule often takes business associates by surprise and can cause compliance problems for them.

(i) Establish the permitted and required uses and disclosures of protected health information by the business associate. The contract may not authorize the business associate to use or further disclose the information in a manner that would violate the requirements of this subpart, if done by the covered entity, except that:

(A) The contract may permit the business associate to use and disclose protected health information for the proper management and administration of the business associate . . . ; and

(B) The contract may permit the business associate to provide data aggregation services relating to the health care operations of the covered entity.

(ii) Provide that the business associate will:

(A) Not use or further disclose the information other than as permitted or required by the contract or as required by law;

(B) Use appropriate safeguards and comply, where applicable, with subpart C of this part with respect to electronic protected health information, to prevent use or disclosure of the information other than as provided for by its contract;

(C) Report to the covered entity any use or disclosure of the information not provided for by its contract of which it becomes aware, including breaches of unsecured protected health information as required by §164.410;

(D) In accordance with §164.502(e)(1)(ii), ensure that any subcontractors that create, receive, maintain, or transmit protected health information on behalf of the business associate agree to the same restrictions and conditions that apply to the business associate with respect to such information;

(E) Make available protected health information in accordance with §164.524;

(F) Make available protected health information for amendment and incorporate any amendments to protected health information in accordance with §164.526;

(G) Make available the information required to provide an accounting of disclosures in accordance with §164.528;

(H) To the extent the business associate is to carry out a covered entity's obligation under this subpart, comply with the requirements of this subpart that apply to the covered entity in the performance of such obligation.

(I) Make its internal practices, books, and records relating to the use and disclosure of protected health information received from, or created or received by the business associate on behalf of, the covered entity available to the Secretary for purposes of determining the covered entity's compliance with this subpart; and

(J) At termination of the contract, if feasible, return or destroy all protected health information received from, or created or received by the business associate on behalf of, the covered entity. . . .

(iii) Authorize termination of the contract by the covered entity, if the covered entity determines that the business associate has violated a material term of the contract. . . .

. . . .

(g) Standard: Requirements for a covered entity with multiple covered functions.

(1) A covered entity that performs multiple covered functions that would make the entity any combination of a health plan, a covered health care provider, and a health care clearinghouse, must comply with the standards, requirements, and implementation specifications of this subpart, as applicable to the health plan, health care provider, or health care clearinghouse covered functions performed. . . .

45 C.F.R. §164.506. Uses and disclosures to carry out treatment, payment, or health care operations

(a) Standard: Permitted uses and disclosures. . . . [A] covered entity may use or disclose protected health information for treatment, payment, or health care operations as set forth in paragraph (c) of this section, provided that such use or disclosure is consistent with other applicable requirements of this subpart.

(b) Standard: Consent for uses and disclosures permitted.

(1) A covered entity may obtain consent of the individual to use or disclose protected health information to carry out treatment, payment, or health care operations.

(2) Consent, under paragraph (b) of this section, shall not be effective to permit a use or disclosure of protected health information when an authorization, under §164.508, is required or when another condition must be met for such use or disclosure to be permissible under this subpart.

(c) Implementation specifications: Treatment, payment, or health care operations.

(1) A covered entity may use or disclose protected health information for its own treatment, payment, or health care operations.

(2) A covered entity may disclose protected health information for treatment activities of a health care provider.

(3) A covered entity may disclose protected health information to another covered entity or a health care provider for the payment activities of the entity that receives the information.

(4) A covered entity may disclose protected health information to another covered entity for health care operations activities of the entity that receives the information, if each entity either has or had a relationship with the individual who is the subject of the protected health information being requested, the protected health information pertains to such relationship, and the disclosure is:

(i) For a purpose listed in paragraph (1) or (2) of the definition of health care operations; or

(ii) For the purpose of health care fraud and abuse detection or compliance. . . .

45 C.F.R. §164.508. Uses and disclosures for which an authorization is required

(a) Standard: Authorizations for uses and disclosures —

(1) Authorization required: General rule. Except as otherwise permitted or required by this subchapter, a covered entity may not use or disclose protected health information without an authorization that is valid under this section. When a covered entity obtains or receives a valid authorization for its use or disclosure of protected health information, such use or disclosure must be consistent with such authorization.

(2) Authorization required: Psychotherapy notes. . . .

(3) Authorization required: Marketing. . . .

(4) Authorization required: Sale of protected health information. . . .

(c) Implementation specifications: Core elements and requirements —

(1) Core elements. A valid authorization under this section must contain at least the following elements:

(i) A description of the information to be used or disclosed that identifies the information in a specific and meaningful fashion.

(ii) The name or other specific identification of the person(s), or class of persons, authorized to make the requested use or disclosure.

(iii) The name or other specific identification of the person(s), or class of persons, to whom the covered entity may make the requested use or disclosure.

(iv) A description of each purpose of the requested use or disclosure. The statement "at the request of the individual" is a sufficient description of the purpose when an individual initiates the authorization and does not, or elects not to, provide a statement of the purpose.

(v) An expiration date or an expiration event that relates to the individual or the purpose of the use or disclosure. The statement "end of the research study," "none," or similar language is sufficient if the authorization is for a use or disclosure of protected health information for research, including for the creation and maintenance of a research database or research repository.

(vi) Signature of the individual and date. If the authorization is signed by a personal representative of the individual, a description of such representative's authority to act for the individual must also be provided.

(2) Required statements. In addition to the core elements, the authorization must contain statements adequate to place the individual on notice of all of the following:

(i) The individual's right to revoke the authorization in writing, and either:

(A) The exceptions to the right to revoke and a description of how the individual may revoke the authorization; or

(B) To the extent that the information in paragraph (c)(2)(i)(A) of this section is included in the notice required by §164.520, a reference to the covered entity's notice.

(ii) The ability or inability to condition treatment, payment, enrollment or eligibility for benefits on the authorization, by stating either:

(A) The covered entity may not condition treatment, payment, enrollment or eligibility for benefits on whether the individual signs the authorization when the prohibition on conditioning of authorizations in paragraph (b)(4) of this section applies; or

(B) The consequences to the individual of a refusal to sign the authorization when, in accordance with paragraph (b)(4) of this section, the covered entity can condition treatment, enrollment in the health plan, or eligibility for benefits on failure to obtain such authorization.

(iii) The potential for information disclosed pursuant to the authorization to be subject to redisclosure by the recipient and no longer be protected by this subpart.

(3) Plain language requirement. The authorization must be written in plain language.

(4) Copy to the individual. If a covered entity seeks an authorization from an individual for a use or disclosure of protected health information, the covered entity must provide the individual with a copy of the signed authorization. . . .

QUESTIONS

1. Given how specific and clear these regulations appear to be, does it surprise you to learn that year after year, the number one issue OCR investigates in HIPAA breaches is "impermissible uses and disclosures"?
2. If a health care provider needs to use PHI, is patient consent required? Under what circumstances, if any?
3. What is the difference between "consent" and "authorization" under the Privacy Rule?
4. Why do certain uses of PHI require specific patient authorization?

Many found HIPAA to be a weak privacy rule until it was amended by section 105 of Title I of the Genetic Information Nondiscrimination Act of 2008 (GINA), Pub. L. No. 110-233, which strengthened protection for genetic information, as well as the Health Information Technology for Economic and Clinical Health (HITECH) Act (enacted as part of the American Recovery and Reinvestment Act of 2009, Pub. L. No. 111-5), which strengthened privacy, security, and breach notification rules under HIPAA, among other provisions to protect health information. For example, the HITECH Act increased enforcement capability, deputizing state attorneys general to pursue privacy actions, as explained by OCR:

> The HITECH Act . . . gave State Attorneys General the authority to bring civil actions on behalf of state residents for violations of the HIPAA Privacy and Security Rules. The HITECH Act permits State Attorneys General to obtain damages on behalf of state residents or to enjoin further violations of the HIPAA Privacy and Security Rules.

This expansion of privacy enforcement authority has made HIPAA compliance and enforcement more prevalent and important to all health care providers. The HITECH Act also established the Office of the National Coordinator for Health Information Technology (ONC), which extends HHs's authority to establish programs to improve health care quality, safety, and efficiency through the promotion of health IT. In other words, ONC oversees the implementation of EHR adoption, which increases the need for HIPAA privacy and security standards.

ONC's Web site provides this brief description of the "meaningful use" rules, which have encouraged use of EHR:

> The Medicare and Medicaid EHR Incentive Programs provide financial incentives for the "meaningful use" of certified EHR technology. To receive an EHR incentive payment, providers have to show that they are "meaningfully using" their certified EHR technology by meeting certain measurement thresholds that range from recording patient information as structured data to exchanging summary care records. CMS has established these thresholds for eligible professionals, eligible hospitals, and critical access hospitals.

When the meaningful use rule was implemented in 2011, physicians could receive incentive payments up to $44,000, and hospitals could receive millions of dollars over the initial four-year phase-in period.

> The Medicare and Medicaid EHR Incentive Programs include three stages with increasing requirements for participation. All providers begin participating by meeting the Stage 1 requirements for a 90-day period in their first year of meaningful use and a full year in their second year of meaningful use. After meeting the Stage 1 requirements, providers will then have to meet Stage 2 requirements for two full years. CMS has recently published a proposed rule for Stage 3 of meaningful use which focuses on the advanced use of EHR technology to promote health information exchange and improved outcomes for patients.

> Eligible professionals participate in the program on the calendar years, while eligible hospitals and CAHs [(critical access hospitals)] participate according to the Federal fiscal year. The Stage 3 proposed rule proposes to change the EHR reporting period so that all providers would report under a full calendar year timeline.

The meaningful use regulations are quite technical and extensive, and anyone representing health care providers that have yet to move to EHR should understand them. The regulations can be found at the ONC and the CMS Web sites. As this book went to press, the ONC suggested that major revisions were likely for meaningful use incentives and rules, and on January 11, 2016, CMS Acting Administrator Andy Slavitt stated, "The meaningful use program as it has existed will now be effectively over and replaced with something better." Stay tuned.

It should be clear by now that HIPAA does not begin to cover all medical privacy or confidentiality possibilities or protect all health information. Thus, the HITECH Act also authorized the Federal Trade Commission (FTC) to regulate personal health records (PHR). Web-based health care–related businesses often collect PHR, but these companies are not health care entities, so they are not subject to HIPAA. Pursuant to the HITECH Act, the FTC protects consumers from misuse of PHR by such companies. The FTC imposes reporting and breach notification rules much like the HIPAA notification rules, discussed below (16 C.F.R. Part 318). Even so, Web-based information often is not secure or private, as evidenced by a 2016 class action lawsuit filed against a variety of medical Web sites such as cancer.org that shared private patient data with Facebook for marketing purposes. Smith v. Facebook, No. 5:16-cv-01282 (N.D. Cal., filed March 15, 2016), 2016 WL 1042966.

PROBLEM

Your client is a regional hospital that wants to solidify relationships with referring physicians by offering a regional EHR. One outcome of this financial support will be improved coordination of care. Can the hospital offer this financial support? (As you answer the question, also consider fraud and abuse rules discussed in Chapter 6.)

2. COMPLIANCE AND ENFORCEMENT

OCR has become more aggressive in enforcing HIPAA privacy, security, and enforcement, encouraged by the modifications in the HITECH Act and GINA. Although OCR once emphasized voluntary compliance, it now subjects noncompliant health care providers to civil fines and pursues other remedial measures such as referrals to the Department of Justice (DOJ) when criminal activity is suspected. This chart, from the OCR Web site, shows how the agencies work together.

HIPAA Privacy & Security Rule Complaint Process

The following is notice of a settlement with an academic medical center pursuant to such an investigation:

Press Release: $750,000 HIPAA Settlement Underscores the Need for Organization-Wide Risk Analysis (Dec. 14, 2015)

The University of Washington Medicine (UWM) has agreed to settle charges that it potentially violated the Health Insurance Portability and Accountability Act of 1996 (HIPAA) Security Rule by failing to implement policies and procedures to prevent, detect, contain, and correct security violations. UWM is an affiliated covered entity, which includes designated health care components and other entities under the control of the University of Washington, including University of Washington Medical Center, the primary teaching hospital of the University of Washington School of Medicine. Affiliated covered entities must have in place appropriate policies and processes to assure HIPAA compliance with respect to each of the entities that are part of the affiliated group. The settlement includes a monetary payment of $750,000, a corrective action plan, and annual reports on the organization's compliance efforts.

The U.S. Department of Health and Human Services Office for Civil Rights (OCR) initiated its investigation of the UWM following receipt of a breach report on November 27, 2013, which indicated that the electronic protected health information (e-PHI) of approximately 90,000 individuals was accessed after an employee downloaded an email attachment that contained malicious malware. The malware compromised the organization's IT system, affecting the data of two different groups of patients: 1) approximately 76,000 patients involving a combination of patient names, medical record numbers, dates of service, and/or charges or bill balances; and 2) approximately 15,000 patients involving names, medical record numbers, other demographics such as address and phone number, dates of birth, charges or bill balances, social security numbers, insurance identification or Medicare numbers.

OCR's investigation indicated UWM's security policies required its affiliated entities to have up-to-date, documented system-level risk assessments and to implement safeguards in compliance with the Security Rule. However, UWM did not ensure that all of its affiliated entities were properly conducting risk assessments and appropriately responding to the potential risks and vulnerabilities in their respective environments.

"All too often we see covered entities with a limited risk analysis that focuses on a specific system such as the electronic medical record or that fails to provide appropriate oversight and accountability for all parts of the enterprise," said OCR Director Jocelyn Samuels. "An effective risk analysis is one that is comprehensive in scope and is conducted across the organization to sufficiently address the risks and vulnerabilities to patient data."

The Resolution Agreement and Corrective Action Plan can be found on the OCR website at: http://www.hhs.gov/ocr/privacy/hipaa/enforcement/examples/uwm/index.html. . . .

The aforementioned security policies are based on the HIPAA Security Rule, which requires that notifications be transmitted to every person affected by a security breach.

45 C.F.R. §164.306. Security standards: General rules

(a) General requirements. Covered entities and business associates must do the following:

(1) Ensure the confidentiality, integrity, and availability of all electronic protected health information the covered entity or business associate creates, receives, maintains, or transmits.

(2) Protect against any reasonably anticipated threats or hazards to the security or integrity of such information.

(3) Protect against any reasonably anticipated uses or disclosures of such information that are not permitted or required under subpart E of this part.

(4) Ensure compliance with this subpart by its workforce.

(b) Flexibility of approach.

(1) Covered entities and business associates may use any security measures that allow the covered entity or business associate to reasonably and appropriately implement the standards and implementation specifications as specified in this subpart.

(2) In deciding which security measures to use, a covered entity or business associate must take into account the following factors:

(i) The size, complexity, and capabilities of the covered entity or business associate.

(ii) The covered entity's or the business associate's technical infrastructure, hardware, and software security capabilities.

(iii) The costs of security measures.

(iv) The probability and criticality of potential risks to electronic protected health information. . . .

45 C.F.R. §164.308. Administrative safeguards

(a) A covered entity or business associate must, in accordance with §164.306:

(1)(i) Standard: Security management process. Implement policies and procedures to prevent, detect, contain, and correct security violations.

(ii) Implementation specifications:

(A) Risk analysis (Required). Conduct an accurate and thorough assessment of the potential risks and vulnerabilities to the confidentiality, integrity, and availability of electronic protected health information held by the covered entity or business associate.

(B) Risk management (Required). Implement security measures sufficient to reduce risks and vulnerabilities to a reasonable and appropriate level to comply with §164.306(a).

(C) Sanction policy (Required). Apply appropriate sanctions against workforce members who fail to comply with the security policies and procedures of the covered entity or business associate.

(D) Information system activity review (Required). Implement procedures to regularly review records of information system activity, such as audit logs, access reports, and security incident tracking reports.

(2) Standard: Assigned security responsibility. Identify the security official who is responsible for the development and implementation of the

policies and procedures required by this subpart for the covered entity or business associate.

(3)(i) Standard: Workforce security. Implement policies and procedures to ensure that all members of its workforce have appropriate access to electronic protected health information, as provided under paragraph (a)(4) of this section, and to prevent those workforce members who do not have access under paragraph (a)(4) of this section from obtaining access to electronic protected health information.

. . . .

(5)(i) Standard: Security awareness and training. Implement a security awareness and training program for all members of its workforce (including management). . . .

(6)(i) Standard: Security incident procedures. Implement policies and procedures to address security incidents. . . .

(7)(i) Standard: Contingency plan. Establish (and implement as needed) policies and procedures for responding to an emergency or other occurrence (for example, fire, vandalism, system failure, and natural disaster) that damages systems that contain electronic protected health information. . . .

(8) Standard: Evaluation. Perform a periodic technical and nontechnical evaluation, based initially upon the standards implemented under this rule and, subsequently, in response to environmental or operational changes affecting the security of electronic protected health information, that establishes the extent to which a covered entity's or business associate's security policies and procedures meet the requirements of this subpart.

(b)

(1) Business associate contracts and other arrangements. A covered entity may permit a business associate to create, receive, maintain, or transmit electronic protected health information on the covered entity's behalf only if the covered entity obtains satisfactory assurances, in accordance with §164.314(a), that the business associate will appropriately safeguard the information. A covered entity is not required to obtain such satisfactory assurances from a business associate that is a subcontractor.

45 C.F.R. §164.310. Physical safeguards

A covered entity or business associate must, in accordance with §164.306:

(a)(1) Standard: Facility access controls. Implement policies and procedures to limit physical access to its electronic information systems and the facility or facilities in which they are housed, while ensuring that properly authorized access is allowed. . . .

Many doctors' offices and hospitals now use rolling carts for laptops so that they can be moved between examining rooms. Is the cart an adequate "physical safeguard"?

(b) Standard: Workstation use. Implement policies and procedures that specify the proper functions to be performed, the manner in which those functions are to be performed, and the physical attributes of the surroundings of a specific workstation or class of workstation that can access electronic protected health information.

(c) Standard: Workstation security. Implement physical safeguards for all workstations that access electronic protected health information, to restrict access to authorized users.

(d)

(1) Standard: Device and media controls. Implement policies and procedures that govern the receipt and removal of hardware and electronic media that contain electronic protected health information into and out of a facility, and the movement of these items within the facility. . . .

45 C.F.R. §164.404. Notification to individuals.

(a) Standard

(1) General rule. A covered entity shall, following the discovery of a breach of unsecured protected health information, notify each individual whose unsecured protected health information has been, or is reasonably believed by the covered entity to have been, accessed, acquired, used, or disclosed as a result of such breach.

(2) Breaches treated as discovered. For purposes of paragraph (a)(1) of this section, §§164.406(a), and 164.408(a), a breach shall be treated as discovered by a covered entity as of the first day on which such breach is known to the covered entity, or, by exercising reasonable diligence would have been known to the covered entity. A covered entity shall be deemed to have knowledge of a breach if such breach is known, or by exercising reasonable diligence would have been known, to any person, other than the person committing the breach, who is a workforce member or agent of the covered entity (determined in accordance with the federal common law of agency).

(b) Implementation specification: Timeliness of notification. Except as provided in §164.412, a covered entity shall provide the notification required by paragraph (a) of this section without unreasonable delay and in no case later than 60 calendar days after discovery of a breach.

(c) Implementation specifications: Content of notification

(1) Elements. The notification required by paragraph (a) of this section shall include, to the extent possible:

(A) A brief description of what happened, including the date of the breach and the date of the discovery of the breach, if known;

(B) A description of the types of unsecured protected health information that were involved in the breach (such as whether full name, social security number, date of birth, home address, account number, diagnosis, disability code, or other types of information were involved);

(C) Any steps individuals should take to protect themselves from potential harm resulting from the breach;

(D) A brief description of what the covered entity involved is doing to investigate the breach, to mitigate harm to individuals, and to protect against any further breaches; and

(E) Contact procedures for individuals to ask questions or learn additional information, which shall include a toll-free telephone number, an e-mail address, Web site, or postal address.

(2) Plain language requirement. The notification required by paragraph (a) of this section shall be written in plain language.

(d) Implementation specifications: Methods of individual notification. The notification required by paragraph (a) of this section shall be provided in the following form:

(1) Written notice.

(i) Written notification by first-class mail to the individual at the last known address of the individual or, if the individual agrees to electronic notice and such agreement has not been withdrawn, by electronic mail. The notification may be provided in one or more mailings as information is available.

. . . .

(3) Additional notice in urgent situations. In any case deemed by the covered entity to require urgency because of possible imminent misuse of unsecured protected health information, the covered entity may provide information to individuals by telephone or other means, as appropriate, in addition to notice provided under paragraph (d)(1) of this section.

45 C.F.R. §164.406. Notification to the media

(a) Standard. For a breach of unsecured protected health information involving more than 500 residents of a State or jurisdiction, a covered entity shall, following the discovery of the breach as provided in §164.404(a)(2), notify prominent media outlets serving the State or jurisdiction. . . .

What is the purpose of notifying the patients and media?

45 C.F.R. §164.408. Notification to the Secretary

(a) Standard. A covered entity shall, following the discovery of a breach of unsecured protected health information as provided in §164.404(a)(2), notify the Secretary.

(b) Implementation specifications: Breaches involving 500 or more individuals. For breaches of unsecured protected health information involving 500 or more individuals, a covered entity shall, except as provided in §164.412, provide the notification required by paragraph (a) of this section contemporaneously with the notice required by §164.404(a) and in the manner specified on the HHS Web site.

(c) Implementation specifications: Breaches involving less than 500 individuals. For breaches of unsecured protected health information involving less than 500 individuals, a covered entity shall maintain a log or other documentation of such breaches and, not later than 60 days after the end of each calendar year, provide the notification required by paragraph (a) of this section for breaches discovered during the preceding calendar year, in the manner specified on the HHS web site.

45 C.F.R. §164.410. Notification by a business associate.

(a) Standard

(1) General rule. A business associate shall, following the discovery of a breach of unsecured protected health information, notify the covered entity of such breach. . . .

QUESTIONS

1. What steps must a covered entity take to notify individuals of a breach of their medical information?
2. When must HHS be notified?
3. When must the media be involved?

The requirement to notify affected individuals of security breaches has been a step up in HIPAA privacy and security enforcement. The notification must occur quickly, directly, and sometimes through mass means of notification. The following is an example of a cyber-attack notification letter sent by an employer affected by the Anthem security breach, mentioned above.

2/5/15 (9:45 A.M.)
Information on Anthem Security Breach

As you may have heard early this morning, our primary health insurance carrier, Anthem, has been the victim of a cyber-security attack. It is unclear at this point whether your data and those of other employees and retirees was compromised by this attack. However, Anthem officials have indicated they have moved quickly to determine the cause of breach and what steps must be taken to protect customers and mitigate any negative impact.

We expect to be briefed by Anthem officials later this morning. In the meantime, Anthem officials have created this website — http://www.anthemfacts.com/ — that contains basic information about what has happened as well as questions and answers.

We are committed to taking all necessary steps to protect your information and we will be back to you as soon as possible when we know more information. Thank you for your patience. We will provide more information as soon as possible.

2/5/15 (4:05 P.M.)
Update on Anthem Cyber-security Attack

This morning, we wrote to you about the notification we received today regarding a cyber-security attack on Anthem. . . . Our commitment to you is to follow up as quickly as possible and as often as necessary with the most up-to-date information. We are vigilantly monitoring this important situation.

Since we first learned of this issue early this morning, we have had several conversations with Anthem officials, including the company's president. They have pledged to keep us informed as they discover more information about what happened, what impacts there may be on customers, and how they will move forward to mitigate any negative impacts.

Moreover, an internal . . . team — comprised of senior officials within Human Resources, Risk Management, Finance and Administration . . . — has met and continued to communicate to ensure that we are providing the most timely information possible, as well as resources. . . .

Here is what we know at this hour:

- Anthem's investigation to date shows that no credit card or confidential health information was accessed.
- Anthem has advised us there is no indication at this time that any of our employees' personal information has been misused.
- All impacted Anthem members will be enrolled in identity repair services. In addition, impacted members will be provided information on how to enroll in free credit monitoring. Anthem will provide that information in a letter sent directly to affected employees in the next two weeks.

- For employees who want to initiate a fraud alert with credit monitoring services in the interim, we suggest using limited-time free services available to anyone who suspects their personal information has been breached. The following companies can provide the service: Equifax; Transunion; or Experian. NOTE: Please be aware that charges may apply beyond the offered free 90-day period. Do not sign up for more than the free period allowed.
- Employees who already have credit monitoring will be covered during the interim period under their current service.
- Once Anthem determined it was the victim of a sophisticated cyber attack, it immediately notified the FBI; began a forensic IT investigation to determine the extent of the breach; and worked to eliminate any further vulnerability and continues to secure all of its data.
- The information accessed includes member names, member health ID numbers/Social Security numbers, dates of birth, addresses, telephone numbers, email addresses and employment information, including income data. Social Security numbers were included in only a subset of the universe of consumers that were impacted.
  - Anthem is still working to determine which members' Social Security numbers were accessed.

The data breach did not include health or credit information about the plan participants, but rather personal identifying and demographic information, which the hackers could use to commit tax and other consumer fraud.

We are continuing to work closely with Anthem to better understand the cyber attack and the impact on our employees. Anthem has created a website — www.anthemfacts.com, and a hotline for its members to call for more information. You can also find more information including frequently asked questions (FAQs) on the HR website.

We will continue to keep you updated on Anthem's ongoing investigation.

2/12/2015 (3:31)

Identity/Credit Protection Offered by Anthem After Cyber Attack

Last week, we made you aware Anthem was the target of a very sophisticated external, cyber attack. Since that time, Anthem has been assisting in the FBI investigation; analyzing the data to understand the impact to members; and securing a best-in-class vendor to provide identity protection services to members as quickly as possible.

Anthem is providing a credit monitoring service for impacted current and former Anthem members. Members can visit AnthemFacts.com to learn how to contact the credit monitoring service. If impacted, members may enroll in two years of free credit monitoring and identity theft repair services, provided by Anthem's vendor — a leading and trusted identity protection provider. Members can access these services starting Friday, Feb. 13, prior to receiving a mailed notification from Anthem, which will be sent in the coming weeks.

The free identity protection services provided by Anthem include two years of:

- Identity Repair Assistance: Should a member experience fraud, an investigator will do the work to recover financial losses, restore the member's credit, and ensure the member's identity is returned to its proper condition. This assistance will cover any fraud that has occurred since the incident first began.

- Credit Monitoring: At no cost, members may also enroll in additional protections, including credit monitoring. Credit monitoring alerts consumers when banks and creditors use their identity to open new credit accounts.
- Child Identity Protection: Child-specific identity protection services will also be offered to any members with children insured through their Anthem plan.
- Identity Theft Insurance: For individuals who enroll, the company has arranged for $1,000,000 in identity theft insurance, where allowed by law.
- Identity theft monitoring/fraud detection: For members who enroll, data such as credit card numbers, social security numbers and emails will be scanned against aggregated data sources maintained by top security researchers that contain stolen and compromised individual data, in order to look for any indication that the members' data have been compromised.
- Phone Alerts: Individuals who register for this service and provide their contact information will receive an alert when there is a notification from a credit bureau, or when it appears from identity theft monitoring activities that the individual's identity may be compromised.

We will continue to monitor the situation and communicate to you any changes as we are made aware of them by Anthem.

QUESTIONS

1. What is the practical impact of a notification of cyber-attack on medical information?
2. Why are frequent updates required?
3. What business implications exist for the entity subject to such an attack and forced to publicly admit it?

Despite the risk of cyber-attacks, as we saw above, the HITECH Act and other laws have pushed health care providers to adopt EHR sooner rather than later.

Mobile health applications regularly collect and share or sell personal health information without seeking consent, according to a study published in JAMA in 2016. "mHealth" is a new front in privacy regulation, demonstrated by the following invitation from HHS:

OCR Invites Developers to Ask Questions About HIPAA Privacy and Security

OCR has launched a new platform [http://HIPAAQsportal.hhs.gov] for mobile health developers and others interested in the intersection of health information technology and HIPAA privacy protection. We are experiencing an explosion of technology using data about the health of individuals in innovative ways to improve health outcomes. Building privacy and security protections into technology products enhances their value by providing some assurance to users that the information is safe and secure and will be used and disclosed only as approved or expected. Such protections are sometimes required by federal and state laws, including the HIPAA Privacy, Security and Breach Notification Rules. Yet many mHealth developers are not familiar with the HIPAA Rules and how the rules would apply to their products.

Anyone may browse the site, which is on the Ideascale cloud-based idea management platform. Users who want to submit questions, offer comments on other submissions or vote on how relevant the topic is will sign in using their email address, but their identities and addresses will be anonymous to OCR. OCR will consider the input provided on this site in developing our guidance and technical assistance efforts.

Stakeholders will use this site to help OCR understand what guidance on HIPAA regulations would be helpful. We are asking stakeholders to provide input on the following issues: What topics should we address in guidance? What current provisions leave you scratching your heads? How should this guidance look in order to make it more understandable, more accessible? Stakeholders can also use this page to submit questions about HIPAA, present a use case, or see what their peers are discussing. Users can comment on the discussions and vote on which topics or use cases would be the most helpful or important.

Posting or commenting on a question on this site will not subject anyone to enforcement action. . . . We appreciate input from stakeholders and will consider comments as we develop our priorities for additional guidance and technical assistance. . . .

C. STATE-BASED PRIVACY PROTECTIONS

State-based protection of patients' confidential information operates in various facets of common law and statutory law. For example, under the doctrine of "physician-patient privilege," courts protect physician-patient confidential information from being discovered in judicial proceedings, unless the value of the information outweighs the need for maintaining confidentiality. Through licensure statutes and regulations, states impose a duty on physicians to keep their patients' medical records in a secure fashion for a minimum period of time, after which physicians are responsible for secure disposal of medical records. And common law doctrines such as those covered in Chapter 8 provide patients recourse if their medical records are improperly exposed, as we see in *Byrne*, below.

> Patient trust is also protected by professional ethics rules pertaining to privacy and confidentiality, the breach of which can lead to sanctions.

HIPAA contains no federal private right of action for individuals harmed by security breaches, whether intentional or negligent. But some state courts have held that HIPAA does not preempt state laws that would allow a patient to pursue wrongdoing under preexisting or separately existing state law doctrines.

42 U.S.C. §1320d-7. Effect on State law
(a) General effect
(1) General rule
Except as provided in paragraph (2), a provision or requirement under this part, or a standard or implementation specification adopted or established under sections 1320d-1 through 1320d-3 of this title, shall supersede any contrary provision of State law, including a provision of State law that requires medical or health plan records (including billing information) to be maintained or transmitted in written rather than electronic form.
(2) Exceptions
A provision or requirement under this part, or a standard or implementation specification adopted or established under sections 1320d-1 through 1320d-3 of this title, shall not supersede a contrary provision of State law, if the provision of State law—
(A) is a provision the Secretary determines—

(i) is necessary —
    (I) to prevent fraud and abuse;
    (II) to ensure appropriate State regulation of insurance and health plans;
    (III) for State reporting on health care delivery or costs; or
    (IV) for other purposes; or
  (ii) addresses controlled substances; or
(B) subject to section 264(c)(2) of the Health Insurance Portability and Accountability Act of 1996, relates to the privacy of individually identifiable health information.

    . . . .

45 C.F.R. §160.203. General rule and exceptions.

A standard, requirement, or implementation specification adopted under this subchapter that is contrary to a provision of State law preempts the provision of State law. This general rule applies, except if one or more of the following conditions is met:

(a) A determination is made by the Secretary under §160.204 that the provision of State law:

  (1) Is necessary:

    (i) To prevent fraud and abuse related to the provision of or payment for health care;

    (ii) To ensure appropriate State regulation of insurance and health plans to the extent expressly authorized by statute or regulation;

    (iii) For State reporting on health care delivery or costs; or

    (iv) For purposes of serving a compelling need related to public health, safety, or welfare, and, if a standard, requirement, or implementation specification under part 164 of this subchapter is at issue, if the Secretary determines that the intrusion into privacy is warranted when balanced against the need to be served; or

  (2) Has as its principal purpose the regulation of the manufacture, registration, distribution, dispensing, or other control of any controlled substances (as defined in 21 U.S.C. 802), or that is deemed a controlled substance by State law.

> This regulation clarifies that state laws that are more protective of privacy are not preempted by HIPAA.

(b) The provision of State law relates to the privacy of individually identifiable health information and is more stringent than a standard, requirement, or implementation specification adopted under subpart E of part 164 of this subchapter.

(c) The provision of State law, including State procedures established under such law, as applicable, provides for the reporting of disease or injury, child abuse, birth, or death, or for the conduct of public health surveillance, investigation, or intervention.

(d) The provision of State law requires a health plan to report, or to provide access to, information for the purpose of management audits, financial audits, program monitoring and evaluation, or the licensure or certification of facilities or individuals.

As you read the following case, consider which state laws or common law doctrines should be saved from HIPAA preemption given HIPAA's preemption provisions and enforcement structure.

Byrne v. Avery Center for Obstetrics & Gynecology, P.C.

102 A.3d 32 (Conn. 2014)

Congress enacted the Health Insurance Portability and Accountability Act of 1996 (HIPAA) as a comprehensive legislative and regulatory scheme to, *inter alia*, protect the privacy of patients' health information given emerging advances in information technology. In this appeal, we determine whether HIPAA, which lacks a private right of action and preempts "contrary" state laws, preempts state law claims for negligence and negligent infliction of emotional distress against a health care provider who is alleged to have improperly breached the confidentiality of a patient's medical records in the course of complying with a subpoena. The plaintiff, Emily Byrne, appeals from the judgment of the trial court dismissing counts two and four of the operative amended complaint (complaint) filed against the defendant, the Avery Center for Obstetrics and Gynecology, P.C. On appeal, the plaintiff contends that the trial court improperly concluded that her state law claims for negligence and negligent infliction of emotional distress were preempted by HIPAA. . . .

> HIPAA, like ERISA §502, expressly preempts state laws. The issue is determining the scope of preemption, analyzing the statutory text and legislative intent.

The trial court's memorandum of decision sets forth the following undisputed facts and procedural history. "Before July 12, 2005, the defendant provided the plaintiff [with] gynecological and obstetrical care and treatment. The defendant provided its patients, including the plaintiff, with notice of its privacy policy regarding protected health information and agreed, based on this policy and on law, that it would not disclose the plaintiff's health information without her authorization.

"In May, 2004, the plaintiff began a personal relationship with Andro Mendoza, which lasted until September, 2004. . . . In October, 2004, she instructed the defendant not to release her medical records to Mendoza. In March, 2005, she moved from Connecticut to Vermont where she presently lives. On May 31, 2005, Mendoza filed paternity actions against the plaintiff in Connecticut and Vermont. Thereafter, the defendant was served with a subpoena requesting its presence together with the plaintiff's medical records at the New Haven Regional Children's [Probate Court] on July 12, 2005. The defendant did not alert the plaintiff of the subpoena, file a motion to quash it or appear in court. Rather, the defendant mailed a copy of the plaintiff's medical file to the court around July 12, 2005. In September, 2005, '[Mendoza] informed [the] plaintiff by telephone that he reviewed [the] plaintiff's medical file in the court file.' On September 15, 2005, the plaintiff filed a motion to seal her medical file, which was granted. The plaintiff alleges that she suffered harassment and extortion threats from Mendoza since he viewed her medical records."

The plaintiff subsequently brought this action against the defendant. Specifically, the operative complaint in the present case alleges that the defendant: (1) breached its contract with her when it violated its privacy policy by disclosing her protected health information without authorization; (2) acted negligently by failing to use proper and reasonable care in protecting her medical file, including disclosing it without authorization in violation of General Statutes §52-146o and the department's regulations implementing HIPAA; (3) made a negligent misrepresentation, upon which the plaintiff relied to her detriment, that her "medical file and the privacy of her health information would be protected in accordance with the law"; and

(4) engaged in conduct constituting negligent infliction of emotional distress. After discovery, the parties filed cross motions for summary judgment.

With respect to the plaintiff's negligence based claims in counts two and four of the complaint, the trial court agreed with the defendant's contention that "HIPAA preempts 'any action dealing with confidentiality/privacy of medical information,'" which prompted the court to treat the summary judgment motion as one seeking dismissal for lack of subject matter jurisdiction. In its memorandum of decision, the trial court first considered the plaintiff's negligence claims founded on the violations of the regulations implementing HIPAA. . . .

The trial court concluded similarly with respect to the plaintiff's common-law negligence claims, observing that, under the regulatory definitions implementing HIPAA's preemption provision to "the extent that common-law negligence permits a private right of action for claims that amount to HIPAA violations, it is a contrary provision of law and subject to HIPAA's preemption rule. Because it is not more stringent the preemption exception does not apply." For the same reasons, the trial court dismissed count four of the complaint, claiming negligent infliction of emotional distress. . . .

On appeal, the plaintiff claims that the trial court improperly determined that HIPAA preempted her negligence based state law claims. Conceding that there is no private right of action under HIPAA, the plaintiff asserts that she is not asserting a claim for relief premised solely on a violation of HIPAA, but rather . . . propos[es] that common-law negligence actions, with HIPAA informing the standard of care, may complement rather than "obstruct" HIPAA for preemption purposes. . . . [T]he plaintiff emphasizes that the use of other state law causes of action to enforce statutes otherwise lacking private rights of action has been upheld by this court in the analogous contexts of the Connecticut Unfair Insurance Practices Act and the federal Occupational Safety and Health Act (OSHA) and its state counterpart. The plaintiff further argues that, under HIPAA and its implementing regulation her state law claims for relief are not preempted because it is not "contrary to" HIPAA to provide for damages under state common-law claims for privacy breaches.

In response, the defendant relies on the long line of federal and state cases establishing that there is no private right of action, express or implied, under HIPAA. See, e.g., O'Donnell v. Blue Cross Blue Shield of Wyoming; Fisher v. Yale University. Observing that "playing word games does not change the underlying theory of liability," the defendant . . . contends that, because there is no private right of action under HIPAA, "a plaintiff cannot use a violation of HIPAA as the standard of care for underlying claims, such as negligence." The defendant further emphasizes that the plaintiff's negligence claim relying on §52-146o is preempted because HIPAA is more stringent than the state statute. . . .

We note at the outset that whether Connecticut's common law provides a remedy for a health care provider's breach of its duty of confidentiality, including in the context of responding to a subpoena, is not an issue presented in this appeal. Thus, assuming, without deciding, that Connecticut's common law recognizes a negligence cause of action arising from health care providers' breaches of patient privacy in the context of complying with subpoenas, we agree with the plaintiff and conclude that such an action is not preempted by HIPAA and, further, that the HIPAA regulations may well inform the applicable standard of care in certain circumstances.

I

PREEMPTION CLAIMS

. . . Whether state causes of action are preempted by federal statutes and regulations is a question of law over which our review is plenary. Thus, we note that "the ways in which federal law may [preempt] state law are well established and in the first instance turn on congressional intent. . . . Congress' intent to supplant state authority in a particular field may be express[ed] in the terms of the statute."

Turning to the HIPAA provisions at issue in this appeal, we note by way of background that, "[r]ecognizing the importance of protecting the privacy of health information in the midst of the rapid evolution of health information systems, Congress passed HIPAA in August 1996. HIPAA's Administrative Simplification provisions were designed to improve the efficiency and effectiveness of the health care system by facilitating the exchange of information with respect to financial and administrative transactions carried out by health plans, health care clearinghouses, and health care providers who transmit information in connection with such transactions. . . .

> Under the HIPAA statute, Congress had the first opportunity to write the Privacy Rule but failed to do so in the statutory time frame.

"Within the Administrative Simplification section, Congress included another provision — [§]264 — outlining a two-step process to address the need to afford certain protections to the privacy of health information maintained under HIPAA. First, [§] 264(a) directed [the department] to submit to Congress within twelve months of HIPAA's enactment 'detailed recommendations on standards with respect to the privacy of individually identifiable health information.' . . . Second, if Congress did not enact further legislation pursuant to these recommendations within thirty-six months of the enactment of HIPAA, [the department] was to promulgate final regulations containing such standards." Because Congress ultimately failed to pass any additional legislation, the department's final regulations implementing HIPAA, known collectively as the "Privacy Rule," were "promulgated in February 2001," with compliance phased in over the next few years.

With respect to the preemptive effect of HIPAA, 42 U.S.C. §1320d-7(a)(i) provides that: "Except as provided in paragraph (2), a provision or requirement under this part, or a standard or implementation specification adopted or established under sections 1320d-1 through 1320d-3 of this title, shall supersede any contrary provision of State law, including a provision of State law that requires medical or health plan records (including billing information) to be maintained or transmitted in written rather than electronic form." . . . The department's regulations, namely, 45 C.F.R. §160.202 (2004) and 45 C.F.R. §160.203, provide additional explication of HIPAA's preemptive effect. Specifically, 45 C.F.R. §160.203 provides as a "general rule" that a "standard, requirement, or implementation specification adopted under this subchapter that is contrary to a provision of State law preempts the provision of State law." A state law is "contrary" to HIPAA if "(1) A covered entity would find it impossible to comply with both the [s]tate and [f]ederal requirements; or (2) [t]he provision of [s]tate law stands as an obstacle to the accomplishment and execution of the full purposes and objectives of part C of title XI of [HIPAA], [§] 264 of [Public Law] 104-191, as applicable." 45 C.F.R. §160.202. The regulations define a "[s]tate law" as "a constitution, statute, regulation, rule, common law, or other [s]tate action having the force and effect of law."

As relevant to this appeal, state laws exempted from preemption include those that "[relate] to the privacy of individually identifiable health information and [are] more stringent than a standard, requirement, or implementation specification adopted under subpart E of part 164 of this subchapter." 45 C.F.R. §160.203(b). A state law is "[m]ore stringent" "in the context of a comparison of a provision of [s]tate law and a standard, requirement, or implementation specification adopted under subpart E of part 164 of this subchapter, [if it] meets one or more of the following criteria:

> HIPAA's statutory preemption language is further interpreted in implementing regulations.

> "(4) With respect to the form, substance, or the need for express legal permission from an individual, who is the subject of the individually identifiable health information, for use or disclosure of individually identifiable health information, provides requirements that narrow the scope or duration, increase the privacy protections afforded (such as by expanding the criteria for), or reduce the coercive effect of the circumstances surrounding the express legal permission, as applicable. . . .
>
> "(6) With respect to any other matter, provides greater privacy protection for the individual who is the subject of the individually identifiable health information."

This statutory and regulatory background brings us to the question in the present appeal, namely, whether HIPAA preempts a state law claim sounding in negligence arising from a health care provider's alleged breach of physician-patient confidentiality in the course of complying with a subpoena. It is by now well settled that the "statutory structure of HIPAA . . . precludes implication of a private right of action. [Section] 1320d-6 [of title 42 of the United States Code] expressly provides a method for enforcing its prohibition upon use or disclosure of individual's health information — the punitive imposition of fines and imprisonment for violations."

Nevertheless, it is similarly well established that, "[o]rdinarily, state causes of action are not [preempted] solely because they impose liability over and above that authorized by federal law." As a corollary, "a complaint alleging a violation of a federal statute as an element of a state cause of action, when Congress has determined that there should be no private, federal cause of action for the violation, does not state a claim 'arising under the [c]onstitution, laws, or treaties of the United States'" for purposes of federal question jurisdiction. . . .

Consistent with these principles, the regulatory history of HIPAA demonstrates that neither HIPAA nor its implementing regulations were intended to preempt tort actions under state law arising out of the unauthorized release of a plaintiff's medical records. As the plaintiff aptly notes, one commenter during the rulemaking process had "raised the issue of whether a private right of action is a greater penalty, since the proposed federal rule has no comparable remedy." Standards for Privacy of Individually Identifiable Health Information, 65 Fed. Reg. 82,462, 82,582 (December 28, 2000). In its administrative commentary to the final rule as promulgated in the Federal Register, the department responded to this question by stating, inter alia, that "the fact that a state law allows an individual to file [a civil action] to protect privacy does not conflict with the HIPAA penalty provisions," namely, fines and imprisonment. This agency commentary on final rules in the Federal Register is significant evidence of regulatory intent. Indeed, "[w]here an agency has authoritatively interpreted its own rule, courts generally defer to that reading unless it is plainly erroneous or inconsistent with the regulation."

Consistent with this regulatory history, the parties' briefs and our independent research disclose a number of cases from the federal and sister state courts holding that HIPAA, and particularly its implementation through the Privacy Rule regulations, does not preempt causes of action, when they exist as a matter of state common or statutory law, arising from health care providers' breaches of patient confidentiality in a variety of contexts; indeed, several have determined that HIPAA may inform the relevant standard of care in such actions. . . .

. . . [W]e conclude that, if Connecticut's common law recognizes claims arising from a health care provider's alleged breach of its duty of confidentiality in the course of complying with a subpoena, HIPAA and its implementing regulations do not preempt such claims. We further conclude that, to the extent it has become the common practice for Connecticut health care providers to follow the procedures required under HIPAA in rendering services to their patients, HIPAA and its implementing regulations may be utilized to inform the standard of care applicable to such claims arising from allegations of negligence in the disclosure of patients' medical records pursuant to a subpoena. The availability of such private rights of action in state courts, to the extent that they exist as a matter of state law, do [es] not preclude, conflict with, or complicate health care providers' compliance with HIPAA. On the contrary, negligence claims in state courts support "at least one of HIPAA's goals by establishing another disincentive to wrongfully disclose a patient's health care record." Accordingly, we conclude that the trial court improperly dismissed counts two and four of the plaintiff's complaint, sounding in negligence and negligent infliction of emotional distress.

> Federal law, such as HIPAA privacy standards and procedures, may be relevant to the state common law duty of care with respect to disclosure of medical records.

QUESTIONS

1. Does HIPAA protect patient information in situations such as the one in *Byrne*, where PHI was disclosed without a patient's permission to someone litigating a case against her?
2. Why doesn't HIPAA provide a private right of action for violations of the law? Consider, by way of comparison, the private actions available under the Emergency Medical Treatment and Labor Act (EMTALA) and Employee Retirement Income Security Act (ERISA).
3. Why is the Connecticut Supreme Court willing to rely on HIPAA as a standard of care in negligence cases?

Not all state courts agree with importation of federal privacy standards into state law. As you read *Sheldon*, contrast the reasoning in *Byrne* and consider whether Ohio is more or less protective of patient privacy than HIPAA requires.

Sheldon v. Kettering Health Network

40 N.E.3d 661 (Ohio Ct. App. 2015)

. . . The complaint alleged common-law tort claims for invasion of privacy, negligence, negligence per se, negligent training, negligent supervision, intentional infliction of emotional distress, and breach of fiduciary duty. The claims stemmed from KHN's alleged failure to protect the privacy of the plaintiffs' electronic medical information and the improper accessing and disclosure of that information by KHN administrator Duane Sheldon, the former spouse of Vicki Sheldon.

KHN responded to the complaint by seeking dismissal under Civ. R. 12(B)(6). In support, KHN argued that each of the tort claims was based on alleged violations of the federal Health Insurance Portability and Accountability Act ("HIPAA"). KHN noted that HIPAA did not provide a private right of action to enforce its terms. There- fore, KHN reasoned that the plaintiffs could not assert common- law tort claims essentially alleging HIPAA violations. KHN argued that the "[p]lain- tiffs should not be permitted to circumvent the bar on private enforcement of HIPAA violations by merely masking alleged HIPAA violations as common-law torts." . . . Because HIPAA does not provide a private right of action, the trial court concluded that the plaintiffs could not state a claim for relief. . . .

> KHN is wielding HIPAA as a shield against tort claims filed in state court.

. . . [W]e turn to the complaint in this case. It contains the following factual allegations:

6. Defendant KHN uses a system of software for storing, maintaining, acces- sing, and protecting electronic medical information. The system is known as "EPIC." When properly used, the system protects medical information from being accessed by unapproved personnel to comply with the federal law Health Insurance Portability and Accountability Act, otherwise known as "HIPAA."

7. The "EPIC" System uses reports to ensure that electronic medical informa- tion is safely protected and remains private. Through a series of reports, known as "CLARITY" reports, the hospital or authorized medical information custodian has the ability to ensure that records are not being improperly accessed through, but not limited to, the following reports: * * * [The com- plaint lists numerous different types of reports that allegedly can be produced to help detect possible security or privacy breaches]. The cumulative effect of the regular running and monitoring of these Epic Clarity reports is to detect and deter improper access. When routinely run and monitored, the Epic Clarity reports provide early detection of privacy breaches of EHRs.

8. Under the HIPAA Security Rule, a covered entity must identify and analyze potential risks to electronic private health information, and it must imple- ment security measures that reduce risks and vulnerabilities to a reasonable level. EPIC reports should be run and reviewed on a consistent and recurring basis, no less than monthly, and preferably weekly, in order to adequately monitor, ensure and protect the privacy of health information to meet the HIPAA Risk Analysis and Management Process. When used properly and effectively, EPIC Software and CLARITY Reports provide auditing and mon- itoring protection for electronic health information.

9. Defendant D. SHELDON, an administrator for KPN under the KHN, had access to the EPIC system but was not authorized to access the health records of the Plaintiffs. Defendant D. Sheldon improperly accessed the health records of Plaintiffs on multiple occasions over a period of at least 15 months, as Defendant KHN failed to take reasonable steps under EPIC and CLARITY to detect his unauthorized access or otherwise to pro- tect such information.

10. Duane Sheldon, as administrator, commenced at least one extramarital affair with certain others in the Kettering Health Network. In order to enhance his affair, Duane Sheldon improperly accessed extremely sensitive medical information belonging to Vicki Sheldon, and shared such information with his paramour, who is an employee of KPN who reported to D. Sheldon.

11. In addition, upon information and belief, Duane Sheldon and other parties in his department created one or more fictitious names that do not represent real parties or real users of health information to improperly access protected health information.

12. These fictitious names accessed Plaintiffs' protected health information.

13. In addition, there were significant other breach incidents by D. SHELDON and his accomplices of Vicki Sheldon's protected health information, and also to the protected health information of H. DERCOLA and [T.D.].

14. The breach of such information would have been prevented (or greatly minimized) had Defendant KHN been taking the reasonable and normal steps to protect Plaintiff's health information by running weekly or at least monthly EPIC CLARITY reports, and monitoring those reports.

15. Defendant KHN eventually revealed to Plaintiffs that there had been multiple breaches of their private and protected health information, in violation of the Health Information Technology for Economic and Clinical Health Act ("the HITECH Act") however, when Plaintiffs requested proper information from the "EPIC" and "CLARITY" reports to examine the nature of the actual breaches, KHN refused to provide them. In fact, Plaintiffs, through counsel, on multiple occasions asked for copies of the "EPIC" reports, by name, that would have shown the exact nature of the privacy breaches, and Defendant refused to provide them and/or stated that such reports did not exist.

16. Instead, Defendant Kettering Health Network provided a "Homegrown" Report (a report designed by KHN employees to control what information to provide) that is inadequate, and then proceeded to provide false and malicious information regarding the parties that are listed on the "Homegrown" Report.

. . . We discern at least two types of tortious activity alleged by the plaintiffs: (1) Duane Sheldon's intentional improper accessing and sharing of their health information and (2) KHN's alleged failure to take reasonable steps to protect that information and to detect Duane Sheldon's breaches. We note that the factual allegations about Duane Sheldon's conduct do not necessarily appear to depend on an alleged HIPAA violation. The statute is invoked only in connection with the plaintiffs' factual allegations about KHN failing to take reasonable steps to protect their health information and to detect his breaches. In particular, the plaintiffs allege that KHN failed to regularly run and monitor CLARITY reports, which they allege was required by HIPAA. . . .

. . . We turn now to the factual allegations in the complaint regarding KHN's own failure to take reasonable steps, as alleged to be required under HIPAA, to protect the plaintiffs' health information and to detect Duane Sheldon's breaches. As noted above, the plaintiffs' allegations are grounded in the notion that KHN failed to regularly run and monitor the EPIC system CLARITY reports in violation of HIPAA. According to the complaint, "the system protects medical information from being accessed by unapproved personnel to comply with the federal law * * * known as

'HIPAA.'" "[T]he cumulative effect of the regular running of these Epic Clarity reports is to detect and deter improper access." "Epic reports should be run and reviewed on a consistent and recurring basis * * * to meet the HIPAA Risk Analysis and Management Process."

Based on the plaintiffs' own specifically-titled headings of the complaint's stated causes of action, they intended to assert common-law causes of action against KHN for invasion of privacy, negligence, negligence per se, negligent training, negligent supervision, intentional infliction of emotional distress, and breach of fiduciary duty. The trial court found these claims subject to Civ. R. 12(B)(6) dismissal because they all essentially alleged violations of HIPAA, or were "HIPAA based," and the statute does not provide a private right of action.

> The plaintiffs seek to find a state law route for holding wrongdoers liable because, as should be clear by now, HIPAA is consistently interpreted not to offer a private right of action that affords standing in federal court. Then state courts must determine whether to continue to allow certain tort claims to exist under a HIPAA regime.

As a preliminary matter, it is beyond dispute that HIPAA itself does not create an express or implied private right of action for violations of its provisions. The cases supporting this holding are legion, and the plaintiffs agree HIPAA provides no private action. Despite the fact that plaintiffs argue that they have asserted common-law claims and not a statutory HIPAA claim, unquestionably the complaint is grounded in the notion that KHN's actions were wrongful because they failed to take steps, consistent with HIPAA, that would have prevented or reduced the risk of disclosure. Nevertheless, at this stage of the litigation we are required to interpret the complaint broadly to determine whether the allegations assert common-law tort claims independent from HIPAA. Thus, the absence of a private right of action under HIPAA does not necessarily resolve the issues before us. For that reason, we find some of the case law cited by KHN to be of little assistance. The Ohio case law upon which KHN relies does not decide whether a plaintiff can bring a common-law tort claim that might also involve a HIPAA violation for which no private statutory right of action exists. KHN cites OhioHealth Corp. v. Ryan, which states: "HIPAA does not allow a private cause of action, according to Ohio law." . . .

Contrary to the language in *OhioHealth Corp. v. Ryan* upon which KHN relies, we find it imprecise to say that HIPAA "does not allow a private cause of action." What we should determine is whether HIPAA prohibits common-law tort claims based on the wrongful release of confidential medical information unrelated to and independent from HIPAA itself. Indeed, the State of Ohio has recognized an independent tort for the "unauthorized, unprivileged disclosure to a third party of nonpublic medical information[.]" Biddle v. Warren Gen. Hosp., 715 N.E.2d 518 (1999). *Biddle*, however, was decided before HIPAA's privacy-rule regulations were published on December 28, 2000 and before its security-rule regulations took effect on April 21, 2003. Therefore, we must first determine whether *Biddle*'s common-law right of action recognized in 1999 survives HIPAA.

. . . HIPAA is a combination of the statute and the regulations adopted under its authority. The HIPAA statute states that it "shall supersede any contrary provision of State law." 42 U.S.C. §1320d-7(a)(1); *see also* 45 C.F.R. §160.203. But the statute specifically directs that any regulations shall not supersede state law that is "more stringent" than the requirements under HIPAA. Section 264(c)(2) of Public Law 104-191. The regulations provide that state law is "contrary" to HIPAA when (1) it is "impossible to comply

> HIPAA is a floor, not a ceiling, on privacy rights.

with both the State and Federal requirements;" or (2) "state law stands as an obstacle to the accomplishment and execution" of the act. 45 C.F.R. §160.202. The "more stringent" exception is adopted in 45 C.F.R. §160.203(b). The regulations also explain that a state law is "more stringent" than HIPAA if the state law provides greater privacy protection, provides the patient greater rights of access or access to more information than HIPAA, or narrows the scope or duration of the use or disclosure of information HIPAA would allow. 45 C.F.R. §160.202. Significantly, "State law means a constitution, statute, regulation, rule, common law, or other State action having the force and effect of law."

Upon review, we conclude that HIPAA does not preempt the Ohio independent tort recognized by the Ohio Supreme Court in *Biddle* "for the unauthorized, unprivileged disclosure to a third party of nonpublic medical information that a physician or hospital has learned within a physician-patient relationship." However, we further conclude that federal regulations — as opposed to an Ohio statute that sets forth a positive and definite standard of care — cannot be used as a basis for negligence per se under Ohio law. Additionally, in our view utilization of HIPAA as an ordinary negligence "standard of care" is tantamount to authorizing a prohibited private right of action for violation of HIPAA itself, and moreover, in specific regard to plaintiffs' allegation that monitoring access to medical records was too infrequent, HIPAA does not provide a standard of care as to the frequency of review of information-system activity.

We determine that a *Biddle* claim is not preempted because we fail to see how such a claim conflicts with HIPAA unless the alleged claim asserts recovery for release of information that HIPAA specifically allows. And although Congress has provided for enforcement of HIPAA by the Secretary of Health and Human Services, and more recently, by State Attorneys General, the allowance of recovery of an individual's damages does not interfere with government enforcement. Therefore, we do not find it is impossible to comply with HIPAA and with state law to the extent we have indicated, and state law is not an obstacle to the accomplishment of HIPAA's purposes. We believe a *Biddle* claim enhances the protection of confidentiality of medical information.

Despite our agreement that a cause of action still exists for "unauthorized, unprivileged disclosure to a third party of nonpublic medical information that a physician or hospital has learned within a physician-patient relationship," plaintiffs have not alleged a set of facts that would entitle them to relief under *Biddle*. . . .

. . . In any event, we decline to recognize the plaintiffs' alleged "Third Count: Negligence Per Se," which undoubtedly is "HIPAA based," for three separate reasons. First, to the extent that HIPAA universally has been held not to authorize a private right of action, to permit HIPAA regulations to define per se the duty and liability for breach is no less than a private action to enforce HIPAA, which is precluded. Second, in Chambers v. St. Mary's School, the Ohio Supreme Court held that "[t]he violation of an administrative rule does not constitute negligence per se; however such a violation may be admissible as evidence of negligence." Therefore, under Ohio case law the HIPAA administrative rules that appellants argue are applicable cannot be the basis of a negligence per se theory of recovery. Third, critical allegations in the complaint state that "Epic reports should be run and reviewed on a consistent and recurring basis, no less than monthly, and preferably weekly, in order to adequately monitor, ensure and protect the privacy of health information to meet the HIPAA Risk Analysis and Management Process." These allegations suggest that had KHN audited its records more frequently it would have discovered Duane Sheldon's intrusion sooner (although, significantly, after he already had accessed the plaintiffs' records at least once). This allegation implies that HIPAA presents some "standard" for when and how information security audits should be performed. We have not found any such regulation. We note that 45 C.F.R. §164.312(b) provides for a hospital to "[i]mplement hardware, software, and/or procedural mechanisms that record and examine activity in information systems that contain or use electronic protected health information." Another regulation, 45 C.F.R. §164.530 (i)(1), provides that "policies and procedures must be reasonably designed, taking into account the size of and the type of activities related to protected health information undertaken by the covered entity, to ensure such compliance." These regulations are flexibly designed to accommodate the vast array of medical providers. The regulations do require auditing of record access, but they do not provide a "standard" for how frequently to do so. In this regard, the regulations do not set forth "a positive and definite standard of care * * * whereby a jury may determine whether there has been a violation thereof by finding a single issue of fact." Accordingly, the regulations at issue are insufficient to support negligence per se liability. . . .

Here, at best, the plaintiffs' claim against KHN is predicated upon KHN's alleged failure to earlier detect Sheldon's intentional, unauthorized access through procedures required by HIPAA. Consistent with *Scott*, we determine that the facts alleged do not constitute "disclosure" for purposes of a *Biddle* breach-of-confidentiality claim. Therefore, we affirm the trial court's dismissal of the claims albeit as a result of a somewhat different analysis.

Despite preemption and the lack of a private right of action, we are aware of three states that have expressed approval of the use of HIPAA regulations as a standard of care. Byrne v. Avery Center for Obstetrics and Gynecology, P.C., 102 A.3d 32 (Conn. 2014), R.K. v. St. Mary's Med. Ctr., Inc., 735 S.E.2d 715 (W.Va. 2012), and Acosta v. Byrum, 638 S.E.2d 246 (N.C. Ct. App. 2006). However, each is dependent on the nuances of applicable state law, the claims pursued, and the unique facts presented. In *Byrne*, the court analyzed state law claims of negligence and negligent infliction of emotional distress resulting from production of records in response to a subpoena without notifying the patient which, for non-judicial subpoenas, is required by HIPAA. The court stated "HIPAA may inform the applicable standard of care in certain circumstances." We perceive the issue in *Byrne* to be more of whether the release was "authorized" not whether the defendant was responsible for its disclosure. In *R.K.*, plaintiff's various state negligent, intentional conduct, and breach of confidentiality claims were asserted without specific HIPAA labeling against a hospital whose employees accessed plaintiff's psychiatric records and disclosed information to his estranged wife. Although reference was made with approval to other cases which addressed use of HIPAA as a standard of care, the holding was "we now hold that common-law tort claims based upon the wrongful disclosure of medical or personal health information are not preempted by [HIPAA]." In *Acosta* a physician gave a subordinate his medical access code, which would be contrary to HIPAA. The subordinate retrieved the plaintiff's psychiatric records. The plaintiff brought claims for invasion of privacy and for intentional and negligent infliction of emotional distress alleging the sharing of the access code violated regulations of "University Health Systems, Roanoke Chowan Hospital, and [HIPAA]." The *Acosta* court determined plaintiff sufficiently pled causes of action separately from the

HIPAA violation, although it also concluded that plaintiff did not bring a HIPAA claim but that HIPAA was only applicable as "evidence of a the [*sic*] duty of care owed by Dr. Faber." To the extent that these cases from other jurisdictions are not binding or that they are distinguishable we choose not to follow them. . . .

QUESTIONS

1. For what reason or reasons does the Ohio common law differ from Connecticut and other jurisdictions?
2. Should varying state standards be permitted given the HIPAA preemption structure?

Consider the following substantial jury verdict, which was also based on state law yet analyzed HIPAA as a guiding privacy principle.

Walgreen Co. v. Hinchy

21 N.E.3d 99 (Ind. 2014)

In this case, a pharmacist breached one of her most sacred duties by viewing the prescription records of a customer and divulging the information she learned from those records to the client's ex-boyfriend. A jury heard extensive evidence during a four-day trial and ultimately found that the pharmacist and her employer are liable for the damages sustained by the customer as a result of the breach. We are loath to disturb jury verdicts and decline to do so in this case.

Walgreen Company raises a number of issues in this appeal. First, it argues that the trial court erred by refusing to grant summary judgment or a directed verdict in Walgreen's favor on Abigail Hinchy's claims based on respondeat superior and negligent retention and supervision of an employee. Second, Walgreen argues that Hinchy's attorney engaged in improper ex parte communication when he filed a trial brief under seal with the trial court and did not provide a copy to Walgreen. Third, Walgreen contends that the jury was improperly instructed on issues surrounding respondeat superior and the tort of public disclosure of private facts. Fourth, Walgreen argues that the $1.8 million jury verdict was excessive and based on improper factors. Finding no reversible error, we affirm.

FACTS

Although the parties dispute the precise beginning and ending dates, at some point between fall 2006 and spring 2010, Hinchy was engaged in an on-and-off sexual relationship with Davion Peterson. During this period, Hinchy filled all of her prescriptions, including oral birth control pills, at a Walgreen pharmacy. At some point in 2009, Peterson began dating Walgreen pharmacist Audra Withers. In August 2009, Hinchy became pregnant with Peterson's child. On an unknown date, Peterson learned that he had contracted genital herpes. Hinchy gave birth to a son on May 22, 2010.

At some point during the week of May 26, 2010, Peterson mailed a letter to Withers informing her about the baby and about the possibility that he may have exposed her to genital herpes. Withers became terrified about the possibility of contracting a sexually transmitted disease. Consequently, during her shift and while at work, Withers looked up Hinchy's prescription profile in the Walgreen computer system to see if she could find any information about Hinchy's sexually transmitted disease. The next day, Withers again looked up Hinchy's profile to confirm that she had spelled it correctly the day before. Withers has consistently maintained that she never revealed to anyone what she had learned about Hinchy's prescription profile, did not look for any information related to birth control, and did not print anything out relating to Hinchy's prescription profile.

On May 29, 2010, Peterson sent the following text message to Hinchy:

> I'm not trying to start any crap but I have a print out showing that you didn't even refill ur birth control perscription for July or august. The last time you filled ur prescription was June. I know uve lied to ur mom and harmony and anybody willing to listen but the printout does not lie. I know you lied to me wth tears and curse words and misplaced righteousness. U really should think about what you did . . . on ur own. You really should think about that FACT before you call me another name. What kind of person does something like that?

Tr. Ex. 1A (internal spelling and grammatical errors original). In response, Hinchy sent the following text to Peterson:

> Print out. It's illegal for u to obtain any kind of information like that regarding me. And if u knew anything about my medical history u would know that I was on multiple types of birth control since I was 15[.]

Tr. Ex. 1B (internal spelling and grammatical errors original). Peterson responded with the following return text:

> Abby, you ddnt refill ANYTHING at all. No type of birth control medication at all. June you did. You did NOT in july and august. Jeezr you really still trying to claim? Again, I'm not trying to start shit. What's done is done, but what's happening was totally avoidable. You are NOT a victim. You did something wrong abby. Very wrong. Ps. . . . it is not illigall for ME to have it. Ime being very technical here but I ddnt break any laws myself.

Be careful what you and your clients communicate by text message; it may end up in a published opinion one day.

Tr. Ex. 1C (internal spelling and grammatical errors original).

It was, in fact, true that Hinchy had not filled her birth control prescriptions in July or August 2009. Unable to understand how Peterson had accessed a printout containing her private prescription information, Hinchy immediately contacted her local Walgreen but was unable to reach anyone. She then called a Walgreen in her mother's hometown of Schererville and was told by the Walgreen employee at that location that there was no way to track whether her records had been accessed. With no idea how to proceed, Hinchy took no further action at that time.

On March 18, 2011, Peterson mailed his son a gift. The package had a return address that Hinchy did not recognize. After conducting an internet search regarding the address, she learned that the address belonged to Withers. She also learned that Peterson and Withers were married and that Withers was a pharmacist at the local Walgreen where she fills her prescriptions. Hinchy immediately contacted her local Walgreen to report her suspicion that Withers had looked at her personal records and disclosed the information she learned to an unauthorized individual.

Over the next three weeks, Hinchy was in regular contact with Walgreen's regional office and loss prevention department. When Withers was confronted about the situation, she admitted that she had accessed Hinchy's prescription profile for personal reasons. On April 15, 2011, Loss Prevention Detective Michael Bryant confirmed to Hinchy that (1) a HIPAA/privacy violation had occurred, (2) Withers had viewed Hinchy's prescription information without consent and for personal purposes, and (3) Walgreen could not confirm that Withers had revealed that information to a third party. As a result of Walgreen's investigation, Withers received a written warning and was required to retake a computer training program regarding HIPAA.

The Litigation

On August 1, 2011, Hinchy filed a complaint against Walgreen and Withers. Against Withers, Hinchy filed claims of negligence/professional malpractice, invasion of privacy/public disclosure of private facts, and invasion of privacy/intrusion. Against Walgreen, Hinchy filed claims seeking liability for the counts she filed against Withers by way of respondeat superior, as well as direct claims for negligent training, negligent supervision, negligent retention, and negligence/professional malpractice.

On July 2, 2012, Walgreen moved for summary judgment. On November 26, 2012, the trial court granted the motion in part with respect to Hinchy's claims for negligent training (against Walgreen) and invasion of privacy by intrusion (against Withers), but otherwise denied the motion. . . .

The four-day jury trial began on July 23, 2013. Among other things, the parties argued about final jury instructions. Walgreen objected to two of Hinchy's three instructions regarding respondeat superior and to two of Hinchy's instructions regarding public disclosure of private facts. Over Walgreen's objections, the trial court permitted the jury to receive those instructions. The jury found in Hinchy's favor and found that the total amount of damages suffered by Hinchy was $1.8 million, that non-party Peterson was responsible for 20% of the damages, and that Walgreen and Withers were jointly responsible for the remaining 80%. Walgreen now appeals.

DISCUSSION AND DECISION

I. Summary Judgment and Directed Verdict

Walgreen first argues that the trial court erred by partially denying its motion for summary judgment and by denying its motion for a directed verdict. Specifically, Walgreen contends that it was entitled to judgment as a matter of law on Hinchy's claims for respondeat superior and negligent retention and supervision, and that those claims should never have been presented to a jury.

. . . .

A. *Respondeat Superior Liability*

Vicarious liability will be imposed upon an employer under the doctrine of respondeat superior "where the employee has inflicted harm while acting 'within the scope of employment.'" To fall within the scope of employment, "the injurious act must be incidental to the conduct authorized or it must, to an appreciable extent, further the employer's business." An act "is incidental to authorized conduct when it 'is subordinate to or pertinent to an act which the servant is employed to perform,' or when it is done 'to an appreciable extent, to further his employer's business.'"

. . . An employer is not held liable under the doctrine of respondeat superior because it did anything wrong, but rather "because of the [employer's] relationship to the wrongdoer." Sword v. NKC Hosps., Inc., 714 N.E.2d 142, 148 (Ind. 1999).

It is well established that whether an employee's actions were within the scope of employment is a question of fact to be determined by the factfinder. Even if some of the actions were unauthorized, the question of whether the actions were within the scope of employment is for the jury. Only if none of the employee's acts were authorized is the question a matter of law that need not be submitted to the trier of fact.

. . . .

Here, . . . Withers's actions were of the same general nature as those authorized, or incidental to the actions that were authorized, by Walgreen. Specifically, Withers was authorized to use the Walgreen computer system and printer, handle prescriptions for Walgreen customers, look up customer information on the Walgreen computer system, review patient prescription histories, and make prescription-related printouts. Withers was at work, on the job, and using Walgreen equipment when the actions at issue occurred. Hinchy belonged to the general category of individuals to whom Withers owed a duty of privacy protection by virtue of her employment as a pharmacist. The fact that some of Withers's actions were authorized, or incidental to authorized actions, or of the same general nature as authorized actions, precludes summary judgment. In other words, Ingram dictates that whether Withers was acting in the scope of her employment was properly determined by the jury rather than as a matter of law by the trial court.

. . . .

B. Underlying Liability

Although Walgreen does not appeal the jury verdict itself, we observe that for respondeat liability to attach, there must also be underlying liability of the acting party. Hinchy proceeded to trial on two separate theories of direct liability against Withers: professional malpractice and public disclosure of private facts. The jury was instructed on both claims. . . .

Without expressing opinion upon the recognition of the tort of public disclosure of private facts in Indiana, we turn to the tort of negligence by virtue of professional malpractice of a pharmacist. Negligence is comprised of three elements: (1) a duty on the part of the defendant to the plaintiff; (2) a breach of that duty; and (3) an injury to the plaintiff resulting from the breach. Indiana law recognizes a relationship between a pharmacist and her customer that gives rise to a duty on the pharmacist's part. Furthermore, Indiana law provides that "[a] pharmacist shall hold in strictest confidence all prescriptions, drug orders, records, and patient information." Ind. Code §25-26-13-15(a). Unquestionably, therefore, Withers had a duty of confidentiality to Hinchy. Also unquestionable is Withers's breach of that duty. Furthermore, Hinchy provided evidence of the damages she sustained as a result of that breach. Under these circumstances, we find that the jury verdict can be affirmed based upon the respondeat superior liability of Walgreen, which attaches via the liability of Withers for her negligence/professional malpractice.

. . . .

III. Jury Instructions

A. *Jury Instructions 8 and 10: Respondeat Superior*

. . . .

2. *Instruction 10*

Final Instruction 10 reads as follows: "You are instructed that [Withers] admits she was acting in the course and scope of her employment with Walgreen Co. when she reviewed [Hinchy's] prescription information."

Walgreen argues that this instruction is misleading because it could have led the jury to find that Withers's admission was binding on Walgreen. Over Walgreen's objection, the trial court removed a second sentence to the instruction: "You are to accept this fact as conclusive and binding as to [Withers]." The trial court removed the sentence because it made it sound as if it only applied to the case against Withers. Walgreen argues that the instruction should not have been given at all, but if it were given, should have at least included the second sentence.

Walgreen overlooks the distinction between Withers's admission being "binding" and being "relevant." While her admission was not binding as to Walgreen, it was relevant to whether she was acting in the course of her employment, which is relevant to the ultimate determination of vicarious liability. Additionally, we note that Walgreen extensively cross-examined Withers and made sure the jury understood that the admission had been made by Withers's attorney and that she did not necessarily understand what it meant. Therefore, any error was cured by Walgreen's own questioning.

B. *Jury Instructions 5 and 11: Public Disclosure of Private Facts*

Walgreen next argues that two of the jury instructions related to the tort of public disclosure of private facts were erroneous. Initially, we note that Walgreen is not appealing the denial of summary judgment on the claim of privacy invasion through public disclosure of private facts. Instead, it is merely objecting to the jury instructions on this claim. Its entire argument with respect to Instruction 5 rests on the position that the tort is not recognized in Indiana and the jury should never have been instructed thereon. This is merely an attempt to make a back-door argument to the trial court's denial of summary judgment on this issue. Inasmuch as Walgreen has not taken the position on appeal that the trial court erred by denying summary judgment on this tort, we will not address this claim of error.

. . . .

CONCLUSION

In conclusion, we have found as follows: (1) the trial court did not err denying Walgreen's summary judgment and directed verdict motions on respondeat superior liability; (2) the trial court did not commit reversible error with respect to an ex parte brief filed by Hinchy; (3) the jury instructions were not erroneous; and (4) the damages award was not excessive or based on improper factors. The judgment of the trial court is affirmed.

PROBLEM

Imagine you are general counsel for Walgreen Co. Write down what steps you would take to prevent this type of disclosure of confidential information. As you write, consider the following: Will HIPAA computer training prevent such rogue behavior? Should your employment policies be altered to facilitate reprimand or contract termination for such circumstances? What steps could you take to avoid being held vicariously liable for an employee's privacy breaches of customer PHI?

D. TELEMEDICINE

CMS defines "telemedicine" as follows:

> For purposes of Medicaid, telemedicine seeks to improve a patient's health by permitting two-way, real time interactive communication between the patient, and the physician or practitioner at the distant site. This electronic communication means the use of interactive telecommunications equipment that includes, at a minimum, audio and video equipment.
>
> Telemedicine is viewed as a cost-effective alternative to the more traditional face-to-face way of providing medical care (e.g., face-to-face consultations or examinations between provider and patient) that states can choose to cover under Medicaid. This definition is modeled on Medicare's definition of telehealth services (42 C.F.R. 410.78). Note that the federal Medicaid statute does not recognize telemedicine as a distinct service.

As this guidance indicates, Medicare contains a more specific regulation pertaining to telehealth for Medicare beneficiaries:

> **42 C.F.R. §410.78. Telehealth services**
> . . . (b) General rule. Medicare Part B pays for office or other outpatient visits, subsequent hospital care services (with the limitation of one telehealth visit every 3 days), subsequent nursing facility care services (not including the Federally-mandated periodic visits under §483.40(c) and with the limitation of one telehealth visit every 30 days), professional consultations, psychiatric diagnostic interview examination, neurobehavioral status exam, individual psychotherapy, pharmacologic management, end-stage renal disease-related services included in the monthly capitation payment (except for one "hands on" visit per month to examine the access site), individual and group medical nutrition therapy services, individual and group kidney disease education services, individual and group diabetes self-management (DSMT) training services (except for one hour of in-person services to be furnished in the year following the initial DSMT service to ensure effective injection training), and individual and group health and behavior assessment and intervention services furnished by an interactive telecommunications system if the following conditions are met:
> (1) The physician or practitioner at the distant site must be licensed to furnish the service under State law. The physician or practitioner at the distant site who is licensed under State law to furnish a covered telehealth service described in this section may bill, and receive payment for, the service when it is delivered via a telecommunications system.

(2) The practitioner at the distant site is one of the following:

(i) A physician.

(ii) A physician assistant.

(iii) A nurse practitioner.

(iv) A clinical nurse specialist.

(v) A nurse-midwife.

(vi) A clinical psychologist.

(vii) A clinical social worker.

(viii) A registered dietitian or nutrition professional.

(3) The services are furnished to a beneficiary at an originating site, which is one of the following:

(i) The office of a physician or practitioner.

(ii) A critical access hospital.

(iii) A rural health clinic.

(iv) A Federally qualified health center.

(v) A hospital.

(vi) A hospital-based or critical access hospital-based renal dialysis center (including satellites).

(vii) A skilled nursing facility.

(viii) A community mental health center.

> Each of the health care providers and sites listed is defined within the Medicare Act or its regulations.

(4) Originating sites must be located in either a rural health professional shortage area as defined under section 332(a)(1)(A) of the Public Health Service Act (42 U.S.C. 254e(a)(1)(A)) or in a county that is not included in a Metropolitan Statistical Area as defined in section 1886(d)(2)(D) of the Act. Entities participating in a Federal telemedicine demonstration project that have been approved by, or receive funding from, the Secretary as of December 31, 2000 qualify as an eligible originating site regardless of geographic location.

(5) The medical examination of the patient is under the control of the physician or practitioner at the distant site.

. . . .

(f) Process for adding or deleting services. Changes to the list of Medicare telehealth services are made through the annual physician fee schedule rule-making process.

QUESTIONS

1. Where must the patient be located for Medicare to pay telehealth service providers?
2. Bearing in mind the rules for Medicare you learned in Chapters 2 and 6, why does it matter if the patient is sitting in a health care facility while telemedicine services occur?

As with privacy and confidentiality, the technology of telemedicine invites both federal and state regulatory efforts. In the next case, a federal court attempted to reconcile gaps between the traditional regulatory mechanisms of a profession-protective medical licensure board and the innovative plans executed by a very large telemedicine company.

Teladoc, Inc. v. Texas Medical Board

2015 WL 8773509 (W.D. Tex. 2015)

I. BACKGROUND

Plaintiffs Teladoc, Inc. and Teladoc Physicians, P.A. (jointly "Teladoc"), Kyon Hood, M.D. ("Dr. Hood"), and Emmette Clark, M.D. ("Dr. Clark") bring this action against fourteen members of the Texas Medical Board ("TMB") in their official capacities challenging recent regulatory changes adopted by the TMB.

The TMB is a state agency "statutorily empowered to regulate the practice of medicine in Texas." Teladoc describes itself as providing "telehealth services," utilizing telecommunication technologies to provide health care services outside the traditional models wherein medical professionals provide[ ] services in an in-person office or hospital setting. According to Plaintiffs, "[t]elehealth providers are generally available 24 hours per day, 365 days per year, for a fraction of the cost of a visit to a physician's office, urgent care center, or hospital emergency room."

Teladoc's services are typically available to individuals whose employer has contracted with Teladoc for a per-member subscription fee. Individuals register with Teladoc either by telephone or online, creating a personal account, including information such as a medical history, physician, contact information, and medical records. Registrants may also upload photographs and medical records to Teladoc's system for inclusion with their medical history.

Registrants seeking a physician consultation can log into Teladoc's web portal or call a toll-free number to place a request for consultation. Teladoc employs board certified physicians who are provided specialized training in treatment and diagnosis via telephone. Once a Teladoc physician accepts the request for consultation, the physician reviews the requesting registrant's information and medical records through the website, then calls the registrant by telephone and consults with him or her. Based on the medical records and history, reported symptoms, and other information the physician elicits during the consultation, the physician dispenses medical advice, including referring the registrant to a physician's office, dentist, or emergency room. When deemed appropriate, the physician can prescribe certain medications. Following the consultation, the Teladoc physician enters notes and findings into the registrant's record, which is available to the registrant and, if the registrant chooses, is forwarded to his or her primary-care physician.

> Teladoc has approximately 11 million subscribers nationwide, and one-quarter of them live in Texas. Various forms of telemedicine, delivered not only directly to patients across state lines — the Teladoc model — but also within the same state via hospitals, clinics, schools, ambulances, and other settings, are increasingly critical to providing access to care in rural areas across the country.

This action relates to the TMB's adoption of revisions to Chapters 174 and 190 of the Texas Administrative Code title which governs the TMB. Chapter 174 regulates the practice of telemedicine medical services in Texas. Chapter 190 sets forth disciplinary guidelines for the practice of medicine in Texas.

As originally adopted by the TMB in 2003, section 190.8(1)(L) ("Old Rule 190.8") prohibits prescription of any "dangerous drug or controlled substance" without first establishing a "proper professional relationship" which requires, in pertinent part, "establishing a diagnosis through the use of acceptable medical practices such as patient history, mental status examination, physical examination, and appropriate diagnostic and laboratory testing." In 2004 the TMB adopted regulations specifically governing "telemedicine."

Effective October 2010, the TMB amended its telemedicine regulations, restricting the definition of "telemedicine" to consultations using "advanced telecommunications technology that allows the distant site provider to see and hear the patient in real time." The amended regulations also made clear that, to establish a "proper physician-patient relationship," telemedicine providers were required to conduct a physical examination of a patient. *Id.* §174.8 ("New Rule 174"). In response to the amended regulations, Teladoc restricted the services it offered in Texas, specifically eliminating the option of video consultation.

In June 2011, the TMB issued a letter to Teladoc, stating the language of Old Rule 190.8 required a "face-to-face" examination prior to prescription of a dangerous drug or controlled substance. Plaintiffs allege the letter was prompted by complaints from Texas physicians about competition from Teladoc.

Teladoc sought legal recourse by bringing suit against the TMB in Texas state court. In July 2011 the state court issued a temporary restraining order barring enforcement of the TMB's interpretation of Old Rule 190.8. In December 2014 the court of appeals held the "TMB's pronouncements in its June 2011 letter are tantamount to amendments to the existing text," finding the TMB had effectively substituted "including" for the actual "such as" phrase. Teladoc, Inc. v. Texas Med. Bd., 453 S.W.3d 606, 620 (Tex. App.—Austin 2014, pet. filed). Thus, the court found the "TMB's pronouncements hardly 'track' [Old] Rule 190.8 . . . rather, they depart from and effectively change that text," rendering the June 2011 letter a procedurally invalid amendment to Old Rule 190.8.

In response, the TMB issued an "emergency" rule on January 16, 2015, amending Old Rule 190.8. The emergency amendment mandated a "face-to-face visit or in-person evaluation" before a physician can issue a prescription. Teladoc sought and obtained a temporary injunction of the emergency rule in Texas state court. The TMB then engaged in a formal rulemaking, resulting in an April 10, 2015 vote by the TMB to adopt section 190.8(1)(L) ("New Rule 190.8") which sets forth practices the TMB deems to be violations of the Texas Medical Practices Act. According to the TMB, that new rule would require a face-to-face visit before a physician can issue a prescription to a patient, regardless of medical necessity.

Plaintiffs filed this action on April 29, 2015, asserting Defendants have committed a violation of antitrust law, as well as the Commerce Clause of the Constitution in adopting New Rule 190.8 and New Rule 174. The TMB seeks to dismiss Plaintiffs' claims, arguing they are barred by the statute of limitations, the TMB is immune from antitrust liability, and Plaintiffs have failed to state an actionable claim under the Commerce Clause. The parties have filed responsive pleadings and the motion is now ripe for review.

. . . .

III. ANALYSIS

Defendants contend the claims asserted by Plaintiffs attacking New Rule 174 should be dismissed as barred by limitations. Defendants also maintain Plaintiffs' claim of an antitrust violation is barred by the doctrine of state action immunity. Finally, Defendants argue Plaintiffs have failed to state a claim under the Commerce Clause.

A. Statute of Limitations

. . . Plaintiffs suggest it would not disserve the public interest to permit their attack to proceed. This suggestion is supported by the fact that in seeking, and obtaining, a preliminary injunction, Plaintiffs presented evidence that consumers will face higher prices for medical care, as well as reduced access as a result of the TMB's restrictions on telemedicine. The TMB provides no rebuttal to these arguments. Accordingly, the Court concludes application of laches is not justified on the facts of this case at this point. The TMB's motion to dismiss on the basis of limitations is, therefore, properly denied.

B. State Action Immunity

The TMB next contends Plaintiffs' antitrust claim is barred by the doctrine of state action immunity. States are generally permitted to regulate their economies in ways they see fit, including "impos[ing] restrictions on occupations, confer[ring] exclusive or shared rights to dominate a market, or otherwise limit[ing] competition to achieve public objectives." Thus, in most situations "federal antitrust laws are subject to supersession by state regulatory programs." As a result, the Supreme Court has "interpreted the antitrust laws to confer immunity on anticompetitive conduct by the States when acting in their sovereign capacity." However, the Supreme Court has also made clear that so-called "Parker immunity" is afforded only if two requirements are satisfied: "first that 'the challenged restraint . . . be one clearly articulated and affirmatively expressed as state policy,' and second that 'the policy . . . be actively supervised by the State.'" FTC v. Phoebe Putney Health Sys., Inc., 133 S. Ct. 1003, 1010 (2013). The Supreme Court has further cautioned that "given the fundamental national values of free enterprise and economic competition that are embodied in the federal antitrust laws, 'state-action immunity is disfavored.'" . . . . . . ' . . .

> The state-action immunity doctrine is applied sparingly by federal courts, as noted in *FTC v. Phoebe Putney* (covered in Chapter 7), because it permits state-imposed constraints on competition.

2. *Supervision*

The parties agree that a showing of active state supervision is required to obtain the protection of the state action doctrine. They disagree as to whether such supervision exists over the TMB.

An important backdrop to the case is the Supreme Court's most recent decision concerning state action immunity. At issue in that case was whether the North Carolina State Board of Dental Examiners ("the Board") was entitled to the protection of the doctrine. As in this case, the Board was largely composed of market participants. The Board argued its members were invested by North Carolina with the power of the State and thus, the Board's actions were protected by state action immunity. The Supreme Court rejected that argument, and made clear that a "nonsovereign actor controlled by active market participants — such as the Board — enjoys Parker immunity only if" it was subject to active state supervision and the challenged restraint was an expression of state policy. While the Supreme Court did not need to decide whether state supervision existed because the Board made no claim that it was actively supervised, the Court did address the issue, stating:

> It suffices to note that the inquiry regarding active supervision is flexible and context-dependent. Active supervision need not entail day-to-day involvement in an

agency's operations or micromanagement of its every decision. Rather, the question is whether the State's review mechanisms provide "realistic assurance" that a nonsovereign actor's anticompetitive conduct "promotes state policy, rather than merely the party's individual interests."

The Court has identified only a few constant requirements of active supervision: The supervisor must review the substance of the anticompetitive decision, not merely the procedures followed to produce it; the supervisor must have the power to veto or modify particular decisions to ensure they accord with state policy; and the "mere potential for state supervision is not an adequate substitute for a decision by the State." Further, the state supervisor may not itself be an active market participant. In general, however, the adequacy of supervision otherwise will depend on all the circumstances of a case. *N. Carolina State Bd.*, 135 S. Ct. at 1116-17. In this case, the TMB argues it is subject to active state supervision because its decisions are subject to judicial review by the courts of Texas and the State Office of Administrative Hearings ("SOAH"), as well as review by the Texas Legislature.

. . . In contrast, the Supreme Court has made clear that to qualify as active supervision "the supervisor must have the power to veto or modify particular decisions to ensure they accord with state policy." *N. Carolina State Bd.*, 135 S. Ct. at 1116. And the TMB has not pointed to any example of judicial review which rejected the validity of a rule on the ground it did not "accord with state policy." In addition, the judicial review on which the TMB relies merely permits a court to determine a rule is invalid. It does not, therefore, meet the Supreme Court's mandate that "the supervisor must have the power to veto or modify particular decisions to ensure they accord with state policy."

. . . Significantly, the TMB does not cite to any case supporting its view that this type of review constitutes active supervision, while Plaintiffs cite to a string of cases concluding the opposite.

. . . [T]he Supreme Court has made abundantly clear that the "mere presence of some state involvement or monitoring does not suffice." Rather, active supervision requires that state officials have and exercise power to review particular anticompetitive acts of private parties and disapprove those that fail to accord with state policy. Absent such a program of supervision, there is no realistic assurance that a private party's anticompetitive conduct promotes state policy, rather than merely the party's individual interests. Accordingly, the Court finds the TMB has failed to show the active supervision required to merit dismissal on the basis of state action immunity.

. . . As the Court has concluded the TMB has failed to show its adoption of the challenged rules is subject to active state supervision, this second requirement of state action immunity need not be addressed.

C. Dormant Commerce Clause

Plaintiffs maintain both New Rule 174 and New Rule 190.8 violate the Commerce Clause because they discriminate against physicians who are licensed in Texas, but are physically located out of state. The "negative" or so-called "dormant" aspect of the Commerce Clause prohibits "economic protectionism — that is, regulatory measures designed to benefit in-state economic interests by burdening out-of-state competitors." Dep't of Revenue of Ky. v. Davis, 553 U.S. 328, 337-38 (2008). The Supreme Court has made clear "[t]ime and again," that state laws violate the Commerce Clause if they mandate "differential treatment of in-state and out-of-state economic interests that benefits the former and burdens the latter." Granholm v. Heald, 544 U.S. 460, 472 (2005). . . .

In pertinent part, Texas law provides that "[t]he Texas Medical Board is an agency of the executive branch of state government with the power to regulate the practice of medicine." This statement clearly indicates the TMB acts on behalf of the state. Plaintiffs correctly point out that the question of immunity from anti-trust liability rests on a different determination. That is, whether the TMB is subject to active state supervision in its decisions which have an anti-competitive effect. In contrast, liability under Section 1983 requires only a showing that the TMB is a state actor. Accordingly, Plaintiffs' Commerce Clause claim need not be dismissed on this basis.

Finally, the TMB maintains Plaintiffs cannot establish more than "an indirect burden on interstate commerce" which does not violate the Commerce Clause. The Fifth Circuit has explained:

> A statute violates the dormant Commerce Clause where it discriminates against interstate commerce either facially, by purpose, or by effect. If the statute impermissibly discriminates, then it is valid only if the **state** "can demonstrate, under rigorous scrutiny, that it has no other means to advance a legitimate local interest." If the statute does not discriminate, then the statute is valid unless the burden imposed on interstate commerce is "**clearly** excessive" in relation to the putative local benefits.

Allstate Ins. Co. v. Abbott, 495 F.3d 151, 160 (5th Cir. 2007).

As Plaintiffs point out, both New Rule 174 and New Rule 190.8 require a physician to provide an in-person physical exam of a patient to create a relationship with that patient. They maintain this requirement constitutes intentional discrimination against physicians located out of Texas and cannot withstand the strict scrutiny applicable to such regulations. Plaintiffs concede the regulation is facially neutral, but contend the regulation is nonetheless subject to rigorous scrutiny because, even though it does "not in explicit terms seek to regulate interstate commerce, it does so nonetheless by its practical effect and design." The TMB, in turn, contends the challenged rules are not discriminatory, and thus not subject to rigorous scrutiny. The TMB further maintains the rules withstand the lower level of scrutiny as Plaintiffs have not alleged facts sufficient to show[ ] any burden imposed is "**clearly** excessive" in relation to the local benefits. . . .

Plaintiffs further argue, even if the challenged rules are not viewed as discriminatory in effect and design, the rules cannot withstand a Commerce Clause challenge under even the lesser standard. In support, Plaintiffs point to their allegations that Teladoc's business model, including obtaining and retaining national clients, depends on being able to provide telehealth in Texas without the requirement of conducting an in-person physical exam before treating patients. Plaintiffs have further alleged the challenged rules do not provide local benefits because the current regulatory scheme mandates that physicians abide by standards of care which dictate when an in-person physical exam is necessary. Further, they have alleged that the current standard of care permits a physician to provide "on-call" services to patients of other physicians without an in-person physical exam. Finally, Plaintiffs have alleged the challenged rules are affirmatively harmful to public health because they reduce access to affordable and convenient treatment.

The Court finds Plaintiffs' allegations sufficient at this early stage of the litigation. Resolution of Plaintiffs' Commence Clause challenge is "one of degree," requiring the Court to determine "the nature of the local interest involved, and [ ] whether it could be promoted as well with a lesser impact on interstate activities." This inquiry is inherently fact-intensive. Accordingly, the Court declines to dismiss Plaintiffs' Commerce Clause claim at this time.

Accordingly, the Court hereby DENIES Defendants' Amended Motion to Dismiss.

QUESTIONS

1. Did the TMB have legitimate concerns that could be addressed by prohibiting the prescribing of controlled substances through a telemedicine consult? Are those concerns related to health privacy, confidentiality, or something else?
2. Teladoc has not won the case, but its claims survived a motion to dismiss on multiple causes of action that are somewhat unusual. Why is the district court willing to allow Teladoc to pursue its federal claims given the long-standing role of states in the regulation of medicine?

Texas is one of many states that have a deep divide between sophisticated health care resources in major metropolitan areas and vast rural areas that suffer perennial shortages of health care providers as well as medical resource challenges. Telemedicine is considered by both federal and state governments to be an inexpensive and generally safe way to facilitate health care access in rural areas, as evidenced by the regulatory authorities at the start of this section. Rural areas have long suffered from health care shortages, and widespread use of electronic resources may increase access to health care, but perhaps at the expense of patient privacy and confidentiality.

CAPSTONE PROBLEM

Find the model business associate agreement on the HHS OCR Web site. Now imagine that you are in-house counsel for a hospital in the state of Hipaadom, and you are about to contract with a new management company for billing and other services. Does the model business associate agreement cover everything the hospital needs in the agreement? Could or should this agreement be combined with any of the contractual writings required by the fraud and abuse laws covered in Chapter 6? What would change in the contract, if anything, when the Hipaadom Court of Appeals permits common law actions to proceed against hospitals that fail to properly supervise privacy practices of business associates?

CHAPTER 11

Regulation of Biomedical Research on Humans

"Well what do you expect from Hopkins?," Bobbette yelled from the kitchen. . . . "I wouldn't even go there to get my toenails cut." . . .

"Back then they did things," Sonny said. "Especially to black folks. John Hopkins was known for experimentin on black folks. They'd snatch em off the street. . . ."

"That's right!" Bobbette said, appearing in the kitchen door with her coffee. "Everybody knows that."

"They just snatch em off the street," Sonny said.

"Snatchin people!" Bobbette yelled, her voice growing louder.

"Experimentin on them!" Sonny yelled.

"You'd be surprised how many people disappeared in East Baltimore when I was a girl," Bobbette said, shaking her head. "I'm telling you, I lived here in the fifties when they got Henrietta, and we weren't allowed to go anywhere near Hopkins. When it got dark and we were young, we had to be *on the steps*, or Hopkins might get us."

The Lackses aren't the only ones who heard from a young age that Hopkins and other hospitals abducted black people. Since at least the 1800s, black oral history has been filled with tales of "night doctors" who kidnapped black people for research. And there were disturbing truths behind those stories. . . .

. . . Many doctors tested drugs on slaves and operated on them to develop new surgical techniques, often without using anesthesia. Fear of night doctors only increased in the early 1900s, as black people migrated north to Washington, D. C., and Baltimore, and news spread that medical schools there were offering money in exchange for bodies. Black corpses were routinely exhumed from graves for research. . . .

—Rebecca Skloot, *The Immortal Life of Henrietta Lacks* 165-166 (2010).

A. INTRODUCTION

Innovation introduces new drugs, devices, biologics, gene therapies, and personalized medicine to health care. Research and innovation offer hope to patients with incurable medical conditions. But the research that leads to breakthrough therapies has a long history studded with cautionary tales about mistreated and injured human research subjects. Research may be therapeutic, meaning it benefits the individual who is participating in a study in addition to the public, or it may be nontherapeutic, meaning it contributes to generalized knowledge.

Clinical trials of drugs and devices intended for marketing to humans test the safety and efficacy of new therapies and typically include four phases following pre-clinical, or laboratory, research. Clinical trials involving humans begin with "Phase I," which involves testing an experimental drug or treatment in a small group of people for the first time. Researchers evaluate the treatment's safety, determine a safe dosage range, and begin to identify side effects. "Phase II" trials assess the experimental drug or treatment in a larger group of people to determine if it is effective and to further evaluate its safety. "Phase III" trials give the drug or treatment to an even larger group of people to confirm its effectiveness, monitor side effects, compare with existing treatments, and collect other information that will allow the experimental drug or treatment to be used safely. "Phase IV" trials are "post-marketing studies" that are conducted after the FDA has approved a drug or treatment to provide additional information on the safety or efficacy of a new therapy. Clinical trials end during Phases I through III if the new therapy proves too risky.

> The Food and Drug Administration regulates clinical trials, but the Office for Human Research Protections is responsible for protecting the individuals participating in clinical trials; both are sub-agencies of HHS.

Whether therapeutic or nontherapeutic, the golden rule of clinical research is that subjects must provide informed consent. Nevertheless, history is littered with examples of researchers flouting ethical and legal rules, sometimes to further the public good, sometimes to line their own pockets, and sometimes for other reasons. Many students will have studied Nazi exploitation of concentration camp prisoners in the name of scientific research; this was perhaps the most widespread and egregious example of using non-consenting human subjects in the name of performing nontherapeutic medical research. But research abuses are neither a thing of the past nor isolated to foreign, wartime, or other settings. Many abuses have been perpetrated by researchers in the United States both on a large scale — for example, in the Tuskegee Syphilis Experiment and the Guatemala Syphilis Experiment — and on an individual scale, such as Henrietta Lacks's cancer cells being taken without her knowledge and used to make HeLa, the most prolific cell line ever established for scientific research. None of the subjects of these experiments knew that they were participating in research. In many of these studies, the individuals subject to research were harmed by the researchers, who knowingly withheld information that would likely have halted participation in the research. In some instances, the researchers withheld medical treatment that would have saved many lives.

> As you read the opinion, contemplate how you would have advised Dr. Golde to perform his research differently.

To begin, consider the classic case of *Moore v. Regents of the University of California*, which many encounter during their first year of law school. This decision offers an example of therapeutic research run amok.

Moore v. Regents of University of California

51 Cal. 3d 120 (1990)

. . . [W]e briefly summarize the pertinent factual allegations of the 50-page complaint. The plaintiff is John Moore (Moore), who underwent treatment for hairy-cell leukemia at the Medical Center of the University of California at Los Angeles (UCLA Medical Center). The five defendants are: (1) Dr. David W. Golde (Golde), a physician who attended Moore at UCLA Medical Center; (2) the Regents of the University of California (Regents), who own and operate the university; (3) Shirley G. Quan, a researcher employed by the Regents; (4) Genetics Institute, Inc. (Genetics Institute); and (5) Sandoz Pharmaceuticals Corporation and related entities (collectively Sandoz).

Moore first visited UCLA Medical Center on October 5, 1976, shortly after he learned that he had hairy-cell leukemia. After hospitalizing Moore and "withdr [awing] extensive amounts of blood, bone marrow aspirate, and other bodily substances," Golde confirmed that diagnosis. At this time all defendants, including Golde, were aware that "certain blood products and blood components were of great value in a number of commercial and scientific efforts" and that access to a patient whose blood contained these substances would provide "competitive, commercial, and scientific advantages."

On October 8, 1976, Golde recommended that Moore's spleen be removed. Golde informed Moore "that he had reason to fear for his life, and that the proposed splenectomy operation . . . was necessary to slow down the progress of his disease." Based upon Golde's representations, Moore signed a written consent form authorizing the splenectomy.

> Why was this written consent insufficient?

Before the operation, Golde and Quan "formed the intent and made arrangements to obtain portions of [Moore's] spleen following its removal" and to take them to a separate research unit. Golde gave written instructions to this effect on October 18 and 19, 1976. These research activities "were not intended to have . . . any relation to [Moore's] medical . . . care." However, neither Golde nor Quan informed Moore of their plans to conduct this research or requested his permission. Surgeons at UCLA Medical Center, whom the complaint does not name as defendants, removed Moore's spleen on October 20, 1976.

Moore returned to the UCLA Medical Center several times between November 1976 and September 1983. He did so at Golde's direction and based upon representations "that such visits were necessary and required for his health and well-being, and based upon the trust inherent in and by virtue of the physician-patient relationship. . . ." On each of these visits Golde withdrew additional samples of "blood, blood serum, skin, bone marrow aspirate, and sperm." On each occasion Moore travelled to the UCLA Medical Center from his home in Seattle because he had been told that the procedures were to be performed only there and only under Golde's direction.

"In fact, [however,] throughout the period of time that [Moore] was under [Golde's] care and treatment, . . . the defendants were actively involved in a number of activities which they concealed from [Moore]. . . ." Specifically, defendants were conducting research on Moore's cells and planned to "benefit financially and competitively . . . [by exploiting the cells] and [their] exclusive access to [the cells] by virtue of [Golde's] on-going physician-patient relationship. . . ."

Sometime before August 1979, Golde established a cell line from Moore's T-lymphocytes. On January 30, 1981, the Regents applied for a patent on the cell line, listing Golde and Quan as inventors. "[B]y virtue of an established policy . . . , [the] Regents, Golde, and Quan would share in any royalties or profits . . . arising out of [the] patent." The patent issued on March 20, 1984, naming Golde and Quan as the inventors of the cell line and the Regents as the assignee of the patent.

The Regent[s'] patent also covers various methods for using the cell line to produce lymphokines. Moore admits in his complaint that "the true clinical potential of each of the lymphokines . . . [is] difficult to predict, [but] . . . competing commercial firms in these relevant fields have published reports in biotechnology industry periodicals predicting a potential market of approximately $3.01 Billion Dollars by the year 1990 for a whole range of [such lymphokines]. . . ."

With the Regents' assistance, Golde negotiated agreements for commercial development of the cell line and products to be derived from it. Under an agreement with Genetics Institute, Golde "became a paid consultant" and "acquired the rights to 75,000 shares of common stock." Genetics Institute also agreed to pay Golde and the Regents "at least $330,000 over three years, including a pro-rata share of [Golde's] salary and fringe benefits, in exchange for . . . exclusive access to the materials and research performed" on the cell line and products derived from it. On June 4, 1982, Sandoz "was added to the agreement," and compensation payable to Golde and the Regents was increased by $110,000. "[T]hroughout this period, . . . Quan spent as much as 70 [percent] of her time working for [the] Regents on research" related to the cell line.

Based upon these allegations, Moore attempted to state 13 causes of action. Each defendant demurred to each purported cause of action. The superior court, however, expressly considered the validity of only the first cause of action, conversion. . . .

III. DISCUSSION

A. Breach of Fiduciary Duty and Lack of Informed Consent

Moore repeatedly alleges that Golde failed to disclose the extent of his research and economic interests in Moore's cells before obtaining consent to the medical procedures by which the cells were extracted. These allegations, in our view, state a cause of action against Golde for invading a legally protected interest of his patient. This cause of action can properly be characterized either as the breach of a fiduciary duty to disclose facts material to the patient's consent or, alternatively, as the performance of medical procedures without first having obtained the patient's informed consent.

Our analysis begins with three well-established principles. First, "a person of adult years and in sound mind has the right, in the exercise of control over his own body, to determine whether or not to submit to lawful medical treatment." (Cobbs v. Grant (1972) 8 Cal.3d 229, 242; cf. Schloendorff v. Society of New York Hospital (1914) 211 N.Y. 125.) Second, "the patient's consent to treatment, to be effective, must be an informed consent." Third, in soliciting the patient's consent, a physician has a fiduciary duty to disclose all information material to the patient's decision.

Physicians earn money by treating patients. How far should the court's fiduciary duty concept reach?

These principles lead to the following conclusions: (1) a physician must disclose personal interests unrelated to the patient's health, whether research or economic, that may affect the physician's professional judgment; and (2) a physician's failure to disclose such interests may give rise to a cause of action for performing medical procedures without informed consent or breach of fiduciary duty.

To be sure, questions about the validity of a patient's consent to a procedure typically arise when the patient alleges that the physician failed to disclose medical risks, as in malpractice cases, and not when the patient alleges that the physician had a personal interest, as in this case. The concept of informed consent, however, is broad enough to encompass the latter. "The scope of the physician's communication to the patient . . . must be measured by the patient's need, and that need is whatever information is material to the decision." . . .

It is important to note that no law prohibits a physician from conducting research in the same area in which he practices. Progress in medicine often depends upon physicians, such as those practicing at the university hospital where Moore received treatment, who conduct research while caring for their patients.

Yet a physician who treats a patient in whom he also has a research interest has potentially conflicting loyalties. This is because medical treatment decisions are made on the basis of proportionality — weighing the benefits to the patient against the risks to the patient. As another court has said, "the determination as to whether the burdens of treatment are worth enduring for any individual patient depends upon the facts unique in each case," and "the patient's interests and desires are the key ingredients of the decision-making process." (Barber v. Superior Court, 147 Cal. App. 3d 1006, 1018-1019 (1983).) A physician who adds his own research interests to this balance may be tempted to order a scientifically useful procedure or test that offers marginal, or no, benefits to the patient. The possibility that an interest extraneous to the patient's health has affected the physician's judgment is something that a reasonable patient would want to know in deciding whether to consent to a proposed course of treatment. It is material to the patient's decision and, thus, a prerequisite to informed consent.

Golde argues that the scientific use of cells that have already been removed cannot possibly affect the patient's medical interests. The argument is correct in one instance but not in another. If a physician has no plans to conduct research on a patient's cells at the time he recommends the medical procedure by which they are taken, then the patient's medical interests have not been impaired. In that instance the argument is correct. On the other hand, a physician who does have a preexisting research interest might, consciously or unconsciously, take that into consideration in recommending the procedure. In that instance the argument is incorrect: the physician's extraneous motivation may affect his judgment and is, thus, material to the patient's consent.

We acknowledge that there is a competing consideration. To require disclosure of research and economic interests may corrupt the patient's own judgment by distracting him from the requirements of his health. But California law does not grant physicians unlimited discretion to decide what to disclose. Instead, "it is the prerogative of the patient, not the physician, to determine for himself the direction in which he believes his interests lie." "Unlimited discretion in the physician is irreconcilable with the basic right of the patient to make the ultimate informed decision. . . ."

Accordingly, we hold that a physician who is seeking a patient's consent for a medical procedure must, in order to satisfy his fiduciary duty and to obtain the patient's informed consent, disclose personal interests unrelated to the patient's health, whether research or economic, that may affect his medical judgment.

> The decision rests with the patient, not the physician; therefore, the physician must disclose conflicts of interest.

1. Dr. Golde

We turn now to the allegations of Moore's third amended complaint to determine whether he has stated such a cause of action. We first discuss the adequacy of Moore's allegations against Golde, based upon the physician's disclosures prior to the splenectomy.

Moore alleges that, prior to the surgical removal of his spleen, Golde "formed the intent and made arrangements to obtain portions of his spleen following its removal from [Moore] in connection with [his] desire to have regular and continuous access to, and possession of, [Moore's] unique and rare Blood and Bodily Substances." Moore was never informed prior to the splenectomy of Golde's "prior formed intent" to obtain a portion of his spleen. In our view, these allegations adequately show that Golde had an undisclosed research interest in Moore's cells at the time he sought Moore's consent to the splenectomy. Accordingly, Moore has stated a cause of action for breach of fiduciary duty, or lack of informed consent, based upon the disclosures accompanying that medical procedure.

We next discuss the adequacy of Golde's alleged disclosures regarding the postoperative takings of blood and other samples. In this context, Moore alleges that Golde "expressly, affirmatively and impliedly represented . . . that these withdrawals of his Blood and Bodily Substances were necessary and required for his health and well-being." However, Moore also alleges that Golde actively concealed his economic interest in Moore's cells during this time period. "[D]uring each of these visits . . . , and even when [Moore] inquired as to whether there was any possible or potential commercial or financial value or significance of his Blood and Bodily Substances, or whether the defendants had discovered anything . . . which was or might be . . . related to any scientific activity resulting in commercial or financial benefits . . . , the defendants repeatedly and affirmatively represented to [Moore] that there was no commercial or financial value to his Blood and Bodily Substances . . . and in fact actively discouraged such inquiries."

Moore admits in his complaint that defendants disclosed they "were engaged in strictly academic and purely scientific medical research. . . ." However, Golde's representation that he had no financial interest in this research became false, based upon the allegations, at least by May 1979, when he "began to investigate and initiate the procedures . . . for [obtaining] a patent" on the cell line developed from Moore's cells.

In these allegations, Moore plainly asserts that Golde concealed an economic interest in the postoperative procedures. Therefore, applying the principles already discussed, the allegations state a cause of action for breach of fiduciary duty or lack of informed consent.

We thus disagree with the superior court's ruling that Moore had not stated a cause of action because essential allegations were lacking. . . . Even if the splenectomy had a therapeutic purpose, it does not follow that Golde had no duty to disclose his additional research and economic interests. As we have already discussed, the existence of a motivation for a medical procedure unrelated to the patient's health is a potential conflict of interest and a fact material to the patient's decision.

2. The Remaining Defendants

The Regents, Quan, Genetics Institute, and Sandoz are not physicians. In contrast to Golde, none of these defendants stood in a fiduciary relationship with Moore or had the duty to obtain Moore's informed consent to medical procedures. If any of these defendants is to be liable for breach of fiduciary duty or performing medical procedures without informed consent, it can only be on account of Golde's acts and on the basis of a recognized theory of secondary liability, such as respondeat superior. The procedural posture of this case, however, makes it unnecessary for us to address the sufficiency of Moore's secondary-liability allegations.

[The court then rejected the conversion claim, which argued that the cells had been stolen and were still Moore's property, despite the patents.]

Society places great emphasis on trust and fiduciary relationships in health care, ideals that are reflected in both legal and ethical standards. As *Moore* demonstrates, these are particularly complex issues when a physician is treating a patient while also studying that patient for research purposes. The fiduciary relationship between doctor and patient is even more complex when external considerations may affect the caregiver's judgment; in some ways, the law here echoes the fraud and abuse laws discussed in Chapter 6.

This chapter introduces the complex field of clinical research on human subjects from the perspective of the regulatory structure an individual or institutional health care provider will encounter. By the end of the chapter, we learn that any systematized conduct that contributes to generalized knowledge, rather than treatment of the individual patient, can be considered research under federal law and requires informed consent. With the designation "research" comes a host of rules designed to protect the human subject that can create liability in torts, contracts, fiduciary duties, and other areas. Before studying national laws and state-based common law, we begin with the vital backdrop of ethical guidelines that predated subject-protective laws in the United States by decades.

B. ETHICAL PRINCIPLES

Before the United States began to regulate research on humans for medical knowledge, international organizations created ethical codes designed to guide researchers and heighten their awareness of the vulnerability of research subjects. The two most important international codes are provided here. The first is the famous Nuremberg Code, written in response to the testimony detailing war crimes and crimes against humanity committed by Nazi doctors. The war crime tribunal's indictment included the following counts:

COUNT TWO—WAR CRIMES

6. Between September 1939 and April 1945 all of the defendants herein unlawfully, willfully, and knowingly committed war crimes, as defined by Article II of Control Council Law No. 10, in that they were principals in, accessories to, ordered, abetted, took a consenting part in, and were connected with plans and enterprises involving medical experiments without the subjects' consent, upon civilians and members of the armed forces of nations then at war with the German Reich and who were in the custody of the German Reich in exercise of belligerent control, in the course of which experiments the

> Note the emphasis on the idea of "consent." Under current legal and ethical standards, a prisoner of war could not provide consent to any human subject experimentation. But at the time, no such legal standards were clearly articulated.

defendants committed murders, brutalities, cruelties, tortures, atrocities, and other inhuman acts. Such experiments included, but were not limited to, the following:

A) High-Altitude Experiments

B) Freezing Experiments

C) Malaria Experiments

D) Lost (Mustard) Gas Experiments

E) Sulfanilamide Experiments

F) Bone, Muscle, and Nerve Regeneration and Bone Transplantation Experiments

G) Sea-Water Experiments

H) Epidemic Jaundice Experiments

I) Sterilization Experiments

J) Spotted Fever (Fleckfieber) Experiments

K) Experiments with Poison

L) Incendiary Bomb Experiments

7. Between June 1943 and September 1944 the defendants Rudolf Brandt and Sievers unlawfully, willfully, and knowingly committed war crimes, . . . in that they were principals in, accessories to, ordered, abetted, took a consenting part in, and were connected with plans and enterprises involving the murder of civilians and members of the armed forces of nations then at war with the German Reich and who were in the custody of the German Reich in exercise of belligerent control. One hundred twelve Jews were selected for the purpose of completing a skeleton collection for the Reich University of Strasbourg. Their photographs and anthropological measurements were taken. Then they were killed. Thereafter, comparison tests, anatomical research, studies regarding race, pathological features of the body, form and size of the brain, and other tests, were made. The bodies were sent to Strasbourg and defleshed. . . .

QUESTIONS

We cannot unlearn ill-gotten information. If members of the military currently benefit from the research knowledge gained by Nazi doctors on unconsenting prisoners, can that knowledge be used ethically? Is there an ethical path forward? (Reconsider this question after reading the Belmont Report, below.)

The Nuremberg Code attempted to address the transgressions perpetrated in the name of research benefitting medical knowledge and military personnel's survival. Though it does not have the same force as domestic law, the Code is influential in many countries' laws addressing research on human subjects.

Nuremberg Code

1. The voluntary consent of the human subject is absolutely essential.

This means that the person involved should have legal capacity to give consent; should be so situated as to be able to exercise free power of choice, without the intervention of any element of force, fraud, deceit, duress, over-reaching, or other ulterior form of constraint or coercion; and should have sufficient knowledge and comprehension of the elements of the subject matter involved, as to enable him to make an understanding and enlightened decision. This latter element requires that, before the acceptance of an affirmative decision by the experimental subject, there should be made known to him the nature, duration, and purpose of the experiment; the method and means by which it is to be conducted; all inconveniences and hazards reasonably to be expected; and the effects upon his health or person, which may possibly come from his participation in the experiment.

The duty and responsibility for ascertaining the quality of the consent rests upon each individual who initiates, directs or engages in the experiment. It is a personal duty and responsibility which may not be delegated to another with impunity.

2. The experiment should be such as to yield fruitful results for the good of society, unprocurable by other methods or means of study, and not random and unnecessary in nature.

3. The experiment should be so designed and based on the results of animal experimentation and a knowledge of the natural history of the disease or other problem under study, that the anticipated results will justify the performance of the experiment.

4. The experiment should be so conducted as to avoid all unnecessary physical and mental suffering and injury.

5. No experiment should be conducted, where there is an a priori reason to believe that death or disabling injury will occur; except, perhaps, in those experiments where the experimental physicians also serve as subjects.

6. The degree of risk to be taken should never exceed that determined by the humanitarian importance of the problem to be solved by the experiment.

7. Proper preparations should be made and adequate facilities provided to protect the experimental subject against even remote possibilities of injury, disability, or death.

8. The experiment should be conducted only by scientifically qualified persons. The highest degree of skill and care should be required through all stages of the experiment of those who conduct or engage in the experiment.

9. During the course of the experiment, the human subject should be at liberty to bring the experiment to an end, if he has reached the physical or mental state, where continuation of the experiment seemed to him to be impossible.

10. During the course of the experiment, the scientist in charge must be prepared to terminate the experiment at any stage, if he has probable cause to believe, in the exercise of the good faith, superior skill and careful judgement required of him, that a continuation of the experiment is likely to result in injury, disability, or death to the experimental subject.

> Today, most interventional human subject research will have an independent safety committee, with the power to terminate the experiment early for safety reasons.

QUESTION

Could research on children with cancer be performed in conformity with the Nuremberg Code?

The second key international document, the Declaration of Helsinki, was a document drafted by the World Medical Association (WMA) in 1964 that has been adopted by branches of the WMA in many countries around the world over the years. Though it, too, does not have the force of law, it ethically obligates physicians to consider their role in research on human subjects and has influenced laws pertaining to medical research.

Declaration of Helsinki ("The Helsinki Accord") (2013 edition)
Preamble

1. The World Medical Association (WMA) has developed the Declaration of Helsinki as a statement of ethical principles for medical research involving human subjects, including research on identifiable human material and data.

The Declaration is intended to be read as a whole and each of its constituent paragraphs should be applied with consideration of all other relevant paragraphs.

2. Consistent with the mandate of the WMA, the Declaration is addressed primarily to physicians. The WMA encourages others who are involved in medical research involving human subjects to adopt these principles.

General Principles

3. The Declaration of Geneva of the WMA binds the physician with the words, "The health of my patient will be my first consideration," and the International Code of Medical Ethics declares that, "A physician shall act in the patient's best interest when providing medical care."

4. It is the duty of the physician to promote and safeguard the health, wellbeing and rights of patients, including those who are involved in medical research. The physician's knowledge and conscience are dedicated to the fulfilment of this duty.

5. Medical progress is based on research that ultimately must include studies involving human subjects.

6. The primary purpose of medical research involving human subjects is to understand the causes, development and effects of diseases and improve preventive, diagnostic and therapeutic interventions (methods, procedures and treatments). Even the best proven interventions must be evaluated continually through research for their safety, effectiveness, efficiency, accessibility and quality.

7. Medical research is subject to ethical standards that promote and ensure respect for all human subjects and protect their health and rights.

8. While the primary purpose of medical research is to generate new knowledge, this goal can never take precedence over the rights and interests of individual research subjects.

9. It is the duty of physicians who are involved in medical research to protect the life, health, dignity, integrity, right to self-determination, privacy, and confidentiality of personal information of research subjects. The responsibility for the protection of research subjects must always rest with the physician or other health care professionals and never with the research subjects, even though they have given consent.

10. Physicians must consider the ethical, legal and regulatory norms and standards for research involving human subjects in their own countries as well as applicable international norms and standards. No national or international ethical, legal or regulatory requirement should reduce or eliminate any of the protections for research subjects set forth in this Declaration.

11. Medical research should be conducted in a manner that minimises possible harm to the environment.

12. Medical research involving human subjects must be conducted only by individuals with the appropriate ethics and scientific education, training and qualifications. Research on patients or healthy volunteers requires the supervision of a competent and appropriately qualified physician or other health care professional.

Which of these provisions were violated several years later by Dr. Golde in *Moore v. Regents*?

13. Groups that are underrepresented in medical research should be provided appropriate access to participation in research.

14. Physicians who combine medical research with medical care should involve their patients in research only to the extent that this is justified by its potential preventive, diagnostic or therapeutic value and if the physician has good reason to believe that participation in the research study will not adversely affect the health of the patients who serve as research subjects.

15. Appropriate compensation and treatment for subjects who are harmed as a result of participating in research must be ensured.

Risks, Burdens and Benefits

16. In medical practice and in medical research, most interventions involve risks and burdens.

Medical research involving human subjects may only be conducted if the importance of the objective outweighs the risks and burdens to the research subjects.

17. All medical research involving human subjects must be preceded by careful assessment of predictable risks and burdens to the individuals and groups involved in the research in comparison with foreseeable benefits to them and to other individuals or groups affected by the condition under investigation.

Measures to minimise the risks must be implemented. The risks must be continuously monitored, assessed and documented by the researcher.

18. Physicians may not be involved in a research study involving human subjects unless they are confident that the risks have been adequately assessed and can be satisfactorily managed.

When the risks are found to outweigh the potential benefits or when there is conclusive proof of definitive outcomes, physicians must assess whether to continue, modify or immediately stop the study.

Vulnerable Groups and Individuals

19. Some groups and individuals are particularly vulnerable and may have an increased likelihood of being wronged or of incurring additional harm.

All vulnerable groups and individuals should receive specifically considered protection.

20. Medical research with a vulnerable group is only justified if the research is responsive to the health needs or priorities of this group and the research cannot be carried out in a non-vulnerable group. In addition, this group should stand to benefit from the knowledge, practices or interventions that result from the research.

Scientific Requirements and Research Protocols

21. Medical research involving human subjects must conform to generally accepted scientific principles, be based on a thorough knowledge of the

scientific literature, other relevant sources of information, and adequate laboratory and, as appropriate, animal experimentation. The welfare of animals used for research must be respected.

22. The design and performance of each research study involving human subjects must be clearly described and justified in a research protocol.

The protocol should contain a statement of the ethical considerations involved and should indicate how the principles in this Declaration have been addressed. The protocol should include information regarding funding, sponsors, institutional affiliations, potential conflicts of interest, incentives for subjects and information regarding provisions for treating and/or compensating subjects who are harmed as a consequence of participation in the research study.

In clinical trials, the protocol must also describe appropriate arrangements for post-trial provisions.

Research Ethics Committees

23. The research protocol must be submitted for consideration, comment, guidance and approval to the concerned research ethics committee before the study begins. This committee must be transparent in its functioning, must be independent of the researcher, the sponsor and any other undue influence and must be duly qualified. It must take into consideration the laws and regulations of the country or countries in which the research is to be performed as well as applicable international norms and standards but these must not be allowed to reduce or eliminate any of the protections for research subjects set forth in this Declaration.

The committee must have the right to monitor ongoing studies. The researcher must provide monitoring information to the committee, especially information about any serious adverse events. No amendment to the protocol may be made without consideration and approval by the committee. After the end of the study, the researchers must submit a final report to the committee containing a summary of the study's findings and conclusions.

Privacy and Confidentiality

24. Every precaution must be taken to protect the privacy of research subjects and the confidentiality of their personal information.

Informed Consent

25. Participation by individuals capable of giving informed consent as subjects in medical research must be voluntary. Although it may be appropriate to consult family members or community leaders, no individual capable of giving informed consent may be enrolled in a research study unless he or she freely agrees.

26. In medical research involving human subjects capable of giving informed consent, each potential subject must be adequately informed of the aims, methods, sources of funding, any possible conflicts of interest, institutional affiliations of the researcher, the anticipated benefits and potential risks of the study and the discomfort it may entail, post-study provisions and any other relevant aspects of the study. The potential subject must be informed of the right to refuse to participate in the study or to withdraw consent to participate at any time without reprisal. Special attention should be given to the specific information needs of individual potential subjects as well as to the methods used to deliver the information.

After ensuring that the potential subject has understood the information, the physician or another appropriately qualified individual must then seek the potential subject's freely-given informed consent, preferably in writing. If the consent cannot be expressed in writing, the non-written consent must be formally documented and witnessed.

All medical research subjects should be given the option of being informed about the general outcome and results of the study.

> How do we know if patients understand the long consent forms that have developed in the years following Helsinki?

27. When seeking informed consent for participation in a research study the physician must be particularly cautious if the potential subject is in a dependent relationship with the physician or may consent under duress. In such situations the informed consent must be sought by an appropriately qualified individual who is completely independent of this relationship.

28. For a potential research subject who is incapable of giving informed consent, the physician must seek informed consent from the legally authorised representative. These individuals must not be included in a research study that has no likelihood of benefit for them unless it is intended to promote the health of the group represented by the potential subject, the research cannot instead be performed with persons capable of providing informed consent, and the research entails only minimal risk and minimal burden.

29. When a potential research subject who is deemed incapable of giving informed consent is able to give assent to decisions about participation in research, the physician must seek that assent in addition to the consent of the legally authorised representative. The potential subject's dissent should be respected.

30. Research involving subjects who are physically or mentally incapable of giving consent, for example, unconscious patients, may be done only if the physical or mental condition that prevents giving informed consent is a necessary characteristic of the research group. In such circumstances the physician must seek informed consent from the legally authorised representative. If no such representative is available and if the research cannot be delayed, the study may proceed without informed consent provided that the specific reasons for involving subjects with a condition that renders them unable to give informed consent have been stated in the research protocol and the study has been approved by a research ethics committee. Consent to remain in the research must be obtained as soon as possible from the subject or a legally authorised representative.

31. The physician must fully inform the patient which aspects of their care are related to the research. The refusal of a patient to participate in a study or the patient's decision to withdraw from the study must never adversely affect the patient-physician relationship.

32. For medical research using identifiable human material or data, such as research on material or data contained in biobanks or similar repositories, physicians must seek informed consent for its collection, storage and/or reuse. There may be exceptional situations where consent would be impossible or impracticable to obtain for such research. In such situations the research may be done only after consideration and approval of a research ethics committee . . . .

The horror of the human rights violations revealed during the Nuremberg Trials created widespread concern for individuals participating in medical research. The Helsinki Declaration followed in 1964. But the United States did not act to protect research subjects through federal laws until the National Research Act of 1974, Pub. L. No. 93-348, created a commission to study the problems internal to the United States. That commission issued the "Belmont Report," reproduced below, which was the United States' first comprehensive attempt to regulate research on human subjects.

The Belmont Report Office of the Secretary Ethical Principles and Guidelines for the Protection of Human Subjects of Research The National Commission for the Protection of Human Subjects of Biomedical and Behavioral Research

April 18, 1979

Ethical Principles & Guidelines for Research Involving Human Subjects

Scientific research has produced substantial social benefits. It has also posed some troubling ethical questions. Public attention was drawn to these questions by reported abuses of human subjects in biomedical experiments, especially during the Second World War. During the Nuremberg War Crime Trials, the Nuremberg code was drafted as a set of standards for judging physicians and scientists who had conducted biomedical experiments on concentration camp prisoners. This code became the prototype of many later codes intended to assure that research involving human subjects would be carried out in an ethical manner.

The codes consist of rules, some general, others specific, that guide the investigators or the reviewers of research in their work. Such rules often are inadequate to cover complex situations; at times they come into conflict, and they are frequently difficult to interpret or apply. Broader ethical principles will provide a basis on which specific rules may be formulated, criticized and interpreted.

Three principles, or general prescriptive judgments, that are relevant to research involving human subjects are identified in this statement. Other principles may also be relevant. These three are comprehensive, however, and are stated at a level of generalization that should assist scientists, subjects, reviewers and interested citizens to understand the ethical issues inherent in research involving human subjects. These principles cannot always be applied so as to resolve beyond dispute particular ethical problems. The objective is to provide an analytical framework that will guide the resolution of ethical problems arising from research involving human subjects.

This statement consists of a distinction between research and practice, a discussion of the three basic ethical principles, and remarks about the application of these principles.

Part A: Boundaries Between Practice & Research

It is important to distinguish between biomedical and behavioral research, on the one hand, and the practice of accepted therapy on the other, in order to know what activities ought to undergo review for the protection of human subjects of research. The distinction between research and practice is blurred partly because both often occur together (as in research designed to evaluate a therapy) and partly because notable departures from standard practice are often called "experimental" when the terms "experimental" and "research" are not carefully defined.

For the most part, the term "practice" refers to interventions that are designed solely to enhance the well-being of an individual patient or client and that have a reasonable expectation of success. The purpose of medical or behavioral practice is to provide diagnosis, preventive treatment or therapy to particular individuals. By contrast, the term "research" designates an activity designed to test an hypothesis, permit conclusions to be drawn, and thereby to develop or contribute to generalizable knowledge (expressed, for example, in theories, principles, and statements of relationships). Research is usually described in a formal protocol that sets forth an objective and a set of procedures designed to reach that objective.

When a clinician departs in a significant way from standard or accepted practice, the innovation does not, in and of itself, constitute research. The fact that a procedure is "experimental," in the sense of new, untested or different, does not automatically place it in the category of research. Radically new procedures of this description should, however, be made the object of formal research at an early stage in order to determine whether they are safe and effective. Thus, it is the responsibility of medical practice committees, for example, to insist that a major innovation be incorporated into a formal research project.

Research and practice may be carried on together when research is designed to evaluate the safety and efficacy of a therapy. This need not cause any confusion regarding whether or not the activity requires review; the general rule is that if there is any element of research in an activity, that activity should undergo review for the protection of human subjects.

Part B: Basic Ethical Principles

The expression "basic ethical principles" refers to those general judgments that serve as a basic justification for the many particular ethical prescriptions and evaluations of human actions. Three basic principles, among those generally accepted in our cultural tradition, are particularly relevant to the ethics of research involving human subjects: the principles of respect of persons, beneficence and justice.

1. Respect for Persons. — Respect for persons incorporates at least two ethical convictions: first, that individuals should be treated as autonomous agents, and second, that persons with diminished autonomy are entitled to protection. The principle of respect for persons thus divides into two separate moral requirements: the requirement to acknowledge autonomy and the requirement to protect those with diminished autonomy.

An autonomous person is an individual capable of deliberation about personal goals and of acting under the direction of such deliberation. To respect autonomy is to give weight to autonomous persons' considered opinions and choices while refraining from obstructing their actions unless they are clearly detrimental to others. To show lack of respect for an autonomous agent is to repudiate that person's considered judgments, to deny an individual the freedom to act on those considered judgments, or to withhold information necessary to make a considered judgment, when there are no compelling reasons to do so.

However, not every human being is capable of self-determination. The capacity for self-determination matures during an individual's life, and some individuals lose this capacity wholly or in part because of illness, mental disability, or circumstances that severely restrict liberty. Respect for the immature and the incapacitated may require protecting them as they mature or while they are incapacitated.

Some persons are in need of extensive protection, even to the point of excluding them from activities which may harm them; other persons require little protection beyond making sure they undertake activities freely and with awareness of possible adverse consequence. The extent of protection afforded should depend upon the risk of harm and the likelihood of benefit. The judgment that any individual lacks autonomy should be periodically reevaluated and will vary in different situations.

In most cases of research involving human subjects, respect for persons demands that subjects enter into the research voluntarily and with adequate information. In some situations, however, application of the principle is not obvious. The involvement of prisoners as subjects of research provides an instructive example. On the one hand, it would seem that the principle of respect for persons requires that prisoners not be deprived of the opportunity to volunteer for research. On the other hand, under prison conditions they may be subtly coerced or unduly influenced to engage in research activities for which they would not otherwise volunteer. Respect for persons would then dictate that prisoners be protected. Whether to allow prisoners to "volunteer" or to "protect" them presents a dilemma. Respecting persons, in most hard cases, is often a matter of balancing competing claims urged by the principle of respect itself.

2. Beneficence. — Persons are treated in an ethical manner not only by respecting their decisions and protecting them from harm, but also by making efforts to secure their well-being. Such treatment falls under the principle of beneficence. The term "beneficence" is often understood to cover acts of kindness or charity that go beyond strict obligation. In this document, beneficence is understood in a stronger sense, as an obligation. Two general rules have been formulated as complementary expressions of beneficent actions in this sense: (1) do not harm and (2) maximize possible benefits and minimize possible harms.

The Hippocratic maxim "do no harm" has long been a fundamental principle of medical ethics. Claude Bernard extended it to the realm of research, saying that one should not injure one person regardless of the benefits that might come to others. However, even avoiding harm requires learning what is harmful; and, in the process of obtaining this information, persons may be exposed to risk of harm. Further, the Hippocratic Oath requires physicians to benefit their patients "according to their best judgment." Learning what will in fact benefit may require exposing persons to risk. The problem posed by these imperatives is to decide when it is justifiable to seek certain benefits despite the risks involved, and when the benefits should be foregone because of the risks.

Ethicists distinguish beneficence, the duty to do good, from nonmaleficence, the duty to do no harm. Thus, there are four core bioethical principles, rather than the three delineated in the Belmont Report.

The obligations of beneficence affect both individual investigators and society at large, because they extend both to particular research projects and to the entire enterprise of research. In the case of particular projects, investigators and members of their institutions are obliged to give forethought to the maximization of benefits and the reduction of risk that might occur from the research investigation. In the case of scientific research in general, members of the larger society are obliged to recognize the longer term benefits and risks that may result from the improvement of knowledge and from the development of novel medical, psychotherapeutic, and social procedures.

The principle of beneficence often occupies a well-defined justifying role in many areas of research involving human subjects. An example is found in research involving children. Effective ways of treating childhood diseases and fostering healthy development are benefits that serve to justify research involving children — even when individual research subjects are not direct beneficiaries. Research also makes it possible to avoid the harm that may result from the application of previously accepted routine practices that on closer investigation turn out to be dangerous. But the role of the principle of beneficence is not always so unambiguous. A difficult ethical problem remains, for example, about research that presents more than minimal risk without immediate prospect of direct benefit to the children involved. Some have argued that such research is inadmissible, while others have pointed out that this limit would rule out much research promising great benefit to children in the future. Here again, as with all hard cases, the different claims covered by the principle of beneficence may come into conflict and force difficult choices.

3. Justice. — Who ought to receive the benefits of research and bear its burdens? This is a question of justice, in the sense of "fairness in distribution" or "what is deserved." An injustice occurs when some benefit to which a person is entitled is denied without good reason or when some burden is imposed unduly. Another way of conceiving the principle of justice is that equals ought to be treated equally. However, this statement requires explication. Who is equal and who is unequal? What considerations justify departure from equal distribution? Almost all commentators allow that distinctions based on experience, age, deprivation, competence, merit and position do sometimes constitute criteria justifying differential treatment for certain purposes. It is necessary, then, to explain in what respects people should be treated equally. There are several widely accepted formulations of just ways to distribute burdens and benefits. Each formulation mentions some relevant property on the basis of which burdens and benefits should be distributed. These formulations are (1) to each person an equal share, (2) to each person according to individual need, (3) to each person according to individual effort, (4) to each person according to societal contribution, and (5) to each person according to merit.

Questions of justice have long been associated with social practices such as punishment, taxation and political representation. Until recently these questions have not generally been associated with scientific research. However, they are foreshadowed even in the earliest reflections on the ethics of research involving human subjects. For example, during the 19th and early 20th centuries the burdens of serving as research subjects fell largely upon poor ward patients, while the benefits of improved medical care flowed primarily to private patients. Subsequently, the exploitation of unwilling prisoners as research subjects in Nazi concentration camps was condemned as a particularly flagrant injustice. In this country, in the 1940's, the Tuskegee syphilis study used disadvantaged, rural black men to study the untreated course of a disease that is by no means confined to that population. These subjects were deprived of demonstrably effective treatment in order not to interrupt the project, long after such treatment became generally available.

Against this historical background, it can be seen how conceptions of justice are relevant to research involving human subjects. For example, the selection of research subjects needs to be scrutinized in order to determine whether some classes (e.g.,

> A contemporary example of a justice issue is whether the fruits of biomedical research are available to low-income populations who are unable to afford expensive drugs.

welfare patients, particular racial and ethnic minorities, or persons confined to institutions) are being systematically selected simply because of their easy availability, their compromised position, or their manipulability, rather than for reasons directly related to the problem being studied. Finally, whenever research supported by public funds leads to the development of therapeutic devices and procedures, justice demands both that these not provide advantages only to those who can afford them and that such research should not unduly involve persons from groups unlikely to be among the beneficiaries of subsequent applications of the research.

Part C: Applications

Applications of the general principles to the conduct of research leads to consideration of the following requirements: informed consent, risk/benefit assessment, and the selection of subjects of research.

1. *Informed Consent.* — Respect for persons requires that subjects, to the degree that they are capable, be given the opportunity to choose what shall or shall not happen to them. This opportunity is provided when adequate standards for informed consent are satisfied.

While the importance of informed consent is unquestioned, controversy prevails over the nature and possibility of an informed consent. Nonetheless, there is widespread agreement that the consent process can be analyzed as containing three elements: information, comprehension and voluntariness.

Information. Most codes of research establish specific items for disclosure intended to assure that subjects are given sufficient information. These items generally include: the research procedure, their purposes, risks and anticipated benefits, alternative procedures (where therapy is involved), and a statement offering the subject the opportunity to ask questions and to withdraw at any time from the research. Additional items have been proposed, including how subjects are selected, the person responsible for the research, etc.

However, a simple listing of items does not answer the question of what the standard should be for judging how much and what sort of information should be provided. One standard frequently invoked in medical practice, namely the information commonly provided by practitioners in the field or in the locale, is inadequate since research takes place precisely when a common understanding does not exist. Another standard, currently popular in malpractice law, requires the practitioner to reveal the information that reasonable persons would wish to know in order to make a decision regarding their care. This, too, seems insufficient since the research subject, being in essence a volunteer, may wish to know considerably more about risks gratuitously undertaken than do patients who deliver themselves into the hand of a clinician for needed care. It may be that a standard of "the reasonable volunteer" should be proposed: the extent and nature of information should be such that persons, knowing that the procedure is neither necessary for their care nor perhaps fully understood, can decide whether they wish to participate in the furthering of knowledge. Even when some direct benefit to them is anticipated, the subjects should understand clearly the range of risk and the voluntary nature of participation.

> Informed consent for treatment may not be sufficient for research. The two forms of consent should be treated differently, and obtained separately, so as not to confuse the patient.

A special problem of consent arises where informing subjects of some pertinent aspect of the research is likely to impair the validity of the research. In many cases, it is sufficient to indicate to subjects that they are being invited to participate in research of which some features will not be revealed until the research is concluded. In all cases of research involving incomplete disclosure, such research is justified only if it is clear that (1) incomplete disclosure is truly necessary to accomplish the goals of the research, (2) there are no undisclosed risks to subjects that are more than minimal, and (3) there is an adequate plan for debriefing subjects, when appropriate, and for dissemination of research results to them. Information about risks should never be withheld for the purpose of eliciting the cooperation of subjects, and truthful answers should always be given to direct questions about the research. Care should be taken to distinguish cases in which disclosure would destroy or invalidate the research from cases in which disclosure would simply inconvenience the investigator.

Comprehension. The manner and context in which information is conveyed is as important as the information itself. For example, presenting information in a disorganized and rapid fashion, allowing too little time for consideration or curtailing opportunities for questioning, all may adversely affect a subject's ability to make an informed choice.

Because the subject's ability to understand is a function of intelligence, rationality, maturity and language, it is necessary to adapt the presentation of the information to the subject's capacities. Investigators are responsible for ascertaining that the subject has comprehended the information. While there is always an obligation to ascertain that the information about risk to subjects is complete and adequately comprehended, when the risks are more serious, that obligation increases. On occasion, it may be suitable to give some oral or written tests of comprehension.

Special provision may need to be made when comprehension is severely limited — for example, by conditions of immaturity or mental disability. Each class of subjects that one might consider as incompetent (e.g., infants and young children, mentally disabled patients, the terminally ill and the comatose) should be considered on its own terms. Even for these persons, however, respect requires giving them the opportunity to choose to the extent they are able, whether or not to participate in research. The objections of these subjects to involvement should be honored, unless the research entails providing them a therapy unavailable elsewhere. Respect for persons also requires seeking the permission of other parties in order to protect the subjects from harm. Such persons are thus respected both by acknowledging their own wishes and by the use of third parties to protect them from harm.

> Parents often make medical decisions on behalf of their minor children, including for research. Many children with cancer are enrolled in research studies.

The third parties chosen should be those who are most likely to understand the incompetent subject's situation and to act in that person's best interest. The person authorized to act on behalf of the subject should be given an opportunity to observe the research as it proceeds in order to be able to withdraw the subject from the research, if such action appears in the subject's best interest.

Voluntariness. An agreement to participate in research constitutes a valid consent only if voluntarily given. This element of informed consent requires conditions free of coercion and undue influence. Coercion occurs when an overt threat of harm is intentionally presented by one person to another in order to obtain compliance. Undue influence, by contrast, occurs through an offer of an excessive, unwarranted, inappropriate or improper reward or other overture in order to obtain compliance.

Also, inducements that would ordinarily be acceptable may become undue influences if the subject is especially vulnerable.

Unjustifiable pressures usually occur when persons in positions of authority or commanding influence — especially where possible sanctions are involved — urge a course of action for a subject. A continuum of such influencing factors exists, however, and it is impossible to state precisely where justifiable persuasion ends and undue influence begins. But undue influence would include actions such as manipulating a person's choice through the controlling influence of a close relative and threatening to withdraw health services to which an individual would otherwise be entitled.

2. *Assessment of Risks and Benefits.* — The assessment of risks and benefits requires a careful arrayal of relevant data, including, in some cases, alternative ways of obtaining the benefits sought in the research. Thus, the assessment presents both an opportunity and a responsibility to gather systematic and comprehensive information about proposed research. For the investigator, it is a means to examine whether the proposed research is properly designed. For a review committee, it is a method for determining whether the risks that will be presented to subjects are justified. For prospective subjects, the assessment will assist the determination whether or not to participate.

The Nature and Scope of Risks and Benefits. The requirement that research be justified on the basis of a favorable risk/benefit assessment bears a close relation to the principle of beneficence, just as the moral requirement that informed consent be obtained is derived primarily from the principle of respect for persons. The term "risk" refers to a possibility that harm may occur. However, when expressions such as "small risk" or "high risk" are used, they usually refer (often ambiguously) both to the chance (probability) of experiencing a harm and the severity (magnitude) of the envisioned harm.

The term "benefit" is used in the research context to refer to something of positive value related to health or welfare. Unlike "risk," "benefit" is not a term that expresses probabilities. Risk is properly contrasted to probability of benefits, and benefits are properly contrasted with harms rather than risks of harm. Accordingly, so-called risk/benefit assessments are concerned with the probabilities and magnitudes of possible harm and anticipated benefits. Many kinds of possible harms and benefits need to be taken into account. There are, for example, risks of psychological harm, physical harm, legal harm, social harm and economic harm and the corresponding benefits. While the most likely types of harms to research subjects are those of psychological or physical pain or injury, other possible kinds should not be overlooked. . . .

Finally, assessment of the justifiability of research should reflect at least the following considerations: (i) Brutal or inhumane treatment of human subjects is never morally justified. (ii) Risks should be reduced to those necessary to achieve the research objective. It should be determined whether it is in fact necessary to use human subjects at all. Risk can perhaps never be entirely eliminated, but it can often be reduced by careful attention to alternative procedures. (iii) When research involves significant risk of serious impairment, review committees should be extraordinarily insistent on the justification of the risk (looking usually to the likelihood of benefit to the subject — or, in some rare cases, to the manifest voluntariness of the participation). (iv) When vulnerable populations are involved in research, the appropriateness of involving them should itself be demonstrated. A number of variables go into such judgments, including the nature and degree of risk, the condition of the particular population involved, and the nature and level of the anticipated benefits. (v) Relevant risks and benefits must be thoroughly arrayed in documents and procedures used in the informed consent process.

3. *Selection of Subjects.* — Just as the principle of respect for persons finds expression in the requirements for consent, and the principle of beneficence in risk/benefit assessment, the principle of justice gives rise to moral requirements that there be fair procedures and outcomes in the selection of research subjects.

Justice is relevant to the selection of subjects of research at two levels: the social and the individual. Individual justice in the selection of subjects would require that researchers exhibit fairness: thus, they should not offer potentially beneficial research only to some patients who are in their favor or select only "undesirable" persons for risky research. Social justice requires that distinction be drawn between classes of subjects that ought, and ought not, to participate in any particular kind of research, based on the ability of members of that class to bear burdens and on the appropriateness of placing further burdens on already burdened persons. Thus, it can be considered a matter of social justice that there is an order of preference in the selection of classes of subjects (e.g., adults before children) and that some classes of potential subjects (e.g., the institutionalized mentally infirm or prisoners) may be involved as research subjects, if at all, only on certain conditions.

Injustice may appear in the selection of subjects, even if individual subjects are selected fairly by investigators and treated fairly in the course of research. This injustice arises from social, racial, sexual and cultural biases institutionalized in society. Thus, even if individual researchers are treating their research subjects fairly, and even if IRBs are taking care to assure that subjects are selected fairly within a particular institution, unjust social patterns may nevertheless appear in the overall distribution of the burdens and benefits of research. Although individual institutions or investigators may not be able to resolve a problem that is pervasive in their social setting, they can consider distributive justice in selecting research subjects.

Some populations, especially institutionalized ones, are already burdened in many ways by their infirmities and environments. When research is proposed that involves risks and does not include a therapeutic component, other less burdened classes of persons should be called upon first to accept these risks of research, except where the research is directly related to the specific conditions of the class involved. Also, even though public funds for research may often flow in the same directions as public funds for health care, it seems unfair that populations dependent on public health care constitute a pool of preferred research subjects if more advantaged populations are likely to be the recipients of the benefits.

One special instance of injustice results from the involvement of vulnerable subjects. Certain groups, such as racial minorities, the economically disadvantaged, the very sick, and the institutionalized may continually be sought as research subjects, owing to their ready availability in settings where research is conducted. Given their dependent status and their frequently compromised capacity for free consent, they should be protected against the danger of being involved in research solely for administrative convenience, or because they are easy to manipulate as a result of their illness or socioeconomic condition.

QUESTIONS

1. Are there circumstances in which civilly or criminally committed individuals would be appropriate research subjects? If so, what steps could ensure their informed consent is not coerced?
2. Is there any definable group of individuals who should never be asked to participate in research?

C. FEDERAL LAW PERTAINING TO CLINICAL RESEARCH ON HUMANS

The "Common Rule" is the set of federal regulations found at 45 C.F.R. §§46.101 through 46.505. The term "Common Rule" indicates that these regulations apply across all federal agencies that fund or otherwise regulate research on human subjects, including not only HHS (of which the National Institutes of Health (NIH) is a sub-agency), but also the Department of Homeland Security, Department of Agriculture, Department of Energy, National Aeronautics and Space Administration, Department of Commerce, Social Security Administration, Agency for International Development, Department of Justice, Department of Labor, Department of Defense, Department of Education, Department of Veterans Affairs, Environmental Protection Agency, National Science Foundation, and Department of Transportation. A portion of the existing Common Rule follows:

> **Basic HHS Policy for Protection of Human Research Subjects**
> **45 C.F.R. §46.101 To what does this policy apply?**
>
> (a) Except as provided in paragraph (b) of this section, this policy applies to all research involving human subjects conducted, supported or otherwise subject to regulation by any federal department or agency which takes appropriate administrative action to make the policy applicable to such research. This includes research conducted by federal civilian employees or military personnel, except that each department or agency head may adopt such procedural modifications as may be appropriate from an administrative standpoint. It also includes research conducted, supported, or otherwise subject to regulation by the federal government outside the United States.
>
> (1) Research that is conducted or supported by a federal department or agency, whether or not it is regulated as defined in §46.102, must comply with all sections of this policy.
>
> (2) Research that is neither conducted nor supported by a federal department or agency but is subject to regulation as defined in §46.102 (e) must be reviewed and approved, in compliance with §46.101, §46.102, and §46.107 through §46.117 of this policy, by an institutional review board (IRB) that operates in accordance with the pertinent requirements of this policy.
>
> (b) Unless otherwise required by department or agency heads, research activities in which the only involvement of human subjects will be in one or more of the following categories are exempt from this policy:
>
> (1) Research conducted in established or commonly accepted educational settings, involving normal educational practices, such as (i) research on regular and special education instructional strategies, or (ii) research on

the effectiveness of or the comparison among instructional techniques, curricula, or classroom management methods.

(2) Research involving the use of educational tests (cognitive, diagnostic, aptitude, achievement), survey procedures, interview procedures or observation of public behavior. . . .

(4) Research involving the collection or study of existing data, documents, records, pathological specimens, or diagnostic specimens, if these sources are publicly available or if the information is recorded by the investigator in such a manner that subjects cannot be identified, directly or through identifiers linked to the subjects. . . .

(c) Department or agency heads retain final judgment as to whether a particular activity is covered by this policy.

(d) Department or agency heads may require that specific research activities or classes of research activities conducted, supported, or otherwise subject to regulation by the department or agency but not otherwise covered by this policy, comply with some or all of the requirements of this policy.

(e) Compliance with this policy requires compliance with pertinent federal laws or regulations which provide additional protections for human subjects.

(f) This policy does not affect any state or local laws or regulations which may otherwise be applicable and which provide additional protections for human subjects.

> When human subject research covered by this policy occurs in foreign countries, the protections must be "at least equivalent" to the Common Rule.

(g) This policy does not affect any foreign laws or regulations which may otherwise be applicable and which provide additional protections to human subjects of research.

(h) When research covered by this policy takes place in foreign countries, procedures normally followed in the foreign countries to protect human subjects may differ from those set forth in this policy. [An example is a foreign institution which complies with guidelines consistent with the World Medical Assembly Declaration (Declaration of Helsinki amended 1989) issued either by sovereign states or by an organization whose function for the protection of human research subjects is internationally recognized.] In these circumstances, if a department or agency head determines that the procedures prescribed by the institution afford protections that are at least equivalent to those provided in this policy, the department or agency head may approve the substitution of the foreign procedures in lieu of the procedural requirements provided in this policy. Except when otherwise required by statute, Executive Order, or the department or agency head, notices of these actions as they occur will be published in the Federal Register or will be otherwise published as provided in department or agency procedures.

(i) Unless otherwise required by law, department or agency heads may waive the applicability of some or all of the provisions of this policy to specific research activities or classes of research activities otherwise covered by this policy. Except when otherwise required by statute or Executive Order, the department or agency head shall forward advance notices of these actions to the Office for Human Research Protections, Department of Health and Human Services (HHS), or any successor office, and shall also publish them in the Federal Register or in such other manner as provided in department or agency procedures.

45 C.F.R. §46.102 Definitions

. . . .

(d) Research means a systematic investigation, including research development, testing and evaluation, designed to develop or contribute to generalizable knowledge. Activities which meet this definition constitute research for purposes of this policy, whether or not they are conducted or supported under a program which is considered research for other purposes. For example, some demonstration and service programs may include research activities. . . .

(f) Human subject means a living individual about whom an investigator (whether professional or student) conducting research obtains (1) Data through intervention or interaction with the individual, or (2) Identifiable private information. Intervention includes both physical procedures by which data are gathered (for example, venipuncture) and manipulations of the subject or the subject's environment that are performed for research purposes. Interaction includes communication or interpersonal contact between investigator and subject. Private information includes information about behavior that occurs in a context in which an individual can reasonably expect that no observation or recording is taking place, and information which has been provided for specific purposes by an individual and which the individual can reasonably expect will not be made public (for example, a medical record). Private information must be individually identifiable (i.e., the identity of the subject is or may readily be ascertained by the investigator or associated with the information) in order for obtaining the information to constitute research involving human subjects.

(g) IRB means an institutional review board established in accord with and for the purposes expressed in this policy.

(h) IRB approval means the determination of the IRB that the research has been reviewed and may be conducted at an institution within the constraints set forth by the IRB and by other institutional and federal requirements.

(i) Minimal risk means that the probability and magnitude of harm or discomfort anticipated in the research are not greater in and of themselves than those ordinarily encountered in daily life or during the performance of routine physical or psychological examinations or tests.

A "federalwide assurance" can be used by one research entity across all federal agencies to indicate compliance with the Common Rule.

(j) Certification means the official notification by the institution to the supporting department or agency, in accordance with the requirements of this policy, that a research project or activity involving human subjects has been reviewed and approved by an IRB in accordance with an approved assurance.

45 C.F.R. §46.103. Assuring compliance with this policy—research conducted or supported by any Federal Department or Agency

(a) Each institution engaged in research which is covered by this policy and which is conducted or supported by a federal department or agency shall provide written assurance satisfactory to the department or agency head that it will comply with the requirements set forth in this policy. In lieu of requiring submission of an assurance, individual department or agency heads shall accept the existence of a current assurance, appropriate for the research in question, on file with the Office for Human Research Protections, HHS, or any successor office, and approved for federalwide use by that office. When the existence of an HHS-approved assurance is accepted in lieu of requiring submission of an assurance, reports (except certification) required by this policy to be made to department and agency heads shall also be made to the Office for Human Research Protections, HHS, or any successor office.

(b) Departments and agencies will conduct or support research covered by this policy only if the institution has an assurance approved as provided in this section, and only if the institution has certified to the department or agency head that the research has been reviewed and approved by an IRB provided for in the assurance, and will be subject to continuing review by the IRB. Assurances applicable to federally supported or conducted research shall at a minimum include:

> An Institutional Review Board (IRB) is a group that ensures that human research complies with federal law and bioethical principles. Hundreds of IRBs exist across the United States. Most universities have at least one IRB, if not an entire office dedicated to clinical research that coordinates many IRBs.

(1) A statement of principles governing the institution in the discharge of its responsibilities for protecting the rights and welfare of human subjects of research conducted at or sponsored by the institution, regardless of whether the research is subject to Federal regulation. This may include an appropriate existing code, declaration, or statement of ethical principles, or a statement formulated by the institution itself. This requirement does not preempt provisions of this policy applicable to department- or agency-supported or regulated research and need not be applicable to any research exempted or waived under §46.101(b) or (i).

(2) Designation of one or more IRBs established in accordance with the requirements of this policy, and for which provisions are made for meeting space and sufficient staff to support the IRB's review and recordkeeping duties.

(3) A list of IRB members identified by name; earned degrees; representative capacity; indications of experience such as board certifications, licenses, etc., sufficient to describe each member's chief anticipated contributions to IRB deliberations; and any employment or other relationship between each member and the institution; for example: full-time employee, part-time employee, member of governing panel or board, stockholder, paid or unpaid consultant. Changes in IRB membership shall be reported to the department or agency head, unless in accord with §46.103(a) of this policy, the existence of an HHS-approved assurance is accepted. In this case, change in IRB membership shall be reported to the Office for Human Research Protections, HHS, or any successor office.

(4) Written procedures which the IRB will follow (i) for conducting its initial and continuing review of research and for reporting its findings and actions to the investigator and the institution; (ii) for determining which projects require review more often than annually and which projects need verification from sources other than the investigators that no material changes have occurred since previous IRB review; and (iii) for ensuring prompt reporting to the IRB of proposed changes in a research activity, and for ensuring that such changes in approved research, during the period for which IRB approval has already been given, may not be initiated without

IRB review and approval except when necessary to eliminate apparent immediate hazards to the subject.

(5) Written procedures for ensuring prompt reporting to the IRB, appropriate institutional officials, and the department or agency head of (i) any unanticipated problems involving risks to subjects or others or any serious or continuing noncompliance with this policy or the requirements or determinations of the IRB; and (ii) any suspension or termination of IRB approval. . . .

45 C.F.R. §46.107. IRB membership

(a) Each IRB shall have at least five members, with varying backgrounds to promote complete and adequate review of research activities commonly conducted by the institution. The IRB shall be sufficiently qualified through the experience and expertise of its members, and the diversity of the members, including consideration of race, gender, and cultural backgrounds and sensitivity to such issues as community attitudes, to promote respect for its advice and counsel in safeguarding the rights and welfare of human subjects. In addition to possessing the professional competence necessary to review specific research activities, the IRB shall be able to ascertain the acceptability of proposed research in terms of institutional commitments and regulations, applicable law, and standards of professional conduct and practice. The IRB shall therefore include persons knowledgeable in these areas. If an IRB regularly reviews research that involves a vulnerable category of subjects, such as children, prisoners, pregnant women, or handicapped or mentally disabled persons, consideration shall be given to the inclusion of one or more individuals who are knowledgeable about and experienced in working with these subjects.

(b) Every nondiscriminatory effort will be made to ensure that no IRB consists entirely of men or entirely of women, including the institution's consideration of qualified persons of both sexes, so long as no selection is made to the IRB on the basis of gender. No IRB may consist entirely of members of one profession.

(c) Each IRB shall include at least one member whose primary concerns are in scientific areas and at least one member whose primary concerns are in nonscientific areas.

(d) Each IRB shall include at least one member who is not otherwise affiliated with the institution and who is not part of the immediate family of a person who is affiliated with the institution.

(e) No IRB may have a member participate in the IRB's initial or continuing review of any project in which the member has a conflicting interest, except to provide information requested by the IRB.

(f) An IRB may, in its discretion, invite individuals with competence in special areas to assist in the review of issues which require expertise beyond or in addition to that available on the IRB. These individuals may not vote with the IRB.

45 C.F.R. §46.108. IRB functions and operations

In order to fulfill the requirements of this policy each IRB shall:

(a) Follow written procedures in the same detail as described in §46.103(b) (4) and, to the extent required by, §46.103(b)(5).

(b) Except when an expedited review procedure is used (see §46.110), review proposed research at convened meetings at which a majority of the members of the IRB are present, including at least one member whose primary concerns are in nonscientific areas. In order for the research to be approved, it shall receive the approval of a majority of those members present at the meeting.

45 C.F.R. §46.109. IRB review of research

(a) An IRB shall review and have authority to approve, require modifications in (to secure approval), or disapprove all research activities covered by this policy.

(b) An IRB shall require that information given to subjects as part of informed consent is in accordance with §46.116. The IRB may require that information, in addition to that specifically mentioned in §46.116, be given to the subjects when in the IRB's judgment the information would meaningfully add to the protection of the rights and welfare of subjects.

(c) An IRB shall require documentation of informed consent or may waive documentation in accordance with §46.117.

(d) An IRB shall notify investigators and the institution in writing of its decision to approve or disapprove the proposed research activity, or of modifications required to secure IRB approval of the research activity. If the IRB decides to disapprove a research activity, it shall include in its written notification a statement of the reasons for its decision and give the investigator an opportunity to respond in person or in writing.

(e) An IRB shall conduct continuing review of research covered by this policy at intervals appropriate to the degree of risk, but not less than once per year, and shall have authority to observe or have a third party observe the consent process and the research. . . .

45 C.F.R. §46.111. Criteria for IRB approval of research

(a) In order to approve research covered by this policy the IRB shall determine that all of the following requirements are satisfied:

(1) Risks to subjects are minimized: (i) By using procedures which are consistent with sound research design and which do not unnecessarily expose subjects to risk, and (ii) whenever appropriate, by using procedures already being performed on the subjects for diagnostic or treatment purposes.

(2) Risks to subjects are reasonable in relation to anticipated benefits, if any, to subjects, and the importance of the knowledge that may reasonably be expected to result. In evaluating risks and benefits, the IRB should consider only those risks and benefits that may result from the research (as distinguished from risks and benefits of therapies subjects would receive even if not participating in the research). The IRB should not consider possible long-range effects of applying knowledge gained in the research (for example, the possible effects of the research on public policy) as among those research risks that fall within the purview of its responsibility.

(3) Selection of subjects is equitable. In making this assessment the IRB should take into account the purposes of the research and the setting in which the research will be conducted and should be particularly cognizant of the special problems of research involving vulnerable populations, such

as children, prisoners, pregnant women, mentally disabled persons, or economically or educationally disadvantaged persons.

(4) Informed consent will be sought from each prospective subject or the subject's legally authorized representative, in accordance with, and to the extent required by §46.116.

(5) Informed consent will be appropriately documented, in accordance with, and to the extent required by §46.117.

(6) When appropriate, the research plan makes adequate provision for monitoring the data collected to ensure the safety of subjects.

(7) When appropriate, there are adequate provisions to protect the privacy of subjects and to maintain the confidentiality of data.

(b) When some or all of the subjects are likely to be vulnerable to coercion or undue influence, such as children, prisoners, pregnant women, mentally disabled persons, or economically or educationally disadvantaged persons, additional safeguards have been included in the study to protect the rights and welfare of these subjects.

45 C.F.R. §46.112. Review by institution

Research covered by this policy that has been approved by an IRB may be subject to further appropriate review and approval or disapproval by officials of the institution. However, those officials may not approve the research if it has not been approved by an IRB.

45 C.F.R. §46.113. Suspension or termination of IRB approval of research

An IRB shall have authority to suspend or terminate approval of research that is not being conducted in accordance with the IRB's requirements or that has been associated with unexpected serious harm to subjects. Any suspension or termination of approval shall include a statement of the reasons for the IRB's action and shall be reported promptly to the investigator, appropriate institutional officials, and the department or agency head.

. . . .

45 C.F.R. §46.116. General requirements for informed consent

Except as provided elsewhere in this policy, no investigator may involve a human being as a subject in research covered by this policy unless the investigator has obtained the legally effective informed consent of the subject or the subject's legally authorized representative. An investigator shall seek such consent only under circumstances that provide the prospective subject or the representative sufficient opportunity to consider whether or not to participate and that minimize the possibility of coercion or undue influence. The information that is given to the subject or the representative shall be in language understandable to the subject or the representative. No informed consent, whether oral or written, may include any exculpatory language through which the subject or the representative is made to waive or appear to waive any of the subject's legal rights, or releases or appears to release the investigator, the sponsor, the institution or its agents from liability for negligence.

> In the research context, waiver of liability for negligence is inappropriate and does not comply with the informed consent rules.

(a) Basic elements of informed consent. Except as provided in paragraph (c) or (d) of this section, in seeking informed consent the following information shall be provided to each subject:

(1) A statement that the study involves research, an explanation of the purposes of the research and the expected duration of the subject's participation, a description of the procedures to be followed, and identification of any procedures which are experimental;

(2) A description of any reasonably foreseeable risks or discomforts to the subject;

(3) A description of any benefits to the subject or to others which may reasonably be expected from the research;

(4) A disclosure of appropriate alternative procedures or courses of treatment, if any, that might be advantageous to the subject;

(5) A statement describing the extent, if any, to which confidentiality of records identifying the subject will be maintained;

(6) For research involving more than minimal risk, an explanation as to whether any compensation and an explanation as to whether any medical treatments are available if injury occurs and, if so, what they consist of, or where further information may be obtained;

(7) An explanation of whom to contact for answers to pertinent questions about the research and research subjects' rights, and whom to contact in the event of a research-related injury to the subject; and

(8) A statement that participation is voluntary, refusal to participate will involve no penalty or loss of benefits to which the subject is otherwise entitled, and the subject may discontinue participation at any time without penalty or loss of benefits to which the subject is otherwise entitled.

(b) Additional elements of informed consent. When appropriate, one or more of the following elements of information shall also be provided to each subject:

(1) A statement that the particular treatment or procedure may involve risks to the subject (or to the embryo or fetus, if the subject is or may become pregnant) which are currently unforeseeable;

(2) Anticipated circumstances under which the subject's participation may be terminated by the investigator without regard to the subject's consent;

(3) Any additional costs to the subject that may result from participation in the research;

(4) The consequences of a subject's decision to withdraw from the research and procedures for orderly termination of participation by the subject;

(5) A statement that significant new findings developed during the course of the research which may relate to the subject's willingness to continue participation will be provided to the subject; and

(6) The approximate number of subjects involved in the study.

(c) An IRB may approve a consent procedure which does not include, or which alters, some or all of the elements of informed consent set forth above, or waive the requirement to obtain informed consent provided the IRB finds and documents that:

> Informed consent may be impractical for research on emergency treatment for unconscious traffic accident victims.

(1) The research or demonstration project is to be conducted by or subject to the approval of state or local government officials and is designed to study, evaluate, or otherwise examine: (i) public benefit or service programs; (ii) procedures for obtaining benefits or services under those programs; (iii) possible changes in or alternatives to those programs or procedures; or (iv) possible changes in methods or levels of payment for benefits or services under those programs; and

(2) The research could not practicably be carried out without the waiver or alteration.

(d) An IRB may approve a consent procedure which does not include, or which alters, some or all of the elements of informed consent set forth in this section, or waive the requirements to obtain informed consent provided the IRB finds and documents that:

(1) The research involves no more than minimal risk to the subjects;

(2) The waiver or alteration will not adversely affect the rights and welfare of the subjects;

(3) The research could not practicably be carried out without the waiver or alteration; and

(4) Whenever appropriate, the subjects will be provided with additional pertinent information after participation.

(e) The informed consent requirements in this policy are not intended to preempt any applicable federal, state, or local laws which require additional information to be disclosed in order for informed consent to be legally effective.

(f) Nothing in this policy is intended to limit the authority of a physician to provide emergency medical care, to the extent the physician is permitted to do so under applicable federal, state, or local law.

45 C.F.R. §46.117. Documentation of informed consent

(a) Except as provided in paragraph (c) of this section, informed consent shall be documented by the use of a written consent form approved by the IRB and signed by the subject or the subject's legally authorized representative. A copy shall be given to the person signing the form.

(b) Except as provided in paragraph (c) of this section, the consent form may be either of the following:

(1) A written consent document that embodies the elements of informed consent required by §46.116. This form may be read to the subject or the subject's legally authorized representative, but in any event, the investigator shall give either the subject or the representative adequate opportunity to read it before it is signed; or

> Compliance with the Common Rule is a condition for receiving federal funds.

(2) A short form written consent document stating that the elements of informed consent required by §46.116 have been presented orally to the subject or the subject's legally authorized representative. When this method is used, there shall be a witness to the oral presentation. Also, the IRB shall approve a written summary of what is to be said to the subject or the representative. Only the short form itself is to be signed by the subject or the representative. However, the witness shall sign both the short form and a copy of the summary, and the person actually obtaining consent shall sign a copy of the summary. A copy of the summary shall be

given to the subject or the representative, in addition to a copy of the short form.

(c) An IRB may waive the requirement for the investigator to obtain a signed consent form for some or all subjects if it finds either:

(1) That the only record linking the subject and the research would be the consent document and the principal risk would be potential harm resulting from a breach of confidentiality. Each subject will be asked whether the subject wants documentation linking the subject with the research, and the subject's wishes will govern; or

(2) That the research presents no more than minimal risk of harm to subjects and involves no procedures for which written consent is normally required outside of the research context.

In cases in which the documentation requirement is waived, the IRB may require the investigator to provide subjects with a written statement regarding the research.

. . . .

45 C.F.R. §46.122. Use of Federal funds

Federal funds administered by a department or agency may not be expended for research involving human subjects unless the requirements of this policy have been satisfied.

. . . .

45 C.F.R. §46.204. Research involving pregnant women or fetuses

Pregnant women or fetuses may be involved in research if all of the following conditions are met:

(a) Where scientifically appropriate, preclinical studies, including studies on pregnant animals, and clinical studies, including studies on nonpregnant women, have been conducted and provide data for assessing potential risks to pregnant women and fetuses;

(b) The risk to the fetus is caused solely by interventions or procedures that hold out the prospect of direct benefit for the woman or the fetus; or, if there is no such prospect of benefit, the risk to the fetus is not greater than minimal and the purpose of the research is the development of important biomedical knowledge which cannot be obtained by any other means;

(c) Any risk is the least possible for achieving the objectives of the research;

(d) If the research holds out the prospect of direct benefit to the pregnant woman, the prospect of a direct benefit both to the pregnant woman and the fetus, or no prospect of benefit for the woman nor the fetus when risk to the fetus is not greater than minimal and the purpose of the research is the development of important biomedical knowledge that cannot be obtained by any other means, her consent is obtained in accord with the informed consent provisions of subpart A of this part;

(e) If the research holds out the prospect of direct benefit solely to the fetus then the consent of the pregnant woman and the father is obtained in accord with the informed consent provisions of subpart A of this part, except that the father's consent need not be obtained if he is unable to consent because of unavailability, incompetence, or temporary incapacity or the pregnancy resulted from rape or incest[;]

(f) Each individual providing consent under paragraph (d) or (e) of this section is fully informed regarding the reasonably foreseeable impact of the research on the fetus or neonate;

(g) For children as defined in §46.402(a) who are pregnant, assent and permission are obtained in accord with the provisions of subpart D of this part;

(h) No inducements, monetary or otherwise, will be offered to terminate a pregnancy;

(i) Individuals engaged in the research will have no part in any decisions as to the timing, method, or procedures used to terminate a pregnancy; and

(j) Individuals engaged in the research will have no part in determining the viability of a neonate. . . .

. . . .

45 C.F.R. §46.302. Purpose

Inasmuch as prisoners may be under constraints because of their incarceration which could affect their ability to make a truly voluntary and uncoerced decision whether or not to participate as subjects in research, it is the purpose of this subpart to provide additional safeguards for the protection of prisoners involved in activities to which this subpart is applicable.

45 C.F.R. §46.305. Additional duties of the Institutional Review Boards where prisoners are involved

(a) In addition to all other responsibilities prescribed for Institutional Review Boards under this part, the Board shall review research covered by this subpart and approve such research only if it finds that:

(1) The research under review represents one of the categories of research permissible under §46.306(a)(2);

(2) Any possible advantages accruing to the prisoner through his or her participation in the research, when compared to the general living conditions, medical care, quality of food, amenities and opportunity for earnings in the prison, are not of such a magnitude that his or her ability to weigh the risks of the research against the value of such advantages in the limited choice environment of the prison is impaired;

(3) The risks involved in the research are commensurate with risks that would be accepted by nonprisoner volunteers;

(4) Procedures for the selection of subjects within the prison are fair to all prisoners and immune from arbitrary intervention by prison authorities or prisoners. Unless the principal investigator provides to the Board justification in writing for following some other procedures, control subjects must be selected randomly from the group of available prisoners who meet the characteristics needed for that particular research project;

(5) The information is presented in language which is understandable to the subject population;

(6) Adequate assurance exists that parole boards will not take into account a prisoner's participation in the research in making decisions regarding parole, and each prisoner is clearly informed in advance that participation in the research will have no effect on his or her parole; and

(7) Where the Board finds there may be a need for follow-up examination or care of participants after the end of their participation, adequate

provision has been made for such examination or care, taking into account the varying lengths of individual prisoners' sentences, and for informing participants of this fact.

. . . .

45 C.F.R. §46.306. Permitted research involving prisoners

(a) Biomedical or behavioral research conducted or supported by DHHS may involve prisoners as subjects only if:

(1) The institution responsible for the conduct of the research has certified to the Secretary that the Institutional Review Board has approved the research under §46.305 of this subpart; and

(2) In the judgment of the Secretary the proposed research involves solely the following:

(i) Study of the possible causes, effects, and processes of incarceration, and of criminal behavior, provided that the study presents no more than minimal risk and no more than inconvenience to the subjects;

(ii) Study of prisons as institutional structures or of prisoners as incarcerated persons, provided that the study presents no more than minimal risk and no more than inconvenience to the subjects;

(iii) Research on conditions particularly affecting prisoners as a class (for example, vaccine trials and other research on hepatitis which is much more prevalent in prisons than elsewhere; and research on social and psychological problems such as alcoholism, drug addiction, and sexual assaults) provided that the study may proceed only after the Secretary has consulted with appropriate experts including experts in penology, medicine, and ethics, and published notice, in the Federal Register, of his intent to approve such research; or

(iv) Research on practices, both innovative and accepted, which have the intent and reasonable probability of improving the health or well-being of the subject. In cases in which those studies require the assignment of prisoners in a manner consistent with protocols approved by the IRB to control groups which may not benefit from the research, the study may proceed only after the Secretary has consulted with appropriate experts, including experts in penology, medicine, and ethics, and published notice, in the Federal Register, of the intent to approve such research.

(b) Except as provided in paragraph (a) of this section, biomedical or behavioral research conducted or supported by DHHS shall not involve prisoners as subjects.

QUESTIONS

1. Under what circumstances must an IRB approve of research?
2. Can an IRB ever approve research that could be physically or mentally harmful to subjects? Under what circumstance?
3. When could a pregnant woman participate in research? A prisoner? Do you think vulnerable populations should ever be participants in biomedical or behavioral research?

In 2015, HHS proposed revised regulations (issued a Notice of Proposed Rulemaking) to amend the Common Rule, the final rule of which was published on January 19, 2017, with an effective date of January 19, 2018. Certain stakeholders sought guidance from HHS and a delay in the compliance date in the absence of guidance. On January 17, 2018, the final rule was delayed until July 19, 2018; on April 20, 2018, HHS proposed an additional six-month delay. By the time the rule was delayed, many researchers and the institutions with which they work had completed revising their programs to comply with the 2017 final rule. As this edition goes to press, the revised Common Rule has been issued but delayed, so the regulations above remain the law. HHS offered the following executive summary of key changes made to the Common Rule:

Federal Policy for the Protection of Human Subjects

82 Fed. Reg. 7149 (Jan. 19, 2017)

Purpose of the Regulatory Action

Individuals who are the subjects of research may be asked to contribute their time and assume risk to advance the research enterprise, which benefits society at large. U.S. federal regulations governing the protection of human subjects in research have been in existence for more than three decades. The Department of Health, Education, and Welfare first published regulations for the protection of human subjects in 1974, and the Department of Health and Human Services (HHS) revised them in the early 1980s. During the 1980s, HHS began a process that eventually led to the adoption of a revised version of the regulations by 15 U.S. federal departments and agencies in 1991. The purpose of this effort was to promote uniformity, understanding, and compliance with human subject protections as well as to create a uniform body of regulations across federal departments and agencies (subpart A of 45 Code of Federal Regulations [CFR] part 46), often referred to as the "Common Rule" or "Protection of Human Subjects Regulations." Those regulations were last amended in 2005, and have remained unchanged until the issuance of this final rule.

Since the Common Rule was promulgated, the volume and landscape of research involving human subjects have changed considerably. Research with human subjects has grown in scale and become more diverse. Examples of developments include: an expansion in the number and types of clinical trials, as well as observational studies and cohort studies; a diversification of the types of social and behavioral research being used in human subjects research; increased use of sophisticated analytic techniques to study human biospecimens; and the growing use of electronic health data and other digital records to enable very large datasets to be rapidly analyzed and combined in novel ways. Yet these developments have not been accompanied by major change in the human subjects research oversight system, which has remained largely unaltered over the past two decades.

On July 26, 2011, the Office of the Secretary of HHS, in coordination with the Executive Office of the President's Office of Science and Technology Policy (OSTP), published an advance notice of proposed rulemaking (ANPRM) to request comment on how current regulations for protecting those who participate in research might be modernized and revised to be more effective.

On September 8, 2015, HHS and 15 other federal departments and agencies published a Notice of Proposed Rulemaking (NPRM) proposing revisions to the regulations for protection of human subjects in research. Like the ANPRM, the NPRM sought comment on how to better protect research subjects while facilitating valuable research and reducing burden, delay, and ambiguity for investigators. Public comments on both the ANPRM and the NPRM have informed the final rule that is now being promulgated.

The final rule is designed to more thoroughly address the broader types of research conducted or otherwise supported by all of the Common Rule departments and agencies such as behavioral and social science research. It also benefits from continuing efforts to harmonize human subjects policies across federal departments and agencies.

Summary of the Major Changes in the Final Rule

The final rule differs in important ways from the NPRM. Most significantly, several proposals are not being adopted:

- The final rule does not adopt the proposal to require that research involving nonidentified biospecimens be subject to the Common Rule, and that consent would need to be obtained in order to conduct such research.

> The treatment of biospecimens as "people" in the proposed rule was highly controversial. HHS withdrew that revision, and some others, in response to public comments.

- . . . .
- The final rule does not expand the policy to cover clinical trials that are not federally funded.
- . . . .

The final rule makes the following significant changes to the Common Rule:

- Establishes new requirements regarding the information that must be given to prospective research subjects as part of the informed consent process.
- Allows the use of broad consent (i.e., seeking prospective consent to unspecified future research) from a subject for storage, maintenance, and secondary research use of identifiable private information and identifiable biospecimens. Broad consent will be an optional alternative that an investigator may choose instead of, for example, conducting the research on nonidentified information and nonidentified biospecimens, having an institutional review board (IRB) waive the requirement for informed consent, or obtaining consent for a specific study.
- Establishes new exempt categories of research based on their risk profile. Under some of the new categories, exempt research would be required to undergo limited IRB review to ensure that there are adequate privacy safeguards for identifiable private information and identifiable biospecimens.
- Creates a requirement for U.S.-based institutions engaged in cooperative research to use a single IRB for that portion of the research that takes place within the United States, with certain exceptions. This requirement becomes effective 3 years after publication of the final rule.
- Removes the requirement to conduct continuing review of ongoing research for studies that undergo expedited review and for studies that have completed study interventions and are merely analyzing study data or involve only observational follow up in conjunction with standard clinical care.

Other minor changes have been to improve the rule and for purposes of clarity and accuracy.

Even when an IRB has performed its role under the Common Rule, researchers with good intentions may still fail to inform vulnerable populations adequately of the nature of their research. One prominent example was Johns Hopkins University, an internationally renowned medical center that performs groundbreaking biomedical research. "[T]he purpose of Hopkins Hospital was to help those who otherwise couldn't get medical care: 'The indigent sick of this city and its environs, without regard to sex, age, or color, who require surgical or medical treatment, and who can be received into the hospital without peril to other inmates, and the poor of the city and State, of all races, who are stricken down by any casualty, shall be received into the hospital without charge.'" Rebecca Skloot, *The Immortal Life of Henrietta Lacks* 167 (2010). Yet the poor community surrounding the university has long mistrusted it; recall the conversation excerpted at the beginning of this chapter between Henrietta Lacks's relatives. In the case that follows, critically consider the value of the court's highly unusual move of starting with a "Prologue" to emphasize the egregiousness of the behavior exhibited by the researchers.

Grimes v. Kennedy Krieger Institute, Inc.

782 A.2d 807 (Md. 2001)

Prologue

We initially note that these are cases of first impression for this Court. For that matter, precious few courts in the United States have addressed the issues presented in the cases at bar. In respect to nontherapeutic research using minors, it has been noted that "consent to research has been virtually unanalyzed by courts and legislatures." Our research reveals this statement remains as accurate now as it was in 1977.

> This is still true; few cases have been litigated regarding research abuses.

In these present cases, a prestigious research institute, associated with Johns Hopkins University, based on this record, created a nontherapeutic research program whereby it required certain classes of homes to have only partial lead paint abatement modifications performed, and in at least some instances, including at least one of the cases at bar, arranged for the landlords to receive public funding by way of grants or loans to aid in the modifications. The research institute then encouraged, and in at least one of the cases at bar, required, the landlords to rent the premises to families with young children. In the event young children already resided in one of the study houses, it was contemplated that a child would remain in the premises, and the child was encouraged to remain, in order for his or her blood to be periodically analyzed. In other words, the continuing presence of the children that were the subjects of the study was required in order for the study to be complete. Apparently, the children and their parents involved in the cases sub judice were from a lower economic strata and were, at least in one case, minorities.

The purpose of the research was to determine how effective varying degrees of lead paint abatement procedures were. Success was to be determined by periodically, over a two-year period of time, measuring the extent to which lead dust remained in, or returned to, the premises after the varying levels of abatement modifications, and, as most important to our decision, by measuring the extent to which the theretofore healthy children's blood became contaminated with lead, and comparing that contamination with levels of lead dust in the houses over the same periods of time. In respect to one of the protocols presented to the Environmental Protection Agency and/or the Johns Hopkins Joint Committee on Clinical Investigation, the Johns Hopkins Institutional Review Board (IRB), the researchers stated: "To help insure that study dwellings are occupied by families with young children, City Homes will give priority to families with young children when renting the vacant units following R & M [Repair and Maintenance] interventions."

The same researchers had completed a prior study on abatement and partial abatement methods that indicated that lead dust remained and/or returned to abated houses over a period of time. In an article reporting on that study, the very same researchers said: "Exposure to lead-bearing dust is particularly hazardous for children because hand-to-mouth activity is recognized as a major route of entry of lead into the body and because absorption of lead is inversely related to particule size." After publishing this report, the researchers began the present research project in which children were encouraged to reside in households where the possibility of lead dust was known to the researcher to be likely, so that the lead dust content of their blood could be compared with the level of lead dust in the houses at periodic intervals over a two-year period.

> Can you think of explanations as to why the researchers would study partial rather than total lead abatement? Keep in mind that they were focused on low-income housing, and the landlords of such rentals are not known for spending a lot of money on their properties.

Apparently, it was anticipated that the children, who were the human subjects in the program, would, or at least might, accumulate lead in their blood from the dust, thus helping the researchers to determine the extent to which the various partial abatement methods worked. There was no complete and clear explanation in the consent agreements signed by the parents of the children that the research to be conducted was designed, at least in significant part, to measure the success of the abatement procedures by measuring the extent to which the children's blood was being contaminated. It can be argued that the researchers intended that the children be the canaries in the mines but never clearly told the parents. (It was a practice in earlier years, and perhaps even now, for subsurface miners to rely on canaries to determine whether dangerous levels of toxic gasses were accumulating in the mines. Canaries were particularly susceptible to such gasses. When the canaries began to die, the miners knew that dangerous levels of gasses were accumulating.)

The researchers and their Institutional Review Board apparently saw nothing wrong with the search protocols that anticipated the possible accumulation of lead in the blood of otherwise healthy children as a result of the experiment, or they believed that the consents of the parents of the children made the research appropriate. Institutional Review Boards (IRB) are oversight entities within the institutional family to which an entity conducting research belongs. In research experiments, an IRB can be required in some instances by either federal or state regulation, or sometimes by the conditions attached to governmental grants that are used to fund research projects. Generally, their primary functions are to assess the protocols of the project to determine whether the project itself is appropriate, whether the consent procedures are adequate, whether the methods to be employed meet proper standards, whether reporting requirements are sufficient, and the assessment of various other aspects of a research project. One of the most important objectives of such review is the review of the potential safety and the health hazard impact of a research project on the human subjects of the experiment, especially on vulnerable subjects such as children. Their function is not to help researchers seek funding for research projects.

In the instant case, as is suggested by some commentators as being endemic to the research community as a whole, the IRB involved here, the Johns Hopkins University Joint Committee on Clinical Investigation, in part, abdicated that responsibility, instead suggesting to the researchers a way to miscast the characteristics of the study in order to avoid the responsibility inherent in nontherapeutic research involving children. In a letter dated May 11, 1992, the Johns Hopkins University Joint Committee on Clinical Investigation (the IRB for the University), charged with insuring the safety of the subjects and compliance with federal regulations, wrote to Dr. Farfel, the person in charge of the research:

> "A number of questions came up. . . . Please respond to the following points[:]
>
> . . . .
>
> 2. The next issue has to do with drawing blood from the control population, namely children growing up in modern urban housing. *Federal guidelines are really quite specific regarding using children as controls in projects in which there is no potential benefit* [to the particular children]. To call a subject a normal control is to indicate that there is no real benefit to be received [by the particular children]. . . . So we think it would be much more acceptable to indicate that the 'control group' is being studied to determine what exposure outside the home may play in a total lead exposure; thereby, indicating that these control individuals are gaining some benefit, namely learning whether safe housing alone is sufficient to keep the blood-lead levels in acceptable bounds. We suggest that you modify . . . consent form[s] . . . accordingly." [Emphasis added.]

While the suggestion of the IRB would not make this experiment any less non-therapeutic or, thus, less regulated, this statement shows two things: (1) that the IRB had a partial misperception of the difference between therapeutic and nontherapeutic research and the IRB's role in the process and (2) that the IRB was willing to aid researchers in getting around federal regulations designed to protect children used as subjects in nontherapeutic research. An IRB's primary role is to assure the safety of human research subjects — not help researchers avoid safety or health-related requirements. The IRB, in this case, misconceived, at least partially, its own role.

> The IRB helped the researchers to bypass stringent rules pertaining to nontherapeutic research on children.

The provisions or conditions imposed by the federal funding entities, pursuant to federal regulations, are conditions attached to funding. As far as we are aware, or have been informed, there are no federal or state (Maryland) statutes that mandate that all research be subject to certain conditions. Certain international "codes" or "declarations" exist (one of which is supposedly binding but has never been so held) that, at least in theory, establish standards. We shall describe them. Accordingly, we write on a clean slate in this case. We are guided, as we determine what is appropriate, by those international "codes" or "declarations," as well as by studies conducted by various governmental entities, by the treatises and other writings on the ethics of using children as research subjects, and by the duties, if any, arising out of the use of children as subjects of research.

Otherwise healthy children, in our view, should not be enticed into living in, or remaining in, potentially lead-tainted housing and intentionally subjected to a research program, which contemplates the probability, or even the possibility, of lead poisoning or even the accumulation of lower levels of lead in blood, in order for the extent of the contamination of the children's blood to be used by scientific researchers to assess the success of lead paint or lead dust abatement measures. Moreover, in our view, parents, whether improperly enticed by trinkets, food stamps, money or other items, have no more right to intentionally and unnecessarily place children in potentially hazardous nontherapeutic research surroundings, than do researchers. In such cases, parental consent, no matter how informed, is insufficient.

While the validity of the consent agreement and its nature as a contract, the existence or nonexistence of a special relationship, and whether the researchers performed their functions under that agreement pursuant to any special relationships are important issues in these cases that we will address, the very inappropriateness of the research itself cannot be overlooked. It is apparent that the protocols of research are even more important than the method of obtaining parental consent and the extent to which the parents were, or were not, informed. If the research methods, the protocols, are inappropriate then, especially when the IRB is willing to help researchers avoid compliance with applicable safety requirements for using children in nontherapeutic research, the consent of the parents, or of any consent surrogates, in our view, cannot make the research appropriate or the actions of the researchers and the Institutional Review Board proper.

The research relationship proffered to the parents of the children the researchers wanted to use as measuring tools, should never have been presented in a nontherapeutic context in the first instance. Nothing about the research was designed for treatment of the subject children. They were presumed to be healthy at the commencement of the project. As to them, the research was clearly nontherapeutic in nature. The experiment was simply a "for the greater good" project. The specific children's health was put at risk, in order to develop low-cost abatement measures that would help all children, the landlords, and the general public as well. . . .

The research project at issue here, and its apparent protocols, differs in large degree from, but presents similar problems as those in the Tuskegee Syphilis Study conducted from 1932 until 1972 (The Tuskegee Syphilis Study, 289 New England Journal of Medicine 730 (1973)), the intentional exposure of soldiers to radiation in the 1940s and 50s (Jaffee v. United States, 663 F.2d 1226 (3d Cir. 1981)), the tests involving the exposure of Navajo miners to radiation (Begay v. United States, 591 F. Supp. 991 (1984), aff'd, 768 F.2d 1059 (9th Cir. 1985), and the secret administration of LSD to soldiers by the CIA and the Army in the 1950s and 60s (United States v. Stanley, 483 U.S. 669 (1987); Central Intelligence Agency v. Sims, 471 U.S. 159 (1985)). The research experiments that follow were also prior instances of research subjects being intentionally exposed to infectious or poisonous substances in the name of scientific research. They include the Tuskegee Syphilis Study, aforesaid, where patients infected with syphilis were not subsequently informed of the availability of penicillin for treatment of the illness, in order for the scientists and researchers to be able to continue research on the effects of the illness, the Jewish Hospital study, and several other post-war research projects. Then there are the notorious use of "plague bombs" by the Japanese military in World War II where entire villages were infected in order for the results to be "studied"; and perhaps most notorious, the deliberate use of infection in a nontherapeutic project in order to study the degree of infection and the rapidity of the course of the disease in the Rose and Mrugowsky typhus experiments at Buchenwald concentration camp during World War II. These programs were somewhat alike in the

> This paragraph provides a quick tour of notorious research abuses.

vulnerability of the subjects; uneducated African-American men, debilitated patients in a charity hospital, prisoners of war, inmates of concentration camps and others falling within the custody and control of the agencies conducting or approving the experiments. In the present case, children, especially young children, living in lower economic circumstances, albeit not as vulnerable as the other examples, are nonetheless, vulnerable as well.

It is clear to this Court that the scientific and medical communities cannot be permitted to assume sole authority to determine ultimately what is right and appropriate in respect to research projects involving young children free of the limitations and consequences of the application of Maryland law. The Institutional Review Boards, IRBs, are, primarily, in-house organs. In our view, they are not designed, generally, to be sufficiently objective in the sense that they are as sufficiently concerned with the ethicality of the experiments they review as they are with the success of the experiments. . . .

. . . Here, the IRB, whose primary function was to insure safety and compliance with applicable regulations, encouraged the researchers to misrepresent the purpose of the research in order to bring the study under the label of "therapeutic" and thus under a lower safety standard of regulation. The IRB's purpose was ethically wrong, and its understanding of the experiment's benefit incorrect.

The conflicts are inherent. This would be especially so when science and private industry collaborate in search of material gains. Moreover, the special relationship between research entities and human subjects used in the research will almost always impose duties.

In respect to examining that special relationship, we are obliged to further examine its nature and its ethical constraints. In that regard, when contested cases arise, the assessment of the legal effect of research on human subjects must always be subject to judicial evaluation. One method of making such evaluations is the initiation of appropriate actions bringing such matters to the attention of the courts, as has been done in the cases at bar. It may well be that in the end, the trial courts will determine that no damages have been incurred in the instant cases and thus the actions will fail for that reason. In that regard, we note that there are substantial factual differences in the Higgins and in the Grimes cases. But the actions, themselves, are not defective on the ground that no legal duty can, according to the trial courts, possibly exist. For the reasons discussed at length in the main body of the opinion, a legal duty normally exists between researcher and subject and in all probability exists in the cases at bar. Moreover, as we shall discuss, the consents of the parents in these cases under Maryland law constituted contracts creating duties. Additionally, under Maryland law, to the extent parental consent can ever be effective in research projects of this nature, the parents may not have been sufficiently informed and, therefore, the consents ineffective and, based on the information contained in the sparse records before this court, the research project, may have invaded the legal rights of the children subjected to it.

I. The Cases

We now discuss more specifically the two cases before us, and the relevant law.

Two separate negligence actions involving children who allegedly developed elevated levels of lead dust in their blood while participating in a research study with respondent, Kennedy Krieger Institute, Inc., (KKI) are before this Court. Both cases allege that the children were poisoned, or at least exposed to the risk of being poisoned, by lead dust due to negligence on the part of KKI. Specifically, they allege that KKI discovered lead hazards in their respective homes and, having a duty to notify them, failed to warn in a timely manner or otherwise act to prevent the children's exposure to the known presence of lead. Additionally, plaintiffs alleged that they were not fully informed of the risks of the research.

In the first case, Number 128, appellant, Ericka Grimes, by her mother Viola Hughes, appeals from a ruling of the Circuit Court for Baltimore City granting KKI's motion for summary judgment based on the sole ground that as a matter of law there was no legal duty, under the circumstances here present, on the part of KKI, owed to the appellants. In the second case, Number 129, appellant, Myron Higgins, by his mother Catina Higgins, and Catina Higgins, individually, appeal from a ruling of the Circuit Court for Baltimore City granting KKI's motion for summary judgment based on the ground that KKI had no legal duty to warn them of the presence of lead dust. The parties, in their respective appeals, presented almost identical issues to the Court of Special Appeals. Prior to consideration by that court, we granted certiorari to address these similar issues. We rephrase the issues in both cases in the language presented by appellants in Case Number 129:

> "Was the trial court incorrect in ruling on a motion for summary judgment that as a matter of law a research entity conducting an ongoing non-therapeutic scientific study does not have a duty to warn a minor volunteer participant and/or his legal guardian regarding dangers present when the researcher has knowledge of the potential for harm to the subject and the subject is unaware of the danger?"

We answer in the affirmative. The trial court was incorrect. Such research programs normally create special relationships and/or can be of a contractual nature, that create duties. The breaches of such duties may ultimately result in viable negligence actions. Because, at the very least, there are viable and genuine disputes of material fact concerning whether a special relationship, or other relationships arising out of agreements, giving rise to duties existed between KKI and both sets of appellants, we hold that the Circuit Court erred in granting KKI's motions for summary judgment in both cases before this Court. Accordingly, we vacate the rulings of the Circuit Court for Baltimore City and remand these cases to that court for further proceedings consistent with this opinion.

II. Facts & Procedural Background

A. The Research Study

In 1993, The Environmental Protection Agency (EPA) awarded Contract 68-D4-0001, entitled "Evaluation of Efficacy of Residential Lead Based Paint Repair and Maintenance Interventions" to KKI. KKI was to receive $200,000 for performing its responsibilities under the contract. It was thus a compensated researcher. The purpose of this research study was "to characterize and compare the short and long-term efficacy of comprehensive lead-paint abatement and less costly and potentially more cost-effective Repair and Maintenance interventions for reducing levels of lead in residential house dust which in turn should reduce lead in children's blood." As KKI acknowledged in its Clinical Investigation Consent Form, "[L]ead poisoning in children is a problem in Baltimore City and other communities across the country. Lead in paint, house dust and outside soil are major sources of lead exposure for children. Children can also be exposed to lead in drinking water and other sources." Lead poisoning poses a distinct danger to young children. It adversely effects [*sic*] cognitive development, growth, and behavior. Extremely high levels have been known to result in seizures, coma, and even death.

Dr. Mark R. Farfel Sc.D., Director of KKI's Lead Abatement Department, testified in his deposition:

> "The scientific goal of the study is to document the longevity of various lead base paint abatement strategies, factored in terms of reducing lead exposure in house dust and the children's blood lead levels.
>
> . . . .
>
> A. Our study design called for collection of blood lead, venous blood lead from participating children.
>
> . . . [S]tudy protocol called for serial blood lead levels corresponding with the dust collection campaigns. . . . [T]he study goal was to get a baseline, two months, six months, twelve months, eighteen months evaluation.
>
> . . . The study protocol, the data collection protocol was to get close in time the environmental measurements and the venous blood lead."

The research study was sponsored jointly by the EPA and the Maryland Department of Housing and Community Development (DHCD). It was thus a joint federal and state project. The Baltimore City Health Department and Maryland Department of the Environment also collaborated in the study. It appears that, because the study was funded and sponsored in part by a federal entity, certain federal conditions were attached to the funding grants and approvals. There are certain uniform standards required in respect to federally funded or approved projects. We, however, are unaware of, and have not been directed to, any federal or state statute or regulation that imposes limits on this Court's powers to conduct its review of the issues presented. None of the parties have questioned this Court's jurisdiction in these cases. Moreover, 45 Code Federal Regulations (C.F.R.) 46.116 (e) specifically provides: "The informed consent requirements in this policy are not intended to preempt any applicable federal, state, or local laws which require additional information to be disclosed in order for informed consent to be legally effective." Those various federal or state conditions, recommendations, etc., may well be relevant at a trial on the merits as to whether any breach of a contractual or other duty occurred, or whether negligence did, in fact, occur; but have no limiting effect on the issue of whether, at law, legal duties, via contract or "special relationships" are created in Maryland in experimental nontherapeutic research involving Maryland children.

This was not "rogue" research but rather was funded by the EPA and Maryland.

The research study included five test groups, each consisting of twenty-five houses. The first three groups consisted of houses with a considerable amount of lead dust present therein and each group received assigned amounts of maintenance and repair. The fourth group consisted of houses, which at one time had lead present in the form of lead based paint but had since received a supposedly complete abatement of lead dust. The fifth group consisted of modern houses, which had never had a presence of lead dust. The aim of the research study was to analyze the effectiveness of different degrees of partial lead paint abatement in reducing levels of lead dust present in these houses. The ultimate aim of the research was to find a less than complete level of abatement that would be relatively safe, but economical, so that Baltimore landlords with lower socio-economical rental units would not abandon the units. The research study was specifically designed, in part, to do less than comprehensive lead paint abatement in order to study the potential effectiveness, if any, over a period of time, of lesser levels of repair and maintenance on the presence of lead dust by measuring the presence of lead in the blood of theretofore (as far as the record of the cases reveals) healthy children. In essence, the study at its inception was designed not only to test current levels of lead in the blood of the children, but the increase or decrease in future lead levels in the blood that would be affected by the various abatement programs. It appears that this study was also partially motivated, as we have indicated, by the reaction of property owners in Baltimore City to the cost of lead dust abatement. The cost of full abatement of such housing at times far exceeded the monetary worth of the property—in other words, the cost of full abatement was simply too high for certain landlords to be able to afford to pay or be willing to pay. As a result, some lower level rental properties containing lead based paint in Baltimore had been simply abandoned and left vacant. The study was attempting to determine whether a less expensive means of rehabilitation could be available to the owners of such properties.

One way the study was designed to measure the effectiveness of such abatement measures was to measure the lead dust levels in the houses at intervals and to compare them with the levels of lead found, at roughly the same intervals, in the blood of the children living in the respective houses. The project required that small children be present in the houses. To facilitate that purpose, the landlords agreeing to permit their properties to be included in the studies were encouraged, if not required, to rent the properties to tenants who had young children.

In return for permitting the properties to be used and in return for limiting their tenants to families with young children, KKI assisted the landlords in applying for and receiving grants or loans of money to be used to perform the levels of abatement required by KKI for each class of home.

. . . .

In summary, KKI conducted a study of five test groups of twenty-five houses each. The first three groups consisted of houses known to have lead present. The amount of repair and maintenance conducted increased from Group 1 to Group 2 to Group 3. The fourth group consisted of houses, which had at one time lead present but had since allegedly received a complete abatement of lead dust. The fifth group consisted of modern houses, which had never had the presence of lead dust. The twenty-five homes in each of the first three testing levels were then to be compared to the two control groups: the twenty-five homes in Group 4 that had previously been abated and the 25 modern homes in Group 5. The research study was specifically designed to do less than full lead dust abatement in some of the categories of houses in order to study the potential effectiveness, if any, of lesser levels of repair and maintenance.

If the children were to leave the houses upon the first manifestation of lead dust, it would be difficult, if not impossible, to test, over time, the rate of the level of lead accumulation in the blood of the children attributable to the manifestation. In other words, if the children were removed from the houses before the lead dust levels in their blood became elevated, the tests would probably fail, or at least the data that would establish the success of the test—or of the abatement results, would be of questionable use. Thus, it would benefit the accuracy of the test, and thus KKI, the compensated researcher, if children remained in the houses over the period of the study even after the presence of lead dust in the houses became evident.

B. Case No. 128

Appellant, Ericka Grimes, resided at 1713 N. Monroe Street in Baltimore, Maryland (the Monroe Street property) with members of her family from the time of her birth on May 30, 1992, up until the summer of 1994. Her mother, Viola Hughes, had lived in the property since the Summer of 1990. In March 1993, representatives of KKI came to Ms. Hughes's home and successfully recruited her to participate in the research study. After a discussion regarding the nature, purpose, scope, and benefits of the study, Ms. Hughes agreed to participate and signed a Consent Form dated March 10, 1993.

Nowhere in the consent form was it clearly disclosed to the mother that the researchers contemplated that, as a result of the experiment, the child might accumulate lead in her blood, and that in order for the experiment to succeed it was necessary that the child remain in the house as the lead in the child's blood increased or decreased, so that it could be measured. The Consent Form states in relevant part:

> "PURPOSE OF STUDY: As you may know, lead poisoning in children is a problem in Baltimore City and other communities across the country. Lead in paint, house dust and outside soil are major sources of lead exposure for children. Children can also be exposed to lead in drinking water and other sources. We understand that your house is going to have special repairs done in order to reduce exposure to lead in paint and dust. On a random basis, homes will receive one of two levels of repair. We are interested in finding out how well the two levels of repair work. The repairs are not intended, or expected, to completely remove exposure to lead.
>
> We are now doing a study to learn about how well different practices work for reducing exposure to lead in paint and dust. We are asking you and over one hundred other families to allow us to test for lead in and around your homes up to 8 to 9 times over the next two years provided that your house qualifies for the full two years of study. Final eligibility will be determined after the initial testing of your home. We are also doing free blood lead testing of children aged 6 months to 7 years, up to 8 to 9 times over the next two years. We would also like you to respond to a short questionnaire every 6 months. This study is intended to monitor the effects of the repairs and is not intended to replace the regular medical care your family obtains.
>
> . . . .
>
> BENEFITS
>
> To compensate you for your time answering questions and allowing us to sketch your home we will mail you a check in the amount of $5.00. In the future we would mail you a check in the amount of $15 each time the full questionnaire is completed. The dust, soil, water, and blood samples would be tested for lead at the Kennedy Krieger Institute at no charge to you. We would provide you with specific blood-lead results. We would contact you to discuss a summary of house test results and steps that you could take to reduce any risks of exposure."

Pursuant to the plans of the research study, KKI collected dust samples in the Monroe Street property on March 9, 1993, August 23, 1993, March 9, 1994, September 19, 1994, April 18, 1995, and November 13, 1995. The March 9, 1993 dust testing revealed what the researchers referred to as "hot spots" where the level of lead was "higher than might be found in a completely renovated [abated] house." This information about the "hot spots" was not furnished to Ms. Hughes until December 16, 1993, more than nine months after the samples had been collected and, as we discuss, infra, not until after Ericka Grimes's blood was found to contain elevated levels of lead.

KKI drew blood from Ericka Grimes for lead content analysis on April, 9, 1993, September 15, 1993, and March 25, 1994. Unlike the lead concentration analysis in dust testing, the results of the blood testing were typically available to KKI in a matter of days. KKI notified Ms. Hughes of the results of the blood tests by letters dated April 9, 1993, September 29, 1993, and March 28, 1994, respectively. The results of the April 9, 1993 test found Ericka Grimes blood to be less than 9 Pg/dL, which placed her results in the "normal" range according to classifications established by the Centers for Disease Control (CDC). However, on two subsequent retests, long after KKI had identified "hot spots," but before KKI informed Ms. Hughes of the "hot spots," Ericka Grimes's blood lead level registered Class III — 32 μ>g/dL on September 15, 1993 and 22 μg/dL on March 25, 1994. Ms. Hughes and her daughter vacated the Monroe Street property in the Summer of 1994, and, therefore, no further blood samples were obtained by KKI after March 25, 1994.

> Note the time lag between the blood test and KKI's reporting results to the Grimes family.

In her Complaint filed in the Circuit Court for Baltimore City, Ms. Hughes sought to hold KKI liable for negligence for failing to warn of, or abate, lead-paint hazards that KKI allegedly discovered in the Monroe Street property during the research study. Specifically, she alleged:

"3. As part of the [Research] Study, [appellant's] mother agreed to allow [KKI] to periodically inspect the Monroe Street property for the presence of lead-paint hazards. Upon inspection, [KKI] discovered the existence of lead-paint hazards within [appellant's] home, but failed to inform and/or warn [appellant] and her mother of such hazards and failed to take any action to abate said hazards. As a consequence, [appellant] and her mother continued to reside in the home unaware of the hazards and unaware of the dangers to which [appellant] was being exposed."

C. Case No. 129 [involving the Higgins family] . . .

. . . .

III. Discussion

A. Standard of Review

We resolve these disputes in the context of the trial court's granting of the appellee's motions for summary judgment in the two distinct cases. The threshold issues before this Court are whether, in the two cases presented, appellee, KKI, was entitled to summary judgment as a matter of law on the basis that no contract existed and that there is inherently no duty owed to a research subject by a researcher. Perhaps even more important is the ancillary issue of whether a parent in Maryland, under the law of this State, can legally consent to placing a child in a nontherapeutic research study that carries with it any risk of harm to the health of the child. We shall resolve all of these primary issues.

. . . .

B. General Discussion

Initially, we note that we know of no law, nor have we been directed to any applicable in Maryland courts, that provides that the parties to a scientific study, because it is a scientific, health-related study, cannot be held to have entered into special relationships with the subjects of the study that can create duties, including duties, the breach of which may give rise to negligence claims. We also are not aware of any general legal precept that immunizes nongovernmental "institutional volunteers" or scientific researchers from the responsibility for the breaches of duties arising in "special relationships." Moreover, we, at the very least, hold that, under the particular circumstances testified to by the parties, there are genuine disputes of material fact concerning whether a special relationship existed between KKI and Ericka Grimes, as well as between KKI and Ms. Higgins and Myron Higgins. Concerning this issue, the granting of the summary judgment motions was clearly inappropriate. When a "special relationship" can exist as a matter of law, the issue of whether, given certain facts, a special relationship does exist, when there is a dispute of material fact in that respect, is a decision for the finder of fact, not the trial judge. We shall hold initially that the very nature of nontherapeutic scientific research on human subjects can, and normally will, create special relationships out of which duties arise. Since World War II the specialness or nature of such relationships has been frequently of concern in and outside of the research community.

As a result of the atrocities performed in the name of science during the Holocaust, and other happenings in the World War II era, what is now known as The Nuremberg Code evolved. Of special interest to this Court, the Nuremberg Code, at least in significant part, was the result of legal thought and legal principles, as opposed to medical or scientific principles, and thus should be the preferred standard for assessing the legality of scientific research on human subjects. . . .

. . . .

Some analysts contend that IRB review tends to focus exclusively on consent requirements, rather than fully evaluating the merits of the research. Yet, it is important to recognize that, even before consent becomes an issue, the scientific merits and the acceptability of risks need to be appraised. As at least one author has argued, this aspect of the review may be jeopardized if members who have institutional allegiances are caught between the desire to promote the interests of the institution and the need to protect the subject.

C. Investigator-Subject Relationship

Another notable difference between treatment and experimentation lies in the relationship between physician-patient and investigator-subject. . . .

Indeed, as discussed in relation to the notion of uncertainty, the nature of the information held by the investigator can be very different from that of the information held by a treating physician. . . .

. . . .

Just recently the research community has been subjected to question as a result of genetic experimentation on a Pennsylvania citizen. Jesse Gelsinger consented to participate in a research project at the University of Pennsylvania's Institute of Human Gene Therapy. After Gelsinger's death, the U.S. Food and Drug Administration ordered a halt to eight human gene therapy experiments at the Institute. Additionally, other similar projects were halted elsewhere. The FDA took the action after a "discovery of a number of serious problems in the Institute's informed consent procedures and, more generally, a lapse in the researchers' ethical responsibilities to experimental subjects."

Gelsinger had a different type of ornithine transcarbamylase deficiency (OTC) disease, than that addressed by the research. His particular brand of the disease was under control. There was no possibility that the research being conducted would directly benefit him. It was thus, as to him, as it was to the children in the case at bar, nontherapeutic; a way to study the affects [*sic*] on the subjects (in the present case, the children) in order to measure the success of the experiment. In Gelsinger's case, the research was to test the efficiency of disease vectors. In other words, weakened adenovirus (common-cold viruses) were used to deliver trillions of particles of a particular OTC gene into his artery and thus to his liver. Gelsinger experienced a massive and fatal immune system reaction to the introduction of the common-cold virus. . . .

Because of the way the cases sub judice have arrived, as appeals from the granting of summary judgments, there is no complete record of the specific compensation of the researchers involved. Although the project was funded by the EPA, at the request of KKI the EPA has declined to furnish such information to the attorney for one of the parties, who requested it under the federal Freedom of Information Act. Whether the research's character as a co-sponsored state project opens the records under the Maryland Public Information Act has apparently not been considered. Neither is there in the record any development of what pressures, if any, were exerted in respect to the researchers obtaining the consents of the parents and conducting the experiment. Nor, for the same reason, is there a sufficient indication as to the extent to which the Institute has joined with commercial interests, if it has, for the purposes of profit, that might potentially impact upon the researcher's motivations and potential conflicts of interest — motivations that generally are assumed, in the cases of prestigious entities such as John Hopkins University, to be for the public good rather than a search for profit.

> The *Gelsinger* case is discussed below. Consider how lead poisoning research may be different from studying a rare liver disease, if at all, in constructing the research and attendant consents.

We do note that the institution involved, the respondent here, . . . is a highly respected entity, considered to be a leader in the development of treatments, and treatment itself, for children infected with lead poisoning. With reasonable assurance, we can note that its reputation alone might normally suggest that there was no realization or understanding on the Institute's part that the protocols of the experiment were questionable, except for the letter from the IRB requesting that the researchers mischaracterize the study.

We shall further address both the factual and legal bases for the findings of the trial courts, holding, ultimately, that the respective courts erred in both respects.

C. Negligence

It is important for us to remember that appellants allege that KKI was negligent. Specifically, they allege that KKI, as a medical researcher, owed a duty of care to them, as subjects in the research study, based on the nature of the agreements between them and also based on the nature of the relationship between the parties. They contend specifically that KKI was negligent because KKI breached its duty to: (1) design a study that did not involve placing children at unnecessary risk; (2) inform participants in the study of results in a timely manner; and (3) to completely and accurately inform participants in the research study of all the hazards and risks involved in the study.

In order to establish a claim for negligence under Maryland law, a party must prove four elements: "(1) that the defendant was under a duty to protect the plaintiff from injury, (2) that the defendant breached that duty, (3) that the plaintiff suffered actual injury or loss and (4) that the loss or injury proximately resulted from the defendant's breach of the duty." Because this is a review of the granting of the two summary judgments based solely on the grounds that there was no legal duty to protect the children, we are primarily concerned with the first prong — whether KKI was under a duty to protect appellants from injury.

. . . As one court suggested, there are a number of variables to be considered in determining if a duty exists to another, such as:

> the foreseeability of harm to the plaintiff, the degree of certainty that the plaintiff suffered the injury, the closeness of the connection between the defendant's conduct and the injury suffered, the moral blame attached to the defendant's conduct, the policy of preventing future harm, the extent of the burden to the defendant and consequences to the community of imposing a duty to exercise care with resulting liability for breach, and the availability, cost and prevalence of insurance for the risk involved.

Tarasoff v. Regents of University of California, 551 P.2d 334, 342 ([Cal.] 1976). . . .

The relationship that existed between KKI and both sets of appellants in the case at bar was that of medical researcher and research study subject. Though not expressly recognized in the Maryland Code or in our prior cases as a type of relationship which creates a duty of care, evidence in the record suggests that such a relationship involving a duty or duties would ordinarily exist, and certainly could exist, based on the facts and circumstances of each of these individual cases. Once we have determined that the facts and circumstances of the present cases, considered in a light most favorable to the nonmoving parties, are susceptible to inferences supporting the position of the party opposing summary judgment, we are mandated to hold that the granting of summary judgment in the lower court was improper. In addition to the trial courts' erroneous conclusions on the law, the facts and circumstances of both of these cases are susceptible to inferences that a special relationship imposing a duty or duties was created in the arrangements in the cases sub judice, and, ordinarily, could be created in similar research programs involving human subjects.

IV. The Special Relationships

A. The Consent Agreement

Contract

Both sets of appellants signed a similar Consent Form prepared by KKI in which KKI expressly promised to: (1) financially compensate (however minimally) appellants for their participation in the study; (2) collect lead dust samples from appellants' homes, analyze the samples, discuss the results with appellants, and discuss steps that could be taken, which could reduce exposure to lead; and (3) collect blood samples from children in the household and provide appellants with the results of the blood tests. In return, appellants agreed to participate in the study, by: (1) allowing KKI into appellants' homes to collect dust samples; (2) periodically filling out questionnaires; and (3) allowing the children's blood to be drawn, tested, and utilized in the study. If consent agreements contain such provisions, and the trial court did not find otherwise, and we hold from our own examination of the record that such provisions were so contained, mutual assent, offer, acceptance, and consideration existed, all of which created contractual relationships imposing duties by reason of the consent agreement themselves (as well, as we discuss elsewhere, by the very nature of such relationships).

By having appellants sign this Consent Form, both KKI and appellants expressly made representations, which, in our view, created a bilateral contract between the parties. At the very least, it suggests that appellants were agreeing with KKI to participate in the research study with the expectation that they would be compensated, albeit, more or less, minimally, be informed of all the information necessary for the subject to freely choose whether to participate, and continue to participate, and receive promptly any information that might bear on their willingness to continue to participate in the study. This includes full, detailed, prompt, and continuing warnings as to all the potential risks and hazards inherent in the research or that arise during the research. KKI, in return, was getting the children to move into the houses and/or to remain there over time, and was given the right to test the children's blood for lead. As consideration to KKI, it got access to the houses and to the blood of children that had been encouraged to live in a "risk" environment. In other words, KKI received a measuring tool — the children's blood. Considerations existed, mainly money, food coupons, trinkets, bilateral promises, blood to be tested in order to measure success. "Informed consent" of the type used here, which imposes obligation and confers consideration on both researcher and subject (in these cases, the parents of the subjects) may differ from the more one-sided "informed consent" normally used in actual medical practice. Researcher/subject consent in nontherapeutic research can, and in this case did, create a contract.

B. The Sufficiency of the Consent Form

The consent form did not directly inform the parents of the fact that it was contemplated that some of the children might ingest lead dust particles, and that one of the reasons the blood of the children was to be tested was to evaluate how effective the various abatement measures were.

A reasonable parent would expect to be clearly informed that it was at least contemplated that her child would ingest lead dust particles, and that the degree to which lead dust contaminated the child's blood would be used as one of the ways in which the success of the experiment would be measured. The fact that if such information was furnished, it might be difficult to obtain human subjects for the research, does not affect the need to supply the information, or alter the ethics of failing to provide such information. A human subject is entitled to all material information. The respective parent should also have been clearly informed that in order for the measurements to be most helpful, the child needed to stay in the house until the conclusion of the study. Whether assessed by a subjective or an objective standard, the children, or their surrogates, should have been additionally informed that the researchers anticipated that, as a result of the experiment, it was possible that there might be some accumulation of lead in the blood of the children. The "informed" consent was not valid because full material information was not furnished to the subjects or their parents. . . .

> It helps to review the language from the consent form reproduced above.

As we indicated earlier, the trial courts appear to have held that special relationships out of which duties arise cannot be created by the relationship between researchers and the subjects of the research. While in some rare cases that may be correct, it is not correct when researchers recruit people, especially children whose consent is furnished indirectly, to participate in nontherapeutic procedures that are potentially hazardous, dangerous, or deleterious to their health. As opposed to compilation of already extant statistics for purposes of studying human health matters, the creation of study conditions or protocols or participation in the recruitment of otherwise healthy subjects to interact with already existing, or potentially existing, hazardous conditions, or both, for the purpose of creating statistics from which scientific hypotheses can be supported, would normally warrant or create such special relationships as a matter of law.

It is of little moment that an entity is an institutional volunteer in a community. If otherwise, the legitimacy of the claim to noble purpose would always depend upon the particular institution and the particular community it is serving in a given case. As we have indicated, history is replete with claims of noble purpose for institutions and institutional volunteers in a wide variety of communities.

Institutional volunteers may intend to do good or, as history has proven, even to do evil and may do evil or good depending on the institution and the community they serve. Whether an institutional volunteer in a particular community should be granted exceptions from the application of law is a matter that should be scrutinized closely by an appropriate public policy maker. Generally, but not always, the legislative branch is appropriately the best first forum to consider exceptions to the tort laws of this State — even then it should consider all ramifications of the policy — especially considering the general vulnerability of subjects of such studies — in this case, small children. In the absence of the exercise of legislative policymaking, we hold that special relationships, out of which duties arise, the breach of which can constitute negligence, can result from the relationships between researcher and research subjects.

D. The Federal Regulations

A duty may be prescribed by a statute, or a special relationship creating duties may arise from the requirement for compliance with statutory provisions. Although there is no duty of which we are aware prescribed by the Maryland Code in respect to scientific research of the nature here present, federal regulations have been enacted that impose standards of care that attach to federally funded or sponsored research projects that use human subjects. *See* 45 C.F.R. Part 46 (2000). 45 C.F.R. Part 46, Subpart A, is entitled "Basic HHS Policy for Protection of Human Research Subjects" and Subpart D of the regulation is entitled "Additional Protections for Children Involved as Subjects in Research." 45 C.F.R. section 46.101(a) (2000) provides:

"Sec. 46.101

(a) Except as provided in paragraph (b) of this section, this policy applies to all research involving human subjects conducted, supported or otherwise subject to regulation by any federal department or agency which takes appropriate administrative action to make the policy applicable to such research. This includes research conducted by federal civilian employees or military personnel, except that each department or agency head may adopt such procedural modifications as may be appropriate from an administrative standpoint. It also includes research conducted, supported, or otherwise subject to regulation by the federal government outside the United States."

As we discussed, this study was funded, and co-sponsored, by the EPA and presumably was therefore subject to these federal conditions. These conditions, if appropriate administrative action has been taken, require fully informed consent in any research using human subjects conducted, supported, or otherwise subject to any level of control or funding by any federal department or agency. 45 C.F.R. section 46.116 provides in relevant part:

"Sec. 46.116 General requirements for informed consent.

Except as provided elsewhere in this policy, no investigator may involve a human being as a subject in research covered by this policy unless the investigator has obtained the *legally effective* informed consent of the subject or the subject's legally authorized representative. *An investigator shall seek such consent only under circumstances that provide the prospective subject or the representative sufficient opportunity to consider whether or not to participate and that minimize the possibility of coercion or undue influence.* The information that is given to the subject or the representative shall be in language understandable to the subject or the representative. No informed consent, whether oral or written, may include any exculpatory language through which the subject or the representative is made to waive or appear to waive any of the subject's legal rights, or releases or appears to release the investigator, the sponsor, the institution or its agents from liability for negligence. . . ." [Emphasis added.]

Subpart D of the regulation concerns children involved as subjects in research. 45 C.F.R. section 46.407 therefore additionally provides:

"Sec. 46.407 Research not otherwise approvable which presents an opportunity to understand, prevent, or alleviate a serious problem affecting the health or welfare of children. HHS will conduct or fund research that the IRB does not believe meets the requirements of Sec. 46.404, Sec. 46.405, or Sec. 46.406 only if:

(a) The IRB finds that the research presents a reasonable opportunity to further the understanding, prevention, or alleviation of a serious problem affecting the health or welfare of children; *and*

(b) *The Secretary, after consultation with a panel of experts in pertinent disciplines (for example: science, medicine, education, ethics, law) and following opportunity for public review and comment, has determined either:*

(1) That the research in fact satisfies the conditions of Sec. 46.404, Sec. 46.405, or Sec. 46.406, as applicable, or

(2) The following:

(i) The research presents a reasonable opportunity to further the understanding, prevention, or alleviation of a serious problem affecting the health or welfare of children;

(ii) *The research will be conducted in accordance with sound ethical principles;*

(iii) Adequate provisions are made for soliciting the assent of children and the permission of their parents or guardians, as set forth in Sec. 46.408." [Emphasis added]

These federal regulations, especially the requirement for adherence to sound ethical principles, strike right at the heart of KKI's defense of the granting of the Motions for Summary Judgment. *Fully informed* consent is lacking in these cases.

The research did not comply with the regulations. There clearly was more than a minimal risk involved. Under the regulations, children should not have been used for the purpose of measuring how much lead they would accumulate in their blood while living in partially abated houses to which they were recruited initially or encouraged to remain, because of the study.

In the case of Whitlock v. Duke University, 637 F. Supp. 1463 (M.D.N.C. 1986), *affirmed*, 829 F.2d 1340 (4th Cir. 1987), the United States District Court for the Middle District of North Carolina decided that in determining what duty a researcher owes to a subject of nontherapeutic experimentation, it would analyze a duty consistent with 45 C.F.R. section 46.116. That court held that a researcher has a duty to inform the subject of all risks that are reasonably foreseeable. *Whitlock* involved a subject who suffered organic brain damage from decompression experiments. The District Court ultimately held (and was affirmed by the Court of Appeals for the Fourth Circuit) that although a heightened duty existed between a researcher and an adult research participant requiring the researcher to disclose all foreseeable risks, in *Whitlock* there was no evidence presented that the risk of organic brain damage was foreseeable.

That result is clearly distinguishable from the present cases, where the risks associated with exposing children to lead-based paint were not only foreseeable, but were well known by KKI, and, in fact, it had to have been reasonably foreseeable by KKI that the children's blood might be contaminated by lead because the extent of contamination of the blood of the children would, in significant part, be used to measure the effectiveness of the various abatement methods. Moreover, in the present cases, the consent forms did not directly inform the parents that it was possible, even contemplated, that some level of lead, a harmful substance depending upon accumulation, might contaminate the blood of the children.

Clearly, KKI, as a research institution, is required to obtain a human participant's fully informed consent, using sound ethical principles. It is clear from the wording of the applicable federal regulations that this requirement of informed consent continues during the duration of the research study and applies to new or changing risks. In this case, a special relationship out of which duties might arise might be created by reason of the federally imposed regulations. The question becomes whether this duty of informed consent created by federal regulation, as a matter of state law, translates into a duty of care arising out of the unique relationship that is researcher-subject, as opposed to doctor-patient. We answer that question in the affirmative. In this State, it may, depending on the facts, create such a duty.

Additionally, the Nuremberg Code, intended to be applied internationally, and never expressly rejected in this country, inherently and implicitly, speaks strongly to the existence of special relationships imposing ethical duties on researchers who conduct nontherapeutic experiments on human subjects. The Nuremberg Code specifically requires researche[r]s to make known to human subjects of research "all inconveniences and hazards reasonably to be expected, and the effects upon his health or person which may *possibly* come from his participation in the experiment." (Emphasis added.) The breach of obligations imposed on researchers by the Nuremberg Code, might well support actions sounding in negligence in cases such as those at issue here. We reiterate as well that, given the facts and circumstances of both of these cases, there were, at the very least, genuine disputes of material facts concerning the relationship and duties of the parties, and compliance with the regulations.

V. The Ethical Appropriateness of the Research

The World Medical Association in its Declaration of Helsinki included a code of ethics for investigative researchers and was an attempt by the medical community to establish its own set of rules for conducting research on human subjects. The Declaration states in relevant part:

"III. Non-therapeutic biomedical research involving human subjects
(Non-clinical biomedical research)
1. *In the purely scientific application of medical research carried out on a human being, it is the duty of the physician to remain the protector of the life and health of that person on whom biomedical research is being carried out.*
2. The subjects should be volunteers — either healthy persons or patients for whom the experimental design is not related to the patient's illness.
3. The investigator or the investigating team should *discontinue the research if in his/her or their judgement it may, if continued, be harmful to the individual.*
4. *In research on man, the interest of science and society should never take precedence over considerations related to the well being of the subject.*" [Emphasis added.]

The determination of whether a duty exists under Maryland law is the ultimate function of various policy considerations as adopted by either the Legislature, or, if it has not spoken, as it has not in respect to this situation, by Maryland courts. In our view, otherwise healthy children should not be the subjects of nontherapeutic experimentation or research that has the potential to be harmful to the child. It is, first and foremost, the responsibility of the researcher and the research entity to see to the harmlessness of such nontherapeutic research. Consent of parents can never relieve the researcher of this duty. We do not feel that it serves proper public policy concerns to permit children to be placed in situations of potential harm, during nontherapeutic procedures, even if parents, or other surrogates, consent. Under these types of circumstances, even where consent is given, albeit inappropriately, policy considerations suggest that there remains a special relationship between researchers and participants to the research study, which imposes a duty of care. This is entirely consistent with the principles found in the Nuremberg Code.

Researchers cannot ever be permitted to completely immunize themselves by reliance on consents, especially when the information furnished to the subject, or the party consenting, is incomplete in a material respect. A researcher's duty is not created by, or extinguished by, the consent of a research subject or by IRB approval. The duty to a vulnerable research subject is independent of consent, although the obtaining of consent is one of the duties a researcher must perform. All of this is especially so when the subjects of research are children. Such legal duties, and legal protections, might additionally be warranted because of the likely conflict of interest between the goal of the research experimenter and the health of the human subject, especially, but not exclusively, when such research is commercialized. There is always a potential substantial conflict of interest on the part of researchers as between them and the human subjects used in their research. If participants in the study withdraw from the research study prior to its completion, then the results of the study could be rendered meaningless. There is thus an inherent reason for not conveying information to subjects as it arises, that might cause the subjects to leave the research project. That conflict dictates a stronger reason for full and continuous disclosure. . . .

While we acknowledge that foreseeability does not necessarily create a duty, we recognize that potential harm to the children participants of this study was both foreseeable and potentially extreme. A "special relationship" also exists in circumstances where such experiments are conducted.

VI. Parental Consent for Children to Be Subjects of Potentially Hazardous Nontherapeutic Research

The issue of whether a parent can consent to the participation of her or his child in a nontherapeutic health-related study that is known to be potentially hazardous to the health of the child raises serious questions with profound moral and ethical implications. What right does a parent have to knowingly expose a child not in need of therapy to health risks or otherwise knowingly place a child in danger, even if it can be argued it is for the greater good? The issue in these specific contested cases does not relate primarily to the authority of the parent, but to the procedures of KKI and similar entities that may be involved in such health-related studies. The issue of the parents' right to consent on behalf of the children has not been fully presented in either of these cases, but should be of concern not only to lawyers and judges, but to moralists, ethicists, and others. The consenting parents in the contested cases at bar were not the subjects of the experiment; the children were. Additionally, this practice presents the potential problems of children initiating actions in their own names upon reaching majority, if indeed, they have been damaged as a result of being used as guinea pigs in nontherapeutic scientific research. Children, it should be noted, are not in our society the equivalent of rats, hamsters, monkeys, and the like. Because of the overriding importance of this matter and this Court's interest in the welfare of children—we shall address the issue.

Most of the relatively few cases in the area of the ethics of protocols of various research projects involving children have merely assumed that a parent can give informed consent for the participation of their children in nontherapeutic research. The single case in which the issue has been addressed, and resolved, a case with which we agree, will be discussed further, infra.

It is not in the best interest of a specific child, in a nontherapeutic research project, to be placed in a research environment, which might possibly be, or which proves to be, hazardous to the health of the child. We have long stressed that the "best interests of the child" is the overriding concern of this Court in matters relating to children. Whatever the interests of a parent, and whatever the interests of the general public in fostering research that might, according to a researcher's hypothesis, be for the good of all children, this Court's concern for the particular child and particular case, over-arches all other interests. It is, simply, and we hope, succinctly put, not in the best interest of any healthy child to be intentionally put in a nontherapeutic situation where his or her health may be impaired, in order to test methods that may ultimately benefit all children.

To think otherwise, to turn over human and legal ethical concerns solely to the scientific community, is to risk embarking on slippery slopes, that all too often in the past, here and elsewhere, have resulted in practices we, or any community, should be ever unwilling to accept.

We have little doubt that the general motives of all concerned in these contested cases were, for the most part, proper, albeit in our view not well thought out. The protocols of the research, those of which we have been made aware, were, in any event, unacceptable in a legal context. One simply does not expose otherwise healthy children, incapable of personal assent (consent), to a nontherapeutic research environment that is known at the inception of the research, might cause the children to ingest lead dust. It is especially troublesome, when a measurement of the success of the research experiment is, in significant respect, to be determined by the extent to which the blood of the children absorbs, and is contaminated by, a substance that the researcher knows can, in sufficient amounts, whether solely from the research environment or cumulative from all sources, cause serious and long term adverse health effects. Such a practice is not legally acceptable.

. . . .

In the case sub judice, no impartial judicial review or oversight was sought by the researchers or by the parents. Additionally, in spite of the IRB's improper attempt to manufacture a therapeutic value, there was absolutely no such value of the research in respect to the minor subjects used to measure the effectiveness of the study. In the absence of a requirement for judicial review, in such a circumstance, the researchers, and their scientific based review boards would be, if permitted, the sole judges of whether it is appropriate to use children in nontherapeutic research of the nature here present, where the success of an experiment is to be measured, in substantial part, by the degree to which the research environments cause the absorption of poisons into the blood of children. Science cannot be permitted to be the sole judge of the appropriateness of such research methods on human subjects, especially in respect to children. We hold that in these contested cases, the research study protocols, those of which we are aware, were not appropriate.

When it comes to children involved in nontherapeutic research, with the potential for health risks to the subject children in Maryland, we will not defer to science to be the sole determinant of the ethicality or legality of such experiments. The reason, in our view, is apparent from the research protocols at issue in the case at bar. Moreover, in nontherapeutic research using children, we hold that the consent of a parent alone cannot make appropriate that which is innately inappropriate.

. . . .

Conclusion

We hold that in Maryland a parent, appropriate relative, or other applicable surrogate, cannot consent to the participation of a child or other person under legal disability in nontherapeutic research or studies in which there is any risk of injury or damage to the health of the subject.

We hold that informed consent agreements in nontherapeutic research projects, under certain circumstances can constitute contracts; and that, under certain circumstances, such research agreements can, as a matter of law, constitute "special relationships" giving rise to duties, out of the breach of which negligence actions may arise. We also hold that, normally, such special relationships are created between researchers and the human subjects used by the researchers. Additionally, we hold that governmental regulations can create duties on the part of researchers towards human subjects out of which "special relationships" can arise. Likewise, such duties and relationships are consistent with the provisions of the Nuremberg Code.

The determination as to whether a "special relationship" actually exists is to be done on a case by case basis. The determination as to whether a special relationship exists, if properly pled, lies with the trier of fact. We hold that there was ample evidence in the cases at bar to support a fact finder's determination of the existence of duties arising out of contract, or out of a special relationship, or out of regulations and codes, or out of all of them, in each of the cases.

We hold that on the present record, the Circuit Courts erred in their assessment of the law and of the facts as pled in granting KKI's motions for summary judgment in both cases before this Court. Accordingly, we vacate the rulings of the Circuit Court for Baltimore City and remand these cases to that court for further proceedings consistent with this opinion.

QUESTIONS

1. Can parents consent to their children's participation in nontherapeutic research at any time in Maryland? What about other states?
2. Does the Common Rule preempt this court's decision?
3. If you were legally advising KKI, what would you tell the researchers to do differently? Can you draft an effective consent for this research, or script a conversation?
4. Do you think the IRB ran afoul of the Common Rule? If so, which section(s)?

The *Grimes* case presents an example of researchers harming research subjects as a result of improper consent procedures and research protocols. The next case offers a different perspective, one in which the human subjects knowingly contributed not only their bodies (in contrast to *Moore*) but also financial support to a researcher, only to find that the research led to a patented process that excluded them from accessing the fruits of their research contributions.

Greenberg v. Miami Children's Hospital Research Institute, Inc.

264 F. Supp. 2d 1064 (S.D. Fla. 2003)

. . . .

I. Background

Plaintiffs Daniel Greenberg ("Greenberg"), Fern Kupfer ("Kupfer"), Frieda Eisen ("Eisen"), David Green ("Green"), Canavan Foundation, Dor Yeshorim, and National Tay-Sachs and Allied Diseases Association, Inc. (collectively "Plaintiffs") brought this diversity action for damages and equitable and injunctive relief to redress Defendants' alleged breach of informed consent, breach of fiduciary duty, unjust enrichment, fraudulent concealment, conversion, and misappropriation of trade secrets. The individual plaintiffs Greenberg, Kupfer, Eisen, and Green are parents of children who were afflicted with Canavan disease. The other Plaintiffs are non-profit organizations that provided funding and information to Defendants to research and discover the Canavan disease gene. Defendants are the physician-researcher, Dr. Reuben Matalon ("Matalon"), Variety Children's Hospital d/b/a Miami Children's Hospital ("MCH"), and the hospital's research affiliate, Miami Children's Hospital Research Institute ("MCHRI").

The Complaint alleges a tale of a successful research collaboration gone sour. In 1987, Canavan disease still remained a mystery—there was no way to identify who was a carrier of the disease, nor was there a way to identify a fetus with Canavan disease. Plaintiff Greenberg approached Dr. Matalon, a research physician who was then affiliated with the University of Illinois at Chicago[,] for assistance. Greenberg requested Matalon's involvement in discovering the genes that were ostensibly responsible for this fatal disease, so that tests could be administered to determine carriers and allow for prenatal testing for the disease.

At the outset of the collaboration, Greenberg and the Chicago Chapter of the National Tay-Sachs and Allied Disease Association, Inc. ("NTSAD") located other Canavan families and convinced them to provide tissue (such as blood, urine, and autopsy samples), financial support, and aid in identifying the location of Canavan families internationally. The other individual Plaintiffs began supplying Matalon with the same types of information and samples beginning in the late 1980s. Greenberg and NTSAD also created a confidential database and compilation — the Canavan registry — with epidemiological, medical and other information about the families.

Disease registries can be valuable research and public policy tools.

Defendant Matalon became associated in 1990 with Defendants Miami Children's Hospital Research Institute, Inc. and Variety Children's Hospital d/b/a Miami Children's Hospital. Defendant Matalon continued his relationship with the Plaintiffs after his move, accepting more tissue and blood samples as well as financial support.

The individual Plaintiffs allege that they provided Matalon with these samples and confidential information "with the understanding and expectations that such samples and information would be used for the specific purpose of researching Canavan disease and identifying mutations in the Canavan disease which could lead to carrier detection within their families and benefit the population at large." Plaintiffs further allege that it was their "understanding that any carrier and prenatal testing developed in connection with the research for which they were providing essential support would be provided on an affordable and accessible basis, and that Matalon's research would remain in the public domain to promote the discovery of more effective prevention techniques and treatments and, eventually, to effectuate a cure for Canavan disease." This understanding stemmed from their "experience in community testing for Tay-Sachs disease, another deadly genetic disease that occurs most frequently in families of Ashkenazi Jewish descent."

There was a breakthrough in the research in 1993. Using Plaintiffs' blood and tissue samples, familial pedigree information, contacts, and financial support, Matalon and his research team successfully isolated the gene responsible for Canavan disease. After this key advancement, Plaintiffs allege that they continued to provide Matalon with more tissue and blood in order to learn more about the disease and its precursor gene.

In September 1994, unbeknownst to Plaintiffs, a patent application was submitted for the genetic sequence that Defendants had identified. This application was granted in October 1997, and Dr. Matalon was listed as an inventor on the gene patent and related applications for the Canavan disease (the "Patent"). Through patenting, Defendants acquired the ability to restrict any activity related to the Canavan disease gene, including without limitation: carrier and prenatal testing, gene therapy and other treatments for Canavan disease and research involving the gene and its mutations.

Although the Patent was issued in October 1997, Plaintiffs allege that they did not learn of it until November 1998, when MCH revealed their intention to limit Canavan disease testing through a campaign of restrictive licensing of the Patent.

Specifically, on November 12, 1998, Plaintiffs allege that Defendants MCH and MCHRI began to "threaten" the centers that offered Canavan testing with possible enforcement actions regarding the recently-issued patent. Defendant MCH also began restricting public accessibility through negotiating exclusive licensing agreements and charging royalty fees.

> A valid patent can exclude others from using the invention during the life of the patent. Here, the patent owner demanded a royalty for the Canavan genetic test.

Plaintiffs allege that at no time were they informed that Defendants intended to seek a patent on the research. Nor were they told of Defendants' intentions to commercialize the fruits of the research and to restrict access to Canavan disease testing.

Based on these facts, Plaintiffs filed a six-count complaint on October 30, 2000, against Defendants asserting the following causes of action: (1) lack of informed consent; (2) breach of fiduciary duty; (3) unjust enrichment; (4) fraudulent concealment; (5) conversion; and (6) misappropriation of trade secrets. Plaintiffs generally seek a permanent injunction restraining Defendants from enforcing their patent rights, damages in the form of all royalties Defendants have received on the Patent as well as all financial contributions Plaintiffs made to benefit Defendants' research. Plaintiffs allege that Defendants have earned significant royalties from Canavan disease testing in excess of $75,000 through enforcement of their gene patent, and that Dr. Matalon has personally profited by receiving a recent substantial federal grant to undertake further research on the gene patent.

. . . .

III. ANALYSIS

Defendants have moved to dismiss the entire Complaint pursuant to Fed. R. Civ. P. 12(b)(6) for failure to state a claim upon which relief may be granted. The Court will discuss each count sequentially.

A. Lack of Informed Consent

In Count I of the Complaint, the individual Plaintiffs, who served as research subjects, and the corporate plaintiff Dor Yeshorim claim that Defendants owed a duty of informed consent. The Complaint alleges a continuing duty of informed consent to disclose any information that might influence their decision to participate or decline to participate in his research. Defendants breached this duty, Plaintiffs claim, when they did not disclose the intent to patent and enforce for their own economic benefit the Canavan disease gene. The duty was also breached by the misrepresentation of the research purpose that Matalon had included on the written consent forms. Finally, the Plaintiffs allege that if they had known that the Defendants would "commercialize" the results of their contributions, they would not have made the contributions.

1. Duty to Obtain Informed Consent for Medical Research

Defendants first assert that the Complaint fails to state a claim because the duty of informed consent is only owed to patients receiving medical treatment. Furthermore, they claim that even if the duty extends to non-therapeutic research, it does not extend beyond the actual research to research results.

The doctrine of informed consent grew out of a treating physician's fiduciary duty to disclose to the patient all facts which might affect the patient's decision to allow medical treatment. The basic principle of informed consent has been embraced by tort law in order to guard a patient's control over decisions affecting his or her own health. *See* Cruzan v. Dir., Mo. Dep't of Health, 497 U.S. 261, 269 (1990). The state common law of informed consent is often fortified by statute. Florida's medical consent law, for example, applies to the patient/treating doctor relationship.

The question of informed consent in the context of medical research, however, is a relatively novel one in Florida. Medical consent law does not apply to medical researchers. Florida Statute §760.40 does require, however, that a person's informed consent must be obtained when any genetic analysis is undertaken on [] his or her tissue.

> *Cruzan* is discussed in the context of end-of-life care and its regulation in Chapter 9, but note that the Florida court is citing it for adoption of basic informed consent principles.

Defendants argue that this statute is inapplicable to the case at bar because the statute does not apply to medical research, only test results. Moreover, none of the individual Plaintiffs have alleged that they were personally tested, just that they donated their genetic material. Furthermore, although Federal regulations do mandate that consent must be obtained from the subjects of medical research, the informed consent does not cover more than the research itself. Other courts in New York and Pennsylvania have dismissed attempts by patient plaintiffs to stretch the informed consent doctrine to cover medical research. Plaintiffs contend these cases are distinguishable because they do not address informed consent in the research setting or the related issue of commercialization.

With Florida statutory law at best unclear on the duty of informed consent relating to medical research, Plaintiffs refer to cases in other jurisdictions where courts have found that researchers face a duty to obtain informed consent from their research subjects. *See* Grimes v. Kennedy Krieger Inst.; In re Cincinnati Radiation Litig., 874 F. Supp. 796 (S.D. Ohio 1995) (non-disclosure to patients about exposure to radiation).

Defendants counter that these cases are inapposite because Plaintiffs miss the crucial distinction between the use of medical research and human experimentation. Each of the cases cited by Plaintiffs as providing a duty of informed consent regarding medical research was based on some egregious practice, which Defendants argue is absent here. Additionally, there was no actual human experimentation as part of an ongoing relationship alleged in the Complaint.

Since the law regarding a duty of informed consent for research subjects is unsettled and fact-specific and further, Defendants conceded at oral argument that a duty does attach at some point in the relationship, the Court finds that in certain circumstances a medical researcher does have a duty of informed consent. Nevertheless, without clear guidance from Florida jur-

> The court does not accept the theory of an automatic fiduciary relationship in human subject research.

isprudence, the Court must consider whether this duty of informed consent in medical research can be extended to disclosure of a researcher's economic interests.

2. Extension of Duty of Informed Consent to the Researcher's Economic Interests

Defendants assert that extending a possible informed consent duty to disclosing economic interests has no support in established law, and more ominously, this requirement would have pernicious effects over medical research, as it would give each donor complete control over how medical research is used and who benefits from that research. The Court agrees and declines to extend the duty of informed consent to cover a researcher's economic interests in this case.

. . . Accordingly, the Court finds that Plaintiffs have failed to state a claim upon which relief may be granted, and this count is DISMISSED.

B. Breach of Fiduciary Duty

The individual Plaintiffs allege in Count II of the Complaint that all the Defendants were in a fiduciary relationship with them, and as such, they should have disclosed all material information relating to the Canavan disease research they were conducting, including any economic interests of the Defendants relating to that research.

As a threshold issue, Defendants argue that if the Court finds that there is no claim for informed consent, then the claim for breach of fiduciary duty evaporates as both claims have the same elements. Courts routinely hold that where a patient's claim that the doctor breached his fiduciary duty arises from the same operative facts and results in the same injury as another claim asserted against the doctor, then the breach of fiduciary claim is duplicative and should be dismissed. Defendants argue that the two claims are virtually identical, because the damages and liability allegations are very similar, and are both premised on the same duty of disclosure. The Court finds, nevertheless, that a full treatment of this claim is still appropriate as the two claims are not fully congruent.

1. Fiduciary Relationship

Defendants have moved to dismiss this count because Plaintiffs did not plead the elements of a fiduciary relationship. Fiduciary relations are either expressly or impliedly created. A fiduciary duty implied in law is premised upon the specific factual set of circumstances surrounding the transaction and the relationship of the parties. Florida courts have found fiduciary relationships in this context when "confidence is reposed by one party and a trust accepted by the other." This is a two-way relationship, and a fiduciary relationship will only be found when the plaintiff separately alleges that the plaintiff placed trust in the defendant and the defendant accepted that trust. In Florida, once a fiduciary relationship is established, a fiduciary has a legal duty to "disclose all essential or material facts pertinent or material to the transaction in hand."

Defendants assert that the Complaint does not allege any facts that show that the trust was recognized and accepted. Plaintiffs allege, however, that Defendants accepted the trust by undertaking research that they represented as being for the benefit of the Plaintiffs. Plaintiffs rely on other state courts which have held that researchers and research institutions are fiduciaries for their research subjects. For example, in *Grimes*, the Maryland Supreme Court held that "the very nature of nontherapuetic scientific research on human subjects can, and normally will, create special relationships out of which duties arise." *Grimes*, 782 A.2d at 834-35.

Taking all the facts alleged as true, the Court finds that Plaintiffs have not sufficiently alleged the second element of acceptance of trust by Defendants and therefore have failed to state a claim. There is no automatic fiduciary relationship that attaches when a researcher accepts medical donations and the acceptance of trust, the second constitutive element of finding a fiduciary duty, cannot be assumed once a donation is given. Accordingly, this claim is dismissed.

C. Unjust Enrichment

In Count III of the Complaint, Plaintiffs allege that MCH is being unjustly enriched by collecting license fees under the Patent. Under Florida law, the elements of a claim for unjust enrichment are (1) the plaintiff conferred a benefit on the defendant, who had knowledge of the benefit; (2) the defendant voluntarily accepted and retained the benefit; and (3) under the circumstances it would be inequitable for the defendant to retain the benefit without paying for it. The Court finds that Plaintiffs have sufficiently alleged the elements of a claim for unjust enrichment to survive Defendants' motion to dismiss.

While the parties do not contest that Plaintiffs have conferred a benefit to Defendants, including, among other things, blood and tissue samples and soliciting financial contributions, Defendants contend that Plaintiffs have not suffered any detriment, and note that no Plaintiff has been denied access to Canavan testing. Furthermore, the Plaintiffs received what they sought—the successful isolation of the Canavan gene and the development of a screening test. Plaintiffs argue, however, that when Defendants applied the benefits for unauthorized purposes, they suffered a detriment. Had Plaintiffs known that Defendants intended to commercialize their genetic material through patenting and restrictive licensing, Plaintiffs would not have provided these benefits to Defendants under those terms.

Naturally, Plaintiffs allege that the retention of benefits violates the fundamental principles of justice, equity, and good conscience. While Defendants claim that they have invested significant amounts of time and money in research, with no guarantee of success and are thus entitled to seek reimbursement, the same can be said of Plaintiffs. Moreover, Defendants' attempt to seek refuge in the endorsement of the U.S. Patent system, which gives an inventor rights to prosecute patents and negotiate licenses for their intellectual property fails, as obtaining a patent does not preclude the Defendants from being unjustly enriched. The Complaint has alleged more than just a donor-donee relationship for the purposes of an unjust enrichment claim. Rather, the facts paint a picture of a continuing research collaboration that involved Plaintiffs also investing time and significant resources in the race to isolate the Canavan gene. Therefore, given the facts as alleged, the Court finds that Plaintiffs have sufficiently pled the requisite elements of an unjust enrichment claim and the motion to dismiss for failure to state a claim is denied as to this count.

> This unjust enrichment claim is the only one that survives the motion to dismiss.

. . . .

E. Conversion

The Plaintiffs allege in Count V of their Complaint that they had a property interest in their body tissue and genetic information, and that they owned the Canavan registry in Illinois which contained contact information, pedigree information and family information for Canavan families worldwide. They claim that MCH and Matalon converted the names on the register and the genetic information by utilizing them for the hospitals' "exclusive economic benefit." The Court disagrees and declines to find a property interest for the body tissue and genetic information voluntarily given to Defendants. These were donations to research without any contemporaneous expectations of return of the body tissue and genetic samples, and thus conversion does not lie as a cause of action.

In Florida, the tort of "conversion is an unauthorized act which deprives another of his property permanently or for an indefinite time." Using property given for one purpose for another purpose constitutes conversion.

First, Plaintiffs have no cognizable property interest in body tissue and genetic matter donated for research under a theory of conversion. This case is similar to *Moore v. Regents of the University of California*, where the Court declined to extend liability under a theory of conversion to misuse of a person's excised biological materials. . . .

. . . .

IV. CONCLUSION

. . . [I]t is ADJUDGED that the motions are GRANTED *in part*. Accordingly, Count I (lack of informed consent), Count II (breach of fiduciary duty), Count IV (fraudulent concealment), Count V (conversion) and Count VI (misappropriation of trade secrets) are DISMISSED *with prejudice*.

ADJUDGED that the motions to dismiss are DENIED as to Count III (unjust enrichment). . . .

QUESTIONS

1. Consider whether the problem in *Grimes* is financial conflict of interest, detrimental reliance, or a different legal or ethical problem. Why is unjust enrichment the only available claim for this set of plaintiffs?
2. Do you agree that informed consent existed?
3. How would you advise a researcher to proceed differently based on the analysis in this decision?

The tragic case of Jesse Gelsinger offers a different perspective on a research subject who volunteered his body to improve the health of others afflicted by an "orphan" disease (an ailment with a small number of affected patients). Like the participants in *Grimes*, Mr. Gelsinger was aware of the need for his genetic material to support research that could help to save the lives of children born with his disease, called "OTC deficiency." Unlike the families involved in the Canavan research, more than genetic material was required of Mr. Gelsinger; the researchers wanted to inject his liver with genetically modified material to determine if the enzyme deficiency could be reversed.

Finding human subjects was extremely delicate and difficult. Understanding this dynamic, Jesse Gelsinger was reported to have said: "What's the worst that can happen to me? I die, and it's for the babies."

Complaint in Gelsinger v. Trustees of the University of Pennsylvania COMPLAINT — CIVIL ACTION

John Gelsinger, as Administrator and Personal Representative of the Estate of Jesse Gelsinger, and Paul Gelsinger in his own right, claim of defendants, both jointly and severally, a sum in excess of Fifty Thousand Dollars ($50,000.00) in compensatory and punitive damages, upon causes of action whereof the following are true statements:

John Gelsinger, Jesse's father.

1. On September 17, 1999, Jesse Gelsinger, an 18 year old young man died while participating in a gene transfer experiment at the Institute for Human Gene Therapy ("IHGT") located at the University of Pennsylvania.

2. At the time of his death, Jesse suffered from a mild form of ornithine trans-carbamylase deficiency ("OTC"), a rare metabolic disorder, which was controlled with a low-protein diet and drugs. Jesse volunteered to participate in the experiment, knowing it would not benefit his condition in the least, because he was led to believe his participation held little risk and would directly benefit yet to be born infants with OTC.

3. While at IHGT, Jesse Gelsinger was infused with trillions of particles of an adenovirus vector, which was developed at the University for the purpose of transferring OTC genes.

4. The adenovirus vector used by the defendants was known to be more toxic than other vectors used in gene transfer.

5. When Jesse Gelsinger received the vector, he suffered a chain reaction including jaundice, a blood-clotting disorder, kidney failure, lung failure and brain death.

6. On September 17, 1999, Jesse Gelsinger died as a direct result of the carelessness, negligence, recklessness and wanton and willful conduct of defendants as described in detail below. . . .

10. Defendant, the Trustees of the University of Pennsylvania ("the University") is an educational institution . . . . IHGT is an institute within and under the control of the University, which conducts substantial, systematic, continuous and regular business in the County of Philadelphia, Commonwealth of Pennsylvania.

. . . .

12. Defendant, Genovo, Inc., . . . currently provides nearly a quarter of the budget for the IHGT, and conducts substantial, systematic, continuous and regular business in the County of Philadelphia, Commonwealth of Pennsylvania.

13. At all times relevant hereto, Dr. Wilson was the founder of defendant Genovo, a biotech company. At all times relevant hereto, Dr. Wilson controlled up to thirty percent (30%) of the Genovo stock.

14. Genovo agreed to provide the IHGT with over four million dollars a year for five years to conduct genetic research and experimentation.

15. In lieu of up-front payments to the University, Genovo transferred five percent (5%) equity ownership to the University.

> The university is a nonprofit, tax-exempt organization known for conducting top-notch scientific research. Consider whether the deal Penn struck with Genovo was consistent with the educational mission of the university (bear in mind governance and tax-exempt entity conversations from Chapters 4 and 5).

16. In return for Genovo's sponsorship of genetic research and experimentation, the University agreed to grant Genovo licenses for the lung and liver applications for existing technologies developed by defendant, Dr. Wilson.

17. Defendant, Genovo, retained an option to negotiate for licenses for any future developments by defendants, IHGT and/or Dr. Wilson.

18. The proposed licenses between the defendants included full patent reimbursement, milestone payments and royalties on product sales.

19. The shareholders of Genovo include numerous past and present University and/or IHGT employees.

20. Dr. Wilson is a duly licensed practicing physician in the Commonwealth of Pennsylvania and, at all times mentioned herein and material hereto, was the director of the IHGT and an attending physician on the staff of the University of Pennsylvania Hospital. At all times mentioned herein and material hereto, Dr. Wilson was an agent, servant, representative and employee of the University.

21. At the time of the occurrence of the incidents described herein, Dr. Wilson was also acting as an agent, servant, workman, and employee of Genovo.

22. Defendant Steven Raper, M.D., is a duly licensed physician in the Commonwealth of Pennsylvania, . . . [and] an attending physician on the staff of the University of Pennsylvania Hospital and the IHGT. At all times mentioned herein and material hereto, Dr. Raper was an agent, servant, representative and employee of both the University and the IHGT.

23. Defendant Mark L. Batshaw, M.D., is a duly licensed practicing physician in Washington, D.C., . . . and, at all times mentioned herein and material hereto, was an attending physician on the staff of the University of Pennsylvania Hospital and the IHGT. At all times mentioned herein and material hereto, Dr. Batshaw was an agent, servant, representative and employee of the University, Children's Hospital of Philadelphia, Children's National Medical Center and the IHGT.

24. Defendant, Children's Hospital of Philadelphia (CHOP), . . . held itself and its agents, servants, workers, representatives, physicians, nurses, staff, contractors, medical personnel and employees out to be skillful and qualified to administer medical care and treatment. . . .

26. Defendant, Children's National Medical Center, is a corporation and medical center, existing by and under the law of the District of Columbia. . . .

27. . . . [D]efendant, Children's National Medical Center, held itself and its agents, servants, workers, representatives, physicians, nurses, staff, contractors, medical personnel and employees out to be skillful and qualified to administer medical care and treatment. . . .

28. Defendant, William N. Kelley, M.D. ("Dr. Kelley"), is the former dean of the University of Pennsylvania Medical School and chief executive of its health system.

29. Dr. Kelley arrived at the University in 1989.

30. At the time of his arrival at the University, Dr. Kelley and two colleagues had already applied for a patent which Dr. Kelley claimed "is a broad gene therapy patent which involves any DNA or piece thereof."

31. This patent enabled Dr. Kelley to collect royalties should gene therapy research using the replication-defective adeno-viral ("RDAd") vectors prove to be effective.

32. In 1992, Dr. Wilson founded Genovo, Inc., a company in the business of gene transfer research and development.

33. In the spring of 1993, Dr. Wilson was recruited by Dr. Kelley to come to the University and be the director of the IHGT.

34. Defendant, Dr. Kelley, approved Dr. Wilson's OTC gene transfer experiments involving a RDAd vector, a vector similar to the one patented by defendants, Dr. Kelley, Genovo and Dr. Wilson.

> The "adenovirus" was a weakened cold virus manipulated by researchers to deliver genetic material designed to be of medicinal benefit.

35. Defendants, Dr. Kelley, Genovo, and Dr. Wilson all stood to gain financially from the successful use of RDAd vectors.

36. Defendants, the University and/or IHGT, stood to gain financially through their equity stake in Genovo from the successful use of RDAd vectors.

37. Defendant, Arthur Caplan, Ph.D., is the director of the Bioethics Department of the University of Pennsylvania. . . .

38. Defendant, Arthur Caplan, was appointed as Trustee Professor of Bioethics in the Department of Molecular and Cellular Engineering, which defendant, Dr. Wilson, chaired. . . .

39. Defendant, Arthur Caplan, was consulted to determine the ethical complications surrounding the OTC gene transfer experiment.

40. The IHGT agreed to provide funding, in the amount of approximately $25,000.00 per year, for a bioethics faculty position.

41. The gene therapy study was initially designed to enroll terminally ill infants as subjects for the experiment.

42. Defendant, Arthur Caplan, advised defendants, Drs. Wilson, Batshaw and Raper, that parents of terminally ill children were incapable of giving an informed consent and suggested that the gene transfer experiment be performed on otherwise healthy, adults with a mild, medically manageable, form of OTC.

43. Defendant, Arthur Caplan, was quoted subsequent to the death of Jesse Gelsinger as saying, "Not only is it sad that Jesse Gelsinger died, there was never a chance that anybody would benefit from these experiments. They are safety studies. They are not therapeutic in goal. If I gave it to you, we would try to see if you died, too, or if you did OK."

44. Defendant, Arthur Caplan, was also quoted in relation to gene therapy as follows, "If you cured anybody, you'd publish it in a religious journal. It would be a miracle. The researchers wouldn't say that. But I'm telling you. If you cured anybody from a phase one gene therapy trial, it would be a miracle. All you're doing is you're saying, I've got this vector, I want to see if it can deliver the gene where I want it to go without killing, or hurting or having side effects."

45. The Internal Review Board (IRB) of defendant, CHOP, reviewed and approved the protocol for the OTC gene transfer experiment.

46. Hematologists for defendant, CHOP, were consulted regarding the gene transfer experiment.

47. In September of 1994, the stock of Genovo was distributed to the founders of Genovo.

48. These founders include Ms. Marian Grossman who became the Director of the Human Applications Laboratory of the IHGT; Mr. Dennis Berman; Dr. Barbara Handelin who was Genovo's Chief Scientific Officer and the wife of a University faculty member in Dr. Wilson's department; and Dr. Wilson.

49. Upon his arrival at the University, Dr. Wilson had numerous patents which, like the patent held by Dr. Kelley, involved the use of the RDAd vector for gene transfer.

50. In late 1994, the University began discussions with Dr. Wilson concerning his being employed by the University. At the same time the University began discussions with Dr. Wilson concerning an arrangement between the University and Genovo.

51. During this time, the University's Conflicts of Interest Standing Committee ("CISC") held meetings during which the issue of what, if any, conflicts of interest would arise if an agreement was entered into between the University, Genovo and Dr. Wilson.

52. During the meeting of the CISC held on February 6, 1995, committee members asserted that a conflict of interest may exist regarding the relationship between the University, Dr. Wilson, and Genovo.

53. The CISC, an agent of the University, was expressly aware that a conflict of interest would exist if Dr. Wilson were permitted to conduct experiments at IHGT which, if successful, would directly benefit Dr. Wilson and Genovo financially.

54. Despite such express knowledge of the dangers such a conflict of interest would present, the University accepted the Genovo arrangement and allowed Dr. Wilson to conduct experiments at IHGT.

55. Jesse Gelsinger was first diagnosed with OTC at the age of two.

56. OTC is a rare metabolic disorder which affects the body's ability to breakdown ammonia, a normal byproduct of metabolism.

57. Over the next sixteen years, Jesse Gelsinger controlled the disease with a low-protein diet and medication.

58. In September 1998, Jesse was told by his treating physician of an OTC gene transfer trial which was being conducted at the IHGT.

59. On June 22, 1999, Jesse and Paul Gelsinger went to the IHGT where they met Dr. Raper who performed blood and liver-function tests to determine whether Jesse was eligible for the gene transfer trial. Jesse was to receive no financial compensation for participating in the trial.

60. Between June 22, 1999 and September 9, 1999, Jesse and Paul Gelsinger reviewed documents and had discussions with Drs. Raper and Batshaw which

purportedly were to provide certain information necessary to make an informed decision as to whether Jesse was going to take part in and was an appropriate candidate for the gene transfer trial.

61. Such documents and discussions were materially misleading and deceptive because, among other things:

    a. the risks of the toxic effects of the injection of the adenovirus particles were understated;

    b. no mention was made that monkeys injected with the virus had become ill and/or died;

    c. no mention was made that patients who had previously participated in the trial suffered serious adverse effects;

    d. the representation was made that IHGT had achieved certain efficacy with respect to the treatment of OTC; and

    e. the extent to which Dr. Wilson and the University had a conflict of interest was not adequately disclosed.

62. The effects of such misrepresentations and nondisclosure were that Jesse and Paul Gelsinger believed the risks of injection of the adenovirus vector were minimal and the potential benefits of Jesse's participation to the future treatment of OTC patients in the study were enormous.

63. On September 9, 1999, Jesse returned to Philadelphia to begin the gene transfer trial.

64. Jesse was scheduled to be the last of three patients in the sixth cohort in the trial.

65. On September 13, 1999, Jesse was taken to the interventional-radiology suite where he was sedated and strapped to a table while a team of radiologists threaded two catheters into his groin.

66. At approximately 10:30 A.M., Dr. Raper drew 30 milliliters of the vector and injected it into Jesse.

67. The procedure was completed at approximately 12:30 P.M.

68. On the evening of September 13, 1999, Jesse was sick to his stomach and had a fever of 104.5 degrees.

69. The following morning Jesse seemed disoriented.

70. When Dr. Raper examined Jesse the morning of September 14, 1999, he noticed that Jesse's eyes were yellow.

71. Blood tests performed on September 14, 1999, indicated that Jesse's bilirubin was four times the normal level.

72. The symptoms that Jesse was experiencing were similar to those defendants had seen in the monkeys that had been given a similar vector.

73. By the afternoon of September 14, 1999, Jesse had slipped into a coma.

Jesse had just turned 18. Jesse's father, Paul, was not present for the procedure because they were led to believe it was virtually risk-free, and Jesse had younger siblings home in Arizona who needed their father's attention. Paul planned to join Jesse for the liver biopsy that was to follow the injection of the adenovirus vector, several days after the injection. When he arrived, Jesse was already in a coma. Jesse's mother was receiving in-patient treatment for bipolar disorder (then called "manic depression") and could not be with Jesse.

74. At 11:30 P.M. on September 14, 1999, Jesse's ammonia level was 393 micro moles per deciliter of blood. The normal level is 35 micro moles.

75. Thereafter, the doctors placed Jesse on dialysis.

76. Initially, Jesse's condition improved but soon began to deteriorate.

77. After consultation between Drs. Wilson, Raper and Batshaw, the doctors decided to perform extra corporeal membrane oxygenation.

78. On September 16, 1999, Jesse's kidneys stopped making urine and he began to suffer from multiple organ system failure.

79. On the evening of September 16, 1999, Jesse was bloated beyond recognition; his ears and eyes had swollen shut.

80. On the morning of September 17, 1999, tests indicated that Jesse was brain dead.

81. On September 17, 1999, the ECMO machine was shut off and Jesse was pronounced dead at 2:30 P.M.

82. The cause of Jesse's death was attributed to acute respiratory distress and multiple-organ failure, both of which were the direct result of injection of the adenovirus vector.

83. After Jesse's death, the FDA determined there were numerous violations of FDA guidelines by the defendants. Some of these violations were:

a. failing to tell the National Institute of Health Recombinant DNA Advisory Committee ("the RAC") of a change in the way the virus was to be delivered to patients;

b. changing the informed consent form from what had been approved by the FDA by removing information concerning the death or illness of several monkeys during a similar study;

c. failing to report to the FDA that patients prior to Jesse suffered significant liver toxicity which required that the study be put on hold;

d. failing to follow the study protocol which mandated that in each cohort at least two women be subject to injection before any male;

e. admitting Jesse in the trial when his blood ammonia level on the day before he received the gene transfer exceeded the limit set out in the FDA protocol; and

f. allowing the vectors to sit and/or be stored on lab shelves for 25 months before being tested in animals, making them less potent then [sic] they could have been. The vectors administered to the plaintiff's decedent were only stored for two months. The 25 month storage in turn, may have resulted in an underestimation of the vectors['] potency in humans. Additionally, the animals who received the vector stored for 25 months would have been given a dose of vector from 52.2% to 65.3% below the vector dose specified in the FDA protocol.

COUNT I—WRONGFUL DEATH

84. Plaintiffs incorporate by reference paragraphs 1 through 83 as if fully set forth at length herein.

85. At all times mentioned herein and material hereto, the defendants, and each of them respectively, jointly and severally, were charged with the professional responsibility of rendering proper care and treatment to Jesse Gelsinger, of properly and carefully examining him in order to determine his condition and eligibility for the gene transfer trial, of properly and carefully administering the gene transfer protocol in a careful and prudent fashion, and of assuring that proper medical care and attention were provided during all periods of time during which he remained under said defendants' care and treatment.

86. As a result of the careless, negligent and reckless conduct of the defendants herein, Jesse Gelsinger was caused to suffer excruciating and agonizing pain and discomfort and ultimately died as a result of defendants' conduct.

87. Defendants together, and each of them respectively, jointly and severally, by and through their separate and respective agents, servants, workmen, representatives, physicians, nurses, staff, contractors, medical personnel, medical assistants and employees were careless, negligent and reckless in:

   a. failing to properly and adequately evaluate Jesse Gelsinger's condition and eligibility for the gene transfer trial;
   b. failing to properly diagnose Jessie Gelsinger's condition subsequent to the administration of the gene transfer;
   c. failing to perform proper and adequate testing for his condition;
   d. failing to properly and adequately treat his condition;
   e. failing to properly and adequately care for his condition;
   f. failing to monitor his ammonia levels both during and after the administration of the gene transfer;
   g. failing to provide and afford proper and careful medical care and treatment;
   h. failing to perform proper and careful medical practices and procedures in accordance with the standards prevailing in the community in which defendants practiced at the time;
   i. failing to properly care for his condition under all of the circumstances;
   j. caring for Jesse Gelsinger in a negligent and improper manner;
   k. failing to properly monitor his condition both prior to and subsequent to the performance of the gene transfer procedure;
   l. failing to use a proper, adequate and safe vector for gene transfer;
   m. failing to inform Jesse Gelsinger of all the risks of performing the gene transfer procedure so as to afford him with the opportunity to make an informed decision as to the performance of said procedure;
   n. failing to properly and timely observe, discover, diagnose, treat and care for his condition;
   o. failing to conform to the standard of care and treatment prevailing in the medical community in which defendants practiced at the time in conducting gene transfer;
   p. failing to exercise reasonable care under all of the circumstances, in accordance with the accepted practices and procedures in the medical community in which defendants practiced;
   q. failing to follow and abide by guidelines set forth by various governmental agencies; and
   r. acting negligently per se.

88. As a direct and proximate result of the carelessness, negligence, gross negligence, recklessness and willful and wanton conduct of defendants, and each of them respectively, jointly and severally, by and through their separate and respective agents, servants, workmen, representatives, physicians, nurses, staff, contractors, medical personnel and employees, Jesse Gelsinger was caused to sustain serious and excruciating personal injuries which ultimately led to his death. Jesse Gelsinger died as a result of acute respiratory distress and multiple-organ failure. He was caused to suffer agonizing aches, pains and mental anguish; he sustained loss of enjoyment of life and loss of life's pleasures. As a result of his wrongful death he has been prevented from performing all of his usual duties, occupations, recreational activities and avocation all to his and his beneficiaries' loss and detriment.

89. By conducting themselves as aforesaid, defendants increased the risk of harm, thereby causing the wrongful death of Jesse Gelsinger. . . .

WHEREFORE, John Gelsinger, as Administrator and Personal Representative of the Estate of Jesse Gelsinger, claim of defendants, and each of them respectively, jointly and severally, compensatory damages in excess of Fifty-thousand Dollars ($50,000.00), delay damages pursuant to Pa. R.C.P. 238, interest and allowable costs of suit. . . .

COUNT IV—INTENTIONAL ASSAULT AND BATTERY, LACK OF INFORMED CONSENT

. . . .

109. Defendants, and each of them respectively, failed to inform plaintiff's decedent, Jesse Gelsinger, of the risks of all treatment, care, therapy and procedures performed upon him so as to afford plaintiff's decedent the opportunity to make an informed decision as to the performance of said procedures.

110. The lack of informed consent includes, but is not limited to:

a. understating the risks of the toxic effects of the injection of the adenovirus particles;

b. failing to inform plaintiff's decedent regarding the fact that monkeys injected with the virus had become ill and/or died;

c. failing to inform plaintiff's decedent that patients who had previously participated in the trial suffered serious adverse effects;

d. misrepresenting the fact that prior participants in the study had achieved certain efficacy with respect to the treatment of OTC;

e. failing to adequately disclose the extent to which Dr. Wilson and the University had a conflict of interest;

> This is the only litigation document available, because the University of Pennsylvania settled the case within two months of the complaint's filing; the defendants' responses were never filed.

f. failing to adequately disclose the financial interest that Dr. Wilson and the University had in relation to the study; and

g. allowing the vectors to sit and/or be stored on lab shelves for 25 months before being tested in animals, making them less potent then they could have been. The vectors administered to the plaintiff's decedent were only stored for two months. The 25 month storage in turn, may have resulted in an underestimation of the vectors['] potency in humans. Additionally, the animals who received the vector stored for 25 months would have been given a dose of vector from 52.2% to 65.3% below the vector dose specified in the FDA protocol.

111. As a result of the intentional tortious conduct of all the defendants named herein, and each of them respectively, by and through their separate and respective agents, servants, workmen, representatives, physicians, nurses, staff, contractors, medical personnel and employees, plaintiff's decedent, Jesse Gelsinger, was caused to suffer severe and agonizing personal injuries and pain and suffering which resulted in his untimely death on September 17, 1999.

112. As a result of the intentional tortious conduct of all defendants named herein, by and through their separate and respective agents, servants, workmen, representatives, physicians, nurses, staff, contractors, medical personnel and

employees, said decedent's heirs-at-law and next of kin have in the past been and will in the future continue to be deprived of the earnings, comfort, society and companionship of their said decedent, all to their great loss and detriment.

113. As a direct and proximate result of the foregoing, decedent's wrongful death beneficiaries suffered, are suffering for an indefinite period of time in the future damages, injuries and losses, including but not limited to, a loss of financial support, and the beneficiaries have been wrongfully deprived of the contributions they would have received from decedent, Jesse Gelsinger, including monies which decedent would have provided for such items as clothing, shelter, food, medical care and education. . . .

WHEREFORE, John Gelsinger, as Administrator and Personal Representative of the Estate of Jesse Gelsinger, claim of defendants, and each of them respectively, jointly and severally, compensatory damages in excess of Fifty-thousand Dollars ($50,000.00), delay damages pursuant to Pa. R.C.P. 238, interest and allowable costs of suit.

QUESTIONS

1. What should the researchers have done differently?
2. What duties did they owe to Jesse Gelsinger, whether ethical or legal?
3. Should an 18-year old have been allowed to consent to a potentially deadly experiment?

As the complaint noted, Jesse Gelsinger could not have benefited from the experiment for his own condition. Consider the Common Rule's special provisions regarding research on children:

45 C.F.R. §46.404. Research not involving greater than minimal risk.
HHS will conduct or fund research in which the IRB finds that no greater than minimal risk to children is presented, only if the IRB finds that adequate provisions are made for soliciting the assent of the children and the permission of their parents or guardians, as set forth in §46.408.

45 C.F.R. §46.405. Research involving greater than minimal risk but presenting the prospect of direct benefit to the individual subjects.
HHS will conduct or fund research in which the IRB finds that more than minimal risk to children is presented by an intervention or procedure that holds out the prospect of direct benefit for the individual subject, or by a monitoring procedure that is likely to contribute to the subject's well-being, only if the IRB finds that:
   (a) The risk is justified by the anticipated benefit to the subjects;
   (b) The relation of the anticipated benefit to the risk is at least as favorable to the subjects as that presented by available alternative approaches; and
   (c) Adequate provisions are made for soliciting the assent of the children and permission of their parents or guardians, as set forth in §46.408.

45 C.F.R. §46.406. Research involving greater than minimal risk and no prospect of direct benefit to individual subjects, but likely to yield generalizable knowledge about the subject's disorder or condition.

HHS will conduct or fund research in which the IRB finds that more than minimal risk to children is presented by an intervention or procedure that does not hold out the prospect of direct benefit for the individual subject, or by a monitoring procedure which is not likely to contribute to the well-being of the subject, only if the IRB finds that:

(a) The risk represents a minor increase over minimal risk;

(b) The intervention or procedure presents experiences to subjects that are reasonably commensurate with those inherent in their actual or expected medical, dental, psychological, social, or educational situations;

(c) The intervention or procedure is likely to yield generalizable knowledge about the subjects' disorder or condition which is of vital importance for the understanding or amelioration of the subjects' disorder or condition; and

(d) Adequate provisions are made for soliciting assent of the children and permission of their parents or guardians, as set forth in §46.408.

. . . [Note: §46.407 is excerpted in *Grimes*, above.]

45 C.F.R. §46.408. Requirements for permission by parents or guardians and for assent by children

(a) In addition to the determinations required under other applicable sections of this subpart, the IRB shall determine that adequate provisions are made for soliciting the assent of the children, when in the judgment of the IRB the children are capable of providing assent. In determining whether children are capable of assenting, the IRB shall take into account the ages, maturity, and psychological state of the children involved. This judgment may be made for all children to be involved in research under a particular protocol, or for each child, as the IRB deems appropriate. If the IRB determines that the capability of some or all of the children is so limited that they cannot reasonably be consulted or that the intervention or procedure involved in the research holds out a prospect of direct benefit that is important to the health or well-being of the children and is available only in the context of the research, the assent of the children is not a necessary condition for proceeding with the research. Even where the IRB determines that the subjects are capable of assenting, the IRB may still waive the assent requirement under circumstances in which consent may be waived in accord with §46.116 of Subpart A.

(b) In addition to the determinations required under other applicable sections of this subpart, the IRB shall determine, in accordance with and to the extent that consent is required by §46.116 of Subpart A, that adequate provisions are made for soliciting the permission of each child's parents or guardian. Where parental permission is to be obtained, the IRB may find that the permission of one parent is sufficient for research to be conducted under §46.404 or §46.405. Where research is covered by §§46.406 and 46.407 and permission is to be obtained from parents, both parents must give their permission unless one parent is deceased, unknown, incompetent, or not reasonably available, or when only one parent has legal responsibility for the care and custody of the child.

(c) In addition to the provisions for waiver contained in §46.116 of subpart A, if the IRB determines that a research protocol is designed for conditions or for a subject population for which parental or guardian permission is not a reasonable requirement to protect the subjects (for example, neglected or abused children), it may waive the consent requirements in Subpart A of this part and paragraph (b) of this section, provided an appropriate mechanism for protecting the children who will participate as subjects in the research is substituted, and provided further that the waiver is not inconsistent with federal, state, or local law. The choice of an appropriate mechanism would depend upon the nature and purpose of the activities described in the protocol, the risk and anticipated benefit to the research subjects, and their age, maturity, status, and condition.

(d) Permission by parents or guardians shall be documented in accordance with and to the extent required by §46.117 of subpart A.

(e) When the IRB determines that assent is required, it shall also determine whether and how assent must be documented. . . .

QUESTIONS

1. When Jesse Gelsinger learned of the gene therapy, he was 17 years old and in stable health. Which of the above provisions would have applied to him?
2. Could Jesse have been protected from researchers' financial conflicts when he was a minor?

In addition to litigation, researchers may face an investigation by the Office for Human Research Protections (OHRP), a sub-agency of HHS, which is not uncommon. OHRP explains the process:

> OHRP's Division of Compliance Oversight (DCO) evaluates, at OHRP's discretion, written substantive indications of noncompliance with HHS regulations — Title 45, Part 46, Code of Federal Regulations (45 CFR 46). OHRP asks the institution involved to investigate the allegations and to provide OHRP with a written report of its investigation. The Office then determines what, if any, regulatory action needs to be taken to protect human research subjects. DCO also conducts a program of not-for-cause surveillance evaluations of institutions, and receives, reviews, and responds to incident reports from Assured institutions.

This letter offers an example of allegations that were determined to be without merit:

January 16, 2015

Paul J. Sabbatini, M.D.
Deputy Physician-in-Chief for Clinical Research
Memorial Sloan-Kettering Cancer Center
1275 York Ave.
New York, NY 10065

RE: Human Research Protections Under Federalwide Assurance FWA-4998

Research Project: Intra-Vitreal Injection for Retinoblastoma

Investigators: Drs. David Abramson, Jasmine Francis and Brian Marr

Dear Dr. Sabbatini:

Thank you for your October 27, 2014 report in response to our September 30, 2014 letter regarding questions about allegations of noncompliance by Memorial Sloan-Kettering Cancer Center (MSKCC) with Department of Health and Human Services (HHS) regulations for the protection of human research subjects (45 CFR part 46). Based on review of your response, we make the following determination:

Determination

The complainant alleges that research on subjects with retinoblastoma involving intra-vitreal injections of digoxin and other chemotherapy into the eye has been conducted without institutional review board (IRB) review and approval. We note the following regarding this matter:

a) A single patient with bilateral retinoblastoma was treated at New York Presbyterian Hospital and MSKCC.

b) Given the clinical state of the patient's open second degree burn, history of pneumonia and bacteremia, and the extensive cost of intra-arterial treatment, it was felt that different treatment options should be offered for each eye. One eye (left) was treated with intra-vitreal melphalan. For treatment of the second (right) eye, it was felt that an option with less potential for immunosuppression was needed. Dr. Abramson proposed intra-vitreal use of digoxin. Digoxin given intra-arterially had been successful in patients with retinoblastoma, but had not been tried by intra-vitreal administration. It was explained that this approach would hopefully have a reasonable benefit to risk ratio by avoiding the potential for immunosuppression (particularly with two doses of melphalan) and offered a reasonable chance at preserving vision. In addition, MSKCC stated "in the event of adverse events, it is not our practice to use the same agent in each eye simultaneously."

c) Dr. Abramson confirms that the patient in question is the only one to receive such treatment. MSKCC performed a search of pharmacy records from January 1, 2011 through October 10, 2014; the Pharmacy results show that only one patient (referenced above) received digoxin via intra-vitreal route.

Based on the documentation provided in your October 27, 2014 correspondence, we have determined that the allegations of noncompliance are unproven. No evidence was presented to us indicating that research on subjects with retinoblastoma involving intra-vitreal injections of digoxin and other chemotherapy into the eye has been conducted without IRB review and approval.

At this time, there should be no need for further involvement by our office in this matter. Please notify us if you identify new information which might alter this determination.

We appreciate the continued commitment of your institution to the protection of human research subjects. Please do not hesitate to contact me should you have any questions.

Sincerely,

Kristina C. Borror, Ph.D.
Director, Division of Compliance Oversight

QUESTIONS

1. Why does OHRP prefer compliance mechanisms rather than litigation?
2. Which values or priorities are promoted in a collaborative process between the researcher and the regulator?
3. If you were asked to participate in a study by your treating physician, would a disclosure regarding her conflict of interest drive your decision regarding whether to participate? Would it matter if the research were therapeutic or nontherapeutic?

In many ways, the OHRP approach looks like the processes HHS/OIG has constructed for fraud and abuse compliance (Chapter 6). OHRP has posted many forms of guidance on its Web site, creating a clearinghouse for clinical research protection to encourage proactive compliance by clinical investigators. Much like the fraud and abuse field, concerns about conflicts of interest are a key policy driver, as is the desire to protect those intended to be benefited by federal funding.

CAPSTONE PROBLEM

In an interesting twist on historical clinical research problems, patients have argued for access to drugs that are not yet approved by the Food and Drug Administration (FDA) when they are terminally ill and the drugs may offer a chance of longer life. The FDA has an extensive regulatory structure for approval of new drugs that includes multiple phases of clinical trials. The FDA's multistep process is designed to ensure that drugs that reach the national market are safe and efficacious. When drugs are tested on humans in this process, the Common Rule applies to the individuals involved in the research as do regulations the FDA has promulgated to ensure collective safety.

Terminally ill patients have been frustrated with the FDA's slow drug approval process, because their physicians are sometimes aware of drugs being developed that may target, for example, a particular type of cancer cell, but the testing is too early for the drug to be available to the public. The plaintiffs in a case called *Abigail Alliance* claimed a fundamental right to access Phase I developmental drugs, and the Court of Appeals for the District of Columbia Circuit rejected their claim. Abigail Alliance for Better Access to Developmental Drugs v. von Eschenbach, 495 F.3d 695 (D.C. Cir. 2007), *cert. denied*, 552 U.S. 1159 (2008). In the years after *Abigail Alliance*, advocates took a different tack, successfully lobbying state legislatures to pass "right to try laws." These laws promise patients access to drugs before the FDA has approved them and relieve doctors of liability for use of such drugs. Some laws also protect the pharmaceutical companies. The laws do not specify particular protections for the patients accessing the drugs and do not require any pharmaceutical manufacturer to offer access to medicines. As of the printing of this book, about a third of states have passed laws facilitating such access, and a similar bill is being considered by Congress.

The FDA changed its rules to allow some seriously ill and terminally ill patients to access drugs, though patient advocates still find the FDA's "compassionate use" rules to be not lenient enough. On its Web site, the FDA explains that a patient may seek access to investigational drugs "for the diagnosis, monitoring, or treatment of a serious disease or condition if the following conditions are met:

- The person's physician determines that there is no comparable or satisfactory alternative therapy available to diagnose, monitor, or treat the person's disease or condition, and that the probable risk to the person from the investigational product is not greater than the probable risk from the disease or condition;
- FDA determines that there is sufficient evidence of the safety and effectiveness of the investigational product to support its use in the particular circumstance;
- FDA determines that providing the investigational product will not interfere with the initiation, conduct, or completion of clinical investigations to support marketing approval; and
- The sponsor (generally the company developing the investigational product for commercial use) or the clinical investigator submits a clinical protocol (a document that describes the treatment plan for the patient) that is consistent with FDA's statute and applicable regulations for INDs or investigational device exemption applications (IDEs), describing the use of the investigational product.

Also under FDA's statute, a sponsor or a physician may submit a protocol intended to provide widespread access to an investigational product."

You are counsel to OHRP. How would you address the needs of terminally ill or seriously ill patients who desire to access drugs before they are approved by the FDA? Statistically, these drugs are unlikely to benefit patients, which may render them participants in nontherapeutic research. Yet these patients are often asked to pay for the drugs that they access before approval. Should they be protected by the Common Rule? Which ethical principles apply to them? Should OHRP consider special rules? If so, what would they be? What role should physicians play here? Do you find the *Abigail Alliance* perspective sympathetic? Who should be responsible if a patient is somehow harmed by early access to a drug? What other legal or ethical problems do you perceive?

Table of Cases

Principal cases are indicated by italics.

Table of Statutes and Regulations

State Statutes and Regulations

Alabama

INDEX